D1117131

# THE WAR
## Illustrated

Complete Record of the Conflict
by Land and Sea and in the Air

*Edited by*

SIR  JOHN  HAMMERTON

Volume  Seven

The SEVENTH VOLUME of THE WAR ILLUSTRATED
contains the issues numbered 156 to 180, covering the period
May 1943 to April 1944. To this volume has fallen the satisfying
task of recording for posterity an almost unbroken series of Allied
successes in the several theatres of war, from the soil of Italy and
the battle-lines of Russia to islands of the Pacific and the " green
hell " of Burmese jungles.

Our Prime Minister declared on June 8, 1943, that " brighter
and solid prospects lie before us." How the course of events
justified Mr. Churchill's words our pages show. In July Sicily
was invaded, the braggart Mussolini fell, and the German summer
offensive at Kursk was smashed. Came then the colossal counter-
blow which for months the Russians had been preparing : its
skilfully directed fury hurled the Nazis from one ineffective
defensive position backward to yet another. In September
Italy, invaded by the 5th and 8th Armies, laid down her arms,
and ships of her Fleet sailed under Allied orders into Malta's
Valetta Harbour.

Visits of H.M. the King and the Prime Minister to the
Mediterranean war zone cheered our fighting men ; and inspiring
was the news of the conference at Teheran, where President
Roosevelt and Mr. Churchill met Marshal Stalin to discuss
measures for the final overthrow of the enemy. The chronicling
of such pregnant events has occupied much of our space, but we
have striven also to pay due tribute to ordinary folk working
for victory, and to the little-publicized efforts of our colonies.

As this volume closes, unprecedented air assaults by day and
by night are in progress against the Reich and Occupied Countries,
grim prelude, maybe, to invasion of the Continent. It will be
for Volume Eight to record progress of the greatest combined
operations in world history.

Published 2000
Cover Design © 2000
TRIDENT PRESS INTERNATIONAL
ISBN 1-58279-106-6  Single Edition
ISBN 1-58279-022-1  Special Combined Edition*
*Contains Volume 7 & 8 Unabridged
Printed in Croatia

# General Index to Volume Seven

*This Index is designed to give ready reference to the whole of the literary and pictorial contents of* THE WAR ILLUSTRATED. *Individual subjects and persons of importance are indexed under their own headings, while references are included to general subjects such as Burma; Tunisia; Pacific; U.S.A., etc. Page Numbers in italics indicate illustrations.*


**Aaron, F/Sgt. A. L., V.C.,** *478*
Abbey Wood, harvest at, *219*
Aberdeen, H.M.S. mascot, *710*
**Abyssinia,** air war in, 266
—Haile Selassie back in, 7
—money spent on, 115
—war cemeteries in, 748
Acasta, H.M.S., sunk, 518
Accra, bomber week in, *322*
A.C.E.S., in India, 566
Achilles, H.M.S., N.Z cruiser, 615
Acland, Sgt., of A.F.P.U., *278*
Acoustic Mine, countered, 454
Acquafondata, Fighting French take, *555*
Acton, Lord, on power, 179
Adam, Gen. Sir Ronald F., *399*
Aderemi I, The One of Ife, *586*
**Admiral Hipper** (ship), returns to Baltic, 550
— —speed, 358
**Admiral Scheer,** returns to Baltic, 550
— —speed, 358
Admiral's Regiment, R. Marines, 628
Admiralty, opposes Air Ministry, 348
Admiralty Is., U.S. in, 678, *761*
Adolf Hitler Canal, *430*
Adrano, Allies take, 199
Adriatic Sea, German forces in, 678
Advanced Dressing-station, Italy, *516*
Adventure, H.M.S., *43*
Aegean Islands, 73
Aeromebolism, measures against, 521
Aeronautical Chamber of Commerce, U.S., 362
**Aeroplanes,** as ambulances, *84, 85, 687*
—British, for Turkey, *526*
—as freighters, *716, 717*
—German, supplies by, *613*
—Italian, salvage from, *14*
—Japanese, down at Tarawa, *594*
—mobility, 477
—U.S., bomb Wewak, *443*
Aesculapius, sanctuary, Cos, 415
**Africa, N.,** Axis evacuation prevented, *41*
— —cost of living in, 63
— —D.R. in, *436*
— —hospital in, *691*
— —invasion, craft used, 110
— —present conditions, 38
— —railway importance in, 238
**Afrika Korps,** demoralisation, 29
— —new weapons, 52
Agricultural Volunteer Camps, 58, 218
**Agriculture,** in N. Africa, 38
—in N. Ireland, 650
—volunteers for, Great Britain, 770
Agrigento, Greek Akragas, 171, *173*
Aikens, Lt. Brian, wins U.S. Air Cross, *94*
Ainsworth, A., aircraft manufacturer, *374*
Air, transport by, development, *362, 363*
**Airborne Troops,** Allied, in Sicily, 130, *152, 156*
— —British, in Burma, 707, 708, 732, 750, *753*
— —luggage for, *546*
— —U.S., in Sicily, *192*
**Aircraft,** Allied production, 284
—Axis, wrecked, Lampedusa, *103*
—German, Russian losses, 257, 284
—Italian, inferiority, 284
—Japanese, Pacific losses, *573*
—pigeons in, 334
—repairing, S. Rhodesia, *322*
—Russian designs, 307
—supplies by, Changteh, 664
—and U-boat campaign, 202
—Ulster makes, 650
—U.S., at Ascension, 682
**Aircraft-carriers,** Allied and Japanese, 262
— —"Woolworth" type, *104, 105*
— —British, escort type, 10
— — —losses, 54
— — —numbers, 40
— —no future, 348
— —Japanese shortage, 582
— —limitations, 636
— —and U-boat war, 200, *274*
**Aircraft-carriers** *(cont.)*
— —U.S., additions to, 582
— — —off Norway, 327
Aircraft Escort Vessels, in U.S.N., 10, *42*
**Aircraft Factory,** British, council, *374*
— — —tea at, *610*
"Aircraft of the Fighting Powers," 542
Aircraft Production, Ministry of, 700
Air Cross, U.S., Aikens wins, *94*
Air Defence, German, latest methods, 316
Air Defence of Great Britain, formerly Fighter Command, 758
**Airfields,** in Ceylon, *788*
—Chinese make, *466*
—flooded, Italy, *785*
—gardens on, *770*
—military, needs, 732
—new Australian, *584, 585*
—in Pacific, importance, 636
—reconstituting, 620
—Sicilian, reconditioned, *184*
**Air Force, Chinese,** successes, 35
— —**Fighting French,** in Russia, *308*
— —**German,** dispersal dangers, 98
— — —failure, reasons for, 22
— — —High Command's mistakes, 118
— — —in Italy, 262
— — —and Pantelleria, 67, 70
— — —in Sicily, change in, 220
— —**Indian,** in Burma, *752*
— —**Italian,** out of war, 284
— — —strength in 1940, 266
— — —Mussolini and, 182
— —**Japanese,** overwhelmed, 284
— —**Royal,** achievements over Germany, 3
— — —Arctic patrol, *317*
— — —armourers, Middle East, *250*
— — —Auster III with, *348*
— — —and Axis transport, 89
— — —in the Azores, *541*
— — —bomb Berlin, 237, *280, 510*
— — —bombing statistics, 284
— — —bomb Pantelleria, 70, *71*
— — — —radio station, 462
— — —bring war to Germany, 206
— — —catafighter unit, 54
— — —and Chindits, 46, 49
— — —cooperation, 355
— — —creation, 86
— — —decorations, *318*
— — —Denmark wears colours, 248
— — —dinghy drill, Italy, *785*
— — —drop leaflets, Italy, 7
— — —and Dunkirk evacuation, 150
— — —first raid, 54
— — —flying ambulances, 84
— — —gardens, 770
— — —and German railways, 662
— — —greets King, *100*
— — —guards Cyprus, *148*
— — —independence value, 22, 477
— — —and invasion barges, 110
— — —in Italy, 669
— — —and Leros, 442
— — —in Malta, *98*
— — —Mountain Service, *439*
— — —Navy and, 54
— — —and Norwegian campaign, 540
— — —nursing sisters, *691*
— — —Observer Corps aids, *758, 759*
— — —offensive on Germany, 765
— — —origin, 477
— — —over Greece, *236*
— — —past struggle, 348
— — —photographic section, *797*
— — —pilots' training, *694, 695*
— — —pre-invasion activity, *620*
— — —P.R.U., *285*
— — —purpose, 380
— — —and Ruhr dams, 430
— — —salvage squads, *14*
— — —on Sicilian airfields, *184*
— — —and Sicilian invasion, 156, *210*
— — —and skip-bombing *670*
— — —slang, 223
**Air Force, Royal** *(cont.)*
— — —test pilots, *470, 471*
— — —tidiness, 191
— — —Transport Command, *363*
— — —Ulster bases for, 650
— — —Ulstermen in, 650
— — —weakness in 1940, 266
— —**R. Australian,** on Australia Day, *578*
— — — —in N. Australia, *446*
— —**R.N.Z.,** Warhawks of, *597*
— —**Russian,** achievements, *380, 692*
— — —in Caucasus, *140*
— — —development, 307
— — —drop flares, *259*
— —**S. African,** bombs Pantelleria, *57*
— —**Turkish,** strength, 526, *528*
— —**U.S.,** attacks Rabaul, *509*
— — — —bombs Tokyo, *154, 155*
— — — —bombs Verona, *636*
— — — —and daylight bombing, 214, *216*
— — — —daylight raids, Berlin, *701*
— — — —Fortresses in flight, *445*
— — — —in invasion practice, *637*
— — — —in Italy, *669*
— — — —offensive in Germany, *765*
— — — —in Philippines, 563
— — — —power, 477
— — — —and U-boats, *263*
**Air Force Regt., Royal,** in Azores, *705*
— — — —exercises, 159
— — — —invasion training, *129*
— — — —pre-invasion activity, 620
**Air Forces,** Allied, in New Guinea, 323
— — —increased bombing-range, *330*
Airmail, to N. Africa, figures, 716
**Airmen,** altitude training, *521*
—British, rescue devices, *235*
—Dutch, squadron with R.A.F., *418*
—German, in British M.T.B., *41*
Air Ministry, past struggle, 348
Air Observation Post Squadron, *598*
Air Offensive, Hammerton on, 575
Air Photography, and bomb damage, *764*
**Air Power,** Allied, in Far East, 118
— —and Cassino, *709*
— —German failure, 86
— —Germany undervalues, 380
— —and Italy's surrender, 266
— —and military evacuation, 227
— —and Pantelleria, *102*
— —strategic use, 22
— —and total war, 348
**Air Raids,** Allied, effect on Berlin, *559-62*
— —Axis, on Algiers, 654
— —D.R.'s in, 436
— —German, on London, 668, *704*
— —on Japan, likelihood, 10
**Air-raid Shelters,** Berlin, *560*
— — —Ceylon, *428*
— — —of Messina, 229
— — —in Portugal, *360*
— — —Sicilian, *149*
**Air-Sea Rescue Service,** Coastguard and, 234
— — — —painting of (Bone), *720*
— — — —R.O.C. and, 758
— — — —Walruses for, *108*
Airspeed Horsa I, glider transport, 542
Airspeed Oxford, as ambulances, *85*
Air Stewardesses, *514*
**Air Supremacy,** in Mediterranean, 2
— —of United Nations, 22
Air Train, first trans-Atlantic, 362
**Air War,** greater height of, *521*
— —Macmillan's survey, 22, 54, 86, 118, 150, 182, 214, 253, 284, 316, 348, 380, 412, 444, 477, 508, 540, 572, 604, 636, 668, 700, 732, 764, 796
**Ajaccio,** Commandos at, *376*
—rejoicings in, *344*
Ajax, H.M.S., Ulstermen in, 650
AK4, Russian bomber, *252*
Akugbene, The Pere of, *586*
Akyab, not for Japan, 3
**Alamein, El,** battle of, artillery wins, 296
— — —D.R.'s at, 436
— — —maps for, 558
— — —smoke used at, 654
— —railway at, 238
Alaska Highway, continuation, 790
Alazon Bay, U.S.S., launched, *42*
**Albania,** history and future, 342
—radio station bombed, *462*
—unrest in, 7
Albanians, in Calabria, 255
**Albert, Harold A.,** on air transport, 362
— —on roadmaking, 790
Alcock, Capt. E. S., ferry pilot, 362
Alcyon, L' (ship) off Corsica, 294
Aldis Lamp, use, *418*
Aleutian Islands, Attu the largest, *53*
**Alexander,** K. of Yugoslavia, Boris and, 270
—death, Pavelitch and, 342
—dictator, 524
**Alexander, Right Hon. A. V.,** and battle of Atlantic, 678
— —and human torpedoes, *775*
— —on minesweepers, 582
— —on Navy off Sicily, 272
— —on U.S. aircraft carriers, 42
— —with U.S. ships, *487*
**Alexander, Gen. the Hon. Sir H. R. L. G.,** with Anderson and Coningham, *32*
— — —brilliant generalship, 2
— — —C.-in-C., Italy, 515
— — —at Council of War, *81*
— — —decorates Keneally, *286*
— — —head of Amgot in Sicily, 180
— — —and invasion of Sicily, 150
— — —and Italian armistice, 265
— — —and Nettuno landing, 579, *580*
— — —proclamation, Sicily, *180*
— — —at Salerno, *293*
— — —in Tunis, *5*
— — —an Ulsterman, 650
— — —uses jeep, 300
Alexandra, Miss Clare, 514
**Alexandria,** French ships at, *40*
—United Nations Day in, *121*
Alfedana, road to, *490*
Algeria, present conditions, 38
**Algiers,** Allied council in, *80-81*
—busy life in, *440*
—smoke screen over, *654*
"Alice Through the Looking Glass," Hammerton on, 703
Alinda Bay, German barge on fire in, *468*
Ali Shah, Syed Edris, on Turkey's attitude, 526
Allen, Gen., on New Guinea campaign, 659
Allen, Capt. Richard, and transport planes, *716*
Allied Military Government of Occupied Territory: see Amgot
Allied Works Council, Australia, *584, 585*
**Allies,** commanders chosen, 515
—Turkey's sympathy with, 526
"Alligator," transport vehicle, 110, *602*
**Allotments,** British increase, 218
—thefts from, 319
Alpheios R., bridge destroyed, *236*
Alpini, in battle of the Pindus, 179
**Altenfjord,** *Scharnhorst* in, 518
—*Tirpitz* damaged in, 327, *776*
Altitude, ice-chamber tests for, *574*
Altitude Sickness, measures against, 521
Amalfi, *305*
Amaron, Douglas, 569
**Ambulances,** flying, *84, 85, 716*
—jeep as, *353*
—of R.A.F. Mountain Service, *439*
—reindeer draw, *425*
—for repatriated prisoners, *402*
—water, for Combined Operations, 492
Ameer, H.M.S., launched, 486
American China Air Task Force, *466*
**Americans,** in Bizerta, 4
—in Burma, *751*
—in D.W.I., *408*
—in New Guinea, 269, *350*
—in Sicily, 162, *166*
—take Rendova, *170*
See *also* Army, U.S.; Navy, U.S.; Air Force, U.S.
Amery, Rt. Hon. L. S., 429
**"Amgot,"** function, Sicily, 180
—and Neapolitan schools, *736*
Ammiraglio Cagni (submarine), 294
Ammunition, men who pass, *494*
**Amphibious Landings,** stages, 579
— —supplies required, 142
Amphibious Vehicles, U.S. types, 110, *114*
Ancient, H.M. Tug, 762
Ancona, Trajan's arch, *306*
**Andaman Is.,** control of, and Burma, 556
— —lost bases, 230
Anders, Gen., in Italy, 786
Anderson, Pipe-Major A., *289*
Anderson, Pte. Eric, V.C., *478*
**Anderson, Rt. Hon. Sir John,** Chancellor of Exchequer, 311
— — —on material aids, 179
Anderson, Maj. J. T. M., V.C., *123*
**Anderson, Gen. Sir Kenneth,** with Alexander and Coningham, *32*
— —in Bizerta, *4*
— —with Churchill, *82*
— —at Thanksgiving Service, *36*
**Andrea Doria** (ship), for Russia, 710
— —at Taranto, 168
Andreanof, Is., 10
Angell, Sir Norman, "Let the People Know," 351
Angling, in war-time, 319
Angra do Heroismo (Terceira) *361*
Ankara, views of, *527*
Ansaldo, Signor, Massock on, 115
Anson, Lord, at Tinian, 646
Anson, Chief Steward G. H., B.E.M., *254*
**Anti-Aircraft Battery,** British, gun-flash board, 258
— — —German, Sicily, 9
— — — Russian, *257*
**Anti-Aircraft Defence,** German, Allies saturate, 214
— — —of London, *375*
— — —in Switzerland, 718
Anti-aircraft Forts, 629
**Anti-aircraft Gunners,** British, Ortona, *537*
— — —Dutch naval, *96*
— — —German, Naples, *118*
— — —Marines as, 174
— — —of Northern Ireland, *651*
— — —Russian, in Karelia, *564*
**Anti-aircraft Guns,** Allied, Nettuno, *631*
— — — —self-propelled Bofors, *783*
— — —E. African crew, *619*
— — —Emplacement, Atlantic Wall, *20*
— — —Home Guard man, *798*
— — —Italian, Germans man, *37*
— — — —on supply train, *37*
— — —Portuguese, *360*
— — —of Russian armoured train, *276*
— — —Russian, at Leningrad, *394, 624-25*
— — —U.S., at Bougainville, *592*
— — —of *Widgeon*, *271*
Anti-aircraft Posts, British, books for, 127
Anti-aircraft Units, of Home Guard, 26
Anti-flash Helmets, *457*
Antimony, in China, 116
**Anti-tank Gunners,** Russian, central front, *141*
— — —at Orel, *187*
**Anti-tank Guns,** Allied, in Italy, *325*
— — —British 17-pdr., *372*
— — — —25-pdr., filmed, *279*
— — —German, Russians under, *645*
— — — —U.S. use, *676*
— — —Russian, *276*
— — — —at Orel, *194*
— — — —U.S. "bazooka," 296, *297*
**Anti-tank Obstacles,** in Atlantic Wall, *20*
— — —in Corsica, *376*
— — —on Volturno, *356*

Anti-tank Regiment, at Thanksgiving Service, 36
Anti-tank Riflemen, Russian, 385
Anti-tank Unit, of S.R. Home Guard, *211*
Antonescu, Michael, 686
**Anzio,** *601*
—Allied beach-head at, 579, *580*
—Allies at, *690*
—cockpit of, *730*
—Cunningham in, *612*
—German attacks at, 643
— —prisoners from, *780*
—new roads to, *790*
—Recce at, 697
—U.S wounded at, *768*
Aosta, Duc d', missed opportunity, 675
Apennines, Allies advance over, *490*
Apron, armoured, of Fortress crew, *370*
Arabis, H.M.S., for R.N.Z.N., 615
Arabs, bribed, N. Africa, 243
**Arakan,** Allied failure in, 3
—British victory in, *683*
—fighting in, 634, 750
—new roads in, *752*
—supplies by air, 757
Arakan Front, in Burma, 556, *557*
Arbutus, H.M.S., for R.N.Z.N., 615
Archer, H.M.S., "Woolworth" carrier, *105*
Archimedes, in Syracuse, 171
**Arctic Circle,** R.A.F. patrol in, *317*
— —ship's survivors in, 537
Ardent, H.M.S., sunk, 518
Aréthuse (submarine) off Corsica, 294
Arghezi, Tudor, 686
Argyll and Sutherland Highlanders, 2nd, Marines with, 628
Armistice Convention, and French army, 404
Armistice Day, Hammerton on, 415
Armitage, Lt.-Cdr., G.C., G.M., *696*
**Armour,** German, in Corsica, *376*
— —destroyed in Russia, *204*
Armoured Cars, British, on Turkish frontier, *69*
Armoured Corps, Royal, and Recce, 697
**Armoured Train,** Italian, on coast, 7
— —Russian, A.A. guns, *276*
— — —inscription on, *645*
— — —on Karelian Front, *564*
**Armourers,** British, with Piat, *621*
—R.A.F., in Middle East, *250*
Armstrong, H. R., of Dover, *534*
Armstrong, John, painting by, *15*
**Army, British,** Auster III its "eyes," 348
— —cooperation, 355
— —help with harvest, *218*
— —and Home Guard, *26*
— —native troops, prowess, 675
— —new type, 19
— —poor equipment, 477
— —treat buildings badly, 191
— —units in Tunisia, 2
—**Chinese,** in Burma, *752*
— —efficiency, 35
— —modern reforms, 116
—**Free French,** N. African troops, 404, *405*
—**German,** deterioration in, 579
— —raising of, 404
— —top dog, 206
—**Japanese,** in control, 435
— —MacArthur on, 563
—**Portuguese,** on manoeuvres, *360*
—**Russian,** good artillery, 296
— —high morale, 35
— —Michel Berchin and Eliahu Ben-horin on, 307
— —reserves' training, *120*
— —upsets theories, 259
— —use reindeer, *425*
—**Turkish,** strength, 526, *528-29*
—**U.S.,** artillery, 296
— —in Ascension, 682
— —battle training, *418, 746*
**Army Cadet Force,** training, 406, *407*
— — —in Ulster, 650
Army Cooperation Command, and Tactical Air Force, 86
Army Film and Photographic Units, 278, 279
**Army Medical Corps Royal,** Cotterell on, 755
— — — —in Italy *687*
— — — —in Melilli, *165*
— — — —in N. Africa, 84
— — — —Canadian, women in, *226*
Army Movement Control, and Dunkirk, 238
Army of Liberation, National, in Yugoslavia, 524
Army Pigeon Service, *334*
Army Service Corps, Royal, and ammunition supply, *494*
Army Survey Directorate, maps by, 558
Army Transportation Corps, U.S., in Britain, *546*
**Arnim, Gen. von,** Alexander outwits, 2
— —arrives in England, *30*
— —held railways, *238*
— —surrenders, 30
**Arnold, Gen. Henry H.,** *319*
— —and bombing of Tokyo, *154*
**A.R.P.,** in Ceylon, *428*
—in Dover, 534
—in Stockholm, *756*
Arras, smoke-screen at (1917), 654
Art, and war, Hammerton on, 607
Artificial limbs, Poles make, *610*
**Artillery,** at Anzio, 643
—British, in Sicily, *197*
— —in Italy, *783*
—Japanese dummy, *591*
—in modern war, 355
—planes spot for, *598*
—**Royal,** at Anzio, *730*
— —epic of 155th Battery, 77
— —with Gun-How No. 1, *247*
—Russian, at Leningrad, *589*
—Russian prowess with, 515
—Turkish, *529*
Aruba, oil refineries in, *408*
Asbeck, Col. C. J. van, *408*
Asbestos, Cyprus produces, 148
Ascension Is., war effort, *682*
**Asdic System,** improvements, 10
— —Nazi methods against, 262
Ashfield, Lord, 122
Asia, S.E. Command, 772
Askern Colliery, "Bevin boys" at, *600*
Asmara, works for Allies, *7*
Aspromonte, scene in, *304*
Assault Course, for U.S. troops, *418*
Assault Troops, mechanized craft for, *231*
Assembly Shed, of R.E.M.E., Middle East, *142*
**Assheton, Ralph, M.P.,** on National Debt, 246
— —on "pay as you earn," 311
Astor, Lt. Col., and air raid damage, 703
Ataturk, Kemal, statue, Ankara, *527*
A.T.C., Ulstermen in, 650, *651*
Athlone, Countess of, *233*
Athlone, Earl of, and Quebec Conference, *232-33*
**Atlantic, Battle of,** air power and, 444
— —Allied victory, 483
— —new facts, *678*
— —successes in, 105
Atlantic Charter, Amgot and, *402*
Atlantic Wall, details, *20*
Atlantis (raider) sunk, 422
Atlantis, S.S., repatriates prisoners, 359, *402*
**Atrocities,** German, in Naples, 324
— —at Orel, 194
—Moscow Conference and, *396*
**A.T.S.,** and Bren-carriers, *258*
—cleaning guns, *514*
—Cypriot girls in, 148
—at fruit-bottling, *386*
—of Jamaica, *661*
—meat carvers, 290
—on searchlight projectors, *706*
—Signals Sections, 436
—smoking regulations, 767
Attilio Regolo (ship), 550
**Attlee, Rt. Hon. Clement R.,** on the Danes, 78
— —Lord President of Council, 311
**Attu,** map, *10*
—U.S. take, 3, 10, 35, *53*
**Auchinleck, Gen. Sir Claude,** his offensive, air power in, 266
— —an Ulsterman, 650
August, holiday travel in, 246
**Augusta,** Allies take, 130, 167
—Amgot in, 180
—history, 171
Augustus, Arch of, Rimini, *306*
Aurora, H.M.S., carries the King, 97, *101*
**Auster,** performance, 542
—III, as artillery spotter, *598*
— —"Eyes of the Army," *348*
**Austin, A. B.,** death, 346
— —last story, *345*
Austin, Robert, painting, *721*
**Australia,** Allied Works Council in, 584, *585*
—invasion danger removed, 67
—Northern, air bases in, *446*
—railways in, 238
—troops training in, *322*
Australia Day, in London, *578*
**Australians,** at Cape Gloucester, 601
**Australians** *(cont.)*
—at Finisterre, N. Guinea, 715
—flying ambulance for, 84
—and Montgomery, 723
—in New Guinea, 269, 323, *350, 596, 659, 793*
—in N. Guinea, air help for, 716
**Austria,** future, Moscow Conference and, *396*
—Italy's struggle against, 179
Authors, war hardships, 319
Automobile Association, patrol in snow, *674*
Ava Bridge (Burma), Allies bomb, 556
Avenger (bomber), sinks U-boats, *326*
Aversa, P.O.W. camp at, *388*
Aviation Spirit, found in Sicily, 185
**Avola,** Allied patrol in, *178*
—British officer at, *181*
Avro 10, in N. Australia, *446*
Avro York, transport plane, *412, 716*
Azalea, H.M.S., 744
**Azores,** Allied bases, value, 483
—British bases in, 360, *361*
—Portuguese troops for, *467*
—R.A.F. in, *541*
—R.A.F. Regt. in, *705*

## B

Babelthuap, importance, 742
**Badoglio, Marshal Pietro,** books on, 627
— —Hitler and, 398
— —and Italian surrender, 265
— —prospects, 163
— —replaces Mussolini, *213*
**Baerlein, Henry,** on Bessarabia, 588
— —on bombing of Ploesti, 186
— —on Bulgaria, 270
— —on Cyprus, 148
— —on Dalmatia, 342
— —on Danes with Merchant Navy, 78
— —on future frontiers, 462
— —on Hungary, 366
— —on Rumania, 686
**Bagpipes,** of Canadians, Calabria, 289
—in Sicily, *164*
**Baia,** *306*
Bain, Capt. D. K., D.S.O., R.N., 520
**Bairiki,** U.S. Marines land on, 475
Baja and Latina, church destroyed at, *389*
Baka Baka, N. Zealanders at, *502*
Baker, Noel, M.P., on holiday travel, 246
Baker, Capt. Valentine, test pilot, *470*
Baldwin, Lord, 671
Baldwin, C. P. O., and magnetic mine, 124
Baldwin, Air Marshal Sir John E., in Burma, *708, 752*
Balkan Entente, Turkey and, 526
**Balkans,** Bulgaria's influence, 270
—Germans plan withdrawal, 206
—German strength in, 526
**Baltimores,** bomb Pantelleria, *57*
—in Italy, 669
—in Malta, *214*
Band, German, in Berlin, *560*
Bandsmen, of R. Marines, 174
Banka Strait, "Blitz Alley," 410
Banner, Ldg. Seaman F., D.S.M., *696*
Barbed Wire, E. Africans erect, *619*
Barbers, British, in Italy, 690, *740*
**Barges,** for coal transport, 674
—for German canals, 430
—German equipment, on fire, *468*
—Invasion : see Landing Craft
—supply, in Burma, *751*
—women manage, *737*
—for wounded, New Guinea, *350*
Bari, bombed, 182
Bark, for food, China, *117*
Barnard, Capt., test pilot, 470
Barnes, Sgt., of A.F.P.U., *278*
Barr, S.-Ldr. A. W., D.F.C., *638*
**Barracuda, torpedo bomber,** 742
— — —attack *Tirpitz, 776, 794*
— — —in *Ravager, 777*
Barrage, Russian, at Leningrad, *589*
Barratt, Air Marshal Sir Arthur, 86
Barricades, in Portugal, *360*
Barrow, Maj. Leonard, 156
Barrow-Clough, Maj.-Gen. C. E., *502*
**Barry, Rear-Adm. C. B.,** on midget submarines, 649
— —on submarine service, 616
"Bart," coal-miner, 246
Bartoli, Pauline, the King meets, *100*
Barwell, Sqd.-Ldr. George C., *216*
Bases, and Pacific War, 454
Basic English, Hammerton on, 287, 735
Baskets, for pigeons, *226*
**Basque** (ship), off Corsica, 294
—for Free French, 40
**Bastia,** *344*
—as evacuation port, 294
—Goumiers enter, 404
Batavia, Singapore refugees at, 410
Bater-Bek, Russian guerilla, *332*
Batov, Lt.-Gen., with Budenny, *459*
"Bats o' Hell," at Los Negros, 761
Battipaglia, 5th Army in, *299*
**Battledress,** for Coastguard Service, *234*
—for Navy, 415
Battler, H.M.S., 10, *42*
Battle-School, value, 403
**Battleships,** air power and, 348
—British, speed, 358
—Italian, for Russia, 710
— —surrender, *336*
—Japanese, new, 40
— —numbers, 262
—U.S., Bofors guns, *487*
Bauxite, from W. Indies, 661
Bawcombe, Philip, painting, *16*
**Bayonet,** Goumier sharpens, *404*
—new, for Marines, *641*
—for Russian marines, *432-33*
Bayonet Charge, by British infantry, *220*
Bayonet Practice, for Russian reserves, *120*
"Bazooka" U.S. gun, 296, *297*
**B.B.C.,** pronunciation, 543
—records Berlin raid, 313
Beach-masters, Allied, in N. Africa, 243
Beauchamp, Tony, with Chindits, *83*
**Beaufighters,** in Biscay battle, 532
—bomb Preveza, *236*
—bomb steamer, Burma, *444, 634*
—bomb train, Burma, *557*
—down JU 88, *215*
—of F.A.A., Gibraltar, *679*
—in Malta, *22*
—over Leros, 442
—sink enemy shipping, *713*
—sink *Monte Rosa, 742*
—torpedo-carrying, *64*
Beaufort Bomber, Australia, *446*
Beaverbrook, Rt. Hon. Baron, 311
Begbie, Harold, 351
Bedfordshire, farming in, *770*
Beirut, patrols in, *469*
**Belfast, H.M.S.,** Belfast built, 650
— —and *Scharnhorst, 518,* 519, 570
Belfast, important port, 650
Belgian Congo, new roads in, *790*
Belgians, in W.A.A.F., *797*
Belgium, minesweepers, *418*
**Belgrade,** from Foggia, *330*
—Partisans' funeral in, *525*
**Bell,** with fox-brush clapper, *393*
—as siren, Ceylon, *428*
Belladonna, for Guy's Hospital, *290*
Belle Isle, Marines take, 628
Belligerent Power, statement on, 348
Belpasso, British radio operator in, *437*
Benedict, St., and Cassino Monastery, *655*
**Benes, Dr. Edward,** and Czech anniversary, *418*
— —and Czech-Soviet Pact, *522*
— —and Moscow, 383
Bengal, famine in, *429*
Ben-norin, Eliahu, on Red Army, 307
Beni Khalid, prisoners in, 29
Bennett, Air Cmdre. D. C. T., *479*
Bennington, Lt.-Cdr. L. W. A., R.N., *616*
Bensley, Capt. Maurice, 116
**Bentinck, Lord William,** in Sicily, 171
— — —frigate named after, 486
Bentley, Capt. Bede, 83
Bentley, W. J., on Pilots' training, 694
Berchin, Michel, on the Red Army 307
Berdichev, Russians take, 547
Bere, Brigadier De La, *721*
Beret, for R. Marines, *226*
Bering Sea, operations in, 10
**Berlin,** air offensive and, 559-62
—battle of, figures, 604, 700
— —history, 412
—bombs on, 284
**Berlin** *(cont.)*
—concentrated bombing, 477
—inland port, 430
—Mosquitoes bomb, 214
—most bombed city, 472, *473*
—pigeons for *334*
—plan, *237*
—raids on, *237*
— — —effect, *280, 510*
— — —recorded, 313
—U.S. daylight raids on, *701*
Berlin Congress and Bessarabia, 588
Berry, S., paintings by, *16, 720*
Bessarabia, Allies' problems in, *588*
Best, Sgt. Dickie, 278
Bethlen, Count, and Secret ballot, 366
Betio Island, Allies take, 474
Betts, Ernest, with Scots Guards, 93
Beveridge, Sir William, 546
**Bevin, Rt. Hon. Ernest,** air prophecy, 575
— —and coal-mines, 600
— —demobilization scheme, 319
— —on German slave labour, 511
— —on mobilization, 311
"Bevin Boys," training, 600
Bianca (ship) scuttled, 518
Bielgorod : see Byelgorod
"Big Inch," oil pipe-line, *76*
Birmingham, Bishop of, 58
Birth-rate, British, decline in, 246
**Biscay, Bay of,** battle in, 518, *532*
— — —survivors, *550*
— —convoy attacked in, 602
— —Liberator crew in, *54*
— —U-boats sunk in, *107, 263, 284, 647*
Bishop Guns, in Italy, *325*
Bisley Planes, for Turkey, *526*
**Bismarck** (ship), crippled from air, 348
—last cruise, 358
—seen from Ulster base, 650
Bizani, storming of (1912) 342
Bizerta, Allies enter, *4*
**Black Market,** in Imperial Russia, 735
— —in U.S.A., 767
Black-out, in Lisbon, 360
Black Sea, Russian M.T.B.s in, *168*
Black Sea Fleet, 390, 774
Blankenberghe, war cemetery, 747
Blaskowitz, Field-Marshal, 398
Blekeoya Island, British submarine off, 616
Blenheim Bombers, *146*
Bligh, Lt., R.N., *41*
Blindfolding, of German prisoners, *329, 571*
"Blitz Alley," Banka Strait, 410
"Block Busters," *349*
Bloggs, Coxswain A. G., B.E.M., *18*
Blood Transfusion, in Italy, 687
Blue Cordillera Mts., roads in, *791*
Boarding Exercises, from *Philante, 203*
Boatman, P/O, escape, 665
**Bock, Field-Marshal von,** character, 398
— —Hitler and, 398
Bode, Cpl., escape, 665
Bodinnar, Sir John, 246
**Bofors Guns,** defend London, *375*
— —of *Imperialist, 681*
— —of *Richelieu, 504*
— —self-propelled, *783*
— —of U.S. battleship, *487*
Bolkhov, Russians take, *205*
**Bologna,** bombed, 182
—the Leaning Towers, *304*
Bolzano (ship) Germans hold, 294
Bombardier, of Fortress, *369*
Bomb-cases, manufacture, *642*
**Bomber Command,** achievements, 572
— —and Berlin, 477
— —bombs N. Italy, 150
— —estimates for, 700
— —July activities, 182
— —losses, 764
— —mine-laying figures, 763
— —origin, 86
— —raids Ruhr and Rhine, 118, *119*
**Bombers, Allied,** lost over Berlin, 284
—**British,** geographical handicap, 316
— —return from Germany, *87*
—**German,** Americans examine, *184*
— —in Russia, 252
—load carried, 412
—**U.S.,** in China, *466*
— —distress signals, *596*
Bomber Squadron, Russian, in Caucasus, *140*
Bomb Flash Protecting Gear, *271, 272-73*

**Bombing,** and invasion, limitations, 67
—pilots trained for, *694*, *695*
Bombing-up, in Middle East, *250*
Bomb-rack, of Halifax, loaded, 22
**Bombs,** British, " block busters," *349*
— —500 lb., dump, *642*
— —12,000-pdr., *700*, 702
—for Fortresses, *368*
—for Mosquito, *620*
—rocket-glider, construction, 454
—smoke by, 654
—from U.S., for Turkey, *493*
Bomb-sight, Mark IX, *477*
Bomb Trolleys, in Malta, *214*
Bon, Cape, prisoners from, 780
— —resistance ends in, *2*
Bondarenko, Ivan, at Peterhof, *633*
Bone, Sir Muirhead, etching, *722*
Bone, Stephen, painting, *720*
**Books,** for A.A. posts, 127
—English, in Finland, *685*
Boom Defence, of Great Britain, *648*
Boothman, Air Commodore J. N., and Photographic Reconnaissance, 285, 620
Boots, repair, difficulties, 415
Boreas, H.M.S., destroyer, 392
Boris, Tsar of Bulgaria, death, 256, 270
Bormann, Martin, *366*
Bornemicza, Hungarian spokesman, 366
Borstal, and agriculture, 374
Bosnia, unrest in, 342
Bosphorus, Istanbul on, *530*
**Boston Bombers,** over Lampedusa, *128*
— —Russian, over Kursk, *141*
Bougainville, Allies invade, 454, 592-93
Boulting, Flight-Lieut. John, 278
Boulting, Capt. Roy, 278
Bourgas, German control, 270
Bowen, Sqn.-Ldr. W. H., *255*
Bowes-Lyon, Capt. B., of *Adventure*, 43
Bowhill, Air-Chief Marshal Sir Frederick, *363*
Bowles, Cdr. R. N., and magnetic mine, 124
Boxing, in P.O.W. camp, *409*
Boyd, Lennox, new appointment, 438
Braces, as fan belt, 460
Bradford, Churchill's speech at, 275
**Bradley, Lt.-Gen. Omar, D.S.M.,** *639*
— —in Bizerta, *4*
Bradstock, Lt.-Cdr. J. R., 158
Brailsford, H. N., on peace terms, 703
Braithwaite, Major T., in prison ship, 61
Brauchitsch, Field-Marshal von, 398
Breadner, Air-Marshal L. S., *232*
Breconshire, H.M.S., last voyage, 762
Bremen, Fortresses raid, *370*
**Bren Carriers,** Allied, in Burma, *752*
— — —in Centuripe, *239*
— — —in Ortona, *516*
— — —of Recce, *461*, *697*
— — —in Sicily, *163*, *165*
— —ploughing with, *147*
— —for Russia, 258
**Bren-Gunners,** British, in Italy, *489*
— —Norwegian, Spitzbergen, *314*
**Bren-Guns,** ammunition used, 494
— —in battle school, *746*
— —British, in Sicily, *220*
— —for Recce, 460, *461*
Brenner Pass, Tiger tanks in, *320*
**Brest,** as raider base, 422
—*Scharnhorst* at, 518
Bridgeman, Lord, 26
**Bridges,** destroyed, Chernigov, *333*
— — —Dnepropetrovsk, *387*
— — —Italy, *389*
—German, Allied war on, 620
—Pontoon : *See* Pontoon
—rope, in New Guinea, *659*
—Russians mine, *564*, *613*
—Sappers build, Italy, *325*
—in Sicily, *163*
—U.S. repair, Italy, *293*
Bridport, Lt.-Cdr. Viscount, D. of Brontë, 256
**Briefing,** of Fortress crew, *367*
—of Japanese pilots, *435*
—of parachute troops, *766*
—for *Tirpitz* raid, *795*
Brigand, class of tug, 744
Briggs, Maj. Gen. H. R., D.S.O., *753*
**Britain, Battle of,** and day-bombing, 214
— —memorial service, Trinidad, *747*
British Empire, native troops' prowess, 675
British Honduras, loggers from, 631
**British Overseas Airways Corporation,** *362*
— — — — —stewardesses, *514*
British Restaurants, Hammerton on, 639
Broad, Capt. H. S., test pilot, *471*
Bromet, Air V/m G. R., *541*
Bromage, Lieut. J. H., in *Sahib*, 665
**Brontë,** Nelson's property at, 171
—refugees return, *256*
Bronzey, carrier-pigeon, 334
**Brooke, Gen. Sir Alan,** in Algiers, *80*
— —and " gun-how," 296
— —at Quebec Conference, *233*
— —at Teheran, *496*
— —an Ulsterman, 650
— —in warship, *79*
Brooke, Rupert, poem, 44
Brooks, Air V/M G. E., *472*
Brookwood, war cemetery at, 748
Brown, Second Off. C. W. A., G.M., 534
Brown, David, on Italy, 627
Brown, Dickson, 761
Brown, Col, E., in Solomons, *502*
Brown, Rt. Hon. Ernest, on birth rate, 246
— —Chancellor of Duchy, 438
— —and farm workers' cottages, *258*
— —housing scheme, 311
Brown, Lieut.-Cdr. F. D., R.N., in *Tanatside*, 392
Brown, Lt. G., R.N.V.R., in Sicilian landing, 158
" Browned off," 223
**Browning, Robert,** on Aegean Isls., 415
— —and Italy, 575
Broz, Josif : *see* Tito, Marshal
Brunhart, Sgt. Joseph, 730
Brush, of fox, bell-clapper, *393*
**Bryansk,** railway junction, 238
—Russians take, *309*
Bryant, Cdr. Ben, submarine officer, 616
Bryce, Gnr. J. G., 77, 125
**Bucharest,** feeling in, 686
—from Foggia, *330*
Buckingham Palace, R. Australian Air Force at, *578*
Buckley, Christopher, at Cassino, 739
— —in Tunis, 28
**Budapest,** Axis names in, 366
—from Foggia, *330*
—an " open city," 366
Budenny, Marshal, with Gen. Batov, *459*
Bug R., Russians reach and cross, 707
Bugler, of R. Marines, 174
Bukovsky, Maj. H., 441
**Bulgaria,** confusion in, 526
—mercantile marine, 390
—unrest in, *270*
Bullard, Sir Reader, 499
**Bulldozers,** on Makin Is., *533*
—in New Guinea, 323
Bullfrogs, by air, 362
Bulow, Lt. Otto von, and *Ranger*, 678
Buna, Japanese land at, 323
Buono Riposo, defence of, 688
Buoys, of boom-defence, *648*
Burgar, Flt. Sgt. Reginald, *312*
**Burma,** airborne troops in, 732
— air reinforcements for, 284
—Allies fail in Arakan, *3*
—Arakan fighting, 634
—campaign in, maps, *773*
—Chindits in, *46*, *48-49*
—conditions in, *751-54*
—fighting in, *464-65*
—Force Viper in, *630*
—14th Army in, *683*
—How we stand in, *750*
—Japanese prisoners in, *762*
—jeeps in, 300
—monsoon effects, 118
—new road from India, *50*
—operations in (Mar. 1944) 707, *708*
—R.A.F. in, *444*
—reconquest planned, 556, *557*
—road-making in, *791*
—R. Marines in, 174
—troops' entertainment in, 566
Burma Road, steps to reopen, 556
Burnett, Gunner, of Maritime Regt., 537-38
**Burnett, Vice-Adm. R. L.,** *Belfast* his flagship, 650
— —*Milne* his flagship, *583*
— —and *Scharnhorst*, 518, 519
Burns, Sir Allan, and bomber week, *322*
Burns, Lt.-Gen. E. L. M., *707*
Burns, Chief Officer R. V., G.M., *254*
**Buses,** blitz plaques, 95
—Utility, London, *674*
Bushido, Pernikoff on, *595*
Bustler, H.M. Tug, 744
Butaritari Beach, U.S. land on, *533*
Buxton, Capt. Sam, 362
" Buzzards," spotter planes, *598*
Byelaya Tserkov, Russians take, 547
**Byelgorod,** fighting at, *187*
—railway junction, 238
—Russian break-through at, 194
—Russians retake, 163
Bykova, O., woman sniper, *420*
Bywater, Hector, on Truk, 646

## C

Cabbage, dehydrated, *386*
**Cable,** electric, women repair, *354*
—Navy salvages, *648*
—submarine, war maintenance, *302*
Cable & Wireless, Ltd., in Ascension Is., *682*
Cadet-linesmen, of R.C.S., *437*
Cadogan, Sir A., at Cairo Conference, *476*
Caesar, Julius, used smoke screen, 654
Cagliari, capital of Sardinia, *8*
**Caio Duilio** (ship), ? for Russia, 710
— —at Taranto, 168
Cairns, J. R., Mayor of Dover, 534
**Cairo,** Allied Conference at, *476*
—United Nations' Day in, *121*
**Cairo Conference,** *498*, *499*
— —Atlantic battle and, 483
— —Churchill on way to, *481*, *495*
— —and Japan, 454
Caissons, for ammunition, 494
**Calabria,** Canadians enter, 289
—description, 255
—mountain village in, *304*
Calabrian Peninsula, invasion target, 73
Calcutta, famine deaths, 429
Caldecote, Lord, 348
Calder, Capt., R.N., at St. Vincent, 486
Caldwell, Wing-Cdr. Clive R., *446*
Calves, price for, 287
Calvi, Citadel of, *344*
**Cameron, Lt. D., R.N.R.,** submarine commander, *327*
— —wins V.C., 649
Cameron Highlanders, Queen's Own, 410
**Camino, Monte,** Clifford at, 505
— —road to, *542*
— —Vasiliev at, *483*
**Camouflage,** for Bofors gun, *783*
—for *Breconshire*, *762*
—German skill in, 620
—for Germans, Russia, *549*
—for Japanese steamer, *444*, *634*
—for map-producing units, 558
—for N. Zealander, Solomons, *502*
—personal, in invasion, *146*
—for " Recce," *460*
—for Russian guns, *589*
—for 75mm. guns, *676*
—snow, for Russian tanks, *693*
—white, at Cassino, *644*
— —for Russians, *613*
**Camouflage Cloak,** of Russian horseman, *548*
Camouflage Netting, women make, 634, *635*
Campbell, Cpl., piper, Cameron Highlanders, *39*
Campbell, Section Officer A. E., G.M., 534
Campbell, Maj. Lorne M., V.C., *123*
Campbell, Sir Ronald, and Italy's surrender, 265
Campbell-Bannerman, Rt. Hon. Sir Henry, 255
Campochiaro, Canadians in, *424*
**Canada,** boys in, 671
—builds Lancasters, *312*
—dehydrated cabbage from, *386*
Canadian Mounted Police, Churchill with, *232*
**Canadians,** airborne, invasion practice, *637*
—in Azores, *541*
—enter Calabria, *289*
—in Campochiaro, *424*
—in French train, story, 238
—in Italy, *260*
—and Nettuno landing, *581*
—in Ortona, *516*, 537
—praise R. Marines, 174
—as prisoners, Ortona, 569
—rebuild Merstham Church, *91*
—in Sicilian invasion, 156-57
—in Sicily, 162, 163, 165, *166*, *178*
Canadian Seaforth Highlanders, war graves, *749*
Canals, German, use, *430*
**Canberra H.M.A.S.,** *Shropshire* replaces, 264
— —sinks *Coburg*, 422
**Cannon,** of Mosquito, *620*
—of Seafire, *12*
Canoes, outrigger, supplies by, *714*
**Canteens,** mobile, in Burma, 556, *557*
— —from W. Indies, *661*
Cant. Z501, at Preveza, *236*
Cape-Cairo Road, 790
Cape Gloucester, U.S. land at, 601, *602*
Capetan, of Greek guerillas, 281-82
Capital Ships, and air attack, 348
" Captain " Class, of frigate, 486
Capua, the Cathedral, *305*
Carabinieri, Germans and, 324
Carbine, Automatic, *548*
Carbon, for searchlights, *610*
Cards, for French airmen, *308*
Careless Talk, Hammerton on, 95
Carlisle, H.M.S., off Crete, 61
Carol's Dyke, in Rumania, 186
Carr, Henry, paintings, *243*, *719*
Carr, Sub. Lt. R. G., R.N., *60*
Carrots, for canning, *386*
Carter, W/O H., in " G for Georgie," *473*
Carter, Chief Stoker J. R., D.S.M., *696*
**Carthage,** Churchill at, *82*
—thanksgiving service in, *36*
Carthage (ancient kingdom) and Sicily, 171
Cartographers, Army, work *558*
Carving (of meat), by A.T.S., *290*
Casabianca (submarine) off Corsica, 294
**Casablanca,** jeeps at, *663*
—Spirfire transport to, *606*
Casey, Rt. Hon. R. G., at Cairo Conference, *476*
— —in Lebanon, 469
**Cassibile,** Sherman tanks in, *167*
**Cassino,** Allies at, 644
—Allies reach, 389
—bombardment of, *612*
—bomber failure at, 764
—fighting for, *709*, *739*
—monastery at, *653*, *655*, 739
— N.Z. patrol in, *769*
—Red Cross flag at, *755*
—scenes in, *784*
Castel Benito, planes salvaged from, *14*
Castel di Sangro, *424*
Castellano, Gen., negotiations, 265
**Castellorizo,** Allies occupy, 294
—sortie against, 148
Castiglione, British take, *491*
**Casualties, civilian,** and war graves, 748
—**German,** in Russia, 707
— —Taman Peninsula, 420
— —in *Tirpitz*, 742
—**Japanese,** at Attu, 53
—**U.S.,** Gilbert Islands, 454
**Cat,** as destroyer's mascot, *393*
—rescued, Dover, *535*
—scarcity, Hammerton on, *767*
Catafighter Unit, successes, 54
Catalina III, performance, *542*
Catalinas, at Spitzbergen, 315
**Catania,** Allied advance on, *130*, *208-09*
—Allies take, *240-41*
—chaos in, *220*
—8th Army takes, *164*, 167
—the harbour, *9*
—history, 171
—mopping up in, *220*
—naval bombardment, *201*
—pre-war view, *172*
—surrender, *198*
Catapults, Hurricanes by, on ships, *11*
Catenanuova, British advance on, *242*
Catherine the Great, 622
**Catroux, Gen. Georges,** in Algiers, *440*
— —and Lebanon, *469*
Cattle, ignore guns, *375*
**Caucasus,** guerillas in, *332*
—Northern, Russian victories in, *432-33*
—Russian bomber squadron in, *140*
Cava, Sherman tanks near, *325*
Cavalry, British, horses for, *449*
Cavalryman, Russian, *548*
**Caves,** destroyer in, 392
—natural, in Atlantic Wall, *20*
C.E.M.A., facts about, 566
Cemeteries, for war casualties, *45*
Census, taking, Jamaica, *661*
Centaur Tank, *738*
Central Pool of Artists, 566
Centurion, H.M.S., at Tinian, 646
**Centuripe,** Allies in, *239*
—78th Div. at, *196*, *199*
Ceylon, Civil Defence in, *428*
—Adm. Mountbatten in, *774*
—war effort, *788*, *789*
Chaddock, Pte. J. O., in Sicily, *410*
Chain of Fire Control, 456
Chalker, Signalman, resource, 436
Chamberlain, Rt. Hon. Austen and Neville, 115
**Chamberlain, Rt. Hon. Neville,** and F.A.A., 54
— —Mussolini hoodwinks, 115
— —and Rumanian oil, 186
Chambers, F./O. H. W., D.F.C., *318*
Chamier-Glyszinski, Gen. von, death, 398
Chamisso, Adelbert von, 398
Chandos, fishing trawler, 680
Chang Chu-Chung, Gen., *117*
Changteh, China retakes, 664
Chaplain, Canadian, *749*
Charger, U.S.S., 10
Charles II, and R. Marines, *641*
Charles XII (Sweden), used smoke, 654
Charlottesville, Va, Amgot trains in, 180
Chaser, H.M.S., 486
Chatfield, Lord, 348
Chaung Fa Kwei, Chinese general, 268
Cheatle, Sir L., 351
Cheesman, Miss L. E., 323
Chekka Bypass, 790
Chelmsford Rotary Club, 681
**Cherbourg,** British sack (1758), 73
—as raider base, 422
Cherkasy, Russian bridgehead at, 451
Chernigov, bridges blown up at, *333*
" Cherry Ripe " : *see* Centuripe
Chervonaya Ukraina (ship), 710
Chesterton, G. K., on Christianity, 767
Chetniks, and partisans, 342
Chiang, Mme., at Cairo Conference, *476*, *498*, 499
**Chiang, Kai-Shek,** Generalissimo, *463*
— —army reforms, 116
— —at Cairo Conference, *498*, 499
— —with Chinese president, *117*
Chicago, flag for London, *482*
Chichagof Harbour, Attu, 10, 53
Children, Sicilian, Tommy and, *181*
Chilliawack, H.M.C.S., and *Woodpecker*, 744
**China,** air support for, 22
—floods in, *117*
—Japanese drive halted, 35
—occupied territory, *116*
—pilots, in U.S.A., *35*
—retakes Changteh, 664
—7th year of war, 116, *268*
—U.S. help for, *466*
**Chindits,** story of, 46, 47, *48-49*
—war correspondents with, *83*
—Wingate's successor, 772
**Chindwin, R.,** Chindits cross, 46, *49*
— —Viper Force at, *630*
Chinese, in Burma, *683*
Chipchase Raft, *11*
Cholera, in Honan, 116
Christian X, of Denmark, 248
Chrome, Cyprus produces, 148
Chumachenko, Capt., at Kiev, 441
Church, dynamited, Italy, *389*
Churchill, H.M.S., attacks island, 392
Churchill, Lord Randolph, 374
**Churchill, Mrs. Clementine,** with Arab princes, *482*
— —with Smuts, *322*
**Churchill, Rt. Hon. Winston Spencer,** and air power, 54
— —Arab sword for, *482*
— —on Azores' bases, 705
— —and Basic English, 735
— —on battle of Salerno, 314, 330
— —Begbie on, 351
— —on bombing raids, 701
— —at Cairo Conference, *476*, *499*
— —Gen. Chiang meets, 463, *476*
— —and Cyprus' strength, 148
— —demands more labour, 311
— —on future plans, 22
— —gas threat, 22
— —and Government's coal policy, 374
— —and Home Guard, 26, 211
— —to Italian people, 149
— — —results, 115
— —and Italian prospects, 182
— —on Kingsley Wood, 311
— —King's message to, 3
— —on little ships, 501
— —at Malta, *481*, *495*
— —and Naval Air Service, 86
— —on new guns, 247
— —in N. Africa, *80-81*, *82*
— —on N. African successes, 700
— —Ottawa portrait, *275*
— —at Quebec Conference, *232-33*

**Churchill** (*cont.*)
——on Reconstruction Ministry, 438
——with Sherman tanks, 738
——on Sikorski, 98
——on sinking of *Scharnhorst*, 519
——69th birthday, 497, 499
——with Smuts, 322
——speeches, Fyfe on, 275
——and strategic bombing, 67
——in Teheran, 495-96
——3rd visit to U.S.A., 65, 79
——on U-boat campaign, 10, 13
———killings, 74
——and U-boats, joint declaration, 615
———statement, 107, 200
——on Ulster, 650
——on war in Russia, 34
**Churchill Tanks,** first action, 442
——mechanism, 567
Church Parade, Carthage, 36
Ciano, Count Galeazzo, 115
**Cigarettes,** ends thrown away, 127
—for Italian prisoners, 166
—for Kachins, 800
—Montgomery distributes, 489
—for R. Engineers, Italy, 259
—for Services, 63
Civil Constructional Corps, in Australia, 584, 585
**Civil Defence,** British, debate on, 122
———help with harvest, 218
———and Home Guard, 26
———with mobile crane, 706
———proposed reduction, 438
——in Ceylon, 428
Civilians, war graves, 44, 748
Civil Servants, in Holland, 447
**Clark, Gen. Mark,** 377
——commands 5th Army, 388
——on Fighting French, 555
——with King, N. Africa, 67
——at Salerno, 293, 314
——uses jeep, 300
Clarke, Capt. C. P., R.N., in Biscay battle, 532
Clarke, Apprentice D.O., G.C., 254
Clarke, Lt.W. A. Sandys, V.C., 123
Clausewitz, Karl von, 371
" Clerkess," Hammerton on, 287
**Clifford, Alexander,** on Monte Camino, 505
——in Pantelleria, 70
Clogs, for women workers, 610
Clothing for men, restrictions, 415
**Clothing Coupons,** Hammerton on, 607
——as present, 319
——statistics, 58
Cnossus, Lipari stone in, 171
**Coal,** British, lower production, 246
——by barge, 674
—in China, 116
**Coal-mines,** Hammerton on, 671
——training for, 246, 600
Coal Situation, Pike on, 374
Coalville, New Lount Colliery, 246
**Coastal Command,** and anti-U-boat compaign, 13, 202, 486, 615
——in Azores, 541
——Beaufighters with, 64, 713
——and Biscay battle, 532
——co operation with Navy, 54
——Halifax sinks U-boat, 107
——ice patrol, 317
——origin, 86
——planes inspected, 732
——and U-boats, 263, 647
——Ulster and, 650
Coastal Defence Batteries, of H.G., 26
Coastguard, flying ambulance saves, 84
Coastguard Service, 234
Cobley, F/O P. C., D.F.C., 318
Coburg (raider) sunk, 422
Cochran, Col. P. G., 772
Coconut Milk, at Bougainville, 592
Coconut Oil, from Ceylon, 788
Coffin, Hayden, 19
Cohen, Sgt., Lampedusa surrenders to, 70, 92
Cohen, W/Cdr. L., D.S.O., D.F.C., etc., 638
**Coldstream Guards,** in Lampedusa, 103
——at Sbiba, 442
Cole, Leslie, paintings, 720-21
Colijn, Dr., house demolished, 340
Collins, Capt. J. A., in *Shropshire*, 264
Colmans, Lt. L., R.N.R., 744
**Colombo,** imperfect base, 230
—Singapore refugees at, 411
Colonies Exhibition, in London, 578
Columbite, Nigerian product, 587
**Combined Operations,** landing exercises, 111-14
——new chief, 415
——water ambulance, 482
" Combined Operations, 1940-42," 31
**Combine Harvester,** in use, 250
——at Windsor, 219
Comet Plane, Mosquito's forerunner, 90
**Commandos,** Allied, at Ajaccio 376
—and Home Guard, 26
—R. Marines as, 174, 628
—Servicing, of R.A.F., 210
Common Cold, Hammerton on, 479
**Communications,** on Karelian Front, 564
—R.C.S. and, 436, 437
Conca Casale, Allied attack on, 517
**Coningham, Air Marshal Sir Arthur,** with Alexander and Anderson, 32
——at Salerno, 293
——with targets, 225
——in Tunis, 5
Conrad, Joseph, 508
Conscience Money, 63
**Conscription,** British, Labour opposes, 211
—in Switzerland, 718
Constanza, Cyprus and, 148
Constellation, transport plane, 716, 717
Consultative Assembly of France, 440
Conte di Cavour (ship), 294
Contoleon, Col., on winter campaigns, 342
**Control-room,** of anti-U-boat campaign, 13
——A.R.P., Dover, 534
**Control Tower,** British, 765
——of R.A.A.F., 446
Convalescence, in Algiers, 440
Convocation of Canterbury, 58
**Convoys, Allied,** frigates escort, 658
——glider bombs on, 602
——at Murmansk, 106
——coastal, attacks on, 390
——U-boats fear defence, 615
—**Axis** air, destruction, 72
—**British,** eternal watch, 352
——for Malta, Marines and, 174
——stronger escorts, 10
Convoy System, and surface raiders, 422
Cookery, Home Guard learn, 798
Cookhouse Fatigue, for A.C.F., 407
Cooks, Army, routine, 415
**Cooper, Rt. Hon. A. Duff,** on Italian ruins, 172
——on Mussolini, 7
——new appointment, 438
**Cooper, Keith,** on R.O.C., 758
——on test pilots, 470
Co-operation, of Services, Gwynn on, 355
Coote, L/Bdr. E. G., 77
**Copenhagen,** German entry, 282
—riots in, 248
—ruins of Forum Hall, 283
**Copra,** in Ceylon, 788
—Fiji exports, 714
**Coral Sea,** air battle, 54, 323, 348
———Johnston on, 659
Cordite, weather effects, 456
Cormorant II, H.M.S., Gibraltar, 679
Corn, Germans preserve, Russia, 204
Cornwall, H.M.S., 422
Cornwall, Capt. C. J. B., of *Empire Brutus*, 474
" Corpse that Walked, The," 569
Corruption, in Japan, 595
**Corsairs,** with F.A.A., 733, 742
—and *Tirpitz*, 794
**Corsica,** Fighting French in, 376
—Germans evacuate, 294
—Goumiers in, 404, 405
—Hammerton on, 319
—liberation, 344
Corvo, Island, Azores, 361
Coryza, the common cold, 479
**Cos,** Allies occupy, 291, 294
—Germans retake, 468
—Greek theatre, 68
—loss, Hammerton on, 415
—McMurtrie on, 422
—soldier's escape from, 377
**Cossacks,** modern style, 244
—at Peterhof, 623
—on Southern Front, 34
—women in Krymskaya, 3
Costa, Capt. Santos, with Salazar, 467
Costa del Ambra, Canadians land at, 156
Cotentin Peninsula, 73
Cotrone, Navy bombards, 168
**Cottages,** for farm-workers, 311
—at Hildenborough, 258
Cotterell, Major Anthony, " R.A.M.C.," 755
Coty, M., a Corsican, 319
Counter-attacks, German use, 259
County Cadet Committees, and A.C.F., 406
Coventry, raid on, comparisons, 764
Coventry, W/Cdr. H. R., D.F.C., 318
**Cowie, Donald,** on Allied guns, 296
——on Amgot, 180
——on Ammunition men, 494
——on Japanese Pacific bases, 590
——on railways' importance, 238
Cranborne, Lord, Sec. for Dominions, 311
Crane, Mobile, for Civil Defence, 706
Crater, filling in, Leningrad, 394
Crawford, Driver R. J., with Eighth Army, 723
Cremation, for German casualties, 44
Crerar, Air Commodore Finlay, and R.O.C., 758, 759
Crerar, Lt.-Gen. H. D. G., Canadian C.-in-C., 707
Cresswell, Capt. A. J. Baker, D.S.O., R.N., 203
Cretans, trade with Sicily, 171
**Crete,** Allied air weakness in, 54
—evacuation, air power and, 787
——importance, 259
——technique, 227
—fall of, and Cyprus, 148
—Marines in, 628
—villages destroyed in, 450
Cricket, future of, 191
**Crimea,** evacuation, 771, 774
—last battle for, 778
—Russians isolate, 387
Cripps, Rt. Hon. Sir E. Stafford, 604
Croatia, unrest in, 340
Croats, in Yugoslavia, 524
Croce, Benedetto, 275
Croft, Lord, on Franco, 339
" Crossing the Line ", in troopship, 553
Crossland Waistcoat, 11
**Cruisers,** British, gunnery in, 456
——officers watch air-attack, 271
——off Italy, 614
——tea for look-out, 272
—Japanese losses, 230
—no need of seaplanes, 486
" Crusader, The," 543
Cryer, Ldg. Telegraphist G., D.S.M., 423
Cuirassiers, " Infantry Officer " on, 147
Cundall, Charles, painting, 719
Cunningham, Lt.-Gen. Sir Alan, in N. Ireland, 651
**Cunningham, Adm. Sir A. B.,** in Algiers, 81
——greets King, 67
——Italy and, 40
——King's message to, 262
——in Mediterranean, 168
——on our air weakness, 266
Cunningham, Pte. George, in Ortona, 570
**Cunningham, Vice Adm. Sir John H. D.,** 95
——in Anzio, 612
——visits Ankara, 73
Curaçao, oil refineries in, 408
Curry, Sgt., of A.F.P.U., 278
**Curtin, Rt. Hon. John,** and Allied Works Council, 584
——and Australia's safety, 67
Curtis Caravan, transport plane, 716
Cyclopes, in Sicily, 171
Cyclorama, in bomber training, 694, 695
**Cyprus,** air base, 266
—invasion preparations in, 73
—and Rhodes, 422
—strategic importance, 148
Cyprus Regiment, record, 148
**Cyrenaica,** Amgot in, 180
—British administer, 7
—postal service resumed, 127
Cyrillic Alphabet, strike about, 270
**Czechoslovakia,** anniversary celebrations, 418
—dissension in, 383
—Hungary and, 366
—Russians reach, 741
Czech-Soviet Mutual Aid Pact, 522


## D


Dakota Planes, tow gliders, 152
D'Albiac, Air V/m J. H., 86
Dallaway, Harry, basket-maker, 226
Dalmatia, strategic importance, 342, 343
**Dalton, Dr. Hugh,** and new ration books, 58
——on Ulster, 650
Daly, Ldg. Seaman R., 570
Damian, secret society, 270
Danes, with Merchant Navy, 78
Danilova, Cpl. Klavdia, 364
Danish Free Corps, and anti-Nazi riots, 248
Darlan, Adm. Jean François, 243
Darley Dale, yew tree at, 738
Davies, Pte. Stanley, in Sicily, 228
Day, Lt. P. A. C., R.N., 60
Daylight Bombing, Allied increase, 214
Dead, German, in Russia, 355, 613
Deafness, deprivation, 159
Deakin, Lt. Col. F. W. D., 698
Deane, Maj.-Gen. John R., 396
Death, Road of, Austin on, 345
Death Duties, and Home Guard, 255
Debra Marcos, S. D. F., at, 675
Decontamination Squad, of *S.R., 482
**De-Gaussing Apparatus,** Borstal makes, 374
——for British ships, 124
——success, 454
De Havilland, Capt. Geoffrey, 470
De Havilland, John, death, 470
**Dehydration,** of food, 246
—of fruits,W. Indies, 661
Delforce, Maj. F. G., D.S.O., 568
Delhi, New, Wavell at, 429
Demobilization, Hammerton on, 319
Democracy, Salazar's type, 467
Demolition, in Berlin, 561
Denmark, riots in, 248
Denny, Harold, " Behind Both Lines," 83
Dépêche Tunisienne, 29
Dépôt Ship, for destroyers, 393
**Depth-charges,** cripple U-boat, 74
——from *Kite*, 711
——from planes, 54, 107
——for U-boat, off Sicily, 201
——thrower, of British destroyer 13
Derbyshire Yeomanry, 2, 28
Derrick, Sgt. T. C., V.C., 707, 760
Desert Air Force, 249
" Desert Rats," in Tunis, 29
" Desert Victory," making of, 278, 279
Desk, salute for, 351
Desna, R., Russians cross, 309
Destroyer Escorts, in U.S.N., 486
**Destroyers,** British, life in, 392 393
—Italian, numbers, 136
——surrender, 337
—Japanese losses, 230
——sunk, 73
**Devers, Lt.-Gen. J. L.,** 159
——with H.A.C., 482
**Devonshire, H.M.S.,** mail carrier, 390
——sinks *Atlantis*, 422
Dewey, Thomas, 703
**De Witt, Robert,** on invasion preparations, 142
——on pigeon parachutes, 334
——on Walrus Amphibian, 108
Dexterous, H.M.S., tug, 744
D'Eyncourt, Capt. T., of A.F.P.U., 278
" D for Donald," 473
Dick, Commodore Royar, 338
Dickens, Lieut. P., in Little Ships, 328
**Dickson, Harriman,** on Army Cartographers, 558
——on U-boat war, 13
**Dieppe,** raid on, Marines in, 174
——news by pigeon, 334
——smoke screens in, 654
Dietl, Gen., Finland and, 684
Diettmar, Gen., on defensive policy, 34
**Dilke, Alexander,** on Allied invasion craft, 110
——on battlefield salvage, 52
——on monitors off Italy, 488
——on smoke screens, 654
——on war graves, 748
**Dill, F/M. Sir John,** at Teheran, 496
——an Ulsterman, 650
Dinapur, 14th Army at, 750
**Dinghies,** rubber, for Chindits, 48
——drill with, 785
——Germans captured from, 41
———escape in, 10, 741
——radio apparatus from, 52
——for Recce Corps, 461
——for Red Army, 307
——self-inflating, 235
——for U-boat survivors, 263
——Walruses carry, 108
Dionysius, K. of Syracuse, 171
Diplomats, Russian, dress, 383
Dishonesty, increase in, 575
**Dispatch Riders,** Allied, Battipaglia, 299
——of R.C.S., 436
——Turkish, 529
District Entertainment Officer 566
Divorce, Hammerton on, 671
**Dnepropetrovsk,** 397
—bridge destroyed, 387
—Malinovsky at, 397
—Russians take, 309
**Dnieper, R.,** fighting in bend, 515
——German danger in bend, 419
———retreat to, 291
———tenacity on, 547
——Kremenchug on, 365
——Red Army reaches, 309
——Russians cross, 387
**Dniester R.,** Russians cross, 707, 739
——Tighina Bridge over, 734
Dobbie, Lt.-Gen., Sir William, 578
Docks, of Tunis, bombed, 5
**Dodecanese Islands,** 68
——Allied threat to, 7
——Allies occupy, 294
——refugees from, 492
**Doenitz, Gross-Admiral Karl,** with sea-scouts, 406
——son killed, 678
——and U-boat war, 10
——unhappy situation, 105
Doerzer, Gen., with Goering, 398
Dog-fight, Spitfire and M E 109, 215
**Dogs,** British, war and, 575
—German police, Anzio, 690
—with Italian prisoners, 162
—as mascots, 312, 661, 710
Donbas, Russians retake, 276
Donno, Rfn. G., M.M., 59
**Doolittle, Maj.-Gen. James,** bombs Tokyo, 154, 155
——and Pacific air war, 636
Dorian Greeks, found Syracuse, 171
Dornoch, H.M.S., 582
Dorsetshire, H.M.S., 422
Dortmund, record raid on, 22
Douhet, Gen., air theory, 214
Dove, Sub. Lieut. R. G., R.N.V.R., 775
Dover, front-line town, 534, 535
Dowding, Air C/m Sir Hugh, 54
Dowling, Lt. Bob, R.A., 378
Downing, Lt. T. W., G.M., 568
Dragoons (25th), in Burma, 754
Drake, Francis, 654
Draughts (game), in pressure chamber, 521
Dressing Station, British, Sicily, 188
Drexler, Gestapo Chief, 270
Dreyfus, Mr. Louis, 499
Dring, William, portrait by, 18
Drogue, Swordfish draws, 12
Drottningholm (ship), 359
Druma, Cpl., B.E.M., 714
Drury, Capt., at Camperdown, 486
Dubourdieu, Commodore, off Lissa, 678
Dubrovnik (destroyer), 136
Dubrovnik (city), 343
**" Ducks," Amphibious,** 657
——as ambulances, 687
——off Anzio, 580
——motor barges, 301
——at Salerno, 314
——from U.S.A., 642
——in use, 301
Duco, Sgt. Lorrain, 666-67
Duff, Lt. A. A., R.N., of *Stubborn*, 730
Duff, Rev. A. Drummond, 400
Duguay-Trouin (ship), 40
Duisburg, importance, 430
**Duke of York, H.M.S.,** refitting, 551
——and *Scharnhorst*, 518, 519, 520, 570-71
Dukws : see " Ducks "
Dunbar-Nasmyth, Adm. Sir M., V.C., 11
**Dunkirk,** evacuation, causes of success, 150, 227
——lesson in air power, 540
——nurses' part at, 691
——railways and, 238
Dunn, Mr. James, at Moscow Conference, 396
Dunn, Pte. L., in Sicily, 178
Dunstan, P/O R. C., D.S.O., 638
Duquesne (ship), 40
Durham Light Infantry, 163
Dutch People, Hammerton on, 447
Dysentery, in Honan, 116
Dyspepsia, in Army, 755
Dzerzhinsky, guns made at, 296
Dzik, Polish submarine, 678


## E


Eaker, Lieut.-Gen. Ira C., 367
East Africa, war effort, 619

Easton, H.M.S., sinks U-boat, 74
Eastwood, Lt.-Gen. Sir Thomas Ralph, 735
Eben-Emael, taken by glider troops, 732
E-Boat Alley, Rescue Tugs in, 744
**E-boats,** fishing trawlers and, 680
— —little ships and, 328
— —M.-L. rams, *329*
— —renewed activity, 390
Echo, H.M.S., off Dodecanese, 422
Eckhardt, Tibor von, 366
Economic Warfare, battlefield information, 52
**Eden, Rt. Hon. Anthony,** in Algiers, *80, 82*
— —at Cairo Conference, *476, 499*
— —and Home Guard, 26, 211
— —at Moscow Conference, *396*
— —at Quebec Conference, *232*
Eder R., dam bombed, 3, 22, *24, 25*
**Education,** in Naples, *736*
—in Stalingrad, *484*
Egerton, Col. F. C. C., on Salazar, 467
**Egypt,** ammunition men save, 494
—Greek refugees in, *492*
—Italians invade, Hitler and, 259
—United Nations Day in, *121*
**Eighth Army,** British troops in, 483
— —at Cassino, *644*
— —in Catania, *240-41*
— —cooperation, 355
— —Engineers with, *491*
— —invades Italy, 265
— —Italian advance, *291, 292, 356*
— —in Italy, *388*
— —Leese commands, 545, *554*
— —needs, 142
— —and Nettuno landing, *581*
— —New Zealanders with, *452-53*
— —occupies Foggia, 330
— —Poles with, *786*
— —progress, *483*
— —in Sicily, 130, *196, 197, 198, 224*
— — — —units, 163
— —takes Ortona, *516, 554*
— —transport to Italy, *298*
— —war graves, 749
**Eisenhower, Maj.-Gen. D. D.,** in Algiers, *81*
— —Allied C.-in-C., 515
— —on Axis prisoners, 1, 6
— —German name, 799
— —greets King, 67
— —and Italian armistice, 265
— —in Messina, *261*
— —Montgomery greets, *515*
— —N. African work, 243
— —and R. Navy, 169
Elaschuk, Sgt. John, 569
Electrician, woman, Stalingrad, *484*
Electric Welding, for pipeline, *76*
" Elementary Flying Training," 31
Elephants, with Chindits, 46, 49
Elizabeth, H.M. Queen, and Women's Institutes, 122
Ellis, Lt.-Col., on R.C.S. in Malta, 436
Elms, cutting down, Windsor, *290*
**Emden** (ship), at Gdynia, 327
—returns to Baltic, 550
Emelyantsev, Sergei, 441
Emeny, Stuart, with Chindits, *83*
Empire Brutus, S.S., 474
Empress Augusta Bay, U.S. Marines at, *592*
Empress of Russia, S.S., 359
Engineers, African, *322*
—E. African, training, *619*
—Royal : see Royal
—Russian, Kanyev, *613*
—U.S., make pontoon bridge, *357*
— —repair bridge, Italy, *293*
—women, repair cable, *354*
England, increased cultivation, *218*
See *also* Great Britain
England, John, on Switzerland, 718
Enna, strong-points near, *166*
Ensa, facts about, 566
Enterprise, H.M.S., in Biscay action, 518, *532*, 550
Epsom, camouflage netting made at, 634
Equipment, German abandoned, Kanyev, *613*
Erebus, H.M.S., monitor, 488
Eremenko, Gen., in Crimea, *778*
Ericsson, John, built *Monitor*, 488
**Eritrea,** British supervise, 7
—and Sudan, 675
Erskine-Hill, A. G., K.C., M.P., 703
Escapade, H.M.S., rescues U-boat crew, *105*
**Escort Aircraft-carriers,** increase, 486
— — —U.S., numbers, 582
Escorts, and U-boat war, 200, *203*, 615
Eskeshir, Air College at, *528*
**Essen,** bombing of, 572
—mass raids on, 182
**Etna, Mt.,** *172*
— —British guns at, *195*
— —in eruption, 171
Eugenie, Empress, and Fifth Column, 607
Eureka Boats, of U.S. Marines, 110
**Europe,** Occupied, scenes in, *450*
—Sicily and, *133*
—war in, Moscow Conference and, 396
**Evacuation,** from Berlin, 237
—military, essentials for, 227
—of Sicily, perils, 163
—of Sicilians, *149*
Evacuees, from Berlin, *562*
Evans, Major David, G.M., 52
Evans, Surg.-Lt. P., G.M., R.N.V.R., *696*
Evans, W. J., of Dover, 534
Evatt, Dr. H. V., 264
Evzones, Greek soldiers, *179*
Exeter, H.M.S., 650
Exodus, smoke screen in, 654
Expeditionary Force Institute, in Italy, *740*

## F

" Factory-busters," 702
Faithful, carrier pigeon, 334
Falls, Capt. Cyril, " Ordeal by Battle," 371
Famagusta, port, Cyprus, 148
**Famine,** in China, 116
—in India, Wavell and, 429
Fantasque, Le (ship), 294
Far East, British submarines in 582
Faria R., New Guinea, *715*
Farmhouse, as hospital, Italy, *785*
Farming, British development, 218
Farm Sunday, in Britain, 218
Farm Workers, cottages for, *258*
Farr, Walter, 220, *221*
Fascism, Italy repudiates, 162, 265
Fastov, German counter-attacks at, 451
Fawcett, Webster, 14
February, Hammerton on, 607
Feisal, Emir, in Downing St., *482*
Ferdinand, of Sicily, 171
Ferrier, Ldg. Signalman A., 775
Ferrington, Doreen, *382*
Ferro, Nurse M., R.R.C., *382*
Ferry, across Kerch Straits, *420*
Ferry Command, uniform, 316
Ferry Control, 298
Ferry Liaison Officer, 298
Fez, Spitfire over, *606*
Fiat CR 42, Italian fighter, 182
Fiduciary Issue, of notes, 374
Fieldcraft, for A.C.F., 406
Field Hospitals, by air, 716
Fielding, Major, on Salerno beaches, *314*
**Field-kitchen,** for gunners, Italy, *783*
— —for Home Guard, *798*
Field Radio, of 5th Army, 740
Field Surgical Unit, details, 755
Field-telephone, Allied, in Burma, *557*
Field-wireless, German, in Yugoslavia, *699*
**Fifth Army,** advance on Rome, *612, 644*
— —British troops with, 483
— —in Cassino, *709*
— —at Conca Casale, *517*
— —enters Naples, *324*
— —Fighting French with, *555, 581*
— —Italian advance, *291, 292, 293, 325, 356-57, 388*
— —lighter side, *740*
— —at Monte Camino, 505, *506, 542*
— —at Nettuno, *688-89*
— —Nettuno landing, 579, *580-81*
— —oil by pipe-line, *652*
— —in Pugliano, *341*
— —Recce with, *697*
— —at Salerno, *314*
— —takes Battipaglia, 299
— —wounded, Anzio, *768*
" Fifth Column," Hammerton on phrase, 607
**Fighter Command,** " Hairpin Squads," 14
— —origin, 86
— —and R.O.C., 758
— —sorties, figures, 284
**Fighters,** German strength, 572
—Italian, antiquity, 182
—modern power, 444
—Russian, overhauled, *432*
Fighter Squadron, French, in Russia, *308*
" Fighting Cocks," R.A.F. fighter squadron, *210*
Fighting France, desert army, *404, 405*
**Fighting French,** in Corsica, *376*
— —in Italy, *581*
— —Italian successes, *555*
— —Normandie squadron, *308*
— —in N. Africa, mystery, 243
— —Senegalese with, *663*
Fiji, war effort, *714*
Films, for Army training, 19
Finisterre Mts., New Guinea, *715*
**Finland,** Hammerton on, 607
—peace overtures, 684, *685*
Finschafen, Allies take, *323*
Fire Control Room, London Region, *706*
Fire Control Tower, of *Rodney*, *457*
Firefly, H.M. Rescue Tug, *615*
Fireguard, wheelbarrow pump for, *122*
Fires, causes, 127
Fireworks, in Moscow, *431*
Fisher, Adm. Lord, and monitors, 488
Fishing Fleet, Graydon on, *680, 681*
Fishing Tackle, scarcity, 319
Fiume, Germans and, 168
" Five Graves, Road of," 537
Flack, Lt., of A.F.P.U., *278*
Flack Chief P/O F. R., in *Sahib*, *665*
**Flag,** exchange, London, *482*
—of N.F.S., *354*
—Norwegian, refugees salute, *414*
—Polish, *418*
—R.A.F., in Trinidad, *747*
—Red Cross, Cassino, *755*
—of Red Guards, *645*
—signalling by, China, *466*
Flag Days, for sailors, 703
Flak, over Berlin, *701*
Flame-throwers, U.S., on Namur, 729
**Flares,** parachute, in German air defence, 316
—in Russia, *259*
—from Yu.2, 726, 727
Flax, Ulster cultivation, 650, *651*
Fleas, in Western Desert, 723
**Fleet Air Arm,** Barracudas of, *742*
— — —Cingalese recruits, *789*
— — —Corsairs of, *733*
— — —in Gibraltar, *679*
— — —gunners' training, *12*
— — —Navy and, 54, 150
— — —origin, 86
— — —R. Marines with, 174
— — —and Walrus Amphibian *108*
Fleetwood, John, on Dispatch Riders, 436
Fletcher, Flt./Sgt. Walrus story, 108
Fletcher, Sub.-Lt. Ronald, R.N.R., 744
Flies, in Western Desert, 723
Florence, the Palazzo Vecchio, *304-05*
Flour, free issue, Sicily, *181*
**Flying-boats,** Japanese, wrecked, *591*
— —as U-boat spotters, 13
Flyte, F/O P. R., story, 249
**Foggia,** the Cathedral, *305*
—fall of, and bombing-range, *330*
Fog Troopers, German, 654
**Food,** " in battledress," 246
—for bombed-out, Berlin, *559*
—for Britain, from Ulster, 650
—Chinese problem, 116
—decontamination, *386*
—for Norwegian refugees, *414*
Food Yeast, in W. Indies, 661
Fookes, Apprentice Colin, G. M., *254*
Forbin (ship), 40
Force Viper, in Burma, *630*
Ford, Wallace, on treatment of prisoners, 780
Forli, the Campanile, *304*
Formidable, H.M.S., Ulster built, 650
Forth, H.M.S., cheers *Stubborn*, *731*
Fort Monmouth (N. J.), 334
Fortress II, tail turret, *542*
**Fortresses,** achievement, 214, *316*
—and air supremacy, 2
—in Australia, *584*
—in Azores, *541*
—bomb Berlin, *701*
— —Gdynia, 327
— —Ruhr, *119*
— —Verona, *636*
—with bomb doors open, *765*
—controls explained, *765*
—crew saved, *235*
—in flight, *445*
—at Goose Bay, *88*
**Fortresses** *(cont.)*
—over Pantelleria, 70
—raids by, *367-70*
**Fortuné, Le** (ship), off Corsica, 294
—for Free French, 40
Foskett, L/Cpl. W., in Burma, *683*
Foster, 2nd Lt. J., in damaged Thunderbolt, *118*
**Fourteenth Army,** in Burma, 556, *557, 683*, 750
— —badge, *772*
— —relieves Kohima, *771*
Fowler, Maj. G. A., R.A.M.C., *212*
Fox Holes, in New Guinea, 323
Foxhound, H.M.S., *392, 393*
Frampton, Bandsman A., with mule-cart, *212*
**France,** anti-invasion exercises, *450*
—battle of, " Infantry Officer " on, 147
— —railways and, 238
—collapse, and Sudan, 675
—Italy declares war on, 7
—Turkey's treaty with, 526
France, Anatole, 607
Francis-Smith, P/O A., in *Breconshire*, 762
Franco, Gen. Francisco, 339
Franklyn, Lt.-Gen. Sir Harold E., 607
Franz Joseph II, Prince, of Liechtenstein, 729
Frascati, Villa Falconieri, *306*
**Fraser, Adm. Sir Bruce,** C.-in-C. Home Fleet, 327
— —coat-trailing expedition, 486
— —and *Scharnhorst*, 518, 519, 520, *543*
— —and *Tirpitz*, 742
— —visits Russia, 551
Frederick, the Great, and palace sentries, 351
Free French : see Fighting French
Free Greece, underground newspaper, 281
Freel, Ldg. Seaman J., *775*
Fremantle, Sir Francis, 246
French Expeditionary Corps, in Italy, *581*
**Freyberg, Lt.-Gen. Sir B. C., V.C.,** with 8th Army, 452
— —in flying ambulance, 84
Friedrichshafen, bombed, 182
**Frigates,** British, latest type, *658*
—Captain class, 486
Fromanteel, John, on airman's training, 521
Fröndenberg-Bosperde, floods at, *25*
Frontiers, of the future, 462
Fruit, A.T.S. bottle, *386*
Fry, Flt./Lt. R. H., *505*
**Funeral,** mock, Norway, *450*
—of Partisans, Belgrade, *525*
—U.S., Marshall Is., *748*
Furneaux, F/O William, escape from Singapore, *378*, 410
Future, The, frontiers of, 462
**Fyfe, Hamilton,** reviews :— Appeasement's Child, 339
— —Air Power and the Expanding Community, 787
— —Behind both Lines, 83
— —books about Italy, 627
— —" Bushido," 595
— —" An Eighth Army Soldier," 723
— —" The End in Africa," 403
— —" The End of the Beginning," 275
— —" Grey and Scarlet," 691
— —" The Home Guard of Britain, 211
— —" Infantry Officer," 147
— —" Italy from Within," 115
— —" The Little Ships," 501
— —Mackenzie's Roosevelt, 531
— —" New Guinea Diary," 659
— —" One Continent Redeemed," 243
— —" Ordeal of Battle," 371
— —" R.A.M.C.," 755
— —" The Red Army," 307
— —" Salazar, Rebuilder of Portugal," 467
— —" They Call it Pacific," 563
— —" Traveller from Tokyo," 435
— —" The Turning Tide," 19
— —" What About Germany ?" 51
— —" Wind of Freedom," 179
Fyfe, Lt. J. P., R.N., submarine's exploit 602,

## G

Gabes, welcomes 8th Army, 191
Gael, Mosquitoes raid, *764*
Gafencu, M., in Moscow, 686
Gafsa, train adventure at, 238
Gallabat, invasion entry, 675
Gallai-Hatchard, Flt. Lieut. D. N. 278
**Gallipoli,** evacuation triumph, 227
— R. Marines at, 628
Gallup Poll, and victory, 543
Gambia, H.M.N.Z.S., 615
**Gander, Marsland,** and Chindits, 46
— —at Leros, 442
Gardner, Lieut. A. G., R.N., 392
Gardner, Lieut. B. J., in Catania, *198*
**Garibaldi, Giuseppe,** curse of, 287
— —5th Army follows, 357
Garnham, Sgt., with A.F.P.U., 278
Garrison, Pte. John, 729
**Gas, Poison,** Churchill's threat, 22
— —and food, decontamination, *386*
— —test, on Southern Rly., *482*
**Gaulle, Gen. Charles de,** meets Giraud, *38*
— —Moorehead on, 403
— —and Normandie Squadron, 308
— —Royalists' view, 243
Gauntlet Bridge, Vietri, smashed, 345
Gayda, Virginio, 627
Gdynia, Fortresses bomb, 327
**Gela,** Allied landing at, 157
—counter-attacks at, 130
—Dorians found, 171
" General Chase," results, *263*
General Grant Tanks, in Burma, *754*
**Genoa,** Germans occupy, 265
—war memorial, *304*
George III, and R. Marines, 628
**George VI, H.M. King,** and A.C.F., 406
— —to Churchill, 3
— —and Dover Fire Brigade, 534
— —with Home Fleet, 272-73
— —with Lalahadur Thapa, V.C., *123*
— —and magnetic mine, *124*
— —message to Cunningham, 262
— —N. African tour, 67, 97, *100, 101*
— —to repatriated prisoners, 359
— —and Ruhr dams, *33*
— —and Stalingrad sword, *495, 499*
— —uses jeep, 300
— —visits " Woolworth Carrier," 104
George Cross, Malta's, replica in London, *578*
Georges Leygues (ship) *43*
**Germans,** plunder Italy, 115
—Russian retreat, *741*
—in Sicily, 162
**Germany,** artillery weakness, 296
—Balkan strength, 526
—blitz on, 122
—bombed city of, *373*
—bomber's return from, *87*
—bombs on, 284
—and Bulgaria, 270
—central reserves, 98
—citadel of, *206*
—Finland joins, 684
—no help for Italy, 40
—and Italian navy, 168
—and Italian surrender, 265
—railway difficulties, 662
—Swiss trade with, 718
Gervasi, Frank, on Cassino Monastery, *653*
**Gestapo,** in Bulgaria, 270
—in Denmark, 283
—Himmler and, *782*
—new orders for, 206
—Oslo arrests, 506-07
" G for Georgie," *473*
Ghale, Havildar Gaje, V.C., *760*
Ghurkas, in Burma, *708*
Gibbs, Flt. Sgt. A. P., D.F.M., 603
**Gibraltar,** capture, Marines at, 628
—F.A.A. at, *679*
**Gibson, Wing-Cdr., V.C.,** King with, *33*
— —and Ruhr dams, *24*
Gibson, Cpl. Chester, at Kwajalein, 729
Gilbert, W. S., 319
**Gilbert Islands,** air power and, 477
— —Allies land in, *474*
— —fighting in, *503*
— —U.S. land in, 454
— —U.S. retake, *591, 594*
Gillard, Frank, in Italy, 346
Gingell, Basil, 346
Gino Lisa Airfield, at Foggia, 330
Girasole, Yolanda, *212*
**Giraud, Gen. H. H.,** in Algiers, *440*
— —character, 243
— —Clark's message to, 555
— —inspects Goumiers, *405*
— —meets De Gaulle, *38*
— —Moorehead on, 403

**Girgenti,** Greek ruins at, 171, *173*
—sulphur mines at, 319
Girl Guides, in Malta, 148
Giuliani, Lt. Arthur, *186*
**Giulio Cesare** (ship), ? for Russia, 710
— —surrenders, *338*
— —at Taranto, 168
Giuseppe Miraglia, Italian seaplane carrier, 168
Glasgow, H.M.S., in Biscay action, 518, *532*, 550
Glasgow, Home Guard training school at, *27*
Gleaner, Frederick, in Liechtenstein, 729
Glider Bombs, Germans use, 602, *603*
**Gliders,** in air-train, 362
—British, and Sicilian invasion, 150, *152*, *154*
—use, Burma, 732
Glorious, H.M.S., *Scharnhorst* and, 518
Gloucester, H.R.H. Duke of, with minesweepers, *418*
**Gneisenau** (ship), commerce raider, 518
—at Gdynia, 327
—probably seaworthy, 105
—and *Rawalpindi*, 518
—reconstruction, 550
Gnôme-le-Rhône Factory, bombed, *702*
Gobeil, Sqdn.-Ldr. F. M., *152*, 362
Godefroy, Adm., joins Allies, *40*
**Goebbels, Dr., Josef,** air threats, 122
— —enforced silence, 206
— —propaganda in Switzerland, 718
**Goering, F.-M. Hermann,** in Berlin, *472*, *561*
— —on Berlin bombs, 559, 575
— —enforced silence, 206
— —as Hitler's successor, 782
— —inefficiency, 479
— —and the Junkers, 398
— —and N. Africa, 38
— —with officers, *398*
— —and Reich's immunity, 214
Gold Coast, bomber week in, *322*
Golden Arrow, mobile wireless unit, *437*, *728*
Golden Horn, *530*
Goldware, Maj. Joseph, 780
Golovko, Vice-Adm. Fraser visits, 551
**Gomel,** battle for, *355*
—Russians take, 451
Gona, air transport at, 716
Goncourt, De, brothers, 627
Gonnessa, *8*
Goodfellow, Lt., invents still, *11*
Goose Bay, air base in, *88*
Gordon, Lt. Quartermaster, R.A., in prison ship, 61
Gordon, Anthony, broadcast, 433
**Gorizia,** Italian cruiser, 168
—Germans hold, 294
Gornalunga R., bridge over, *207*
Gorrell, Henry, in Naples, 324
**Gort, F/M Viscount, V.C.,** Churchill with, Malta, *495*
— —decorates Nurse Ferro, *382*
— —King bestows bâton, 97
— —the King with, *101*
Gosling, Lt. Ronald, 77
Gotha, Messerschmitt factory bombed, *668*
**Goums,** in Ajaccio, *376*
—French African troops, *404*, *405*
Govorov, Gen., artillery expert, *589*
G.P.O., and submarine cables, 302
**Graf Zeppelin,** aircraft-carrier, a failure, 105
— —rumours about, 550
Graham, Flt. Lieut. G. D. of Mountain Service, *439*
Graham-White, Claude, 383
Grain, silos for, *770*
Granny-ships, cable ships, 302
Grant, Albert, and Leicester Sq., 607
Grant, Capt. H. T. W, R.C.N., 532
**Graves,** German, in Italy, *388*
— —unnamed, 44
—of Lt. Lord Lyell, *286*
Graves, Charles, on Home Guard, 211
Graves Registration Service, 748
Gray, Eric, and Col. Deakin, 698
**Graydon, John Allen,** on British submarines, *616*
— —on Coastguard Service, 234
— —on Dover, 534
— —on Fishing Fleet, 680
— —on flying ambulances, 84
— —on Recce, 460
— —on R. Marines, 174
**Graziani, Marshal Rodolfo,** invades Egypt, 259
— —Mussolini with, *627*
Grazzanise, Sherman tank at, *388*
**Great Britain,** aircraft production, 284
— —Air Defence of, new command, 758
— —Azores bases for, 360, *361*
— —Germany's invasion plans, 150
— —Home Front, 58, 122, 246, 311, 374, *438*
— —and invasion barges, 110
— —Italy declares war on, 7
— —transport in, *674*
— —Turkey's treaty with, 526
**Great War, First,** Italy in, 627
— — —U-boats sunk in, 200
— — —use of aircraft in, 86
**Greece,** Bulgars police, 270
—dissension in, 383
—evacuation, technique, 227
—Guerillas in, 281
—invasion of, Mackenzie on, 179
—Middle East and, 259
—R.A.F. over, *236*
Greeks, in Sicily, 171
Green, R. J., lectures to Coastguards, *234*
Green Howards, in Italy, *608*
Greenland, Danish seaman on, 78
Greenland, Lt. R. T. G., R.N.V.R., 775
Green Mountain, Ascension Is., *682*
Greg, Sir Robert, *498*
Grenades, Home Guards use, *27*
Grenadier Guards, at Nettuno, *688-89*
Grenadiers, German, in Russian retreat, *548*
Grenfell, Capt. Russell, R.N., 127
Gretton, Charles, on A.F.P.U., 278
Greyhound, H.M.S., sunk, 61
"Grid Iron," Naval manoeuvre, *203*
Griffiths, J., on birth-rate, 246
Grigg, Sir James, 671
Griggs, Lieut. G. P., R.N., "Destroyer at War," 31
Grimwood, Mrs. St. Clair, 447
Grinshaw, Capt. W. H., O.B.E., *254*
**Ground Crews,** N.Z., Guadalcanal, *597*
— —R.A.F., and Ruhr bombing, *151*
— —Russian, in Caucasus, *432*
Growler, H.M. Tug, *744*
Gruenther, Maj.-Gen., 377
Grundy, Rev. George, *409*
Grune, Philip, on U.S. manoeuvres, *666*
**Guadalcanal,** Allies take, *350*
—U.S. land at, 454
—Warhawks at, *597*
**Guam,** U.S. raids on, 646
—value, *590*
**Guards, The,** beat Retreat, Hyde Park, 226
— —Hammerton on, 639
Guderian, Gen., Hitler and, 398
**Guerillas,** Chinese, 116
—in Greece, 281
—Russian, in Caucasus, *332*
— —near Kiev, *459*
— —story of, *251*
—Yugoslav, *699*
— —women as, 609, *618*
Guerter, J. V., 44
**Gun Crews,** British, Catania welcomes, *241*
— —of escort aircraft-carrier, 42
— —Russian, Ukraine front, *397*
Gun-flash Board, *258*
"Gun-how," story, 296
**Gunners,** British, Italy, *781*, *783*
—of Churchill tanks, *567*
—Dutch naval A.A., *96*
—of F.A.A., training, *12*
—of Fortress *369*
—Home Guard, London barrage, 632
—R. Marines at, 174
Gunnery, Naval, technique, 456
**Guns, Allied,** camouflaged, *635*
— —at Cassino, *644*
— —in D.W.I., *408*
— —in New Guinea, 269
— —new types, 296, *297*
**—British,** at Anzio, *730*
— —4.5, in Italy, *292*
— — —in Sicily, *208*
— —5.5 howitzer, *247*
— —of monitors, *488*
— —naval, care, *457*
— —17-pdr., A.T.S. clean, *514*
— —75 mm., St. Angelo, *676*
— —25-pdrs., Sicily, *228*
— —in Sicily, *195*, *197*
—feeding the, *494*
**—Free French,** Italy, *688*
**—German,** multiple-rocket, *485*
**—Italian,** British use, *209*
— —dummy, *169*
**Guns** *(cont.)*
—Japanese dummy, *591*
— —naval, Tarawa, *594*
—new German, capture, 52
—of *Richelieu*, *504*
**—Russian,** on Neva, *434*
— —at Orel, *205*
— —on White Russian front, *741*
—of *Shropshire*, cleaning, *264*
**—U.S.** of mountain battery, *350*
— — —naval, at Rendova, *170*
**Gurkhas,** in Burma, 750
—with Chindits, 46
—roadmakers, *791*
—Wavell inspects, *772*
Gusev, M. Feodor, *447*
Gustav Line, Italy, Allies pierce, *581*
Gustavus Adolphus, 654
Guy's Hospital, grows belladonna, *290*
Guzzoni, Gen., in Sicily, *131*
Gwynn, Maj.-Gen. Sir Charles Battle Fronts, 2-3, 34-35, 66-67, 98-99, 130, 162-63, 194-95, 227, 259, 291, 323, 355, 387, 419, 451, 483, 515, 547, 579, 611, 643, 675, 771

## H

H.A.C., at Mansion House, *482*
Hackney, rubbish dump in, 31
Hackworth, Green, *396*
Hague, The, German destruction in, *340*
Haig, F/M. Earl, 86
Haimes, Pte. Wilfrid, 570
"Hairpin Squads," of R.A.F., 14
Halder, Col. Gen. Franz, 398
Half-track Vehicles, *676*
Halifax, Lord, and Mussolini, 115
**Halifax Bombers,** in Biscay battle, 532
— —bombs for *151*,
— —loaded up, *22*
— —new type, *86*
— —sink U-boat, *107*
— —start for Hamburg, *182*
— —and U-boat chase, 263
Hamburg, devastating raids on, 182, *190*
Hamilcar, invades Sicily, 171
Hamilton, Curtiss, 154
Hamilton, Thomas J., "Appeasement's Child," 339
Hammerton, Sir John, postscripts; 31, 63, 95, 127, 159, 191, 223, *255*, 287, 319, 351, 383, 415, 447, 479, 511, 543, 575, 607, 639, 671, 703, 767, 799
Hampshire Regt., 77
Handleman, Howard, in Kwajalein, 729
Harding, L/Sgt., with police dog, *690*
Harmer, Chief Officer E. H., G.M., 534
Harpe, La, in Bessarabia, 588
Harper, Lieut. Jim, 443
Harries, Acting Sq./Ldr. R.H., D.F.C., *318*
**Harriman, Averill,** at Cairo Conference, *476*
— —at Moscow Conference, *396*
**Harris, Air Chief-Marshal Sir Arthur,** and Bomber Command, 54
— — —bombing programme, 214
— — —and Ruhr dams, *24*, 430
Harrison, Ada, "Grey and Scarlet," 691
Harrison, Gnr. F. L., 77
**Harvest,** British, in E. Anglia, 250
— —help for, 58
— —magnitude, 438
— —triumph, *218*, *219*
Hatfield, Cpl. Eadie, B.E.M., *382*
Hats, from Leghorn, 447
Hawkins, Lieut. F. W., R.N., of *Woolston*, 392
Hawtrey, Charles, 671
Hay-stacks, dispersal, Hammerton on, 479
Headquarters, Montgomery's travelling, *158*
Health, Ministry of, 311
Hearse, on Road of Death, 346
**Heinkel III,** in Russia, *252*
—177, glider bombs from, 602, *603*
Heissmeyer, S.S. Obergruppenfuehrer, 782
Helicopters, for U-boat spotting, 10
Hellcats, and *Tirpitz*, 742
Helldivers, attack Rabaul, *604*
Helmets, Japanese, Chinese take *268*
Helmsdale, H.M.S., *658*
Helsinki, Russians raid, *685*
Henderson, Sir Nevile, flag on car, *510*
Henrichenburg, ship elevator at, 430
Henty-Creer, Lt. H., *327*
**Hermann Goering Division,** demoralisation, 29
— — —prisoners from, *162*
— — —in Sicily, 130, 410
Herring, Lt.-Gen. Sir Edmund, *323*
Hertfordshire, harvest in, *219*
Hesperus, H.M.S., rams U-boat, 392
**Hess, Rudolf,** and Adolf Hitler Canal, 430
— —German questions about, 570
— —R.O.C and, 758
Hichens, Lt.-Cmdr. R. P., in Little Ships, *328*
Hide, Mrs. Dorothy, B.E.M., *382*
**Highland Division,** its commander, *193*
— —no ammunition, 494
— —at victory parade, *39*
Hildenborough, new cottages, *258*
**Hill, Air-Marshal Sir R. M.,** *703*
— —head of Air Defence, 758
Himera, Carthaginians besiege, 171
Himmler, Heinrich, 686, *782*
Hindman, 2nd Lieut. Ruth, 633
Hippocrates in Cos, 415
**Hitler, Adolf,** on bombing prospects, 575
— —and command of sea, 40
— —and Egypt, 259
— —fear of British, 150
— —and Finland, 684
— —and German Badoglios, 398
— —and German railways, 662
— —German slogans about, 206
— —Himmler and, *782*
— —and Home Guard, 211
— —and Italian surrender, 265
— —and King Boris, *270*
— —plots against, 307
— —and Spanish Civil War, 339
— —theories about, 191
— —tours West wall, *51*
**Hitler Youth,** A.C.F. contrasted, 406
— —training, 19
"H.M.V." *Aberdeen's* dog, *710*
**Hoare, Sir Samuel,** and Italy's surrender, 265
— —in Spain, 339
Hoel, Dr., Rector of Oslo Univ., 506
Hoffman, Col. R. H., and war graves, 748
Hogben, Prof. Lancelot, 287
**Holidays,** British rush for, 246
—and travel, Hammerton on, 223
**Holland,** destruction in, *340*
—salvage work, 744
Holman, Gordon, "The Little Ships," *501*
Holt, Commodore R. V., in Azores, *541*
Homan, Paymaster Lieut. T. B., 519, 570
"Home and Beauty," 671
**Home Fleet,** George VI with, *272-73*
— —Northern sweep by, 327
Home Front, British, Pike on, 58, 122, 246, 311, 374, 438
**Home Guard,** A.A. gunners of, *632*
— —fourth birthday, *798*
— —Graves on, 211
— —legal status, 255
— —man rocket-guns, 706
— —Swedish, *756*
— —third birthday, 26, *27*
— —trains with Scots Guards, 93
— —in Turkey, *493*
Honan, famine and disease in, 116
Hongkong, escape from, *222*
Hooper, Sub.-Lt. A. C., R.N.R., 744
Hooper, Duncan, flight over Russia, 538
Hoover, Herbert, 531
Hopkins, Harry, 430
Hopkins, Capt. R. E., O.B.E., *254*
Hopkinson, Sgt., of A.F.P.U., *278*
Hop-picking, in Kent, *258*
Hordyk, Lt. Roel, 222
Hornet, U.S.S., and bombing of Tokyo, *154*, *155*
Horsa Gliders, for Sicily, *152*
**Horses,** for British cavalry, *449*
—of Don Cossacks, *244*
—for German transport, Russia, *741*
—killed by blast, 29
Horta, (Fayal) clipper base, *361*
Horthy, Adm. Nicholas, and Axis, *366*
Horthy, Stefan 366
**Horton, Adm. Sir Max K.,** on board *Philante*, *203*
— —and U-boat campaign, *13*
Horwood, Lt. A. G., V.C., 760
Hosfield, Geoffrey, *125*
**Hospitals,** British, in N. Africa, 691
—Dutch, demolished, *340*
—of Naples, Germans and, 324
—new Australian, 584, *585*
**Hospitals** *(cont.)*
—voluntary, Hammerton on, 735
(See *also* Field-Hospital)
Hospital ship, Germans sink, *633*
Hoste, Capt. William, R.N., 678
Hosyo, aircraft-carrier, 582
Hotel Porters, women as, 703
Hough, Lt. Col. C. S., *221*
House Naval Affairs Committee. 110
**Houses,** fortified, France, *20*
—numbering of, Japan, 435
Housing, plastics and, 543
Howie, Col. Robert, 300
**Howitzers,** British 4.5, Sicily, *197*
— —5.5, *247*
—Italian, British use, *197*
—U.S. 105 mm. in Italy, *356*
Hsien, Chinese city, *268*
H.T. Batteries, salvaged, 14
Huanuco-Pucallpa Road, 790, *791*
Hubbard, P/O Cook J. H., D.S.M., *474*
**Hudson, Rt. Hon. R. S.,** appeal for volunteers, 218
— —on harvest of 1943, 438
— —and Women's Institutes, 122
Hudsons, on ice patrol, *317*
Hughes Hallett, Capt. J., *518*, 520
Hull, raid on, 122
Hull, Cordell, at Moscow Conference, *396*
Hulls, L/Cpl. Lewis, with Paiforce, 346, *347*
**Hungary,** Germans occupy *707*, *734*
—Rumania and, 686
—situation in, *366*
Hunter's club, in Turkey, *493*
Hunton, Lt.-Gen. Sir Thos., *629*
Huon Gulf, coastline of, *323*
Huon Peninsula, Allies clear, 454
Hurlingham, food decontamination at, *386*
Hurren, Lieut.-Cdr. B. J., "Eastern Med." 266
**Hurricane, II D,** 542
**Hurricanes,** over Cyprus, *148*
—in the desert, 266
—for Merchant Navy, *11*
—as tank busters, 620
—for Turkish Air Force, 526
"Hush Operation" (1917), 110
**Hussars (4th),** in Cyprus, 148
—(*11th*), in Tunisia, 28
Hustvedt, Rear-Adm. Olaf. M., 486
Hutchinson, Capt. J. S., R.A.M.C *212*
Hyde Park, Retreat in, 226
Hymn of Hate, 511

## I

Ibadan, war council at, *586*
Ice-chamber, tests in, *574*
Iceland, nurses in, 691
Ice Pack Patrol, *317*
Identity Cards, checking, *738*
Identity Disk, German, 44
**Illustrious, H.M.S.,** on fire, *413*
— —and Taranto, 266
**Imperial Defence Committee of** (1936), 348
— — —and Capital Ships, 54
Imperialist, H.M. Trawler, *681*
Imperial War Graves Commission, 748
**Impero** (ship) Germans hold, 294
—at Spezia, 168
Imphal, Japanese and, *750*, 773
**Incendiary Bombs,** for Ruhr, *151*
— —U.S., for Tarawa, *475*
Independent Air Force, 86
**India,** air-communication with, 284
—cost of living in, 63
—famine in, Wavell and, 429
—Japanese invade, 750
—new road to Burma, *50*
—railway importance, 238
—troops' entertainment in, 566
**Indian Ocean,** Japanese strength in, 230
— —surface raiders in, 422
— —U-boats in, 294
**Indians,** with 8th Army, 453
—escort prisoners, Italy, *489*
—with 14th Army, *683*
—in Italy, *513*
—and Montgomery, 723
Indo-China, U.S. Transport Command in, 716, *717*
Indomitable, H.M.S., Seafire of, *794*
**Industry,** British, wages, 122
—Chinese, development, 116
—Russian, development, 426, *427*
**Infantry,** British, enter Vizzini, 209
— —near Cassino, *581*
— —in Sicily, *132*, *134*, *135*, *220*
—Russian, in Kuban, *21*
—U.S., in Attu, *53*

Inglefield, H.M.S. sunk, 678
**Inniskilling Fusiliers, Royal,** at Centuripe, *199*, 239
— — —move up to Catenanuova, *242*
— — —from Ulster, 650
**Inonu, President Ismet,** Ataturk's successor, 527
— —at Cairo Conference, *499*
Inshore Squadron, off Libya, 488
Inskip, Sir Thomas, 412
Intelligence, British, and new weapons, 52
Intelligence Officer, British, in Cos, *291*
Interviews, press Hammerton on, 543
Intruder Squadrons, successes, *55*
**Invasion,** airborne, Allies practise, *637*
—Allied, craft for, *110*, *111-14*
— —Axis anxiety, 73
—bombing and, limitations, 67
—exercises against, France, *450*
Invasion Barges : see Landing-craft
Ionian Greeks, in Sicily, 171
Iowa, U.S.S., in commission, 40
**Iraq,** air power in, 266
—R.A.F. in (1922), 86
**Ireland, Northern,** road-making in, *791*
— —war effort, 650, *651*
Irish, workers in England, 575
Irish Fusiliers, Royal, 650
Irish Rifles, Royal, in France, *147*
Iron Ore, on British train, *674*
Irrawaddy R., R. Marines on, *174*
"Is He Popenjoy?" by Trollope, 383
Iskanderun, bombs unloaded at, *493*
**Ismay, Lt.-Gen. Sir Hastings,** at Moscow Conference, *396*
— —at Quebec Conference, 232
Istanbul, *530*
Italian Empire, lost, 7
Italians, mass surrender, *189*
**Italy,** air power struggle in, 284
—as Allied air base, *284*
—Allied air support in, 669
—Allies advance in, *291*, 292, *293*, *424*
— —land in, *260*
— — —Nixon's story, *281*
—ammunition supply in, *494*
—and Anglo-Egyptian Sudan, *675*
—battle-line, *356*, *483*
—British artillery in, *781*
— —horses in, *449*
— —monitors off, *488*
—campaign in, *388-89*
— — —Gwynn on, 483
— — —progress, *325*
—enters war, Sudan and, 675
—famous ruins, 172, *173*
—fears invasion, 7, *37*
—5th Army in, *356-57*
—future, Moscow Conference and, *396*
—Germans' contempt for, 206, 259
—hatred of Germans, 168
—Hungary and, 366
—and the Mediterranean, 136
—"Monty's Highway" in, *331*
—Nettuno-Anzio thrust, *579*
—R.A.M.C. in, *687*
—relief map, 267
—rocket shells in, *485*
—strange weapons in, *676*
—surrender, air power and, 266 636
— —Hammerton on, 287
— —Switzerland and, 718
— —unconditional 265
—from within, Massock on, *115*
—her islands, *35*
—no German help for, 40
—not a naval power, 40
—struggle against Austria, 179
—Transport Command and, *363*
—two books on, 627
—views of, *304-05*
"It's a Piece of Cake," 223
Ivanin, Capt., at Kiev, 441
Izzard, Spr. R. W., B.E.M., *59*

## J

Jaluit, Japanese base, 590
Jam, British manufacture, *386*
Jamaica, H.M.S., and *Scharnhorst*, *518*, 519, *520*, 550, 571
Jamaica, war effort, *661*
James II, raised R. Marines, 628
James, Lt., of A.F.P.U., *278*
Jannings, Emil, 703
Janus, H.M.S., sunk, 678
**Japan,** air defeat, 380
—air threat to, 22
—apprehensions, 40
—bombing of, difficulties, 253
—Cairo conference and, 454, 499
—naval strength, 230
—Pacific bases, *590*
—Prof. Morris on, 435
—schemes to bomb, 636
**Japan** *(cont.)*
—shipping losses, 710
— —shortage, 294
—to be bombed, 412
—two-Service air force, 700
**Japanese,** in China, industrial result, 116
—cremation for, 44
Javelin, H.M.S., destroyer, 392
Jeanne d'Arc (ship), 294
**Jeeps,** as ambulances, *353*
—amphibious, 110
—in Avro York, *716*
—at Cape Gloucester, *602*
—on Indo-Burmese road, *50*
—in invasion training, *146*
—for Senegalese, *663*
—Spencer on, 300
Jenkins, Celia, B.E.M., *382*
Jennings, P./O. Tom, D.S.M., *423*
Jerusalem, Roosevelt over, 499
Jeschonnek, Col.-Gen. Hans, *398*
**Jews,** massacred, Kiev, 441
—water-queue, Warsaw, *450*
Jibuti, Italian advanced base, 675
**Johns, Howard,** on "Little Ships," 328
— —on rescue tugs, 744
Johnson, Pte. Edgar, at Kwajalein, 729
Johnston, George H., "New Guinea Diary," 659
**Jolly Roger,** for *United*, *423*
— —for *Unrivalled*, *617*
— —as U.S. plane signal, *596*
Jones, L.-Cpl. C. A., in Sicily, *178*
Jones, Lt.-Cdr. E. L., in *Boreas*, 392
Jones, Flight-Lieut. L. L. "Slim," *362*
Jordan, Sgt., of A.F.P.U., *278*
Juin, Gen., in Italy, 555
**Jungle,** Burmese, *465*
—of N. Guinea, bomber down in, *596*
Jungle Commando, the Chindits, 46, *48-49*
"Jungle" Practice, in Australia *322*
Junior Training Corps., and A.C.F., 406
**Junkers 52,** destruction, Sicilian Channel, *72*
—on Sicilian airfield, *184*
—wrecked, Lampedusa, *103*
—88, Beaufighter shoots down, *215*
— —model, as target, *12*
Junkers Class, in Germany, 398
Juno, H.M.S., sunk, 61
Junta, of German generals, 398
**Jutland,** Germans fortify, 73
—battle of, tactics and strategy, 444

## K

K42, German locomotive, 662
Kaafjord, midget submarines in, 649
—*Monte Rosa* in, 742
Kachins, in Burma, *751*, *800*
Kalewa, Viper Force at, *630*
Kalfoff, Christo, and Simeon II, 270.
Kandanos, destruction, *450*
Kandy, S. E. Asia H-Q, 796
Kanyev Pocket, German defeat in, *613*
Kapingamarangi, Japanese base, 590
Karachev, devastation at, *538*
Karelia, communications in, *564*
Kari, slave in Poland, 125
Karlsruhe, block-busters on, 702
Karpov, portrait of Stalin, *417*
Kasatin, Russians take, 547
Kashmir, H.M.S., sunk, 61
Kassala, invasion entry, 675
Katsonis (submarine), sunk, *358*
Kavieng, Japanese use, 454
Kawabe, Lieut.-Gen. Matakasu, 556
Kay, Chief P./O. S., *423*
Keitel, F.-M. Wilhelm, Horthy with, *366*
Kelleher, A. B. J. F., in Crete, *61*
Kelliher, Pte. R., V.C., *568*
Kelly, H.M.S., sunk, 61
Kelly, Adm. Sir Howard, 422
Kelly, H. W. K., and magnetic mine, 124
Kelly, Maj. J. V., D.S.O., *209*
Kelvin, H.M.S., 392, *393*
Keneally, Sgt. John Patrick, V.C., *286*
Kennedy, Capt. James, O.B.E., *254*
Kent, H.M.S., on China Station, 422
Kent, H.R.H. Duchess of, 321
Kenya and Uganda Railways, engineer of, *322*
Kerch, Russians evacuate, 227
Kerch Straits, ferry across, *420*
Kerr, Sir A. Clark, 396
**Kesselring, F./M. Albert,** Anzio attacks, 643
**Kesselring, F./M.** *(cont.)*
— —and Nettuno landing, 579, 611
Ketley, Capt. E. M., O.B.E., *568*
Keyes, Adm. Lord, 534
Keys, Henry, at Betio Island, 474
Khalid, Emir, in Downing St., *482*
Kharkov (ship), father and son in, *422*
**Kharkov** (city), air view, *282*
—German danger at, 419
—past and present, *245*
—recapture, *227*, 249
—reconstruction, 277, 282
—tank manufacture at, 693
Kherson, Russians take, 707
Khoury, M. Bechara, *469*
**Kiel Canal,** first R.A.F. raid on, 54
— —importance, 430
**Kiev,** Pechersk Abbey destroyed, *420*
—Russians take, 387, *431*, *441*
—success exploited, 451
Kiev Salient, Russian advance in, *515*
Killearn, Lord, *476*
Killinger, Baron von, *686*
Kimmins, Cdr. Anthony, R.N., 794
King, Flt.-Lt. D. F., D.F.C., *318*
King, Group-Capt. Patrick, 95
King, Rt. Hon. Mackenzie, *232*
King, Lt. Philip, of 155th Battery, 77
King Edward VII, H.M.S. sunk, 422
King George V, H.M.S., *456*
Kingisepp, Russians take, 589
Kinkaid, Vice-Adm., *761*
**Kipling, Rudyard,** and British Tommy, 19
— —on R. Marines, 628
— —Wavell and, 735
Kirovograd, Russians take, 547
Kishinev, soap factory at, 588
**Kiska,** evacuation secrecy, 227
—heavy raids on, 182
—U.S. bombard, 10, 53
Kitchener, F/M. Lord, 83
Kitchens, model, Hammerton on 479
Kite, H.M. Sloop, 710, *711*
Kites (birds) in W. Desert, 723
Kiwi, H.M.N.Z. Corvette, 615
Kjesater Manor, refugee camp, *414*
**Kleist, F/M. von,** dangerous position, 771
— —supersedes Manstein, 724
Klopper, Maj.-Gen. H. B., escape, *351*
Knatchbull-Hugessen, Sir Hughe, 499
Knight, Dame Laura, painting by, *15*
**Knox, Col. Frank,** on capture of Attu, 53
— —on Japanese shipping losses, 294
— —and Woolworth Carriers, 104
Kobe, U.S. bomb, 154
Kohima, relieved, *771*
**Kokoda,** air transport and, 716
—Japanese defeated at, 323
Kola Peninsula, reindeer transport in, *425*
Kollantay, Mme. Alexandra, 684, *685*
Köln (ship) returns to Baltic, 550
Kolombangara, Japanese threatened in, 99
Kolomyja, Russians take, 739
**Koniev, Marshal,** brilliant strategy, 611
— —new offensive, 707, 771
— —recaptures Kharkov, *227*
— —successes, 739
Königberg (cruiser) sunk, 742
Korcula, Yugoslavs take, *343*
Kormoran (raider) sunk, 422
Koror, in Palau Islands, *590*
Korosten, Russians take and lose, 451
Korsun, German 8th Army at, *610*
Korten, Gen, disappearance, *398*
Kotor, Dalmatian port, *343*
Krasni Krim (cruiser), 710, *774*
Krause, Gen., surrenders, 30
**Kremenchug,** Russians break through at, 387
— —take, *309*, *365*
Kremenets, Russians take, 739
Kreuger, Lt.-Gen. in S.W. Pacific, 99
Krishnan, Lt. M., D.S.C., R.I.N., *696*
Krivitsky, Gen., on purge of 1937, 307
**Krivoi Rog,** Russian take, 643
— —Russian thrust against, 387
Kronprinz Wilhelm, raider, 422
Kronstadt, Soviet fleet at, 550
Krueger, Lt.-Gen.W., *761*
Krymskaya, Russians take, *3*, 21
Krzemieniec, Russians take, *677*
**Kuban,** German danger in, 34
**Kuban** *(cont.)*
—possible German evacuation, 98
—Russian offensive in, *21*
—Russians clear, 387, 420
Kupres, partisans take, 618
**Kursk,** railway junction, 238
—Russian Bostons over, *141*
Kutznetzov, Adm., inspects German mortar, *725*
**Kwajalein,** Allies take, 729
—bombarded, 636
—Japanese prisoners from, *780*
—pontoons at, *743*
Kyauktaw, British take, 750

## L

Laboratories, emergency Britain, *546*
Labour, and conscription, 211
Labrador, air base in, *88*
Laddering, in gunnery, 456
Ladoga L., Russian supplies cross, *626*
**Ladrones Islands,** attacks on, 646
— —Japanese bases in, *590*
**Lae,** Allied drive on, *269*
— —troopship for, *391*
—Allies take, 323, *350*, 454
Lagg-3, Russian fighter, *252*
Lahovary, Antonescu recalls, *686*
Lamb, Maj. J. C., R.A., *683*
Lambert, E. G., drawing by, *490*
Lambrick, Mrs. Dulcie, portrait by, *470*
Lamerton, H.M.S., exploit, 392
**Lampedusa,** Allies occupy, *70*, *103*
—Bostons attack, *128*
—Cohen takes, *92*
Lampione surrenders, 70
**Lancasters,** bomb Berlin, *472*, *473*
—bomb-sight, *477*
—over Berlin, 313
—ploughing land under, *770*
—in production, *312*
—repaired, *381*
—and Ruhr dams, 22, *24*, *25*
—use factory-busters, *702*
—York an adaptation, *412*
Land Army, and harvest, *219*
Land Clubs, and harvest, 218
Land Defence Force, of M.N.B.D.O., 628
**Landing-craft,** Allied, at Nettuno, *580*
— — —at Salerno, *295*
— — —off Sicily, *134*
— — —types, *110*, *111-14*, *656-57*
— —British, Marines handle, *672*
— —building, *138*
— —Materials, in Manchester, *674*
— —mechanized, *231*
— —at Mono Is., *569*
— —N.Z., Vella Lavella, *502*
— —troops boarding, *298*
— —U.S., at Bougainville, *592-93*
— — —for Sicily, *137*, *139*
Landing Ship, Tank, *640*
**Land-Mines,** detecting, Nettuno, *580*
— — —Russia, *673*
— —new, precautions, 52
— —Sicilians reveal, *242*
Larsen, O. T., 362
Latham, Hubert, 383
Lauder, Sir Harry, 275
Laundry Service, mobile, *91*
Lausanne, Red Cross Exhibition at, *718*
Lavenko, Sgt. Andrei, *565*
Lavrinenkov, Vladimir, 697
Law, Mr. R. K., Minister of State, 311
Lawson, Will, M.P., and coal situation, 374
Lawther, Will, M.P., 186
Laycock, Maj.-Gen. R. E., *415*
Leaflets, British, on Italy, 7
League of Nations, 447
Leahy, Adm.W. D., at Teheran, *496*
**Leander, H.M.S.,** N.Z. cruiser, 615
— —sinks raiders, 422
Lease-Lend, and Turkey, *493*
Leathers, Lord, *476*
Lebanon, crisis in, *469*
Le Brun, Jim, on A.F.P.U., 278
**Ledo Road,** construction, *464-65*
— —romance of, 790
— —story of, *665*, *666*
Lee, Clark, "They Call it Pacific," 563
**Leeb, F/M. Ritter von,** Hitler and, *398*
— —implacability, 398
**Leese, Lt.-Gen. Sir Oliver,** commands 8th Army, 545, *554*
— —in Italy, *581*
**Leghorn,** bombed, 182
—name, Hammerton on, 447
**Leghorn** *(cont.)*
—Torre del Marzocco, *305*
Legion of Merit, for Montgomery, 261
Leicester Square, Hammerton on, 607
Leinster, Hospital Ship, 633
Leipzig (ship), 550
Leith, repatriated prisoners at, *359*, *399-402*
**Leningrad,** contrasts in, *394*, *395*
—naval support at, 582
—Red Guards at, *645*
—relief of, *622*, *624-26*
— —strategic results, 579
—Russian offensive at, *589*
—as St. Petersburg, 622, *623*
—Siege of, details, 622
—steel manufacture, *427*
—threat to, Finns and, 684
Lentaigne Maj.-Gen. W. D. A., *772*
**Leros,** air power and, 444
—Cyprus and, 148
—defence of, *442*
—in Dodecanese, *68*
—Germans retake, *468*
—loss, McMurtrie on, 422
—naval base, *294*
Letford, Flt.-Lt. K. H. F., *313*
Lever Bros, mobile laundry service, *91*
Lewis, Maj.-Gen. H. A., invented "gun-how," 296
Lewis, Capt. Neville, portrait by, *16-17*
Lewis, Lt.-Cdr. Roger C., and magnetic mine, 124
Lexington, U.S.S., refitted, 550
**Liberators,** achievements, 214, *216*
—in Biscay battle, 532
—bomb Lae, *269*
— —Madang, 284
— —Ploesti, *186*
—defend convoy, 602
—destroy blockade runner, *540*
— —Japanese planes, *573*
— —U-boats, *486*
—new types, 542
—overhauled, *732*
—servicing, *719*
—spot U-boats, *263*
—Sunderland rescues crew, *54*
—as transport planes, 716
Liberi, U.S. trucks at, *389*
**Libya,** Arab farms in, 7
—Inshore Squadron off, 488
—tank-driver's grave, *44*
—Wavell's offensive, railways and, 238
Licata, Allies take, *132*
Life-Saving Rocket Company, and *Nordale*, 234
Light, Hammerton on, 223
Light Coastal Forces : see Little Ships
Light Naval Craft, Allied, activities, 390
**Lightning Planes,** in Berlin raids, *701*
— —destroy air convoy, 72
— —at Madang, 284
— —power-dive in, *221*
Limoges, R.A.F. bomb, 702
Lindsay, Maj. M. in Italy, *449*
Linen, Ulster industry, 650, *651*
Liner, as trooper, *552*, *553*
Linkomies, E, Finnish premier, *685*
Link Trainer, use, *694*, *695*
Linlithgow, Marquess of, *429*
Linnell, Air-Marshal Sir Francis, knighted, *100*
Linney, Sqd.-Ldr. A. S., and Walrus, *108*
Linosa, surrenders, 70
Lin Sen, Chinese president, *117*
Lipari Islands, and Cnossus, 171
Li Pei-Chi, on Honan famine, 116
Lipovani, Russian people, 588
Lisbon, black-out in, 360
Lissa, reported seizure, 678
Lithgow, Lt. J. A., D.F.C., *318*
**Little Ships,** functions, 328, *329*
— —Holman, on *501*
— —on night patrol, *500*
Litton, A./B., on sinking of *Scharnhorst*, 570
Littorio (battleship), at Spezia, 168
**Litvinov, Maxim,** on Finnish war, 307
— —at Moscow Conference, *396*
**Liverpool,** mobile canteens for, *661*
—repatriated prisoners at, 359, *402*, *416*
Lizards, 8th Army pets, 723
Ljubljana (destroyer), 136
Llewellin, Col. J. J., Minister of Food, *438*
Lloyd, Lieut. H. L., R.N.V.R., in Little Ships, 328
Lloyd-George, Major G., 374
Loadstar Plane, as ambulance, *85*
Loats, Station-Sgt., letter from, 607
Local Defence Volunteers, now Home Guard, 26, 211

Lochner, Louis P., "What about Germany?" 51
Locke, Skipper J. C., honour for, 680
Lockett, Lieut. Jeffrey, in Burma, 46
Lockheed Bomber, *Samsonia* rescues, 744
Locomotives U.S., in Britain, *238*
Locust Bean, in Cyprus, 148
Lofoten Isles, civilians evacuated, 73
Loftus, Ruby, portrait, *15*
"Logistics," Hammerton on, 735
Löhr, Gen., in Sofia, 270
Lombardy, airfields, importance, 284
**London,** A.A. defence, *375, 632,* 668
—air-raids on, *704*
—clean streets, 31
—Fire Control Room, *706*
—flag for Chicago, *482*
—Guards beat "retreat" in, *226*
—St. Paul's exposed *217*
—scenes in, *578*
—Trunk Telephone Exchange, *58*
—United Nations Day in, *91*
London and N.E. Rly., woman worker on, *514*
Londonderry, important port, 650
London Irish Rifles, at Centuripe, *199,* 239
London, Midland & Scottish Rly., volunteers in, *226*
London Transport, 10th birthday, 122
Long, Geoffrey, painting by, *17*
Longhurst, Flt.-Lieut. W. S., 362
Long Island, U.S.S., 10
Longstop Hill, "Buzzards" at, 598
Long Tom, U.S. 155-mm. gun, *676*
Longyear City, Spitzbergen, *315*
Loot, in Denmark, *248*
Looting, in Catania, 220
Lorengau Airfield, Allies take, 710
Lorraine (ship), 40
Lorries, Russian, cross L. Ladoga, *626*
Lotus-eaters, in Sicily, 171
Loud, P./O. W. W. J., D.F.C., *318*
Loud-speakers, at railway stations, 639
Low, David, cartoons by, *191, 396*
Lowestoft, E-boats off, 390
Lowry, Rear-Adm., U.S.N., *612*
Lozovsky, M., and Czech-Soviet Pact, *522*
Lucas, Philip C., test pilot, 470
Luck, Russians take, 611
Ludwig Canal, modernisation, 430
Luftwaffe: see Air Force, German
Lumsden, Maj.-Gen. H., D.S.O., *59*
Lutyens, Sir Edwin, 607
Lutze, Victor, death, 782
**Lützow** (ship), probably at Gdynia, 327
—returns to Baltic, 327, 550
Lvov, Russian threat to, 611
Lyell, Lt. Lord, V.C., *286*
Lyons, Sgt., first in Tunis, 29
Lyons, Neil, "Kitchener's Chaps," 19
Lysander Planes, as ambulances, 84
**Lyttelton, Rt. Hon. Oliver,** on increased production, 246
— —on Ulster, 650

## M

Mabane, William, M.P., 58
**MacArthur, Gen. Douglas,** on capture of Lae, 391
— —Clark Lee on, *563*
— —experience, 253
— —at Los Negros, *761*
— —and New Guinea campaign, 323
— —New Guinea drive, *269*
— —new offensive, 118
— —no strategic air force, 412
Macartney, Maxwell, on Mussolini, 627
McCleod, Piper N. A., in Sicily, *178*
Macdonald, Angus, on Canadian cruisers, 678
Macdonald, Maj. David, of A.F.P.U., *278*
Macdonald, Ramsey, 383
Macdonald, Roderick, on Tunisian surrender, 29-30
McDonnell, Sgt. T. J. J. D.C.M., *59*
Machine-gun Carts, Russian, *458*
Machine-gunners, German, in Russia, *549*
Machine-gun Post, German, in Russia, *141*
**Machine-guns,** of aeroplane, cleaning, *87*
— —Allied, in bombers, 316
— —of Cpl. Mekhalev, *645*
— —French, in Italy, *581*
— —Japanese light, *297*
— —of Mosquito, *620*
— —of Thunderbolt, *23*
Macintosh, Charles, patented mackintoshes, 735
McIntyre, Peter, work of, *17, 787*
Mackensen, Gen. von, at Anzio, 643
**Mackenzie, Compton,** on Roosevelt, 531
— —"Wind of Freedom," 179
Maclean, Brig. F. H. R., in Yugoslavia, *524*
**Macmillan, Rt. Hon. Hugh,** at Cairo Conference, *476*
— —greets King, 67
**Macmillan, Capt. Norman,** on Air Power and Italy, 266
— —on air war, 22, 54, 86, 118, 150, 182, 214, 253, 284, 316, 348, 380, 412, 444, 477, 508, 540, 572, 604, 636, 668, 700, 732, 764, 796
— —on increased bombing-range, *330*
Macmillan, House of, Hammerton on, 479
**McMurtrie, Francis E.,** on the War at Sea, 10, 40, 73, 105, 136, 168, 200, 230, 262, 294, 327, 358, 390, 422, 454, 486, 518, 550, 582, 615, 646, 678, 710, 742, 774
**MacNaughton, Lt.-Gen. A. G. L.,** Crerar succeeds, *707*
— —vigorous language, 159
McNeil, Lt. John Alexander, 697
Macpherson, Lieut.-Cdr. R. A., at Betio Island, 474
McSherry, Brig.-Gen. Frank J., and Amgot, 180
**Madagascar,** R. Marines in, 174
—war cemeteries in, 748
**Madang,** bomb tonnage on, 284
—enemy planes burning at, *109*
Maffei, Gen. Achille, in Pantelleria, 70
Magdepur, S.S., sunk, 124
Maginot Line, weakness, 51
Magister Plane, Turkish, testing, *493*
**Magnetic Mine,** mastery of, *124*
— —secret weapon, 454
Magpie, H.M.S., with Second Escort Group, 710
Mahratta, H.M.S., *583*
Maida, battle of, 73
Maidenhead, fruit-bottling at, *386*
Mails, passed at sea, *390*
Main, R., canalisation, *430*
Maingkwan, Chinese take, 750
Maintenance Craft, of boom defence, *648*
Maisky, Ivan, 255
"Make Smoke," in cruiser, 456
Makin Atoll, U.S. storm, *533, 591*
**Malaya, H.M.S.,** guns, *457*
— —and *Scharnhorst*, 518
Malaya, Allied air weakness in, 54
**Malinovsky, Gen.,** defeats Manstein, *397*
— —new offensive, 707, 771
— —Stalin to, 276
**Malta,** and air power, 266
—Beaufighters at, 22
—bomb trolleys in, *214*
—*Breconshire* at, *762*
—Churchill at, *481, 495*
—and Colonies' Exhibition, *578*
—fighter cover from, *35*
—George VI in, 97, *101*
—Italian fleet at, 294, 327, *335, 338*
—Mosquitoes in, *98*
—nurses in, 691
—as submarine base, 616
—*Terror* off, 488
—Transport Command's mileage for, 362
Maluinov, Capt., Russian airman, *140*
Manchester, invasion craft in, *674*
Manchuria, Japanese oppression in, 595
**Manipur,** Hammerton on, 447
—Japanese invade, 750, *773*
**Mannerheim, Field-Marshal Gustav,** 684
Manoeuvres, in Portugal, *360*
**Man-power,** Chinese, 116
— —German, in Russia, 35
**Manstein, Col.-Gen. von,** critical position, 419
— —good communications, *771*
— —and Kanyev disaster, 643
— —reserves exhausted, 483
— —in retreat, 547
— —in Russia, 387
**Manstein, Col.-Gen.** *(cont.)*
— —Russians outwit, *397,* 451
— —superseded, *724*
— —and Vatutin's offensive, 611
— —against Zhukov, 707
Mapping Unit, Mobile, *558*
**Maps,** Army prepares, *558*
—for Sicilian invasion, 142
**Marat** (battleship), damage to 710
—at Kronstadt, 550
**Marauders,** down M.E.323, *215*
—and M.E. 109F, *153*
—over Adriatic coast, *462*
Margriet, Dutch plane, *418*
Marienburg, Fortresses raid, *369*
**Marines, Javanese,** at Curaçao, *408*
—**Royal,** beret for, *226*
— —in Force Viper, *630*
— —guard shipping, *629*
— —gun crew, *43*
— —history and record, 174
— —invasion training, *143-46*
— —in landing-craft, *672*
— —in landing exercises, *110, 112-13*
— —Pike on, *628*
— —in smoke-screen, *641*
—**Russian,** in Caucasus, *432-33*
—**U.S.,** at Betio, 475
— — —at Bougainville, *592-93*
— — —at Cape Gloucester, *602*
— — —in Gilbert Islands, 454, *591*
— — —at Guadalcanal, 454
— — —landing-craft, 110, *114*
— — —at Marshall Is., 646, *660*
— — —on Namur, *729*
— — —in New Britain, 678
— — —in Rendova, *170*
— — —in S.W. Pacific, 99
— — —Tarawa, *503, 512*
Maritime Regt., gunners' story, 537-38
Mark IV Tanks, secret discovered, 52
Markham R., fighting on, 269
Markham Main Colliery, *600*
Mars, Lieut. A., D.S.O., R.N., *423,* 616
Marsala, Sicily, 9
Mars, flying boat, *508,* 716
**Marshall, Gen. George S.,** in Algiers, *81*
— —on the jeep, 300
**Marshall Is.,** pill-boxes cracked on, 729
— —pontoons in, *743*
— —transport planes for, *716*
— —U.S. attack, 454
— — — —gains in, *646, 660*
— —war cemeteries in, *747*
Martin, Capt. C. A. J., G.C., M.C., *59*
Martin, Denis, and Sydney Cohen, 92
Masai, chiefs broadcast, *619*
Mascalucia, looting in, 220
**Mascots,** of destroyers, *393*
—dog, of Aberdeen, *710*
—of Lancaster bomber, *312*
—of W. Indian squadron, *661*
Masego, Job, M.M., Lewis's portrait, *16-17*
Massacre Bay, Attu Is., *53*
Massock, Richard G., "Italy from Within," *115*
**Matchless, H.M.S.,** destroyer, *392*
— —and *Scharnhorst*, 518, 519
— —and *Scharnhorst* survivors, 571
Mathers, Flt./Sgt. F. E., C.G.M., *638*
Matilda Tanks, in New Guinea, *596*
Maton, Cdr., and magnetic mine, 124
Maugham, Somerset, 671
Maungdaw, Allies retake, *557*
Mauritius, H.M.S., mail for, *390*
Maxton, James, M.P., 246
May, Capt. W. S., air-train driver, *362*
M.C.C., committee, 639
**Meat,** in N. Africa, 38
—in Paris, 543
—Swiss shortage, 718
Mecca, new roads to, 790
Mechanic, of F.A.A., adventure, *793*
—R.A.F., in Azores, *541*
Mechanized Forces, of Turkey, *493*
Mechanized Transport, Turkish, *529*
Medals, modern view, 383
**Mediterranean Sea,** Allied targets in, *66*
— —Allies control, 262
— —freed for Allies, 2
— —Italian islands in, *35*
Medjez el Bab, Recce H.Q. at 460
Mehar Singh, Sqd. Ldr., *752*
Mekhalev, Cpl., *645*
Melilli, Allies take, *165*
Melitopol, Tolbukhin at, *397*
Melitopol Line, Russian offensive against, 387
Menemenioglu, M., 499, *511*
Menin Gate, inscription, 44
**Mechant Navy,** Danish ships with, 78
— —honours for, *254*
— —life-saving devices, *11*
— —Oilers for, 712
— —R. Marines with, 174
— —and troop-transports, 552, *553*
**Merchant Ships,** as aircraft carriers, *104, 105*
— —German, Liberator sinks, *540*
Merrill, Brig.-Gen. F. in Burma, *772*
Merrill's Marauders, in Burma, 773, *800*
Merrimac (ship), duel with *Monitor*, 488
Merstham, church rebuilt, *91*
Messenger, Capt. L. V., ferry pilot, *362*
Messent, Pte, parachute training, 92
Messerschmitt, Prof., and high flying, 521
**Messerschmitt M.E. 109,** abandoned, Sicily, *210*
— —in dog-fight, *215*
— —salvage from, *14*
— —details, *153*
— —F. G., remnants presented, *378*
— —**323,** shot down, *215*
— — —transport plane, *542*
— —**410,** shot down, England, — — *412*
Messerschmitts, factory bombed, *668*
Messervy, Maj.-Gen. F. W., 772
**Messina,** A.A. battery near, *37*
—Allied chiefs in, *261*
—Allies welcomed in, 229
—Duce slogan in, *229*
—earthquake destroys, 171
—German evacuation, 227
—pre-war view, *172*
Meta, Monte, Allies near, *490*
Metaxas, Gen., Mackenzie on, 179
Meteorological Corps, W.A.A.F. in, *151*
Meteorological Officer, and intruders, *55*
Meteorological Reconnaissance, distance and, 330
Mevagissey, sea-harvest thanksgiving, *354*
Meyrick, Cdr. M. D. C., and *Scharnhorst*, *518,* 519
Mice, 8th Army pets, 723
Microphones, for gunners, Italy, *781*
**Middle East,** importance, 259
— —new roads in, 790
Middlesex Regt., in Battle of France, 147
**Midway Is.,** battle of, air victory, 348
— — —results, 54
M I G 3, attacks Heinkel, 252
**Mihailovitch, Gen. Draza,** and the Italians, 524
— —support for Allies, 342
**Milan,** bombed, *195*
—devastation in, 287, *288*
Milazzo, U.S. reach, 195
Mili, Japanese base, 590
Militella, Allied troops in, *164*
Militia, of Moscow, *434, 448*
Milk, value, Hammerton on, 287
Mill, John Stuart, 311
Mills Grenade, Canadians use, Italy, *424*
Milne, H.M.S., *583*
Milne, Lord, 77
**Milne Bay,** Japanese land at, 323
— —U.S. land at, 323
Minefields, guerillas sow, *459*
Minelayers, aircraft as, Coastguard and, 234
Minelaying, by Polish squadron, *763*
Miners, "Bevin boys" as, *600*
Mines, Land: see Land Mines
Mines, Magnetic: see Magnetic
**Minesweepers,** Belgians in, *418*
—keep sea-lanes open, *582*
—trawlers as, *792*
Mineworkers' Federation, 374
Misterbianco, British in, 242
**Mitchell B-25,** *150,* 477
**Mitchell Bombers,** bomb Madang, 284
— — —Tokyo, *154, 155*
— —destroy air convoy, *72*
— —for Dutch squadron, *418*
— —in Italy, *669*
— —at New Gloucester, 602
— —as tank-busters, 620
Mitcher, Rear-Adm. Mark, 646
Mizpah (trawler), adventure, 680
Moa, H.M.N.Z. Corvette, 615
Moana Nui-A-Kiwa Ngarimu, V.C., *123*
Mobile Commandos see Reconnaissance Corps
Mobile Naval Base Defence Organization, 628
**Mobilization,** in Great Britain, 311
—Swiss methods. 718
Models, for Home Guard, *27*
Modica, Canadians in, *166*
Moelders, Col., death, 398
Mogaung, Chinese advance on, *750*
Mogaung Valley, relief map, *773*
Möhne R., dam bombed, 3, 22, *24, 25*
Molotov, Russian cruiser, 774
**Molotov, Viatscheslav,** and Czech-Soviet Pact, *522*
— —at Moscow Conference, *396*
— —and Russian diplomats, 383
— —warns Rumania, 739
Monakhova, Nina, *426*
Monkey, destroyer's mascot *393*
Monks, Noël, with Gen. Clark, 377
Monnet, Jean, on Committee of Liberation, *38*
Mono Island, Allies land at, 569
Monocle, demoded, 511
Monowai, H.M.N.Z.S., 615
Montcalm (ship), off Corsica, 294
Monte Rosa (ship), 742
**Montgomery, Gen. Sir Bernard,** on air power, 540
— —commands 8th Army, 388
— —at Council of War, *81*
— —distributes cigarettes, 489
— —and 8th Army, 723
— —at Fossacesia, *545*
— —greets Eisenhower, *514*
— —his highway, *331*
— —inspects Marine Commandos, *628*
— —in Messina, *261*
— —offensive, air power and, 266
— —praises Canadians, *175*
— —on Sicilian invasion, *130*
— —travelling H.-Q., *158*
— —an Ulsterman, 650
— —uses jeep, 300
— —with Wavell, *160*
"Monty's Highway," *331*
Moore, Arthur, Fyfe and, 83
Moore, Vice-Adm. Sir Henry, 742, *794*
Moore, Martin, and the Chindits, 46, *83*
Moore, Fusilier T., M.M., *568*
**Moorehead, Alan,** "The End in Africa," 403
— —and Nixon, *281*
— —in Tunis, 29
**Morale,** German collapse, Tunisia, 2
—of U-boat crews, 34
Morley, Harry, portrait by, *18*
Morris, Gen., on Port Moresby, 659
Morris, Sgt., of A.F.P.U., *278*
Morris, Capt. Colin, *189*
Morris, Prof. John, "Traveller from Tokyo," *435*
**Morrison, Rt. Hon. Herbert** and Civil Defence, 438
— —on prison workshops, 374
— —on Ulster bases, 650
Morse Code, for Recce, 460
**Mortars,** A.C.F. train with, *407*
—British 4·2, *227, 291, 785*
— —at Pugliano, *292*
— —range-finder on, *19*
— —Spigot, for Home Guard, *27*
—demonstrating, China, 466
—German, in Italy, *489*
— —mobile, *610*
— —in Moscow, *522*
— —multi-barrelled, 296, 297
—Russian, at Orel, *205*
—2-in., for Recce, *461*
Mortar Support Company, in Italy, *785*
Morton, Maj. Desmond, 476
**Moscow,** Civil Security Force, *448*
—Czech-Soviet Pact in, *522*
—firework display, *431*
—Foreign Office, 383
—German mortar in, *725*
—normal life in, *434*
—victory salutes in, *249, 309*
Moscow Conference, results, *396*
Moskva R., traffic control over, *434*
Moslems, in Sicily, 171
Mosley, Sir Oswald, 479
Mosquitoes (insects) protection against, Burma, *465*
**Mosquito Planes,** in Biscay battle, 532
— —bomb Berlin, 214
— —bomb doors open, *764*
— —fighter-bombers, *620*
— —for intruders, *55*
— —in Malta, *98*
— —manufacture, *90*
— —for P.R. units, 285
— —secrecy about, 52
Motor-boat, Wren at helm, *321*
Motor-car, in harbour, Singapore, *411*

Motor-cycles, for D.Rs., *436*
Motor Cyclists, in Beirut, *469*
**Motor Gunboats,** British, sunk, 390
— — —work, 328, *500, 501*
Motor Highways, German, and railways, 662
**Motor-Launches,** British in Burma, *630*
— — —on patrol, *13*
— — —under sail, *329*
— — —work, 501
— —German, by *Tirpitz*, *776*
Motor-sleighs, Russian, 724
**Motor - Torpedo - Boats,** British, *328*, 501
— — —German, destroyed, 390
— — — —in Venice, *450*
— — —Russian, in Black Sea, *168*
Motor Transport Companies, of H.G., *26*
Mountain Battery, U.S., *350*
Mountains, strategic use, 342
Mountain Service, R.A.F., *439*
**Mountbatten, Vice-Adm. Lord Louis,** against Japanese, 262
— —in Ceylon, 774, 788
— —inspects Chinese troops, *752*
— — —Indians, *683*
— —new appointment, 230
— —at Quebec Conference, *232*
— —and reconquest of Burma, 556
— —reinforcements for, 796
— —with Sir R. Peirse, *577*
Movements Officer, Ferry Control, *298*
Möwe, German raider, 422
Mozzagrona, war cemetery at, *749*
Mozyr, Russians take, 547
Mtsensk, Russians retake, 66
**Mud,** in Italy, 543, *554*
—in New Guinea, *793*
**Mules,** for airborne troops, Sicily, *192*
—Allied in Apennines, *490*
— —in Burma, *754*
—of Cyprus, 148
—drag ammunition, Italy, *494*
—fording stream, Assam, *50*
—German, 8th Army captures, *228*
—Italians tend, *740*
—at Monte Camino, 506
—for transport, Sicily, *132*
Muleteers, Indian, in Italy, *513*
**Munda,** Allied attack on, 99, 105, 109
—U.S. bombard, *200*
— — —take, 220
Munday, Ralph, test pilot, *471*
Munday, William, death, *346*
Munitions, in U.S. trucks, Russia, *364*
**Munro, Ross,** on Sicilian invasion, 156-57
— —in Sicily, 188
**Murmansk,** attack on, Finns in, 684
—convoys arrive at, *106*
Murray Capt. A. A., of *Ravager*, *777*
Murray, Sqd.-Ldr. Ernest, 716
Murray, Lt. H. R., R.N., *60*
Murray, Ldg. Telegraphist P. J., *423*
Murray-Jones, Lt. P., R.N., *60*
Musketeer, H.M.S., and *Scharnhorst*, 518, 519
**Mussolini, Benito,** declares war on Allies, 7
— —disappearance, 159
— —and Girgenti, 319
— —inspects defences, *37*
— —invades Albania, 342
— —and Italian disaster, 627
— —and Italian fleet, 136
— —and Pantelleria, 66, 70
— —and Pavelitch, 342
— —resignation, 162
— — —cause, 182
— — —and German morale, 206
— — —Italian rejoicings, *213*
— — —Sicily and, 188
— — —and Skopa, 686
— — —slogan in Messina, *229*
— — —and Spanish Civil War, 339
— — —tyranny, 115
Mustang, P 51 B, *572*
**Mustangs,** in Berlin raid, 701
—train-busters, *89*
Mutiny, in German Navy (1918) 358
Muzio Attendolo, cruiser, 168
Myers, Sister Muriel, R.R.C., *382*
Myitkyina, Chinese advance on, *750*

## N

Nagano, Adm. Osami, 646
Nagoya, U.S. bomb, 154
**Namur** (Marshall Is.), flame-throwers on, *729*
**Namur** *(cont.)*
— —U.S. take, *660*
Nankan, fighting at station, 46
**Naples**, *304-05*
—airfields taken, 330
—Allies occupy, *324*
—block-busters on, 702
—bombed, 182, 214
— —Doolittle and, 154
—British raids on, 7, *266*
—Fortress over, *316*
—German A.A. defence, *118*
— —atrocities in, 324
—schools reopen, *736*
**Napoleon I,** birthplace, *344*
— —a Corsican, 319
Napoli Division, in Sicily, 410
Narvik (destroyer) *Stubborn* with, *731*
Nassau Bay, U.S. land at, *109*
National Assembly, of Portugal, 467
National Book League, 799
National Debt, past and present, 246
**National Fire Service,** in air raids, *704*
— — —flag, *354*
— — —numbers and efficiency, 122
— — —tanks abused, *578*
— — —women in, *706*
Naval Air Service, 86
Naval Bases, Allied, Eastern shortage, 230
Naval Reserve, Royal, fishermen in, 680
**Naval Volunteer Reserve, Royal,** mans landing craft, 110
— — — — —mans Little Ships, 328
— — — — —and submarine service, 616
— — — — —Ulster Division, 650
**Navy, Bulgarian,** strength, 774
**—Danish,** losses, 248
— —ships of, *230*
**—Dutch,** with Allies, 96
**—French,** at Alexandria, joins Allies, *40*
**—German,** air power and, 444
— —disaffection in, 327
— —in last war, 136
— —remaining tasks, 358
— —reported mutinies, 136
— —ships still available, 105, 742
**—Italian,** importance, 168
— —and Pantelleria, 67
— —and Sicilian invasion, 136
— —surrenders, 262, 265, *335-38*
— — —figures, 294
— — —units at Malta, 327, *335*
**—Japanese,** methods, 105
— —must be destroyed, 136
— —strength, *202*
**—Polish,** with Allies, *418*
**—Royal,** and air power, 54
— —battle dress, 415
— —bombards Catania, *201*
— — —Pantelleria, *56, 57, 70, 71*
— —and boom defence, *648*
— —co-operation, 355
— —destroyer activities, *392, 393*
— —and evacuations, 227
— —Fleet Oilers, *712*
— —growing strength, 40
— —human torpedoes, *775*
— —landing-craft, *656-57*
— —the Little Ships, *328, 329*
— —and Malta's defence, 266
— —mans landing craft, 110, *111-14*
— —neatness, 191
— —Nettuno losses, 678
— —in Northern waters, *583*
— —prevents African evacuation, *41*
— — —invasion, *271-74*
— —rescue tugs, 744, 745
— —at Salerno, 294
— —and Sicilian evacuation, 200
— — —invasion, 130, *136, 137,* 156, 168, *169*
— —trails coat, 486, 508
— —training for, Ceylon, *789*
— —and Tunisia escapes, *10*
— —Turkish Mission with, *526*
— —U.S.N. helps, *487*
— —Wrens' work with, *321*
**—R. Australian,** in Eastern theatre, 262
— — —*Shropshire* for, *264*
**—R. Canadian,** expansion, 678
**—R. New Zealand,** in Eastern Theatre, 262
— — —history of, 615
**—Rumanian,** strength, 774
**—Russian,** German precautions against, 550
**—Turkish,** strength, 526, *528*
**—U.S.,** in Eastern theatre, 262
— — —growing strength, 40
— — —and Marshall Is., 646
— — —Pacific purpose, 636
— — —Pearl Harbour disaster, 40
— — —at Rendova, *170*
— — —trails coat, 486, 508
— — —*Victorious* with, *422*
Naxos, Ionian colony at, 171
Near Islands, Aleutians, *53*
Neckar, R., canalization, *430*
Nectarines, price, 191
Neditch, Serb Quisling, 524
Negroes, grand language, 735
Negros, Los, U.S. land on, *761*
Nelles, Vice-Adm. Percy, *232*
**Nelson, Horatio, Viscount,** at Calvi, 344
— — —Duke of Brontë, 171, 256
— — —and methods today, 508
Nepszava, Hungarian paper, 366
**Nettuno,** A.A. defence at, *631*
—Allied landing at, 579, *580-81*, *601*
— — —Gwynn on, 611
— — —naval losses at, 678
— — —naval support, 582
— — —warships cover, *614*
—Fifth Army at, *688-89*
**Neva R.,** A.A. guns on, *394, 624-25*
— —field guns on, *434*
Nevel, Russians take, 387
Nevis, mobile canteens from, *661*
Newall, Lieut.-Col. C. L. N., 86
**New Britain,** L.S.T. for, *640*
— —U.S. land on, *601, 602*
New Caledonia, U.S. supplies for, 99
Newcastle-on-Tyne, club for Danish seamen, *78*
**New Georgia,** Allies invest, *350*
— —battle area, 99, *109*
— —Japanese driven from, 253
— —Rendova taken, *170*
— —U.S. destroyers off, *455*
**New Guinea,** airman lost in, 443
— —air superiority in, 284
— —Allied drive in, *269*
— — —offensive in, *109*
— — —successes in, *596, 597*
— —Australians in, *793*
— —campaign in, survey, 323
— —Huon Gulf coastline, *323*
— —Japanese conquest, Johnston on, 659
New Jersey, U.S.S., in commission, 40
Newspapers, Russian, in Kharkov, 277
New Statesman, The, 703
Newton, Flt.-Lieut. W. E., V.C., *478*
New Year, Hammerton on, 511
**New York,** Danish ships at, *78*
— —and Italian surrender, *265*
New Zealand, H.M.S. 615
**New Zealanders,** in Cassino, 709, *739*, 769
— —with 8th Army, 452-53
— —at Mono Island, *569*
— —in snow camouflage, *644*
— —in Solomons, *502*
Ngakyedauk Pass, fighting in *754*
Nicastro, Sherman tanks at, *293*
Nicholas II, Tsar, 383
Nicholls, Capt., of *Penelope*, 762
Nicholson, Haig, in Sicily, 157
Nicholson, W. A., and Rev. G. Grundy, 409
Nickel, German shortage, 52
Nicobar Islands, lost bases, 230
Nicolson, Hon. Harold, M.P., 639
Niederfinow, ship-elevator at, 430
Niedermeyer, Gen. von, 398
Niels Iuel, Danish ship, *230*
Nigeria, war effort, *586-87*
Nikolai, Bishop, 62
Nikolayev, Russians take, 739, *771*
Nikopol, Russian success at, 611
**Nimitz, Adm. Chester,** on bombing Japan, 636
— —and Marshall Is., 646
Nissen Huts, Hammerton on, 639
Nixon, Lieut. John, Commando, *281*
Noah's Ark, the Avro York, *716*
Noise, modern love of, 703
Nolte, Col., Arnim's Chief of Staff, 30
Nordale (trawler), Coastguard and, 234
Norfolk, H.M.S., and *Scharnhorst* *518, 520*
Norfolk, mechanized harvest in, 250
Normandie Squadron, in Russia, *308*
Normans, in Sicily, 171
Northern East-West Highway, Australia, 584
Northern Territory, "jungle" practice in, *322*
North Sea, little ships in, *500*
North-South Trans-continental Road, 584
**Norway,** Allied air weakness in, 54
— —evacuation, 227
**Norway** *(cont.)*
—German invasion, reasons, 540
—invasion target, 73
—little ships off, 394
—sailor, with Aldis lamp, *418*
—submarine officers in, 616
**Norwegians,** escape to Britain, *75*
— —to Sweden, *414*
—as slaves, Poland, 125
Notes, hoarded, 374
**Noto,** Alexander's proclamation, *180*
—Fascist H.Q. at, *188*
Nova, Joao de, discoverer, 682
Novi Sad, massacre at, 366
**Novorossisk,** naval base, 390
—Russian advance on, *21*
Nubian, H.M.S. *70*
Nuffield, Lord, generosity, 735
Nugent, Driver John, 537
Numbers, for civil population, 511
Nunn, Group Captain, in Batavia, 410
Nuremberg, raid on, planes return, 765
Nürnberg (ship), 550
Nursery, for workers' children, *290*
**Nurses,** British, "Grey and Scarlet," 691
— —of Guy's Hospital, *290*
— —in Sicily, *212*
— —utility uniforms for, *514*
—Chinese, on Salween front, *465*
—Tamil, Ceylon, *428*
Nymphe (ship), guards *Tirpitz*, 550

## O

Oasis, The, desert newspaper, 29
Obituary Notices, Nazis ration, 44
**Observer Corps, Royal,** *758, 759*
— — —Coastguards and, 234
— — —women in, *514*
Ochey, in First Great War, 86
Octopus, Arabs catch, 250
**Odessa,** port for Bessarabia, 588
—Russians evacuate, 227
—Russians retake, 771, *778, 779*
Offa, H.M.S., endurance, 392
Offamil, Archbp. Walter, 171
Offensive, German cult, 259
**Oil,** in Dutch W. Indies, *408*
—on fire, Burma, *630*
—for Sicilian invasion, 142
—in Texas, *76*
—from Trinidad, 661, 747
Oil (Olive), as Arab bribe, 243
Oilers (ships), work, *712*
**Oktiabrskaya Revolutia** (ship) at Kronstadt, 550
— —at Leningrad, 582
Old Moore, Hammerton on, 287
Oliva, Adm. Romeo, surrenders, *338*
Oliver, Mrs. Sarah, at Cairo, 499
Olley, Arthur E., 63
Omrin, Chief, *586*
Omurtak, Gen., with Mediterranean Fleet, *526*
One Hundred and Fifty-fifth Field Battery, in Tunisia, 77, *125*
Operating Theatre, improvised, 755
Operation, on troopship, *553*
Opportune, H.M.S., and *Scharnhorst*, 518, 519
Oran, *Richelieu* returns to, *504*
Orange-peel, Hammerton on, 639
Ordnance, Royal, bombs by, *349*
**Orel,** battle of, German armour in, *204*
—fighting round, 66, *187*
—railway junction, 238
—Russian gains at, *131*
—Russians retake, 163, *194, 205*
Oribi, H.M.S., operation in, 392
Oropesa Float of minesweeper, *792*
Orphans, of Leningrad, *395*
**Ortona,** Amazon at, 569
—battle school in, *746*
—8th Army takes, *516, 554*
—fight for, *537*
—German parachutists in, 709
—refugees from, *599*
Osaka, U.S. bomb, 154
Osbourne, Lt.-Cdr. Harold, R.N.R., 744
Oslo, German arrests at, 506
Osset Grammar School, adopts *Imperialist*, 681
Ostia, Temple of Vulcan, *306*
Otter Control, in minesweeper, *792*
Outcrop Coal, for Army transport, *546*
Ouvry, Lt.-Cdr. John G. D., and magnetic mine, *124*, 454
Ovruch, Russians take, 451
Owen Stanley Mts., fighting in, 323
Oxen, ploughing with, Rome, *115*
Oxy-acetylene Torches, for butt-welding, *610*
Oxygen Apparatus, for draughts playing, *521*

## P

Paasikivi Juho, 684, *685*
**Pachino,** Allies take, *132*
—British tanks in, *166*
—Spitfire at, *184*
"Pacific Charter," 499
Pacific Fleet, U.S., trails coat, 486
**Pacific Ocean,** air war in, 636
— —Japanese bases in, *590*
— —Japanese reverses in, 742
— —S.W., Allied offensive in, 99, *109*, 118
— — — —Japanese danger in, 678
— — — — —withdrawal in, *350*
— — — — —new air technique in, 670
— —U.S. submarines in, 294, 582
— —Western, sea-power in, 646
Paddington, travel conditions at, *159*
Padua, St. Anthony's Church, *305*
Paestum, Temple of Poseidon, *306*
Paget, Gen. Sir Bernard, 515
**"Paiforce,"** Churchill with, 499
—Hulls with, 346
Palace Cavalry, of Bey of Tunis, *29*
Palau Islands, Japanese bases in, *590*
Palazzolo, Allied troops in, *165*
**Palermo,** beauty, 191
—human torpedoes at, *775*
—Mitchells bomb, 150
—pre-war view, *172*
—wall news-sheet, *149*
Palmer, Richard, Bishop of Syracuse, 171
Panormus, now Palermo, 171
**Pantelleria,** Allied air attacks on, 2, *505*
—Allies take, *56, 57,* 66, 70, *71, 102*
Panzer Troops, German, *548*
Papagos, Gen. Alexander, 179
Paper, from wood, 255
Parachute Brigade, British, war graves, *749*
Parachute Regiment (1st German), 709
**Parachutes,** for bombs, Rabaul, *509*
—for carrier-pigeons, *334*
—for magnetic mines, 124
—and self-inflating dinghy, *235*
—supplies by, Burma, *757, 753*
—training with, 92, *93*
—for Turkish pilots, *526, 528*
Parachute Surgical Units, 755
**Parachute Troops, Allied,** in Dodecanese, 294
— — —at Salamaua, 284
— — —in Sicily, 130
— — — —take Primo Sole bridge, *163, 207*
**— —Australian,** in New Guinea, 323
**— —British,** in action, 766
— — —and Canadian, descent, *637*
— — — —dropping, *719*
— — — —Recce rescues, 460
— — — —in Sicily, 150, 156, 188
— — — —in Yugoslavia, 699
**— —German,** in Cassino, 739
— — — —in Crete, *787*
— — — —on Leros, 442
**— —Polish,** *480*
**— —Russian** lead, 307
**— —Turkish,** *493*
**— —U.S.,** Sicily, *156*
Parcels, for H.Q. Tunisia, *100*
**Paris,** meat shortage, 543
—today, 799
Paris, Count of, 243
Paris, Treaty of, and Bessarabia, 588
Pariskaya Kommuna, battleship, 390, 774
Parker, Sgt. William, of Recce, 697
Parliament, Houses of, vaults searched, *798*
Parry, Rev. H., M.C., *59*
**Partisans,** and Chetniks, 342
—Yugoslav, achievements, *618*
— —politics, 524, *525*
*See also* Guerillas
**Pathfinder Force,** adventures, 473
— —Air-Cdre. Bennett and, *479*
— —a member (by J. Berry) *720*
Patourel, Capt. H. W. Le, V.C., *59*
Patrimonio, welcomes Allies, *376*
**Patrols,** British, in Bizerta, 4
— —in Pugliano, *341*
—Russian, at Kanyev *613*

**Patrols** *(cont.)*
— —Ukraine front, 397
— —U.S. in Bizerta, 4
—of Yugoslav partisans, *618*
**Patton, Lt.-Gen.,** enters Messina, *229*
— —U.S. commander, Sicily, *130*
Paul, Prince, Regent, 524
Pauses, between attacks, need, 142
Pavelitch, Anton, leads Ustachi, 342, 524
Pavesi, Adm. Gino, 70
" Pay-as-you-earn " Plan, 311
PE 2, Russian bomber, *252*
Peanut, *Witch's* mascot, *393*
**Pearl Harbour,** air attack on, 348
— —base impotent, 454
— —disaster at, 40
— —Japanese pilots briefed for, *435*
Pears, Charles, paintings by, *18, 722*
Peat, Mr., on paper waste, 31
Peder Skram, Danish ship, *230*
Peenemunde, raid on, *253*
Peirse, Air Chief Marshal Sir Richard, *577*
Pella, Vespasian, at Berne, 686
Pelorus Sight, *393*
**Penelope, H.M.S.,** *Breconshire* and, 762
— —sunk, 678
— —Ulster built, 650
Penguin, type of jeep, 300
Penman, Wing Cdr. W. M., D.F.C., *318*
Pensions, increase, 255
—for Home Guard, 798
Percy, Capt. J. T., ferry pilot, *362*
Perle (submarine), off Corsica, 294
Pernikoff, Alexander, " Bushido," 595
Persano, Adm., off Lissa, 678
Persia, railway importance, 238
—roads made in, 790, *791*
Pert, P./O R. S., D.S.M., *423*
Peru, roadmaking in, 790, *791*
Perugia, Mandoren Gate, *304*
Pester Lloyd, Hungarian paper, 366
**Peter, the Great,** built Peterhof, 633
— —and the Lipovani, 588
— —and St. Petersburg, 622
Peter II (Yugoslavia), *524*
**Peterhof,** destruction at, *633*
— —past and present, *623*
Peterman, Ivan, 156
Peters, Capt. F. T., V.C., *123*
Peter Strasser (aircraft carrier) 105
Petlyakov-2, Soviet dive-bomber *420*, 692
Petrol, U.S. Black Market in, 767
Petrol Station, Sicily, *185*
**Petropavlovsk** (ship), at Kronstadt, 550
—at Leningrad, 582
Petrovitch, Maxim, in *Kharkov*, 422
Peyer, Hungarian Socialist, 366
Peyer, Sergt., of Maritime Regt., 537-38
Philante, H.M.S., *203*
Philip, André, on Committee of Liberation, *38*
Philippine Is. loss, Clark Lee on, 563
Phillips, Sir Frederick, 255
Phoenicians, in Sicily, 171
Phosphorus, for smoke screens 654
**Photographic Reconnaissance Units,** activity, 620
— — —of R.A.F., *285*
Photography, Aerial, and map-making, *558*
— —W.A.A.F's and, 797
Phrase-books, Hammerton on, 415
Piarco Airfield, Trinidad, 747
Piat, anti-tank weapon, *621*
Pick, Frank, and London Transport, 122
Pidsley, Reginald, records Berlin raid, 313
Piedmonte, civilians clear débris, 389
**Pig,** abandoned, Tunisia, 29
—wears slogan, Ceylon, *428*
**Pigeons,** baskets for, *226*
—bombers carry, *87*
—parachutes for, *334*
**Pike, E. Royston,** on Britain's harvest, 218
— —on Finland's peace efforts, 684
— —on the Home Front, 58, 122, 246, 311, 374, 438
— —on Italy's situation, 7
— — —surrender, 265
— —on R. Marines, 628
— —on Sicilian history, 171
— —on Teheran and Cairo Conferences, 499
— —war survey, 707, 739
— —on war in Yugoslavia, 524
Pikemen, of H.A.C., *482*
Pile, Gen. Sir Frederick, *378*
Pilfering, increase, 511
**Pillboxes,** deserted Italian, Sicily, *178*
—floating, *231*
—Italian, dummy gun in, *169*
—of Kwajalein, capture, 729
**Pilots,** Chinese, in U.S.A., *35*
—Japanese, for Pearl Harbour, *435*
—of R.A.F., training, *694, 695*
—Russian, in Caucasus, *433*
—testing for altitude, *521*
—Turkish, of Bisley plane, *526*
Pindar, on Akragas, 171
Pindus, battle of, 179
Pinguin (raider), sunk, 422
Pioneers, in Sicily, *176-77*
**Pipe-line,** oil by, Italy, *652*
— —from Texas to Illinois, 76
Pipers, welcome prisoners, Leith, *402*
Pisa, the Leaning Tower, *304*
Pitch, from Trinidad, *747*
Pitt, Lt. Arthur J., R.N., *60*
**Place, Lt. B. C. G.,** submarine commander, *327*
— —wins V.C., *649*
Place Names, language differences, 447
Plastics, future of, Hammerton, on, 543
Platt, Gen. SirWilliam, 675
**Ploesti,** airfields bombed, 214, *216*
— —Bucharest and, 686
—from Foggia, 330
—oil refineries bombed, *186*
**Ploughing,** with Bren-carrier, *147*
—at R.A.F. station, *770*
—in Rome, *115*
Plumbago, from Ceylon, 788
" Plymouth Argylls," The, 628
Pockets, Hammerton on 415
Pola, Germans and, 168
**Poland,** Navy with Allies, *418*
—Norwegian slaves in, 125
**Poles,** make artificial limbs, *610*
—in mine-laying squadron, 763
—with 8th Army, *786*
Police, R.A.F., with damaged bomber, *381*
Polo, Marco, and Silk Road, 790
Poltava, Russians take, *309*
Pompeii, Temple of Apollo, *306*
Pompey, used smoke-screen, 654
Ponape, details, 590
Ponomareva, Senior Sgt. Valentina, *364*
Ponta Delgada (São Miguel), *361*
Ponomartsev, Lt.-Col., 441
**Pontoon Bridge,** over Volturno, *357*
— —Russian, across Desna, *309*
— — —on Dnieper, *365*
Pontoons, at Kwajalein, *743*
Porpoise, H.M. Submarine, Bennington in, *616*
Porpoises, as torpedoes, 392
**Portal, Air Chief Marshal Sir Charles,** at Quebec Conference, *232*
— —in warship, *79*
Porters, Native, New Guinea, *793*
**Port Moresby,** defence of, 659
— —Japanese attack on, 323
Porto Paglia, Gulf of, Sardinia, *8*
Portsmouth (Eng.), invasion barges built at, 110
Portsmouth (N.H.), submarines launched at, 582
Portugal, tries out defences, *360*
Posters, Russian, Leningrad, *394*
Potato Harvest, *386*
Potenza, 8th Army takes, *291*
**Pound, Adm. Sir Dudley,** with Churchill, *79*
— —death, *358*
— —First Lord on, 678
— —at Quebec Conference, *232*
Powell, Sqn. Ldr., at Goose Bay, *88*
Powell, Sgt. G., in Tunisia, *442*
Prang, To, Hammerton on, 95, 223
**Pre-fabrication,** in Australia, 584
—for M.L's, 501
Premuda (destroyer), formerly *Dubrovnik*, 136
**Pressure Chamber,** cold, *574*
— —for testing pilots, *521*
" Pretty," misuse of word, 159
Preveza, R.A.F. bomb, *236*
**Priestley, Mark,** on destroyers, 392
— —on transport planes, *716*
Primo Sole Bridge, Allies take, *207*
— — —Sicily, *163*
Prince of Wales, H.M.S., 348
Printing-press, by parachute, 716
Prinz Eitel Friedrich, raider, 422
**Prinz Eugen** (ship), possibly at Gdynia, 327
— —returns to Baltic, 550
— —speed, 358
— —*Trident*, damages, 617
Pripet R., Germans cross, *741*
**Pripet Marshes,** Germans retreat to, 291
— —Russian offensive near, 515
**Prisoners-of-War, Allied,** life in Germany, *409*
— — —released from ship, *61*
— —**Axis,** in Italy, *388*
— — —Mihailovitch and, 342
— — —problem of, 142
— — —Tunisian numbers, 1, 2, 6
— —**British,** from Cos, *468*
— — —repatriated, *359, 399-402*, 409, *416*
— — —in Tunis, 28
— — —dealing with, *780*
— —**German,** at Anzio, 730, *780*
— — —of *Georges Leygues*, *43*
— — —on horseback, *29*
— — —in Italy, *489*
— — —in Leningrad, *394, 624*
— — —of M.L., *329*
— — —from Nettuno, *580*
— — —Ortona, *516, 537*
— — —of R. Navy, *10*
— — —at Salerno, *292*
— — —in Scafati, *346*
— — —from *Scharnhorst*, 571
— — —in Sicily, *162*
— — —in Tunisia, *1*
— — —Tunisian numbers, 29
— — —wounded, Italy, *353*
— —**Italian,** in Lampedusa, *71, 103*
— — —at Licata, *132*
— — —in Sicily, *161, 162, 166, 207*
— —**Japanese,** in Burma, *683*, 761, *762*
— — —from Changteh, *664*
— — —Kwajalein, *780*
— — —Tarawa, *512*
**Prisons,** in Franco Spain, *339*
—war work in, 374
**Proclamation,** by Gen. Alexander, Sicily, *180*
—German, in " Roma," 324
Projector, anti-tank, Piat, *621*
Promotion, in Army, Hammerton on, 767
Pronunciation, by B.B.C., 543
Propaganda, German, sows dissension, 40
Prophecies, falsification, 575
Proteé (submarine), 40
Pruth R., Russians reach, 739
Pryse, Cdr. H. L., R.N.R., 744
**Pskov,** past history, 383
—Russian advance on, *643, 684*
Psyche, H.M.N.Z.S., in First Great War, 615
Psychiatry, and the Army, 319, 755
Public Health, emergency laboratories, *546*
**Pugliano,** British mortar at, *292*
—Fifth Army in, *341*
Pulborough, harvest at, *219*
**" Punch,"** on army officers, 351
—Hammerton on, 447
Punjab Regt. (1st) in Burma, *708*
Puppies, of Normandie Squadron, *308*
Purcell, Rev.—, of Dover, 534
Pursuer, H.M.S., 486
Pushkin, Leningrad suburb, *625*
Pyjamas, for soldiers, 479
Pyramids, air-transport over, *717*
Pyramus, H.M.N.Z.S. 615

## Q

" Q for Queenie " bombs Berlin, *473*
" Quack," amphibian Jeep, 300
Quebec Conference, *232-33*
Queen Alexandra Imp. Nursing Service, in Sicily, *212*
Queen Mary, R.M.S., as transport, *552*
Queen Olga (ship) off Sicily, 201
Queensland Inland Road, 584
" Queue Feet," 58
Quill, Jeff, test pilot, 470

## R

**Rabaul,** air attacks on, *509*
—Allied threat to, *350*, 454
—helldivers bomb, *604*
—intensive bombing of, 668
—strategic importance, 253
—U.S. designs on, 99, 105
— — —in harbour, 678
Rack-rent, Hammerton on, 575
Radio, and U-boat hunting, 615
Radio Apparatus, from German bomber, *52*
**Radio Operator,** Canadian, in Azores, *541*
— —of R.C.S., *437*
Raditch, Stephan, death, 524
Radzinsky, Stanislav, 251
**Raeder, Adm. Erich,** Hitler and, 398
— —and surface raiders, 105
**Rafts,** life-saving devices, *11*
—Russian pontoon, on Dnieper, *365*
Raiding Party, Russian, on tank, *187*
Rails, wooden, for Russian mud, *420*
**Railways,** British, women's work on, *514*
—Burmese, Chindits blow up, 46
—of Germany, strain, 662
— —weak spot, 51
—for invasion, 642
—Italian, civilians repair, *292*
—repairing, N. Africa, 142
—thefts from, 767
—strategic importance, 238
Railway Station, Sicilian, British attack, *220*
Ramb I, (raider) sunk, 422
Ramsay, Adm. Sir Bertram, *137*
Ramsay, Capt., M.P., on Franco, 339
Ramsden, Jack, cameraman, 278
Ramsey, Guy, " One Continent Redeemed," 243
Ramu Valley, Australians in, *793*
Randazzo, wrecked transport at, *228*
Range-finder, of British mortar, *19*
Ranger, U.S.S., *678*
Rangers, U.S., training, *144-45*
**Rangoon,** important objective, 556
—jeeps retreat from, 300
Rangoon-Bangkok Rly., 556
Rashleigh, Capt. Vernon, R.N., 234
Rastrelli, designed Peterhof, 633
Rathborne, 1st Off. M. R., M.B.E., *382*
Ration Books, new British, 58
Rats, war against, 251
Ravager, H.M.S., and *Tirpitz*, *777*
Ravenna, S. Apollinare Nuovo, *305*
Raviscanina, peasants of, *389*
Rawalpindi, H.M.S., 518
Rawlings, Cyril, fisherman, 680
Raworth, Maj. J. S., of 155th Battery, 77
Razjelnaya, Russians take, 771
**Razor Blades,** production, *91*
— —salvaged, 14
Rearguard, and evacuation, 227
Recce : see Reconnaissance Corps
**Reconnaissance Corps,** at Anzio, *697*
— — D. Rs. of, 436
— —work and training, *460, 461*
Reconstruction, Min. of, 438
Recruits, Russian, *120*
Red Banner Guards, at Kiev, 441
**Red Cross,** British, convalescent homes, *354*
— — —in Ceylon, *428*
— — —hospital, Anzio, *784-85*
— — —and repatriated prisoners, *400*
— — —in Sicily, *212*
— —International, Suva carnival for, *714*
— — —Switzerland's work for, *718*
— — —vehicles, Cassino, *709*
— — —and war graves, *747*
— — —work for prisoners, 409, 410
Red Guards, relieve Leningrad *645*
**Refugees,** bombing of, technique, 51
—Chinese, from Honan, *117*
—Greek, in Egypt, *492*
—Italian, at San Vito, *599*
—return to Brontë, *256*
—Russian, return, *276*
Regents, Bulgarian, illegal choice, 270
Regent's Canal, coal barge on, *674*
Reggio, Allies take, *260*
Regimental Aid Post, Anzio, *784*
Regulation 18B, 543
Reid, Flt. Lt. W., V.C., *760*
Reilly, Pte. William, escape from Cos, *377*
Reinbold, Lt. Richard, 761
Reindeer, Russians use, *425*
R.E.M.E. and invasion of Sicily, *142*
Rendova Is., U.S. take, 99, 105 *109, 170, 350*
Rennell, Lord, *180*
Renown, H.M.S. and *Scharnhorst*, 518
Rescue Tugs, British, work, *615* 744, *745*
**Reserves,** German, in Italy, 483
— —in Russia, 483
— —weakness in, 163
Restaurant, underground, Dover 534
Retreat, Guards beat, Hyde Park, *226*
Reveillé, for A. C. F., *407*
Reynolds-Hale, Lieut., 329
Rezhitsa, Russians take, 451
Rhine R., bridges over, 662
Rhineland, R.A.F. raids, 118
**Rhodes,** Cyprus and, *148*
—the harbour, *68*
—Italian failure at, 422
Rhodesia, Southern, aeroplanes repaired in, *322*
Ribbentrop, Joachim von, *366*
Rice, Changteh a centre, *664*
Richardson, Lieut. J., in Italy, *449*
**Richelieu** (ship) Danish ships and, 78
— —returns to Oran, *504*
Richthofen, Marshal von, 149
Rimini, Arch of Augustus, *306*
Rionero, on fire, *490*
Ripley, H.M.S., in cave, 392
Ritchie, S/Ldr. P. J. E., D.F.C., *638*
Rivets, for landing craft, *138*
**Roads,** Allies, make, New Guinea, 323
—new Australian, 584, *585*
— —making, *790, 791*
Roberts, H.M.S., monitor, *488*
Robinson, Rear - Adm., in D. W. I., *408*
Rochester, Bishop of, on British morals, 58
Rocket-glider Bomb, Macmillan on, 454
**Rocket Guns,** British, over London, *668*
— — —Home Guard man, *706, 798*
— —German, in Russia, *724*
Rocket Shells, German use, *485*
Rodgers, Lt. Cdr. B. H. Craig, *681*
Rodney, H.M.S., firing, *457*
Roe, A. V., aviation pioneer, 383
Roehampton, Q. Mary's Hospital, 610
Roehm, Capt. Ernst, fate, 782
Rogachev, Russians take, 643
Roi Island, U.S. take, *660*
**Rokossovsky, Gen. Konstantin,** *223*
— —drive on Orel, *194*
— —Gomel offensive, 451
— —takes Mozyr, 547
— — —Rogachev, 643
Rolleston Hall, spinning at, *354*
Rolls-Royce Merlin Aero-Engine, *738*
Roma (paper) German proclamation in, 324
**Roma** (ship) sunk from air, 348
—torpedoed, 262, *336*
Roman Empire, and Sicily, 171
**Rome,** Allied advance on, *325, 388, 489, 490, 612, 644*
—to be bombed, 7
—bombed, Doolittle and, 154
—first raid on, 182, *183*, 214
—Germans occupy, 265
—Hammerton on, 383
—an " open city," 115
—ploughing in, *115*
—rejoicings in, *213*
—views of, *303*
**Rommel, Field Marshal Erich,** and Denny, 83
— —at Salonika, *371*
Roosevelt, Mrs. Eleanor, *42*
**Roosevelt, Pres. Franklin D.,** on Azores bases, 705
— —and bombing of Japan, 253, 412
— — —of Tokyo, *154*
— —at Cairo Conference, *476, 499*
— —on fall of Foggia, 330
— —on invasion of Sicily, *129*
— —to Italian people, 149
— —Mackenzie's biography, *531*
— —at Quebec Conference, *232-33*
— —and ships for Russia, 710
— —at Teheran, *496*
— —on U-boat war, 200
— —and U-boats, joint declaration, 615
— —uses jeep, 300
**Roosevelt, Theodore,** on hero-worship, 531
— —and Russo-Japanese peace, 435
Rope, Ulster makes, 650
Rorqual H.M. Submarine, *617*
Rose Hip Syrup, manufacture, *354*
Roslavl, Russians take, *309*
Ross, Capt. Marion, *226*
Rotterdam, war graves in, 44
Roundel Hat, in Denmark, *248*
Rovno, Russians take, 611
Roxborough, Lieut. J. G. Y., R.N., *423*
Royal Canadian Engineers, in Sicily, 157
**Royal Engineers,** build deck-craft, *356*
— —in Italy, 259, 483
— —and map-making, *558*
— —repair road, Vasto, *491*
— —roadmakers, *790, 791*
— —in Sicily, *176-77*

**Royal Engineers** *(cont.)*
——with U.S.A.T.C., *546*
——at Waterloo Bridge, *311*
Royalists, French, in N. Africa, 243
Royal Marines Mobile Naval Base Defence Organization, 174
See Marines, Royal
Rubber, from Ceylon, *788*
Rudnik, Russian leader, 249
Ruffini, Cardinal, built Villa Falconieri, *306*
**Ruhr,** bombing of, preparations, *151*
—bombs on, figures, 284
—dams bombed, 3, 22, *24*, *25*
——King with pilots, *33*
—R.A.F. raids, 118, *119*
Rum, from Trinidad, *747*
**Rumania,** affairs in, 686
—Bessarabia and, 588
—fear in, 707, *734*
—mercantile marine, 390
—oilfields, Boris and, 270
—oil refineries bombed, 186
—Russian offensive in, *739*
Rummy, Hammerton on, 671
Rumour, Hammerton on, 351
**Runway,** Chinese make, *466*
—R.A.F. Regt. unload, *129*
Russell, D. A., and modern aircraft, 542
**Russia,** advance in Kiev Salient, *515*
——on Pskov, *643*
——on Rumania, *686*
—and armistice for Finland, 684, *685*
—armour manufacture, *426*
—battle-line (June 1943), *34*
———(Aug. 27), *227*
———(Nov. 4), *387*
———(Dec. 3), *451*
———(Jan. 14, 1944), *547*
—and Bessarabia, *588*
—Bren-carriers for, *258*
—brilliant organization, 194
—Bulgarian sympathy with, 270
—Central front, *131*
—continuous advance, 739
—devastation seen from air, *538*
—fighting in (Dec. 1943), *458*
—German aircraft and, 668
——cemetery in, *45*
——locomotives in, 662
——mass graves in, 44
——plans for, 206
——strength in, 34
—Horthy's doubts about, 366
—Japanese hatred, 595
—Junkers' negotiations with, 398
—Korsun pocket, *611*
—? lost opportunities, 419
—Manstein defeated in, *397*
—and Moscow Conference, *396*
—new German offensive, 131, *141*
—new Red offensive, 163
—Orel-Bielgorod Front *163*
—R.A.F.'s debt to, 355
—railway importance in, 238
—reserves' training, *120*
—rocket-shells in, *485*
—Russian advances in, 677, 707
—ships for, 710
—Smolensk - Bryansk - Kharkov line, *194*
—Southern offensive, *364-65*
—Soviet offensive continues, 276, 277, 291, *309*
—steel manufacture, *427*
—Turkey's pact with, 526
—vaccines for, by air, 362
—victories of, *420*, *421*
Russky, Gen., at Pskov, 383
Russo-Japanese War, peace after, 435
Russ-plywood, the Yu. 2, 726, *727*
Rutherford, Sir Thomas, with Wavell, 429
Rymer, Sub-Lieut. K. W., R.N., 392
Ryti, President Risto, 684
Ryuzyo, Japanese aircraft carrier, 582
Rzhev, Bishop Nikolai in, 62

## S

Saadabad Pact, 526
Saamis, reindeer owners, *425*
Saarbrücken, Germans leave, 51
Saba, vineyards at, 588
Sabang, Allied raid on, 774
Sahib, H.M.S., survivor's story, 665
Sailors, flag days for, 703
St. Andrew, hospital ship, 633
St. Angelo, British guns at, *676*
St. Christopher, canteens from *661*
St. David, hospital ship, *633*
Sainte-Beuve, Charles Augustin, 319
S. Giles', Cripplegate, service in ruins, *258*
St. Helena, and Ascension Is., *682*
St. Nazaire, M.L.s at, 501
St. Paul's Cathedral, *217*
**Saipan,** Japanese base, *590*
—U.S. raid, 646
Salamaua, Allies take, 269, 284, 323, *350*, 454
Salarino, Allies in, *181*
**Salazar, Dr. Antonio d'Oliveira,** *383*
——Egerton on, *467*
——and Portugal's defences, *360*
Salcano, railway viaduct, *343*
Sale, Stewart, death, 346
**Salerno,** *304*
—Allied advance on, *293*
—Allied landing craft at, *295*
—battle of beaches, Shapiro on, 314
——monitors and, *488*
—beaches, map, *292*
—Bomber Command at, 604
—escort carriers at, 486
—German prisoners at, *292*
—Tedder at, 515
Salis, Prof. von, 718
**Salonika,** from Foggia, 330
—Rommel at, *371*
**Salute,** for C.O.'s desk, 351
—to U.S. dead, Marshall Is., *748*
"Salute the Soldier," 735
**Salvage,** by naval tugs, 744, *745*
—R.A.F. and, *14*
— by R. Navy, *648*
Salween, R., fighting on, *464-65*
Samos, Allies occupy, 294
Sampan, as ambulance, Burma, *708*
Samsonia, H.M. Tug, 744
San Casimiro (ship), 518
San Clemente, stretcher-bearers at, *506*
Sandstorms, in Western Desert, 723
San Elia, Fighting French take, *555*
San Giorgio, port, Lissa, 678
San Giuliano, Marquis di, 220
**Sangro, R.,** ammunition for, *494*
——Indians, on, *513*
——N. Zealanders on, *453*
——Recce on, *461*
Santa Maria Ridge, 8th Army takes, *453*
San Vito, refugees at, *599*
San Vittore, Allies reach, 517
Sao Miguel, in Azores, *361*
**Sappers, Allied,** in Italy, *325*
——make roads, *790*
——repair Italian roads, *388*
—**British,** mine-detecting, *580*
——in Sicily, 157
—**German,** in Russia, *459*
—**Russian,** detecting mines, *673*
——mine bridge, *564*
*See also* Royal Engineers
Saratoga, U.S.S., refitted, 550
**Sardinia,** Germans abandon, 294
—invasion target, 73
—strategic importance, *8*
Sarny, Russians take, 547, *549*
Saseno, Italians occupy, 342
"Satchel Charges," in Marshal Is., 729
**Sattelberg,** Allied attack on, *596*
—Union Jack over, 707
Saucy, H.M. Tug, 744
**Saumarez, H.M.S.,** in Northern waters, *583*
——and *Scharnhorst*, 518
Saunders, Hilary St. G., 31
Saunders-Roe, build transport planes, 716
Savage, H.M.S., 518, 519
Savikov, Senior Lieut., *385*
Savoia (ship), surrenders, *336*
Saxtead Mill, in use, *770*
Sayer, P. E. G., death, 470
Sbiba, Churchill tanks at, 442
Scafati, German prisoners in, *346*
Scafati Bridge, battle for, *345*
Scavenius, overthrown, 248
Schammer-Osten, Reichs Sports-Fuehrer, 406
**Scharnhorst,** diagrammatic drawing, *519*
—sinking of, *518*, *722*
——aircraft and, 540
——eye-witness stories, 570, *571*
——plan, 550
—work for, 358
Schell, Gen. Adolf von, 662
Schlesien, coast-defence ship, 550
Schleswig-Holstein, coast-defence ship, 550
School Children, help with harvest, 218
Schools, of Naples, reopened, *736*
Schuster, Cardinal, 289
Sciacca, Greek remains near, 171
"Scorched Earth," in Italy, *490*
**Scorpion, H.M.S.** and *Scharnhorst*, 518, 519
———survivors, 571
Scott, Lt. Cdr. Peter M., on Little Ships, *328*
Scottish Troops, in Sicily, *208*
Scouts, Kachin, Burma, *751*
Scrap Metal, for Japan, from Australia, 659
**Sea,** Command of, German bid for, 40
—War at, Mc Murtrie on, 10, 40, 73, 105, 136, 137, 168, 200, 230, 262, 294, 327, 358, 390, 422, 454, 486, 518, 550, 582, 646, 710, 742, 774
Sea Cadet Corps, Ulstermen in, 650
**Seafire Planes,** landing, *12*
——mechanic caught on, 793.
——and *Tirpitz*, 742, *794*
Seagrim, Maj. D. A., V.C., *59*
Sea-Harvest, thanksgiving for, *354*
Seamen, Danish, club for, *78*
Seaplanes, cruisers cease to need, 486
**Sea Power,** air power and, 444
——and invasion, 73
——and Japan, 136
——and military evacuation, 227
**Searchlights,** airborne, in Germany, 316
—carbon for, *610*
—Projectors, A.T.S. work, *706*
—round Lisbon, *360*
Sea-Scouts, in Germany, *406*
Sea-sickness, and landing parties, 110
Sebastopol, Russians evacuate, 227
Sebenico (destroyer), 136
Second Escort Group, destroys U-boats, 710, *711*
Secrecy, and evacuation, 227
Secret Weapon, German talk, 454
Security, Post-war, Moscow Conference and, 396
Seeadler, German raider, 422
Segesta, Greek remains at, 171
Seip, Prof. Didrik Arup, *507*
Selassie, Haile, restoration, 7
Selborne, Lord, 52
Selby, Gen., at Teheran, 499
**Self-propelled Gun,** British, in Sicily, *197*
———German, in Russia, *204*
———Russian, Leningrad, *589*
———U.S., Salerno, *293*
Selinus, remains of, 171
Senegalese, jeeps for, *663*
Senglea, George VI at, *101*
Senior Training Corps, and A.C.F., 406
**Sentry,** German, Novorossisk, *21*
—Italian, Germans kill, 28
—of R.A.F. Regt., Azores, *705*
—Rumanian, Tiraspol, *734*
—stamping, theories, 351
Seraph, H.M. Submarine, *617*
Serbs, in Yugoslavia, 524
Servaes, Lt., of Ferry Control, *298*
Services, The, showmen of, *566*
Seven Years' War, Marines in, 628
Sewing-machine, for tents, Italy, *690*
Seys, Sqn. Ldr. R. G., *152*, 362
Sferro, Allies take, 240
Sforza, Count, Hammerton on, 447
Shaggy Ridge, New Guinea, *715*
Shah, of Persia, greets Churchill, 497
Shakespeare, H.M.S., refitting, *722*
**Shakespeare, William,** misquoted, 31.
——use of "rack," 575
Shakirova, Rashida, electrician, *484*
Shapiro, L. S. B., on Salerno beaches, 314
Sharpshooters, U.S., in Burma, *772*
**Shaw, Capt. Frank H.,** on aircraft and U-boats, 202
——on Fleet oilers, *712*
——on naval gunnery, 456
——on submarine cables, 302
——on transport ships, 552
**Shaw, George Bernard,** and Macmillans, *479*
———and spelling reform, 511
Shaw, W. F. B., and magnetic mine, 124
**Sheep,** by bomb dump, *642*
—in N. Africa, 38
Sheffield, H.M.S., *518*, *519*
Sheherbina, Ivan, in *Kharkov*, 422
Shell-cases, empty, from London barrage, *578*
Shell Fuses, Home Guard sets, *632*
Shelling, warning of, Dover, *534*
**Shells,** for British submarines, 274
—German, for Atlantic Wall, 20
—Russian, placing, *741*
—smoke by, 654
Shell-shock, drug for, 351
Sheludenko, Junior Lieut., 441
Shepherd, P/O G. E., D.S.M., *696*
Sheppard, Maj. E. W., "The Army," 95
**Sherman Tanks,** bogged, Italy, *494*
——in Cassibile, *167*
——in Catania, *240-41*
——Churchill with, *738*
——ford river, Italy, *388*
——in Italy, *489*, *612*
——on manoeuvres, 666, 667
——near Cava, *325*
——at Nicastro, *293*
——U.S., in Sicily, *134*
Shikari, H.M.S., gale adventure, 392
Shiozawa, Adm. Koichi, 422
Shipbuilding, in Northern Ireland, 650
Ship-Elevators, Germany's use, 430
Shippigan, H.M.S., minesweeper, *582*
**Shipping, Allied,** reduced sinkings, 34
——R. Marines guard, *629*
—for amphibious operations, 142
—**Axis,** in Greek canal, *236*
—**Japanese,** bombed, *350*
——diminution, 284
——Pacific losses, 582
——skip-bombing against, *670*
—losses compared, *678*
Ships, replanning, seaman on, 351
Shoes, repair, difficulties, 415
Shoe Shop, in Berlin basement, *561*
Shore-landing Deckcraft, *356*
Showmen, of the Services, *566*
Shropshire, H.M.S., for Australian navy, *264*
Shropshire Light Infantry, *408*
Shrypnikova, R., woman sniper, *420*
Shultz, Capt., at Goose Bay, *88*
Sicani, ancient Sicilians, 171
Siceli, invaded Sicily, 171
Sicilian Straits, Axis air convoy destroyed, 72
Sicilian Tip, battle of, *162*
**Sicily,** air cover in, 182
—airfields reconditioned, *184*
—Allied invasion, *130*, *132*, *133-35*, *176-177*, *178*
———air power and, 150
———commanders, 131
———eye-witness stories, 156-58
———Gwynn on, 162
———maps for, 558
———Marines in, 174
———Navy and, *169*
———preparations, *142*
———training, *129*, *143-46*
———U-boat failure, 200
—Allied occupation, 180, *181*
—bombing of, *149*
—campaign in, *161*, 162-63, *164-67*, *207-10*, 224, *228-29*, *239-42*
——last stages, *195*
—defence, Tunis and, 2
—8th Army in, *196*, *197*, *198*
—German evacuation, Navy and, 200
—Goums in, 404, *405*
—Greek remains in, *173*
—h story, Pike on, 171
—invasion target, 73
—Italian armistice signed, 265
—Recce in, 460
—Red Cross in, *212*
—scenes in, 9
—sulphur miners in, 319
—Tactical Air Force and, *225*
Sidi Barani, and Italian morale, 675
Sidi Nsir, 155th Battery at, 77, *125*
Sidney, Maj. W. P., V.C., *760*
Siebel Ferry, submarine sinks, 602
Siege guns, German at Leningrad, *625*
Siege Mortar, German, Russians take, *725*
Siegfried Line, Lochner on, 51
Siena, the cathedral, *304-05*
**Signaller,** Canadian, wounded, *260*
—of *Ravager*, *777*
Signalling, with flags, China, 466
Signalmen, of Ferry Control, *298*
**Signals,** International, Coastguards learn, *234*
—R.A.F. and Transport Command, 362
—from U.S. bomber, *596*
**Signals, Royal Corps of,** *436*, *437*
——and Golden Arrow, *728*
Signals Section, R.N., Sicily, *169*
Signposts, British, at Anzio, *690*
Sikhs, as snipers, Arakan, *3*
Sikorski, Gen. W., death, *98*
Silk Road, development, 790
Silos, for grain storage, *770*
Silvaplana (ship), scuttled, *43*
Simeon II, K. of Bulgaria, *270*
Simeto, R., bridges over, *163*, *207*
Simi, in Dodecanese, *68*
Simonds, Maj.-Gen. Guy, lands in Sicily, *175*
Simonov, Konstantin, on Yu, 2, 726
Simpson, Capt. G. W. W., R.N., 616
Simpson Haven, now Rabaul, 454
**Sinclair, Rt. Hon. Sir Archibald,** air estimates, 700
——and A.T.C., 651
**Singapore,** advantage to Japan, 230
—fall of, nurses at, 691
—Furneaux' escape from, 379, 410
Singer, P/O A.M., D.F.C., *318*
Singer, P/O P. L., D.F.C., *318*
Singh, Havildar Parkash, V.C., *123*
Sinkiang, roads in, 790
Siren, Ceylon version, *428*
Sixth Army, German, destruction, 387
Skanderbeg, Albanian patriot, 342
Skate, H.M.S., dismasted, 392
Skeaping, John, bust by, *696*
Skis, for Yu. 2, *727*
Skip-bombing, diagram, *670*
Skold, Dr., *756*
Skopa, Bova, Mussolini and, *686*
Skymaster, transport plane, *363*, *717*
Slang, of R.A.F., 223
Slessor, Kenneth, 601
Slim, Lt.-Gen. W. J., *671*, 772
Slovenes, in Yugoslavia, 524
Smart, Norman, 377
**Smith, Gen. Bedell,** at Betio, 475
——and Italian armistice, 265
Smith, Ben, M.P., new appointment, *438*
Smith, Ldg. Signaller J., *423*
Smith, Surgeon-Lieut. Thomas, operates, 392
Smith, Sgt. William, invades Italy, *281*
Smoke, for offence and defence, 654
Smoke-rockets, Germans use, *296*
**Smoke-screen,** in battle school, *641*
——Blenheims lay, *146*
——for British landing craft, *295*
——by Valentine tank, *113*
Smoking, for women, Hammerton on, *767*
**Smolensk,** Germans withdraw from, 192
—Russians take, *309*, *333*
Smuggling, Coastguard and, 234
**Smuts, Field-Marshal Jan C.,** at Cairo Conference, 499
——election victory, 255
——and strategic air force, 86
——on Teheran Conference, 496
——at 10, Downing Street, *322*
Smuts, Capt., at 10, Downing Street, *322*
Smuts Report, and R.A.F., 477
Sneath, Pte., barber, *690*
**Snipers,** 8th Army deal with, *356*
—German, dead, *5*
—Indian, in Arakan, *3*
—Kachin, Burma, *683*
—N.Z., Cassino, *784*
—Russian, in Caucasus, *433*
——training, *565*
——women as, *420*
—search for, Torre Annunziata, *384*
—in Sicily, Americans and, *166*
**Snow,** in Derbyshire, *674*
—guns camouflaged with, *589*
—tanks camouflaged for, *693*
Snowden, Lord, on coolies' clothing, *671*
Snow White, Sqn. Ldr., carrier pigeon, 334
Soap Factory, at Kishinev, 588
"Sobbing Sisters," German mortars, *297*
Socialism, definition, 639
Socks, care of, 5th Army, *740*
**Sofia,** from Foggia, 330
—Nazi H.Q., *270*
Sokol, Polish submarine, 678
Sola, La, destroyer attacks, 392
**Soldiers,** British, learn welding, *610*
——demobilised, suits for, *671*
——help with potato harvest, *386*
**Solomon Is.,** air superiority in, 284
——Allies in, *569*
——New Zealanders in, *502*
——U.S. success in, *592-93*
Solon, S. L., and Capt. Colin Morris, 189
Soloveytchik, George, on St. Petersburg, 622

Somaliland, British, evacuation, 227, 675
**Somerville, Adm. Sir James,** C.-in-C., Eastern Fleet, 230
— —fresh ships for, 262
— —raids Sabang, 774
Soong, Dr. T. V., 268
Sorpe Dam, bombed, 24, 25
Sorrell, Ldg. Seaman L., D.S.M., 696
Sosynov, Senior Lieut. N., 257
Soup, for *Trident* seamen, 617
Sourabaya, bombed, 182
South Africa, British generosity to, 255
South Africans, and Montgomery, 723
South African War, soldiers of, 19
Southall, Sapper R., M.M., 568
**Southern Rly.,** gas test on, 482
— —Home Guard, 211
Souvenirs, from battlefield, 52
Spaatz, Gen. Carl, and Pantelleria, 70
Spaccaformo, surrender, *Roberts* and, 488
**Spain,** and Italian ships, 550
**—to-day,** Fyfe on, 339
Sparanise, skirmishes in, 424
Spartan, H.M.S., sunk, 678
Spears, Maj. Gen. Sir E., 469
Spectator, The, and Brailsford, 703
Spelling Reform, Hammerton on, 511
Spencer, U.S. Cutter, 74
Spencer, Patrick, on the Jeep, 300
**Spezia,** 304
—bombed, 182
—Italian naval base, 168
Spinning, for convalescent men, 354
Spinning-wheels, for Chinese refugees, 117
Spit and Polish, Hammerton on, 575
**Spitfires,** bomb radio station, 462
—camera in, 285
—with Coastal Command, 713
—in dog-fight, 215
—at Pachino, 184
—Seafire an adaptation, 12
—in Sicily, 210
—transport to N. Africa, 606
—XII, 796
**Spitzbergen,** German dash to, 358
— —raid on, 314
Splinters, *Kelvin's* mascot, 393
**Split,** boats in harbour, 342
—Germans take, 342
Sprigge, Cecil, on Modern Italy, 627
Spring, in Russia, vital question, 547
Spruance, Adm. R. A., in the Pacific, 646
**S.S.,** in Denmark, 248
—generals weaken, 206
—Himmler and, 782
**Stalin, Joseph Vissarionovitch,** and Czech-Soviet Pact, 522
— —Karpov's portrait, 417
— —generalship, 387
— —Order of Day (Sept. 8), 276
— —picks commanders, 307
— —plots against, 307
— —receives sword, 495
— —and Russian successes, 771
— —at Teheran, 495, 496, 499
— —on war production, 426
Stalin Avenue, English depôt, 258
**Stalingrad,** artillery saves, 296
—recovery, 484
—6th Army isolated, 419
—Yu.2s at, 726
Stalingrad Sword, presentation, 495, 499
Stanford, Graham, 761
Stannard, Pte. M. D., 382
**Starling, H.M. Sloop,** with Second Escort Group, 710, 711
— —in U-boat chase, 263
Stalino, Russians retake, 276
Stamboul, district of Istanbul, 530
Staniland, Christopher, death, 470
Stark, Adm., Harold R., First Lord with, 487
Stars and Stripes, over Tarawa, 594
Staustufen, in German canals, 430
Stayner, Capt., 486
**Steamer,** Japanese, bombed, 444
— —camouflaged, 634
Steel, Russian manufacture, 427
Steele, Rev. J., conducts service, Carthage, 36
Steinhardt, Mr. L., 476
Sten Guns, for Home Guard, 27
Stephenson, Capt., R.N., of *Battler*, 42
**Stern-Rubarth, Dr. Edgar,** on Hitler and Badoglio, 398
— —on Hitler's last stand, 206
— —Watch Himmler, 782
Stevens, Commissioned Engineer J., D.S.C., 60
Stewardesses, for air liners, 514
Stewart, Andrew, on French desert army, 404
Stewart, Sgt. J., M.M., 568
Stewart, Maj. Oliver, on Air Power, 787
Stiffkey Stick Sight, 783
Still, portable, for ships, 11
**Stilwell, Gen. Joseph,** and air transport, 636
— —battle schools, 466
— —in Burma, 750, 772, 773
— —in China, 665
Stimson, H. L., 109
Stirbey, Prince Barbu, in Cairo, 686
**Stirlings,** bomb Berlin, 237
—Fortresses over, 370
—loading mines, 763
Stockholm, street-fighting in, 756
Stockings, utility, 290
Stord (destroyer) and *Scharnhorst*, 518
Stormking, H.M. Tug, 744
Stormovik Planes, in Caucasus, 140
Strang, William, at Moscow Conference, 396
Straorina, Canadians in, 289
**Strategic Air Force,** achievements, 700
— — —German lack, 118
Strategic Bombing, time factor in, 604
Strategy and Tactics, in air war, 444
Straw, Pte. Sonia, G.M., 382
Street, Capt. G. W. L., M.C., 59
**Street-fighting,** in China, 268
— —in Italy, 424
— —in Ortona, 554
— — —and England, 746
— —in Stockholm, 756
— —training in, for Home Guard, 27
— —in Tunis, 28
Streicher, Julius, 511
**Stretcher-bearers,** Chinese, in Burma, 683
— —at Monte Camino, 506
— —native, New Guinea, 715
— —R.A.M.C., in Italy, 687
**Stretcher-case,** at Anzio, 784
— —from Ortona, 516
Striker, H.M.S., 486
Strong-points, Axis, in Sicily, 166
Stuart, Maj. A. M., 378
Stuart, Frank S., on pre-invasion activity, 620
Stuart, Sir John, in Calabria, 73
Stuart, Lt. Gen. R., at Quebec Conference, 232
Stubborn, H.M.S., adventures, 730, 731
Stuttgart (liner), bombed, 327
**Submarines, British,** achievements, 616, 617
— —decorations won, 423
— —depôt ships for, 536
— —in Far East, 582
— —midget, 649
— — —and *Tirpitz*, 327
— —shells for, 274
— —and Siebel ferries, 602
**—German** : see U-boats.
**—Italian,** Germans and, 168
— —losses, 168
**—Japanese,** losses, 230
— —sunk off Aleutians, 10
**Russian,** of Black Sea Fleet, 774
— —**U.S.,** achievements, 710
— — —in Pacific, 582
— — —Pacific successes, 294
— — —sinks Japanese destroyer, 73
— — —successes and losses, 73
Sudan, defence importance, 675
Sudan Defence Force, 675
Suffisant (D.W.I.), S.L.I. in, 408
Suffren (ship), for Free French, 40
Sugar, Fiji cultivates, 714
Sugar-beet, British development, 218
Sugiyama, Gen., resignation, 646
Sullivan, Capt. C. P., lost in New Guinea, 443
Sulphur, Sicilian mines, 319
**Sumatra,** air importance, 796
—Japanese bases in, 774
Summers, Capt. "Mutt," 470
Sun, The (Sydney), cartoon from, 575
**Sunderland Flying Boats,** in Biscay battle, 532
— — — —survivors, 550
— — —duel with U-boat, 284
— — —and Liberator crew, 54
— — —tug rescues, 744
— — —as U-boat killers, 202, 263, 647
Sunflower, H.M.S., convoy-escort, 74
Sunflower Seeds, as food, 767
Sun Yat-Sen, Dr., and Chinese army, 116
**Supplies,** by air, 664, 757
—Allied, in troopship, 391
—for Allies, New Guinea, 269
—German, by plane, 613
—for invading army, 142
—for London's A.A., 375
—by outrigger canoe, Fiji, 714
—and Pacific War, 454
Supply Train, Italian, 37
**Surface Raiders,** flying boats and, 202
— —possible revival, 422
— —Raeder and, 105
Surplice, Wing-Cdr., Wilfred, 654
**Surprise,** in Sicilian invasion, 130
—Tollemache on, 19
Surrender, of Germans, in Russia, 549
Surry, Eleanora Dayton, 63
Survivors, German, Bay of Biscay, 550
Susak, 343
Sutherland, Flt. Lieut. Hugh, 602
Suva, carnival in, 714
**Sweden,** and German morale, 200
—home defence, 756
—Navy, strength, 550
—refugees in, 414
—and supplies for Germany, 327
Swinton, "Bevin boys" at, 600
Switchboard, women operators, N.F.S., 706
Switzerland, dilemma, 718
**Sword,** Arab, for Churchill, 482
—of Stalingrad, presentation, 495, 499
**Swordfish Planes,** in *Battler*, 42
— —of escort aircraft-carrier, 274
— —at Taranto, 266
— —as trainers, 12
Sydney, H.M.A.S., sunk, 422
Syokaku, Japanese aircraft-carrier, 582
**Syracuse,** Allies take, 167, 171, 189
—harbour, pre-war, 172
—history, 171
—street scene, 9
**Syria,** roadmaking in, 791
—Turkish frontier closed, 69
Syriam, oil-tanks fired at, 630


## T


Tacitus, on British taxpayers, 246
Tactical Air Force, formation, 86
Tactics, strategy and, in air war, 444
Taku, H.M.S., escapes, 60, 454
Taman Peninsula, battle of, 420
Tamils, as nurses, Ceylon, 428
Tanaka Memorial, 127
Tanatside, H.M.S., 392
Tank-busters, Allied types, 620
Tank-driver, Libyan grave, 44
Tank Corps, Royal, refuelling, Sicily, 185
Tankers, work, 712
Tank Recovery Vehicle, U.S. M25, 666
**Tanks, Allied,** on Italian hill, 740
— —at Kwajalein, 729
**—British,** in Cassibile, 167
— —in Catania, 241
— —in Sicily, 166
— —in Torre Annunziata, 384
— —8th Army commanders, 723
**—German,** abandoned in Russia, 724
— —British Intelligence and, 52
— —destroyed at Orel, 204
— —on fire, 458
— —hit by Piat bomb, 621
— —German miniature, 676
— —at Sidi Nsir, 125
— —in Ukraine, 459
— —wrecked in Italy, 388
—landing-craft for, 110, 112-13
—make smoke, 654
—new, information about, 52
**—Russian,** camouflaged, 397
— —Kharkov makes, 245
— —in Kiev, 431
— —in Kuban Peninsula, 21
— —massed attack, 310
— —practice test, 120
— —for raiding-party, 187
— —repair, 426
— —snow-camouflaged, 693
— —Stalingrad makes, 484
— —in Ukraine, 459
**—U.S.** amphibious, Bougainville, 592-93
— — —in Attu, 53
— — —destroyed, Tarawa, 503
— — —for N. Zealanders, 452
—wounded in, 755
*See also* Churchill Tanks : Sherman Tanks, etc.
Tannabashi, Gen., 761
Tanner, Vaino, 684
**Taormina,** 9
—beauty, 191
—bombed, 150
—British take, 195
—Greek theatre at, 173
—*Roberts* and, 488
**Taranto,** Italian ships at, 168
—N. Zealanders in, 452
**Taranto, battle of,** an air attack, 348
— —Italian fleet crippled at, 266
— —Marines at, 174
**Tarawa,** battles for, 503
—Japanese prisoner on, 512
—U.S. bomb, 474, 475
—U.S. retake, 591, 594
Task Force, U.S., with British Home Fleet, 487
Taurus Express, searched, 69
Taxpayer, Chancellor praises, 246
Taylor, Sgt., of A.F.P.U., 278
Tchicherin, M., as Foreign Minister, 383
**Tea,** for aircraft workers, 610
—from Ceylon, 788
—for cruiser look-out, 272
—for R.O.C., 759
Teano, Allies take, 424
Tebbutt, Geoffrey, in Arakan, 750
Tebourba, war grave at, 45
**Tedder, Air Chief Marshal Sir Arthur William,** 576
— —in Algiers, 80
— —and bombing of Sicily, 149
— —and bombing policy, 54
— —Eisenhower's deputy, 515
— —greets King, 67
Tegetthoff, Adm., at Lissa, 678
**Teheran Conference,** 495, 496-97
— —Atlantic battle and, 483
Telegraph Wires, repaired, Karelia, 564
Telephone Operators, women needed as, 58, 63
**Telephones,** in N. Africa, transport for, 716
—R.C.S. and, 436, 437
Telephone Service, Japanese, 435
Tempête (ship), off Corsica, 294
Tennyson, Lord, Wavell and, 735
**Tents,** making, Anzio, 690
—of U.S. Army, Ascension, 682
Terceira Island, Allied base in, 541
Terrible, Le (ship), 294
Terror, H.M.S., monitor, 488
Test Pilots, Cooper on, 470, 471
Texas, oil in, 76
Thackeray, W. M., démodé, 383
Thames Patrol, Home Guard with, 798
Thanbyuzayat, U.S. bomb, 556
Thapa, Subadar Lalahadur, V.C., 123
Theft, from railways, 767
Theocritus, in Syracuse, 171
Theodore, Hon. E. G., and Allied Works Council, 584
Thermometer, Wing, 471
Thetis (ship) guards *Tirpitz*, 550
Thomas, Bert, Hammerton on, 95
Thomas, Lieut. J. O., R.N.V.R., 329
**Thomas W. Vaughan,** on Berlin raid, 313
— —on Nettuno landings, 601
Thompson, J. R. Fawcett, on Home Guard, 26
Thompson, Chief Steward R., B.E.M., 254
Thomson, Flight-Lieut. C. W. H., air-train driver, 362
Thomson, Dr. M., M.B.E., 382
Thornborough, Capt., R.N., 486
**Thornhill, Capt. Martin,** on A.C.F., 406
— —on showmen of Services, 566
Three Powers, Declaration of, 499
Thucydides, on Peloponnesian War, 171
**Thunderbolt Fighters,** in Berlin raid, 701
— —damaged, return, 118
— —details, 23
— —escort Fortresses, 370, 445
**Tiger Tanks,** in Brenner Pass, 320
— —British intelligence and, 52
— —British 17-pdr. and, 372
— —Churchill inspects, 82
Tighe, Desmond, 158
Tighina Bridge, over Dniester, 734
Tikhomirov, Deacon Feodor, 62
Time Factor, in strategic bombing, 604
Timoshenko, Marshal, on army defects, 307
Tin Hat, for Coastguard Service, 234
**Tinian,** Japanese base, 590
—U.S. raid, 646
Tiraspol, Rumanian sentry at, 734
Tires, for 8th Army, 142
**Tirpitz** (ship), Barracudas bomb, 742, 776, 794
— —damaged, Altenfjord, 327, 550
—midget submarines and, 649
Tissandier (balloonist), on altitude sickness 521
Titanium Oxide, for smoke screens, 654
**Tito, Marshal,** and British Mission, 698
— —partisan leader, 343, 524, 618
— —women in army, 609
—wounded, 699
Titulescu, Nicolas, Russian policy, 686
Titus, arch of, Rome, 303
Tivoli, 305
Tjilatjap, refugees at, 411
**Tobruk,** 8th Army tanks at, 723
—relief of, 227
—surrender, cause, 403
—war cemetery near, 45
Todt Organization, and Vitebsk defences, 515
**Tojo, Gen. Hedeki,** 595
— —on "acute situation," 710
— —and Chinese campaign, 67
**Tokyo,** distance, 253
—U.S. raid on, 154, 155
Tokyo Road, construction, 556
**Tolbukhin, Gen.,** in Crimea, 771, 778
— —defeats Manstein, 397
— —Stalin to, 276
Tollemache, Maj.-Gen. E. D. H., "The Turning Tide," 19
Tomalin, Wing-Cdr. C. D., 55
**Tommy-guns,** British, in Italy, 293
— —camouflaged, 644
— —in Russian attack, 21
Tom-tom, for air-raid practice, 428
**Torpedo-Boats,** Dutch, 96
— —Russian, in Kuban R., 21
**Torpedoes,** aerial, for Beaufighters, 64
—German acoustic, failure, 358, 454, 678
— —guided to submarine, 74
—human, 775
—submarine rearms, 536
Torre Annunziata, British troops in, 384
"Tour," W.O use, 159
Tourville (ship) 40
Tracer Bullets, German, in Russia, 549
Tracer Shells, Allied, Nettuno, 631
Tracker, H.M.S., 10
**Tractors,** British use, 218
—Kharkov makes, 245
—U.S., at Bougainville, 592-93
Traders, small, case for, 703
Trades Union Congress, and Home Guard, 211
Trade Unions, and Socialism, 639
**Traffic Control,** by girl, Kharkov, 277
— — — —Moscow, 434
— —by militiaman, Moscow, 434
Tragone, orphans at, 389
Trailer, H.M.S., 486
Trains, bombed in Burma, 557
Trajan, arch of, Ancona, 306
Tram-cars, in Portuguese manoeuvres, 360
Trandafilo, Signor, at Bucharest, 686
Trans-Canada Air Lines, 362
Trans-Canada Highway, 790
**Transport,** by air, development, 362, 363
—Axis, R.A.F. war on, 89
— —at Randazzo, 228
—British, work, 674
—German, Allied war on, 620
—miracle of, 159
—by plane, 716, 717
—Polish, in Italy, 786
—reindeer for, Russia, 425
—some figures, 238
Transport, Ministry of, 447
**Transport Command, Royal Air Force,** 316
— — — —scope, 363
— —U.S., in Indo-China, 716 717
Transport Planes, in Arakan, 757
Transport Ships, responsibility, 552, 553
Transylvania, dispute over, 686
Travers, Capt. F. Dudley, 362
Trawlers, British fishing, perils, 680, 681
—as minesweepers, 792
Treasury Island : see Mono
**Trenchard, Marshal of the R. Air Force, Viscount,** 86
**Trident, H.M. Submarine,** members of crew, 617
— —and *Prinz Eugen*, 327
Trieste, Germans and, 168
Trigg, F/O L. R., V.C., 478
Trigno, R., 8th Army crosses, 356

Trincomalee, imperfect base, 230
**Trinidad**, Flight Sgt. from, *661*
—war effort, 747
Tripoli, advance on, railways and, 238
Tripoli (Syria), war graves in, 747
**Tripolitania**, British administer, 7
—postal service resumed, 127
Triquet, Actg. Maj. P., V.C., *760*
Triumphal Arch, at Cassibile, *167*
Trobriand Islands, U.S. occupy, *109*
Trollope, Anthony, 383
Troop-Carrying Aircraft, construction, 110
Trooping the Colour, Prussian ritual, 351
Troops, Allied, entertainment for, *566*
Troopship, Allied, for Lae, *391*
Troposphere, flight in, 521
Trotsky, Leon, and Red Army, 307
Troubridge, H.M.S., 103
Troubridge, Adm., at Nettuno, *580*
**Trucks**, U.S., near Liberi, *389*
— — —near Smolensk *364*
Trufanov, Maj. Gen., in Kharkov, 282
**Truk**, Allied threat to, 710
—coat-trailing off, 486, 508
—Cowie on, 590
—Japanese base, 454
—U.S. raid on, 646, 668
Trunk calls, higher rate, 63
Tsolakoglou, Gen., a quisling 179
Tucker, Major, in Boulogne, 409
Tudor, transport plane, 716
"Tugboat Annie," 744
Tui, H.M.N.Z. Corvette, 615
Tukachevsky, Marshal, removal, 307
Tuke, Wing-Cdr. B. D. S., in Azores, *541*
Tulagi, war cemetery at, *45*
Tulan, Mai. Jean Louis, 308
Tungsten in, China, 116
**Tunis**, prisoners' camp at, 6
—strategic importance, 2
—street-fighting in, *28*
—victory parade in, *39*
—welcomes Allies, *5*
**Tunisia**, fighter cover from, *35*
—final Axis surrender in, *1*, 2
—George VI in, *100*
—mass capitulation in, *403*
—New British guns in, *247*
—relative distances, *8*
—surrender, eye-witness stories, 28-30
—won by artillery, 296
Tunis Telegraph, The, 29
Tunnels, Japanese, Arakan, 750
**Turkey**, air bases in, 422
—and Bessarabia, 588
—Bulgaria approaches, 270
—favours Allies, 526-30
—ready for action, *493*
—Syrian frontier closed, 69, 73
Turner, C. E., drawings by, *500*, *501*
Tyne, H.M.S., George VI in, *272-73*

**Typhoon Planes**, Lucas tests, 470
— —manufacture, *605*
— —Monday tests, *471*
— —use, *89*
Typhoons (storms) from Truk, 590

## U

**U-boat Campaign**, aircraft and, 202
— —air-power and, 54
— —British H.Q. against, *13*
— —check to, 40
— —failure, 10, 105
— —good news of, 615
— —R.A.F. and, 700
**U-boats**, aircraft destroy, 284, *486*, 508
— —alleged new campaign, 294
— —Allied successes against, 200
— —*Archer* destroys, 105
— —in Black Sea, 168
— —boom defence against, *648*
— —carrier-plane sinks, *200*
— —chart of sinkings, *202*
— —crews depleted, 105, 200
— —cut in half, 174
— —depth-charged, off Sicily, *201*
— —destroyers ram, 392
— —escort aircraft-carriers and, 274
— —"General Chase" against, *263*
— —Halifax destroys, *107*
— —losses, 358, 678
— — —in two wars, 390
— —more sunk, 34, *74*
— —personnel wastage, 390
**U-boats** *(cont.)*
— —Russian planes sink, *380*
— —six destroyed, 710, *711*
— —Sunderland sinks, *647*
— —sunk by R. P. Williams, *326*
— —victory over, 262
Udet, Col.-Gen. Ernst, 398
**Ukraine**, Kiev, the capital, *431*
—Russian guerillas in, *459*
Ukrainets, Col. S., in Bryansk, 309
Ula, Norwegian submarine, 678
Ulpio Traino, sunk, 775
Ulster, strategic importance, *650*
Ulster Rifles, Royal, *650*
Umberto, Crown Prince, 115
Umbra, H.M.S., decorations for, *423*
Unalaska, Dutch Harbour in, 10
Underground Railways, as shelters, Berlin, *560-561*
Union Jack, over Sattelberg, 707
United, H.M.S., achievements, *423*
United Kingdom, at Moscow Conference, *396*
United Nations : *see* Allies
**United Nations' Day**, Egypt keeps, *121*
— — —in London, *91*
**United States of America**, aircraft production, 284
— — —air requirements, 214
— — —black market in, 735, 767
— — —Chinese pilots in, *35*
— — —Germans minimise help, 35
— — —Germany and 2
— — —helps China, *466*
— — —landing craft, 110
— — —and Moscow Conference, *396*
— — —Presidential Election, 703
— — —two-Service air forces, 700
— — —warns Finland, 684
Unrivalled, H.M.S., Jolly Roger for, *617*
Upper Yangtze, battle of, *268*, 465,
**Ustachi**, and Italian surrender, 342
—terrorist organization, 524
Utility Buses, in London, *674*
Utility Uniforms, for nurses, *514*

## V

Vaccines, for Russia, by air, 362
Vaduz, capital of Liechtenstein, 729
Vakuf, partisans take, 618
Valcov, Lipovani in, 588
Valencia, prison in, *339*
Valentine Tank, landing, *113*
**Valetta**, Churchill in, *481*
—George VI in, *101*
—Italian fleet at, 262, *335*
**Valiant, H.M.S.**, leads Italian fleet, *337*
— —at Salerno, 294
Vallene, Gen., and Normandie Squadron, *308*
Vancouver (Washington), aircraft carriers at, 42
Vanessa, H.M.S., destroyer, *392*
Vansen, Lt. H. A., in Burma, *683*
**Varna**, Cyprus and, 148
—German control, 270
Vasiliev, Maj.-Gen., in Italy, *483*
Vasto, bridge destroyed, *491*
Vatican, The and S. Peter's, *303*
**Vatutin, Col.-Gen. Nikolai Fedorovitch**, abilities, 515
— —advances (Nov. 1943), 451
— —captures Zhitomir, *523*
— —death, *771*
— —Kanyev offensive, 611
— —offensive, weight, 547, *549*
— —victor of Kiev, *419*, 431
Vearncombe, A/B, and magnetic mine, 124
**Vella Lavella**, landing-craft off, *502*
— —U.S. destroyers off, *455*
Venafro, Allies take, 517
Vengeance (dive-bomber), in Arakan, *708*
**Venice**, Bridge of Sighs, *305*
—m.t.b.s in, *450*
Vernon, H.M.S., and magnetic mine, 124
**Verona**, Fortresses bomb, 636
—the Old Bridge, *305*
**Vesuvius**, A.A. guns near, *118*
—anti-tank gun under, *325*
—in eruption, *306*
Viaduct, railway, at Salcano, *343*
**Victor Emmanuel III**, loses title, 342
— —Macmillan on, 182
— —and Mussolini, 115, *213*
— —new titles, 7
— —and Sicily, *149*
Victoria Cross, The, *478*
Victorious, H.M.S., in S. Pacific, *422*
**Vienna Award**, Hungary's gains, 366
— —and Transylvania, 686
Vietri, Gauntlet Bridge at, 345
Villa San Tommasso, Indians at, 513
Viminale (transport), 775
Vineyards, in Bessarabia, 588
Vinnitsa, Russians outflank, 547
Virago, H.M.S., 518, 519
Vitebsk, Russian threat to, 515
Vittorio Veneto (battleship), 168
Vimy, H.M.S., exploit, 392
Vivian, Sir Sylvanus, 58
Vizzini, British troops enter, *209*
**Volturno R.**, Clark prepares attack, 377
— —5th Army crosses, *356-57*
— —Sherman tank fords, *388*
Voluntary Land Camps 58
Volunteers, for harvest, arrangements, 218
Voodoo, Waco glider, *152*
Voroshilov, Russian cruiser, 774
**Voroshilov, Marshal K. E.**, and Czech-Soviet Pact, *522*
— —inspects German mortar, *725*
— —at Moscow Conference, *396*
— —at Teheran, *496*, 499
Vrij Nederland, pigeon story, 334
V-sign, Churchill makes, *65*
Vulnerability of Capital Ships, 508
Vyazma, Bishop Nikolai in, 62
Vyshinski, M., at Moscow Conference, *396*
Vysokostrovsky, Lt. Col. Leonid, 282

## W

**W.A.A.F.**, in air ambulance, *85*
— — — —and air photos, *285*, *797*
— — — —meterologists, 151
— — — —and returning bomber, *87*
Waco CG4A, U.S. glider, *152*
Wade, Wing-Cdr. Lance, prowess, *716*
Waffen S.S., Himmler and, 782
Wagg, Alfred, on Italy, 627
Wahba, Sheik Hafiz, *482*
Wakikuyu, in Nairobi, *619*
Walawbum, U.S. take, *800*
Walcott, Capt. C., and Rescue Tugs, 744
**Walker, Capt. F. J., R.N.**, with Second Escort Group, 710, *711*
— —in U-boat hunt, 263
Walls, A. C. F. scale, *407*
Walrus Amphibian, qualities, 108
Walter, Henry, *578*
Wang, Chung-hui Dr., *476*
"Wang-ho Main Royal," 329
Wanklyn, Lt. Cdr. M. D., V.C., Morley's portrait, *18*
Wansey, Rev. P., M.C., *59*
War Artists, work, *15-18*, *719-22*
War Cemeteries, 748, *749*
War Criminals, Moscow Conference and, *396*
Ward, Edward, and Denny, 83
Ward, Patricia, on the harvest, 250
Ward-Jackson, Sqd. Ldr. "It's a piece of cake," 223
Ware, Maj.-Gen. Sir Fabian, and war graves, 748
War Graves Commission, Imperial, 44
Warhawks, at Guadalcanal, *597*
**War Loan**, in Cyprus, 148
— —interest arrangements, 63
War Office, and Home Guard, 211
**War Savings**, in Ulster, 650
— —in Russia, *426*
Warsaw, Jews' water queue in, *450*
War Songs, lack, Hammerton on, 511
**Warspite, H.M.S.**, refuelling, *712*
— —at Salerno, 294
— —sees Italian fleet surrender, *336*
**Water**, in devastated Naples, *324*
—for 8th Army, 142
—Jews queue for, Warsaw, *450*
—queue for, Berlin, *560*
—salt, still for, *11*
Waterloo, Bridge, steel from, *311*
Water-tanks, N.F.S., public abuse, *578*
Watkins, Capt., the Rev. R. T., *188*
Watson, F/O R. C., ferry pilot, 362
Watt, Apprentice, A. V., B.E.M., *254*
Wau, Japanese attack at, 323
**Wavell, Field-Marshal Sir A.**, and Burma raids, 3
— —and the Chindits, *48-49*
— —decorates Ghale, *760*
— —on Inshore Squadron, 488
— —Lentaigne with, *772*
— —with Montgomery, *160*
— —N. African campaign, 259, 266
— —poetry lover, 735
— —railway communications, 238
— —reinforces Cyprus, 148
— —and Sudan, 675
— —Viceroy of India, *127*, *429*
— —in warships, *79*
Weather, in modern warfare, 371
Webb, Inspector, R.S.P.C.A., *535*
Wedding presents, new type, 319
Wehrmacht, building of, 404
Welding, soldiers learn, *610*
**Wellingtons**, in Azores, *541*
—bombing-up, Middle East, *250*
—bomb Preveza, *236*
—lay mines, 763
Wells, H. G., and Stalin, 307
Werbiski, Flt. Sgt. M. N., D.F.M., 603
Werth, Dr. Ernrst, on German railways, 662
Werth, W., on Germany's canals, 430
Westermann, Carl, Danish sailor, 230
**West Indies**, war effort, *661*
— —Dutch, oil guarded in, *408*
Weston, Maj.-Gen. E. C., M.N.,B.D.O., 628
Westwall : *see* Siegfried Line
**Wewak**, Allies raid, 454
—Japanese blockaded, 710
—shipping bombed at, *350*, *443*
Wheelbarrow Pump, *122*
Wheels, for invasion rlys., *642*
Whirlwind, Fighter-bomber, use *89*
Whisky, manufacture stopped, 159
Whitaker, W. G., drawing by, *490*
**White**, as camouflage, Cassino, *644*
— — —, Russia, *613*
White, Mrs., with A.F.P.U., 278
**White Ensign**, at Reggio, *260*
— —at Syracuse, 171
White Flag, of Italians, *189*
Whitehead, Sub.-Lieut. E. H., in motor-launch, *329*
Whiteside, Gunner, of Maritime Regt., 537, *538*
Whitley Bombers, tow gliders, *152*
Whitshed, H.M.S., 390
Whittaker, L/C W., parachutist, 188
Whitworth, Vice-Adm., and *Scharnhorst*, 518
Wickham, F/O A. T., D.F.C., *318*
Wideawake Birds, in Ascension, *682*
Widgeon, H.M. Corvette, *271*
Wiener-Neustadt, bombed, 214
Wieninger, Dr., on Hamburg raids, 182, 190
Wildcats, and *Tirpitz*, 742
**Wild Goose, H.M. Sloop**, with Second Escort Group, 710, *711*
— —in U-boat hunt, *263*
Wilhelmina, Queen, 174, 628
**Wilhelmshaven**, block-busters on, 702
—first R.A.F. raid on, 54
Wilkinson, Wing-Cdr., with S/Ldr. Linney, *108*
Wilkinson, Lieut. (A) David, *793*
**Wilkinson, Ellen**, and cigarette ends, 127
— —on Civil Defence, 122
William IV., and R. Marines, 628
Williams, Lieut.-Cdr. Derek, in *Shikari*, 392
Williams, Maj. E. B., *378*
Williams, Lt. Robert Pershing, *326*
Williamson, **Mrs.**, railway volunteer, *226*
Willink, Rt. Hon. H. U., *438*
Wilkie, Wendell, Presidential candidate, 531
Wilmer, Miss M., makes camouflage, 635
Wilson, Wing-Cdr., test pilot, *470*
**Wilson, Gen. Sir H. Maitland**, in Cairo, 121
— — —C.-in-C. Mediterranean, 515
Wilson, President T. Woodrow, 531
Wimberley, Maj.-Gen. Douglas, *193*
Winant, J. G., *476*
Windmills, save fuel, *770*
Windsor, H.M.S., mileage, 392
**Windsor**, elms cut down at, *290*
—harvest at, *219*
Windsor Uniform, 383
**Wine**, Algerian, price, 191
—for Allied troops, Militella, *164*
—British shortage, 159
**Wingate, Brigadier Orde Charles**, and the Chindits, 46, 47, *48*
— —columns' exploit, 3
— —death, 753, 767
Winrow, Artificer, escape, 665
Wireless, mobile, "Golden Arrow," *728*
Wireless Sets, Norwegians surrender, *450*
Wireless Waves, German experiments, 454
**Witch, H.M.S.**, dismasted, 392
— —monkey as mascot, *393*
Wolf (ship), German raider, 422
Wollaston, Sir Gerald W., and N.F.S. flag, *354*
"Woman's Road," in China, 790
**Women**, as bargees, *737*
—of B.O.A.C., *362*
—**British**, decorations for, *382*
— —Home Guard auxiliaries, 26
— —make camouflage netting, *634*, *635*
— —make typhoons, *605*
— —older, call up, 311
— —in R.O.C., *759*
— —as telephone operators, *58*, 63
— —war work, *514*
—in German internment camps, 409
—as hotel porters, 703
—**Russian**, in Army, *394*
— —as electricians, *484*
— —in front line, *364*
— —as snipers, *420*
— —unload ships, *106*
—smokers, Hammerton on, 767
—**Yugoslav**, as guerillas, *609*, *618*
"Women at War," Hammerton on, 287
Women's Institutes, National Federation of, 122
Women's Services, war graves for, 748
Wood, paper from, 255
Wood, Dr., and magnetic mine, 124
**Wood, Rt. Hon. Sir Kingsley**, death, 311
— —and trunk calls, 63
Wood, F./O. P. D., D.F.C., *318*
Woodlark Is., U.S. occupy, 109
Woodpecker, H.M. Sloop, 710, *744*
Woolston, H.M.S., 25th birthday, 392
**Woolton, Lord**, Minister of Reconstruction, *438*, 671
— —and new ration books, 58
Woolwich Arsenal (painting), *721*
Woolworth Carriers : *see* Aircraft Carriers, Allied.
Worsley, John, painting, *720-21*
Worthington, J. Hubert, 748
**Wounded, Allied**, air transport for, 716
— —in New Guinea, *350*
— —barges for, New Guinea, *350*
—**British**, Anzio, *784*
— —mule transport for, 513
—**Canadian**, signaller, *260*
—**Chinese**, in Burma, *683*
— —on Salween front, *465*
—**German**, prisoner, Italy, *353*
—**Indian**, in Burma, *708*
—**Italian**, in Sicily, *166*
—in tanks, *755*
—**U.S.**, at Anzio, *768*
— — —in Rendova, *170*
— — —Tarawa, *594*
**Wright**, Group-Capt., on birth rate, 246
Wright, P/O J. E. F., D.F.C., *638*
**W.R.N.S.**, Boarding Officer, *514*
— — — —with F.A.A., *12*
— — — —service, *321*
W.V.S., make camouflage netting, *635*
Wynne-Edwards, Cdr. C. J., 392
**Wynter, Philip**, in Arakan, 634
— —on Ledo Road, 665

## X

X6 and X7, midget submarines, *649*
XYZ submarine story, 616

## Y

Yak I, for Normandie Squadron, *308*
Yampol, Russians take, 707
Yangtse R., Chinese counter-attack on, 67

Yavuz, Turkish cruiser, 526
Y boats, of U.S. Marines, 110
Yeats, A/B H. T., D.S.M., 696
Yerofayev, Nikolai, foreman, 426
Yew Tree, of Darley Dale, *738*
Y.M.C.A., and A.A. posts, 127
Yokohama, U.S. bomb, 154
Yorabaiwa, Japanese counter-attack at, 323

Yorkshire, outcrop coal in, 546
Young, Robert E., M.B.E., 191
Youth Corps, of Portugal, *360*
Yu. 2, Russian plane, *726, 727*
**Yugoslavia**, British Mission to, 698
—Bulgars police, 270
—dissension in, 383
—destroyers, 136
—fighting in, *524, 525*

**Yugoslavia** (cont.)
—Hungary and, 366
—partisans of, *618*
—women guerillas in, *609*
—undercurrents in, *342, 343*

**Z**

Zafferana, British guns near, 228
Zanuck, Col. Darryl, 278

**Zaporozhe**, on Dnieper's left bank, 291
—Russians take, 387
Zero Bomber, destroyed, Pacific, *573*
**Zhitomir**, Russians take and lose, 451
—Russians retake, *523*
**Zhukov, Marshal**, break-through at Orel, 194

**Zhukov** (cont.)
— —generalship, 387
— —new offensive 707
— —successes, 739, *741*
Zivkovitch, Gen., Yugoslav C.-in-C., 524
Zmerinka, Russians take, 707
Zogu, K. of Albania, 462
Zuikaku, Japanese aircraft-carrier, 582

# List of Maps and Plans

**Africa**
North, Anglo-Egyptian Sudan, strategic importance, 675
Tunisia, fighting round Sbiba, 442
— —relative distances, 8
**Atlantic, Battle of**
Chart of shipping losses, 202
Ascension Island, 682
Azores, The, 361
**Balkan States**
Bessarabia, political importance, 588
Rumania, Russian advance on, 686, 739
**Burma**
Battle front, 556
—campaign in, Kohima relieved, 771
—Chindits' campaign in, 46
—Japanese advance on Imphal, 750
—Mogaung Valley, relief map, 773
**China**
Japanese occupied territory, 116
**Europe**
Fortification walls, 133
—Germany's " Citadel " in, 206
—Occupied, vital railways, 662
**Finland**
Frontiers, 684

**Germany**
Berlin plan, 237
canal system, 430
Ruhr, position of great dams, 24
**Great Britain**
Areas under cultivation, 218
Ulster's strategic importance, 650
**India**
Ceylon, 788
Kohima relieved, 771
Manipur State, relief map, 773
**Italy**
As air base, 284
—Allied advance on Naples, 325
—Allied advance on Rome, 388
—Allied invasion of, 260
—battle line (Oct. 22, 1943), 356
—battle line (Dec. 15), 483
—capture of Potenza, 291
—Foggia as air-base, 330
—and her islands, 35
—Nettuno-Anzio thrusts, 579
—physical map, 267
—R.A.F. targets, 183
**Mediterranean Sea**
Allied targets in, 66

**Mediterranean Sea** (cont.)
Corsica, 344
Leros, 442
Pantellaria, 2
**Pacific Ocean**
Japanese bases in, 590
—North, Attu Is., 10, 53
—South West, Admiralty Islands, 761
— —Gilbert Is., Betio, 474
— —Japanese withdrawal in, 350
— —main Allied objectives, 109
— —New Georgia, battle area, 99
— —New Guinea. Allied offensive in, 269
— — —Huon Gulf Coastline, 323.
—U.S. gains in, 646
**Russia**
Advance on Pskov, 643
—battle-front, early June (1943), 34
— —(Aug. 27, 1943), 227
— —(Sept. 23), 309
— —(Nov. 4, 1943), 387
— —(Dec. 3, 1943), 451
— —(Jan. 14, 1944), 547
—campaign in, June 1941-Nov. 1943, 421

**Russia** (cont.)
—central front, 131
—changing battle-lines (Mar. 1943-Mar. 1944), 677
—the Dnieper Line, 309
—fighting in Kiev salient, 515
—the Korsun pocket, 611
—Kuban Peninsula, 21
—Orel-Bielgorod Front (July 27, 1943), 163
—Orel Front, 66
—Smolensk-Bryansk-Kharkov front, 194
—Soviet offensive in Donbas, 276
—Soviet offensive in South, 365
—Soviet thrusts in Crimea 778
**Scharnhorst**, sinking of, 518
**Sicily**
Allied advance on Catania, 130
—battle of the Tip, 162
—communications and air bases, 133
—last stages of campaign, 195
**Texas**, the Big Inch pipeline, 76
**Turko-Syrian Frontier**, 69
**West Indies**
British, Trinidad, 747
— —Netherlands, 408

# Index of Special Drawings and Diagrams

Fighters and Fighter-Bombers, R.A.F., 89
Frigate escorts Allied Convoy, 658
German Bomber Unit in Russia, 253
Landing-craft Varieties, 656-57

Little Ships on Night Patrol, 500
Messerschmitt 109F, 153
Minesweeping Trawler saves ships, 792
Mountain Villages Ablaze in Italy, 490

Pantellaria Bombarded, 56
Scharnhorst, The, 519
Skip-bombing in S.W. Pacific, 670
Submarine Depôt Ships, 536

Tanks of the Red Army, 310
Wardroom of a Motor-Gunboat, 501
Winter's Approach in Apennines, 490
" Woolworth " aircraft-carriers, 104

# Errata and Addenda

P. 140, illustration No. 3. Plane shown is P.E. 2 bomber, not Stormovik.

P. 227, bottom picture. For 2 lb. *read* 20 lb. ; for 4,000 ft. *read* 4,000 yards.

P. 567, last sentence. For 28-30 tons *read* 37 ; for 50 m.p.h. *read* about ten.

P. 639, col. 1 top of paragraph 3. For Nicholson *read* Nicolson.

Printed in Great Britain by The Amalgamated Press, Ltd., London

'WE ARE CLOSING DOWN FOR EVER,' was Von Arnim's final message to Hitler just before the great Tunisian surrender. By May 13, 1943 not a single Axis soldier was left fighting in N. Africa, and a week later Gen. Eisenhower announced that the number of Axis prisoners taken in Tunisia since the break-through on May 5 was 224,000. Carrying sundry trophies, map-cases, and a pistol, his bayonet decorated with a white flag, this 1st Army man leads in his captives—Germans from the 334th Artillery Regiment. *Photo, British Official*

# THE BATTLE FRONTS

## by Maj.-Gen. Sir Charles Gwynn, K.C.B., D.S.O.

PANTELLERIA, Italian island situated about 60 miles from the Sicilian coast, and 45 miles from Cap Bon (see map, page 8), was repeatedly attacked by Allied aircraft following the end of the African campaign.

SINCE the collapse of the Axis in North Africa there has been a more complete cessation of land operations than at any time since the months following the fall of France. The lull is not likely, this time, to last so long, but there is a curious resemblance in reverse between the two situations.

Then, we were awaiting the invasion of Britain and Egypt; now it is the invasion of Europe that is expected, with Britain and Egypt providing offensive bases. Then, while the armies remained inactive, the air war intensified with the battle for air supremacy being fought out across the English Channel, and with London and British industrial centres targets for bombers. Today the air war is again the main feature in the news; but the targets for bombers are Berlin and the war industries of Germany and Italy, while the battle for air supremacy as a prelude to invasion is being fought across the Mediterranean. Now it is the attacker not the defender that is winning. Now it is the Allies who have captured a great line of naval and air bases for their operations.

During the lull of 1940 Germany's Eastern front gave her no cause for anxiety, but now it is precisely there that her armies are most deeply committed. Then, she scoffed at the idea that American material aid could reach Britain in time to affect the issue even if it could run the U-boat blockade. Now she has learnt to her cost that it is not material aid alone that America can give, and in spite of all her efforts the U-boat is becoming a dwindling asset.

TUNISIA When I last wrote we had not yet fully learnt the extent of the Tunisian victory, nor about some of its most amazing features. It seemed probable then that the Axis forces might be found to have been weaker than had been estimated and that a proportion of their troops might have been evacuated.

Yet, on the contrary, it has now been proved by the numbers of prisoners and booty captured that the enemy's numerical strength was greater than expected, that he was not seriously short of munitions or supplies, and that, far from having evacuated part of his force, he had received substantial reinforcements shortly before disaster overtook him.

It is true that some of his detachments were isolated, and may have run short of supplies, after Alexander's initial breakthrough had dislocated central control. But a large section of his force, facing the 8th Army, was intact and had not been heavily engaged.

Von Arnim had undoubtedly been misled and outmanoeuvred by Alexander and had lost control: but that does not excuse the astounding collapse of German morale or the lack of initiative shown by almost all subordinate commanders.

In spite of the magnificent energy and dash displayed by our armour in exploiting

---

### THEY FOUGHT IN TUNISIA

The Lancashire Fusiliers, Hampshire Regiment King's Own Yorkshire Light Infantry, Argyll and Sutherland Highlanders, The Black Watch, London Irish Rifles, Buffs, Royal Irish Fusiliers, Seaforth Highlanders, Lincolnshire Regiment, East Surrey Regiment, York and Lancaster Regiment, Royal Inniskilling Fusiliers, Gordon Highlanders, Northamptonshire Regiment, Cameron Highlanders, and Royal West Kent Regiment.

Both Regular and Territorial units of various regiments have been fighting, and it must not be forgotten that the Brigade of Guards took a great part in the campaign, as well as the Royal Regiment of Artillery in all its branches; the Royal Engineers, the Royal Armoured Corps, including the Derbyshire, Staffordshire, and Nottinghamshire Yeomanry, the R.A.S.C., R.E.M.E., R.A.O.C. and R.A.M.C.—*Lord Croft, Under-Secretary of State for War, May 18, 1943*

---

success in the capture of Hammamlif and the drive to Hammamet it is abundantly evident that, but for the breakdown of morale and failure in initiative, the Germans might still be holding a very strong position in the Cape Bon peninsula. Whether the collapse of morale was due to the withdrawal of the Luftwaffe and the consequent undisputed air supremacy established by the Allies, or to a refusal to make ruthless sacrifice of life on the Stalingrad pattern, is not yet clear. It may have been due mainly to a sudden loss of faith in German invincibility.

German failures, however, in no way detract from the amazing achievements of the Allied Army or from the brilliance of Alexander's generalship.

The extent of the Axis disaster is not measured solely by the loss of men and material. Tunis was the bastion relied on to close the Sicilian Channel and to protect Sicily and Italy from invasion. Even partially to effect those two objects, and whether or not we intend to attack Sicily, another army at least equal in strength to the one that has been lost will be required with a Luftwaffe component of undiminished size. Unless Germany is prepared to leave the task to the Italians, she must produce that force at a time she needs every available man in Russia.

ITALY The battle for air supremacy in the central Mediterranean has now shifted northwards and the whole Allied air force based on North Africa and Malta, liberated from the task of cooperating in land operations, can devote itself exclusively to securing complete supremacy in the air over the Sicilian Channel and to making the enemy's bases from which that supremacy might be disputed as far as possible unusable.

Whether it is intended to invade Sicily, Sardinia, or Italy itself or not, it is obvious that we must take advantage of the newly acquired African air bases to make the Mediterranean route as safe as possible for the passage of convoys, and the attack is naturally being pressed home while the enemy is still weakened by his losses in Africa.

Not long ago it would have been difficult, if not impossible, to establish air supremacy, or even a marked degree of air superiority, beyond the orbit of short-range fighter aircraft based on North Africa and Malta; but it would seem from the results obtained, especially by the American Flying Fortresses, that we have in the bomber which can operate without escort an ideal weapon for pressing home the attack on a weakened enemy. If the Luftwaffe had possessed such a weapon in the Battle of Britain the results might have been disastrously different.

Obviously, the greater degree of air superiority we establish in the central Mediterranean, the more vulnerable to invasion Sicily, Sardinia, and Italy become; and whether they are attacked or not the enemy is bound to provide troops for their protection on quite a new scale. The enemy is therefore forced into the dilemma of becoming weak everywhere in the attempt to be strong everywhere.

CAPE BON—FINAL AXIS STRONGHOLD IN AFRICA. These two infantrymen stand on the edge of a cliff in the Cape Bon peninsula, overlooking the sea from which the enemy was debarred from staging a Dunkirk Thousands of prisoners and an enormous quantity of military stores of every kind fell into the Allies' hands when this last centre of resistance was overwhelmed.

*Photo, British Official: Crown Copyright*

**RUSSIANS ENTER KRYMSKAYA.** This important railway junction, 25 miles N. of Novorossisk in the Kuban (see map p. 21), was captured on May 4, 1943, after four days of sustained Soviet attacks. German forces then withdrew W. of the town. These Cossack women welcome Red Army men as the latter march into the place
*Photo, U.S.S.R. Official*

## GERMANY

If the Allied air forces are achieving great results in the Mediterranean the recent successes of the Home-based aircraft have been even more remarkable with the attack on the Mohne and Eder dams, an outstanding achievement —incomparably the greatest blow in its lasting effects German war industries have yet received.

The captious may ask why it was not done before; but that implies ignorance of the problems the destruction of the dams involved. It is evident that no ordinary bombing attack could have shifted such a great mass of masonry. To achieve the results obtained an exceptionally large and concentrated weight of explosives had to be placed with absolute accuracy, and detonated at a correct depth to obtain the maximum effect of water pressure. That in the face of powerful flak defence. The amazing thing is that the attack in two cases was completely successful. The highest standard of training, skill and courage to give effect to precise calculation was clearly necessary, as well as aircraft of suitable type to deliver the load. Seldom can an experiment involving an untried technique have justified itself so completely.

## RUSSIA

The last week of May came without either side making a major move, though feverish preparations were clearly in progress. Inaction was the more intriguing because the ground in the south, where preparations were most apparent, had for some weeks been in a condition favourable to mobile operations. It had

seemed probable that the Germans would strike first, before the Russians could completely restore communications in recaptured territory.

Possibly the very effective and intensified air attacks made by the Russians on German communications may have caused delay, or events in North Africa, with their implications, may have caused the Germans to hesitate to commit themselves. Reports were current that sections of military opinion opposed offensive action in Russia which might lead to an inescapable entanglement, and advocated a defensive policy.

There were few definite indications as to the exact points at which major action might be taken; but the probability seemed to be that the Germans might, as an initial move, attempt a two-pronged offensive from the Briansk-Orel salient and from the neighbourhood of Bielgorod against the Russian salient west of Kursk.

The Russians, on the other hand, were expanding their bridgeheads across the Middle Donetz which might indicate an offensive against the Germans in the Donetz Basin.

The Russian attack in the Kuban had not been abandoned, but had been brought almost to a standstill by the very strong German positions covering Novorossisk.

The Russians probably benefit by delays in view of their inferior communications; and the successes gained by their air forces are very encouraging, especially now that the Luftwaffe is so widely dispersed. It must be expected, however, that if and when the Germans take the offensive they will again be able to support it with a strong concentration of air power and will almost certainly have initial successes.

## FAR EAST

It is now frankly admitted that our operations in the Arakan district of Burma failed in their offensive object; but they gave valuable training and achieved the defensive object of denying Akyab to the Japanese as a base from which to bomb India. We have now withdrawn practically to the Indian frontier, and if we cannot claim success the situation has not materially deteriorated.

The exploits of Brigadier Wingate's raiding columns were remarkable. They are encouraging as revealing elements of weakness in the Japanese position; and no doubt they were something more than disconcerting to the enemy. But they were more than ever make plain the difficulties Burma presents to military operations. The enterprise inspired by Field-Marshal Wavell himself recalls, and may have had the same purpose as, the reconnaissances and raids carried out by his covering troops on the Libyan frontier in 1940. They, it will be remembered, acquired much valuable knowledge of the conditions of the desert terrain and the military use that could be made of them.

## PACIFIC

The American capture of Attu island in the Aleutians marks the loss to the Japanese of yet another of their defensive outposts. It is difficult at present to assess the importance of the capture, but clearly it makes the situation of the Japanese on Kiska island more precarious; and the experience gained in landing operations will be valuable.

**INDIAN SNIPERS IN THE ARAKAN JUNGLE,** like Brigadier Wingate's " Chindits " in the forests of Central Burma, have inflicted considerable losses upon the Japs. This guerilla warfare, carried out in inaccessible country, has been maintained in spite of difficult conditions. These vigilant Sikhs are shown amid typical surroundings. *Photo, Indian Official*

# British and Americans Enter Bizerta Together

**ALLIES IN BIZERTA.** The U.S. 2nd Army Corps occupied this great base on May 7, 1943 and, as at Tunis, resistance had to be overcome in the streets. So swift was the advance upon the city that the enemy was unable to complete the destruction of the port. I, Lt.-Gen. Anderson, commander of the 1st Army, with Maj.-Gen. Bradley, in command of the American troops. 2, U.S. patrol awaits order to advance during a street battle. 3, British patrol moves forward in search of enemy snipers.

*Photos, British Official: Crown Copyright*

# With Unbounded Joy Tunis Greeted the Allies

ALLIED OCCUPATION OF TUNIS. 1, Gen. Alexander and Air-Marshal Coningham drive into the city, taken by the 1st Army on May 7, 1943. 2, A German who had been sniping at our men from a garden lies dead. French civilians step cautiously from their hiding-places. 3, Inhabitants give the Allied troops a tumultuous welcome. Day after day our bombers strafed the dock area (5), but the commercial and residential quarters (4) were hardly damaged.

*Photos. British Official*

FANTASTIC SCENES OF SURRENDER AND DEFEAT were enacted during the last battle of Tunisia when the hopelessly disorganized and shattered Axis forces were rounded up in their thousands. At one prisoners' camp alone, Germans and Italians flowed in at the rate of 1,000 an hour, and so overwhelming was the Allied victory that the roads were choked with what appeared to be never-ending streams of captives. On May 19, 1943 Gen. Eisenhower, Allied C.-in-C., N. Africa, announced that the total number of prisoners taken in Tunisia since the Battle of Mareth was 267,000, while in addition 30,000 of the enemy were killed and 27,000 seriously wounded. A vast crowd of soldiers, sailors and airmen is here seen at a prisoners' camp near Tunis.

# Italy Trembles at the Thunder of the Guns

Now that the Allied armies are in full control of all the North African coast, now that their bombers are disrupting Italy's social and industrial system, the Italians are hearing already in fearful anticipation the tread of the invader. How are they bearing up in their hour of trial?

A T six o'clock on the evening of June 10, 1940—just three years ago—Mussolini appeared on the balcony of the Palazzo Venezia, the No. 10, Downing Street of Rome, and announced that Italy's declaration of war had been handed to the Ambassadors of Britain and France, those "plutocratic and reactionary democracies of the west." Proletarian and Fascist Italy, barked Il Duce, was on her feet. She had only one watchword : "To conquer !" Up went the bully's chin. From below came the sound of delirious cheers uttered by the crowd of giddy young Fascists.

Swift in reply came the voice of Mr. Duff Cooper, in a broadcast speech from London.

"Mussolini," declared the Minister of Information, "will bring misery and starvation upon his people. He will leave nothing behind him but the curses of those whom he has betrayed. *He will increase the number of ruins for which Italy has long been famous.*"

A T the time this remark about ruins was considered by the political purists to be not altogether nice, as being slightly indecorous. But few of our latter-day prophets have been so signally and so speedily justified in their predictions as Mr. Duff Cooper in his grim warning to Italy, then inflated almost to bursting-point at the prospect of a victory on the cheap. Italy has always been a land of ruins, but never have the ruins been so numerous as now. The Italian Empire is a ruin. Italy herself, her military establishments, her industrial system, her social complex, her intellectual ideology—in all and everything she displays

      ruin upon ruin, rout on rout.
Confusion worse confounded.

Only three years have been added to history since "Sawdust Caesar" uttered his frantic boasts and foolish words. Where is he now?

Mussolini still sits in his great room in his Roman palace, behind the desk placed in the far corner so that he has a long and clear view of his visitors. He is still the Pooh-Bah of Pooh-Bahs, holding nearly all the portfolios of the Italian Cabinet in what he likes to think is still a masterful hand. He still overshadows little Victor Emmanuel, keeps his eye on Crown Prince Umberto ; he still plays musical-chairs with his subordinates, frequently sacking not a few to encourage the others. But unless he has lost his one-time shrewdness, he may suspect in the uneasy watches of a sleepless night that all around him the rats are nibbling at the foundations of the Fascist house that he so proudly built and dreamed of as his eternal monument. Maybe he suspects that king and courtiers, army generals and Fascist chiefs allow him to remain where he is because it may be convenient to have a scapegoat for the crimes and follies of more than twenty years. And where could they find a better one than the man who willed that he should give his own name to his age ?

T HE Italian Empire: you may look for it now in vain and find it only in atlases the sword has made out of date. Genially condescending, Benito Mussolini, the blacksmith's son, bestowed on his king, whose ancestors have been dukes and princes for a thousand years, the titles of King of Albania and—still better sounding—of Emperor of Ethiopia. Victor Emmanuel still keeps his titles, but—well ! According to the Almanach de Gotha he is King of Cyprus, King of Jerusalem, King of Armenia. His writ runs just as effectively in Abyssinia as in Cyprus —or in the moon.

In Addis Ababa, Haile Selassie sits again on the throne from which he was driven by Italian bombs and poison gas. Tripolitania and Cyrenaica in North Africa are now being administered by a handful of British officers under the Civil Affairs Branch of G.H.Q.,

Middle East, in Cairo. The farms in Libya which were carved out of the desert with such toil and expense are now being worked by Arabs. So, too, with Eritrea. The Italian officials still function, but they do so under British supervision. Asmara's extensive machine-shops, reputed to be almost as good as Birmingham's, are now working for the Allies ; and British officials see that the 20,000 grass-widows left behind in the Italian débâcle get the supplies of fresh milk for themselves and their children.

With all the Italian Empire in Africa in Allied hands, Emperor Emmanuel is left with Albania (boiling with unrest, always on the verge of open revolution) and the Dodecanese Islands, now definitely threatened by the ever-

**READY FOR INVASION ?** This Italian armoured train, equipped with naval guns, is placed in position near the coast. Following the spectacular and devastating defeat of the Axis in Tunisia in May 1943, tension in Italy steadily mounted in the face of an Allied invasion. A state of emergency was proclaimed throughout the country. *Photo, Associated Press*

growing British power in Cyprus. And, of course, Italy . . .

Looking out on the Italian scene the king and the Duce can discover little to gladden their eyes, to raise their leaden spirits.

They take up their newspapers, and they find complaints about this, that, and the other. Here is a cardinal denouncing the growth of atheism and irreligion. Pilfering and forgery are the subjects of frequent leading articles. Profiteering and the black market are the objects of constant denunciation. The luxury of the rich, the idle living, the untimely elegance of the well-to-do provide a congenial theme for journalistic Jeremiahs. Particularly scathing are the comments directed against the bomb-dodgers who crowd the hotels and boarding-houses of the seaside and mountain resorts. Why, some of these women have flaunted themselves in trousers . . .

B EYOND a doubt the prevailing mood is one of intensest depression. And who can wonder at it, when every morning and every night bring news of yet further defeats, yet greater losses ? Not all the chicanery of the communiqué-mongers can hide the blackness of the outlook from the coffee-house politicians, the peasants driving their ox-teams across the stony soil, the husbandmen tending their vineyards on the mountain slopes, the

housewives gossiping beside the village well or in the churchyard after Mass.

Occasionally their fears are heightened by the news that filters through the walls of censorship. A broadcast from London or New York is picked up surreptitiously. A leaflet, urging the Italians to surrender before they are blasted into nothingness, is retrieved from the dust where it was dropped during the night before by an R.A.F. plane.

On the other side of the leaflet is a map, on which the cities which are to be bombed are indicated. Among these, we may well believe, is Rome, since it is inconceivable that it may be maintained much longer that Rome, the metropolis of the totalitarian state of antiquity, contains relics of greater cultural importance than our own Canterbury or Exeter, Westminster or York—or the Athens which, after giving to the world ages ago the deathless trinity of goodness, truth and beauty, is today polluted by the barbarians.

W HAT of the future ? Will Victor Emmanuel abdicate and Umberto reign in his stead ? Will the Duce flee, or push himself forward in the role of a Darlan ? Or will the inheritors of Mazzini's dream of a liberal Italy rise again as from the dead ?

It is almost idle to speculate, but it may be doubted whether in the post-war world there will be a place for Italy as a great power. She has not got the resources for that, the industrial organization, the economic wealth, the population, the imperial urge. As colonizers Italian men and women have their virtues, and as civil engineers Italians are first-rate. But their shoulders are not broad or strong enough to carry Caesar's mantle.

But it is not yet tomorrow. It is still the grim and gloomy present, when Italy's state is summed up in a sentence penned by a Milanese journalist in a description of Naples after a recent raid. "It is a voiceless city, in which are seen only pale, thin-faced inhabitants, turning their faces to the sky as if they expected it to rain death until the end of the world."    E. ROYSTON PIKE

# Will Invasion Follow the Bombs on Sardinia?

SARDINIA, some 120 miles N.N.W. of Bizerta, has felt the full weight of Allied air power. The island has four main airfields with a seaplane base at Cagliari and a number of satellite landing-grounds. With the final collapse of the Axis in Tunisia, Sardinia became an important target in our campaign against Fortress Europe. Top left, map showing relative distances between N. Tunisia and enemy key-points. Top right, Cagliari, capital and chief port of Sardinia; after being devastated by Allied bombers it was evacuated by the civilian population, Rome Radio announced on May 25. Below, Gonnesa, with the Gulf of Porto Paglia in background.

PAGE 8          *Map by courtesy of The Daily Telegraph; Photos, E.N.A., Topical*

# Only 100 Miles Divide the Allies From Sicily

SICILY, chief stepping-stone to Italy, is separated by the 95-mile-wide Sicilian Channel from Cap Bon (see map in opposite page). The island is held by a number of Italian divisions, supported by Luftwaffe and Regia Aeronautica Squadrons. 1, Marsala, heavily raided on May 11, 1943. 2, A street in Syracuse. 3, Taormina. 4, Member of a German anti-aircraft battery paints a sign among cacti, indicating the way to the A.A. site. 5, A glimpse of Catania's harbour.

*Photos, E.N.A., Pictorial Press, Keystone*

# THE WAR AT SEA

### by Francis E. McMurtrie

ATTU, N. Pacific, Jap base in the Aleutians, was the scene of bitter fighting when U.S. forces launched a triple drive against remnants of the enemy in mid-May 1943. (See below.) *By courtesy of The Daily Telegraph*

AN even more serious portent for Germany than the loss of her armies in Tunisia is the failure of the much-advertised U-boat offensive in the Atlantic. Grossadmiral Doenitz, who superseded Grossadmiral Raeder early this year in consequence of the latter's inability to prevent Allied convoys getting through to Russia, must have disappointed Hitler sadly.

In his address to the United States Congress on May 19 Mr. Churchill revealed that in the early months of this year, and especially during the first three weeks of May, the number of U-boat killings has broken all previous records. Though this may to some extent be connected with the fact that in recent months there have been more enemy submarines at sea than ever before, the primary factor is undoubtedly the much stronger escorts which it is now possible to provide for convoys. In the case of one convoy that was exposed to a series of attacks by about 25 U-boats from April 30 to May 6, escort vessels mentioned as taking part in repelling the U-boat packs numbered no fewer than ten. These comprised two destroyers, a sloop, two of the new frigates, four corvettes and an ex-U.S. Coast Guard cutter. It is quite likely that there were other vessels besides in the escort, which in any case was much stronger than has been usual in the past. It is this strengthening of escorts that counts for most in defeating the U-boats, though there are other contributory causes.

A VALUABLE aid which should not be overlooked is the escort aircraft-carrier, as the type is termed in the Royal Navy, though in the United States Navy the expression " aircraft escort vessel " is preferred. Scores of these have been built in American shipyards, and photographs have so far appeared of four of them, H.M.S. Battler and Tracker and the U.S.S. Charger and Long Island. All were laid down as merchant vessels, but flight decks have been superimposed on the original hulls, with lifts to bring up aircraft from the extensive hangar space below. Varying numbers of planes, up to a maximum of 30 fighters, can be carried. Some of these ships are propelled by Diesel engines at speeds in the region of 16 knots, but others, including the Battler, have geared turbines and high pressure water-tube boilers, so are probably faster.

To provide a continuous air patrol around a convoy as it proceeds on its way is the important duty carried out by these extremely useful ships. Smaller, cheaper and more rapidly built than the big fleet aircraft-carriers, they have done much to help in overcoming the U-boat menace, as a submarine is obliged to keep under water when an aircraft is overhead.

Mention in Press reports and in the Prime Minister's speech of "new weapons" for combating submarines has given rise to sundry conjectures as to their nature. Improved Asdic methods, heavier depth charges and radio-location of submarines on the surface are amongst these. Another is the use of helicopters, of a type which can rise and descend almost vertically, and hover over a target if desired. Carried on the decks of merchantmen, helicopters add a fresh terror to the various dangers which threaten the U-boat's existence today. (See illus. p. 728, Vol. 6.)

Everything, then, points to the fact that the U-boat attack is being held, but that our adversaries will use every means in their power to intensify the attack, rather than submit to defeat, may be taken for granted.

### AMERICA'S Sea Power in the Aleutians

Though to people in this country it may seem a very remote theatre of war, the operations in the Bering Sea, between Alaska and the coast of Asiatic Russia, are of considerable importance, and may have a far-reaching effect on the struggle with Japan.

It was in July 1942 that it first became generally known that the Japanese had sent an expedition into the Bering Sea. Forces of uncertain strength were landed in the islands of Attu and Kiska, where airfields were in due course laid out. These islands are amongst the westernmost of the chain known as the Aleutians, extending from the south-west coast of Alaska along the southern fringe of the Bering Sea in the direction of the Kamchatka peninsula. In one of the easternmost of these, Unalaska, is situated the American naval base of Dutch Harbour.

For a considerable while hostilities in this region were mainly confined to sporadic air raids on Attu and Kiska by United States forces, and on various American islands by the Japanese. In August 1942 a naval bombardment of Kiska was also carried out, causing some damage to enemy shore installations. This interference had the effect of delaying, but not stopping, Japanese efforts to consolidate their positions; and in October, as a counter-move, American troops landed in the Andreanof Islands, thus providing a base somewhat nearer to the enemy-occupied territory.

For the greater part of the year weather conditions in the Bering Sea are so bad that warlike operations can only be undertaken intermittently, and are subject to unforeseen interruptions. Fog is seldom absent; and gales which make it impossible to fly spring up without much warning. All the islands of the Aleutian chain are more or less encumbered by rocks and shoals.

It is not surprising, therefore, that no operations were reported in this region during the winter. In February there was a naval bombardment of Attu; and at the end of April it was announced that a Japanese submarine had been sunk by an American bomber off the Aleutians.

IN May strong forces of U.S. troops were landed at two points in Attu and, after bitter fighting drove their opponents into a small area around the village of Attu, on Chichagof Harbour. This is in the northeast of the island, and is often incorrectly referred to in transatlantic news reports as " Chicago Harbour." It is actually named after a Russian admiral who died in 1849.

Attu having been reconquered, the Japanese garrison of Kiska, further to the eastward, is left between two groups of American-held islands. Their relief is thus rendered difficult if not impossible, and surrender should be only a question of time.

Undoubtedly this end to the Bering Sea expedition is a serious defeat for Japan, whose obvious intention in intruding was to divide American forces in Alaska from a possible future junction with Soviet allies on the western side of the Bering Sea. Now the position will be changed to the disadvantage of Japan, which will be exposed to air attack from Siberian bases should Russia join the nations at war with Tokyo.

From the Kamchatka peninsula or from the Siberian Maritime Province, behind Vladivostok, destructive raids could be directed against Japanese bases in Hokkaido and the Kurile Islands to the north-eastward. This is a danger which the enemy had hoped to avert by moving first in this direction.

AXIS TROOPS ESCAPING FROM TUNISIA by sea fared badly. On May 24, 1943 it was stated that during the previous fortnight some 900 Germans and Italians escaping in small craft had been captured by the Royal Navy. This photograph shows a party of Germans who set out in rubber dinghies to reach Pantelleria being put into the Royal Navy's " bag " some 20 miles from land. *Photo. British Official: Crown Copyright*

# Our Merchant Seamen Should Be Safer Now

**LIFE-SAVING DEVICES IN THE SEA WAR.** I, Hurricane fighter on its catapult mounted in the bows of an Allied supply ship. 2, Crossland waistcoat has a cord attached which forms a loop behind wearer's back to facilitate rescue. 3, A portable still for converting salt water to fresh water. 4, Lt. Goodfellow (left), the inventor of another type of still, demonstrates it to Adm. Sir M. Dunbar-Nasmyth, V.C. 5, Chipchase raft: stores, sail and anti-frostbite bag are fitted into the lockers.

*Photos, British Official; Keystone, Central Press, Daily Mirror*

# Sailors with Wings Are Taught Their Job

*Photos, Pictorial Press Exclusive to* THE WAR ILLUSTRATED

**FLEET AIR ARM GUNNERS**, operating in carrier-based aircraft, receive a magnificent training. These photographs show phases of their instruction at a Naval Air Arm station in Britain.  I, Gunnery instruction officer coaches a trainee.  2. Fleet Air Arm gunners train mostly in Swordfish planes.  Here one Swordfish draws a drogue—sleeve target towed by a plane—while the other aircraft attacks it.  3, A Wren gathers up the drogue.  The score is calculated from the number of bullet-holes in the sleeve.  4, Instructing the pilot of a Seafire to land by signals.  This method is practised by all naval air pilots.  An experienced pilot is in charge of the bats.  5, Gunner takes aim at a "Junkers 88."  The model, tilted in several positions, is moved up and down a runway to give the effect of varying distances and backgrounds  6, Fixing the cannon in a Seafire—a Spitfire adapted for taking off and landing on deck.

# Where They Plot the War Against the U-Boats

More and more the Nazis are coming to rely upon the U-boat to win them the victory denied their armies on land. Yet here, too, they are finding increasing difficulty in holding their own. This article by HARRIMAN DICKSON tells of the underground H.Q. whence our campaign against the U-boats is directed.

PRACTICALLY the whole of this large room is covered with charts. The precise nature of the areas covered by these charts I cannot reveal, but I can tell you something of the fascinating things which go forward in this room day and night. For this is the headquarters in the tremendous battle against the U-boats.

ADM. SIR MAX K. HORTON, C.-in-C. Western Approaches (see accompanying text), recently inspected escort vessels under his command which are engaged in fighting U-boats. He is here aboard a destroyer; the device in the foreground is a depth-charge thrower. *Photo, British Official : Crown Copyright*

There are clusters of pins and tiny flags scattered about the wall charts. They show the precise position of battleships, cruisers, and destroyers in the Atlantic. They trace the course of our convoys as they plough through the hazards of the ocean's millions of square miles.

A thousand miles away a great argosy of ships is suddenly attacked by U-boats. The sirens wail, the destroyers swerve in their tracks, the depth charges begin to go down . . . It is past midnight when the attack begins, and nearly one before it is over. Back in the chart-room some small pins put in an appearance on one map. They are the pins used to indicate U-boats. They have increased considerably in the last nine months. Germany is staking a large part of her war effort on the U-boat, and every action which takes place in the Atlantic is reflected on the charts at H.Q.

The room is underground. You need very special credentials before you can so much as approach it. In fact, it is, of course, barred to everyone who has not urgent and official reason for being there. Petty officers and ratings with fixed bayonets guard the room.

The enormous charts are the first things that catch your eye. Then you notice something like an enclosed glasshouse at one end. This is

"air operations." Here, once again, messages are filtering through day and night from the steadily increasing Coastal Command patrols. Giant flying-boats have given the U-boat commanders a new type of headache. They can spot submarines more easily than the surface observer. They can also bring terrible destruction to bear.

Dominating both these sections again is a second glass compartment. This is the room of the Commander-in-Chief Western Approaches, Admiral Sir Max Horton. Sir Max was one of our most distinguished submarine officers in the last war, and has an intimate knowledge of U-boat campaigns. He won considerable fame amongst the Germans, who regarded him with deep respect. The Russians also thought highly of him: his submarine fought side by side with their submarines in the Baltic, and he frequently came back with German ships to his credit.

From this higher, glass-fronted room Admiral Sir Max Horton can see all the details on the charts below without getting up from his desk. Next to his office is a small cubicle. It has a bed in it where the Admiral can sleep. Actually, in these days, complete relaxation is rare. Any hour of the day or night the C.-in-C. is liable to be called. It is a twenty-four-hour job directing the war against the U-boats.

When you first enter the underground H.Q. the atmospherics from wireless sets of various calibres are disturbing, but that, and the ringing of small bells, eventually

make up a hardly noticeable background.

Historic messages have come over these wireless sets, messages which have subsequently reached the public and thrilled the whole nation. When the Bismarck was relocated and under attack in May 1941, the first news came through to this room. All kinds of ships are continually sending messages, all kinds of dramas are reflected

here. Even a lifeboat picked up by a warship may set things humming in the underground H.Q.

As every new anti-submarine device comes into operation the first intimation of its effectiveness is received here. It is indeed a fascinating business.

FULL SPEED AFTER THE ENEMY! Earlier in the War, when U-boats were operating in narrow waters, fast motor launches were employed for anti-submarine work. For this purpose they carried depth charges, in addition to the latest type of A.A. gun and machine-guns, and had small but highly trained crews. This photograph shows a motor launch on patrol.

*Photo, Planet News*

# What Are These 'Hairpin Squads' of the R.A.F.?

Salvage drives are a frequent occurrence in our cities and villages, and it is good to know that Servicemen are just as keen and eager as civilians to save every scrap of paper, metal, etc. which may contribute something to the national war effort. This article by WEBSTER FAWCETT tells of the really splendid activities of the R.A.F. salvage squads.

AN R.A.F. train-busting ace of Fighter Command, fully alive to the vital necessity of salvage, exultantly returned from a recent railway raid with a chunk of Nazi locomotive embedded in the fuselage of his plane. The fragment had been blown sky-high by his own delayed-actions just as he wheeled for a second attack, and the pilot gleefully promised himself to extract it in person and bestow it upon the appropriate salvage dump with full honours. Thirty minutes later, when he returned with the tools to finish the job, the tell-tale hole in his fuselage remained, but the trophy had vanished. The "Hairpin Squad" of his station had whisked it away.

Every morning, when the bombers return from the night's offensive, the Hairpin Squads bear down upon the machines, as one pilot put it, "like a swarm of locusts," and toothcomb them for spent bullets, flak fragments, or cannon-shell shrapnel. After technicians have analysed the material it goes to salvage ; and a single station has wrested enough metal from Hitler in this way to make 75,000 rifle barrels. In addition, in a matter of nine months, Hairpins of Fighter Command alone have retrieved as much as 2 tons of silver paper, 27 tons of ethylene glycol, 120 tons of rubber, 14 tons of cement paper bags —enough to make 8,000 bomb interior containers—and 160 tons of aluminium and non-ferrous metals.

Who are Hairpins ? They are sections of the maintenance ground crews who work in their spare time from other duties to ensure that nothing is wasted. Headed by a full-time salvage officer—usually a flight-lieutenant from the Equipment Branch—they have made a name for themselves because, from derelict steam rollers to W.A.A.F. hairpins, they make use of everything.

Thanks to Hairpins, the toughened glass from wrecked Dornier bombers brought down over this country has helped to make denture plates and even false teeth for the Army Dental Corps. Thanks, too, to their "waste not" policy, the R.A.F. has salvaged and

**SMASHED AXIS PLANES** at Castel Benito airfield, near Tripoli (occupied by the 8th Army last January), provided a vast quantity of material for the R.A.F. Hairpin Squads.
*Photo, British Official : Crown Copyright*

refined enough engine oil in the past six months to save a tanker a trip across the Atlantic.

Fighter Command units are still augmenting this total by 10 tons a week. Oil from rags, as well as from engine sumps, is not overlooked ; and R.A.F. rag-waste itself accumulates to 100 tons of salvaged wool annually. In a single month recently, after Hairpins had made mincemeat of confidential reports and secret orders, over 900 tons of waste paper and cardboard were returned to the mills for conversion to fresh uses.

At one airfield the Hairpin Squad—let us call them Hairpin I—heard with envy that a rival group at another drome (Hairpin II) had donated a derelict bus to salvage. Hairpin I, pleading that the invasion risk was over, received permission to disinter an obsolete tank which had been originally placed near the perimeter track as a defence post. Hairpin II responded with a couple of steam rollers. Hairpin I—and here the issue rests at present—knew that their station had been a civil airport in peacetime, and discovered some disused boilers under a building. Cut up, these provided 20 tons of first-class boiler steel, and Hairpin I gained a lasting satisfaction from the fact that the boilers had been made in Germany.

In another instance, a Hairpin Squad worked in its own off-duty time to take three blitzed cars to pieces and finally construct one sound vehicle. Duly camouflaged, this was presented to the C.O., who, feeling very proud of his men, mentioned the feat to higher authorities. " You are not entitled to an official car," was the response, " only a motor bicycle "—and the treasured car is now being used by . . . the higher authorities !

BLITZED R.A.F. timber has been made into 12,000,000 ammunition boxes ; and this takes no account of the timber salvaged by the Hairpin Squads for further constructional purposes. A condemned hangar presented a tough proposition in face of a lack of labour to tear it down ; but Hairpins dynamited first one wall, then the other, with such skill that the 40-ton wooden roof was brought down without damage.

In similar Syd Walker style, a salvage officer faced the problem of what to do with 350 old motor-cars which had been dumped as obstructions on one airfield before it became operational. The cars were real derelicts, for all useful metal such as aluminium, and every instrument, had been removed. A Hairpin man suggested piling them in heaps and burning the woodwork for the metal residue— and £100 worth of scrap metal was forthcoming.

These facts are all the more remarkable when it is recalled that before the War private contractors cleared R.A.F. rubbish at a cost of between £100 and £800 for each unit. The little-known work of the Hairpin Squads has enabled three-fourths of these scavenging contracts to be cancelled and many others to be reduced substantially, effecting a saving to the taxpayer of £40,000 a year.

Collecting 1,400,000 razor blades alone, the Hairpins accumulated four tons of scrap, and the sale realized £570 for the R.A.F. Benevolent Fund. A plane crashes—and within a few hours, when Hairpins have stripped all usable materials, the aluminium of the twisted fuselage becomes a neat stack of ingots ready for dispatch to an aircraft factory. Or a Messerschmitt falls in the Channel—and the local Hairpins go all out to wrest it from naval salvage and send it to the 20-acre scrap pile, the funeral pile of the Luftwaffe, where the wings of crashed aircraft fence off the various salvage heaps as tidily as any housewife sorts the salvage from her own kitchen.

Salvaging 6,000 tons of scrap in a year from Fighter Command alone, the Hairpin Squads took time off to rescue the H.T. batteries which had outlived their usefulness in aircraft. And thanks to this, soldiers in the Orkneys—where H.T. batteries were unobtainable—now are enabled to enjoy their radio programmes.

**TRAIL OF WRECKAGE** from El Alamein to Bizerta has yielded tons of salvage which will be used against the enemy. Anything resembling a completed aircraft can be employed by the R.A.F. for experimental purposes. These men of an R.A.F. Salvage Unit are examining instruments in the cockpit of a broken ME 109, lying derelict in the desert.
*Photo, British Official : Crown Copyright*

**BURNT-OUT AEROPLANE**

John Armstr

**RUBY LOFTUS SCREWING A BREECH-RING**

Dame Laura Knight, R.A.

## Artists and the War

MUCH well-merited praise is often bestowed on the fine output of the Army Film and Photographic Unit and that of the official photographers attached to the other Fighting Services. The notable work of the official war artists, however, is much less widely known and appreciated, though it has been regularly displayed at the National Gallery, London, since early 1940 and exhibitions have toured the provinces and the Dominions, as well as South America.

A number of outstanding examples have already been reproduced in THE WAR ILLUSTRATED (see pp. 545-8, Vol. 3, and 322-3, Vol. 4), but an important and distinctive feature of the interesting selection given in this and the three following pages is that several of those included are vivid impressions recorded on the actual scene of battle. Such are the admirable Western Desert subjects executed by the South African artists Geoffrey Long and Philip Bawcombe, and the New Zealander Capt. Peter McIntyre. Portraiture is represented by the vigorous works of Capt. Neville Lewis, another South African, and two British exponents of the art, Harry Morley, R.A. and William Dring.

*(Top) Exhibited at the National Gallery, London, and (bottom) at the Royal Academy Summer Exhibition, 1943. Painted for the Nation's War Records. Crown Copyright reserved*

25-POUNDER GUN AND TEAM IN ACTION ON THE ALAMEIN FRONT    J. Berry

JOB MASEGO, M.M.

RAILWAY STATION, ALAMEIN    Philip Bawcomb

*(Top centre, bottom left and right) Reproduced by permission of the Government of South Africa, and (top righ*

16

NEW ZEALAND ANTI-TANK REGIMENT AT SIDI REZEGH          Peter McIntyre

AXIS ROAD, CROSSROADS IN THE DESERT          Geoffrey Long

*...vernment of New Zealand. (Top left) Crown Copyright reserved. Exhibited at the National Portrait Gallery, May 1943*

**CONVOY TO RUSSIA**        Charles Pears

Lt.-Comdr. M. D. WANKLYN, V.C., D.S.O.      Harry Morley, R.A.      Coxswain A. G. BLOGGS, B.E.M.      William Dring

*(Top and bottom right) Exhibited at the National Gallery, London. Crown Copyright reserved. (Bottom left) Exhibited at the Royal Academy Summer Exhibition, 1943. Copyright reserved for Artist or Owner by " The Royal Academy Illustrated."*

# VIEWS & REVIEWS
### Of Vital War Books

*by Hamilton Fyfe*

"To give the public an idea of the new type of Army which has been built up out of the failures and defeats of the first part of the war." That is the object Major-Gen. E. D. H. Tollemache set before him when he wrote The Turning Tide (John Murray, 4s. 6d.).

The phrase "new type of Army" set me thinking. My mind went back forty-four years to the time of the South African War, when I first made the acquaintance of "the British Tommy," as he was then called. He was certainly a strikingly different type from the soldier of today.

Kipling drew him in Soldiers Three—at any rate, in the persons of Ortheris and Learoyd (Mulvaney I could never believe in). Hayden Coffin sang the universal popular notion of him in a catchy musical comedy number:

It doesn't matter what he was before,
Or what his parents fancied for his name,
Once he's pocketed the shilling
And a uniform he's filling,
We call him Tommy Atkins all the same.

It was a nickname used in a way that was half affectionate, and half—not contemptuous, but condescending. The idea that soldiers were, as the Duke of Wellington put it, "the scum of the earth," still haunted a good many minds. A lot of people—especially "chapel folk"—thought a family was disgraced if a son enlisted. Some places of entertainment still put up the notice: "Soldiers in uniform not admitted."

It was the South African War which began to break down the notion that the private soldier was a drunken, foul-mouthed, none too moral blot on society. Kipling rhymed the change in Tommy:

I went into a public-'ouse to get a pint of beer,
The publican 'e up and sez, "We serve no redcoats 'ere" . . .
I went into a theatre as sober as could be,
They gave a drunk civilian room, but 'adn't none for me !
They sent me to the gallery or round the music-'alls,
But when it comes to fightin', Lord ! they'll shove me in the stalls !

The lilting refrains caught the public ear :

Oh, it's Tommy this, and Tommy that, and "Tommy, wait outside,"
But it's "Special train for Atkins" when the trooper's on the tide.

It's Tommy this, and Tommy that, and "Chuck him out, the brute ! "
But it's "Saviour of 'is country" when the guns begin to shoot.

Today if a rhymester were putting words into a soldier's mouth, as Kipling did in Tommy's, the h's would not be dropped: it would not be suggested that a private soldier was more "common" in his speech than an officer. It was still considered correct to do this when Neil Lyons during the last war wrote that masterpiece of humour, Kitchener Chaps. Now it would seem out of date, old-fashioned, insulting.

General Tollemache does not touch on this social change which has come over "Other Ranks"

in the last half-century or so. He deals with soldiers solely as fighting men ; "killers" he insists on calling them. He shows how they are being trained to kill, and how this training differs from that of the past. The essential aim now is " to harden physically, to develop personality and speed of thought in action, and to produce a specialist to take his part in the team of killers." The old drill of the parade ground is, the general says, completely superseded (I wish all British officers agreed with him). Its object was to weld the troops into a solid mass which could be hurled against the enemy.

Theirs not to reason why,
Theirs but to do or die.

No initiative was permitted, no trace of individuality encouraged. The soldier was

## A New Type of British Army

moulded into an automaton ; he became part of a machine.

Steadily, shoulder to shoulder ;
Steadily, blade by blade . . .

That was how the Boys of the Old Brigade did it.

Well, the South African War stopped all that—or ought to have stopped it. Campaigning on the veld caused all rules of warfare based on the campaigns of Marlborough and Napoleon to be scrapped as obsolete. Individuality had to be fostered instead of being stamped out. The chief reason why the Boers made it a three years', and not, as we were led to expect, a three months' job, was that they had this quality and our men had it not.

From 1914 to 1918 it was not often called for. Trench warfare doesn't give the individual much chance, though trench raids

brought out personal qualities and special aptitudes. In this war it is called for as it never has been before, except in Red India fighting or such guerilla warfare as went on for many years in the mountains of Spain. Now, says Gen. Tollemache, " there is no room for the amateur." The soldier must not rely solely on orders. He must be " quick-thinking, self-reliant and supremely confident in his own powers."

The Hitler Youth Movement, copied from "our own Boy Scout organization," develops these qualities.

The strong morale of the Nazi soldier is the direct result of deliberate youth training. At the approved age it presents the army with a trained soldier, one who can start at once to specialize in whichever branch of warfare he has already proved himself to be most suited.

Specialization is the keynote of soldiering today.

Former wars did not require the employment of large numbers of specialists, but rapid strides have been made in the art of killing. Inventions require continued increases in specialization. It extends to all soldiers in accordance with the nature of the country in which they are fighting. It is estimated that three months' training and seasoning are required for desert fighting, and six months' for jungle fighting before a soldier ceases to be a liability in battle.

Thus we couldn't throw into the battle, as we did in 1918, totally untrained youths and middle-aged men scarcely knowing one end of a rifle from the other. They were a " liability " indeed. I know, for I saw them, and sick at heart I was to think of their plight. What Gen. Tollemache looks forward to is " the permeation throughout the Army of the Commando standard of training." It is the aim of all commanders, he states, " to teach their units to reach this high degree and to emulate the inspiring example of the Commando troops." I wonder.

Tribute is paid to the value of Army films for training purposes. They are created by " a combination of military expert and film technicians." They teach almost as well as actual demonstrations of attack and defence, which are not easy to arrange.

The film can portray the general idea of the whole manoeuvre and teach the object, the scope, and the result, or demonstrate the wrong way and the right way of carrying it out, and finally each distinct little phase can be shown and described separately.

The soldier in training can see how every operation of war and the handling of war machines and equipment are carried out by experts, with the help of an expert commentary.

Surprise, in the General's opinion, is the element "in which lies our chance of earlier victory." All the Nazi successes in the first three years of the War have been due to it. The United Nations surprised the world when they landed armies in North Africa. Unfortunately, they did not follow this up when the enemy in the Bizerta region had only 20,000 men to pit against us. Inadequate preparation allowed Rommel and Von Arnim to accumulate 200,000, and we have had to advance "inch by inch," as the radio commentators frequently emphasize. To be able to take advantage of a surprise move is more important, recent experience has proved once again, than the surprise itself.

**FIGHTING MEN IN THE MAKING.** The Turning Tide, Gen. Tollemache's book reviewed in this page, stresses the necessity for specialization among all branches of the Army in warfare today. These 18-year-old youths are learning to use the rangefinder on a mortar.

*Photo, Daily Mirror*

# Will the Atlantic Wall Prove Another Maginot ?

THE ATLANTIC WALL, supposed to extend from Norway to the Bay of Biscay, comprises " a concrete belt 5,000 miles long to defend the Fortress of Europe." How much has been actually built, and how much is just propaganda, remains to be seen. These photographs were recently published in the German press. 1, Fortified houses in a French coastal town. 2, Natural caverns "invulnerable to air attack." 3, Alarm signal: Germans carrying heavy shells run towards their guns. 4, A.A. gun emplacement. 5, Anti-tank obstacles.

*Photos, Associated Press, Planet News, Keystone*

# Yet Nearer to Novorossisk Drive the Russians

**HUNTING THE NAZIS FROM THE CAUCASUS.** On April 29, 1943, our Ally launched an attack against the German bridgehead in the Kuban peninsula, facing the Crimea (see map inset) ; and by May 4, had captured Krymskaya, powerful German base 25 miles from Novorossisk. 1, Soviet infantrymen attack in this area. 2, Russian tanks advance with tommy-gun detachments. 3, German sentry on guard at Novorossisk. This Soviet Black Sea naval base was taken by the enemy on Sept. 6, 1942. Engagements have also taken place between light naval craft in the Kuban River ; in (4) Russian torpedo boats are seen on patrol.

*Photos, U.S.S.R. Official, Planet News, E.N.A., Keystone*

# THE WAR IN THE AIR

## by Capt. Norman Macmillan, M.C., A.F.C.

UNTIL Churchillian-Roosevelt war policy consequent upon the outcome of the Anglo-American staff talks becomes evident in the form of strategic moves, it would be idle to predict what tactical forms the war in the air will take. Mr. Churchill has laid emphasis upon British help to America against Japan, and upon the pressing urgency of giving relief both to China and to Russia. That predicates coming greater pressure upon the Japanese by the forces now in the zones commanded by Field-Marshal Wavell and General MacArthur; but where the blows will fall which will ease from Russia the pressure of the present 190 German divisions and 38 Axis-allied divisions arrayed against her, is not likely to be disclosed until the stroke begins.

One thing is certain. That is, that the air pressure which will be brought to bear against the Axis contained within Europe and exerting a tremendous attrition against the air power of Germany, Italy and Japan—destroying their aircraft on the ground, in the air, and in course of manufacture. The third method of destruction of enemy air power has yet to be carried to Japan. Its delivery has been promised by both President Roosevelt and Mr. Churchill. There is every reason to believe that the great man-power of China will be strengthened by the addition of air power and ground mechanized power at no very distant date. Meanwhile, the bases of Italy and industry of Germany are being pulverized from the air with ever-increasingly powerful strokes by day and night.

### STRATEGIC Significance of the Raid on the Ruhr Dams

The loss of eight out of 19 Lancasters to effect the rupture of the Eder and Mohne dams in Germany was a small price (however

**LOADED UP FOR A RAID ON GERMANY, this Halifax's bomb-rack is packed with H.E.s and incendiaries. N.C.O.s check over the fuses before the bomb-doors are shut. The R.A.F.'s record raid on Dortmund on May 23-24, 1943 brought the total weight of bombs dropped on Germany to 100,000 tons.**
*Photo, Keystone*

the Japanese forces outside Japan and the Japanese within Japan will be stepped up to ever-increasing power and frequency. For there is today no doubt in the minds of those who hold absolute directional power over Anglo-American war effort that air supremacy and the power of the bomber form a war weapon of unparalleled force, and there is expressed determination to make the utmost of the Allies' air superiority.

THE turning of the tide in the air war is one of the most outstanding features of the World War. At the beginning Germany wielded great superiority in the air, 20 to one at least against Poland, 100 to one against Norway, 40 to one against Holland, 25 to one against Belgium, 10 to one against France, five to one against Britain. That superiority has gone. Britain alone exceeds in air strength the Axis and Japan. Add American and Russian air strength, and the United Nations must possess a two to one ratio in their favour against all their enemies combined. This ratio is rising rapidly to a flood. The present air strength of the combined air force of the United Nations is regrettable) to pay for a blow of such outstanding strategic significance. It is the first time in history that such a stroke has been effected from the air. It is a use of air power which I among others have long since prophesied. Its significance lies in the fact that it points the way to the fulfilment of many other uses of air power or to their capacity for fulfilment. One was specifically stated by Mr. Churchill when he said that if Germany used gas against the Russians we would immediately employ gas against her cities and factories. That is one of the aspects of the air weapon which too many in Britain did not accept before the War began—I mean, the strategic conception of its use; how, but by air power, could we hope to deter Germany from using gas against Russia? Only by the threat, nay, the certainty, of swift retribution, would Germany be held back from the employment of any means which held out hope of victory. Dare she try the use of gas against the spoken word of Mr. Churchill, knowing (as at least her leaders know) that she is inferior in air power, and especially in the kind of aircraft

which would deal most havoc in air gas warfare? Nothing that sea or land power could do today to Germany could have the slightest restraining influence. Air alone may restrain, and, if that fails, answer.

Here we have the reply to those who, even a short time ago, having noted Germany's failure to end the War with her then predominance in air power, proceeded to argue that the strategic conception of air power was false and that all air power should be "integrated" with land and sea power: or, in other words, handed over in a sub-servient capacity to Army and Navy Commanders. The independent nature of the R.A.F. as a Service was challenged by these theorists.

HOW wrong they were! It has been precisely the independent nature of the R.A.F. which saved Britain. If it had been an Army service, we might have had far too many squadrons in France, and too few for the Battle of Britain. No Army air service could have rendered greater help than the R.A.F. and the associated air forces in the Battle of North Africa. The truth is that air power is a specialist's job; and that its employment can be deflected by that specialist where he wills, strategically or tactically, according to the current necessities of political, military, or naval situations.

The failure of the Luftwaffe is the failure of a service which, although ranked as independent, was nevertheless the vassal of the German Army. The beginning of its failure was in the tactical conception of the Battle of Britain by responsible German commanders, and in the kind of equipment they provided for the purpose.

The reservoir of Allied air power that was stored in North Africa is now released and is rushing towards Southern Europe, battering the islands with its flood, creating havoc and alarm in Italy. That is one price the Italians have had to pay for-defeat in Africa.

### WHEN a Beaufighter Was Shot Down off Malta

Recently, I heard an interesting story of the earlier days of the Mediterranean struggle in the air. A Beaufighter squadron which was moved from Scotland through England to Malta to help to provide protection for the convoys to North Africa once had two Beaus. out on patrol from George Cross island. They shot down two German aircraft. One of the Beaus. came down and its crew of two got into their dinghy. The other Beau. circled and radioed back to base. Two more aircraft of the squadron came out, took over, and circled in patrol over the dinghy.

The only seaplane in Malta at the time was a captured Italian machine. It took off to go to the rescue of the two British airmen, only to be shot down by a Spitfire.

Two more Beaus. went out to circle the dinghy. One returned with engine trouble. The other relieved the two who were there.

FOUR F.W.190s appeared and circled above the solitary Beaufighter but did not attack it. A Dornier flying-boat then came along and circled with the Beau. The British pilot called up Malta and asked what he should do. He said he could shoot down the Dornier, but then the F.W.s would attack him and the dinghy.

Malta replied that if the Dornier would rescue the dinghy's crew, let it do so. The Beau. pilot then dived repeatedly over the dinghy. The Dornier pilot understood, went down, landed alongside and took the two men on board. It rose again. The Beau. flew alongside it, and the pilot saluted. The German pilot saluted in return and then turned off on a course for Italy. The solitary Beaufighter turned on to a course for Malta, and the four F.W.190s retired.

# For Reasons Enough It's Named Thunderbolt

THUNDERBOLT, America's latest fighter (P.47) now operating from British bases, has a span of 41 ft., length 32 ft., and weighs 13,500 lb. Its powerful armament consists of eight 0·5 in. machine-guns, having a combined rate of fire of 6,400 rounds a minute. A single-seat, low-wing monoplane, it is designed for high altitude performance and is powered by a 2,000 h.p. engine giving a speed of about 400 m.p.h. 1, Thunderbolts in flight. 2, Four guns in each wing give this plane a deadly punch. 3, The Thunderbolt's nose. 4, Taking off.

*Photos, New York Times Photos, Central Press, Associated Press*

# Lancasters Breach Ruhr Dams by Moonlight

DESTRUCTION OF MÖHNE, SORPE AND EDER DAMS by R.A.F. Lancasters on May 17, 1943, launched the War's greatest industrial disaster against Germany. 1, Position of targets in relation to Ruhr centres. 2, Sir A. Harris, A.O.C.-in-C. Bomber Command (standing on left), listens to a crew being interrogated after the raid. 3, Wing-Cmdr. Gibson, D.S.O. and bar, D.F.C. and bar, who led the attack ; his V.C. was announced on May 28. 4, Möhne Dam with valve chambers in foreground and control-room on crest, and (5) seen from the air before the raid. 6, Water pouring through the 300-ft.-wide gap made by the R.A.F.'s mines.

*Map by courtesy of The Daily Telegraph : photos, British Official ; Barratt's.*

# Floods Complete the Havoc Wrought by Bombs

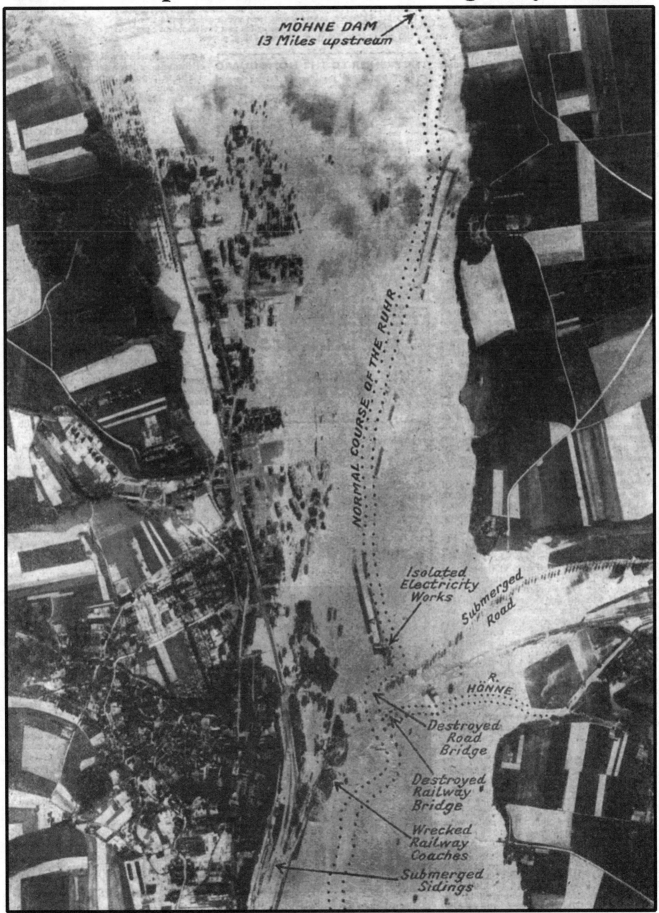

MÖHNE DAM
13 Miles upstream

NORMAL COURSE OF THE RUHR

Isolated
Electricity
Works

Submerged
Road

R.
HÖNNE

Destroyed
Road
Bridge

Destroyed
Railway
Bridge

Wrecked
Railway
Coaches

Submerged
Sidings

**IN THE RUHR VALLEY :** An R.A.F. reconnaissance photograph showing the inundations at Fröndenberg-Bosperde, 13 miles from the Möhne dam (see map in opposite page) following the breaching of the Möhne and Sorpe dams by 19 R.A.F. Lancasters on May 17, 1943. Two days after the attack it was stated that flood waters from the Möhne reservoir had swept more than 100 miles along the Ruhr and Rhine rivers to Emmerich, a few miles from the Dutch frontier.

*Photo, British Official : Crown Copyright*

# Aggressive Defence Is the Home Guard's Duty

On the completion of its third year's service, on May 14, 1943 the Home Guard was signally
honoured by a broadcast from Mr. Churchill, salient points from which are given in this page.
Here, also, is a comprehensive review of the force's work during the past twelvemonths ; previous
articles will be found in Vol. 4, p. 570, and Vol. 5, p. 760

THREE strenuous years have gone by
since that well-remembered evening
in May when Britons in their hundreds of thousands rallied to Mr. Eden's
stirring call for Local Defence Volunteers.
Years of increase, these, increase in training,
in arms and equipment, in fighting efficiency ;
and their expiration finds the Home Guard—
changed in name but not in spirit—a vital
part of the formidable defence forces now
gathered against the danger of invasion.
More than this, the time is at hand when the
Home Guard must take a great deal of the
burden of home defence on to its own
shoulders and so release the regular troops
for the impending onslaught on Europe.

What has Britain's citizen army done
during the past year to fit itself for this great
and responsible task ? Firstly, it has widened
and developed the scope of its activities, as
foreshadowed early in 1942. Thus in
addition to the main body of General Service
battalions, there are the much augmented
A.A. units, the Coastal Defence batteries,
and the recently formed Motor Transport
companies which already number over one
hundred. The primary function of the last-
named, some of which are troop-carrying
and some load-carrying, is to undertake
general transport duties for the Army in
case of emergency. Secondly, by a progressive stiffening up of training, continual
practice and improved knowledge of operational duties, all branches of the Home Guard
have attained a notably higher standard of
proficiency. Finally, the supply of all-
important arms and equipment has at last
met the insistent demand, even practice
ammunition being now available in quantity.

Though the chief task of the General
Service battalions—the aggressive defence of
their towns and villages—has not changed,
certain far-reaching innovations have been
made in training methods. The adoption
of battle procedure and battle drill on a
modified Army model, necessitating the
reorganization of units into battle companies
and platoons, has on the whole effected
an undoubted improvement in operational
efficiency. In some instances this form of
training may have been too uniformly
employed without due consideration for the
capabilities of the older members of the
force, but the obvious results of this over-
enthusiasm have tended to correct such
mistakes. The attempt to train some units
on Commando lines was, however, a more
serious error, upon which Lord Bridgeman,
the Director-General, recently made forceful
comment. " I would like to make it quite
clear," he said, " that Commandos train
for certain special duties which the Home
Guard does not share with them . . . Commandos are not Home Guards and Home
Guards are not Commandos."

THE general speeding up of training so
marked in the past year has been immensely
facilitated by the substantial extension of
instructional centres. There are now three
G.H.Q. schools, twenty-six travelling wings
and one Town Fighting wing, all staffed by
regular officers and N.C.O.s familiar with
Home Guard requirements. In addition,
courses are run at Command Weapon
Training Schools where the use of Home
Guard weapons is taught, together with
certain specialist subjects such as signalling,
anti-gas and intelligence. All this is but a
part of the invaluable help being given by the
Army, to which must be added the regular
officers and Permanent Staff Instructors
allotted to battalions for training and
administrative work and, of course, the

## THE PREMIER TO THE HOME GUARD

GREAT BRITAIN is the advanced fighting base of
the United Nations, and is still under constant
siege and assault by air and sea. It is in a very large
measure the powerhouse and directing centre of the
whole British Commonwealth and Empire. It is
the source of a vast output of war equipment. It is the
home and cradle of the Navy . . . In this zone there
burns the light of freedom—Guard it well, Home
Guard . . .

We have now nearly 2,000,000 resolute, trained and
equipped men, all of whom do their daily work in field
or factory, and add to it, free gratis and for nothing but
honour, the last and proudest duty of a citizen of the
Empire and a soldier of the King . . . You Home Guardsmen are specially adapted to meet that most modern
form of oversea attack—the mass descent of parachute
troops. The Home Guard might well share the motto
of the Royal Artillery—' Ubique '—for they are
everywhere.

And if the Nazi villains drop down upon us from
the skies, any night on a raid or heavy attack upon the
key production centres, you will make it clear to them
that they have not alighted in the poultry run, or in the
rabbit farm, or even in the sheepfold, but that they have
come down in the lions' den at the Zoo.

Here is the reality of your work. Here is that
sense of imminent emergency which cheers and
inspires the long routine of drills and musters
after the hard day's work is done . . . Just in the
same way as the Home Guard render the regular
forces mobile against an invader, so the Home
Guard must now become capable of taking a great
deal of the burden of home defence on to themselves and thus set free the bulk of our trained
troops for the assault on the strongholds of the
enemy's power.

It is this reason which, above all others, has
prompted me to make you and all Britain realize afresh
. . . . the magnitude and lively importance of your duties
and of the part you have to play in the supreme cause,
now gathering momentum as it rolls forward to its goal.
—In a broadcast from The White House, Washington,
U.S.A., May 14, 1943

ever-welcome cooperation in exercise and
training so readily extended to individual
units by the Field Army itself.

It is no small satisfaction to the Home
Guard to know that it is returning thanks
to the Army every day in the form of
"recruits" who are already well-trained
soldiers at the moment they join the colours.
A member of the Home Guard does in fact
start his Army career many weeks ahead of
the raw recruit ; moreover, every man who
passes the proficiency test provided for in
Home Guard Regulations is now to be given

L.D.V.s ON PARADE during the anxious
summer months of 1940. These eager volunteers, ill armed and equipped though they
were, established the great tradition of
service that inspires the Home Guard today.
Photo, Fox

a certificate which will guarantee the standard
of training he has attained when he joins up.

The man-power problem, steadily growing
more acute, has created many difficulties
for the Home Guard in general and the
General Service battalions in particular.
Not only have the latter had to replace the
continual drain imposed by the Services, but
also fill the gaps left in their ranks by the
numerous transfers to A.A. units, Coast
Defence batteries and M.T. companies.
These losses have to a large extent been
offset by the intake of "directed" men
under the compulsory enrolment scheme
introduced in 1942, and the lowering of the
joining age to 17. Other demands have
been those of agriculture and vital war
industries crystallized by a suggestion, put
forward in February 1943 by the T.U.C.,
that members of the Home Guard engaged in
such essential work who had reached a
reasonable degree of efficiency should have
their training and duties lightened to the
minimum absolutely necessary. This was in
accordance with War Office policy and was
immediately given effect.

YET another outcome of the increasing man-
power shortage was the greatly improved
co-ordination between the Home Guard and
the Civil Defence Services. Although the
former cannot be called upon for Civil
Defence duties if the local Military Commander deems such employment detrimental
to military requirements, it has in fact been
found practical in many places for the two
forces usefully to interchange certain branches
of their training. The value of this has been
abundantly proved in many major and minor
air raids when the Home Guard has rendered
good service to the Civil Defence authorities.

A year ago the newly-formed A.A. units
had scarcely found their feet ; today many
of the batteries have mastered the hard
training called for and are now operational.
Their success is fittingly summed up in a
terse communiqué issued on January 18,
1943 : "The Home Guard turned out and
manned A.A. guns during last night's raids.
The muster was very satisfactory. More
than one regular battery commander stated
that they came fully up to expectations and
did a 'good job of work.' "

Progress has also been good in communications and transport. To the already
competent signalling sections, portable wireless sets are now being issued ; while the
number of W.D. vehicles in use, ranging from
motor-cycles to 8-cwt. trucks, has passed
the 9,000 mark. Feeding and medical
arrangements, too, have been greatly improved. On mustering, the Home Guard is
now in a position to provide its own food.
Every battalion and most companies have
their own medical officers and specially
trained N.C.O.s, while a high percentage of
the rank and file has qualified in first aid.

Finally, after much agitation, the useful
help long given unofficially by women has
been properly recognized, and women
auxiliaries have now been authorized to
perform service with the Home Guard in
non-combatant duties. They will wear a
specially designed badge, but no uniform.

The question is sometimes asked : "Is too
much being put on the Home Guard ?"
In answer let me again quote the Director-
General. " Never yet," he said at a Press
Conference on May 6, 1943, "has the
Home Guard turned back from any job
which they realized was necessary, and was
in their power to perform and they were the
right people to perform it."

J. R. FAWCETT THOMPSON

# 'If the Nazi Villains Drop Down Upon Us'

HOME GUARD TRAINING has made vast strides during the past year—the third of the Force's existence. The supply of arms and equipment, also, is now keeping pace with the demand. These photographs taken during training show how Home Guardsmen are preparing themselves for the serious responsibilities that lie ahead. 1, Model for teaching street-fighting tactics at a Glasgow school. 2, Crossing open ground under live fire. 3, Sten machine-carbine as fired from the shoulder. This useful weapon has been issued to the Home Guard in increasing quantities. 4, Scaling walls by means of toggle-ropes at a street-fighting school. 5, Firing a grenade from a discharger cup attached to a Service rifle. 6, The spigot mortar, part of the Home Guard's sub-artillery.

*Photos, British Official, G.P.U., Sport & General, Central Press, Topical*

# I WAS THERE!

## We Were in at the Death in Tunisia

*Told in vivid dispatches from front-line war reporters in Tunisia, here is the story of the final dramatic stages of the brilliant campaign which, culminating in the capture of General von Arnim, leader of the vaunted Afrika Korps, now demoralized and broken, freed North Africa of Axis domination.*

So here we are in Tunis (May 7). We are in the town and fighting is still going on in the streets. In friendly rivalry, armoured cars of the First and Eighth Armies have gone in side by side—the Derbyshire Yeomanry from the former and the 11th Hussars from the latter. I can tell you just what the first hour or two after our entry was like. With other correspondents I had been all day close on the heels of our armoured cars, through Massicault and St. Cyprien. In front of us were a couple of Sherman tanks, some half-dozen armoured cars, and a solitary jeep.

We had topped the rise beyond St. Cyprien and seen the wide expanse of Tunis lying before us under a thick pall of black smoke from burning enemy petrol dumps. This sombre spectacle was pricked out with brightly burning fires in one part or another of the city as we began to descend the hill. Eagerly we counted the kilometre stones that brought us ever nearer to the city—six, five, four. The nearer we got the louder grew the cheering of the freed people.

GAILY-DRESSED women lined the streets as we passed through. Elderly men were cheering with the gusto of schoolchildren. Outside a villa appropriately named the Villa de la Victoire a pretty girl in a light blue jumper impulsively thrust a bottle of wine into our hands. A few paces farther on other women threw flowers into our car. The cheering swelled to a roar as we approached the centre of the city. Everyone seemed to be waving the Tricolor. There were shouts of "Vive la France ! Vive l'Angleterre !"

Then at 4.30 we drew up behind the advanced armoured cars, our car the only Allied "soft-skinned" vehicle in Tunis. The capital of Tunisia was taken. Then began a crowded half-hour of life. One hardly realizes how it started. One moment we were standing up in our car among a cheering throng. The next there was a sudden crackle of machine-gun fire, loud and repeated.

There were German snipers in the town, and they were firing from the windows of houses. In a moment we were out of the car and down flat on the ground, under the shelter of the nearest house. It was a strange sensation. Against the wall overhead machine-gun bullets were pattering in quick succession. We were in the very midst of a street battle. I can only describe it by saying that it was all more incredibly Hollywood than anything I could possibly have dreamed.

SUDDENLY a voice called out, "There is a German firing from the house above you." Whether it was so or not we did not wait to discover. We crawled along the ground some distance, and then got to our feet and made quick going for a couple of hundred yards perhaps. Here we were on "dead ground," and fantastic scenes were taking place. I had been present at the entry of British troops into Benghazi, Tripoli, Kairouan and other towns and each was generally an affair more or less conforming to a set pattern. Here it was different. British troops, German troops, French civilians, all seemed mixed up in indescribable confusion.

Out of numberless side streets more and more Germans were appearing. Some were under escort, but the majority were coming in to surrender themselves freely. They tramped stolidly along in twos and threes or fours, sometimes with their hands up and sometimes not. Anyhow, they seemed to have no fight left in them. And yet a hundred yards or so away heavy street fighting was still continuing. Elsewhere a group of Germans had surrendered to a couple of British Bren-gun carriers. The troops manning the carriers were under orders to go forward to take part in routing out the remaining nests of enemy snipers in the town. They did not know what to do with the numbers of prisoners. They simply piled them into the carriers, where they considerably outnumbered their captors. The troops then went forward into action, taking their prisoners with them.

Not the least remarkable feature was the fate of the British prisoners. Some 800 of them had been housed in a large covered-in cattle shed on the outskirts of the town. On Wednesday of this week 380 of these had been removed by sea to Italy. The bulk of the remainder were due to go today or tomorrow. I found these 400 in their improvised prison just as the street battle was dying down in their immediate neighbourhood. They greeted us with cheers and began spontaneously singing any music-hall catch that came into their heads.

Most of them had been there about a fortnight. They had suffered severely from dysentery. All were weak from hunger. They had not been positively ill-treated, but the administration of the prison camp had simply broken down in the last few days, and sanitary arrangements had been practically non-existent.

WHEN I entered the prison I saw lying on the floor, soaked in blood, a badly wounded Italian soldier. He died within a few minutes. His fate is a grim illustration of the attitude of the Germans towards their allies. He had been on sentry duty outside the prison and had wandered perhaps some dozen yards from his sentry box to talk to a group of civilians. Suddenly a German armoured car swept through the town. Its occupants saw the sentry apparently fraternizing with the civilians. With one swift round of machine-gun fire they mortally wounded the sentry, who had to be dragged in and succoured by the very men whom he had been set to guard. That was how the last German panzers behaved as they fled.

What an amazing 48 hours it has been since our final blitz attack started with the

**CLEARING OUT ENEMY STRONGPOINT in Tunis. Street fighting, described in this page, was quickly dealt with by our men.**
*Photo, British Official*

attack on Djebel Bou Aoukas on Wednesday evening (May 5)! In this last act of the Tunisian drama the climax seemed to come with amazing swiftness. What happened was that we brought an immense superiority in man-power and every sort of material to bear in the final decisive battle. And that was a matter of supreme organization. The result was that, having weathered the earlier storms, when the final phase of the attack started on Wednesday evening the battle developed with such clockwork precision and punctuality as have scarcely been equalled since Wavell's first great battle at Sidi Barrani nearly three years ago. Our infantry went slap through their objectives right up to time, and the armour were up ready to exploit them.

When it is realized that we had in the air frequently well over 100 planes at a time over a single small sector and that for the final infantry attack on Wednesday night there was one gun to every several yards of front it will be seen how immensely powerful was the blow which we were able to strike. And that was why the enemy front collapsed so suddenly and abruptly.

AT first light we all went forward nourishing the hope that we might perhaps reach the suburbs of Tunis or at any rate look over the city from the adjacent hillside before evening.

By 2.45 in the afternoon the first armoured cars of the Derbyshire Yeomanry were reported in the outskirts, and at 4.30 the 11th Hussars broke into the town itself.—*Christopher Buckley, The Daily Telegraph*

## How We Did Rejoice in Liberated Tunis!

IT is a wonderful thing seeing a city come to life after the Germans have gone. Tunis has given itself up to three days of rejoicing, and there are no signs of it ending yet. Shouts, cheers and yells keep coming up to this hotel bedroom window from the main street, where 1st and 8th Army units are flowing through the crowds.

For two days before we arrived all French people were confined to their houses, and for six months before that they could not go beyond the city limits. Now, as though the whole war were finished, they have burst out on the streets, waving flags, throwing flowers on every passing truck.

The singing and shouting have not stopped since dawn.

Only the military curfew put a stop to festivity last night. A broadcasting truck passed through the streets at 7.30 p.m., and in French and English it was announced that "everyone, including military personnel, must be off the streets in half an hour." They melted away reluctantly and made up for the loss of time today. At dusk I went into a music hall, which carried on in spite of the fact that the Germans smashed the electric power plant before they left. A notice outside said : "Despite Adolf and Benito the show goes on."

Footlights were a row of candles, and

an oil lamp kept exploding through the performance. But four or five hundred people deliriously sang "Madelon," and roared over the comedians' wise-cracks against Hitler and "Macaroni"—wise-cracks which would have meant death three days ago. There was a tumult of clapping when the principal comedian announced that he had composed a new song "without any kind of collaboration whatever." The word "collaboration" to all Frenchmen has come to mean "pro-German."

WHEN I came out into the street a much better show was going on. Four "Desert Rats" were standing on the balcony in an almost Romeo and Juliet setting, roaring English songs to a fascinated crowd of French people who swarmed across the street below.

Suddenly three motor lorries filled with Germans and Italians who had tardily been routed out of some houses came round the corner and passed the crowd. The thing that took my attention was not the tide of boos and hisses, not the wave of hate, but the stony look on the face of the last German in the last car. I have seen some 20,000 prisoners in the last two days, but this youth was the expression of them all. He had such a look of balked fanaticism, of weariness and bewilderment that it was clear that he was on the point of breaking down, and saying: "Why do they hate me so much ? Have we been wrong all along ? Is Hitler a fraud ?"

But this crowd is in no mood for finesse, nor has it any time for worrying over German feelings. French and Allied officials are making a clean sweep through the Administration. Refugees from Bizerta, Sousse, Sfax and France itself are being sorted out. Already young Frenchmen are being called up. The food situation is being taken care of at once. It is announced this morning that everyone is to have 500 grammes (more than a pound) of bread daily, and the new coffee ration starts this week.

I went into the offices of the local newspaper, *Dépêche Tunisienne*, where the Germans printed most of their propaganda. Just before they left a party of German saboteurs entered the building, smashed the linotypes and poured nitric acid on to the paper rolls. "They just left these," said the head compositor, showing me a great pile of anti-British cartoons and printing blocks. With a superb gesture he swept them off the table into a rubble heap.

There were stacks of the last issue of the German desert newspaper The Oasis, which was started for the Afrika Korps two years ago. This is one German paper that will never be published again. This issue was dated May 9, the day after the Germans had left. In place of The Oasis a newspaper for British troops appeared off the same presses today—The Tunis Telegraph. The first man to get in here was a Sergeant Lyons, who was the first man to get into Tripoli, the newspaper says.— *Alan Moorehead, The Daily Express.*

**PRISONERS ON HORSEBACK. These cheerful Germans in Tunisia come in unassisted. A description of our round up of the enemy is given in this and the following page.**
*Photo, British Official*

denied them their débâcle has been utter, complete and devastating.

As we drove down into the Cape Bon peninsula from Tunis we met the first number of refugees returning homeward, then gorgeously dressed horsemen of the Palace Cavalry of the Bey of Tunis, who are guarding the furniture and ornaments which are being hauled back to his Tunis residence. In a yard outside the town of Hammam Lif were eleven dead horses without a mark of injury on them, but all killed instantaneously by bomb blast. Swollen by gases, they lay in fabulous attitudes, their feet in the air.

German 88-mm. guns, sometimes destroyed, sometimes still complete, lay abandoned along the roadway, and away to the right of the highway an occasional shell was plopping as our men dealt with an obstinate pocket of Germans. We raced down miles of empty road, hardly knowing whether a German ambush lay ahead, for every building in the fields was flying the white flag and an occasional strange figure melted into the bushes as our solitary car approached.

We went north-east from the middle of the peninsula to the town of Beni Khaled, where we found a squadron of Churchill tanks clanking through the narrow winding streets, seeking to catch up with the First Army reconnaissance units which were reported to be pushing right down toward Cape Bon itself. Here were gardens being improvised into prison cages, and in them Germans who smoked, played accordions, even sang as they awaited transport up the road. Most of them were decorated, and many had seen a year's fighting in Russia.

## For 60 Miles I Drove Past German Prisoners

TODAY (May 11) I have seen what must be the greatest collapse of German arms since Adolf Hitler, as Chancellor of the German Reich, began ten years ago to lead his nation into war.

For sixty miles I have been driving past German vehicles crowded with German soldiers, driven by Germans flying the white flag. More than 40,000 additional German troops have surrendered and are coming back unguarded except for an occasional British private.

Perhaps nothing could more clearly highlight the utter cracking in German morale than the fact that thousands of men have been sitting down beside the road merely awaiting someone to accept their surrender.

Three hundred men, led by officers, surrendered to myself and one other correspondent near the end of the peninsula. And these were not slovenly Italians, but men of the Afrika Korps and the Hermann Goering Regiment.

In the race back through the darkness to catch the courier plane we have had to order to a side road German staff cars crowded with officers. Lumbering along the road back to Tunis we have seen hundreds of German trucks, cars, volks-wagons, and troop carriers containing, as far as my rapid count can be regarded as accurate, between 20,000 and 25,000 crack German troops—accompanying them were not more than a few dozen British soldiers. With evacuation

THERE was a large store of Axis equipment in this town, and from now on we were to see deserted enemy camps left crammed with material, abandoned dumps, munitions, transport in working order with petrol still in the tanks and loaded trucks beside the road. In one was a great miserable pig in a crate which grunted piteously as we approached. That was in the early afternoon, and from then on only two things were monotonously repeated—the burning vehicles beside the road and Germans driving toward Tunis in long dusty columns.

When we first saw truck after truck with black German crosses on the sides and filled with German soldiers, with an occasional staff car or tractored troop carrier, roaring past us, this might have been a nightmare, for there wasn't a sign of any British escort. If it had not been for the absence of weapons it was like an ordinary enemy troop movement behind the lines. It appeared that those German units who hadn't enough petrol to run their vehicles were setting them afire or wrecking them, for pillars of smoke were

**CELEBRATING OUR VICTORY IN TUNIS. Delirious with joy, citizens turn out en masse in carnival mood to greet the victorious Allied troops. As told in this and the preceding page the streets of the city were thronged with singing and cheering multitudes.**
*Photo, British Official; Crown Copyright*

rising blackly, and others were driving themselves into captivity.

As Allied planes in their last bombing of the day on the northern side of the peninsula —down which we were now following an armoured car reconnaissance squadron— began low attacks on the country ahead we halted for lunch.

News began to come back a little later from an armoured division that they were pushing on and meeting practically no resistance but taking thousands of prisoners. We realized that organized resistance had ceased. The prisoners are mainly German, and the extraordinary thing is that they seem relieved to be captured. They are docile and not aggressive, stopping at each corner in order to inquire which way they turn for the prison cages. They came out from woods, attaching white flags to their vehicles or carrying them on sticks.

Groups of officers, smartly uniformed and smoking cigarettes, drove in sleek cars with their men. Others stood at attention beside the roadway, saluting every British officer who passed. In Tunis as I drove through in the moonlight there was the grotesque scene of Germans reoccupying the streets which they had been driven out of last Friday, but this time they were not men of war but mere wayfarers whom I saw asking in broken English which route they were to take to the prison camp.—*Roderick Macdonald, The News Chronicle*

Gen. **VON ARNIM**, defeated Axis C.-in-C. in Tunisia, steps from the plane which landed him in Britain on May 16, 1943. He was brought by air from Gibraltar. *Photo, British Official*

## How Von Arnim Surrendered at Last

OUR brigade columns of the Fourth Indian Division were working their way through hilly country in the St. Marie du Zit zone, 28 miles south of Tunis, on May 12 (said an officer of this famous unit), when some German lorries came forward with white flags flying. The lorries brought Col. Nolte, Arnim's Chief of Staff, with other officers and interpreters. Nolte said that he had been authorized by Arnim to seek terms of surrender for the supreme commander of the Axis forces in Tunisia, for Gen. Krause, German Panzer general, and their Staffs.

Nolte was taken to our divisional headquarters, near Ainel Asker, where he was shown a typewritten note setting out terms for the unconditional surrender of the Axis forces and the immediate cessation of hostilities. He reiterated that Arnim was surrendering only himself, Krause and their Staffs, and that they had no power to accept other terms. The Major-General commanding our Division and a Corps Commander went off with Nolte to German H.Q. Arnim greeted the British generals outside his caravan, stiffly saluting each one before inviting them inside. Arnim and Krause then talked with the British generals through an interpreter.

The Axis commander declared that his forces were too widely scattered for him to order them to cease fire even if he wanted to. Nothing more could be done, and Arnim's surrender was accepted. He and Krause gave up their revolvers, and later in the afternoon, when arrangements had been made for their removal, Arnim emerged from the caravan. His Staff Officers, lined up outside, sprang to attention and remained at the salute for nearly half a minute. Arnim acknowledged the salute and then walked down the ranks of his officers, shaking hands with each one of them.

The officers clicked their heels and some of them gave the Nazi salute. All were dressed in their best uniforms with full decorations and gave a remarkable display of military etiquette. Arnim entered an open car and stood holding the windscreen with his left hand in Hitler fashion while he gave the final salute to his Staff. The car rolled slowly away to the H.Q. of the British 1st Army, followed by other cars carrying Krause and other German officers, along a road packed with Italians and Germans driving themselves into captivity in their own vehicles.

Arnim stood up in his car practically all the way acknowledging the salutes and cheers of his defeated soldiers. He dined with other captured German generals in a small tent at 1st Army H.Q. Then he had a talk with General Anderson. — *Reuters Special Correspondents in Tunisia*

# OUR DIARY OF THE WAR

**MAY 12, 1943, Wednesday**    1,348th day
  **Air.**—Duisburg bombed in R.A.F.'s heaviest attack to date ; 34 bombers missing. Soviet Air Force raided Warsaw railway station.
  **North Africa.**—Organized resistance in Tunisia ceased ; Gen. von Arnim, commander of Axis forces, captured.
  **Mediterranean.**—Naples docks and railway yards raided by Allied bombers.

**MAY 13, Thursday**    1,349th day
  **Air.**—R.A.F. made very heavy night raids on Bochum in the Ruhr, Berlin and Czechoslovakia ; 34 bombers missing.
  **North Africa.**—Last Axis forces in Tunisia surrendered.
  **Mediterranean.**—Pantelleria bombarded by naval force. Allied bombers raided Sardinia and Sicily.
  **Russian Front.**—Soviet Air Force raided rly. junctions at Orel and Lozovaya.

**MAY 14, Friday**    1,350th day
  **Air.**—Heavy force of U.S. bombers raided Kiel, Velsen, Antwerp and Courtrai.
  **Mediterranean.**—Fortress bombers made heavy attack on port of Civita Vecchia, nr. Rome.
  **Australasia.**—Sixteen Jap aircraft shot down out of 45 raiding Oro Bay, New Guinea. Australian hospital ship Centaur torpedoed by submarine off Brisbane.

**MAY 15, Saturday**    1,351st day
  **Air.**—Strongest force of U.S. bombers to operate from Britain to date attacked Emden in daylight.
  **Russian Front.**—Soviet Air Force raided Briansk, Kremenchug and Dnepropetrovsk.

**MAY 16, Sunday**    1,352nd day
  **Sea.**—Admiralty announced loss of submarine Splendid.
  **Air.**—During night of May 16-17 Lancaster bombers breached with mines the Moehne and Sorpe dams in the Ruhr valley and the Eder dam in the Weser valley, causing great floods ; eight out of 19 Lancasters lost.
  **Mediterranean.**—Seaplane base at Lido di Roma, near Ostia, bombed.
  **Burma.**—In Arakan British troops raided Maungdaw from the sea.

**MAY 17, Monday**    1,353rd day
  **Sea.**—Admiralty announced scuttling of two German blockade runners from the Far East, intercepted by cruisers Adventure and Glasgow.
  **Air.**—U.S. heavy bombers raided Lorient and Bordeaux in daylight.

**MAY 18, Tuesday**    1,354th day
  **North Africa.**—Announced that number of Axis prisoners taken between May 5 and May 18 exceeded 200,000.
  **Mediterranean.**—U.S. bombers gave Pantelleria its heaviest raid of the war.

**MAY 19, Wednesday,**    1,355th day
  **Air.**—U.S. heavy bombers (unescorted) attacked U-boat yards at Kiel and Flensburg by day. At night Mosquitoes attacked targets in Berlin.

**Mediterranean.**—In Allied raids on Sicily and Sardinia 29 Axis fighters were reported destroyed in combat and 44 enemy aircraft on the ground.
  **General.**—Mr. Churchill addressed both Houses of Congress in Washington. Mr. Joseph Davies, President Roosevelt's envoy, arrived in Moscow.

**MAY 20, Thursday**    1,356th day
  **Air.**—Mosquitoes again bombed Berlin.
  **Mediterranean.**—Flying Fortresses attacked airfield at Grosseto, on Italian mainland, destroying 58 aircraft on the ground.
  **Burma.**—Announced that long-range jungle force of British, Indian and Burmese troops had returned from three months wrecking operations in enemy-occupied territory.

**Australasia.**—Japanese bombers made abortive raid on Exmouth Gulf, Western Australia.

**MAY 21, Friday**    1,357th day
  **Air.**—U.S. heavy bombers (unescorted) bombed submarine yards at Wilhelmshaven and Emden at midday ; 12 bombers missing ; 74 enemy aircraft destroyed. Mosquitoes again over Berlin at night.
  **Mediterranean.**—U.S. heavy bombers made heavy daylight attacks on airfields in Sardinia and Sicily ; San Giovanni and Reggio, in toe of Italy, also raided.
  **Australasia.**—Japanese bombers again attempted to raid Exmouth Gulf.
  **General.**—Announced that Adm. Yamamoto, C.-in-C. of Japanese fleet, was killed in April " in air combat."

**MAY 22, Saturday**    1,358th day
  **Mediterranean.**—Airfields in Sicily again attacked by day. R.A.F. raided San Giovanni, Italy, at night.
  **India.**—R.A.F. Hurricanes destroyed or damaged nearly half force of Japanese aircraft raiding airfield at Chittagong.
  **General.**—Moscow announced that Communist Third International (Comintern) was to be dissolved.

**MAY 23, Sunday**    1,359th day
  **Air.**—R.A.F. made heaviest air attack of the war on Dortmund by night ; over 2,000 tons of bombs dropped in an hour ; 38 aircraft missing.
  **Mediterranean.**—Three daylight air attacks on docks and airfields on Pantellaria, followed by night attack.; Messina also raided at night.
  **Home Front.**—Sharp daylight attacks by F.W. 190s on two south coast towns.

**MAY 24, Monday**    1,360th day
  **Mediterranean.**—Day and night attacks by Allied bombers on ports and airfields in Sardinia. U.S. heavy bombers also attacked San Giovanni and Reggio, in toe of Italy, by daylight.

**MAY 25, Tuesday**    1,361st day
  **Air.**—R.A.F. made very heavy night attack on Düsseldorf.
  **Mediterranean.**—Very heavy air attacks on Sicily (especially Messina), Sardinia and Pantelleria. R.A.F. made daylight raid on seaplane base at Preveza, Greece.
  **U.S.A.**—American warships bombarded Chicagof area of Attu Island.

★ ————————————————— *Flash-backs* ————————————————— ★

### 1940

May 14. *Rotterdam heavily bombed by Luftwaffe ; Dutch Army on mainland surrendered ; Govt. moved to London.*
  *Mr. Eden announced formation of "Local Defence Volunteers" (later Home Guard).*
May 15. *Germans broke through French lines south of Sedan.*
May 17. *Brussels occupied by Germans.*
May 19. *Gen. Weygand became C.-in-C. of Allied forces.*
May 21. *Germans reached Amiens and Arras, cutting off Allies in north. Gen. Giraud, commander of French 9th Army, captured.*
May 23. *British troops withdrew from Boulogne.*
May 25. *Germans announced closing of ring round Belgian Army, B.E.F., and part of French army.*

### 1941

May 19. *Italian troops under Duke of Aosta surrendered at Amba Alagi, northern Abyssinia.*
May 20. *German airborne troops landed in Crete.*
May 21. *Maleme aerodrome, Crete, captured by Germans. British naval forces destroyed seaborne convoy.*
May 22-23. *Cruisers Gloucester and Fiji and destroyers Juno, Greyhound, Kelly, and Kashmir sunk by enemy aircraft off Crete.*
May 24. *H.M.S. Hood sunk off Greenland when engaging German battleship Bismarck.*

### 1942

May 13. *Timoshenko launched offensive in Kharkov sector.*
May 16. *Germans occupied town of Kerch in the Crimea.*

SURELY, I thought the other day, London streets have never been so clean as now, when traffic has been reduced to a minimum, when careful passengers on bus and tram drop their tickets in the boxes provided, so that the stopping-places are no longer strewn with a rich collection of evidences of journeys done; and when the morning's newspapers no longer clutter up the gutter but are "posted" in special receptacles. (For the benefit of posterity let me record that they are collected every evening and distributed free to the canteens, etc., of the men and women in the Services.) Yet only a day or two after I had mentally congratulated my fellow-citizens on their advancement towards litter-consciousness, I read that Mr. Peat, Joint Parliamentary Secretary to the Ministry of Supply, had declared that tons of paper are still being wasted daily through people throwing away cigarette cartons, bus tickets, and other odds and ends. "Our streets are littered with presents to Hitler," is one of the statements he is reported to have made.

LONDON is a big place, and only a taxi-driver of long standing can profess acquaintance with more than a very few of the multitude of nooks and corners that make up its vastness. But I cannot help feeling that Mr. Peat has gone somewhat beyond his brief. He was opening the "Private-Scrap Builds a Bomber" Exhibition at Charing Cross Underground Station, and he may well have felt the necessity for putting a little stimulus into our waste-paper collections. Undoubtedly there is plenty of paper being wasted, every day, every hour. But Mr. Peat should look nearer home. Perhaps he will take note of such an absurdity as the instruction printed on the front of an O.H.M.S. envelope just received from the National Savings Committee. "War Economy," it begins, in black capitals. "Open by slitting along the flap edge. Re-use envelope by sealing with Economy Label." Now this is one of those foolscap envelopes so preferred by Government departments (though to my mind they are most inconveniently shaped) in which the flap is on the long edge. So in order to cover up the slit as directed, an economy label or piece of paper 8⅞ inches in length is required. Surely it would be more sensible to urge that the short edge, which is only 3¾ inches, should be the one to be slit open? A little thing doubtless, but not only a Scot knows that many a mickle makes a muckle.

THEN it was unfortunate, to say the least, that on the very day that Mr. Peat was denouncing the paper-wasting habits of the people at large, the newspapers should be carrying richly detailed and illustrated accounts of a certain rubbish dump in the North London district of Hackney. Before the War, it appears, the site of this dump was liable to flooding, and so it was chosen as a suitable place on which to dump the refuse left behind by the months of blitz. The level of the ground would be raised; the unsightly litter got rid of, buried out of the sight of man. But, according to report, included among the materials dumped are such things as small shell-casings with copper bands and brass ends, bolts and washers, lengths of iron and brass piping, copper wire, brass screws, strips of aluminium and duralumin, even iron house railings. For weeks past the "totters," as the men are called who rake over refuse dumps and sell their findings to waste-metal merchants, have been reaping a rich harvest. Where all the stuff has come from no one seems to know; and when the reporter of The Star, which first gave publicity to the matter, inquired of the Directorate of Salvage and Recovery, he says an official told him, "We have no comment to make." It is an extraordinary story; and it wasn't cleared up at all satisfactorily when the matter was raised in the House of Commons. Moreover, the Hackney dump is not the only one, it seems, on which valuable metals are being thrown to waste. Yet it is still an offence to throw away a bus ticket, or the cap off a milk-bottle.

NOW here is a book which cannot but make a very strong appeal to all who are in the least degree air-minded—Elementary Flying Training, published by H.M. Stationery Office, price 9d. It is the manual used in the Royal Air Force by cadets learning to fly elementary trainers, and it is expected that it will make its strongest appeal to young men who aspire to take up air-crew duties in the R.A.F. But it is issued by the Air Ministry and placed on public sale so that all who are interested in flying may have access to an authoritative work on the subject.

ANOTHER of the books that take us "behind the scenes" is Destroyer at War, by Lieut. G. P. Griggs, R.N. (Hutchinson, 5s.). Mr. Griggs tells us that his object in writing was to present a destroyer from within, and to recapture the kind of lives men lead in her—to convey an atmosphere of truth and reality, a portrait of little ships. There I should say he has succeeded. Life on his imaginary H.M.S. Valcarron must be very much the kind of life that is lived on those destroyers you and I are most interested in. So this little book may help to fill some of those gaps in our knowledge of which we are sometimes painfully aware.

COMBINED Ops., we are reminded in Combined Operations 1940-42, recently published by the Ministry of Information (H.M. Stationery Office, 1s.), are no new development in our history, since they are the inevitable consequence of sea-power. Drake in the West Indies in 1585, Essex and Howard at Cadiz in 1596, the capture of Gibraltar in 1704, of Quebec by Wolfe in 1759, and of Cape Town in 1795, were all "conjunct expeditions," to give them the name used in olden times. But never in our history have they been so numerous and so widespread as those which are chronicled in the 144 pages of this excellently illustrated Government publication. The unnamed author—it is understood he is Mr. Hilary St. G. Saunders, who wrote the text of Battle of Britain and other official bestsellers—describes the origin of the Commandos, their training and the most outstanding of their exploits. They began immediately after the fall of France, and since that summer of 1940 Commandos have been in action many a time in places separated by thousands of miles. The French coast and the Channel Islands, Vaagso, Lofoten and Spitzbergen, Tobruk, and the crossing of the Litani River in Syria, Colonel Keyes' superbly audacious and daring raid on Rommel's headquarters, the attack on the radio location station near Bruneval, the Campbeltown's rendezvous at St. Nazaire, the storming of Diego Suarez in Madagascar, the reconnaissance in force at Dieppe, and the landing in North Africa last November—these are all described in this remarkable shillingsworth.

WHEN the official scribe sat down to write the story, the Chief of Combined Operations, we are told, gave but one order: "Bearing considerations of security in mind, see to it that the account is accurate and truthful." That order has been obeyed, no doubt. But, all the same, one wonders why we have had to wait until now for the details of these gallant exploits, when if they had been revealed earlier they would have had the greatly added interest of topicality. It is difficult to see how security could have entered into the matter to any extent, since the Germans must know quite as much as is told here—possibly very much more, since there are gaps in some of the narratives, e.g. that of the St. Nazaire raid, which can be filled in only when the Commandos who are now kicking their heels in German stalags come home again. Surely we have a right to complain when the bare bones of glorious deeds of daring are not clothed with flesh until they have passed into history.

IN my last notes I quoted a story going to show that the Navy knows its Shakespeare. Alas, the same cannot be said of those responsible for the production of Combined Operations. Hardly had the first copy reached this office when a colleague of mine with a sharp eye and a retentive memory reported a misquotation in the line of Shakespeare given in the concluding paragraph. As printed it runs, "To win bright honour from the palefaced moon." But what Hotspur really said—you can check the reference for yourself in the First Part of Henry IV, Act I, Scene 3—was not win, but pluck. This is obviously the right word; it is difficult to see how "win" in this context makes any sense at all. Only a small matter, I know; but I make no bones of declaring that a Government publication ought not to misquote the national poet.

# They Led the Triumphant Host in Tunisia

Photo, British Official: Crown Copyright

**VICTORS IN CONFERENCE.** The three men whose brilliant leadership contributed in so great a measure to our overwhelmingly successful campaign in Tunisia, are here shown conferring at First Army H.Q. in Tunis. In the centre stands Gen. Alexander, Deputy C.-in-C. to Gen. Eisenhower; left is Gen. Anderson, C.-in-C. 1st Army, and right Air Marshal Coningham, A.O.C. Tactical Air Force.

Printed in England and published every alternate Friday by the Proprietors, THE AMALGAMATED PRESS, LTD., The Fleetway House, Farringdon Street, London, E.C.4. Registered for transmission by Canadian Magazine Post. Sole Agents for Australia and New Zealand: Messrs. Gordon and Gotch, Ltd.; and for South Africa: Central News Agency, Ltd.—June 11, 1943. S.S. Editorial Address: JOHN CARPENTER HOUSE, WHITEFRIARS, LONDON, E.C.4

*Vol 7* The War Illustrated *Nº 157*

Edited by Sir John Hammerton

SIXPENCE

JUNE 25, 1943

H.M. THE KING learns details of the R.A.F. raid on the Ruhr dams on May 17, 1943 from Wing-Cmdr. Gibson, D.S.O. and bar, D.F.C. and bar, who was awarded the V.C. for the part he played in the daring exploit. During his visit to a station at which Lancaster crews trained for the raid, his Majesty is examining photographs showing havoc caused by the attack.

*Photo, British Official: Crown Copyright*

NO. 158 WILL BE PUBLISHED FRIDAY, JULY 9

# THE BATTLE FRONTS

## by Maj.-Gen. Sir Charles Gwynn, K.C.B., D.S.O.

JUNE 1, 1943 found the lull in land fighting still practically unbroken, and the air offensive against Germany and Italy proceeding with increased violence and effectiveness. But the most important war news was that in May sinkings of Allied merchantmen had reached a new low, and killing of U-boats a new high, level.

Nothing will contribute more towards increasing the all-round war potential of the Allies than the defeat of the U-boat. The menace can never entirely be eliminated, but once counter-offensive measures establish a definite mastery, the situation must progressively improve. It is, therefore, the success achieved in destruction that is particularly encouraging; and this is evidently due both to the greater offensive strength of the surface escorts and to the wide range and increased effectiveness of air escorts.

The U-boat now prefers to meet air attack on the surface instead of seeking safety by crash diving—clear proof that we have produced a new and more powerful underwater weapon. These tactics indicate a certain loss of morale, for they have evidently been adopted because even an unsuccessful fight on the surface provides a chance of escape from what may be a lingering death.

In the last war, until the convoy system was adopted the hunt for U-boats in the wide spaces of the ocean was an unprofitable task; but convoys lured the game to the hunter. Now, however, that we have aircraft of great range and in adequate numbers, the U-boat can also often be spotted and attacked when leaving or returning to its base. In this war the enemy has, of course, offset the higher rate of U-boat destruction by great increase of construction. But that does not help him to sustain morale; it may even add to his difficulties of finding men of sufficiently tough moral fibre.

## RUSSIA

Complete reliance cannot be placed on General Diettmar's announcement that the Axis has definitely adopted a defensive policy and has no intention of attempting major offensive operations this year in Russia. His statement certainly does not exclude offensive operations with a defensive purpose, and should they meet with an unforeseen measure of success opportunities to exploit them would probably not be neglected. In view of offensive preparations that Germany had undoubtedly made in Russia, the statement may, however, safely be accepted as an indication of change of plans.

In my last article (see page 3) I recorded that a section of German military opinion was opposed to offensive action, and suggested that the threatening offensive might have, initially at least, a limited objective only. I have all along taken the view that to commit herself to a really major offensive would have been a desperate gamble for Germany, involving the danger of an entanglement from which it would be almost impossible to escape.

On the other hand, the German front in Russia is not well suited for defensive purposes. It is considerably longer than the front on which the Russian offensive of the winter of 1941-42 was stopped, and it offers salients dangerously exposed to attack—the Leningrad region, the Orel salient, and the Donetz basin being the principal. The line might be shortened either by withdrawal or by limited offensives undertaken for the elimination of the Russian salients in the Veliki-Luki and Kursk regions, while the Donetz basin could be made more defensible by the capture of the line of the middle Donetz. Defensively the Kuban bridgehead has little value and would seem to be rather a dangerous commitment. There is, however, yet no sign of withdrawal from it.

On the whole, adoption of a defensive policy might include withdrawal on certain parts of the front, and limited offensives on other parts; the former being timed to elude Russian offensive projects on the precedent of the withdrawal to the Hindenburg Line in March 1917, and the latter to forestall them if practicable. If, however, there has been a sudden change in German policy owing to the Tunisian disaster and the growing danger of a major second front, the Russian offensive may be launched before a defensive policy can be fully matured.

**LENINGRAD TO NOVOROSSISK**
In the early summer of 1943 three great Axis Army groups (comprising, said Mr. Churchill on June 8, 190 German and 28 satellite divisions) faced the Russians on a front of some 2,000 miles. This map shows the line at the beginning of June. *By courtesy of The Daily Mail*

Furthermore, there is the question whether Germany can maintain a sufficient force in Russia to carry out an offensive-defensive policy such as the present alignment of her front would seem to necessitate. She is reputed to have some 200 divisions there—an impressive number.

But considering the length of the front and the necessity of holding strong local reserves widely scattered for purely defensive reasons, the number of divisions available for an

**COSSACKS OF THE RED ARMY** are among the toughest fighters of the Soviet forces. As cavalrymen, infantrymen, sappers or artillerymen they are living up to their reputation. This radio photograph from Moscow shows Cossack guardsmen on the Southern front firing point-blank at German panzers. *Photo, U.S.S.R. Official*

offensive role may be inadequate. Last year, when her commitments were so much less, her defensive front stronger and she had much larger and more reliable contingents of satellite troops with which to eke out her resources, she had to limit her offensive operations. Large elements of the offensive force she then employed have been destroyed ; and to replace them she has had to make heavy drafts on her available man-power.

It is, therefore, not only a question of whether at the moment she has sufficient troops available for offensive purposes, but whether she has a residual reserve of manpower to replace losses which active operations throughout the year in Russia and other theatres are bound to entail.

On the whole, there would seem to be indications that Germany has fallen between two stools if she has definitely abandoned all idea of a major offensive, for the defensive stool is not ready to receive her. To hold her present front defensively would, on account of its length, be wasteful of her resources and be dangerous on account of the shape of its alignment. To undertake offensive action in order to gain a shorter and less vulnerable position might involve costly operations with, in view of her limited resources, no certainty of substantially improving the situation.

The third alternative, withdrawal to a shorter and more defensible line, would seem to be more consistent with a defensive policy. But is it now too late to adopt such a course ? It might have been adopted safely during the thaw lull, but now the Russian Army is in a state to resume the offensive and is well equipped to exercise pressure, perhaps to an irresistible degree, on an army engaged in a hastily organized and complicated withdrawal. It is easier to proclaim a defensive policy than it is in practice to switch from one policy to another.

In justification of their new defensive policy German military authorities say that what Germany needs is a quiet year in which to train and organize the new recruits and formations which she requires to make good her losses and give her strength for a supreme effort. That, no doubt, is true ; but it is a remarkable case of wishful thinking and a typical example of German inability to look on any question from a standpoint other than her own. The chances that the Allies will give her a quiet year are, I hope, small.

To reassure the German public German authorities have attempted to minimize the part the American Army can play in this war as compared with the last because the U.S.A. is engaged with Japan. They conveniently ignore the fact that America has on the fringe of Europe a more effective army than she produced in the last war, and has many others to come. They would have their public forget, too, that it was only in the last half of 1918 that the American Army appeared in strength on the battlefields, and that even then it was largely dependent on French and British tanks, guns, and aircraft. The German public may be ignorant and gullible, but it presumably knows something of Flying Fortresses and Sherman tanks and of the existence of American armies in North Africa and in Britain.

Apart from what the Western Allies may do, are the Germans satisfied that Russia will be content to give them a year for recuperation ? The Red Army has certainly suffered

ITALY AND HER ISLANDS present an almost bewildering choice of landing-places in the event of an Allied invasion. Heavy bombings of Pantelleria, Sicily and Sardinia presaged a climax in this theatre of war. This map shows range of fighter cover from Tunisia and Malta.      *By courtesy of The Daily Express*

terribly both in the summer campaigns when it was meeting attack and in the winters when it was attacking. But in spite of its losses, its spirit has never been broken ; and there is little doubt that today its morale is higher, and its training and equipment better than in any previous period. It has acquired a wealth of experience and has, by reliable accounts, large reserves of armaments received from the Allies, still untouched because their design was unsuitable for Russian winter conditions. For a summer campaign, however, they are equal or superior to anything the Germans possess.

But, above all, what is likely to make the Red Army even more formidable than it has already proved and to drive it into attack is the spirit of revenge. To know that great areas of your country have been occupied by the enemy provides a stimulus ; but when the soldier has seen with his own eyes, and has heard from the lips of the men and women whom he has helped to liberate from Nazi tyranny, what happens in a country occupied by Germans the stimulus acquires new strength.

## FAR EAST
With the capture of Attu there is likely to be a lull in the war in the Pacific Islands, though it may be only for a short period. Events in China should, however, not escape attention.

The Japanese recently started a drive from the inland port of Ichang, far up the Yangtse, which they announced would lead to the capture of Chiang Kai-shek's capital at Chungking. In spite of the handicap of armament shortage, the Chinese offered determined resistance and after heavy fighting initiated counter-offensive action, evidently with considerable success. The Japanese have undoubtedly suffered a heavy reverse, and 5 or 6 of their divisions are in danger of being surrounded. The American-trained and -equipped Chinese air force has evidently played a large part in the success, and the Japanese no longer retain the air supremacy on which they formerly so much relied.

Yet perhaps the most encouraging feature of the operations was the behaviour and offensive attitude of the Chinese ground troops. It gives clear proof that deficiencies of equipment have not interfered with their progressive training ; and though deficiencies may necessitate the suspension of major offensive operations in China, it is evident that Chinese armies will be able to play a very important part when the general Allied offensive operations, foreshadowed at Washington, open. For China may be the main base from which an air offensive against Japan's war industries and home bases will eventually operate.

Meanwhile it must be recognized that the capture of Attu Island does not provide such a base since it is too far away, though it may serve other useful purposes.

CHINESE PILOTS undergoing advanced operational training at an Eastern air base "somewhere in America" are here shown being inspected by their U.S. Army instructors. These men, many of whom have seen service in their own country, will return to China on completion of their training. Their ages range from 21 to 39.      *Photo, Associated Press*      PAGE 35

# Church Parade Where Roman Gladiators Fought

**FIRST ARMY THANKSGIVING AMID THE RUINS OF ANCIENT CARTHAGE**—attended by Gen. Anderson and his men after their N. African victory —was a simple and moving ceremony. The service was held within the scanty remains of the old Roman Amphitheatre, near Tunis, and was conducted by the Assistant Chaplain-General, the Rev. J. Steele. The Anti-Tank Regiment provided the band and choir. Top, Gen. Anderson reading the lesson. Below, the service in progress.

# Are You Quite Sure Everything Is Ready, Duce?

**ITALY PREPARES FOR INVASION. 1,** Mussolini takes a long view of Mediterranean defences. **2,** A.A. gun aboard a supply train ready for action against Allied bombers. In the background another train is transporting oil. Germans recently took over Italian air-bases in bomb-stricken Sicily. **3,** Watched by local children, Nazi crew mans A.A. gun-site near Messina. **4,** Steel and concrete fortifications on which big guns are mounted defend one of Italy's island bases in the Mediterranean.

*Photos, Fox, Keystone, Planet News*

# In North Africa Now: A Correspondent's Picture

Since the dramatic collapse of Axis resistance in Tunisia, the B.B.C. and the newspapers have had little to tell of North Africa. All the more reason then for this first-hand account from a special correspondent in Algeria of social and economic conditions shortly before and after the triumph of the Anglo-American army of liberators.

WITHIN forty-eight hours of the capture of Tunis, on May 7, 1943, a train entered the terminus. The driver was brought to the microphone to tell the world that he had come straight through from Algiers as the track was already repaired at all points where it had been damaged by the Luftwaffe. The freight he brought in was foodstuffs, exclusively for the civilian population.

What war damage North Africa has suffered may soon be repaired. From the Atlantic Coast to Tunis gangs are at work to retrieve and improve the transport vehicles and communications by road and rail, by sea and air. The whole country is covered with an excellent network of wide roads, and there is an uninterrupted railway starting from Gabès and following the Tunisian, Algerian and Moroccan coasts down to Marrakesh. There is also a well-arranged combine of both passenger and goods air transportation.

The worst damage is that inflicted by air raids on the Tunisian ports of Bizerta, Tunis, Sousse and Sfax, and on the Algerian ports of Bône, Philippeville, Bougie, Algiers and Oran. The Tunisian ports before the War were equipped with the most modern devices. They are now cleared of all wreckage and may be in full use again within a short while.

WHAT will be the contribution of French North Africa to the war effort of the United Nations ? It can hardly be industrial. Although the country has been surveyed and its rich mineral resources recognized, with the exception of phosphates none of these deposits is exploited. There is practically no industry. Coal deposits are scarce, and the programme of hydro-electric power development is far from completed.

But agriculture is well developed. The country exports wheat, oats, barley, rye, wine, olive oil, oranges, lemons, fruits and vegetables. The cultivation of *primeurs* (earlies) is extended to the fertile fields along the coast ; and regular fast services of merchantmen ran from Algiers, Oran, Bône, Bougie and Philippeville to Marseilles, whence express trains rushed the early fruits and vegetables to Paris, Brussels, the Channel ports for England, and across the Rhine to the big towns of Germany. That was in peacetime, and the Germans did not forget it. After the armistice in 1940 they had special commissions in North Africa charged with the requisitioning of all foodstuffs. Soon all stocks disappeared, so that not enough was left for local consumption. As one of the biggest wine merchants in Algiers has put it :

It seemed that we were ridden by locusts. We were soon left without flour, sugar, coffee, milk, olive oil, leather and dress materials. We could not get the usual imports ; we ran short of shoes, linen, garments, and indeed, of all kinds of goods and articles. It was reported that that porky Goering said that if people were going to starve during the winter, it would not be the Germans. And so it proved. They made a clean sweep, everything was swag for the thieves. But now we are free again to deal with our produce as we think fit. The English a nd the Americans are doing their best to set us going again, and no doubt the situation will improve rapidly.

**M. JEAN MONNET**
Appointed by Gen. Giraud to the French Committee of National Liberation at Algiers on May 31, 1943, in the new " cabinet" he became Minister for Armament and Supplies.

**M. ANDRE PHILIP**
Having played a great part in the underground movement in France, he escaped to De Gaulle in London in 1942. On the new committee he is Minister of the Interior and of French Resistance.

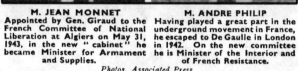
*Photos, Associated Press*

But my friend the wine merchant was not concerned only for material prosperity. Having expressed his confidence in the Allies he adds :

But above and before everything, we must have arms, so that we can give our maximum effort with our Allies to expel the Boche from Africa, and then follow on and fight him farther on. My three sons and my son-in-law are in the forces, and I can assure you they are game. They escaped being arrested last year when the Gestapo became specially active and deported as many men as they could to Germany.

MEAT is neither very good nor luscious in North Africa. There are hundreds of thousands of sheep grazing on the highlands, but they never get nice and plump. It is said of them that it seems as if they had trudged their way from Timbuktu across the Sahara. In peacetime they were shipped over to France, where they were distributed over the grazing pastures of the Alps before being sent to market. The Boche tried to raid as many of the large flocks as he could ; but the natives kept them away from his reach, and meat became rare in the towns. A pound of mutton cost from 100 to 150 francs, while the bread ration was $\frac{1}{2}$ lb. a day for adults, and a $\frac{1}{4}$ lb. for children under sixteen. To quote again from our Algerian wine merchant:

Now it is improving, and we shall soon be again a land of plenty. Food supplies and other goods rushed into the country have brought swift relief to the market situation. Housewives who had been on short rations since December are now buying commodities, and fresh vegetables are piled high in the shops. You remember those thousands of acres of artichokes, tomatoes, potatoes, and every kind of early vegetable, the groves of orange and lemon trees ? Well, they are for us now : the Boche and Italboche locusts have been swept away. I happened to be present when their leaders were cooped and packed up by the English and the Americans. How crestfallen they were, these swaggering uniformed officials and officers of the so-called armistice commissions, walking down the steps of the big hotel where they had established their headquarters, carrying their heavy luggage themselves ! How sheepishly they clambered into the lorries that were taking them to less luxurious quarters !

North African produce is not going " to fatten Goering and his swine any more," he tells me. His only regret is that he and his neighbours had not more to share with their British and American friends, "who have so thoroughly cleansed our land of the arrogant Nazis and Fascists who infested it too long."

**GENERAL GIRAUD** (left) greets **GENERAL DE GAULLE** as the latter arrives at Algiers airport on May 30, 1943. For six months the two generals had been negotiating the terms of their collaboration. Now their efforts were soon crowned by the establishment of what is in effect a French Government. *Photo, Planet News*

# They Kept Right On to the End of the Road

AT THE VICTORY PARADE IN TUNIS on May 20, 1943, the salute was taken by Generals Eisenhower, Alexander, Anderson and Giraud. This photo shows regimental pipe bands heading the 51st (Highland) Division at the march past. The bearded piper in the leading files behind the pipe major is Cpl. Campbell of the Camerons. For 1,700 miles from Alamein the Highlanders fought their way, and so, in the words of Sir Harry Lauder's song, " right on to the end of the road."

*Photo, British Official: Crown Copyright*

**FRENCH SHIPS AT ALEXANDRIA.** It was announced on May 31, 1943, that the French squadron, under Adm. Godefroy, immobilized at "Alex" since 1940 (see p. 456, Vol. 6), had joined Gen. Giraud's forces on May 7. The squadron comprised the 10,000-ton cruisers Duquesne and Tourville and the 9,938-ton cruiser Suffren (all shown in this photo), each mounting four 8-in. guns ; the 22,189-ton battleship Lorraine, the light cruiser Duguay-Trouin; destroyers Fortune, Basque, and Forbin ; and the submarine Protée.
*Photo, British Official : Crown Copyright*

# THE WAR AT SEA

### by Francis E. McMurtrie

Since the tide began to turn against the Axis, each of the enemy countries has reacted in a different way.

Germany has done little or nothing for her vassal partner, Italy. It is plain, in fact, that Italian losses mean nothing to her, so long as German interests remain intact. What Hitler most urgently needs is a respite sufficient to enable his forces to recuperate, and if that can be gained by sacrificing Italy, the end is all that matters.

Germany has plenty of troubles of her own to worry about, without concerning herself about those of Italy, Japan, or smaller satellites like Hungary, Finland, Rumania and Bulgaria. The U-boat offensive has received a very definite check ; many of the manufacturing centres on which the German forces rely for their munitions are being shattered by incessant air raids ; and reserves of soldiers and aircraft are so low that the prospects of renewing the campaign in Russia do not look bright.

As a provisional measure, Germany is seeking every opportunity, however unpromising, to sow dissension between the Allies. Thus when Russia and Poland were induced to break off diplomatic relations, something was gained by the enemy ; even the encouragement of disagreement between the various groups of patriotic French people is reckoned worth while ; and if, by underground machinations on the other side of the Atlantic, American distrust of Britain can be fomented, the Germans imagine there may yet be a chance of the war terminating with a negotiated peace, which would be in reality nothing but a truce, enabling them in due course to renew their efforts to achieve world domination.

Though these plots may seem to have little hope of success, the history of 1918-1933 shows that the danger is a real one. In those years of divided counsels and empty gestures, the rulers of this country and of the United States were so shortsighted as to allow their navies to be reduced to a fraction of their former strength. It was this more than anything else that encouraged Hitler, when he came to power, to resume the building of submarines, with the deliberate intention of using them against seaborne trade. Aided first by Italy and later by Japan the Germans made a bold bid for sea control. Only one thing stood in their way in 1940-41 :

the indomitable spirit of the Royal Navy, whose officers and men never faltered under a strain more severe than was ever before imposed upon it.

Japan's entry into the conflict might well have proved the last straw, especially as, by the surprise attack at Pearl Harbour, the United States Navy was dealt a stunning blow. It is now known that on that occasion the American fleet was deprived instantly of five out of its 15 capital ships, though three of them have since been salved and refitted. At the time the full facts were cleverly concealed, and with surprising rapidity the United States Navy recovered from the shock. It has since inflicted even heavier losses on the Japanese fleet.

### AXIS Battle-fleets are now at Increasing Disadvantage

The rulers of Japan now appreciate the fact that it is only a question of time before the Allied fleets, having finished with Germany and Italy, will be able to devote their undivided attention to their Eastern foe. Warnings from Tokyo to the people of Japan that they are likely soon to be facing a crisis have taken the place of the boasting of a year ago. As some small consolation it is also asserted that two new 45,000-ton battleships have been completed. This may be true, since several were believed to be building ; but it may be mere propaganda, concocted to set off the fact that the new U.S. battleships Iowa and New Jersey have recently been commissioned.

As always, Italy continues to show herself the least astute of the three confederates. Mussolini would never have entered the War in the summer of 1940 had he not imagined that it would be a walk-over, with plenty of plunder to be had for the taking. When it became a matter of hard fighting, the weakness of Italian fibre became manifest. The actions of Calabria, Taranto and Matapan, with sundry smaller fights, have demonstrated that, wherever Italy's future may lie, it is not upon the water !

Yet now that the last has been seen of Italy's African Empire, and an Allied invasion of Italian territory in Europe is obviously imminent, the panic which has already affected the poorer strata of the population appears to be spreading upwards.

Vapourings about the Italian Navy, now less than ever equal to coping with the British Mediterranean Fleet under its tried leader, Sir Andrew Cunningham, are intermingled with wild and foolish threats towards British airmen. These threats ignore the fact that Italy is in no position today to risk reprisals by committing further breaches of international law even more atrocious than her past bombings of hospital ships. It would be surprising, too, if at this stage the Italian fleet were to offer any formidable resistance. By the time these words are published this will perhaps have been put to the test.

At the same time it may be well to point out that, compared with 1940, Allied superiority at sea has grown very considerably. Three years ago the Germans had not lost the Bismarck, and Italy had not seen one of her battleships, the Conte di Cavour, reduced to a wreck by the torpedoes of the Fleet Air Arm. Japan had not lost two battleships of the Haruna class, nor five out of her nine aircraft-carriers. In the same period all three Axis countries have also suffered heavy losses in smaller ships, such as cruisers, destroyers and submarines.

In June 1940 this country had 14 capital ships in service. Today there are 15, four of which have been completed since the earlier date. In aircraft-carriers the position is even better. There were five aircraft-carriers at the former date ; today the exact number is unknown, but, including the new escort type, there are certainly more than three times as many. But it is in the smaller craft, so valuable for escort duties, that the biggest expansion has been seen. Destroyers, sloops, frigates and corvettes have been turned out in gratifying numbers, and continue to be added to the fleet at frequent intervals. It is this accretion of strength, together with the advent of the escort aircraft-carrier already mentioned, that has worn down the submarine attack on Atlantic convoys.

With the United States Navy the rate of increase is even more amazing. Today there are probably 21 battleships and as many aircraft-carriers in service, compared with 15 of the former and six of the latter category in June 1940. Cruisers are being turned out at a rate that has more than kept pace with losses ; and new destroyers, both of the fleet and escort type, are being completed by the hundred.

Since it is sea power that is the factor which counts most in ensuring victory—for important though the air arm has become, its fuel, spares, etc., still have to travel across the oceans in ships—these figures should give encouragement to all who hope for victory in the not too distant future.

# There Was No 'Dunkirk' for the Axis in Africa

THE ROYAL NAVY PREVENTED AXIS EVACUATION during the final phase of the enemy's Tunisian defeat; very few even attempted to escape by sea. 1, Luftwaffe prisoners aboard a British M.T.B. and 2, Lt. Bligh, the vessel's captain. When his ship struck a sandbank, he ordered the crew to swim to another M.T.B., staying behind to fire the petrol. He was wounded in the ensuing explosion. 3, Italian lies dead beside the boat in which he hoped to escape, while a comrade who attempted to get away supported only by an inflated inner tube (4) is hauled aboard a British warship. 5, Fleeing Germans captured in their rubber dinghy.

*Photos, British Official : Crown Copyright ; Keystone*

# More Killers of U-Boats Take the Water

ESCORT AIRCRAFT-CAR-RIERS are being built in America; already, said Mr. Alexander, First Lord of the Admiralty, on June 2, several are in service and have proved their worth. 1, Three of these carriers are shown in a Kaiser yard at Vancouver, Washington. The crowd on the waterfront is waiting to welcome Mrs. Roosevelt, who named the vessel on the right The Alazon Bay.

The American-built H.M.S. Battler, which joined the Royal Navy recently, was converted from a merchant-man. She was laid down early last year, and carries a number of Seafire and Swordfish aircraft. 2, Gun crew at action stations. 3, The Battler afloat. She is commanded by Capt. Stephenson, R.N., who served in the Ark Royal. 4. Swordfish brought up to the flight deck.

*Photos, Associated Press, Key-stone, Planet News*

# Two Enemy Ships Tried to Run the Blockade

IN THE SOUTH ATLANTIC on May 13, 1943, the French cruiser Georges Leygues sent an enemy supply ship to the bottom. Ninety German survivors were rescued. 1, Some are seen coming alongside; 2, prisoners step ashore from the Fighting French ship. A month earlier, on April 10, H.M.S. Adventure (Capt. R. Bowes-Lyon, M.V.O., R.N.) intercepted the German Silvaplana (4,793 tons). The Germans scuttled their ship 200 miles off Cape Finisterre. 3, Adventure's crew watch the scuttling. 4, R.M. gun crew which fired at the enemy. *Photos, British Official; Central Press*

# How Many Germans Rest in Unnamed Graves?

In the great battles on the Russian front hundreds of thousands, nay millions, of German soldiers have died. But very few have had their obituary notices in the German newspapers, and in a host of instances their resting-places are completely unmarked. This article by J. V. GUERTER throws some light on this example of Nazi reticence.

WHAT has happened to the millions of Germans who have fallen on the great battlefields of Eastern Europe? Nowhere else in this war have the dead and wounded approximated in number to the casualties to which we became accustomed in the battles of the Great War of 1914-18.

The Germans have said very little about the graves containing " the flower of their manhood," to use Hitler's words. And for good reason. They dare not let the people at home know that the number killed exceeds a few hundred thousand. To ensure the true extent of their dead being kept secret, they have " rationed " notices of deaths on active service in the newspapers. Each newspaper has a " ration " of so many obituaries a day. The Nazis fear that if more were published readers might start doing sums in arithmetic and reach the unpleasant truth. During the present comparative " lull," newspapers are being allowed to catch up with arrears to a small extent. But the Germans have not during the present war published a single official casualty list. And they have said very little about how they are burying their dead.

At least half, perhaps more, of the Germans killed on the Russian front lie in unmarked graves. This is only partly due to the methods of modern war, which result in large numbers being marked " Missing—believed killed." It is also due to the desire to hide the true number of dead. When the Russians advanced during last winter they passed many German cemeteries varying from a handful of graves at the wayside to very extensive ones covering some acres, like that near Stalingrad. Most of the graves were neatly marked with crosses, some of which appeared to have been produced by mass-production methods and sent to the front with typical German thoroughness. All bore the name of the soldier, and in many instances his unit. Some of the crosses were Maltese, bearing a swastika, and others the ordinary cross.

BUT the interesting point was this. When it became necessary for the Russians to open a number of graves for reburial of the bodies elsewhere, they found that many of the graves marked with a single cross bearing a single name were in fact " mass graves " containing the bodies of from 30 to 60 German soldiers. The orderliness of the small cemetery suggesting to German soldiers passing for the first time that some small patrol action had taken place in the neighbourhood, was a complete deception.

It might well be concluded that it was a planned deception. For when from the grave of " Private Karl Schmidt " the Russians recovered thirty to sixty bodies and re-buried them, they found that the mass graves had been used not for men shattered beyond recognition, but for soldiers still wearing round their neck their identity disk. It would have been simple, even if speed demanded burial in a single grave, to have removed these disks and noted the names of the men buried on a cross or headstone above. But for the Russian opening of the grave, this deception would never have been discovered.

Nor was this an isolated instance. Its repetition many times must make us presume that it was the result of official instructions. The Russian explanation is that the Nazis feared the sight of the endless graves would affect the morale of troops going towards the front, and that this dishonest idea was devised to permit burial and yet hide the numbers buried.

The German identity disk, incidentally, is a small piece of paper enclosed in a special metal container like a cartridge case with a sealed top.

Cremation has been used by the Germans in some instances, and mobile crematoriums have been devised for the purpose. But except in emergencies these seem to have been used chiefly for the many victims of their terrorist methods and for the bodies of their enemies. The Germans are a curious blend of scientists and sentimentalists. The scientists know that cremation is a speedy, hygienic and effective way of disposing of bodies after a big battle. But there is still a deep sentimental aversion to it in Germany. Before the War, prisoners who died in concentration camps and victims of " mercy deaths " were cremated, but earth burial was the more usual method of disposing of the dead. The great number of their dead

**BATTLEFIELD GRAVE IN LIBYA.** A small mound surmounted by his helmet and a rough cross marks the resting-place of the driver of an enemy tank. *Photo, British Official*

they have buried in Russia suggests that even the Nazis are uncertain of the effects of wholesale cremation on morale. Cremation seems to have been more extensive during the first hard winter, when burial was impossible with the ground frozen for months.

Cremation, incidentally, is the universal method of disposal of their dead by the Japanese, the ashes being sent home in little boxes to the relatives. But thousands of Japanese who will perish in the eastern jungles will have no grave.

RUPERT BROOKE'S famous poem, " If I should die . . . " contains the phrase, " some corner of a foreign field, That is forever England." Few people realize how uniquely English is that conception. The Germans have a horror of being buried in foreign soil. One of the stimulants that Nazi propaganda has been applying to the Russian campaign is the idea that soil in which Germans are buried must be made literally German—that is, enclosed for ever in the German frontiers, in contrast to the poetical conception of Rupert Brooke.

Britons who have fought the world over for centuries have no feeling like this. Some 725,000 dead of the First Great War whose names are known are buried in 15,000 different places abroad. How uniquely British is the idea is shown by the fact that even our American cousins carried back for burial in the U.S.A. 50,000 of their soldiers who died in France, the result of a pledge given when the U.S. entered the war that not a single American soldier would be buried in foreign soil without the express consent of his next of kin. The fear of being buried in foreign soil has undoubtedly played its part in creating the dread of the Russian Front

which seems to be planted in so many German soldiers.

The great majority of the two million or more Germans who have died in Russia have nothing to mark their graves. Many were buried in the ruins of Russian towns, many blown to pieces, many buried in temporary graves marked with bayonet and helmet in areas which have been fought over in later battles. German mothers and wives at the end of the war will receive a horrible shock.

The work of the Imperial War Graves Commission, which at the end of the First Great War was faced with the formidable task of re-arranging the remains of 1,100,000 dead buried in 100,000 different places, will seem simple compared to that of regularizing the graves on the still unfinished Russian battlefields.

THE massed battles in Russia have been nearer the type of those in 1914-18, which resulted in 300,000 of the British dead in France having no known graves. The more open warfare in which the British armies have been engaged in this war has resulted in fewer " to whom the fortune of war denied the known and honoured burial given to their comrades in death," to quote the Menin Gate Memorial. The work of marking graves with a temporary wooden cross is carried out overseas by the fighting Services, and in the United Kingdom by the Imperial War Graves Commission. The number marked is now about 40,000. In many cases comrades of the dead man have themselves carved beautiful crosses or headstones and erected them. Probably after the War many of these temporary cemeteries will be collected, and the graves marked with a standardized headstone like that of the First Great War.

The present war has presented another problem, the identification and burial of civilians who die in air raids. Some 13,000 men and women died in London during the great raids, and all but a very small proportion were identified and buried. Where large numbers have perished together, a single grave has not only been necessary but has appealed to the sentiments of relatives who have found unity in their common sorrow at the graveside. On the Continent, where thousands of civilians died in towns and by the roadside as the result of the German attacks, hundreds have not been identified and even lie in unmarked graves. Perhaps the most beautiful memorial is in Rotterdam, where 30,000 are believed to have perished in the most criminal raid of the War. The citizens have planted seeds secretly, so that now flowers blossom amid the ruins. As they pass the survivors lift their hats, to the intense annoyance of the Germans.

Long after this war is over men will be found buried on the battlefields and perhaps identified. For years after the First Great War unmarked graves of some of the 3,000,000 men who died in France were found, the bodies disinterred and buried again in the war cemeteries. Watches, pencils, the remains of notebooks, often enabled next of kin to identify the remains. One little " cemetery " of British soldiers was found years later when a French youth, talking to English visitors, said he recalled as a small boy seeing Germans burying British soldiers after a skirmish. He led the English visitors to the spot he remembered. Digging revealed the remains, which were in due course identified. The Kaiser's soldiers, at any rate, generally buried their enemies decently; and there is reason to believe that the Nazi soldiers of today are also whenever possible discharging this time-honoured duty with care.

# For Friend and Foe 'Last Post' Has Sounded

**WAR GRAVES ON FAR-FLUNG FRONTS.** 1, One of the innumerable German cemeteries in Russia. 2, First Army artillerymen place flowers on the grave of a comrade who fell at Tebourba, Tunisia, in last November. 3, Resting-place of British and Imperial troops near Tobruk. Each grave has been enclosed to resist the encroachment of desert sand. 4, Cemetery in Tulagi, N. of Guadalcanal, where lie many of those who were killed in our naval battles in the Solomons.

*Photos, British Official: Crown Copyright; Planet News, Keystone*

# Jungle Commando: The Story of the Chindits

What Lawrence of Arabia was in the last war, Brigadier Orde Wingate may well be in this. Below is the story of his latest exploit. Our account is based on the dispatches to The Daily Telegraph by its correspondents Martin Moore and Marsland Gander. Some of the only photographs taken of the expedition will be found in pages 47 to 49.

A REMARKABLE man this Brigadier Wingate —the man who led the "Jungle Commando" in its raid behind the Japanese lines in Burma. Martin Moore, The Daily Telegraph Special Correspondent on the Burma front, who was one of the two or three newspapermen privileged to accompany the raiders on the first stage of their journey, says that he has the lean face of an intellectual, with small, piercingly blue eyes, and a jutting chin as aggressive as his bony nose. Though he is only 38, his lank, untidy hair is already grey. But for his uniform you would put him down as a university professor or a barrister destined for the Bench.

After the expedition had set out, Martin Moore made further discoveries concerning this remarkable personality. Wingate, he tells us, a gunner by training, is a student of war, but a student also of life and art. Round the camp-fire at night, deep in the green heart of the jungle, he discussed literature, music, painting, films, economics, the organization of the post-War world. The Brigadier quoted Shakespeare and Plato, Leonardo da Vinci, and Gray's Elegy. He talked of the art of detective fiction and the psychology of comic strips in the newspapers. From Jane of the Daily Mirror he would pass on to outline his ideas for a new League of Nations.

Wingate, it was soon made clear, has studied his enemy. "The Jap isn't a superman," he used to impress upon the little group sitting round the camp-fire; "but the individual soldier is a fanatic. Put him in a hole, give him a hundred rounds, and tell him to die for the Emperor, and he will do it. The way to deal with him is to leave him in his hole, and go behind him. If this operation of ours is successful it will save thousands of lives."

He has studied, too, the Burmese tribesmen, whose hostility to the Japanese he was hoping to fan into a flame just as, two years ago, he raised the Abyssinian guerillas against the Italians. Before he left India he had a manifesto prepared, in which he called his force the Chindits (the Burmese name for the griffin or lion-like figures which stand guard round the temples to ward off evil spirits) and described them as "mysterious men who have come among you who can summon from afar mysterious powers of the air, and who will rid you of the fierce scowling Japanese." Very shortly he was famed as the Captain of the Chindits, as well as the Lord Protector of the Pagodas.

FOR many months the Chindits—or Wingate's Circus as they called themselves —were specially trained in India under conditions of strict secrecy. They were a very mixed bunch. Among the British soldiers, drawn from twenty or thirty different regiments, there were some Commandos who had already taken part in sudden descents on the French and Norwegian coasts; but many more were married men from the North of England, men between twenty-eight and thirty-five, who, before they began their training, would have been described as second-line troops. (In England they had been a coast defence unit.) Then there were wiry, keen-eyed little Gurkhas from the hill-country of the Indian North-West Frontier, and soft-spoken Burmans, patriots who refused to bow the knee to the Japanese invader. All were trained together; and so well trained that (as was soon to be discovered) the Japanese could teach them nothing in the difficult subject of junglecraft.

Early in February the Chindits crossed the mountains from Tamu in Assam into Burma. Martin Moore accompanied them as they left their last halting-place in "safe" territory. Here is his vivid picture of their setting out.

We marched at night. Elephants carrying mortars, machine-guns and ammunition, plodded on ahead, silent-footed, but brushing their way with rending sounds through overhanging bamboos and low branches. Uphill or downhill they took gradients of one in two with slow majestic ease. With the delicate step of a tight-rope walker they picked their way along rocky tracks, no wider than their own feet.

One lost his balance. He rolled ponderously backwards and crashed through the trees down

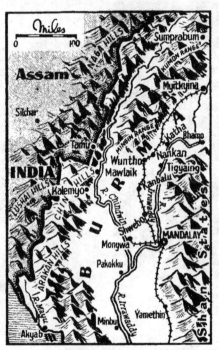

**STRIKING INTO BURMA, the Chindits (see accompanying text) penetrated to within 50 miles of Mandalay. This map depicts the mountainous terrain in which this force so effectively operated.**

*By courtesy of The News Chronicle*

a precipitous slope. His howdah was smashed and his load scattered, but he came meekly back and waited while the mortars and ammunition-boxes were collected.

Next came the mules and men, platoon after platoon, laden with all the varied paraphernalia of this strange unit. In rear were the slower-moving oxen. They dragged their sturdy little carts until the track became so narrow and steep that they could go no farther. Then the carts were abandoned and oxen became pack animals like the mules.

For three months the Chindits were in operation against the Japanese in the Burmese jungle. Beating the enemy at his own game of infiltration in the dark solitudes of the tropical forests, they penetrated between 200 and 300 miles into enemy-infested territory. In numerous jungle clashes they killed at least 200 Japanese; and a whole Japanese division of 15,000 men was kept busy hunting them and trying to prevent them reaching the Lashio railway.

Arrived at the Chindwin, Moore watched the Chindits cross the 300-ft.-wide river.

Several Burmese boats had been obtained and were drawn up on the shore awaiting us. While some men swiftly loaded them, others were inflating rubber boats which we brought with us.

The elephants plunged straight across, deposited their loads, and swam back for more.

A strongly armed party went over to guard the bridgehead against possible enemy attack. Then, while the main body of troops rested, hidden in the thicket, platoons went forward one by one with their animals to make the crossing. Most of the men easily swam across, despite the swift current; but the transport of arms, ammunition and supplies, with so few small craft, was a slow process.

When the first light streaked the eastern sky a large proportion of the force were still on this side of the river. By then, however, there was no further need for secrecy. Our patrols had made sure there were no Japanese in the vicinity; the troops came out of their concealment in the thicket, and the sun rose on a scene which seemed to belong rather to the seaside on Bank Holiday in England than to a military operation in the Burma jungle. Hundreds of men awaiting their turn to cross sat breakfasting on the shore. Naked figures splashed through the shallows and raced over the sands in pursuit of recalcitrant mules. Some were swimming across leading lines of plunging animals. Rubber boats piled with arms and kit were being towed.

AFTER crossing the Chindwin the Chindits split up into separate columns, each charged with a special task. That they were successful was very largely due to the support of the R.A.F. Each man carried six days' rations on his back; but for the rest they were dependent on supplies dropped by plane. Each column had an R.A.F. unit with its own radio to act as spotters for the bombers, but still more as liaison with the aircraft dropping supplies. The R.A.F. made it a point of honour to drop everything that was asked for; and so to these little bands of wandering fighters there came down from the sky such things as monocles, false teeth, a kilt, a copy of a recent life of Bernard Shaw, and a will form for signature by an officer who was temporarily surrounded by Japanese. Once two volunteer wireless-operators were landed by parachute: they came down in the middle of a scrap, and had to hide in the jungle until it was over.

One chief objective was the Mandalay-Myitkyina railway, which the column charged with its destruction reached on March 6, just a month after they had marched out of India. So far they had not seen a single Japanese soldier, but after they had blown up the line north of Wuntho with seventy charges placed over a distance of 4½ miles they had a successful clash with lorry-borne Japanese at Nankan railway station; and on March 14, when bivouacked on an island in the Irrawaddy, just south of Tigyaing, they had another brush with the enemy. Still they pushed on till at Pargo they received orders to disperse into parties and return to India.

"The Japanese," Lieut. Jeffrey Lockett told Marsland Gander, The Daily Telegraph correspondent in New Delhi, "were now straining every effort to close in on us, and we moved with the utmost caution, hitting back hard by ambushing one of their platoons. Rations were dropped from the air for the last time. For the rest of the time, relentlessly pursued by the Japanese, we existed on rice, fruit, tomatoes, a few coconuts, eggs and chickens. Once we shot a water-buffalo, and we also ate our mules. We delayed the enemy by constantly planting booby traps on the trail."

On April 15, weak, almost exhausted, but in jubilant spirits, they made contact with Indian soldiers and knew they were home. "I had been imagining all the wonderful things I would eat and drink," said Lt. Lockett, "but found, in fact, that I could eat nothing of civilized fare and drink only a quarter of a bottle of beer."

## *Wingate, Captain of the 'Chindits*

The man whom the Burmese villagers know as " Lord Protector of the Pagodas " is a 38-year-old professional soldier who combines the dreamer, almost the mystic, with the man of action. Brigadier Orde Charles Wingate saw service in Palestine in 1937, and was one of the little band of British officers who stirred up the Abyssinian revolt in 1941. His most recent exploit is the leadership of a force of British, Indian, and Burmese troops—called Chindits after the griffin-like figures placed on guard outside Burmese temples—in a three-months' raid behind the Japanese lines in Burma.

## *First Photographs of the Jungle Commando*

It was in the early part of this year that the Chindits set out on their 200-mile-deep penetration of the Japanese positions in Burma. 1, The Chief Chindit, Brigadier Wingate (right), making his final plans. 2, Field-Marshal Sir Archibald Wavell, who was largely responsible for the expedition, inspects the men just before they cross the frontier from Assam into Burma. 3, Chindits rest in a Buddhist temple, the first of many passed in their long and dangerous expedition.

Pho

## *Behind the Japanese Lines in Burma*

On and on the Chindits raided, hunted by a much more numerous enemy, but, such was their new-found jungle-craft, evading them or beating off their attacks. The country they passed through was difficult in the extreme. 4, Crossing a stream in rubber floats they took with them. 5, Passage of the Chindwin river ; note elephant transport (left). 6. The sole means of communication between the raiding columns and their base was radio, operated by R.A.F. signal sections.

# A New Road Links India and Burma

Photos, British Official: Indian
Official; Crown Copyright

Before the War land communications between Assam and Burma were none too satisfactory, since athwart the frontier lies a great mass of jungle-covered mountains. But military necessity admits no insurmountable obstacle. Top photo, a convoy of Jeeps passing along a two-way motor-road which our Army engineers have built in less than six months: a whole division of troops, equipped with bulldozers and other up-to-date machinery, was used for digging the track, uprooting trees and blasting rocks. Bottom, troops with supply mules crossing one of the many jungle streams on the route.

# VIEWS & REVIEWS Of Vital War Books

## by Hamilton Fyfe

Most people would dismiss Burns's couplet about the "best-laid schemes of mice and men ganging aft agley" as a commonplace. "Everybody knows that," they would say contemptuously. Yet how few bear it in mind!

The Maginot Line was a grand scheme. The French believed it guaranteed them against invasion. They sat behind it, foolishly confident, for eight months after war began. Then they found it had "gone agley."

Hitler's Westwall is an even more elaborate affair. It is better "laid" than the Maginot Line. In his book What about Germany? (Hodder & Stoughton, 12s. 6d.), Mr. Louis P. Lochner gives a detailed description of it. He saw it from end to end in 1939. It was then 375 miles in length, all on German soil. Now it is a good deal longer; it extends deep into France and far into Holland.

Hitler is said to have put on the table, when he was explaining it to some General Staff officers, a large china plate and a small copper coin. "Which is the harder to hit, gentlemen?" he asked them. That, Mr. Lochner tells us, illustrates one of the basic differences in the French and German fortifications.

The Maginot Line was made of one piece, so to speak. It was one gigantic, continuous and interconnected system. Hitler decided to lay out his Westwall in the form of innumerable smaller units, of which one or other might be captured or destroyed without endangering the rest. Just as the modern steamer has its hold subdivided into bulkheads that are each watertight, thereby permitting of damage to one without danger to the next, so the Siegfried Line has its various sections, interconnected, but constructed independently of each other.

At strategic points there are steel-plated fortresses which left on Mr. Lochner a most unpleasant impression. There were turrets to spit forth liquid fire, other turrets with heavy machine-guns. He saw "periscopes, electric kitchens, shower-baths, radio sets, complete telephone plants, air purification machinery, bunks for officers and men—all in the bowels of the earth." Usually these vast subterranean fortifications are built into huge mountain sides.

From each end of long corridors machine-guns ominously peered at us. The officers guiding us claimed that if "by miracle" an enemy should get in through some steel door machine-guns would finish him. Even if they failed, the enemy would probably get no further. All the German soldier needs to do is to push a button whereupon a trap-door opens and the enemy drops into a dark hole.

It sounds terrible, and the whole system of defences is 35 miles in depth, with four lines arranged to keep out tanks and infantry, and to escape hits from guns on the ground and bombs from the air. The cost was enormous. "In order to construct the Westwall Hitler literally stopped the nation's business and diverted the energies of 80 million people." But does any sane German military leader imagine the United Nations will be so mad as to attack either the Siegfried or the Maginot Line (which is now manned by Nazis)? There are other ways of getting into Germany than those which lead from France and Holland and Belgium. The Westwall scheme will be found to have "gone agley," like its counterpart in France.

Mr. Lochner was astonished and rather shocked, when he was on the frontier between France and Germany, to see that, while the German Army was "forever kept in fit condition and taught offensive tactics," the French "apparently settled down to a winter of card-playing, reading and chatting inside its fortifications." They did not seem to care what was happening only a short distance from them. A group of journalists with a German general, several colonels and other officers, stood on a hill only 250 yards from a French post : not a shot was fired at them. The general, who had broad red lapels to his coat and red stripes in his trousers, said he had been there the day before, watching the French through field-glasses, and nothing had happened.

Even worse was the liberty accorded to the Germans in September 1939 to clear out of Saarbrücken and take with them thousands of car-loads of most valuable machinery and war material. As many as 200 railway wagons were moving in and out daily. "We saw big trucks, loaded to the top, leaving across a

## The Line That Hitler Built

bridge which the French might easily have destroyed. Yet not a shot had been fired at the city." Mr. Lochner does not explain this inactivity. It was due to the anxiety of the French leaders to avoid reprisals. That has been clearly established by other witnesses.

From his shrewd observations on several German fronts as a war correspondent Mr. Lochner draws some very useful lessons. One is the necessity of brainwork in the smallest details of campaigning. The Germans, for instance, always use one type of car on any road by which the army is advancing into enemy country. This means that only one sort of "spares" need be carried, only one type of tire, only mechanics who have specialized on the car used and probably worked in the factories where it is made.

The problem of road repair is tackled with the same care. All cars in eastern and south-eastern Europe, where the highways are soon broken up, carry a load of thin logs for "corduroying" bad places (that is not new ; we did it in France last time), and the troops also use steel "mattresses" for covering morasses in places where roads would otherwise be impassable. But for moving both men and materials the enemy relies mainly on rail transport, the author says. He has therefore been glad to notice a growing realization in the United States that :

One of the most important tasks for the United Nations' air forces to perform is that of interfering with enemy railway communication. It is of great military importance to wreck plants that manufacture goods, parts and materials for war use. But isn't it putting the cart before the horse to do this first and leave the railways for later attention ? If transportation is wrecked first, finished goods cannot reach their destination.

So, when we hear or read that a dozen locomotives or several freight trains have been bombed, as we do frequently now, we can consider that "a hit, a palpable hit" has been scored. The railway is a vital artery. With the railways tied up, generals would be helpless, no matter how magnificent their strategic plans might be.

One trick of German bombing is mentioned that I have not heard of before. When Nazi airmen bomb roads with troops or refugees on them, they aim at the sides, not at the road itself. This has two advantages. One is that the road is not made useless for their advancing columns. The other is that " the natural tendency, when enemy bombers heave into sight, is to get off the roads and seek shelter in the ditches."

There is a great deal in the book about life in Berlin as well as in the battle areas. I have read nowhere a more convincing account of Hitler's personality—that of a very skilful actor as well as a fanatic believing he is inspired and his country destined through him to enjoy world domination for a thousand years. But it is the war part that concerns us most in these pages ; and there is no more heartening statement by this able and experienced newspaperman than that which he makes about the method that secured the German successes in 1940 and 1941.

No time is given for rest. The army keeps hammering away without pause in the hope that the enemy will crack up because of battered nerves.

We have adopted that method, the method of all great commanders since the earliest times. We have played the Germans' own game, and beaten them at it. "No time was given them for rest" in Tunisia. They did crack up because of their exhausted nerves.

**HITLER'S SIEGFRIED LINE, as the Westwall is sometimes called, was visited by the author of What About Germany? reviewed in this page. Accompanied by staff officers, the Fuehrer is here shown leaving the camouflaged entrance to a subterranean fort during a tour of the Westwall in May, 1939.** PAGE 51 *Photo, New York Times Photos*

# Souvenirs from the Battlefield May Save Lives

On both sides of the war fronts there is an understandably intense anxiety to find out as soon as may be the details of any new weapon or article of military equipment used by the enemy. In this article ALEXANDER DILKE shows that this curiosity has a practical basis.

DURING one of the innumerable air battles fought off and over the North African coast a German plane was brought down close to the shore; and as it sank its crew climbed into a rubber dinghy and made for the beach. A " reception committee " was waiting to take them prisoners; but there soon appeared on the scene an R.A.F. officer who was more interested in the plane than in the prisoners. He wanted some " souvenirs " from it; and, taking the rubber dinghy the German crew had used, he paddled out to the plane.

Looking down fifteen feet through the clear water, he could see it. Blocking the air-pipe of his gas-mask and using it as a diving helmet, he went down, got a grip on the cockpit, and had a look. What he saw evidently only increased his determination to secure souvenirs. Returning to the shore, he borrowed a shallow water diving-suit from a naval unit; and, weighting himself with pieces of heavy iron, managed to make a series of dives long enough to get the equipment he wanted from the sunken plane, bringing it ashore in the dinghy.

Just what that equipment was and where the incident took place must remain secret. But the " souvenirs " obtained by this officer, one of many in the R.A.F. whose duty is to inspect every enemy machine brought down, were probably the means of saving the lives of many British pilots at a later date. Experts carefully examined his find, discovered its purpose, and issued guidance on tactics based on their deduction from it.

After every battle in the air or on land, " souvenirs " are deliberately collected for examination by experts, so that the most exact information may be available for our own men about enemy equipment. Where it is known that the enemy is using new equipment—a new tank, mine, or gun—extreme efforts may be made to capture one intact, so that tactics can be altered to minimize the damage it does. The determination and courage of intelligence officers in obtaining information about the Afrika Korps' new weapons contributed to the succession of defeats inflicted upon them.

As an example, not long ago it was believed that the Germans were using a new 75-mm. gun, and instructions were given to get one undamaged as early as possible. A British unit saw one of the guns, attempting to take up a new position, fall a victim to one of the Germans' own mines. They found the gun abandoned in the middle of the minefield, with one wheel blown off. Without hesitation, they began to lift mines to clear a path to it, temporarily patched up the wheel, and pulled it out for handing over to experts for examination. Within a short time new instructions, based upon examination of the gun and estimation of its possibilities and limitations, were being issued.

In an effort to hinder the enemy, both sides are constantly producing variations of anti-tank and anti-personnel mines. Securing a specimen of a new mine and " broadcasting " instructions about it, may save dozens of lives and hours of valuable time. The work is, of course, dangerous—comparable, indeed, to the remarkable efforts of

the Mine Experimental Department of the Royal Navy in securing specimens of the magnetic mine, the full story of which has just been told. (See page 779, vol. 6.)

Given a specimen of a new weapon, scientists and ordnance experts can soon lay bare its secrets and tactical specialists deduce the ways in which it may be used. Knowledge of the radius of fire, " blind spots " and " soft spots " of a new tank, for instance, may enable new tactics to be developed in meeting it; and so hundreds of valuable lives may be saved which would have been

ENEMY SECRETS are sometimes laid bare when aeronautical experts hold post-mortems on captured aircraft. Here is an ingenious apparatus found in a rubber dinghy from a German bomber which had crashed into the sea. It comprises kite, aerial and transmitting set used for sending out S O S signals.
*Photo, Topical Press*

lost if these facts had had to be found out " the hard way " in battle.

Both sides have made special efforts to capture intact specimens of new tank types as soon as they have made their appearance. The British have been very successful in this. The German Mark VI tank (Tiger) was not the surprise that was generally supposed. British intelligence officers had obtained exact information about it weeks before it was used in strength in the North African battles. Defences and tactics were altered to meet its expected appearance. The result was that, instead of being the decisive weapon expected by the Germans, it attained only local successes of limited importance, and did not stop the drive on Bizerta and Tunis.

THE " classic " story of intelligence regarding German tanks goes back to the first appearance of the German Mark IVs in the Western Desert, and was revealed when Major David Evans was awarded the George Medal for rescuing a tank from a burning liner at Suez. The tank was the first specimen of the Mark IV captured intact, and it was brought back from the front for shipment to Britain under immense difficulties. The tank, travelling under its own power with a British crew, was attacked several times by German

aircraft on its way back—whether because the Germans recognized it and so made every effort to prevent it reaching our experts, or bombed it simply because it was a tank behind our lines.

The tank was put aboard a homeward-bound ship. During an air raid the ship was fired and the tank was in danger of complete destruction, when Major Evans went aboard and finally rescued the " souvenir " when it was nearly red hot. Examination of this tank by our experts resulted in considerable modification of our armour and defences.

Every new article captured from the enemy is minutely examined. If it does not yield information of direct military value, it may provide tips for our own designers and manufacturers who are not above learning from the enemy if he has something better.

IT may also be of value to our economic warfare experts in revealing shortages of certain materials in Germany. Thus through the long chain of intelligence a " souvenir " captured in the desert may lead to an R.A.F. raid on a new objective " recommended " by economic warfare experts. The proportion of cotton and wool in enemy uniforms, the use of certain alloys in aircraft, even the packings used for rations, may indicate where the enemy is feeling the pinch. Only a short time ago, Lord Selborne revealed that minute examination of a shot-down German bomber had shown it was built completely without the aid of nickel, so that its metallic parts had a tensile strength of 10 per cent less than previous types. The fact that British experts have repaired crashed German aircraft and flown them to discover their tactical possibilities is well known.

Intelligence does not, of course, work only on captured material. In one battle in North Africa, it was asked: " Who was the fool standing up in the middle of the battle making notes? " The " fool " was an intelligence officer studying the rate of fire and manoeuvrability of a new German gun.

The enemy, of course, is equally anxious to capture " souvenirs " from us for the same purpose. For that reason full descriptions of new pieces of equipment have to be kept secret even after it is well known to the public that they are in use. For instance, it was not until long after Mosquito bombers had come into use that any details about speed, armament, bomb load, etc., were published. The Germans had shot down a certain number, but there was no certainty that they had been able to probe their secrets. How much they wanted a Mosquito more or less intact was shown by the efforts they made to salvage one of the bombers that came down in a lake after the raid on Oslo last September.

The official silence on the technical details of our new weapons until it is certain beyond question that the Germans have specimens is due not to obstinacy but to the desire to make the Germans find out about them "the hard way." If one of our intelligence officers making an examination at great risk under fire can save hundreds of lives by learning the enemy's technical secrets, any man or woman working in a war factory or simply seeing something on the road can endanger an equal number of lives by gossiping about it so that the enemy learns " the easy way."

# Americans Triumph Over the Japs in Attu

ATTU, westernmost of the Aleutian Isles, 196 miles W. of Kiska (another Aleutian island occupied by the Japanese in 1942), was the scene of a landing by American forces on May 11, 1943.

"In spite of their numerical inferiority, our men put up fierce resistance," declared Tokyo. By May 18 American troops had gained possession of a ridge at the end of the island—the enemy's main defence position. U.S. troops, landing at Massacre Bay, advanced N. and joined their comrades who had likewise landed in the Holtz Bay area. The Japs withdrew towards Chichagof harbour, where they established positions. The battle of Attu then entered its final phase, the enemy having been split up into three groups.

Right, U.S. infantry firing at Japanese from behind improvised cover. Below, map showing position of vital Attu areas, and points at which the Americans landed. Attu is the largest of the group of Aleutian islands given the name of Near because of their proximity to Kamchatka. See also map on page 10.

JAP FORCES IN ATTU were relentlessly pressed back against the N.E. extremity of the island. On May 25 Col. Knox, Secretary of the U.S. Navy, stated that the enemy was being "corralled." Jap pockets of resistance were being mopped-up by the Americans. After 19 days of hard fighting in severe weather conditions, victory was assured for our Ally, the whole island subsequently falling into her hands. The way was thus paved for landings on Kiska, and ultimately for a drive that would follow the island-chain towards Japan itself.

Kiska was heavily raided by U.S. aircraft as Jap resistance came to an end on Attu, enemy bases being vigorously bombarded. On June 3 a U.S. Navy communiqué announced that 1,791 Japanese were killed in the Attu fighting.

Above, American tank rumbles through the snow at an advanced base in the Aleutians. Left, U.S. troops disembark from landing-barges on to the beach at Massacre Bay.

*Map by courtesy of The Times; photos, Planet News, Keystone, Associated Press*

# THE WAR IN THE AIR

### by Capt. Norman Macmillan, M.C., A.F.C.

**AIR CHIEF MARSHAL SIR H. DOWDING** commanded fighter pilots in Battle of Britain, 1940. On June 2, 1943 it was announced that he had been created a Baron.
*Photo, Topical Press*

PERHAPS the most salutary lesson of this war is that air power is amphibious. It is almost revolutionary. As with all revolutions there were those who believed in the new ideas before they were proven, while others denied their likelihood. We have seen a tremendous growth in the power of the air weapon over armies in the field, and when employed against industrial targets which constitute the latent war potential of a nation. We have seen an increasing use of air power against ports, dockyards, in the laying of mines, and in direct attacks against enemy shipping and warships. In the essentially maritime division of air operations now lies most opportunity for development. The implications of air supremacy over the oceans are so immense as to leave no room for doubt that air power over the sea will have a momentous influence on the outcome of the war and bear largely upon the future status of nations in world affairs.

There is wisdom in looking back for a moment or two upon the course air-sea war has so far taken.

The very first R.A.F. raid was made against German warships in Wilhelmshaven Roads and at the Brunsbüttel end of the Kiel Canal. In Norway our land and sea operations could not be covered by adequate fighter protection, and against the enemy's superiority in air power we had to withdraw. The same applied in Crete. It happened again in the Far East when we lost Malaya, and the Prince of Wales and the Repulse were sunk by air attack.

Here let us turn to the report of the sub-committee of the Committee of Imperial Defence on the Vulnerability of Capital Ships to Air Attack, signed on July 30, 1936, from which I take the following:

It has been argued that the functions of the capital ship can at least equally well be carried out by aircraft . . . since if the enemy possesses battleships they will be destroyed by our own air forces, properly distributed in advance to deal with such a situation. We do not consider that the conditions prevailing today or likely to prevail in the near future justify these opinions, nor do we consider that there is sufficient evidence to affirm that aircraft can perform the role of our own capital ships by holding in check, and if possible destroying, enemy capital ships.

The war provides sufficient evidence to modify some of the findings of that sub-committee, and clear up many of the doubts expressed in their report.

The air-sea battles of the Coral Sea and Midway Island saved Australia and Hawaii from invasion. Those were true air-sea operations, with two opposing fleets, accompanied by aircraft-carriers, meeting for the first time in history. The air decided the issue in each case; and the ships' guns had to fight, not the guns of other ships, but the bombs and torpedoes of aircraft. The actions were fought outside the range of interchange gunfire.

## AIR Support Essential for Ocean-going Fleets

It has been usual for large-scale air-sea operations to take place during daylight hours. It does not follow that this will always be the case, but when it is so it is probable that fighter aircraft will provide the most efficacious defence against attacking torpedo and bomber aircraft.

The lessons of the Coral Sea and Midway Island actions are that fleets steaming out of range of shore-based fighter protection must possess their own fighter protection in sufficient strength to combat the air attacks of the enemy's carrier-borne aircraft, and at the same time have sufficient torpedo-bomber-reconnaissance aircraft to damage or destroy the enemy's ships, especially his aircraft-carriers, capital ships, and submarines.

Experience in the war against the submarine shows, too, the necessity for close air protection at all times. The increased range of the modern ocean-going submarine left a blank spot in mid-ocean which was outside the cover-range of shore-based aircraft, and over such areas convoy escorts must be able to provide their own anti-submarine air umbrellas.

THE R.A.F. catafighter unit, which provided fighter aircraft to be catapulted from merchant ships (see illus. p. 11), was able to give material assistance against air attack, and did valuable work during passages to North Russia in protecting the convoys from the shore-based German aircraft operating from high-latitude Norway. But this method of air operation at sea does not meet the threat of submarine warfare, except by driving off enemy reconnaissance aircraft which might otherwise put submarines in the path of the moving ships.

The destruction of submarines demands the employment of depth charges, for which fighter aircraft are unsuitable. Small escort carriers carry torpedo-bomber-reconnaissance aircraft for that purpose, and the slow, short-range Swordfish is a good sub-hunter. In the Great War of 1914–18 the convoy system ended the submarine menace. In this war it is the air-protected convoy system which is bringing that about. (See illus. p. 42.)

British sea-borne air power was assigned to the Royal Navy by Mr. Neville Chamberlain in 1938, and in that year of taking over

full control of the Fleet Air Arm, naval experts prophesied that the future navy would operate one-third of its strength on the surface, one-third submerged, and one-third in flight. Hitherto one weakness of Britain's air-sea power has been lack of carriers. We have lost five—the Courageous, Glorious, Ark Royal, Eagle, and Hermes. Without sufficient carriers, air power cannot always be placed where sea power wants it to be.

NOW that there is sufficient evidence from which to draw conclusions, it is certain that even the most conservative naval opinion will no longer withhold from the air its place and its power in sea operations.

But there is a real danger that conservative naval opinion still wants to devour part of the separate third Service, the R.A.F., subordinate it to its own needs, and give the remainder to the Army.

But the admirable dovetailing of the air operations in North Africa with those of the land forces, and the fine work of Coastal Command with the Navy, show that the air can cooperate with land or sea as efficiently as the two older Services have in the past joined forces in combined operations.

We have travelled a long way from the time when the sub-committee to which I have referred issued its report. And Mr. Churchill, who, almost as soon as he became Prime Minister, turned the Coastal Command over to the operational control of the Admiralty, appears to be satisfied with the present allocation of British air power, for in his speech to the United States Congress on MAY 19, 1943, he said:

Opinion . . . is divided as to whether the use of air power could by itself bring about the collapse in Germany and Italy. The experiment is well worth trying so long as other measures are not excluded.

Air Chief Marshals Harris and Tedder are trying the experiment. If they succeed, even in " softening " these two enemies, theirs are the British elements which will assuredly be the principal factors in bringing Japan also to account for her crimes.

THE British effort in the war is not helped by the maintenance of the pre-war naval feud against the R.A.F. In any case, I believe this reactionary outlook represents a minority view today. The Air Branch of the Royal Navy and its enthusiastic officers and men have a full-time job ahead of them in developing the Fleet Air Arm into its full proportion of specialized air power for intrinsically naval purposes. And the R.A.F. has done too well to be politically assailed. But for the fact that the R.A.F. was a separate Service we might have lost the Battle of Britain, and the war.

**SUNDERLAND FLYING-BOAT** of the Coastal Command recently picked up two survivors of a Liberator which had crashed in the Bay of Biscay after being attacked by five Junkers. Survivors approaching the Sunderland in a dinghy.
*Photo, British Official: Crown Copyright*

# They've Made a Fine Art of Night 'Intrusion'

R.A.F. INTRUDER SQUADRONS, equipped with Mosquito aircraft, have scored innumerable successes in Germany and the occupied countries. Airfields, goods trains, barges and road transport have been repeatedly shot up, and enemy planes intercepted on their return from attacks on Britain. These photographs were taken at an Intruder station when operations were in progress. 1, Meteorological Officer gives this crew a last-minute weather report. 2, Wing-Cmdr. C. D. Tomalin, O.C. an Intruder Squadron. 3, Pilots compare notes as they wait beside their planes on a clear moonlit night. 4, About to take off for an important raid.

*Photos, Planet News, The Times*

# Mussolini Boasted This Was Another Malta

PANTELLARIA HARBOUR: N.W. corner of island

MAGNA GRANDE Central crater peak.

MT GIBELE

PANTELLERIA—Italy's island stronghold—was at one time the base for enemy fighters and bombers, submarines and surface craft which attacked our Mediterranean convoys. Now the tables have been turned. In addition to being repeatedly bombed, the island received a devastating naval assault on May 15, 1943; the above drawing gives a vivid impression of this 20-minute bombardment. It was reported that as a result of this and subsequent naval and air poundings, the island was " out of commission " and its airfield wrecked (see photo opposite page). Left, part of the rocky coastline. Below, the harbour from the air.

*Drawing by courtesy of The Sphere;*
*Left-hand photo, Keystone*

# Pantelleria's Only Airfield Blasted by Bombs

MUSSOLINI'S ISLAND-FORTRESS in the Sicilian Straits, the little island of Pantelleria, has an area of only 31 sq. miles. But it occupies a key position in the Mediterranean, and so day after day the Allied air forces and the Royal Navy have been punishing its much-vaunted defences. Here is Pantelleria's only airfield during an attack by S.A.A.F. Baltimore bombers. Clouds of black smoke indicate two oil fires. Arrows show entrances to underground hangars and workshops at the far end of the airfield.　PAGE 57　　　　　*Photo, British Official : Crown Copyright*

# THE HOME FRONT

*by E. Royston Pike*

LOOKED at from beneath a bishop's mitre Britain is in a very bad way. "Bishops deplore wartime morals" ran a headline in The Daily Telegraph of May 27; and the report that followed, of a meeting of the Upper House of Convocation of Canterbury, contained many a fine example of episcopal fault-finding. The bishops were discussing a resolution noting with deep concern a widespread decay of truthful speaking. The increasing disregard of truth, said the Bishop of Birmingham, Dr. E. W. Barnes, can be observed throughout the community; and, taken with the "concurrent increase in theft and a growth of sexual licence," it is among those signs of degeneration "which shows itself among large sections of our people in lower standards of personal hygiene and self-discipline." The ultimate cause of this degeneration is war, the present conflict which is reinforcing the social disorder of twenty-five years ago. Family disruption exists on a scale unparalleled in our national history. The worst stocks of the community are now earning high money, and there are cases where this has been wasted on stupid luxuries. "I have heard of people buying mushrooms at 10s. a pound."

But not only the war is to blame. "You cannot expect cleanliness, truth and honesty," went on Bishop Barnes, "from people brought up in houses which are damp, verminous, and without sanitary decency. There must be a million such houses in this country. Sexual morality fails when there is deplorable overcrowding in filthy houses. For fifty years after the present war we shall be struggling to regain the moral and social level which our people reached at the end of the Victorian era . . .'"

OPINIONS may, indeed will, differ over this encomium on the moral and social standards of our grandparents; behind the heavily-curtained windows of the Victorian façades there were many disreputable goings-on from which the bishops of the time found it expedient to avert their gaze, that the historians have found it just as well not to mention. Still more provocative were some sentences that fell from the lips of the next speaker.

After an outburst, "I wish to God that if we cleared bugs out of houses then everyone would tell the truth," Dr. Chavasse, Bishop of Rochester, continued: "We are on the verge of something like a sex war. Decent young women are beginning to say that it is unsafe to go out with eleven out of twelve young men; and young men are tending to look upon young women as potential prostitutes."

Mathematics and morals have little in common; and some will ask, How does the bishop *know*? That the war has brought a change in the moral code and practice of great numbers of men and women herded together in uncomfortable quarters, far from their homes and friends and usual ways, is too obvious to need stressing; but it may be doubted whether there is any such sexual promiscuity as would deserve the bishops' wholesale censure.

NEW manners and morals, new complaints—physical ones this time. "Queue feet" is the latest of the ills to which the flesh is heir in wartime: victims say that they got it by standing for hours in tremendously long queues outside the food offices, waiting for their new ration books. Last year the new ration books were delivered by post; but this year the economy-minded gentlemen in Whitehall thought that a wonderful lot of time, trouble and expense might be saved if new identity cards, clothing coupons for the next period, and the new ration books should be issued all in one go.

In theory the scheme was excellent, but in practice it broke down into a colossal muddle. The newspapers' mailbags were filled with letters from readers complaining not only of the long waits outside the food offices selected as centres, but still more because of such instances of official blindness as the requirement that villagers should travel ten or twelve miles to the food office in the nearest town—often on foot, since in the fourth year of war bus services not only cost money but are few and far between, and practically every private car is laid up in the garage for duration.

**WOMEN PHONE OPERATORS, as stated in page 63, are wanted by the thousand within the next 12 months to fill the gaps made by marriage, the call-up, etc. This photo shows girls at a main switchboard of the London Trunk Telephone Exchange.**
*Photo, Keystone*

What with the queues and the difficulties in travelling, a great number of war workers lost a day's pay—and the country lost their day's work. Then at the outset the alphabetical arrangement was strictly adhered to, so that if a householder whose name begins with B, has living with him his mother-in-law Mrs. D— and a married daughter Mrs. F— and perhaps a lodger Mr. L— (not to mention two evacuated children from London whose names begin with S and W), he would have to go or send to the food office as many times as there are surnames in the household.

GREAT and growing was the uproar following the launching of the scheme in the middle of May. Outside every food office there were long queues. People stood for hours on end. Some fainted and gave useful practice to the first-aid squads. Many went home in disgust. Some waited so long for the coming year's ration books that they found the shops closed when they went to get the rations for today. From a thousand directions the Ministry of Food was shot at, although in truth the Registrar-General, Sir Sylvanus Vivian, and Dr. Dalton of the Board of Trade, shared the responsibility with Lord Woolton. On May 25 Mr.

Mabane, Parliamentary Secretary to the Ministry of Food, made a tour of a number of centres in London and Surrey; he reported that things were not as bad as had been feared, and were getting better. But all the same, swift changes followed.

BROADCASTING on the evening of May 28, Lord Woolton told the public: "I am sorry you are being put to some trouble."

He explained that this time, "We are not just issuing ration books; we are having a national check-up"; and he admitted that, aiming at perfection in the matter of national security, they had over-centralized it. "It was too tight, and we have had to loosen it. But don't let us waste time bothering who was to blame. There are 43,000,000 books and cards to be delivered to people who have a right to them, and to no one else, before July 25." Then he gave a pat on the back to the food executive officers and to the local authorities—he was particularly grateful to the school authorities and the children in the Highlands, where every child had become an agent covering the most remote spots—and wound up by announcing certain concessions. "If there are several families in one house with different surnames, don't all go," he said; "let one member of the family do the job for the rest—and remember to go on the call-up of the last letter." Local authorities were authorized to open sub-offices, particularly in rural districts; the ever-useful Women's Voluntary Service was called in to assist; and a system of block distribution of ration books in factories, etc., was authorized.

BELIEVE it or not, women are not "borrowing" clothing coupons from their menfolk. No doubt some husbands have been stripped of their coupons by their wives, says the Board of Trade, but the reverse must have happened too. During the first rationing year men spent 68 coupons, women 70; during the second year, however, up to the end of last March, men had spent 46½ and women 50. All along, the biggest "spenders" have been the children of 14 to 16. A number of coupons have been returned to the Board of Trade or destroyed; such patriotic gestures are welcome, since if everyone cut one coupon from the book and returned it or threw it away, 5,000 tons of raw material would be released for other purposes, or its transport space saved. The ban on trouser turn-ups and certain pockets on suits has resulted, we are told, in five million yards of cloth being released for the war effort. Another interesting fact is that each set of R.A.F. parachutes and harness takes up the silk that might have been used in making 130 pairs of ladies' stockings.

ALL the signs go to show that we are going to have a bumper harvest, but ten pairs of hands are required to reap what one pair has sown. So to assist the men and women whose job is agriculture and the Women's Land Army, tens of thousands of volunteers are required to work for four days or a week, a week-end, or a number of summer evenings on the country's farms. In every county an organizer has been appointed, whose name and address can be obtained from the announcements in the newspapers or the Ministry of Agriculture in London. All over the country Agricultural Volunteer Camps have been established, as well as Voluntary Land Clubs for small groups of helpers. Some schools are organizing harvest camps; the National Union of Students is doing the same, and the Youth Organizations. To a town-dweller work in the country must prove a welcome change, but it is *work*. The sort of volunteer the Ministry of Agriculture does *not* want is the man who asks: "Can you put me on to a comfortable farm where I can take the wife and kids for a holiday?"

# Decorated for Gallantry : Some Army Awards

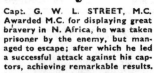

Capt. G. W. L. STREET, M.C. Awarded M.C. for displaying great bravery in N. Africa, he was taken prisoner by the enemy, but managed to escape; after which he led a successful attack against his captors, achieving remarkable results.

Capt. (temp. Maj.) H. W. LE PATOUREL, V.C., awarded the Victoria Cross for most gallant conduct and self-sacrifice in the Tebourba area, Tunisia, on Dec. 3, 1942. His brilliant leadership and tenacious devotion to duty in the face of a determined enemy were beyond praise. On June 2, 1943 it was stated he was among 435 repatriated British captives.

Maj. (temp. Lt.-Col.) D. A. SEAGRIM, V.C. Posthumously awarded V.C. for leading his battalion of the Green Howards in a desperate attack on the Mareth Line on Mar. 20-21, 1943. His valour and disregard for personal safety enabled the objective to be captured. Major Seagrim subsequently died of wounds. He accounted for some 20 Germans.

Rev. H. PARRY, M.C. Held daily service during the eight-months' siege of Tobruk, and was wounded in the battle at Knightsbridge, Libya.

Maj.-Gen. H. LUMSDEN, bar to D.S.O. Displayed fine leadership in armoured operations in the Western Desert. Succeeded late Gen. Gott as commander of 13th Army Corps in Libya.

Rev. P. WANSEY, M.C. He attended to wounded in fierce fighting in Tunisia, and by his courageous action under fire helped to save many lives

Capt. (temp. Maj.) C. A. J. MARTIN, G.C., M.C. An electrical engineering expert, he displayed utmost gallantry in carrying out most hazardous work.

Spr. R. W. IZZARD, B.E.M. Without thought of personal risk, he saved valuable petrol tanks during outbreak of serious fire in the North of England.

Rfm. G. DONNO, M.M. He operated radio transmitter in the face of enemy advance amid blazing lorries in N. Africa. Before the war he was a chimney-sweep.

Sgt. T. J. J. McDONNELL, D.C.M. He took prisoner 39 Germans in Tunisia, after holding off savage enemy attacks with two of his men for a matter of two hours.

*Photos, Daily Mirror, H. Jenkins, Vandyk, Associated Press, Planet News, Topical Press*

# I WAS THERE!
Eye Witness
Stories of the War

## Under the Sea I Gave the Order—Fire!

Our men who hunt their quarry underseas live a life apart : a life of almost unrelieved peril and uneasy suspense. What it is like to be in action in these circumstances is vividly described by Lieut. Arthur Pitt of H.M. submarine Taku. His story is reprinted here from The Listener.

WE were on patrol in the Aegean Sea off Athens. I was looking through the periscope on a lovely sunny day; good for submarine attacking because there was a nice little breeze making a few small white horses. That's very good covering for your periscope; the feather isn't seen so easily. We could see the coast all round : a beautiful rocky coast, the sort of place for pleasure cruisers in peacetime. And then I saw some smoke, and aircraft circling, the first warning of an enemy convoy coming. It slowly materialized into a supply ship. Then we saw its escort, an armed yacht, and still these two aircraft overhead. It was about five miles away.

I passed the order for diving stations. Everyone closed up to his station. There's a great bustle on the boat for a minute or two after that. They bring the torpedo tubes to the ready and everybody checks up their own particular station that everything is correct. This bustle settles down very soon to absolute quiet. No talking is allowed at all in a submarine ; there's coming and going through the control-room when diving stations are ordered and then it's absolutely quiet. You are concentrating on the attack all the time. There are one or two working the attack instruments and the rest are quietly doing their jobs, and a lot of them have nothing to do except wait. Everybody is tensed up, but looking round at them you wouldn't think it.

I found I had turned in to attack too soon and so I had to run right across its bows, and the escort never knew I was doing it. I turned round completely 180 degrees and landed on the other side, on the starboard side. When she passed right in front of my sights, I could see the ship standing out like a great big haystack. I could see the people on the bridge. I watch her come in the sights at the last minute and then fire as she crosses the wire in the periscope. I gave the order : "Fire."

IT was a certain shot. There was no doubt that one of the torpedoes would hit. We felt we couldn't miss. You just feel a little jar as the torpedoes go out. It sort of gives the submarine a push. The man at the hydrophone reported torpedoes running correctly, and we speeded up to try to get away a little, knowing the counter-attack would come. Shortly afterwards we heard a very loud explosion as the torpedoes hit. We all heard the explosion, not only the man on the hydrophone. It's a hard, cracking noise. I asked him, "Can you hear the target's engines ?" And he said, "Engines have

stopped." Again very loud noises, and he told me : "Sounds as though she's breaking up." I think she must have sunk very quickly. Now it's very quiet again in the submarine, waiting for the counter-attack from the escort. Nothing happened for about 20 minutes. He was either picking up survivors or he was listening round and wondering where we were. Then the hydrophone operator reported he had started up his engines. We knew he was starting to run for his first attack.

Then the depth charges came. As they drop the whole boat jumps, all the indicating needles leap madly. The corking which absorbs the moisture came down all over us in a cloud from overhead. Small gratings over fan intakes and covering fuse panels shook loose and flew through the air right across the small control-room. One battery grating hit one of my sailors on the head. By the look on his face he thought the end had come. All this muck coming down from overhead : I saw the navigator stolidly sweeping it off his charts. And then he carried on, plotting our position. They dropped eleven depth charges, and we felt each one like a great thundering roar.

THEN there was a period of quiet for a bit, and we knew he was listening round to get our position. More depth charges were dropped in batches of two or three during the next half-hour. You feel extremely helpless all this time. You just have to sit and wait. Sometimes you speed up, alter the depth, alter course and try to dodge him. Once or twice he was very close. He never actually

went over the top of us but just up and down the sides. It's a crunch-crunch noise that the screw makes.

Then there wasn't a sound for half an hour, and just as I'd decided he wasn't about we suddenly heard him start his engines up very close, very fast. He thought he had made absolutely certain where we were this time, and he dropped another line of eleven charges. The navigator came up to me ; he was writing down details of the attack quite calmly and he wanted some details about the supply ship—whether she had two masts and one funnel or one mast and two funnels. I was too astonished to be angry that he could ask me this question in the uproar.

The enemy dropped one more, and the engineer officer said to me, " I think that's his last." We came up and had a look. Yes, we had definitely slipped him. He was about three miles away, still searching round.

Three days later they were on to us again, and still near land where it is hard to manoeuvre : two M.T.B.s and a grey motor-launch. They had run into us early in the day, had made two attacks and then seemed to run out of depth charges. We were continually hearing their engines. They were going to stay with us till they could call up more depth charges ; or maybe wait till we surfaced and try to torpedo us. They stayed close to us all day, and that night they were still with us. We couldn't get up to the surface long enough to get the blowers working to get fresh air.

I went round explaining to the crew the situation we were in. You know all the men well because you live pretty close to each other. And though the jokes were a bit grim, they were all cheerful. I explained we should probably be down all night. We had to keep down all the next day too. And the air was getting bad. From mid-day onwards everyone was breathing very heavily through their mouths. We moved as little as possible so as not to waste the air. We couldn't cook anything ; but we didn't feel like eating very much. Towards the second evening some of us—especially the big

H.M.S. TAKU, one of the Royal Navy's most elusive submarines (see text), has an astonishing record of hairbreadth escapes. No submarine has been hunted more relentlessly than this ship. She is seen above, trying out a few practice rounds as she sets out on an important patrol. Top, officers of the Taku. Left to right : Commissioned Engineer J. Stevens, D.S.C., Lt. P. Murray-Jones, Lt. Arthur J. Pitt (Commander), Lt. H. R. Murray, Sub-Lt. R. G. Carr, and Lt. P. A. C. Day.

PAGE 60

*Photos, British Official*

and burly ones—were lying down and nearly out. The second day we couldn't see the enemy, but it was out of the question to surface in daytime near their coast. We were all watching the clocks and longing for the night. Looking through the periscope at a red sunset, I came up just a quarter of an hour before dusk, and we got the blowers working at last.

DAYS later we got our revenge. We were again very close to the shore and spotted a small supply ship. Not worth a torpedo, I thought, but just right for gun action. The crew always like gun action ; it cheers them up after days of being hunted. But I was doubtful about going in. Ten minutes before six aircraft had been over. Then I had a closer look. I could see she was flying a little swastika flag at the mast. And German soldiers were lolling about on the guard rail. We couldn't resist it. We surfaced about half a mile away and opened fire. The second round hit her and we saw the Germans jumping over the side. We got about fifteen hits on her and left her still afloat but afire. It was all over in ten minutes. Then we had to dive in case the aircraft came back.

The next morning we moved in close to an enemy-occupied port. It was stormy and enemy supply ships were crowded together in the harbour. We surfaced about a mile from the shore and lobbed a number of shells into the mass of tightly packed shipping. The moment we dived we heard several loud cracks. They had brought their guns into action just too late.

ALLIED PRISONERS IN A GERMAN SHIP were released when, preceding the fall of Tunis, the vessel was damaged and beached in Allied air attacks—described in this page. Here the men are making for the beach, from which flies the French Cross of Lorraine. *Photo, British Official*

## Off Tunis Our Prison Ship Was Riddled

During the Allied bombing which preceded the fall of Tunis 700 British soldiers, 200 American airmen and 35 officers imprisoned in an Axis ship had a hair-raising experience. Major T. Braithwaite relates below how they were attacked by our own fighter-bombers.

ONE bomb fell so near that it started our plates. We leaked so badly that we had to turn back. We anchored in shallow water at La Goulette, where the vessel settled on the bottom, a helpless target for raid after raid. The Italians and Germans on board abandoned the ship, and the British and Americans took charge of it.

Our fighter-bombers attacked us continually, dropping bombs uncomfortably close and riddling the ship with cannon shells. Particularly fine work was done by a British officer, Lieut. Quartermaster Gordon, of the Royal Artillery. He stood at the entrance to the hold where all the British and American troops gathered for protection and gave them a running commentary on the attacks by our own machines. He was very quick at shouting down to them the direction from which the next attack was coming. That gave them time to rush to the opposite side of the hold so that they had a better chance of escaping the cannon fire. He was a big tall fellow and his cheerfulness

and alertness helped to keep everyone's spirits up.

All behaved magnificently in what was quite an ordeal. We tried everything to let the airmen know that the ship was filled with Allied troops. We tried using the wireless. It wouldn't work. We tried flashing the "V" sign and draped the guns

with white sheets. There were about 100 sick and wounded men on board. We fashioned big red crosses on the deck with signal flags and red leather from the settees in the passenger quarters. We also marked out the initials P.O.W. in four places.

Then the raids stopped. An Italian officer in charge of the ships came aboard on his own with a solitary soldier to see that the wounded and sick were taken off. He knew he was bound to be our prisoner, and he handed over his revolver, and shortly afterwards boats came out to take us ashore. Tunis was in our hands.

## In Crete's Bomb Alley We Fought Terrific Odds

Wounded whilst serving in the anti-aircraft cruiser Carlisle during naval operations covering the evacuation of our forces from Crete in 1941, Able Seaman J. F. Kelleher wrote this story of his experiences specially for THE WAR ILLUSTRATED during his recent convalescence in hospital.

WE sailed from Alexandria on one of our toughest jobs on a Thursday morning two years ago this May. Together with other cruisers and destroyers of the Mediterranean Light Forces, acting as anti-aircraft escort vessels, we were to assist ships of the Merchant Navy to bring away from Crete as many of our Marines and other troops as possible (so terminating their heroic but ill-fated rearguard actions against thousands of airborne Nazis) and conduct them safely back to Alexandria.

The sun shone brightly and there was not a cloud in the sky as gun crews stood about the Carlisle's deck, alert for enemy planes. The sound of "rattlers" suddenly called us to gun stations. A reconnaissance plane was shadowing us. My job was Loading Number at a 4-inch gun, and perspiration streamed from my brow as I loaded shell after shell into the breech. But we were unlucky, and the plane made off—having noted our position and almost certainly guessed at our destination.

It was not long before rattlers again sounded, and from the bridge came a warning that enemy aircraft had been reported on our detecting gear. We were now approaching the Aegean Sea, commonly known as Bomb Alley, and it was here we were to expect big trouble. It was 6.30 a.m. when

the aircraft were sighted : nine Stuka dive-bombers and a half-dozen Messerschmitts. Our guns started to bark. As quickly as I could get a shell from the "ready- use" locker, fuse it, and insert it in the breech, my gun was fired. The Stukas were sorely damaging the ships of our fleet, and I saw two of our medium cruisers, the Gloucester and the Fiji, go down with guns firing to the last. More enemy planes were coming in from all directions, and some of our destroyers received direct hits ; from my gun position I saw at least six of these, including the Kelly, Kashmir, Juno and Greyhound, go down battling to the last moment.

BUT I hadn't much time for looking around, especially when six Junkers dived on us from out of the sun, straddling the Carlisle with bombs. I was wounded by shrapnel entering my right thigh, and I placed myself at the disposal of the First Lieutenant for any job that was going and that, hampered as I was by my wound, I might be able to manage.

Then our "ready" ammunition lockers were set ablaze, and along with other personnel mustered by the First Lieutenant I helped to fling the ammunition overboard. That done, I went with the First Lieutenant to the bridge, where we were greeted by a hail of machine-gun bullets, the skipper being killed outright. With the skipper gone

A.B. KELLEHER, who tells his story in this and the following page, was wounded in the evacuation of Crete in 1941, while serving in H.M.S. Carlisle.

and no more ammunition in our lockers it was up to the First Lieutenant to try to get the Carlisle back to Alexandria.

It was not going to be an easy task, our speed having been reduced by the heavy bombing ; and it was an easy guess that we would be under constant air attack until we were in sight of Alexandria again. But the worst didn't happen, and at midday on the Saturday we steamed past the boom and dropped anchor in the "home" harbour. We of the Carlisle hadn't completed our mission, unfortunately, but we had done all that any ship's crew could do in such murderous circumstances.

## What Horrors I Saw In Vyazma and Rzhev!

One of the most distinguished figures in the Russian Orthodox Church and a member of the Soviet State Commission established to investigate the crimes of the German-Fascist invaders of his country, Bishop Nikolai of Kiev has recorded the cruelty and destructiveness wrought in Vyazma, recaptured by the Russians on March 12, 1943, and Rzhev, recaptured nine days earlier. His description is here condensed from Soviet War News.

VYAZMA is an ancient Russian town. It was built solidly, lastingly, with walls an arm's span thick. The Germans had to work hard to destroy it. There was no fighting in Vyazma itself, yet for three days the town was filled with the continuous thunder of explosions. The Germans did not spare dynamite ; they spent it without stint.

And the town was razed to the ground. Of its 5,500 buildings, only some 50 timber houses on the outskirts still survive. Such splendid edifices as the theatre, the history museum and the market are piles of ruins.

We arrived in Vyazma the fifth day after its liberation, but the explosions still continued. The Germans had laid delayed-action mines everywhere, and our fearless Red Army men did not always succeed in detecting them in time to avert an explosion. The commander of the Soviet troops advised us not to linger there, as our forces were passing through the town, and Vyazma was still being bombed by hostile aircraft. Nevertheless, the inhabitants were streaming back. The day the Red Army entered Vyazma there were only some 300

persons left there. During our stay the number increased to 3,000. But let it not be forgotten that before the war Vyazma had a population of 75,000. Today the town is a vast graveyard.

I climbed a hill and looked around. Nothing could be seen but piles of brick and rubble, gutted houses. My mind could not conceive the reason for this insensate destruction. Only a frenzy of despair could have prompted such insanity. They destroyed not only the town. They also destroyed the inhabitants. We were taken to the cemetery. The fence surrounding it had been pulled down, and an enormous trench dug. Into this trench the Germans cast non-combatant citizens they had shot or tortured to death. Women, children and old folk were flung higgledy-piggledy into it and covered with only a thin layer of earth mixed with snow. A medical commission is now busy exhuming corpses to determine how they died. Many bodies bear signs of torture.

The Germans wrecked Rzhev as thoroughly as Vyazma. But there are no streams of people

flocking back to Rzhev. They have either been carried off to Germany or exterminated. We arrived there seventeen days after the Germans withdrew. Even then there were hardly 1,500 people in the town. When the Red Army arrived there were only about 200. I had a long talk with sixty-year-old Deacon Feodor Tikhomirov. I asked him how he had lived under the Germans.

"How I lived ? At first I kept count of how many times the Germans beat me, but after thirty I stopped counting. They beat me because I could not carry heavy loads. They beat me when they harnessed me to a cart or when I dropped from fatigue or hunger. Every other day they issued me with a handful of boiled rye. Sometimes the church people who still had some stocks of food left would give me something to eat. Many in the town died of starvation."

Terrible is the impression left by this dead city. On the left bank of the river, where the shopping and residential quarters lay, a few people could still be seen wandering about, but on the right bank not a soul was to be seen. Yet before the war the town had a population of 55,000.

Some streets are still not fully de-mined, and it is dangerous to walk through them. But the horror of these streets is not due only to mines. We glanced into some houses and saw harrowing sights. Murder after murder, monstrous and senseless murder. In one house on Vorovsky Street lay the dead bodies of a husband and wife and five children. The head of the family had been trampled to death. He was unrecognizable. The wife had been shot. The 18-year-old daughter had been raped, then strangled. The eldest son had been shot through the right eye. Even a tiny infant had been slain and thrown out of its cradle. In the house next door were six more corpses.

## OUR DIARY OF THE WAR

**MAY 25, 1943, Wednesday** 1,362nd day
**Mediterranean.**—Airfields in Sicily again bombed by Allied aircraft ; in Sardinia hits scored on Tirso power-station.
**U.S.A.**—American aircraft attacked main Jap camp on Kiska island.
**Australasia.**—Allied bombers made heaviest recorded raid on Lae, New Guinea.

**MAY 27, Thursday** 1,363rd day
**Air.**—Mosquitoes made low-level raid at dusk on Zeiss works at Jena ; after dark heavy bombers made strong attack on Essen.
**Mediterranean.**—Airfields in Sardinia attacked by Allied aircraft ; harbour defences on Pantelleria also bombed.
**Russian Front.**—Soviet long-range aircraft raided railway junctions of Mogilev, Karachev and Roslavl.

**MAY 28, Friday** 1,364th day
**Sea.**—In night action near Dunkirk our light coastal forces set four trawlers and two coastal craft on fire ; one of our gun-boats was lost.
**Mediterranean.**—More than 100 Flying Fortresses made daylight raid on Leghorn from N. Africa without loss.
**Russian Front.**—Heavy fighting still in progress N.E. of Novorossisk, Kuban.

**MAY 29, Saturday** 1,365th day
**Sea.**—Admiralty announced loss of submarine Regent.
**Air.**—Large force of Fortresses and Liberators raided St. Nazaire, Rennes and La Pallice by day ; at night R.A.F. made first attack on industrial area of Wuppertal in the Ruhr.
**Russian Front.**—Soviet aircraft made night raids on Gomel and Karachev.
**China.**—Supported by U.S. aircraft, Chinese forces launched counter-offensive on Yangtse front.

**MAY 30, Sunday** 1,366th day
**Sea.**—Sinking of five U-boats in ten days by Coastal Command aircraft announced.
**Mediterranean.**—More than 100 Flying Fortresses bombed aerodrome and docks at Naples ; aerodrome at Foggia, S.E. Italy, again raided. Naval forces bombarded Pantelleria during the night.
**Russian Front.**—Heavy fighting continued N.E. of Novorossisk.
**U.S.A.**—Navy Dept. announced that Japanese organized resistance had ceased on Attu island.
**Home Front.**—Sharp daylight raid on S.W. coast town by fighter-bombers.

**General.**—Gen. de Gaulle arrived in Algiers for talks with Gen. Giraud. Announced that French fleet at Alexandria had joined the Allies.

**MAY 31, Monday** 1,367th day
**Air.**—Daylight raid by R.A.F. on Cherbourg, Flushing, Zeebrugge and Caen.
**Mediterranean.**—Another heavy attack by Flying Forts on Foggia, S. Italy.
**Russian Front.**—Night attacks by Soviet Air Force on rly. junctions of Briansk, Polotsk and Rezhetza.
**Australasia.**—Liberators made heavy raid on Lae airfield and waterfront.

**JUNE 1, Tuesday** 1,368th day
**Mediterranean.**—Naval forces again bombarded Pantelleria ; air attacks on Naples, Sicily and Sardinia. At night Allied destroyers routed enemy convoy off Cape Spartivento, S. Italy.

**Russian Front.**—Soviet aircraft made night raids on Smolensk and on Karachev, on Briansk-Orel railway.
**U.S.A.**—American and Canadian airmen raided Jap base on Kiska.
**General.**—British air liner shot down while flying from Lisbon to Ireland.

**JUNE 2, Wednesday** 1,369th day
**Mediterranean.**—Allied aircraft again raided Pantelleria and island of St. Antioco off Sardinia ; Pantelleria also bombarded by Navy during the night.
**Russian Front.**—Out of force of 500 German aircraft raiding Kursk, 162 were shot down for loss of 27 Soviet planes.
**China.**—Announced that, as result of Chinese victory on the Yangtse, threatened Jap drive on Chungking was averted.

★ ═══ *Flash-backs* ═══ ★

### 1940
**May 28.** Belgian Army under King Leopold surrendered.
**May. 30.** Evacuation of troops from Dunkirk began.
**June 3.** First German air raid on Paris ; over 1,000 bombs dropped.
**June 4.** Evacuation from Dunkirk completed ; 335,000 British and French troops brought out.
**June 5.** Opening of "Battle of France" ; new German offensive along Somme and Aisne.
**June 8.** French Cabinet reconstituted under M. Reynaud ; M. Daladier dropped ; Gen. de Gaulle Under-Secretary for Defence.

### 1941
**May 26.** German reinforcements landed at Maleme, Crete.
**May 27.** German battleship Bismarck sunk in Atlantic after pursuit of 1,750 miles.
**May 30.** Evacuation of British troops from Crete began.

**June 1.** Clothes rationing came into effect in United Kingdom.
**June 8.** British and Free French troops crossed Syrian frontier.

### 1942
**May 26.** Anglo-Soviet Treaty was signed in London by Mr. Molotov and Mr. Eden.
Rommel launched new attack in Libya to outflank Bir Hacheim.
**May 27.** Attack on Heydrich, Deputy-Protector of Czechoslovakia, which led to his death on June 4.
**May 30.** R.A.F. raided Cologne and Ruhr with 1,130 bombers.
**May 31.** German "reprisal" raid on Canterbury.
**June 1.** Essen and the Ruhr raided by 1,036 bombers.
**June 4.** Battle of Midway Island began ; Japanese naval attack beaten off with heavy losses.
**June 5.** Germans launched heavy attack on Sevastopol.

**JUNE 3, Thursday** 1,370th day
**Mediterranean.**—Pantelleria again bombarded by naval forces by day and bombed at night.
**Russian Front.**—During the night of June 2-3, Soviet bombers attacked rly. junctions of Kiev and Roslavl.
**General.**—Agreement reached in Algiers between Gens. Giraud and de Gaulle on formation of French Committee for National Liberation.

**JUNE 4, Friday** 1,371st day
**Mediterranean.**—Pantelleria again attacked by Allied aircraft.
**Russian Front.**—During night of June 3-4, 500 Soviet long-range aircraft attacked railway junction of Orel.
**General.**—Army revolution broke out in Argentina against pro-Axis Government of President Castillo.

**JUNE 5, Saturday** 1,372nd day
**Mediterranean.**—Large force of Flying Fortresses from N. Africa made daylight attack on warships at Spezia, N. Italy.
**General.**—Mr. Churchill arrived back in England from the U.S.A. and N. Africa.

**JUNE 6, Sunday** 1,373rd day
**Mediterranean.**—U.S. heavy bombers made daylight raids on railway ferry termini at Messina and in toe of Italy. Air attacks on Pantelleria continued by night and day.
**Russian Front.**—Soviet long-range aircraft made mass raid on rly. centre of Unecha, in Orel region ; German bombers raided Gorki, on the Volga, 200 m. E. of Moscow.

**JUNE 7, Monday** 1,374th day
**Mediterranean.**—Pantelleria again bombed several times. British Commando patrol made scouting raid on Lampedusa island.
**Russian Front.**—Soviet long-range aircraft raided enemy aerodromes in Orel and Briansk area. Germans again raided Gorki.

**JUNE 8, Tuesday** 1,375th day
**Mediterranean.**—Pantelleria called on to surrender by leaflets dropped from Allied aircraft ; bombardment from sea and air continued.
**Russian Front.**—German aircraft raided Volkhov, E. of Leningrad, by day.
**General.**—President Roosevelt issued formal warning of retaliation in kind if Axis began gas warfare.

WHICH is the most expensive country to live in just now? India, writes a young naval officer of my close acquaintance ; India, where a tube of toothpaste costs 6s. 9d., and razor blades are 10d. each ! I have had similar complaints of exorbitant charges for the necessities of civilized existence from a correspondent in Ceylon ; and no doubt many candidates could be listed for the unenviable distinction. How the men in the Services manage to keep themselves so spick and span is a perpetual wonder, and it is surprising that, with razor blades at such a price, we don't see many more beards beneath the peaked hats, berets and forage caps. But I believe there is a ban on beards. In the Army and R.A.F. only moustaches are permitted ; while in the Navy, although it is " beard or nothing," few save submarine crews seem to wear them. And then, as often as not, they shave them off when they come into port.

NORTH AFRICA is another place where the British soldier has had to face a barrage of high prices. But here the military authorities have promptly put a stop to profiteering by publishing official price lists of the drinks, smokes, toilet goods, etc., which enter most prominently into the Serviceman's shopping. Thus I read the other night in The (London) Star that the Tripoli Times (the newspaper that was started on January 1st as a single sheet in Italian and English, but is now extended to 4 pages in English only) contains a long list of articles with the prices against each. Razor blades are five for 1s. 3d. ; toilet soap 6d. per tablet ; a tooth-brush 1s. ; woollen socks 2s. 6d. a pair. Synthetic coffee is a 1d. a cup if you drink it standing, or 1½d. if you drink it sitting down ; with milk it is 3d. and 3½d. respectively. You can get a glass of brandy for 1s., an aperitif for 3d. or 3½d., and a glass of punch costs 6d. Shops selling items in the list are required to display a price list, and each article is to be ticketed with the price.

ALL cigarettes sold in the Navy's canteens afloat bear the inscription " H.M. Ships Only " ; very shortly cigarettes sold in the Services' canteens will be similarly labelled " H.M. Troops Only," Mr. Arthur E. Olley, editor of the trade journal Tobacco, tells me. It is illegal to sell a Navy cigarette in a shop (goes on Mr. Olley), since it has paid no duty to the wartime revenue ; on board ship at sea a twenty of cigarettes costs 6d. In Army and R.A.F. canteens in this country the price of a twenty is still 1s. 6d., as compared with the 2s. 4d. which we civilians have had to pay since the last Budget. Because of this difference of price there has been a considerable leakage of Service supplies to civilian smokers, often at a cut-price even after several profits have been raked off. Officially there is no free issue of cigarettes to soldiers in this country, though our men in Tunisia get one since they are on active service. Hitler's soldiers still have a cigarette issue when at the front ; but the moment he goes on leave Fritz comes on the civilian ration card for cigarettes. This means he now gets only two a day.

ARE you one of the 1,250,000 holders of 3½ per cent War Loan ? If so, a further question : Did the postman on the morning of June 1 drop a " Bank of England " envelope into your letter-box ? Some 550,000 stockholders have their share of the £33 million half-yearly interest paid direct into bank, Post Office or Trustee Savings Bank accounts, but there are still 700,000 who have their warrants sent direct to their homes. The Bank of England is now urging the 700,000 to follow the good example set by the 550,000. If they do so, it is estimated that 3½ tons of paper—154 miles of 5-inch-long warrants—will be saved every year on dividend warrants alone. Envelopes consume another 4¼ tons ; and if, as is probable, half the holders concerned post their warrants to their banks for crediting, another 2 tons of paper are used. Altogether, it is calculated that 10 tons of paper could be saved each year ; while 72,000 man-hours would be saved in clerical work, in addition to relieving the hard-pressed Post Office of the work of sorting and delivering close on a million envelopes each half-year. To play your part in this eminently desirable economy, all you have to do is to ask your banker or Post Office for a dividend request form, spend a minute or so in completing it, then hand it back. The bank or the Post Office will do the rest.

IN his last Budget Sir Kingsley Wood included an increase in the charges for trunk telephone calls—not because he was looking for increased revenue therefrom, but because it was desired in the interest of labour economy to discourage people from making all but really important trunk calls. But, in fact, the increased rates have had next to no effect on the number of calls. So now the Post Office has invited the support of the Press in bringing home to telephone-users the utmost importance of cutting down the number of calls, particularly the trunk calls, they make. As was recently made plain to us when the London Trunk Exchange was " at home " to the Press, labour shortage is acute and is steadily becoming more so.

NEARLY 9,000 women are employed as telephone operators in London, and for one reason or another some 1,500 resign each year (to get married, as often as not). At the present time there are about 500 vacancies waiting to be filled, while another 500 girls are made necessary by normal expansion. In 1939 the London Trunk Exchange was handling about 30,000 originating calls a day ; now the figure is well over 40,000, and there was one day in April last with a peak load of 46,000.

FOR full-time employment girls between the ages of 16 and 18½, and women between 31 and 50 are urgently needed. Hours are normally 48 a week ; every attention is paid to welfare, and so far as possible telephonists are employed at exchanges within easy reach of their homes. While learning—the course takes six or seven weeks—new entrants are paid £1 0s. 6d. a week, or £1 3s. if they are eighteen ; when trained, a girl of sixteen receives £1 14s., and at 21 she gets £2 18s., after which there is an annual increment of 2s. per week.

HIDDEN behind the walls of their exchanges, heard but not seen, the telephonists have their part in the battle (we have been asked to emphasize) equally with their sisters in the auxiliary services and the munition factories, and with their brothers on the sea, in the air, and in the fighting line on land. The vital importance of their work is well brought out in these lines by Eleanora Dayton Surry. She is one of the Bell Company's telephone-girls in Washington, U.S.A., but her sisters over here would echo every word.

We are the unseen, ever watchful, never sleeping,
Binding the atoms together.
Not ours the glory nor applause,
We wear no uniform and yet are part of our
    land's destiny,
Guarding her secrets well.
We are the unseen, loyal, true to an ideal,
One God, one country, one flag :
We want no praise, knowing, out there,
Men have shed their blood that we might live . . .
With others soon to follow them.
Our reward shall be, one day, with the touch of
    magic at our finger-tips
To send across the quivering wires
One far-flung cry—" Ours is the Victory ! "

DOES conscience prick as often and so sharply as it used? A correspondent, whose letter is quoted in The Manchester Guardian's amusing Miscellany, asks if we are right in thinking that the comparative disappearance of those once familiar acknowledgements by the Chancellor of the Exchequer of "conscience money" denotes an increase in honesty among income-tax payers, rather than conscience dulled by the size of demand ? There seems to be some ground for the more optimistic view, answers the Miscellanist, in stories of the Inland Revenue's having to return cheques lately to people who imagine that notification of sums put to their post-War credit were additional income-tax demands. But perhaps, too, the Income Tax people must be credited with an ever-increasing keenness, which makes it more difficult to conceal anything from them, so that conscience does not have the opportunities it enjoyed years ago. " Perhaps the Inland Revenue eye has attained that power of penetration mentioned by Mr. Samuel Weller, in Bardell v. Pickwick."

# Relentless Scourge of the Enemy's Ships

**TORPEDO-CARRYING BEAUFIGHTERS,** it was disclosed early this year, have been operating with Coastal Command, and have scored great success in attacks against enemy shipping. Armed with four cannon and carrying their " tin fish " under their fuselage, these planes were originally used in the Mediterranean. Two pilots are here shown with a Beaufighter and its torpedo in position. *Photo, British Official: Crown Copyright*

Printed in England and published every alternate Friday by the Proprietors, THE AMALGAMATED PRESS, LTD., The Fleetway House, Farringdon Street, London, E.C.4. Registered for transmission by Canadian Magazine Post. Sole Agents for Australia and New Zealand : Messrs. Gordon & Gotch, Ltd. ; and for South Africa : Central News Agency, Ltd.—June 25, 1943. S.S. *Editorial Address :* JOHN CARPENTER HOUSE, WHITEFRIARS, LONDON, E.C.4.

*Vol 7* The War Illustrated N° *158*

Edited by Sir John Hammerton

SIXPENCE

JULY 9, 1943

**MR. CHURCHILL GIVES THE V-SIGN** to cheering members of the ship's crew as he walks down the gangway of the vessel that took him to America. The Prime Minister returned to this country on June 5, 1943, after nearly a month's tour that took him to Washington, Gibraltar, Algiers, and Tunis. "Brighter and solid prospects lie before us," declared Mr. Churchill in his address to Parliament on June 8.
*Photo, British Official: Crown Copyright*

**NO. 159 WILL BE PUBLISHED FRIDAY, JULY 23**

# THE BATTLE FRONTS

## by Maj.-Gen. Sir Charles Gwynn, K.C.B., D.S.O.

OREL FRONT. On or about June 14, 1943 the Russians recaptured Mtsensk, N.E. of Orel, and German counter-attacks failed to dislodge the Red Army from its gains. This map shows the fighting-line at June 17.
*By courtesy of The Times*

WITH the exception of the capture of Pantelleria, the implications of which are discussed below, no event of outstanding importance took place in the period under review (June 6 to 20, 1943). There was even a slight lull in the air attacks on the German industries and on Italian targets.

That the Allies did not follow up the victory in Tunisia as quickly as was popularly expected was presumably due partly to the necessity of reorganization and partly to the complexity of the preparations for any great amphibious enterprise. There may also have been a modification of plans influenced by the unexpected suddenness of the Tunisian victory and to greater quantities of shipping becoming available owing to the marked improvement in the war against the U-boats.

By this time last year all the enemy's preliminary operations were either complete or well under way, though his major thrust on the Kursk front was not delivered till June 28. The lateness of that date no doubt contributed to his ultimate undoing ; and if he intends to take the offensive in Russia again it is not clear why he delays Is it because he wishes to be certain as regards the strength and direction of the blows of the Western Allies before committing himself ?

The period has been marked by an increase in the number and weight of local engagements in Russia, in which the Russians seem as a rule to have taken the initiative, with the Germans counter-attacking fiercely where they have lost ground, particularly at Mtsensk in the Orel salient. But on the whole there has been no change in the Russian situation since I last wrote.

## PANTELLERIA

**PANTELLERIA** With the capture of Tunisia and the establishment of air superiority over the Sicilian Channel, the strategic importance of Pantelleria had largely disappeared. Its airfield could at any time be made practically unusable, and it could be closely blockaded by the Royal Navy. Its value as a base from which the Allied convoys might be attacked had therefore been lost, and its ultimate fate was hardly in doubt.

There were obvious reasons, however, why its immediate capture was advisable. Its airfield would provide a useful base for fighter aircraft protecting the passage of convoys from attacks made from other enemy bases, and for supporting amphibious enterprises or bombing attacks against western Sicily. Moreover, its capture would relieve the Navy and Air Forces of the task of neutralizing the island, and its harbour would be of use to naval light craft. Since the island was known to be heavily armed and had a substantial garrison, its capture by

a landing might, however, prove costly, particularly as the beaches where it could be effected were few and restricted, giving no alternative points of attack. There were, therefore, good reasons for trying experimentally whether the island could be compelled or induced to surrender by a concentrated bombing attack, combined with naval bombardments and a strict blockade.

The readiness of German troops in Tunisia to surrender when they found themselves in a hopeless situation made it not improbable that the garrison of Pantelleria in an even more hopeless position would set a limit to the sacrifice it was prepared to make. The island during the Tunisian battle had experienced heavy bombing attacks, and an immense bombing force was now available to make a devastating attack on so small a target. The only question was whether stubborn endurance by the garrison might necessitate prolonging the experiment to an extent that would interfere with other developments of the Allied plans. It was believed to have

ample food supplies and plenty of bomb-proof shelter.

Great as the effect of bombing would undoubtedly be on morale, it was calculated to induce rather than to compel surrender. To introduce the element of compulsion and a time factor, it was therefore intended to effect a landing, after the garrison had been softened by bombing and naval bombardment, should it still refuse to surrender.

The experiment proved entirely successful, with a minimum cost in lives and apparently without involving delays disturbing to plans. The garrison refused for a time to surrender ; but Mussolini, unlike Hitler, did not insist on a supreme sacrifice, and no doubt the Italian commander had already practically decided to give in, when the appearance of the invasion flotilla eliminated any hesitation he felt. The few shots fired did not indicate any strong determination to resist,

**ALLIED TARGETS IN THE MEDITERRANEAN.** After the fall of Pantelleria on June 11, 1943, air attacks on Sardinia, Sicily, and the Italian mainland increased in violence. The Allied air offensive—a prelude to invasion—disrupted southern Italy's transport system. Key-points such as Spezia, Messina, Naples, Reggio di Calabria, and San Giovanni received shattering blows. Meanwhile, British submarines operated in enemy waters, and sank Axis shipping from the French Riviera to the Tyrrhenian Sea.

*By courtesy of The Daily Telegraph*

break the blockade of the island is not surprising in view of its past record. But there is something in the Italian argument that while the fleet remains in being it compels the Allies to retain a number of battleships in the Mediterranean ; and that may be of more importance than the damage that might have been done them in an engagement.

It would be unwise to deduce, because the garrison of Pantelleria left their posts to take shelter and finally surrendered, that Italian troops would not display much determination in case of invasion under circumstances more favourable to defence. For one thing, the garrison was mainly composed of indifferent second-line troops ; and in any case there was little object in manning defences, other than anti-aircraft weapons, except under immediate threat of a landing. In fact, keeping guns silent with a view to concealment till the critical moment is a course that has plenty of good precedents ; and the fact that some of the troops did offer sporadic resistance on their own initiative tends to show that demoralization was not complete.

On the whole, it is wiser to look on Pantelleria as a unique episode. Lessons to be

but they sufficed to show that a measure of resistance was still possible. (See page 70.)

The success of the methods adopted gave rise at first to a belief that this was what Mr. Churchill had in mind when recently he spoke of an " experiment worth trying," and that a new technique had been discovered for eliminating or reducing the difficulties and dangers of a landing in face of opposition. Actually, Mr. Churchill was referring, I think, to the strategic bombing of Germany as a possible method of forcing her to unconditional surrender ; and that there was a widespread failure to realize that the methods employed would be inapplicable to most large-scale landings. It is, for instance, obvious that a prolonged bombing of a particular section of the enemy's coastline would give definite indication of the point selected for a landing, thus eliminating the element of uncertainty, which is one of the main advantages held by amphibious enterprises.

Nor would the prolonged concentrated bombing of a small section of the enemy's defences deprive him of power to bring up fresh troops and reserves for counterattack : to meet which successfully is one of the main problems of a landing-force. Undoubtedly, heavy bombing would force the enemy's troops to take shelter, but even prolonged bombing might fail to destroy many of his well-protected weapons—which might then be remanned at a critical moment. Concentrated bombing at the moment of landing and in cooperation with subsequent attacks by the landed force would be, of course, of the utmost assistance—practically an essential. But its object would be to neutralize rather than to destroy the enemy's weapons. Prolonged preliminary bombing would be apt to be subject to the same objections and to produce the same disappointing results as the prolonged bombardments of the last war ; which towards its end were superseded by short hurricane bombardments immediately preceding assault.

The bombing at Pantelleria was on the whole analogous to the reduction of a closely-besieged city by bombardment, and is rather a case of employing a new weapon than a new method.

Correspondents on the spot have been at pains to remove any early misapprehensions, and to emphasize the fact that a landing on an enemy coast remains a very formidable undertaking. In any case, the initial landing is only the first step towards the building up of an invading force adequate to conduct a long and heavily contested campaign.

THE KING VISITS N. AFRICA. After a 1,200-miles flight from Britain, his Majesty arrived in N. Africa on June 12, 1943. Above, he is greeted by (left to right) : Gen. Eisenhower (behind the King), Air Chief-Marshal Tedder, Adm. Cunningham, and Mr. H. Macmillan. Top, the King with Gen. Clark inspects U.S. guard of honour.
*Photos, British Official : Crown Copyright*

There were,, apart from these considerations, many interesting features about the operations which would seem to bear on the general situation.

Why did the Luftwaffe, from their numerous airfields in Sicily, make practically no serious attempt to interfere with our bombing aircraft ? I think it must be presumed that it was considered that the attempt would prove too costly, and that it was deemed preferable to husband air strength rather than expend it in the defence of an island recognized to be in a hopeless position. It would be a mistake therefore to assume that little air opposition will be encountered in future operations. After the surrender the Luftwaffe did make various counter-attacks in order to interfere with the restoration of the airfield and harbour facilities (characteristically without any consideration for the unfortunate Italian prisoners awaiting evacuation). Such attacks would naturally have had some element of surprise and been much safer to carry out than attacks on bombers with fighter protection.

The failure of the Italian battle fleet to put in an appearance or to make any attempt to

learnt from it are chiefly minor points affecting tactical technique.

FAR EAST Here also there has been an absence of outstanding incidents, and operations have been almost all confined to air and submarine activities. A heavy air attack made by the Japanese on Guadalcanal met with a striking reverse.

The Chinese counter-offensive on the Yangtse goes ahead, and Tojo's admission that the Japanese army is engaged in large-scale operations in China is interesting.

Mr. Curtin, the Australian Prime Minister, has also made the very interesting statement that Australia may now be considered secure from danger of invasion. It may be remembered that not long ago he made a somewhat alarming appeal for reinforcements, and he is not suspected of being unduly optimistic. We may therefore conclude, I think, that substantial reinforcements have been received, and that the reorganization of Australian defences has been completed. It is even more reassuring that Mr. Curtin looks forward to Australia playing an important part in offensive operations to come.

# Maybe These Are Next on Our Invasion List

**THE DODECANESE,** twelve islands in the Eastern Mediterranean off the coast of Turkey, were first occupied by the Italians in 1912 (see pages 552-553, vol. 4). They were the scene of feverish counter-invasion preparations in June 1943. 1, Town of Leros on the island of the same name. 2, Rhodes harbour. 3, Ancient Greek theatre on the island of Cos. 4, The clock tower is a prominent feature of the harbour at Simi. The position of the island-group will be clear from the map.

*Photos, E.N.A., Pictorial Press*

# Why Did We Close the Frontier With Turkey?

MYSTERY MOVES IN THE NEAR EAST. Following reports of Allied concentrations in Cyprus and Syria, the frontier between Turkey and Syria was temporarily closed on June 15, 1943. The Taurus Express, the one link between Axis and Allied countries, runs from Tripoli (Syria) to Ankara. 1, Officials search the train at the frontier. 2, British armoured car crews fraternize with Turkish soldiers at a border post. Map showing the position of frontier. 3, War supplies are handed over to Turkish troops at the frontier. *Photos, British Official. Map by courtesy of The Daily Telegraph*

# Why the White Flag Went Up on Pantelleria

The fortress island of Pantelleria, compared by Axis propagandists with Gibraltar and Malta, surrendered to the Allies on June 11, 1943—the first instance in history of a heavily fortified territory of the greatest military value being forced to submit solely as the result of bombardment. The account that follows is mostly from the dispatches of ALEXANDER CLIFFORD, who represented the combined British Press on this historic occasion.

AFTER the occupation of Tunisia by the Allies, it was obviously Pantelleria's turn. The little island, of whose fortifications Mussolini had been wont to boast in the days before the War, lay in the very middle of the Sicilian Channel, blocking the free passage of the Allies' convoys. Everyone expected it to be attacked; almost everyone, even in Italy, expected it to fall. But few can have expected that it would be taken at the cost of some 40 airmen, who were in the 20 planes that the defenders were able to shoot down—20 out of hundreds.

Preliminary bombing of the island began on May 9, and each day that passed saw a stepping-up of the aerial and naval bombardment. One by one the little houses of Pantelleria village were pounded into dust. Jetties were smashed, roads blocked. A water-distilling plant was broken, and it became more and more difficult to distribute supplies. The 15,000 troops in the island —chiefly the Fifth Infantry Regiment and Fascist Militia—had to spend most of their time crowded into tunnels and trenches and the huge subterranean hangars on the airfield. The civilian population scattered to isolated houses on the hillsides.

By June 8, said Rome wireless, the island had had four naval bombardments and at least a hundred distinct air attacks, recently at the rate of 12 a day. But the answer of the admiral commanding the island and the garrison (Admiral Gino Pavesi) to a call for surrender contained in leaflets signed by General Spaatz (commander of the Allied North-West African Air Forces) could be imagined. "The stout defenders of Pantelleria are still standing upright, ready to exact a high price for the expected attempt at a landing." Later it transpired that Admiral Pavesi had radioed to Rome: "Bombing bad, but the island can hold out if it gets no worse. I need not surrender."

But it did get worse. Two days later (Thursday, June 10) there was a tremendous tornado of bombs. The island simply stopped functioning. Roads were blocked, all communications were ruined, workshops were destroyed, and the airfield was pock-marked with craters. Everybody spent that dreadful day underground. One German Luftwaffe sergeant, who was watching from a safe loophole, counted more than 1,800 bombers over the island in the course of the day.

That night General Achille Maffei, commander of the Italian troops, contacted Rome by radio. Speaking directly to Mussolini he told him, "The situation is unendurable. If this happens again we cannot carry on. Everything is destroyed.

We cannot even resist invasion now." The Duce sadly agreed. There was nothing else for him to do. He told Maffei to do the best he could, and not let Italy's honour down.

Bombing went on all night, and started again on Friday morning. And at ten minutes to ten the look-out on the island's highest point spied the Allied armada approaching. A little later he was able to report that the armada included assault craft. Pantelleria's hour had come. Once more Admiral Pavesi called up Rome: "I cannot oppose landing," he said; "now I must surrender." And Rome gave permission. At eleven o'clock the Admiral got into radio communication with Malta and surrendered. He said he had no water and must surrender. In fact, there was plenty of water—in bottles and wells and cisterns; but he wanted to salve his pride by finding some non-military excuse. About the same time the Italians laid out a white linen cross on the airfield.

SOON after 11.30 the Allied general heard that there was a white flag flying from a brown conical peak, just behind the town. But the attack was already under way. The whole tremendous process had been put in motion. Wave after wave of Flying Fortresses were approaching the target. Fifty, eighty . . . when their number got into three figures the men in the assault craft, rapidly approaching the island, stopped counting. They had never seen anything like that bombing; they looked at one another in amazement, imagining what they would feel if *they* were beneath it.

At last the planes flew away. The British cruisers were still firing, but the one brave Italian gun, which had been replying, was silent now. Pantelleria was just one mass of dust and smoke. At noon, zero hour, the attackers disembarked. On one of the beaches there were a few bursts of machine-gun fire, but they were short and ineffectual.

Not a shot was fired in the harbour. As the assault craft came skimming in, shabby, dusty Italian troops began popping out of ruined houses and hoisting white flags. They were waiting to surrender. Assault craft pushed straight up to the little jetty, and men ran ashore exactly as they had done it in the exercises. Within a couple of minutes their little radio sets were sending back news that the landing had been made. In my boat they began to have a little lunch before going ashore. Soon empty bully-beef tins were sinking like silver caskets through the clear blue Mediterranean water, and people were handing round huge bread-and-cheese sandwiches.

The Italians had left their surrender so late that our invasion had to roll on for

some time by its own momentum. The bombing programme was dragged finally to a halt, but not before several Italian positions had been raided superfluously and Admiral Pavesi, apparently bewildered by the situation, fled into the hills. They did not find him till six o'clock. The commander sent an emissary with an interpreter to chase him, and finally he consented to walk down to the airfield. There—a handsome, elderly man with grey hair and plenty of gold braid on his uniform—he waited with General Maffei. They gasped with astonishment when the British general drove up in a tank; they had never dreamed that tanks could be got ashore so swiftly and manoeuvred up to the airfield. Gathered in a subterranean office, the Allied Commander produced a sheet and a half of typewritten conditions, and gave it to Pavesi to read. After querying several items the Admiral signed. And so Pantelleria was surrendered.

Pantelleria village, where 3,000 fisherfolk used to live and kept their boats, was a rubbish heap. There were big stretches of the countryside practically covered with bomb craters. The "main road," down which poured a stream of merry and relieved Italian prisoners, carrying cardboard suitcases or wooden boxes already packed with their pathetic trivial belongings, was a grotesque sea-sawing track with a diversion every few yards. The airfield, to which it led, was littered with bits and pieces of Italian fighters. But the superb underground hangar remained untouched beneath its artificial hill, and its great white-washed interior was crammed with an incredible collection of junk. A couple of hundred Italian prisoners squatting on the ground and chattering like magpies. Some fifty Germans standing aloof, cutting the Italians dead; they were Luftwaffe technicians, and their opinion of the Regia Aeronautica was practically unprintable. A dozen absurd little tanks. Two biplanes of astonishing antiquity. Then a couple of hundred two-decker beds littered with clothing, books and letters, cartridges and razors and bottles of ink. Upstairs in a tunnel-like gallery was the Luftwaffe mess and store-room. Great 7-pound tins of butter from Holland or Denmark, excellent tinned pears, 40-pound cheeses, brandy, wine and beer, crates of cigarettes, real coffee. The Luftwaffe, at any rate, is still eating luxuriously.

NINETY minutes after Pantelleria's fall the blitz was switched to Lampedusa, a smaller island to the south. It surrendered on June 12 to Sgt. Cohen, an R.A.F. pilot who landed on the island through engine trouble in the middle of the bombardment (see page 92). Linosa followed suit on June 13; as soon as the British destroyer Nubian appeared, its garrison of 140 Italians raised the white flag. A fourth island, Lampione, was occupied on June 14.

LAMPEDUSA, the little Italian island lying about 100 miles S. of Pantelleria, is some seven miles in length and about two miles wide, with an area of nearly twelve square miles. It was occupied by our forces on June 12, 1943, after being subjected to heavy air and naval bombardments. There were some 4,000-5,000 Italian military, naval and air personnel on Lampedusa at the time of our occupation. This photograph shows the harbour which had been used by the Axis as an E-boat base.

*Photo, The Times*

# Never Such a 'Blitz' on So Small a Target

**BOMBED AND BATTERED PANTELLERIA** was occupied by our forces on June 11, 1943 at a cost of 40 Allied casualties, and after an attack lasting 24 days. 1, One of the many scenes of devastation that confronted our landing-parties. 2, White cross marked out on the airfield was the first indication that the island had surrendered. About 11,000 Italian troops were taken. 3, Prisoners washing in the oil-covered waters of the harbour, while a British sentry keeps an eye on the proceedings.

*Photos, British Official: Crown Copyright ; Associated Press*

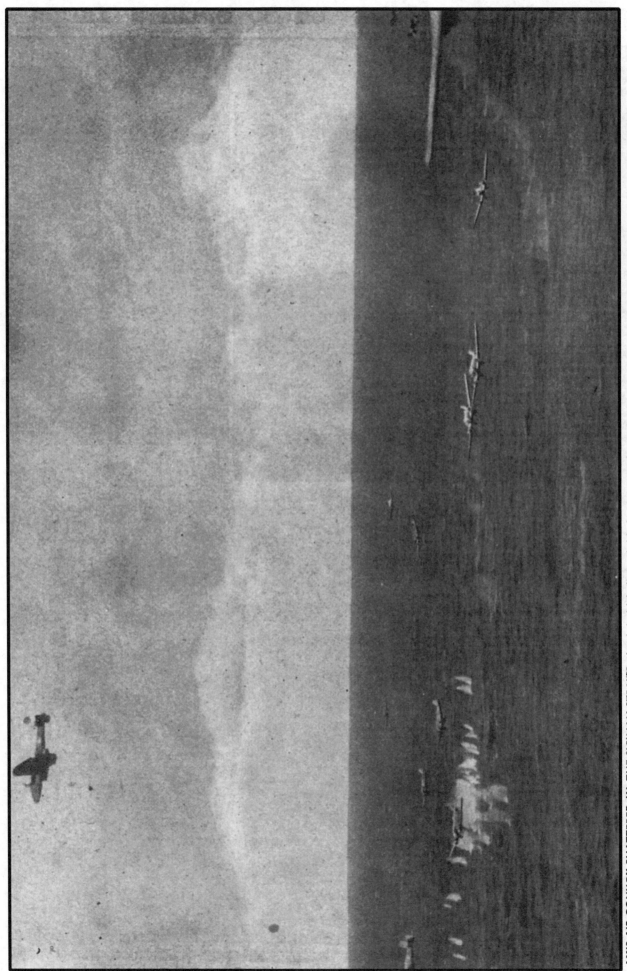

AXIS AIR CONVOY SHATTERED IN THE SICILIAN STRAITS. Loaded with badly-needed fuel and supplies for the hard-pressed Axis forces in Tunisia, 35 giant air transports (Ju 52s), flying at low-level in the vain hope of eluding attack, were pounced on by U.S. Mitchell bombers and Lightnings of the N.W. African Air Force over the Sicilian Straits on April 10, 1943. Twenty-five of these transports were shot down; ten only reaching their destination. This remarkable photograph, taken in the heat of the sea-level battle, shows eleven of the Ju 52s under their assailants' withering onslaught. The splashes are caused by machine-gun bullets. On the same day another large enemy formation of Ju 52s with fighter escort was effectively dispersed by Mitchells and Lightnings.

*Photo, Associated Press*

# THE WAR AT SEA

## by Francis E. McMurtrie

For some time past there has been much talk of invasion possibilities. Undoubtedly the enemy are growing increasingly nervous as the signs of preparation for such an enterprise on the part of the Allies grow more numerous.

One of the greatest worries that beset the Axis rulers is that there is no saying where the principal blow will fall. However anxious they may be to leave no likely point uncovered by strong defending forces, it is manifestly impossible to be strong everywhere. Moreover, when a landing is made it may prove a mere feint designed to draw attention from the real danger-point.

It is the fact that the United Nations control all the sea approaches to the enemy coasts, with the trade routes across the ocean by which supplies and reinforcements must travel, that constitutes the real problem. With these advantages, it is possible to strike almost anywhere, meanwhile keeping the enemy guessing in vain. There is no surer method of baffling and confusing an opponent than by making use of sea power to cloak the coming attack.

On the face of it, the islands of Sicily and Sardinia, garrisoned by the dispirited Italians and lying at no great distance from the ports of North Africa, offer the most tempting targets to the invader. Yet there are many other openings concerning which the Axis have shown acute anxiety. The temporary closing of the frontier between Syria and Turkey, following on the visit to Ankara of Admiral Sir John Cunningham, the newly-appointed Commander-in-Chief in the Levant, has given rise to a suspicion that the islands of the Aegean may be in danger.

### WILL the Navy Attack the Aegean Islands?

These islands form the outer ramparts of the enemy position in the Balkans and Greece. The largest and most important are Crete, Scarpanto and Rhodes in the south, and Lemnos, Mitylene and Khios in the north. Strategically, Crete and Lemnos hold the most valuable positions. With air superiority added to control of the sea, it should not be difficult to recapture these islands one by one. For this purpose, it is suggested in enemy broadcasts (evidently designed to extract information), that big preparations are on foot in the British island of Cyprus. Though Cyprus is nearer to Syria than it is to the Axis islands, its situation should make it a valuable base for attacks on either Crete or Rhodes. Much money is reported to have been spent on the construction of airfields in the island.

With the Aegean Islands in Allied hands, the enemy forces in Greece would find their position outflanked. Moreover, passage of the Dardanelles would then be easy for Allied shipping. Germany is clearly afraid that Turkey would in that event join the ranks of her enemies, affording a clear route for supplies to the Russian forces in the Black Sea. In fact, the possession by the Allies of the Aegean Islands would inevitably be the prelude to enemy evacuation of the Balkans and South Russia.

Almost as exposed to attack as Sicily is the Calabrian peninsula, forming the "toe" of Italy. Not many people remember that in 1806, when Italy was mainly occupied by Napoleon's armies, British infantry under Sir John Stuart were landed in Calabria and defeated a superior force of French troops with heavy loss at the Battle of Maida. History has sometimes a trick of repeating itself when circumstances are similar.

It is not only in the Mediterranean that Axis nervousness of invasion has become apparent. All along the western shores of Europe, from Tromsö to Bordeaux, similar apprehensions appear to be entertained. Norway, with its long sea coast abounding in harbours, offers a favourable field for an invader, to say nothing of the readiness with which the persecuted population of the country would furnish aid and information. Another advantage would be that bases from which convoys proceeding to North Russia can be attacked would be wrested from the enemy.

Precautions taken by the Germans include the evacuation of the civilian population from the Lofoten Islands, the group that has been raided on three occasions by Anglo-Norwegian expeditions, and the concentration in Norwegian ports of German surface warships. The latter are not numerous enough to constitute a real obstacle, even though they may be more formidable opponents than the Italian fleet.

In Denmark the Germans have recently been fortifying parts of the Jutland peninsula, in fear of an invasion on its western coast. Dutch and Belgian coastlines have also been extensively fortified.

Nearest to this country of all the more probable landing-places is the Cotentin peninsula, jutting out northward from the mass of Normandy. In 1758 a British expedition landed here and sacked the naval base at Cherbourg, a fact which has never been forgotten by the inhabitants of that city. To seize this peninsula and hold it as a bridgehead for an advance into France would be a perfectly feasible enterprise.

With all these possibilities in view, it is easy to understand why Hitler hesitates to renew his attack in Russia. While he waits, the forces of the United Nations grow stronger each week ; and the failure of the U-boat onslaught in May and June has added to the shipping resources upon which so much depends.

By the time these comments appear, some indication may have been given of the direction of the invasion ; but it must still be remembered that it is in the power of the Allies to invade at more than one point. For this reason the enemy may hesitate to commit too great a force to defending any single area.

Some figures released recently by the United States Navy Department in Washington provide encouraging news of the progress of submarine attacks on Japanese commerce and supply routes in the Pacific. Altogether not less than 181 and probably over 200 ships have been sunk by American submarines since December 1941. Quite a number of these casualties are warships, including at least three cruisers and 20 destroyers, the total approaching, if not exceeding, 40 units.

With the rapid construction in U.S. yards of more submarines of the latest type, this drain on Japanese resources is likely to become more severe. It is understood there are now nearly 200 American submarines in service, the majority ocean-going craft. Losses to date have been but eight altogether.

**END OF A JAP DESTROYER** as seen through the periscope of the U.S. submarine that recently torpedoed her off Formosa. Top, the ship just after the torpedo struck, apparently severing the bow from the rest of the vessel. Centre, the stern tilts up, and (below) the destroyer plunges to her death.

*Photos, Planet News*

# Two More U-Boats Sent to Their Doom

**OUR U-BOAT KILLINGS** in May, stated Mr. Churchill on June 8, 1943 exceeded the enemy's output. 1, U.S. cutter Spencer's depth charges cripple a U-boat. 2, Rescuing the crew. 3, Germans guide a torpedo from their supply-ship to their submarine in mid-Atlantic. 4, Crew of the Corvette Sunflower, recently a convoy-escort. 5, In the Mediterranean, destroyer Easton closes in to sink the U-boat on right.

*Photos, British Official; Associated Press, Planet News, Barretts*

# Norwegian Patriots Give the Nazis the Slip

SINCE Norway was occupied by the Germans in 1940 increasing numbers of patriotic Norwegians have escaped to Britain. These photographs were taken by a party of 10 Norwegians who recently arrived on these shores. They managed to outwit the Gestapo and German coastal guards under pretext of a fishing expedition. Their ship was a large, seaworthy motor vessel, and their trip was uninterrupted by enemy patrol boats. 1, Two men—the last of the party—row out to the waiting vessel. 2, A conference is held before the party finally sets off. 3, Keeping a sharp look-out in the North Sea. 4, Unknown vessel appears. Is it friend or foe? 5, It's British, so the escapees hoist the Norwegian flag.

*Photos by courtesy of The Royal Norwegian Government*

# Texas Makes Sure We Won't Run Short of Oil

'BIG INCH,' the world's largest oil pipeline, speeds oil for U.S. and Allied war needs at the rate of 300,000 barrels a day. This 24-in. line runs some 531 miles from the vast oilfields of Texas to the mid-west state of Illinois ; from thence a second pipeline (scheduled to be completed by June 1943) will cover 857 miles to the New York City-Philadelphia oil refining region. This enormous project will form the principal source of oil for the war industries of America's eastern seaboard and the United Nations war machine in Europe and Africa:

1, Laying a section. 2, Map showing area traversed by "Big Inch." 3, Sections of line are joined together by electric welding. 4, Tractor-cranes lower a 200 ft. section into position. 5, One of the 4,500 h.p. pumping stations.

*Photos, Pictorial Press*

# The Glorious 155th Battery Fought to the End

Long and glorious is the history of the Royal Regiment of Artillery, but it may be doubted whether it contains any finer story than that of the stand of the 155th Field Battery on Feb. 26, 1943, in Northern Tunisia. Here is the official account, with photographs of one of the nine survivors and five others of the heroic band reported to be prisoners-of-war in Italy

Maj. J. S. RAWORTH     Lt. PHILIP KING

LORD MILNE, veteran general of the last war, was filled with indignation. Rising from his seat in the House of Lords he criticized in severe terms the propaganda department of the War Office, and pointed out one or two notable omissions —the Rifle Brigade, the Royal Corps of Signals, and the cavalry regiments—from Lord Croft's recent statement giving the names of the regiments which had been fighting in Tunisia. Why were we told so little about our units and their leaders, he asked. Today wonderful deeds were being done about which people were told nothing. He would give one example. A battery of artillery was told to cooperate with an infantry regiment. At the end of the battle, when morning broke, every officer and 95 per cent of the men were lying round their smashed guns. The Germans knew what had happened ; the Army knew what had happened ; but when the report came to the colonel of the regiment it was marked " secret." Secret from whom ? It was one of the things that ought to have been read by every unit of the British Army.

That was on June 3. Two days later the Ministry of Information issued an official account of a field battery's most gallant action in the Tunisian fighting. There could

Lt. RONALD GOSLING     L/Bdr. E. G. COOTE

be no doubt that this was the incident to which Lord Milne had referred. The date was February 26, 1943. The place was Sidi Nsir, in the hills twelve miles east of Hunts Gap, near Beja. The battery was the 155th who, with a battalion of the Hampshires, had been ordered to hold the place. If Sidi Nsir fell Beja, the key to the northern Allied line, already threatened by a strong German force, would fall too. With Beja in their hands the enemy would soon have made the Medjez el Bab salient untenable, and transport to and from the Algerian ports extremely difficult. They did not get Beja, because the time won by the 155th Field Battery and the Hampshires at Sidi Nsir sufficed to put Beja into a state of effective defence. But the artillerymen paid the price.

ON the evening of February 25 no signs were visible of enemy movement. The Divisional Commander, his Commander Royal Artillery, and the C.O. of the Field Regiment to which 155 Battery belonged spent two hours examining the countryside from a dominating observation post and could detect nothing ominous. But during the night Verey light signals began to go up in the hills around Sidi Nsir, and at 6.30 next morning heavy mortar fire opened on the British guns. After 45 minutes' shelling came a direct assault. German tanks drove down the road from Mateur. Four 25-pounders leapt into action, No. 1, specially placed at the top of a slope to cover the Mateur approach, firing over open sights. Three tanks were hit as they attempted to

pass through a minefield and the road was blocked. Checked in their initial thrust, the enemy sent in lorried infantry who turned the battery's southern flank under cover of a hill.

THINGS began to look serious. The highest observation post, from which the whole countryside could be surveyed, was heavily attacked, its wireless transmitter was smashed, and its telephone lines were cut. Eight Messerschmitts swooped down on the guns and raked each in turn with machine-gun and cannon fire, inflicting heavy casualties. This manoeuvre was repeated many times. Several vehicles on the road back to Hunts Gap were wrecked and left burning, and the precious ammunition they carried had to be salvaged at imminent risk by the gunners. Bivouac shelters and dumps were in flames. Many men were wounded or killed. But the C.O. of the Regiment, visiting the battery, found all ranks cheerful and determined. Their offensive spirit was completely undaunted. None of the wounded complained.

By midday 30 German tanks, with self-propelled guns and infantry in support, had worked round both flanks and were within 600 yards. A little later the enemy opened small arms fire at close range. At 3 o'clock strong detachments of infantry were across the road to the rear and no more ammunition could pass. For several hours every round had been manhandled forward under heavy fire.

The battery might have saved itself many losses had it concentrated throughout the fire of all its eight guns at a range of 1,300 to 2,000 yards on the German tanks and artillery whose columns were cluttering the way up from Mateur. But its first duty was to protect the Hampshire companies by all means in its power, and it put first things first, by concentrating in support of the infantry.

About 3.30, on every ground of military probability, the battle was almost over. So at least the German Command reasoned. What was meant to be the death blow was struck by a column of tanks which raced along the road into the heart of the battery position. Thirteen other tanks gave covering fire with guns and machine-guns from hull down positions. A Mark VI led the attack. This was holed three times in the turret by shells from No. 1 gun of F Troop. A Mark IV tried to pass round the wreckage, but it also was knocked out by No. 1 gun. The same gun set on fire another tank. Then the surviving tanks drew back and shelled and machine-gunned both F and E Troops, whose positions were easily spotted, for they were now engaging the enemy over open sights. Hull down, the enemy tanks had a great advantage. Concentrating on one gun at a time they killed the detachments,

smashed the guns and set the remaining ammunition on fire. When all seemed finished the Germans advanced again. But a surprise awaited them. At its dying gasp, the 155th Field Battery could still hit back. No. 1 gun of F Troop, whose crew had showed themselves heroes among heroes, destroyed the leading tank. A moment later a direct hit killed all the survivors ; without a man left, No. 1 was silenced. Nos. 2, 3 and 4 fought on. One officer, batmen, cooks, all who could stand, ran from gun to gun, serving each in turn. Although the issue was decided they fought out the day to the last man and the last round at ranges which shrank from 50 yards to 10 yards.

At 5.30 the Germans, heavily mauled, moved on to crush E Troop as they had crushed F. At nightfall one 25-pounder and several Bren guns were still engaging at ranges of from 10 to 20 yards German tanks which were lumbering through the position, smothering the last resistance, swivelling round on their tracks and crushing in slit trenches. A few minutes earlier the last message had come over the wireless " Tanks are on us," followed by the single V tapped out in Morse.

When the battle began there were at the guns in the command posts and observation

Gnr. J. G. BRYCE     Gnr. F. L. HARRISON

posts nine officers and 121 other ranks. But only nine survivors managed to make their way back to the British lines, and of these two were wounded. One of the nine was Gunner J. G. Bryce, who described in a letter to his wife, published in the News Chronicle, the closing scene :

We withstood the brunt of a powerful German attack—all on our own, with no support whatever, under continuous dive-bombing, mortar fire and eventually tanks (the latest German Mark VI). We knocked out seven of them.

Everyone showed perfect calm and coolness, even when it was obvious the end was in sight. One gun crew were actually singing that song " Praise the Lord and Pass the Ammunition " when their gun was hit. But we held them all until all our guns were knocked out, and we were finally overrun by the enemy.

Then in the pitch darkness, through heavy rain and bitter cold, he managed to get past the German tanks and infantry on to the mountains. After four days in the open, sustained only by his water-bottle and a bar of chocolate, he struggled back to his base.

OF the men who did not come back some were taken prisoner. Their wives then learned at last the meaning of a sentence in a letter received from an enemy prison camp : " I was taken by the Germans on Feb. 26. See if the papers have any account of the battle on that day." They had to wait for three months. But for Lord Milne they— and we, and the world—might have had to wait perhaps for years before this was added to the immortal stories of British valour.

# Proudly We Danes Serve Under the Red Ensign

In earlier pages HENRY BAERLEIN has told how serving beside and with our own fighting men and merchant mariners there are many drawn from the countries on the Continent at present overrun by the enemy. In this article he describes the gallant Danes who have taken their place in ships flying the Red Ensign of the Mercantile Marine.

"THE captain summoned us to a conference," said a big, jovial Danish seaman in the very pleasant club which has been established by the British authorities in a certain port for these friends of ours who have no Government of their own in this country, but who, as Mr. Attlee has expressed it, are Allies in all but the name; "and the captain told us what had happened, that Denmark had been invaded. What did we want to do ? Not a single man was for going back to be under the Germans. We went to the Faroes and a few days later a British warship arrived and asked if we would like to serve under the Red Ensign ; and, of course, we said yes."

heard from their families since the outbreak of the War. "I have not written to my parents," said one young man, "because of the Gestapo, but they know about me." I asked how that was possible. "They know," he said, "that I am doing my duty." When the Danish Minister at Washington made an arrangement with the American Government whereby some 26 Danish ships in New York harbour were placed at the disposal of the Allies and, instead of remaining safely in port, would now be facing all the perils of the sea, shipping shares rose the next morning on the Copenhagen bourse—to the rage of the Nazis, for the Danes were making it clear that they knew who was going to win the War.

member of her crew, "by German radio from Copenhagen to sail for home. Of course we refused, and for eleven days we stayed in that place—every now and then a German plane used to fly around and signal to us that we had to go back. When they saw that we had no intention of obeying them they bombed our ship, killing one man and wounding seven. In the night we got a fisherman who knew the fjord very well ; he took the ship far in, so that under the shelter of the land she could not so easily be hit. Something had to be done at once, because we heard that the Norwegian Army and the British troops were leaving that part of the country. So we repaired the ship and a few Norwegian airmen arrived. They knew where some Germans were interned— their plane had once bombed England and had to come down in Norway with engine trouble. We took the Nazis on board ; they protested that it was against International Law. We reminded them that they had broken it every day since September 1939. What about those 450 Danish seamen who had been drowned when they sank our neutral ships ? They said that Germany and Denmark were not at war. "Maybe," we replied, "but we, the men of this ship, we are at war with you."

"As for my ship," said an elderly seaman, "in the middle of a great storm she ran ashore on Holy Island. I think there are 200 people there, and we were quite sorry when we had put the ship right again and had to leave. They paid us a compliment, those people, saying that we were the best drinkers of whisky they had seen. We emptied the island. Perhaps I'll get a little drunk on the day of victory, but until then no more."

CLUB FOR DANISH SEAMEN in Newcastle serves as a splendidly-equipped meeting-place for Danes who, leading a strenuous life at sea, can enjoy a game of billiards amid comfortable surroundings. As told in this page, these men are waging a gallant fight against the enemy for a free Denmark.
*Photo, Courtesy of Danish Legation*

"That was democratic of the captain, when he asked you," I said.

"But he knew the answers beforehand. We are a people who have had and must have freedom. We have the sea in our blood."

A DIFFERENT sort of captain was in command of another Danish ship, as I was told by a fair-haired fellow who sat beside us. This man hailed from the part of Denmark that was recovered from Germany after the last war—it had been stolen by Bismarck in 1864. The captain was a Danish subject, but retained his German sympathies ; and a very unsympathetic person he must have been, for when the ship lay in an Argentine port, unable to leave as they had no money for the harbour dues, he gave the men such short commons that they nearly starved, and when Danish farmers on shore sent money for them, he sent it back without telling them of it, but informed the farmers that the men had all they wanted. So they sold the electric fittings to Americans and the captain knew nothing of it, as he was too wise to venture into their part of the ship.

It is not generally realized how large a merchant fleet Denmark possesses ; and practically all of it, with several thousand officers and men, are ceaselessly sailing in the common cause. Many of them have not

When France collapsed in 1940 several Danish ships were at Dakar, where they were interned, as the crews refused to be repatriated and have their ships sent to Marseilles. Some of the Danish vessels were placed as a screen round the Richelieu by the French authorities ; but the small British craft which damaged the Richelieu's propeller dived under them and did them no harm. "One Sunday morning," said a burly fellow, "three of us took a rowing-boat and went out through the minefield that was open then. We pretended to be fishing and when the Richelieu, which could then only steam at 9 knots, was far enough away, we hoisted our sail and on the next afternoon we arrived in a British colony, where the wife of the Governor went shopping with us and she actually spoke some Danish. That was all right."

The Germans have attempted to side-track the enthusiasm of the Danes by telling them on the wireless that Britain has seized these ships, but they know very well that an accurate account is kept and that after the War all the profits earned by the ships will be paid to their rightful owners.

Very varied have been their experiences. One tanker chanced to be off the coast of Norway. "We were ordered," said a

ANOTHER Dane told me how he had hoped to lead an idyllic life in Greenland, whither he had gone just before the invasion of Denmark in one of the ships sent every year with clothes, food and so forth by the Danish Government. "As we sailed up the coast of Norway," he said, "we saw some German ships with cargo on deck ; but they were very high in the water. Some of us suspected they had Germans down below —as indeed they had, hundreds of soldiers. Well, after we had passed the Shetlands we heard what happened and went on to Greenland. The people there are so friendly, they never lock their doors ; I only heard of one Eskimo who had been stealing and they made him load and unload ships for a time without being paid. Even in winter it is good, because of the Northern Lights, and the stars and the moon are very near. They love Denmark so much that they paint their houses red and white, which are our colours. Now I am at sea again ; but after the victory I want to live for ever in Greenland."

A comrade of his had joined us while he was talking. "In the last war," he said, "we made a lot of money, for the country stayed neutral. But we are all glad to be like the Britishers now, fighting for the right side, so that our children may live in a free Denmark, as it always was and must be."

And these excellent sons of the Vikings have installed over here a school where prospective mates and engineers are trained. They pass the examination in English without trouble ; and one of them showed me, not without modest pride, his certificate which mentioned that he had passed ahead of everyone. "Thank God for everything," said he ; and we can be thankful that these sturdy fellows are so whole-heartedly with us in the common struggle today.

## On the Way to America

That Mr. Churchill had arrived in Washington on his third visit to the American President at the White House since the U.S.A. came into the War, was announced by Mr. Roosevelt's secretary on the evening of May 11, 1943 ; not until his return on June 5 was it revealed that he had crossed the Atlantic by sea.  1, Mr. Churchill on the bridge of the warship ; 2, with a British and American gun crew ; 3, at a conference on board ship with (left to right) Air Chief Marshal Sir Charles Portal, Admiral of the Fleet Sir Dudley Pound, General Sir Alan Brooke, and (right) Field Marshal Sir A. Wavell.

## Council of War in Algiers

On the way home from his visit to Washington, Mr. Churchill "thought it well to go to North Africa . . . in order to deal more particularly and precisely on the spot with the problems of the Mediterranean theatre." For a week discussions went on in Algiers, and "the most complete concord and confidence prevailed (the Premier told the House of Commons on June 8) amongst those charged with the 'application upon the enemy of force in its most intense and violent form.'"

Photo
C

### Mr. Churchill with his Captains

At Algiers, in the H.Q. of the Allied Armies in North Africa, sits the Prime Minister. On the left is Mr. Anthony Eden, and next is Sir Alan Brooke, C.I.G.S. On the other side of Mr. Churchill are Gen. Marshall, U.S. Chief of Staff, and Gen. Eisenhower, C.-in-C. in North Africa. Standing just behind are (left to right) Air Chief Marshal Sir Arthur Tedder, Admiral of the Fleet Sir Andrew Cunningham, Gen. Sir Harold Alexander, and Gen. Sir Bernard Montgomery.

# Home Via the Battlefields

Photos, British Official:
Crown Copyright

It was at the end of May that Mr. Churchill, his talks in Washington being concluded, flew from the United States to Gibraltar and thence to Algiers. Here he was joined by Mr. Anthony Eden, the Foreign Secretary, and together they visited Tunis and the British and American armies in North Africa. In the ancient Roman amphitheatre at Carthage he found awaiting him a great and enthusiastic audience of fighting men (1), and with Lt.-Gen. Anderson and Mr. Eden at his side he gave them an inspiring address (2). 3, The Premier is seen making a personal inspection of a German Tiger tank.

# VIEWS & REVIEWS Of Vital War Books

*by Hamilton Fyfe*

NEVER before, since war reporting was controlled and organized, have Press correspondents been able to get near enough to the front to be taken prisoner. "Just as well for them," many people will mutter. But that is not the view journalists take. They want to get as near the news as they can.

In the last war, the war of 1914-1918, the times when I got nearest were those in which I was free-lancing, roaming about in battle-areas without official sanction—indeed, with severe official disapprobation. Lord Kitchener told a friend of mine, the late Capt. Bede Bentley, one of the many who claimed to have invented tanks, that if he could catch me (this was while I was in France soon after war began in August, 1914) he would have me shot. He was feeling sore at the moment, for the day previous he had announced in Parliament that there were no correspondents in the field—and that morning he had read in the Daily Mail a page from me about the arrival of the first trains of wounded at Rouen. However, he didn't catch me, though a patrol of Uhlans did; and with Arthur Moore, a Times man, I had a very narrow escape of being shot by the enemy, or at any rate being interned in Germany for four years.

**MR. HAROLD DENNY, of The New York Times, author of Behind Both Lines, reviewed in this page.** *Photo, New York Times Photos*

I was luckier than Harold Denny of the New York Times, who was captured by Germans in Libya and who gives in a book he has just brought out, Behind Both Lines (Michael Joseph, 8s. 6d.) a vivid account of his experiences as a prisoner of war. He was right in the middle of a tank engagement, a place where, to my thinking, no correspondent has any right to be. I was taught that the newspaperman's first duty, whether in peace or in war, is to his employer. He must not avoid exposing himself to danger, when that is necessary, in order to get news. But he should take care to keep his line of retreat open, so that he can slip off and send his message in time for the next day's issue. That is his chief obligation.

WELL, Denny had no line of retreat available. He and Edward Ward of the B.B.C. were crouching in a slit trench in the desert sand when enemy tanks overran them and they had to surrender. The South African brigade they were with was, except for a handful of men who managed to escape, wiped out. A Hun officer "motioned them to the rear with his pistol." Then another told them to double, so they "broke into a trot, holding our hands awkwardly in the air and feeling more silly than frightened," although they "half expected to be disposed of with machine-guns, for the simple reason that a large group of prisoners such as the Germans were then rounding up is a serious hindrance to a flying column in the thick of a battle."

However, they were trotted off for a mile or two, and no harm happened to them, though, when they halted, they had a gun turned on them and an officer said : "Everything will be all right if no one makes any trouble. If one man tries to escape we will mow you all down." That seemed fair enough, but what did appear hard was that they got nothing to eat and scarcely a mouthful of water to drink for a matter of thirty hours. The Germans had nothing to give them, they said.

Perhaps for this reason the prisoners were turned over to the Italians next day. But not before they had been looked over by Marshal von Rommel, " burly, unshaven, in a dirty overcoat," who abused the German soldiers for " wasting their time gaping at the Englishmen and so delaying the war."

Rommel, says Mr. Denny, was very talkative with captured officers. He asked one why the British spread out their tanks " and let me smash them in detail ? " Mr. Denny has no doubt that " violation of the fundamental military law of concentration of forces was a major cause of the British failure in the 1941-42 offensive in Libya."

# Behind Both Lines

When the journalists were handed over to the Italians, soldiers tried to rob them under pretence of searching for weapons. They got a watch and a pocket-knife from Mr. Denny ; he only just managed to keep his fountain-pen and lighter. In their new " pen " the prisoners got the water they so badly needed ; and some inferior bully beef was served out, which British soldiers warmed up. The officers were accommodated in small tents : the rank and file " lay sleepless with cold on the sodden bare ground."

NEXT, the American correspondent with an American officer-observer, who had diplomatic status, was sent to Benghazi. At a place on the way they were put into the local prison, a little private house furnished scantily, where they met two very suspicious and inquisitive young men who said they were Maltese and had been captured in a Commando raid. They had evidently been planted there by the Italians to wheedle information. They got none. Nor did an Italian pressman who made a friendly offer of wine and cigarettes, and then asked a question about the British forces—something he had for the moment forgotten ! His memory received no help ; he did not send the cigarettes or wine.

At Benghazi there were a great many prisoners in unfinished Italian barracks, " barnlike buildings with only a few dozen cots among a thousand or more men, and straw mattresses and blankets for a few score more. Most of us had to sleep in inadequate clothing on the concrete floor. . . Many officers gave their blankets to their men, pretending they had others, and then slept coverless themselves."

THE Italians, Mr. Denny thinks, did their best, but there were many hardships to endure. On the ship going across the Mediterranean to Italy he was in the wardroom where " the space was too small for all to lie down at once, so at night some of us dozed standing, like horses in a stable." When the sea got rough, the water poured in : " We were drenched and shivering." But at Taranto they were given a good meal on a liner, which was brilliantly lighted inside, the crew standing to attention in the passages.

" We were shown into the glittering first-class dining-room. Wet, dirty, bearded and tattered, we were ushered to snowy tables, decorated with flowers and bottles of good wine. Italian waiters served us as attentively as if we had been de luxe passengers bulging with tips. We had a rich minestrone, liberal cuts of cold meats, vegetables, salad and fruit. A spokesman for the ship apologized that conditions did not permit the serving of a better meal. Our cruiser's captain had felt badly over our miserable voyage, we learned, and had wirelessed ahead asking this service. Brigadier Sterling, senior British officer present, made a little speech of thanks on behalf of all of us."

Later, in Rome, conditions were good ; but for a time Mr. Denny was in a Gestapo prison in Berlin, where he had many bad hours, being questioned and confronted with things he had written, or had not written, about Hitler and the Huns. Eventually he was exchanged and got back to New York, with the conviction that " the Italians are fundamentally a decent people, too individualistic and cultivated to fit into the Fascist mould."

Well, they had better show it—quick !

**WAR CORRESPONDENTS WITH THE 'CHINDITS.' Several newspapermen accompanied Brigadier Wingate into the Central Burmese forests (see page 46). Here we see (left to right) Stuart Emeny of the News Chronicle, Martin Moore of The Daily Telegraph and Tony Beauchamp, press photographer.** *Photo, Indian Official*

# Flying Ambulances Save Many a Soldier's Life

The 8th Army's great advance from Egypt into Tunisia was marked by many outstanding features, of which the speed of the advance is perhaps the most noticeable. But a fact which appears to have escaped attention is the small number of dead. Below, JOHN ALLEN GRAYDON explains why the mortal casualties have happily been so few.

THAT we have suffered so few fatal casualties in North Africa is due in large measure to the brilliant work of the R.A.M.C., and the splendid manner in which they have cooperated with the "Flying Ambulances" of the R.A.F. During the Polish campaign of 1939 the Germans utilized aircraft in this way and so kept down the number of fatal casualties. Over the past two years we have improved considerably upon the German method.

It can now be revealed that nearly 3,000 badly wounded British and Empire soldiers were saved from death by the speed of the Flying Ambulances. The planes have shock-and sound-proof cabins, equipped with nursing and medical stores, special blood-transfusion gear and heating apparatus. Aboard these aircraft, doctors, when a patient was in danger of dying, have been known to perform emergency operations while flying through the air at over 200 miles an hour.

In past campaigns head wounds were a source of special worry to the medical services. Unless a badly wounded man suffering from an injury of this kind was rushed to a base hospital and given the best possible treatment, he usually died. In the Middle East, however, only one-tenth of the men suffering from head-wounds have so far failed to survive. The speed of the Flying Ambulances, which rush men from the front line to hospitals well in the rear, has made this great achievement possible.

That is why, from the point of view of the medical services, the Egyptian and Libyan campaigns were so successful. Similarly, in Tunisia, the Air Ambulances speedily conveyed those who needed urgent treatment from the front-line dressing stations to the hospitals at base.

General Freyberg, New Zealand's V.C. leader, who always goes into action with his men, was saved from possible death when wounded in the neck. Only prompt action by a Flying Ambulance enabled him to be tended by specialists before it was too late.

Our Australian comrades, who first saw the possibilities in air ambulances 14 years ago —they used one in Queensland—have supplied three for the use of their own troops in the Middle East.

The British machines have trained medical orderlies aboard who, in their quiet way, have performed some of the War's greatest deeds. Never forget that for the most part these hospital planes travel back to base unescorted, often over enemy-held territory. On more than one occasion, when attacked by Axis aircraft, these orderlies have had to carry on their normal duties in a " care-free manner." One lad with whom I talked had two bullets enter his left leg—but he said nothing until they reached base and the last of his patients had been taken into a ward. Then, weak from loss of blood, he collapsed.

ON one occasion a young pilot, assisting to take aboard the wounded men, had something of a shock when he saw amongst them his own father, a major in an infantry regiment. The wounded man was in a dangerous condition, and the pilot, when he took the air, knew that everything depended upon his ability to get to base in record time. Is it to be wondered at that he piloted his machine like a man inspired?

Enemy fighters twice got on to his tail, but on both occasions the youngster, with his precious cargo safe, eluded the enemy by taking cloud cover. He landed at base several minutes ahead of the previous record time for the trip ; his father was rushed to the operating theatre, and today, thanks to his son's skill, is once more on duty.

Not so long ago two Boston bombers were forced down after attacking an enemy-held drome in the desert. Several men were wounded, but the observer of one machine walked 22 miles in 30 hours and reached an airfield. He notified the authorities of his comrades' position, and a doctor was flown to the scene aboard a Lysander.

Quickly he tended to the sick and wounded, and by the time an ambulance plane arrived the stranded airmen were ready to be taken aboard and flown to base. Thanks to the Flying Ambulance's prompt action only one man, killed by German fighters, was lost.

On many occasions the R.A.F.'s ambulances have performed some outstanding deeds on the Home Front. Sometimes, when a sick man needed special treatment, these craft have flown him through the night so that he might reach a specialist. Nothing is too much trouble for the R.A.F. when it means saving a human life.

I CAN recollect hearing, when in the Shetlands, how the Flying Ambulance attached to a certain R.A.F. station flew to the rescue of a coastguard who was badly injured by a cliff fall. The doctor who examined him was of the opinion that he needed special treatment, but that the journey over 40 miles of rough road might prove fatal. A signal was flashed to the nearest R.A.F. base, and the C.O. ordered a Flying Ambulance to proceed to the coastguard's assistance. Touching down near the station, the ambulance quickly took aboard the injured and unconscious coastguard, and he was flown 300 miles to Edinburgh. Today that coastguard is back at his important task.

When the moment arrives for the Second Front to be opened the Flying Ambulances will play a vital role. By their speed they can assure wounded of the best possible treatment far from the dangers of the front line. Surgeons, without the thought of the enemy being near, can concentrate all the better on their immediate task, and satisfaction is assured all concerned.

The Flying Ambulances, when first constructed, were considered something of a "stunt." Modern war has proved them to be, however, one of the greatest successes on the " Medical Front."

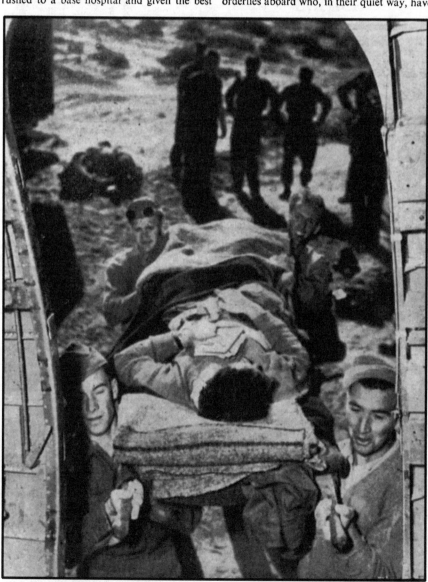

**U.S. FLYING AMBULANCE, bound for a base hospital on the N. African front, receives a badly-wounded 8th Army man. Within a matter of minutes he will be receiving expert surgical attention. Such aircraft have saved the lives of many wounded soldiers (see accompanying text).**
*Photo, British Official ; Crown Copyright*

# From Battlefield to Hospital Ward by Air

TRANSPORTING the wounded by air is one of the finest developments in the saving of human life brought about by this war. A Lockheed Loadstar in Tunisia (1) stands-by while a wounded man is prepared for a journey to hospital at a British field-base.

Air Speed Oxford aircraft in service as flying ambulances carry two stretcher-cases in addition to a doctor and fully trained staff. (2) Two of these machines, marked with the International Red Cross, fly above the clouds. (3) W.A.A.F. air ambulance orderlies attend to a patient aboard a plane en route to hospital. (4) A British sergeant who has been wounded in the head, cheerfully assists a comrade from an ambulance aircraft.

*Photos, British Official: Crown Copyright; Central Press*

# THE WAR IN THE AIR

## by Capt. Norman Macmillan, M.C., A.F.C.

THE decision to form a Tactical Air Force in the United Kingdom to operate in conjunction with the land forces is the logical outcome of the experience of war in North Africa. The section of the R.A.F. hitherto known as the Army Cooperation Command has been embodied in this Tactical Air Force; and Air Marshal Sir Arthur Barratt, who has commanded the Army Cooperation Command since its inception after Dunkirk, now goes to the Technical Training Command. Air Vice-Marshal J. H. D'Albiac, who commanded the R.A.F. in Greece, assumes command of the Tactical Air Force

Looking back for a moment to the Great War of 1914-18 makes it possible readily to visualize how the organization to employ air power to its fullest extent is still evolving. Practically all the aircraft we, possessed during the first three years of the Great War were employed tactically. The few that were otherwise engaged belonged to the Royal Naval Air Service, and under the inspiration of Mr. Winston Churchill, then First Lord of the Admiralty, made strategic raids against Zeppelin sheds at Cuxhaven and Friedrichshafen and the railway station in Cologne. But it was not until we had had considerable experience of Zeppelin and Gotha raids against British towns and cities, that the true idea of a real strategic air force was mooted. It sprang up in the mind of General Jan Smuts, and was embodied in his Memorandum to the Cabinet in the early autumn of 1917. So the 41st Wing of the Royal Flying Corps was sent to Ochey, near Nancy, then the most convenient point behind the 400-miles-long trench front from which to bomb strategic points behind the enemy lines. In command was Lieut.-Col. C. L. N. Newall, now Marshal of the R.A.F. and Governor-General of New Zealand. From this first strategic wing of four squadrons, set up in France in October 1917, grew the Independent Air Force of 1918 commanded by Major-General H. M. Trenchard, now Marshal of the R.A.F. Viscount Trenchard.

FIELD-MARSHAL Earl Haig (then Sir Douglas Haig) bitterly opposed the idea of a separate strategic air force, and contended that all available aircraft in France should be directly under Army control. This was contrary to the whole idea of the Smuts' Memorandum, which visualized the strategic air force as a power controlled by the Cabinet for the purpose of smashing the German war organization at distant, selected points behind the front which could not be attacked in any other way.

Before the Independent Air Force was formed in June 1918, the Royal Air Force had been created under a separate and independent Air Ministry.

WHEN the Great War ended in 1918, and disarmament cut the R.A.F. to a shadow of its wartime strength, a decision had to be reached about the policy which would govern the activities of the R.A.F. Five main branches of activity emerged. These were: (1) to keep in being at least the nucleus of a fighter force which would be able to fight for the mastery of the daylight air, and at the same time to explore the possibilities of night-fighter defence; (2) to provide an Empire-control and defence force; (3) to cooperate with the Army; (4) to cooperate with the Navy; and (5) to maintain an independent offensive bomber force.

From Nos. 1 and 5 came Fighter and Bomber Commands of the present R.A.F.; from 3 came the Tactical Air Force; from 4 the Fleet Air Arm (air side) and Coastal Command; and from 2 came the defence units overseas, the establishment of the practical nature of air control in the experiment made in Iraq in 1922, when for the first time in history the R.A.F. became the senior and controlling Service on the spot, and the experience of aircraft, aero-engines, terrain and methods which contributed so handsomely to the victory in North Africa.

### TACTICAL Air Force as a Separate Command

What is happening in the organization of the R.A.F. today in the midst of war is not change, but the welding together of all past experience into the strongest and most resilient framework of air power. This does not threaten the R.A.F. with disintegration. On the contrary, it makes it stronger than ever; for the methods by which the maximum effect of air power can be applied in the field for the benefit of military operations have been established in accordance with current needs, and they have produced marvellous results under the controlling hands of senior air officers working harmoniously as a part of the co-ordinated team under Army officers holding still higher directive appointments.

Why, it may be asked, should it be necessary to separate the tactical and strategic air forces into distinctive commands?

Air Vice-Marshal J. H. D'ALBIAC, C.B., D.S.O., whose appointment as commander of the Tactical Air Force of the R.A.F., based in Britain, was announced on June 14, 1943. He is 49.  *Photo, British Official : Crown Copyright*

In a short article it is not possible to go into the whole question, but it may be readily understood that the planning of strategic operations differs from the planning of tactical operations. A force may be sited in a given base for strategic operations long before there is any need for a tactical force; this was indeed the case in the United Kingdom. The higher control of the two distinct types of force may be vested in different authorities—the one political and the other military—yet the two forces must be capable of fusion of effort when the appropriate moment comes.

The types of aircraft may differ in many respects in the two forces, and their equipment may vary in such important items as guns and bombs. While the basic air training must be the same, there will of necessity be a veneer of specialization in each case. And, not least important, there is the team work of the commanders of the surface and air forces; these men must work together harmoniously if they are to achieve a common result, and they must know one another intimately and get on well together.

IN every age the military processes which have been evolved by war have left their traces behind when the need for them ceased. The evolution of transport by land, sea, and in the air has been greatly developed by war. In England we still drive over some of the old Roman military roads. The Panama Canal was primarily a military project. Wars left us a legacy of income tax, passports, identity cards, artificial frontiers. The present period of this war is pregnant with possibilities in the realm of the air. And the amazing fact is abundantly clear that the United Nations have learned how to use the air, whereas the Germans, who began the war with what was then a tremendous advantage in air power, have failed to use it properly. They nailed it down entirely to the demands of their Army; and the German Army generals; not comprehending because they did not have the training or instincts of the engineer, believing that aeroplanes could be thrown away as they were accustomed to throw away German lives in infantry regiments, staked everything on a grand slam and did not pull it off.

The United Nations have beaten the Germans in the use of air power. They have swept through all North Africa. They have seized the Italian islands in the Sicilian Narrows almost without resistance following the use of air power. By its power in scientific combination with other arms they can conquer Italy, Germany and Japan; and when the war is over there will be in the hands of the United Nations a means to govern such as has never been seen before.

NEW HANDLEY PAGE HALIFAX BOMBER is even deadlier and faster than its predecessors. The power-operated gun turret in the nose has been replaced by a large perspex nose; and instead of the dorsal turret which carried two ·303 guns, there is a Boulton-Paul Defiant-type four ·303 gun turret. Inset, the old nose.  *Photo, British Official : Crown Copyright*

# Safe Back From an Uninvited Visit to Germany

OUR BOMBER CREWS RETURN AFTER A RAID. 1, W.A.A.F. sergeant gives a pilot permission to land. 2, These airmen make out detailed reports of their operations immediately they have landed at their base. 3, Aircraft is towed away by a W.A.A.F. Bombers have carrier-pigeons aboard to take an S O S in the event of their radio being put out of action ; 4, pigeon released from its container on reaching home. 5, Member of ground staff cleans an aircraft's machine-guns. 6, The officer on the right has an egg for his back-from-the-raid meal. On June 22, 1943 a new phase opened in the Battle of the Ruhr, when Fortresses attacked in daylight.

*Photos, Daily Mirror*

# At Labrador's Port of Call for U.S. Bombers

**AT GOOSE BAY, LABRADOR,** has been built one of the world's largest air bases, with full repair and maintenance facilities for aircraft. Here U.S. bombers arrive from the West, refuel, and continue their flight to Britain. 1, Workers photographed against Save for Victory posters. 2, Capt. Shultz and (3) Sqdn. Ldr. Powell, veteran fighter pilot of the Battle of Britain, two members of the Goose Bay garrison. 4, Flying Fortresses waiting to fuel up for their trip to this country.

*Photos, Canadian Official: Crown Copyright*

# Cross-Channel Sweeps Are Their Speciality

BESIDES the major bombing of enemy heavy industries, the R.A.F. wages a continual conflict against Axis war potential of a more ordinary description. The constant attacks against locomotives, trucks, barges, etc., mean that the enemy is faced by a stream of damaged road and rail vehicles and rivercraft into already overcrowded repairshops. The Germans must now be finding it difficult to organize repairs on anything like the necessary scale. The drawing above shows three types of plane often mentioned as being engaged in this form of nuisance attack.

THE HAWKER TYPHOON (1). This is the latest and most powerful of our single-engined fighter planes. The 24-cylinder Napier Sabre engine with large radiator beneath (A) gives the plane a formidable appearance, which is well borne out by the punch power of the 4 wing-mounted cannon (B). Twelve machineguns are fitted on other models of this aircraft.

Two Typhoons are seen making an attack upon a German Dornier Do 217 E, which has been located whilst being prepared for operations. A petrol bowser (C) is being used to re-fuel the wing tanks with petrol, whilst maintenance platforms used by the ground crews to service engines and fuselage are seen in position (D).

WHIRLWIND FIGHTER BOMBER (2). This beautifully-streamlined plane is powered by two R.R. Peregrine engines of over 800 h.p. each. The radiators are within the wings: the air intakes to them are seen at (E). The four nose-cannon are a feature. The highly-placed tailpiece with Acorn fairing (F) is characteristic. The pilot of the Whirlwind has dived low across a busy river estuary to attack an enemy cargo vessel which is taking on supplies from a river barge (G). Bombing attacks of this kind often smash barge derricks —as here seen—and other deck fittings, with

resultant delay while cargoes are unloaded, and still further delay when repairs have to be undertaken.

MUSTANGS (3). These planes have long been known as train-busters. The number of enemy locomotives put out of action has now reached a high figure. This, together with the attacks by heavy bombers on locomotive repair centres, has created a serious transport problem for the Germans.

In this attack Mustangs are seen firing their eight machine-guns into an enemy goods train. Two of the Mustang's guns are synchronized to fire through the propeller (H). When the bullets rip through the thin metal boiler skin they play havoc with the network of high and low pressure steam-pipes within. The Germans are now using flak trains to defend their rail systems. These consist of 88-millimetre and smaller guns mounted on railway wagons. One of the smaller, quick-firing guns is at (J).

# Mosquitoes on the Bench and in the Air

MOSQUITOES, the world's fastest bombers (see p. 344, vol. 6) are unique among operational types of aircraft. The work done by the de Havilland Co. on the Comet, with which the England-Australia race was won in 1934, bore fruit in the Mosquito—put into service in 1942. 1, Mosquito in flight. 2, Soldering small parts in tail sections. 3, Fitting oxygen pipelines during fuselage assembly. 4, Machines nearing completion. 5, The nose bristles with machine guns.

*Photos, P.N.A., Planet News, Central Press*

# To Town and Country Goes Our Roving Camera

CANADIAN SOLDIERS HAVE REBUILT A SURREY CHURCH which was destroyed in an air raid in 1941. Above we see the soldier-builders putting the roof on the building at Merstham, that they have erected in their spare time, out of materials taken from the original edifice. The church was consecrated at Easter 1943.

MOBILE LAUNDRY SERVICE, touring the Home Counties, has greatly assisted busy war workers with the weekly washing. This National Emergency Laundry Service includes washing, ironing and airing. Staffed by Messrs. Lever Bros., the vans wait outside factories. Women workers are here shown in the laundry queue.

RAZOR BLADES, of which there has been an acute shortage for many months, are now being produced at half the pre-war rate. In 1939 2½ million blades were produced every day, but in 1943 the output is less than a million blades a day. The machine shown above perforates and stamps 540 blades every minute.

UNITED NATIONS DAY was celebrated in London on June 14, 1943. Along Whitehall and the Mall great crowds paid homage to the fighting-men and war-workers of Britain and to the 31 flags of the United Nations. Right, part of the procession passing under Admiralty Arch.

*Photos, Keystone, L.N.A., Topical Press, Planet News*

# I WAS THERE!

## Now They Call Me 'The King of Lampedusa'

When R.A.F. Sgt.-Pilot Sydney Cohen, 22-year-old Londoner, forced-landed his Swordfish plane on Lampedusa, June 12 (see page 70), the Italians offered immediate surrender of their island. Here is his astonishing story, as told to Denis Martin, Reuters Special Correspondent at Allied Headquarters in North Africa.

**Sgt.-Pilot SYDNEY COHEN, to whom the Italians on Lampedusa offered to surrender the island, was formerly a tailor's cutter. His story is told in this page.** *Photo, G.P.U.*

DURING an air-sea rescue mission the plane got a fit of Gremlins. I swept down on a landing-field and saw a few burnt-out aircraft, but we were still not sure that it was Lampedusa.

Then we saw white objects being waved by figures on the edge of the field. Two Italian officers came up to our aircraft, followed by civilians. We were vastly intrigued by the leader of the deputation. He was wearing a Tyrolean hat with a large plumed feather (headdress of the crack Bersaglieri), a leather jacket, shorts and high boots, and he burst forth into voluble Italian. We gathered that the Italian was offering the island's surrender.

In view of the accidental nature of my mission it was a bit of a shake-up, but I put on a bold heart, and asked to see the Commandant of the island. I was taken to the Commandant's villa and presented to a high ranking officer. We were joined there by a further contingent, including our Tyrolean friend.

Our session was interrupted when everybody suddenly made a dash from the room. The reason was that an air raid was starting, but there was no sound of gunfire or bombs. I concluded that the nerves of my hosts were wearing a bit jagged. We followed them down a steep flight of steps into an operational room 75 feet below ground-level.

I tried to explain that I was not an Allied emissary; but they asked me to return to Malta and inform the authorities of the offer to surrender. They gave me a scrap of paper with a signature on it. We decided to make for Tunis. We returned to our aircraft and were about to crank her up when four of our fighter-bombers zoomed over at zero feet. Two more fighters sheered off when they spotted the markings on our plane. Twelve single-engined bombers next began bombing the harbour.

Our Tyrolean friend reappeared and advised us to leave at once, as the heavy bombers would probably be coming over very soon. He urged us to leave before the raid started, and we took off, reached Tunisia and landed, and I went to an American camp nearby and produced the Italian surrender chit. My crew, Peter and Les, now call me "The King of Lampedusa."

## 'Happy Landings!' Said the Sergeant with a Grin

From Private Messent comes this entertaining account of high spots in paratroop training. His practice jumps from a balloon and from a bomber did not seem so funny to him at the time. Onlookers got the laughs.

"RIGHT, lads—I want four of you," said our instructor, Sergeant T., having lined us up and inspected our harness. We had been issued with rubber helmets and parachute-packs. Half an hour had been spent in adjusting our cumbersome equipment, then we had waited while two big captive balloons were got ready. Now four of us shambled forward and followed Sergeant T. into the cage suspended beneath one of the balloons. This small, open cage consists mainly of a hole around which four fellows have just room to sit—one with his legs dangling through it. The instructor stands in a corner.

Sergeant T. gave us our jumping numbers —I was Number Four —then clipped the static lines from our chutes to a bar above our heads. "All right, lads?" he asked. We nodded, and he called over the side to a man operating the winch. "Up to 700 feet, four to drop." The balloon started to rise rapidly. Anxiously we watched the ground receding. We were beginning to feel giddy when the sergeant

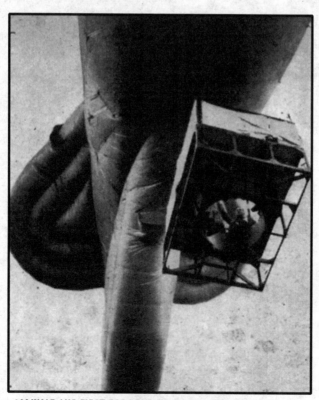

**MAKING HIS FIRST PARACHUTE JUMP, this trainee prepares for action as he ascends in the basket attached to a balloon. This photograph was taken at an R.A.F. station where the R.A.F. and Army collaborate in training. A description is given in the text.** *Photo, British Official: Crown Copyright*

called out, "Don't look down, lads!" For four minutes we continued to rise, and Sergeant T. kept up a stream of jokes. But we didn't laugh.

Suddenly the balloon stopped, with a swaying motion, and we sat there looking dumbly at each other as the wind whistled through the wires. "Action stations, Number One!" Sergeant T.'s yell made us jump. Number One tensed. "Go!" A slight hesitation, and Number One slipped through the hole. Then there were three of us. I sat back, somehow imagining that it was next week and not today that I was jumping. Two more disappeared, then, "Action stations, Number Four!"

"What, me?" I exclaimed, rather foolishly, for I was the only one left—other than the instructor. Reluctantly I swung my legs into the hole—and saw Sergeant T. grinning fiendishly at me. "Go!" I gave a push, and my breath was snatched away. I gasped as I hurtled down, and I remembered I had 175 feet to drop before my chute opened. There was a loud roar above my head, and for a moment, as my descent was checked, I seemed to shoot upwards. I looked up, and it was good to see that canopy of silk above me.

I looked down and gasped again, at a few square inches of water—really a large lake. I turned this way and that, staring at the amazing panorama. A mighty voice from nowhere roared, "A nice exit, Number Four—now watch that landing!" Although I could not see anyone, I realized it must be the officer on the ground giving instructions over the loudspeaker. "Make a turn, Number Four!" Obediently I grabbed the lift-webs above my head and, pulling them, managed to make a turn. Looking down again I saw the ground rushing up at an alarming rate.

I tried to remember Sergeant T.'s instructions about ascertaining drift, when bump!— I sat with my behind tingling, and no doubt wearing an expression of idiotic surprise. "Number Four, that was an awful landing!" Without warning, the wind billowed my chute and I was dragged along the ground at ever-increasing speed until, with a vicious bump, I was airborne again for a moment. As I smacked the ground once more I desperately banged my quick-release box, and after much fidgeting, and being dragged

**DROPPING INTO SPACE** is always a thrilling and dramatic experience for the parachute-jumper. In practice jumping a static line is fastened from the parachute to the plane. As this line becomes taut the cover is ripped off the chute and the latter immediately opens. *Photo, British Official*

another 25 yards, I struggled out of my harness, stood up, galloped after my chute and collapsed it.

So much for the balloon jump. The day came for his first jump from a plane.

WE had been waiting half an hour on the tarmac. Our chutes seemed to be getting heavier, and our backs began to ache. At last our big bomber (" C " for Charlie) came taxi-ing up, and we climbed aboard through the hole in the side and took our places. Sergeant T. hooked the static lines from our chutes to the straps and these, in turn, were hooked to a ring on the side of the plane. There was a terrific roar, and the plane began to move.

I was jumping Number One this time, and was able to watch the ground rushing past as I sat on the very edge of the hole. Suddenly I saw the ground start to leave us. I tried to edge away from that alarming hole now several hundred feet above the ground, but I was not able to move—I was pressed tightly against my companions—so I had to grin and bear it. It was the first time I had been in a plane, and as it dipped from time to time like a boat in a rough sea I managed to complete the illusion by feeling sea-sick. " Happy landings to you all ! " shouted Sergeant T. ; then, as a red light above my head glowed, " Action stations ! " I swung my legs into the hole and sat with an awful sinking sensation in my stomach. The red light changed to green. " Go ! "

I jumped, and gasped as the slipstream hit me. I felt myself jerked about like a marionette. I seemed to turn a somersault. I had no idea whether I was on my head or my heels. Then, in a flash, I was whipped out of the slipstream. It was a relief to be away from that fierce buffeting, though I was swinging violently from side to side as I went down, like a pendulum.

AT this point I should have looked up to see if my parachute was properly opened, because it is often the case when you are spun by the slipstream that your rigging lines become twisted. This can be corrected by kicking out wildly until you start to turn slowly in the opposite direction, thus unravelling your twists ; the canopy can then open fully. But I forgot all about that and became absorbed in the amazing view around and below me. In order further to appreciate it, I decided to put on my glasses. I managed to wriggle my hand underneath my harness and succeeded in withdrawing my spectacle case from my pocket.

Suddenly there came a bellow from a loudspeaker below, "Number One ! What the blazes are you doing ? " Hastily I looked down and saw the ground swooping up. I shoved my specs down the front of my jumping-jacket and grabbed my lift-webs. The ground seemed to rush up and envelop me. I felt my feet touch and immediately went into a roll, thus spreading the shock of impact evenly over my body.

It was a fairly soft landing, but as I lay there the wind caught my chute and I was dragged

along. Unfortunately the ground was very muddy, and there were patches of water. I was dragged faster and faster, trying desperately to get out of my harness. I ploughed through a large puddle, and just as I arrived on the shore I came away from my harness. A spectator told me, when I was free to listen, that I looked exactly like a speedboat as I shot through the water.

As I got to my feet a big plane came over and dropped several instructors. It was meant to be a demonstration drop, to show us how to do it. But the pilot misjudged, and with one exception those instructors were dumped in a line of trees at the side of the dropping-zone. The exception landed in a pond. No one was hurt, but I marvelled at the flow of language that came from the trees as the instructors tried to free themselves. They looked like dolls in giant Christmas trees.

I tried to wring some of the dampness out of me, then rolled up my chute and made for a welcome cup of tea. Sipping it, it suddenly occurred to me that the very first time I had been up in an aeroplane I had hurled myself out !

## I Went 'Square-Bashing' with the Scots Guards

*"' I have just spent a week's ' holiday ' in camp which left me at the end of it scarcely able to stand on my two feet," says Home Guard Ernest Betts. His lively story appears here by arrangement with The Daily Express, in which it was first published.*

I WAS one of a London Home Guard company who volunteered for a week's intensive training with a battalion of the Scots Guards. " You will enjoy it," headquarters said. " We should like to have you with us," said the Guards. It was the first time they had invited a H.G. company to spend a week's holiday with them and enjoy the pleasures of sleeping on a stone floor, of parades at 6.20 a.m., breakfast at 7.15, attacks under fire, and a succession of non-stop exercises at high speed until six in the evening.

Those who were still conscious in the evening moved off at a smart pace to the nearest pub about a mile away, drank beer at the N.A.A.F.I. canteen, or tea at the Y.M.C.A., or went to the films. In my " Old Bill " and " Young Bert " platoon were tailors, barristers, factory workers, butchers, cooks, businessmen, mechanics and clerks. Some of them had taken the week off without pay or closed their businesses. There were boys of 16 and old soldiers of more than 50, with ribbons up and memories of bloody battles in France.

The sergeant in charge of my section was a magistrate. The fierce-looking warrior lying opposite me in the hut was a plumber. At the end of the holiday, he said : " Blimey, I feel like ten men today—nine dead and one paralysed." Every morning we went " square-bashing " (drill on the square), digging our heels into a parade-ground where thousands of men have been lashed into an exact mechanical piston-rod drill by glittering sergeant-majors with backs like pokers and feet like machinery. I have seen a lot of sergeant-majors. But I have never seen anything like the square-bashing sergeant-majors and the sergeants under them on this parade ground.

Probably they had never seen anything like us. Sometimes they said so. An incorrect movement, a man fidgeting with a button, affected them like the loss of a battle. One guilty Home Guard, moving an inch without an order, brought curses and damnation on the whole company. " D'you want to look like a lot of apes ?

Apes walk like this—with their hands splayed out." (The sergeant-major gave a demonstration). "Now get going. Move ! When you get off this parade, your bones have got to be sore, and I'll see that they *are* sore ! "

THESE words had a wonderful effect on the whole company. They were polite words to Home Guards not in the Scots Guards. Dimly, as we "swung them arms" and bashed the square, we realized that thus were the battles won in Tunisia—on this square, on the playing-fields of the sergeant-majors.

All day we were fanatically on the move, doubled off our feet, hurled into assault courses in which Bren guns spat live ammunition over our heads. And if you were on guard after all this, you spat and polished your way towards a sergeant-major who said : " The acid test of a soldier is that he should be able to stand still." That was easy. But how do you stand *up* ? " Blimey," said the plumber after we'd routed the enemy, " my feet are so stuck together tonight, they can't ——well stand at ease ! " But he never missed a parade. As the course became more strenuous and the sweat poured down our backs, we warmed up to the pattern and meaning of it all.

These Scots Guards, moving up from a long tradition of split-second discipline and hard fighting, had an incomparable efficiency and dash, a brilliant common sense in the conduct of war. To us amateurs they were inspiring. For the best we could do was a mere shadow of what they normally did as trained infantry ready for battle. Their

**WHEN A PARACHUTIST LANDS** he releases the harness as speedily as possible to prevent himself being dragged along the ground. Landing is by no means an easy operation—as this photograph clearly shows. *Photo, British Official : Crown Copyright*

officers and N.C.O.s had been in action and were bang up to date with information from the battle front and the dirtiest tricks of the enemy.

They had an extraordinary patience. Chesty sergeants and sinewy corporals, with voices like klaxons and muscles of steel, did everything themselves which they expected us to do. Faster. Better. They shot across the ground like electric hares. When it came to square-bashing they were miracles of smooth, harmonious movement. In the field they had the aggressiveness of tanks. Most of our exercises were carried out in hot, green, Surrey fields to a sound of guns, rifle fire, cuckoos and bees, and the order to "Move, move, it isn't a funeral."

Here, for example, is the programme for one day's holiday at Government expense : Reveille: 06.00 hrs. P.T., 06.20 hrs. Breakfast : 07.15 hrs. Hut inspection : 08.00 hrs. Training : 08.15 hrs. (fieldcraft ; drill with arms). Dinner : 12.15 hrs. Fire and movement (an attack in which ball ammunition is fired to within 30 yards of the objective) : 13.15 hrs. Tea : 18.00 hrs. Guard mounting: 18.45 hrs.

During all this sweating around on stomach and feet the grub was lovely A typical dinner menu consisted of roast beef, baked potatoes, swedes, bread, apricots and custard. Supper (when it took the place of tea) was : Beans on fried bread, gravy, tea, marmalade, bread, margarine. There was always tons of food, and it was always boiling hot. I had the best porridge I have ever eaten.

No doubt the Guards had a good laugh at us now and then. We were always parading in front of them, always under their cool, informed, practised scrutiny. But it got around, all the same, that we had done quite a good job for a bunch of amateurs. And we packed more training into the week than we

ever had in months of crawling across Golders Green or Kilburn or Hampstead Heath. And the Scots Guards paid us the highest compliment as citizen soldiers ; they admitted us to a ceremonial parade.

At the end of it some one said to the plumber : "And what do *you* know about soldiering ? " "Nothing, mate," he grinned. "If I did, I wouldn't have come down to this ―― place !" He looked at his feet. "Blimey, they'd go on parade now without my even askin' them," he said. He spoke for a lot of feet—feet better for a tough, tactical holiday.

## They Gave Me the United States Air Cross

*A former London policeman, now a British naval observer with the U.S. Air Force in North Africa, Lieut. Brian Aikens, of Ealing, has been honoured by America for courageous action in mid-air. Here is the story, as told by him to Reuters Correspondent*

A FORMATION of about 24 Flying Fortresses was ordered to attack a convoy. The aeroplane in which I was stationed in the nose with the bombardier was in the rear formation, which was unescorted.

Lieut. BRIAN AIKENS, who tells here the story of how he won the U.S. Air Cross. He displayed great gallantry during an attack on an enemy convoy. *Photo, J. O'Brien*

When we got near the enemy ships we were heavily attacked by enemy fighters. Between 30 and 35 of them put in about a dozen attacks in all. A minute before we got over our target to drop our bombs a 20-mm. cannon shell tore through the Fortress and hit the back of the bombardier's seat. It exploded, blew his parachute into tiny pieces and wounded him badly in the back.

A few shell fragments hit me, but they only caused cuts. I got behind his seat and propped him up in my arms. He was losing blood, but he never complained. He kept his eyes on the bombsight, and only when he had reported by the inter-telephone to the captain, "Bombs away, doors closed," did he relax, but only for a moment.

Then he turned to me and said : " Don't bother about me. Look out for fighters." I grabbed a gun and fired when anything came into my sights. I don't know if I hit anything.

When the enemy fighters made off after a few minutes I went back to the bombardier, dressed his wounds and gave him some dope tablets. He is one of the pluckiest chaps I have ever met. Though our Fortress was badly shot up, we got it home safely.

# OUR DIARY OF THE WAR

**JUNE 9, 1943, Wednesday**    *1,376th day*
**North Africa.**—Announced that prisoners taken during the Tunisian fighting total 291,000.
**Mediterranean.**—U.S. heavy bombers attacked Sicilian airfields of Catania and Gerbini. Allied air forces concentrated on Pantelleria.
**Russian Front.**—Loss of Oranienbaum, 20 m. W. of Leningrad, admitted by Berlin radio.
**General.**—Vice-Adml. Sir John H. D. Cunningham appointed C.-in-C. the Levant.

**JUNE 10, Thursday**    *1,377th day*
**Mediterranean.**—Bombing of Pantelleria continued ; 37 enemy aircraft destroyed in these and Wednesday night's attacks.
**Russian Front.**—Over 700 Russian aircraft raided enemy aerodromes, destroying or damaging 150 German aircraft on the ground.
**Australasia.**—U.S. Fortresses and Liberators dropped nearly 40 tons of bombs on Rabaul, New Britain.
**General.**—Germany and Italy recognised new Argentine Govt. Moscow announced dissolution of the Comintern.

**JUNE 11, Friday**    *1,378th day*
**Air.**—200 U.S. Flying Fortresses (unescorted) attacked Wilhelmshaven and Cuxhaven U-boat bases ; 8 bombers missing. At night, R.A.F. heavily attacked Düsseldorf (more than two sq. miles devastated) and Munster ; 43 bombers missing.
**Mediterranean.**—After 13 days' intense bombardment, Italian island of Pantelleria surrendered with 15,000 troops ; enemy reports indicated 1,000 aircraft took part in final attack. Lampedusa bombarded from the sea.
**Australasia.**—Liberators dropped 28 tons of bombs on Kupang, Dutch Timor.
**Burma.**—R.A.F. attacked Rathedaung, Buthidaung and Jap H.Q. on the Chindwin.
**General.**—New Argentine Govt. recognised by Britain and U.S.A.

**JUNE 12, Saturday**    *1,379th day*
**Air.**—R.A.F. bombed Bochum (Central Ruhr) in severe night attack.
**Mediterranean.**—Lampedusa, again bombarded, surrendered. U.S. bombers attacked Sicilian airfields.
**Australasia.**—25 Jap planes shot down near the Russell Islands by U.S. fighters.
**Burma.**—U.S. bombers attacked Man-

dalay by day ; the R.A.F. attacked by night. Other objectives bombed by R.A.F. in Arakan.
**China.**—Chungking announced that Chinese had pierced Jap line on the Yangtse.
**Russian Front.** — Soviet bombers attacked Gomel, Briansk and Karachev by night.
**General.**—H.M. the King, accompanied by the Sec. of State for War, Sir James Grigg, and the Sec. of State for Air, Sir A. Sinclair, arrived in N. Africa from England.
Mr. Churchill announced Axis lost 137 ships in the Tunisian campaign, totalling 433,400 tons.

**JUNE 13, Sunday**    *1,380th day*
**Air.**—U.S. heavy bombers (unescorted) raided Kiel and Bremen ; 26 machines lost. Reconnaissance showed fires still burning in Düsseldorf after Friday's attack.
**Mediterranean.**—Destroyer Nubian accepted surrender of Italian island of Linosa. U.S.A. heavy bombers raided Catania and Gerbini in Sicily.

★ ━━━━━ *Flash-backs* ━━━━━ ★

### 1940
June 10.  *Announced Allied forces withdrawn from Narvik and King Haakon and Norwegian Govt. were in London.*
   *French Govt. left Paris for Tours. Italy declared war against Britain and France.*
June 11.  *Italians bombed Malta.*
June 14.  *Germans entered Paris. French Govt. moved to Bordeaux.*
June 16.  *British offer of Anglo-French union rejected.*
June 17.  *Marshal Pétain asked Germany for an armistice. Evacuation of B.E.F. from France completed.*
June 18.  *In a broadcast from London, Gen. de Gaulle appealed to all Frenchmen to fight on.*

*Heavy air raids on Britain began.*

### 1941
June 11-12.  *R.A.F. raids on the Ruhr, Rhineland and N.W. Germany began.*
June 21.  *Damascus (Syria) occupied by the Free French.*
June 22.  *Germany invaded Russia.*

### 1942
June 9.  *British and U.S. Air Force units arrived in China.*
June 10.  *Prague announced Lidice massacre.*
June 17.  *El Adem and Sidi Rezegh (Libya) abandoned by British.*
June 18.  *Mr. Churchill arrived in U.S.A.*
June 21.  *Rommel captured Tobruk.*

**JUNE 14, Monday**    *1,381st day*
**Air.**—R.A.F. raided Oberhausen (Ruhr); 18 bombers lost.
**Mediterranean.**—Island of Lampione occupied by Allied naval party.
**Home Front.**—Creation announced of a Tactical Air Force of the R.A.F., based on this country ; Air Vice-Marshal J. H. D'Albiac appointed to the command.
**General.**—H.M. the King reviewed U.S. 5th Army in N. Africa.

**JUNE 15, Tuesday**    *1,382nd day*
**Australasia.**—Allied aircraft raided Rabaul, New Britain. Beaufighters strafed the Markham Valley, New Guinea.
**General.**—Turkish-Syrian frontier closed on Syrian side. Reported that the Germans had evacuated the Lofoten Islands.

**JUNE 16, Wednesday**    *1,383rd day*
**Air.**—Cologne bombed for 115th time.
**Mediterranean.**—Naples bombed.
**Australasia.**—Ninety-four Jap aircraft destroyed over Guadalcanal by Americans.

**JUNE 17, Thursday**    *1,384th day*
**Mediterranean.**—U.S. Liberators pounded Sicilian airfields of Biscari and Comiso ; R.A.F. hit Comiso again at night. Naples again bombed.
**Burma.**—Liberators bombed Lashio.
**General.**—Turco-Syrian frontier reopened.

**JUNE 18, Friday**    *1,385th day*
**Mediterranean.**—Bombers from N.W. Africa and Middle East bases continued attacks on Sicily, Sardinia, especially town of Messina. Reported that Naples and Sicilian towns were being evacuated.
**General.**—Announced Field-Marshal Sir A. O. Wavell to be Viceroy of India (from Oct.) in succession to Lord Linlithgow ; Gen. Sir C. J. E. Auchinleck to succeed Wavell as C.-in-C. India ; East Asia Command to be set up.

**JUNE 19, Saturday**    *1,386th day*
**Air.**—R.A.F. heavily bombed Schneider arms works at Le Creusot, S. of Paris ; 3 bombers missing.
**Pacific.**—Announced that Liberators and Catalinas had successfully raided Jap-held Nauru Island.
**General.**—H.M. the King inspected the 8th Army in N. Africa.

**JUNE 20, Sunday**    *1,387th day*
**Air.**—R.A.F. Lancasters, without loss, smashed Germany's largest radiolocation factory, at Friedrichshafen, after which they flew on to N. Africa.
**Sea.**—Admiralty announced biggest U-boat offensive took place during 5 days in May ; 97 per cent of convoyed ships got through ; 2 U-boats sunk for certain, and a number of probables.
**Australasia.**—22 Jap planes destroyed or crippled in enemy attack on the Darwin area, Australia.
**General.**—H.M. the King visited Malta ; journeyed from N. Africa aboard the cruiser Aurora.

**JUNE 21, Monday**    *1,388th day*
**Air.**—Krefeld (10 m. W. of the Ruhr) blasted by R.A.F. ; 44 bombers missing out of more than 700.
**Mediterranean.**—U.S. heavy bombers attacked Reggio di Calabria and San Giovanni.

**JUNE 22, Tuesday**    *1,389th day*
**Air.**—Huls, Antwerp and Rotterdam docks bombed. Concentrated attack on Mulheim by R.A.F. ; 35 bombers missing.
**General.**—H.M. the King returned from Malta to N. Africa.

**W**HAT is the real meaning of this word "prang" that crops up so often in our airmen's accounts of their flying experiences? Recently the subject has been given considerable space in the correspondence columns of The Daily Telegraph; but alas, the explanations are as varied and contradictory as they are numerous. "No one will deny that the engaging expression 'to prang a target' is vivid in the extreme," wrote the initiator of the discussion; "when and how this word came into use in the R.A.F. I do not know, but I hazard a guess that it is derived from the Scots word *pran* or *prann*, meaning to hurt or wound (Gaelic, *pronn*, to pound or mash). Another possible origin, although in my opinion less likely, is from the Norwegian *prange*, meaning to make a parade or great show."

**A** FEW days later a Flight-Sergeant in the R.A.F. stated that the word first came into use after the Norwegian evacuation, when it was used to describe the effects of a few 500-pounders on the invasion ports and enemy naval bases. "A three-pronged fork or trident pins anything down most effectively," he wrote; "so does a heavy bombing raid. When completed efficiently the pranging is known as a 'wizard prang'." Another correspondent pointed out that in Devonshire "pranging" is one of the oldest known methods of fishing; "to prang is to stab from above, and a prang is a multi-pronged barbed fork attached to a ten-foot pole." Yet another declared that the word was introduced into this country by members of the R.A.F. who have seen service in Malaya, since *pérang* is the Malay word for war and *perangi* means to attack. But already it had been stated that "our South African cousins who gave us this word will confirm that 'to prang' is the Zulu for 'to spear.'"

**U**NFORTUNATELY I have neither a Malay nor a Zulu dictionary on my shelf, so am unable to confirm these etymologies; and the many English dictionaries that lie within reach have not proved to be very helpful. From Skeat I learn, however (under the entry Prong), that in Middle English there was a verb *pranglen*, to constrain, derived from a Teutonic base, prang—to compress, nip, push, pierce. Related words are the Dutch *prangen*, to press, and the German *pranger*, a pillory. But this derivation is not very helpful—though it would be nice to know that, since it is the Germans who are being most effectively pranged, we have chosen a good old German word to describe their ordeal. I am convinced, however, that we are making a mystery out of nothing. Here, I feel sure, is the one and only explanation worthy of acceptance.

I take it from another letter in The Daily Telegraph's correspondence; it is from Group Capt. Patrick King, who writes:

The first time I heard the word "prang" I asked the pilot officer who used it, "Why prang?" His reply was, "Well, what else could you call it?" In other words, prang is an onomatopoeia derived from the sound of the impact of a metal aircraft with the ground. Its usage in connexion with enemy targets is a natural and obvious extension, but the word was coined as being more expressive than "crash," which was adequate in the days of wooden aircraft. So please may the experts refrain from devising far-fetched explanations for this simple word. We are not experts in either Gaelic or Norwegian in the Royal Air Force; but we retain the knack of

coining the right word without thinking how we do it. Prang is a worthy successor to joy-stick and all the other flying slang of long ago.

**M**R. BERT THOMAS, best remembered of the caricaturists of the last War, is still going strong in this one. The numerous lively and telling posters he has thrown off as propaganda for the home front need no signature, his style is so individual. But in a delightful little portfolio of 16 pp. that has just come to my table from Raphael Tuck (price 1s. 6d.) the signature is essential, as Bert has broken out in a new place with Close-ups Through a Child's Eyes. The

**VICE-ADM. SIR JOHN H. D. CUNNINGHAM, K.C.B., M.V.O.,** whose appointment as C.-in-C., Levant (with acting rank of Admiral) was announced on June 10, 1943. In command of the 1st Cruiser Squadron at the beginning of the War, he was until recently Fourth Sea Lord of the Admiralty. *Photo, Topical Press*

coloured portraits of Mr. Churchill, Mr. Roosevelt, "Premier Stalin" and other familiar figures, including "Five Bad Men," are all highly amusing and might well have been drawn by a child with a touch of genius. They are instinct with life and the humour of life and the letterpress, which gives a good imitation of infantile calligraphy, is nearly—but not quite—as funny as the pictures. Stalin and "Eleanor" (Mrs. Roosevelt, if you please!) are masterpieces. Young and old alike will enjoy this little artistic *jeu d'esprit*—if they are able to get a copy.

**T**HERE comes from a reader in Preston a letter which will be of interest to those who live in London. "On reading back the articles in THE WAR ILLUSTRATED on the blitz (he writes), I came across a caption to a photograph which said that London had borrowed 2,000 buses from the Provinces; and I recalled that one day last week, while travelling on a Corporation bus in Preston, I noticed that inside, behind the driver's cab, there was a small brown plaque lettered London 1940-41. This bus must have been one of those which Preston sent to London at that time. It would be interesting to know

if this practice is general amongst all the 2,000 buses concerned." On inquiry at the headquarters of London Transport I am informed that 2,000 buses were offered to London in those difficult days, but it was found necessary to accept the loan of only 500. They came from 44 provincial cities and towns, from Inverness to Plymouth, from Manchester (88 came from here) to Southend. All have now been returned, and with each was supplied a plaque such as my correspondent describes. It was a thoughtful little tribute to good friends of London which all good Londoners will be glad to know was paid.

"**I**NVASION" is very much in the air just now. Vast military movements are in progress, and it is but natural that we should feel some curiosity as to the destination of the men in khaki, navy, and Air Force blue whom we see setting out. But we must not express our curiosity in words—unless we are willing to expose our informant to a court-martial for having imparted secret information to an unauthorized person. These courts-martial are held in secret—necessarily so; but here are officially-released details of several that will show how seriously the offence is regarded.

A senior officer, after taking part in a combined operations exercise, went on leave. He asked a friend to dinner, told her that he was going abroad, and that he believed the opening of a Second Front was imminent. He gave dates, and particulars of the forces involved, including the First Army. Details were also given of the equipment issued, which gave some indication of the probable theatre of operations. The lady passed on this information, and it came to the notice of the authorities. Notwithstanding evidence of excellent character and service, the officer was sentenced to be cashiered and imprisoned for a year. In another case a man employed on clerical duties which gave him access to secret information of troop movements, met a stranger in a public house. Drinks were stood, and the stranger asked him about his work. He implied that he was a confidential clerk with important duties, and went on to substantiate this impression by telling the stranger that a named division was going abroad to Egypt and was to be replaced by another division which he also named. For this disclosure of troop movements the man was sentenced to 112 days' imprisonment.

Then there was a man about to go overseas who posted a letter on shore to his wife, giving a code which he would use, so as to enable her to identify the places at which his ship touched. Thus "Brenda" stood for Gibraltar, and "Cissie" for Malta. The man realized that this was wrong since he added, "Whatever you do you must tell no one; you might become a widow if you do." For this and for sending other information he was sentenced to 6 months' imprisonment. In yet another case an officer, whose work concerned equipment for operations abroad, discussed with a friend the destination of a relative on embarkation leave. This relative was a doctor, and expert in tropical diseases. The officer said to his friend that this pointed towards an African operation and that this fitted in with the work on which he was engaged, mentioning a certain class of equipment. The officer was severely reprimanded.

Each of these stories is true; each conveys the one, all-important moral: In wartime we all must belong to the Silent Service.

**F**ORMING the second volume of their Britain at War series, Messrs. Hutchinson have just published Major E. W. Sheppard's The Army (from January 1941 to March 1942). Priced at a guinea, it is a well-produced and lavishly-illustrated volume — there are 490 photographs, etc., and a number of maps. As for the text, Major Sheppard has done justice to a great theme

# Sailors of the Netherlands Navy in Action

*Photo, Topical Press*

**HOLLAND FIGHTS ON.** Aboard a Royal Netherlands Naval torpedo-boat, this A.A. gunner and officer spotter are fully prepared for enemy attack. Their small but fast vessel of 325 tons, brought to this country by its crew in 1940, performs important night patrols off our coasts. The torpedo-boat's armament includes 2-in. guns.

Printed in England and published every alternate Friday by the Proprietors, THE AMALGAMATED PRESS, LTD., The Fleetway House, Farringdon Street, London, E.C.4. Registered for transmission by Canadian Magazine Post. Sole Agents for Australia and New Zealand : Messrs. Gordon & Gotch, Ltd. ; and for South Africa : Central News Agency, Ltd.—July 9, 1943. S.S. *Editorial Address :* JOHN CARPENTER HOUSE, WHITEFRIARS, LONDON, E.C.4

Vol 7     The War Illustrated     N° 159

Edited by Sir John Hammerton

SIXPENCE                                          JULY 23, 1943

REGAL SMILE FOR MALTA'S DEFENDER.   H.M. the King arrived at Malta from N. Africa aboard H.M.S. Aurora on June 20, 1943.
Amid the right royal welcome accorded him by the delighted George Cross Islanders (see p. 101) he drove to the Governor's Palace in
Valetta, and this photograph, taken in the palace's Hall of St. Michael and St. George, shows His Majesty presenting Viscount Gort, Malta's
Governor and C.-in-C., with his Field-Marshal's baton.   Viscount Gort was created Field-Marshal on Jan. 1, 1943.          *Photo, British Official*

NO. 160 WILL BE PUBLISHED FRIDAY, AUGUST 6

# THE BATTLE FRONTS

## by Maj.-Gen. Sir Charles Gwynn, K.C.B., D.S.O.

ON July 5 the prolonged lull in land fighting was broken. At the time I am writing it is impossible to give a definite opinion as to the scale and object of the German offensive. If it achieved greater success than there is any reason to expect, it might develop into a threat to Moscow. It seems more probable, however, that it has the limited double object of forestalling Russian offensive plans and of shortening the front by ironing out the Russian salient in the Kursk region.

The exposed position of the Orel salient has also probably influenced German action. Failing an offensive to straighten the front a difficult withdrawal from the salient would probably have been necessary, a course which might have aggravated German depression.

These objects would be consistent with a defensive policy on the Russian front necessitated by the growing threat of Allied offensive action in the Mediterranean and on the Western seaboard.

It would not surprise me if the intensification of Russian air raids on both sides of the Kerch straits is an indication that signs have been observed of a German intention to evacuate the Kuban—a probability if the Germans aim to shorten their front.

The German offensive in Russia opens again the possibility that Japan might seize it as an opportunity to attempt to eliminate the latent threat to Tokyo from Vladivostok.

The Allied offensive in the Pacific has made a good start, and the scale on which it has been undertaken is a welcome sign of the improvement in the shipping position. Rapid sensational results cannot be expected, however, unless the Japanese fleet seeks decisive action in an attempt to restore her naval situation before it becomes worse.

**EUROPE** Threatened at many points on the immense length of perimeter she has to defend, but so far only actually engaged on land on one front—the Russian—Germany's strategic problems, as they affect the dispositions of her armies, are very different from those of the last war. Then her Western and Eastern forces were fully deployed, each with its quota of reserves behind it, and they were engaged with armies also deployed.

The theatres of war were, in fact, well defined and there was no necessity to maintain a strong central reserve to meet unforeseeable emergencies. The distances between the two fronts and the strategic railways connecting them were such that, as the situation developed, it could be met by transferring strength from one front to the other and by adapting the attitude, offensive or defensive, on each to circumstances.

In this war, under present conditions, a fairly strong central reserve is essential to Germany. On her active Russian front she must maintain a fully deployed army with its quota of reserves, but greater distances and a much less conveniently laid-out system of strategic railways make it impracticable to transfer troops rapidly from this front to

points of danger on the threatened sectors of her perimeter. She cannot, of course, in these threatened sectors employ, without gross waste of power, fully deployed armies, nor can she leave the sectors without adequate forces to meet the first brunt of an attack should one be made. Obviously the forces deployed must therefore be kept to a minimum, with sufficient reserves immediately available to meet an attack in its initial phase.

But it is an irreducible minimum entailing waste of power in all sectors not actually attacked. Germany, in fact, has a very considerable part of her army dispersed inactive and yet non-transferable. The forces thus employed might be able to repel an overseas invasion, but they would have little offensive power to counter-attack an enemy who had once established a substantial footing. For counter-offensive purposes, and to avoid transfers from the active Russian front, which would probably have a very disturbing effect on the strategic situation there, a strong central reserve would clearly be the only possible solution.

Moreover, since the threat exists at a number of points on the perimeter, without good lateral communication between them, the reserve would have to be of sufficient

GEN. W. SIKORSKI, Polish Prime Minister and C.-in-C., who was killed in an air crash near Gibraltar on July 4, 1943. In one of the last photographs taken of him, Gen. Sikorski is here seen acknowledging the salute at a march past of Polish troops in Iraq. Paying tribute to the memory of this great Polish patriot and staunch ally, Mr. Churchill described him as "a man of remarkable pre-eminence both as a statesman and a soldier."
*Photo, U.S. Official*

strength to reinforce several points simultaneously. Presumably the central reserve would not be highly concentrated but disposed in groups which would facilitate rapid reinforcement of any sector under attack; so that a counter-attacking force could be concentrated before the enemy was fully deployed and established, but when he was sufficiently committed to make his defeat a much more important success than the mere repulse of an initial landing.

The comparatively slow process of deploying an army invading from overseas undoubtedly opens exceptional opportunities for successful counter-blows. The weakness of the Axis situation is that the central reserve would be earmarked for a particular role and it could no longer safely be employed to effect a great concentration for offensive purposes in Russia, as was apparently done last year when risk of a large-scale invasion in the West was practically non-existent, and when no threat had developed on the Mediterranean front.

So far as the Russian front is concerned, the main use that could be made of the central reserve would be to treat it as a pool in which fresh formations could be exchanged for those that had become exhausted in active fighting. The effect of being compelled to retain so much of her army in a state of inactive suspense over long periods, in addition to being a waste of force, may be seriously damaging to the morale of troops, especially at a time when the morale of the civil population is showing signs of weakness; for it is among those least actively employed that rumour spreads.

From the foregoing considerations I would conclude that Germany is unlikely to attempt a major offensive on the Russian front this summer; and that her main hope of achieving an important success would be, not so much by repulsing attempts at invasion, as by inflicting a disastrous defeat on a force which had landed and was fully committed, though not yet at great enough strength to meet successfully the counter-attacks Germany's available reserves could deliver.

The dispersion of the Luftwaffe over so many areas may be an even more serious matter for Germany than the dispersion of her armies, because there is a constant drain on its strength on threatened sectors before

**R.A.F. MOSQUITOES IN MALTA** have taken a prominent part in many sorties over Italy and Sicily. They have repeatedly shot up trains, airfields, and attacked shipping in the Mediterranean. Soldiers while working with the R.A.F. on a Maltese airfield are here shown helping to move a Mosquito in order to check compass errors. *Photo, British Official: Crown Copyright*

NEW GEORGIA BATTLE AREA includes Rendova Island, the scene of U.S. landings on June 30, 1943. The Jap garrison was destroyed and the island occupied. Top relief map shows strategic points in this vital war centre. By July 5 Jap garrisons were seriously threatened on Kolombangara and New Georgia itself. Left, supplies for U.S. forces on New Caledonia are lowered from a freighter into a 2½-ton amphibious lorry. Right, American troops disembark at a base in the S.W. Pacific. Lt.-Gen. Kreuger, commanding the U.S. 6th Army, is seen on the left.

*Photos, Associated Press, New York Times Photos; map by courtesy of The Daily Express*

the threat matures on any one. The maintenance and protection of airfields in all menaced areas must also entail a heavy drain on resources even if the aircraft using them can normally be kept to a low figure.

## S.W. PACIFIC
The American and Australian offensive that started in the first week of July has so far evidently had the object of getting within striking distance of the more important Japanese advanced bases. This to some extent necessitates a step-by-step capture of the Japanese outpost islands in order to secure airfields from which a further advance could be supported. (*See map p. 109.*)

In the process it is no doubt hoped that the Japanese air power will suffer from attrition, and still more that the Japanese fleet will be induced to come into action. It may, however, be safely assumed that the Allies have not undertaken the interminable task of clearing out the Japanese systematically from all their island footholds. The main objective of the present operation is presumably Rabaul, the base that is so important to Japan both for offensive and defensive purposes.

The ultimate object of all amphibious operations in the Pacific must, however, be the destruction of Japanese sea power, without

which the card house she has built must collapse. The Japanese fleet cannot be compelled to come into action, though it may be induced to seek decisive battle. Neither fleet is likely to risk an engagement outside the cover of its own shore-based air umbrella and within that of its opponents; but where the umbrellas overlap, as they do in the Solomons, a decisive naval engagement might take place.

The operations at Guadalcanal and in New Guinea have shown how long it may take to clear each Japanese nest; but with the growing strength of the Allies it will not be necessary to complete the clearance of one before another is attacked. The manner in which these latest landings have been accomplished is very encouraging. Not only have the equipment and preparations been of a much higher standard than at Guadalcanal, but the troops have evidently been much better trained and consequently quicker in action. The magnificent American Marines have again shown their value as a spearhead in amphibious operations.

THE Munda base cannot be expected to fall with the same rapidity as the small post on Rendova island; for the Japanese, in considerable force and strongly entrenched,

are certain to fight with their accustomed tenacity. Under artillery fire and bombing attacks they should, however, have no offensive power to interfere with further enterprises.

The capture of Salamaua, in New Guinea, may prove even more difficult than that of Munda; but the experience the Australian troops have gained should be of immense value and may help to expedite matters.

On the whole it would be unwise to expect any rapid or sensational successes, and the main points of interest are whether the Japanese will continue to sacrifice large numbers of aircraft while they are in a position of air inferiority and, more important, whether their navy will intervene in the struggle, risking again the serious losses they suffered at Guadalcanal. Obviously the Japanese could in a short time assemble heavy concentrations of both air and sea power if they considered the retention of their advanced outposts was worth the risk, and if they felt so good an opportunity for a counter-stroke might not occur again when the Allies had multiplied the number of their air bases and in general increased their strength. The longer they postpone decisive action the more will they feel the effects of the wide dispersion of their forces.

# His Majesty's Triumphant N. African Tour

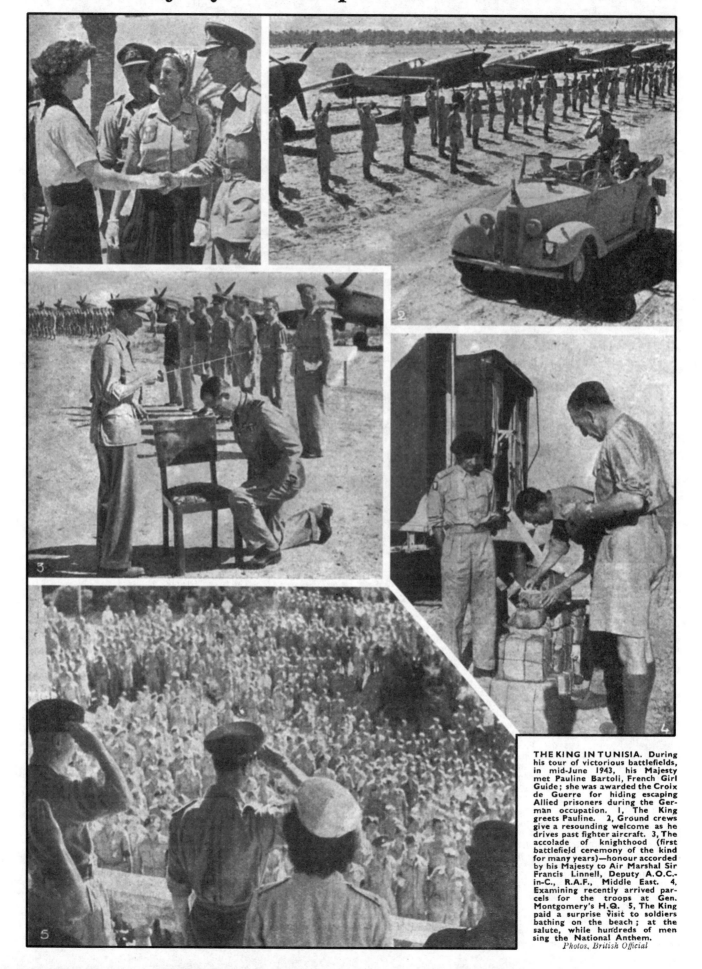

THE KING IN TUNISIA. During his tour of victorious battlefields, in mid-June 1943, his Majesty met Pauline Bartoli, French Girl Guide; she was awarded the Croix de Guerre for hiding escaping Allied prisoners during the German occupation. I, The King greets Pauline. 2, Ground crews give a resounding welcome as he drives past fighter aircraft. 3, The accolade of knighthood (first battlefield ceremony of the kind for many years)—honour accorded by his Majesty to Air Marshal Sir Francis Linnell, Deputy A.O.C.-in-C., R.A.F., Middle East. 4, Examining recently arrived parcels for the troops at Gen. Montgomery's H.Q. 5, The King paid a surprise visit to soldiers bathing on the beach; at the salute, while hundreds of men sing the National Anthem.

*Photos, British Official*

# Joyously the Maltese Welcomed Their King

THE KING IN MALTA. Arriving from N. Africa for a visit to the George Cross island on June 20, 1943, his Majesty is seen (1) saluting Britain's Mediterranean fortress as the cruiser Aurora enters Valetta harbour. 2, A young Maltese girl presents a bouquet. Accompanied by Lord Gort, the King toured badly bombed districts; here (3) he is conversing with his guide, the parish priest of the devastated city of Senglea. 4, The Royal car passing through the packed streets of Valetta. 5, In Kingsway, Valetta's main thoroughfare, the King received a tumultuous welcome. On the right is seen the bombed opera house. Malta will long remember this Royal visit, concluded by the King's return to N. Africa.

*Photos, British Official: Crown Copyright reserved*

# Air Power Alone Claims Its First Real Triumph

**ALLIED OCCUPATION OF PANTELLERIA** was carried out on June 11, 1943 (see pages 70, 71) after an unprecedented air assault. The landing force consisted of troops of the British 1st Division. Some of our men are seen amid the ruins (1) after the Italian island's surrender, enjoying a brief rest. 2, The General in charge of landing operations (smoking pipe) is shown with other officers; in the background the Union Jack flies triumphantly. 3, Devastation in the harbour testifies to our terrific preliminary pounding of the port. The shattered hulk in the foreground was once an enemy invasion barge.

*Photos, British Official; Crown Copyright*

# Over Lampedusa's Battlements Our Flag Unfurls

**CAPTURE OF SECOND ITALIAN ISLAND.** When the British destroyer H.M.S. Troubridge escorted landing-craft to Lampedusa, 70 Coldstream Guardsmen were among the troops who took possession of the former Axis U-boat base (see page 70). 1, Two Guardsmen proudly hoist the Union Jack above the Italian battlements. The airfield suffered great devastation; 2, wrecked Ju 52s were among the smashed aircraft that littered the ground. 3, Italian prisoners pile captured weapons and ammunition in the square of the little port after our forces occupied the battered island, June 12, 1943, following the fall of Pantelleria (opposite page). PAGE 103 *Photos, British Official: Crown Copyright*

FLIGHT DECK

AIRCRAFT LIFT

ENGINE EQUIPMENT

UPPER DECK

(MAIN (OR 1ST) UPPER DECK)

(LOWER (OR UPPER) TWEEN) DECK

(ORLOP (OR LOWER) TWEEN) DECK

AS SHE APPEARS BOW

**WOOLWORTH CARRIERS** — so called because of their speedy mass-production — are now operating with the British and American Navies, giving vital air cover to our convoys in mid-Atlantic. These ships constitute one of the new weapons which have helped to turn the U-boat war in our favour.

In March 1943, when Colonel Knox, Secretary of the U.S. Navy, referred to new auxiliary aircraft-carriers, it was stated that these were ex-merchant vessels of more than 17,000 tons, with a speed of 18·5 knots, armed with light A.A. weapons and machine-guns, and carrying up to 30 fighter-aircraft, or from 15 to 20 torpedo-bombers.

The carrier shown in the above drawing is one of these converted U.S. merchantmen and was visited some time ago by H.M. the King. She is driven by Diesel engines, without funnels. Bridge and masts are placed outboard, thus leaving a clear flight deck connected by a lift to a hangar below. Outstanding features

include commodious cabins for officers and extensive quarters for the crew.

Details: 1, Laundry; 2, Sick Bay; 3, Operating Theatre; 4, Stores; 5, Aviation Stores; 6, Cafeteria; 7, Aircraft Hangar; 8, Cinema Projector; 9, Wireless Room; 10, Photographer; 11, Stores; 12, Hold; 13, Officers' Cabins; 14, Aero Fitters' Shop; 15, Diesel Engines; 16, Stokers' Mess; 17, Chief Engineer's Office; 18, Fans; 19, Captain's Cabin; 20, Ward Room; 21, Officers' Galley; 22, Soda Fountain; 23, Shop; 24, Gyro Room; 25, Engineers' Stores; 26, , Stores; 27, Pumps; 28, Hold; 29, Parachute Compartment; 30, Passage; 31, Aircraft Pilots' Cabins; 32, Quarter Deck; 33, Communications; 34, Crew's Reading Room; 35, Crew's Berthing; 36, Bulk Stores; 37, Deep Ballast Tanks; 38, Loud Hailer; 39, Flying Control Officer; 40, Bridge; 41, Coding Rooms; 42, Deck Offices; 43, Crew's Mess and Berthing; 44, Bulk Stores; 45, Hold; 46, Ballast; 47, Passages; 48, Stores.

*Drawn by G. H. Davis, from sketches made in an escort carrier by permission of the Admiralty. Reproduced by courtesy of The Illustrated London News*

# THE WAR AT SEA

## by Francis E. McMurtrie

EVIDENCE accumulates to show that the defeat of the U-boats in the Battle of the Atlantic is more far-reaching than at first supposed. Endless excuses have been made by Axis propaganda agencies to palliate the fact that the enemy submarines are no longer able to carry out a really dangerous attack on a convoy provided with adequate escort. Thus the long-established and well-tried principle of convoy for merchant ships in wartime has once more been vindicated.

One of the earliest excuses, which to some may have sounded plausible, was that U-boats had to be withdrawn from the Atlantic trade routes and concentrated in waters nearer home, so that they might resist the coming invasion of Europe. Apart from the reduced effectiveness of submarines operating in coastal waters, the feeble opposition offered by them when N. Africa was occupied demonstrates the fallacy of this theory.

Another report was that German submarines were being taken in hand for re-arming with a preponderance of anti-aircraft guns, owing to the increased number of planes now used for convoy protection. Though there may be some truth in this, it falls far short of an adequate explanation of the greatly reduced scale of attack in June.

That U-boats are being strengthened to enable them to withstand the shock of heavy depth-charge explosions is also improbable. Short of complete rebuilding, it is difficult to see how any appreciable addition could be made to the present resisting power of a submarine hull. It is much more likely that it has been decided to re-design the standard type of U-boat, a task that must inevitably result in the whole submarine building programme being held up for a number of months. What this must mean to the enemy at the present crisis in the war can be imagined. It goes far to explain the doleful tone of recent Axis utterances.

### AVAILABLE U-Boat Crew Reserves Depleted

Apart from this possibility, it is obvious that heavy losses at the rate of more than one submarine a day, extending over the month of May and probably part of the following month, are bound to have disorganized the routine of regular reliefs on which the U-boat campaign against commerce relied. The sudden loss of so many submarine crews must have depleted the available reserves to the point of extinction ; and it is probable that drafts have had to be made on the battleships and cruisers lying in Norwegian waters and in the Baltic in order to fill the gaps.

It is barely six months since Karl Dönitz, advocate of intensive submarine warfare to the practical exclusion of other naval activities, was made Commander-in-Chief of the German Navy in place of the veteran Raeder. Today the former's position must be an unhappy one, since his big new offensive against Allied convoys, of which so much was expected, has proved a disastrous failure. It is not in Hitler's nature to tolerate failures ; but to supersede Dönitz immediately would merely heighten the dismay already felt by the German public. It is probable, therefore, that Grossadmiral Dönitz may last a little longer ; but his advice is hardly likely to be listened to with the same attention by the Nazi rulers.

A possibility is that in these circumstances Hitler may revert to Raeder's ideas, and seek to attack commerce afresh by means of surface warships. Prospects of success by this method are by no means bright, but so long as the people of Germany can be persuaded that some results have been achieved, it would suffice for the purpose.

What ships has Germany available for a sortie into the Atlantic ? There is the big battleship Tirpitz, of over 40,000 tons ; two smaller battleships, the Scharnhorst and Gneisenau, of 26,000 tons ; two so-called pocket battleships, the 10,000-ton Lützow and Admiral Scheer ; two heavy cruisers, the Prinz Eugen and Admiral Hipper ; and at least three smaller cruisers, the Leipzig, Nürnberg and Emden. Destroyers and sea-going torpedo boats may number 40, but their fuel endurance would hardly be equal to a lengthy cruise. There is also the 19,000-ton aircraft carrier Graf Zeppelin, but she has never left the Baltic since she was commissioned and is clearly regarded as a failure. Her sister ship, the Peter Strasser, has not been completed and her construction may have been abandoned.

A REPORT from a neutral source avers that the Gneisenau was found to be so severely injured when taken in hand for refit that she could not be made thoroughly sea-worthy again, and has therefore been relegated to the duties of an anti-aircraft harbour defence ship. This story has a suspicious flavour, and has probably been put out by the enemy in a clumsy attempt to hide the fact that the Gneisenau has been completely refitted and is ready to proceed to sea.

It is doubtful whether the two pocket battleships would be sent out after the fiasco of their sister ship the Admiral Graf Spee in 1939, which discredited the design.

If a squadron of uniform speed were considered essential, it would probably be made up of the Tirpitz, Prinz Eugen and Admiral Hipper, to which might perhaps be added one or more of the small cruisers. Should such a desperate step be undertaken the cruise will be a short one, designed to bring the ships back to port before they can be intercepted by a superior Allied force. Even so, there is the danger that British naval aircraft may get in an attack with torpedoes and cripple one or more of the German ships, enabling her to be overtaken and sunk. For these reasons it is extremely doubtful if any considerable force will be sent to sea ; but Hitler is in such need of better news (even if falsified) to cheer his disheartened people, that it may be thought worth the risk.

THE American seizure of Rendova, followed by an attack on Munda airfield, in New Georgia Island, took the Japanese by surprise. They are fighting hard to retain their foothold in the latter island and will not willingly relinquish it. To assume that the reduction of Rabaul, the main enemy base in this area, will speedily follow, is too optimistic. Still, the systematic reconquest of the chain of islands leading towards Rabaul, which has now begun, is a good step in this direction (see map p. 109).

There seem no solid grounds for expecting a major naval battle in defence of Rabaul. In my opinion its position is too remote from Japan for the enemy to consider it necessary to throw their main fleet into the contest. Even if Rabaul falls sooner than expected, and the New Guinea bases are isolated and rendered innocuous, there are still some 800 miles of enemy-patrolled ocean between Rabaul and Truk, the most important Japanese harbour in the South Seas. An attack on that base might bring about a major naval action ; but the Japanese policy is to hold back their fleet as a last reserve, hoping meanwhile to wear down the Allied assault.

H.M.S. ARCHER (top), first " Woolworth " escort carrier to join the Royal Navy, was also the first converted merchant-ship carrier to have " killed " a U-boat. On July 5, 1943 it was stated that H.M.S. Archer's planes, Swordfish and Martlet, had attacked U-boats menacing an Atlantic convoy. One U-boat was sunk, another probably destroyed, and others damaged. Lower photo, a blindfolded U-boatrating aboard the destroyer H.M.S. Escapade, which rescued the U-boat survivors. (See illus. p. 104.)

*Photos, British Official*

# Great Convoys Dock in Russia's Front-Line Port

**MURMANSK, RUSSIA'S ARCTIC PORT,** has aptly been described as a front-line city. Here the great convoys arrive laden with arms, ammunition and stores from Britain and America. By day and by night the work of unloading goes on, and train after train leaves for the battlefronts. 1, Trainload of structural engineering parts. 2, Women volunteers help to fill the waiting wagons. 3, Travelling crane expedites the discharging of cargo. 4, British and U.S. ships in port. 5, Unloading vessels anchored in the roads.

*Photos, K. Moiseyev, by courtesy of Soviet War News*

# Thirteen was a Lucky Number for this Halifax !

**R.A.F. COASTAL COMMAND HALIFAX** deals with a U-boat in the Bay of Biscay. Heading for the Atlantic when she was spotted, the enemy submarine was destroyed within three minutes. This was the 13th U-boat to be attacked in seven weeks by the Halifax's squadron. Depth charges are here shown straddling the enemy's deck, while one of the aircraft's wheels is seen at the top of the photograph. Mr. Churchill announced on June 30, 1943 that more than 30 U-boats had been destroyed in the Atlantic during May.

*Photo, British Official : Crown Copyright*

# 'Good Old Walrus!' Say the Fleet Air Arm

Compared with the Spitfire, for example, the Walrus may seem a figure of fun. Sometimes, as ROBERT DE WITT writes here, the men of the Fleet Air Arm themselves laugh at it. But they would not be without it : for many of them—not to mention quite a number of Nazi flyers—have been saved from a watery grave by the Walrus planes of the Air-Sea Rescue Service.

THERE is one plane which even the most amateur "spotter" can identify immediately it drones into view. The rather ponderous lines of the Supermarine Walrus amphibian are unmistakable. They recall the Schneider Trophy races of the 'twenties rather than the Spitfire of which the Walrus is a "blood relation." But the Walrus, for all its "old-fashioned" appearance, can do things which are impossible for the up-to-date 400 m.p.h. fighter, or even the four-engined flying-boat designed with the wealth of experience gained during this war.

The lines of the Walrus may not be as pretty as those of the Spitfire, but it can fly in weather that would keep its cousin—or, for that matter, any other plane—on the ground. With its biplanes and rigging it may seem clumsy beside a modern flying-boat, but it can come down on the open sea and stay afloat when the most daring pilot in any other craft would be inclined to think it suicide. Many people have laughed at the Walrus. The Fleet Air Arm themselves laugh at it. But they would not be without it, for scores of R.A.F. and German pilots owe their lives to it.

AIR-SEA rescue is the speciality of the Walrus. Its all-weather flying qualities enable it to continue searching in just the bad conditions which are likely to force down damaged bombers returning from the Continent. After a big raid on Germany the Walruses go out and patrol the Channel, looking for the dinghies of planes reported missing. In some instances they are helped by messages from the pigeons carried on all bombers, or by the distress signals used by the R.A.F. But in others they have to patrol an area, their slow speed enabling the crew to "spot" the speck which is a rubber dinghy more easily than it could be seen from a fast plane.

The rescue planes themselves carry well-stocked dinghies and smoke signals to drop to any airman in distress on the water. In some instances when airmen are found they may be able to guide the fast, specially-equipped rescue launches to them. In many cases the Walrus just goes down, alights on the water, taxies to the raft and picks up the air crew. The Walrus is not a large plane, and its normal complement is three.

Modern bombers carry large crews, and prodigious stories are told of the loads with which Walruses have staggered into the air from the sea after a rescue. Some of them are probably apocryphal. The Walrus has a whole mythology, or perhaps one should say anecdotage, of its own : it is that kind of plane. But at a seaside resort "somewhere in Britain" I have myself seen a Walrus, apparently unable to rise with its heavy load of rescued men, calmly taxi several miles through seas which I would not care to have ridden in a rowing boat, and then nonchalantly put the airmen ashore on an open beach.

Recently a Walrus came down on the sea to rescue the crew of a Polish bomber. Perhaps there was some misunderstanding owing to the difficulties of the language, possibly the pilot had Nelson's "blind eye."

Anyway, the Walrus lurched into the air with the whole crew of seven on board in addition to its own crew and made a perfect landing at its base.

The capacity of the Walrus for taxi-ing is astonishing. It is amphibian in the fullest sense, apparently equally at home on the surface or above it. On one rescue flight last year a Walrus, unable to rise because of the heavy seas, taxied 14 miles to the shore. And when the Walrus cannot fly any more, it is quite at home being towed like a small boat. On one occasion a Walrus accompanying a convoy was unable to find its "mother" ship and ran out of petrol. It alighted, taxied up to a merchant ship, was taken in tow until the coast was reached and then, after re-fuelling, flew home as if travelling a few hundred miles on the sea was as normal as flying them in the air !

Here is a typical story of the Walrus at

S/Ldr. A. S. LINNEY, O.B.E., leader of an Air-Sea Rescue squadron, the Walrus crews of which recently effected their 100th rescue. Standing beside his Walrus amphibian aircraft, Linney is being congratulated by Wing-Cdr. Wilkinson (right). His squadron operates off the S.E. and south coasts of England. *Photo, G.P.U.*

work on air-sea rescue. It is all the more interesting because the men rescued were Germans. Walrus planes on the water trying to pick up survivors have been attacked by German aircraft who thought them "sitters" in the fullest sense; but the rule runs that men in the water are rescued, whatever their nationality.

A WALRUS manned by three sergeants of the Air-Sea Rescue Service found a raft some fifteen miles from the coast. The sea was rough, and the pilot guessed that once he put the Walrus on the water he would not again be able to take off. But he went down, turned the flying-boat and came up to the raft. Flight-Sergeant Fletcher, D.F.M., a commercial traveller before the War, found his "customers" were German sailors from a torpedoed ship. He passed the boathook with the idea of making fast the raft to the plane while the men were transferred. But the German who grabbed the boathook was apparently not worrying about his companions. He just held on and was pulled in through the rear hatch of the Walrus as the raft was swept past by the seas.

The pilot made a difficult turn. (Another advantage of the Walrus in rescue work is its manoeuvrability on the water.) It came up to the raft again. The remaining

Germans on the raft failed to catch the rope thrown to them. The seas carried the Walrus right into the raft, damaging the hull and throwing two of the Germans into the water. A rope was thrown to them, but they were too weak to catch hold and were swept away in heavy seas. It was getting dark and they were not seen again. But before the Walrus and raft were parted the rear gunner managed to grab one of the men on the raft and haul him into the plane.

ONCE more the Walrus turned and came towards the raft on which one man remained. The pilot aimed straight at the raft and, as the plane hit, the front gunner grabbed the German and pulled him aboard. The plane taxied round searching for the men who had been swept away, while the two gunners pumped and baled. The water in the hull was 18 inches deep at one time. No sign was seen of the sailors, and the growing darkness made the search hopeless. There was a danger of fire from the electrical equipment, which was shorting owing to the water.

The pilot turned the Walrus towards the coast and taxied mile after mile at full throttle until, a few yards from the shore, he was able to put the rescued men aboard a trawler. It was only then that he learned he had been running over minefields large enough to blow a whole navy to pieces. But it is doubtful whether prior knowledge would have made any difference to his actions. The three flight-sergeants forming the crew had all won the D.F.M. and had 11, 21 and 10 rescues to their credit in the "good old Walrus."

This story is typical of hundreds of rescues made by Walrus planes during this war. The Channel sees particular activity after a big raid on the Continent, but at all times there are Walrus planes patrolling or standing by, ready to rescue any airmen who may be in the sea.

Air-sea rescue is only one of the many tasks given to the Walrus, which is a "utility" plane in the best sense. When it comes to the Walrus as a fighter we enter the realm of mythology rather than history. The Walrus is armed, but its low speed and large hull make it a vulnerable target. Normally, when engaged in rescue work in an area where enemy fighters might be expected, it is protected by fighters above. Nevertheless, Walrus planes have shot down German planes and sent many home with bulletholes in the fuselage, a greater respect for the good old Walrus and, no doubt, a story of a fierce encounter with a Spitfire or Hurricane ! German airmen would consider being shot down by a Walrus much as a county cricketer would regard being bowled by an amateur, underarm bowler !

The anecdotes about the Walrus include stories of a half-hour battle with a Messerschmitt, outwitted by the Walrus, keeping so low that the German could never get in a decent burst ; and of a Walrus that "led" its opponent into a church steeple which it swerved aside itself to miss.

The Walrus was not built to attack the fast modern fighter or the very heavily-armed bomber ; but it is a grand plane, very robust and versatile, and the best of its kind anywhere.

# America Seizes the Initiative in the Pacific

ALLIED OFFENSIVE IN S.W. PACIFIC. In New Guinea, where the Americans landed at Nassau Bay at the end of June 1943, bombing raids caused great damage to Jap airfields and aircraft. Above, burning enemy planes at Madang, north-west of Lae. Left, Rendova Island (New Georgia), on which U.S. forces landed on June 30. By July 12 the Allies had closed in on Munda, largest Jap air base in the Solomons, and the Japanese garrison was isolated.

VITAL U.S. INVASION POINTS included the Trobriand and Woodlark groups of islands off the eastern tip of New Guinea. These had been ignored by the Japs, and their occupation by American forces on June 30 was effected without opposition. Presumably both Trobriand and Woodlark will provide valuable aerodrome bases from which Allied planes can increase their range. Mr. Stimson, U.S. Secretary for War, declared on July 1 : " our forces have reached the outer defences of Japan and strong enemy reaction may be expected." Above, village in the Trobriand Islands. Centre right, native huts in New Georgia. Right, map showing main Allied objectives.

*Photos, News Chronicle, E.N.A., map by courtesy of the Daily Herald*

# What Sort of Invasion Craft Are We Using?

With "invasion" the subject of so much of our reading and conversation, there is a distinct topicality about this article: an account by ALEXANDER DILKE of the invasion craft which we and our American allies have prepared in readiness for the all-out assault on Europe.

WHEN three years ago Hitler, like Napoleon, shivered on the brink of the Channel, we read almost daily of R.A.F. assaults on "invasion barges." These barges were the 2,000-ton Rhine lighters, the smaller steel or oak *péniches* of Belgium, varying in size from 75 to 600 tons, and a collection of miscellaneous craft from all the rivers and canals of western Europe. Not one of them was specially built for invasion, although many were hastily adapted to take tanks. The R.A.F. and possibly large-scale practice invasions persuaded the Germans that these craft would never successfully assault Britain's beaches; and so, as with Napoleon, the historic chance faded.

The story might have been very different if Hitler had had an invasion fleet of specialized craft even one-quarter the size of that now available to the Allies. Whether for once German thoroughness forgot to prepare, or whether Hitler really believed that he would not have to fight Britain and therefore did not contemplate armed invasion, will remain for future historians to discover.

They will also discover that at the very time when Britain was daily expecting invasion, her High Command set its own designers to work on craft that really would carry infantry, vehicles and tanks across the choppy English Channel and land them fighting. Before the danger of invasion from the Continent had passed, Britain was already producing craft for the invasion of the Continent. Today those craft, with the craft of different types but similar purpose from our American allies, constitute the most imposing invasion fleet ever known.

MOST people credit the invention of the "invasion barge" to Germany. But in fact Britain with her tradition of amphibious warfare was far in front of Germany in design even before the War. Landing-craft for carrying Marines of a type still used today were built at Portsmouth in 1936. Flat-bottomed, steel-sided for protection, and with a ramp that could be lowered for rapid disembarkation, they were very satisfactory for short journeys. As a matter of fact, the first tank landing-craft in the world were built in Britain in 1917 for what was known as the "Hush operation." Few people have heard of them because the operation was postponed; but the craft were built and carried out practices in the Thames estuary. They were pontoons 600 feet long, which were to be lashed between two monitors and taken across the Channel to assault the Belgian beach defences at Ostend.

Very different are the tank landing-craft of today. Many of their details, especially of the later types, are secret; but it is known that they are shallow-draught vessels, powered by Diesel engines producing 1,000 h.p. and driving twin screws. Except for their very square bows containing the tank ramp, they look like oil-tankers, as, for ease in driving the tanks on and off, the bridge and all accommodation is well at the rear. According to German reports, the vessels at Dieppe which landed 30-ton tanks were grey, about 800 tons, and each carried six to eight tanks.

The vessels are capable of making considerable ocean voyages, as their presence at the North African landings showed. They are manned by the Navy, mostly by officers of the R.N.V.R. and Navy recruits who have undergone special training. Controlling one of these craft at sea, putting it on the beach, and then getting it off again is quite unlike navigating an ordinary small ship. Each tank landing-craft has a crew of about twelve.

TROOP-CARRYING aircraft, now generally armoured to give protection against small-arms fire, are smaller but built on the same principles—flat-bottomed to enable them to be run up on sloping beaches and Diesel-engined for self-propulsion. They have little in common with the "barge" except the flat bottom. The smaller invasion craft are given a "lift" to a pre-arranged point near the beach by larger vessels. The methods of launching them and hoisting them aboard again are secret.

How many of these landing-craft we have is also a secret, but we may be sure that they are being turned out very fast. Many of them are being built by women.

The United States became very interested in barges in 1940, and long before she entered the War was practising amphibious operations with specially-constructed craft. Recently the House Naval Affairs Committee approved the construction of 1,000,000 tons of naval craft for amphibious warfare at a cost of £425,000,000—an indication of the scale upon which the U.S. contemplates the invasion of her enemies in the East and in the West. Many details of the types of invasion craft which will form this million tons must be secret, but photographs and official accounts have already shown some of the advances made in recent years.

In the invasion of North and West Africa, the U.S. forces used sea-going craft carrying tanks, lorries and cars. These were able to go right through the surf on to the beach, when the bows dropped down and formed a landing ramp along which the vehicles were able to drive ashore under their own power.

The U.S. have always taken considerable interest in amphibious vehicles. They have the amphibious Jeep for fording rivers and lakes, a little open four-seater which seems as much at home in the water as on the road. Then there is the Roebuck "Alligator," which looks like a low tank with the top removed. The caterpillar treads have special cleats which give a good grip on land and act like paddles in the water. They can carry men or supplies, and have the advantage that they "come in shooting"—there is no need to disembark at the water's edge. At manoeuvres in Florida before the U.S. entered the War these amphibious vehicles showed they were capable of climbing an embankment of 55 degrees with ease and of crashing their way through both surf and jungle.

The U.S. marines use Eureka or Y boats, which are similar to our own personnel landing craft. In the Solomons they produced some supply barges with outboard motors the size of tractors, probably the noisiest and also the most manoeuvrable craft which are on the sea.

Not only invasion craft, but also men have to be specially prepared. The naval crews are, of course, specialists; but even the soldiers must have constant practice in embarkation and disembarkation. To help this, dummy craft have been built ashore. Securing vehicles and tanks so that they will not shift in heavy seas yet will be instantly released when the craft touches the beach, calls for ingenious design and special training.

Invasion craft, being flat-bottomed, are apt to roll, especially in the swell just off the beach; and this can cause sea-sickness at a critical time. The theory has been put forward that it was sea-sickness that led the Germans constantly to postpone their invasion. Britain and the U.S. have made some progress in the conquest of this exhausting complaint, and their invasion craft land men not only quickly but in good condition.

An invasion fleet consists of more than flat-bottomed craft in great variety. There must be motor-boats for protection, minesweepers to clear the way, destroyers, cruisers and so on up to battleships. These ships of every kind Britain and the U.S. now have in numbers sufficient for any conceivable number of landing craft. That is another advantage we enjoy over the Germans of 1940 who were never able to guarantee that a superior naval force would not appear.

On the facing page and the three following pages of our special gravure section are a number of photographs which have recently been released, showing various types of invasion landing-craft adopted by the Allies for their onslaught against the European stronghold of the Axis.

PREPARING FOR THE REAL THING, these Royal Marines, carrying out invasion exercises on the English south coast, are ready for instant action as the ramp of their dummy landing-craft is lowered. As pointed out in the text, embarking and disembarking practised ashore are part of their highly specialized training. *Photo, Fox*

## All Set for Invasion

In Britain, in North Africa and elsewhere overseas, great numbers of the Empire's fighting-men have been training for months past for the day when the host of the United Nations will descend on the Continent of Europe to do battle with and utterly destroy the Axis in the very seat of its power. In that greatest of amphibious enterprises air, sea and land forces must cooperate as never before, and for this they have been trained. These photographs of personnel landing-craft at full speed were taken during "Combined-ops" exercises.

# When the Battle of Europe Opens

Wherever the blow may fall, the invasion of the Continent must be made from across the sea. Great fleets of transports and supply-vessels, guided and guarded by warships and aircraft, will approach the enemy coast. When near enough the troops will embark in landing-barges and, crouching low to avoid hostile fire, speed for the shore, as shown in (1). This type of craft is of such shallow draught that it lands them (2) on the very beach.

### How the Invaders Will Get Ashore

Not one or two but scores of landing-craft, each in charge of the Navy's "assault troops," will speed for the disembarkation beaches (3). Vessels of a larger type are shown turning in (4). Safely beached, the landing-craft disgorge their load of heavily-armed invaders—in (5) they are Marines—who rush on to engage the defenders. Close behind them arrive special tank-conveying craft: in (6) a Valentine makes its own smoke screen as it takes to the land.

## Americans on the Invasion Wave

Photos, Associated Press

Like Britain, the U.S.A. has an ever-increasing number of men trained in the exacting art of land-sea warfare, and they have devised landing-craft of patterns suited to their own particular requirements. Here, for instance, we see (top) an amphibious 2½-ton lorry : right, running along the sand in Florida ; left, it takes the water. Below, U.S. Marines nearing the shore in their landing-craft.

# VIEWS & REVIEWS
### Of Vital War Books

## by Hamilton Fyfe

READERS of Meredith's novels (there are some still, including the editor of this journal, who once wrote a book about them) recollect vividly the scene in the Scala opera house at Milan when Sandra Belloni, who has become a prima donna, defies the Austrian oppressors of Italy by singing " Italia, Italia shall be free ! " Englishmen thrilled to that as well as Italians. The Austrians were hated in England (hard to think of them now as tyrannizers !). Garibaldi and Mazzini and Vittorio Emmanuele were heroes here and in America. They liberated their country. Italia, Italia was at last free.

But not for long. After fifty years of freedom they submitted tamely to another tyrant, this time one of their own race and a worse ruffian than any of the Austrian rulers. For twenty years now they have been governed with contemptuous brutality by Mussolini, who has reduced them to a state which can only be called sub-human.

There is in Italy " no free speech, no free writing, no free association, no free industry. All is sacrificed to the material interests of a political party. The retail shopkeeper has to obtain a Fascist licence. No doctor, lawyer, teacher or journalist can practise without the enrolment of his name by a Fascist committee, after it has looked into his conduct to see if it has been politically irreproachable. The Press is purely Fascist, with editors actually appointed and removed by the Ministry of Popular Culture."

THAT is what Mr. Richard G. Massock, author of Italy from Within (Macmillan, 15s.), says after living there as an American correspondent. He saw the effect of Fascism on the nation.

It embittered them and made them a cynical race that would welcome foreign deliverance, but were too disheartened to do anything about it except complain among themselves and to the democratic foreigners they could trust.

They know how news is systematically falsified before it is allowed to reach them. They know that high-up Fascist officials are mostly "incompetent, if not always dishonest, adventurers." They are aware that Ciano, Mussolini's son-in-law and "sedulous ape" (he tries to stick out his chin and copy the Duce's posturing)—they are aware that he has become rapidly one of Italy's richest men. He owns—for the moment—vast quantities of valuable property, including "great areas of rich Tuscany farmland in the famous Chianti wine country." His poorer countrymen attempt to imitate him by buying property " from trinkets to real estate " because they have no faith in the value of the lira, which has dropped already from 10d. to 2½d. ; but here even they are balked by the Nazis who are everywhere in Italy and have "stripped it like a swarm of locusts."

The Italians have got used to justice being turned into a mockery. Here is an illustration. An American clergyman, rector of a church in Rome, was arrested and accused of receiving a letter from an Italian officer containing military information. Washington protested energetically; the ridiculous charge had to be dropped. It was dropped in this way. The clergyman was brought to trial on a Monday and sentenced to 30 years' imprisonment. On the Tuesday he was pardoned by the King. On the Wednesday he was released and allowed to leave for the United States.

That sort of humbug pervades the whole Fascist system. Mussolini wears round his neck a religious medal, though he is a notorious atheist. He pretends to have had the Government offices removed from Rome, so as to make it an open city which should not be bombed. But "it was all a fiction. The Government offices and the headquarters of the High Command remained in the city, troops were encamped there, and camouflaged warplanes hidden under straw matting huts."

## The Canker at Italy's Heart

Mussolini and his gangsters are like Italians of the Elizabethan age, when they were reputed to be "as false as hell." He completely took in the innocent Mr. Neville Chamberlain, as he had before taken in his brother, Sir Austen. Mr. Massock was in Rome when the former as Prime Minister, with Lord Halifax as Foreign Secretary, visited the Duce and complimented him on "the new Italy, powerful and progressive, that had arisen under his guidance and inspiration." No British Prime Minister had ever been at the same time so fatuous and so fulsome as that. The visit was futile for the reason, Mr. Massock says, that the French Foreign Office forbade ours to attempt intervention between France and Italy. Another humiliation !

When Mussolini decides that one of his crew is too incompetent or too dishonest—or too popular—the victim is thrown overboard without hesitation. One morning he finds a note on his desk. It is in the Duce's own handwriting. "I accept your resignation and thank you for your services," it says. A cheque is enclosed, usually for about £100. The sacked man disappears without delay.

"Delays have dangerous ends." The King is treated in much the same unceremonious fashion. He is reported to have said to a friend "Be careful what you tell me, for I have to repeat everything to—you know who." He was made to pray at the graves of "you know who's" parents. After Mr. Churchill had made his radio appeal to the Italian people in December 1941 the King was ordered to issue an army order saying, "No obstacle can halt the rise of Italy" ; and one of the princesses had to announce that she had become a member of the Fascist Party.

The appeal, according to Mr. Massock, and indeed according to events since it was made, turned out "a complete fiasco." The Italians were too dispirited, too listless, to do more than shrug their shoulders and ask "What can we do ?" They needed no telling of the mess they were in. During Mussolini's attempt to govern Abyssinia he spent £450 million sterling. The roads on which our troops advanced to wipe out the Italian garrisons cost thirty millions. Private firms' investments of 70 millions were a total loss. Italians are poorer now than in the days when they shipped hundreds of thousands of workers to the U.S. every year. They have little food and little warmth in winter ; life is hard for all but the rich people and the Fascist officials.

As an example of the wages earned by a skilled worker in wartime the book mentions a foreman bricklayer who is paid fifty shillings a week, lives in a slum, and has to let his wife go out as a charwoman to earn the rent. Yet when any of them venture to make the smallest complaint Mussolini calls them "a lot of bastards incapable of feeling the grandeur of this unique moment in human history" (March 1942). He evidently knows there are a good many such "bastards," for he goes about surrounded by guards, who also look after the safety of the King ; there are 350 of them and they are kept busy.

FROM the King, who is seventy-three and chiefly interested in collecting coins, Mr. Massock thinks there is nothing to expect. Nor has he much opinion of the Crown Prince Umberto, who "busies himself with inspections, reviews, and similar military ceremonies, and has little personality." What he heard in Italy, before he was imprisoned and then turned out made him believe that "the liberation and future system of government is primarily the business of the Italians in Italy." Those who have gone to other countries are forgotten. All the political parties seem to have been "buried so profoundly that not even their ghosts are abroad in the land." He says Ansaldo, the radio talker, was a Socialist, but went over to the Fascists "with the ardour which Italians describe as more Catholic than the Pope."

That sort of transformation makes Italians distrust all politicians. But where are they to look for leadership now that the theatrical glamour of Mussolini has worn through and revealed merely a nasty old man ? That is the phrase which describes the distaste felt for the numerous love affairs of this fat, repulsive-looking man of sixty. He transfers his affections very quickly, making no attempt to hide his "affairs." That they have weakened his mind and constitution are, in Mr. Massock's view, "sheer nonsense." More's the pity !

**PLOUGHING IN ROME** and other Italian cities has long been a familiar wartime sight. Flower-beds in the heart of the Eternal City are here being ploughed by oxen. Italy from Within, the book reviewed in this page, gives a vivid picture of present conditions in that unhappy country. PAGE 115

*Photo, Keystone*

# China Can Mobilize Fifty Million More Men

*The seventh day of the seventh month marked the opening of China's seventh year of struggle against Japanese aggression. And still great armies are at grips over a tremendous battlefield. The issue is not yet decided, but Capt. MAURICE BENSLEY gives reasons in this article for the belief that, sooner or later, China's almost illimitable man-power must win the day.*

BEFORE the Japs went on the warpath, nowhere was military service such an uncertain profession as in China. A soldier's pay was often months in arrears. In return for big risks, terrific hardship, and precious little relaxation, he was lucky if he received a few shillings a month—half in cash maybe, the rest in rations. There was nothing much in the way of uniform, no pension, no allowances for disablement, no compensation for his family if he died. His employers might discharge or demobilize him any day, without reason, without prospects, his wages still unpaid.

Pauperism, however, was—still is—the lot of millions of Chinese, and to many soldiering meant at least food and clothing. Possession of arms was an added attraction. But primarily the Chinese were strictly civilians. They had little fighting spirit; went into battle with umbrella, crickets and birdcage; fraternized and traded with the enemy, soldiers themselves passing to and fro between the lines as carriers of merchandise. That was China's army of a very recent yesterday. And there had been no recognizable change when young Chiang, who, soldier-trained in Japan, returned to his homeland with 100 followers and set up the revolutionary standard against the despotic Manchu Emperor. With Dr. Sun Yat-sen, Chiang fed the revolution until it was strong enough to end for ever the tyrannies of the 4,000-year-old Chinese Empire.

WHEN Dr. Sun died of cancer in 1925 powerful war-lords did their best to hinder the subsequent work of unification, and Chiang Kai-shek was forced to flee to Japan. But he was soon back again, and formed a new government by promising regional tolerance to those disgruntled provinces which were reluctant to join his confederation. By 1936 Chiang had pacified most of the recalcitrant states, achieving a national unity never before dreamed of in China. The Marshal was not alone a great general, his eventual success was not due solely to clever military leadership. To Chiang the soldier should go the credit for implementing most of the civic reforms which sprang out of the partnership of this young Chinese rebel from Japan with that great friend of China's people, Dr. Sun.

And when total war hit the China he had re-made, threatening to sabotage the most remarkable industrial reconstruction ever crammed into a quarter-century, nobody realized better than the Generalissimo the vital need to save the precious organism. Slowly but with a sure hand he applied himself to the task.

Coal had been used as a fuel in China for 2,000 years. Her huge below-earth reserves gave her third place after the U.S.A. and Canada in this all-important source of mineral wealth. But with the invader's approach new workings had to be opened up in the interior. In the supply of tungsten, essential component of steel, China led the world. With Burma, China's co-producer of four-fifths of the world production, lost to the Japs every effort had to be made to maintain maximum output. It was anything but easy. Kwangtung province, one of China's own big sources of supply, was being greedily gobbled up by the invaders. But there was still the vast province of Kiangsi, and by developing new mines in west Honan, well out of Japanese reach, China had been able to keep her own

and the United Nations' war industries essentially supplied with this vital commodity. The same applies to antimony—a metal essential to munition-making—in which China heads world production.

The remarkable migration of heavy industry began when the Japs first set foot on China's seaboard. As Nippon's hordes advanced, a mass exodus of literally millions of workers poured into and began to develop the once isolated western provinces of Shensi, Szechwan, Honan, Kweichow, Kwangsi and Yunnan. In addition, vast new factories were established—cotton and silk mills, sugar and paper plants, as well as hospitals, universities and schools. With them came new highways, new railroads. Concentration of new industries and regulation of output led to increased efficiency. China is now turning out rifles and machine-guns, artillery and mortars, bombs and mines, shells and explosives. She is making steam turbines, gas engines, oil burners, scientific and precision instruments. Vegetable oils are made to pro-

CHINA has suffered tremendous set-backs, as related in this page, but in spite of all she valiantly fights on. The shaded portions in this map indicate Jap-occupied territory.

duce urgently needed motor fuel. Four-fifths of the more urgent medical supplies that China needs are now home-produced.

## Magnitude of China's Handicaps

It is in locomotives, tractors, aircraft and motor-cars that China's war machine is so pitifully deficient. She has not yet the facilities to produce these war primaries, and she still has to rely on America and Britain for high-grade tools and steels, aviation spirit, and the heavier military equipment. The value of Jap-destroyed properties alone is put at £300,000,000 to £400,000,000. It is largely to replace these and their industries that industrialization of the western provinces was undertaken. The magnitude of the task would be best understood by the Russians, faced with a similar need when they transferred vast war plants in the west to safe areas east of the Volga.

But, despite her new hospitals and public health centres, her agricultural stations and farm credit organizations China's social and economic revival has been slower to progress than that of the more up-to-date Soviet Union. Her basic need—food for 450,000,000

souls—is almost as much a problem today as ever it was. Once again there rages with unabated fury in the Honan province, bordering the north-eastern battle-front, one of the worst famines in China's recorded history. The blighted area is approximately 20,000 square miles, and some of the worst stricken districts are along the Yellow River, near Chengchow, only ten miles from the Japanese lines.

" I saw," says a vivid dispatch from a Times correspondent, " train after train encrusted with humanity which was huddled on the slippery roofs of the cars . . . They were jammed between the cars, and many fell from the speeding trains." Weakened by seven months of starvation diet of millet husks, straw, cotton seeds, slimy weeds, and even the bark of trees, a million people in Honan are facing an epidemic of cholera and dysentery. But worse: before the harvest can relieve the situation, states the Provincial Governor, Li Pei-Chi, millions of destitute Chinese will die unless aid speedily arrives.

Yet with problems of this magnitude spiking her war effort, China manfully fights on. No expense was spared by Japan in equipping the forces she sent against her peaceable foe. But China's Army, raised from a German-trained nucleus of troops equipped with pikes and spears, has only in the last five or six years even approached the efficiency of modern-trained and -armed troops. For years peasant soldiers, fed on a handful of rice or millet, performed astounding feats of endurance against a soundly-trained well-led, admirably-equipped enemy. Incomplete in everything except infantry, it was man-power alone that saved China from destruction.

BUT slowly, inevitably, Marshal Chiang has been building up an increasingly formidable force of all arms. Nearly 200 divisions, though poorly armed, were in the field a year after the Japs had consolidated their coastal conquests. Now the Chinese army numbers well over 300 divisions; 5,000,000 soldiers hold a battle-line 1,500 miles long, and reserve and training units are at full strength with a further 15,000,000 men. Japanese strong points and garrisons are constantly harassed by nearly a million stubborn guerillas, widely disposed. Over 600,000 regular troops operate in organized bands on the enemy's side of the long irregular battle-front. Completely without a military tradition a few years ago, the whole Chinese population now accepts military training as part of its very life. Seven years of total war and Jap domination of a third of the population have turned the most peace-loving people in the world into a nation whose army training now begins at school.

And behind her huge armies of fully-trained soldiers are 50,000,000 able-bodied men of military age. Japan's total falls short of this by at least four-fifths. This fact, with the present casualty ratio of one Jap to one Chinaman, must be a prospect that is anything but rosy to the military chiefs in Tokyo.

For it must inevitably spell defeat when China's new factories are at top production; when American and British war industries can fill all the gaps; and when Japanese man-power, now sprawled throughout the whole of the Pacific area, becomes stretched to exhaustion point.

# Floods Add to China's Wartime Load of Trouble

GREAT floods in the Chinese province of Honan drove some 3,000,000 people from their homes in August 1942. The Chinese Government, the Y.W.C.A. and relief agencies did all in their power to alleviate the sufferings of the starving refugees; clinics, hostels, equipment and, above all, food, reduced the misery of thousands. In May 1943 the Honan Relief Committee sent to Loyang over 30,000 bags of cereals for distribution. At Sian spinning-wheels were provided. 1, Refugees bring in spun thread in exchange for cotton wool. 2, This photograph tells its own terrible story. 3, Left to right, Pres. Lin Sen of China, Marshal Chiang Kai-shek and Gen. Chang Chu-Chung, Minister of Military Operations. 4, Women strip tree-bark for desperately needed food. 5, A train crowded with refugees from stricken areas.

*Photos, Y.W.C.A., Topical, Keystone, The Times*

# THE WAR IN THE AIR

## by Capt. Norman Macmillan, M.C., A.F.C.

AFTER the conquest of North Africa and the capture of the Italian islands of Pantelleria, Lampedusa and Lampione in the Sicilian Narrows, a strange hush descended upon military operations over all Europe. While the armies waited, and doubtless while new dispositions were being made, the war in the air continued with undiminished fury and, indeed, in some areas of operation, with increasing power.

Intensive attacks were made upon the Italian peninsula from Leghorn southwards; upon the islands of Sicily and Sardinia. The smashing blows of Bomber Command upon the industrial towns of the Ruhr and Rhine descended with shorter pauses between each raid. Repeatedly, day after day, the broadcast news bulletins stated that the principal news was of the war in the air. There could be no better illustration of the cardinal principle of war in the air, which is this : war in the air cannot pause, it is ever on the offensive, and must continue upon the offensive or fail.

The men who fly never let up. From the night following May 11, 1940, Bomber Command has never ceased to maintain its offensive against Germany and German-occupied Europe. It may have had to miss a night now and again on account of weather. But that is all. The battle waged by Bomber Command is continuous, and will continue without cessation until the war ends. The work of this Command may prove to be, ultimately, when the whole history of this long and widespread air war can be calmly assessed, the classic example of the employment of air power.

By keying the Luftwaffe to the tactical assault needs of the German Army, the German High Command made one of its fundamental errors in this war. By doing so it failed to provide a Strategic Air Force. The Luftwaffe as a whole was a tactical force ; when strategic operations in the air were demanded, part of the tactical force had to be detached for this employment, thereby weakening the parent body. Nor can it be claimed that the equipment of a tactical air force is necessarily the same as that of a strategic air force : on some occasions it may be the same, but on others it must be very greatly different.

IT does not appear that anything that Germany can now do can correct the great and basic mistake that the German generals of the Army and Luftwaffe both made. The German troops that were halted by the snows and soldiers of Russia and by the seas and fighter pilots of Britain discovered that the way for further advances could not be prepared for them by a tactical air force.

When the German armies' advances were brought to a standstill, the paramount need of the German High Command was for a strategic air force which could prepare the

way for a further advance. There was no such force. They had not foreseen the demand and for that reason it could not be met.

Now the United Nations' armies have come to a temporary halt—faced, as the German armies were faced, by a sea crossing (and in Russia by a vast plain whose characteristics presented problems as great and grave as those presented by the sea). And, in the similar circumstances which they have to face, the United Nations are possessed of a

GERMAN A.A. GUNNERS DEFEND NAPLES. This Nazi naval A.A. battery is seen in action against Allied aircraft during a heavy attack on the much-bombed Italian city. Mount Vesuvius appears on the extreme left, and the outline of city buildings on the right. *Photo, Planet News*

powerful Allied strategic air force whose blows grow mightier with each passing month, preparing the way for the next onward move of the surface forces, so that, in effect, the grand offensive role never ceases by day or night.

While this air pressure continues from Britain, from North Africa, from Malta, from aircraft carriers, from Russia, beating like gusts upon the long, indented line of the German-Italian military perimeter, the situation in relation to Japan becomes increasingly important.

In Burma the wild violence of the monsoon breaks in fierce storms that flood the rivers, churn the soil to mud, beat the waters of the Bay of Bengal to angry violence. I have seen it and flown through it and I know how hard a natural enemy to airmen the monsoon is. So, in the theatre of the eastern gateway to India, the season spells stalemate upon the ground. But it does not mean the end of air attack.

There is greater risk and strain upon the air crews, greater hardship upon the

ground crews, discomfort in the tossing flight of aircraft passing through the turbulent air ; but these things are all swept aside by military necessity, and the air war goes on while the front line troops maintain their uncomfortable positions and are stuck by mud.

In the Far East a new offensive has begun, initiated by General MacArthur. It is an offensive designed apparently with the main object of securing more air bases throughout the chains of islands that lie scattered upon the tropic seas between Australia, China and Japan. In those vast seas any advance to reconquest demands imperatively the possession of full air cover.

For by possession of that air cover transport aircraft can operate to carry supplies to the forward troops, to provide them with arms and ammunition, food, water, medical supplies, hospitals, Red Cross tender aircraft. Without superior air power the reconquest of the lost lands of the Far East might become interminable. But when we have, as we now have in steadily growing measure, air superiority over the Japanese, the ability of the yellow race to maintain its hold upon the lands it has overrun diminishes with every fresh blow that United Nations' air power strikes. Each forward move of the ground forces in concert with the unified plan of air, sea and land operations brings into the realm of the United Nations territory wherein new air bases can be sited, and wrests bases for their air forces from the Japanese.

AT the moment, this process has taken its first forward movement, and during this period is fraught with many difficulties ; but as the process continues the power of the United Nations will steadily expand, while that of the Japanese will continually contract—for, as the Japanese are forced northward, a zone will be reached wherein the islands available to them are smaller, the air bases fewer, the capacity for defence slighter, and the geographical opportunities for the United Nations to engage them become more suited to the application of our strategic air power.

But it is not strange that the offensive against the Japanese in the South-West Pacific began during the lull over the German-Italian zone and the monsoon stalemate on the Indo-Burmese front. Germany and Italy would naturally hope that Japanese pressure in the Far East might draw away from them some of the terrible air pressure which they now face. General MacArthur's offensive in the Pacific anticipates the possibility of Japanese intervention there to succour the Axis partners in their European imbroglio.

U.S. THUNDERBOLT, piloted by 2nd Lt. J. Foster, was recently singled out for attack over France by German fighters. Five 20-mm. shells ploughed into the right wing of the aircraft. Its pilot managed to fly the damaged plane to England and crash-land. *Photo, U.S. Official*

# Fortress-Eye View of a Raid on the Ruhr

**U.S. FLYING FORTRESSES' FIRST DAYLIGHT ATTACK ON THE RUHR** was carried out on June 22, 1943. At Huls a big synthetic rubber factory
—the second largest of its kind in Germany—received a devastating weight of bombs, no part of the target escaping damage. This photograph, taken
from a Fortress at the height of the raid, shows one of the attacking planes. At bottom right, great clouds of smoke and columns of flame almost
obscure the whole of the target area.

*Photo, United States Official*

# How Russia Trains Her Mighty Reserve Armies

TAKING ITS FIRST OBSTACLE during a practice test, this Soviet tank is watched by Red Army men undergoing intensive training in tank warfare. The inscription on the turret reads: "Crush the Fascist viper!" Great battles, involving formidable numbers of tanks, were taking place N. and S. of the Kursk salient from July 5, 1943.

RUSSIAN RECRUITS include all types of workers. Above, a group arriving for military training. Below, after training, a youthful soldier fully equipped and eager to fight for his country.

FIGHTING POWER OF THE U.S.S.R. has grown to gigantic dimensions since that fateful June 22, 1941, when Hitler treacherously marched into Russia. Now, while Germany is experiencing a shortage of man-power reserves, Russian re-inforcements are being continually brought up to the fighting fronts, equipped with the most effective means of destroying the enemy. The Soviet war industry is not only able to re-place considerable material losses, but, with the help of Britain and America, to keep the Red Army—with its constant influx of recruits—supplied with an ever-increasing flow of arma-ments. Above, young Russians receiving their first lesson in bayonet fighting, for which the Red Army is mightily renowned. Left, under the guidance of keen instructors, trainees carrying full kit are being toughened by arduous marching - drill in column of fours.

*Photos. Pictorial Press, Exclusive to* THE WAR ILLUSTRATED

# Egypt Salutes Flags of Thirty-Four Allied Nations

**UNITED NATIONS DAY IN EGYPT** was celebrated in Cairo and Alexandria on June 14, 1943 by impressive parades. In Cairo 5,000 troops, sailors and members of the women's Services took part, while R.A.F. fighter squadrons swooped low over the city to salute the flags of 34 Allied nations. Top, soldiers bearing their national flags halt at the saluting base; the salute was taken by Gen. Sir H. Maitland Wilson, C.-in-C. Middle East Forces. Lower photo, Army detachments march along the promenade at Alexandria. PAGE 121    *Photos, British Official: Crown Copyright*

# THE HOME FRONT

### by E. Royston Pike

Two years have passed since the great blitz ended in 1941. Now it is the Germans whose Civil Defence forces are being stretched to the utmost; and their plight (on their own confession, as made by war reporters who have visited the Ruhr, Cologne, and other sorely battered cities of the Reich) is so terrible that one would think that, as Miss Ellen Wilkinson put it the other day, " either the Germans must hit back at us or confess to the world that Bomber Command can make rubble of their vital industries while they are helpless to do more than defend themselves." So far the Germans have not renewed their " blitz "; quite a number of our coast towns have been visited by hit-and-run raiders, and (according to German accounts) Hull has been severely attacked. But there is plenty of sound and fury in the enemy camp; and Goebbels and his propagandists are trying to bolster the morale on their own home front by blood-curdling threats of what they are going to do to us before many weeks have passed.

Altogether, then, it was not inopportune that the House of Commons should debate the state of our Civil Defence organization. Opening the debate on June 30, Miss Wilkinson, Parliamentary Secretary to the Ministry of Home Security, viewed the question as one of the amount of insurance that we should carry against the possibility and, indeed, the probability, of the Nazis carrying out their threats. As regards the Civil Defence general services, the insurance today falls below that of its peak in 1941, although the insurance against fire is considerably higher. In the whole-time personnel the C.D. establishment has been cut by about a third in the last twelve months, and further cuts are to be made before very long. So far as possible whole-time personnel are being replaced by part-timers, but already there are rather more than ten part-timers to one whole-timer; to make up the rota, about three part-timers are required for every whole-timer relieved. It is remarkable how much the whole-time personnel are doing to help the war effort in their stand-by periods. They have helped in salvage work, the clearance of debris, and in harvesting, while the women have given a great deal of clerical help to the local authorities—among other things, they wrote out millions of the new ration books recently issued—and they have also assisted in the running of day nurseries and maternity and child-welfare clinics.

While a raid is on, Miss Wilkinson continued, the biggest single problem is fire. Photographs from Germany have shown that it is not only the fire inflicted during the raid which does damage, but insignificant bombs which get lodged in gutters, and little pieces of phosphorus which cause blazes after the raid is over. But our precautions against fire are far superior to what they were two years ago. The National Fire Service, consisting of 42 large fire forces instead of, as formerly, 1,451 local brigades, is something of which the country can be really proud; and there are, in addition, about five million fireguards.

Somewhat earlier in the month the National Federation of Women's Institutes held their conference at the Albert Hall in London. Mr. R. S. Hudson, Minister of Agriculture, addressed one of the sessions; during the last four years, he said, the countryside has been reborn and has resumed its rightful place in the life of the nation. Without the countrywomen—in particular the 300,000 included in the 6,000 Women's Institutes—this could not have happened; it was they who had made the miracle possible. The high-light of the Conference was a surprise visit from the Queen.

Today (she said) our villages are sadly empty The young men are away fighting for the land they love so well. The girls, too, are at their war-work, and the great responsibility of carrying on rests with the older women. How gallantly they are doing this, shouldering every sort of job with such a grand and cheerful spirit, and planning and praying for the day when their dear ones come home again!

Sometimes, when I go through our villages and

**FIREGUARDS' NEW WEAPON, the "wheelbarrow pump," is a petrol-driven appliance intended to replace the familiar stirrup pump. Several have already been sent to important target areas. A crew of two men and a woman is shown with their new machine, ready for action.** *Photo, Keystone*

look at the gardens, so full of colour as well as of vegetables, I think of the hard work that goes to the making of them, and of Kipling's lines :

> Our England is a garden, and such gardens
> are not made
> By saying " How Beautiful! " and sitting
> in the shade.

No, indeed, you country-folk have allowed yourselves no sitting in the shade. . . .

And what sort of work have the Women's Institutes been doing! In their last report there is a list of activities showing that ten Government departments are very much in their debt. Here are some of the items:

Encouragement of schemes for the production of vegetables, fruit, rabbits, poultry, pigs, etc. Help in the repair of rubber boots for agricultural workers, and in the organization and supply of part-time labour on the land. Hospitality for the Women's Land Army. Help in the school meals, cod-liver oil and fruit juice schemes. Administration of rural section of the Fruit Preservation Scheme. Production and collection of culinary herbs; also medicinal herbs. Making toys for refugee children. Propaganda and educational work for diphtheria immunization and V.D. campaigns. Hospitality to American troops. Salvage of scrap iron and paper Establishment of hundreds of War Savings Groups. Welfare work for A.T.S., A.A. units, W.A.A.F.s and Home Guard, etc. . . . What a list! And the etc. at the end covers a multitude of good things and deeds

London Transport was ten years old on July 1. This is not the place to give the history of the huge organization—it is the greatest urban transport system in the world—which does for Londoners what was formerly done by 5 railways, 17 tramways and 136 bus and coach undertakings; but at least we may recall some of the wartime achievements of the London Passenger Transport Board. An unco-ordinated system of transport could never have faced, without serious risk of breakdown, the tremendous difficulties which the Board has successfully surmounted. Among its war tasks are the training of 6,000 employees as specialists in air-raid work, the construction of shelters for passengers and staff, the blacking-out of thousands of vehicles, the evacuation of 450,000 children, the conversion of the fleet of express coaches into ambulances, the development of a system of road spotters to warn drivers of imminent danger from aircraft, the provision of sleeping accommodation and the making of feeding arrangements at 79 Underground stations for those seeking shelter during air raids. (As many as 160,000 men, women and children found shelter in the Tubes at one time.)

Throughout the ten years Lord Ashfield has presided as the Board's chairman (as for many years before 1933 he presided over the " Underground " group of companies). Associated with him until 1940 was Frank Pick, who was not only a great man of business but a man with a fine artistic sense—as the posters which used to adorn the Tube stations in peacetime bear eloquent witness. But while gladly acknowledging the work of such men of superlative ability and achievement. let us not forget the tens of thousands of employees who, in good weather and in bad, before the blitz, during it, and since, have kept running the buses, the trams and trolley-buses, the Tubes and the local railways. And we must not forget to record the fact that many of them today are women. We have got quite used to women porters and ticket collectors; and the " conductorettes "—among the best-paid of women war-workers—rival in their perky humour their predecessors, those Cockney friends of ours who have been telling the Germans and Italians to " pass along "—without the " please."

What are the actual earnings of those engaged in industry at the present time? Every six months the Ministry of Labour and National Service sends out a questionnaire to some 55,000 employers. The latest inquiry was made in January last, and the results have just been published. The figures relate to those employed in a number of the most important industries—textiles, clothing, food, drink and tobacco, building, transport, public utility services and Government industrial establishments—but do *not* include coal-mining, agriculture, railways, merchant shipping, the distributive trades, catering, and domestic service. The average earnings in the last pay week of January 1943 of the 6¼ million workpeople covered by the returns received were as follows :

| | | |
|---|---|---|
| Men, 21 years and over | .. | 114s. 5d. |
| Youths and boys under 21 years | .. | 45s. 0d. |
| Women, 18 years and over | .. | 59s. 0d. |
| Girls, under 18 years | .. | 32s. 3d. |

These are general averages, and it will be understood that they are affected by the fact that different industries with varying levels of wages were not represented in equal proportions in the returns received. And, of course, the actual figures for the different industries vary widely.

# Awarded the Little Bronze Cross—For Valour

**Maj. J. T. M. ANDERSON, V.C., D.S.O.**
Led attacks on Longstop Hill, Tunisia, on April 23, 1943, and though wounded carried on and captured the position with a small force of men. For this he was awarded the V.C. He won the D.S.O. last May.

**Lt. W. A. SANDYS CLARKE, V.C.**
Dealt with two sniper posts single-handed during an enemy attack at Guiriat el Atach, Tunisia, on April 23, 1943, and recaptured three-quarters of the position before he was killed. He was posthumously awarded the V.C.

**Maj. (temp. Lt.-Col.) LORNE M. CAMPBELL, V.C.**
Formed an important bridgehead for a brigade of the 51st (Highland) Division at Wadi Akarit, Tunisia, on April 6, 1943, and subsequently captured some 600 prisoners. He was awarded the V.C. for this gallant deed.

**Act. Capt. F. T. PETERS, V.C., D.S.O., R.N.**
Completed an "enterprise of desperate hazard" when his ship rammed and shattered the boom of Oran Harbour on Nov. 8, 1942. He was killed in an air-crash the same month. In addition to the V.C. he was awarded the American D.S.C. for his heroic exploit.

**2/Lt. MOANA-NUI-A-KIWA NGARIMU, V.C.**
This Maori officer led his men to capture a vital position on Tebaga Gap, Tunisia, on March 26, 1943. In a violent Nazi counter-attack "he was killed on his feet, facing the enemy with his tommy-gun at his hip," and was posthumously awarded the V.C.

**SABADAR LALAHADUR THAPA, V.C., and HAVILDAR PARKASH SINGH, V.C.**
This valiant Gurkha officer (left) displayed remarkable leadership during crucial fighting at Wadi Akarit last April. He is seen being congratulated by H.M. the King after the latter had decorated him with the V.C. (the fifth to be awarded to a member of the Indian military forces in this war) in N. Africa in June 1943. Of the 8th Punjab Regt., Havildar Parkash Singh (right) earned his V.C. by great gallantry on Jan. 6 and 19, 1943, in hard fighting in the Mayu Peninsula, Burma.

*Photos, British Official: Crown Copyright, Indian Official: Catherine Bell, Daily Mirror Keystone, News Chronicle*

# I WAS THERE! Eye Witness Stories of the War

## How We Mastered the Infernal Magnetic Mine

Hitler boasted of a "secret weapon" which would sink our ships and leave us guessing. The story (written specially for THE WAR ILLUSTRATED) of how a small party of R.N. personnel tackled this serious challenge is here told in full, for the first time, by Lieut.-Commander John G. D. Ouvry, D.S.O., R.N., of H.M.S. Vernon. He received his decoration for the part he played on that occasion. Lieut.-Commander R. C. Lewis, R.N., also was awarded the D.S.O., and Chief Petty Officer Baldwin and Able Seaman Vearncombe the D.S.M. (See illus. p. 779, vol. 6.)

O N September 10, 1939—seven days after the outbreak of war—the steam vessel Magdepur was sunk in low water off Orford Ness. The casualty was attributed to an enemy mine; and minesweepers stationed at Harwich were sent out to clear that area. For hours they swept, but no mines were forthcoming. Later, another vessel was seriously damaged by a mysterious explosion while passing down the same channel.

A significant fact came to light. The hull of this ship had not been pierced, yet the underwater explosion had been severe enough to put her machinery out of action. This suggested to the experts that a non-contact type of mine—magnetic, or acoustic, or actuated by some other means—was being used by the enemy. Casualties continued to occur round our coasts, usually at the entrance to big ports. By the first week of November it was apparent to the authorities that if the Germans could lay this mine in sufficient numbers in our seaways the result to this country would indeed be serious.

On the night of November 21, 1939 German aircraft flew up the Thames and other estuaries, dropping into the water long cylindrical objects attached to parachutes. This, then, was the Nazis' method—or one of their methods—of depositing their infernal "secret weapon." As one of the staff of the Mines Department of H.M.S. Vernon (the R.N. Torpedo and Mining School) I was awakened at 3 a.m. the following day and instructed to catch the first available train from Portsmouth to London. I went direct to the Admiralty, where I was informed that I was required to remain at immediate notice to endeavour to discover the type and mechanism of these mines. Speed in this task was of the very greatest importance, for our sea traffic was in danger of being brought to a standstill.

Late that night, tired out with the strain of hours of waiting, I went to a London hotel to sleep. I was wakened soon after midnight to receive an urgent message from the Admiralty instructing me to return there at once. I did so, and met Lieut.-Commander Roger Lewis, R.N. He told me that aircraft had again flown over the Thames estuary, that night, and had dropped an object, probably a mine, off Shoeburyness. Low-water there was at 4.30 a.m., and it was likely that the mine would then be exposed.

O UR orders were to locate it, attempt to render it "safe," then collect it for further investigation at the Mine Experimental Department of H.M.S. Vernon, at Portsmouth. We went by fast car to Southend, through the darkness and the rain. At Southend we joined up with Commander Bowles, R.N., on the staff of the Naval Officer in Charge, Southend. We continued our journey to Shoeburyness, where Commander Maton (attached to the Experimental Department), who was to provide guides and all facilities, had already collected a small party of helpers.

Together we headed seaward, filled with excited anticipation. Guided by torches, we slithered for about 500 yards over slimy mud and sand. Occasionally we splashed knee-deep through pools. We strained our eyes in the darkness. Suddenly one of the guides, a private soldier who had seen the airborne object drop into the water in the early hours of the night, shouted, "There it is, sir!" It was a very thrilling moment when the light from the torches, concentrated in the direction he indicated, revealed a glistening object—with horns. It was our intention to carry out a preliminary examination, take flashlight photographs, then lash the mine down until the daylight low-water period, when we would do our best to render it "safe."

Lewis and I, having divested ourselves of metal items likely to influence the mechanism of the mine, approached it, leaving the remainder of the party in the rear. The external fittings of the aluminium alloy cylinder—it was seven feet long and 26 inches in diameter—were secured by screw rings requiring a special type of pin-spanner to remove them. We took paper rubbings, to serve as patterns from which suitable tools (of non-magnetic metal) could be fashioned.

### If We Were Unlucky . . .

Having lashed the mine securely and obtained our flashlight photographs, we set off back to our quarters. Confirmation that we really had found what we had been sent to look for came with the discovery of a parachute stretched out on the mud: a parachute fitted with an automatic-release device which came into operation after the mine had entered the water. Lieut.-Cmdr. Lewis and I had a very early breakfast, but it was not until early afternoon that the state of the tide permitted us to return to the scene of operations. Petty Officer Baldwin and Able Seaman Vearncombe, who had been with me on previous expeditions, had now arrived from Portsmouth; and soldiers with a caterpillar tractor waited inshore to cart off the mine as soon as we had finished.

We decided that Chief Petty Officer Baldwin and I should endeavour to remove the vital fittings; Lieut.-Cmdr. Lewis and Able Seaman Vearncombe to watch from what we considered to be a safe distance and make detailed notes of our actions and progress—for reference in case of accident. There was a possibility that the mine had devices other than the magnetic one, which added to the hazard. If we were unlucky, the notes which the two watchers had taken would be available for those who would have to deal with the next available specimen.

I first tackled an aluminium fitting sealed with tallow. In order to use one of the special spanners which had been rushed through (by Cmdr. Maton) in the local workshops for us, it was necessary to bend clear a small strip of copper. That done, we were able to extract this first fitting. Screwed into its base, when we drew it clear, we found a small cylinder—obviously a detonator, for in the recess from which the fitting had been withdrawn were disks of explosive. These I removed. This mysterious fitting proved, to be a delay-action-bomb fuze; it was necessary for the airman to tear off the copper strip referred to (before releasing his load) if bomb not mine was the requirement.

Before we could proceed further we had to call on Lieut-Cmdr. Lewis and A.B. Vearncombe for assistance to roll the mine over, this being firmly embedded in the hard sand and held fast by the tubular horns. The fact that the mine did not, and was not intended to, float explains the non-success of our minesweepers in their efforts to secure a specimen. Lieut.-Cmdr. Lewis and A.B. Vearncombe from then onwards lent a hand with the stripping-down. Dr. Wood, Chief Scientist of the Mine Design Department, H.M.S. Vernon, arrived in time to witness

H.M. THE KING listens to Lt.-Cdr. Ouvry's description as he inspects a German magnetic mine (see accompanying text). Hitler's "secret weapon" bore the date 1938.
*Photo, Topical*

the later stages. We were somewhat startled to discover yet another detonator and priming charge. Having removed all the external fittings, we signalled for the caterpillar tractor and soon had the mine ashore.

We had a shock—and a laugh when the shock wore off—before we had stowed away all the removed gadgets. We stopped for a breather on the foreshore, and one of the helpers carrying a rather heavy fitting put it down on a stone. It immediately commenced to tick noisily. The company dispersed like lightning! That most disturbing ticking, we presently discovered, came from clockwork mechanism within the heavy fitting; actuated by pressure, it happened to rest on its starting spindle. This proved to be a delay-action device, designed to keep the mine safe until the clock setting had run off.

N EXT day the body of the mine and the components we had removed were sent to H.M.S. Vernon. When we arrived there we were conscious of a somewhat tense atmosphere. The complete specimen had been locked up in a laboratory outside which stood a sentry with fixed bayonet. Responsibility for further investigation—searching of the actual interior—now passed to Dr. Wood and his two assistants, Mr. W. F. B. Shaw and Mr. H. W. K. Kelly. These experts worked on into the night, until they had laid bare the final secret of this destructive device. They found in the mine's interior an intricate and beautifully made piece of electro-magnetic apparatus; this, actuated by the passage above it of a steel hull, would fire a detonator which in turn would "set off" the 660 lb. of high explosive packed into the forepart of the 1,130-lb. mine. It was not long before a counter-measure was devised; our metal-hulled ships were fitted with de-gaussing coils—anti-magnetic cables—which rendered Hitler's "secret weapon" innocuous.

## I Was One of the Nine Who Came Back

The closing scene in the glorious stand of the 155th Field Battery R.A. on Feb. 26, 1943, in Tunisia, was briefly described in page 77 of THE WAR ILLUSTRATED by one of the nine survivors who got back to the British lines. The conclusion of Gunner Bryce's story (contained in a letter to his wife) appears here, by arrangement with the News Chronicle.

WHEN we were finished at last I found myself alone and surrounded by Germans on all sides. It was dark. A miracle happened and it poured with rain, making it pitch-black so that you could not see in front of you.

Some Germans passed within one yard of me. My only means of getting away was to crawl through a river, over a field (Germans occupying this spot), and then over a road where German tanks were spaced every 20 yards apart. After taking four hours to crawl through the river (I was so weary I nearly fell asleep lying in it) I came to the road where the tanks were.

My heart was in my mouth as I slowly began to wriggle across the road with both the sentries on each tank looking at me. To me it seemed ages before reaching the other side, although it was only four yards wide. Every second I expected one of them to take a shot at me. After getting across the road I rolled in a ditch on the other side. Another four yards on I had to cross a single railway track which, being higher up, was more exposed.

That was also quite a job, as the stones which the track lay on were all loose (a couple did roll down and it sounded to me like the world crumbling). While halfway over the track a Very light shot up—right from the spot I had been in on the other side of the road. I thought I was sure to be spotted, but my luck held.

Getting over the road and the railway was a hell of a job, as my clothes were squelching with mud and water every time I moved. Anyway, after the railway, I continued crawling in the stream until the dark blacked me out (it was only the pitch-black night and rain that enabled me to do it). I was able then to get up and start hiking to the nearest mountains. I thought once up in them I would be fairly safe.

I did intend to lay up during daytime and move by night, making for a British base about 40 miles away. Anyway, during that night, clambering over rocks, etc., made so many wild dogs (Arab ones) start howling that I decided to keep going during daytime.

This I did and after four days—from Friday till Tuesday—I arrived at our base, just a bit worn out, dirty, etc., but after a wash, shave and some food was as right as rain again. Luckily I had my water-bottle with me and a bar of chocolate—which kept me going those four days (the chief thing I missed was a nice cup of tea).

I'll always remember on the Sunday afternoon around dinner-time I laid down to rest and, a bit peckish, thought of you back home and pictured you just having dinner—and all the lovely dishes I could be eating.

I went over several lots of ranges before sighting our base. At first it was very disheartening to keep on seeing more hills in front of you after you had just climbed one, but when I looked down on the spot I was making for I moved quicker than at any other time. That first night in the hills I felt like crying when I thought of all our fellows who are now missing. They were very brave and didn't care two pins.

## A Norwegian Girl, I Was a Slave in Poland

Dreadful conditions are imposed on Norwegian boys and girls, between the ages of 14 and 18, sent by the Nazis to work on the land in Poland. Here Kari, who recently escaped to the safety of Sweden, tells her own grimly pathetic story.

UNDER German pressure I was weak enough to join the Quisling Youth Service in Oslo. I soon found out what type of organization it was, and tried to get out of it. My punishment was an order to work in Germany. In June of last year I left Oslo, with about 40 other girls who had also "volunteered" for German land work. We did not go to Germany, however, but to Poznan in Poland. Constantly under the observation of Nazi "fuehrerinner," or girl leaders, there was no opportunity to escape from the train as we went through Sweden. On arrival in Poznan

SIDI NSIR, NORTHERN TUNISIA, scene of the 155th Field Battery's glorious resistance in February 1943, which has been described as one of the most gallant actions in the Battle of Tunisia. Gunner Bryce (whose portrait appears in page 77) tells his dramatic story in the accompanying text. Taken just N. of Sidi Nsir, near Beja, the above photograph shows a knocked-out German tank, one of the many used by the enemy in overpowering force to crush the heroic British defence.

*Photo, British Official*

we found nine camps for Norwegian boys and girls, but I was sent farther afield with 18 others to a camp about 20 miles from Rosshöhe.

We were led into a school building which was filled with beds, with straw mattresses and one blanket. We were afterwards issued with working clothes, and set to work almost immediately filling in trenches. Our day began at 4.30 a.m., when we had breakfast consisting of skimmed milk soup, ersatz coffee, and two pieces of bread. Then followed a Nazi parade, after which work began. We had just a short time for a dinner of vegetable soup and potatoes, and after we finished work at 6 o'clock we were given a similar meal. Once a week we got meat, but never any fish. We were made to go to bed at 8.30, but it was almost impossible to sleep because of the rats, which ran over the beds all night, and the bugs and lice.

LATER in the year we worked in the fields and never had any free time for ourselves, with the exception of Sundays. One evening a friend and I met a Polish boy, but he was afraid of us at first because he thought we were German. We soon convinced him of his mistake, and went with him to his home, where we learned that the Poles' rations consisted of five pounds of potatoes a week, a small amount of bread, and no milk. We crept back to the camp thinking that our illegal visit had not been noticed, but a girl Nazi heard about it, and both of us were confined to our room for 14 days. We had three meals a day. But each of them consisted only of dry bread, ersatz coffee and unpeeled potatoes. We heard afterwards that, because of what we had done, collective punishment was imposed on the whole camp, the girls being set to work to dig field latrines after their normal day's work.

After the 14 days' punishment was up I was ill, and laid up for a week with a high fever ; but no doctor came nor was any attention paid to me. When I was well again it was decided that my friend and I should be separated, and I was sent to another camp, at Pappelhausen, where there were 17 others living in a rat-infested school building. There was no paraffin for the lamps and after we had finished our work we had to sit about in the darkness. We repeatedly had lectures on Quisling, and sometimes were sent to the nearest town to hear lectures on Hitler and his new order.

We Norwegians were strictly forbidden to speak to the Jews and Poles who were also working on the land, and we were told that if any of them failed to salute us when they saw us we had to report the matter. But none of us ever did that. If any of them were late for the parade in the morning they were beaten with sticks. They nearly all lived in the near-by farms, the owners of which had been torn away from their families and sent to other parts of the country. These workers received no pay and worked 11 hours a day. The Polish children went to German schools, but they were not allowed even to speak with the German children there.

I was sent to Poznan shortly afterwards for an operation for appendicitis. Then I was sent back to work too soon, and became seriously ill and was in hospital for another two months. When I returned to the camp it was bitterly cold. We had no extra clothes, and we could not have done much work in the fields, anyway, because of the snow. So work stopped for the time being, although the Poles and Jews were made to go out in the usual way. I had to visit the hospital again one day, and a young Pole came with me, both of us in the charge of a Nazi. But the Pole had no money to pay his hospital fees, so they sent him back. On the way he died.

Then I was told that because of my illness I might go home to Norway for a month's leave. I went to Oslo, and at the end of the time was summoned to return to Poland. As the train passed through Sweden, however, I was able to evade the Nazi leaders and jump off the train. I gave myself up to the Swedish authorities, and now (it seems like Heaven !) I am at last safe from the Nazis.

**GEOFFREY HOSFIELD, 20-year-old Merchant Navy engineer, returning to England from a Calcutta hospital, was suffering from spinal injuries and was encased from hips to shoulders in plaster of Paris. His voyage was almost over when his ship was torpedoed in the Atlantic at midnight. In spite of his terrible handicap Hosfield helped to lower a boat, but this subsequently turned over and he swam back to the sinking ship. The last boat was just pulling out, but he managed to reach it before the doomed ship finally sank.**

# OUR DIARY OF THE WAR

**JUNE 23, Wednesday.** 1,390th day
**Air.**—Spezia, Italian naval base, raided by Lancasters returning from N. Africa to England.
**Mediterranean.**—Pozzallo (Sicily) attacked by Malta-based fighter-bombers ; Catania attacked by Wellingtons.
**Pacific.**—Macassar, Jap base in Celebes, attacked by Allied bombers.

**JUNE 24, Thursday** 1,391st day
**Air.**—Elberfeld, W. half of Wuppertal (Ruhr), heavily raided.
**Mediterranean.**—Sedes airfield, 6 miles S. of Salonika, attacked by Liberators. Targets in Sardinia attacked by 300 bomber-fighter force.

**JUNE 25, Friday** 1,392nd day
**Air.**—Bochum-Gelsenkirchen (Ruhr) district very heavily bombed by R.A.F.
**Mediterranean.**—Messina (Sicily) battered by more than 100 Flying Fortresses. Naples again raided by R.A.F.
**U.S.A.**—Kiska (Aleutians) subjected to six U.S. air attacks.
**General.**—H.M. the King arrived back in England (by air) from N. Africa.

**JUNE 26, Saturday** 1,393rd day
**Mediterranean.**—Naples target for concentrated R.A.F. night assault.
**Burma.**—Jap positions near Kalemyo attacked by R.A.F. Blenheims ; U.S. bombers raided targets N. of Shwebo.
**U.S.A.**—U.S. bombers made seven attacks on Kiska (Aleutians).

**JUNE 27, Sunday** 1,394th day
**Mediterranean.**—Eleusis and Hassani airfields, near Athens, pounded by U.S. bombers. Malta-based aircraft attacked Gerbini airfield, Sicily. Wellingtons attacked San Giovanni in toe of Italy.
**U.S.A.**—Hammering of Kiska (Aleutians) continued with six attacks by U.S. aircraft.

**JUNE 28, Monday** 1,395th day
**Air.**—St. Nazaire U-boat base bombed, and airfield of Beaumont le Roger. Cologne heavily bombed (117th attack), also Hamburg.
**Mediterranean.**—Leghorn, N. Italy, subjected to concentrated nine-minute attack. Reggio di Calabria and Messina bombed.
**Australasia.**—Darwin received its 56th Jap raid.
**Burma.**—Akyab attacked by R.A.F. Wellingtons

**JUNE 29, Tuesday** 1,396th day
**Air.**—Le Mans (France) attacked by large force of Fortresses.
**Mediterranean.**—Comiso airfield (Sicily) attacked by Malta-based fighter-bombers ; Messina (Sicily) bombed.

**JUNE 30, Wednesday** 1,397th day
**Mediterranean.**—Palermo and airfields in Sicily attacked by Fortresses ; Cagliari (Sardinia) bombed.
**Australasia.**—Americans landed at Nassau Bay, nr. Salamaua, New Guinea. Trobriand and Woodlark Islands, N.E. of New Guinea, and Rendova Island, in New Georgia group of Solomons, occupied. Munda, on New Georgia Island, bombarded from Rendova, from the sea and from the air. Allied warships shelled Vila on Kolombangara Island, and Faisi (Shortland Islands). Darwin raided by 27 Jap bombers.

**1940**
June 23. Mr. Churchill announced Britain to fight on.
June 24. French armistice with Italy signed.
June 25. Hostilities in France ceased.
June 28. Gen. de Gaulle recognized as "Leader of all Free Frenchmen."
July 1. Announced French Government established itself at Vichy. Jersey and Guernsey taken over by Germans.
July 3. French warships in British ports taken over.
July 4. Italians occupied Kassala and Gallabat on Sudan frontier.
July 5. Pétain Government broke off diplomatic relations with Britain.

**1941**
June 23. Germans crossed River Bug (Poland).
June 24. Germans took Brest-Litovsk, Kaunas and Vilna.

June 26. Russians bombed Bucarest, Ploesti and Constanza (Rumania).
June 30. Germans captured Lwow (Poland).
July 3. Palmyra (Syria) captured by British.
July 4. General Gazzera, supreme commander of remaining Italian forces in Abyssinia, surrendered.
July 5. Germans claimed to have reached River Dnieper (Russia).

**1942**
June 24. British withdrew from Sollum and Sidi Omar to Mersa Matruh (Egypt).
June 25. Russians evacuated Kupiansk, S.E. of Kharkov.
June 27. Mr. Churchill arrived back in London after week of conferences in U.S.A.
June 29. Mersa Matruh evacuated by our troops.
July 1. Sebastopol captured by the Germans.

**General.**—Mr. Churchill received Freedom of the City of London at the Guildhall ; in his speech he predicted heavy fighting in Mediterranean and elsewhere "before the leaves of autumn fall." Award announced of Viscounty to Field-Marshal Sir A. Wavell, Viceroy-designate of India.

**JULY 1, Thursday** 1,398th day
**Mediterranean.**—Palermo (Sicily) and Cagliari (Sardinia) bombed ; Biscari airfield attacked by Malta-based fighters.
**Australasia.**—Viru Harbour, New Georgia, captured by Americans.

**JULY 2, Friday** 1,399th day
**Mediterranean.**—Trapani (Sicily), Olbia (Sardinia), and Castelvetrano (Sicily) bombed. Airfields of Lecce, Grottaglie and San Pancrazio (Italy) bombed.
**Australasia.**—American troops landed on Vangunu Island, and captured Vura.

**JULY 3, Saturday** 1,400th day
**Air.**—Kalk and Duetz, Cologne industrial districts, bombed ; Hamburg and Ruhr targets also attacked.
**Mediterranean.**—Sardinian and Sicilian airfields bombed.
**Australasia.**—Allied warships, supported by dive-bombers, bombarded Wickham Anchorage, Vangunu Island, in New Georgia. Jap raids on Nassau Bay and Bena Bena (New Guinea) ; Kendari (Celebes) heavily raided by Liberators ; Kupang (Timor) attacked by medium bombers. Australians and U.S. forces linked up in New Guinea.
**U.S.A.**—Kiska (Aleutians) again bombed by U.S. aircraft.

**JULY 4, Sunday** 1,401st day
**Air.**—Le Mans, Nantes and U-boat base of La Pallice (France) attacked by U.S. Fortresses.
**Mediterranean.**—Small British land-forces raided airfields in Crete at night destroying aircraft on the ground, before withdrawing safely.
**General.**—General Sikorski, Polish Prime Minister and C.-in-C., among 18 people killed in a Liberator which crashed just after leaving Gibraltar.

**JULY 5, Monday** 1,402nd day
**Air.**—Announced first air train (fully-loaded glider) to cross any ocean towed from Canada to Britain by a plane of R.A.F. Transport Command.
**Australasia.**—Allied warships bombarded Bairoko Harbour (New Georgia) and Vila Harbour (Kolombangara Island). American forces landed at Rice Anchorage, New Georgia Island, and at Zanana, near Munda, after American warships had shelled Jap bases on both sides of Kula Gulf.
**Russian Front.**—Germans launched offensive in Kursk, Orel and Bielgorod sectors ; 586 German tanks and 203 aircraft disabled or destroyed.

**JULY 6, Tuesday** 1,403rd day
**Australasia.**—Japs suffered considerable damage in naval battle in Kula Gulf (Solomons). Announced that Americans captured Vangunu Island.
**Mediterranean.**—Gerbini airfield (Sicily) pounded by Liberators. Palermo bombed by Wellingtons.
**Russian Front.**—433 more German tanks and 217 aircraft damaged or destroyed by Russians. Enemy made slight advances in Bielgorod area.

At the time of writing the Second Front has not been launched —at least there has been no invasion of the Continent, which is what is meant, I understand, by the phrase we so often see scribbled on the walls or above those oh so ancient photographs in the railway carriage! But quite a number of people seem to be expecting it daily, almost hourly. June 22 was the date given out by the Germans a short time ago as being that on which we were going to attack them. But when the anniversary of Hitler's invasion of Russia came and went, "the day" was moved on to July 3. That day too has gone by; but if the German prophets are at all like our own, they will have swallowed their disappointment with a perfectly good grace.

You must be hardened to that sort of thing if you set up in business as a rival of Old Moore, and you cannot but be cheered by the reflection that prophecies are forgotten almost as soon as they are uttered. Only those who keep a file of newspapers, or a folder of clippings, can realize how wrong—how generally wrong—the prophets have been. And the "armchair critics" are in the same boat, if I may be forgiven the mixture of metaphors. I happened recently to come across an article cut from one of the London evening papers, bearing a date in last January, in which the writer, a well-known commentator, makes the statement that "not many more than 150,000 men are holding at arm's length in Africa the flower of British and American strength, perhaps 900,000 men." I do not know how near or wide of the mark the latter figure is; but I do remember that the final count revealed that 291,000 Germans and Italians were put "into the bag" in Tunisia. Just one instance of many in which our "well-informed critics" have been—shall we say, misinformed.

Two hundred million cigarette ends are thrown away every day. You must take the figure on trust: the only authority given by Miss Ellen Wilkinson, when she made the statement recently, was an "investigation." But there is no doubt plenty of evidence to support her further statement that of the thousand fires which are reported every day half are caused by the careless disposal of cigarette ends and used matches. Naturally enough, Miss Wilkinson, as Parliamentary Secretary to the Ministry of Home Security, is deeply concerned over this matter of fires caused through sheer carelessness. Never have people been so keen on anything as getting the War won at the earliest possible moment, yet (she points out) there are all too many cases of factories being destroyed by fire, not to mention commodities in private homes, to replace which takes up valuable shipping space. Non-smokers may smugly boast that in this respect their record is a blameless one, but, as a fourth leader in The Times put it delightfully a few days ago, the cigarette ends themselves are at least guilty of contributory negligence. "They cling to life with astonishing tenacity," it read. "We may grind them underfoot, squash them and crush them, reduce them to their very elements, and yet 'rough hew them how we will,' they will not say die. The vital spark refuses to quit their frame, and several minutes after their presumed decease an unmistakable and pungent odour and a little coil of smoke proclaim that mangled they still live."

Lonely indeed is the life of the men and women in khaki who man our A.A. and searchlight sites all over the country; and good is it to know that a regular distribution of books is now being made to scores of the more isolated stations. More than fifty library vans are now in use, driven for the most part by volunteers wearing the red triangle of the Y.M.C.A. The vans are equipped with an initial stock of 1,000 volumes; and a typical day's run entails calling at ten sites on a 70-mile tour and distributing 150 books. Seventy per cent of the books borrowed are Wild West and detective yarns, but there are often some surprising demands. One librarian received request after request for "heavy" political books from two sergeants on separate A.A. sites; eventually she found that they were carrying on a long-distance argument with the help of information from the borrowed books. There are also library and music vans, the sides of which can be lowered to form a stage; and a piano, microphone, loudspeaker and gramophone are fitted. A small record library is carried from which the men can make their choice. One woman driver, we are told, arranges music "quizzes," and gives cigarettes as prizes.

How does the pay of a man in the Services compare with that of his contemporary in civilian life? That's a very difficult question to answer; how difficult was shown by Capt. Russell Grenfell, R.N. in a recent issue of the Sunday Times, of which paper he is the Naval Correspondent. In a White Paper published last August it is stated that it is "reasonable to suppose" that the provision of the Service man's board, lodging, clothing, laundry, health and unemployment insurance costs the country 35s. a week, which can therefore be brought into the total of his gross emoluments. But this figure is

considerably higher than the corresponding assessments made in 1914 and 1923, even when corrected for differences in cost of living, and it is noteworthy that the billeting charge allowable against the highest-paid Civil Servant is only 21s. This evidence of the Treasury's solicitude for its own people is supported by the fact that in making up the ex-Civil Servant conscript's pay there is no deduction in respect of emoluments in kind.

In the estimate of the soldier's cost of living the item "accommodation" works out at 12s. a week. As Capt. Grenfell says, "it seems rather high rent to levy on men living under water in a submarine or on a long Atlantic patrol in an aircraft, to say nothing of those drifting about on a raft, in a rubber dinghy, or sleeping under a ground sheet on land. For the wealthier officer the place on the raft or in the dinghy is naturally more expensive, the charge being in the region of 45s. In both cases the faithful watchdogs of the Treasury have remembered to include the estimated income-tax charge on these benefits."

But in spite of all the Treasury's ingenuity the Service man's pay cannot be made to approximate to that of a civilian. Comparing the White Paper's estimate of the total earnings of the Service man of three years' standing, married with two children, with those of the average workman over 21, married or single, in Government industrial establishments, we get the figures are for July 1942, the latest available): Service man, £4 12s. 9d., of which £3 9s. 9d. is received in cash; workman, £6 2s. Moreover, between October 1938 and July 1942 the workman's earnings increased by 46s. 9d. a week—more than double the whole cash pay of the unmarried Army conscript. The latter receives 21s., representing an increase of 14s. a week since 1797, a matter of 146 years. Another interesting fact unearthed by Capt. Grenfell is that the pay of most Naval lieutenants (under £6 a week for the unmarried officer) has increased by 45s. 6d. a week since 1840. Again, while the average of civilian remuneration has risen by 40 per cent in the last four years, the basic pay of full admirals has not quite reached that degree of increase since 1816.

Everyone who takes an interest in Far Eastern affairs must have heard of the Tanaka Memorial—the document which is supposed to contain the recommendations of the then Japanese Prime Minister to his Emperor following a conference of civil and military chiefs at Mukden in July 1927. The authenticity of the Memorial is not beyond question, but it is a fact that the events of recent years have often shown a close resemblance to what has been described as a "blueprint of Japanese expansion." Its publication in this country—Japan's Dream of Empire: The Tanaka Memorial, Edited with an Introduction by Carl Crow (Allen & Unwin, 4s. 6d.)—is, then, not inopportune.

From the General Post Office came the other day the announcement that civil postal services have now been restored to the occupied territories of Tripolitania and Cyrenaica. The announcement can be regarded as of historical importance, since it means that postal communications are now possible to the whole of the African continent. As a matter of interest, postal communications were never entirely severed with Tunisia.

FIELD-MARSHAL SIR A. WAVELL, G.C.S., C.M.G., N.C., whose appointment in succession to Lord Linlithgow as Viceroy of India was announced on June 18, 1943. He will take over his duties in October. On June 30 the King approved the conferring of a Viscounty upon him. *Photo, Topical*

# Air Onslaught on a Stepping-Stone to Italy

*Photo, British Official: Crown Copyright*

**R.A.F. BOSTON BOMBERS ATTACK LAMPEDUSA,** the little Italian island S.E. of Pantelleria (see p. 70), which surrendered on June 12, 1943. This photograph reveals the twelve square miles of the island—site of an important Axis submarine base—at the height of the aerial bombardment. Dense smoke-clouds billow from fiercely burning targets.

Printed in England and published every alternate Friday by the Proprietors, THE AMALGAMATED PRESS, LTD., The Fleetway House, Farringdon Street, London, E.C.4. Registered for transmission by Canadian Magazine Post. Sole Agents for Australia and New Zealand : Messrs. Gordon & Gotch, Ltd. ; and for South Africa : Central News Agency, Ltd.—July 23, 1943. S.S. *Editorial Address :* JOHN CARPENTER HOUSE, WHITEFRIARS, LONDON, E.C.4.

Vol 7 · The War Illustrated · Nº 160

Edited by Sir John Hammerton

SIXPENCE

AUGUST 6, 1943

'THE BEGINNING OF THE END!' declared Mr. Roosevelt when he spoke of the Allied invasion of Sicily on July 10, 1943. Many months of arduous training made Britons, Canadians and Americans irresistible when at length the day of the Sicilian adventure arrived. First sea-borne troops landed on Sicily before it was light, and this night scene shows men of the R.A.F. Regiment unloading runways from a landing-craft during a dawn rehearsal at a training centre.

*Photo, Daily Herald*

# THE BATTLE FRONTS

## by Maj.-Gen. Sir Charles Gwynn, K.C.B., D.S.O.

THE invasion of Sicily is an accomplished fact, and although the complete occupation of the island and the annihilation of the Axis forces defending it may take time, the issue is no longer in doubt. Moreover, clear proof has been given that amphibious operations on a great scale are practicable and that the Allies possess the resources, organization and leaders to carry them through successfully.

In Russia the German offensive (which had just started when my last article went to the press), whatever it was designed to achieve, has evidently failed conspicuously. The Russian counter-offensive has compelled the enemy to adopt a defensive attitude. It may result in the Soviet forces regaining the initiative which they had temporarily lost at the close of their great winter campaign. The situation will be discussed more fully below, for it is one on which there has been great diversity of interpretation.

In the Far East the American operations in New Georgia are proceeding steadily, but the Japanese force at Munda is strongly entrenched and is certain to fight like rats in a trap. In their attempts to assist the Japanese Navy has twice suffered serious losses; and the expenditure of Japanese aircraft has been high. These results are more important than the rapid annihilation of the detachment. The New Guinea operations also are bound to go slowly, but the capture of the Mubo post by the Australians is an important step towards closing in on Salamaua.

**Lt.-Gen. PATTON, commanding the U.S. 7th Army in Sicily, personally led the decisive attack which threw back two regiments of German tanks at Gela on July 12, 1943, after the Americans themselves had been driven back twice.** *Photo, Fox*

SICILY The amazing completeness of the success with which the invasion of Sicily was accomplished should not suggest the idea that the difficulties and dangers of amphibious operations on a great scale have been exaggerated. Rather should we be astonished that it was possible to organize an armada of such unprecedented size and to bring it safely and in secrecy to its appointed theatre of action.

The success of the operation depended primarily on thorough preparation and

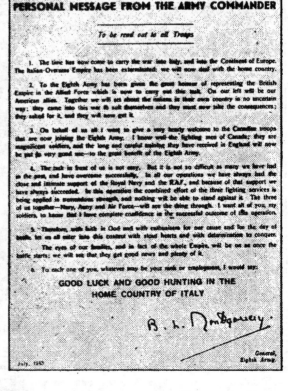

**STRIKING TOWARDS CATANIA, second largest city of Sicily, the 8th Army had breached German defences at Lentini on July 15, 1943. Four days later (July 19) they had captured an important defence position on the outskirts of Catania itself. (See also map in page 133)**
*Map by courtesy of The Daily Telegraph*

wonderful organization on the part of all three Services, but especially by the Navy. But we should not lose sight of the other factors which contributed to success, some of which were due to mistakes made by the enemy, unlikely always to be repeated. Control of sea communications by the Navy and mastery in the air were clearly essential preliminaries; they did not imply action by those two Services outside their normal role, but the conditions were favourable for their attainment owing to great numerical and qualitative superiority and the possession of suitable bases.

THE first phase of the actual operation—the sea passage—could therefore be carried through in fundamentally favourable circumstances. The immense size of the armada and the fact that Sicily was a clearly indicated objective made it seem, however, that surprise in the fullest sense would be unobtainable. That surprise was achieved is perhaps the most remarkable feature of the whole operation.

It was due primarily to the amazing accuracy in time and direction with which the various components of the convoy reached their disembarkation points along the 80 miles of coast on which landings were to take place. That the armada escaped observation either by aircraft or by the enemy's light surface vessels or submarines may be accounted for partly by the completeness of our sea and air control; but the gale which sprang up during the time of the passage may have induced the enemy to relax precautionary reconnaissance.

It would certainly be unwise to count on similar attainment of surprise in future operations. Disembarkation of the troops, also the responsibility of the Navy, was evidently carried out with the greatest speed and absence of confusion, much helped, of course, by the perfection of the landing-craft employed. The first phase of the operation gave a triumphant display of Naval efficiency, but it rested on the Army and the Royal Marines to take full advantage of the wonderful start given them. Clearly they displayed immense dash, sustained energy and initiative as they drove rapidly inland.

FIRST the beaches were firmly secured; then, without a pause, the troops pressed on to establish a bridgehead. Within 24 hours one had been gained, of a size adequate for the deployment of large forces, containing three airfields and, even more important, the port of Syracuse. The Italian troops first encountered were chiefly local coast defence militia, and on the whole their resistance was feeble, though at points they fought with determination. Airborne troops, landed by parachutes and gliders during the night some hours before the arrival of the main body, contributed to the success, though, owing to the stormy weather, parties got separated and were not in every case put down at the points intended.

Full information as to what they achieved is not yet available, and some parties were certainly overwhelmed and captured; but it is undoubted that their appearance helped to distract attention and to give rise to the impression that only a sabotage raid was in progress. They must, therefore, have given valuable assistance to the main operation. The well-timed and heavy bombing of the Headquarters of the defence added

to the confusion and accounted largely for lack of co-ordination in the resistance offered.

The second phase of the invasion, the capture of a bridgehead, had therefore been unexpectedly easy and great energy was shown in exploiting this success. A counter-offensive was expected within 72 hours after the first landing. A measure of caution consequently was necessary, and in any case lack of transport limited the size of advanced parties and the distance to which they could penetrate in order to enlarge the bridgehead. But no counter-offensive came, and, except for local counter-attacks at Augusta, after its capture by our advanced troops, and at Gela against the Americans, the Axis was concerned mainly in defence.

The two counter-attacks mentioned were carried out by parts of the Herman Goering Division, a new division under an old name.

They had some temporary success, but were eventually driven off with heavy loss. Why the great opportunity for counter-attack, which must always exist in the few days immediately following a landing in any region where the enemy has substantial forces, was not seized is difficult to explain. It was more surprising than the failure of the Italian fleet to interfere with the landing operation, and the failure of the Luftwaffe to act vigorously against shipping and congested beaches.

### WHY Did the Axis Fail to Counter-attack?

It appears probable that the enemy was convinced that the landing would be made at the Western end of the island and had disposed his counter-offensive reserves on that assumption. The assumption would not have been unwarranted, for there are more and better harbours at the Western end, and it lies closer to the air bases and harbours of Tunisia. The Allied air forces had also paid special attention to that end of the island.

THE enemy may also have considered that a landing in the south-east of the island close to his air bases on the Italian mainland was improbable. With his reserves wrongly disposed the Allies were given a chance of exploiting the unexpected, and the bombing of defence Headquarters combined with the bombing of roads must have added greatly to the difficulty of readjusting faulty dispositions. Having lost his opportunity the enemy was compelled to fall back on a purely defensive strategy in view of the rapidly increasing Allied strength. Henceforward the campaign is bound to develop on normal lines, with Catania and the main Axis east and west communications passing through Enna, as the chief immediate objectives.

The struggle may be protracted in view of the mountainous and defensible nature of the country, but the Axis forces with little hope of reinforcement or of successful evacuation are clearly in danger of disaster comparable to that of Tunisia. Since the naval and air

Gen. GUZZONI, Axis C.-in-C. in Sicily, who, on July 19, 1943, removed his H.Q. to Reggio di Calabria on the Italian mainland. He reported to King Victor Emmanuel that he was unable to guarantee prolonged resistance in Sicily. *Photo, Associated Press*

superiority is well established there should be few of the difficulties which caused delay in bringing the Tunisian campaign to a climax.

## RUSSIA

When their offensive opened the Germans, presumably in order to mislead, announced that it was merely a local counter-attack which had unintentionally grown in scale on the initiative of local commanders ; and that it was the Russians who had made the first move. This pretence was not kept up, but at no time have the Germans claimed that their attacks amounted to more than operations to forestall a Russian offensive.

When, however, they were able to announce the penetration of the Russian defences they admitted that the battles raging were of unprecedented violence and promised to produce results of decisive importance. In Moscow it seems to have been thought that an all-out offensive had been attempted. To me personally it seemed inconceivable that the Germans, with danger threatening in the west and south, would risk entangling themselves in an all-out offensive entailing long advances and the employment of constantly increasing numbers.

That the offensive had been carefully prepared and was on an exceptional scale cannot be doubted. The very large number of Panzer divisions employed was sufficient proof of that. But the probabilities seemed to be that territorially it had a limited objective and that its main object was to forestall and disrupt Russian offensive plans. Its immediate object was evidently, by simultaneous attacks, southwards from Orel and northwards from Byelgorod, to pinch out the Russian salient west of Kursk, encircling and annihilating the strong Russian Army within it.

The very high proportion of Panzer divisions in the two thrusts made it clear that blitzkrieg action was aimed at in order to make Russian withdrawal difficult. Obviously, if rapid decisive results could be obtained not only would Russian offensive power be greatly

reduced, but a shorter and more defensible front could be established, giving, especially, security to Orel which would no longer stand in an exposed salient. With these results achieved, greater freedom to divert forces to meet the threat of the western Allies would be attained.

From the first the German plan, whatever it was, miscarried. The thrust south from Orel failed, after heavy losses, to make any substantial progress. The thrust northwards from Byelgorod after some days of desperate fighting did succeed in driving wedges through the Russian defences and emerged into open country. It is impossible yet to say how deep the penetration was, but it is clear that ferocious fighting continued and the Panzers never succeeded in establishing freedom of movement. Both sides threw in reserves, and the Germans claimed that a great battle of attrition was in progress in which Russian reserves would be exhausted.

It was, in fact, a case of victory going to the side which could conserve its last reserves. After nine days of furious fighting it became

evident that it was German reserve strength that was becoming exhausted, and the intensity of the fighting died down. At the same time Stalin and Zhukov again proved that they were masters of the principle of conservation of reserve power. They had demanded the utmost tenacity from their defending troops and had refused to divert reserves intended for an attack on Orel.

WONDERFULLY well timed, the attack was launched before the Germans at Byelgorod had recovered sufficiently to renew their efforts. Both Orel and its railway communications with Bryansk are threatened, and the Germans have been forced to withdraw the Orel arm of their pincer plan to meet the danger. It would probably be too much to expect that Orel will be captured or even be completely isolated, for it has been strongly fortified as a hedgehog position. It is certain however to become too restricted an area to retain its value as an offensive spring-board.

The Germans claim that the Russian attack on Orel is merely a diversionary operation to relieve the danger to their Kursk position, and that the Byelgorod battle has actually destroyed Russian power of conducting a major offensive. Even if that were so it would hardly compensate for the immense losses suffered by their own picked troops. It could not be expected that the Germans would admit failure, but their complaints that bad weather prevented them achieving a decisive victory is tantamount to an admission.

CENTRAL RUSSIAN FRONT. By July 20, 1943 the Russians had made further important gains in the Orel sector. The white line and white arrows in this map show the German front at mid-July ; black arrows indicate Soviet attacks.

# Swift Advance Follows Landing on Sicily's Coast

PUSHING ON INTO SICILY, Allied forces had occupied one half of the island by July 21, 1943. British infantry (1) advance from Pachino, capture of which was announced on July 12, towards Augusta, which fell two days later. Two infantrymen (2) enter a street in Pachino. Army pack-mules (3) for use in mountainous areas are led ashore from landing-craft, and (4) not unwilling Italian prisoners are marched into the main square of Licata, capture of which, by the Americans, was announced on July 12. Only 11 days after the landing, the Axis forces in central and Western Sicily were retreating towards Messina, in the north-eastern tip of the island, facing the "toe" of Italy. But the struggle for Catania—some 20 miles north of Augusta—was still proceeding, with General Montgomery's men of the 8th Army making steady progress towards the conquest of the town.

*British Official photographs by radio from Algiers*

# After Sicily Comes the European 'Fortress'

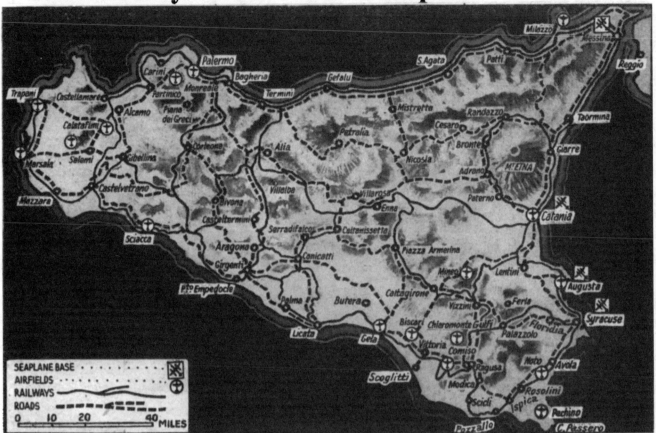

**SICILY—AND THE LARGER TARGET.** Stiffer enemy resistance encountered by July 19, 1943, indicated that the first phase of the Sicilian conflict was over. By then we had occupied all that part of the island south of a line drawn from Empidocle to the outskirts of Catania. The upper map shows Sicily's communications and air bases. The lower one, outer and inner fortification "walls" of Hitler's European "Fortress." Solid black arrow indicates our Sicilian thrust; broken arrows, directions of further possible invasion blows.

*New York Times and News Chronicle*

# The United Nations Attack Europe's Under-Belly

AMERICAN SHERMAN TANKS are seen in the top photograph splashing their way towards the Sicilian shore during the Allied landings on July 10, 1943.] By July 19, U.S. forces had advanced westward from Gela to Porto Empedocle (see map on page 133). Below, infantrymen have just disembarked from the landing-craft on the left. This new type of vessel has shaped instead of square bows, resulting in greater speed and it is fitted with ladder-gangways to facilitate disembarkation. (See also illus. page 139.) PAGE 134 *Photos, British Official : Crown Copyright ; Keystone*

# Our Invaders Set Foot on the Sicilian Shore

JUST OUT OF THEIR LANDING-CRAFT, Allied infantry wade up the Sicilian beach, the foremost of them heading in the direction of the sand dunes seen in the background. The Italian shore defences "folded up like a concertina," and within a few hours after the landings on July 10, 1943 our troops had penetrated several miles inland. By July 13 Allied forces were firmly established in the S.E. corner of the island, and by July 19 one-third of Sicily was in our hands, together with more than 35,000 prisoners.

**LANDED BY THE ROYAL NAVY** on a beach in Sicily on July 10, 1943, British troops, wading keee-deep, have here formed a chain to pass the ammunition. In the background a tank from one of the landing-craft is ploughing through the shallow water. An almost unending flow of vessels, escorted by the Allied Navies and further protected by aircraft, has kept our increasing invasion forces fully equipped with guns, tanks and other supplies essential to the successful prosecution of the great task in hand.
*Radio photo from Algiers*

# THE WAR AT SEA

## by Francis E. McMurtrie

As this is written, reports of the internal condition of Italy suggest that the end of Italian resistance cannot be so far away as was thought before the invasion of Sicily began. In these circumstances it is perhaps hardly surprising that the Italian Navy has shown no sign of coming out of port to fight. That this is due to any lack of courage no one who knows the Italians is going to believe. Neither should it be ascribed solely to inadequate air support, though this may be a contributory reason. Another explanation that has been presented is that there are no longer enough destroyers in the Italian fleet to provide an anti-submarine screen. This is hardly supported by the facts.

It is true that fully fifty of his destroyers have been sunk since the Duce decided to take the fatal plunge in June 1940. Probably about a dozen more have disappeared in various ways, so that the total wastage may be assessed at something over 60. Yet there were 130 destroyers or large seagoing torpedo boats in the Italian Navy at the start of the war, with 12 more under construction.

In addition, there are at least two Yugoslav destroyers, the Dubrovnik and Ljubljana, which are reported to have been taken over by the Italians and renamed Premuda and Sebenico respectively. It would seem, therefore, that there may be quite 70 still in service ; enough to afford ample screening to a bigger battle-fleet than ever Italy has been able to muster, even if some deduction be made for destroyers under refit.

This leads to the conclusion that the object in keeping the Italian fleet out of action is mainly a political one. Mussolini doubtless considers that the retention under his control in two different ports of some six or seven battleships, over a dozen cruisers, some 70 destroyers, and an uncertain number of submarines and other warships, is equivalent to the possession of a certain number of bargaining counters. But he will find it difficult to bargain with adversaries whose only terms are unconditional surrender.

Whether similar ideas are entertained by the Nazi rulers of Germany it is impossible to tell. At the end of the last war, when the situation became desperate for the Germans, their fleet was ordered to proceed to sea and fight, but broke out into mutiny instead. This mutiny did not affect the submarines, being confined mainly to the big ships at first. Long periods of idleness in port, with the gradual picking out of key ratings for duty in U-boats, led to discontent and insubordination.

There is always the possibility that similar conditions will produce the same results. Germany's big ships in the present war are by no means so numerous as in the last, but they must have had an even duller time. Several of them have been stationed for over a year in Norwegian waters, far removed from their homes and with a definitely unfriendly population around them. They have the added discomfort of knowing that the homes of many of them are in nightly danger of being wiped out by Allied bombing, which was not the case in 1918. Thus it is possible there may be some element of truth in the stories from Sweden of sailors in the German squadron at Trondheim becoming restive under the strain.

## MIGHT Have Won War For the Axis

One of the principal objects with which Germany dragged Italy into the war was connected with the fact that Italy's geographical position, aided by the possession of a powerful fleet, gave her the opportunity of cutting British communications with the East through the Mediterranean. Until quite recently, indeed, it has been necessary to send the bulk of our shipping via the Cape of Good Hope instead of through the Suez Canal, involving an enormous addition to the distance to be covered and consequently to the time occupied in the voyage.

From London to Aden via the Mediterranean and Suez Canal is just over 4,600 miles ; by way of the Cape of Good Hope it is 10,200 miles. This extra strain on our already overtaxed shipping resources, combined with the greatly improved opportunities given to the U-boat attack on commerce by the simultaneous withdrawal of France from one side and the entry of Italy on the other, might well have won the war for the Axis.

It must be admitted that it was a close thing.

Had Japan come in sooner the situation would have been even more desperate. As it was, the United States had been given a certain amount of time to prepare for the danger which ultimately materialized at Pearl Harbour. This second crisis of the war was almost as acute as the first, and but for the experience gained in dealing with the earlier emergency it is questionable whether it would have been possible to struggle so successfully with the second.

After the war is over in Europe there will remain a tremendous task still to be accomplished in the Pacific and Far East. It will require all the resources of the United Nations to overcome the stubborn resistance which the Japanese are accustomed to offer even when there is no hope of relief from a desperate position. Not until the Japanese fleet has been induced to fight it out and has been completely annihilated will the ultimate victory be in sight. Nor is it to be expected that surrender will follow immediately ; for the real rulers of Japan are the soldiers, who do not grasp the implications of sea power.

Had it been left to the Japanese naval chiefs, it is to be doubted whether the decision to challenge the united sea power of the British Empire and the United States would ever have been taken. But with the army holding the controlling influence, wielded by Tojo, it was not to be expected that naval views would receive much attention.

By this time it is possible that some glimmering of the truth is beginning to penetrate into Japanese Army circles. Their troops are being sacrificed freely in endeavours to hold back the Allied advance in the Solomons and New Guinea, but without complete command of the sea it has proved impossible either to prevent landings in New Georgia or Nassau Bay or to reinforce the threatened garrisons. Already severe losses have been inflicted on the Japanese naval forces that have vainly attempted to escort transports to New Georgia.

Though there seem to be plenty of cruisers and destroyers left in the Japanese Navy, the supply cannot be inexhaustible, and sooner or later the time will come when there are not enough to go round. At the same time, the Allied superiority in all classes of warships continues to grow with increasing speed. When the European situation has been cleared up, the naval reinforcements immediately available should be sufficient to turn the scale in the Allies' favour.

# Allied Navies Do a Mighty Job Magnificently

SUCCESS OF OUR LANDING OPERATIONS in S.E. Sicily on July 10, 1943 was due largely to the faultless efficiency of the Allied Navies. The invasion armada was composed of about 2,000 vessels of all sizes, from cruisers to "little ships," and the troops were put ashore dead on time. Top, en route for Sicily ; inset, Adml. Sir Bertram Ramsay, K.C.B., M.V.O., Naval Commander Combined Operations in the Mediterranean. Bottom, American L.C.I. landing-barges laden with troops ready for departure. PAGE 137 *Photos, British Official ; Daily Mirror*

# They Helped to Make the Invasion Possible

BRITISH INVASION CRAFT which played so successful a part in the assault on Sicily on July 10, 1943 represented many months' work in our shipbuilding yards. These boys (1) heated the rivets which the riveters (2) are seen driving home. A great side-plate (3) being moved into position for riveting. Finished invasion barge (4) being transported seawards by means of a lorry. The dinner-hour (5) is welcomed after a hard morning's work well done. The smiles became even broader when these Home Front workers learned of the great results of their arduous labours. Another type of invasion craft is shown in the opposite page.

*Photos, Fox*

# How Our Assault Troops Crossed to Sicily

NEW TYPE OF INVASION CRAFT that greatly increased the speed with which assault troops gained the Sicilian beaches. Built in U.S.A. from Anglo-American designs, it has several interesting features, including the ladder-gangways (see also page 134) which are lowered as soon as the vessel enters shallow water, enabling troops to disembark from both sides. Top, U.S. troops clambering up one of the gangways during rehearsal in Britain. Bottom, one of the new craft with gangways raised. *Photos, British Official: Crown Copyright*

# With a Red Bomber Squadron in the Caucasus

SOVIET AIR FORCE CREWS assembled at their base (1) for the take-off ; they are about to set out on an important sortie ; Capt. Maluinov, the Squadron's Commander, is seen on the right. 2, Stormovik dive-bombers swoop low among the mountain valleys as they attack enemy ground targets entrenched on the precipitous hillsides. 3, In close formation the Stormoviks roar above snow-clad peaks. 4, The Commander, smiling and confident, gives the signal for yet another take-off.

*Photos, S. Kafafyan, Exclusive to* THE WAR ILLUSTRATED

# The Germans Drove a Wedge—At What a Cost!

**ON THE CENTRAL RUSSIAN FRONT**, in the Byelgorod-Kursk-Orel sectors, battles began on July 5; three days later German tanks drove a wedge into Soviet positions at Byelgorod. By July 14 the enemy had little to show for his terrific onslaught. In the first six days of the offensive he was reported to have lost 2,609 tanks and 1,037 planes. Bottom, Russian anti-tank gunners fire at a Panzer unit across a river in the Byelgorod area. Centre, U.S. Boston Bombers flown by Soviet aircrews operate over Kursk. Top, German machine-gun post in the marshes of the Kuban bridgehead, where the Russians took an important position on July 18, 1943.

*Photos, Pictorial Press and Associated Press*

# What Goes On in the Lulls Between Attacks?

Intensive planning and material preparation on a colossal scale—with nothing left to chance and always with an eye on the clock—are in progress when there is "nothing in the news." Here ROBERT DE WITTE explains what tremendous thought and labour are involved in the preparations to move an attacking force, such as that which descended upon Sicily.

Two thousand ships laden with men, equipment, lorries, armoured cars, tanks—these and more formed the spearhead of the invasion force which struck at Sicily in the early hours of Saturday, July 10, 1943. They will be followed by more ships, more men, more materials every hour until the island is conquered.

To have assembled this great force with its equipment down to the last bootlace and sent it off according to a split-second time-table within two months of the last major battle securing the ports in North Africa is a remarkable feat, exceeding anything that the Germans, for all their reputation for organization, have been able to do. Just what the preparation of such an invasion armada involves is not appreciated even by those who see loaded ships in endless procession leaving port.

When the last Axis soldier in North Africa stopped fighting many people expected that they would pick up their newspapers in two or three days and read that Allied forces had landed in Europe and were continuing the chase of Axis armies where they had left off in Tunisia. As days passed there was a sense of anti-climax. There was " nothing happening," as the man-in-the-street put it.

In fact a very great deal was happening, more perhaps than at the height of the battles in Tunisia. Victories in modern war must be succeeded by " pauses " while preparations are made for the next battle. And where the victory has been on the beaches the pause is likely to be a long one, for completely new kinds of equipment have to be brought up for the next operation, which is necessarily amphibious.

### Planning Delivery

A modern army requires a fantastic amount of equipment. A modest figure is 12,000 tons per division for " warlike stores." Put this in another way and you find that moving a comparatively small army of 100,000 men will require a convoy of perhaps 100 large merchant ships. Bringing the stores to the dockside needs several hundred trains or perhaps 40,000 lorries. And mere numbers is only half the problem. The men, materials, weapons, food, medical supplies and so on must be brought in the right order to the right place at the right time.

Remember that the British army uses 3,500,000 different items of equipment, from small instruments to 30-ton tanks, and you will appreciate that planning delivery, much of it under fire, makes the transport problem of a West End store in a peace-time Christmas week seem simple.

But the piling up of supplies in anticipation of an attack is only the first stage. The attacking armies have to be fed and supplied while they fight, and preparations for this must be made long before they go into action. A successful landing in, say, Italy would end in disaster if the arrangements for perhaps 400 tons of supplies a day per division were not completed to the last detail. Actually, the Eighth Army advancing across North Africa required 520 tons a day per division; but one-fifth of this was water, a difficulty that might not be found in better-watered battlefields.

Before giving battle preparation must be made for exploiting success. This means having ready materials for repairing railways, roads and ports and for setting going again public utilities such as power-houses and waterworks which might have been damaged. Before the Eighth Army struck at El Alamein

specialists had made plans for repairing everything between Egypt and Tunisia ! The result was that the railway destroyed in 208 places was completely repaired in 28 days, and ports like Benghazi and Mersa Matruh, which the Axis thought they had utterly destroyed, were handling hundreds of tons every 24 hours within a short time.

The final battle of North Africa was not amphibious, as any future operation against the Axis must be. To get some idea of the complexity of large-scale amphibious operations, take some of the figures which it is now permitted to give about the American landings in Morocco and Algeria. The complete preparations to move the modest armies took 15 weeks. During this time

MAIN ASSEMBLY SHED at an R.E.M.E. Middle East depot where thousands of transport trucks and other vehicles are assembled, serviced and delivered in record time for use by the Allied armies. *Photo, British Official*

700,000 different items were assembled and packed. They included over 20,000,000 lb. of food, 38,000,000 lb. of equipment and 10,000,000 gallons of petrol and oil.

The fuel was conveyed partly in tankers, partly in small drums which could be carried ashore by two soldiers. The " logisticians " —as the U.S. call the men who plan the movements of men and materials—also worked out and set in motion the machinery for the replacement of all this material as required. Experience shows how long a pair of boots or a set of tires will last. Replacements must be there. And the period varies with the pace of the fighting and the terrain. The Eighth Army required 2,000 tires a day. U.S. soldiers were expected to wear out boots at the rate of seven pairs in three months. In kinder terrain tires, caterpillars, boots and " spares " of all kinds are not required in such numbers.

Shipping is the determining factor in amphibious operations, and upon the number of ships available may depend the size and formation of the invading force. Long experience enables the experts to say very precisely what materials and men they will

transport, not such a simple matter when you remember that the order in which materials are packed, the unloading facilities at both invasion port and attacking points, and the proportion of material to be packed ready for action, all have to be forecast and taken into account. The most economical method of packing is in cases, but where weapons will be required immediately on landing this is not possible. The normal calculation is very nearly 180,000 packing-cases for a division.

Many of the calculations have, of course, been standardized so that all the experts have to do is to multiply the standard equipment by the number of units which have to be transported. The usual basic unit is the division. But even the simplest operation calls for an immense amount of additional material. For instance, if the area to be attacked is infested by mosquitoes or suffers from extremes of heat and cold, special additional materials will be required in large quantities—mosquito nets, sun glasses, furs, skis or whatever it may be, in thousands.

### Prisoner Problems

Then there are maps and photographs. The experts will prepare them first for themselves, so that they may not only make a general calculation on the tonnage that can be handled on every beach and harbour, but a really detailed one, down to the exact berth to be taken up by each ship with its special cargo. The invading army will require maps and photographs in thousands. Over 1,000 different maps and 5,000 different air photographs were printed, some of them in hundreds, for the invasion of Morocco and Algeria. The more detailed maps have to show, if possible, the minutest features, on a scale of nearly one inch to the furlong.

Even this very condensed account of some of the preparations that have to be made for a major amphibious operation will explain the " pauses " that must occur. The Germans had six years to prepare for their attack on Poland, Holland and Belgium and France. Yet even they required a long pause for preparations after the initial successes in Flanders, and they waited nearly two months after their conquest of France before considering the time to be ripe for the aerial attack that was to precede the sea invasion of Britain.

One of the reasons for their delay when immediate assault might have caught Britain virtually unarmed was that they were choked with the prisoners and booty they had taken. They had made elaborate preparations for clearing prisoners rapidly; but weeks had to be spent in " digesting " their booty.

We have been faced with something like the same problem in North Africa. The 291,000 Axis prisoners, taken at the end of very overloaded lines of communication, have been a major problem, absorbing transport and manpower.

Plans, perhaps in some detail, may exist for all the major battles which the Allied High Command anticipate will end the war. The movement experts have probably worked out to the last cartridge just what will be required for anticipated operations far ahead of the speculations of even the boldest amateur prophets. But the actual carrying out of these huge movements of men and materials is a three-dimensional operation in which the time factor cannot be compressed beyond a certain point, even with the help of air transport being increasingly used by the Allies. Hence the pauses.

Photos, Fox, Planet News

## Our Sea-Soldiers Storm the Beach

The recent landings on Sicily owed much of their success to the toughness, efficiency and skill of our assault troops, the result of months of most rigorous training. The first British officer to step ashore in Sicily was a Royal Marine—and here are men of that famous Corps of sea-soldiers carrying out a grim rehearsal. At top they are seen gaining the crucial initial foothold on land, while below a section is providing covering-fire for its advancing comrades.

143

## Swift Work Follows the Landing

Clothes and equipment bundled in a ground-sheet and pushed before them as cover and gun-rest (1) Marines of the advanced landing-party negotiate a river a short way inland, to work round to the enemy's rear. A concrete sea-wall backing the beach (2) proves no insurmountable obstacle with disciplined hauling and pushing, and a jetty (3) is rope-scaled with incredible speed, whilst a rifle group sees to it that the brisk proceedings shall not be unduly interrupted.

*Photos*

## Stiff Hazards are Taken at a Stride

Even a vertical cliff (4) gives the "Jollies" foothold, burdened as they are with battle equipment. At the top of the rope sudden action may develop—but the men above are speedily protected by comrades with light machine-guns. A cross-river scramble and a downward climb (5) are tackled as coolly by these U.S. Rangers who have trained with their British allies; they are swinging down netting into their waiting boats to carry the inland advance a stage farther.

## *The Attack is Pressed Home*

A dense smoke-screen to cover the advance (1) is put down by low-flying Blenheims, whilst a Jeep (2) summons Spitfire support by radio to aid the foremost units. Ultimate success is largely dependent on uninterrupted and rapid intercommunication, and this is provided and maintained by men of the Royal Corps of Signals; here (3) an A.A. gunner protects cable layers. Personal camouflage, especially at dawn and dusk, is vital and in (4) two Marines prepare to rush an enemy reconnaissance patrol and with bayonet-work ensure that news of the advance shall not leak back that way.

# VIEWS & REVIEWS
### Of Vital War Books

### by Hamilton Fyfe

THE P.B.I.! I suppose everyone knows what the letters stand for. The phrase was invented, I believe, during the last war. The poor b—— infantry invented it themselves. It is an example of that half-jocose, half-pathetic humour in which the English, Cockneys especially, excel. I feel sure it must have been a Cockney who first spoke of the P.B.I. And after reading Infantry Officer (Batsford, 6s.) I am more than ever convinced that those initials exactly fit the case.

As the author is a serving soldier he cannot put his name to the book. All we are told about him is that he is a young man, about twenty-four; but what he writes reveals a stubborn, obstinate character and a lucid, observant mind. He needed them both in France during those catastrophic weeks between the opening of the Hun offensive in May 1940 and evacuation via Dunkirk.

Of the first eight months—he went out at the beginning—little is said; but there is one painfully significant, casual remark: "During those eight months I don't think I took part in one field exercise." We have learned since then the absolute necessity of practising over and over again the operations the infantry will be called on to undertake. Was there no general on our side who saw it in those months of "digging and drinking"? Alexander must have known; it was he who started intensive field training after Dunkirk; but he was not high enough up at the time. The truth was the commanders-in-chief did not know their job. We know the Germans were being put through the most realistic rehearsals of what they were to do when the offensive started. We did next to nothing in that line. Fortunately the commanders-in-chief today are of very different mentality.

Educated French people the author found friendly and understanding. With the peasants he had some trouble. One day a piece of anti-aircraft shell made a small hole in a farmhouse roof. He went to ask if men should be sent to mend the tiles. "All the thanks I got from the old woman of the house was a hysterical tirade on England's responsibility for the war, and a pewter mug hurled at my head."

No more helpful was the French General of a division who later was encountered in a village near Lille. "He had lost his division. He didn't seem to care very much. In fact, the only thing that worried him was ourselves. He hated our intrusion and tried to order us out. But we stayed." He refused stupidly to have anything to do with the British or to help in any way the miserable refugees who arrived in streams. The mayor of the village and the one policeman had bolted. "So we British were left to deal with the pathetic and ever-increasing lines of waifs." A food counter was set up and a tin of something with a packet of biscuits given to each person. Their gratitude knew no bounds.

It was not easy to spare these rations. They had to be protected against a company of French Moroccans or they would all have been stolen. One-fifth of the little force was on constant duty "guarding our stores, hiding what liquor there was in the village, stopping fights, and carrying home drunks." Very different was the squadron of Cuirassiers that was in support—for a few hours. "They were as good as only good French troops can be. We had seen so much of the rottenness of France, the selfishness and gutlessness of it all, that it came as a great joy to meet the real France again."

If there had been more of that "real France" the invasion would not have taken the army so completely unawares. I well remember how surprised some of us were when the Germans struck at France and Belgium on the morning after Chamberlain had dismissed Parliament for a fortnight's holiday. How was it possible, we asked, that he did not know what was coming? At the front they were equally in the dark. Our Intelligence failed criminally. "To say we were caught with our pants down would not be a misstatement," says Infantry Officer. We were utterly unprepared for the astonishing sequence of events which followed.

# Infantry Officer in the 'Phoney' War

The author was actually on his way to the coast for ten days' leave which had been granted as a matter of course, with no anticipation of the war suddenly becoming real instead of "phoney." He hurried back, and found his battalion in Belgium. The Belgians were in panicky retreat. When it was suggested to a Belgian Guards colonel that he might "forget about escaping and try to defend Brussels," the capital of his country, he retorted furiously, "You English teach me how to fight a battle! Pah, I spit in your eye!"

How chaotic the Battle of France was many incidents illustrate vividly. Here is one. While the battalion was moving away from Brussels towards the enemy, some of it came under machine-gun fire. "It was very frightening to see red-hot tracer bullets flashing past our ears in the darkness. We flopped down quick and started to reply with our Brens." Then it was discovered that the machine-gunners were not German,

but belonged to the Middlesex Regiment! Here is another episode that shows how mixed-up everything was. A regimental policeman was directing traffic at a cross-roads in Flanders. The nearest German troops were supposed to be twenty miles away. An armoured car came hurtling along the road. While it was still some distance away the policeman waved it on.

Suddenly a burst of machine-gun fire came from it and bullets spat on the ground at his feet. He took a flying leap on to his motor-bike, which by the grace of God was ticking over at the side of the road, and went off hell for leather with the armoured car, a Hun, after him, firing for all it was worth.

He got away, but "the incident shook him." No wonder! "What the car was doing twenty miles behind the lines, God alone knows," the book says piously.

Really there were no "lines." No "front" lasted for more than a few hours. The best account of a battle in the Napoleonic wartime can be found in Stendhal's novel, _Le Rouge et le Noir_: it is better even than Tolstoi's descriptions in War and Peace. The book under review gives an excellent idea of a modern battle, fluid and confused, small separate engagements going on in many places far distant from one another, small bodies of troops compelled to act on their own initiative: that is to say, on the initiative of some completely junior officer or sergeant —or private, maybe.

IN "the first real fight we had with the enemy" it was the author who did most of the commanding. The chief incident was the knocking-out of an enemy tank which was left "stuck bottom-down and belly-up in a ditch." Some motor-cycle combinations were also smashed and a dozen Germans put to flight by six of our fellows. It is minute affairs of this kind that make up the infantryman's battle today, in open warfare.

His worst ordeal is being bombed or shelled without much chance of cover. But a lot of artillery fire can be sent over without much result. For an hour "Jerry pumped shells at us and not one man did he kill. In fact, only two or three were hit and those not badly." Yet at one time they were marching "in full view of his guns." Luckily "he could never quite get the range."

If he had done we should have missed a piece of writing that both depresses and thrills—and makes one think.

**BEFORE THE BATTLE OF FRANCE commenced—when our men out there were largely inactive —the troops eagerly jumped at any chance to relieve their boredom. Having no better use for their Bren gun carrier, these men of the Royal Irish Rifles went 'back to the land' with it and hitched it to a French farmer's plough. A first-hand description of life in the B.E.F. in France when there was as yet no real war, and after, is given in the book Infantry Officer, reviewed above.**

*Photo, British Official*

# Cyprus—A Thorn in the Side of the Axis

Impending Allied operations may bring Cyprus well into the limelight, and the part it may perhaps play in our invasion strategy is sorely puzzling the Axis at this moment. In this page HENRY BAERLEIN throws considerable light on this small island in the Eastern Mediterranean.

A LITTLE larger than the counties of Norfolk and Suffolk combined, and with a population of some 380,000, the famous island of Cyprus occupies today a very important strategic position in the Eastern Mediterranean. Since the beginning of the war the role of Cyprus has oscillated more than once from the offensive to the defensive and back. It is not generally known that up to the French collapse it was partially garrisoned by French troops from Syria, no doubt with offensive designs on the Italian islands of the Dodecanese.

Thereafter, with the fall of Crete and with Rommel's advance, Cyprus lived through critical days; but, although the necessary naval and air operations could be better carried out from Alexandria and Malta, General Wavell (as he then was) made the

But Rhodes, the obvious first objective in this area, is less than 300 miles from Cyprus, as against nearly 400 miles from Alexandria. Not far from Rhodes is Leros, whose port between lofty hills and with a winding entrance from the sea has been turned by the Italians into their most powerful base in the Dodecanese. Farther afield are the Black Sea ports of Varna in Bulgaria, and Constanza in Rumania, not to speak of the oilfields in the latter country.

These objectives, which lie between 600 and 800 miles from the nearest Allied-occupied territories, are all closer in a direct line to Cyprus than to any available alternative base. Whether, with a neutral Turkey intervening, the United Nations contemplate using Cyprus aerodromes for such raids is one of the many questions, answers to which are being vainly

Mr. Churchill has referred to the not inconsiderable body of troops in Cyprus, including many Indians and his own former regiment, the Fourth Hussars. The Germans have stated that the island is crowded with American troops, which may or may not be the case. There are some thousands of refugees from Greece, and of course the one desire of all the able-bodied men amongst them is to oppose the oppressors of their native land. The Cyprus Regiment, comprising transport and pioneer companies, came into being on a voluntary basis in the first months of the war. It has served in Greece, Crete, Egypt, Libya, Syria and Abyssinia. (In Greece, owing to the difficulties attending the evacuation, some 2,000 officers and men fell into the enemy's hands and are now prisoners of war in Italy or Germany.)

FOR home defence there has been formed the Cyprus Volunteer Force, while several detachments of Cypriot girls, some of whom are now in Palestine, have been recruited for the A.T.S. This is a distinct innovation, for the local ideas on the subject of chaperonage are traditionally not less strict than those prevailing in Malta, where Girl Guides, until very lately, were constrained to march through side streets in order not to offend the susceptibilities of their menfolk.

When Cyprus launched her War Loan, the first of its kind in the colonies, over £200,000 was subscribed in the first week. Wartime conditions have raised the price of the good local white wine from 3d. or 4d. a bottle to about 1s., while olive oil, which used to be 3s. 6d. a litre, is now 10s. These increases have benefited a number of farmers, who have taken the opportunity to pay off their mortgage debts.

## Source of Supplies

Their chief product, the locust bean, after being a drug in the market for a year or two (in this country it forms the staple diet of the giraffes at the Zoo !), came with the war into good demand as fodder for military and civilian transport animals throughout the Middle East. Cyprus, by the way, has an admirable breed of mules that have done excellent war service. They can be more recalcitrant than ordinary mules, but for the men who understand them they will perform incredible tasks. Among the war materials produced in Cyprus are asbestos and chrome, while a great many men in the various Services are today wearing buttons manufactured in Cyprus, without being aware of it.

R.A.F.'s CEASELESS VIGIL OVER CYPRUS. This British outpost in the E. Mediterranean (see page 404, Vol. 6) has for many months held itself in readiness to face an imminent assault. Recently there has been every indication that the island may play a vital role in our offensive warfare. A Hurricane squadron is shown patrolling above the mountains. *Photo, British Official*

bold and, as it turned out, very wise decision to send to the island substantial reinforcements from his hard-pressed forces.

To such a degree was this done that the Germans, in spite of repeated Allied radio warnings of invasion, became rather shy of attempting to capture what they and the Italians are now constantly speaking of as a strong base, whose possibilities are only diminished by the German base at Crete, but which has, say the Germans, a friendly Turkey on its flank.

No one now seriously expects that Cyprus will be invaded; it is clearly for offensive purposes, and especially for the air offensive, that preparations have been made. A glance at the map may suggest what targets can most usefully be attacked from Cyprus. Not Crete, which is much closer to the Libyan aerodromes, nor even the greater part of Greece, although the airfield six miles south of Salonika which we bombed on June 6, 1943 is equidistant from Cyprus and Benghazi.

fished for by German radio propaganda.

If we decide upon an offensive in the Aegean it may be that the Dardanelles will be open to the Royal Navy. The passage of merchant shipping by day is now unrestricted, while warships would be allowed to pass if giving assistance to a State which is the victim of aggression, which the Soviet most certainly was two years ago. It should be remembered that Cape St. Andreas in Cyprus is a mere 52 miles from the Asia Minor mainland.

IT is common knowledge that Famagusta, the island's chief port, does not bear comparison with Malta or Alexandria; on the other hand, the great Mesaorian plain in Cyprus, celebrated in ancient times for its crops of cereals and now being brought back by irrigation works to its former prosperity, is much more desirable from an airman's point of view than the restricted and rocky area of Malta.

IT must not be imagined that Cyprus has been immune from air attack. On April 29, 1943 her gunners shot down their fifth enemy bomber. These hostile visits have, if anything, increased the war zeal of the people. They are as sturdy today as were their ancestors in the fourth century, when a separate branch of the Eastern Church was founded there, and the archbishop was given the privilege, which he still enjoys, of signing his name in red ink !

After the French collapse, even when the forces in Cyprus were reduced to a minimum garrison, a spark of the offensive appeared in the sortie against the Italian seaplane base of Castellorizo, which is generally assumed to have been made from Cyprus. We have lately been informed by Axis radio that this small island has been " abandoned by the enemy." One can understand their apprehension as Cyprus becomes to them a more and more formidable opponent.

# As Handed Out to Others by Mussolini

ALLIED BOMBING OF SICILY steadily mounted in intensity during the weeks between the Axis collapse in Tunisia, in May, and our invasion of the island in July 1943. Every target of military or strategic importance was heavily attacked. Futile attempts by Marshal von Richthofen, the Luftwaffe chief in S. Italy, to halt the Allied offensive cost him tremendous losses in aircraft.

For a week preceding the invasion, day and night attacks by the N. W. African and Middle East Air Forces were maintained. Air-Marshal Tedder (who planned the heavy day-light raid on military objectives in Rome, on July 19) threw into the onslaught every type of aircraft, from Fortress to fighters. Axis communications were paralysed and their air forces neutralized during this "softening" of the island.

THE SICILIANS had full and overflowing draughts of the "medicine" as prescribed for others by Mussolini. During our pre-invasion onslaughts they sheltered (1) in cellars and caves. Inspecting new fighter aircraft brought up to meet the offensive, the King of Italy (2, centre) personally encouraged his pilots. Evacuation of civilians (3) from target areas proceeded hurriedly. The wall news-sheet (4) in Palermo, the sea-port capital, was anxiously scanned from hour to hour.

A stirring message to the Italian people, signed by Pres. Roosevelt and Mr. Churchill, was broadcast from Algiers on July 16, 1943 : " We take no satisfaction in invading Italian soil and bringing the tragic devastation of war home to the Italian people. But we are determined to destroy the false leaders and their doctrines which have brought Italy to her present position."

*Photos, Planet News, New York Times Photos, Keystone*

# THE WAR IN THE AIR

## by Capt. Norman Macmillan, M.C., A.F.C.

It has become axiomatic in the course of this war that air superiority is essential to the success of surface forces. Up to the present this has been the more readily conceded in relation to land than to sea operations, due partly to the influence of old-inherited traditions upon the British outlook on sea power, and partly to the fact that the naval side of our war organization persists in carrying the nomenclature of the sea into the air, calling aerodromes H.M.S. So-and-so, and attributing the success of sea-borne air forces to the parent carrier ship rather than to the aeroplane.

This naval outlook upon the air relegates the aeroplane to the category of the torpedo, or the shell, or the man with a telescope aloft upon the crow's nest; but in effect it merely bends the new method of war to conform to the physical restrictions of the older method with which it is associated, because to operate outside those restrictions would benefit but little the functions of ships in war.

I remember before the war began, in the year 1938, when the Admiralty took over full control of the Fleet Air Arm, it was prophesied by some of the senior sailors that the future navy would operate one-third of its strength on the sea, one-third beneath the sea, and one-third in the air. It is impossible during war to state what the proportions actually are, but it is certain that all naval developments have moved in this direction since the war began.

It is a fact clearly brought out in retrospect, but not properly perceived at the time, that the success of the evacuation of Dunkirk was due to four primary causes. These were (1) that characteristic of the British soldier which refuses to accept defeat; (2) the superb handling of the rescue craft; (3) the weather conditions which prevailed during the " Operation Dynamo "; (4) the covering operations of fighter, bomber and coastal aircrews of the R.A.F. No skill in organization upon the part of the officers commanding the naval, land, and air sides of the evacuation could have achieved success without having had that skill inalienably allied with the four characteristics I have mentioned.

In the invasion of Sicily we have seen the obverse side of the Dunkirk operation: the British soldier going forward into battle from small craft supported by the Navy and Air Force; all the same characteristics were exhibited; and there was the same general on the spot, General Alexander. This time there was no lack of material, and there was something which was absent at Dunkirk—the heavy guns of the big ships in support to provide artillery against the coastal batteries defending the Sicilian coast; during the evacuation of three years ago there was but the relatively light field artillery of the B.E.F. to counter the gun-crews of the Wehrmacht, and at night the bombers of the Royal Air Force.

### HITLER Betrayed His Fear of the British

At Dunkirk and after, all the cards were apparently on the side of the Germans. They had gliders for carrying troops. We had none. They had transport aircraft. We had none. They had dive-bombers. We had none. They had parachute troops. We had none. They had superiority in tanks, aircraft, guns of all kinds, trained men. They had the military loot from Czechoslovakia, Holland, Belgium, France, Poland. They had thousands of barges gathered from all the inland waterways of Europe. How, then, did they come to fail?

It was because they believed that the capture of the United Kingdom could be made easy by its preliminary reduction (in the military sense) through the bombardment of the Luftwaffe. That bombardment over, the troops would just be able to sail over and walk in. Upon that, apparently, their whole strategy hung. Why? Because they were afraid. The German as an individual suffers from an inferiority complex towards his British counterpart. It shows itself in divers ways—in some Germans as arrogance, in others as an attitude of cringing. There are exceptions, but they are in the minority.

Hitler betrayed his fear of the British as a fighting race in Mein Kampf. One German who was a colonel before the war, and whose name I last saw reported with the rank of major-general somewhere in south-eastern Europe, came to London for his first visit to England about six years before the war. He witnessed the changing of the guard at Buckingham Palace. And this is what he afterwards said to me: " You British are not a military people, but you are a martial race ! "

The Germans, on the contrary, have been for generations a dragooned military people by compulsion, but they have never been, in the inner British way of taking to war (when the need arises) as a duck takes to water, a martial race. That is why we defeat them and how victory over us eludes their grasp. It is not in the spirit of the power of the German people to defeat the power of the spirit of the British people.

And so we have come to learn something of the meaning of air power and its application to war. We have applied it for the first time in its completest form to the invasion of Sicily. In the night before the morning when the assault was launched, glider-borne troops plunged through the darkness of the stormy air above the Mediterranean between North Africa and Sicily, on an indirect course which would bring them to landfall from an unsuspected direction, and their tow-ropes cast off from the Douglas air-tugs, descended to landings and crash-landings in the light of a half-moon.

### BOMB-BLASTED Almost Without Cessation.

The bands of lightly-armed men who emerged from the gliders moved forward towards strategic objectives with the purpose of seizing them and holding them, by this means to aid the subsequent advance of the sea-borne assault forces who would follow before the dawn. Parachute troops dropped through the darkened air silently. They came down in an island which had been blasted from the air for seven days and nights almost without cessation, by the might of a United Nations' Mediterranean air force of great superiority over the Axis combined air force. The enemy's Sicilian headquarters and its communications nerve centre in the telegraph and telephone building in Taormina had been struck by direct bomb-hits the day before.

With daylight on July 10 came the waves of fighters, fighter-bombers and bombers bringing, in endless succession, support to the landing troops and the advancing troops, and protecting the sea-borne vessels of all kinds. Quickly the advance went on; airfields were captured and put into use with scant delay in spite of their having been ploughed over. The push north along the coast to Messina, and westwards along the south coast, moved with a rapidity beyond normal expectation. The bridgehead established was large enough to guarantee the power to disembark all troops and supplies with the utmost facility; while strategic bombers ranged to Palermo, Messina, Naples, Turin, and the hydro-electric power stations of northern Italy, these last two targets being attacked by Bomber Command from Britain.

We have demonstrated to the world that the United Nations can achieve what Germany, under more favourable circumstances, failed to do in 1940. And for the opportunity extended to us to give that demonstration we must thank, first, all those who conducted themselves so well in Operation Dynamo; second, the boys of Fighter Command who defeated the Luftwaffe in the Battle of Britain; and third, Adolf Hitler who turned east because he was afraid of Britain !

U.S. MITCHELL B.25s, seen here flying to Italy, were the first American medium bombers to raid the Italian mainland, on June 21, 1943. It was announced on July 16 that bombs had been dropped by these planes on Palermo, Sicilian capital, and on July 19 they took part in the first air attack on military objectives in Rome. *Photo, U.S. Official*

# Preparing Our Bombers to Batter the Ruhr

NON-FLYERS OF THE R.A.F.—the ground staffs—do tremendously important work behind the scenes. At a base from which our giant aircraft make devastating and almost nightly attacks against industrial targets of W. Germany, incendiaries are taken from an immense dump (1) and loaded into waiting planes. A W.A.A.F. meteorologist (2) gets a last-minute weather report before the raiders set off. This bomb (3) is given an appropriate inscription. A formidable bomb-load (4) is being prepared for the waiting Halifax. PAGE 151 *Photos, Fox*

# Our Gliders Made History in Sicily's Skies

AIRBORNE TROOPS LED THE INVASION. Towed by twin-engined bombers, Horsa gliders landed Allied troops in Sicily on July 9, 1943; Horsa glider (1) towed by a Whitley aircraft at a training-station; at (4) after a night flight. It was announced on July 5 that a freight-carrying glider, the U.S.-built Waco CG4A "Voodoo", had been towed by a Dakota plane from Montreal to Britain, captained by (2) Sqdn.-Ldr. R. G. Seys, D.F.C., R.A.F. Transport Command (right), with Sqdn.-Ldr. F. M. Gobeil, R.C.A.F., as co-pilot (3) The "Voodoo" being unloaded through the hinged nose; it carried 1½ tons of medical and war supplies. (5) An amphibious U.S. transport-glider skims the water. *Photos, British Official; Planet News*

# 'Given the Works'—Germany's ME 109F Dissected

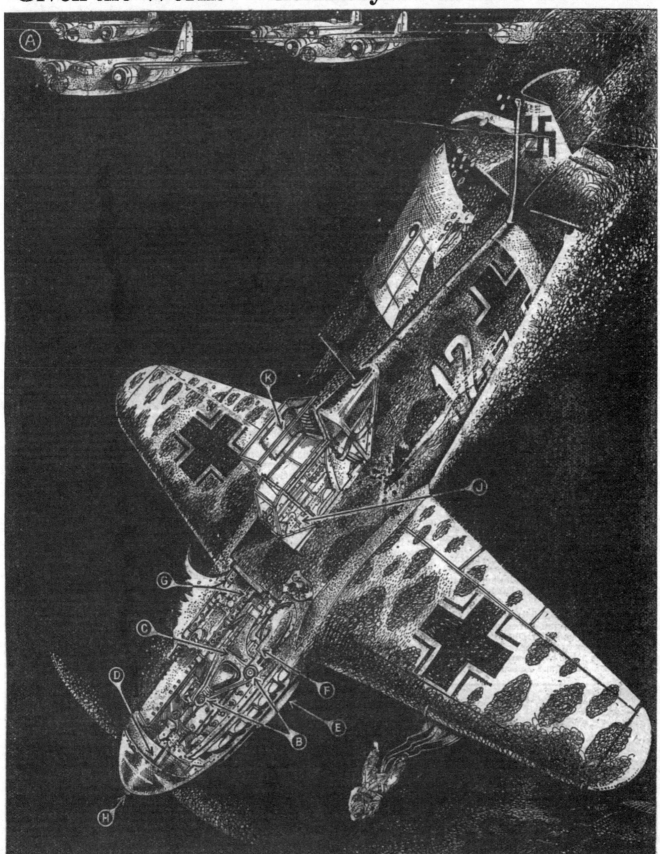

NAZI FIGHTERS IN THE MEDITERRANEAN have vainly attempted to check the overwhelming Allied offensive. These aircraft include large numbers of ME 109s, which in one form or another have been in service with the Luftwaffe since the outbreak of war.

The above drawing shows an ME 109 F which has been shot down while trying to intercept a raid by Martin Marauder bombers (A). The German pilot has baled out. Interesting features of the plane can be identified in the drawing. The engine is a Daimler-Benz DB 601 N 12-cylinder inverted V type, developing 1,200 h.p. at about 16,000 feet. It is mounted by means of shock-resisting pads (B) on two large brackets (C). The oil tank is at (D) and oil cooler at (E). Air is taken into the supercharger at (F).

Armament includes two 7.9-mm. machine-guns (G) and a 15-mm. cannon mounted between the cylinder banks and firing through the spinner (H). The pilot fires these weapons by means of separate buttons on the control stick (J). Armour protection for pilot's back and head is provided; of 8-mm. thickness, it is seen at (K) fixed to open cockpit cover.

Over 80 gallons of petrol are held in the tank behind and beneath the pilot, giving a range of about 440 miles at over 300 m.p.h. Maximum speed is 370 m.p.h. and greatest height 37,000 ft. Wing span is 32 ft.

*Specially drawn for* THE WAR ILLUSTRATED *by Haworth*

# He Flew From 'Shangri-La' to Bomb Tokyo

Before very long Tokyo and other cities in the Japanese homeland will be feeling the weight of Allied air-power. But so far only one raid has been made on Tokyo—that led by "Daredevil" Doolittle, the subject of this article by CURTISS HAMILTON

ON an April morning of last year a small man, with shrewd eyes and going a little bald, walked along the deck of the U.S. aircraft-carrier Hornet for the start of the greatest adventure of his life. This man, now in his middle forties, had spent twenty-five years as test pilot and stunt flyer; this was his first combat operation. It was more than that; it was his own idea, conceived at the moment he heard of the Pearl Harbour attack four months earlier, and he was personally to lead the raid on the capital of Japan on April 18, 1942.

If he looked a little preoccupied it was because the Hornet, steaming within 800 miles of Tokyo and far from its base, had been spotted by enemy forces. Plans had had to be hurriedly changed and the take-off made 10 hours in advance. What was to have been a night raid was now to be a day raid, with a strong possibility that ground and air defences, warned by radio, would be in full operation. Maj. James Doolittle and the 80 men he had personally selected for this task were not worried about the danger. They were worried that they might be driven from their targets and that months of careful preparation and rehearsal might be spoiled.

The Hornet turned into the wind and the plane piloted by Major Doolittle flew from its deck, circling until it had been joined by the other bombers. Then, with the Hornet turning at full speed for its base, the bombers flew towards the Japanese capital. They went in low to escape observation.

HOW the bombs raining down not only on Tokyo, but also on Yokohama, Nagoya, Kobe, and Osaka brought the Japanese the greatest shock in their military history; how Doolittle and his men completely deceived the defences; and how 64 of them, after making forced landings because of the unexpected distance they had had to travel, reached the Chinese lines and found their way back to America—all this is now a matter of history. For a year the world knew no more than that U.S. planes had bombed Japan from a base which President Roosevelt called "Shangri-La" in playful allusion to the mythical country of James Hilton's novel, Lost Horizon.

Now it has been officially confirmed that the base was an aircraft-carrier, and that the planes were led by Major Doolittle, who for twenty-five years had astonished and thrilled the American public by his spectacular flying. As the whole daring and well-conceived plan was revealed, it became evident how well Major Doolittle deserved the Congressional Medal of Honour and the rank of Brigadier-General given him a month after the raid. It made him "American Hero No. 2," second only to General MacArthur in popularity with the public.

A few months later "Daredevil" Doolittle was in London on a mission, the nature of which the Axis was left to guess. Few recognized him at the West End hotel where he stayed, for indeed Doolittle bears little resemblance to the hatchet-faced, hawk-eyed air ace of fiction. Presently Axis curiosity was satisfied about Doolittle's mission. Hundreds of tons of bombs from 100 Fortresses fell on Naples in April last in the first attack made by U.S. planes on Europe from North Africa. They were under the command of Maj.-Gen. Doolittle.

U.S. planes followed that up with the first air raid on Rome, in full daylight on July 19, 1943, the North-West African Strategical Air Force—of which Maj.-Gen. James Doolittle is commanding general—combining with Middle East based bombers to pound the carefully chosen military targets for 2½ hours. Of more than 500 planes which took part only five failed to return.

## Doolittle Takes the Helm

His bombers have operated in many different places, with only minor losses. On one occasion Doolittle himself had a narrow escape, the Flying Fortress in which he was travelling with a number of staff officers being attacked simultaneously by four enemy aircraft. The co-pilot was hit, and Doolittle took his place; and after two of the enemy planes had been damaged the Germans gave up the attack.

The success of Gen. Doolittle, who, as pilots go, is a veteran, is due to his unusual combination of talents. That he has courage, daring and boldness goes without saying. Since he went to North Africa he has been awarded the Silver Star, the third highest U.S. award for gallantry. But a general requires more than this. Doolittle is not only one of the most skilled pilots in the world in anything from a fighter to a multi-engined transport—he has set up world records in both—he is also a most careful planner, a man who realizes that all the courage and skill in the world are not enough without the most careful preparation. He does not hope for luck; but he courts it by overlooking no detail or possibility beforehand. It is a safe guess that the alternative plan of a daylight raid on Tokyo which was put into execution was no emergency make-do, but a scheme which had been as carefully rehearsed as the attack which the planes had been practising over American cities two months previously.

Maj.-Gen. DOOLITTLE was awarded the Congressional Medal of Honour on May 19, 1942; President Roosevelt is presenting it to the intrepid airman, whose wife looks on. On left, Gen. H. H. Arnold.     *Photo, Topical*

All through his long career as test-pilot and stunt flyer, Doolittle's preparations have equalled the daring of his conceptions. The public had heard only of his breath-taking flights across America and his daring pioneer blind landings in fog. They heard little of his "going back to school" for a refresher course before preparing for a record-breaking flight, or his rigorous physical self-discipline and training before attempting some new feat in blind-flying or altitude flying.

The bare facts of Doolittle's career which made him the hero of American civil aviation in the years between the wars are quickly told. He learned to fly in the last war, and was denied combat experience in France only because his skill made him so invaluable as an instructor that the authorities kept him in the U.S. With the coming of peace he turned to racing and record breaking. There were few important races he did not win, from the Schneider Trophy Race in 1925, when he beat the British, to the Bendix Trophy Race, when he became the first man to cross the U.S. in less than 12 hours.

DOOLITTLE rejoined the U.S. Army Air Force before America entered the War, and was engaged in research when Pearl Harbour, which gave America a shock, gave him an idea. The Tokyo raid was already in rehearsal in less than a month. It was his own idea, and he converted experts and chiefs in the services to his viewpoint that it was possible not only by his enthusiasm but also by hard facts and figures. The raid was not intended as a decisive military action, but as a "reply" to Pearl Harbour, a demonstration that the U.S. also had original ideas, as a "lift" for morale in the U.S. and an operation to keep the Japs guessing for months afterwards. After the raid Doolittle addressed a series of meetings of aircraft workers in California, and it is probable that his talks resulted in extra production more than equivalent to the number of planes lost (still secret) in the raid.

FIRST TO TAKE OFF from "Shangri-La," Doolittle's Mitchell bomber headed for Tokyo. This was the first time in the history of warfare that a raiding force of normally land-based bombers had taken off from an aircraft-carrier for a full-scale raid.     *Photo, Associated Press*

# Before and After the Attack on Japan's Capital

ON THE HORNET'S FLIGHT DECK (above) U.S. Mitchell bombers assembled in readiness for the Tokyo raid ; escort ship is seen in background. Right, Yokosuka naval base, Tokyo, viewed from one of the attacking planes ; Japanese warships are shown in foreground.

AFTER THE RAID some of the pilots crash-landed in China. Above, they are being carried in rough conveyances to a village. Left, they are seen entering the village street on foot. Below, wreckage of Gen. Doolittle's bomber on a Chinese hill-top.

FAMOUS U.S. RAID ON TOKYO and other important Japanese cities which took place on April 18, last year (see opposite page and pages 680-681, vol. 5), was carried out by Mitchell medium bombers, it was disclosed on April 20, 1943. Sixteen of these aircraft, commanded by Maj.-Gen. (then Major) J. Doolittle, took off from the aircraft-carrier Hornet, 800 miles from the Japanese capital. The machines were to fly on to specified landing-fields in China after completion of the operation ; but they were unable to make the distance. One landed unharmed on Russian soil, others force-landed in China or in Chinese waters. Two were forced down in Japan, and the crews, consisting of eight men, were taken prisoner.

# I WAS THERE!

## By Air and Sea We Swooped on Sicily

The Allied invasion of Sicily—main stepping-stone to Italy—began with the landing of glider-borne troops on the night of Friday, July 9, 1943. Large-scale landings from the sea began early next day. Here front-line reporters tell vivid stories of the initial operations by air, sea and land.

IT was exactly 10.22 on Friday night, July 9, when I heard Major Leonard Barrow, our pilot (I was in one of the U.S. tow-planes taking gliders packed with British troops to Sicily), speak into the inter-plane phone—"Calling glider, calling glider. Are you ready ? I repeat are you ready ? We are casting off." Then, before releasing the 300-ft. towline, the Major added: "And lots of luck, fellows."

I jumped on the navigator's table and looked out through the "blister" atop of Helen B, as our plane was called. For a moment the glider seemed to follow, then its wing dipped and it slipped to Sicily—its cargo of Britons braced and ready. Right and left it looked as if we were on top of Dante's "Inferno." The port we were over was throwing up heavy, light and medium flak, trying to clip the darting ships. The coast defences chimed in. I watched it coming at us, my face wet with sweat.

We were doing 187 miles an hour and driving out to sea when a big shell exploded beyond the tail and I saw a stream of tracers diverging like a garden hose towards our trailer companions. "It missed them, too," the radio sergeant breathed, dropping his earphones on the floor. Then Helen B banked into the darkness as Barrow "poured on some coal," and one night's ride I shall never forget passed its crisis.

On the way out to Sicily, on all sides were fires started by explosions. They spread as we watched, as fires will when nobody is around to put them out. Flashes sometimes indicated ground fire as the first airborne troops struck, and then a gun would stop firing and another beacon would go dark. Strangest in the blinking panorama were regularly spaced "street lights" the defenders sent up—suspended starlike for as much as fifteen minutes, they extended for miles. Searchlights probed between them like a policeman's seeking torch.

Crouched at the window of the squadron-leader's ship I watched our planes ahead and their trailers climb to the desired altitude and saw the gliders cast off. Drifting noise-lessly to earth the glider boys rallied and went to work at their job of seizing a beach-head, striking the enemy from the flank and rear, cutting communications and causing general consternation. I could sense it there in the plane as the first ones landed—a sudden darkening of lights and the cessation of A.A. fire at certain spots. It was a little weird and a whole lot exciting.

The paratroops in the transports had their weapons strapped to their sides. The British were in gliders with British pilots— eager, laughing Tommies who couldn't wait to land in Mussolini's acres. They were the spear-head.—*Ivan H. Peterman, American representative of the Combined Press.*

## We Battled Ashore Through Waist-Deep Water

I LANDED alongside the first wave of assault companies of a famous Canadian regiment on the sandy beach of Costa del Ambra, four miles, south-west of Pachino, at 5.15 on Saturday morning, July 10, and the Canucks have been rushing ahead ever since. It is a tough job keeping up with them on two feet.

The Italian beach defences, which folded up like a concertina, were merely barbed wire and some machine-gun posts which fired a few bursts and then gave up. On our beach the enemy were evidently counting on the sand bar, 15 feet off shore, as a natural defence. But the Canadians surprised them completely by coming in in the heavy surf, and battling ashore through rough water up to the waist.

Coastal batteries shelled the boats, but the firing was erratic. The Canadians went through the beach defences in a matter of minutes, cleared them and struck inland, mopping up groups of Italians en route. More than 700 prisoners, including 15 officers, have been captured already. All day columns of prisoners poured down from the front, a happy-looking crowd guarded by one or two soldiers.

The Royal Navy has been giving the troops magnificent gun support, and big and small warships lying close inshore bombard targets with thundering salvos. During the day we did not see an enemy aircraft. It seemed eerie not having any about. The beach looked like a Cup Final traffic jam with tanks, guns and trucks ploughing through the sand to the roads leading inland. It was almost unbelievable to the Canadians that this first stage could be so easy.

I started this story of the first day in a slit trench on my cliff-top position, and it is being finished now in the early morning aboard headquarters ship. Last night bombers attacked troops near the beach and tried to hit ships under the glare of flares. The raid lasted only about 30 minutes and was not effective. Our A A. from ships and shore was terrific.

The troops were well dug in ashore, and the bombers could not touch them except by direct hits. The R.A.F. have been giving us fighter protection, and you hear the drone of Spitfires nearly all day. The ships have barrage balloons up, and it looks like part of London. Thousands and thousands of troops poured in on the bridgehead after the successful assault, and vehicles, guns and ammunition have been rushed to the beaches.

### Secrecy Maintained

The day before the attack we started to head in the general direction of Sicily, and everyone was keyed to high pitch. In the morning the wind started to kick up white-caps on the sea. The wind rose steadily and our spirits sank, for we thought the operation would have to be postponed. Our small boats could not have lived in that sea. But there was bright burning sunshine and no message came telling us the job was off. The colonel told us the attack was to go on. At last we were on our way.

During the evening we learned from H.Q. ship that Pachino airfield had been ploughed up. Some thought that perhaps the Italians had got wind of our attack, but secrecy had been maintained 100 per cent. The attack was a tactical surprise. The officers met in the lounge. "We are on the eve of a night in the history of the world which will never be forgotten," said the colonel. "We will look back on this night and our children will." Then everyone repeated the Lord's Prayer, and shook hands all round. The meeting broke up.

I went out on deck and watched our convoy in the moonlight. Darkness fell and we were still heading towards Sicily. The High Command gambled on the wind falling—and they won. Then the big convoy broke up. The Americans headed off for the Gela beaches.

'YOUR DESTINATION IS SICILY, and you will be the first American troops to land! the U.S. officer (standing) is saying to his paratroops, in their transport plane. A story by Ivan Peterman, American correspondent, who accompanied British glider-borne troops to Sicily on the night of July 9, is given in this page.

*Radio photo, Planet News*

We sailed right ahead under the first-quarter moon that gilded the ocean.

I was going in with the naval commander in the naval motor-launch which guided the assault troops to the right beaches. At 1 a.m. we went down the side. Slowly the assault landing-craft gathered around us for the run-in. Many troops were seasick in them. It was a thrilling moment. Tremendous explosions boomed out in the night. I think it was bombing far inland.

Some Royal Canadian Engineers from Nova Scotia and two companies of an Ontario regiment were touching down ahead of us. There were spurts of machine-gun bullets at their boats and along the beach, and then I heard our Bren guns.

Some of the beach defences were still pegging away with their final shots before being wiped out. A coastal battery, half-way between the beach and Pachino, was firing with six-inch guns. Shells crashed into the sea around us, too close for comfort, but they did not hit a thing.

I cleared off down the beach with one thought in my mind—to dig in against dive-bombing, which I thought was certain to come. I had no spade, so I scooped out the sand with my hands and my tin cup. The sun was now up. Infantrymen with fixed bayonets were prodding the bushes on the dunes. The first prisoner had been taken—a soldier in a pillbox; apparently others had run.

Canadians moved up the hill to the right of the beach and occupied it. There was some firing at farmhouses among the vineyards of the gently rising land. There are stone walls around most of the fields. For half an hour I waited tensely for enemy planes, as did many others, but they never showed up. The beach was organized now and special British beach groups had the whole situation well in hand.

### First Italian Prisoners

Canadian infantry were now racing up the road leading to Maucini, a mile and a half from the beach. In an old monastery on the hill-top they surprised nearly 200 Italian soldiers and captured the lot of them. Troops of an Ontario regiment by now were about three miles inland and pushing ahead at top speed with Royal Canadian Engineers and British sappers going ahead through the fields with mine detectors. They located several large minefields and dug up scores of the latest model German mine.

On the right flank a British formation had equal success in landing and taking out beach defences. They occupied the tip of the peninsula, and I believe captured Pachino. Vancouver and Winnipeg regiments virtually walked in standing up and infiltrated inland, cleaning out pocket resistance and occupying high ground with British troops on their left.

After about half an hour on the beach I began to trudge up the Maucini road. At the first turn I met a batch of Canadians who had made the initial assault. They told me that the first civilian they ran into was a Sicilian who had lived in Toronto for seven years. Bren gun carriers were ashore now and they clattered along the hard dusty roads on their way to the Pachino area. Long columns of troops followed up the assault infantry. The beach was a conglomeration of soldiers, vehicles, landing-craft, radio sets, and beach-markings indicating where craft could come in.

About 400 yards from the beach I went round a sharp turn in the road and saw the

MOVING TOWARDS THE LANDING-CRAFT at a base from which Allied sea-borne attacks were launched against Sicily, these British troops are all keyed-up and fighting-fit for the great adventure—complete subjugation of the island.
*Photo, British Official*

first prisoners coming in. Two hundred Italians taken at Maucini were marching down the road with three Canadians escorting them with fixed bayonets.

Canadians and British troops were in their tropical kit and wearing shorts. They looked like veterans; by noon all were covered with white dust. A frequent comment to us, as we passed them was: "Say, where's the war?" This whole advance seemed so unreal, and was nothing like what the troops expected. They'd got over the first hurdle in good style, and many had been in action and they were feeling like kings of Sicily.—*Ross Munro, Combined British Press, with the Canadians, S.E. Sicily.*

## Gela Beach Was Like a Fourth of July Display

THE ships in the invasion fleet joined up on the night before the invasion (a young naval officer in charge of a naval craft which led the landing-barges into the beach at Gela, on the south coast of Sicily, told me). It was a rough night (he went on) and I thought the soldiers were going to be sick, but they weren't—possibly through excitement. We slipped slowly in shore, and about 11 o'clock saw our airmen busily bombing. There was a good

deal of A.A. fire. We thought the whole show had been given away, but we were mistaken. There were a lot of searchlights about, and we thought they were looking for us.

One searchlight flashed out to sea and we tried to put it out. We were out of range, but an American cruiser in the vicinity put it out with its first salvo. It was some shooting. There were many fires on shore. There was little coastal battery fire by the enemy,

either because he had no powerful guns at the spot or our airmen had knocked them out.

We saw the landing-craft go in. There was a certain amount of opposition, but they got in safely. The surprise seemed to be complete. I don't think the enemy thought we were going to assault that particular beach. There was a good deal of machine-gun fire. There were also numbers of explosions and a lot of noise. It was something like a Fourth of July display.

We stayed inshore for an hour and a half, giving what help we could with our guns. There was a good deal of shooting going on, but it came mostly from the sea. If the enemy had had sufficient and large enough guns he could have given us a lot of trouble.

We returned to our parent ship and some enemy planes came over, but only just a few. From beginning to end we had complete air superiority. Whenever we looked up into the moonlit sky or heard a plane it was five hundred to one that it was an Allied one. We screened our parent ship for some time and were then asked to take more landing-craft to the beach. When we drew close in enemy shells were falling some yards away, so we said to the landing-craft: "That's the way. Step in and help yourselves."

There must have been some casualties

among the landing forces from machine-gun fire, but I don't think there were very many. I saw no ships lost during the landing, and I don't think that any were even hit. Casualties throughout were smaller than even the greatest optimist could have hoped for.

I knew there were mines in the vicinity, but I didn't tell my crew. They were in action for the first time, but they behaved like veterans. Quite frankly, I didn't expect to come back.— *Haig Nicholson, Reuters Special Correspondent in North Africa*

the young officer in charge of the assault craft —Lieut. G. Brown, in peacetime a Bristol business man, who handled his boat with the skill and confidence of a seasoned veteran.

## Italian Prisoners Helped Us Land Our Guns

ONLY a few hours after they were captured, Italian prisoners were cheerfully helping to unload stores and ammunition from Allied landing-craft on the Sicily beaches. The first prisoners were made at dawn on the first day of the landing. They came down from the hill where they had been fighting and surrendered.

Greyish brown columns of smoke drifted over the sun-drenched hills and the air resounded with the bark of field guns and the booming of ships' broadsides as I watched the most gigantic combined operational assault ever concentrated on a single island. It was exactly midnight when we arrived. The sky was illuminated with the flashes of bombs. Dozens of fierce fires were burning and flares hung suspended in the sky.

I sailed in with British infantry on a troop-landing ship which had done service at Lofoten, Dieppe and Boulogne, and in North Africa. A wind had risen and high seas were running. By the dim light of a sickle moon one could pick out the other ships of the convoy forming into line. Tank-landing craft, little trawlers, and M.T.B.s plunged and wallowed in the deep trough of the sea. Escort destroyers circled on the watch for submarines and enemy surface craft.

Midnight came—zero hour. The troops were piped from the mess decks into the assault craft. " Away, landing-craft ! " came the order, given by Lieut.-Commander J. R. Bradstock. We slithered over the tops of the waves. It took some time to reach shore. A searchlight suddenly lit up and

swung towards us and miraculously went out again just before reaching us.

To our right, where other assault craft had already hit the beach, streams of red tracer bullets seared the blackness of the night. The thunder of the surf grew louder as we passed a small island. Then we saw the shore—a white lighthouse and some concrete pillboxes. "Get ready to land," whispered

**SIGNBOARD OF MONTGOMERY'S H.Q.**
Here is a notice being fixed to the side of the General's travelling Headquarters at a North African port shortly before the commencement of the Sicilian invasion.
*Photo, British Official*

The assault craft slithered and bumped over the rocks. The forward gangway was swung down and the men, heavily loaded with kit and weapons, plunged into the surging sea and stumbled ashore. Led by their colonel, they moved ahead calmly, in Indian file. Suddenly the silence was broken by the sharp crack of rifle and machine-gun fire. Bullets sang over our heads and twanged into the metal sides of the assault craft. There was still heavy equipment to be disembarked, so we backed the barge and headed for a more promising landing spot. Here Jeeps and motor-cycles were ridden through the breakers and pushed up the beach. Men stumbled back and forth through the surf with boxes of ammunition.

The snipers were getting more accurate. " We'd better get clear back to the ship," said Lieut. Brown, and we moved ponderously seaward while a hail of small arms fire whistled overhead.

A dull, tawny light was creeping over the sky and revealing an amazing sight. As far as the eye could see were craft of every imaginable type, riding proudly barely two miles from the shore ; tank-landing craft chugged towards the beaches while British cruisers and destroyers covering them slammed shells into enemy positions. Suddenly Lieut. Brown spotted the grey-green wreckage of a floating aircraft. We altered course and pulled aboard nine nearly exhausted paratroops. They had been in the water since 11 o'clock the previous night, when they landed just short of the shore.

As the morning wore on we waited for what we thought was the inevitable Luftwaffe attack —but none came. Only once two Me109s came sweeping low over the beach, but they were driven off by small arms fire. Meanwhile reports started to arrive : "Enemy posts on high ground captured" ; "Contact established." We had suffered no casualties and had landed every man from the ship.— *Desmond Tighe, Reuters Correspondent*

# OUR DIARY OF THE WAR

**JULY 7, 1943, Wednesday**  1,404th day
**Sicily.**—Gerbini and other airfields bombed.
**Russian Front.**—On Orel-Kursk front, reported that 520 German tanks put out of action and 229 aircraft destroyed.
**General.**—China entered 7th year of war with Japan.

**JULY 8, Thursday**  1,405th day
**Air.**—Cologne attacked for 118th time ; over 1,000 tons of bombs dropped.
**Sicily.**—Catania and other airfields bombed.
**Russian Front.**—Germans penetrated Soviet line in Bielgorod area ; 304 German tanks destroyed or disabled and 161 aircraft shot down.
**General.**—Gen. Giraud and President Roosevelt reached agreement for equipment of French Army of 300,000 to be supplied by U.S.A.

**JULY 9, Friday**  1,406th day
**Air.**—Gelsenkirchen (Central Ruhr) heavily bombed.
**Sicily.**—Allied glider and parachute troops invaded Sicily before midnight.
**Australasia.**—Munda (New Georgia) bombarded from air and sea and from Rendova Island ; bombers attacked Jap naval force off Choiseul Island (Solomons).

**JULY 10, Saturday**  1,407th day
**Sicily.**—Invasion armada of 2,000 vessels landed British, Canadian and American troops on Sicilian coast. Syracuse captured by 8th Army units.
**Australasia.**—Munda again bombarded.

**JULY 11, Sunday**  1,408th day
**Sicily.**—Announced Allied forces had captured 3 airfields, including one at Pachino. Reported that British and Canadians linked up on Cape Passero. Pozzallo and Noto captured.
**Russian Front.**—Concentrated German attacks repulsed in Orel-Kursk area.
**Australasia.**—Salamaua (New Guinea) and Munda (New Georgia) heavily raided.

**JULY 12, Monday**  1,409th day
**Air.**—Turin (N. Italian armament centre) bombed by strongest force of aircraft ever sent from Britain to an Italian target.
**Sicily.**—Announced towns of Avola, Pachino, Scoglitti, Gela, Ispica, Licata, and Rosolini captured.

**Australasia.**—Rabaul (New Britain) raided by Liberators. Second naval action within a week fought in Kula Gulf.

**JULY 13, Tuesday**  1,410th day
**Air.**—Aachen (W. Germany) raided.
**Sicily.**—Fall of Floridia and Palazzolo announced.
**Russian Front.**—Fighting in Bielgorod area continued with utmost ferocity.

**JULY 14, Wednesday**  1,411th day
**Sicily.**—Augusta captured by a British and a Greek destroyer. Ragusa and Naro occupied. Announced fall of Comiso and Ponte Olivo to Americans, Modica to Canadians, Priolo to British. Capture announced of Gen. Davet, commander of Italian 206th Division, together with his H.Q. ; 12,000 prisoners taken to date. Disclosed that French troops were operating with Allies.

**JULY 15, Thursday**  1,412th day
**Air.**—Poix and Abbeville airfields (France) attacked by Typhoon and Boston bombers. Halifaxes attacked Peugeot vehicle works at Montbéliard (France). Lancasters attacked N. Italian electrical transformer stations.

**Sicily.**—Announced Melilli, Biscari airfield, Vizzini, and commander and staff of 54th Naples Division, captured.
**Russian Front.**—N. of Orel, Soviet troops advanced 28 m. on 25 m. front ; and E. of Orel, 12-15 m. on 20 m. front ; five enemy divisions routed and strong enemy defences pierced ; claimed 12,000 German troops killed and 2,000 taken prisoner, 104 tanks and 294 aircraft destroyed in course of offensive to date. Enemy assaults in Bielgorod area continued without success ; in Orel-Kursk area enemy went over to defensive.
**Australasia.**—Announced Mubo (New Guinea) encircled, and Greenhill, important point in Mubo defence system, captured. 45 Jap aircraft destroyed over Rendova Island.

**JULY 16, Friday**  1,413th day
**Air.**—N. Italian switching and transformer stations at Milan and Bologna bombed by Lancasters.
**Sicily.**—Announced capture of 13 places, including Canicatti and Canicattini.
**Russian Front.**—Soviet forces advanced 6 to 9 miles in Orel sector.
**Australasia.**—Capture announced of Mubo (New Guinea) ; Munda (New

Georgia) pounded by 100 U.S. aircraft. Jap aircraft bombed Guadalcanal.

**JULY 17, Saturday**  1,414th day
**Air.**—Amsterdam and N.W. Germany bombed by Fortresses.
**Sicily.**—Announced Scordia, Lentini, Caltagirone and Grammichele taken by 8th Army, Agrigento and Porto Empedocle by Americans. Catania in flames as result of air and sea bombardments. Gen. Alexander appointed Military Governor of Sicily. Anglo-American Military Government (AMGOT) set up, headed by Maj.-Gen. Lord Rennell.
**Russian Front.**—Soviet troops advanced 8 miles in Orel-Kursk sector.
**Australasia.**—Jap shipping in Buin-Faisi area of Solomons struck by 200 aircraft in greatest air attack yet launched in this area. 7 Jap ships sunk.

**JULY 18, Sunday**  1,415th day
**Sicily.**—One-third of island in Allied hands along with 30,000 prisoners.
**Australasia.**—Jap shipping in Buin-Faisi area and Kahili airfields (Solomons) heavily attacked. Munda bombed.

**JULY 19, Monday**  1,416th day
**Sicily.**—Announced capture of Caltanisetta by Americans and Piazza Armerina by Canadians. 8th Army reached Gerbini area and point 3 miles from Catania ; Randazzo raided by Mitchells ; 35,000 prisoners taken to date.
**Mediterranean.**—Rome military targets bombed for first time, by U.S. Fortresses, Liberators, Marauders and Mitchells ; warning leaflets dropped on city before raid.
**Russian Front.**—Soviet troops advanced in Orel sector.

**JULY 20, Tuesday**  1,417th day
**Sicily.**—8th Army bridgeheads established south of Catania held against strong enemy counter-attacks. Enna fell to joint U.S. and Canadian attack.
**Russian Front.**—Russians advanced 3 to 5 miles in Orel sector, repulsing 10 enemy counter-attacks ; in Bielgorod area advances of 6 to 8 miles made ; in Donetz basin Soviet troops forced crossing of Donetz and Mius rivers ; Mtsensk and Voroshilovo captured. ¶
**General.**—Gen. Giraud arrived in Britain.

★ ~~~~~~~~~~~~ *Flash-backs* ~~~~~~~~~~~~ ★

**1940**
July 11. *Marshal Pétain announced formation of new Government, with himself as " Chief of the French State."*

July 14. *British garrison of Moyale (Kenya) withdrew after prolonged resistance to Italians.*

July 19. *Italian cruiser Bartolomeo Colleoni sunk in Mediterranean by Australian cruiser Sydney.*

**1941**
July 15. *Allied troops occupied Beirut (Syria).*

July 16. *Four-week battle of Smolensk opened.*

July 19. *Col. Britton announced on radio the formation of " V for Victory " army.*

**1942**
July 14. *Germans attacked Tel El Eisa (Egypt), British secured objectives on Ruweisat Ridge. Gen. de Gaulle's " Free French " Movement became " Fighting France."*

July 19. *Russians announced evacuation of Voroshilovgrad, 100 miles N. of Rostov.*

Few people realize what a marvel of human ingenuity there is in supplying a country with all that its inhabitants need, even in peacetime. How vastly greater is the miracle of keeping huge armies fed at a distance from their bases, and munitioned as well, and kept going with armaments of every kind! If you begin to think of the process in detail, it is positively bewildering. All the movements of the stuff to be carried, perhaps thousands of miles, have to be most carefully timed and co-ordinated. The hours taken in loading and unloading must be calculated to a minute. The arrivals at ports must tally with the readiness of ships to take cargo. The transfer from rail to hold, and from hold to rail again at the other end, has to be done with the least possible delay.

The labour to do it has to be on the spot whenever needed. Day by day, night by night, this endless chain of transport goes on. One broken link might throw it all out. It goes on without ceasing for an instant, thanks to the toil and calculations of great numbers of unknown men and women in offices and railway yards, on quaysides, and on board ships. They deserve our deep gratitude as much as the fighting men. Perhaps more, for their job is never exciting, though it often is dangerous, and its faithful accomplishment is essential to winning the war. I could expand considerably on this fascinating subject, a special aspect of which has been dealt with in page 142 of this issue.

I LIKE the up-to-date vigour and forthright language of Lieut.-General A. G. L. McNaughton, famous G.O.C. in Chief, 1st Canadian Army, as expressed in statements which he made when he visited Sicily shortly after the opening of the invasion. Commenting on that operation, he said, " It was a pretty remarkable feat . . . The ships were marshalled in perfect order. They made the correct rendezvous to the minute, they carried out the intricate manoeuvres as planned, and they landed on the right beaches at the right time. I call it a marvellous achievement." But why, I wonder, did this forceful Army Chief elect to use the word "pretty" in that connexion? To me, it does not seem to fit. "Truly," perhaps, or even "amazingly." But that colloquialism of "pretty" I like it not. It falls short of doing justice to the tremendous occasion. However, the most captious critic could find no fault with his declaration, "The operation as a whole was the most perfect example of combined operations the world has ever seen." He went on, "It must shake the Japs as well as the Germans to know that an overwhelming force can be brought to bear whenever and wherever the Allied leaders give the order."

BOTH the Admiralty and the War Office cling to old-time phrases that have an odd sound to modern ears. For instance, in announcing the retirement of a general officer, the W.O. stated that "the tour of duty for which he had been recalled had been completed." Most readers of that must have wondered what a "tour" meant in this connexion, and probably put it down to a misprint (when in doubt, blame the printer!). It is used in its French meaning, which is "turn." Probably it has been a military expression in Britain since the days of the great Duke of Marlborough.

Then, the Admiralty always insists on the B.B.C. adding to news of reverses or ships lost the statement that "the next-of-kin of casualties have been informed." That is done as a matter of course, not only by the Naval authorities but by those of the Army and the Air Force. Yet the expression continues to be used, just for old sake's sake. I dare say old naval men would feel something valuable was missing if they did not hear it always tacked on when "regrettable incidents" are made known to the nation: That phrase, by the way—"regrettable incident"—was so frequently included in Boer War communiqués that it became a joke and was hastily dropped.

IN several Continental countries they used to help railway passengers to get trains without having to ask questions of harassed

Lt.-Gen. J. L. DEVERS, whose appointment as Commander U.S. Forces in the European Theatre of Operations was announced on May 6, 1943, is one of America's foremost tank experts ; he was Chief of the American Armoured Force from August 1941.
*Photo, U.S. Official*

officials. No one was allowed on the platforms before a train came in. All who were waiting for trains sat in a big comfortable waiting-room. When a train was signalled a porter put his head in and called out the names of the places it was going to. All who were bound for those places filed out. This applied only to long-distance trains. For suburban services it was not required. It certainly was of great assistance ; more so, I think, than the loudspeakers now installed at many of our stations which often produce merely a blare of incomprehensible sound.

I was reminded of that Continental method while I sat on Paddington Station waiting for a train to the West, where business took me a few days ago. As the hour at which it was expected drew near, we lined up on the edge of the platform. Many who had not waited got even better places than some who had. As the train slowed down we grabbed the handles and scrambled in. In the North passengers queue for trains, which is a much better plan ; and safer, too, for boarding a train before it has quite come to a standstill is a risky business.

MOST men of the R.A.F. Regiment, formed last year to protect airfields, are glad they are to have exercises of a useful military character by way of training for their very important duties. They have been in many parts of the country (unless they were on A.A. duty) fed up with having nothing to do. One R.A.F. Regiment private I know attached himself to one of his officers as an extra batman, just to fill up his time. He said that polishing silver and Hoovering carpets was preferable to hanging about. Now they will not so often find time hang heavy on their hands.

WHEN one opens one's morning paper and scans the headlines, " Rome is Burning ! " comes easily first as an eye-catcher. Back to Nero ! Musso may be fiddling for all we know, but whatever he's doing is " on the strict Q.T.," as the old music-hall ditty had it. More than ever can we repeat today the words of Mr. Churchill that Italy owes all her present and impending tribulations to " one man, and one man alone." Soon we may have the satisfaction of seeing the puffed-up maker of the new Roman Empire as completely defeated as Nero, the short-lived tyrant of Old Rome, who gave him a lead by doing the deflation himself in the manner of the honourable harakirists of Japan.

TO the news that no more whisky is to be made has been added the announcement that stocks of wine are nearing exhaustion. It looks as if we might have Prohibition forced on us by circumstances, instead of being jockeyed into it by crazy fanatics and dishonest politicians, as were the Americans. Since North Africa was freed from Vichy rule some small amount of Algerian wine has been arriving, but it is grotesquely dear considering what its price used to be : fifteen shillings a bottle for what sold before the war at about one-and-ninepence—if you knew where to buy it. Plenty of purchasers seem to be found for it, though.

While five shillings is the authorized limit for a hotel or restaurant meal, it is possible to have a very costly dinner at home. Salmon at 5s. 6d. a pound to start with and peaches at 3s. 6d. each to finish with (they have been as much as 9s. each), with what used to be known as cheap wine at nearly £10 a dozen. Chickens at 12s. 6d. apiece could be added.

IT is a terrible affliction to be deaf. Many people say they would rather be blind, if they were compelled to choose between the two disabilities. Blind people have their other faculties sharpened, and everyone is kind to them. Deafness has a dulling effect on the mind and arouses very little sympathy ; it is regarded by the thoughtless as a nuisance rather than a misfortune. It is painful, therefore, to know that shortage of shipping space is causing a number of deaf persons to be without the aids to hearing on which they have been accustomed to rely.

These, I am told, came from the United States. It may be that they required some material that is now more urgently needed for armament production. Anyway, they don't come ; and this causes much suffering among folk whose lot is hard enough at all times. It is just "one of those things."

OUR next issue will be mainly devoted to illustrating the Battle of Sicily, of which a fine selection of photographs is in hand.

# Two Far-Famed Warriors Seen at Ease

**MEETING IN LONDON** last May, Gen. Montgomery (left), C.-in-C. 8th Army, is here seen in conversation with Field-Marshal Viscount Wavell of Cyrenaica and Winchester, Viceroy-Designate of India. The General had returned from N. Africa, while the Field-Marshal had come back from the U.S.A., where he had been present at the Churchill-Roosevelt conferences at Washington. *Photo, Planet News*

Printed in England and published every alternate Friday by the Proprietors, THE AMALGAMATED PRESS, LTD., The Fleetway House, Farringdon Street, London, E.C.4. Registered for transmission by Canadian Magazine Post. Sole Agents for Australia and New Zealand : Messrs. Gordon & Gotch, Ltd. ; and for South Africa : Central News Agency, Ltd.—August 6, 1943.    S.S.    *Editorial Address :* JOHN CARPENTER HOUSE, WHITEFRIARS, LONDON. E.C.4.

Vol 7 *The War Illustrated* Nº 161

*Edited by Sir John Hammerton*

SIXPENCE

AUGUST 20, 1943

PASSING FROM BATTLE in Sicily to a prisoners' cage, these Italians, for whom the war is at an end, are but a handful of the upwards of 90,000 Axis prisoners taken by August 2, 1943 when all but the north-eastern tip of the island had passed into Allied hands. Cigarette in mouth, the British soldier and his comrades on the wall watch the motley throng with good-humoured smiles as it leaves the dust of conflict for the peace and comparative comfort of captivity.

*Photo, British Official : Crown Copyright*

NO. 162 WILL BE PUBLISHED FRIDAY, SEPTEMBER 3

# THE BATTLE FRONTS

## by Maj.-Gen. Sir Charles Gwynn, K.C.B., D.S.O.

JULY fulfilled its promise of being one of the most eventful months of the war. The collapse of Mussolini and of the Fascist regime was the most sensational event of the month, certainly accelerated if not brought about by the military events. The opening of the German summer offensive in Russia, which for a few days looked dangerous, revived Axis hopes, but they were quickly damped by the remarkable Russian defence.

While the battle in the Kursk salient was at its height and its results still uncertain, came the amazingly successful invasion of Sicily, marked by the wonderful perfection of the Allied preparations and the skill shown in the planning and execution of one of the most difficult operations in warfare.

Then followed the Russian offensive on the Orel front to prove how completely the German offensive had failed. There had been Russian offensives in the summer in previous years, but they had all had a defensive or diversionary purpose to check the full development of German offensive strategy. Here, however, was a Russian summer offensive which marked a definite recovery of the initiative lost temporarily at the end of the winter campaign.

It is not surprising that Hitler had no reserves to send to Mussolini's assistance, nor that in the circumstances Mussolini decided to quit the sinking ship leaving Badoglio the task of saving what he could from the wreckage.

**ONE MAN AND HIS DOG.** Cherished personal possessions, including pets and musical instruments, were carried by many Italian prisoners, one of whom waits on the beach with his dog for the boat that will carry him captive from Sicily.
*Photo, British Official : Crown Copyright*

## SICILY

At the time I am writing (at the end of July) the military situation in Sicily is clear enough, but the further development of political events in Italy may affect immensely the normal course of military action before this article is published.

Up to the present the Allies have to their credit the great achievement of having in the course of three weeks successfully landed a large army in Sicily and of having secured possession of more than three-quarters of the island. What they occupy provides them with an admirable base for further operations, having several good ports and a considerable number of airfields.

But the enemy, having deliberately abstained from risking German troops in defence of the western part of the island, has concentrated them in its North-East corner, where they are holding a very strong position covering approaches to the Straits of Messina. With three and a half German divisions and two or three Italian divisions which may be of better quality than most of those met with in Sicily the enemy should have sufficient

troops to offer determined resistance on a front which is little over fifty miles long in a straight line; especially as much of the front could probably be lightly held on account of the nature of the terrain. The position also affords excellent observation.

THE Allies are now in contact with the enemy almost along his whole front: British troops on the right and Canadians in the centre after having been engaged in stiff fighting with the Germans in their advance. The Americans on the left who have just come up into line have had less fighting,

**BATTLE OF THE SICILIAN TIP, showing how the Allied Armies moved off on August 1, 1943.** During the following week Catania, Alderno and Bronte had fallen to the Eighth Army; the Americans had taken Troina and advanced beyond S. Agata.
*Courtesy of The News Chronicle*

**THIS YOUNG OFFICER** of the famous Hermann Goering Division was included in the first batch of prisoners from Sicily to be landed in Britain. Note the distinctive armlet on his sleeve. *Photo, P.N.A.*

but much larger distances to go and have presumably to develop new bases at the ports captured in the west of the island; in fact, they are ready to take part in a major operation. It is clear that should the enemy continue to hold his ground here a full-scale, carefully prepared attack would be required to dislodge him, and days or even weeks may elapse before it could possibly achieve decisive results.

Meanwhile, the enemy is being subjected

to heavy artillery and air attacks with probably numerous local operations to secure favourable starting positions and better observation. Up to the present the enemy has been receiving reinforcements, probably at least sufficient to replace casualties. That, owing to developments in Italy, may become more difficult, but it is safer to assume that the numerical strength of his forces will be maintained though the morale of his troops may deteriorate under bombardment.

The enemy obviously is accepting the risk of a large-scale disaster ; for evacuation as a last resort would, under concentrated air attack and under pressure of Allied pursuit, be a very different matter from dribbling in reinforcements. It might be altogether impracticable and at the best extremely costly. Yet the Germans were almost bound to accept the risk, for at no other point in Italian territory could they hope to meet us on comparatively equal terms. The number of German troops in Italy is small, and Germany has no central reserve from which the numbers can be increased materially, nor can reserves be safely transferred from other sectors.

CLEARLY, with such limited numbers, Germany could not consider holding the whole of Italy without Italian cooperation, and that, in any case, would have entailed the danger of German troops becoming involved in an Italian débâcle. Withdrawal of German troops to Northern Italy would have antagonized the Italians, and left them, even if they made the attempt, incapable of

**OREL-BIELGOROD FRONT** on July 27, 1943. Von Hunersdorff's push from Bielgorod to Kursk had been smashed, and the Soviet advance on Orel neared its conclusion. Orel and Bielgorod were retaken by the Red Army on August 5. *By courtesy of The Times*

holding the southern part of the peninsula, which would then become an Allied base.

In fact, the north-east corner of Sicily alone offered a sufficiently restricted front on which a small, exclusively German force might check Allied progress and at least gain time to see what policy under Badoglio's leadership Italy would follow. But even should the Germans be able to hold this position for some time it will not prevent the further development of Allied plans nor interfere with intensified bombing of Italy. Germany cannot escape the dilemma in which her lack of a strong central reserve places her.

It is interesting to note that all the German divisions in Sicily are new formations under old names of divisions lost in Africa or at Stalingrad. They might therefore have been expected to be of second-class quality con-

stituted from the inexperienced and inadequately trained personnel produced by Hitler's call-up of all Germany's available man power. Yet actually they are evidently first-class troops probably with a high percentage of recovered wounded and invalids who have all the advantages of experience and thorough training. Their loss would therefore make disaster all the more serious.

If Badoglio fails to rally the Italian nation and army and is forced to accept the Allied terms, the Germans may hope that he would be able to give them an opportunity of withdrawing such parts of their force as they can succeed in evacuating from Sicily. But if Badoglio is able to continue the struggle it seems probable that the Germans will fight for their bridgehead in Sicily to the last possible position, and a quick, decisive success such as was won in Tunisia should not be expected when our attack is delivered.

**PRIMO SOLE BRIDGE** over the Simeto River in Sicily—which this Bren carrier is crossing—was the scene of grim fighting when British parachutists seized it on July 13, 1943, and then were forced back. With the arrival of Durham Light Infantry reinforcements the bridge—vital for our advance towards Catania—was again captured and held successfully against counter-attacks. Our positions were finally consolidated on both banks of the river. See also parachutists' story in page 188.
*Photo, British Official : Crown Copyright*

## RUSSIA

Events of the past month in Russia have been of even greater importance than those in the Mediterranean and have been no less favourable to the Allies in their effect on the general war situation. In their abortive offensive the Germans made prodigal use of their best and most formidable troops, and it is certain they could not have been brought to such an abrupt standstill unless they had suffered losses on an immense scale. The Germans themselves admitted that the intensity of the fighting was unprecedented.

The Russian offensive against the Orel salient, although its progress has not been rapid and on small-scale maps would seem to affect a comparatively insignificant area, must be costing the Germans heavily.

An area so highly fortified cannot be easily overrun, and so long as it is defended with determination it must be dealt with by a series of well prepared concentrated attacks. But the defence has little chance of retreat, and the capture of each successive locality implies the practical annihilation of its garrison. The cost to the defence is therefore very high. The Germans appear determined to hold the salient at all costs and have again used their reserves of mobile troops prodigally in counter-attacks which when unsuccessful are liable to prove desperately expensive.

The drain on German reserves must therefore during the past have been exceptionally high. We know from bitter experience in the last war that it is the intensity of the fighting rather than the extent of the area covered by operations that rapidly reduces reserve strength. Germany's great weakness is the lack of a central reserve available to reinforce threatened points on her immense defensive front.

If she had hoped to be able to build up such a reserve by adopting a defensive attitude in Russia, that hope must by now be rapidly vanishing. Having failed to disrupt Russian offensive plans by her own offensive, her Russian front is now threatened throughout its length and needs reserve strength behind it as much as or more than her fronts in the south and west of Europe. No reserves can be spared for it.

UNDER Russian pressure the Orel salient has diminished in size, but it would still be practicable for the Germans to withdraw from it, although probably only with great loss of material. There are, however, no signs that this is yet their intention, and they may hope that the Russians will exhaust their offensive strength in their efforts to effect its reduction. But there is little reason to believe that the development of Russian plans depends entirely on the elimination of the Orel salient or that Zhukov would make Hitler's mistake of allowing the desire to capture a city to divert him from his main object. Desirable as the capture of Orel undoubtedly is, it should not be looked on as the test by which the success of Russian strategy can be judged.

### THE EIGHTH ARMY IN SICILY

Units serving in the Eighth Army in Sicily are :
\*The 5th, 50th, and 51st United Kingdom Divisions and the following Canadian regiments, their places of origin, when not obvious, being given in parentheses.
**Hastings and Prince Edward** (Eastern Ontario).
**Royal Canadian** (London, Toronto, Montreal).
**48th Highlanders, Canada** (Toronto).
**Princess Patricia's Canadian Light Infantry** (Winnipeg, Vancouver).
**Seaforth Highlanders** (Vancouver, B.C.).
**Edmonton, West Nova Scotia, Royal 22nd** (French Canadian : Quebec).
**Carleton and York** (New Brunswick).
\*[On August 4, 1943 Mr. Churchill announced that the 78th United Kingdom Division was operating in the Centuripe Sector.]

# Skirl o' the Pipes on the Road to Catania

SCOTTISH TROOPS in Sicily march to the music of the pipes (top) in the hills north of Vizzini, towards Catania, some 31 miles distant as the bomber flies. These are some of the men who broke the Lentini "bottle-neck" and deployed into the Plain of Catania on July 16, 1943. Catania fell to the 8th Army on August 5. At Militella (bottom), a few miles from Vizzini, our men receive gifts of wine. War correspondents, commanders and troops agreed on the warmth of their reception by a people weary of Fascism.    PAGE 164    *Photos, British Official; Crown Copyright*

# Approach to the 'Bottle-neck'—Key to the Plain

A BREN CARRIER (above) passes through the hilly Sicilian countryside of Palazzolo (see map in p. 133), which was occupied by Canadian units of the 8th Army on July 13, 1943. The town stands astride the only railway and road to the west from the port of Syracuse, which fell three days earlier. Thus was closed one of the avenues through which the enemy might have sent forces for the relief of the port—the capture of which, with its harbour facilities undamaged, was one of the outstanding gains of the first days of the invasion. Success in this area enabled the 8th Army to press on to the town of Melilli (right) and thence through the Lentini "bottle-neck" to the Plain of Catania.

Soon after Melilli fell, on July 15, the Royal Army Medical Corps, who had been with the forward troops, took over suitable buildings as hospitals and parked their ambulances in the main square in the shadow of the undamaged Church of St. Sebastian, while British infantry and armoured units passed on.

*Photos, British Official: Crown Copyright*

# Three Allied Forces Sweep on With One Aim

PERFECT CO-ORDINATION crowns the efforts of British, Canadian and American troops in Sicily with outstanding success. Having conquered the centre and west, Americans and Canadians turned east, to form with Gen. Montgomery's Britishers on July 29, 1943, the Catania-Agira-San Stefano line in preparation for clearing the last of the Axis forces from of the island.

During the advance to Caltanisetta the Americans dealt with many a sniper's hide-out (1), but bitterness of fighting was forgotten when a wounded Italian prisoner (2) wanted a cigarette and a light. British tanks were passing through Pachino (3) by July 12; in the hills around Enna our men became accustomed to strong-points disgorging Axis troops (4) complete with white flag. At Modica, a town clinging to the side of an impressive gorge, with a population of 40,000, men of the Western Canadian Infantry (5) encountered no opposition on July 15; they found the gates of the town wide open and scores of Italian soldiers begging to be captured.

*Photos, British Official: Crown Copyright; Associated Press*

# Eighth Army Armour In Triumphal Setting

A SHERMAN TANK passes through an imposing arch into the town of Cassibile, on the coastal road between Syracuse and Avola, a sector over-run by the 8th Army on July 10, 1943. Syracuse fell on July 10, Augusta surrendered without a fight on July 14, and following the establishment of a bridgehead at Primo Sole (see p. 163) our troops deployed into the Plain of Catania for the crucial battle. On August 1 the 8th Army launched the assault, and Catania fell four days later.

# THE WAR AT SEA

## by Francis E. McMurtrie

THOUGH the Italian surrender is still delayed at the time of writing, there is good reason to suppose that it cannot be long deferred. When it comes it will take the form of a complete capitulation, for nothing less will be accepted by the Allies. Apart from the immense strategical value which the Italian peninsula will possess as an Allied base from which to attack Germany and her remaining satellites, there is much important war material in Italian hands which can be turned to good account when handed over to the victors.

First and foremost is the Italian Navy, with its valuable bases at Spezia, Naples, Taranto, Venice, and Pola, including dockyards and other facilities. There are also important private shipyards, gun factories, armour-plate foundries and rolling mills, marine engine works, and other establishments, of which the Odero-Terni-Orlando and Ansaldo undertakings are the largest.

IT is known that the Germans are extremely anxious that none of these should fall into Allied hands, yet how they are to prevent this occurring—except possibly in the case of the ports of Trieste, Pola, and Fiume—it is hard to see. There are reports that already steps have been taken to occupy the three ports named, though how far the matter has gone is not clear. Even assuming that these particular prizes are bagged by the Germans (who have long cast a covetous eye upon them, as they were formerly part of the Austro-Hungarian Empire), they are believed to contain an insignificant proportion of the Italian fleet. There are a semi-complete new battleship, a heavily damaged old one under refit, and a couple of cruisers of 4,200 tons laid down for the Siamese Navy in 1939, but not believed to have been finished. There may also be some smaller craft, such as destroyers and submarines, under refit.

IT has been reported that the Germans are endeavouring to appropriate a flotilla of submarines in the Dodecanese, but this story should be received with caution. In Italy, as in most other countries, the Germans are cordially detested, and it is probable that the average officer of the Italian Navy would prefer to destroy his vessel rather than surrender her to the hated Tedeschi, even as the French decided to scuttle their ships at Toulon in the last resort.

At the moment the portion of the Italian fleet in the greatest danger of becoming Allied property is the squadron at Taranto, composed of three old but rebuilt battleships, dating from 1911-13, some cruisers, destroyers, submarines and auxiliaries. Once Sicily is entirely conquered there is nothing to stop the invasion of Calabria (the "toe" of Italy), followed by that of Basilicata, the adjoining province in which Taranto is situated. Already the Royal Navy has bombarded Cotrone, a port half-way between the Strait of Messina and Taranto, without encountering any opposition worth mentioning.

A dash for the Adriatic is still a possibility; but so little enterprise has been shown by the Italian Navy in this war that it by no means follows that such a venture need be contemplated. It is unlikely that all the ships would escape were it to be attempted, for the British Mediterranean Fleet, under Admiral of the Fleet Sir Andrew Cunningham, is certain to be on the watch for some such move; and in the sure knowledge has been shown by the Italians may prefer to stay in harbour and wait on events. Such an attitude would be consistent with their conduct of the naval war to date.

## HOW United Nations Could Use the Italian Fleet

Similarly, it is doubtful whether the squadron at Taranto, comprising three new battleships with a number of cruisers, destroyers and submarines, will elect to seek another refuge, either at the ill-omened port of Toulon or in some neutral harbour such as Barcelona. Thus it may be assumed that with Italy's complete collapse, her fleet will mostly fall into the Allied lap. It remains to be considered to what extent that fleet could be utilized for our purposes.

Of the battleships, the three at Spezia—the Impero, Littorio and Vittorio Veneto—are fine new vessels of 35,000 tons, armed with 15-in. guns. With certain alterations there is no doubt that good use could be made of them, as in the analogous case of the French battleship Richelieu, refitted at New York. But the same can hardly be said for the three at Taranto, understood to be the Andrea Doria, Caio Duilio and Giulio Cesare, of 23,622 tons. Though renovated and made to look like new, their hulls are fully 30 years old and in one or more cases have been considerably strained by torpedo hits. Their main armament of 12·6-in. guns could only be used if a sufficient stock of shells could be made available, as this calibre does not exist anywhere outside Italy.

Italian cruisers may number a dozen, of which only one, the battered Gorizia, is of a heavy type. Her main armament comprises eight 8-in. guns. She has been torpedoed as well as damaged by bombs and is still under repair. Seven smaller cruisers, of from 7,874 to 5,000 tons, armed with 6-in. guns, would be more useful, though one of them, the Muzio Attendolo, has been heavily damaged and is being refitted at Naples. There are three or four of the new fast cruisers of the Regolo class, of 3,362 tons, armed with 5·3-in. guns; one of them has been badly mauled. They are really glorified destroyers, very lightly constructed, everything having been sacrificed to enable engines to be installed of sufficient power to produce a speed of 41 knots.

Two obsolete cruisers, dating from the last war, of low speed and small fighting value, may still exist, but are not worth taking into account. They were relegated to colonial service some years ago, and one of them may have taken refuge in Japanese waters. How many destroyers remain in serviceable condition is doubtful, but there may be 50 or 60. Good use could be made of these for operations in the Mediterranean or Black Sea, though the fuel supply of the majority would probably be insufficient to enable them to undertake ocean convoy work.

THERE are an uncertain number of submarines, losses having been heavy; indeed, the names of over 40 of those sunk have been reported. Perhaps as many as 50 may be in a seagoing state, though the total may well be less. Considerable internal modification would be needed before any of these could be manned and operated by Allied crews.

There remain the numerous auxiliaries, which would be particularly useful for all the subsidiary work which falls to the lot of a navy in wartime. There is a small seaplane carrier, the Giuseppe Miraglia, together with sundry minelayers, minesweepers, trawlers, transports, oil tankers and water-carriers. Though the number of these has doubtless been curtailed by the heavy toll taken of Axis convoys by H.M. submarines, there should be a useful residue which, together with the remnant of the Italian mercantile navy, ought to constitute a valuable reinforcement to Allied resources.

**BLACK SEA POLICE.'** The Russians are now policing the Black Sea with motor-torpedo boats. Crews are here running to man four of these craft moored off-shore as an alarm is sounded. Necessity for such constant vigilance is emphasized by the German claim of July 31, 1943, that a U-boat had sunk a 7,000-ton Soviet tanker in this Sea. PAGE 168 *Photo, Associated Press*

# The Royal Navy Lends a Powerful Hand Ashore

TRANSPORTED BY THE ALLIED NAVIES, our troops got to work directly they reached the Sicilian beaches—some with more fruitful results than fell to this Tommy (1) who investigated an Italian pill-box and found the gun was a dummy! This Signals Section (2) of the Royal Navy, dug in ashore, maintained contact with vessels landing stores and armour (3) on July 10, 1943 (see also pp. 176–177). Of the naval men Gen. Eisenhower said, "Their comrades of the air and ground forces unite in an enthusiastic and grateful 'Well done!'"

*Photos, British Official*

# Americans Subdue Rendova in the Solomons

RENDOVA ISLAND, in the New Georgia group of the Solomons, was the scene of one of the heaviest air defeats ever inflicted on the Japanese ; on June 30—July 1, 1943 they lost 123 planes in two days at a cost to the Allies of only 25 aircraft. In that period American Marines occupied the island, wiped out the Japanese garrison, and from Rendova itself U.S. artillery proceeded to pound the adjacent enemy-held Munda airfield.

Under cover of darkness, big guns of the U.S. Navy's task force (1) reached the Kolombangara area (see map, p. 99) and softened-up Rendova for the landing-party, one of whom (2) is having his injured leg dressed by a comrade after the attack. Troops are manhandling a light field gun (3) through the water to the island, and a little farther out (4) a 10-wheeled truck is unloaded on to a waiting lighter—one of the indispensable " invasion ferry " fleet.

*Photos, Planet News*

# For 3,000 Years History Has Been Made in Sicily

"A museum of cultures, a picture-book of history," the author of this revealing article calls the battle-scarred island which we invaded on July 9-10, 1943. With its chronicle of battles and conquerors, of past glories—and a future freed from oppression—the story makes fascinating reading : and place-names in the war communiqués come to life.

Is there another island in the world in which so many races and generations of men, through such a succession of centuries, have left so many traces as Sicily ? Set in the very middle of the sea which was itself for two thousand years the centre of the known and civilized world, gifted by Nature with a fertile soil and a pleasant climate, it has acted like a magnet on those whose wanderings and excursions have given a backbone to European history.

Prehistoric men of the caves, workers in stone, bronze and copper, Cretans and Mycenaeans, Greeks, Phoenicians and Carthaginians, Romans and Vandals, Saracens and Normans, English—yes, our sailors were there a hundred and fifty years ago—Garibaldi's patriots and Mussolini's ruffians. . . . And now British, Canadians and Americans, engaged in one of the greatest ventures in human history. Sicily has received them all. Her soil retains and will long retain their footprints. She is a museum of cultures, a picture-book of history, containing many a gory or glamorous page.

## On the Prowl for Slaves

According to the traditions of the ancient Greek mariners, Sicily was inhabited in the long, long ago by lotus-eaters and the wild, lawless and wicked race of one-eyed Cyclopes. But flint implements and fragments of pottery are more reliable evidence of human habitation in the very dawn of European history. The earliest inhabitants of whom anything definite is recorded were the Sicani, who, about 1500 B.C., were driven into the western part of the island by the Siceli, invaders from the Italian mainland, who, judging from the weapons that their graves have revealed, were in the bronze age of culture.

Not long after came Cretan traders, if it be true that the great blocks of liparite stone to be seen in the ruins of Cnossus came—as is most likely since it is the nearest possible source—from the Lipari islands, just off Sicily's northern coast. Then came the Phoenicians, on the prowl for slaves and choice trading-sites ; they founded many a little colony on the coast.

And next the Greeks. In 735 B.C., when Rome was still little more than a collection of shanties, Ionian Greeks, probably from what is now Asia Minor, founded a colony at Naxos (near the present-day Taormina), the north-eastern corner of the island within sight of the Italian "toe." Shortly afterwards, some say the next year, Dorian Greeks from Corinth founded Syracuse, and they laid the foundation-stones of Gela in 729 B.C. Between them the Ionians and Dorians made themselves masters of the greater part of the island, pushing the Phoenicians back into the western parts, where Panormus—we know it as Palermo—was one of their strongholds. The Phoenicians were men of commerce rather than of the sword, but they had powerful relatives, and in 480 B.C., in response to an appeal for help, Carthage, the great Phoenician city-empire in what is now Tunisia, sent an army under Hamilcar to succour the hard-pressed Phoenicians.

Advancing along the north coast, the Carthaginian host besieged Himera, a few miles west of the present Cefalu ; and here it was met by the Greek levies and in a surprise attack routed utterly. The battle was indeed the "Salamis of Sicily" ; and in Sicily, as in Greece after the defeat of the Persian invader, the victory was followed by a remarkable flowering of Hellenic culture.

All over the island there are still to be found architectural relics of this wonderful age, fortifications and aqueducts, theatres and tombs, houses and, most notable of all, Doric temples of the Greek gods. One of the most important sites is Girgenti—Agrigentum the Romans called it, and as Agrigento it was mentioned often enough in the communiqués recently ; to the Greeks it was Akragas, "the most beautiful city of mortals," according to Pindar. Here are the remains of the Temple of Zeus, a vast structure, the largest temple in all Sicily, 372 feet long (the Parthenon at Athens is 228 ft. in length), the Temple of Concord, one of the best-preserved

**BRITISH ENSIGN** hoisted in Syracuse, fifth most important town in Sicily, after its capture by the 8th Army on July 10, 1943. Since its foundation in 734 B.C. many despots have ruled the town. A new era of freedom now begins. (See also article in page 180.)
*Photo, Canadian Official.*

in existence, the Temple of Juno Lacinia, situated above a steep precipice, and the Temples of Ceres, Hercules, and Castor and Pollux. (See ilus. p. 173.) Near Sciacca, 50 miles west of Girgenti, are the remains of the ancient Selinus, farthest west of Greek settlement in the island ; its ruins are described as the grandest ancient temples in Europe. Twenty miles inland, between Calatafimi and Castellamare, is Segesta, with many a relic to show the sight-seeing soldier from Canadian prairies or American Middle West. Then there is Syracuse.

Volumes have been written on this, the first of the Sicilian cities which fell to the British invader a few weeks ago. Since its foundation in 734 B.C. by a little band of Greek colonists from Corinth it has been warred for and over many times. For years it was Europe's finest city. Here, 400 years before Christ, Dionysius ruled as a "philosopher-king" ; before its walls the power of would-be imperial Athens was shattered in what Thucydides described as the most important event that befell the Greeks in the Peloponnesian War ; here Theocritus wrote

his verses and Archimedes, most famed of ancient mathematicians, invented machine after machine to defend the city when the Romans besieged it in 212 B.C. According to tradition he was seated in the public square lost in thought, studying a variety of geometrical figures he had drawn in the sand before him. As a Roman soldier approached with drawn sword, he loudly called to him "not to spoil the circle !" But the Nazi of those days cut him down.

The fall of Syracuse brought the whole of Sicily beneath the Roman rule, and Roman it remained for more than a thousand years, until the Saracen invasions in the ninth century of our era. Syracuse fell to the Moslems in A.D. 877, but two hundred years later, its capture by the Normans put the seal on their Sicilian conquests. Those Normans were near relations of the men who fought and won at Hastings, and on Sicily they left an indelible mark just as their fellows did on England. Mighty castles and magnificent churches still bear witness to their power and genius. Palermo Cathedral, we may care to recall, was built by an Englishman, Archbishop Walter Offamil (Walter of the Mill). Many an American and British soldier must have gazed of late weeks upon his tomb in the Norman crypt. Another Englishman, Richard Palmer, was bishop of Syracuse.

## Latest Conquerors Welcomed

Augusta, another of General Alexander's recent captures, was founded by the Normans in 1232 on an ancient site. Several times during the Middle Ages it was conquered and destroyed ; it has made the latest in the long line of its conquerors welcome, since they come not to destroy but to liberate. Catania, which for a time held the 8th Army at bay, was the second of the Greek colonies in Sicily ; their name for it was the same but without the "i." Its cathedral was begun by a Norman duke in 1091 ; its amphitheatre is Roman and its theatre, too. Then, overshadowed by the cone of Etna, lies Messina. It is one of Sicily's most ancient cities, yet the remains of antiquity are few.

Not for the first time Etna boiled up in 1908, and the city was practically wiped out by the earthquake, some 77,000 lives being lost. On Etna's western slopes is the little town of Bronte. Englishmen should be welcome here, for an English "milord" (Viscount Bridport, descendant of Nelson's niece) owns the estates roundabout. They were given to Nelson by King Ferdinand of Naples and Sicily in 1798, in recognition of the great sea-captain's help against the French Jacobin invaders. Nelson was made Duke of Bronte, but it is unlikely that he ever found time to visit his new domain ; he preferred to spend his leaves at Palermo, where were the royal court—and Lady Hamilton.

Ferdinand called the British in again in 1808, and for several years the island was guarded against Napoleon by British troops. Their commander was Lord William Bentinck, and under his guidance the Sicilian Estates (local parliament) in 1812 set up a constitution on the English two-chamber model. (It was swept away by Ferdinand, soon after Bentinck, whose name is still honoured in the island, left Sicily in 1814.)

Now we are adding yet another page to the massive volume of Sicilian history. And in all the age-long record is there anything to compare with this conquering progress in which we, the "enemy," are met with the V-sign of our coming victory ?  **E. ROYSTON PIKE**

# 'Mussolini Will Increase the Number of Ruins—

**PROUD OF HER ANCIENT RUINS,** Italy is seeing the fulfilment of the prophecy made by Mr. Duff Cooper on the day—June 10, 1940—of Italy's entry into the war ; speaking of Mussolini—the inglorious dictator who resigned on July 25, 1943—he said, " He will increase the number of ruins for which Italy has long been famous." Taken before the onslaught on Sicily by Allied bombers, these photographs show the harbour of Syracuse (1), captured by the 8th Army on July 10, 1943; (2) Palermo, taken on July 22 by the U.S. 7th Army ; Messina (3), terminus of the Axis " ferry " to the mainland ; Catania (4), captured on August 5, and (5) front-line Etna.

*Photos, Pictorial Press, E.N.A., Topical Press*

# —For Which Italy Has Long Been Famous!'

THESE VENERABLE PILES are among the show places of Sicily. Beside them now lie other ruins—of very recent date. The Temple of Concord (1) built in the 5th century B.C., and the Temple of Castor and Pollux (2), dating from the end of the 4th century B.C., are at Agrigento—ancient Girgenti (see article in page 171)—which fell on July 16, 1943 ; the hill-road to the town and the administrative buildings were destroyed by our naval bombardment. From the Greek Theatre at Taormina (3), where the Axis H.Q. was destroyed by Allied bombs on July 9, the view includes the road to Catania.

*Photos, Topical Press, E.N.A.*

# They've Been Our Commandos For 300 Years

No higher honour could have been paid to the Royal Marines than their selection as the first seaborne troops to make the assault on Sicily, on July 10, 1943. They are the Empire's super-shock troops, without peer. JOHN ALLEN GRAYDON outlines briefly below some stirring achievements which will make the name of this proud Corps of sea-soldiers live for evermore.

At 1 a.m. on July 10, 1943, assault craft packed with Royal Marine Commandos left the parent ship, lying some eight miles off the Sicilian coast. The task of these tough "Jollies" was to gain and establish the first foothold on the island and destroy the shore defences to the west of the main landing beaches of the First Canadian Division . . . By dawn the job was done ; the infantry could " go in."

On land, sea. and in the air, Britain's Royal Marines, since the war commenced in 1939, have fought in more engagements, and on more fronts, than any other Corps in the world. They were the last to leave Norway, France and the Low Countries. Last out of Crete and Burma. And always able to inflict more damage upon the enemy than he upon them.

At the outbreak of war the Royal Marines, who have been the Empire's Commandos for three hundred years, were well below their 1918 strength. Slowly but surely, for the " Royals " demand men of high mental as well as physical standard, the Corps was built up to its present superlative standard.

Aboard our warships Royal Marines—in every ship from a cruiser to a battleship—help to man about one-third of the guns, supply guards, and furnish the bands. On most of the big " convoy runs " Royal Marine bandsmen have excelled, for besides tending the delicate fire-power instruments, they undertake secret work which calls for a high degree of intelligence. During many of the Malta convoys these bandsmen have suffered heavily ; but when the George Cross Island was neared the Marines donned their " blues," and, with their march, A Life on the Ocean Wave, played the convoy, loaded with essentials for Malta's defence, into Valetta Harbour.

At home, too, you will see Royal Marine Police patrolling the various dockyards and the Admiralty ; and when Britain was threatened with invasion they manned the long-range guns at Dover. At the same time, when the story of their deeds can be told in full, it will be found that the " Jollies " rank among the greatest anti-aircraft gunners in the world.

Aboard merchant-ships Royal Marine gunners are also showing that skill for which they are famous. Certain is it that many U-boats have suffered serious damage as the result of these always-ready gunners.

Many Royal Marines are also revealing their ability as pilots with the Fleet Air Arm. They were well to the fore in the famous attack upon the Italian battle fleet at Taranto, and many of the Duce's most-prized naval units have consistently been attacked by pilots of the Royal Marines.

## Submarines Were Cut in Half

It was a young Royal Marine, leading a flight of three torpedo-carrying aircraft, who was responsible for one of the War's most sensational operations. Two enemy submarines, a destroyer, and a supply ship lay at anchor off the Libyan coast when the Marine commenced the attack. Two torpedoes cut the submarines completely in half ; another fired the destroyer. Before the crews could prevent the flames from spreading the supply ship had caught fire, and photographs later revealed that the men under the leadership of the Royal Marine had destroyed four enemy warships with only three " tin-fish " !

It is as the spearhead to land operations, however, that the Royal Marines excel.

Without touching the pride of any other force, it can truthfully be said that the " Jollies," when it comes to making a landing on enemy-occupied territory, are the finest in the world.

When that assault landing craft left the parent ship at 1.0 a.m. on July 10, flares of the R.A.F. lit up the horizon, silhouetting the dark coastline while the thud of their bombs could be heard on the ships. The glare grew brighter as the flat, black landing-craft drove in through a heavy ground swell, spray drenching the tightly-packed silent Marines. Several craft shipped a good deal of sea. A machine-gun suddenly chattered. Already knee-deep in water in the craft, men jumped in succession into the warm, waist-deep sea, each holding up his weapons and ploughing forward with his allotted load of ammunition, mortar bombs or water . . . There were sharp, brief engagements, the Marines inflicting on the enemy five times the number of casualties that they

**BUGLER BOY of the Royal Marines, the magnificent Corps instituted by the Admiralty in 1664 as " land souldgers prepared for sea service " and whose mighty achievements—down to the Sicilian landing—are dealt with in this page.** *Photo, Topical*

themselves suffered. As the sun came up, more landing craft were streaming to the beach, while patrols of Marines and Canadians exploited inland. Thus was the first foothold in Sicily established.

When Britain was reeling, following the Dunkirk set-back, the " Royals " were actually practising for an invasion of Europe ; and the first man to organize raids upon enemy territory was a high officer of the Royal Marines, who later gave way to Sir Roger Keyes and became his assistant.

When the Queen of Holland was in danger of capture by the enemy, the Adjutant-General phoned the Chatham establishment at seven o'clock one evening and ordered that 200 men should be taken to The Hook and assist in the rescue of the Queen. An hour later the men were equipped, had food enough to last for three days, and climbed aboard a motor-coach which drove them through the night to Dover. Here they boarded a destroyer and reached the Dutch coast just before midnight.

For reasons of security I cannot reveal in detail all that happened during the hectic hours that followed. Fifth Columnists, German parachutists, and dive-bombers—all attempted to prevent the Royal Marines from achieving their purpose. But the Royal Marines brought the Dutch Queen to Britain —and returned with *all* their equipment : a fact of which they are justly proud.

In the sweltering jungles of Burma, when General Alexander organized his masterly withdrawal, Royal Marines, far away from their cruisers and battleships, displayed that Commando training which has made their Corps world-famous.

### Great Honour Earned at Dieppe

With a small force of river-craft they made the Japanese Army commanders believe that a formidable flotilla of Royal Navy gunboats was on patrol. By this method they prevented the enemy from using the Irrawaddy. At night, taking advantage of their superb training, they crept into the jungle, taking food, water and ammunition to isolated units, often passing within a few yards of the enemy. On their return journey these Marines brought back with them wounded, and provided medical attention.

When the main units had reached India, the Royal Marines took their small boats into the centre of the river, fired them, then lined up in front of their commanding officer. Their ranks had thinned, but the spirit of a great Corps was still with them ; and they marched, as only the Royal Marines can march, the two hundred miles into Assam.

As a war correspondent I have many opportunities of meeting the men who come to this country from outposts of the Empire to fight ; and of the many Canadians with whom I have talked, all were full of praise for the Royal Marines. You see, because of the Royal Marine Commandos' feats at Dieppe and in Sicily, a great bond of friendship has grown between the men of the Maple Leaf and the " Jollies." Before the Dieppe raid Canadians tell me that dozens of Marines, just to help their cousins from the New World, pointed out to them the best method of forcing a landing and taking cover. With a determination that was magnificent to behold, Royal Marine Commandos, who wear the famed green beret, side by side with Canadians earned great honour at Dieppe.

At Madagascar, too, fifty Royal Marines, landing in the rear of the enemy defences, created such havoc by their daring that very much stronger enemy forces continually offered to surrender ! In the end the Royal Marines had more prisoners than they could possibly cope with, and it was with a great deal of satisfaction that " reinforcements " arrived and took over from them.

When the forces of freedom decide to assail the mainland of Europe the Royal Marines Mobile Naval Base Defence Organization may well prove of very great value. Designed originally for the purpose of enabling any weak or unprotected naval base to repel a surprise attack, its purpose altered as the unit developed in strength. Today this, the first of Britain's amphibious forces can be relied upon to capture a harbour, and also provide and install all the shore defences needed for a fleet base. Tradesmen, such as carpenters, electricians, builders, etc., all of them Royal Marines, then follow up and repair the damaged cranes, docks and harbour installations, while their comrades can be trusted to hold that which they have captured.

## Invasion General Wades Ashore

In the early hours of July 10, 1943 Maj.-Gen. Guy Simonds, commanding the First Canadian Division, splashed through the surf from a landing-craft to join his men pushing inland from the Sicilian shore. At 40 he is the youngest Canadian general, and he has imbued his troops with the magnificent fighting spirit which is carrying them to such great conquests. Gen. Montgomery, leader of the invincible 8th Army—of which Maj.-Gen. Simonds' command forms a part—declared, " The Canadians were terrific on the beaches and in attack inland."

## *As the Sun Came Up On Invasion Day*

Our ships and men crowded the Sicilian beaches as dawn broke on July 10. Coastal batteries had been silenced and shore defences vanquished, and troops and naval beach parties up to their waists in water could work unhindered at the task which was to occupy them without pause through the coming day—the landing of vast quantities of stores, all the varied paraphernalia of war brought for the invaders' use by the Royal Navy.

## *With Pick and Shovel the Way is Cleared*

Beach roads had to be prepared without delay.   As Royal Engineers and Pioneers laboured to level a way through boulders and rocks of the landing ground, vessels with bows wedged in the shallows prepared to disgorge heavy traffic that would presently pour in that direction to the firm island roads : guns, tanks, trucks, cars, ambulances, jeeps almost without number, for a speedy link-up with the fighting troops thrusting victoriously inland.

## Advance of the Liberators

Photos, Canadian and British Official

Past a deserted Italian pill-box (top), infantry—among the first Canadians to set foot on Sicily—push inland from the beach. They are (right to left) Piper N. A. McLeod, L/Cpl. C. A. Jones and Pte. L. Dunn, all from Vancouver. Below, on the road to Syracuse, a patrol passes the bodies of Italian soldiers at Avola, the capture of which by the 8th Army was announced on July 12. As the advance continued the people of Sicily greeted their liberators with the V-sign and with flowers and wine.

# VIEWS & REVIEWS
### Of Vita War Books

### by Hamilton Fyfe

THERE is, after all, a limit to the power of the purely mechanical over the human element in warfare. It is not true to say, as Sir John Anderson once did in a broadcast, that " men can never be defeated by the want of material aids"—and he said it just at the moment when the Spanish Republicans had been so defeated ! But it always has been and still is true that men fighting for some cause they believe in, to defend their country's soil or throw off an oppressor's yoke, can stand up against great odds, can beat a foe armed with better weapons, can overcome the soulless might of machines.

When the Italians were struggling to rid their country of the Austrians, who ruled despotically, and cruelly too (which is not easy to believe of Austrians now), Italian courage, Italian endurance, Italian readiness to meet enemies who seemed on paper to be superior in every way, aroused the admiration of the world. They struggled successfully because their hearts were in the fight. They were thrice armed because their quarrel was just.

How different their behaviour when they were flung into battle against the Greek nation in 1940 ! Gone the spirit they had shown under Garibaldi ! Gone the belief in themselves which had given them victory over the Austrians, the Croats, the Poles ! They went into battle with reluctance. They were beaten from the start. They were chased out of the territory they invaded, not perhaps like "intruding puppy-dogs," as Mr. Compton Mackenzie writes in Wind of Freedom (Chatto and Windus, 15s.), but in a manner which brought contempt on them and especially on the braggart leaders who made such a mess of their campaign.

THIS book is a History of the Invasion of Greece by the Axis Powers, covering the period from the end of October 1940 to the evacuation of Crete in May 1941. It sketches briefly, too, the events of the between-wars epoch in Greece, when General Metaxas made himself dictator with the support of Athenian "society" and Big Business and was defeated by all lovers of liberty. Of the general's decision to resist the Fascist demand for the subjugation of his country Mr. Mackenzie writes lyrically. "He unified Hellas" (the old name for Greece) "beyond his most sanguine hopes as a political craftsman, expunged the blots upon his own career, and added to the world's oldest and richest roll of honour another immortal name."

On the next page but one, however, this judgement is revised and we are told that, if he had answered Yes to the Italian demand "he would have been swept away by the wrath of a proud people within a day." So he really acted less as a great patriot than as a prudent "political craftsman," and later on we get hints that he was all for keeping in with Hitler, if he could do that while he fought Mussolini—which, of course, was impossible ; and that "society" in Athens was behaving in a suspicious way.

The fact seems to have been that Metaxas was an illustration of Lord Acton's saying: "All power corrupts and absolute power corrupts absolutely." His mind had got so twisted and weakened by the exercise of uncontrolled tyranny that he could not think straight. It was fortunate for him that he died in the odour of patriotism. Another turn of the wheel of destiny might have made him a Quisling, ready to collaborate with the Nazis when they overran the country, as Gen. Tsolakoglou, of Turkish descent, did later on.

METAXAS made the same mistake as the Belgian and Dutch Governments—the mistake was made also by Mr. Chamberlain —of thinking that Hitler "might mean well in spite of appearances." If he had turned to Britain instead of to Hitler when Mussolini began the war against Greece, we might have been able to plan help that would have been really worth while.

As it was, the appeal, made only when the Nazis had to go to Italy's assistance, caught us when we were busy in Libya. We had to suspend operations there. Wavell had to

## So Bravely the Greeks Fought

send some of his troops to do no more than make a noble gesture. We left things no better for the Greeks and a good deal worse at the moment for ourselves.

One of the high lights of Mr. Mackenzie's book is a fuller account than we have had before of the action which stopped the Italian advance less than a fortnight after it had begun and which started the complete rout of the invaders. This was the Battle of the Pindus, named after the mountain region between Epirus and Thessaly.

Here three battalions of Evzones, who "should be compared to the Highland regiments of the British Army," the soldiers who wear starched kilts sticking out like frilled ballet skirts, were falling back before one of the best Italian Alpini divisions. I was with one of these in 1917 and I know how good they can be. A vital pass through the Pindus range seemed as if it must be taken by the enemy. That would have been a very serious disaster.

Then the Greek commander, Gen. Papagos, recollected the tactics of Marathon. He ordered the Evzones to take up positions on the mountain sides.

This manoeuvre was to be carried out urgently at all costs and it was to be carried out regardless of whether supplies could reach the men entrusted with so desperate a task.

They got supplies. They were dragged up from the villages at night by old men, women and children. They lacked neither food nor ammunition. Then at dawn they rushed down on the flank and rear of the Alpini, who were toiling through the defiles. Nothing could withstand their impetuous attack.

The Italians, caught at a disadvantage, offered little resistance. The celebrated Julia Division became a mob of fugitives thinking only of how to save their lives.

The retreat became a rout. The renowned Alpini flung away their arms and abandoned their wounded. Many were drowned in the swollen waters of a river. Those who could not run fast enough surrendered, and surrendered crying " Bella Grecia ! " to appease with a pretty phrase and compliment the redoubtable foes by whom they had been broken.

This affected the whole Italian plan. There had to be retreats everywhere. From that moment the invaders were driven back rapidly and with very heavy losses. Only the help sent them by the Nazis saved them from annihilation.

HOW did the Greeks do it ? What accounted for their victories which astonished the world ? Where do we find the explanation of this overwhelming defeat of a large nation by a small one ? First of all in "the fighting hearts of the entire Greek people and their extraordinary unity." That overstates it a little. There were elements which would have preferred to subside quietly under the Nazi yoke, but they were few.

As a whole, it was resolved to resist to the last possible effort, and so it did. Next the Greek success is attributed to the ability shown by the General Staff and the inefficiency of the Italian High Command. Finally, the "pronounced lack of combative spirit and an understandable lack of conviction (even respect for what they were commanded to do) on the part of Fascist soldiers," contributed to their discomfiture and disgrace.

The Italians, in a word, were fed up, while the Greek troops by their self-denial, audacity, endurance and valour "offered the world an example of military virtue which has never been surpassed. They fought from icy dawn to icy dusk on a handful of olives and a chunk of bread. For warm clothing they had to substitute the warmth of their love for Hellas. For shelter from the wind night after night they had nothing except holes dug in the drifted snow. They had to drag guns up precipitous slopes on which the pack-mules lost their footing."

So bravely the Greeks fought, so skilfully were they led, that it seems a pity to exaggerate what they did. Mr. Mackenzie has developed a turgid style which indulges in such phrases as Germany's "final plunge into eternal infamy" (meaning the occupation of Greece) ; Gayda, "the wind-galled hack" of Mussolini ; the Nazis "meeting their doom in the land where democracy was born." The Greeks, he says, were the first to "shatter the legend of Axis invincibility."

**EVZONES, hardy Greek mountain troops—kilted like Scottish Highlanders—were in the thick of the Albanian fighting during the winter of 1940–41. In Wind of Freedom, reviewed in this page, Compton Mackenzie pays tribute to their gallantry at the Battle of the Pindus. Here is one of them with a comrade from a line regiment.** *Photo, Bosshard*

# We Have Taken New Life and Hope Into Sicily

A word new to most of us is springing into prominence : Amgot, short for Allied Military Government of Occupied Territory. This new form of government is creating order out of chaos in Sicily and substituting new and humane laws for the bad old regime, as explained below in this special article by DONALD COWIE. Amgot will assume vast proportions as more and more enemy territory is occupied by the Allies—for the good of all men of good will.

HERE is one of the most remarkable stories in modern history. Soon after the first troops landed in Sicily a man came ashore with a knapsack. Asked what it contained, he replied jokingly : "'Oh, that's the new government !'" Whether or not that story is true, it is a fact that Sicily's liberators brought with them a system of civil administration for the island no less efficient than their military organization— Amgot, the 1943 streamlined government to succeed the guns.

Hitherto, most conquerors have been content to impose the rule of the jack-boot ; an elderly officer and some second-line men are left behind in each occupied town to perform the functions of mayor, town clerk, treasurer, superintendent of police, and sanitary inspector combined. What muddle and what bitterness among the townsfolk ! But no sooner are our troops marching out of captured places in this war than a real, up-to-date civil administration marches in.

CONSIDER the scene in Augusta, Italy's prize naval base on the Sicilian east coast, after our mighty tongue of avenging flame had licked it and the area had capitulated. Here was a ghost town, stark, battered, and desolate. Hardly a pane of glass remains in the windows, rubble is everywhere ; a few frightened Italian faces peer from under shawls out of grim cellars. Where are the Italian A.R.P. officials, the police, all of those who should be working selflessly to restore order amid the chaos ? Well, there might be one or two native heroes ; but most have fled or have been whisked away by the retreating Fascists.

If our Eighth Army had left that ghost town to its own sorry devices it would soon have become a plague-spot and a wilderness. But here is a familiar figure, a young fellow of the Royal Engineers in battledress. He is disentangling great coils of bomb-twisted telephone wires. And there is a smart Red-Cap, already directing traffic among the ruins with Oxford Street precision. Then two businesslike men, one an Englishman and the other an American, walk swiftly by with sheaves of papers in their hands. "I have got those two bakeries working," says one ; and the other replies : "Good. Now I'll just paste up these notices about the taxation order." Already Amgot is operating.

What does Amgot mean ? The full title is Allied Military Government of Occupied Territory. When founded ? Some time after the entry of America into the war ; details worked out at one of those Roosevelt-Churchill inter-staff conferences. Object : To make an efficient job of the civil as well as the military side of victory this time. But there is more to it than that, quite one of the most intriguing secrets of the war as it is now gradually being revealed.

About a year ago the local inhabitants of a South of England town and America's Charlottesville, Virginia, began to notice queer activities. Scores of intelligent-looking men and women, usually with portfolios under their arms, appeared in those districts and were given billets. Scraps of foreign languages were continually overheard in conversations. Then it leaked out, though without much credence at first, that people were being trained hereabouts to help administer enemy territories as soon as they were occupied. "Thousands of folk are learning German down Virginia way," wrote one Washington columnist—and, of course we took that with a grain of salt.

PERHAPS it did seem rather premature in those dark days. But we now know, and are extremely glad to know, that our Governments did begin to make preparations so early, and on a scale hitherto unprecedented. At those training establishments, the Civil Affairs Centre, the School of Military Government, Charlottesville, and the Occupational Military Police School, Michigan, carefully chosen recruits, most of them with professional experience of central and local government, many of them with knowledge of European countries, were given courses in modern proconsulship. That is, they were, and still are, taught how to apply the Atlantic Charter practically to occupied territories. The weapons they learned to use ranged from by-laws to public health devices, from tele-communication systems to full-scale state governorships. They had to master not only the technical side, but also a variety of foreign languages; the lay-out of foreign towns and, above all, tact and humanity.

**LORD RENNELL** of Rodd who, as head of Amgot, is Chief Civil Affairs Officer in Sicily.
*Photo, Press Portrait Bureau*

Fortunately it was not entirely a theoretical course. Quite early in the war we had opportunities of trying-out the new system. Many of us are unaware that Abyssinia, Eritrea, Italian Somaliland and Madagascar have been run along Amgot lines for a year or more. Cyrenaica has several times seen these scientific administrators march in, and now knows them permanently, as also do Tripolitania and Tunisia. A young man who has a big future in British politics, Major-Gen. Lord Rennell of Rodd is at the administrative head of the Sicilian team.

Let us glance at that Amgot team as it is working in Sicily this moment. Titular head is General Alexander, appointed Military Governor of the island. But that is a formal rather than an executive appointment. General Alexander is directing all the Sicilian military operations on the spot, and must have titular control of every phase ; but Amgot works directly under Lord Rennell as Chief Civil Affairs Officer, Son of our most famous Ambassador to Italy, closely acquainted with the country from childhood, once manager of the Bank for International Settlement at Basle, and a Sahara explorer in his vacations, this square-jawed young man of 48 strides about in a little white town somewhere in Sicily today and introduces an Order that is humane as well as New. His second-in-command is Brig.-Gen. Frank J. McSherry, U.S. Army.

Lord Rennell has beneath him a Civil Affairs Officer for each captured province and for each city down to 12,000 inhabitants. These are men trained in every branch of the work, but they are provided with officials who have specialized in single departments, chiefly Legal, Financial, Civilian Supply (comprising food, water, fuel, transport, clothing, building), Public Health and Public Safety. Order is kept by a special corps of civil police organized for Sicilian purposes on the basis of the local Carabinieri, while there are garrisons and a system whereby reinforcements could be rushed to any area.

ALL these special Sicilian arrangements were worked out at a "school" high in the Algerian mountains before the invasion. They say that the only aspect which has not conformed to the plan has been the almost excessive willingness of the local Italians to cooperate in the scheme. It has been found possible in many cases to retain Sicilian mayors and officials. Special immediate jobs for Amgot, however, have been the firm "pegging-down" of prices and the control of crops, food supplies, banks and purchases by Allied troops. It is an experiment in Anglo-American world rebuilding which, from all the evidence, most hopefully works.

**GENERAL ALEXANDER'S PROCLAMATION** which dissolves the Fascist Party in occupied Sicily, annuls discriminatory laws and guarantees personal and property rights, being read by police and civilians of Noto, a town in the extreme S.E. of Sicily. *Photo, British Official : Crown Copyright*

# Welcoming Smiles for the Armies of Liberation

AS LIBERATORS, NOT DESPOTS. Scenes reminiscent of the triumphal landing at Marsala on May 11, 1860, of the great Italian patriot " Garibaldi the Deliverer " occurred in Sicilian towns taken by Allied troops 83 years later. Our Tommies made a fuss of the children of Salarino (1) and the children loved them. A British officer found time to chat with peasants (2) near Avola, and a free issue of flour (3) in the Palazzolo area delighted the people ; a happy mother (4) carries off her flour while a Britisher carries her kiddie.

Photos, British Official : Crown Copyright

# THE WAR IN THE AIR

## by Capt. Norman Macmillan, M.C., A.F.C.

THE air war has now reached its most intricate pattern. Great strategic and tactical blows are being dealt out to the enemy in every theatre of war. The homeland of Japan alone remains untouched, for it lies as yet too distant from the nearest Allied air bases to make the bombing of Nippon a practical operation, although token bombing, like that effected by the Mitchells under Maj.-Gen. Doolittle (see pages 154-155), could be brought about now.

But there is a world of difference between token bombing and real hard bombing blows. All the evidence points to the former method being worthless in the military sense, however valuable it may be in the political sense.

It is probably impossible to assign the precise cause to the resignation of Benito Mussolini as the leader of the Italian people.

Undoubtedly the whole course of the war, adverse to Italy as it has been, has shown up all the defects of the system so lauded by Mussolini in its military aspect ; and, as a result, the steed he bestrode dropped under him, and he was unsaddled. But why should it have happened at the precise moment it did ? Is it not significant that it followed within a week of the first, and (at the moment of writing), only bombing raid on military targets within the area comprised by Rome ?

AND let it be remembered that during the interval between July 19, when the railway marshalling yards of San Lorenzo and Littorio and the airfields of Littorio and Ciampino were bombed in daylight by American Fortresses, Liberators, Mitchells and Marauders, and July 25, when Mussolini tendered his resignation to King Victor Emmanuel, the progress of the war in Sicily, from the area of Catania towards Messina, was virtually at a standstill, meeting with terrific opposition from the German troops resisting the Eighth Army.

For many years Mussolini appraised the Regia Aeronautica as one of the foremost air forces in the world. Undoubtedly it was fairly well equipped around about 1935, when our Royal Air Force was definitely backward in the types of aircraft it possessed. But once production of modern aircraft improved, when the change from "string-bag" types to all-metal, stressed-skin monoplanes took place, Italy could not keep up the pace and fell behind technically.

THE only fighters she ever sent against Britain in 1940 were Fiat CR 42s, at that time almost antique biplanes which were easy meat to the Hurricanes and Spitfires that met them over the Channel and the Thames Estuary.

The bombing raid on Roman targets met with little opposition, and undoubtedly great damage must have been caused to the Italian railway systems which, on that side of the peninsula, bottle-neck through Rome. The loser of a jerry-built Empire was then faced with the fact of the impotence of his own air defence to protect Italy. There was no Italian fighter command comparable to that of the R.A.F. which saved Britain in 1940 to save Italy in 1943. The Luftwaffe could not make good the Italian deficiency.

It was the first writing in the sky of the power of the United Nations in the air. And against such power, organized as it is organized today, and associated with the sea and land forces possessed by the United Nations, there is no ultimate defence. It is but a matter of time. Defeat is certain to be the fate of the nations who have lost the mastery of their own sky.

The bombing of Rome was therefore a psychological as well as a material success. Its date-line was probably chosen with that object in view. It put the final screw on Mussolini, made him rush into whatever pact he agreed with Hitler, and then came up against the implacable veto of his king backed by the veteran Marshal Badoglio.

CANADIAN HALIFAX BOMBERS taking off in the moonlight of a late July night to hammer Hamburg, now the worst-bombed city in the world. Contrast the serenity of this setting "somewhere in England" with the scene of havoc shown in p. 190 (together with an eye-witness story). By August 3, 1943 over five square miles of the city had been devasted in the ninth raid on the port in 8 days—an unprecedented intensity of bombing.
*Photo, Barratts*

I remember the King of Italy visiting Istrana aerodrome behind the Piave River early in 1918. I was senior officer of No. 45 Squadron R.F.C. on the aerodrome at the time of his visit, and it was my duty to receive him and present the officers. I found him a pleasant conversationalist, with a marked sense of humour, a fluent command of English, and a real power of dignity despite the handicap of small stature. From that brief contact I can well imagine his personality clashing with Mussolini and coming out on top, even if it has taken him 21 years of forbearance to achieve that result.

Time and again it has been said that bombing only hardens the thoughts of the people bombed against those who bomb and that no victory can be achieved by means which produce that psychological effect and do not at the same time occupy a country. That may be true under circumstances when (as with Britain in 1940) there was air defence. It may have been true of Germany during the preliminary years of the war.

But it is certainly not true during the declining period of a war. Mr. Churchill has promised that Italy will be hotted up if that process is necessary to produce the capitulation which is the price of peace. If that process is required it will display perhaps for the first time in history the real effect of bombing upon a people. The choice must rest mainly with the King of Italy.

No less important in the air war is the effect of the air cover provided to the forces which attacked in Sicily. The island was swept from end to end, and air cover maintained over land and sea at a peak which has perhaps not previously been realized by the United Nations. The early capture of Sicilian aerodromes helped this process.

### GERMANY'S Harvest of Bombs is Far From Garnered

Meanwhile, the strategic operations were linking up from all directions. Bomber Command bombed the radio-location producing plant at Friedrichshafen, and the aircraft which did the job flew on to a landing in North Africa. On their return flight they bombed Leghorn. Spezia naval base took a hammering. The railway yards at Bologna, important junction in Italy, were raided. Naples, Bari and other centres in what the Italians themselves used to call their "African colony" were bombed.

In Germany, Hamburg suffered a terrific blow with a raid that dropped 2,300 tons of bombs in 50 minutes on the night following July 24. Essen came next on the programme for a big-scale raid, while the Hamburg raid was kept stoked up by visits by day bombers—Venturas and Mosquitoes, and Fortresses. Dr. Wieninger, German commentator, said in a broadcast after the Hamburg raid (see page 190) that the whole area surrounding the Binnen Alster was on fire.

Well, that was a lovely part of Hamburg. Germany is now reaping where she sowed, and her harvest is far from garnered.

Hamburg was again mass-raided by Bomber Command's heavy night bombers on the nights following July 27 and 29. The port of Hamburg was virtually wiped out in one week during which the R.A.F. and U.S. Army Eighth Air Force dropped more than 10,000 tons of bombs on Germany by day and night.

IN the Far East the aeroplane is wresting triumph from the Japanese. Amid the fogs and gales of the north Pacific, Kiska is being bombed in increasing strength. In the south Pacific, a large raid on Sourabaya took the Japanese by surprise ; as well it might, when the nearest United Nations base was 1,000 miles away.

# First Bombs Crash Down on Military Rome

**MILITARILY IMPORTANT,** Rome is the focal point of Italy's inland communications; through it every railway passes, save the 'ine along the Adriatic shore. So on July 19, 1943 the Italian capital experienced a bombing raid, the first it had known, 500 American planes dropping 700 tons of bombs in the course of 2½ hours.

Our map shows the targets: the marshalling yards at San Lorenzo and Littorio (which bottle-neck traffic to southern Italy and Sicily), and the Ciampino airfields. Official photos show the accuracy of the Allied bombing; (top) the San Lorenzo yards, and (bottom) a longer-range view of the same target, as bombs were falling.

Warning leaflets were showered on Rome before the raid, and pilots were instructed: "Bomb accurately or don't bomb at all."

*Photos, U.S. Official. Map, British Official*

SAN LORENZO MARSHALLING YARDS

COLISEUM

# R.A.F. Spreads Its Wings From Sicilian Airfields

RAPID RECONDITIONING of captured Sicilian airfields has been a notable achievement. Operations Unit R.A.F. (1) plan the clearing-up of Comiso aerodrome, while Servicing Commandos (3) examine a wrecked German Ju52 on the flying field ; damaged buildings are evidence of previous R.A.F. visits. A Spitfire takes off at Pachino (2) while an R.E. steam-roller is still consolidating the ground which the enemy had ploughed up. Americans service a Spitfire (4) and inspect a Nazi bomber (5), the pilot of which (foreground) has made his last flight.

*Photos, British Official ; Planet News*

# Gift From Sicily to Thirsty British Transport

AT A WAYSIDE PETROL STATION, taken intact in Sicily, troopers of the Royal Tank Regiment refuel their scout car before continuing their advance. Retreat of the enemy was so hasty in some areas that he could not pause even to destroy his petrol supplies, recklessly abandoning them as a welcome "windfall" for British transport pressing hard on his heels. At one of the airfields taken over by the R.A.F. (see opposite page), millions of gallons of aviation spirit were found—ready for our use.

*Photo, British Official: Crown Copyright*

# At Last We Have 'Struck Oil' in Rumania

One-third of Germany's fuel for her war machines has been coming from the oilfields and refineries of Rumania. Now Ploesti, centre of that supply, has been very heavily bombed by the Allies. HENRY BAERLEIN discusses in this article possible reasons for our delay in assaulting this vital target.

THE Russians have once or twice bombed the oil refineries at Ploesti, the centre of the Rumanian oil industry and an important railway junction to the north of Bucharest. Five of the fourteen refineries are situated in a straight line along the Ploesti-Buzau railway, and are the kind of target of which bombers dream; nor are any of the others difficult to spot.

It has been argued that it is difficult to transport the oil to the German Army, but then Hitler has sent his Army to the Rumanian

PLOESTI RAIDERS report to an intelligence officer, Lieut. Arthur Guiliani, on their return from the daylight raid on the Rumanian oilfields on August 1, 1943. The biggest low-level mass raid to date—more than 175 American planes participated—it had as its targets refineries, storage plants and distilleries. *Photo, U.S. Official*

oil, basing his operations in the Balkans on those supplies. We were likewise told that oil production in Rumania was decreasing and, therefore, bombing was not worth while; the fact is that Germany is not anxious to produce more than she needs at the moment, as oil in storage tanks is more vulnerable to air attacks than oil below the surface. When it is said that Rumanian oil is of low grade, the answer is that any low-grade oil can be treated by chemical processes to produce high-grade petrol.

At the outbreak of the war only 7 per cent of the oil production was contributed by Rumanian companies, whereas 93 per cent came from foreign companies: British, American and so forth. At a critical point in the

last war the British-owned wells were dealt with quite effectively; and I am told by an Englishman who had long lived in Rumania and did not leave till the last moment that this time these wells had been mined, but that for some reason unknown to him nothing further was done. One remembers that French and German electricity companies were selling each other power across the frontiers even after the outbreak of war. And did not Mr. Will Lawther, the President of the Mineworkers' Federation, protest at Swansea in June 1939 at the huge exports of scrap metal which we were allowing to be sent to Germany?

It appears that the British and French companies in Rumania transferred their rights at the outbreak of war to the companies of countries not as yet involved, such as the United States and Holland, these in their turn transferring the rights to neutrals—which does not in the least prevent the Germans from helping themselves to this commodity. And when they are compelled to quit Rumania they will not leave in a nice condition what still remains of the wells and refineries.

Until 1939 most of the Rumanian Budget was based on oil taxes, and any decrease in the amount pumped-up created Budget difficulties. Foreign shareholders held the whip-hand and could take decisions that would affect the daily bread of a country. It was to remedy this unbearable situation that the nationalization of the subsoil was brought about.

Ex-King Carol planned to use his country's oil as a barrier against Hitler's marauding hordes. Throughout the winter of 1939–40 " Carol's Dyke," which was to be better than the Maginot and Siegfried Lines, was being constructed at the frontiers. Instead of reinforced concrete and steel it was made of mud, and was to be flooded with oil and set on fire if Hitler should attempt to invade the

country. Carol felt he could rely on powerful potential allies in Britain and France. But his confidence was killed by a message from London: why, it was asked, was Rumania selling more oil to Germany than to Britain?

Mr. Chamberlain must have known that Rumania badly needed both money and armaments. Britain had told her that she was not much interested in Rumanian oil, as she could get better quality elsewhere and at a cheaper rate. Germany, on the other hand, was willing to pay anything—guns, tanks or gold. Headlines began to appear in our papers: " Scotland bombed by German planes using Rumanian oil," or " British merchantmen sunk by German planes using Rumanian oil." The general verdict was that Rumania had been treacherous.

BUT who sold this Rumanian oil to Germany? Was it the Rumanian people? Was it Carol? Or was it the foreign oil companies? The Rumanian Government could control quotas, but the selling was managed by those who actually held the concessions. The Government collected taxes on production and exports, but did not act as a selling agency. Carol established a Board whose duty it was to keep a strict watch on the dealings of the foreign companies, but this only made matters worse for Britain, as this Oil Board was considered a further infringement of the property rights of the companies.

And now, happily, the Allies have very thoroughly attended to Ploesti. On August 1, 1943, in full daylight, a force of Liberators flew 2,400 miles in all, and wrought destruction there from tree-top height. The Astro-Romana refinery, the biggest plant of its kind in Europe, was heavily damaged. The Creditul Minier refinery, the only one producing high-octane aviation fuel, was completely covered with bombs; there was a direct hit on Colombia Aquila, the fourth largest refinery; many explosions were reported from the pumping-station of the Giurgiu pipe-line. But the greatest damage of all was inflicted on the Americana Romana and Orion refinery.

It is known that for three months' offensive in Russia the Germans require about a million tons of oil; the maximum refinery capacity of all Rumania is 32,000 tons a day, of which nearly 25,000 were until the other day refined at Ploesti. Now this vital supply has been almost closed down and German engineers in Rumania will be as unemployed as those who went towards the Caucasus with Hitler's army.

FIRST OF THE LIBERATORS coming home to their base in the Middle East after the 2,400-mile there-and-back flight to bomb Ploesti, Rumanian oilfields centre. They swept in at less than 500 feet to drop nearly 300 tons of high explosives, mostly delayed-action bombs, and several hundred incendiaries, over seven major targets in this immensely important oil area. They left all the major refineries burning, and long after the Liberators had passed there were reports of continued explosions in the neighbourhood. Months of planning preceded the attack, and rehearsals included the bombing of a reproduction of Ploesti in miniature—a model town built in the Libyan Desert. *Photo, U.S. Official*

# Hitler's Greatest Defeat Followed This Fighting

**VICTORS AND VANQUISHED** of Orel and Bielgorod. After a month of some of the most savage fighting of this war, the tremendous Russian push on the Orel-Bielgorod front reached its climax on August 5, 1943 with the recapture of both these key towns. It was Hitler's most significant defeat so far. A Russian tank-borne raiding party (1) waits in ambush near Bielgorod. . On the Orel sector Nazi infantry take cover from a Soviet shell-burst (2) and Russian anti-tank gunners (3) pound at enemy armour.

*Photos, Pictorial Press, Associated Press*

# I WAS THERE! Eye Witness Stories of the War

## 'Down With Mussolini and Death to the Duce!'

*Extraordinary scenes of jubilation were witnessed by Ross Munro, Canadian Press Correspondent in Sicily, when news of the resignation on July 23, 1943 of the Pinchbeck Caesar—Benito Mussolini, Dictator of Italy—reached the ears of the islanders.*

THIS battered front-line town of poverty-stricken Italian citizens received the news of Mussolini's resignation with shouts of " Bravo, bravo ! " The people shook hands and cried, " Down with Mussolini and Death to the Duce ! "

They swarmed in the main street gesticulating wildly, laughing and shouting with relief at the Italian leader's fall. It was one of the most unexpected and spontaneous scenes I ever witnessed.

Early in the morning Canadian war correspondents heard the news in a B.B.C. broadcast and headed for the town. I found a signaller from Cochrane, Ontario, who spoke Italian fluently, and he came as my interpreter.

I stopped with him in the main street, which was a centre of bloody fighting when the Canadians assaulted the place, and we walked up to a group of civilians. The signaller asked them if they had heard the news. No, they had not. Then he told them.

I had seen civilians in every town give our troops the "V" sign in the march from the coast and sometimes heard them cheer. But I never really expected to see a group of people in a Fascist country expressing their relief at the collapse of their dictator and the chance of freedom they saw ahead.

In a few minutes the news spread through the town, and it changed from a miserable, down-trodden place into a place of high excitement and enthusiasm for our cause. Overjoyed Sicilians vented their hatred of their Fascist overlords by tearing down Italian propaganda posters of Mussolini. They threw stones at Fascist emblems.

A Canadian patrol came up to me, asking anxiously if a riot was brewing. I told them they need not worry, because they were seeing the Italian reaction to the best news they had had for years.

The people told me they had been taxed to the hilt, reduced to dire poverty and forced to fight while the Fascist group at the top had indulged in Roman luxury in Sicilian country mansions. I talked to a grey-haired distinguished Italian, mayor of the town 22 years before, when the Fascists established their rule. He had been thrown out then, but was in great spirits now. The citizens said that they would make him mayor again, for he knew their wants and would work for them.

## I Ran a Field Hospital for Our Parachutists

*Here is a truly epic story of the superb courage of British parachutists who dropped from the skies in Sicily in the early hours of July 14, 1943, and captured a vital bridge in the Catania plain. It was told by a Methodist padre, the Rev. Capt. R. T. Watkins, of Leeds, who dropped with them, to Ronald Monson, representing the Combined Press.*

I WAS with the medical dressing station and so wandered all over the place seeing a good bit of what was going on. Part of the plan was for some parachutists to hold the hill south of the bridge, and it was there that I landed. We knew the Germans had put in a heavy attack on the bridge at three p.m. with machine-guns and artillery, but the attack was not pressed home and the defenders held on until their ammunition had run out, and the anti-tank guns had started blasting them out.

Under a heavy mortar and artillery barrage, the bridge defenders drew back as darkness came on. Those dropped in the hills southwards did a good job, holding important positions on both sides of the road and preventing the enemy in that area from falling back to assist the defence of the bridge. Our field ambulance came down well out of its proper zone, but we mustered 30 men. We reached a farmhouse and took goats and horses and cattle from their stalls and cleaned them up and set up a hospital behind the enemy lines.

We had the services of the best medical specialists and all apparatus required, including a bloodbank from which we carried out blood transfusions for both the enemy and our wounded. We captured a German ambulance with medical supplies and obtained the services of an Italian doctor. An operating theatre was set up, and by 8.30 a.m. the first operations were being performed. The last was completed at 9 p.m.

Altogether 30 operations were carried out. We rounded up enemy transport, commandeered horses and carts, and brought back our wounded from the bridge. At one time all the stables were choked with wounded, 90 German and Italian as well as our own. A captured German tent served as a ward for the lightly wounded. We even painted a Red Cross and put up Red Cross flags on the barns.

*Lance-Corporal W. Whittaker, of Macclesfield, Cheshire, who dropped two miles south of the bridge, takes up the story :*

There was a lot of tracer and heavy ack-ack flying up as we came near our objective at 400 feet. Gliders ahead of us were being shot up. I landed about 4 a.m., picked myself up and moved towards the bridge, which was about two miles away. The Brigadier formed us up under a culvert and led us towards the attack. The bridge was well defended by Italians and men of the German regiment. After a sharp fight we drove the enemy off and established ourselves on it.

About a quarter of an hour later we saw an enemy convoy approaching the bridge from the north side. A few of us went

FASCIST H.Q. AT NOTO, Sicilian town captured on July 11, 1943, displayed beneath a huge portrait of Mussolini a notice : " The Italian people have created an empire with their blood . . . and will defend it against anyone with their arms." The British soldier is examining some of the weapons the Italians will never use again. *Photo, British Official*

REV. CAPT. R. T. WATKINS, of Leeds, who dropped with our parachutists in Sicily to hold the vital bridge on the road to Catania, tells his story above. *Photo, Daily Express*

across and joined the others on the far side and attacked the convoy with bombs. It consisted of five ammunition wagons. We blew three of them sky high ; the others turned and got away. While the party removed the charges, the rest of us took up positions in pillboxes guarding the southern approach to the bridge.

There we stayed all day fighting it out with the enemy. There were about 300 Italians our side of the bridge, but we had them pinned down. They had the wits scared out of them when a glider crashed among them, early in the attack. Many of them came to our pillboxes and gave themselves up. We couldn't hold them, but others on the far side had established a small prisoner-of-war cage. We took them across, but the Germans started shelling them heavily just after we left them. We could hear them squealing.

About 6 p.m. we were still in the pillboxes when anti-tank guns caught us in a heavy fire and blasted us out. We crept away and met the glider party. We turned the gun on the enemy and belted them properly. Their mortars caught us and finally we were driven back. Then we linked up with our tanks, who went on to cover the bridge.

BRITISH TROOPS IN SYRACUSE. A war correspondent describes below his arrival in this captured Sicilian port, which before our occupation was badly battered from the air.
*Photo, British Official*

## Syracuse Was Like Margate in Holiday-time

A British newspaper correspondent who accompanied the assault troops from Africa records his impressions of the Sicilian port of Syracuse, which fell to the 8th Army on July 10, 1943. His story is reprinted here by arrangement with The Evening Standard.

WHEN I landed at the port of Syracuse, in Eastern Sicily, this morning the atmosphere was a bit like Margate during a summer week-end before the war. One or two local policemen wearing dark blue uniforms with peak caps and red-stripes down the sides of their riding breeches, looked rather sour as they watched men, guns and vehicles pouring out of landing-craft that had brought them from Africa without incident, and spilled us out right on to one of the main streets, but everybody else seemed pleased to see us.

Landing-craft emptied us into the street already crammed with vehicles and onlookers. Barefooted boys ran around with baskets of tomatoes and lemons. Some of them kept yelling to the British Tommies, " Johnny ! cigarette ! " Soldiers swapped cigarettes ;

the rate of exchange seemed to be one cigarette one lemon.

Old men and women in park chairs watched lorries driving right out of our craft down ramps into the street. They chattered excitedly as the vehicles streamed out at a surprising pace. They stared at us as new arrivals, and seemed thoroughly interested in the vehicles clattering down the ramp at a brisk pace.

Opposite our landing-craft where we crossed the road to shelter beneath some trees was a mural tablet commemorating the " Unknown Hero " of Syracuse. There was a flamboyant inscription relating to the virtues of the Italians who fell in the last war. On a ledge beneath was a glass torch with a glass flame. But the electric bulb inside was out.

A few yards away was a wooden shack with a signboard bearing the legend " Caffe." Near this place—which was shuttered up—a gang of children were playing at soldiers. They were lanky and high-spirited boys. Several of them were wearing paper caps in shape exactly like the caps worn by Italian prisoners.

Away from the waterfront things were much quieter. British soldiers clomped about

CAPT. COLIN MORRIS, of Wallasey, tells below how he captured 130 Italians single-handed, challenging them with pidgin-Italian and armed only with a Service revolver.
*Photo, Burrell & Hardman*

the streets, but there were not many civilians if I leave out the children still begging for cigarettes. This morning only the barber shops were open. They were filled with elderly middle-aged men sprucing up and gossiping as without doubt they have done for years and years.

WHITE FLAGS FLUTTERED as Italians surrendered in droves in almost every sector of the fighting in Sicily. By August 8, 1943, about 125,000 Axis troops had been captured, mostly Italians. *Photo, British Official*

## 'Advanco Pronto!'—and a Mob Surrendered!

Capt. Colin Morris, of Wallasey, an observer with the assault troops in Sicily, found himself alone Hearing that enemy troops were concealed near by he proceeded to investigate, with astonishing results. He told the following story to S. L. Solon, representing the Combined Press.

I FIGURED there were a couple of Italians there so I took my revolver and went up the hill to the stone house. I kicked the door open and yelled out " Advanco mucho pronto suos bastardos ! " For a moment there was silence. So I yelled louder. " The Potentes Alliados are here ! "

It worked ! One by one they filed out. My eyes bulged as the line grew longer and longer. Finally, there were a hundred and thirty lined up on the left-hand side of the ruins of the Greek amphitheatre in Syracuse. They carried automatic arms, grenades, machine-guns, rifles, revolvers.

I yelled harder, and motioned to them to

put all the arms in a pile. They threw them down and ranged themselves against a wall. There was nothing left to do except to take the lot down to the prisoners' cage on the beach.

I got on my motor cycle and marshalled them like a flock of geese down the road. It took hours to get them there. There was no one to help, but the prisoners behaved.

At the entrance of the prisoners-of-war cage I was stopped by the corporal in charge. He didn't bat an eyelash, but just said, " Have you searched them ? " When I said " No," he seemed peeved. So I went and had a mug of tea.

# My Night of Terror in Bomb-Battered Hamburg

On the night of July 24, 1943, in an attack lasting 50 minutes, the R.A.F. dropped 2,300 tons of bombs on Hamburg, greatest port in Germany. Dr. Wieninger, a Nazi war reporter, described his night of terror in the following broadcast, published here by arrangement with The Daily Mail.

MOUNTAINS of broken glass can be seen about the streets. Bomb craters are everywhere and wherever one turns there are burning buildings. Loud crashes from time to time denote the collapse of damaged houses.

Among the buildings destroyed are the State Library, the Phalia Theatre, the Opera House, the City Hall, St. George's Church, the Nicolai Church, and the St. Matthew Church. All the amusement centres have gone. It is difficult to ascertain the losses among the population and the full extent of the damage, but they are very heavy.

Standing in the Reeperbahn (the main road leading to the suburb of Altona) I saw great burning façades. Driving through the streets, through piles of glass, splinters, rubble and debris ; past bomb craters with flaming timber crashing down and barring the way, was not easy.

Often enough we had to turn back. We went to the Lombard Bridge and looked across to the Alster basin, where we saw a frightful sight. Everywhere smoke rose from where the buildings of the commercial centre of the town once stood.

Time bombs are still exploding all over the place. Everywhere, in the streets, there are sticks of incendiaries. Smoke hangs over the town like a gigantic black storm cloud. There is only a thin, red slice of the sun. It is as dark this morning as it was at midnight.

SMOKE PALL OVER HAMBURG, most bombed city in the world, as Allied bombs burst on the Howaldtswerke shipyards, where U-boats were built. In eight days approximately 10,000 tons of bombs were rained on the city.
*Photo, U.S. Army Air Force*

# OUR DIARY OF THE WAR

**JULY 21, Wednesday**      1,418th day
**Sicily.**—Castelvetrano captured by Americans.
**Mediterranean.**—Cotrone (Italy) bombarded by Royal Navy ; Grosseto airfield N. of Rome heavily raided.
**Russian Front.**—Soviet troops advanced 4 to 9 miles in Orel sector.

**JULY 22, Thursday**      1,419th day
**Sicily.**—Palermo taken by Americans. Places taken included Sciacca, San Stefano and Rammacca.
**Russian Front.**—Soviet advance of 4 to 5 miles in Orel direction ; Bolkhov captured.
**Pacific.**—Surabaya (Java) bombed by Liberators from Australian bases for first time since its occupation by Japanese.

**JULY 23, Friday**      1,420th day
**Mediterranean.**—Italian airfields of Aquino, Cotrone, and Leverano bombed. Over 100 R.A.F. and Greek aircraft bombed Crete.
**Russian Front.**—Marshal Stalin in Order of the Day revealed that gains of German July offensive were everywhere liquidated.

**JULY 24, Saturday**      1,421st day
**Sicily.**—Announced Marsala occupied. Taormina bombarded from the sea.
**Mediterranean.**—Bologna (Italy) bombed.
**Australasia.**—Announced that Japanese 9,000-ton seaplane-carrier attempting to reach Buin (Solomons) sunk by Allied bombers.
**Air.**—Trondheim and Heroya bombed by U.S. Fortresses in their first attack on Norway. Hamburg battered at night in heaviest raid of the war to date ; 2,300 tons of bombs dropped in 50 minutes.

**JULY 25, Sunday**      1,422nd day
**Sicily.**—Capture of Trapani announced.
**Italy.**—Mussolini, Fascist Dictator of Italy, resigned. King Victor Emmanuel assumed supreme control of Italian armed forces ; Marshal Pietro Badoglio became Premier.
**Russian Front.**—Russians made further advances on Orel.
**Australasia.**—Munda (New Georgia) heavily bombed.
**Air.**—Hamburg and Kiel attacked by American bombers. Essen, Krupps armament centre, subjected to 2,000-ton bomb-attack. Mosquitoes raided Cologne and Hamburg.

**JULY 26, Monday**      1,423rd day
**Sicily.**—Over 70,000 prisoners in Allied hands to date.
**Italy.**—Marshal Badoglio formed new cabinet ; martial law proclaimed throughout the country.
**Russian Front.**—Kurakino and Erovkina captured in Soviet Orel advance.
**Australasia.**—Vila (Kalombangara Is.) bombed by 200 Liberators. Salamaua and Komiatum (New Guinea) heavily raided.
**Air.**—N.W. German cities, Hanover, Hamburg, Wilhelmshaven and Wesermunde, bombed by U.S. Fortresses in daylight. Hamburg raided at night by Mosquitoes.

**JULY 27, Tuesday**      1,424th day
**Air.**—In fourth successive night raid Hamburg received greatest battering of the war to date ; bomb-load, exceeding previous record, dropped in 45 minutes.
**Italy.**—New Italian cabinet dissolved the Fascist Party and swept away powers of Fascist Grand Council. Mr. Churchill said of Italy that he would "let the Italians stew in their own juice for a bit and hot up the fire to accelerate the process."
**Australasia.**—Announced 500-yd. advance along whole U.S. line in Munda (New Georgia) area.

**JULY 28, Wednesday**      1,425th day
**Sicily.**—German defence line defined as running from San Stefano on N. coast through Nicosia to the River Dittaino. Gangi captured by Americans.
**Australasia.**—Cape Gloucester airfield (New Britain) bombed by Allied aircraft.
**General.**—M. Maisky, Soviet Ambassador to Britain, appointed Deputy Commissar for Foreign Affairs.

**JULY 29, Thursday**      1,426th day
**Sicily.**—Announced Pollina, Castelbuono, Nicosia, and Agira captured ; 75,000 prisoners taken to date.
**Italy.**—Disclosed that in Rome raid of July 19, 700 U.S. bombers dropped 1,100 tons of bombs.
**Air.**—Hamburg again plastered in great night attack.

**JULY 30, Friday**      1,427th day
**Mediterranean.**—Grottaglie (Italy) bombed by Fortresses.
**Russian Front.**—Germans opened large-scale attacks in the Donetz basin ; Russian Orel advance continued.
**Air.**—Kassel (Central German arms centre) and Remscheid (between Ruhr and Rhine) heavily bombed.

**JULY 31, Saturday**      1,428th day
**Sicily.**—Announced islands of Favignana, Levanzo and Marettimo occupied by Allies. Capizzi captured by Americans. Coastal road at Taormina, and Cape

Molini 17 miles to the S. bombarded by British destroyers.
**Air.**—French airfields of Merville, Poix, Tricqueville, Abbeville, St. Omer, Amiens and Lille attacked by Allied aircraft.

**AUGUST 1, Sunday**      1,429th day
**Sicily.**—Milazzo, Messina, Paterno, and Randazzo bombed. Allies opened general offensive along whole line.
**Mediterranean.**—Cotrone (Italy) heavily bombarded by British warships. Naples bombed.
**Russian Front.**—Soviet troops continued advance on Orel.
**Air.**—Ploesti, Rumanian oil centre, raided in daylight by more than 175 U.S. Liberators based on Middle East ; nearly 300 tons of bombs dropped.
**General.**—Announced M. Feodor Gusef to succeed M. Maisky as Soviet Ambassador to Britain. Gen. Giraud became C.-in-C. of united French armies, Gen. de Gaulle chairman of National Committee for political purposes.

**AUGUST 2, Monday**      1,430th day
**Sicily.**—Canadians captured Regalbuto. 90,000 prisoners taken to date. Announced opening of Allied general offensive along whole front.
**Russian Front.**—In the Donbas, S.W. of Voroshilovgrad, German attacks made no headway ; Russians continued to advance on Orel.
**China.**—President of China, Lin Sen, died ; Gen. Chiang Kai-shek became Acting President.
**Air.**—Hamburg again bombed. Reconnaissance revealed 1,700 acres of the city devastated.

**AUGUST 3, Tuesday**      1,431st day
**Sicily.**—Announced capture of Assoro, Nissoria, Mistretta, San Stefano, and Catenanuova ; fall of Centuripe to British 78th Div., Troina and Cerami to Americans. 8th Army entered Catanian Plain in the west.
**Australasia.**—Fortresses and Liberators attacked Japanese supply and ammunition dumps S. of Mandang (New Guinea.) Progress made against stiff opposition at Munda (New Georgia) and Salamaua (New Guinea).
**Russian Front.**—Bitter fighting continued round Orel ; Russians captured Stish ; enemy ceased attacks in Donetz area due to heavy losses.
**Sea.**—Announced that in the Atlantic recently a concentration of 25-30 U-boats had been dispersed, two being destroyed.

★════════ *Flash-backs* ════════★

**1940**
July 25. Vichy Govt. announced special court to try those responsible for the war.
July 29. Dover Harbour heavily raided.

**1941**
July 21. First German air raid on Moscow.
July 24. German battleships, the Gneisenau at Brest, and Scharnhorst at La Pallice (France), bombed by British.
July 28. Japanese troops landed in French Indo-China.

July 29. Mr. Churchill announced in House of Commons, "all armed forces have been warned to be at concert pitch by Sept. 1 " —ready for invasion.
Aug. 2. R.A.F. bombed Kiel, Hamburg, and centre of Berlin.

**1942**
July 21. Japanese landed at Gona (New Guinea).
July 27. Russians announced evacuation of Rostov and Novocherkassk.
July 31. Düsseldorf very heavily raided.

EVERYONE who has delightful memories of sunny holidays in Sicily must have watched the progress of operations there with mixed feelings. I recollected, when Palermo was captured, how I once described it in an article as "a pearl in an emerald cup," the "pearl" being the town of gleaming and glittering white houses, while the "cup" is the green valley running up between the mountains that shelter the bay. Reading of Taormina being a scene of war made me think of its long, cool, grey medieval street running round a sort of arena whose sides plunge sheer down to the sea hundreds of feet below. It was a lovely place at any time of year, but best of all I liked it in very early spring; when the red-gold oranges glowed amid greenery, and the sun at noon drove one beneath the shade of dark cypresses and pines, and double red geraniums were in full flower, and the scents of thyme and jasmine mingled deliciously, and one had no difficulty in understanding why Sicily has been a theme for poets since earliest times. It is also said to possess an atmosphere specially good for irritable folk. Contentment was in the very air Sicilians breathed.

A FAMOUS school I know was used for a time by the Army. It was abominably treated. The soldiers left it dirty, with the marks of their destructive behaviour all over it. The Navy took it over and now, as the saying goes, "you could eat your dinner off the floors." The whole place is well-kept, tidy, clean. Why this difference? I think the explanation is that on board ship space is so restricted, and the comfort of the crew so dependent on the order that is maintained and upon everything being "ship-shape," that no departure from decent, thoughtful conduct can be tolerated. Sailors get the habit of living like reasonable beings. I am afraid that does not always apply to soldiers. Any house they occupy is liable to show signs, not merely of neglect to keep it in good trim, but of wanton damage. No reproach of this sort can be levelled at the R.A.F., whose members are acquainted with intricate machinery and alive to the necessity of protecting it from harm and keeping it clean. They dislike, therefore, any mess or muddle; they take no pleasure in destruction; they are careful tenants.

I HAVE had a letter about some recent remarks on the waste of paper. My correspondent comments caustically on the amount Income Tax officials use—much of it, he thinks, unnecessarily. But they are not so bad as they were a year or so back. He mentions an amusing instance of punctiliousness on the part of one of these gentry. He received a letter in which the typist had begun "Dear Sir." That evidently seemed to the bureaucrat to be too friendly. He crossed out the "Dear"! Another reader supplies another illustration of the readiness of some people—fortunately very few in number—to spend extravagantly on luxuries. He knows of a case in which nectarines were sold by the grower to a wholesaler in Covent Garden at 96s. a dozen. As both wholesaler and retailer would have to make a profit on them, I leave it to the reader to estimate the price at which these nectarines would be sold to the public. I see someone has been asking

a question in the House of Commons about Algerian wine. It is said to cost threepence a bottle in North Africa. Why, the M.P. inquires, is its price fixed at 8s. a bottle in Britain? What sort of Britons are they who pay that much for it, is what I should like to know.

I CAN'T think of anything that requires more real courage, more intrepid disregard of danger, than making live bombs harmless. When I saw that a Canadian Pilot Officer, Robert E. Young, had been given the M.B.E. for his bravery, I couldn't help thinking he ought to have some very much higher distinction. Here is what he did in the course of four days this summer. On the airfield where he is stationed a 500-lb. bomb was dropped accidentally. He was

*Courtesy of The Evening Standard*

called and in a few minutes it had been dismembered. A couple of days after that a bomber crashed as it was taking off; it had two live mines in it. Out went Young and dealt with them. Next day a bomber came down heavily with a 4,000-lb. "block buster" on board. If this had exploded, it would have done a vast amount of harm. But it didn't explode. The same cool saver of lives and property was on hand in time. The bomb was dismantled in a few minutes, the Pilot Officer showing, as the official record puts it, "little regard for his personal safety." I should call that an under-statement. The truth is that three times in four days he was ready to "lay down his life for his friends."

IT surprises me to find how many people there are among us who believe that Hitler is dead, or in an asylum, and that he is now being impersonated by one of those famous doubles who have been talked about for so long. Whether they fancy that Mussolini was taken in when they met, or that he was let into the secret, I cannot say: possibly their theory is that the ex-Duce was being impersonated also. What is not unlikely, it seems to me, is that the throat affection from which the Fuehrer has suffered for many years may have got

worse. That would account for his speaking so seldom, and for the raucous tone of his voice the last time it was heard on the air. There is always something rather harsh and uncouth about it. A German compared his accent to me the other day with that of the Northumbrian "Geordies." He is not considered by educated people to speak German properly. That is not surprising, seeing that he is not German but Austrian, and from a part of Austria where the people speak a dialect which almost always leaves traces in their speech long after they have left their villages or little towns.

I READ a few evenings ago that "the all-important question whether first-class cricket matches shall be of two days or three days has not yet been settled at Lord's. A sub-committee has been appointed to investigate and report on this problem." Do the panjandrums of the M.C.C. suppose that cricket is ever going to resume the place it once held in English (note that I do not say in British) national life? I don't ask this question derisively. I really should like to know. For years the interest in the championship games has seemed to me to be very much on the wane. The days when huge crowds were drawn to Lord's, the Oval, and the big county grounds to sit for many hours watching a match are now far away behind us. Like certain other games, cricket was over-professionalized, over-elaborated. Cricket on village greens is a capital pastime. Matches there last for a few hours, and I know few pleasanter ways of spending a hot afternoon than playing in or looking on at one. But when pitches are so carefully perfected that the bowlers get little chance, and batsmen stay in for hours, playing cautiously so as not to run the risk of spoiling their averages, there is not much enjoyment either for players or spectators. And without large numbers of spectators on frequent occasions to pay gate money professional cricket is doomed. This is only a personal opinion, however.

I PUBLISHED at the end of April a photograph of British troops entering the town of Gabès after the Eighth Army had driven the enemy out of it. "Gabès Greets the Victors with Smiles and Flowers" was the headline over the picture. Now I have a letter from "one of the Highland Division boys who were on that armoured car," asking if the six of them could have copies of the photo or of the issue in which it appeared, and assuring me that our headline told the exact truth. "It was one of our biggest thrills," the writer says, "when we drove into that little white town and were met by the cheering populace. Their enthusiasm was genuine, and we could not help but feel that the fighting and hazards of battle were well worth while—just to see the joy and happiness in those French people's faces was enough to spur us on to greater efforts than before. Now the job out here is done and the Eighth Army is ready for new fields to conquer back from the Nazi hordes." That was written on the first of June. Now, as I write, it is the first of August, and the Eighth Army have shown that the above was no empty boast.

# Airborne—But Not Above Riding in Carts

*Photo, British Official: Crown Copyright*

**GAILY DECORATED MULE CARTS** have here been commandeered by American airborne troops after they landed in Sicily, to carry them in pursuit of the enemy. The invasion glider-fleet was towed by two-engined bombers which, based in North Africa, flew 200 miles to the eastern beaches of Sicily, arriving at 10.10 p.m. on July 9, 1943, in advance of the seaborne landings.

Printed in England and published every alternate Friday by the Proprietors, THE AMALGAMATED PRESS, LTD., The Fleetway House, Farringdon Street, London, E.C.4. Registered for transmission by Canadian Magazine Post. Sole Agents for Australia and New Zealand : Messrs. Gordon & Gotch, Ltd. ; and for South Africa : Central News Agency, Ltd.—August 20, 1943.     S.S.     *Editorial Address :* JOHN CARPENTER HOUSE. WHITEFRIARS. LONDON. E.C.4.

Vol 7    # The War Illustrated    Nº 162

Edited by Sir John Hammerton

SIXPENCE                                              SEPTEMBER 3, 1943

**COMMANDER OF THE 51st (HIGHLAND) DIVISION,** Major-General Douglas Wimberley, D.S.O., M.C., hails from Inverness. His men, mostly desert veterans, have been winning new laurels since they landed in Sicily, as part of the 8th Army, on invasion day, July 10, 1943. They were among the first to enter Catania on August 5, having fought magnificently through every stage of the great advance. Maj.-Gen. Wimberley won his D.S.O. in the fighting against Rommel, and his M.C. in the 1914-1918 war.                        *Photo, British Official*

NO. 163 WILL BE PUBLISHED FRIDAY, SEPTEMBER 17

# THE BATTLE FRONTS

*by Maj.-Gen. Sir Charles Gwynn, K.C.B., D.S.O.*

WHEN I wrote last it was clear that the initiative had passed to the Russians and that the Germans were in danger of a major disaster if they decided to cling to Orel at all costs ; the capture of Orel constitutes a notable Russian victory, and though the German retreat was carried out skilfully it cost them heavy losses and necessitated the use of all available reserves to keep the Russian pursuit in check. Doubtless this involved a transfer of formations from the Byelgorod front and gave Zhukov a chance of delivering one of those brilliantly timed blows which had been such a feature of his winter offensive.

It looks as if it took the Germans by surprise and the resulting break-through has placed them in a position even more critical than it was when the exceptionally early thaw came to their aid in the winter. The attack cannot have been merely a brilliant improvisation, which could hardly have been exploited so rapidly and fully. But it is amazing that Zhukov after the great defensive battle waged for the Kursk salient should have been left with a force sufficient to seize the opportunity. It will be disappointing if the Byelgorod break-through does not presage ultimate decisive victory.

The week that saw the fall of Orel, Byelgorod, Catania and Munda may prove to have opened up new vistas which will lead to modification of Allied plans. The capture of Sicily can be regarded only as a preliminary step.

## RUSSIA

Once again Russia has surprised both the enemy and her friends in falsifying all expectations. Last winter the initial success of her offensive, though surprisingly great, was to some extent due to the strategical mistakes of the enemy which presented a great opportunity, and winter conditions were in her favour. What really amazed military observers all over the world was the astonishing competence of the administrative organization which enabled the momentum of the offensive to be maintained with the most inadequate communications, far beyond the range at which it was thought it must be lost. The campaign gave convincing proof of how formidable the Red Army was under winter conditions ; but it did little to shake the belief that in summer the Reichswehr would assert its superiority when it regained its mobility.

When the German Kursk offensive opened there was an almost universal expectation that the belief would be justified, and the complete failure of the attack, in spite of the formidable character of the force employed,

had to be explained by the admitted courage and tenacity of Russian troops in defence. Nevertheless, the success of the defence, especially after the defences in the Byelgorod area had been penetrated, caused great surprise ; and for the first time German invincibility in offensive action became open to doubt. Few, however, believed that the Russians would be capable of repeating in the summer their winter successes.

The comparatively slow progress of the attack on the obviously exposed Orel salient seemed to indicate the limits of their offensive capacity and gave little hope that they would ever be capable of breaking through the main German defensive positions. Even so, the fact that the Germans, in spite of great efforts, were unable to bring the Russians to a standstill caused surprise.

Then came the greatest surprise of all— the break-through at Byelgorod followed by its rapid exploitation. Here was something entirely new, vitally affecting prospects in the remainder of the summer campaigning season. It was a success which could only be explained

by a definite superiority of the Russians both in generalship and in power of manoeuvre.

It could hardly be argued that the Germans must have been caught on the rebound, after the failure of their offensive, for Byelgorod had for months been a strongly-defended position and formed an ideal rallying line. Even if the Germans had weakened their hold on it by transferring picked formations to the Orel front, there should have been ample reserves available to relieve them ; for there must certainly have been a considerable concentration of less mobile troops assembled to support the original offensive spearhead. The break-through was effected, therefore, not at a weak but at a strong point in the enemy's front, and was, consequently, all the more important in its implications. It was a soft spot, only in the sense that a successful break-through reached a particularly sensitive area in the enemy's rearward organizations, and had major strategical results.

When the Byelgorod break-through was followed by the penetration of the German defences between Smolensk and Bryansk, again a sector where they might have been expected to be exceptionally strong, a still further proof was given of Russian offensive power.

In the winter campaign, when the German situation was at its most critical, the Russians were desperately handicapped

SOVIET ANTI-TANK ARTILLERY, vanguard of Gen. Rokossovsky's army, at the gates of war-devastated Orel. The city—key to Moscow and second only to Smolensk in importance as a citadel—was relieved by the Russians after 23 days' costly fighting. (See also pp. 204-5.) Evidence of horrors perpetrated on the civil population by the Nazis during their 22 months' hold on the city is reported to rival that at Lidice and Krasnodar. *Radio photograph by Pictorial Press*

BRITISH GUNS IN ACTION among the lava-rock foothills of Mount Etna. The fall of Randazzo on August 13, 1943 and Castiglione on August 16 (see map below) completed the Allied encirclement of the mountain, last pivot of the Axis defences in Sicily. *Photo, U.S. Official*

anyone without the fullest knowledge of resources available, of the political factors involved, and of the full scope of the Allied plans, to offer any explanation of the apparent inaction.

The occupation of the island has clearly caused a notable disturbance of the dispositions of the enemy's troops ; and it must be realized that it would have been quite impracticable to forestall the German occupation of the Lombardy plain. Whether it was ever the intention of the Allies to undertake a complete occupation of Italy, involving immense demands of shipping, is, I think, doubtful ; and it is possible that the success of the Russian offensive may make it less, rather than more, advisable.

The actual fighting in the island followed the course expected, once it was apparent that the enemy, though he had failed to counter-attack in strength, was determined to play for time. The terrain gave exceptional opportunities for delaying action and made it impossible to take full advantage of the Allied superiority in numbers and armament. Only highly-trained and determined infantry could have overcome the especially difficult obstacles encountered.

Catania might possibly have been taken by a frontal attack, under cover of an artillery barrage ; but the cost would have been heavy and the chances of failure were considerable. In any case, the greater portion of the garrison would almost certainly have escaped to continue their resistance in the defiles beyond. It was, therefore, in this case, undoubtedly correct to evict the enemy by manoeuvre.

What the enemy's object was in fighting so desperately for time is still not quite clear. Possibly it was merely to gain time to assemble craft for evacuation, and for the concentration of anti-aircraft defences ; but probably there were other political and strategic motives which presently will be revealed in yet more triumphant action.

in their attempts to give the decisive blow by the immense length their lines of communication, entirely dependent on motor transport, had reached, and by the retarding effects of snow on movement. The weight of their forward thrusts was consequently reduced. Moreover, the approaching thaw gave the Germans prospects of a period of respite, and encouraged them to hold on at all costs to dangerously exposed positions, rather than attempt difficult retreat which might otherwise have been inevitable.

Now the Russian base of operations has been immensely advanced and has a restored railway system to supply it. They are, therefore, in a much better position to exploit initial successes, both by weight of blows and by speed of movement over firm ground ; and the Germans can expect no respite.

With the initiative lost, and their lateral lines of communication threatened, the German problem, always inherent in defensive operations, must be that of moving reserves to the threatened points, and unless they can concentrate reserves for counter-attack on a great scale their situation is extremely precarious. If they are compelled now to carry out a withdrawal to a shorter defensive line, the evacuation of warlike stores from their forward areas will be immensely difficult. Moreover, they must be saved, not merely to prevent them falling into Russian hands but in order to fill the depots on a new defensive line. It is highly improbable that any position far in the rear is well stocked, and to stock it rapidly from home bases would, on account of the great distances and limited railway facilities, be a slow business. Retreat on a large scale would in particular involve an immense expenditure of petrol supplies difficult to meet.

SICILY The capture of Sicily, giving us ·············· practically complete control of the Mediterranean route, proving the practicability of large-scale amphibious operations and providing us with new air bases, was undoubtedly a vitally important preliminary step. There has been some disappointment that, during the time required to clear the island, further operations for which preparations had obviously been made were not undertaken. It is, however, impossible for

DEVASTATION IN MILAN, wrought by the R.A.F. on the night of August 7, 1943, is typified by this huge block of buildings utterly wrecked. Three further attacks were carried out in 72 hours, August 13-15. "One gigantic ruin" is an eye witness description of the city's centre. *Photo, Planet News*

NEARING THE END IN SICILY. By August 16, 1943, Taormina was taken by the British 8th Army, the U.S. 7th Army were on the outskirts of Milazzo, and Allied units were advancing from Milazzo on Messina which fell on August 17. *By courtesy of The Daily Telegraph*

# Our Infantry Show Their Mettle in Sicily

BRITISH FOOT-SLOGGERS soon found ample scope in Sicily for demonstration of their superb skill, daring and endurance. The mountainous interior of the island presented a problem with which they alone could deal—for after all the bombing and strafing from the air had been completed it was the men on foot who had to effect the actual conquest of town after town.

Up steeply-rising hill roads, across gorges and swift-flowing rivers they had to fight their way almost yard by yard, exposed to enemy snipers and strongpoints favoured by the terrain.

What Gen. Montgomery called "the wonderful feat of arms" by the 78th Division at Centuripe (see also page 199) was one of the infantry's most remarkable achievements in the course of the whole Sicilian campaign.

*Photos, British Official : Crown Copyright*

EIGHTH ARMY troops are shown tackling a Sicilian railway station converted into a strong point by the enemy.

From the shelter of a stationary truck (1) a Bren gunner fires at the defenders strongly entrenched in the station. Then comes the moment for a bayonet charge (2). Foothold gained on the platform, bolted doors are smashed open with rifle butts (3) and skulking Nazis routed out. The initial phase of this vigorous action is illustrated in page 224.

"Mopping up" is one of the urgent jobs requiring attention after a town has been taken. No sooner had Catania fallen to units of the 8th Army on August 5, 1943, than our infantry set about mopping up amid the ruins of the devastated city (4). They found no Germans : the enemy had pulled out the night before, having spent most of the previous three days mining buildings, including the post office, the Bank of Sicily and a big hotel. See also eye witness story in page 220.

# British Artillerymen Back Up the Infantry

A GUN FOR EVERY JOB, expertly handled, was a major factor in our Sicilian triumph. Varied terrain called for a variety of artillery.

Working a self-propelled gun (1) is a manoeuvre calling for agility and alertness, exemplified by this gun-crew, all "on their toes."

Following the taking of the Primo Sole bridge (see p. 207) the 8th Army found progress hampered by the Germans' 88-mm. artillery. A battery of 25-pounders was brought up to deal with the situation (2). Different methods were called for in the hill fighting: (3) gunners loading a 4·5 howitzer, which proved invaluable in the difficult mountainous country of the interior.

Near Catania our troops captured an Italian howitzer intact, and very shortly it had been turned round and was punishing its former owners during a night artillery operation (4).

*Photos, British Official: Crown Copyright*

# Gaily the 8th Army Marched Into Catania

MONTGOMERY'S MEN GET THERE! Patrols of the 8th Army enter Catania (top) on August 5, 1943, and find the Cathedral intact.—evidence of the accuracy of our air bombing and naval bombardment. Lieut. B. J. Gardner, of the Durhams (inset), received the Mayor's surrender, while our troops were welcomed by the liberated townsfolk (bottom).

*Photos, British Official; Planet News*

# The 78th Division Plucked Sicily's 'Cherry Ripe'

CENTURIPE, 'FAIRY TALE TOWN' of Sicily, on the higher slopes of Monte Calvoria, had lost some of its picture-postcard glamour when the vanguard of the British 78th Division entered it after three days' hard fighting. Royal Inniskilling Fusiliers and London Irish, famed as mountain fighters in Tunisia, stormed their way across jagged gorges and high-banked rivers to the town—"Cherry Ripe" to them—and occupied it on August 3, 1943, on which day also Catania fell. Adrano was taken two days later.   PAGE 199   *British Official photo, radioed from Algiers*

# THE WAR AT SEA

## by Francis E. McMurtrie

THE latest results of the war against the U-boats, announced in a joint statement by the Prime Minister and President Roosevelt on August 14, are the equivalent of a great sea victory.

Over a period of three months enemy submarines have not only failed to inflict any serious losses on our convoys, but have themselves been incurring casualties at the record rate of one U-boat sunk every day. During the first seven months of 1943 Allied shipping was increased by 3,000,000 tons, losses notwithstanding.

These figures eclipse anything accomplished in 1917-18. During those years the worst period for the U-boats was the month of May 1918, when 16 were destroyed. In no other month were so many accounted for, the next most successful being September 1917, when we destroyed 10, and the following November, when the total was nine. Thus there was no continuous run of heavy losses for the enemy to face, such as has been revealed recently. Nor was the shipbuilding output of this country and the United States in 1917-18 comparable with that of the present war.

ALREADY it is evident that the Germans are at a loss to meet the situation which confronts them. Their first reaction was to alter the tactics of the U-boat flotillas, which found that the wolf-pack system of preying upon convoys had ceased to pay them. Instead, as indicated by the reference in the official announcement to recent sinkings having taken place in distant areas, enemy submarines have had to seek targets in remote seas, where there is a chance of finding merchantmen unescorted. This policy is not going to yield any rich returns, such as might have been expected when a heavy attack was launched on an inadequately escorted convoy.

No secret has been made of the fact that the defeat of the U-boats is mainly due to a more abundant supply of escorts. From such accounts of convoy actions in the past three months as have appeared, it would seem that 10 to 12 warships, comprising destroyers, sloops, frigates and corvettes, is no unusual total for a convoy escort. In addition, the mid-Atlantic gap between the extreme operating ranges of shore-based aircraft on either side has been bridged by the employment of carriers of the escort type, whose planes are able to patrol the waters around the convoy routes and drive beneath the surface any submarines encountered. Not infrequently the patrolling aircraft are able to drop depth-charges which damage the U-boats and leave them an easier quarry for the warships that are immediately directed to the spot by signal.

Though no figures of shipping losses have been released since the middle of 1941, an indication of the improvement during the present year is contained in the official statement that in the first six months of 1943 the number of ships sunk per U-boat was only half that in the second half of 1942, and only a quarter of that in the first half of 1942. (See chart in p. 202.)

An excellent opportunity appeared to be offered to the U-boats when the Allies invaded Sicily. Over 2,500 vessels were involved in the operation of invading the island and landing reinforcements and supplies, yet the total losses the enemy succeeded in inflicting were only about 80,000 tons, and that at heavy cost to the attacking submarines.

### GERMANY Faces a Dearth of Experienced U-boat Crews

In spite of these discouraging results the Nazi propaganda agencies are working manfully to keep up the courage of the German people, who are regaled at frequent intervals with imaginary figures of the tonnage which is claimed to have been destroyed, even while it is admitted that the submarines' task is becoming harder.

However many U-boats remain in service, they cannot continue operating freely in the face of such severe losses as have been incurred in the past three months. Doubtless there are sufficient submarines in reserve or completing to make good the casualties, but the training of crews will need to be accelerated to man them all. An even greater difficulty will be to provide experienced captains, since it is usually the daring and enterprising ones whose submarines run into trouble. The slower and more cautious captains do not as a rule accomplish very much destruction, as analysis of the results of the last war's submarine campaign showed plainly enough.

LAST MOMENTS OF A U-BOAT, at the mercy of an escort carrier plane. Two bare-legged Nazi seamen duck as a huge spray of water rises alongside an Allied depth-charge, which is just about to spell doom for the enemy submarine—one of the 90 sunk by the Allies during the quarter May-July 1943. *Photo, Planet News*

In these circumstances the Germans are obviously batting on a losing wicket. They are endeavouring to retrieve the situation by increasing the force of air attacks on shipping, but the area within which their aircraft can operate effectively is less than it was earlier in the war. For the Luftwaffe to be required to provide fresh squadrons for war against seaborne commerce may well prove the last straw.

How is the morale of U-boat personnel likely to stand the severe losses inflicted upon it? Judging from the last war's experience, it is improbable that it will be affected to any serious extent, though more hurried training may result in some loss of efficiency. In 1918, it will be recalled, it was the crews of the German heavy surface ships, and not those of the destroyers and submarines, which became discontented and ultimately broke out into mutiny. There are far fewer big ships in the German Navy today, and their influence on the situation is correspondingly less.

At the same time, the fact that those ships are mostly in Norwegian waters, and that their crews must be feeling acute anxiety for their homes and families in the Reich as the Allies' bombing programme continues to extend, is a factor whose importance must not be overlooked. The less friendly attitude which is now being adopted by Sweden must also have a depressing effect on their spirits.

IN connexion with the evacuation of German troops from Sicily across the Straits of Messina, I was recently asked: "What is the Navy doing to prevent this?"

Those who raise such questions would do well first to examine the geographical position. The Straits of Messina are narrow and tortuous, as a glance at a large-scale map will show. There are strong currents and whirlpools, to two of which the ancients gave the names of Scylla and Charybdis. To cross in power-driven boats at night is a simple matter, as the distance to be covered is not more than two or three miles.

For heavy warships to venture into such narrow waters would be to risk destruction by mines, to say nothing of heavy guns in coastal batteries on either side of the Straits. Light draught vessels such as motor torpedo-boats and motor gunboats have more than once, under cover of darkness, delivered attacks upon enemy vessels sheltering there.

Even aircraft found it difficult to interfere effectually with the traffic across the Straits, as the Germans had assembled there a mass of anti-aircraft artillery whose incessant fire made it extremely hard to hit small craft in motion.

THE POUNDING OF MUNDA by U.S. warships contributed heavily to the capture of this important Japanese air base in the Central Solomons. After a fiercely fought campaign of little over a month Munda fell to Gen. MacArthur's troops on August 6, 1943. (Above) A light cruiser during a bombardment in which 19,000 shells were fired. (See also story and illus., pp. 220-21.) *Photo, Associated Press*

# Catania Softened-Up by Allied Navies' Big Guns

**NON-STOP NAVAL SHELLING** of Catania—probably the most prolonged naval bombardment in history—preceded the 8th Army's assault on the city. When our men entered it (see p. 198) they found ample evidence of the accuracy of the shelling. A British battleship led the firing (top and bottom) with broadsides at from 15,000 to 11,000 yards range. During the engagement—in which the warship Queen Olga of the Royal Hellenic Navy participated—destroyers depth-charged a U-boat (centre) that attempted to interfere.   PAGE 201       *Photos, British Official*

# Will Allied Planes Spell the U-boats' Doom?

Step by step the U-boat menace is being met and mastered. And in that process a great and growing part is being played by aircraft. Indeed, as Capt. FRANK H. SHAW tells below, the men of the R.A.F.'s Coastal Command are of the opinion that, given the planes, they can provide the best answer to the enemy's much-vaunted submarine.

My pilot claimed no fewer than seventeen aerial attacks on enemy U-boats during recent months; and he expressed the opinion that in the long-range Sunderland or Liberator or Catalina—or the Whitley, for that matter—the Allies had the best answer to Hitler's savage U-boat threats. Over the Bay of Biscay, in the Sunderland's wardroom, he intelligently expressed his views; and, though a child in years, he was a sagacious veteran in experience, which counts more than many years of theorizing.

It seems enemy submarines, when attacked, vary in behaviour according to their nationality. Italians usually surface, Germans as usually crash-dive, when spotted from the air and in danger of attack. Just why this should be so my pilot had no opinion to offer, unless it was that the "Itie" commanders were more humane to their crews than the Huns, and gave them an extra chance of survival. Better to jump overboard than die, poisoned and drowned and suffocated, in the clammy dark of the Biscay deeps.

Our long-range, weight-carrying aircraft have one main advantage over surface war-ships—speed. The increased range of vision is also worth taking into account. The Sunderland in which I travelled recently attacked and badly damaged a U-boat that was just coming into position to scatter torpedoes among a convoy; and the destroyers and corvettes shepherding the freighters didn't even know of the killer's proximity. He had probably detected the escort's precise whereabouts by his listening devices and had planned a quick hit-and-run assault on the unguarded part of the convoy. Instead there was this young pilot, with depth-charges.

"We shook up that custard!" grinned the pilot. "It was a picnic; he tried to dive—hard; but the depth-charges lifted him so high out of the water that we saw his keel as he rolled. We gave him a pretty bracket; he wallowed like a harpooned whale. The escort ships hadn't even turned about by the time our attack was over."

The corvettes found just oil and a smear of debris; and the Sunderland's crew were allowed a "probable." If they hadn't spotted him, two, three or four—even more—of that very valuable convoy might well have been lost, ships and cargoes alike. A U-boat can crash-dive in 20 seconds, and can cruise on the surface at round about 20 knots. He has the entire ocean in which to hide; and the range of vision from a warship's bridge is limited. My pilot backed the aircraft against the surface ship every time.

"It will be better when the anti-submarine aircraft are trebled in number, of course," said Young Sagacity. "I know we're not exactly limiting our output. Assume that one aircraft attacks one submarine—to be relieved by another the moment it's got rid of its load of d.c.s (depth-charges)—the good old Merchant Navy would have a better chance. As it is, a man hesitates to unload everything on a single target in case another and even more urgent target shoots up just as he has disarmed himself. You can attack with machine-guns, cannon even, if fitted; but these U-boats are tough and can take a lot of punishment; and that sort of fire is wasted when they submerge."

To drop heavy depth-charges across the U-boat swirls more than doubles the hope of destroying him; the sea-disturbance following the big burst is bound to shake him up more than somewhat, set his batteries leaking, jolt the machinery; and when that happens he simply must surface to avoid asphyxiating his crew. That emergence gives the surface escort its chance.

Quite recently this pilot was cruising southwards not far from the course taken by enemy submarines from Lorient. The Bay of Biscay is a fruitful stalking-ground for Coastal Command.

Hanging immediately below cloud, in order to be able to climb to cover if attacked by the almost ubiquitous Ju 88s, he sighted some French trawlers down below. At that height they looked toylike, innocent. As the Sunderland passed over, the rear-gunner called through the inter-com: "There's one, Captain!" The U-boat had mingled with the trawlers as soon as it spotted our aircraft.

"Maybe he thought I wouldn't attack with a chance of sinking so-called friendly craft. It was a real Hun trick; like driving women before an advancing army to stop hostile fire. But the trawlers simply scuttered away like scared porpoises, so the Hun started to dive. We shot down on him like a thunderbolt and followed his swirl. Crossing him, we dropped a couple of d.c.s, and nothing happened beyond the bursts. But after a bit the look-outs—and every member of the crew turns into a look-out at such times—reported a small quantity of oil. That mightn't have meant anything; it's simple to squirt a gallon of oil out through a valve. But presently a little more oil seeped up—at about the same spot."

The pilot's face glowed. He was seeing it all again; that victory which means so much to our airminded youth.

The aircraft then circled the swirls. Everyone was keyed up, with the gunners watching in case of air-attack. The pilot went in and dropped another brace of depth-charges; these exploded precisely. Up came the Hun, rolling hard. Before his conning-tower was rightly up, men opened the hatches and began to jump over the side. Others, better disciplined, manned their A.A. guns and opened fire; but a spraying from the Sunderland's armament either laid them out or caused them, too, to leap overboard.

With the flying-boat going at full speed, it wasn't too easy to distinguish details; but the U-boat appeared to be tilted the wrong way, down by the stern. The commander appeared in the conning-tower and must have tried to recall his crew; but they swam away all the faster, whereupon the German shot them up with a machine-gun. Another charge dropping close to the hull caused it to fold like a pocket-knife; the wreck went down hump-backed. All that remained was to go lower and signal the trawlers to pick up survivors.

Coastal Command has no desire to steal the Navy's thunder; but the impression is growing strongly in the Command that big, long-range aircraft provide the best antidote to the marauding submarine. The radius of action is wide; with an adequate number operating, aircraft relieving aircraft without gaps, there need be no single moment, day or night, when a convoy is not covered by an efficient air-umbrella.

"We feel we cannot do enough to help the Merchant Navy," said my pilot. "The way they carry on, come hell or high water, they deserve the best protection they can get."

Two of this youth's best attacks occurred at night. Once the moon helped; the Northern Lights flared usefully the other time. A corvette collected survivors from No. 1, but no corvette was handy in the second case.

These long-range flying-boats are usefully employed against enemy surface ships. This one in which I travelled caught one blockade-runner fairly west of Finisterre, hurrying for a Biscay port. As no answer was given to the private signal, the Sunderland went down to investigate; whereupon the blockade-runner opened fire with everything he carried. Had the Hun kept quiet he might have had the benefit of the doubt, being disguised as a Spaniard; as it was, evasive action became immediately necessary. With the run-in, two depth-charges dropped almost against his paint. As the ship was not divided into innumerable water-tight compartments, he promptly disintegrated. The opinion was that his magazine had exploded. "Only H.E. could have created such a Brock's benefit!" said my pilot.

I foresee a time when the air will be full of flying "destroyers." When that time comes Hitler's dreams of final victory will fade into distorted nightmares.

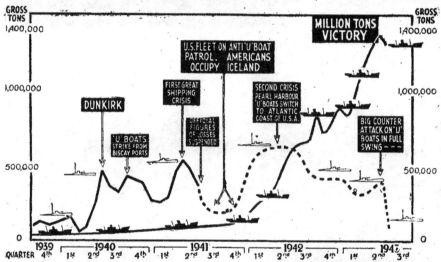

**CHART OF MOUNTING VICTORY**, showing the trend of sinkings (heavy line marked with U-boats, changing to dotted line when official figures were withheld) and new building (heavy line marked with merchant ships), from the outbreak of war. Allied output in June 1943 had reached 1,300,000 gross tons, and sinkings had fallen almost to the lowest recorded level.
*Courtesy of The Evening Standard*

# Behind the Scenes in Waging the Atlantic Battle

GREATEST BATTLE of the Atlantic in this war was fought during May 1943. The U-boats were routed and our losses were the lowest since 1939. Much of this success is due to Capt. A. J. Baker Cresswell, D.S.O. (3), Escort Training Captain, Western Approaches, and his staff aboard H.M.S. Philante, who are constantly trying out new methods of detection and destruction of U-boats and conducting training courses based on their researches. Among the exercises taught are the art of boarding an enemy vessel (2) and the manoeuvre known as the "Grid Iron" (4). Adm. Sir Max K. Horton (1), C.-in-C. W. Approaches, goes aboard the Philante.

# Vanquished German Armour on the Road to Orel

METAL MONSTERS met in terrific conflict in the historic Battle of Orel. The capture of this city—hinge linking Hitler's central and southern armies—on August 5, 1943, followed 23 days of progress by the Russians through more than 40 miles of successive fortified belts reinforced with all the devices of military science by the Nazis during their 22 months' occupation.

Smashed German tanks (1 and 4) marked the line of the Soviet advance. Other enemy armour—of which this tank and self-propelled gun (2) are examples—was taken in perfect condition and sent to the Russian rear, later to play a further part in the concluding stages of the battle.

While on the way to the front line the Russians were careful not to encroach upon growing corn (3) or other crops, so vital for their continued drive, which by August 16 had taken them to Malye Luki, 16 miles east of their next objective—Bryansk—also menaced by Soviet forces thrusting from Zhizdra, 35 miles to the north-east.

*Photos, U.S.S.R. Official; Pictorial Press*

# A Dagger at Russia's Heart Torn from Nazi Hands

**CAPTURE OF OREL**—followed in a few hours by the taking of Bielgorod—was the most heartening and significant development since war flared up on the Eastern Front. It exploded the myth of the inferiority of the Red Army to the Wehrmacht in summer fighting; it finally removed any German threat to Moscow; and it "hacked out the strongest molar in the jaw of the Nazis' southern defence line."

The fall of Bolkhov (1) on July 22 marked the last phase of the campaign, for it was then the strongest remaining outpost of Orel facing the Russian lines. A regimental gun follows Soviet infantry through fields that only a day before were held by the Nazis (2), while a battery of medium mortars gives powerful support (3).

Inside the Orel citadel at last, a spokesman of the Commanding Generals of the Red Army talks to inhabitants of the charred and shattered town (4), which was second only to Smolensk in importance in the Nazi defence system.

*Photos, U.S.S.R. Official; Pictorial Press*

PAGE 205

# From 'Fortress Europe' to 'Citadel Germany'

With Germany reeling under terrific blows and reverses, Hitler is preparing his last stand—or it is being prepared for him. DR. EDGAR STERN-RUBARTH explains here the reactions of the bewildered German people, and outlines the possible plans of the military Junkers who now see plainly enough what stands at the end of Hitler's road.

For exactly 130 years the Germans have never seen war within their own frontiers —until the R.A.F. carried it there. Gifted with imagination as they undoubtedly are, this lack of experience, fostering some sort of superstition as to the safety of their own homes, has contributed not a little to their acceptance of risk and odium of Hitler's predatory campaigns. The realization of what it now means to them, to their families and homesteads, is more bewildering, exasperating, and demoralizing by far than the same experience for Frenchmen, Russians, Italians, Balkan peoples and any other of the nations whose soil, within living memory, was swept by war.

Gestapo and concentration camps, for a while, were able to deal with the consequences of that sudden realization, as long as the Nazi leaders could explain away his predicament to the German man-in-the-street as a transitory hardship to be borne for the sake of ultimate victory. After all, there was something "heroic," some patriotic duty in suffering the loss of house and home, limbs and life if it contributed to the alluringly painted glorious future of the fatherland and the creation of a German-dominated world cleansed of Bolsheviks, Jews, Plutocrats, and whatever other bogies Goebbels's inventive brain had created for the Nazi dupes.

But this stage of the war is past; the enormous credit given to Hitler and his gang by a people that wanted to be convinced of their being right, and the rest of the world wrong, is exhausted. Under the blows of the R.A.F. and U.S.A.A.F., of the utter failure of the third, but relatively limited summer offensive in Russia, the loss of all Africa, the successful invasion of Sicily, the dwindling U-boat campaign, that huge, obedient but greedy Gulliver, the German people, is beginning to turn and twist in the fetters applied by the Nazi dwarfs; Mussolini's sudden downfall, and the defection from the Axis cause of all Hitler's puppets afraid of retaliation from their own and the oppressed peoples, are completing the drastic cure.

Significant posters have turned up in Berlin and elsewhere in Germany: "Hitler hat Achsenbruch gehabt—entzieht ihm den Fuehrerschein!" In German "Axis" and "axle" are identical, while "Fuehrer" (leader) means "driver" in the official designation of a driver's licence; thus this slogan, rapidly spreading all over Germany, implies that Hitler has incurred a break of his axle (Axis), so withdraw his driver's (Fuehrer's) licence! A few months ago the repetition of such blasphemy, or any other public criticism of the Nazi leaders and their policy, would have meant the execution of scores of careless talkers, and the concentration camp for many more.

This, too, is at an end; the Gestapo and the S.S., wherever demonstrations have arisen, of late have been ordered to stay put, to let popular wrath exhaust itself, whether in the case of the looting by desperate masses in devastated Wuppertal, or of joint Italian-German demonstrations in armament

plants when Mussolini's elimination was celebrated with bonfires into which both the dictators' pictures went indiscriminately. Hitler, Goering, and of late even glib-tongued Goebbels keep astonishingly quiet and invisible—and not merely from prudent considerations, or in order to devise some new devilry, but in consequence of pressure exercised by powers stronger now than their own.

In fact, the generals have won their fight which, with interruptions, was going on between them and what they contemptuously call "Hitler's circus" ever since the first of their own bosses, Field-Marshal von Brauchitsch, C.-in-C. of the Forces, to begin with, was dismissed early in Hitler's disastrous winter campaign of 1941. They fight now, clearly, for their own narrow caste and professional interests —not for Hitler's ambitions, which they shared only as long as victory seemed possible.

They know, these military Junkers, that no victory, total or partial, but utter ruin and destruction stands at the end of Hitler's road; and they see a slender chance for themselves— the preservation of a smallish German army, with themselves as the leaders of the nation, if only they can make the war last another year or two so as to weary the Allied nations and exploit what dissensions might ensue. Their plan has been for some time a wholesale German withdrawal from the widespread and indefensible lines of Hitler's fantastic "Fortress Europe" into the "Citadel of Germany."

Long before our invasion of Sicily their main strategists had written off their Italian ally as "more of a liability than an asset"; and after a fierce 48 hours' row (July 24 and 25), they had enforced upon Hitler the ultimate and ridiculous offer of sacrificing eight divisions only for supporting the defence Italy to the last.

They now envisage, with the cool mathematics of professionals, yet with disastrous disregard for the political consequences, the taking back of their lines in Russia so as to shorten them by at least one third, the giving up of the Balkans, indefensible without the 29 to 34 Italian divisions and the wholly unreliable 23 Bulgarian —they want to keep, at least for the time being and in view of their value for Doenitz's fading U-boat campaign, the shores of France and Norway, but to provide also for their evacuation in an emergency.

For their lines of defence are clearly mapped out already; they embrace Germany proper, with a glacis surrounding her rugged and ill-defensible frontiers, from the tip of Jutland to the Straits of Dover, along the Maginot Line, the Swiss and Austro-Italo-Yugoslav mountain-border to the eastern tip of Slovakia in the Carpathian mountains; from there straight north across Poland to the eastern border of East Prussia—thus including some 60 to 70 million foreign people, instead of the 250 million they at present hold down.

There is a rather fantastic element of political speculation in that scheme, too: the hope of coming to terms with Russia by evacuating her devastated and looted soil! While this concentration to within a stringently reduced territory would facilitate some of their, at present, most difficult tasks: transportation, exchange and reinforcement of fighting units, food-distribution, etc., and make heavily depleted fighting forces do for a longer period, the plan seems bound to miscarry because (a) it affords the same advantage of shortened lines to the United Nations, plus the active support of liberated nations thirsting for revenge, and (b) it would expose at one fell swoop the whole of that "Citadel" to our bombs, from Vienna to Koenigsberg, from Krupp's to Skoda's, from Upper Silesia to the Ruhr, and turn Germany proper into an ant-hill of desperate men, women, and children trying to escape destruction.

Yet, better strategists than Hitler as Brauchitsch, Bock, Rundstedt, Manstein—all of them, characteristically, belonging to the old Prussian nobility—undoubtedly are, they are clumsy politicians. What they are now preparing for the ultimate emergency is therefore hardly better than a parallel to the Italian transitional Savoy-Badoglio régime: a non-Nazi, then to be stamped "anti-Nazi," government of the one-time Papen-Schleicher brand, with a blend of less compromised high officials screening their own military regime.

They have systematically weakened Hitler's Pretorians, the real S.S., now largely replaced by unreliable bullies recruited all over occupied countries, by pushing their units into the most sanguinary spots of the Russian front; the military governors all over Europe have interfered with all political measures decreed by the Nazi authorities. They would not hesitate to enforce the fate of Mussolini upon Hitler and his henchmen, when they decided that they have served their purpose in taking the blame for present disasters. There may be a last, bitter fight between desperate gangsters and cold-blooded military chess-players, before that.

- ⋯⋯⋯ PRESENT GERMAN LINE IN RUSSIA.
- ‑ ‑ ‑ PRELIMINARY DEFENCE LINE.
- ‑‑‑‑ DEFINITE DEFENCE LINE, "CITADEL OF GERMANY."
- ▨ GERMANY BEFORE MARCH 1938.
- ANNEXED OR OCCUPIED TERRITORY TO BE HELD AS GLACIS OF "CITADEL".
- FRONTIERS BEFORE MARCH 1938.

Leningrad · Moscow · Minsk · Kiev · Berlin · Warsaw · Paris · Metz · Strasbourg · Prague · Vienna · Odessa · Budapest · Venice · Belgrade · Bucharest · Sofia

Statute Miles
0   200   400   600

**WHAT GERMANY HOPES TO HOLD** in Europe is suggested in this map, specially drawn for THE WAR ILLUSTRATED. Territory within the solid black line embraces Germany proper, with a glacis (shaded) surrounding her vulnerable frontiers. Note that Metz, Prague and Warsaw are included in the "German Citadel," as forecast by Dr. Stern-Rubarth in this page.

## *British Paratroops Seized This Bridge*

Here was fought one of the grimmest battles of Sicily. The 400-ft. long Primo Sole bridge (top) spanning the confluence of the rivers Simeto and Gornalunga, and key to our successful advance on Catania, was seized on the night of July 13–14, 1943, by British paratroops, changed hands again and again, and was finally held by the Durham Light Infantry. German prisoners (below) taken during the prolonged and bitter fighting there included many paratroops.

## *Pressing on From the Bridgehead*

The Primo Sole bridgehead (see p. 207) made secure, our men pressed onward along the arrow-straight, six-mile road towards their objective—Catania.   A British 4·5-in. gun (1) pounds enemy positions in the city's southern outskirts.   Scottish troops (3) move up towards the grim fighting which awaits them ;  in the opposite direction go carts laden with Sicilian families and their goods, returning now that the fighting from which they fled has passed beyond the area of their homes.

Pho

## *Rifles and Shore Batteries Triumphant*

The shadow of defeat already loomed darkly over Catania when British infantry (2) moved up to Vizzini, scene on July 15
of yet another 8th Army triumph. Three weeks later Catania itself was occupied. Meanwhile, Sicilian coastal defence
batteries had been overcome and the guns, captured in good order, manned by the British (4) : these men, under Major
J. V. Kelly, D.S.O., are overlooking Syracuse (which fell on July 10) ; Allied invasion ships are seen in the background.

## R.A.F. Contributes Its Magnificent Quota

With amazing speed captured Sicilian airfields were reconditioned for use by the R.A.F. A Spitfire (top left) is overhauled by the side of an abandoned German ME 109. R.A.F. Servicing Commandos (top right) repair radio equipment within a stone's throw of a Spitfire revving-up for onslaught on enemy transport ; while pilots of " The Fighting Cocks "—a famous North African fighter squadron—perch on yet another unlucky ME 109 (below) while waiting orders for a fresh sortie.

# VIEWS & REVIEWS
### Of Vital War Books

*by Hamilton Fyfe*

WHO first thought of a Home Guard for Britain? There are many claimants to this honour, one of them, oddly enough, the Trades Union Congress.

From the Trade Unions, and from the Labour Movement as a whole, there came for as many years as that Movement has existed, the most determined opposition to a Citizen Army. I can remember having many heated arguments with Labour men when I was doing my best to support Lord Roberts' appeal for national military training.

"No conscription" was the Party's slogan; it was opposed equally to the raising of a vast volunteer force. Yet, according to Mr. Charles Graves, who has written a very full and most interesting history of The Home Guard of Britain (Hutchinson, 10s. 6d.), it was the T.U.C. which, after the War Office had turned down a scheme put up to it by two highly-placed army officers, took the matter up "and very shortly afterwards the scheme went through."

It is a pity this sudden conversion was so long delayed. At an earlier date the arming of two million men for defence, leaving the regular army free to undertake operations overseas, would probably have convinced Germany, whether in the Kaiser's time or after Hitler took his place, that we really meant business and sabre-rattling must stop.

I think there is little doubt that the response to the Prime Minister's call (made through Mr. Eden) for Local Defence Volunteers in May 1940 had a great deal to do with making Hitler postpone the attempt to invade this island. It was a sign, for one thing, that our national unity was complete; that there was no Fifth Column here to help him; that, even if Mosley, the potential British Quisling, had not been clapped into jail, any attempt to do here what had been done by traitors in Holland and Norway, and probably in France, would have been instantly and bloodily crushed.

IT was on receiving help from sympathizers in our midst that Hitler counted when he planned his invasion. Ribbentrop had misled him, just as Prince Lichnovski misled the Kaiser's Government before 1914. When hundreds of thousands of men from all classes hurried to join the L.D.V. the Nazis quailed at the thought of the reception an invading force dropped from the air would get. Their plan was hurriedly changed.

If they had known more about this new element in the war situation they might have stuck to their original idea. When I joined it a week or two after recruiting began, it was in a condition which could almost be called in the language of the Book of Genesis "without form and void." We had no officers, we had no arms, we had no notion what our duties were to be.

After some weeks we got a few rifles which we shared, much to the disgust

of the "old sweats" among us, who looked on a rifle as a soldier's most treasured personal possession. Gradually the force took shape. By the time its name was altered to Home Guard, in the late summer of 1940, it was settling down to its job.

The War Office was taken by surprise when the decision to enrol a citizen defence army was made. Suggestions had been put up to it that such a supplement to the regulars might be necessary in view of the probable use of parachute troops by the enemy. These were waved aside. The official attitude was "We are doing all that is required." Even when Mr. Churchill forced its hand, it took a long time to carry out his

## Why Hitler Changed His Plan

wishes. Mr. Eden as War Minister was sent to tell Parliament there would be no commissioned ranks nor even real N.C.O.s.

AS late as November 1940 the headquarters of the force were "a scene of mild pandemonium." There was not then the same urgency as there had been in May, when the organizers were told the L.D.V. "must be ready to fight in two weeks." But it was incredible that after six months there should still be so much uncertainty and muddle.

Finance was one great difficulty. The Treasury were very sticky about it. However, the obstacles to the efficient and smooth working of the force were smoothed away until it became what we know it to be today—the most remarkable example in history of what the French call a *levée en masse*, the uprising of the manhood of a nation in face of danger, the manifestation of a will to victory that has never been surpassed.

It was the complete mix-up of all sorts and conditions of men in the recruiting of the L.D.V. that puzzled and worried Hitler when he was shown translations from British newspapers of reports about the rush to join. The War Office had said that, if the country was appealed to, "it did not think the men would come forward for volunteer local defence." That shows how utterly bureaucrats are out of touch with the public. Recruits began coming forward even before Mr. Eden had finished speaking on the wireless that memorable evening of May 14, 1940.

The police stations experienced a busy night. Young men, old men, the fit and the invalids gave

in their names. Statements as regards age were taken on trust, except in those cases in which those who were obviously in the seventies and eighties wanted to pass as under sixty-five, and those recently out of the nursery who pretended they had reached the age of seventeen.

In the ranks were many who had fought well and even become famous as soldiers. One commanding officer, a V.C., looked at a recruit and said, "Haven't I seen you before somewhere?" "Yes, sir, at Buckingham Palace, an investiture," was the reply. "What decoration did you get?" the officer inquired. "The same as yours, sir," the recruit answered. He was a V.C., too; his name, J. Leach.

When a brigadier was inspecting Home Guards, he stopped before a man with a long row of medal ribbons on his tunic and said patronizingly, "You seem to have seen a lot of fighting, my man. Tell me, which campaign did you enjoy most?" The private thought a moment, then replied, "I think, sir, it was the one in which I was second-in-command to General Allenby."

Though Mr. Graves has written a serious history with full details (though not quite full enough dates), he is not above telling a story whenever the chance comes in his way. Here is a good one about a sentry in Scotland. His company commander came round and asked if he had ever fired his rifle. The answer was No. Was it loaded? Yes, five rounds in the magazine. Had he got a cartridge in the breech, ready to be fired? No. He opened up and showed the breech empty. "All right," said the officer. Then the private "closed the bolt smartly, thereby sending a round into the breech, pressed the trigger, and—missed his commander by a couple of inches!" There was the silence of consternation for a moment. Then the sentry remarked, "Aweel, I've fired ma rifle noo, sir."

CHANGING from a volunteer to a conscripted force has not altered the spirit of the Home Guard. They are keener now than at any time, Mr. Graves claims.

No country in the world could have provided so many men able to maintain so much enthusiasm over so long a period of so much relative inaction. But for the Home Guard England would almost certainly have been invaded. But for the Home Guard it would have been impossible to envisage the invasion of the Continent. Two million men fully armed and trained, knowing every inch of their district, well led and in good heart, form a sure guarantee of victory. It is a force which has given courage to all the United Nations. It has survived its haphazard origin, its temporary lack of arms, its critics, and its greatest potential enemy—boredom. It has been and continues to be the most inexpensive force ever raised.

The average age of the Home Guardsmen is now slightly under thirty. The old and unfit have been weeded out "stringently," says Mr. Graves. Those who remain are alert, proficient, keen. He has a word for their wives, too. "They could not do it if their womenfolk did not encourage them." A word that is thoroughly well deserved.

ANTI-TANK UNIT of the Southern Railway Home Guard at gunnery practice. Trained for garrison defence duty in Kent, they are a gallant few of the 2,000,000 members of Britain's Citizen Army whose proud and chequered story is told in the book reviewed in this page.

*Photo, Planet News*

# Healing Hands of the Red Cross in Sicily

SUCCOURING THE WOUNDED are Major G. A. Fowler and Capt. J. S. Hutchinson, of the R.A.M.C., assisted by an Italian Red Cross nurse, Yolanda Girasole (1). Bandsman A. Frampton, of the Isle of Wight, employs a Sicilian mule-cart (2) to take medical supplies to a forward dressing-station. Nursing Sisters of the Queen Alexandra Imperial Nursing Service were serving in Sicily three or four days after the invasion started. (3), British nurses resting barely an hour's ride from the front.

*Photos, British Official*

# Italians Applaud the Fade-Out of Mussolini

JUBILATION IN ROME followed the resignation of Mussolini, self-appointed Dictator of Italy and Fascist Number One, on July 25, 1943. From an improvised platform, a portrait of King Victor Emmanuel is displayed, flanked by the Italian flag (top), while a bus conveys a cheering mob flourishing the national standard through a street of rejoicing citizens (bottom). Marshal Badoglio replaced the Duce as Governor of the country, with full powers. See also story in page 188.

*Photos, Associated Press*

ON A MALTA AIRFIELD a chain of bomb trolleys delivers its load to R.A.F. Baltimores. These light bombers have recently been operating from Malta against enemy positions in Sicily and the toe of Italy for the first time since Italy entered the war. To them must go part of the credit for the destruction of some 2,000 Axis aircraft during the Sicilian campaign, and they were well represented in the 12,500 sorties made by Allied aircraft over Sicily in July, 1943.

*Photo, British Official: Crown Copyright*

# THE WAR IN THE AIR

## by Capt. Norman Macmillan, M.C., A.F.C.

PERHAPS the most important aspect of the rising air offensive of the United Nations against the European end of the Axis is the increasing scale of daylight bombing. For this we have to thank principally the foresight of American Air officers and American aeronautical and armament engineers.

Indeed, the team work of the British and Americans in the air is one of the most remarkable current features of the war. Where the Americans were least advanced (as in heavy night bombers) the British were ahead of the world. And where the British were backward (as in heavy day bombers) the Americans were ahead of the world. This happy combination of circumstances has made it possible to stage the most complete air offensive the world has yet seen. It is a condition of things which the Axis failed to foresee, a failure they must bitterly regret.

When Goering boasted that the Reich—and especially the Ruhr—would be safe from bombs he must have placed his faith in gunfire to keep back the night bombers and in the (then) superior numbers of German fighter squadrons to defend the daylight sky. But nothing the German air generals ever did in the way of night bombing approached in the slightest degree the overwhelming of the defences that is achieved in every big raid by Sir Arthur Harris's Bomber Command. The guns and searchlights, massed though they are, are battered into semi-silence and blinded by the sheer weight of the air bombardment and by the smoke that rises from the smashed and burning target.

ALWAYS the Germans learn much in theory, but seldom enough in practice. Their own theory of war before they plunged the world into this second and greater global conflict was that mobile attack would defeat static defence. How then did it come about that Goering and the German air generals failed to perceive that air attack is mobile while air defence is largely static and especially so at night? My own view is that they never got as far as that in thought. They knew that they possessed great superiority in numbers of aircraft and they assumed that victory would be theirs because the enemy would never get an opportunity to recover. In June 1941 Hitler departed from the German theory by turning his forces against Russia and thereby giving us the opportunity to recover. Finding himself up against a tougher proposition than he evidently expected, he had need to embroil Japan to keep us and the Americans too busy to bother him while he remained preoccupied with his Asiatic adventure.

We never believed seriously in the daylight bombing offensive. It was thought that no day bomber forces could survive the losses that would be inflicted by modern fighter aircraft. And so we concentrated on night bombers and day fighters. This theory was vindicated in the Battle of Britain, and Hitler's forces (and theories) met their first defeat.

## AMERICAN Long-Range Planes Surprise Axis Air Strategy

In the Western Hemisphere, however, the conditions were so different from those obtaining in crowded Europe with its relatively small countries and cheek-by-jowl frontiers, and thinking of the wide spaces of the Atlantic and Pacific Oceans—the jump from San Francisco to Honolulu is 2,400 miles with no intervening island—and the 2,650 miles overland crossing from the east to west seaboards, and the 3,000-mile trip from San Diego to the Panama Canal Zone, not to mention the mountain and desert nature of some of the territory, American points of view coincided neither with the British nor the German. The Americans built long-range flying boats and long-range daylight bombers to meet their own hemisphere's requirements. The extensive nature of the operations which they had to provide for made it imperative that they should provide their bombers with the elementary defences of height and speed and powerful armament, rather than design them to take advantage of the strategic cover of night.

Bombers that operate by night are handicapped by the variations in the hours of darkness in the higher latitudes throughout the year. That is why it is easier for some of our bombers to operate from the southern side of the European front, rather than the western side represented by the British Isles, and why some of the bombers taking off from Britain in the summer months for distant targets, situated several degrees to the south, fly on to land in Africa, instead of attempting to return to Britain, where their return flight would discover them in daylight over German-occupied Europe.

Hitler's early successes in this war gave Germany possession of a continent and introduced conditions which were not dissimilar from those which naturally belonged to the Western Hemisphere. And American long-range, heavily armed, high-flying day bombers brought to these new conditions equipment which neither Britain nor Germany possessed, and a phase of the air war began which was unexpected by the Axis.

Daylight raids by Fortress and Liberator bombers began with short-range attacks against targets in Western Europe. The crews required operational experience. But the ability of these aircraft to fight their way was soon demonstrated, and gradually they were sent to tackle targets sited at greater ranges.

There came the raid against the Ploesti oilfields of Rumania, when 177 Liberators flew from the south of the Mediterranean up to Corfu and then turned in eastward across the Balkans. They shot down 51 enemy fighters. They flew through the balloon barrage that protected (or rather was supposed to protect) the oil region. Fortresses and Liberators bombed the marshalling yards in Rome, Naples came under their frequent assault. Hamburg felt their bombs. So did Gelsenkirchen. Liberators bombed Wiener-Neustadt's shadow factory for Messerschmitt fighter aircraft on August 14, Austria's first raid. Fortresses bombed the Messerschmitt plant at Regensburg, Germany, three days later. Mitchells and Marauders bombed the Rome airfields of Ciampino and Littorio. All these and many other raids were made by day. Heavy night bombers from Britain were raiding Milan and Turin; Mosquitoes night-bombed Berlin.

So, with the dove-tailing of American day methods and British night methods of bombing, the power of the United Nations to create havoc within the Axis-controlled ring of Europe has risen to proportions beyond the capacity of the Luftwaffe to counter.

These powerful blows are strategically fitted into the general strategy of the war, so that they aid the land offensive in Europe and Russia and the offensive against the U-boat. They are the nearest approach to the application of the theory of General Douhet, the Italian air theorist, that any nation or group of nations has yet reached. It would be the height of irony for Britain and America in combination to prove to the Axis partners that the theory of an Italian general was correct, after Germany and Italy, having tried to carry out the theory, thought that it could not be applied in practice. But war is always paradoxical. Air war is no exception.

# Last Moments of Service in the Luftwaffe!

DEATH STRUGGLES in the air, caught by the camera, provide some of the most dramatic photographs of the war. A German ME 323 transport plane (1) is hit by a stream of cannon shells from an American Marauder, near Cape Corse, Corsica; gunfire from the victim's windows suggests that it was a troop-carrier.

The end awaiting it is as inescapable as that of this Junkers 88 shot down by a Coastal Command Beaufighter in the Bay of Biscay (5); all that remains of the Junkers is a blaze of oil and petrol on the water.

A dog-fight between a Spitfire and an ME 109 over Northern France concludes with a burst at 200 yards, which causes fire in and around the cockpit of the ME 109 (2), resulting in an explosion in the èngine (3) and pieces of the aircraft falling away. A moment later (4) the port wheel drops off and the smoke trail almost blinds the Spitfire's camera vision as the Nazi machine hurtles to destruction.

*Photos, British Official*

# Funeral Pyre of Hitler's Rumanian Oil Hopes

**PLOESTI OILFIELDS ABLAZE** as 177 Liberators of the 19th U.S. Army Air Force pressed home their daylight attack on August 1, 1943 (see also p. 186.) Bombers sweep in low above swirling smoke and flame (2). Smoke clouds thicken as another releases its bomb-load on the refineries (3), which suffered very heavy damage (4). Sole Englishman among the 2,000 airmen who took part was Squadron Leader George C. Barwell, D.F.C. (1), R.A.F. gunnery expert, since awarded the American D.F.C. and Air Medal.

*Photos, U.S. Official; Planet News*

# Demolition Gives Us a New View of St. Paul's

**WHERE STEEP LITTLE DORSET RISE** takes you from Tudor Street by historic Salisbury Square to Fleet Street, this unique view of St. Paul's has recently been opened up by the demolition of bombed property. The Cathedral may now be seen in a setting comparable to that which inspired Sir Christopher Wren—standing on an eminence and islanded in space—with room enough even for the open-air fête and sports meeting which was held on August Bank Holiday, 1943.

*Photo, Topical Press. Copyright, Amalgamated Press, Ltd.*

# This Harvest Will Live in the Memory of Man

*Between summer and what the Americans call the fall half a million additional workers are required to help the farmers in the British countryside. This article tells something of the magnificent achievements of our agriculture under the stress of war, and of the yet greater achievements within reach—if the labour is forthcoming' and the weather is not too unkind.*

HIGH summer has come and gone, and in all the counties from Cornwall to Caithness those whose job it is to make things grow for the filling of hungry mouths are toiling from before the dawn to after the bedding of the sun. As summers go it has not been above reproach, but then the weather is not and never has been what the farmer would like it to be. And after two thousand years or so of making the best of it, our British agriculturists have learned to make it a very good best indeed. Moreover, in time of war they do very much better than in peacetime—not so much because they work harder or more enthusiastically, but because they have the happy confidence that what they have sowed, that will they not only reap but be able to sell. Compared with the pre-War position the total production of food from the soil of this country has increased by 70 per cent. Here are some figures recently released by the Ministry of Agriculture which indicate the tremendous advances made in farming practice since the War began. They show the percentage change in the acreage of land under cultivation and given over to some of the most important crops, and the livestock population, in 1942 compared with 1939 :

| | | | |
|---|---|---|---|
| Arable tillage | + 33·7 | Potatoes | + 80·4 |
| Tillage .. .. | + 52·8 | Vegetables | + 55·1 |
| Cultivated area | − 2·0 | Cattle .. | + 4·6 |
| Wheat .. .. | + 35·6 | Sheep .. | − 17·8 |
| Oats .. .. | + 72·0 | Pigs .. | − 51·9 |
| Cereals .. .. | + 65·7 | Poultry .. | − 24·2 |

The small reduction in the cultivated area—in spite of the increased acreage of arable land and that devoted to tillage—is due to the conversion of farm land to military and industrial uses ; in other words, it reflects the vast growth of aerodromes, war factories, training-grounds and the like, that our mounting war effort has called forth. The decline in stock, with the exception of cattle—in itself an indication of the valuable encouragement given by the Government to milk production—is largely accounted for by the fall in imported feeding-stuffs, from the pre-War figure of 8,500,000 tons to 1,300,000 tons in 1942-3.

BEFORE the War we produced from home-grown beet 23 per cent of our total sugar requirements ; we are now producing 35 per cent. Last year Britain's farmers were using 150,000 tractors, against only 55,000 before the War. Another comparison made by the Ministry's statisticians is in the number of allotments : 1,700,000 as compared with 930,000. In the same period the number of gardens cultivated for vegetables has increased from three millions to five millions.

Every year since the War began has seen a good harvest, but this year's is expected to out-top them all. (And very necessary is it that it should do so, in view of the immense strains on our shipping, to be inevitably intensified tremendously as soon as the Battle for Europe opens in real earnest.) But the greatest hindrance to still further increased production is the shortage of labour, and this in spite of the vast strides in mechanization

suggested by the tractor figures just quoted. For potato-planting in the spring, for root-hoeing, for the corn harvest in the summer, and for potato and beet lifting in the autumn, additional hands are always wanted. For the regular work the " professionals," supplemented by the Women's Land Army, Italian prisoners and other wartime additions to the rural labour supply, have somehow managed to cope with the ploughing and cultivations. But at the peak points, these varying with the crop, the district, and the weather, scores of thousands more are wanted even in ordinary times. Under war conditions there is no reservoir of casual labour that may be tapped, while the need for extra hands is greater than ever.

## Volunteers Lend a Welcome Hand

Where are they to come from ? The people who are of the greatest value are those living in the countryside who are not normally workers on the land but are available in an emergency. These are particularly welcome, since in their case there is no question of transport or accommodation. Most County War Agricultural Committees prepared registers of these potential volunteers long ago ; and last year probably some 30,000 people, mostly women and young folk, made themselves available under the scheme. This year it is hoped that the figure will be doubled. Then thousands of men and women, chiefly sedentary workers engaged in the smaller towns, have been rendering more or less regular part-time help in agriculture through Land Clubs—bodies of individuals prepared to work on odd jobs at week-ends or during the long evenings.

BUT though the countryside and the small towns can do a lot, they have not been able to provide all the extra labour required on the farms at the peak periods. So the call has gone out to the town-dwellers proper, to the great mass of people whose contacts with the country are few and far between yet who have the love of the country still in their hearts. During the summer months a number of Agricultural Camps has been set up in many parts of the country, under the auspices of the County Agricultural Committees ; and to these many thousands of men and women, youths and girls, have been proceeding, to spend four days or a week in work on the neighbouring farms. These camps have been extensively advertised as holiday camps ; and so they are, although they cater for guests who both pay and work.

Other camps have been run for school children, a two-year-old development. In 1941 about 12,000 children attended these camps ; in 1942 the number grew to 30,000, including some three or four thousand girls ; this year it is hoped to pass the 50,000 mark. Public and secondary schools have sent out parties in term-time, and many elementary schools have had their holidays altered so that the children can help in the fields. Civil Defence workers have been prominent among the volunteers, both in their spare time and during duty hours. Last year a vast amount of assistance was rendered by the Army—during September, for example, there was a daily average of nearly 45,000 soldiers working on the land, and throughout October and November and well into December some tens of thousands were engaged in lifting potatoes and sugar beet. But it may be that in the final months of 1943 the Army and the Air Force will have another task to do.

JULY 4, American Independence Day, was also celebrated as " Farm Sunday " throughout Britain. For most of the farmers and their helpers it was a day of hard work, but those who could attended the demonstrations that were held in many districts that were to emphasize the tremendous importance of the coming harvest. In a speech broadcast from Ormskirk, Mr. R. S. Hudson, the Minister of Agriculture, made an appeal for half-a-million volunteers to help with the harvest. " We are now nearing the climax of the year when," he said, " those long hours spent in all weathers in the fields reach their fulfilment. After Dunkirk, when every shipload of munitions gained meant the difference between life and death, the farmers of Britain, with equipment little better than what our armies had, grew a tonnage of food that staggered the world. Again this year we have sown to good purpose. We should reap a harvest which will live in the memory of man. We are starting this month on the toughest harvesting job in our history, a harvest which the farmers and their workers cannot hope to lift unaided. It will need the united efforts of all. From first to last it will probably mean the best part of 100,000,000 tons . . .''

E. ROYSTON PIKE

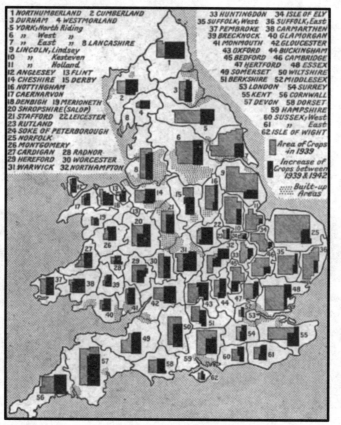

1 NORTHUMBERLAND  2 CUMBERLAND
3 DURHAM  4 WESTMORLAND
5 YORK, North Riding
6  ,,  West
7  ,,  East  8 LANCASHIRE
9 LINCOLN, Lindsey
10  ,,  Kesteven
11  ,,  Holland
12 ANGLESEY  13 FLINT
14 CHESHIRE  15 DERBY
16 NOTTINGHAM
17 CAERNARVON
18 DENBIGH  19 MERIONETH
20 SHROPSHIRE (SALOP)
21 STAFFORD  22 LEICESTER
23 RUTLAND
24 SOKE OF PETERBOROUGH
25 NORFOLK
26 MONTGOMERY
27 CARDIGAN  28 RADNOR
29 HEREFORD  30 WORCESTER
31 WARWICK  32 NORTHAMPTON

33 HUNTINGDON  34 ISLE OF ELY
35 SUFFOLK, West  36 SUFFOLK, East
37 PEMBROKE  38 CARMARTHEN
39 BRECKNOCK  40 GLAMORGAN
41 MONMOUTH  42 GLOUCESTER
43 OXFORD  44 BUCKINGHAM
45 BEDFORD  46 CAMBRIDGE
47 HERTFORD  48 ESSEX
49 SOMERSET  50 WILTSHIRE
51 BERKSHIRE  52 MIDDLESEX
53 LONDON  54 SURREY
55 KENT  56 CORNWALL
57 DEVON  58 DORSET
59 HAMPSHIRE
60 SUSSEX, West
61  ,,  East
62 ISLE OF WIGHT

Area of Crops in 1939
Increase of Crops between 1939 & 1942
Built-up Areas

**INCREASE IN AREAS UNDER CULTIVATION in Britain, 1939-1943—prime factor in this year's bumper harvest. Total food production from the soil of this country has increased by 70 per cent since the outbreak of war—substantially easing the strain on Allied shipping resources.**
*Specially drawn for* THE WAR ILLUSTRATED *from information supplied by the Ministry of Agriculture*

# How Britain Reaped Her Record Victory Crops

BRINGING IN THE SHEAVES of this year's phenomenal harvest. A combine-harvester on the Crown Estate at Windsor (1) cuts, thrashes and sacks in one operation. The corn then goes to the mill (5). Horses have a stiff pull up the slope of a Hertfordshire barley field (2). At Abbey Wood, London office workers stook the corn crop (3). Sun-hatted Land-Girls stack oats at Pulborough, Sussex (4), and another raises drooped stalks to ensure the corn will be cut properly and not an ear be wasted (6).

*Photos, Fox, E. W. Tattersall, Keystone*

## Catania Was a City of Chaos and Desolation

*Both before and after the Germans fled from Catania astonishing scenes were witnessed in the city. As this front-line Sicilian pen-picture (dated August 6, 1943) by a Special Correspondent of The Daily Telegraph reveals, chaos reigned supreme. Not until some time after the entry of our troops on August 5 was order fully restored.*

CATANIA has all the air of a town that has been frozen into immobility. Of all the conquered towns I have seen there has been none where the machinery of civic life has so completely come to a standstill. There were no signs of any shop or hotel being open. It was a complete contrast to Tripoli, where within five hours of the arrival of the first British troops British officers were booking bedrooms and being served lunch by white-coated waiters in restaurants.

But Catania is a city of desolation. Of its 250,000 population only 50,000 still remained when we arrived, and of these 30,000 habitually slept in air-raid shelters. Such has been the effect of our bombing—far severer than one had anticipated. This remnant population had been living a hand-to-mouth existence.

The departure of the last of the enemy troops signalized the breakdown of all semblance of order in Catania and the looting of shops began. It was worst in the Via Vittore Emanuele, immediately bordering on the central square, the Piazzo del Duomo.

Here the population had broken into the shops. Standing on a balcony outside the first-floor windows I saw men throwing down bale after bale to the populace below. There were women carrying armfuls of silk stockings, and their drab working-class clothes—only the poorest were left in Catania—were in sharp contrast to the newly-acquired gay silk scarves they wore around their heads or shoulders.

I had a long talk yesterday morning with the Mayor of Catania, the Marquis di San Giuliano, immediately after the formal surrender of the town. Troops made a peaceful advance into the place. There was no street fighting, despite reports to the contrary. The Mayor is a nephew of the Marquis di San Giuliano, formerly Ambassador to Britain, who as Foreign Secretary under Signor Salandra in 1914 was largely responsible for holding back Italy from entering the war on the side of Germany.

The Mayor had received many insults from Germans during their occupation of Catania. On one occasion his car had been stopped in the street and he had been covered with a machine-gun while the contents of his car were looted by German soldiers. On another occasion a number of German officers entered his house at 4 a.m. and insisted on billeting themselves there. As there were not enough beds for all they turned out three women relatives of the Mayor.

Finally, that very morning, as he drove into the town from his villa on the northern side of Catania, the Mayor was held up by German soldiers, who turned him out of his car, telling him that it was wanted for carrying the ammunition to a battery near by. He had to walk into town.

"Fortunately," he added, "it was only a few minutes before I met an officer commanding your advance troops, and I think I was able to give him some useful information about the location of that battery."

This deterioration in the conduct of German soldiers towards the civilians of a technically allied country has become very marked in recent months, particularly since the end of the Tunisian campaign. But the change in their behaviour towards civilians seems to have gone hand-in-hand with their realization that the war could no longer be won.

"When the Luftwaffe first came to Sicily early in 1941," said the Mayor, "they were a cheerful, laughing, jolly people. They enjoyed listening to the radio, which always recounted fresh German victories. The date they gave us then for the end of the war was July 1941.

"Then came the Russian campaign, and presently the Germans began to admit that they had miscalculated the strength of Russia. But they were still convinced of victory. Tunisia was the real shock. They had told me that they would keep their foothold in Africa. They were dumbfounded at the completeness of their defeat.

"After that their attitude was quite different. You never heard any more laughing and joking, and they did not seem to listen to the radio so much. Then they began to blame us Italians because the war was coming to Sicily."

During the last days of occupation the Germans unashamedly began looting. There was little food available by this time, so they carried off furniture, beds, blankets, sheets, pictures, knives, forks and household utensils.

As may be expected, tension between the Italians and Germans has become very marked. In another day or two fighting would probably have broken out between them in the streets of Catania. In the neighbouring village of Mascalucia the population forcibly opposed an attempt by German troops to requisition their mules. Several civilians were shot in resisting before Italian carabinieri arrived and drove off their allies.

## I Saw the Americans Storm Munda Field

*Munda, in New Georgia, fell to the Americans on August 6, 1943. How its much-bombed airport—of immense importance to the occupying Japanese—was stormed by U.S. infantry is vividly told by Walter Farr, Special Correspondent of The Daily Mail, from which this story is reprinted.*

FIFTY yards ahead, through the tropical trees, I can see a crowd of ragged-looking Jap soldiers running wildly away in three directions and firing back at us with light machine-guns and rifles as they go. Stumbling over mounds of fallen coconuts and among American-made bomb craters, they dash back into temporary safety on high ground near Munda Point, where their mortars are firing to cover the retreat.

This is the end of Munda Field. Ignoring the mortar fire, we rush on to see whether our infantry unit or another, pouring down Bibolo Hill on our right, shall be first to step on to the aerodrome. We cross a bare, cratered ridge where heaps of dead Japs lay near their mangled guns and rifles.

Breathlessly we hurry over a Jap burial place where our last torrent of bombs a few hours ago threw up skeletons from their graves. On through scores of pillboxes and lines of trenches. Then comes a final stream of enemy machine-gun fire, throwing up clouds of coral near us and killing one of our officers.

Americans on either side of me advance with fixed bayonets. Here and there a man drops flat to fire at the fleeing Japs, or to fling grenades into a pillbox entrance, or into ruined native shacks—just to make sure. A rifle barks near me, and one Jap who could not run as fast as the others drops dead. More American riflemen pause to pump a few more rounds into the prone figure in case he is pretending death.

Someone shouts, "A plane, a plane! Look, there's a grounded plane right ahead of us!" Suddenly through the shell-torn trees there looms the tattered outline of a wrecked Zero. More Japs are running frantically away from it. Our main body halts in case of some last-minute enemy traps, but we move on.

**HOW WIDESPREAD LOOTING** by the civilian population followed the taking of Catania by our men is described by an eye witness in this page. After hours of amazing scenes British security troops restored order where the local police had been helpless. Here looters on balconies of houses throw booty to the clamouring crowd, most of whom look half-starved and unkempt.

*Photo, British Official: Crown Copyright*

MUNDA POINT, vital Japanese air base in the Solomons, the first major objective to fall to the United Nations' forces in their offensive, begun on June 30, 1943 on a 680-mile front from New Guinea to New Georgia, where Munda is situated. How this much-bombed airfield fell (on August 6) is told in this and the facing page.
*Photo, Associated Press*

noise of it like the roaring and rushing of a sea past my cabin and the shrill screaming of the propellers. When I judged that I had reached the limit of possible velocity with the engines full on I thought I would "feather" the propellers to give me even a little more speed.

But as I began to reduce power the nose of the plane started to turn inwards on an outside loop. That cured me pretty quick of any desire to "feather" the propellers. I held on to maximum speed for 10 sec. I had no sensation of speed at all, for there was nothing to impress it on my notice. If I had passed anything going down or could have kept my eyes on the earth leaping up to meet me, it would have been different. When I had got to within 18,000 ft. of the ground I guessed it was time to let the old instinct of self-preservation have its way. So I started to flatten out. This was the really exciting part.

I had only 18 sec. to go before reaching the ground, and I had to act quickly and at the same time very carefully. If I had pulled out suddenly I wouldn't have been here to tell the tale. However, I got her out in a nice curve—and that was unpleasant enough. I didn't black out—I just greyed out. Everything went grey, but I didn't for an instant lose consciousness. I felt as if some hefty fellow was sitting tight on my head and pushing me back from the way the plane was going, and when I tried to move my arm it was so heavy I thought I'd need a crane to lift it.

My whole body felt like lead. Now I could see the ground and the neatly divided fields—and all at once I became conscious of speed. After flattening out I did a little climb that eased matters a bit. A few seconds later I landed. How did I feel? Oh, fine. I just breathed a little prayer of thanksgiving and went into the office to write my report.

I undertook the test dive in the ordinary course of my research work. In fact I decided to go up quite suddenly—and only half an hour before. I had my usual breakfast—toast and coffee and a cigarette.

You see, it sort of helps a fighter pilot to know just how much his plane can stand.

Another wrecked Zero comes into view, then another, and another. Twenty of them in all. Four of us move forward, clear the under brush, skirt three huge bomb craters, and run towards the planes—straight on to Munda Field.

There, stretching 3,000 yards before us to Munda Point, is what is left of one of the

world's most bombed airports. There are acres and acres of craters and practically every installation has been ground to pieces by the fury of our bombardment. Only an occasional window frame or doorway or a few charred papers mark the place which the Japs thought would be the nerve centre of a huge aerial armada which would drive us back towards Australia.

## I Power-Dived Faster Than Sound Can Travel

The fastest man alive, Lieut.-Col. C. S. Hough, of Michigan, Technical Director of the 8th Fighter Command, tells how he power-dived vertically at 780 m.p.h. from more than eight miles above the English countryside to test a fighting machine. His story appears here by arrangement with The Daily Mail.

I GUESS I shall remember more than anything else the wonderful experience of seeing from that height of 43,000 ft. practically the whole of England spread out under me on a perfect English day. I stayed up there for a little while just to look around. I saw right across to the Bristol Channel on one side and away to the Wash on the other. I saw the Mersey gleaming, and the brighter Bristol Channel.

I took a glance at the North Sea and then at the English Channel and away across to Calais and the Cherbourg peninsula. Gee! What a thrill it was to see the whole of one country at once! Well, then I had to get along, for my cabin wasn't supercharged for climbing so high, and I wasn't getting enough oxygen. It was pretty cold up there too—60 degrees below zero (Fahrenheit), and all the

heat I got was from the twin engines of my Lightning plane. So it was time I really got moving.

I didn't think about taking the plunge—I just put her nose down and went for the earth, gradually gaining maximum speed. I suppose it was about five seconds after reaching my ceiling that I started to make the power dive and I was diving for 25 seconds at 1,000 ft. a second. In the middle 15 seconds my hands were off the controls—it was a bit risky, I admit—and I was diving with my eyes glued to the instruments that told me of my speed and other things. It sure was a thrill when I realized at one point that I was travelling faster than the sound of my engines and faster than the speed of my propellers.

I wasn't conscious of any sensation in particular—only the rather comfortable feeling of going through *solid* air. There was the

LIEUT.-COL. C. S. HOUGH, of Michigan, with two of his ground staff and the plane in which he flew faster than sound. He describes his unique exploit in this page.
*Photo, Planet News*

# From a Prison Camp We Tramped 1,000 Miles

Two Dutch submarine officers escaped from Hongkong and tramped 1,000 miles across China to a British Army outpost in Burma. One of them, Lieut. Roel Hordyk, tells their story, given here by courtesy of The Observer.

WE were taken prisoner in December, 1941, when our submarine was sunk during an attack on an enemy convoy at the time of the Japanese invasion of the Malay peninsula. But within two days of being put in the prison camp we escaped.

How we escaped must still remain secret, but shortly before dawn on the third morning we were on the outskirts of a town. By hiding in ditches and behind bushes we eluded the Japanese patrols and reached the hills, where we stayed for seven days, and then, because we were getting weak from want of food, we decided to try to find a boat to take us to the mainland.

I had copied a map of China and knew roughly where we wanted to go. So on the seventh night we went down to the coast and luckily found a boat. The fifty-mile row to the mainland took three or four days, as we had to make our way from island to island by night.

Right from the start the Chinese helped us. They were wonderful. One island was inhabited by a small community of poor fishermen. After sharing their rice and fish with us they had a collection and gave us half a Chinese dollar. And that was all the money we had throughout our trek (when we finally arrived at our destination we still had it). We reached the mainland at a place occupied by Chinese guerillas. Their sentries surrounded us and took us to their leader.

We explained who we were and he gave us a " safe conduct "—a small piece of paper with Chinese characters written on it. It worked like a charm. Whenever we showed

it people fell over themselves to help us. I pointed out to the guerilla leader on my map where I wanted to go, and he sent a man to put us on the road. And then our trek began in earnest.

There were a lot of evacuees on the road and we followed them. Mostly they were rich Chinese travelling with twenty or more coolies carrying their belongings. The Chinese walk fast and they never seem to tire. We must have averaged about 20 or more miles a day. The roads they took led up into the mountains. They were 'little more than rough, rock-strewn tracks, twisting and curling for mile after mile.

Cold and boredom were the two worst things with which we had to contend. The pace was fast, but after a few days we got used to it. We walked in silence most of the time, just concentrating on walking.

Our route led from hamlet to hamlet, clusters of two or three poor wooden huts perched precariously on the mountain rocks. Misty rain soaked our clothes—khaki battle-dress—and tennis shoes, and icy winds cut through them. On the bare heights we had to rely on the kindness of the villagers to feed us. Nothing could grow in such wild country. We ate practically nothing but rice throughout the journey.

Most of the towns and villages through which we passed had been bombed, and many of the Chinese had rebuilt their houses three or four times, only to have them shattered again by Japanese planes. Ultimately, after nine weeks, we reached a British Army outpost. There we were taken to a hotel, where

LIEUT. ROEL HORDYK, of the Royal Netherlands Navy, who tells in this page the story of his 1,000-mile trek to freedom across Japanese-occupied China.
Photo, British Official : Crown Copyright

we had our first bath and European food since our capture more than three months before. Then we were flown to Calcutta.

# OUR DIARY OF THE WAR

**AUGUST 4, Wednesday** *1,432nd day*
**Sicily.**—Capture announced of Caronia by U.S. troops.
**Russian Front.**—Soviet troops launched big offensive on Byelgorod front.
**Australasia.**—Revealed that American troops had reached Munda airfield and had occupied part of Bibolo Hill.

**AUGUST 5, Thursday** *1,433rd day*
**Sicily.**—Catania and Paterno captured by 8th Army ; island of Ustica occupied by Americans.
**Mediterranean.**—Naples pounded.
**Russian Front.**—German bastions of Orel and Byelgorod taken by storm ; Marshal Stalin ordered the firing of 12 salvoes of 120 Moscow guns in celebration.

**AUGUST 6, Friday** *1,434th day*
**Sicily.**—Troina, erroneously reported taken on Aug. 3, fell to Americans ; fall of Gagliano announced ; 125,000 prisoners taken to date.
**Russian Front.**—Announced in three days of Byelgorod offensive to date, Russians penetrated enemy defences to depth of 15-37 m. on 44-m. front. Kromy, 25 m. S.W. of Orel, captured.
**Australasia.**—Munda air base captured. Jap cruiser and two destroyers sunk in naval engagement with U.S. ships between Kolombangara and Vella Lavella.

**AUGUST 7, Saturday** *1,435th day*
**Sicily.**—8th Army captured Adrano and Belpasso.
**Russian Front.**—Graivoron captured by Soviet troops in Kharkov advance.
**Burma.**—Maungdaw raided by R.A.F.
**Air.**—N. Italian cities of Milan, Genoa and Turin heavily bombed.

**AUGUST 8, Sunday** *1,436th day*
**Sicily.**—San Fratello and Sant' Agata captured by Americans ; amphibious U.S. force landed east of Cape Orlando, capturing 1,500 prisoners. Announced fall of Biancavilla to 8th Army.
**Russian Front.**—In Bryansk sector Russians captured 130 places ; advances of 8-10 m. made in Kharkov direction.

**AUGUST 9, Monday** *1,437th day*
**Sicily.**—Announced capture of Acireale by 8th Army. Fortresses pounded communications in Messina area.
**Mediterranean.**—Castellammare di Stabia in Gulf of Naples and railway bridges at Cape Vaticano (Italy) bombarded by Royal Navy.

**Air.**—Twin Rhineland towns of Mannheim-Ludwigshaven heavily attacked.

**AUGUST 10, Tuesday** *1,438th day*
**Sicily.**—Announced Bronte captured, and union made between 7th U.S. Army and 8th Army near Bronte and Cesaro. Second U.S. amphibious force landed east of Cape Orlando, establishing a bridgehead.
**Russian Front.**—In Bryansk sector, Khotinets captured by Russians.
**Air.**—Nuremberg (S. Germany) plastered with over 1,500 tons of bombs.
**General.**—Announced arrival in Canada of Mr. Churchill, Lord Leathers and British Chiefs of Staff.

**AUGUST 11, Wednesday** *1,439th day*
**Sicily.**—Announced fall of Guardia. Reported German evacuation of Sicily in progress covered by A.A. barrage.
**Russian Front.**—Soviet troops cut the Kharkov-Poltava railway line and took Akhtyrka and Krasnokutsk.
**General.**—Mr. Churchill attended a session of the Canadian War Cabinet.

**AUGUST 12, Thursday** *1,440th day*
**Russian , Front.**—In Kharkov drive Russians captured Chuguyev ; advances of 10-12 m. made in Bryansk region.
**Air.**—Gelsenkirchen (Ruhr), Wesseling

and Bonn (nr. Cologne) heavily raided by Fortresses. Milan (over 1,000 tons dropped) and Turin heavily raided. Berlin attacked by Mosquitoes.

**AUGUST 13, Friday .** *1,441st day*
**Sicily.**—U.S. troops entered Randazzo, Naso and Brolo ; announced capture of Riposto, Giarre, and Milo by 8th Army. Floresta and Piraino by Americans. U.S. warships bombarded Milazzo.
**Mediterranean.**—Rome bombed in daylight by U.S. Fortresses led by Maj.-Gen. J. H. Doolittle ; 400-500 tons of bombs dropped.
**Russian Front.**—Russians announced opening of new offensive drive against Smolensk in which Spasdemensk fell. In Briansk sector Navlya occupied.
**Australasia.**—Balikpapan (Borneo) was raided by Liberators in 2,500-mile round trip. Heaviest raid to date on Salamaua (New Guinea).
**Air.**—Wiener Neustadt works, 27 m. S. of Vienna, bombed by Liberators.

**AUGUST 14, Saturday** *1,442nd day*
**Sicily.**—Taormina taken by 8th Army.
**Italy.**—Badoglio Govt. declared Rome an open city.
**Russian Front.**—German tanks and infantry counter-attacked at Kharkov.

**Air.**—Milan target for heavy attack by Lancasters ; Breda armament works main objective. Mosquitoes bombed Berlin.
**Sea.**—Announced in three months May-July 90 U-boats destroyed and that during 1943 new shipping completed by Allies exceeded all sinkings by 3,000,000 tons.

**AUGUST 15, Sunday** *1,443rd day*
**Sicily.**—Announced occupation of Fiumefreddo, Piedimonte and Mazzara ; U.S. troops reached Oliveri.
**Russian Front.**—In Bryansk area Russians captured Karachev.
**Australasia.**—Vella Lavella (Solomons), captured.
**Air.**—Milan bombed in longest duration raid ; over 100 4,000-pounders dropped. Mosquitoes raided Berlin.
**General.**—Mr. Churchill returned to Quebec from visit to President Roosevelt.

**AUGUST 16, Monday** *1,444th day*
**Sicily.**—Announced fall of Kaggi and Castiglione ; 8th Army landed near Messina, U.S. force near Milazzo.
**Russian Front.**—In Bryansk area, Russians captured Zhizdra and Malye Luki. In Smolensk sector Tserkovshchina taken.
**Air.**—French engineering works at Denain, Le Bourget (Paris airport) and other airfields raided by Fortress, Ventura, Typhoon and Marauder bombers. Turin heavily bombed at night.

**AUGUST 17, Tuesday** *1,445th day*
**Sicily.**—Island completely conquered after 38-day campaign. Messina captured by Americans ; gun duel began across Messina Straits.
**Mediterranean.**—Istres and Salon airfields near Marseilles raided by Fortresses —first time targets in France attacked from Mediterranean bases.
**Australasia.**—Wewak (New Guinea) airfields bombed ; 120 enemy planes destroyed.
**Air.**—Schweinfurt, E. of Frankfert, and Regensburg, S. of Nuremberg, pounded by Fortresses. Peenemünde research works N.W. of Stettin blasted ; Berlin attacked by Mosquitoes.
**General.**—Revealed that H.M. the King in H.M.S. Duke of York led the Home Fleet to battle practice in the North Sea during a 4-day visit. Announced arrival of President Roosevelt at Quebec.

★ ══════ *Flash-backs* ══════ ★

### 1940
*August 4. Italians invaded Brit. Somaliland.*
*August 5. Hargeisa captured by Italians.*
*August 8. Battle of Britain opened ; 60 German aircraft down.*
*August 15. 180 German planes destroyed over Britain. First R.A.F. raid on Turin and Milan.*

### 1941
*August 7. First Soviet air raid on Berlin.*
*August 12. Six Blenheim squadrons raided Cologne by day.*

*August 14. Announced that Atlantic Charter formulated in Churchill-Roosevelt meeting aboard H.M.S. Prince of Wales and U.S. cruiser Augusta.*

### 1942.
*August 7. U.S. troops landed on Guadalcanal.*
*August 11. Aircraft carrier Eagle sunk in Mediterranean convoy action.*
*August 12. Mr. Churchill arrived in Moscow.*
*August 17. First all U.S. raid on Rouen.*

**F**OUR Years! Do they seem to have been more like forty? Or do you ask yourself, "Can it really be four years since we heard Mr. Chamberlain on Sunday, September 3, 1939, tell us we were again at war with Germany?" That is rather how I feel myself. Crowded with events as these four years have been, there seems to have been an emptiness about them when I compare them with periods of peace. War stops so many activities. It reduces us to a dead level. One day is so much like other days. I felt between 1914 and 1918 as if a slice was being cut out of my life. I haven't had that feeling this time, but, as I look back to that Sunday I have mentioned, the years appear to have slid by quickly and to have left few outstanding memories behind them. There was the night when Chamberlain announced his resignation, the week during which it became plain that France was out of it, the days that saw the magnificent evacuation from Dunkirk, the June evening when we heard that Hitler had invaded Russia, the December morning that brought the news of Pearl Harbour. But mostly the triumphs, like the Battle of London and Tunisia and Stalingrad, had been so long anticipated that their effect when they came was blunted. Now there is a wave of optimism bearing people up. Things look good certainly. But I fear the end is not yet.

**W**AR teaches us to value many benefits we take for granted at other times. Light, for example. Have you ever before set so much store by it as you do now? We used to take it as a matter of course. It was always there. It always would be there. Now we know we were wrong. We look back longingly—and forward hopefully as well—to the days when we could have all we wanted. That extra second hour of Summer Time, which we have recently had to knock off, seems a terrible deprivation. Instead of being able to do without artificial light till nearly ten, we have to black out and switch on before nine. It's no use complaining; it has to be done. But the prospect of the days shortening steadily, until we have to get up in the dark and must draw black curtains or fix screens between four and five in the evening, is not a pleasant one. As usual, Shakespeare supplies the appropriate comment:

It so falls out,
That what we have we prize not to the worth
Whiles we enjoy it; but being lack'd and lost,
Why, then we rack the value, then we find
The virtue that possession would not show us
Whiles it was ours.

We feel that about daylight; but there are vast numbers on the continent of Europe who now value freedom as they never valued it before. It seemed to them part of the natural order of their world. They would not lift a finger to safeguard it. They kept on repeating parrot-like that no one meant them any harm. Now they realize what they have lost and look to the United Nations to restore it to them.

**I** MUST say I thought some of the harsh comments on the unfortunate folk who crowded the railway stations during the early part of last month were ill-considered and unnecessary. The Minister, for instance, who remarked "they deserved all they got," showed himself unable to imagine how factory workers, toiling in grime day after day and going home to little stuffy rooms in city streets, long for the freshness and space of the countryside and the countless smiles, as the Greek poet put it, of the blue sunlit sea. I think these war workers have the hardest lot of all the millions who are putting their effort towards victory. In the Services there is always the possibility of death or wounds, but there are change of scene, adventure, robust health, and the chance of winning distinction. The need of the factory workers for holidays ought to have been foreseen and provided for. It could have been done. I heard one of the harsh critics say that holidays are a "modern craze." His grandparents "never took one in their lives." But there is no resemblance between the conditions even of sixty or seventy years ago and those of today. It was then easy to get into fields and woods. Work

**GENERAL KONSTANTIN ROKOSSOVSKY, victor of Orel. His appointment to the Kursk front three months ago was preceded by his routing of the Nazis before Moscow in December 1941, and his sensational triumph over Field-Marshal von Paulus at Stalingrad in January, 1943. He is 45.** *Photo, Pictorial Press*

was more interesting and less wearisome. Most workers made "things," not bits of things. Now a little regular relaxation is essential to a contented life.

**I**N these times it is easier than at others to distinguish between people who know how to behave and those who don't. Especially in shops. At other times all who serve in them have to be polite. They would lose custom or get the sack if they were not. Now the positions are reversed. The customer has to ingratiate himself, even to fawn and flatter sometimes. The sales-people have the upper hand. Many still bear themselves courteously and kindly, but some do the opposite. They seem to take delight in saying they have not got what you want, and even laugh at you for expecting to find it. They refuse haughtily to let you have what is concealed under the counter. I don't fancy they will be very popular when things are normal again. These are, however, only a small number. On the whole, British people manage wonderfully well to keep their tempers sweet as well as their upper lips stiff.

In Germany appeals have been made for a long time past for less irritability, less rudeness in public. Goebbels has begged them to show a stronger spirit of comradeship. But when one is afraid one is always nervy and perturbed. And the Germans have been afraid for at least two years now. A Polish prisoner of war who escaped and got to America reports that in the summer of 1941 they were saying, "It must be over soon. Another year of this would be impossible." What must they be saying now?

**I** HAVE often been asked the origin of the expression "browned off," which was heard so constantly among soldiers and R.A.F. men during the first two years of war. Into every article about them it was introduced. What did it mean? In a little book on R.A.F. slang (It's a Piece of Cake, by Squadron-Ldr. Ward-Jackson, published by Sylvan Press, 2s.) I find the statement that "it has been used in the Service for at least 25 years," and that its origin is "problematical." I suppose that means it started among airmen. Another booklet on Service Slang generally (compiled by J. L. Hunt and A. G. Pringle, published by Faber & Faber, 2s. 6d.) says "it has long been the approved answer to any inquiry as to one's health," and treats it as being common to the Services generally. As a verb active it can be used in such a sentence as "The sergeant-major browned him off proper"; but to be "browned off" is usually to be "fed up," or bored with something or somebody. The metaphor is said to be taken from cooking. This sounds more likely than the suggestion that it refers to "the notable lobster-tan which all soldiers, sailors and airmen seem to acquire."

**A**NOTHER term of mysterious origin is "to prang." This, I gathered from the conversation of pilots, meant, as the R.A.F. book says, "to damage, destroy or wreck." Hamburg was badly "pranged." But the other book defines "prang" as being used when a pilot crashes or smashes his plane. It is apparently a sound-word, expressing the sort of noise that metal aircraft make when they hit the ground too hard. Then it extended to enemy targets. "It's a piece of cake" explains itself—to anyone who likes cake. "In a spot" is clearly abbreviated from "spot of bother." An aircraft is a "kite"; bombs are "groceries" to be delivered; an R.A.F. officer is a "gussie"; a perfect landing on an airfield is a "daisy-cutter." If you make a forced landing in the sea, you fall into "the drink"; barrage balloons are known as "pigs"; "scran" and "rum" in the Navy signify "good" and "bad." The naval expression which means "quite correct" is given as "tiggerty-boo;" it more often has the sound of "tickety-boo;" it comes from a Hindustani word. Service Slang ignores it. Was "wangle" originally an Army word? It is a perfect example of meaning expressed by sound. Not many new words or phrases have come out of this war. Probably this is accounted for by things being taken more seriously, grimly even, than they were last time. You have to be light-hearted to invent slang.

A reminder may be given here that previous references have been made, at some length, to this subject of Service terms and slang in page 95 of this volume of THE WAR ILLUSTRATED and in page 767, volume Six.

# Our 'Desert Rats' Capture Sicilian Railway

**MEN OF THE '8th ARMY** are here charging across a railway cutting in Sicily to join in the attack on an enemy-held station. Just one striking example of several ways in which our veterans of N. African desert fighting adapted themselves to quite different conditions entailed by Sicilian terrain. How the station was taken at the bayonet point is shown in other photographs in p. 196. *Photo, British Official*

Printed in England and published every alternate Friday by the Proprietors, THE AMALGAMATED PRESS, LTD., The Fleetway House, Farringdon Street, London, E.C.4. Registered for transmission by Canadian Magazine Post. Sole Agents for Australia and New Zealand : Messrs. Gordon & Gotch, Ltd. ; and for South Africa : Central News Agency, Ltd.—September 3, 1943. S.S. *Editorial Address :* JOHN CARPENTER HOUSE. WHITEFRIARS, LONDON, E.C.4.

Vol 7    *The War Illustrated*    Nº 163

*Edited by Sir John Hammerton*

SIXPENCE                                                      SEPTEMBER 17. 1943.

**HE KNOCKED OUT THE LUFTWAFFE IN THE MEDITERRANEAN**—Air Marshal Sir Arthur Coningham, commander of the North-West African Tactical Air Force, here indicating targets on a map during a Press conference in Sicily. Main contribution of his men to our triumph there was the pounding of the island's airfields in June and early July and methodical destruction of the Axis air fleet. Up to August 12 a total of 1,691 enemy aircraft had been shot down or captured on the ground in Sicily.

*Photo, British Official*

**NO. 164 WILL BE PUBLISHED FRIDAY, OCTOBER 1**

# Into War's Background With Our Roving Camera

Capt. MARION ROSS, of Toronto, first woman to be commissioned in the Canadian Army as a Medical Officer. With a contingent of Sister Nurses attached to the Royal Canadian Army Medical Corps she accompanied the Dominion's Sicily-bound troops to the Middle East. A bacteriologist, she joined the R.C.A.M.C. in November 1942.

ROYAL MARINE BERET, replacing the field service cap for all ranks except certain specialists, is of navy blue with a scarlet patch behind the regiment's famous Globe and Laurel badge. The beret will not displace the blue peaked cap with scarlet band worn with the blue service dress—the traditional Marine uniform. (See also article in p. 174.)

ONE OF 800 VOLUNTEERS who work for 10 hours on a Sunday in 38 L.M.S. Railway depots cleaning engines, polishing wheels, oiling, and doing other maintenance jobs for which man-power is in short supply, Mrs. Williamson needs no assurance from anyone of the importance of her part time war work.

Photos, British Official: Crown Copyright; Canadian Official, Daily Mirror, Topical Press.

BASKETS FOR PIGEONS (left) is the war effort of 80-year-old Harry Dallaway, of Herne Bay, Kent, who has followed the craft of basket-making for 60 years. Carrier pigeons taken on bombing raids are confined in baskets such as these until released for emergency message-carrying to the base. (See also pp. 122 and 686, Vol. 6.)

BEATING RETREAT in Hyde Park—a thrilling spectacle provided for home-holidaying Londoners on August 24, 1943, by massed drums and fifes of the Grenadier, Coldstream, Irish and Welsh Guards, together with pipers of the Irish Guards. This ancient ceremony, normally performed at sundown, has nothing to do with retirement from battle. It indicates, for the troops whose band is playing, that general activities are over for the day, and in peacetime it is part of the ordinary routine.

# THE BATTLE FRONTS

## by Maj.-Gen. Sir Charles Gwynn, K.C.B., D.S.O.

ALTHOUGH it is now generally understood why the Germans were able to carry out the Messina evacuation with a considerable measure of success, there is still some feeling of disappointment that the bag was not complete. That, I think, is because many people expected that our greatly superior air power would be able to make evacuation of any considerable force, and heavy equipment in particular, impracticable.

Previous experience did not, in fact, warrant that expectation, and it may therefore be of interest to analyze the conditions which make for successful evacuations or which, conversely, render them impracticable, and to recall the strikingly numerous precedents which may be studied.

The primary essential for successful evacuation is, of course, that the sea passage can be made in reasonable safety. That postulates, in the case of passages too long to be made under cover of darkness, control of sea communications in the vital area. Where passages are short, control may, however, be effected by air cover or, as at Messina, by coastal batteries keeping the enemy's surface warships at a distance. At the worst, fast craft may be able to evade the enemy and escape by night.

Time and opportunities to assemble the necessary sea transport are important factors affecting the sea passage, and where it is over long distances, necessitating the use of comparatively large vessels, the difficulties in this respect are greatly increased. Moreover, large vessels afford good targets to the enemy aircraft. The shortness of the passage is on all counts, therefore, obviously of vital importance where control of sea communications is not assured by naval and air strength.

Air protection of points of embarkation and disembarkation and during passage presents special difficulties. The force embarking can never have air bases within its final bridgehead, and to maintain an adequate flak cover entails almost certainly the abandonment of a large amount of heavy equipment. The situation is, of course, immensely eased when the sea passage is so short that fighter aircraft can operate from the disembarkation side, and more so where, as at Messina, flak cover can be provided from both sides.

YET even when such protection was not available air power in great superiority has proved incapable of preventing evacuation, though it has caused very heavy losses. This is probably due to the fact that air attack is bound to a great extent to be intermittent and that at night it lacks precision. Actually, when naval conditions render evacuation at all practicable, the only decisive way of preventing it being carried through is by land attack.

Wherever rearguards have held out, evacuation has been carried through with a considerable measure of success, in spite of air attacks. Where land protection fails the result is decisive, especially if armour effects a rapid break-through. When it is possible

to maintain secrecy evacuation may be, as at Gallipoli, completely successful. Even if the intention to evacuate can for a time be concealed much may be saved.

Secrecy at Gallipoli was surprisingly maintained, in spite of the close observation the enemy had over embarkation beaches; and Kiska has now proved that secrecy, in spite of air reconnaissance, may under certain circumstances still be achieved. Even at Messina there is little doubt that the enemy had withdrawn a large part of his equipment and part of his personnel before his intention to evacuate was fully revealed. Secrecy in the critical final disengagement of rearguards is quite possible to attain unless the enemy is prepared and able to break down all rearguard resistance with a violent attack.

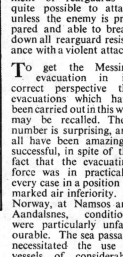

**RUSSIAN FRONT, August 27, 1943. Kharkov fallen, the Russians thrust towards Kiev and Poltava, with no hint of a threat to Taganrog, which fell three days later.**
*By courtesy of The Daily Telegraph*

To get the Messina evacuation in its correct perspective the evacuations which have been carried out in this war may be recalled. Their number is surprising, and all have been amazingly successful, in spite of the fact that the evacuating force was in practically every case in a position of marked air inferiority. In Norway, at Namsos and Aandalsnes, conditions were particularly unfavourable. The sea passage necessitated the use of vessels of considerable tonnage which took time to load and presented good targets to an air force enjoying complete superiority.

Anti-aircraft defence was mainly what could be provided by warships, themselves targets for attack. Yet the enemy's air efforts, though very damaging, were indecisive. Fortunately, the Germans had not sufficient strength on land to break through our ill-

**NEW BRITISH 4·2-in. MORTAR in action near Adrano, Sicily, where it proved as useful as in Tunisia. The 4·2-in. throws a 2-lb. bomb 400 yards, reaching a height of 4,000 ft. at the peak of its trajectory.** *Photo, British Official*

**GENERAL KONIEV, one of the victorious Soviet triumvirate of generals who recaptured Kharkov on August 23, 1943, reading of the progress of the campaign from a tape-machine at his H.Q.** *Photo, Pictorial Press*

equipped and exhausted rearguards. For that, no doubt, we owe a debt to Norwegian troops, who helped keep the enemy at bay.

Then came Dunkirk, a miracle of naval improvisation. Fortunately, distances allowed all sorts of craft to be employed on the sea passage and aircraft based on England to afford a degree of cover. Essentially, however, it was a race against the time our extensive and weak bridgehead position could hold back the German Army. Somaliland was another case in which everything depended on rearguards, and the air factor was of little importance. Greece and Crete, again, found the enemy with absolute air supremacy; yet the Navy, accepting immense risks and suffering heavy losses, got the Army away. It was a desperate race against time, won before the enemy's army could deliver a decisive blow.

IT should be remembered too, that in Russia the garrisons of Odessa, Sebastopol and Kerch were successfully evacuated by the combined action of Russian rearguards and naval forces, in spite of the enemy's great air superiority. During the siege of Tobruk, although the port was subjected to constant air attack, the relief of a division was successfully accomplished. In all these cases it should be noted that success depended on control of sea communications and the protection afforded by rearguards, and that the enemy's air supremacy failed to give decisive results.

At Hong Kong, Singapore, on the second occasion at Tobruk, in Tunisia, at Pantelleria and in the Pacific islands, no attempt at evacuation was made.

Now to compare the situation at Messina with these previous experiences. The shortness of the distance across the Straits enabled the passage to be covered by coastal batteries assisted by an admittedly inferior air force. That practically eliminated the possibility of decisive naval interference such as the naval blockade of Tunisia established.

The terrain presented the enemy with special opportunities of holding up the attacking army with mines and demolition. A rapid and decisive break-through by armour such as sealed the fate of the German Army in Tunisia, therefore, was impracticable.

Under these circumstances practically the whole responsibility for preventing the evacuation was thrown on the Allied air forces, and the conditions were exceptionally unfavourable. The enemy, owing to the shortness of the crossing, could make the fullest use of the cover of darkness, could use craft which took a minimum time to load and discharge, and which presented tiny targets.

# When the Axis in Sicily Was Nearing Its End

**ON THE LAST LAP** of the 39 days' campaign which freed Sicily, Pte. Stanley Davies, of Bramley, Leeds (1), is seen with one of many useful packmules captured from the enemy by the 51st (Highland) Division in the 8th Army's advance on Biancavilla ; note the swastika branded on the mule's neck. Under the walls of the Cathedral at Randazzo lies the wreckage of enemy transport (2) which fell victim to our accurate road-strafing. British 25-pounders in action (3) near Zafferana.

*Photos, British Official : Crown Copyright*

# Old Order and New Spirit in Sicily's Messina

THE MAN RESPONSIBLE for the horror which overtook Messina was lauded in slogans such as this one overlooking the battle-scarred streets (1), but a citizen's open-armed welcome of the Allied liberators (3) expressed the change of heart of the many, some of whom emerge with tremendous relief from their tunnel-shelter (4) knowing their long nightmare to be ended. Lieut.-Gen. Patton, commander of the American 7th Army, rode into the captured town on August 17, 1943 (2).

*Photos, British Official ; U.S. Official*

FLAGSHIP OF THE DANISH NAVY, the 3,800-ton Niels Iuel, followed by her sister vessel, the 3,500-ton coastal defence ship Peder Skram. While trying to escape to Sweden on August 29, 1943, after the Germans had taken over the government of Denmark, the flagship, which mounted 36 guns and two torpedo tubes, was scuttled by her captain, Carl Westermann, in Helsingoer (Elsinore) harbour. The Peder Skram was one of 20 Danish war vessels which were also scuttled in Copenhagen harbour before the Nazis could seize them—two new destroyers, four torpedo boats, nine submarines, and minesweepers and smaller craft.                *Photo, Pictorial Press—Exclusive to* THE WAR ILLUSTRATED

# THE WAR AT SEA

## by Francis E. McMurtrie

FROM the appointment of Vice-Admiral Lord Louis Mountbatten to be Supreme Allied Commander, South-East Asia, for charge of operations based on India and Ceylon against Japan, it is evident that greater activity in that quarter may be looked for within the next few months. It is not generally realized that Lord Louis, in addition to being a fine leader, is also an extremely astute planner, who leaves nothing to chance if it can be avoided. As Chief of Combined Operations, he has proved his worth ; and the new appointment should give further scope for his abilities.

Up to now the only operations against the Japanese in this area have been purely local ones, designed to drive the enemy out of Akyab. Their failure should have taught some valuable lessons for the future campaign.

One of the handicaps from which our Eastern Fleet is undoubtedly suffering is lack of good bases within reach of enemy-occupied territories. Colombo has no dock able to take anything bigger than a cruiser, while Trincomalee possesses few resources beyond its excellent natural harbour. The Japanese seizure of Singapore deprived us of our finest base in the East. Moreover, the enemy has taken care to occupy the Andaman and Nicobar Islands, in the Bay of Bengal, which possess more than one good harbour capable of being converted into a naval base.

To drive the Japanese out of Burma, Siam, Malaya, and the Dutch Indies is going to be a long and arduous task, which will need careful planning. Before an effective blow can be struck, the enemy defences must be studied and possible weak spots investigated. Every available item of information concerning climate, natural resources, and transport facilities has to be accumulated and subjected to careful examination before any decision is reached on the plan of campaign. As the approach has to be made by sea, the problem in the first instance is a naval one, involving the passage of the attacking armies to the most suitable landing place.

Our Eastern Fleet under the command of Admiral Sir James Somerville is believed to have been reinforced of late. Its strength must depend upon that of the forces which it may be expected to meet. Here there is

scope for speculation, since it is uncertain whether the Japanese will be willing to gamble any considerable proportion of their naval force on the defence of outlying conquests. Most probably they will endeavour to keep their main fleet intact, unless and until Japan proper is threatened by the gathering strength of the Allied attack.

After allowing for losses, Japan has probably still at her disposal ten or twelve battleships, at least two of which are large new units of over 40,000 tons. In aircraft carriers, strength has been seriously affected by the losses at Midway Island ; but there may be as many as four fleet carriers available if the work of replacing sunken ships has gone ahead as rapidly as might be expected.

### JAPANESE Cruiser and Destroyer Losses Assessed

Cruiser strength is in dispute, for though U.S. Navy and Army claims at their maximum would account for almost every Japanese ship in this category, it has been suggested by American writers that there has been too much optimism about these claims. One correspondent has assessed Japanese cruiser losses at anything from 15 to 25 ships, the lower figure being the more likely. It would therefore seem reasonable to assume that Japan can still dispose of between 20 and 30 cruisers.

In destroyers the position is somewhat similar, but after allowing for a reasonable proportion of the losses claimed and adding something for new construction, it is probable that Japan can muster fully 80 or 90 destroyers. In submarines her losses are not believed to be heavy, and have probably been replaced in full ; a total of 70 or more seems a reasonable estimate, midget submarines being excluded.

From these forces the Japanese might allot a squadron comprising say four battleships, two aircraft carriers, a dozen cruisers, and appropriate numbers of destroyers and submarines to oppose any Allied assault from the Indian Ocean. Seaplane carriers may also be employed to economize in the use of fully-equipped aircraft carriers, following the practice adopted in the past.

This would still leave the enemy with quite

a formidable fleet for defence in the Pacific, while the mobility of modern warships would always enable the Indian Ocean contingent to be withdrawn to reinforce it if required, provided action on terms likely to endanger its survival were avoided. It may be argued that such cautious strategy scarcely accords with Japanese methods in 1941-42 ; but it has to be remembered that today our Eastern opponents are no longer in a position to launch a big offensive, and must content themselves with trying to hold what they have already taken.

Undoubtedly the possession of Singapore confers considerable advantage on its holders. From this point it is possible to strike at Allied sea forces either through the Straits of Malacca or the Strait of Sunda, while any approach it may be sought to make to Singapore by sea is likely to be detected long before it gets near. Indeed, it is questionable if it will be possible to attack Singapore at all from the southward or westward until the islands of Java and Sumatra have been reconquered.

It would seem preferable to follow the same course as the Japanese did in 1941, and retake Malaya first. Singapore would then be open to attack from the north, across the Johore Strait, and, failing superiority at sea, it is difficult to see how Japan could retain the base for any length of time.

IT may be assumed that any attack launched from India and Ceylon would synchronize with other Allied attacks from the direction of Australia on the Dutch Indies, and from the Solomons on Japanese positions in the Caroline and Mariana Islands. With the enormous growth of the British and United States Navies during recent months, sufficient cover should be available for expeditions against outlying islands, enabling a gradual but methodical approach to be made to the seas surrounding Japan itself.

Then, and only then, is it likely that Japanese naval strength will be concentrated in a supreme effort to win a sea victory and so save the situation. Though the issue of such a conflict can scarcely be in doubt, the enemy may be relied on to fight hard.

Such immense distances separate the various islands which are in Japanese hands that all this will inevitably be a lengthy process. To seek to hasten it unduly would be to risk a set-back which might prolong the struggle unnecessarily. Experience has already demonstrated, in the Solomons more particularly, the best method of dealing with Japanese armed forces.

# Floating 'Pillboxes' Escort Our Armadas Now

**MECHANIZED LANDING CRAFT** are the carriers of modern assault troops, whether it be on a Commando raid or full-scale invasion, such as Sicily, where they did great service in ferrying and landing men, armour and supplies. Some of these craft at exercise "in line ahead" (1) are escorted by their landing-craft support ships (marked L.C.S.) and protected by indispensable air cover (3). L.C.S. vessels are floating pillboxes (2), equipped with five machine-guns, Lewis gun and mortar.

*Photos, News Chronicle, Fox*

# 'Decisions are Taken for the Forward Action—

QUEBEC CONFERENCE, AUGUST 1943.
At Hotel Frontenac (1): (front left) Lord Louis Mountbatten, Chief of Combined Operations ; Adm. of the Fleet Sir D. Pound, Chief of Naval Staff ; Gen. Sir A. Brooke, Chief of Imp. Gen. Staff ; Air Chief-Marshal Sir C. Portal, Chief of Air Staff ; Lt.-Gen. Sir H. Ismay, Chief of Staff to Min. of Defence ; Air Marshal L. S. Breadner, Canadian Chief of Air Staff (just visible) ; Vice-Adm. Percy Nelles, Canadian Chief of Naval Staff; Lt.-Gen. R. Stuart, Canadian Army Chief of Staff.

Earl of Athlone and Mr. Mackenzie King watch Mr. Eden greet Mr. Roosevelt (2). Canadian Mounted Police on duty (3) when Mr. Churchill arrived at Quebec ; crowds cheering him (4) on his way there.

*Photos, British Official! ; Keystone*

# —Of Our Two Fleets, Armies and Air Forces'

**FOURTH CHURCHILL-ROOSEVELT CONFERENCE** since America entered the war ended on August 24, 1943 with the inspiring announcement : " The necessary decisions have been taken to provide for the forward action of the fleets, armies and air forces of the two nations." Conference had for its setting the historic Citadel of Quebec, on the terrace of which are Prime Minister and President, with Mr. Mackenzie King, Premier of Canada (extreme left) ; Earl of Athlone, Governor-General of Canada : and Countess of Athlone.

*Photo, British Official*

# The Coastal Eyes of Britain Never Close

Every yard of our 6,000-mile coastline is under the surveillance of sentinels of the Coastguard Service, founded over 100 years ago with the suppression of smuggling as its primary duty. As revealed here by JOHN ALLEN GRAYDON, in an interview with Capt. Vernon Rashleigh, Chief Inspector of Coastguards, the war has brought these men many new and important tasks.

"WITH the enemy sending over hit-and-run raiders Coastguards, who rarely take their eyes off the sea, are often able to give warning as aircraft sweep towards the coast, just above the waves"—hoping to avoid our radiolocation—"and have on several occasions passed on information, through the Royal Observer Corps, which has resulted in the destruction of the raider," Captain Vernon Rashleigh, C.B.E., R.N., Chief Inspector of Coastguards, told me when I recently talked with him in his office at the Ministry of War Transport.

"Not so very long ago," he continued, "one Coastguard, having seen an enemy machine heading for the coast, hurried into his look-out hut and seized the telephone to the Observer Corps. As he was phoning the German plane machine-gunned the Coastguard look-out. So he dived beneath the table, taking the telephone with him, and there completed his report. I know you rarely hear of the work of the Coastguard Service, but I assure you there is not a yard of our 6,000-mile coastline the approaches to which are not under constant watch."

THE tasks carried out by the Coastguards are many and varied. Today they are more than six times stronger than at the outbreak of war, and they work in close cooperation with the Royal Navy, the Army and the Royal Air Force. When invasion closely threatened this country the Coastguards, who carried arms, never ceased their vigilance ; and now, though the threat of invasion has receded, they are taking no chances.

In the course of my duties as a war correspondent, I have made extensive travels around Britain and had opportunities of seeing these Coastguards at work. Having a great interest in the Dover area—which I named "Hellfire Corner" during the Battle of Britain—I asked Captain Rashleigh which, in his opinion, was the busiest locality. "It's not hard to answer that," he said. "Those stations on the East and South-East coast, closest to the enemy shores, have probably seen as much action as any others in the country."

The Coastguards know every danger to shipping around the coast of the United Kingdom, and are ready, day and night, to bring aid to a stranded vessel or plane forced down into the sea. These khaki-clad sentinels, to be successful at their job, must possess keen powers of observation, initiative and resource, and the ability to size up a situation rapidly. In addition, the Coastguardsman must be something of a detective. At least, I gathered that these qualifications were necessary for success when I heard a few stories of the deeds of these men.

"ALTHOUGH the Coastguard Service was formed over a hundred years ago for the purpose of running smugglers to earth, this is no longer one of our duties," Captain Rashleigh told me. "Our principal peacetime duty, although not by any means the only one, is the provision of a watch on the coast for the safeguard of shipping. The war, so far from diminishing our duties, has added many new ones, which, for security reasons, I cannot disclose.

"One which can be mentioned, however, is that of watching for enemy minelayers. As you know, the Germans use aircraft in large numbers for this purpose. The Coastguard, in conjunction with other Services, plot the positions in which mines are laid, and report to the nearest Naval authority.

"I know one Coastguard who for several weeks used to watch a German plane dive low and drop its mines—a cargo worth anything up to £500. Not a shot was fired by either the anti-aircraft guns in the district or by fighter planes. They just allowed the German to waste his precious mines while the Coastguards marked on a map the spot mined. Next morning the sea-lanes were again swept successfully ! This went on for some considerable time, until the enemy machine was one afternoon surprised and shot down into the sea," Capt. Rashleigh went on. "Our men can be relied upon to spot the majority of planes that crash into the sea within telescopic range, and by a close understanding with the Air-Sea Rescue Service have helped to save many airmen."

I asked Captain Rashleigh if there were many veterans among the men of the Coastguards. "Yes," he answered, "quite a number of men have returned from retirement

OLD AND THE NEW. Coastguards now wear battledress in place of the peacetime "navy cut," and on duty a steel helmet replaces the peaked cap (see photograph below).
*Photo, Sport & General*

to play a part in the war. I know one old fellow of seventy-two who still rides on horseback three miles to and from his station every day. He's as keen as any youngster.

"Our Coastguards, when patrolling the various beaches, often make some very interesting discoveries," he continued. "It should not be forgotten that the contents of the pockets of a dead German airman or sailor, washed ashore, can sometimes provide interesting information about the enemy. But then, as I told you earlier, the Coastguards have so many jobs."

I THINK one of the best stories of the Coastguard Service is connected with the steam trawler Nordale when she ran ashore in Scotland. The local Life-Saving Rocket Company, under very difficult conditions, landed seven of the trawler's crew and hauled them over a ridge 850 feet above sea-level to safety. They were then conveyed by a farmcart, through a blinding storm, to a shepherd's cottage, where they were given warmth and refreshment. Most of the rescuers gave the seamen some of their own clothing, and every man of those rescued lived to put to sea again.

In the past year life-saving appliances were in action at various parts of the coast on 56 occasions, and 458 lives were saved by these means. On 700 occasions life-saving action has been taken to assist vessels or aircraft in distress. It can be said that the "Eyes of Britain" never close, for, to quote Captain Rashleigh : "Whatever takes place off the shores of this island interests the Coastguard Service." When the full story of its work can be told, the public will learn to what a tremendous extent this Service is assisting in the national effort.

INTERNATIONAL SIGNALS is the subject of the lecture to which these Coastguards are listening. The lecturer, Mr. R. J. Green, made the models in his spare time. Wartime work of the Coastguards—now under an Order in Council, ranking as members of the Armed Forces—is described above.

*Photo, Keystone*

# Self-Inflating Dinghy Is Airmen's Life-Saver

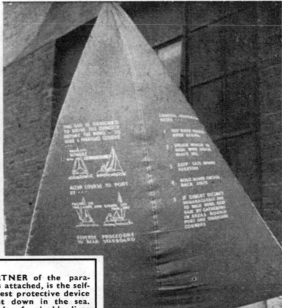

LIFE-SAVING PARTNER of the parachute, to which it is attached, is the self-inflating dinghy, latest protective device for airmen brought down in the sea. Typical of thousands of valuable lives saved by these dinghies are those of the Flying Fortress crew (6 and 7) who kept afloat in the North Sea until an Air Sea Rescue plane could drop them a lifeboat equipped with an engine and borne by three parachutes.

Behind such a rescue are much ingenious designing and brilliant factory work : cutting out the parts in several thicknesses (1), testing the inflation of the buoyancy chamber (2) and final checking of the finished dinghies (4).

The sail, with its clearly imprinted and very simple instructions for use (3), and the hood with apron attached to give protection from weather and sea (5), are further evidence of painstaking planning.

Deflated, the complete dinghy goes into a small canvas bag fitted beneath the parachute harness. The airman normally sits on it, and in emergency pulls a rip-cord, similar to that of his 'chute, thus opening a cylinder of compressed air inside the dinghy; this bursts the canvas bag and inflates the dinghy, which takes shape automatically and rests on the sea awaiting the dropping airman.

*Photos, British Official ; Pictorial Press.*

# R.A.F. Is Loosening the Axis Grip on Greece

**GREECE GETS A SHARE** of the Allied air offensive on Europe, now surpassing anything the Nazis dreamed of. Preveza, enemy seaplane base on the west coast of Greece, had a visit from R.A.F. Wellingtons and Beaufighters on August 12, 1943; there is much smoke from the base and enemy planes are on fire (1), while fate is approaching this moored Italian Cant Z501 flying-boat (4) about to be attacked by Beaufighters.

To a famous Middle East fighter squadron was allotted the job of destroying by bomb and cannon an important bridge across the River Alpheios, near Pyrgos: smoke obscures the result (2).

Enemy shipping in the canal between Levkas and Acarnania is a target for Beaufighters (3).

The four months' air blockade of the Aegean and Ionian Seas has practically stopped Axis shipping plying between Italy and Greece.

*Photos, British Official : Crown Copyright*

# These Boys Gave Berlin Its Fiercest Battering

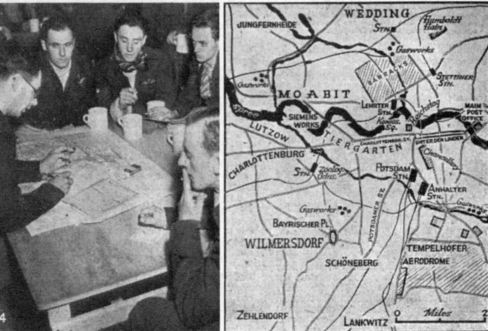

**HEAVIEST R.A.F. RAID** on Berlin was carried out on the night of August 23-24, 1943, at a cost of 58 bombers out of a fleet of some 700—highest price Bomber Command has ever paid for an assault on the Nazi war machine. Late reports indicate that about one tenth of the German capital's area was severely damaged.

R.A.F. men detailed to participate in this epic raid hear a few last words from their commander before setting out (1). Some of their machines—Stirlings—are silhouetted against the darkening sky as they take off (2). The 1,200-mile trip completed, air-crews report (4) on their achievements over the target shown on the map (right). Heaviest damage was inflicted in the Charlottenburg and Wilmersdorf districts.

Berliners, who had been fearing such a visitation, are hastily evacuating (3).

*Map by courtesy of The Daily Telegraph; Photos, British Official; Fox, Planet News*

# Railways Are Vital in Our Invasion Schemes

Swift transport by railway will be to us a matter of supreme importance when we invade the mainland of Europe. Why, then, are we battering Axis rail communications? The answer is supplied by DONALD COWIE, who explains also why an efficient "steel road" is regarded almost as a trump card by commanders in the field.

SOME folk may have been puzzled by our perpetual bombing of European railways, by preparations to send British and American rolling-stock to Europe, by references to the inadequacy of rail facilities. Aren't modern armies mechanized and independent of fixed lines of communication, they ask?

Consider these facts. To move a modern infantry division by road 4,165 three-ton lorries are required; 1,216 trucks will do the same job by rail. One steam locomotive will haul as much as 66 petrol engines could pull. Much less fuel is required for rail transport per ton of freight. It might be difficult to believe, but railways are less susceptible to bombing than roads: such has been the experience so far in this war. Damaged portions of the permanent way can be quickly repaired with sectional parts, whereas great craters in and around roads

every truck. With throttle wide open the train tore past the dangerous area and did not stop till safety was reached at an unoccupied Channel port. The Canadians said afterwards that they were more scared of missing the points or colliding with another train than of German shells and bullets.

THREE years later the incident was repeated in S. Tunisia. But this was a more daring exploit. An American officer heard there were a number of locomotives and wagons in Gafsa, then occupied by Rommel. He took a few men and a truck, dashed past enemy patrols to Gafsa Station, hooked-up thirteen locomotives and a good many wagons, and steamed back to safety with them! During this return journey the train continually ran the gauntlet of Germans with guns; once some tanks fired on the racing procession at close range. But a railway train was again shown to be a tough moving target.

single line crossing the border from Bône to La Calle, and after that only road—hundreds of miles of bad road. The Germans could convey their troops and heavy material swiftly to the various fronts on smooth lines. We had to accumulate supplies painfully, each convoy a long-distance expedition.

Nevertheless, that campaign followed the railways to the end. Will our men ever forget the fighting which swept up and down the north coast-line, beginning at Tabarka and passing through Tamera and Sejenane to Mateur? The Eighth Army came up another railway via Gabes, Sfax and Sousse to Enfidaville. Of 1,200 miles of track in Tunisia some 800 miles was held by Von Arnim to the last, 200 miles was our meagre portion, and the other 200 was in no man's land.

YET such is the ease with which railways can be repaired that within periods varying from two hours to ten days all the Axis and no man's land lines were restored to full working order by our engineers after the victory. Observers described the repair work as similar to Meccano construction. All the spare parts had been brought forward in readiness and just had to be bolted together; 350 freight wagons and 64 locomotives had been imported from the United States, 50 wagons and six locomotives from Britain, to make up for rolling-stock held by the Germans that we had very accurately bombed.

## Vital Strategic Arteries.

A study of the Russian war map will reveal how both German and Russian strategy has consistently followed the railways since the beginning of the struggle. The recent German offensive was aimed primarily at Kursk, one of the most important railway junctions between Moscow and Kharkov. Orel is another Clapham Junction of those parts, also Bryansk and Byelgorod, and nearly all the familiar names.

Follow the war East and you will find that the most important feature of Persia today is a railway whereby British locomotives and British engineers enable supplies to reach Russia via the Persian Gulf and the Caspian Sea. The Indian line from Calcutta to Sadiya in remote Assam right up against the Himalayas and near China is now one of the most vital strategic arteries in the world. A tenuous line across the dead heart of Australia from the populated parts to Darwin enables the defenders of Northern Territory to maintain their defences.

WHEN it is realized that Army Movement Control was running 1,000 special trains a month to the South Coast prior to Dunkirk, and 2,000 during that disaster (one every ten minutes from Dover), some idea will be obtained of the extent of tomorrow's traffic—when the Army proceeds towards France again. For ambulance purposes alone several hundred passenger trains have already been converted. Scores of locomotives stand ready, possibly to replace on French railways those that our fighter pilots have been shooting up so assiduously during the last three years. We are on our way to smashing the railway system of north-western Europe, causing the Germans much confusion; but we must be ready tomorrow to effect a speedy restoration, or be stuck ourselves.

LEASE-LEND LOCOMOTIVE on a British railway : one of a large number that have reached us from U.S.A. It is specially intended for use on the Continental lines when we land our armies in Nazi-held Europe. The tremendous importance of efficient rail facilities in connexion with military operations is explained in this page.

*Photo, Keystone*

sometimes take a long while to fill, especially in bad weather.

It is as fallacious to think that modern armies can do without railways as to believe that the modern infantryman never has to perform long marches. Each major campaign so far has—partly at least—been a battle for rail communications, and lines and stations have often attracted the fiercest fighting. Battle of France accounts gave us the impression that tank columns on roads won the day; they certainly struck the decisive blows, but hundreds of German tanks were brought forward by railway, and the campaign followed the principal French lines, even to Dunkirk, Calais and Abbeville.

THIS is the sort of thing that often happened. A body of Canadians journeyed halfway across France in a commandeered train, hoping to take part in the fight. They stopped at one station, to discover that the town was surrounded by Germans. The French driver refused to make a dash through the cordon, so the Canadians restarted the locomotive themselves. A rifle was poked out of every window in readiness, and A.A. guns pointed skywards from the tender and

Why could Wavell mount that amazing Libyan offensive in 1940? The answer is that he had rail communications with Alexandria and Cairo leading right up to his starting-point at Mersa Matruh. The Italians, who had neglected to construct a railway through Cyrenaica, could never bring heavy supplies forward so quickly. Afterwards, the Libyan campaigns always came back to that all-important tentacle of desert railway. Alamein was one of the final railway stations before the Nile Valley, and the stand and the battle there were conditioned by the presence of the steel road. (See illus. p. 16 and p. 101, Vol. 6.)

Then the advance to Tripoli was greatly assisted by an extension of that Libyan line across the 200 miles from Mersa Matruh to Tobruk. (See illus. p. 713, Vol. 5.) But the Tunisian campaign nearly foundered on the railway problem.

Study a railway map of North Africa and you will see why Von Arnim could hold us at bay for so long. From Bizerta and Tunis he had several good lines running to such places as Mateur, Medjez-el-Bab and Pont du Fahs—and there petering out. We had a

It will be seen, therefore, that railways do remain one of the most important transport factors in modern war. Motor transport is an indispensable auxiliary—but no more than an auxiliary as yet.

## *Sicilian Mountain Stronghold Stormed*

The steep, rocky slopes of picturesque Centuripe were desperately defended by Axis troops, and the struggle for this town at the top of a mountain was waged furiously for days. It was finally taken by assault on August 5, 1943 by men of the 78th Division—Royal Inniskilling Fusiliers and the London Irish, who had learned their mountain fighting in Tunisia and perfected their street fighting in Centuripe. Above, Bren carriers are taking supplies into the captured town.

239

## From Sferro Station to Triumph in Catania

Commanding an important crossroad leading to Catania, Sferro was shelled by Allied artillery before our troops marched in; two 8th Army men are patrolling the battered railway station (1). Catania itself fell on August 5; Sherman tanks are passing through the Via Garibaldi (2), while farther down the same thoroughfare an infantry patrol negotiates welcoming crowds (4), some of whom, carrying bundles of personal belongings, are once again returning to their homes.

## *No Fear of the British in Their Hearts*

Happy Sicilian youngsters swarmed unchecked over 8th Army tanks (3) in Catania's crowded streets, delighted with the free and novel entertainment and the cheery good humour of British tank-crews. Every gun team that entered the town, now freed of Nazi and Fascist taint, was greeted with hand-clapping and cheers from onlookers (5) overjoyed at the appearance of their liberators—conquerors of the last great Nazi stronghold on the east coast road to Messina.

# *Hot on the Heels of the Enemy*

Photos, British Official:
Crown Copyright

On August 5 British troops passed through the town of Misterbianco (top left), beyond Catania, in pursuit of the retreating enemy ; Sicilians who knew where German mines had been placed to delay the 8th Army's progress revealed the presence of these death-traps and watched—and admired—whilst our men skilfully removed them (top right). Inniskilling Fusiliers (bottom) move up to Catenanuova, whence they launched their successful assault on Centuripe (see p. 239).

# VIEWS & REVIEWS Of Vital War Books

## by Hamilton Fyfe

ALMOST everyone in this country is still puzzled and uneasy about the French in North Africa. This puzzlement began when Admiral Darlan "ratted" from Vichy and was accepted as a collaborator by General Eisenhower. It was heightened by the mystery kept up about the Admiral's assassination. It is still being deepened by inability to understand what are the differences between Generals de Gaulle and Giraud, and which of the two the British and American Governments prefer.

It is useful, therefore, to have some first-hand information on this subject. Mr. Guy Ramsey, one of the News Chronicle's war correspondents, went to North Africa with the expedition last year and stayed there for some time. He knew all the parties concerned. He is able to tell us in his book One Continent Redeemed (Harrap, 8s. 6d.—ready shortly) a good deal that helps to make the situation more intelligible. He quotes Gen. Eisenhower as saying that the whole of the French authorities in North Africa looked to Darlan for orders and would not act unless he told them to do this or that.

The General declared he hated politics; he has no feeling in the matter except that he wished to arrange matters so as to help and not hinder the Allied war effort. All who had been in Algeria for any length of time agreed that Darlan was a pill, not a pleasant pill, which must be swallowed.

HE himself was under no illusions as to what sort of reputation he had, not only with the Allied commanders but among the populace. He turned his coat because he saw it would pay him best to do so, just as he worked for Hitler when that seemed the most profitable line for him to take. He was easy to get on with because he was ready to do anything asked of him. He wanted to show that he was really earning his money. No one, says Mr. Ramsey, could compare Darlan with Giraud, who succeeded him.

Their very photographs make it plain that one was a time-server, while the other is a man of unshakable and unbreakable integrity. But it was easier to work with Darlan than with Giraud, and there was genuine regret among the authorities when Darlan was killed. The crime was committed, according to Mr. Ramsey, by a Royalist, that is a Frenchman who would like to see a king in France again. The pretender to the throne is the Count of Paris; he is said to be not far away when the murderer fired his shots. He lives usually in the outskirts of Tangier.

THE Royalists are described as being numerous in the French army of North Africa, especially among the higher officers. It would be interesting to know whether Gen. Giraud has any sympathy with the Bourbon cause. The Royalists call Gen. de Gaulle "traitor," "outlaw," "careerist," and other abusive names. They say he put himself outside the law when he set up a sort of government opposed to Vichy. Dissensions among the French in Algeria make it hard to believe they can ever agree about anything.

Many of those who were loudest in their welcome of the Allies would have given just as warm a reception to the Nazis. They had no motive but self-interest. But for several months American consular officials had been making inquiries and keeping in close touch with everything that went on, so we had a good idea, when the invasion started, as to who were our real friends.

Gen. Eisenhower struck Mr. Ramsey as a man of understanding, a skilful negotiator, conciliatory and endowed with the gift of making people who talk to him think they must be extremely intelligent and well-informed. He talks a great deal himself, with the intelligence of a University don and the fluency of a Rotarian speaker. At first he was distrusted as a military commander. The Guards and the Hampshire battalions were sent forward in a hurry without adequate supply arrangements. There was relief when Gen. Alexander was associated with him in the high command. But he is a favourite with the correspondents because he takes them into his confidence, treats them as Moulders of Public Opinion (the tones of his voice supply the capital letters!) and, unlike most British generals, he thinks that News really matters.

## After Darlan: What Has Happened in North Africa

Of Gen. Giraud Mr. Ramsey gives a vivid sketch that brings him before the reader in clear outline. He is in appearance the typical French cavalry officer. His uniform verges on foppishness. He is tall and slight, very straight still. But his moustache is not so "swashbuckling and ferocious" as it looks in pictures, a smile plays round the corners of his mouth, his voice is high and light, he has a courteous, friendly manner.

His reason for maintaining that he was the man to lead the French in Africa amounted simply to this: he knew the country and the people, also he was known by the people; De Gaulle was not.

In Giraud's view they looked on De Gaulle with the gravest suspicion. That was wrong. The British were right in their support of De Gaulle. "I myself admire him, not only for his abilities as a soldier, but for what he has done from London. For two years he has spoken with the voice of France. That must never be forgotten."

De Gaulle apparently wanted a purge of all Vichy officials. In Giraud's view that would have caused a revolution with, he feared, slaughter on a vast scale—"the gutters of Morocco, Algeria, Tunisia, would have run with blood." It is significant that two of the very high officials whom he described to Mr. Ramsey as indispensable have since

been dismissed and without any untoward consequences. Now that he has agreed to share the leadership, we must hope that all the energies of the French in Africa will be applied to winning the war.

The whole lay-out in this part of the world is difficult to understand, still more difficult to manage. The Arabs have to be bribed to turn against the Germans, who for so long bribed them to be on their side. They won them over chiefly by letting them have oil, which is essential to Arab cookery, when it was scarce. We pay them £40 for handing over a live spy, parachutist, or airman forced to land; £24 each for dead ones. That is the officer tariff; it is less for other ranks.

THE Arabs are not much good for hard, continuous labour—on getting damaged airfields into a usable state again, for example. They are slower and lazier than Europeans or Americans, and the language difficulty makes it a long business teaching them what to do. Also they are, in spite of their reputation for calm resignation to fate and disregard of danger, terrified of being killed. "They're quite undependable," a Royal Engineers colonel told Mr. Ramsey; "one bomb thirty miles away and they're off to the hills for a week!"

The account the book gives of our landing as seen from a ship is picturesque and lively. The writer especially admired the beachmasters for their magnificent organizing skill. They landed first in the dark and, waist-deep in water, worked for seventeen hours, using megaphones and shaded torches to guide the troops coming ashore, showing infinite patience and unbreakable good humour.

They lent their arms to soldiers weighed down by their heavy equipment, they carried burdens ashore which would otherwise have been lost in the sea, they pushed off craft that ran aground. It was largely due to them that the operation was carried out so smoothly and with very small losses.

**GENERAL EISENHOWER,** Commander-in-Chief of the Allied Forces in the Mediterranean theatre of war, tribute to whose work in resolving Free French differences in North Africa is paid in the book reviewed in this page. This striking portrait, by Mr. Henry Carr, is one of several new war pictures recently on view at the National Gallery, London.

*Crown Copyright reserved*

# 'The Cossacks Are Coming!' the Nazis Cry

'KOSSAKEN KOMMEN!' cried the Germans fleeing from Taganrog to Mariupol on August 30, 1943. Formidable horsemen warriors from the Don territory in S. Russia, the Kuban, the Urals and the Caucasian foothills, armed with modern guns in place of their traditional sabres, Cossacks are the terror of the harassed enemy. Don Cossacks take aim from the shelter of their superbly-trained horses (1), ford their native river, which is 1,160 miles long (2 and 4), and enter a village recaptured from the Nazis (3).

*Photos, Pictorial Press—Exclusive to* THE WAR ILLUSTRATED

# Four Times In Battle Kharkov Changes Hands

**VIOLENTLY CONTRASTING SCENES** from the second city of the Ukraine, now once again in Russian hands. Before it first fell to the Nazis, in October 1941, Kharkov was Russia's greatest tank-producing centre. It also produced some 50,000 tractors a year and over 900,000 workers thronged its tree-lined streets (bottom). Before abandoning it to the enemy the Russians scorched it, and since then the city has changed hands three times in battle. The top photograph shows a tragic result : one of Kharkov's main squares as the Russians found it when they returned on February 16, 1943, to hold the city for a month only. See also p. 249.

*Photos, Planet News, Pictorial Press*

# THE HOME FRONT

### by E. Royston Pike

Aᴜɢᴜsᴛ is the traditional month of holidays; and this year, more than any of the previous wartime summers, it saw a great rush to the country and those parts of the coast where a strip of beach is open for picnics and bathes. They are hardy spirits, these holiday-makers, ready to put up with a deal of inconvenience and downright discomfort in order to have their break, their bit of fun, a change from the everyday routine and surroundings. Wireless and newspapers have told terrible tales of thousands of holidaymakers standing for hours in long queues, missing the last train, sleeping on the station platform. Such a holiday is not everybody's "cup of tea," but can we find it in our hearts to blame those who feel that they must "get away from it all for a bit"? Fifty-one weeks, perhaps seven days a week for a long stretch: so much work—then a week's play !

Yes, it's understandable enough ; and more's the pity that apparently little or nothing can be done to make travelling a little easier for those who have decided that their journey *is* really necessary. The Government (Mr. Noel Baker, Parliamentary Secretary to the War Transport Ministry, has said) have every sympathy with the desire for holidays, fresh air, and change of scene, but they can provide extra trains only if they give up the priority accorded to essential military traffic. This, of course, they are not prepared to do. So far from victory abroad reducing the demands on our internal transport (he said on August 30), it increases them. To North Africa and Sicily we have to send from this country, along roads and railways to our ports, a constant stream of military and civilian supplies in addition to the large tonnage needed for the new and greater battles that lie ahead.

Hᴇᴀᴠᴇɴ knows, the workers —most of them—have well deserved their break. "We are now producing a greater volume of goods than ever before in the history of our country, whether in war or in peace," declared Mr. Oliver Lyttelton, Minister of Production ; and on August 30 he revealed that Britain's total output of munitions showed an increase of 25 per cent in the second quarter of 1943 over the same quarter of 1942, and the increase in structural weight of aircraft was 44 per cent compared with the previous year. Altogether, the combined war production of the United Nations is now three times that of the Axis —and next year it will be four times.

Usᴜᴀʟʟʏ workers on the Home Front are anonymous, but in a wireless talk given not long ago by a Colliery Manager there was a mention of "one man, known to his friends as Bart." He is a miner, standing 5ft. 4in. high in his socks, and weighing just 9½ stone, "a cheerful little fellow, full of the joy of life." In 1,205 shifts, 84 of them on Sundays, Bart has produced 21,511 tons of coal : every day he has worked he has produced only a fraction below 18 tons, which is equal to 300 times his own weight.

" Let's look at it in another way,"·went on the Manager. " In four years Bart has loaded the equivalent of 2,200 railway trucks of coal, or one whole train-load every four weeks. The vast quantity of coal raised by this one man is sufficient to provide the finished steel for the production of one heavy cruiser and two destroyers of the Tribal class. During the whole period of the War Bart

has lost only one shift voluntarily. He has worked 7 days a week for 84 weeks, and his average for the whole war is 6 days per week, including holiday periods." Bart works in a North Midland pit. If he worked in Russia, he would be hailed enthusiastically as a Hero of Socialist Labour !

But in spite of such Herculeans as Bart, coal production is once again giving rise to acute anxiety, and it is now the official view that the industry is very much under-manned. So efforts are being made to recruit fresh workers for the pits. At the end of August the Ministry of Labour announced that the age limit of 25 for the exercise of the option for underground work in coal-mines was being abolished, and that men of all ages, unless they are in certain skilled categories, may volunteer for coal-mining when called up for service.

A week or so later an appeal for 30,000 volunteers for the mines was directed to men between 16 and 41 at present engaged in other civilian jobs. At this stage of the War it has been made clear that before we can win the Battle of Europe we must win the battle for coal, coal, and yet more coal.

**COAL ARMY RECRUIT learns from an experienced miner at the New Lount Colliery, Coalville how to drill a shot-hole preparatory to inserting powder for blasting the coal face. The Battle for Coal is an indispensable complement to the Battle of Europe.** *Photo, The Daily Telegraph*

Tʜᴀᴛ much-discussed subject the declining birth-rate came up for debate in the House of Commons a few weeks since. When this country entered the War in 1939 we had fewer children than in any year since 1876, when the population was only 24 millions, said Group-Capt. Wright ; in 1971, when the population will be about the same as today, there will be 50 per cent more people over 45 than now and 100 per cent more over 65. On the other hand, the number of people of 45 and under will be only three-quarters of what it is today.

It does not require a super-intellect to appreciate the almost intolerable burden (went on Group-Captain Wright) of supporting this ever-increasing proportion in the higher ages, which is the inescapable destiny of the young people who are now fighting so gloriously for a better future. What is the reason for the fall ? Mr. J. Griffiths, a Labour member from Wales, adduced the fear of poverty, insecurity and war ; mothers are in revolt, he said, and motherhood must be made safer. " To be a mother in this country is more dangerous than to be a miner."

By way of contrast a Conservative stalwart, Sir F. Fremantle (he has since died), blamed women for wanting to earn money and have a career instead of stopping at home and raising a family. Mr. Maxton professed to

be a little disgusted at the tone of the debate : much of the discussion concerning intimate and sacred human relations had been of the type which (he declared) he had heard from Ayrshire farmers talking about their Ayrshire cows ! But he rebutted the charge that there was something unpatriotic or any dodging of responsibility in men not reproducing their species in the same degree as formerly.

Winding up the debate Mr. Ernest Brown, Minister of Health, said that he didn't think very much of the call for more babies : what we want is *better* babies. After all, a check in the growth of population was inevitable sooner or later.

Aᴍᴏɴɢ the credit items in the balance sheet of war is the immense stimulation it affords to invention, not only of mechanical contrivances, but of industrial processes. Thus of late we have been learning a lot about what Sir John Bodinnar, Commercial Secretary to the Ministry of Food, has described as "putting food into battledress." By importing boned and moulded beef and telescoped mutton carcasses the shipping space saved last year compared with pre-War amounted to 41,000,000 cubic feet ; by importing dried, instead of shell, egg, to about 22,500,000 cubic feet ; and by importing milk powder, instead of tinned condensed milk, to about 1,000,000 cubic feet.

These figures represent a saving of about 750,000 tons, or the carrying capacity of seventy-five 10,000-ton ships—" a phantom convoy that did not sail." Still more interesting developments are in hand. Bacon from the U.S.A. will occupy less space in future, since it is to be sent across the Atlantic in bales weighing 5 lb. instead of packed in wooden boxes weighing 70 lb. More space will be saved by substituting chests made from Indian jute fibre instead of plywood in the carriage of tea.

Then, several dehydrated foods can be pressed into blocks without affecting their use or value. Thus dried egg can be reduced in volume by 30 per cent. Dried carrot, cabbage and potato are being similarly treated ; dehydrated cheese, mixed with potato flour and compressed into blocks, is now being supplied to the troops. Dried meat has its storage life doubled by compression.

Wʜᴇɴ the Budget was given its third reading in the Commons, the Chancellor of the Exchequer gave a well-deserved pat on the back to the taxpayer. There never has been a time, he said, when the people of this country paid their taxes so willingly and so promptly. Nearly two thousand years ago Tacitus, the Roman historian, recorded of the inhabitants of Britain that they were good taxpayers unless they were exasperated by official insolence. That, declared the Chancellor, is true today. His lieutenant, Mr. Assheton, Financial Secretary to the Treasury, announced that the National Debt now stands at £17,700 millions.

We are borrowing as much money every eight weeks now as was borrowed during the whole period of the Napoleonic wars. At the end of the wars conducted by the great Duke of Marlborough the National Debt had reached a figure in the neighbourhood of £53 millions, a sum which we should spend, said Mr. Assheton, between then and the end of the following week. One of the principal objects of high taxation is to minimize the burden of the Debt after the War ; what is not being raised by taxation is being borrowed, and the Chancellor might well remark on "the wonderful effort made by the people of the country in voluntary savings."

# Our New 5·5 Gun-Howitzer is Now an Open Secret

A TUNISIAN secret was revealed when official details of the new British 4·5-in. and 5·5-in. medium guns were made available.

"On the six-mile front of attack we had a 25-pounder gun, or better, to every 23 yards," Mr. Churchill declared in his statement to the House of Commons at the beginning of our victorious sweep through North Africa. The world now knows what the words "or better" implied. They meant these new guns, which both fit the equally new dual service gun-carriage.

We had waited a long time for these splendid products of British engineering, and it was fortunate that they were available just when they were needed. For at the beginning of the war Germany outclassed us in this type of field gun, and after Dunkirk, when the British Army had to be almost completely re-equipped with artillery, second place had to be allotted to the medium gun for the time being; anti-aircraft weapons took priority.

But research went on—and now the 4·5-in. and 5·5-in. "gun-hows" are proving their worth against enemy armour and entrenchments. In four days of the Tunisian campaign, for example, the 5·5-in., which is illustrated in this page, accounted for 17 tanks destroyed and 24 probables—signal service indeed !

*Photos, British Official: Crown Copyright*

'GUN-HOW NO. 1' in our present armament is the, new 5·5-in., details of which have just been revealed.

Like the 25-pounder (see p. 460, Vol. 5,) it combines the functions of a howitzer and a high-velocity field gun, but it embodies vast improvements on the 25-pounder. The 5·5-in. can throw a 100-lb. projectile with devastating effect at a maximum range of over eight miles, exceeding its German counterpart by nearly 1,500 yards—a triumph of invention which has reversed the position at the beginning of the war, when we were quite outclassed by the Germans in medium artillery.

Royal Artillery men prepare to limber up their new gun to a backing lorry (1). On the practice range they have the 5·5-in. in position (2) ; the rammer is thrown back after the shell has been plunged home. When the gun is fired, like this one in Tunisia (3), note how the crew turn away to lessen the effect of the blast on their ear-drums—evidence of the gun's immense power.

# Denmark Struggles to Break the Nazi Shackles

GIRL WITH ROUNDEL HAT—the colours are red, white and blue, a tribute to the R.A.F.—is questioned by a Danish policeman (centre) and a Nazi S.S. man.

**THE DANES REVOLT** after three years' passive subservience to the Nazi invader. Never has underground resistance, encouraged by the Allies, altogether ceased, but not until now has there been an uprising so spontaneous and widespread, demanding all the German resources of tyranny to suppress it, as these photographs show.

Traffic is at a standstill in the capital, Copenhagen (above), while police disperse crowds after a street fight. A policeman and two civilians were wounded in this disturbance.

*Photos, Danish Council Information Office, Planet News, Associated Press, Topical Press*

**LOOT FROM THE DANES** weighs down a Nazi soldier (below) as he goes on leave. German currency trickery enables the invaders to purchase (if they cannot otherwise acquire) luxuries unobtainable in their own country.

COPENHAGEN CITIZENS CHARGED by black-uniformed S.S. men—minions of the terror specialist, Himmler—assisted by members of the so-called Danish Free Corps. The Forum Hall, largest in the city, an ideal barracks for some of the 50,000 Nazi troops poured into Copenhagen on August 20, and Denmark's largest aluminium factory are both reported to have been destroyed by saboteurs.

IN DENMARK the Nazis have thrown off the mask they have worn since they entered the country on April 9, 1940. When even the pro-German Premier Scavenius was unable to meet their demands they overthrew the Danish Government, imprisoned King Christian and imposed martial law. Denmark now joins her sister-nation Norway in servitude.

This Nazi move on August 29, 1943 was the culmination of a wave of strikes, riots and sabotage. Thus came to an end the three years' farce that Denmark was a perfect example of willing cooperation in the Nazi New Order—Hitler's "Model Protectorate." The German demand for the death penalty for patriotic saboteurs was the final outrage: Danish 'cooperation' would not go to that shameful length. And so at last the velvet glove came off to reveal the Nazi mailed fist.

The Navy resisted to the last. Part of the fleet got away to the neutrality of Swedish ports, but the flagship Niels Iuel and the Peder Skram did not manage to escape (see p. 230).

DANISH WORKER BEATEN UP by German soldiers. A sight only too familiar in cities under the Nazi heel, and one that is now stirring even good-tempered, once passively resistant Danes to active fury against their oppressors.

# I WAS THERE! Eye Witness Stories of the War

## Fire and Ruin Marked the Road to Kharkov

*After one of the greatest battles of this war Kharkov, city of the Ukraine, was finally wrested from the Germans by the Red Army on August 23, 1943. Stories of scenes along the approaches to and in the town, given in Soviet broadcasts, appear here by arrangement with The Evening Standard.*

IT is a clear, sunny August day. We are moving along the road to Kharkov. Only a few months ago there were factories working over there. There were people in the houses about the factories. Nothing is now left either of the factories or the houses. There are fires and ruins and more fires springing up even now.

There is the wreckage of tanks and guns on this road—the road to Kharkov. Masses of twisted metal, the burnt debris of war. There is a great cloud of smoke over the town. The special German detachments have set fire to many more buildings. Now we reach a signpost. It is yellow, with great black letters written on it. It is written in German, but we can understand what is written. It is the boundary post: THIS IS KHARKOV.

*In another broadcast a Pravda correspondent described how the Russians occupied the fortified area around Kharkov :*

Through this gateway our troops began to pour and advanced at the rate of nine to eleven miles a day. Our tanks, infantry and artillery worked together. Two hundred guns were together in action over a distance of little more than half a mile. If the infantry were held up the artillery opened with a withering fire. If there was a further hold-up, our aeroplanes came swooping in to blast the enemy positions.

OUR main forces concentrated in a forest area. Sometimes our men had to work their way through with an axe. They carried their ammunition in their hands. One of our flanking units worked through the forests for 18 hours to make a surprise attack. The vanguard, with their commander, Rudnik, at the head, broke through to the northern area of Kharkov after covering a distance of more than 130 miles. Street fighting started immediately and then began the third, the most heroic and the most intense phase of the battle for the city.

While the vanguards fought on the outskirts, our main forces were encircling the city in a wide out-flanking movement. Gradually they enclosed Kharkov in a grip of iron which the enemy could not break.

The achievements of Orel, Byelgorod and now Kharkov were made possible by two things—the extraordinary gallantry and endurance of our troops and the qualities of leadership of our officers. The skilful movements of the Stalin school defeated the old German methods.

*Another Soviet broadcaster said :* The Germans mined every yard of the city. They sent 10,000 civilians to make tank ambushes. Houses inside the city were bristling with machine-guns and trench mortars. Our troops had to fight hard—for every yard, for every house. When we drove the Germans from the ground floors of the houses they retreated to the first floors and then to the second floors and so on.

## I Fly With a Middle East Bomber Squadron

*"Sometimes we see our eggs hatch down there in the darkness," says Flying-Officer P. Flyte, writing specially for THE WAR ILLUSTRATED of desert warfare and all that accompanies it. The day's work is hot and hard, the night's exploits filled with peril. Yet the life fascinates him.*

THE heavy bomber squadron with which I fly has been in the Middle East a very long time, hauling "eggs" to drop on the Italian and German armies. In those dark moments of the early days when the enemy was almost at the gates of Alexandria the hauls were long ones, across the Western Desert to Tobruk, Benghazi and beyond, and because of their regularity we used to call them the "mail-runs." Things changed when the Eighth Army began to roll the Germans back and we moved farther and farther into the desert close on the heels of the Army.

All ranks of the Desert Air Force did heroic work then keeping up the battering from bases which in many cases were taken over and used within a few hours of the enemy having "vacated the premises." All the airfields had been mined and left with wrecked equipment, poisoned water supplies, and so on, so that we had to work hard to make them serviceable and keep our bombers in the air. Often it was only a matter of minutes after landing at a new base before we were bombed-up and out for yet another "party."

Often we would be at a drome only a few days before being moved up another hundred miles or so. We would take-off from the old airfield loaded up with all kinds of gear, and in a few hours would be joined at the new base by the rest of the squadron personnel and equipment travelling by truck. Several hundred men and their kit,

tents, oil, water, fuel, food, bombs, spares, trucks and planes moved in an hour or two across hundreds of miles of desert—not once but many times ! The air offensive went ahead in ever-greater strength until the enemy was out of Africa for good.

Now the Desert Air Forces—British, American, and all the others who fly with us—are operating from a hundred bases along the African coast, hitting hard at German and Italian industrial targets, ships, ports and railways from Sardinia to Salonika.

**FLYING-OFFICER P. R. FLYTE,** who gives a first-hand account of desert warfare from the airman's viewpoint in this page. Note the petrol drum serving as a table, and the empty bottle used as a lamp-glass in his tent.

Outside of operational duties men of the Desert squadrons live a somewhat simple and unexciting existence. My squadron, for example, is just a cluster of tents grouped alongside a hard-packed stretch of sand which is glorified by the term "airfield," and all around is a flat brown waste which stretches until it dips over the hazy horizon. I live, sleep, eat and work in tents, and find I miss the flapping of those canvas walls when I enter a place built of bricks and mortar. And, of course, we have to make our own amusements.

THE day's work usually starts early, so that as much as possible can be done before the searing heat of the sun makes us lie on our camp-beds and gasp for air. By midday the metal of the aircraft is hot enough to blister unprotected hands, and any movement in the open is an effort. I find the great open spaces of the desert foster man-size appetites, and even the heat doesn't keep us away from the mess at mealtimes. Cooks do wonders with the rations and open-air field kitchens. Eggs are usually plentiful as we keep a few chickens scratching about the place, and wandering Arabs are always ready to barter eggs for cigarettes.

Most squadrons are within a half-hour's run of the Mediterranean, and mine is no exception. We organize swimming parties and go bumping off over the desert in an open truck, leaving behind us a wake of swirling sand. We waste no time in diving into those warm, tideless waters once we arrive. The sea is unbelievably clear, with fantastic rock shapes showing at the bottom. Once someone yelled that an octopus was swimming around with us, and I don't think I have ever

**MOSCOW SALUTES KHARKOV VICTORS** with 20 volleys from 224 guns on the night of August 23, 1943. It was the city's second tribute to the Red Army, for on August 5, 120 guns fired 12 salvos in celebration of the capture of Orel and Byelgorod. Exactly a week after the recapture of Kharkov 12 salvos from 124 guns marked the occupation of Taganrog on August 30. See also p. 245.

*Photo, Pictorial Press*

**R.A.F. ARMOURERS are kept busy bombing-up the air-fleets that now operate a deadly shuttle service from Middle East bases : here Wellingtons are being loaded. See story in this and preceding page.** *Photo, British Official*

swum faster than I did on that occasion. Sure enough it was an octopus, but only about two feet across, and the local Arabs collected it. They threw a sort of hand-grenade into the sea close to the visitor and the resulting explosion stunned or killed it. The Arabs than waded in and hauled out the body, departing with it in high glee to I know not what messy end.

One of our greatest needs is reading matter, and Cairo newspapers are a boon, even though they are often a week old when we get them. Many men are keeping up with their peacetime careers as well as they can, by taking correspondence courses run by English technical schools with overseas branches and by the Royal Air Force educational organization. We are fortunate in having several ex-schoolmasters among our air-crew personnel and they hold classes in languages, mathematics, and other subjects. I have just completed studying for a certain examination in engineering, and in a few weeks, when my examination papers arrive from England, I shall "sit" in the Desert with my commanding officer to vouch that I abide by the rules !

I LIKE the life, the friendship, the ruggedness, the sense of teamwork in all that goes on about the squadron ; above everything I like the quiet of the desert night in those rare moments when we are not flying. A deep silence settles over the desert then—a silence you can almost feel. But that does not happen very often, for on most nights there is work to do. Early in the day I am busy with maps and charts for the long trip ahead. The afternoon slowly passes, and as we struggle into flying gear we hear the great bombers coughing into life down there on that sun-baked strip of sand. The ground crews are giving the "kites" a last-minute check. Perspiring in our thick gear, we bump out to "Miss Blandish"—our particular machine—and tumble out under the shadow of her wing. By tomorrow she will have another orchid painted on her side—we hope.

We file aboard, and then far off down the runway winks the take-off signal. Bill the pilot opens up our engines, and in a moment we are bumping down the flare-path leaving behind us a streaming wake of wind-lashed sand. Soon we fly into the darkness and head out to sea on yet another " party." We climb as we rumble on, and soon the falling temperature makes us glad of our heavy flying kit. The hours tick away and at last we arrive. Like a giant bat we swoop down the skies, and in the under-belly of the machine the long, black bomb-doors are gaping wide. Flak is streaking up now, but the target is in sight and we weave our way in.

Back over the inter-com comes the drone of the bomb-aimer as he squints through his bomb-sight : " Left, left, steady, left, left, steady, steady now . . ." We all tense as we level out on that

last run, and then— "Bombs gone ! " yells the bomb-aimer, and Bill pulls up and away out of the flak belt. Sometimes we see our eggs " hatch" down there in the darkness. Sometimes we are too busy twisting and turning to observe results, but we feel we " made it " O.K. and turn for home. As the grey of dawn brings a lighter streak to the East we circle over the airfield and get the welcome green signal from control. Bump, bump, and we are down again with the usual blinding swirl of sand as we touch.

We climb out and plod over to the Ops. tent for the usual reports, and then off to the mess for eggs and ham. I drain a third mug of tea and say one word to Bill across the plain wood table. " Bed ! " Usually there is a brief dispute between several spiders and myself as to who shall use the camp-bed ; it ends in our bedding-down together. And I dream of Cairo, and a bath.

# I Saw Victory on the Land Army Battle Front

Touring the harvest fields, Patricia Ward of The Evening Standard (from which this story is reprinted) wrote in late August how farmers are rejoicing at the rich yield of Mother Earth : reward for our land-workers' toil, and aid to Britain's ultimate victory. See also pp. 218-219.

THROUGHOUT East Anglia three weeks ago the corn was standing high ; today, all but a few of the fields are stubble and innumerable stacks bear testimony to a record harvest completed in record time. There is rejoicing among the farmers. Not only because the cereal crop was a "bumper" one and is threshing out even better than it looked. But as one of them put it to me : "An early harvest means a good start to the year ; now we can get ahead with the ploughing and early sowing."

Already many of the fields have lost the

last trace of gold, for the stubble has either been treated with cultivator or given a shallow ploughing to clear it of weeds. One of the reasons, the farmers reckon, that they are so well in advance of the year is that Norfolk is so highly mechanized. Much of the cutting has been done by combine-machines.

I watched one at work on one of the still uncut areas. It was a self-propelled machine, one of the latest types to arrive in the country. The farm worker who drove it said: "Wonderful job, isn't it ? And it saves a

**COMBINE HARVESTER which has its knives adjusted so that only the ears of the corn are reaped. The straw will be ploughed in for manure—an example of how our farmers strive to get the utmost from the land, typical of the thorough husbandry which has made this year's harvest so richly abundant.** *Photo, Picture Post*

lot of time and labour. Of course, when anything goes wrong, it's a job to get it fixed.'' Through the chute and into the row of sacks slung behind the driver's seat barley poured forth in a golden stream.

The man who was handling the sacks picked up a handful to show me. '' I've farmed in Norfolk for a lifetime,'' he said, '' and I've never seen better-looking grain.'' The extra labour which has enabled the farmers to gather this ''extra'' harvest has been, I learned, almost entirely unskilled, provided by holiday camps and part-time

volunteers from town and village.

'' Farming is in the blood of every man and woman and child in the county,'' explained one white-haired farmer. I asked him what, apart from the question of labour, the main farming difficulties had been throughout the season. ''Transport,'' he said, ''though the Services have helped us a lot over that. Shortage of spare parts for machinery. And rats—but the War Agricultural Committee are doing a good job there. This year 500,000 acres have been cleared of them.''

our armies' retreat, of the brutality of the Germans and of the devastation of our towns, I asked to be allowed to join the regular army. I was refused. Then came news of the development of the partisan movement in the Ukraine. After that I couldn't bear to remain in Moscow any longer.

I AM an old partisan and a Ukrainian. I know the country and the people. Twice already I had punched the savage visages of the Germans, and I felt I would not find rest until I had cracked their skulls for the third time and for all. My chief opposed my idea. At first he wouldn't hear of my leaving the factory. But I am a man of determination Then my friends attempted to dissuade me.

## From Factory Manager to Guerilla Fighter

A wounded Ukrainian partisan, who had fought the Germans before, in 1918, tells Stanislav Radzinsky (in Soviet War News, from which this story is taken) how, wanting to crack enemy skulls again, he left a comfortable job and became commander of a detachment in the German rear.

You ask why I joined the partisans? There are thousands like myself. Can you understand our psychology —the psychology of elderly people who certainly could make themselves useful in the rear, but who feel bound to share actively in the struggle?

I am 55. I have worked in factories for twenty years. My last job was manager of a factory. You will be even more surprised if I tell you that ours was a munition factory, and that I am a graduate of the Academy of Industry—in short, I worked in one of our most essential industries.

I did not live in a place that has since been occupied by the Germans. I lived in Moscow. I had a good flat. I am married to a woman I dearly love, and am the father of two children—a daughter who is working in a munition factory, and a younger child. I was well provided for and had everything a man could want. I am an old soldier. I fought the Germans in the last war. I fought

them again in the Ukraine in 1918, in the first partisan detachments. In those days we made our own weapons.

When, soon after the declaration of war, our communiqués informed the country of

**SOVIET GUERILLAS, typical of thousands of soldiers without uniform who harry the retreating Germans and destroy enemy communications.** *Photo, British Official*

'' I realize everything,'' I told them. '' I know I can't sit happily in my comfortable office any more, or read my favourite books of an evening, or play with my children. I know that the partisan movement has just begun to develop, that at first we shall feel like hunted beasts, that I shall live in the cold forest, in open fields or in bears' haunts, and that a German bullet will dog my every step, and, even worse, that a traitor may deliver me into the hands of the enemy. I know I may be tortured to death. I have weighed everything in my mind, and have come to the conclusion that I shall be more useful as the organizer of a partisan detachment than as manager of a factory.''

That was how I came to be in the German rear and began organizing a partisan group. Later on this group grew into a detachment, and I was chosen as its commander.

The British Prime Minister was right when he said that the Hun either clutches you by the throat or rolls at your feet. At the beginning of the war they clutched us by the throats, but you should see how they roll at your feet, begging for mercy, when they are taken prisoner !

# OUR DIARY OF THE WAR

**AUGUST 18, Wednesday** *1,446th day*
**Mediterranean.**—Toe of Italy bombed continuously by Allied air forces ; Gioia, Tauro and Palmi shelled from sea.
**Russian Front.**—In Kharkov area, Russians captured Zmiev ; Berezovka and Mylinka fell in Bryansk drive.
**Australasia.**—Wewak (New Guinea) raided ; 64 enemy aircraft destroyed on the ground and 28 in the air.
**General.**—Mr. Eden and Mr. Brendan Bracken (Min. of Information) arrived in Quebec.

**AUGUST 19, Thursday** *1,447th day*
**Sicily.**—Stated that Italian Sixth Army (300,000 men) lost (dead, wounded, captured), during Sicilian fighting.
**Mediterranean.**—Day and night raids on Foggia and Salerno ; Gioia and Tauro (Italy) again shelled.
**Air.**—French and Dutch airfields attacked by escorted Fortresses and other bombers ; 41 enemy fighters destroyed. Mosquitoes bombed Berlin at night.

**AUGUST 20, Friday** *1,448th day*
**Mediterranean.**—Announced that on August 17 Lipari and Stromboli Islands surrendered to American warships.
**Russian Front.**—In Kharkov area, Russians captured Lebedin.

**AUGUST 21, Saturday** *1,449th day*
**Mediterranean.**—Villa Literno, Battipaglia, Cancello and Aversa bombed ; Cotrone marshalling yards raided.
**China.**—Americans bombed Hankow.
**U.S.A.**—Japanese abandonment of Kiska (Aleutians) announced.

**AUGUST 22, Sunday** *1,450th day*
**Mediterranean.**—Rail communications at Salerno (nr. Naples ) attacked.
**Australasia.**—Allied forces occupied Komiatum, Orodubi, Mt. Tambu and Goodview Junction in New Guinea.
**Air.**—Leverkusen, N. of Cologne, and other Rhineland objectives attacked at night.

**AUGUST 23, Monday** *1,451st day*
**Mediterranean.**—Italian railway yards at Bagnoli and Battipaglia bombed, airfield at Bari attacked. Wellingtons bombed Lindos, in Is. of Rhodes.
**Russian Front.**—Kharkov retaken by Russians. New Soviet offensive S.W. of Voroshilovgrad.

**China.**—First Japanese raid on Chungking for two years.
**Air.**—Heaviest raid to date on Berlin ; 1,700 tons of bombs dropped in 50 minutes ; 58 bombers lost.
**General.**—U.S. and Canadian troops landed on Segula Island (Aleutians).

**AUGUST 24, Tuesday** *1,452nd day*
**Mediterranean.**—Torre Annunziata (nr. Naples) railway yards bombed by Wellingtons ; Locri in toe of Italy bombarded by British naval force.
**Australasia.**—Wewak (New Guinea) heavily attacked by Liberators.
**Burma.**—Banguna, S. of Buthidaung, attacked by Vengeance dive-bombers
**Air.**—Fortresses attacked Bordeaux. Berlin raided by Mosquitoes.
**General.**—Quebec Conference ended ; joint statement issued by President Roosevelt and Mr. Churchill indicated that Japan was main subject of discussions. Himmler appointed Minister of the Interior in Germany.

**AUGUST 25, Wednesday** *1,453rd day*
**Mediterranean.**—Foggia airfields (Italy) heavily bombed.

**Russian Front.**—Zenkov, N.W. of Kharkov, captured by Russians.
**Australasia.**—Hansa Bay shipping base (New Guinea) attacked by nearly 100 Allied aircraft.
**Air.**—French airfields of Tricqueville, Beaumont-le-Roger and Bernay St. Martin attacked by Allied aircraft. Mosquitoes raided Berlin at night.
**General.**—Formation of S.E. Asia Command for operations against Japan, based on India and Ceylon, announced ; Lord Louis Mountbatten, Combined Operations Chief, to be Supreme Allied Commander.

**AUGUST 26, Thursday** *1,454th day*
**Mediterranean.**—Taranto attacked by Wellingtons. Capizzi and Grazzanise (Italy) bombed by Fortresses.
**General.**—French Committee of National Liberation recognized by Britain, Canada and America.

**AUGUST 27, Friday** *1,455th day*
**Mediterranean.**—Sulmona, Benevento and Caserta railway yards in Rome-Naples area heavily bombed ; Cotrone attacked.

**Russian Front.**—Soviet troops captured Sevsk, S. of Bryansk.
**Australasia.**—Arundel Is. (one mile from Kolombangara) occupied by U.S. forces.
**Air.**—Targets in France attacked by U.S. Fortresses. Nuremberg pounded at night for 45 mins. with 1,500 tons of bombs.
**General.**—Soviet Govt. recognized French Committee of National Liberation.

**AUGUST 28, Saturday** *1,456th day*
**Sicily.**—Announced that British naval losses during the campaign were 2 submarines, 3 M.T.B.s and one motor-gunboat.
**Mediterranean.**—Canello, Aversa, Terni and Taranto railway yards heavily raided.
**Australasia.**—Announced that all organized resistance at an end in New Georgia, and Bairoka occupied. Kahili airfield in Buin bombed.
**General.**—King Boris of Bulgaria died.

**AUGUST 29, Sunday** *1,457th day*
**Mediterranean.**—Orte, Lamezia, Cosenza and Torre Annunziata marshalling yards bombed.
**Russian Front.**—Lyubotin, in Kharkov area, occupied by Red Army.
**General.**—Fighting broke out in Denmark ; Germans declared martial law ; Danish warships escaped to Sweden, others scuttled. King Christian interned.

**AUGUST 30, Monday** *1,458th day*
**Mediterranean.**—Viterbo airfield, Aversa and Civitavecchia rly. yards (Italy) heavily bombed.
**Russian Front.**—Germans evacuated Taganrog, on Sea of Azov. Elnya fortress in Smolensk area seized by Russians in renewed offensive ; penetrations made into N. Ukraine on 60m. front ; Rylsk and Glukov taken.
**General.**—Germans in complete control in Denmark.

**AUGUST 31, Tuesday** *1,459th day*
**Mediterranean.**—Pisa and Pescara bombed. H.M.S. Rodney and Nelson shelled enemy coast defences N. of Reggio and S. of Cape Pellaro. Announced Italian liner Conti di Savoia sunk.
**Air.**—Berlin attacked by night with great weight of bombs for 45 minutes.

★────── *Flash-backs* ──────★

**1940**
August 18. 152 German aircraft brought down over Britain.

**1941**
August 18. Russians announced evacuation of Nikolaiev. Mr. Churchill arrived in England after a meeting with the U.S. President at sea.
August 21. Russians evacuated Gomel.
August 27. Attempt made to assassinate Laval, the Quisling of France, leading collaborator with the Germans. '' Cease fire '' ordered in Iran.

August 28. Russians announced evacuation of Dnepropetrovsk.
August 31. Flying Fortresses bombed Bremen.

**1942**
August 19. Combined Operations raid, lasting 9 hours, on Dieppe. Krasnodar (Kuban) evacuated by Russians.
August 22. Brazil declared war on Germany and Italy.
August 26. Japanese landed at Milne Bay, New Guinea.
August 31. Germans opened offensive at El Hemeimat (Egypt).

**THE LUFTWAFFE IN RUSSIA** is now said to be so deficient in fighter planes that bomber formations operate with little fighter escort; our Ally claims to have destroyed 100 Nazi machines a day since June 5, 1943.

Above, a Nazi bomber unit is attempting to cover a river-crossing for the retreating German forces, whilst the Russian bombers, operating in support of the Red Army, have attacked dumps and concentrations on the German-held river bank; meanwhile, the Soviet fighters break up the enemy attack.

A German Heinkel 111 (1), almost obsolescent but still much used on the Russian front, has had its starboard engine cowling torn open by cannon fire and the power unit is beginning to flame. The pilot (2) and the gunner-bomb-aimer (3) are seen through the plexiglas panels, the latter training his 7·9-mm. gun on the Soviet MIG-3 fighter (4) as it flashes past. These gull-wing planes have a 1,200 h.p. liquid-cooled engine and a speed of over 350 m.p.h.; armament is one heavy machine-gun or cannon and two other machine-guns. Close by is a later Soviet fighter type, the Lagg-3 (5), now in production and of all-wood construction. Later models are said to fly in excess of 350 m.p.h. with a 1,600 h.p. engine and 20-mm. cannon, plus machine-guns. They are reputed to be a match for the Focke-Wulf 190.

Seen through the smoke, upper left, are two types of Russian light-reconnaissance bomber, the AK 4 (6) and the PE 2 (7). Both these types fly at 300 m.p.h., with two 1,100 h.p. engines. The former has a crew of two; the PE 2 carries a 1,700-lb. bomb load and a crew of three.

*Specially drawn for* THE WAR ILLUSTRATED *by Haworth*

# THE WAR IN THE AIR

## by Capt. Norman Macmillan, M.C., A.F.C.

THE constrictor-like grip of the United Nations' air forces continues to tighten round the Axis in both hemispheres. By combined operations, wherein the air arm has played a redoubtable part, the Japanese forces have been driven out of New Georgia in the Solomon Islands. Kolombangara and Vella Lavella islands are the next stepping-stones to the islands of Choiseul and Bougainville, themselves stepping-stones to the still more important islands of New Ireland and New Britain, in the second of which lies the strategically important harbour of Rabaul.

Rabaul, used by the Japanese as their principal base for operations in that part of the South Seas, has been the target for numerous United Nations air raids, and the waters around about Rabaul have become the graveyards of many Japanese ships sunk by air attack.

THE capture of Rabaul would turn the Japanese flank in New Guinea, mark the beginning of the end of Japanese occupation of any part of Melanesia, and remove entirely all threat from Japan against the Queensland territory of Australia, curtailed although that threat already is by the United Nations' recapture of Papua and the peninsular area of North-East New Guinea.

Rabaul—although a strategic objective on the immediate horizon—is itself 40 degrees south and about 12 degrees east of Tokyo, so that even when Rabaul is captured there will still lie about 2,800 English statute miles between the Melanesian base and the heart of Japan. And that means that the capital of Nippon will be too far-distant to fall within bombing range of Rabaul.

Thus we must regard the action of General MacArthur's forces in the Solomon Islands and New Guinea as the preliminary moves necessary to secure suitable bases—principally for seaborne lines of communication—from which to launch further campaigns against the Netherlands East Indies and the Philippine Islands. The selection of General MacArthur for this long-term operation is sound, for he had unrivalled experience during the Philippine defence action against Japan; he is thus fighting towards a known terrain, always an advantage.

NEVERTHELESS, capture of Rabaul would open up another aspect of combined operations, for it would place in the hands of the United Nations a suitable base from which to employ aircraft carriers against the numerous islands under Japanese mandate and occupation between Melanesia and Japan—the Marshalls, Carolines, Palau, Marianas, and the archipelago running north to Nippon.

It would mark the beginning of the closing of the Pacific ring around our Far Eastern foe, from Kiska and Attu in the north-east, Midway in the east, and Rabaul in the south. And the process that was applied to Germany

in relation to expansion *westward* towards the Americas would then be equally applied to Japan in relation to expansion *eastward* towards the Americas.

Thus the fundamental necessity of world strategy would be secured to the United Nations, namely, the absolute security of the base represented by the land mass of the Western Hemisphere. Then, with the ring tightening ever more effectively around our enemies, the outcome of the war would be assured, because, whatever else might happen, one nation could certainly not be defeated and

**PEENEMUNDE BY NIGHT**—the night of August 17, 1943, when Bomber Command visited this Baltic coast town for the first time. Bright moonlight favoured the raiders, two of whom are silhouetted against the glare of fires as they run over the target—the largest and most important aircraft research and radiolocation station in Germany.
*Photo, British Official: Crown Copyright*

victory must go to the Allies of that nation—which is America. That is the geographical interpretation of the war today.

Thus, with America as the main world base; Britain as the main advanced base against Europe (with Africa as a subsidiary base); Australia as the main base against Japanese occupation in the South-West Pacific; and India as the main base against Japanese occupation of the Asiatic mainland (with China as the advanced base): we can observe the general strategic lay-out of the war, and the vital part that aircraft must play therein, on all fronts.

In view of the great distances that lie between Japanese industry and Allied bomber bases, it is important to observe the indica-

tion that President Roosevelt at the time of the Ottawa Conference gave of the intention to utilize air transport as a line of communication to keep a forward bomber force operating in China against Japan proper.

China and aircraft carriers are the only bases from which bombs can fall upon Japan at present. The difficulty with the carrier method is the small load of bombs which carrier-borne aircraft can carry on a longish flight because of the restrictions imposed upon the aircraft by the relatively small flying-off deck, even when the carrier is under way and making its own half-gale breeze to aid the aircraft to take off.

So we must presume that the staff have figured things out and have come to the conclusion that with a force of bomber boys pushed well forward in Chinese-held China (where they can get within about 1,200 miles of Tokyo even now) and air transports to feed them with bombs, fuel, food, oil and all the requirements of a modern air force unit on active service, a greater load of bombs can be brought to bear upon Japan than can be achieved by carrier methods. Even then, the use of both methods would keep the Japanese guessing, and would make it far more difficult for them to provide adequate defence against attacks which would come from both east and west of Japan.

IN Europe the Axis forces are steadily being hemmed in and pinned down. With the Russians driving slowly but steadily westward from the steppes into the Ukraine, and destroying German military equipment, including aircraft, on a great scale, the demands upon German factories must be redoubled to drive the output up to meet the incessant requisitions of the German general staff.

As a counter to the power of German industry to deliver the goods which the German army must have if it is to maintain even defensive fighting effectively, fall the blows of Bomber Command, descending upon German industry and communications with ever-rising force. The 1,500-ton raid is now a standard-scale stroke. Raids of this size have recently fallen all over the Ruhr, on Peenemünde radio-location and experimental plant, Hamburg, Berlin, Nuremberg, and in Italy upon Milan and Turin. Some of the loads dropped in these raids were in excess of 1,500 tons, the greatest being about 2,300 tons.

The air defences of the Luftwaffe have been unable to inflict losses upon the British bombers which would be sufficient to deter them. On the contrary, the flood grows. Night fighters rise against the bombers in increasing numbers. But still the rate of loss seldom reaches five per cent, rarely exceeds it, and is mostly only a fraction of that loss rate.

Added to these devastating night raids are the American day raids against appropriate targets, such as the Messerschmitt factories at Wiener-Neustadt and Regensburg. Bomber Command and the American Army Eighth Air Force are beating down the power of Germany to defend herself against the air blows. The crest of the wave of German air defence may have been already reached. If so, Germany is sinking into the trough. The real bombing war is only now beginning.

# Superb Courage Earns Merchant Navy Honours

**CAPT. JAMES KENNEDY, O.B.E.**
Skipper of a merchantman torpedoed 300 miles from land, he and his crew exhibited "outstanding courage and endurance." Some were washed ashore on an uninhabited island, others reached safety on rafts.

**CAPT. R. E. HOPKINS, O.B.E.**
Master of a merchantman torpedoed and shelled by a U-boat, he returned the enemy's fire, brought his ship to harbour, then went again through submarine-infested waters for essential repairs.

**CAPT. W. H. GRINSHAW, O.B.E.**
He brought his ship into port after three days of almost continuous attacks by aircraft and submarines, repairing the damage and improvising so promptly and rapidly that the ship never lost speed.

**APPRENTICE D. O. CLARKE, G.C.**
For two hours he rowed a boatload of survivors from the blazing hulk of his torpedoed ship, with his hands burned to the bone. He died singing to cheer the hearts of the shipmates he helped to save.

**CHIEF OFFICER R. V. BURNS, G.M.**
With complete unconcern for his own safety he led a volunteer party to tackle an unexploded heavy bomb which had hit his ship during an air attack. They carried out the difficult and dangerous job with success.

**APPRENTICE COLIN FOOKES, G.M.**
When the magazine of his oil tanker was set ablaze by a bomb he grabbed smouldering boxes of cordite and unexploded shells and threw them overboard, regardless of burns and the very great danger.

**CHIEF STEWARD G. H. ANSON, B.E.M.**
In harbour in the Mediterranean his ship was subjected to heavy aerial attack. Together with the Chief Officer and the cook he plugged holes below the water-line, enabling the ship to carry on an hour later.

**CHIEF STEWARD R. THOMPSON, B.E.M.**
When a member of the crew suffered a torn knee-cap, "something had to be done." The necessary operation was carried out by this amateur surgeon while the ship was rocked by enemy bombs.

**APPRENTICE A. V. WATT, B.E.M.**
This nineteen-year-old seaman helped to save 32 shipmates who had been adrift for seven days in an open boat in the Arctic after the convoy had been attacked and his ship had been torpedoed.

*Photos, L.N.A., Daily Mirror, Planet News, Northern Press Agency*

"MAN, am I no a bonny fighter?" asked Alan Breck in Stevenson's great story, as he wiped his sword after a combat. The Russians can without any boastfulness lay that same flattering unction to their souls. How enormously they have improved since those summer and autumn battles of 1941, in which they were rolled back and back until the enemy was very near Moscow and Leningrad! How few were those who believed they would be able to hold out much longer! Our good friend Maisky told me once that distrust of the Red Army in the highest circles here was the "most unkindest cut" he had to bear during his long ambassadorship in London. He never doubted its recovery. He knew the men who would reorganize the defeated armies and at the right moment throw them into battle again. He kept up a continual storming of the Foreign Office and the American Embassy in order to hasten and increase the supply of tanks and planes to the Russian troops. He echoed Mr. Churchill's "Give us the tools and we will finish the job." They have not done it yet, but it is quite on the cards that they may do it. If they can beat the Nazis in summer, they should be able to rout them utterly in winter. The war might well be ended by the Cossacks sweeping into Berlin; the fear of that has haunted the Germans since 1914.

ANY fighting that might take place in Calabria would tax the energies and temper of the troops taking part in it more than either the Desert or Sicily has done. Few people know this almost uninhabited part of the Italian kingdom. I say "almost uninhabited" because one so seldom sees anybody. The villages are many of them approachable only by paths. Roads are not numerous, railway facilities less so; there is little water, the soil is arid, the summer fiercely hot, the winter cold. Snow stays on the mountains six months in the year. The population are mostly a poor-looking lot. Malaria is endemic on the coast strip. Cultivation is unenterprising, if not primitive. The million and a half Calabrians grow grapes for wine, olives for oil, rice, tobacco of a low grade, oranges, lemons, figs. If you like sucking liquorice jujubes, they probably came from there. I never was in a part of the world that seemed less attractive. The most interesting discovery I made was that Albanians have lived in certain little Calabrian townships of their own for five centuries, and still remain Albanian, speaking that language and wearing their national dress. They are a finer race than the Italians of this area, who mostly seemed to me degenerates of a low type.

AN attempt is to be made to get a legal decision as to what exactly Home Guards are. They have reckoned themselves part of the armed forces ever since they were given uniforms in 1940. Now they are under military discipline this view is taken more strongly. Yet it appears the authorities do not share it. Recently there have been one or more cases of Home Guards being killed in discharging their functions and their estates not being relieved of Death Duties, as are, I understand, the estates of men killed on active service. This seems a most unsatisfactory position. It ought to be cleared up. If a volunteer who is under no compulsion to risk his life does so of his own free will and loses it, the community may treat him as it does other civilians who die in their beds. But if the community conscripts us and treats us as soldiers, even if we only serve as such in our spare time, then it is bound, it seems to me, to put us on the same footing as other soldiers in every way. What a difference between the Local Defence Volunteers of the summer three years ago and the compact, well-trained, military Home Guards of today! As the song of South African War days said of Tommy Atkins, they're "a credit to their country and to their native land."

THAT pensions for total disablement have been increased from 37s. 6d. to 40s. a week is all to the good, but how meagre that

SQUADRON-LEADER W. H. BOWEN, Officer Commanding R.A.F. High Speed Launch Base, Dover. His men's job is to rescue airmen shot down in the Channel. They operate in fair weather and foul, constantly endangered by German gunfire from the French coast, mines, E-boats and enemy armed trawlers.
*Photo, News Chronicle*

extra half-crown seems when you consider how little it will buy nowadays! Also when you compare it with the money spent by some people on meals. Five shillings is the limit for the price of a meal, but it is possible to expand this to a couple of pounds when you add oysters and unrationed food and wine. Lots do pay as much as that. More attention is being paid to the inequality of incomes than this matter ever attracted before. But there is no way to check it that I can see. The Russians tried, and had no success. A few years ago (it may be so still) the man with the largest income in the U.S.S.R. was a dance-band leader. If that is Socialism, it is absurd. Yet on the principle that those whose services are most in request by the public should get the highest pay it is, on paper, equitable. But how could anybody justify remunerating a man who provides jiggery music for dancers more highly than statesmen, historians, doctors and surgeons of distinction, men and women engaged on important research work? Logically all who contribute their best efforts to the national service should be paid alike. Will they ever be? I doubt it.

THE world, it has been said, does not know its greatest men until they are dead. I should alter that to "most useful men." The "great" are seldom useful. Frederick was not, Napoleon was not (except for his codification of French law and construction of French ports); Alexander and Alfred have better reputations, but the former gave himself away by his silly grievance of having no more worlds to conquer and the other couldn't even keep the cakes from burning. But here and there are scattered about sparsely men who are of signal use to humanity and yet never come into the public eye. One of these was Sir Frederick Phillips of the Treasury, who has had such enthusiastic tributes from many quarters since he died a week or two ago. I doubt whether more than one person in a hundred thousand of us had ever heard his name. He had much to do with making and operating the Lease-Lend arrangements between this country and the United States, and was so much respected and liked in Washington that it is hard to find anyone to take his place. To the credit of the British Civil Service, when it finds such men, it employs them usually to the best advantage.

I RECOLLECT seeing, when I was a small boy at an exhibition in Edinburgh, what was then a novelty—paper made from wood. It was considered almost a miraculous novelty. To me it all seemed wrong. I remembered a sentence read out for translation by the old Polish teacher from whom I learnt French. "Books are preented on paaper, ant paaper ees made of rags." That was true, but the amount of paper required so vastly increased (and is still increasing) that it was essential to find some other substance from which to make it. Unfortunately, we have scarcely any trees in this country that can be turned into wood pulp. The United States are luckier. I have had sent to me copies of publications issued by the American Ordnance Department. "Prodigious!" is the word for them. Thick and beautifully shiny pages, lots of them. No crowding of type or use of small print. "Battlenecks" is just the thing to catch the conscience of the war factory worker. Another is "Tremendous Trifles" with its pages laid out so as to impress their lessons on the most infantile minds. The producers understand that appeal to the eye is not less important than appeal to the intelligence.

IN the comments on the great victory won by Field-Marshal Smuts in the South African general election I have seen no suggestion that it is a result, long delayed, of Britain's wise generosity in handing the country back to the Boers as well as the British inhabitants and conferring full self-government upon them. "Cast thy bread upon the waters, for thou shalt find it after many days." Since we "cast our bread" in 1906 (when Campbell-Bannerman took the statesmanlike decision to wipe out war bitterness which led to the foundation of the Union of South Africa), there have been periods in which it seemed that the hostile critics of that act were right. At times the enmity between British and Afrikanders has been almost savage. But they came together when their country was in danger, and the German invasion of Holland swung the Dutch over to the side of the United Nations. South Africa has difficult problems which can be solved if the Dutch and British elements pull together, as they look like doing

# Going Home Again in Liberated Sicily

**BACK TO THEIR WAR-SHATTERED TOWN** return refugees of Bronte, following its occupation by British troops on August 8, 1943. The priest is one who stayed behind and gave valuable help to Amgot officials (see p. 180). Nelson was created Duke of Bronte by the King of Naples in 1799 for services rendered, and a descendant, Lt.-Comdr. Viscount Bridport, is now holder of the title to this estate (see p. 171).

*Photo, British Official*

Printed in England and published every alternate Friday by the Proprietors, THE AMALGAMATED PRESS, LTD., The Fleetway House, Farringdon Street, London, E.C.4. Registered for transmission by Canadian Magazine Post. Sole Agents for Australia and New Zealand : Messrs. Gordon & Gotch, Ltd. ; and for South Africa : Central News Agency, Ltd.—September 17, 1943. S.S. *Editorial Address :* JOHN CARPENTER HOUSE, WHITEFRIARS, LONDON, E.C.4.

**Vol 7** _The War Illustrated_ **N° 164**

_Edited by Sir John Hammerton_

SIXPENCE

OCTOBER 1. 1943

**THIS RUSSIAN ANTI-AIRCRAFT BATTERY, commanded by Senior Lieut. N. Sosynov, has shot down five enemy aircraft. Accurate marksmanship of such men as Sosynov's, in conjunction with brilliant work by the Soviet Air Force, has played great havoc with the Luftwaffe on the Eastern Front. A competent observer estimates total German losses in Russia to be some 40,000 planes, leaving the Luftwaffe there a mere shadow of its former self, and consisting largely of obsolescent types.**

_Photo, Pictorial Press_

# Our Roving Camera Goes on Home Front Tour

IN STALIN AVENUE, aptly named corner of a depot "somewhere in England," many hundreds of armoured vehicles are gathered prior to shipment to Russia. Above, A.T.S. girls put the finishing touches to a consignment of Bren-gun carriers. Thus is our promise of aid to Russia being generously fulfilled.

ST. GILES'S CHURCH, CRIPPLEGATE, one of the many lovely old City of London churches which suffered in the 1940 raids, was the scene of a special service on the Day of National Prayer September 3, 1943—fourth anniversary of our declaration of war on Germany.

THE GUN-FLASH BOARD' is a bright idea at a Mixed Heavy A.A. site near London. Crews compete for the honour, here enjoyed by an A.T.S. spotter, of chalking up their winning slogans.

FIRST TWO OF THE 3,000 farm workers' cottages to be built by the Ministries of Health and Agriculture were formally opened by Mr. Ernest Brown, Minister of Health, on September 15, 1943. Erected at Hildenborough, Kent, in only eleven weeks, at a cost of £950 each, they will be let at 14s. 6d. per week.

HOP-PICKING SEASON IN KENT offers a working holiday to all comers. Above is a family of pickers, representative of the army of 100,000 who from 7 a.m. till dusk strip the hop vines. Such a family, or two energetic friends working briskly, can pick 40 bushels of hops in a day, paid for at 6d. a bushel. The pickers live in their own communities—and receive an extra ration of cheese, being temporarily regarded as "agricultural workers."

   Photos, British Official: Crown Copyright; Fox, Planet News, Associated Press, Keystone

# THE BATTLE FRONTS

## by Maj.-Gen. Sir Charles Gwynn, K.C.B., D.S.O.

I HAVE always held that one of Hitler's greatest blunders was his failure to insist on taking part in the original invasion of Egypt in 1940. At the time I was desperately anxious that Graziani's slow movements might indicate that he was waiting for reinforcement by German Panzer Divisions, and possibly by contingents of the Luftwaffe.

Wavell's little army could have had little chance of successfully resisting a determined attack, and it was obvious that the Western Desert, with the mechanization of armies and development of air power, had lost its value as a defensive obstacle. Admiral Cunningham's Fleet, boldly as it was being used, was greatly inferior in material power to the Italian Navy, and it could not be expected to prevent the passage of transports from Italy to Tripoli or Cyrenaica. Malta had at the time no offensive value; it possessed no aircraft and could not be used as an operational naval base.

Why did Hitler neglect to seize the opportunity? The fall of France had left him with an army of much larger size than he could use for the invasion of Britain, even if he soon realized that he would need the whole strength of the Luftwaffe in connexion with his invasion project. He stood in no danger of attack from any quarter—not even from Russia, for before invading France he had taken precautions on the new frontier in Poland.

HE could therefore have spared at least two of his Panzer divisions and a few motorized infantry divisions which would have sufficed to give Graziani overwhelming strength; and German advisers would no doubt have supplied the drive which Graziani lacked. One can only assume that Hitler considered that the war was already won, and was obsessed with the vision of seeing himself leading a triumphal march into London.

He may have thought that would in itself settle the fate of the Middle East, and have considered that division of the spoils would be easier if Italy had not already staked her claim. When eventually he dispatched Rommel and his Afrika Korps to Graziani's assistance the opportunity of securing a decisive victory had passed and North Africa had become an ulcer which was by degrees to fester and burst.

To appreciate the magnitude of our escape and its bearing on the development of the war situation as a whole, let us recall the sequence of events and their implication.

In the first instance, Wavell's victorious campaign was a blow to Italian morale from which it never recovered; a result that contributed to the contempt in which the Germans held their partners, not without its effects on the ultimate dissolution of the partnership. It made possible the elimination of Italian East African possessions, which had notable effects on the naval situation in the Indian Ocean and Red Sea. It paved the way for the subsequent North African campaigns, which, after varying fortune, culminated in the Tunis victory and the invasion of Italy.

Without the retention of our Middle East base the Allied landing in North-West Africa would probably have never been contemplated, for the cooperation of the Eighth Army was an essential element in the plan. The success of the African land campaign resulted first in the retention of our naval bases in the Eastern Mediterranean, and later in the capture of the new naval and air bases which re-established our control over the Mediterranean route.

But it was not only in the war with Italy that our retention of the Middle East was of vital importance. It enabled us to intervene in Greece; and although intervention led to a severe temporary reverse it had an immense effect on delaying and upsetting German plans for the conquest of Russia. Even the Crete disaster called for an effort by Germany which defeated Hitler's plan for securing control of Syria and Iraq and for isolating Turkey.

All through the campaigns based on the Middle East the diversion of Luftwaffe strength was sufficient to have a considerable effect on other theatres of war, and the diversion of Reichswehr strength, if it did not reach so high a proportion, was far from negligible. All the more because the crushing defeat of the German troops engaged did much to shake belief in German invincibility.

### GERMAN General Staff Lost Great Opportunity

Taking this series of events and their far-reaching results into consideration, one may admit that Wavell's claim that the victories of the Army of the Nile would prove a turning point in the war has been amply justified, although it has often been derided by the cynical. It should not be forgotten, however, that Wavell's achievement was made possible by the bold decision of the Government to send him reinforcements, ill as they could be spared from Britain.

I have often wondered if the German General Staff has ever realized what a great opportunity they had lost, and whether they will excuse themselves by claiming that their Panzer divisions and their troops in general were not trained or equipped for desert warfare, about which little was understood till Wavell demonstrated its possibilities.

THEIR FIRST SMOKE IN ITALY is hugely enjoyed by these men of a Royal Engineers Field Company, who landed near Reggio.
*Photo, British Official : Crown Copyright*

While events in the Mediterranean were reaching a climax, the Russian Army was upsetting many preconceived beliefs and theories. The widely held belief that the Red Army's offensive power could only be developed under winter conditions has gone by the board, and with it a belief that the German theorists had devised an impregnable system of defence.

Surprising were the Russian successes when their summer offensive was launched. The presumed impregnable German defensive line was penetrated, not at one point only but at many, in spite of stubborn resistance and the employment of every available reserve in fierce counter-attacks. It was expected that the Russian onslaught would exhaust itself and lose its momentum. But in spite of temporary checks the impetus of the attack increased rather than diminished, till the German front over a distance of some 600 miles was reeling back, seeking a still shorter and more defensible rallying line.

At the time I am writing a shorter front has not been found, for though the distance between the terminal points of the front of retreat has been shortened the front has actually lengthened, owing to the bulges formed in it. The failure of the German defence is certainly not due to the fighting quality of their troops, but it is the more remarkable since it has occurred in Africa and now, when for the first time seriously tested under summer conditions. in Russia.

I am of the opinion that the failure has been largely due to the cult of the offensive carried to extremes. All soldiers agree that to be successful defence must be active with constant counter-strokes; but counter-attacks must be used with discretion or they may lead to excessive losses and the rapid expenditure of reserves; and German defensive theories tend towards their reckless use. I suspect that is why the Germans in the crisis of the battle have so frequently been left without the necessary reserve power to tip the scales.

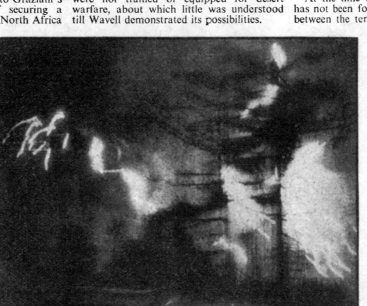

AN EERIE SCENE on the southern Russian front as flares are dropped by bombers of the Soviet Air Force during a night attack. The Luftwaffe, first mastered in the Battle of Britain, has again been cowed by mighty air-fleets the Russians have mustered.
*Photo, Planet News*

# Twilight of the Axis Gods Descends on Italy

THE SCENE IS ITALY, the day September 3, 1943, when General Montgomery's magnificent 8th Army had the honour of being the first Allied troops to set foot on the mainland of Europe. Italy had accepted the United Nations' demand for her unconditional surrender; an armistice would be effective on September 8; but troops who confronted our invading army swarming across the straits (2) from Messina were not aware of the Italian Government's submission. This Canadian signaller (1) was one of the few casualties, but he remained at his post; two of his comrades, though out of the fight, were able to wade to safety (3). On September 3 Reggio fell: the Royal Navy's ensign was hoisted over the harbour (4). By September 8, our troops had established a bridgehead (see map) extending north and south of Reggio and well into the interior. See aslo pp. 265 and 267.

*Photos, British Official: Crown Copyright;*
*Map by courtesy of The News Chronicle*

# 8th Army Objective Clear to Conquerors' Eyes

**GENERALS MONTGOMERY AND EISENHOWER** view from a balcony in Messina the Italian mainland, only three miles distant. Bright is the outlook. Across the narrow strait the 8th Army would—five days later, as they had planned—successfully land on Calabria, even as it had invaded Sicily. Occasion of this meeting, on August 29, 1943, was the bestowal on Gen. Montgomery of the highest distinction America can confer on a soldier of another nation—Chief Commander of the Legion of Merit.

*Photo. British Official: Crown Copyright*

SURRENDER OF THE ITALIAN FLEET took place at Valetta Harbour, Malta, on September 10, 1943. These cruisers, seen from an escorting R.A.F. plane, had steamed from Spezia together with two battleships, three other cruisers and four destroyers. By September 12 all the Italian fleet had been accounted for. H.M. the King, congratulating Admiral of the Fleet Sir Andrew Cunningham, C.-in-C. Mediterranean, said : " Throughout the Empire we are all proud of this glorious chapter in the history of the British Navy."
*Photo, British Official : Crown Copyright*

# THE WAR AT SEA

### by Francis E. McMurtrie

IT was in August 1943 that the Prime Minister and President Roosevelt, in a joint statement, announced a great victory over the U-boats in the preceding three months. In the weeks that followed the standard of success was evidently well maintained, for in August the number of enemy submarines destroyed was greater than the total of merchant vessels sunk.

German efforts to restore the position by mounting more anti-aircraft guns in submarines have failed to make any difference. It is now alleged that all U-boats are to be re-engined with silent machinery, giving no clue to the Asdic detectors which at present are able to trace a submarine's movements under water. This story need not be taken too seriously, since in the first place it is a tremendous undertaking to replace the machinery of every U-boat, and in the second, it may well be doubted whether silent-running engines such as described have yet been perfected.

It will be recalled that before the war the Germans were stated to have evolved a new method of propulsion by which only a single type of engine would be used for navigating their submarines, both on the surface and when submerged. The method was said to be based on an invention which had already been tested in this country without yielding the results desired. This marvellous engine has since proved to be a myth.

A FURTHER naval victory has been won with the surrender of most of the Italian fleet, an occasion comparable with the arrival of the German fleet in the Firth of Forth in November 1918. The consequences of this victory should be far-reaching, since it will enable the naval situation in the Mediterranean to be controlled by far smaller forces than the Allies have recently considered it necessary to maintain there. There should no longer be any occasion for all the six battleships—H.M.S. Howe, King George V, Nelson, Rodney, Valiant and Warspite—to remain on the station ; and there should be less need of aircraft carriers and cruisers. Ships so released can be utilized to reinforce the Eastern Fleet under Admiral Sir James Somerville, expected to play the leading part in the campaign against the Japanese which is now being planned by Admiral Lord Louis Mountbatten, the new supreme Commander-in-Chief.

For convoy work in the Mediterranean the surrendered Italian ships—or at any rate, some of them—should be quite useful. At the time of writing it is not clear whether the Germans have succeeded in detaining any important ships, though it is believed that at least one battleship was under refit at Pola, where she may have been seized. In any case, it is a heavy blow for the enemy, whose position at sea is rapidly becoming hopeless. Despite its hasty sortie to Spitsbergen, it is to be doubted whether the German Navy will ever again proceed to sea as a fleet, while Hitler's chosen weapon, the U-boat, has become so blunted that its blows are easily parried.

Its chances of accomplishing much in the Mediterranean are poor, for that sea is not well suited for submarine operations, in spite of the remarkable successes gained by our own underwater craft there. If the U-boats were unable to interfere effectively with the Sicilian landings, there is little hope of their being able to fill the gap left by the defection of the Italian Navy.

### ITALIAN Warship Design Aimed At High Speed

One solitary success at sea was gained when the Luftwaffe torpedoed the Roma, of 35,000 tons, Italy's newest battleship. No information is available concerning the number of hits secured, but the only eye witness account received suggests that a magazine exploded. This is hardly a good advertisement for Italian warship design ; but for more than half a century this has been governed by the principle of sacrificing all other considerations to high speed. It may well be, therefore, that in order to secure more powerful engines, magazine protection against underwater attack was neglected.

So far as the Allies are concerned, it made little difference whether the Roma was sunk or surrendered. She would have been valueless to the enemy in either case ; and fortunately the United Nations already possess as many battleships as are needed to overcome Japan while keeping a watch over the remnant of the German fleet.

German hopes of dominating the Mediterranean by means of aircraft have long vanished. Inferior in strength to the Allied air forces, the Luftwaffe is now waging a losing battle in Italy, the odds against it becoming even greater as fresh airfields are acquired by the advancing 8th and 5th Armies. It should not be long, therefore, before the main interest in the war at sea is centred in the Eastern theatre. There the United States Navy, with aid from the Royal Australian and Royal New Zealand Navies, has been steadily gaining ground as its losses at Pearl Harbour have been made good and new ships added to its strength. With the accession to our own Eastern Fleet of those ships that can be spared from the Mediterranean, the time is fast approaching when Japanese sea power will be challenged to a trial of strength.

ASSUMING that as many as six battleships are retained in British waters to counterbalance the German force of three, there will be available to the East a maximum of 32 capital ships. This does not include the French Lorraine, Courbet and Paris, nor any of the surrendered Italians.

At the opening of hostilities the Japanese possessed ten battleships, two of which have since been lost. They are believed to have completed at least two new ones, and may have two more almost ready for sea. This gives a potential total of 12, or considerably less than half the Allied strength in this category.

It may be argued, however, with some show of truth, that in the wide Pacific aircraft carriers may count for more than battleships. In that case, the position still remains an unpromising one for Japan. It has been officially stated that by the end of the year the United States Navy will include 14 first-line carriers. How many the Royal Navy will have at that date has not been disclosed ; but the present total is not less than six, and judging from what has been published concerning ships under construction, there ought to be at least eight in service by December 31 next. This makes 22 in all, without counting escort aircraft carriers, which have been built in large numbers.

Japan began the war with nine aircraft carriers. Five or six of these have been destroyed, leaving possibly four, perhaps only three. New construction may have added something to this, but it is questionable if it can have doubled the figure in view of Japan's limited shipbuilding resources. Thus, the odds are again fully two to one, even if it is considered necessary to leave a couple of Allied carriers in European waters.

Japan's great advantage is, of course, her unique strategical position, which renders it extremely difficult to strike at her vital spots. In time this difficulty is bound to be overcome, and the margin of strength outlined above ought to be adequate for the task. The Allies' chief handicap is lack of suitable bases within reach of Japanese possessions, but this obstacle is not insuperable.

# 'General Chase' Signal Spells U-Boats' Doom

THREE U-BOATS are spotted by a Liberator (above), first act in the Bay of Biscay drama related at the foot of this page. The U-boats were proceeding in close order on the surface at full speed : note how their wash is unmistakable from the air. A Sunderland flying boat accounted for the first of the trio, also getting this photograph (right) of the survivors bunched together in the water around a rubber dinghy that was dropped to them by the plane.

VETERAN N. ATLANTIC U-boat hunters participated in the action—an escort group of Royal Navy sloops under the command of Capt. F. J. Walker, D.S.O., R.N., once of H.M.S. Starling, now of H.M.S. Kite ; below, right, Capt. Walker addresses men of H.M.S. Wildgoose, one of his group. Below, left, H.M.S. Wildgoose and (nearer camera) H.M.S. Starling in port again after a foray. On September 14, 1943 Capt. Walker was awarded the C.B for his exploits while in command of H.M.S. Starling.

GREATEST ONE-DAY TRIUMPH of the war against U-boats in the Bay of Biscay was recently won by aircraft of Coastal Command and the U.S.A.A.F. cooperating with sloops of the Royal Navy commanded by Capt. F. J. Walker, D.S.O., R.N., one of the most successful anti-submarine officers of the war. In less than six hours three U-boats were destroyed. A Liberator spotted them moving in close order at full speed on the surface. Within an hour and a half wireless signals brought six more planes to the scene, and Capt. Walker's sloops were steaming full-speed towards their enemy. The U-boats made no attempt to submerge, trusting themselves to a barrage of anti-aircraft fire. An R.A.F. Sunderland destroyed the first of the enemy trio with depth charges. A Halifax of Coastal Command played a great part in the sinking of the second, with anti-submarine bombs and shell-fire. The third crash-dived, but the sloops had now arrived. Capt. Walker hoisted the "General Chase" order— historic signal which opened the attack on the Spanish Armada in 1588— and for more than three hours his ships patterned the area with depth charges. Suddenly oil and wreckage floated to the surface—the last of the preying trio had gone to its doom. This action was one of five which took place within a few days. In all, nine U-boats were spotted and seven destroyed. Announcing these achievements on September 6, 1943, the Admiralty and Air Ministry called them " a notable victory.'

*Photos, British Official*

# Royal Australian Navy Proud of New Cruiser

H.M.S. SHROPSHIRE, 9,830-ton cruiser, is the latest acquisition of the Royal Australian Navy, presented by the Royal Navy to replace the flagship H.M.A.S. Canberra, which sank in the Battle of the Solomon Islands in August 1942. It was announced on Sept. 7, 1943 that the Shropshire had left a British port, after extensive refitting and modernization.

Repainting the ship (1) was, of course, necessary, and certainly the guns had to be cleaned (2) to perfection, preparatory to the ship being inspected by Dr. Evatt, Australian Minister for External Affairs (5), before leaving for her new scene of action : the cheer-leader is the skipper, Capt. J. A. Collins, C.B. (4). The Australian ensign hoisted (3), the Shropshire sailed away.

*Photos, Fox, Planet News, Barratt's Photo Press*

# Unconditional Surrender: Italy Pays the Price

With blaring bands, boastful orations and much flag-wagging Italy entered the war on June 10, 1940. Some three years later, on September 8, 1943, she abandoned the struggle against the United Nations, though not yet is she out of the War. The story of the capitulation, so far as it may yet be told, is the subject of this article by E. ROYSTON PIKE.

HARDLY had Mussolini slipped, or been kicked, from his commanding position on a reeling world when Marshal Badoglio, his successor as the chief of the Italian state, entered into negotiations with the United Nations. He knew that the position was desperate, that the Italian armies could not be expected to continue the fight for more than a brief space, one to be measured in weeks and days.

So in the first week of August Badoglio sent two Italian generals as his emissaries to contact the British representatives in two neutral countries. Each stressed the desperate character of Italy's plight, and asked for the conditions under which an armistice might be granted. To each the reply was the same: unconditional surrender.

In the middle of August General Castellano presented himself to Sir Samuel Hoare, the British Ambassador in Madrid, and the next day to Sir Ronald Campbell, our ambassador in Lisbon. Castellano told Sir Ronald that he had come with Marshal Badoglio's full authority to say that when the Allies landed in Italy itself the Italian Government was prepared to switch its alliance and join the United Nations in the war against Germany. The message was at once transmitted to the British Government, and in reply the American and British Governments declared that Italy must first surrender unconditionally and then accept the Allies' further terms. These terms were embodied in a document which was handed by Sir Ronald Campbell to General Castellano and taken by him to Rome.

It consisted of 13 clauses, the most important of which demanded the immediate cessation of all hostile activity by the Italian armed forces; that Italy should use her best endeavours to deny to Germany facilities that might be used against the United Nations; that all Allied prisoners should be handed over immediately; that the Italian fleet, aircraft and merchant shipping should be transferred immediately to the Allies; that Corsica, together with all Italian territory, both mainland and islands, should be surrendered at once to the Allies for them to use as operational bases and for any other purposes they thought fit; that the free use by the Allies of all Italian airfields and ports should be guaranteed forthwith; that Italy should withdraw immediately all her forces engaged in other theatres of war; that the Italian Government should guarantee that it would, if necessary, employ all its armed forces to ensure exact and prompt compliance with all the provisions of the armistice.

MEANWHILE, at home in Italy the old Marshal looked on at, perhaps actively encouraged, the liquidation of the Fascist regime. Mussolini disappeared for the time being on July 25, and all the men who had risen to greatness with the Duce were involved in his disgrace and fell with him. The Fascist organizations were swept away, with every material expression of the Fascist creed. There was a grand clearance of ideological rubbish, a cleansing of the filth engendered and accumulated by twenty years of dictatorship. After long years of suppression, years during which newspapers and schools and local councils were the ready vassals and convenient tools of the Fascist State, the Italian people began to find their tongues, to criticize, to

assail, to *act*. They were tired to death of Mussolini's imperialism, of the endless defeats, of being trailed in the wake of Hitler's war machine. They hated the Germans. They wanted to get out of the war as quickly and as completely as possible.

Even in the police-state of Mussolini's making the dissatisfaction had been widespread—as was seen at once when Fascism collapsed like a child's balloon at the touch of a lighted cigarette. Six anti-Fascist parties, ranging from Liberals through Christian Democrats and Socialists to Communists, emerged from the underworld in which they had been forced to operate hitherto, and organized or supported strikes in the northern cities launched with the political purpose of securing an immediate armistice. On August 12 a committee of these parties published their disapproval of Badoglio's continued prosecution of the war, and saddled him with the responsibility of allowing yet more German troops to enter the peninsula.

## Armistice Signed in Sicily

By now Badoglio's reply had been conveyed to the Allied advanced H.Q. in Sicily: it was to the effect that the Italian Government was under the control of the Germans and considered it impossible to announce the armistice before the Allied main landing in Italy. The Italian general who had brought the Marshal's reply was sent back to demand an acceptance of the terms within 24 hours, while Castellano remained behind in Sicily to make known the fact of the armistice if the Germans by occupying Rome should prevent Badoglio from doing so. Within 24 hours the Marshal's message of acceptance was received, and on Sept. 3 the armistice was signed in Sicily in the presence of Gen. Eisenhower and Gen. Alexander by Gen. Bedell Smith, representing the Allied C.-in-C., and Gen. Castellano on behalf of Marshal Badoglio. That same day Montgomery's 8th Army had crossed the narrow channel from Sicily and landed on the Italian " toe."

It was stipulated that the armistice should come into force at the moment most favourable to the Allies. That moment was deemed to have arrived on Sept. 8; at 5.30 B.S.T. on

that afternoon the " cease fire " was given to the 8th Army.

The Italian capitulation was announced by General Eisenhower from Algiers Radio:

This is Gen. Dwight Eisenhower, Commander-in-Chief Allied Forces: The Italian Government has surrendered its armed forces unconditionally. As Allied Commander-in-Chief I have granted a Military Armistice the terms of which have been approved by the Governments of the United Kingdom, United States and Union of Socialist Soviet Republics. I am thus acting in the interests of the United Nations. The Italian Government has bound itself to abide by these terms without reservation. The Armistice was signed by my representative and the representative of Marshal Badoglio, and becomes effective this instant. Hostilities between the armed forces of the United Nations and those of Italy terminate at once. All Italians who now act to help to eject the German aggressor from Italian soil will have the assistance and support of the United Nations.

FEW were surprised at the news—unless it were the Germans. At first Berlin professed that the Reich government had already taken " precautionary measures necessary for the safeguarding of the continuation of the war until victory by Germany and her allies," but the hollowness of this bravado was soon exposed by none other than Hitler himself. Breaking a silence of many months, the Fuehrer on Sept. 10 presented the world with the nauseous spectacle of Satan rebuking sin. It was indeed a chastened, sobered Hitler who whiningly complained of the tactics that had been " used against an ally who had fulfilled his duty with blood and sacrifices beyond the letter of the treaty."

The same night a communiqué from Hitler's H.Q. gave the news of the German occupation of Rome and Genoa and much of Northern Italy, of clashes with Italian soldiers and the disarming of the Italian garrisons in the Balkans and France.

As a result of the armistice the Allies obtained the Italian fleet, but the delay in negotiating it had enabled the Germans to pour so many troops into Italy that the peninsula rapidly became a battlefield. The Italians have not finished paying yet for the infamous "stab in the back " of 1940.

**NEW YORKERS CELEBRATED** the capitulation of Italy with traditional Manhattan ticker-tape carnival. Jubilant crowds thronged the main streets of the city; strangers shook hands and congratulated one another; and from the windows of skyscrapers office-workers hurled hastily-made confetti and streamers. In the Italian quarter, men, women and children wept for joy.

*Photo, Associated Press*

# How Air Power Contributed to Italy's Fall

It is impossible to discriminate in awarding laurels for the triumphs of North Africa, Sicily and Italy. But it does not minimize in any way the contributions thereto of the strategists, the sailors, the artillerymen and infantrymen and other branches of the Services to appraise the magnificent achievements of the Air Arm, as CAPT. NORMAN MACMILLAN, M.C., A.F.C., does here.

WHEN Mussolini and King Victor Emmanuel threw Italy into the war on June 10, 1940—with France almost prostrate under the apparently all-conquering German troops—the air position of the British and Imperial forces in North Africa was fraught with danger.

The R.A.F. in Egypt and Palestine had then 168 first-line aircraft— 40 Gladiator fighters, 70 Blenheim bombers, 24 Lysander Army cooperation aircraft, ten flying boats, and 24 Bombay and Valentia transport aircraft. The Italians in Libya opposed us with 400 fighters and bombers of modern types in equal proportions, plus further obsolescent aircraft. Their lines of supply across the Mediterranean were short ; ours were long—round the Cape of Good Hope.

We evacuated British Somaliland as the Italians marched in, but even then we had begun the campaign against the Italian forces in Abyssinia. The latter were cut off. They were too far from Italy to receive reinforcements by air, and the British Navy barred reinforcement by sea while we held Alexandria and the Suez Canal. Bold, and above all swift, action in the Mediterranean by Italy might have carried the day for the Italian forces in Abyssinia.

A determined onslaught by land and air upon our combined forces in the Eastern Mediterranean might have altered the whole course of the war. Admiral Cunningham himself said : " When the war started we were at the mercy of Italian bombers."

But the Italians were incapable of making the necessary effort. Instead, David struck at Goliath. In November 1940 the main Italian fleet was crippled where it lay in Taranto harbour by ten Swordfish which, armed with torpedoes, flew from the aircraft carrier Illustrious at night from the sea somewhere west of Crete.

Two Hurricane squadrons joined the R.A.F. in Egypt during the autumn of 1940. Greek resistance, aided by the R.A.F. and the Fleet Air Arm, held up Italy ; Graziani dilly-dallied in the desert at Sidi Barrani. Then Wavell struck. In a brilliant desert campaign, with a numerically inferior force and a minimum of air support, he drove the Italians right back through Cyrenaica and took whole armies prisoner during the winter of 1940-41. This forced Germany to send troops to North Africa.

MEANWHILE, Italian fighter aircraft in Abyssinia were destroyed by British fighters. Bereft of fighter support the Regia Aeronautica in Abyssinia was unable to ward off attacks made by British bombers of relatively obsolescent type—the only kind we could spare at the time. Thus air superiority over Italian North East Africa was obtained without depleting too seriously the demands of Fighter Command in Britain for its life-and-death struggle with the Luftwaffe over England and the Low Countries.

My friend, Lieut.-Commdr. B. J. Hurren, of the Naval Air Branch, in his interesting personal narrative, Eastern Med, recalls how his convoy sailed up the Red Sea in December 1940 with more than 35,000 troops. Eighteen ships of 20,000 tons and more were escorted by one cruiser and two corvettes. Five miles to west lay the Eritrean coast. Hurren's particular ship carried only four Lewis guns to defend herself against air attack. But Mussolini's North-east African airmen were short of bombs.They dropped 4-inch shells in lieu of bombs when raiding Aden !

Italian intervention in the war became a nuisance to Germany instead of a help. The checks and reverses suffered by the Italians at the hands of forces much inferior in numbers of men, ships, guns, tanks, and aircraft brought Germany precipitately into the Balkans, through Greece, and into Crete to guard the right flank of what was to become her Eastern Front against Russia. Simultaneously German and Italian forces drove us out of Cyrenaica back into Egypt. Malta's long ordeal began. Cyprus became an important air base.

But behind the thin screen of men and ships protecting Egypt, which the German and Italian armies could not penetrate, and which the Italian forces had lost the opportunity to prise open, our small and specialized forces retook British Somaliland, captured Italian Somaliland, Eritrea, and Abyssinia.

IN the spring of 1941 the R.A.F. played a vital part in quelling the Irakian revolt. Soon afterwards the R.A.F. and the Fleet Air Arm provided skilful cover for the entry of British forces into Syria. Before the Syrian campaign ended Hitler struck at Russia. But we had direct access to Iran. British and Russian troops met. The first arc of the circle was drawn around Germany, from Murmansk to the eastern frontier of Egypt. The load of air attack on the United Kingdom was reduced.

By this time the trans-African route from the Atlantic West Coast was in full operation, and fighter aircraft, fitted with extra fuel tanks, were able to fly to Egypt, thus saving the long sea voyage round the Cape. American aircraft, in addition to British, were pouring into Egypt, and by the time Auchinleck struck at Rommel in November 1941 the British forces in Egypt possessed numerical and technical air superiority over the opposing enemy forces.

Part of this achievement of air superiority must be attributed to gallant Malta, which proved a veritable death-knell to enemy aircraft (and ships) in the Mediterranean ; part of the credit for the defence of Malta must go to the Royal Navy, which ran the convoys to the beleaguered island against enemy bombers and submarines. Fighter aircraft from the aircraft carriers played a valiant part in that dangerous task. Would the essential supplies have got through without the aid of aircraft carriers ?

In June 1942 the tide of battle swung us back to El Alamein, 80 miles from Alexandria. Came again the vast preparations. Still greater superiority was built up in the air. Tank-buster Hurricanes came to the desert. Rommel's fighter opposition was beaten down by fighters killing it in the air, and bombers blasting it to destruction on the ground.

MONTGOMERY's forces swept forward after a terrible blizzard of bullets, shells, and bombs ; broke through, and preceded continuously by air power, on a scale never before seen in the desert, took Cyrenaica, Tripolitania, and, with Anderson's 1st Army and the Americans from Algeria, took Tunisia, Lampedusa, Pantelleria, and Sicily.

Still the air blizzard blew ahead of the armies—over the south of Italy, over Rome, Naples, Taranto, and a hundred other places—while in the north cascades of bombs from Britain fell upon the arms towns of Turin and Milan, and lesser loads upon Genoa, Spezia, Leghorn, and Pisa—military legacy of the first small raids that were made upon the Lombardian arms towns two nights after Italy declared war. North of the Alps more bombs fell upon railway centres and the arms towns of Germany and Austria, destroying latent military power and the means by which it might pass to the aid of the Italians.

Mussolini fell. Marshal Badoglio surrendered unconditionally, and the Armistice was signed on September 3, 1943 (the day on which the Eighth Army landed in Italy). Aircraft brought Italian representatives to Sicily to conclude the Armistice.

**NAPLES, weakly-beating heart of the network of railways in southern Italy, was by September 7, 1943 the centre of a 100-mile arc of destruction wrought by bombers of the Strategic Air Force. Here, in the harbour, lies a 20,000-ton ship, one of our targets, now a blazing hulk.**
*Photo, New York Times Photos*

# The Achilles Heel of Hitler's Ambitions

CONFIGURATION OF ITALY simplifies strategy but favours the enemy. The mountainous interior compels the main railways to follow the coasts, with but few traversing lines running along valleys, thus limiting the points at which transport can be dislocated—such as Bologna, Rome, Naples and Foggia, all of which have been pounded by our bombers. The inhospitable hinterland encountered by our men who have landed in the neighbourhood of Reggio, Taranto and especially Salerno, makes even a mile's advance an achievement. *Specially drawn for* THE WAR ILLUSTRATED *by Félix Gardon*

# China Undaunted In Seventh Year of Battle

SINCE JULY 1937 our ally China has striven valiantly against Japan. So much so that Mr. T. V. Soong, Chinese Foreign Minister, was able to reveal on Sept. 14, 1943 that peace overtures by the enemy were "persistent."

Street fighting (1) is the last stage in the retaking of a "Hsien," or provincial city, one of the occasional gains made from the enemy by the Chinese, led by such brilliant generals as Chaung Fa Kwei (2), of "The Ironsides." Indomitable fighters, our Allies rush headlong to attack when they can, as in this episode (3) from the Central Front. They are justly proud of their trophies, such as these Japanese helmets (4) captured during the Battle of the Upper Yangtze, where the Chinese defended the approach to their wartime capital. See also pages 116-117.

*Photos, Chinese Official, Keystone*

# Japanese in New Guinea Lairs Get No Respite

**LAE, CAPITAL OF NEW GUINEA,** and Salamaua, main Japanese advanced base on that island, are objectives of Gen. MacArthur's latest drive. By September 13, 1943 Salamaua had fallen and Lae was being invested by Allied "pincers" (see map). On September 5 Australian artillerymen dropped from the skies with American infantry in the upper reaches of the River Markham; Australian troops advanced from the south to join them; another contingent was landed to the north-east of Lae, completing the trap. Campaigning in this territory is formidable: guns are man-handled into position (1) and supplies must reach jungle front lines (2). A Liberator (3) has just bombed the airfield at Lae (marked **X**) and adjacent targets indicated by arrow. Map in p. 109 shows how Rabaul, great Jap base, is menaced by our progress here and by our recent gains in New Georgia.

PAGE 269      *Photos, Australian Official, Sport & General, News Chronicle.  Map by courtesy of The Daily Mail*

# Nazis' Balkan Cornerstone—Bulgaria—Is Loose

The death of King Boris of Bulgaria on August 28, 1943, removed Hitler's most powerful vassal in the Balkans. The possible strategic consequences, here discussed by HENRY BAERLEIN, may well include an open rupture between the pro-Nazi Government and the pro-Russian people. Definitely the Nazi cornerstone in the Balkans has been loosened.

"TELL me," said King Boris on one occasion as we sat in his tawny-coloured palace, "tell me, how is my colleague in Belgrade?" In that very democratic fashion did he refer to Alexander, his colleague in the art of kingship. It was regrettable that his democratic sentiments were not powerful enough to keep him out of the clutch of the totalitarian rulers and bring Bulgaria, like all the other Slav countries—Russia, Poland, Czechoslovakia and Yugoslavia—into the democratic fold.

He would have liked to do so when Hitler attacked the Soviet and thereby antagonized the vast majority of Bulgars, but when you sup with the devil you cannot get up till you have had your dessert. Now that Boris has gone one naturally asks what will be the political and military consequences.

Hitler telegraphed to the Bulgarian Queen that he was "shattered" by the tragic news of the death of Boris, which he himself had probably caused by making such further demands for collaboration that in view of the rising Bulgarian discontent Boris could only escape from the *impasse* by suicide. What is certain is that German plans in the Balkans will be shattered if Bulgaria now refuses to support them.

HITHERTO all has gone according to the Nazi desire—Boris urged us to refrain from bombing the Rumanian oilfields and refineries, on the ground that the passage of our planes over his country would give Hitler an excuse to occupy it; the time thus gained was used by Hitler to reinforce his defences of the oilfields, whereupon Boris threw off the mask and allowed Bulgaria to be overrun by the Germans. Sofia became the seat of the anti-invasion General Staff, with the German General of the Air Force, Löhr, at its head; its members included ten German generals, three Italians and one Bulgar.

There has been feverish activity in those parts of the Balkans controlled by the Nazis, because they know very well that in other parts an Allied landing will have the assistance of the population. And the presence of so many German troops in Bulgaria has become more than ever necessary since the reverses they have suffered in Russia.

Large areas of Greece and Yugoslavia are being policed by the Bulgars; but Hitler demanded in addition that Bulgaria should be fully mobilized, economically and mili-

tarily, to supply German needs; also that a considerable Bulgarian army should at once take up its position on the Turkish frontier and the Gestapo should have perfect liberty of action throughout Bulgaria.

The growing discontent has been manifested by the murder of various Bulgarian sympathizers with the Nazis; and in spite of all the police raids and house searches it has been impossible for Drexler, the Gestapo chief in Sofia, to discover the executioners.

THERE exists in the Bulgarian army a secret democratic and pro-Russian organization known as "Damian." Not long ago numerous officers belonging to it were dismissed at Drexler's orders. But Damian has by no means been blotted out, and one asks whether, with the help of the Bulgarian man in the street, it will be able to save the country before it is too late. Of course, the Germans will spare no effort to prevent this awkward satellite from breaking away; all the airfields are in their possession and it is very difficult for a Bulgar to visit the Black Sea ports of Varna or Bourgas.

There was a time, early in the war, when the natives of those ports might have awakened one day and found to their surprise that Bulgaria had quite a navy, for an inquiry was addressed by Boris to Ankara as to whether a fleet of his warships might come through the Straits. Once in the Black Sea they would have hoisted their true Italian colours and, manned probably by German sailors, have been employed against the Russians. The Turks were not helpful; the plot petered out, and now the Germans, on the defensive, look anxiously from the Bulgarian shore in the direction of Russia.

## Pro-Russian Sentiment Prevails

It is likely that for some time the Germans will be able to maintain themselves in Bulgaria with their own resources, certain politicians and those officers, a diminishing band, who still believe in German invincibility, because that was an axiom at the war academies they attended in the Reich. The Bulgars are an obstinate, dour people, and, while they acknowledge that in the second Balkan War and in the war of 1914-1918 they backed the wrong horse, a fair proportion of the older officers are still of opinion that this cannot happen again. Others are to such an extent compromised that they have

A SMILE FROM HIS MASTER, Hitler, greeted King Boris of Bulgaria on a recent visit to the Fuehrer's headquarters. Rumour associated the death of Boris with certain decisions taken at this meeting.
*Photo, Sport & General*

no choice but to continue. Thus it will probably take some time before the pro-Russian majority in the country can make its influence felt. This pro-Russian sentiment, indeed, not only prevails among the masses, irrespective of the regime in Russia, but is cherished by the intelligentsia; there was a proposal to eliminate from the Cyrillic alphabet three rather redundant letters, but as these letters were being retained in Russia the students of Sofia University went on strike until the proposal was shelved.

Human nature being what it is, an act of benevolence does not invariably cause the recipient to be eternally grateful, but the statue in front of Sofia's Parliament building of the Tsar who liberated the Bulgars in 1878, and the splendid white cathedral presented by Russia to the capital, have not caused the Bulgars to swerve from their traditional devotion. German life insurance companies would do well to remember that the red pavement of Sofia's central square has often been turned a darker red by the two Macedonian factions, as to whom one's only regret is that some of them managed to escape. It will be less easy in the case of Germans.

WHAT emerges out of the present uncertainties is that the state of things in Bulgaria is a good deal less favourable to the Nazis than it lately was. The strategic advantages we shall in due course gain are very obvious: the Turks freed from a menace to the north, the Russians more in control of the Black Sea, and the whole Balkan Peninsula, as in the last war, the avenue through which our armies will march into Central Europe.

It is extremely significant that the three pro-Nazi Regents have been illegally appointed; they should have been chosen by the Great Sobranje, a numerous assembly elected *ad hoc* by the whole people, but the Germans and their Bulgarian collaborators knew very well what would happen if this had been permitted. Certainly the death of Boris has loosened the Nazi cornerstone in the Balkans and frantic efforts are being made to provide a buttress.

BOY KING SIMEON II, who succeeded to the throne of Bulgaria on the death of his father, Boris, attends a parade of his troops. "His Majesty faces stormy days and many trials," said Christo Kalfoff, President of the Bulgarian Chamber, proclaiming him. The background of impending events in the young Simeon's dissension-torn land is authoritatively examined in this page.
*Radio Photo by Keystone*

## Royal Navy Makes Invasion Possible

Keeping the ocean highways open is vital to our building-up of supplies, accomplishment of which helps to make possible the mounting of such gigantic amphibious operations as the invasions of Sicily and Italy. Typical of smaller vessels that get the convoys through is the corvette Widgeon, about to go into action with her A.A. guns (bottom). Note the bomb-flash protecting head and hand gear. Officers of a cruiser (top) on convoy duty tensely watch dispersal of an enemy air attack.

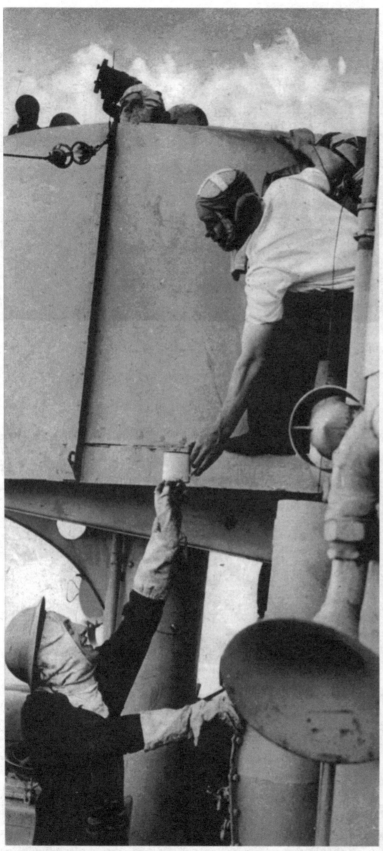

## Italy's Hour Was Approaching

When the Sicilian campaign was ending and the shadow of invasion loomed over Italy itself, H.M. the King led the Home Fleet to sea for battle practice, and inspected destroyer crews aboard the depot ship Tyne (right). The work of the Royal Navy in destroying the enemy's power to resist invasion is being magnificently carried out; from the first landing until the final conquest the Navy subjected Sicily to more than 50 organized bombardments, these extending also to the Italian mainland. Mr. Alexander, First Lord of the Admiralty, said: " I doubt whether there has ever been a more concentrated attack on land targets by warships in the history of warfare." A cruiser's look-outs (above) welcome tea during a lull in action.

*Photos, British Official: Crown Copyright; Fox*

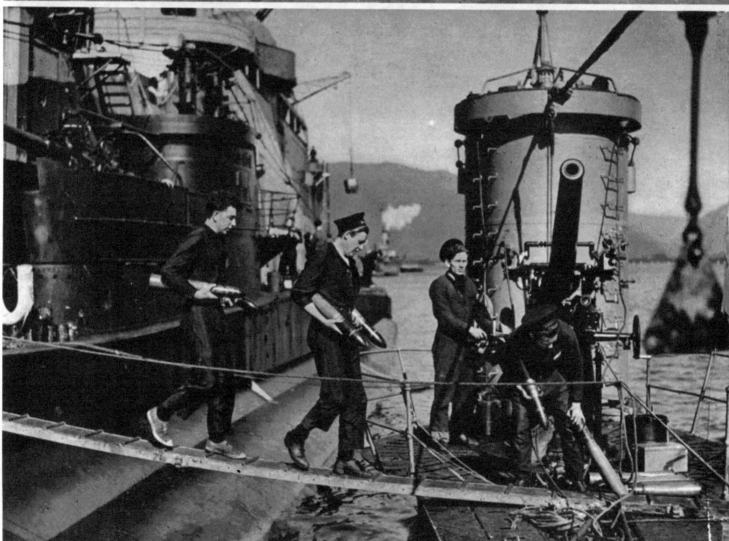

## *Air and Sea Power in Invincible Harmony*

Photos, British Official.
Crown Copyright

Effective counter-weapon to the diminishing U-boat threat is the Navy's mass-produced escort aircraft-carrier (see p. 104). A Swordfish—torpedo-spotter-reconnaissance biplane of the Fleet Air Arm—is seen (top) going down the flight deck lift of one of these carriers.   Subduing the sea challenge also are our submarines, which during the Sicilian operations sank or damaged more than 20 enemy transports and supply ships.   Submarine personnel are taking shells on board (bottom).

# VIEWS & REVIEWS
Of Vital War Books

### by Hamilton Fyfe

How many statesmen in history called upon to deal with crises in their countries' lives have fulfilled, and more than fulfilled, their countrymen's hopes and expectations as Mr. Churchill has done? Very few indeed. Most of them have been disappointments. Some have crumbled away under their great tasks. I can think of hardly a single other who at the end of more than three years was higher in estimation and more gratefully regarded than he was at the beginning of them.

Mr. Churchill has done that. In spite of mistakes made in the strategy of the war (Greece one, Crete another, Dakar a third), he has today the whole nation at his back more solidly than in any previous hour. Indeed, he has the trust and admiration of all the nations of the British Commonwealth; of a large part of the American people too. Throughout the world he is respected and honoured as a man who possesses very rare gifts of inspiration and leadership.

This is largely due to his speeches. As to what he has actually done since May 1940 the world knows little. We ourselves do not know very much for certain. How far he has been the supreme director, how much the Service chiefs have done, we shall not be sure about until fighting is over and books are written to inform us. But his speeches we have all read. Many we have listened to on the air. It is from his speeches that the world has formed its judgement of him. Therefore, it is interesting to go through a book of those which he delivered last year, just issued under the title The End of the Beginning (Cassell, 11s. 6d.), and to analyse the qualities which distinguish them from the usual rigmarole droned out by politicians and not considered by newspapers to be worth more than a few lines.

Churchill has never been that kind of politician. To begin with, he took his career very seriously. He wrote his speeches from the time I first knew him, which is forty years ago; he learned them by heart; he rehearsed them. Even at that date, when he was in his twenties, they had quite a different sound and quite a different effect on the mind from those of his fellow-M.P.s. Then, to go on with, he was never really a Party politician. He formed a Party of his own. It has always consisted of himself alone. Its motto might have been "I am I."

Though he has at all times been loyal to whatever Party he happened for the moment to be in, though he has repeated their slogans fervently and supported their policies with vigour, he was never a dyed-in-the-wool Party man. First he was a Conservative, then a Liberal, then a Conservative again, next an Independent, and now he is titular leader of those whom he once described as "Tories standing for vested interests, trickery and tyranny, dear food for the million, cheap labour for the millionaire; for the rich against the masses, the strong against the weak," and so on.

Many think he would have done better to remain a national leader instead of identifying himself with one Party. But he is no more a bigoted Conservative now than he was when in 1924, a few weeks before he left the Liberals, he described them as the only people who could "open the path of real progress to the whole nation with the golden key of their culture, their toleration, their humanities." This can be proved by his speech to the Central Council of the Conservative Party in which he merely threw in at the end a few sentences about that Party being "the main part of the rock on which the salvation of Britain was founded and the freedom of mankind retained." Then "the rt. hon. gentleman resumed his seat amid loud cheers." He had so far relaxed his usual practice as to wind up after the manner of politicians playing for applause.

## Winston Churchill 'Lord of Language'

He does not seem as a rule to mind in the least whether he is cheered or not. That is part of his "I am I" complex. He is supremely sure of himself. I remember one day in 1903, just after Joseph Chamberlain had proclaimed his Tariff Reform campaign, meeting Winston in the Lobby of the House of Commons. I was editing a London daily paper then. He said he wished he could advise me what line to take about this new

**DOGGED DETERMINATION is apparent in every line of this portrait of the Prime Minister, taken in Ottawa on the occasion of his 1941 visit to Canada (see pp. 414–415, 435, Vol. 5). Mr. Churchill's speeches since he became Premier in the dark days of May 1940, have enshrined his unshakable will to victory.** PAGE 275 *Photo, Karsh*

and unexpected political development. I said I had taken a line already. He looked surprised: one of the very few occasions on which I have known him to hesitate.

He even believes, as so many resolute personalities have done, that he is under some sort of divine protection. This is not religiosity. "Religiosity," the famous Italian philosopher Benedetto Croce has written, "is vague. Religion is clear-cut." Churchill gets his definiteness of view from "his strong feeling that some guiding hand" is in charge of him, that "we have a guardian because we serve a great cause, and shall have that guardian as long as we serve that cause faithfully." This puts him far above the general run of politicians.

No ordinary Prime Minister would refer back to a past in which he was opposing most of his Parliamentary supporters today. Churchill did this at Bradford—"I say to you what I said when I was here nearly 30 years ago: Let us go forward together and put the great principles we support to the proof." When he used that phrase before, he was about to launch his attack on Ulster! Yet he recalled it without confusion, even with a sort of impish amusement.

It is the literary quality in his speeches that sets them apart. He is a master of words. There are no vain repetitions, no rodomontade, no slipshod phrasing. When he is abusive, you feel he has carefully chosen the terms in which to assail Mussolini as a hyena or to twit the Huns with giving out "the low, dull, whining note of fear." No one who knows his capacity in this direction believed him when he said he had "exhausted the possibilities of the English language" in his descriptions of Laval. However long he kept up his denunciation, he would always have a shot left in his locker.

That he is an author rather than an orator is made clear when he is caught unawares. A speech he made at Tunis—or was it Tripoli?—which was heard over the radio, surprised many by its halting, disconnected character. He has said that he cannot speak without preparation, though he can answer questions with pungency and wit. Even then he is the literary artist.

"I am certainly not one of those who need to be prodded .... I am a prod" was delightful, and who else could have put such malignity into a retort to adversaries who had not been quite fair as there was in his ejaculation that he could believe the name of the Churchill tank "afforded a motive to various persons to endeavour to cover it with their slime"? Again, the choice of the term "minstrel" gave his reference to Sir Harry Lauder a charm and dignity which "singer" would have missed.

How genuine a Parliamentarian the Prime Minister is comes out over and over again. He is "the servant of the House and is liable to dismissal at a moment's notice"; he is "refreshed and fortified by its inflexible steadiness." It is "these ideas of parliamentary government, and the representation of the people upon franchises, which .... constitute at this moment one of the great causes which are being fought out." When he arranges a three-day debate on the war's progress, he asks if there could be "any higher expression of democracy than that."

# Awe-Compelling: the Vast Red Tide Unstemmed

## MARSHAL STALIN'S ORDER OF THE DAY

**Issued on September 8, 1943**
**Addressed to General Tolbukhin and Army General Malinovsky**

The Order of the Day named the towns taken during the six days' offensive in the Donbas, and stated :

" Troops of the Southern and South-Western fronts, as the result of a determined offensive, have won a great victory over the German invaders in the Donetz Basin.

The important industrial region of the Donetz Basin has been wrested from the hands of the invaders and returned to our people."

The generals of troops who had distinguished themselves were then named.   To commemorate their successes three divisions are to receive the name of Stalino Divisions.   Fifteen other divisions, a brigade and two regiments will bear the names of other towns captured.

The Order concludes : " Today, at 6 p.m., Moscow will, in the name of the Motherland, salute with 20 salvos from 224 guns the gallant troops who liberated the Donbas.   I express my gratitude to all the troops commanded by you which participated in the fighting. Eternal glory to the heroes who fell fighting for our Motherland. Death to the German invaders."

The above is typical of Marshal Stalin's inspiring Orders of the Day, which since the Soviet counter-offensive began on July 13, 1943, have recorded new glories for the Russian Army.

SOVIET ARMOUR is turning the German retreat into a rout.   This A.A. armoured train (above), which recently added 14 enemy planes to its credit, has played an outstanding part in the destruction of the Luftwaffe.   Right, an anti-tank gun unit advances towards the enemy under cover of a smoke screen. Below, right, women and children return to their liberated village, on the road to Bryansk.   The wreckage of humble homes is a familiar feature of Nazi occupation and frenzied retreat.

'A SPRING TIDE OF RUSSIAN UNITS is storming our positions,' the Nazis confessed on August 23, 1943.   By September 13 there still seemed no stemming of the Red Army's advance along the whole front from Leningrad to the Sea of Azov.   In the south, particularly, they had recaptured the entire Donbas, their wealthiest industrial region, following the taking of Stalino (see map) on September 8, and swept through the rich wheatfields of the Ukraine, seeking to invest Kiev.

*Photos, U.S.S.R. Official, Associated Press.   Map by courtesy of The Daily Mail*

# Soviet Life Flows On Again in Freed Kharkov

GETTING BACK TO 'NORMAL' after the triumphant entry into Kharkov of the Russians on August 23, 1943. A Red Army girl directs street traffic (top), while citizens eagerly scan hastily-printed newspapers stuck up on a wall (bottom). For the fourth and almost certainly last time the ravaging tide of battle has swept over this town of the Ukraine; from here the apparently irresistible Red Army in three days enveloped Taganrog and seemed at last to be able to sweep the enemy from the entire area between the Dnieper and the Sea of Azov. See also page 282. *Photos, Pictorial Press*

# Movie-Cameramen in the Front Line of Battle

Those who saw Desert Victory, the film of the 8th Army's triumph in Italian North Africa, cannot but have been impressed by the plentiful evidences of the movie-men's daring. This article by CHARLES GRETTON and JIM LE BRUN tells of some individual cameramen who "took" this and other war documentary films. (See also opposite page.)

"FIRE!" yells the officer. "Fire!" yells another mouth in gigantic close-up; and the silence is shattered by such a tempest of fire and fury as seems incredible even now. Guns tear the night to red ribbons; not one a second, but scores simultaneously. The effect on the enemy is dazing. The miracle is that anyone lived through it. In the making of these dramatic war films on the battlefront, cameramen certainly risk their lives to put the war on the screen.

No. 1 unit of the A.F.P.U., comprising twenty-six photographers, including movie and still men under Major David Macdonald, the film director, carrying special portable 35-mm. cameras, raced forward with the front line to film Desert Victory. They shared the soldiers' hardships and brought back pictures of all arms in action which are magnificent in their realism and revelation of stark courage. This triumph of art and valour was not bloodless. Seven A.F.P.U. cameramen were killed or missing (including one still cameraman); four are prisoners of war.

Major David Macdonald, of the Army Film Unit, responsible for some of this war's best movie-making, went out to Cairo in November 1941, when Rommel thought he was going to throw us out of Egypt.

"I took with me thirty-two cameramen," Macdonald said. "They were allotted to the various divisions and ordered to go into action with the troops and film what they could. The terrific barrage, the tank battles and bayonet charges you see in the film were taken from every possible angle—in front of the men, behind them, at the side of them. Of course, we couldn't help having casualties. They occurred after Benghazi, mostly from mines, dive-bombers and anti-personnel artillery fire. Four of us were taken prisoner.

"One of my cameramen was formerly a salesman at a Bond Street photographer's; another was a projectionist at a West End cinema; a third—Sergeant Garnham, who used to work with the L.M.S.—was my Number One camera mechanic. He used the Western Desert as his back room. When the cameras came back from the show, clogged with sand, he always had another one ready. But for that sergeant there would have been no picture of the Eighth Army.

"The Army perhaps do not regard us as combatant troops. But we were often ahead of the fighting. We were first in Tobruk. On one occasion a senior officer, questioned whether a certain town had fallen, said: 'Yes, the Army Film Unit photographed it this morning!'

"I hope this doesn't sound too like a puff for ourselves, but the forward positions of the camera crew accounted for three of four sergeants being killed by mines.

"After the fall of Benghazi I came back to assemble the miles of film we had taken; but most of the credit goes to the editor, Captain Roy Boulting—he made Thunder Rock—whose all-round brilliance will make him one of the biggest film men one day. Sergeant Dickie Best, his first assistant, also did great work.

"And there was a woman who helped—Mrs. White—the only woman on our staff. It was she who, time after time, found us the one shot we needed out of thousands and thousands."

## Killed in Air Operations

Unluckily not all of our war movie heroes live to see their films screened. For instance, some of the war's most vivid news films of R.A.F. exploits were shot by Flight-Lieut. Donald N. Gallai-Hatchard, of the R.A.F. Film Unit, who later was killed in air operations in Tunisia. His area shot of the Dieppe raid, the R.A.F. big daylight raid on Lille, and others on north-west Germany, thrilled countless cinema goers. Some of the most recent news films of the aerial war in Tunisia were also his work.

Formerly an operative cameraman for the London Film Production Company, he helped to film Private Lives of Henry the Eighth, Shape of Things to Come, and The Citadel—the last picture on which he was engaged before joining the R.A.F. as an ordinary aircraftman. He was 32 when he was killed.

Still alive and defying the Nazis to harm him is another tough war cameraman, Jack Ramsden. The Eighth American Air Force and the Eighth British Army fill with their exploits the latest news reels. Jack Ramsden, British Movietone News cameraman, went with Flying Fortresses bombing railway yards at Rouen. His film and pictures of other raids by Forts make fitting companions to scenes from the Mareth Line.

Then there is Flight-Lieutenant John Boulting, who is going to America to make a film about the air training scheme there. He is 29. Before he was posted to the R.A.F. Film Unit, he served as an A.C.2

mechanic. His twin brother, Captain Roy Boulting (praised by Major Macdonald), served in a tank regiment for more than a year before joining the Army Film Unit. He has made several short documentaries. One, Via Persia, showed the southern supply route to Russia. Another, The Army Lays the Rails, told the story of the Royal Engineers. Roy also filmed the Vaagso raid landing.

Some of the latest war films are not just documentaries for entertainment. They are for Service instruction. A technicolour film of the actual fighting between American and Axis forces in North Africa is to be shown to United States and British troops in England for training purposes.

THE film, now being made in the United States, is similar to Desert Victory and records the initial phase of the North African campaign, covering the occupation of Algiers, Casablanca and Oran and the first American action on the Tunisian front. Produced by Colonel Darryl Zanuck, U.S. Army Signal Corps and former executive of 20th Century-Fox, it was made largely in the height of battle. It shows Axis troops in retreat under terrific anti-tank fire, Lockheed Lightning fighters attacking Messerschmitts, and ships being loaded under extreme difficulties.

Of course, we are not the only ones who make this kind of film. Nazi Ufa film studios are busy with war subjects; the Japanese are making war films too. Thousands of British prisoners-of-war took part in making a film, The Siege of Singapore, according to Tokyo radio. Actual battle sites have been used.

Films, in the making of which men have given their lives, often have a happy ending. Here is a typical story—vouched for by the Army cameraman concerned.

The picture flashed on the screen for a moment—a line of troops embarking for a raid. As the camera moved along one soldier turned and smiled at it—smiled out into the packed cinema to his mother sitting watching him. It was the last smile she will have from him until the end of the war. He was taken prisoner. The film was a special wartime "short." The mother wrote to the Ministry pleading for the picture of her boy smiling as he left on his last raid.

There was little to identify him. The mother had not noticed that almost every one of that long line of British troops had smiled at the camera!

However, the war-film laboratory experts found the single frame in the film where her soldier-son appeared, and duly sent her a photograph from it.

CINE-TEAM WHO MADE DESERT VICTORY and Battle for Egypt: Front row, l. to r., Sgt. Acland, 8th Army F.P.U. (camera 1st), first Tommy to meet the Americans at the historic link-up in Tunisia, April 7, 1943; Lt. Flack, Movietone News (camera 1st); Lt. James, Daily Mirror (script); Sgt. Hopkinson, Warner Bros. (camera 2nd). Back row, l. to r., Sgt. Curry, London Films (camera 2nd); Sgt. Taylor, London Films (camera 2nd); Sgt. Barnes, Olympic Film Labs. (processing); Sgt. Jordan, M.G.M. and British Lion Films (camera 1st); Sgt. Morris, Ealing Studios (camera 1st).

# 'Shooting' the War for the Cinema Screen

THEY BRING THE WAR HOME—the British Army's own Film and Photographic Unit, working under the Army Public Relations Directorate. Specialists all, they live and work as part of the fighting forces to which they are attached (see opposite page). When this 25-pounder anti-tank gun (2) fired at the enemy the cameraman was hard by "shooting" the action; a colleague recording a bombardment (3) had a watchful bodyguard A portable workshop (1) cf the Unit accompanies the team everywhere.

# Blitzers Blitzed: Driven from Home By R.A.F.

IN HITLER'S CAPITAL, after one of the new series of large-scale Allied aerial assaults, culminating in the great raid (the 78th on Berlin) of September 3, 1943, in which 1,000 tons of bombs were dropped in 20 minutes.   Some 500,000 of the normal population of 4,250,000 take to the  woods (1) and live in hastily-built shacks.   Others in the shattered city eat amid the devastation (2), fetch water in buckets from emergency supply points (3). and queue up (4) for such food allowance as is available.

*Photos, Planet News, Keystone, New York Times*

# I WAS THERE!

## I Led the British Commandos Into Italy

*Days before the main British Army landed their shock troops (September 3, 1943) Commandos were put ashore in the darkness on the toe of Italy. The first man ashore—the leader, in fact—was Lieut. John Nixon, who told his story to Alan Moorehead, representing the Combined British Press.*

I KEPT thinking the shore was closer than it was. At least half a dozen times I said, "It's only another couple of hundred yards." The shore was absolutely silent. We came in perfectly on the beach, a dry landing. The ramp went down and we stepped ashore, Sergeant William Smith, of Faversham, Kent, following me.

We seemed to have landed beside some sort of factory that smelt abominably. Beyond that was the bridge we were making for, and I heard someone coughing up there in the dark. There were no mines or barbed wire on the beach, but under the bridge itself there was wire. We clambered up the embankment. There was no one in sight.

THEN an Italian came down the road. We had landed at 2.40 a.m., and heaven knows what he was doing walking about at that hour. Anyway, we grabbed him and when he protested we propelled him down to the boat. He seemed to think he had got mixed up in some sort of manoeuvres.

After that we swarmed on to the bridge, and found it unguarded and unmined. I had noticed one light away to the left and it had been my intention to make for it. But now it became apparent that we had landed in the middle of a town and I decided to abandon the light and concentrate on the town itself.

We set grenades on the bridge—enough to blow a truck in the morning—and then started towards the houses and the shops. The silence was uncanny. We heard or thought we heard voices and scuffling in the houses, but when we broke into them they were empty. We shouted and yelled. We blew the locks off the doors and tramped inside through the bedrooms and the shops.

We fired bursts down the main street. Still nothing, no sign of anyone. I ordered a flare to be sent up but it was a dud. The second one lighted up the town as though it were daytime. Still no one answered our fire. We started to set fire to one or two of the houses. Then down in the railway yards we put incendiary bombs in the trucks, but for some reason they didn't burn very well. There seemed to be no mines, no wires, no blocks in the town anywhere, and I will guarantee there were no enemy troops.

The place was deserted by civilians as well as Germans. If there had been Germans with guns in the hills behind, surely they would have fired. It was money for rope. We went on shouting and making as much disturbance as we could.

By now it was getting near to dawn. I got my party back to the boat and at four a.m.—just one hour and twenty minutes after we landed—we put to sea again, bringing our

**LIEUT. JOHN NIXON, of Brasted, was one of our Commandos who landed in Italy several days before the actual invasion. Leader of the party, he tells his story in the adjoining columns.** *Photo, Daily Mirror*

prisoner with us. No enemy motor-boat or shore battery opened up on us, but in the darkness we lost the mother ship, and we were forced to come back under our own steam.

## Here in Liberated Greece the Guerillas Rule!

*In a large area embracing Roumeli, Thessaly and Central-Western Macedonia the Greek guerillas have won victory over the Axis invaders, and under their authority hundreds of thousands of Greek citizens are now living a free existence. This remarkable account of the victorious guerilla fighters comes from the underground newspaper Free Greece.*

A FEW hours' journey from the towns on the Athens-Salonika railway (Thebes, Livadia, Lamia, etc.) and you tread the sacred soil of Liberated Greece, finding yourself under the protective shadow of our guerillas. That is how I found myself, a few days ago, in a little village close to Parnassus. The authority of the guerillas was quickly revealed when I was challenged by a group of young men in the outskirts. They were members of the fighting unit of the village, a kind of armed civic guard which constitutes the reserve force of the guerillas. Only after a thorough and exhaustive cross-examination was I allowed to proceed.

Imagine my emotion when I saw the Greek flag, with the motto "Liberty or Death" embroidered across it, waving over a balcony. I saw the villagers free to work, to argue, to sing, without the nightmare of the carabinieri or the looter or the cattle thief constantly hovering over them. I saw the village brightly lit at night and the inhabitants free to move about in the evening as they pleased.

IT was against this background I saw our guerillas for the first time. They were tall, sunburnt men with determined features, long beards and moustaches—except the young lads, and there were many of them, whose faces haven't even begun to grow a beard. They all wore military uniforms of different kinds and from all sources; some wear Greek uniforms, some British, others German or Italian or a little of everything.

Slung over their shoulders they carry bandoliers filled with cartridges and bullets, and they carry them with a certain pride, although they avoid the ornamental pistols and daggers which our guerillas used to fancy in olden times. They all wear a forage cap with the badge of their organization embroidered on it. Their armament is usually completed with a dagger slung by their side or thrust through their belt.

These fighters have an organization which is amazingly democratic. Each band is usually composed of 15 men and is commanded by a "Capetan," who is their leader. These "Capetans" are the officers

**GREEK GUERILLAS now control whole mountain ranges of Northern Greece and territory between Salonika and Athens; and they have created an efficient civil administration—under which thousands of their liberated countrymen are living—with this village as its centre. They publish their own underground newspaper, from which the story on the right is reprinted.** *Photo, The Evening Standard*

of the bands, but they do not carry any distinctive badge—a fact which is consistent with the completely equal life they lead with their men. The "Capetan" will share his cigarette with the simple ranker guerilla, and will do his spell of sentry duty at night. There is a common mess for all, without discrimination, just as there is common sleep, common danger, common duty. At any moment the guerilla has the right to express his opinion, except of course when in action or on duty, when discipline and blind obedience are rigid. These men have an instinctive sense of discipline, which is the real source of their strength.

THESE guerillas are not only comrades among themselves, they are on brotherly terms with the villagers too. I have seen this brotherly intercourse with my own eyes; it is sincere and reciprocated as has been proved time and again. The behaviour of the guerillas is exemplary. Drunkenness and brawling are unknown; any abuse would be ruthlessly punished by the governing body. No guerilla band has ever taken food or anything else from villagers without permission.

Under these conditions the population carries on its normal life in complete security and confidence. All the villagers are governed by civil councils elected by the inhabitants, and any differences are dealt with by judicial committees elected by the people. Other elected committees deal with victualling, refugees and equipment for the guerillas.

A visit here is a lesson in optimism, a new baptism of faith. If only those who live in the slavery and bitterness of Athens could come here to Liberated Greece for a few days, for a few hours! When I left the village a

**KHARKOV FROM THE AIR.** Once the linchpin of Hitler's entire southern front in Russia, the great city was reoccupied by Soviet forces on August 23, 1943, and—to make the devastated area habitable again—street clearance and similar work was at once commenced, as told in the story below.
*Photo, Pictorial Press*

very young guide came with me. He would return at night with the mules after he had taken me to the next village.

"Aren't you afraid to go back by yourself at night?" I asked him. "Friend," he said to me gravely, "all those things we had to put up with are finished now. There are no Italians or Germans or any other vermin in the mountains now. Here the guerillas rule!"

## Remaking Their Homes in Kharkov's Ruins

Even before the last of the Nazis in Kharkov were rounded up, restoration work had been put in hand. Lieut.-Col. Leonid Vysokostrovsky, Special Correspondent of Red Star, Journal of the Russian Army, describes his visit to this great but sorely battered city of the Ukraine, two-thirds of which, according to its civic chief, is in ruins. See also p. 277.

I ENTERED Kharkov by the Lipetsk high road on the morning of August 23. By this same road there had already entered the 3rd Rifle Division, which by Stalin's orders has since been renamed the 93rd Kharkov Division. Here and there rifle and machine-gun fire could still be heard and German shells were still bursting in the streets. The division's artillery had hastened forward to the centre of Kharkov to support their infantry.

The first big thoroughfare I entered was Pavlov Avenue. All the finest houses on it had been blown up by the Germans and people were rummaging in the ruins salvaging whatever they could of their household goods.

When I stopped my open car to light a cigarette two little girls came running up and presented me with a bouquet of red dahlias. A crowd quickly gathered round us, and the bouquets steadily increased until my driver had his work cut out garlanding the car with them. On Stalin Avenue we overtook a column of artillery. The guns and limbers were likewise decked with flowers.

We went on our way and reached the river. The bridge across it had been blown up, but the sappers had already restored it sufficiently to permit of one-way traffic. We soon reached the centre of the city and drove to Dzerzhinsky Square. Here the Germans had given full vent to their destructive proclivities.

Every large building had been blown up or burned. The city park had been laid waste. Here German shells were still bursting, but nobody paid any attention to them. The inhabitants loudly and enthusiastically greeted the Red Army, and crowds gathered round the portable loudspeakers listening to

Moscow broadcasts. Streets and side-walks were being quickly cleared of rubble, broken glass, barbed wire, and tank obstacles.

I paid a visit to Major-Gen. Trufanov, Commandant of Kharkov, at his headquarters near the city's centre. He had just entered on his duties. I congratulated him on his appointment and asked him to register me as an army man come to Kharkov for a short stay. A sergeant entered my name and rank in a book while the General himself made a note on my identity papers, "arrived in Kharkov, August 23, 1943."

I was the first person he had registered in his capacity as commander of Kharkov, he said. The Commandant told me that his first concern on entering on his duties was to restore bridges, clear the city of hidden mines, and regulate the traffic. How successful his efforts were I had an opportunity to judge before I visited him. Virtually all footbridges were repaired, although hastily and provisionally. Traffic regulators were posted at crossings, and signposts indicated the roads to various points. Squads of sappers were looking for mines and removing them.

While we were talking an officer entered and reported that patrols had just brought in several Germans caught in the city. I went out to look at them. They were gazing around wildly, unable to realize what had happened. They related that the day before they had been given an hour's leave. They met some comrades and decided to have a drink. They drank in a cellar, got thoroughly drunk, and fell asleep. Their comrades abandoned them. They were awakened in the morning by Red Army men and children of the town. The Germans could not understand how the Soviet troops could have captured the city so soon.

When I emerged into the street I observed that the German bombardment had markedly subsided. Dusk was gathering. I spent the night with a friendly and hospitable family in a house which had not suffered.

Next morning I bade farewell to Kharkov and hurried to overtake our advancing and victorious troops.

## I Was in Copenhagen When the Germans Came

Here is the story of Black Sunday in Copenhagen—August 29, 1943, the day the German army marched in (see p. 248). It was told to the B.U.P. Stockholm correspondent by a 20-year-old Dane who witnessed armed clashes with the Germans in the streets of Denmark's capital where the nation-wide wave of revolt found its natural focus.

ON Sunday morning I got up very early to see what was going to happen, as I heard the proclamation of the state of emergency on the radio. Rosenberg Castle and the Royal Guards Barracks are not far from where I live. When I walked out to Solv Gade (Gade means street), towards Rosenberg, I suddenly saw two tanks coming in the opposite direction, with their guns pointing at me.

I jumped out of the street and threw myself flat on the ground in some bushes in the Botanic Gardens on my right hand. Immediately the tanks began firing at the barracks, which I could see through the trees

about 300 yards away. I could clearly see the flashes of the guns and hear the crackling of the machine-guns. The fire was answered from the barracks, but only with rifles and machine-guns—not with any artillery.

Soon I could hear the blast of field-guns which the Germans had posted right in front of the barracks on the Norre Vold. I could not see the guns, however. Shooting was still going on when I went home, carefully taking cover behind whatever trees and bushes happened to be available.

When I returned to the scene of the fighting the following day I saw gaping holes in the walls of the barracks, blasted by the field-guns. How many of the Royal Guards were

**THE FORUM HALL, COPENHAGEN, after Danish patriots had blown it up on August 24, 1943, to prevent it being used as barracks for some of the 50,000 troops Germany poured into the city four days previously to deal with the nation-wide outbreak of sabotage. Before it was reduced to ruins the Forum Hall could accommodate 16,000 people.** *Photo, Associated Press*

killed nobody knew. I returned to Copenhagen about 9 p.m. on the same day—Sunday—after spending the afternoon with friends in the country near the city.

To get a railway ticket was something of a problem. I had to stand in a queue for nearly two hours and fill in several forms, before an ill-tempered German soldier gave me the necessary permit. When I stepped out of the station (on my return) I could hear shooting from practically every part of the city. In the dark I couldn't tell where the shooting was coming from exactly, and because of the curfew I got home as quickly as possible.

Naturally, I couldn't sleep, so I kept the window open all night. I heard one big blast, probably sabotage, but I couldn't tell where it came from. Sporadic shooting went on throughout the whole night. There was also another sound—that of ambulances rushing through the pitch-black streets with their sirens screaming. They made for the Municipal Hospital near by, delivering their loads and returning quickly to fetch fresh victims. Then it was the Germans who were doing all the shooting.

The garrison at Rosenberg and Amalienborg surrendered early on Sunday morning and there was no other organized resistance except from people disregarding the curfew. All public buildings, including the Town Hall and the police stations, were taken over by the German troops and the Gestapo by that time.

I SAW for myself how quickly the Germans let fire. The following morning I was standing in the middle of the Town Hall Square when a German tank came down the Vester Gade, approaching the crossing of this with the main street. At that moment the traffic light changed, causing an involuntary gathering of about twenty people on the far side of the street. The tank immediately let fire with its guns, and I saw five people fall. The others scattered. This took place at about eleven in the morning.

The same evening I cycled to the shore opposite Haelsingborg, where I met the rest of my party, including a naval officer who acted as our captain. Shortly after 10 p.m. we pulled out as quickly as possible. After an hour and a half's rowing we saw the lantern of a German patrol boat—probably an armed trawler—coming rapidly towards us.

We all threw ourselves on the bottom of the boat, fearing that the light from the Swedish lighthouse on the Island of Ven would betray us. Four of us had guns and we got ready to defend ourselves if necessary. Fortunately, the Germans passed, and we made a quick dash for the Swedish coast. All went well for us!

# OUR DIARY OF THE WAR

**SEPTEMBER 1, 1943, Wednesday** 1,460th day

**Italy.**—Enemy wireless station wrecked on Cape Spartivento on toe of Italy.

**Pacific.**—American task force began attack on Marcus Island, halfway between Tokyo and Midway Island.

**General.**—Arrival of Mr. Churchill in Washington announced.

**SEPTEMBER 2, Thursday** 1,461st day

**Italy.**—Two British battleships bombarded Cape del Armi.

**Russian Front.**—Sumy, on Voronezh front, captured by Red Army; whole of Kursk area liberated. In Donetz Basin, Voroshilovsk and Lisichansk taken.

**Australasia.**—Announced Japanese surrounded on Roosevelt Ridge near Salamaua. Three 7,000-ton Japanese freighters sunk in escorted convoy with balloon protection off Wewak (New Guinea).

**Air.**—Airfields and marshalling yards in N. France raided in biggest single Fighter Command operation of the year.

**SEPTEMBER 3, Friday** 1,462nd day

**Italy.**—British and Canadian troops of 8th Army invaded toe of Italy. Reggio, Catona, Villa San Giovanni and Gallico Marina captured. Fortress bombers blocked Brenner Pass. Sulmona marshalling yards bombed by Liberators. Capua and Capodichino airfields attacked. Armistice with Italy signed on neutral territory, but fact not disclosed (for military reasons) until Sept. 8.

**Burma.**—Nicobar Island group in Bay of Bengal attacked by U.S. heavy bombers in 2,000-mile round trip.

**Australasia.**—Lae and the Markham Valley (New Guinea) heavily raided by Mitchells and Liberators. Vila (Kolombangara) and Kahili in Buin-Faisi area bombed.

**Air.**—Fortresses raided repair works near Paris and 5 French air bases. Lancasters attacked Berlin in 20-min. raid with 1,000 tons of bombs.

**SEPTEMBER 4, Saturday** 1,463rd day

**Italy.**—Bagnara captured. By nightfall 40 miles of coast in our hands. Road and rail communications in Naples area heavily attacked.

**Russian Front.**—Merefa captured in Soviet Kharkov advance; Gorlovka, Nikitovka and Debaltsevo in Donbas taken.

**Australasia.**—Australian troops landed in force on coast of Huon Gulf, east of Lae, New Guinea.

**Air.**—French airfields of Rouen, Amiens, Abbeville, Lille and St. Pol, rly. yards at Hazebrouck (France) and Courtrai (Belgium) bombed.

**SEPTEMBER 5, Sunday** 1,464th day

**Italy.**—Viterbo, Grazzanise, Aversa and Capua airfields bombed; Villa Literno marshalling yards near Naples raided.

**Russian Front.**—Artemovsk, Dzerzhinsk and Khartsyzk in Donbas captured by Russians; Khutor-Mihailovsky in Bryansk sector taken.

**Australasia.**—Announced Japanese abandonment of seaplane base at Rekata Bay, Isabel Island. U.S. paratroops dropped in Markham Valley, New Guinea, completing encirclement of 20,000 Japanese.

**Air.**—Ghent (Belgium) marshalling yards, Woensdrecht airfield (Holland) and Mardyck airfield (France) attacked by Allied aircraft; Mannheim-Ludwigshafen (1,500 tons of bombs dropped) heavily raided at night.

**SEPTEMBER 6, Monday** 1,465th day

**Italy.**—Capture of San Stefano announced; Naples area bombed by day.

**Russian Front.**—Konotop, on Bryansk-Kiev railway, and Makeevka, Slavyansk and Kramatorsk in Donbas, captured by Red Army.

**Air.**—Stuttgart and targets in S.W. Germany raided by Fortresses. Munich heavily attacked at night.

**SEPTEMBER 7, Tuesday** 1,466th day

**Italy.**—Foggia, Viterbo, San Pancrazio, and Muduria airfields, rail yards at Benevento, Metaponto, and Potenza bombed. Capture of Palmi and Delianuova announced.

**Russian Front.**—Baturin in Bakhmach region, Navlya in Bryansk sector, Tarasovka, Shurovka, and Zvenkov in Kharkov area captured by Russians.

**Australasia.**—Lae (New Guinea) heavily bombed; Mitchells strafed the Markham Valley.

**Air.**—Airfield and factories at Evere, near Brussels, attacked by Fortresses.

**SEPTEMBER 8, Wednesday** 1,467th day

**Italy.**—Gen. Eisenhower broadcast unconditional surrender of Italian Armed Forces; military armistice (terms agreed upon by United Nations) came into operation at once. German H.Q. at Frascati, near Rome, destroyed. 8th Army made fresh landing 30 m. behind enemy at Vibo Valentia.

**Russian Front.**—Whole of Donetz Basin cleared of Germans. Stalino, Krasnoarmeisk, Yasinovataya captured. Moscow saluted victory with 20 salvos from 224 guns.

**Australasia.**—Capture of Nadzab airfield (New Guinea) by U.S. paratroops announced.

**SEPTEMBER 9, Thursday** 1,468th day

**Italy.**—U.S. 5th Army, including British troops, landed near Naples. Ventotene Island, 40 m. S. of Naples, captured. British occupied naval base of Taranto. In toe of Italy lateral road from Giogi to Locri in Allied hands. Italian battleship Roma sunk by German bombs in Straits of Bonifacio, while fleeing with other vessels from Spezia.

**Russian Front.**—Bakhmach captured by Russians in Kiev drive.

**Air.**—In conjunction with amphibious exercise in Channel, 3,000 Allied bomber and fighter sorties flown over France.

**SEPTEMBER 10, Friday** 1,469th day

**Italy.**—Italian commander in Rome capitulated to Germans in area of 30 miles round city. Germans reported fighting at "isolated points" with ex-allies, claimed surrender of 50,000 Italians at Trieste and of Italians stationed abroad, and capture of Genoa, Spezia, Bologna, Verona, and Cremona. 2 Italian battleships, 5 cruisers, and 4 destroyers arrived at Malta.

**Russian Front.**—Mariupol, on Sea of Azov, captured by Russians, and landing made west of Mariupol.

**SEPTEMBER 11, Saturday** 1,470th day

**Italy.**—Capture of Salerno (near Naples) and Brindisi, on heel of Italy, announced. Roosevelt and Churchill urged Italians to rise against Germany and aid in "the great surge of liberation."

**Australasia.**—Allied troops drove all Japanese from southern bank of Francisco River (New Guinea).

**Air.**—Le Trait shipbuilding yards and airfield at Beaumont-le-Roger (France) bombed.

**SEPTEMBER 12, Sunday** 1,471st day

**Italy.**—Mussolini said to have been freed by German paratroops. Italian Battle Fleet in Allied hands, excepting one incomplete battleship at Trieste. 5th Army continued to fight grim battle near Salerno.

**Mediterranean.**—Liberators raided 2 airfields on Rhodes.

**SEPTEMBER 13, Monday** 1,472nd day

**Italy.**—Capture of Cotrone by 8th Army announced.

**SEPTEMBER 14, Tuesday** 1,473rd day

**Italy.**—Capture of Cosenza and Bari by 8th Army announced.

**Australasia.**—Capture of Salamaua (New Guinea) announced.

★══════ *Flash-backs* ══════★

**1939**

September 3. *Liner Athenia sunk by U-boat.*

September 4. *German warships in Kiel Canal bombed by R.A.F.*

September 14. *Germans claimed capture of Gdynia, Polish port.*

**1940**

September 3. *Anglo-U.S. agreement whereby Britain leased to U.S. bases in British possessions along Atlantic sea-board.*

September 11. *Mr. Churchill warned country of German invasion preparations.*

September 13. *Italians captured Sollum (Egypt).*

**1941**

September 12. *Russians announced evacuation of Chernigov on River Desna.*

**1942**

September 4. *Rommel withdrew his forces after failure of assault on British line at Alamein.*

# THE WAR IN THE AIR

### by Capt. Norman Macmillan, M.C., A.F.C.

EVERYWHERE the air war goes well for the United Nations. Indeed, the air situation has never looked better than at this phase of the war—on the fighting fronts, in Western Europe, over the Atlantic, and in the factories producing aircraft.

With the unconditional surrender of Italy on September 3, 1943, the Regia Aeronautica is removed from the war. The United Nations have theoretical use of all Italian aerodromes, but they will have to fight the German Wehrmacht and the Luftwaffe on the Italian mainland for possession of those retained in enemy hands. The position of the air bases in Rhodes and the Dodecanese Islands is obscure, and may remain so until the United Nations' strategic advance includes within its orbit that part of the Aegean Sea.

There have been accounts of gallant fighting by Italian pilots even when they were mounted in aircraft hopelessly inferior to British Hurricane and Spitfire fighters. That personal gallantry is much as I found it among the Italian pilots when I fought with them during the 1914-1918 war, when they were our allies. But because the general run of Italian aircraft were unable to stand up to the latest British and American machines the Regia Aeronautica must have been badly mauled before the signing of the Armistice.

Nevertheless, the elimination from the fighting fronts of the Italian aircraft that remained means a direct gain to the United Nations air forces in relative strength which can be applied to other purposes to increase the air pressure upon Germany and Japan.

ONE important aspect of Italy's surrender is the opening of almost direct air communication between England and India. As stepping-stones we have Gibraltar, Sicily, Brindisi, Taranto, Malta, the North African aerodromes to Alexandria, Cairo, Iraq, and Iran. It should now be possible to provide quickly by air strong reinforcements to the air command confronting the Japanese in Burma. This is important, because the advent of new squadrons on that front will coincide with the ending of the monsoon, when the ground will again become possible for surface action.

The effect of air superiority upon the Japanese has been seen in the Solomon Islands and New Guinea. The myth of Japanese stoicism and invincibility has been crushed by bombs. Everywhere within the zone commanded by General MacArthur the air war has risen in power; Japanese shipping moves in deadly peril from the air, and the attrition of the merchant tonnage of the Japanese wears on to its appointed end.

The Japanese Army and Navy air forces are quite unable to provide the requisite strength to defend the danger points about the periphery of the undigested lands which the glutton of the Far East has tried to swallow. Wherever we choose to concentrate we can outfight and outbomb the Japs. And they do not like it. Moreover, we can move our convoys under adequate air protection, by-pass Japanese garrisons and so surround them. Our paratroops descended on the farther side of Japanese strongpoints in the Salamaua area and cut off the defenders there. During the second week-end of September 1943 Salamaua airfield fell to our forces—a serious loss to the enemy.

Over that vast archipelagic region airfields form the vital strategic holding points. Who holds the airfields holds the islands. It is already clear that the Japanese—like the Germans—altogether underestimated the size of the air force required to conduct the type of campaign upon which they entered.

The cardinal facts which both these enemies overlooked were these : (1) that the mobility of aircraft in flight is so great that concentrated attack can be made in a variety of places against an enemy occupying a vast area ; (2) that defence aircraft cannot be moved swiftly enough to meet these widespread attacks ; and (3) that a tremendous air force is therefore required to hold a great area, with numbers of aircraft out of all proportion to the size of the air force required to attack the same area.

### DEFENCE of the Lombardy Airfields Vital to the Nazis

These fundamental factors are operating to the advantage of the United Nations both in the Far East and in Europe, for in both war zones we choose our salients and make wedge-like attacks, but the enemy dare not denude his other fronts too greatly to provide reinforcements because he fears the extension of our surface and air attacks upon him. As the deployed combined Services of the United Nations increase in strength the anomaly of the situation will grow, and the rate of acceleration of the war will roll ever more rapidly to its climax. Meanwhile, the destruction of German aircraft is unending as the Red Army advances into the Ukraine.

For the moment, however, the peninsula of Italy offers to Germany a breathing space in the west, be it long or short, for on the Italian mainland both they and we must concentrate. The defence of the Lombardy airfields is vital to the Germans (because their

## HUGE GROWTH OF R.A.F. BOMBING ON GERMANY

The following official R.A.F. totals, issued recently, reveal an amazing increase in Bomber Command's attacks during the last four years.

### BOMBS ON GERMANY

| | | | | | |
|---|---|---|---|---|---|
| 1940 | ... | ... 3,500 tons | 1942 | ... | ... 33,000 tons |
| 1941 | ... | ... 20,000 tons | 1943 | ... | ... 96,000 tons |

### BOMBS ON THE RUHR

1943 ... ... 50,000 tons

By comparison, the entire weight of bombs dropped on Britain during the four years was slightly over 63,000 tons.

### PRINCIPAL GERMAN OBJECTIVES

The seven German towns which have been subjected to the heaviest attacks during 1943 are :

| | | | | |
|---|---|---|---|---|
| HAMBURG ... | 11,000 tons | BERLIN | ... | 6,000 tons |
| ESSEN | 9,000 ,, | DUISBURG | ... | 6,000 ,, |
| COLOGNE | 8,000 ,, | DUSSELDORF | | 5,000 ,, |
| | NUREMBERG | 5,000 tons | | |

During 11 months of heavy raids on London the enemy dropped 7,500 tons of bombs.

### SORTIES BY FIGHTER COMMAND

During the four years Fighter Command has made numerous sorties in addition to the above totals ; the figures are :

| | | | | | |
|---|---|---|---|---|---|
| 1940 | ... | ... 65,000 tons | 1942 | ... | ... 145,000 tons |
| 1941 | ... | ... 173,000 ,, | 1943 | ... | ... 145,000 ,, |

Note.—The figures in each case refer to years ending September 2.

capture by us must lay all Europe open to devastating air attack), and bitter fighting will occur before the German army in Italy is defeated. It will be aided on our side by the struggle for supremacy over the air of central and northern Italy.

The prelude to the battle is the conquest of the air above it. It is the core of the struggle, the path to victory. We shall have to knock their fighters out of the Italian sky and smash them on the ground as we did in Libya, Tunisia, and Sicily.

OVER the Atlantic, and nowhere more than in the Bay of Biscay, the war goes well against the U-boat. Air and sea operations are so knit together that it becomes increasingly hard for submarines to slip through the net. The relative figures are not disclosed, but there seems to be small doubt that the aeroplane is the chief enemy of the underwater-boat. As with the duel between the gannet and the pilchard, the diving bird is the victor in most encounters. In one strange episode a Sunderland sank a submarine which almost simultaneously made the flying-boat crash. The survivors of the U-boat and those of the Sunderland were picked up together by a destroyer. Recent U-boat sinkings have averaged one a day.

The factories continue to produce aircraft rapidly. A total of 7,333 aircraft came from U.S. factories during July, making a four per cent rise on June figures. Britain's second quarter output for 1943 was 44 per cent greater in structure weight than the same quarter of 1942.

On September 1 Liberator and Mitchell bombers with Lightning fighter escort dropped 206 tons of bombs on South-West Pacific Madang and neighbourhood—a record for that theatre of war. Berlin received its baptism of concentration raids on the nights following August 31 and September 3. The enemy used flares, airborne searchlights, and round-cones of searchlights with 500 (estimated) fighters to try to kill the raid. The defences did not keep the bombers out ; but 69 bombers were lost in the two raids. Over France day sorties rose to new high levels of thousands per day.

WITH ITALY AS AN AIR BASE no part of Germany would be outside our bombing range, as this map-diagram shows. Not only so, our bombers, operating from Italian airfields, would be able to attend to industrial centres in Southern Germany with fighter cover for the first time.

*By courtesy of The Daily Mail*

# Flying Scouts Record Our 'Target for Tonight'

FROM START TO FINISH of a Photographic Reconnaissance Unit expedition over enemy territory : a giant camera is installed in a Spitfire (1), which is soon soaring above the clouds and bound for its target (2) ; the round-trip safely completed, exposed film from the camera is placed in the developing machine (3) by a W.A.A.F., then transferred to the drying drum (4), and finally scrutinized (5).

*Photos, British Official.*

PHOTOGRAPHIC RECONNAISSANCE UNITS of the R.A.F. are among the most remarkable developments in aerial warfare. Reconnaissance was one of the first responsibilities allotted to aircraft when military possibilities of the aeroplane were exploited 30 years ago ; and though the imagination is most caught by the work of the mighty bombers of today and their accompanying fighters, modern reconnaissance has reached such a pitch of efficiency that it can be said to be quite indispensable to the successful prosecution of the war.

These P.R. units use either Spitfires or Mosquitoes, the latter for really long-range jobs. Their long-focus cameras are fitted in the body of the machine ; Spitfires carry three, Mosquitoes five. From portholes in the floor of the machine photographs are taken horizontally or obliquely, as the pilot directs from appropriate switches. Each camera takes 500 pictures.

Used in pairs, they overlap one another slightly and so produce an unbroken mosaic of the target about which information is wanted—maybe a bombed town, an enemy front line, a movement of troops, or an entire area such as the Ruhr, the whole of which had been photographically covered by March 1940.

Through an Air Ministry channel all branches of the Armed Forces submit their requests for reconnaissance photographs, and the work is carried out by a comparatively small number of specialists under the command of Air-Commodore J. N. Boothman, A.F.C., who won the Schneider Trophy outright for Britain in September 1931.

# Gallantry and Self-Sacrifice Merit the V.C.

SGT. J. P. KENEALLY was one of a company of the Irish Guards who on April 28, 1943, were holding a ridge of the Bou—a feature dominating the region between Medjez El Bab and Tebourba, Tunisia. Theirs was the task of maintaining a precarious hold until a major British attack could be launched to capture the whole position, an essential preliminary to the final assault on Tunis. A company of the enemy was seen forming up to attack. Keneally—then a lance-corporal—decided that this was the moment to act. Alone, he charged down the bare slope straight at them, firing his Bren gun from the hip. This so demoralized the enemy that they dispersed in disorder.

Two days later Keneally, this time accompanied by a sergeant of the Reconnaissance Corps, again charged the enemy forming up for an assault. Inflicting many casualties, he so harassed them that the threatened attack was abandoned. His purpose achieved, he went to the support of another company; and it was only when he was noticed hopping from one firing position to another, his gun in one hand and supporting himself on a fellow Guardsman with the other, that it was discovered he had been wounded. But, refusing to give up his gun—he said that only he himself "understood it"!—he continued to fight throughout the day with great courage, devotion to duty and disregard for his own safety. As the official citation states, "his was an achievement that can seldom have been equalled."

'AN INSPIRATION TO ALL RANKS' is the official summing up of the exploits of Sergeant John Patrick Keneally, Irish Guards, seen here being decorated with the V.C. Ribbon by General Alexander. How Keneally earned his V.C.—the 73rd to be awarded in this war—by routing single-handed a massed body of the enemy and breaking up an attack on two occasions, is told on the right. His actions in Tunisia influenced the whole course of battle.

*Photos, British Official: Crown Copyright; Bassano*

LIEUT. (TEMP. CAPT.) LORD LYELL, posthumously awarded the V.C., commanded his company of Scots Guards with great gallantry, ability and cheerfulness during difficult and dangerous operations in Tunisia, between April 22 and 27, 1943.

On April 27 Lord Lyell's company was held up in the foothills of Dj Bou Arada (65 miles from Tunis) by heavy fire from an enemy 88-mm. gun and a heavy machine-gun in separate pits. Realizing that until this post was destroyed the advance could not continue, Lord Lyell collected his only available men not pinned down by fire—a sergeant, a lance-corporal and two Guardsmen—and led them to attack the post. He lobbed a hand grenade into the machine-gun pit, destroying the crew, just as his sergeant was killed and his two Guardsmen wounded.

Given covering fire by his lance-corporal, Lord Lyell then ran towards the 88-mm. gun-pit so quickly that he was among the crew and bayoneting them before they had time to fire more than one shot. He killed a number of them before he himself was overwhelmed. The few survivors of the gun-crew fled, some of them falling to our fire. Both guns silenced the company was able to advance and take its objective.

IN THE GUN-PIT WHERE HE FELL, Lieut. (Temp. Capt.) Lord Lyell, first peer to be awarded the V.C. in this war, was buried with honours. A simple cross and his helmet mark the last resting-place of a great hero, whose feat of valour is related on the left. In the background is the German 88-mm. gun which he put out of action at the cost of his life.

THE photograph of the Galleria Vittorio Emmanuele at Milan, which I reproduce in the back page of this issue by way of a change from photographs of bomb destruction in our own cities, I looked at—on its arrival at my desk—with somewhat mixed feelings ; for it shows a spot familiar to me for many years, one where I spent many happy hours with Italian friends. This fine arcade was the centre of life in Milan, something very different from any of those English arcades which are usually short-cuts from one street to another. Some of the leading publishers had their showrooms there, and these were open till about the closing time of English pubs, and usually busy with book-lovers examining their attractive exhibits. There were several excellent restaurants in the Galleria, and it was here in the happy days of peace that one could see the impresarios sauntering back and forth discussing terms with the operatic stars for engagements in London or Paris, Buenos Aires or New York — a continuously changing scene of liveliest interest. That our essential bombing of Milan should have brought it to ruin and that it will be many a day before I may have a chance again to sit at one of the restaurant terraces there, sipping a Strega with some of my Milan friends, were the first sad thoughts that occurred to me as I looked at the photograph; but when, a few minutes later, I had to make my way through some of the devastated areas of the City to catch my train at London Bridge, I felt that it was foolish to sentimentalize.

THOSE who backed Mussolini rejoicing in the destruction of so many of London's historic landmarks must take all they have got and all that is coming to them, and on the whole my last impression of that particular photograph as it goes to press is one of satisfaction that, like the grateful people we British are, we are always ready to give as good as we get . . . And as I write, the news that Italy has surrendered is being broadcast ! Though long and confidently expected, the announcement is breath-taking. Here indeed is the beginning of the end, and Anglo-American bombers had no small part in its achievement. The devastating of Genoa, Turin, Milan and Naples may yet prove to have been the most merciful way to eliminate the junior partner of the Axis ; Sir Arthur Harris will have a good many more bombers liberated now for smothering the pest-holes of Nazidom.

I FEEL that I ought almost to apologize for not having kept my readers in touch with the prophecies of Old Moore, to which in the past I have made many references, as by chance I have just looked at his prognostications for September and discovered this gem from the reading of the stars : " This month reveals Japan in a very parlous position indeed. With the decisive defeat of the Japanese Fleet, the bombing of Tokyo and other centres, the isolation of islands occupied by Japanese troops, who have to be blasted out of their strongholds, the ' Rising Sun ' sinks in hopeless surrender. Rumour will be rife relative to the fate of the Japanese

emperor. Hara-kiri is more than hinted at." Greatly encouraged after reading this unexpected news, I ventured to peep at what is to happen in October, and read the following with mingled feelings of horror and surprise : " An aviation disaster about this time will cause widespread regret. Much interest is aroused by the adoption for military and civil uses of a new type of aeroplane, driven by compressed air, and an experiment, conducted with a view to broadcasting perfumes by wireless, will excite general curiosity. The occupation of Berlin by Allied Forces causes general satisfaction." But don't you think it is rather an under-statement that the complete collapse of Nazidom which would be involved by our occupation of Berlin this October should cause only " general satisfaction " ? If I had read this in the stars I would have foretold a much more exciting reception for such important news. It may be that Old Moore is only a year out and those tremendous events which he had catalogued for September and October 1943, will be realities in 1944. The disparity in dates may be attributed to prophet's licence.

THAT "the women are splendid" is a commonplace nowadays. We all know how much they have contributed to the War effort and how badly off we should be without them. But it is a pity there should be any tendency to limit the praise which all British women deserve to Englishwomen alone.

In a book just published, called Women at War, the authors say, "no one who is at all familiar with England can be surprised at the courage displayed by Englishwomen in this War." Probably this was not in the least intended to be a slur on Scotswomen and Welsh women and the women of Northern Ireland. It is due no doubt to the still far too common use of the word England to describe what should properly be called Britain. The Prime Minister is now always very careful about this. It would be interesting to know what his comment would be on another remark in the book to the effect that the valuable contribution of women should be kept separate from that of men ; they should not walk side by side, for then women would inevitably get ahead and this would have a disruptive effect on society. This is the opinion of the Chief Controller in the A.T.S. She must have felt in a provocative mood when she expressed it like that.

ONE of the new words that have cropped up during the War is " clerkess." I see a number of advertisements for women clerks under this title in a Scottish newspaper and feel inclined to ask, as the posters do about railway journeys, Is this " really necessary " ? We don't call women doctors "doctoresses" or women lawyers "barrister-esses." Salesladies we have accepted because their male counterparts are known as salesmen, but where one term serves to cover both men and women there is no need to use another. We ought to be careful not to complicate the English language any further than is needful now that there is so much likelihood of its becoming an international tongue. The Ministers for Education of the Allied Governments in this country have recommended its adoption. More people than ever before are learning it and more still will be doing so after the War. It is suggested that we shall have to alter our spelling and make it conform to our pronunciation, but that will not be required if Basic English is used as the world language. This would be much easier to master as a means of ordinary communication, while we could keep English as we have it today unchanged for our own use. Invented languages have little chance of success, not even the very ingenious one which Professor Hogben has put together lately.

HERE is an instructive contrast. The woman convicted of using milk to clean her doorstep has been generally repro-bated. Few, I fancy, realize the value of the food she was so recklessly wasting. A cow-keeper of my acquaintance sent to market two fine bull calves. They were to be sold by auction and he expected to get from £7 to £10 for the pair. The highest bid was one pound ten shillings. He had to accept this—fifteen shillings apiece for his beasts that had cost him far more than that to bring up. In the same week that this misfortune befell him he had to pay £65 for a cow in milk. Cleaning doorsteps with milk is an exceptional case of misusage, but it is wasted in other ways. The facts I have given should be a lesson for the wasters to take to heart.

---

## THE CURSE OF GARIBALDI

### By the Editor

TO none of the Western Powers more than to Britain does Italy owe her existence as a State. Thanks to the intellectual leadership of Mazzini and Cavour and the military energy of Garibaldi, Italy ceased to be "a geographical term" and under Victor Emmanuel II, so recently as 1861, achieved unity as a kingdom. So conscious was Garibaldi of Italy's debt to Britain, for all that our statesmanship and goodwill had contributed to the founding of the Italian state, that he called down a curse upon any Italian Government of a future day that would ever take up arms against the country that had stood by her in the struggle for inde-pendence which culminated in the year 1861.

Anglo-Italian friendship suffered no set-backs from that time until the sinister figure of Mussolini arose out of the economic and political confusion of the post-war years. It was to "that man alone" who saw in the fall of France the chance that, as a jackal serving the Nazi lion, he might secure some of the kill for himself and his Fascist-ridden country. From that day the curse of Garibaldi became operative, and we are witnessing its fulfilment.

This is not the moment to criticize the dispositions that made it possible for the Germans to snatch Mussolini from the custody of the Badoglio Government : the internal convulsions that followed the dismissal of that arch-disturber of European peace made this surprising stroke of the enemy the less surprising. It will but little delay the final fulfilment of Garibaldi's curse. Indeed, it may help Italy eventually to a better clean-up.

Mussolini (no longer il Duce) as the Quisling of Italy can never regain the leadership he has lost : he can never again harangue the mob from a window in the Palazzo Venezia at Rome, or from a window anywhere else in Italy, without the high probability of being shot. At best he will be somewhat more useful to Hitler as a broadcaster than his own *alter ego* Hess, whom we hold prisoner in Britain.

The transference of Mussolini's custody will not vitally retard the progress of our occupation of Italy to the full extent of the Armistice terms, but in whatever measure it may hamper that progress Italy will be the sufferer : and as the Nazi threat to " make Italy a battlefield " is carried out, it will only increase the hatred with which the Italian people for centuries to come will regard the name of Mussolini.

Meanwhile, a dreadful alternative is presented to the Fascists : to stand up again for Mussolini and Hitler, or for an Italy freed from both Fascism and Nazism. There is little doubt of the direction to which the sympathy of the Italian people, after three years of cumulative disaster, trends today.

# Milan will carry Such Scars for Many Years

**IN THE ITALIAN 'CITY OF THE DEAD'** called Milan, which in the period August 12-15, 1943, suffered three heavy night raids by R.A.F. bombers, gaunt ruins stand where once were fashionable shopping centres and humming war factories. Above, all that remains of the Galleria Vittorio Emmanuele, arcade joining the Piazza del Duomo—Milan's Piccadilly—with the Piazza della Scala, site of the famous opera house. "Thirty years will not suffice to rebuild Milan," its Archbishop, Cardinal Schuster, is reported to have said. (See also page 287.) *Photo, Planet News*

Printed in England and published every alternate Friday by the Proprietors, THE AMALGAMATED PRESS, LTD., The Fleetway House, Farringdon Street, London, E.C.4. Registered for transmission by Canadian Magazine Post. Sole Agents for Australia and New Zealand : Messrs. Gordon & Gotch, Ltd. ; and for South Africa : Central News Agency, Ltd.—October 1, 1943. S.S. *Editorial Address :* JOHN CARPENTER HOUSE, WHITEFRIARS, LONDON, E.C.4.

Vol 7

# The War Illustrated

Nº 165

SIXPENCE

*Edited by Sir John Hammerton*

OCTOBER 15, 1943

**CANADIANS IN CALABRIA.** Led by Pipe-Major A. Anderson of Toronto, Canadians of General Montgomery's 8th Army march through Straorina, near Reggio di Calabria. It was on the beaches around Reggio, at 4.30 a.m. on September 3, 1943, the fourth anniversary of our declaration of war on Germany, that our men landed to establish their major bridgehead for the invasion of Italy. Hands on hips, a young Italian girl watches and wonders whilst the Canadians pass.
*Photo, Associated Press*

NO. 166 WILL BE PUBLISHED FRIDAY, OCTOBER 29

# War Work and Play Seen by Our Roving Camera

BELLADONNA, powerful and useful drug, being in short supply, Guy's Hospital, London, now produces its own. Nurses (above) collect leaves of the drug-yielding plants grown in the hospital grounds.

ART OF CARVING the Tommies' Sunday joint (right) is acquired by girls of the A.T.S., who learn everything about meat from carcass to menu.

WHILE MOTHER IS AT WORK the war time kiddies are well cared for. In a corner of a modern nursery (below) a shallow bathing pool provides engrossing enjoyments.

VICTORY HOSE : last stages in the manufacture (above) of the Utility stocking. Girls put the stockings on metal shapes, which revolve into a wetting chamber and then travel 60 ft. to a drying chamber, finally being removed, ready for wear.

THE LONG WALK at Windsor, famous elm-lined approach to the Castle, is losing its ancient trees. As felling and sawing-up (below) of the diseased elms proceeds—providing valuable timber and firewood—chestnut saplings will replace them.

*Photos, Fox, Topical Press, Sport & General*

# THE BATTLE FRONTS

## by Maj.-Gen. Sir Charles Gwynn, K.C.B., D.S.O.

DURING the month of September the progress of the Russian offensive was so astonishing that, whatever the original intentions of the Germans may have been, they were left with no alternative but retreat to the Dnieper at least as far north as the Pripet marshes, the eastern extension of which encroaches on the river some 50 miles up stream of Kiev (see map p. 309).

The loss to them of Bryansk and the line of the Desna River will also inevitably compel them to retreat to the upper Dnieper. That has entailed withdrawal from Smolensk, probably to be followed by the swinging back of the whole of their northern front. On what line the Germans will try to stabilize the front, either temporarily or for winter occupation, becomes a matter for speculation.

CAPTURE OF POTENZA by the 8th Army, announced on September 22, 1943, placed them in line with the 5th Army attacking north and east of Salerno. Patrols of the two armies had already linked up on September 15.
*By courtesy of The Daily Mail*

So far, though Smolensk has been abandoned in order to escape another Stalingrad, there are no indications of retreat from the front north of Veliki Luki. Withdrawal from the Leningrad-Lake Ilmen front to the Estonian frontier and to a line running roughly from Pskov at the south end of Lake Peipus would, however, give a somewhat shorter front, and probably one that could be more economically held than the position required for the investment of Leningrad. There would also be a considerable shortening of lines of communications, reducing traffic and releasing troops now employed on protection of railways against guerilla activities.

IT seems improbable that at this stage the Germans would abandon Estonia and Latvia and fall back to the line of the Dvina, as some have suggested, for that would mean the isolation of Finland and give the Russian Baltic Fleet greater liberty of action. Nor would it mean much shortening of the front so long as the line of the upper Dnieper is held. The chief advantage to be gained by such a drastic withdrawal would be a great reduction in the length of lines of communication. Any withdrawal on the northern front would, of course, release large Russian forces —not only the garrison of Leningrad but also the field army which keeps open the city's lifeline.

Much, however, must depend on whether the Germans will attempt to establish their winter front on the line of the Dnieper if they are able to halt the Russian offensive on the river during the autumn. This seems more than doubtful, but since there are as yet no signs of withdrawal from the Crimea the

Germans may not have given up hope of checking the pursuit. Already the German public has been warned that a defensive line may be established much farther to the west ; that may be either because the General Staff is not confident that the Russians can be stopped on the Dnieper, or it is considered that the Dnieper does not provide either a sufficiently short or suitable winter position.

We have yet to see whether the impetus of the Russian offensive will carry them across the Dnieper, but, assuming it will not, as far as I can judge, the river would not give the Germans a good winter position, although it would obviously be desirable to hold it for a time to cover further withdrawal. If it could be held as an intermediate position it would cover the withdrawal of much heavy material and a gradual thinning-out of troops. It would provide a means of escaping a general retreat during the autumn rains over long distances and with roads reduced to a quagmire.

### RETENTION of the Crimea or Nazi Withdrawal From It

At the best, river lines are never easy to defend. Their windings increase the length of front which has to be kept under observation, and they present innumerable alternative points at which the enemy can concentrate for attack. Furthermore, they provide a screen beyond which patrols of the defence cannot easily penetrate, increasing the difficulty of discovering the enemy's intentions.

Air reconnaissance, unless supplemented by ground observation, may prove misleading, and has definite limitations. The right bank of the Dnieper, like that of all rivers in south Russia, is high and commands the low ground on the opposite side. As a natural consequence, practically all the large towns, Zaporozhe being an exception, are situated on the right bank. These conditions obviously give the defence considerable advantages, but they are advantages which favour temporary rather than permanent defence ; and they make it more difficult to maintain bridgeheads across the river covering the main approaches to it.

The most obvious weakness of the Dnieper as a winter defence line is the great bend in its lower reaches, which lengthens the front to be held and forms an exposed salient. To obviate this weakness and to enable them to retain the Crimea (or to cover withdrawal from it), the Germans are evidently holding in force a front from Zaporozhe to the

ISLAND OF COS, in the Dodecanese, was reported occupied by the Allies on September 21, 1943. An Intelligence Officer of the Middle East Command is here questioning Italians who saw German ME109s shot down by the R.A.F. over the island. German sea and airborne troops launched a counter-attack on October 3. *Photo, British Official*

BRITAIN'S NEW 4·2-IN. MORTAR is proving highly effective in action. Manned by a crew of four, it can throw a bomb no less than 20 lb. in weight to the remarkable distance of 4,600 yards. This corrects the performance figures previously given in page 227.
*Photo, British Official : Crown Copyright*

western end of the Sea of Azov—but this may only be a temporary measure, at best a dangerous one. A greater weakness is, I think, the lack of good lateral communications west of the river. In particular, the Pripet marshes interpose a wide obstacle between the forces holding the middle and upper reaches of the river. There are no roads across the marshes usable by vehicles and only two railways cross them from north to south, one 70 miles and the other 170 miles behind the front.

Even in the sectors north and south of the marshes lateral communications are not good, and especially in winter this would delay concentration for counter-attack of an enemy who had effected a crossing and would greatly add to the difficulty of keeping the troops holding the front supplied. The fact that most of the large towns of the region are situated on the river exposed to artillery fire from the opposite bank, and to bombing attacks against which complete aircraft defence could not be provided, would add greatly to the difficulty of providing comfortable winter quarters. Too much of the defence organization would in fact of necessity have to be in the front window.

THE conclusion I come to is that, though the Germans will fight hard to use the obstacle of the Dnieper as an intermediate defence line to cover a further withdrawal, they will retreat much farther west before winter sets in. I should expect their main object would be to place a considerable part of the Pripet marshes in front of the line on which they decide to halt, the object being to secure good lateral communications for themselves while imposing on the Russians the disadvantage of advancing in two separated bodies—a situation which affords possibilities for a counter-stroke.

Should the Germans retreat from the Dnieper and abandon the Vitebsk-Orsha defences it would, however, open to the Russians the passage between the basins of the Dnieper and Dvina. It should be noted that on this sector Russian railway gauge has by now been restored, providing a good base for winter operations.

The truth is that a comparatively short front which could be economically held is not easy to find in Russia, and in looking for it I should expect the Germans to be influenced more by a desire to secure good lateral communication and to shorten their supply lines than to gain the protection of a physical obstacle to direct attack. On the whole, it would seem that, though it would not be the shortest line, the Russian frontier prior to the occupation of Poland and the Baltic states may indicate approximately the zone where the Germans will attempt to establish a winter position. It remains to be seen, however, whether Russian action will leave them much, if indeed any, freedom of choice this autumn or winter.

# 5th and 8th Armies Take a Firm Grip on Italy

FIRST GERMAN PRISONERS come running in (above) soon after the landing of the Fifth Army at Salerno on September 9, 1943. From this British mortar position at Pugliano (below) shells are being fired into German positions at Torello, ten miles east of Salerno. See also opposite page and page 295.

ROUNDING A HAIRPIN BEND in the hills between Scilla and Palmi, in Calabria, is no easy proposition for this 8th Army 4·5-in. gun (above), which went into action on September 7. Italian civilians (below) volunteered to help our troops repair damage to a railway line where German demolition squads had been busy.

THE SALERNO BEACHES and other points of the 5th Army invasion front where our positions were for a time extremely critical (see story in page 314). Black arrows indicate direction of powerful enemy thrusts aimed at pushing our forces back into the sea. Only after 16 days' bitter fighting was our Salerno-Agropoli bridgehead made secure.

*Photos, British and U.S. Official*

# From the 'Heel' to Salerno Our Men Advance

A SHERMAN TANK of the 8th Army, pushing northwards to join the hard-pressed 5th Army, passes through a road barrier of stone masses at Nicastro, in Calabria.

HASTENING THE RETREAT of German forces, Tommy-gun fire directed by an observer with binoculars from this 5th Army forward observation post is proving effective.

SELF-PROPELLED ASSAULT GUN (left) enters a town occupied by U.S. forces in the Salerno area.   British and American leaders (centre) confer on a Salerno beach:  right to left, Gen. Mark Clark, commanding 5th Army, Gen. Sir Harold Alexander, Chief of Operations on the Italian mainland, and Air Marshal Sir Arthur Coningham.   American engineers (right) speedily erect a wooden trestle structure, to span a gap blown in a bridge by the enemy with the object of delaying our advance as long as possible.

*Photos, British and U.S. Official, Fo:*

**LEROS, ISLAND IN THE DODECANESE,** capture of which by British forces was announced on September 21, 1943, was used by the Italians as a naval base and will now, of course, be at the disposal of the Royal Navy. Chief importance, however, of its occupation—together with two other Greek islands Cos and Samos, on the same date—is that this constitutes a definite breach of the German outer circle of defences in that region. *Photo, E.N.A.*

# THE WAR AT SEA

### by Francis E. McMurtrie

FIRST-FRUITS of the elimination of the Italian fleet from the Mediterranean conflict were gathered within a fortnight of the submission of its principal units at Malta. Without a battle the Germans abandoned the great island of Sardinia to the custody of its Italian garrison and retired into Corsica. In that retreat they were not long left undisturbed, for the French patriots in the island, reinforced by troops from Algeria, lost no time in attacking them. By desperate efforts they succeeded for a time in keeping open the port of Bastia, in the north-east of the island, from which they evacuated men and supplies to Elba and Leghorn. Enemy losses in this operation were by no means light, as Allied aircraft and light naval forces struck heavily at transport planes and evacuation vessels.

Able to move their forces freely by sea, the Allies are at a very great advantage in these insular operations. Transport of supplies and troops to Corsica was carried on under the escort of French warships, of which the cruisers Montcalm and Jeanne d'Arc, the destroyers Le Fantasque, Le Terrible, L'Alcyon, Le Fortuné, Basque and Tempête, submarines Casabianca, Perle and Aréthuse, have been mentioned officially.

FARTHER east there have been interesting developments. As practically the whole of the Italian squadron in the Levant had proceeded to Haifa or Cyprus, the Dodecanese and other Aegean islands were left without sea defence. Airborne troops, presumably from the Ninth Army, therefore, descended on the large Greek island of Samos, and on the smaller islands of Leros, Cos (see illus. p. 291), and Castellorizo, in the Dodecanese. Warmly welcomed by the Greek inhabitants and by the Italian army formations stationed there, the invaders proceeded to secure the airfields and harbours, after defeating attacks made by the Luftwaffe from Rhodes. From the naval point of view, Leros is a particularly useful prize, as its excellent harbour was developed by the Italians as a minor naval base, with a floating dock and a seaplane station.

Without doubt, the remaining enemy-occupied islands in the Levant will by degrees fall into Allied hands. Deprived of any naval force, and lacking their former superiority in the air, the Germans will find it impossible to hold even such important islands as Crete and Rhodes when these, in turn, are assailed. Once deprived of these outlying bulwarks, the mainland of Greece, and especially the peninsula of the Morea (or Peloponnesus), will be open to attack from more than one quarter, and evacuation will become imperative.

### DECISIVE Intervention of Royal Navy at Salerno

All these benefits flow from the submission of the Italian Navy, for though that force was never actively employed in offensive operations, its existence in harbours within easy reach constituted a threat which could not be ignored by the Allies when planning the invasion of enemy-held territories. Another effect has been to make the Germans nervous about their line of retreat through Italy, as evidenced by references in Berlin war commentaries to the probability of the Allies landing forces at points in the rear of Marshal Kesselring's armies. Those armies, it is admitted, owed their sudden reversal of fortune at Salerno to the decisive intervention of ships of the Royal Navy, notably the Warspite and Valiant, whose 15-in. shells created havoc in the enemy ranks.

Corsica should be of considerable value to the Allies as a base from which not only air attacks but even invasion operations can in due course be launched upon Northern Italy and Southern France, a fact of which the enemy must be well aware.

In the latter part of September the Germans endeavoured to cheer up their dispirited civilian population by a highly-coloured account of a fresh campaign opened against Atlantic traffic by U-boats. Doubtless these submarines have been undergoing alterations and improvements in recent months with a view to some such fresh attack ; but it is hardly to be expected that, after suffering such a decisive defeat, accompanied by heavy losses, they should renew their operations with any great measure of enthusiasm. Nor is it likely that they will accomplish any large destruction of shipping, for not only are our escorts stronger than ever they were, but they have been gaining further experience of working together during the lull in the U-boat campaign.

In the Pacific American submarines continue to operate with a far more consistent degree of success than those of Germany have experienced in the Atlantic. Colonel Knox, the United States Secretary of the Navy, revealed recently that fully one-third of the Japanese mercantile fleet had been destroyed, including all the additions made to it since Pearl Harbour. It is shortage of shipping that is likely to undermine the Japanese scheme of defence, for her forces are so widely dispersed between her various conquests that adequate sea communications are of vital importance.

In the Indian Ocean enemy submarine attacks on shipping have been reported from time to time, but these do not appear to have assumed the serious proportions of U-boat depredations in the Atlantic. Some considerable reduction in the number of targets afforded may be expected now that supplies for the East are passing through the Mediterranean instead of going by the longer route round the Cape of Good Hope. It is evident that the Italians were contributing their quota to this sphere of operations, for in September the submarine Ammiraglio Cagni entered the port of Durban in accordance with the terms of the Armistice. She is one of the largest submarines in the Italian Navy, with a displacement of 1,461 tons. What is more remarkable is that she is armed with no fewer than 14 torpedo tubes instead of the normal maximum of ten. These are of 18-in. calibre instead of the standard 21-in. Presumably she was designed to prey on merchant shipping, for which purpose a smaller torpedo was considered sufficient. This allowed the number of tubes and of torpedoes carried to be increased to a corresponding extent.

A RECENT Rome broadcast cleared up to some extent uncertainty that had existed concerning various Italian warships. It was stated in this broadcast that ships in ports under German control comprised the battleships Impero, of 35,000 tons, and Conte di Cavour, of 23,622 tons, and the cruisers Bolzano and Gorizia, of 10,000 tons. At the same time it was admitted that the Impero is incomplete and that the other three ships are so badly damaged that they are no longer seaworthy. It will be recalled that the Cavour was sunk in Taranto Harbour by torpedoes from British naval aircraft in November 1940 and was not refloated for a long time, while the Gorizia was badly injured by American bombers in April 1942. It is believed that the Bolzano was torpedoed by a British submarine.

# Modern Horse of Troy on the Beaches of Salerno

**HUGE LANDING-CRAFT** of new design carried the British-American 5th Army to the Salerno beaches on September 9, 1943. Here is one disgorging men and transport through great doors in its hull, under cover of its own smoke-screen—effectively shielding from the enemy's eyes the scene of tremendous activity. Wheel-grip for the motor vehicles is ensured by a track of wire netting laid on the sandy shore. Salerno port was occupied on September 10. See also pages 292, 293, and story in page 314.

PAGE 295

*Photo, British Official*

# Battlefield Gunfire Now Defeating the Nazis

In pre-war days official Germany clamoured for "guns before butter." The Nazis got their guns, but today they lack both the butter and effective artillery power. DONALD COWIE explains how and why Germany has no effective answer to the Allied gunfire now blasting her armies and driving the Wehrmacht back to "Citadel Germany." See also opposite page and pages 247, 291.

DURING seven long years, from 1928 to 1935, a certain Englishman had locked up in his desk the plans of his lifetime's invention—the perfect light field-gun. He knew that not only the British Army but also the German, Russian, French and American lacked such a weapon, but could this Major-General H. A. Lewis get anyone interested ? Not a soul.

It was by the merest chance that Sir Alan Brooke, now Chief of the Imperial General Staff, found himself in a position in 1935 to put a recommendation forward on behalf of his old friend's invention. Thus we got the 25-pounder "gun-how" and our principal means of winning land battles in this war.

To which the reader may well retort, "But surely the Germans built a gun of equal effectiveness and, what's more, built it in greater numbers ! Wasn't it guns before butter in Germany before the war ?" Now the answer to that is most interesting, and contains perhaps the secret of why Germany, for all her preparations, has failed: she has lacked both the butter and the guns.

By studying our major battles so far we can now see that the Wehrmacht, however well equipped in other ways, has consistently lacked the wherewithal to effect large-scale artillery concentrations. On the other hand, that huge army, when defeated, has nearly always been defeated by our own or our Allies' superior gunfire. Glance back over the great events : defence of Moscow, Voronezh, Stalingrad, Alamein, Tunisia, Kharkov—each has been a triumph for the last-war style of artillery barrage.

We can consider the actual gun-work in those battles presently, but first we had better explore the matter of defective German artillery a little farther. To do this it is necessary to imagine ourselves present at a meeting of the German General Staff about 1937. They're mostly young, super-efficient

men, greatly impressed by the work of bombers in Abyssinia and Spain, equally enthusiastic about panzer possibilities. One and all they agree that the static battles of the last war, with their great artillery barrages, will not be known again.

Therefore, regarding the manufacture of new guns they decided that these should be confined to : (1) weapons to be carried on tanks ; (2) anti-aircraft ordnance ; (3) highly-mobile self-propelling pieces to accompany panzer divisions ; (4) anti-tank guns and (5) single and multi-barrelled mortars.

OF course, that is to over-simplify the matter ; but, broadly speaking, it appears now that the Germans made their great mistake in that way. They concluded too soon that old-style artillery methods were finished ; they put their faith in aerial artillery as represented by bombers and mobile artillery as provided by tanks ; and they got away with it during those campaigns, such as the Polish, the Norwegian, the French and the Greek, wherein their opponents had few modern guns of any type. And they got nearly to Moscow with their first mad thrust of tanks and aircraft.

But a few miles from Moscow, as a few miles from Leningrad—and later a few miles from Voronezh and Stalingrad—they came up against the Russian guns. The Red Army had not made the same mistake. During the preparatory years this silent force had probably indented for more guns than any other army in history. The fire power of one of its corps had been raised to 70 tons a minute, compared with 54 tons and 53 tons respectively for French and German corps. So Hitler was foiled before Moscow by such a barrage as prevented his spearhead from ever advancing a yard farther in that direction. It was consistently the same elsewhere. Russian guns on the heights over the city and on the Volga islands saved Stalingrad.

One of the artillery marvels of this battle was how the gunners continually received new weapons, hot from the Dzerzhinsky works at their rear. Next, the Red Army surged forward from Stalingrad, as they have not ceased surging yet ; and the guns always paved the way. In a few days of the Donetz battles one of Zhukov's artillery regiments fired 35,000 shells. Asked to explain subsequent victories, a Russian general said : "Our artillery. It was so accurate and deadly that the Russian infantry advancing behind the barrage took their objectives with losses of less than a dozen men. There was no resistance left after the barrage." Even as we write we hear that Russian guns are "softening-up" the last Nazi defences at Kiev.

Now over to Egypt, and the all-important battle of Alamein. Montgomery's massed guns undoubtedly won that day, the first occasion of the war that we had employed 1914-1918 artillery tactics with modern improvements. And note how Tunisia dragged on till Alexander was transferred to that front, and the break-through to Tunis was achieved by the concentration of no fewer than 400 guns in one place, one to every eight yards. Sicily gave no such opportunities, because the enemy had speeded out before we could bring sufficient big guns forward ; but tomorrow the artillery will prove a decisive factor again.

TO clinch the argument it will not be said the Germans have possessed no good guns. On the contrary, they have developed some magnificent pieces. But the point is that these have been "specialist" weapons, built not for massed artillery work but for accompanying panzers "under their own steam," and for anti-tank and anti-aircraft purposes ; whereas we and our Allies have developed our artillery as primary weapons, for employment as concentrated "rubbers-out" of enemy positions. And here the long-neglected invention of Major-General Lewis —a world's foremost artillery expert who retired on age-limit from the War Office only the other day—has served us particularly well.

The 25-pounder "gun-how" is essentially a light weapon, and we have many other guns. For instance, details have recently been released (see page 247) of the B.L. 4·5-in. and the B.L. 5·5-in., heavy field pieces which strikingly outclass their German equivalents. But our possession of vast numbers of the "little" 25-pounders has enabled us, in swift-moving "pocket" campaigns such as those of the Mediterranean theatre, repeatedly to mount artillery barrages that have swept the Germans off their feet. Prisoner after prisoner has testified to the demoralizing effect of these ubiquitous guns.

And the Americans ? Well, they have been able specially to supply our most conspicuous lacks, which have been "specialist" weapons of the German type, from self-propelling pieces to new inventions such as the "Bazookas" and multi-barrelled mortars. They have also developed a fine range of heavy artillery.

Probably an unbiased vote of all nations would elect our 25-pounder the best gun of this war, as the French "75" was the best of the last war. But the Germans have produced some excellent weapons, and are being beaten on the battlefields chiefly by their failure to have them assembled in sufficient quantities at the right places—by their failure, that is, to use them properly. There is such a thing as being too eager to be off with the old love and on with the new, and if it is a matter of 25-pounders or Stukas the modern soldier will know which to choose.

SMOKE-ROCKETS, such as are here being loaded into a six-barrelled mortar (a variation is shown in opposite page), are among the latest " secret weapons " claimed by the Nazis ; a novel method of projection, dispensing with heavy barrels and affording fast manipulation, is one of the special features. A weapon of this type is said to project smoke and explosive shells simultaneously.

*Photo, Keystone*

# 'Bazooka' & 'Sobbing Sisters'—Secret Weapons

MOST DEADLY AND EFFICIENT weapons being used in this war are mainly developments of tried types with established reputations, but here we show some new and unusual examples. 1, Japanese light machine-gun fitted with bayonet, presumably for use when gun is held on the hip. 2, German five-barrelled "nebelwerfer," used both in Russia and Sicily, which projects smoke- or artificial fog-producing rockets. 4, A battery of these mortars in action they are called "Sobbing Sisters" by the Red Army from the noise made during the projectiles' flight. 3, American anti-tank rocket thrower (background), known as the "bazooka."

*Photos, U.S. Official, New York Times Photos, Associated Press*

# Ferry Control's Great Job in Invasion of Italy

**TRANSPORTATION OF 8TH ARMY TROOPS** and all their vehicles and material to the Italian mainland on September 3, 1943, was the colossal organization job of Ferry Control. This unit consists of a Movements Officer, who fixes beach assembly areas, a Ferry Liaison Officer, and Naval Ferry Control, which supervises sea transport. Lt. Servaes phones (1) to Movements Office (2 and 5) that his men are assembled for the crossing. Troops board an invasion craft (3); the sky is scanned for enemy aircraft (4), and signalmen maintain communications (6). *Photos, British Official*

# Battipaglia Added to Fifth Army's Triumphs

IN A WAR-TORN STREET amidst the desolation that was Battipaglia, on the Salerno front, a dispatch-rider of the 5th Army asks his way of British and U.S. military police. Possession of this Italian town, bitterly contested by the Nazis, was announced on September 19, 1943. The Allies will now repair the damage done to the important railway junction there by our bombers before and after the Salerno landings on September 9. Battipaglia junction is on the routes to Naples from Taranto and Reggio di Calabria.　　　PAGE 299　　　*Photo, British Official*

# Meet the Blitz Buggy, the Quack and Penguin

Italy is the latest portion of the earth's surface to receive the impress of the bullet-proof tires of the Jeep, famous blitz buggy, which, since it came off the drawing-board two years ago, has poked its blunt, adventurous nose into nearly every battlefield. Told by PATRICK SPENCER, here is the story of this amazing mechanical midget which Gen. George S. Marshall, U.S. Chief of Staff, has described as America's main contribution to modern war.

THE ubiquitous jeep's latest progeny, an amphibian which treats land and water alike with equal contempt, has already earned for itself in action the affectionate nickname of the Quack. The comment of one American soldier who first saw a Quack side by side with its cousin, a Penguin—of which more later—was: "Give them babies a couple of wings and a tail, and the next thing you know they'll be goin' upstairs to smack at the Stukas!"

Not such a surprising suggestion when you realize how much the jeep has accomplished since the earliest models bucketed into action in the campaign in Burma. Some of their feats are almost unbelievable. Indeed, when two newspapermen who had driven from Burma into India in a jeep met an officer and told him so, he as good as intimated that they were liars. "There isn't a single road across these jungles and hills," he protested vehemently.

"Sh-h-h! Don't talk so loud," replied one of the correspondents. "Our jeep hasn't found out about roads yet, and we don't want to spoil her!"

THEY were jeeps which rescued rearguards in that epic of heroism, the retreat from Rangoon. Loaded down to their axles with weary troops, they tackled the world's worst road, from Rangoon to Lashio, and got through with their precious cargoes. But Burma is only one of the campaigns in which the jeep has played a big part since it emerged from the mind of its inventor.

It was in 1939 that Major (later Colonel) Robert Howie, of the U.S. Army, visualized an entirely new army vehicle—a fighting midget that would fill the gap between the motor-cycle and the larger armoured units: By March 1940 a pilot model was actually in existence.

Then the fun began! Month after month of gruelling tests, rebuilding, more tests, more rebuilding, and finally an "impossible" six weeks' test imposed by the Army over obstacles never before attempted by any kind of motor vehicle.

THE jeep came through those tests and production began in the autumn of 1941. The following year something like 100,000 of the tough little mechanical warriors poured off the lines. This year the figure is expected to reach a quarter of a million!

Not many people know how the jeep got its name. The early models had a big "G.P." (General Purposes) painted on their sides, and an American soldier seeing one standing in the parking ground of a training camp said, "Jeep, eh?" He didn't know it, but he had performed the christening ceremony of an infant prodigy whose name is now famous throughout the world.

If you haven't seen a jeep, it is a squat, purposeful little vehicle with a flat square-faced bonnet, beneath which is packed an engine that produces more than 60 horse-power. The jeep is only eleven feet long by about five feet wide—lightest of all army vehicles bar the motor-cycle—but it carries three soldiers and their equipment and a machine-gun at more than 70 miles an hour on its bullet-proof tires. It has six forward speeds and two reverse, the power in the land version being transmitted to all four wheels and hauling and shoving the jeep across rocks, sand, mud, jungle, and almost any sort of hopeless surface you can imagine.

And the jeep is almost indestructible. A Jap plane once dropped a 500-lb. bomb within ten yards of one, turning it tail-over-bonnet in a series of somersaults which killed its driver and threw the officer, riding as a passenger, out into a ditch. The officer picked himself up, heaved the jeep on to its wheels, slid into the driving seat, and—having recovered his breath—pushed on!

**ADAPTABILITY OF THE JEEP,** midget general-purposes vehicle, is illustrated by this astonishing scene. With crew aboard, and suspended from a wire cable attached to trees, a quarter-ton jeep is being pulleyed across an otherwise impassable ravine to negotiable ground on the far side.    *Photo, New York Times Photos*

So it is not surprising that this gallant little vehicle holds a revered place not only in the U.S. Army but among those of our own troops who are handling it. The soldiers of today treat their jeeps with a sort of rough affection akin to that displayed by the old cavalrymen for their horses. It is not only loved—it is honoured!

Generals ride in jeeps as a matter of course. Mark Clark and Montgomery are using them to tour Allied positions in Italy. You have seen pictures of Gen. Alexander in his jeep in North Africa (see p. 678, vol. 6). The King rode in one in Northern Ireland. President Roosevelt, when he inspected American troops during the Casablanca conferences, chose to ride in a jeep in preference to the usual limousine. If that isn't an honour for a mechanical hero-of-all-trades, what is?

One can only touch on the multiple uses to which the jeep has been put in the two brief years of its existence. Among other things, jeeps have dragged ploughs to make airfields in Australia and elsewhere; they were the first vehicles to conquer precipitous heights and dense jungle on the new India-China supply route which replaces the Burma Road; they have been used for towing artillery, for mounting anti-aircraft guns and searchlights, as radio cars, snow-ploughs, fire engines, farm tractors—and a host of other thoroughly unlikely purposes. There isn't a battlefront in the world where the jeep's blunt snout hasn't pushed into the thick of the fighting.

AND now they've taught it to swim and ski! The Quack, with its boat-like hull, is merely our old friend the jeep with modifications. Built around the original chassis the hull is a completely nautical affair, with decked-over space fore and aft in which to store ammunition and equipment, and a power-operated nigger-head capstan in the bows which enables the Quack to haul itself up steep banks without calling on outside help. A bilge pump bales out water, and a 30-calibre machine-gun bales out bullets for the discouragement of any-one foolish enough to attempt to interfere with the Quack's brisk progress.

Completely amphibious, the Quack can roar up on its bullet-proof tires to a stretch of water, plunge in and froth across it, emerging on the opposite bank and continuing its journey across land without a perceptible pause. It can do this by reason of a lever which instantaneously switches the engine power from the wheels to a propeller beneath its stern, and vice versa as required.

Before the appearance of the Quack one jeep driver produced his own emergency amphibian—in this case an improvised submarine! Bound by ship to an enemy beach, he took the precaution of soldering a vertical air-intake pipe to his carburettor in case of accidents. He had every cause to be mightily thankful for his prevision.

When he drove off the ramp of the landing craft he dropped up to his neck in the waves. But the jeep, gurgling and coughing spasmodically, clawed its way under the water, rising like Aphrodite from the foam of the sea and roaring into action across the beach.

EARLIER in this article I made a passing reference to the Penguin, cousin to the Quack. This is yet another version of the jeep, designed in this instance for use in sub-zero regions. Detachable skis fit over the front wheels, and a half-track attached to the rear axles gives it a caterpillar action. A small stove and special canvas blanket keep the engine sufficiently warm to give almost instantaneous starting even when the vehicle has been standing overnight in 40 degrees below zero. A Penguin recently under test skimmed over frozen snow at 30 miles an hour, dragging a whole platoon of ski troops in its wake.

Yes, the jeep has been almost everywhere, and it will be one of the first vehicles into Berlin and Tokyo. One of the very few things it hasn't done in this war is to collect a medal—and if machinery could win a V.C. then surely this gallant little blitz buggy would be entitled to it!

# Equally at Home on Sea and Land—the 'DUKWS'

'DUCKS' THEY ARE CALLED in soldier slang, and it is easy to see why. In the first place there is something duck-like about these queer motor-barges-cum-trucks which are as much at home on the sea as on the land ; and then their factory serial letters placed together spell 'DUKWS.' It was in the Sicilian campaign that these strange craft first came into prominence, but they were used before that by the Americans in the S.W. Pacific. Manned by personnel of the Pioneer Corps, they were used to convey supplies from ships moored offshore to inland dumps. They were used later in the invasion of the Italian mainland.

A typical duck — this one is a 3-tonner— is embarked at a North African port to play its part in the invasion of Sicily (1). And here it is on the job (2), alongside a Liberty ship—wartime-built cargo vessel— being loaded up. Its cargo delivered where the bridgehead men desire it, perhaps on the shore itself, perhaps farther inland, the duck returns for more (3). All stores landed, the duck can become a troop-carrier, like these (4), manned by British Tommies, proceeding inland from Reggio.

*Photos, British Official: Crown Copyright*

# Theirs the Job to Keep the Cables Mended

In spite of the development of wireless, submarine cables are still of immense importance, particularly in time of war. Here Capt. FRANK H. SHAW tells of the ships whose job it is to keep the cables functioning in face of enemy attack as well as the wear and tear of Nature.

SINCE no wireless code is absolutely safe from solution, our deep-sea cables have an added importance in, wartime; and since the armoured wires are vulnerable to enemy action, and even to chance mishap, their maintenance is a matter of utmost concern to those responsible. So the cable-ships play no small part in our island war-plan; and, notwithstanding the risk of U-boat and aircraft attack, they carry on their job, day in, day out, without advertisement. Indeed, the less advertisement they get the better pleased their crews are. No need to invite hostile attack unnecessarily!

With so many depth-charges bursting in their vicinity, under-sea cables are liable to "faults" on a far greater scale than ever before. Mines explode in startling proximity too; and airborne bombs are no respecters of locality, any more than is a hurrying destroyer in chase of a U-boat. No self-respecting destroyer-commander is going to miss an opportunity to "put-paid" to a submarine through any consideration for the sea-cables. If such wires happen to be in the way of the bursting charge, so much the worse: it's just too bad. Hurriedly dropped anchors, too, might easily foul a cable and drag it to breaking-point; and it has been known for enemy vessels to grapple for, and cut, the submarine links with the outer world, just to prevent secret messages being transmitted from one ally to another. So the ring-nosed cable-ships are kept constantly under steam, ready for action at a moment's notice, prepared to go any-where and take heart-stopping risks in fulfilment of their duty.

CABLE-SHIPS—Granny-ships they are styled—are fitted both to lay and repair the cables. Internally they are fitted with vast tanks, capable of holding a thousand miles of armoured wire. They are also mobile workshops; for when a cable is parted the break may well be a thousand miles from shore, and repair work must be carried out on the spot where the fault is discovered.

Needless to say the enemy does his best to frustrate such attempts; since, by breaking a line of communication, a tactical plan of campaign might well be thwarted. So, if it is at all possible, the "Grannies" are given armed pro-tection, both against aircraft and against U-boats. Being defensively armed, too, they are able to play a part in their own protection; and the expert cable-mender of one minute may well become the determined gunlayer of the next.

Peacetime life in a cable-ship, though tending to monotony, is apt to be pleasant. There are no up-to-the-minute schedules to which to adhere, and there is ample society aboard; for the technical experts are always carried in addition to the actual crew. More-over, if the cable-laying causes the cable-ship to, use ports frequently, good contacts are made with desirable acquaintances ashore. The work is well-paid, food and accom-modation are up to liner standard; and since such a ship may be sent to any corner of the world, the opportunities for varied travel are frequent. But war brings changes.

The ship, lying in a snug port, is suddenly warned that a fault exists in such and such a cable; she must stand by for instant service. An immediate hurry starts. Last-minute necessities are got on board. If the fault persists, off goes the Granny-ship. The break has probably been located to within a dozen

miles, more or less; but, electricity being so instantaneous in action, only an approximate position can be given beforehand. The ship steams fast along the charted line taken by the cable when laid. She has to avoid mines and suchlike dangers, and she has to maintain tireless vigilance against air attack. Every object breaking the sea's surface is naturally cause for suspicion; it might be a U-boat's periscope—and U-boats sink at sight, irrespective of the nature of the target.

BAD weather is not permitted to interfere: cables are vital. Arrived at the approxi-mate position, the grapnels are let go to the depth at which the cable is supposed to lie. When laid in deep ocean the electric link might stretch fairly tightly across from sub-marine mountain peak to mountain peak;

**WORK ON A CABLE-SHIP** in wartime is as dangerous as it is important. Here cable is being taken aboard—over the vessel's bow-sheaves and engine-drum—for coiling in one of the vast tanks below deck. From that store it will later be "fed" to the sea-bed as a new subterranean link, or used, in part, for replacement of a faulty length of existing cable.
*Photo, Keystone*

but normally it follows the contours of the sea-floor. If an old cable, it is probably so overgrown with weed or coral formation as to be practically a part of the underwater geography. The ship zigzags systematically across the charted course of the wire; the many-tined grapnel dragging steadily. Maybe that grapnel fouls a solid body: if the rope is not paid out sufficiently quickly, or the engines are stopped too late, the grapnel and much of its rope may well become a total loss.

Sometimes it means days and nights of slow groping before the cable is discovered. It can be a tiring, exasperating toil. Even when the armoured wire is found, bringing the bight aboard is no light task. If the strain of three thousand miles of cable is considered, to drag a bight of that weight up from several thousand feet is heroic work. It sometimes happens that the dead drag breaks off the tines of the grapnel, thus releasing the enor-mously heavy catch; whereupon the long, slow, tedious sweeping has to recommence.

When the snared cable is got aboard, it is immediately cut for testing. This is no small matter. The deep-sea cable is a formidable affair, sheathed in protective coverings varying from rubber to hardened copper—this latter to resist the attack of undersea creatures, which gnaw through rubber as mice gnaw through cheese. Once cut, sparks are sent both ways of the wire: presently the fault is more or less precisely located. This done, the cut is repaired, the bight of the cable is passed over the wheel in the ship's bows, and the cable itself is "under-run"—being picked up, passed over the wheel, and dropped, clear of the propellers, until the scene of the fault is reached. This may take days. There may be more than one fault. The fault may be so distant from the point where the first pick-up was effected as to make it unprofitable to under-run all the way; whereupon the cable is thrown overboard, the ship steams back, grapples again until successful, and then carries on repair-work. Maybe a whole damaged section of cable needs to be cut out and replaced. Cable-splicing is an expert's job. Each cable might carry scores of individual wires, and the right ends must be brazed to those corresponding. Then the armouring has to be renewed.

NOT until signals have been tapped from one end of the line to the other is the task completed. Once the repairs are satisfactory the connecting link between great nations is lowered again to its ocean-bed for further functioning. The Granny-ship steams home, unless a wireless call deflects her to another fault in another line.

In dangerous seas, where air attack is frequent, repair work is preferably carried on by night, though the sweeping is a daylight task. Cases have been reported where enemy ships have them-selves grappled the cables—their routes being marked on international charts—and either cut them for good, or tapped them to read the vitally secret messages constantly flashing to and fro. To grap-ple and cut a submarine cable also tends to bring a vitally important ship within range of the lurking U-boat that did the damage. So cable-ship men must work under similar conditions to the Biblical men of old who toiled with a spear in one hand and a spade in the other—only for spade substitute brazing iron and for spear an Oerlikon A.A. gun.

All cables in wartime are under G.P.O. control; and the Granny-ships are run under G.P.O. instructions. In peacetime the cable companies concerned with ownership maintain their own repair and laying ships.

IT may be, of course, that the chances of war demand entirely new cables shall be laid from land to land. If, say, Norway were occupied, an early movement would be to effect invulnerable communications between this country and that—across the stickiest stretch of water in the world, perhaps. The cable-ships would have to perform this service, notwithstanding the enemy's most vicious attacks. But their crews were trained well in peacetime; and they show no sign now of shrinking from the important, hazardous duty. It is doubly hazardous because of the slow pace at which a cable must be laid: this makes the ship a sitting shot for attack, though her escort naturally does its best to safeguard her in her precarious occupation. Many sensational victories are credited to these ships and men. They do great honour to the flag under which they sail.

**1.** Via dell' Impero from an arch of the Colosseum; in the distance the Victor Emmanuel II monument.

**2.** Arch of Titus, commemorating defeat of the Jews (A.D. 70). It spans the Via Sacra not far from the Colosseum.

**3.** Forum Romanum showing the only three columns that remain of the Temple of Castor and Pollux.

**4.** Church and Square of St. Peter, showing the Vatican on the right.

**5.** The Colosseum near the eastern end of the Via Sacra. It dates from A.D. 80 and was completed by the Emperor Titus.

**6.** The Palazzo Venezia seen from the Victor Emmanuel monument. Until recently it was Mussolini's official home in Rome.

*Photos, E.N.A.*

# Rome Ancient and Modern at the Mercy of the Hun

It is to be hoped that the modern Hun as he is driven from Italy's historic soil may be prevented from devastating its priceless memorials of antiquity as Hun and Goth and Vandal loved to do when raiding the lands of Ancient Rome. But as the new Barbarians are more bestial than the old who can say what havoc they may work among monuments of the past of which Italy is the world's treasure house?

## A Little Panorama of the Storied Italy—

In presenting our readers with this selection of world-famous landmarks in Europe's loveliest land, which British and American soldiers are at present endeavouring at great personal sacrifice to restore to the possession of the Italian people, we feel there will be a general desire on the part of the United Nations that, despite the determination of Nazi Germany to make Italy a battlefield, there will be no destruction which it is in the power of Anglo-American arms to prevent.

Photos, E.N
Press, Paul

7. Salerno.
8. Scene in the Aspromonte.
9. Padua, St. Anthony's Church.
10. Amalfi, near Salerno.
11. Forli's 12 Cent. Campanile.
12. Siena Cathedral.
13. Leghorn, the 15 Cent. Torre del Marzocco.
14. Perugia, Mandoren Gate.
15. Genoa, Memorial to the First Great War.
16. Ravenna, S. Apollinare Nuovo.
17. Verona, the Old Bridge.
18. Mountain village in Calabria
19. Pisa, the Leaning Tower.
20. Florence, Palazzo Vecchio.
21. Tivoli.  22. Spezia.
23. Bologna, Leaning Towers.
24. Naples.
25. Foggia Cathedral.
26. Venice, Bridge of Sighs.
27. Capua, 11 Cent. Cathedral.

*Associated*
*gh, Keystone*

## —Our Soldiers Will Admire and Try to Save

The sites and scenes here illustrated are likely to be witnessed with pleasure and pride as our armies work their way northward to Lombardy, where between the Apennines and the Alps these German invaders with their puppet Duce will probably have to make their last stand, and the heaviest fighting will surely be witnessed. Italy has known many invaders, but Mussolini and his Fascists had never envisaged the country they have betrayed becoming the latest Cockpit of Europe.

28. Pompeii, the Temple of Apollo, largely restored after A.D. 63.
29. Paestum: the Greek Temple of Poseidon dating from 5 Cent. B.C.
30. Ancona, the Triumphal Arch of Trajan, erected in A.D. 115.
31. Baia, favourite resort of Imperial Rome, remains of the Great Hall of the magnificent baths.
32. Ostia, the Temple of Vulcan; once the pride of Rome's seaport.
33. Frascati, the Villa Falconieri, built by Cardinal Ruffini in 1546.
34. Vesuvius in eruption.
35. Rimini, a side view of the Arch of Augustus.

## *Majestic Ruins of Time's Own Making*

Photos, E.N.A.

The most impressive ruins of Greek architecture in Southern Italy are to be seen at Paestum, and already many of our soldiers have had the rare privilege in beholding these to get a "close-up" of what Greco-Roman culture achieved when men's minds were bent on creating beauty instead of destroying it. At Tivoli the beauty of nature will appeal to them when our armies of relief have got to the neighbourhood of Rome;. at Ostia they will see what remains of Rome's imperial port, a flourishing city once; at Baia beyond Naples, once the luxury resort of Imperial Rome, only a vestige of the great domed hall of the magnificent baths endures. Everywhere in Italy these time-made ruins will turn the thoughts of the men who compose our armies of relief to the wonder and the beauty of "the grandeur that was Rome."

# VIEWS & REVIEWS Of Vital War Books

### by Hamilton Fyfe

ONE of the mysteries that historians may in time be able to clear up is how far Trotsky deserved credit for the creation of the magnificent fighting force which is driving the Nazi invaders out of Russia and has won the admiration of the world—not to mention its gratitude as well. So long as he remained in favour Trotsky was given this credit. Directly he fell into disgrace, through his own obstinacy in wanting to stir up "world revolution," his name was erased from any connexion with the building-up of the military might of the U.S.S.R.

A year or two after his fall I went through the museum and picture gallery at the War Office in Moscow. The only trace of him was as a figure in a large group, an inconspicuous figure which I felt the Soviet officials would have obliterated if it could have been done without spoiling the photograph.

The authors of The Red Army (Allen & Unwin, 16s.) do not discuss this question. They make very little reference to Trotsky. Apparently Michel Berchin and Eliahu Ben-horin are content to leave it to history. They are both Russian, but they do not claim personal knowledge of the facts they assemble about the formation, training and exploits of the Soviet forces. They leave unsolved also the problem of the 1937 purge which removed Tukhachevsky (a Deputy Marshal of the Red Army) and so many more of the ablest Russian commanders.

THEY do not even mention the circumstantial stories that have strongly suggested, if not actually revealed, the plot hatched between some of these (at any rate) and German military chiefs to upset Stalin—and possibly Hitler too. They show Tukhachevsky as immensely vain, believing in Fuehrer-rule (by himself, no doubt), hating democracy, preferring barbarism to Christianity—in short, a Nazi by conviction as well as by temperament. Just the man for cunning Germans to get hold of and infect with treason !.

The authors have an extremely high opinion of his professional ability. "The real brain of the Red Army," they call him. But it has managed to do very well without him and without those who were liquidated at the same time. The number of them is quoted from the writer known as "General Krivitsky," who puts it at 35,000. The book admits this is "probably exaggerated" and expresses a doubt as to Krivitsky's general trustworthiness. But their quoting him at all shows how carefully all their sources of information must be examined.

THEY do not mention, in their account of the Finnish campaign, in which the Russians began so badly, the belief among the Kremlin rulers that the Red troops would only have to march in and be welcomed with enthusiasm by the mass of the Finnish people. That is the explanation of the ineffective start, the absence of any prepared plan of operations, the lack of winter clothing for the troops, the delay in putting ski units into the field. The Soviet leaders were misled, their information was incorrect, they were astonished when the Finns showed fight. Of this the authors seem to be unaware. Though they quote Litvinov's admission that "the Red Army had not prepared for war against Finland," they "find it difficult to understand why the Soviet Government decided on war." It did not so decide ; it blundered into it under a disastrously wrong impression.

Whether Litvinov was right in surmising that "Hitler drew incorrect conclusions from initial setbacks of the Soviet Army during the Finnish campaign" is doubtful. If that was so, both Hitler and those who were his military advisers at the time must have been wishful thinkers of the most credulous type. For twenty years the Red forces had been not only growing in numbers, but steadily increasing their efficiency.

Heavily handicapped at first by the demoralization of the Tsar's regiments and by the crack-brained zeal of many Bolshevik organizers, they rapidly improved in fighting quality and by the end of 1919 there were three millions of them, far superior in every way to the Tsarist troops, whose equipment and spirit filled me with dismay when I joined them on the Galician front in 1915.

By 1917 they had lost the dogged, bull-headed courage they were showing then. "They run away in panic, throwing away

## Background of the Red Army

their arms, as soon as a German helmet appears on the horizon," their commander-in-chief reported. Their one desire was to quit fighting and get back to their homes. A new army had to be called into being.

What the rulers in the Kremlin decided was that it should be as different as possible from the old army. In that, what passed for discipline was mere brutality. I have seen officers strike men in the face furiously for trifling faults. I have seen sergeants and corporals kicking and beating unfortunate peasants because they were not quick in understanding orders bawled at them. I knew of cases in which officers were shot by their men.

If some of the higher-ups, whose muddling and dishonesty sent men into battle with sticks in their hands instead of rifles, and limited batteries to half a dozen shells a day, and provided equipment far inferior to that of the enemy in many respects—if some of them could have been shot also, justice would have been done.

I remember going up in a battle-plane in 1916 and marvelling at the way it held together. "Flying coffins" aircraft were nick-named then ; it wasn't much of an exaggeration, either. The new Government resolved to develop civil aviation as quickly and competently as possible, and "never lost sight of the use to be made of it in a future war." The result was that when war came the Red Air Force was as good as any, and in some ways ahead of all the rest. It led the way, for instance, in the training of paratroops.

I have mentioned in THE WAR ILLUSTRATED before, I think, how I saw at a Russian Embassy party, in 1936 a film showing the descent of hundreds of soldiers with parachutes from aircraft. This had been already practised then for three years at least, and at that time no one else was doing it. The Soviet Air Force designers led the way also in giving it both the "flying tank" and the anti-tank plane. The coffins are now required for the other side !

THOSE who imagined the Germans would drive Soviet troops before them as they had driven French, Belgian and Dutch had no idea of the leadership under which the Red Army was trained. Leadership both in the field and in the rear have been of the highest quality during the war. Stalin has picked his commanders for their initiative, their enterprise, their readiness to do and dare. He wants men, he told H. G. Wells, "who understand that the enemy is not going to surrender ; he must be crushed," but, he added, boldness in itself is not enough. "When your offensive is successful, forces must be regrouped, positions taken must be secured, reserves must be brought into play to follow up the success and bring the offensive to its triumphant conclusion."

It is clear that Stalin found men who could grasp and act upon this idea, one of the oldest and truest of war maxims, yet one that is very often neglected. By just these tactics the Russian victories have been won. And they were won in advance on the manoeuvre grounds, where the troops had "true rehearsals for real war."

And in the way that Stalin lectures his nation when he has fault to find, so did Timoshenko after the 1940 manoeuvres tell off the armies that had been engaged in them. He pointed out many defects, he blamed officers who did not take the exercises seriously enough, he demanded better organization, better Intelligence service, more initiative for small units, and so on. In all ways the Russians prepared for war, in which the whole population should take part. That explains their success, as this book with its numerous very fine photographs so lucidly and fully explains the preparation.

CROSSING WATER BY RUBBER DINGHY is an essential part of the training of Red Army recruits, for the Russian battle front has numerous wide rivers and spacious lakes. When the Russians reached and crossed the Dnieper in late September 1943, thousands of their stormboats were in action on the river ferrying the victorious Soviet troops to its western bank. PAGE 307

# French Air Squadron Fights on Russian Front

VICTORIOUS PILOTS of the French Normandie Squadron (see text at foot of page) return to their well-equipped Soviet base (1) after yet another operational flight against the Nazis on the Russo-German front.

These bright puppies (2) were born at the aerodrome and, as well-loved pets, have accompanied the pilots on numerous flights. Testifying to successful combats are these swastikas painted on the side of a French pilot's machine (3); they are a proud reminder of Nazi aircraft shot down.

The pilots' scanty leisure moments are sometimes devoted to a game of cards outside a squadron dug-out (4), and good-fellowship is furthered by draughts of Russian beer—taking the place of the Normandy cider for which these valiant flyers doubtless long: and, with luck, will taste again some day.

*Photos. Pictorial Press—Exclusive to* THE WAR ILLUSTRATED

FRENCH Fighter Squadron, formed on the initiative of Gen. de Gaulle and known as the Normandie Squadron—the title was conferred by Gen. Vallene, then head of the Fighting French Air Force—has been in almost constant action against the enemy on the Soviet-German front since December 1942.

Most of these specially selected pilots are veterans of battles in the skies of Britain, France and Libya, and some have been decorated and mentioned in Soviet communiqués. The squadron is commanded by 31-year-old Major Jean Louis Tulan, recently awarded the Soviet Order of the Patriotic War, First Class. Invited to the Red Air Force Headquarters, Moscow, he himself chose the sector on which his squadron was to fight. The fact that it was a "hot" sector naturally made these French air-warriors very popular with the Russians.

Its steadily mounting score of German fighter and bomber aircraft pays eloquent testimony to the squadron's skill and tenacity of purpose and to its fast, highly manoeuvrable and well-armed Yak I planes.

# Triumphant Red Army Reaches the Dnieper Line

MOSCOW'S VICTORY GUNS have thundered almost nightly in acclamation of victories since the fall of Orel and Byelgorod on August 5, 1943; the Kremlin, symbol of Soviet might, is silhouetted (2) by their flashes. On September 23, Poltava, last German stronghold before the Dnieper River, fell, and the Red Army was threatening Smolensk, Kiev and the whole of the Crimea peninsula (see map).

Smolensk and Roslavl were stormed two days later, and by September 27 Red Army Guards Divisions had forced crossings of the Dnieper north and south of Kiev; the latter was being abandoned and the Red Army was within 80 miles of Poland.

In the German Desna bastion of Bryansk, freed on September 17, citizens welcome their liberators (3) led by Col. S. Ukrainets; (1) Russian engineers build a pontoon bridge across the Desna.

On September 29 the Red Army captured Kremenchug; two days earlier Soviet troops had entered a suburb of Dnepropetrovsk, farther down the Dnieper.

*Photos, U.S.S.R. Official Pictorial Press. Map by courtesy of The Daily Express*

# RED ARMY TANKS IN MASSED ATTACK

*Specially drawn for*
*THE WAR ILLUSTRATED*
*by Haworth*

MIGHTY TANK FORCES have been in the forefront of battle at most points of the vast Eastern front throughout the amazingly sustained Russian offensive of 1943. Clashes of armoured vehicles on a scale that almost defeats the imagination have gone on in our Ally's favour, aiding sensational advances. Above is a representative group of Russian tanks crossing a shallow river, almost on the heels of retreating German troops. In the foreground one of the heavier types (1) is grinding its way up the muddy bank; the weight of low-built, heavily-armed monsters such as this is between 30 and 40 tons. Farther back (2) is another heavy tank, with even larger turret and gun; the punching power of this type being very great, it is used to reduce obstinately defended and heavily fortified strong-points. Crossing the wooden bridge in the background are two smaller types: a cruiser tank (3) with powerful quick-firing gun and massive armour, and (4) a fast-moving general purposes vehicle. One notable feature of all Russian tanks is the exceptionally wide track to facilitate movement through mud, snow, slush, and forest swamps." Large numbers of tanks in action on the Soviet front have, of course, been supplied by Britain and America as replacements of inevitable casualties. The latter are, naturally, on a high scale—higher, it would appear, in the case of German tanks. For example, in a special Moscow communiqué giving details of losses inflicted on the enemy on the Orel and Byelgorod front during one month alone—the period July 5, 1943, when the German summer offensive began, to August 5, the day on which the Russians definitely turned the tables and took Orel and Byelgorod—it was claimed that 4,605 German tanks had been destroyed and 521 captured. But mere numbers and weight of metal are not alone accountable for all the Red successes in the tank battles that have now become almost a commonplace. The tank crews are the heart and soul of the metal monsters; with their unquenchable spirit, and the superb leadership with which they are blessed, the impossible in battle has frequently been shown to be possible.

# THE HOME FRONT

*by E. Royston Pike*

MOBILIZATION has reached a stage in this country that has not been excelled by any other country in the War. This was the proud claim of Mr. Bevin, Minister of Labour, made on the occasion of a debate on man-power in the House of Commons on September 23, 1943. In one and the same war Britain has provided a great continental army, a great navy and a great air force, and supplied and maintained all the mechanical equipment needed for a mechanized war. Any expert who had been asked before the War if such a thing were possible would have answered, No. Yet "we have had to do it and we have done it," and we can take credit for a triumph of British organization.

"I have registered every man from 18 to 51," went on Mr. Bevin, "and all women from 18 to 47—10 million men and 10 million women . . . I began with a population between the ages of 16 and 64 of 33 million people. Of these, 22,750,000 are in the Services, Civil Defence, or paid employment either in the munitions industry or carrying on the civil life of the community. That includes 700,000 part-time women. There are nearly 16 million males between 14 and 64, and 15 millions are in the Services or paid employment. Of the 17 million women between 14 and 64, 7,750,000 are in the Services or paid employment, and over a million are doing unpaid voluntary work which, if they were not doing it, I should have to find paid persons to do."

OF single women between 18 and 40, ninety-one per cent are working. Over 80 per cent of married women of that age-group without children are engaged in the war effort. "More than a million men and women over 65 are doing full-time paid employment in the war effort," said Mr. Bevin. "In Merseyside and Manchester, the great mouth of England at the present moment, the average age of the docker is nearly 51, and he is giving a remarkable turn-round of ships under present circumstances. I saw a man there the other day aged 83 wheeling 3 cwt. bags of Cuban sugar. I do not think I have been hard on other people when these examples are borne in mind"—a reference to the many complaints voiced in the debate against the registration and call-up of women between 45 and 50. Over 2,500,000 women have been recruited to the Forces and industry from the non-manual and non-industrial classes ; and of the million persons added to the Forces and munitions between July 1942 and June 1943 two-fifths were drawn from the non-industrial classes. Today we are employing 2,250,000 more people on munitions than at the end of the last war.

BUT great as has been the national effort, a greater is called for. Examining the strategy of the war that lies ahead, the Prime Minister, as Minister of Defence, has made a demand for more labour. So it is that in what is left of 1943 and half of 1944, Mr. Bevin has to find 700,000 more workers. As a result, the intake to the women's Services has been reduced to a minimum (much to the disappointment of many of the girls affected), women are being registered up to 50, ex-cotton operatives up to 55 are being brought back to the mills, boys and girls of 16 and 17 are to be directed into the aircraft industry, surface workers are being sent down the mine.

It was against this background of great need and as great effort that the Minister justified his call to the middle-aged woman to take up work of a definite "war" description. And let it be said that there were few criticisms from the women themselves ; it was the men-folk who did most of the protesting. They feared the effect on home life if the presiding genius were withdrawn ; they urged—with much force—that the Civil Service might well do with a thorough combing, and alleged that many of the women already enlisted in the Services and at the work-bench were not fully or properly occupied.

A few hours before he was due to introduce into the Commons his eagerly-awaited "pay-as-you-earn" income-tax plan, Sir Kingsley Wood, the Chancellor of the Exchequer,

**3,000 TONS OF STEEL** will be released for the war effort when London's temporary Waterloo Bridge is demolished. Of this, 95 per cent will be utilized by the War Office. The remainder will go to make shells and bombs. Here, railway construction men of the R.E.s, who are helping in the demolition, are lowering one of the steel trusses. *Photo, Fox*

collapsed and died in his London flat. His passing was sincerely mourned, not least by those who sat on the opposite benches ; and in the Commons on September 23 many a tribute was paid to his memory and achievements. At the Treasury he was an unexpected success. His Chancellorship, said Mr. Churchill, will be historic, since it represents by far the greatest financial effort in our history. The last of his three Budgets in particular was a triumph.

Out of £5,700 millions, half was raised by taxation, the most severe taxation (said the Premier) ever imposed by a Government and loyally accepted by the taxpayers. "All the greatest economists, John Stuart Mill at their head, have always spoken of the evils of borrowing for the purposes of war, and have pointed out that so far as possible posterity should be relieved and that the cost of what is consumed in the war should be met at the time. That is a counsel of perfection, but nobody has ever come nearer to it than the late Chancellor of the Exchequer."

The "pay-as-you-earn" plan will be regarded as Sir Kingsley Wood's monument, and it was an unkind fate that prevented him from explaining the scheme to which he had devoted intense thought and all the ingenuity of his mind. As it was, it was introduced by Mr. Assheton, Financial Secretary to the Treasury, and a full explanation was published in a White Paper. Briefly put, from the first pay-day after April 5 next the great majority of income-tax payers will pay tax, not as heretofore on their previous year's income, but on the income that is actually earned each week. In order to give the scheme a good send-off, income-tax that will have accumulated for the present year—representing ten months' tax for some ten millions of workers—will be excused by the Government, which means a loss to the Treasury of £250 millions (but about half this sum would have been returnable in the shape of post-War credits).

Small wonder that the proposals were most gladly received by all who were affected by them, the only grumblers being those—small shopkeepers, for instance, and those wage and salary earners who are paid on a monthly or yearly basis—who were excluded from the plan. Within a few hours the postbags of M.P.s were bulging with appeals from those left outside the plan, urging most strongly that the whole body of income-tax-payers should be given the benefit of the new proposals.

TWO days after Sir Kingsley Wood's passing the announcement was made from No. 10, Downing Street that Sir John Anderson was to be his successor at the Treasury. The appointment was well received, for Sir John has not only held such high positions as Home Secretary and Governor of Bengal, but he was for a number of years a prominent Civil Servant. His experience as Chairman of the Board of Inland Revenue for several years after the last war should serve him in good stead in his new post. It may be remarked, too, that he sits in the House as a "National," without prefix or suffix. At the same time it was announced that Mr. Attlee, while still remaining Deputy Prime Minister, was to succeed Sir John Anderson as Lord President of the Council, and Lord Cranborne was to follow Mr. Attlee at the Dominions Office. Furthermore, Lord Beaverbrook rejoined the Government—this time as Lord Privy Seal (vice Lord Cranborne) ; and Mr. R. K. Law, son of the Conservative Premier of a generation ago, became Minister of State, it being understood he would continue as Mr. Eden's principal lieutenant at the Foreign Office.

Many months ago the Ministry of Health announced that it was about to build 3,000 cottages for farm-workers (the critics said that 30,000, or even 300,000, were actually needed). By August 1, 644 of the 2,730 houses for which tenders had been approved were actually under construction (see illus. p. 258), and on September 24 Mr. Ernest Brown, Minister of Health, said that work was in progress on 1,974. Two had been completed, but were not yet occupied. This statement gave rise to laughter of a rather ribald kind, since, the week before these two cottages had been opened by the Minister with what one member called a great flourish of trumpets. "If it takes seven months to produce two cottages, how many centuries will it take to build 3,000?" asked another, to the accompaniment of further derisive laughter and cheers. As for the cottages themselves, they look charming enough, but their lay-out has come in for criticism. Insufficient cupboards, and hot-water pipes going through the larder. Well, well ! Are there no domesticated males in Whitehall ?

# This British Night Bomber Drops 18,000-lb. Load

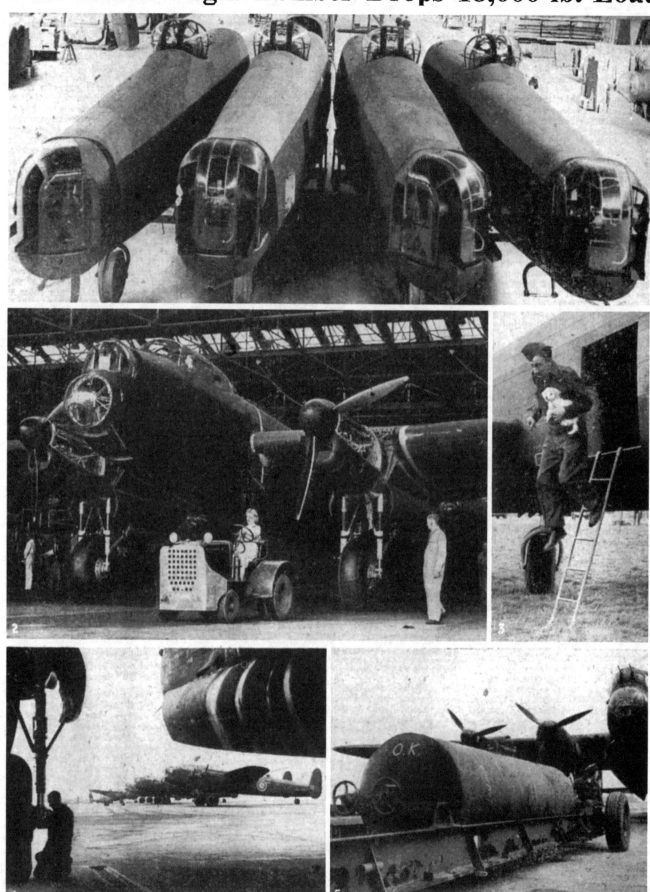

THE FOUR-ENGINED LANCASTER, one of Bomber Command's most potent weapons, carries a greater weight and flies faster than any other British night bomber. We are building these planes in impressive numbers. On the assembly lines (1) fuselage sections await fitting to the body of the machine, which when completed (2) is hauled from the shop to the runway (4) for its first flight by the test pilot. Found flawless, it is ready to take aboard an 8,000-lb. bomb (5); the full bomb-load is 18,000-lb. Flight Sgt. Reg. Burgar, with mascot, leaps from the first Canadian-built Lancaster to be flown to Britain (3). See Berlin raid story, opposite page.

*Photos, British Official; P.N.A., Fox*

# I WAS THERE! Eye Witness Stories of the War

## We Recorded a Big Bombing Raid on Berlin

*Two B.B.C. men and recording gear went with the R.A.F. Lancasters that bombed Berlin on the night of September 3, 1943. Recording Engineer was Reginald Pidsley; the Observer was W. Vaughan Thomas, who in an enthralling broadcast the following day (published here by courtesy of the B.B.C.) introduced the records they made on their perilous trip.*

THAT'S the roar of the four powerful engines of F for Freddie—a Lancaster with 42 raids to its credit. And Reg Pidsley, our Recording Engineer, and I can still hear it drumming in our ears, just as we heard it all last night on those eight long hours on our way to Berlin. F for Freddie roared down the long runway of the aerodrome and then lifted with its heavy bomb-load into the evening sky.

Ken, our Captain, headed F for Freddie in between the searchlights from the Dutch coast, and we set course over the cloud-covered land for Berlin. We were lucky. We were flying with a crew that knew every trick of the trade. Ken, the pilot, was a veteran, and so was Bill, our bomb-aimer. Then there was Con, the Australian navigator, and Jock, the Scottish Flight Lieutenant.

They'd done the trip before, while Sparky—our wireless operator—well, to make certain he had brought along a small white doll as a mascot for luck. Then the two vitally important men—we could hardly see forward in the aircraft—Fieldhouse in the mid-upper and Dev, our rear-gunner, in their turrets: the men who guarded us as we flew deeper and deeper into Germany.

SUDDENLY, Jock gave me a nudge. Over the clouds ahead I could just see a dull red glow. We heard Ken's voice then on the inter-com, " That's it, lads, the big city ! " There was our target—Berlin. So Reg Pidsley made his last preparations for recording as the glow just started to resolve itself into a hedge of searchlights woven criss-cross over the night sky. Now the cloud below us started to thin out. Berlin was right ahead, and we were going in to bomb.

Now what follows are the recordings we made on the run over the target. Our voices will sound strange and slow, and certainly a bit forced now and then, but remember we were talking in oxygen masks thousands of feet up. You'll hear a bump and a crack half-way through. That's where our Lancaster leapt upwards as our huge four-thousand-pound bomb was released. But these recordings mirror exactly what we and the crew felt and did on that run over Berlin. Ken, our Captain, gave the signal, we started our run in, and at the same time started this recording :

FIRST thing we can see now is a wall of searchlights—not the thirty that we saw as we came in from the coast ; they're in hundreds, in cones and clusters. It's a wall of light with very few breaks, and behind that wall there's a pool of fiercer light. It's glowing red and green and blue, and over that pool there are myriads of flares hanging in the sky. That's the city itself.

And there in the heart of the glow, there goes a bigger, a red flash—the biggest we've yet seen—that must be the first of the big four-thousand-pound bombs going down. There's flak coming up at us now. All we see is a quick red glow from the ground—then up it comes on a level—a blinding flash. One went then, and it was pretty near ; our aircraft rocked. But it's pretty obvious as we're coming in now through the searchlight cones that it's going to be hell over the city itself. There's one comfort, it's going to be quite soundless, because the roar of our engines is drowning every other sound.

We're running straight into the most

gigantic display of soundless fireworks in the world. We're due over our target in about two minutes' time, and Bill, our bomb-aimer, is forward ; he's lying prone over his bomb sight. And the searchlights are coming nearer now all the time. There's one cone split again and then it comes together. They seem to splay out at first like the tentacles of an octopus waiting to catch you. Then they stop, they come together again, and this time as they come together they've got a Lancaster right in the centre. It's up to us.

IT's getting too hot with these searchlights and we've starting weaving. Our pilot's put the nose of the Lanc down and we're pelting away at a furious angle. Up comes our starboard wing. It's hidden that Lancaster now. But light flak is coming to us as we're coming out of the searchlight belt, coming up more towards the inner defences. That light flak starts slowly. There they come—just a series of red dots—starting at the ground—as it comes up it's leaping past us —going right past our starboard wing—starting slowly and then whipping past in red flashes. They're being pumped up at us in a steady stream.

Now a flare drops right ahead, and from it breaks a fantastic shower of green lights, scintillating as they fall. That was a near one ; that must have been heavier flak, because it gave us a flash that sent us rocking. The skipper's just called out on the inter-com, " We've got a long bomb run-in ; it's going to take us some time, but the bomb-aimer's ready ! " So I knock off as he goes over to the inter-com. And here we go to drop our bombs on Berlin.

" Hullo, skipper."
" Hullo, navigator."
" Half a minute to go."
" O.K. Thanks for reminding me. Keep weaving, Ken. There's quite a lot of light stuff coming up as well—falling off a bit low."
" Hullo, engineer, skipper here. Will you put the revs. up, please."
" O.K. Keep weaving. A lot of searchlights and fighter flares, skipper, there now."
" O.K. boys, O.K."
" Left—bomb doors open ! Hullo, bombardier. O.K. when you are—bomb doors open."
" Bomb doors open, bombardier."
" Right—steady, steady—there's a long time yet—a little bit longer yet. O.K. steady. Right a little bit —steady."
" Bombs going in a minute."
" Two, three. Bombs still going. Jerry tracer behind us, boy."
" Where is he, rear-gunner ? Can you see him ? "
" Down. Down. He's shot down ! "
" Did you shoot him down ? "
" Yes, we've got him, boys, right in the middle ! Bloody good show ! "
" Keep weaving. There's some flak coming up."
" O.K. Don't all shout at once."
" Photograph taken."
" O.K. photograph taken."
" Hullo, skipper, will you turn on to Zero 81."
" Right, Zero 81, navigator. Don't all speak at once now. Keep quiet, it's O.K."
" Hullo, mid-gunner, did you recognize that fighter you shot off ? "
" No, I didn't recognize it, but it's definitely going down now."
" Good, Jimmy, I can see it, boys. Good show ! I can see it now. I can see him burning. Don't he look lovely ! "
" Good show, lads ! Now keep your eyes open."
" O.K., cap. Keep steady. All O.K."

FLT. LIEUT. K. H. F. LETFORD, of Plumstead, London, piloted the Lancaster which figures in the Berlin bombing raid story in this page. He has since been awarded the Distinguished Flying Cross. *Photo, G.P.U.*

Now we can see him too. He's going down all right. He's burning in a huge flare. And the searchlights get on to him—a cone of twenty swing on to him. We can see him falling now right into that central glow. As he drops the whole searchlight cone is swinging back, swinging on to us. The main searchlight is probing for us all the time. Its beam swings past us now. Our pilot's weaving—he's getting out of it. Down goes the nose of the Lancaster.

We feel ourselves being flung around. The wings dip. We're swinging away. That main beam's getting farther and farther away. We're out of it, and once we're through that searchlight, as we weave, I've got a glimpse of that furious glowing carpet of light that's all we can now see of Berlin. We're beating out of it for home as fast as we can. . . .

*Yes, we set course for home, and all the way I kept looking back at the glow in the sky until miles away I recorded our last glimpse of Berlin :*

At last we're out of the searchlights. We've left the whole boiling cauldron behind us, and as soon as our run-out was finished we all heaved a heartfelt sigh of relief. And now I'm looking back, right over the giant tail fin. And that's our last sight of it— just a great glow in the sky, and around that glow a feathery spray of searchlights, and all that's fifty miles away, and now we've six hundred miles to go for home.

WELL, that six hundred miles was covered in a very different spirit from the outward journey, for everybody was light-hearted again. I remember cracking a joke and drinking a very welcome warm cup of tea with Jock, our Flight Engineer—by the way, I promoted him to Flight Lieutenant earlier on in this commentary—but everyone was light-hearted, and then, as we approached the English coast, Ken, our pilot, spoke to the navigator :

" Hullo, bombardier, English coast should be coming up now. Will you tell me when we cross it, please ? "
" O.K., navigator, I'll let you know when we cross it. I can see it coming up ahead now."
" Thank you."
" Nav. lights on, skipper."
" O.K. navigator, nav. lights on."
" Hullo, navigator, I can just see it coming up now. We shall be directly over it in a few minutes—a few seconds."
" Thank you. O.K. Yes, it's coming up. We're right over it now, navigator."

We were home, Pidsley and I, from a single trip, but the crew of F for Freddie and thousands of others like them may be preparing to set out again tonight. Well, I can only say that next time we both of us hear the roar of English bombers over the countryside we'll feel a new and a very deep respect for the crews who man them !

## I Saw the Fateful Battle of Salerno Beaches

*From the third to the seventh day the issue of the nine days' battle for the beaches of Salerno, Italy, hung dangerously in the balance. How the Fifth Army finally won what Mr. Churchill called " an important and pregnant victory " is told by L. S. B. Shapiro, Combined Press reporter.*

Now that the Battle of the Salerno bridgehead has been won it is possible to reveal details of the 12 tortured hours on the night of September 13-14, when the Fifth Army only held on by the skin of their teeth. Fewer than 100 men and half-a-dozen cleverly placed anti-tank guns stood between the Germans and the sea on that desperate night.

The heroism of these men and the coolness of the Fifth Army's High Command, which directed operations virtually under the guns of the German tanks, averted disaster and turned a moment of German hesitation into an eventual victory for the Allies.

Toward sunset on that fateful night the Germans had gathered enough strength to strike furiously down the dead centre of the Allied bridgehead at the confluence of the Sele and Carlore rivers, where they were only three miles from the sea.

Allied forward troops, exhausted after four days of continuous fighting, were ill-prepared for the onslaught. All day Monday our High Command hoped that the Germans would not make the expected counter-attack before Wednesday, by which time we should have been safely entrenched.

At nightfall the Germans drove through our loosely-held front line between the rivers, at first only with infantry, then with tanks. As the full moon lighted their path they thundered on a three-mile front towards the sea from which we were landed.

I was bivouacked near the junction of the rivers when word was received at 9 p.m. that enemy tanks were within 500 yards of us. There was nothing to stop them. The camp was quickly organized for the last-ditch defence. Cooks, clerks and orderlies, with armed patrols, were sent out behind us. At that critical moment a reconnaissance car armed with only light anti-tank weapons arrived to survey the situation.

Close behind the lines Gen. Clark coolly directed the scant organized forces at his disposal. He rushed a handful of heavier field guns to cover German exits from the bottleneck of the two rivers and to protect the main avenue of Allied reinforcements.

We waited breathlessly for the German onslaught, but it did not come. The Germans hesitated to make the gamble, and our guns, though pitifully few, opened up on them. Gun crews loaded and fired without pause. Off-shore, naval guns joined in.

The German tanks, on the brink of success, failed to rush our scanty defences. Apparently puzzled, they dug into new positions to await daylight. Behind our furious gun-fire we frantically reinforced a new defence line. When dawn broke the German chance of success had gone. Then we began the painful process of pushing them back.

**NORWEGIAN BREN-GUNNER of the Spitzbergen garrison, which was raided by a German naval force on September 8, 1943. Story by a Norwegian officer is given below.**
*Photo, Royal Norwegian Govt.*

## I Was a 'Sitting Target' in the Arctic Sea

*Evacuated to Britain with the rest of the Norwegian population when the Allies raided Spitzbergen in September 1941, the writer of this story joined the Norwegian Army, and when he returned home in 1942 his exploits won him the M.B.E. His story has now been released for publication, following the German attack on the Spitzbergen garrison on Sept. 8, 1943*

I was selected as one of the force of 82 Norwegian soldiers who were to re-establish Norwegian sovereignty over Spitzbergen and set up meteorological stations again. The journey to Spitzbergen in our two little ships—an ice-breaker and a sealer—was uneventful. Our destination was the now deserted Russian mining town of Barentsburg, and our ice-breaker set to work to break through the two miles of ice that lay between us and our goal. Before we could reach it, however, a German reconnaissance plane spotted us,

and a line of four four-engined bombers swept down suddenly out of the "midnight sun" and raked our ships with cannon shells and machine-gun bullets. Then the planes turned, broke formation and came over us singly, dropping bombs. We were a sitting target, held in the ice as we were. But the gunners kept on firing until they were killed, or unconscious from wounds.

In a few minutes the ice-breaker was sunk and the sealer, which was carrying most of the fuel oil, was blazing furiously. Some of the men jumped into the water where the ice had been broken, others scrambled on to the ice. There was no cover, so we lay flat on the ice, shamming dead. The German planes hovered round for an hour trying to wipe out the whole force, and did not depart until they considered they had achieved their object.

Twelve men had been killed, two were fatally wounded and twelve more were seriously injured. I was one of the less seriously hurt, with a wound in my back. The doctor had lost all his equipment and instruments, and the wounds could only be bandaged with field dressings. It was a

desperate situation. Here we were stranded in the Arctic, without food, arms, medical equipment or radio. One of the cooks, however, found some driftwood lying around on the shore, lit a fire and made Russian tea. We began to make plans for the future.

Some of the men formed a "suicide squad," as we called it at the time, and climbed on board the blazing sealer. Ammunition was blowing up all around, but they managed to rescue some rifles and ammunition. A radio receiving set was also saved, but what we wanted most was a transmitter. We then headed for the houses on the shore which had been left by the Russians in 1941, and there we spent our first night. But in the morning the Germans came back again and spotted our tracks in the snow. There was more machine-gunning, but no harm was done.

Meanwhile, we split up into search-parties and discovered in the houses some Russian biscuits, raisins and tins of sprats. Now we held a council of war, and a number of our men afterwards set out on a 32-hour journey across glaciers and snow to a safer part of the island where food might be found. On one of these trips another man was lost through falling into a crevasse.

We who stayed behind continued to search the houses and found blankets, clothing and food which kept us going. I was one of the few who spoke Russian, and because I had lived in Spitzbergen for so many years I knew the Russian ways. I knew that the Russians had had many pigs and also that they would not have had time to do anything with them when they were evacuated in 1941. I guessed the pigs must have been shot.

I had a good idea where we might find them buried beneath the snow, where the cold might have preserved them. I was wounded, and the men had to carry me in our search for them. At last, after a good deal of digging, about 20 carcasses were brought to light.

Much of the meat looked good to eat, and the commanding officer and I ate the first of it as a treat. It tasted all right, and as we suffered no ill effects it seemed safe to use it. Afterwards we all enjoyed plenty of boiled and roasted pork.

Our patrols had been out to locate the enemy, who we knew must be garrisoned on the island somewhere, and discovered a German H.Q. at Longyear City. They had insufficient arms to attack, of course, so our men kept watch and then returned to report. Meanwhile, the German planes had continued to attack us, and day after day they flew over the town, bombing and machine-gunning and firing the wooden buildings. The wounded were carried into a cellar which was used as a "hospital." I had recovered sufficiently by this time to get about on my own, and when one day during a low-level enemy attack a bomb skidded along the snow and crashed against the side of the hospital without exploding, I managed to drag it away, assisted by another soldier, to a safe distance from the wounded.

Our position was not improving by any means, although we did still have food. Then one day we had the surprise of our lives. A Catalina flying boat flew over us and we were able to make contact with it.

Not long afterwards—early in June, when the ice had melted—another Catalina landed in the fjord. Seven of our most seriously wounded returned with it. We had been given sufficient supplies to carry on for a few weeks longer, and 50 days after we first reached Spitzbergen a British Naval force arrived with reinforcements. We now had arms again and so set off to meet the Germans in Longyear City. But when we got there on July 14 last year the Germans had fled.

**CHIEF MINING CAMP OF SPITZBERGEN,** Longyear City was reoccupied on July 14, 1942, by Norwegian forces, whose story is narrated here. Ten months previously the Allies had destroyed all meteorological stations and coal mines in the Spitzbergen archipelago, to prevent these being used by the Germans, and had taken off all the Norwegian population. *Photo, Royal Norwegian Govt.*

# OUR DIARY OF THE WAR

**SEPTEMBER 15, Wednesday** 1,474th day
Italy.—8th Army capture of Belvedere announced. First patrols of 8th and 5th Armies linked. Islands of Procida and Ponsa occupied. Gen. Alexander visited 5th Army front.
Mediterranean.—Ten Italian warships, including two battleships, arrived at Alexandria from Malta.
Russian Front.—Nezhin, 78 m. from Kiev, taken by Red Army.
Air.—Fortresses attacked ball-bearing works in Paris area. At night Montluçon rubber factory, 40 m. N.W. of Vichy, raided. Berlin bombed.

**SEPTEMBER 16, Thursday** 1,475th day
Italy.—5th Army resumed offensive at Salerno and wiped out German salient between Sele and Colore Rivers. Island of Ischia, off Gulf of Naples, surrendered.
Russian Front.—Novorossisk, on Black Sea, Novgorod-Seversky on River Desna, Lozovaya, Romny, Valki, and Glinsk captured by Soviet troops.
Australasia.—Lae (New Guinea) captured.
Air.—Nantes, La Pallice and airfields of Cognac and La Rochelle (France) attacked by Fortresses. Modane marshalling yards near opening of Mont Cenis tunnel, and viaduct near St. Raphael in the Riviera bombed at night. Mosquitoes raided Berlin.

**SEPTEMBER 17, Friday** 1,476th day
Italy.—British troops advanced 2 miles at Salerno. Fall of Albanella announced.
Mediterranean.—Announced Yugo-Slav patriot troops had captured Split, on the Adriatic.
Russian Front.—Bryansk, Trubchevsk and Bezhitsa on River Desna, Berdiansk on Sea of Azov, captured by Russians.

**SEPTEMBER 18, Saturday** 1,477th day
Italy.—Mussolini broadcast for first time since rescue by Germans. Capture of Rocca d'Aspide by 5th Army announced.
Russian Front.—Pavlograd in Dnepropetrovsk sector and Pologi on Dnieper Steppe captured by Red Army. German supply line to Kiev cut.

**SEPTEMBER 19, Sunday** 1,478th day
Italy.—Arrival of Marshal Badoglio behind Allied lines announced, and capture of Altavilla and Battipaglia on 5th Army front.
Mediterranean. — Revealed that Italians had forced Germans to evacuate

Sardinia and French patriots had occupied Ajaccio, capital of Corsica.
Russian Front.—Fall of Dukhovschina and Yartsevo on Smolensk front announced.
General.—Mr. Churchill returned to London from America.

**SEPTEMBER 20, Monday** 1,479th day
Italy.—Fall of Gioja to 8th Army announced. Marshal Badoglio appealed to Italians to resist Germans. Venice and Pescara bombed.
Russian Front.—Velizh, 75 m. N.W. of Smolensk, captured by Red Army.

**SEPTEMBER 21, Tuesday** 1,480th day
Italy.—Eboli captured by 8th Army. Reported that Germans were sacking Naples. Leghorn attacked by Liberators.
Mediterranean.—Capture announced of Greek Islands of Cos, Leros and Samos. Announced that all western Corsica freed by French troops. British M.T.B.s raided Valona (Albania).
Russian Front.—Russians crossed River Desna and occupied Chernigov in upper reaches. Enemy driven from Desna Line throughout its length. Demidov, 40 m. N.W. of Smolensk, captured.
Air.—Beauvais airfield and Lens cokeovens (France) bombed.
General.—Mr. Churchill declared to Parliament in his war review that arrangements had been made for conference of Foreign Ministers of Soviet Russia, Great

Britain and U.S.A., and promised "mass invasion" of western Europe.

**SEPTEMBER 22, Wednesday** 1,481st day
Italy.—San Cipriano, Montecorvino, Rovella and Campagna announced captured by 5th Army, Potenza and Altamura by 8th Army.
Russian Front.—Anapa, N.W. of Novorossisk in the Kuban, captured by Red Army. Novomoskovsk in Dnieper bend occupied.
Mediterranean. — Maritza (Rhodes) and Eleusis (Athens) airfields bombed by Liberators.
Australasia.—Allied troops landed 9 m. N. of Finschafen (New Guinea). Capture by airborne troops of Kaiapit, 60 m. up Markham Valley, announced.
Air.—Hanover pounded in concentrated 30-min. attack. Oldenburg and Bremen bombed.

**SEPTEMBER 23, Thursday** 1,482nd day
Italy.—Ginosa, Avigliano and Acerno announced captured by 5th and 8th Armies.
Mediterranean.—Bonifacio and Porto Vecchio, Corsica, captured.
Russian Front.—Poltava, S.W. of Kharkov, captured by Russians ; Unecha, rail junction between Bryansk and Gomel also taken.
Air.—Twin Rhineland towns of Mannheim-Ludwigshafen heavily bombed at night. Darmstadt and Aachen also raided.

**SEPTEMBER 24, Friday** 1,483rd day
Italy.—Matera and Oliveto Citra announced captured by 8th Army.
Mediterranean.—19 Junkers transport machines destroyed while evacuating German troops from Corsica, making total of 28 in two days.
Russian Front.—Karelli, on Smolensk front, captured by Red Army.

**SEPTEMBER 25, Saturday** 1,484th day
Italy.—Announced that 5th Army troops had captured heights overlooking Naples Plain. Molfetta, 15 m. from Bari, announced occupied by 8th Army. Boizano, Verona and Bologna raided.
Mediterranean.—Oletti, Olmetta and Valletalle in Corsica occupied by French troops. Kalamaki airfield (Greece) attacked by Liberators and Halifaxes.
Russian Front.—Smolensk and Roslavl taken by storm.
Australasia.—Finschafen airfield (New Guinea) announced captured.

**SEPTEMBER 26, Sunday** 1,485th day
Italy.—Spinnozzola and Atella taken.
Russian Front.—Russian troops reached Dnieper near Dnepropetrovsk, Kremenchug and Kiev.

**SEPTEMBER 27, Monday** 1,486th day
Italy.—Foggia air base captured by 8th Army. Fall of Cerignola and Muro to 8th Army, capture of Calbritto and Cassaro by 5th Army, announced. Lioni and Castelnuovo occupied.
Mediterranean.—Corfu (off Greece) occupied by German troops.
Russian Front.—Temryuk, last German port in the Kuban, captured by Soviet troops. Red Army entered suburb of Dnepropetrovsk.
Air.—Emden and Aurich attacked by Fortresses ; 1,000 tons of bombs dropped. Hanover heavily bombed at night.

**SEPTEMBER 28, Tuesday** 1,487th day
Russian Front.—Soviet forces advanced 11-14 miles in Kremenchug direction, and occupied localities on west bank of Dnieper in Kiev region. Germans admitted a Soviet force had crossed the Dnieper at junction of Dnieper and Pripet rivers.
Australasia.—Announced that 7 Japanese ships and 29 barges sunk by Allied bombers at Wewak (New Guinea).

★ ══════ *Flash-backs* ══════ ★

**1939**
September 19. Soviet troops at Polish-Hungarian frontier.
**1940**
September 15. 185 German planes shot down over Britain.
September 17. City of Benares, evacuating children from England to Canada, sunk by U-boat.
September 27. 133 German planes brought down over Britain.
**1941**
September 18. British and Russian

troops entered Teheran, Iran.
September 27. Italian garrison of Wolchefit (Abyssinia) surrendered.

**1942**
September 15. Germans launched mass air attacks on Stalingrad.
September 18. Tamatave, Madagascar, occupied by British.
September 23. Antananarvo, capital of Madagascar, captured by British.
September 25. R.A.F. Mosquitoes raided Gestapo H.Q. in Oslo.

# THE WAR IN THE AIR

### by Capt. Norman Macmillan, M.C., A.F.C.

IF you saw an officer dressed in a dark blue uniform, with plain buttons, rank braid around his cuffs like that of the R.A.F. but in a darker colour, with a star above the three rings that correspond to a Wing Commander's rank badges, and wearing small silver R.A.F. wings in metal on his left breast, would you know what he was? Probably you wouldn't, and you would simply dismiss the subject with a shrug of your shoulders and the thought that here was another of the many new uniforms which have blossomed in this war.

I met one of these officers the other evening in a London club. It happened to be one of the tip-and-run raid nights when about 15 German aircraft crossed the coast and a few got through to London. The structure of the building was trembling slightly with the vibration of the guns in and around the neighbourhood of Hyde Park, and occasionally in the distant rumble of the slight aerial storm that was breaking over the great city you could hear the low boom of an exploding bomb. No one paid any attention to the intermittent racket outside. Conversation never slackened. One resident member of the club was out in his dark blue civil defence uniform on duty in his sector. Fire guards were on watch.

The noise was just dying away in the distance when in came the officer in the R.A.F.-like but distinctive uniform, a senior captain of Ferry Command, now absorbed in R.A.F. Transport Command. He had left Newfoundland that same morning. Next day he would be away from London again. His home was the world—at least, the part of it that comes under the control of the United Nations. Los Angeles, New York, London, Cairo, New Delhi, Melbourne, Auckland, Honolulu are to these men as bus stops or railway stations to most people. They never know the schedule of their next run until they receive their orders.

They pack a bag for Australia, and get instructions to fly to Newfoundland.

They move about so fast they never have time to catch up with the changes of climate they encounter. They are developing a new accent, which is not that of any part of Britain, or of the United States, nor yet of Canada or any of the great Dominions. There is an international flavour about the way they speak, a levelling-out of all the different accents into one, with slang gathered from all the English-speaking world.

The pilots, navigators, radio operators, and flight engineers who wear this uniform are not soldiers, or sailors, or rafiers (to coin a word in which the Air Service is lacking). They are civilians attached to the R.A.F., with none of the privileges of the serving officers, but with all the responsibilities of an arduous job. I don't think for a moment that any of them would change to complete military status if they were offered it. They are probably happiest as they are, free from the discipline and job-shifting system of the Service, but with their own iron discipline ruling their lives, and keeping their schedule in the air from continent to continent, flying in any long-range aircraft that have to be ferried over the oceans and over the land masses.

THE senior pilots are of different nationalities. Some are on the reserve of the forces of their native country. But while they do the job they do now, Ferry Command has priority on their services. For this is an important war job, one which requires great flying skill and experience, the right kind of temperament and, surely, lots of guts, and physical stamina of a high order.

Next time you happen to see men dressed in this uniform you will know that they are civilians in a special category doing a tough flying job with a nonchalance and an esprit de corps that make them take the whole world in their stride and look the whole world in the face; although they are rarely honoured and their praises seldom sung, just because they fight the elements instead of fighting man. And their work will increase as the big aircraft pour out of the United Nations' factories in greater numbers.

German air defences against Bomber Command continue to follow the tactics adopted during recent weeks, of concentrating upon defence by night fighters operating in skies illuminated by cones of searchlights formed by as many as fifty lights per cone, with additional single lights or smaller cones to follow the aircraft that fly through and out of the lit-up zones. Above the level of the British bombers German defence aircraft fly for the purpose of releasing parachute flares, while others have been reported carrying airborne searchlights. In places the sky has been lighted almost as brightly as if it were day. In these conditions the German night fighters have been able to engage our bombers and cause casualties.

### GEOGRAPHICAL Handicap That Will Be Overcome

Three factors have contributed to the results gained by the enemy night fighters. One is that our bombers when operating over enemy territory must come under hostile action for long continuous periods. This geographical handicap can only be overcome when Europe is invaded from the west or when we capture the northern Italian airfields. A second factor is the original 1936 design of our night bombers to carry heavy loads over considerable distances employing the cover of night for safety. For night air defence has progressed, and a method which was sound three years ago is not necessarily sound today.

The fact that our night bombers operate at medium height and medium speed makes it possible for them to be illuminated fairly effectively from above and below, and thus trailed fairly readily by the faster fighters. The third factor is our employment of rifle-calibre defence machine-guns in these bombers. These guns have an effective range of about 300 yards (although aircraft have been brought down by them at half-a-mile in daylight on rare occasions). Cannon-guns and half-inch machine-guns have twice the effective range. German fighters, armed with the heavier weapons, can shoot effectively at normally longer ranges than our night-bomber air-gunners. So it looks as if present types of night bombers must carry heavier defensive weapons, even at the sacrifice of some bomb load.

THIS does not mean the doom of the night bomber, as some might think. In time the night bomber will become a far larger aircraft with a greater range and carrying capacity; it will be armoured and have much heavier armament. But that time has not yet arrived, and we may not reach it during this war. We have to fight at the moment with the aircraft we possess, and modify them as little as possible, for every modification means delay. (Using more of our faster, smaller aircraft—such as the Mosquito—means easier evasion of the fighters, but entails severe loss of bomb load.)

Perhaps the best answer may prove to be the sending of a long-range fighter force with our night bombers, composed of aircraft like the Fortresses which have shown their ability to fight enemy day fighters on equal terms. Certainly if the war goes on for long without the capture by the Army of Continental airfields close to Germany there will have to be a change in our night-bombing tactics if we are to maintain their efficiency at the highest level. Meanwhile, we should remember with gratitude that the night bombers of Bomber Command are the only branch in all the Services who have had to fight for four years without any aid whatever from other land, sea or air forces.

PART OF ITS WING BLOWN OFF by flak, and turned completely over by the terrific force of the flak explosions, after having dropped its bombs on Naples (before the capitulation), this B.17 Flying Fortress was levelled out by its pilot 1,500 feet below the height at which the hair-raising incident occurred—and five parachutes were seen to open. PAGE 316 *Photo, Associated Press*

# Seaways of Frozen North Patrolled by R.A.F.

ICE FLOES DRIFTING SOUTHWARDS from the Arctic Circle have always constituted a grave menace to North Atlantic shipping. But owing to the unceasing vigilance of R.A.F. Coastal Command patrols based on Iceland, which chart the positions of floes for the information of all shipping concerned, not one of our vessels has been lost through collision with drift-ice since the war began. Thus are our Northern supply routes kept open. Typical bergs (1 and 2) were photographed by R.A.F. Hudsons, and this equally perilous field of broken ice (3) was snapped by another plane of the little publicised but indispensable Ice-Pack Patrol.

*Photos, British Official : Crown Copyright*

# These Airmen Win Distinguished Flying Cross

**W/CDR. H. R. COVENTRY, R.A.F.**
Berlin, Duisburg, Düsseldorf and Essen have been among the targets of this "outstanding captain."

**F/O A. T. WICKHAM, R.A.F.V.R.**
His award was for his part in the daylight raid on Berlin on January 30, 1943—a mission which achieved "complete success."

**F/O P. D. WOOD, R.A.F.V.R.**
Described as "a navigator of high merit," he contributed to the destruction of 3 enemy aircraft. He has given "valuable service."

**ACTG. F/LIEUT. D. F. KING, R.A.F.V.R.**
Has served both Bomber and Coastal Commands "with marked ability, courage and devotion."

**ACTG. SQ./LDR. R. H. HARRIES, D.F.C., R.A.F.V.R.**
"A fine leader" who has now been awarded a second bar to his D.F.C.

**P/O P. L. SINGER, R.N.Z.A.F. (left), and P/O A. M. SINGER, R.N.Z.A.F.**
Twin brothers, they have led many successful bombing sorties, common targets including Berlin and Hamburg.

**F/O P. C. COBLEY, R.A.F.V.R.**
"A fearless pilot and a relentless assailant," has engaged in varied operations, destroying 5 of the enemy.

**LIEUT. J. A. LITHGOW, S.A.A.F.**
"Has displayed qualities of courage and determination . . . and set a high example to the flying personnel of his squadron."

**F/O H. W. CHAMBERS, R.N.Z.A.F.**
"A skilful and determined pilot" who has "invariably displayed great courage and devotion."

**P/O W. W. J. LOUD, R.A.F.V.R.**
He has shown "courage and skill" in operational flying, including reconnaissances, always showing "exceptional keenness."

**W/CDR. W. M. PENMAN, A.F.C., R.A.F.**
Has flown on a number of successful attacks on Germany, Italy and the Occupied countries.

*Photos, British Official: Crown Copyright; Canadian Official*

THERE is clearly going to be a lot of discussion over the process of demobilizing men and women from the Services when peace comes. Mr. Bevin's "first in, first out" formula has been severely criticized. It would be foolish, say the critics, to release people in the order they joined up or were conscripted, regardless of their value to the nation for the after-war effort. The rule ought, they suggest, to be "The most useful first." They mean most useful for the particular tasks we shall be faced with after the war. To defer the discharge of skilled building workers, for instance, and to let go men without capacity for anything but pick-and-shovel labour would certainly appear to be bad economy, considering the enormous amount of building work that will be needed. Proclaiming his private idea brought Mr. Bevin a round of unthinking cheers, but it is unlikely the War Cabinet will endorse his proposal. No broad principle can be applied to demobilization. Cases must be judged on their merits —and according to national benefit.

A "SEMI-SAVAGE island" the famous French essayist Sainte-Beuve called Corsica. But that was a long time ago. No one would use such a description today. This sweet-scented isle, covered with shrubs whose fragrance can be enjoyed many miles out at sea, has civilized itself; become a delightful holiday ground in peacetime (though few British visitors went there); and even given up its vendettas (family feuds) which provided fiction-writers with sensational episodes. I have walked all over Corsica, enjoying the ever-changing views and the ever-present flowers, and finding the people interesting, though not much interested in anything but their own concerns. They are neither French nor Italian, but a mixture. Like their two most famous fellow-islanders, Napoleon and Coty (the Paris perfumer), they have to go to the mainland if they want riches or fame. They will never get either by hotel-keeping. They do not take nearly enough trouble.

CAN any thefts be meaner than those of the sneaks who creep among allotments at night and pilfer the onions or the fruit or the cabbages (now that this homely vegetable, usually so cheap, has become for the moment scarce and dear)? The allotment holder works hard, he plans carefully, he raises crops for home consumption. To have these stolen by criminals too lazy to dig and plant and hoe themselves, too utterly lacking in decent feeling to be ashamed of their despicable robberies, is hard indeed. I am surprised that magistrates should be satisfied if they pay fines. They ought to be made to suffer punishment more drastic. To send them to prison would be a pity. Their wives and children would suffer, they would pick up evil notions, for prisons create more criminals than they cure. Why not make them wear some mark or costume that would show everybody what they had been doing? I believe it would have a reforming effect.

A GIRL acquaintance of mine who is going to be married is begging her relatives and friends not to give her fish-servers or salt-cellars or rose-bowls. What she would like are saucepans, kettles, strainers, frying-pans. These are at times so difficult to get that many young couples find it next door to impossible to set up homes. You can do without a great many things, but to prepare meals without those indispensable kitchen utensils is out of the question, unless you are content to live on cold stuff out of tins, which, by the way, needs so many points that you simply can't do it for more than a few days at a time. Present-giving of all kinds has become much easier, I find. One used to be compelled to choose among a lot of things mostly useless. They all seemed equally futile—and equally dear. Now one tries to buy something that will be really welcomed, no matter how humble its character. One wife I know gave her husband for his birthday present twenty-one of her clothes coupons. He needed shirts badly, but had used all his coupons on the necessary purchase of a suit and overcoat. He said he had

GEN HENRY H. ARNOLD, Commanding-General of the U.S. Army Air Forces, now conferring with British Service chiefs. On September 4, 1943 he gave as his "timetable for victory . . . First, supremacy in the air and then crushing invasion by land and sea." He added: "So far we are on schedule, and we are not going to pull our punches." *Photo, Planet News*

never been given anything he liked better—or that he really needed more!

ONE of the most pathetic of the "war casualties" that have come to my notice on the Home Front is an author who has written a number of books and made quite a reputation in his own subjects. He finds, of course, that his market is severely restricted. Paper scarcity reduces the quantity of books that publishers can bring out. The small size of newspapers has the effect of squeezing out articles which used to be accepted from outsiders. But diminished income has for this writer one most unhappy consequence—he cannot find any quiet place in which to write. His one room is too cramped and does not possess a table steady enough to write at! His club has been partly wrecked; the Silence Room, where he could spend hours undisturbed, is no more. If he tries to work in the room where writing must be done now, he is continually interrupted, he complains wryly, by kind inquiries after his health or remarks about the weather. "They mean well," he says, "but it makes concentration impossible." I suggested to him that many Public Libraries have good Reference Rooms where writing can be done. He did try the Reading Room at the British Museum, but could not find a seat. It is now always full, it seems, for many foreigners are doing research work there.

WHEN W. S. Gilbert in one of the Savoy operas (was it The Pirates of Penzance?) introduced a patter song about "the modern major-general," he endowed the ideal type of this rank with all sorts of learning. He did not include psychiatry, because this branch of mental study was at that time unknown. Now it has become part of the regular army routine. At the Selection Centres which examine soldiers to see what their special aptitudes may be, psychiatrists are on the staff for consultation, if desired, and a number of the examinees take advantage of the opportunity to have their "psyches" analyzed. This term used to be translated as "soul." It has come to mean "character" in a general sense; and part of the task undertaken by the Selection Boards is to discover what are the characteristics of the men who appear before them. Intelligence tests are applied, inquiry is made into mechanical knowledge, every possible endeavour is used to find out the attainments and experience of each individual so that each may be given the job for which he is specially fitted. The centres do all they can to make the soldiers sent to them comfortable and care-free, so that they may be at their best. This seems to me one of the most valuable of the many innovations in military training which this war has brought about.

I HOPE the British and American occupation of Sicily will make the lot of the sulphur mine-workers at Girgenti more bearable than it has been, not only under the rule of Mussolini, but long before that. Musso ordered that this place should be called, as it was in Roman times, Agrigentum, but it had been Girgenti for centuries when I was there some time before the Fascist tyranny gained sway. There are some magnificent ruins of Greek architecture there and for them it was worth taking a tedious journey across the island by a very slow, dusty, hot little train. And while I was there I saw the sulphur mines close by. These are tunnels driven into the soil diagonally and entered from the surface. Seldom have I seen any sight as painful as that of the undersized, gnome-like Sicilian miners toiling through these low-roofed tunnels, in which I could not stand upright, with grievously heavy sacks of sulphur on their shoulders. Their conditions were those of slaves. They were allowed to die off like flies from the effects of sulphur and excessive toil.

ANGLERS are finding fishing tackle difficult to buy. This hits them particularly hard at a time when they have been making unusually good catches. In the Thames and other rivers barbel, bream, dace, grayling and carp have been biting eagerly. They are a welcome addition to the wartime larder, and numbers of men who have never fished before have taken to what is now not so much a sport as a means of increasing food supply. That, of course, partly accounts for the shortage of fishing requisites. But gut for lines is also scarce; a great deal of it is used in Service hospitals for the treatment of wounds. Thus a check is given to a recreation particularly soothing to jangled nerves as well as useful for filling hungry bellies.

# Hitler's Alpine Highway to Northern Italy

**THROUGH THE BRENNER PASS** thunders a column of Tiger tanks on its way to reinforce Nazi contingents holding down the war-weary people of the Plain of Lombardy. When Italy entered the war the Brenner became her lifeline to Germany; now, instead of coal and oil, this famous Alpine highway brings to the Italians ruthless oppressors.

*Photo, Planet News*

Printed in England and published every alternate Friday by the Proprietors, THE AMALGAMATED PRESS, LTD., The Fleetway House, Farringdon Street, London, E.C.4. Registered for transmission by Canadian Magazine Post. Sole Agents for Australia and New Zealand: Messrs. Gordon & Gotch, Ltd.; and for South Africa: Central News Agency, Ltd.—October 15, 1943.      S.S.      *Editorial Address:* JOHN CARPENTER HOUSE, WHITEFRIARS, LONDON, E.C.4.

Vol 7 # The War Illustrated Nº 166

Edited by Sir John Hammerton

SIXPENCE
OCTOBER 29, 1943

**WREN AT THE HELM** of a motor-boat. Harbour work with the Royal Navy, such as this girl is engaged upon, is one of a variety of important duties under the White Ensign now being performed by members of the Women's Royal Naval Service. With H.R.H. the Duchess of Kent as their Commandant, the Wrens are brilliantly maintaining Britain's proud sea traditions and justifying their distinction as the senior Women's Service.
*Photo, Keystone*

**NO. 167** WILL BE PUBLISHED FRIDAY, **NOVEMBER 12**

# Empire War-Tour With Our Roving Camera

SOUTH AFRICA'S Premier, General Smuts, is the advance guard of Dominion Prime Ministers expected in London early in 1944 for the first full-dress Empire Conference of the war. Gen. Smuts is accompanied by his son and A.D.C., Capt. Smuts; they are here seen (right) with Mr. and Mrs. Churchill in the garden of No. 10, Downing Street. While in Britain General Smuts will act as a member of the War Cabinet, where his experience of affairs of State will be of immense value.

NORTHERN TERRITORY, Australia, is the scene of this exercise (below) by bearded Navy men advancing with fixed bayonets through tall grass. They are taking part in a "jungle" practice aimed at toughening them for possible land defence. Though General MacArthur's men are gradually ousting the Japanese from New Guinea, the enemy is still strongly enough entrenched in adjacent Timor and the Netherlands East Indies to require great vigilance along the northern coast of Australia (see map in page 350)

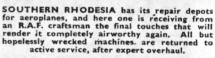

SOUTHERN RHODESIA has its repair depots for aeroplanes, and here one is receiving from an R.A.F. craftsman the final touches that will render it completely airworthy again. All but hopelessly wrecked machines are returned to active service, after expert overhaul.

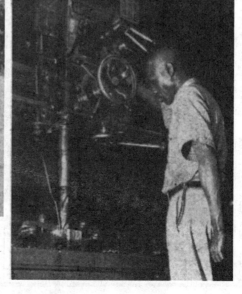

GOLD COAST of West Africa staged a bomber week parade at Accra, as part of the town's drive to raise to £150,000 West Africa's present total of £113,474 subscribed towards Bomber and Spitfire Funds. Above, fire fighting units passing the saluting point, where the Governor of the Gold Coast, Sir Allan Burns, K.C.M.G., is standing. Right, this African engineer in a Kenya and Uganda Railways and Harbours workshop is one of many natives who have temporarily abandoned an outdoor life to learn munition-making and thereby assist the war effort.

*Photos, British Official, New York Times, Pictorial Press*

# THE BATTLE FRONTS

### by Maj.-Gen. Sir Charles Gwynn, K.C.B., D.S.O.

**HUON GULF COASTLINE has been the scene of some of the fiercest fighting in the New Guinea campaign. Finschafen, last enemy base in this area, fell on Oct. 2, 1943. See also p. 350.** *Map by courtesy of The Times*

THE campaign in New Guinea which has been in progress for over 18 months has attracted less attention than it deserves. Yet it has been of extraordinary interest, not only on account of the astonishing courage and tenacity displayed by the Australian troops under appalling conditions, but also by reason of the enterprise and ingenuity with which a technique has been developed for dealing with the problems of jungle warfare. This technique promises also to provide a key to the even more difficult strategical problem of evicting the Japanese within a reasonable period from the innumerable footholds they have secured.

Information about the campaign, till recently, has been scanty, and I know of no better description of the difficulties encountered in its earlier phases than that given by Miss L. E. Cheesman in the Geographical Journal of March 1943 (E. Stanford, Ltd.).

LET me recall briefly the main features of the campaign. By the middle of March 1942 the Japanese had occupied the principal harbours and airfields on the north coast of New Guinea as far east as Salamaua. With these bases they could dominate sea communications (and none other existed) leading to the north-eastern coast of the island. Now at this time almost all the fully trained troops of Australia were serving in Malaya or the Middle East, and the U.S. were still reeling after Pearl Harbour.

An attack on Port Moresby therefore seemed to the enemy good strategy ; and in fact in July they landed a force at Buna with the object of capturing Port Moresby on the south coast from the land side—the battle of the Coral Sea in May having frustrated hopes of reaching it by sea. During August they worked their way across the Owen Stanley Mountains and came to within 30 miles of Port Moresby. But difficulties of the mountain track and air attacks made it impossible for them to supply a force strong enough to overcome the Australian defence reinforced and within easy reach of its base

At the end of the month they attempted to open a new avenue of approach by landing troops at Milne Bay, whence an advance along the south coast would turn the mountains. The attempt had, however, been foreseen and a brilliant counter-attack threw the invaders into the sea. The failure of this attempt and difficulties of supply then compelled the Japanese to withdraw their main body across the Owen Stanley, leaving only a rearguard in the southern foothills at Yorabaiwa.

THIS brought the defensive phase of the campaign to a close, and at the end of September the offensive phase was initiated with a counter-attack on the Yorabaiwa position. The Japanese retreated, offering only slight resistance, until the crest of the Owen Stanley was reached ; but it was now the Australians who were faced with the immense task of crossing the range by a barely usable track and of debouching on the the other side in sufficient numbers to defeat an enemy within easy reach of his bases. It was a desperate and laborious business, made all the more difficult for the Australians by the greater quantity of supplies they required as compared with the Japanese, and by the greater care they took of their wounded.

Yet progress was steadily made ; not a little owing to the loyal service rendered by native carriers. Here, and throughout the campaign, the good relations the Australian Administration had established with the natives earned its reward. Japanese resistance stiffened during the descent of the

northern side of the mountains, but the Australians by now had mastered the Japanese in jungle tactics. Space does not permit an adequate description of the difficulties of the terrain which had to be overcome or of the insects, leeches, diseases and weather conditions which combine to make New Guinea the most trying theatre for military operations that could be found.

HAVING reached the low ground larger Japanese forces were encountered, but they were out-manoeuvred and out-fought at Kokoda and at the rivers on the track to Buna, to the defences of which they retreated. Here they were strongly fortified, and in November the long battle of Buna began in which an American force, landed at Milne Bay, took part. Fought in the height of the monsoon season, deep mud, insects and malaria made conditions more appalling than ever. The Japanese, in fox holes, revetted and covered with coconut logs (proof to anything but a direct bomb hit), had to be dug out one by one by infantry attacking through deep mud.

Not till a few guns, brought by air, were available could much progress be made. Tanks also appeared, but at few points could they be used. The Japanese were in a hopeless position, attempts to reinforce or evacuate them having been defeated with disastrous losses by Allied air attacks ; yet they were

**LT.-GEN. SIR EDMUND HERRING, C.B.E., D.S.O., M.C., commander of Australian troops in the forward areas in New Guinea. On Oct. 7 it was announced that his men were within 50 miles of the Japanese base at Madang, about 140 miles north-west of Lae.** *Photo, British Official ; Crown Copyright*

determined to fight to the death, and not till the end of January were the last remnants annihilated. The campaign so far had been a wonderful achievement, but it left the impression that the capture of all the Japanese strongholds in the Island would be an interminable process. Nevertheless, airfields had been secured, and, with the growing strength and improved quality of the Allied air arm, sea communications could be used to bring forward heavy weapons and material which could not be transported by land or air

A long lull in land operations ensued, during which the enemy showed signs of attempting a new offensive. But in this interval the Allied air force was active, scoring great successes against his convoys

attempting to reinforce his New Guinea detachments and against the base he was attempting to develop at Wewak on the northern coast. The only land fighting of consequence that occurred was when the Japanese attacked the small Australian force at Wau, 40 miles inland from Salamaua. This detachment, supplied by air, had been maintained in the settlement which had grown up round the neighbouring goldfield, itself developed, equipped and supplied entirely by air transport. Reinforced, the detachment repelled the attack, and later played a part in the recapture of Salamaua.

Not till the beginning of July was MacArthur ready to exploit the advantages secured by the capture of Buna, and to start the series of amphibious operations which, at a constantly increasing pace, led to the successive captures of Salamaua, Lae and Finschafen. First came a landing of Americans south of Salamaua which, after hard fighting, and with the cooperation of the Australians from Wau, led to the encirclement of the Salamaua inner defences.

A SITUATION similar to that at Buna developed, but this time more guns could be used and the enemy could be more completely cut off from supplies; his resistance, therefore, though stubborn, was not so prolonged. Still it was not till the second week of September that the place was completely captured. Before it finally fell, another landing had, however, been made north of Lae, on Sept. 4, 1943, thus turning the obstacle of the Markham River. At the same time an Australian parachute force (some of the men making the jump for the first time) descended in the Markham valley to cut off the enemy's escape. Surprise was complete, but to supply and reinforce the parachutists MacArthur's new equipment had to be brought into action.

Bulldozers landed by American engineers and operated by Australian sappers attacked the jungle, and roads over which jeeps and guns could move came into existence at an amazing pace, in many places surfaced with logs laid corduroy-fashion. Supply, the crucial problem of jungle operations, had been solved, and impenetrable jungle had been conquered by the engineer and his modern tools. It will be seen that sea and air power had provided strategic lines of communication, and the engineer those required for the tactical operations of the infantry and artillery. Lae was captured in two weeks, and Finschafen fell to attacks of similar character in even shorter time.

These were great achievements, but it must be realized that, though modern equipment had made them possible, the results could not have been attained without skilful and daring planning and by a wonderful display of human energy and courage.

# In Naples the Nazi Reign of Terror Ends—

THE GERMAN TERROR lasted for five days. In those five days the Germans must have realized that all hope of holding Naples was gone, and they did their worst in the time they had left to them. They killed and wounded thousands of people, set fire to buildings they knew would burn easily, and dynamited those that would not. The result is that the hospitals are full of wounded Italians—men, women and children—and in some of the parks they are making cemeteries for the dead. The Germans attacked hospitals, knowing they had supplies of food and water, and the staffs manned rifles and machine-guns and fought them off.

I saw more than 100 bodies of men, women and children killed in the miniature civil war that raged in the city, and I passed through a hospital ward containing 600 wounded, most of them Italians who had fought it out with the Germans. The dead in this hospital had been piled up in one huge room, and because of the fighting there had been no opportunity to dispose of them.

The Germans dynamited all the large buildings. Naples University was set on fire—and left a burned-out shell. The Germans, and Blackshirts, burned and destroyed the most valuable works of art, including famous paintings, and tried to set the Opera House on fire. A large number of Italians were rounded up and herded into a building. While sentries held them in, mines were laid under the building. More than 100 Italians were killed when the mines exploded. On one of my tours of inspection I was accompanied by a colonel who had seen some Russian battlefields : "But never have I seen anything like this on any battlefield," he told me.

One of the toughest nests of resistance our troops had to overcome was in the area of the hospital I have just mentioned, overlooking the Strada Capodichino. There, Germans and Blackshirts fought it out with the civilians until their ammunition ran out. Nurses carried on with their work all the time under fire. Germans shot down scores of Italians for refusing to report for service in German labour camps or with the army.

THE director of one hospital proudly showed me an ambulance which had been captured from the Germans by civilians armed with machine-guns. "They stole one of ours, and we needed them," he told me. "They were besieging the hospital, because they knew that we had supplies of food and water. They wanted completely to demoralize the town by leaving the wounded unattended, but my doctors and nuns stuck to their posts. The Germans even shelled our dispensary, hoping to destroy our medicines." When they saw the battle was lost, they became panic-stricken. They took prisoner large groups of Italians, tied their hands, and forced them to form a cordon round their armoured cars, so that they should not be shot at as they (the Germans) returned.

A colonel of the Carabinieri told me that the Germans were particularly angry with the Royal Police. If a member of the Carabinieri shot a German,

NEAPOLITANS gathered outside the Municipal Buildings show their curiosity and appreciation as units of the 5th Army enter the town on the morning of October 1, 1943. The Nazi reign of terror was over.

they would shoot scores of the police as a reprisal In the village of Aversa, near Naples, 80 Carabinieri and 20 civilians were shot on the spot in reprisal for the death of one German. I have before me a copy of the newspaper Roma containing a German proclamation published on September 13, stating: "Every German soldier killed or wounded will be avenged 100 times. A state of siege exists. Anyone violating the rules will be shot outright."
—*Henry Gorrell, British United Press Correspondent*

REJOICING seemed almost out of place in the once beautiful city, now plundered and laid waste. But the entry of our troops meant to the citizens of Naples bread and liberty. The Germans, before retreating, had perpetrated atrocities and destruction on an appalling scale. People were reduced to drawing drinking-water as best they could from broken mains (top left). The street scene above was a repetition of joyful demonstrations by Italians that greeted General Mark Clark's victorious Anglo-American army as it advanced along the road from Torre Annunziata to Naples to crown with success the operation which began at Salerno.

*Photos, British and U.S. Official*

# —And Our Men Sweep on to Italy's Capital

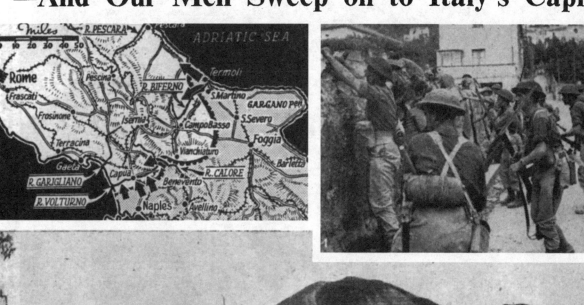

**BITTER FIGHTING, AND DELAY** due to systematic demolition by the retreating Germans, marked our advance to Naples. Sappers had arduous tasks to complete ; these troops (1) have just crossed a bridge erected in only 50 minutes. With Vesuvius as background (2) an anti-tank gun goes into action. Near Cava Sherman tanks (3) pause for a few moments before continuing through difficult mountain country in which self-propelled Bishops (4) give powerful support. From Naples the 5th Army forged on (see map, showing line on **October 8**) towards Rome, aware that a wing of the 8th Army was cutting across the Apennines to join them in the assault on the Italian capital. *Photos, British Official. Map by courtesy of News Chronicle*

**ANOTHER U-BOAT GOES DOWN**, but it is no ordinary "kill." This was the last of a trio sent to the bottom by one American pilot—Lieut. Robert Pershing Williams—in four days during a recent convoy action in the Atlantic. Lieut. Williams was in charge of a carrier-borne Avenger torpedo-bomber. He was accompanied by a wireless operator and a turret gunner. All three U-boats were accurately straddled with bombs through the expert cooperation of the three airmen. The third U-boat is here seen as she was settling down by the stern, her prowling days over for ever. Day by day, through such skilful operations—by Allied seamen as well as by airmen—the U-boat menace is being effectively countered.

*Photo, U.S. Navy Official*

# THE WAR AT SEA

### by Francis E. McMurtrie

**ITALIAN NAVAL UNITS AT MALTA**

Lying off Malta under the guns of this island fortress, on September 12, 1943, Italian warships numbered 20, including 5 battleships. In addition to the battleships there were 8 cruisers and 7 destroyers. The list is as follows :

**Battleships :** Caio Duilio, Andrea Doria, Italia, Vittorio Veneto, Giulo Cesare.

**Cruisers :** Luigi Cadorna, Pompeo Magno, Eugenio di Savoia, Giuseppe Garibaldi, Emanuele Filiberto Duca d'aosta, Raimondo Montecuccoli, Luigi di Savoia Duca degli Abruzzi, Scipione Africano.

**Destroyers :** Nicoloso da Recco, Vittorio Alfieri, Velite, Arcigliere, Fuciliere, Grecale, Legionario.

See pages 335-338.

WITH the Italian Navy eliminated, it was inevitable that the German Fleet would receive a fuller share of the Allies' attentions. First intimation that something untoward had happened to the enemy squadron in Norwegian waters came from a neutral source. It was stated by a Swedish newspaper that acts of sabotage were believed to have been committed by members of the crews of German warships in a certain Norwegian harbour. This belief appears to have been based on the fact that salvage pumps had been observed being taken alongside one of the ships.

This is not the first report of disaffection amongst German crews in Norway. Although such stories should always be received with great caution, the situation of these German sailors is by no means a happy one. They are stationed at a long distance from their homes, with a hostile population around them, while their wives and families in the Reich are exposed to a steadily mounting campaign of heavy bombing.

A hint of the truth was given a little later when it was officially admitted in Berlin that on Sept. 22, 1943, an attack had been made on the German squadron in Altenfjord, near Hammerfest, by submarines of a small type. It was claimed that this attack had been a failure, but soon afterwards it became known that the "pocket battleship" Lützow, of 10,000 tons, had proceeded back to the Baltic. Following the Swedish statement that the use of salvage pumps had been called for, this suggested that there had been an attack which had damaged at least one of the ships.

ON October 11 the significance of all these reports was explained. In an Admiralty communiqué the story was told of a "very gallant enterprise," in which a number of midget submarines penetrated the farthest recesses of the Altenfjord, some 50 miles from the open sea, and delivered a successful attack on the German squadron. A series of very heavy detonations following on the discharge of the submarines' torpedoes proved that some of them had scored hits. Subsequent photographic reconnaissance showed the 42,000-ton Tirpitz, Germany's biggest battleship, still lying at her anchorage, surrounded by fuel oil which covered the part of the fjord in which she lay and extended over a distance of more than two miles from

her berth. A number of small craft, probably repair ships or vessels to provide light and power, could be seen alongside the battleship.

Three of the midget submarines which executed this daring attack failed to return and must be presumed lost ; but the Germans claim that some of the personnel were taken prisoners. Commanding officers of the missing submarines were Lieut. G. Place, D.S.C., R.N., Lieut. D. Cameron, R.N.R., and Lieut. H. Henty-Creer, R.N.V.R.

To reach the enemy anchorage the midget submarines had to pass through minefields and navigate an intricate series of channels without being detected by patrols ; and the same obstacles had to be surmounted on the return passage. As the Altenfjord is 1,000 miles from the nearest British base, it is obvious that these submarines must have been brought most of the way by a mother-ship of some kind, in the same way that the Japanese midgets were taken to within striking distance of Pearl Harbour, Sydney and Diego Suarez in 1941 and 1942.

It was not long before the Germans in Norway received a further shock. In the first week in October the Home Fleet, under the command of Admiral Sir Bruce Fraser, made a sweep towards the northern shores of Norway, to cover the approach of a United States aircraft carrier. From this carrier a number of aircraft proceeded to raid the shipping in the "leads," or deep-water channels, between the Norwegian coast and the chain of islands fringing it. Altogether, eight vessels of various types, including an oil tanker, were sunk or badly damaged. All or most of them were undoubtedly engaged in transporting supplies to the German forces in the north of Norway.

These two attacks have shown that the German squadron in those waters can no longer expect immunity from attack, or to

**Lt. H. HENTY-CREER, R.N.V.R.** One of the three midget sub. commanders who did not return from the Tirpitz attack. In civilian life he was a film-producer, and was only 23.

**Lt. D. CAMERON, R.N.R.** Another of the valiant trio who displayed "the highest qualities of courage, enterprise and skill." Aged 27, he was formerly of H.M.S. Sturgeon.

**Lt. G. PLACE, D.S.C., R.N.** Aged 22, he won his D.S.C. for "bravery and devotion to duty," and also held the Polish Cross of Valour. He was a close friend of Henty-Creer.

*Photos, British Official: Crown Copyright; The Daily Mirror*

receive its supplies regularly, for Sweden now forbids their transit by rail. It is to be doubted whether the enemy can spare sufficient aircraft to maintain the full reconnaissance required to give warning of such raids. Two German planes which attempted to shadow the American carrier were destroyed. These tribulations must add to the discontent of German naval personnel, who may sooner or later demand to be brought back to a home port.

Since its occupation in the early weeks of the war, the Polish naval base of Gdynia has been increasingly utilized by the German Navy. Its distance from this country has hitherto rendered it raid-free, but on October 9 "strong formations" of American Flying Fortress bombers made a heavy pattern attack on the dockyard. Apparently the enemy must have been taken by surprise, for the anti-aircraft fire was light and negligible in its effects. It is probable that most of the warships in the port had been paid off for refit and that there were few if any ratings on board to man the guns. Pilots reported, however, that as the Fortresses approached the Germans sent up a great smoke screen.

IT is believed that the ships at Gdynia include the battleship Gneisenau, of 26,000 tons, which has been under repair ever since she was badly damaged by torpedoes on her passage from Brest to Germany last year ; the aircraft-carrier Graf Zeppelin, of 19,250 tons, of which no use has been made since her completion in 1940, so that she is generally regarded as a white elephant ; the "pocket battleship" Lützow, whose doleful return from Norway has been related in a previous paragraph ; the old cruiser Emden, of 5,400 tons, formerly in use as a seagoing training ship ; and possibly the 10,000-ton cruiser Prinz Eugen, torpedoed by H.M. submarine Trident last year.

Reconnaissance photographs show that the raid resulted in four ships being set on fire, including the 13,387-ton liner Stuttgart, while oil storage tanks were hit and the naval yard, docks and railway yards were damaged. The "very successful completion" of this 1,600-miles bombing mission makes it clear that Gdynia can no longer be regarded by the German Navy as a safe harbour of refuge for its lame ducks.

**GERMAN BATTLESHIP TIRPITZ**—42,000-ton sister-ship of the Bismarck, which was sunk in action on May 27, 1941—lies damaged at anchorage, and surrounded by a two-mile-long mass of thick oil, in the sheltered and well-guarded Altenfjord, Northern Norway, following a magnificently daring attack by British midget submarines on September 22, 1943. "It is difficult to realize the skill and determination necessary . . . to carry out such an attack," the Admiralty commented.

*Photo, British Official: Crown Copyright*

# These Little Ships Excel In High-Speed War

Cutting into the enemy's coastal lifelines and shipping reserves, harrying the E-boats and preventing them attacking our convoys, enabling our Commandos to make vital raids about which we do not always hear: these, writes HOWARD JOHNS, are some of the gallantly performed tasks of the Royal Navy's Little Ships and their indomitable leaders. See also opposite page.

IN their quiet way Light Coastal Forces of the Royal Navy, operating off the coasts of Norway, the Low Countries, France and Italy, have been responsible for some of the most successful attacks in modern war. Their prey, for the major part, consists of numerous German supply ships and tankers that attempt to run the gauntlet of British sea and air power by hugging close to the coasts of occupied Europe.

Precise figures of their successes are not to hand; they will have to wait until after the war. But it can be stated that dozens of tankers have been either sunk or seriously damaged by the Royal Navy's speed-boat fighters, and that has meant that squadrons of the Luftwaffe, based on Western Europe airfields, have gone short of essential oil supplies. Enemy troops, too, stationed in France, the Low Countries and Norway, receive a large proportion of their supplies by sea. German merchantmen, using Brest, Dunkirk, and other French ports as bases, are being called more and more into service by the enemy in an effort to free the railroads for more important traffic.

This has presented our Light Coastal Forces with more opportunities of showing their skill and daring; and with the aid of minelaying craft enemy convoys are often forced into lanes in which our motor-torpedo-boats and motor-gunboats are waiting.

The gunboats, most heavily armed craft for their size in the world, act as "Spitfires" to the torpedo-boats, which, with their "tin fish," might be described as the light bombers of Light Coastal Forces.

ALTHOUGH the Germans would not admit this, men of the little ships are blockading the enemy. It is becoming increasingly difficult for Germany to ferry supplies round to her scattered forces, and in a desperate effort to make things easier the number of escorts to each merchantman or tanker has been strengthened. Recently one tanker had an escort of five E-boats and two armed minesweepers—but that did not prevent our little ships from registering hits upon her.

It has been my pleasure to meet many of the young leaders who are responsible for this day and night—especially night—offensive against the enemy. The greatest was the late Lieut.-Cmdr. Robert Hichens, D.S.O. (and Bar), and triple D.S.C. "Hich," as he was known to all who served with our small craft flotillas, was the modern Drake

of the North Sea. A born leader, he took part in 148 operations and 14 actions before a chance shot cut short his brilliant career.

In peacetime he was a solicitor at Falmouth. In his spare moments he used to sail his own yachts. He became an expert on the Channel and its approaches, and before the war joined the R.N.V.R. When war came

and he was not called for Service, "Hich" wrote a letter of protest to the Admiralty—and eventually got his own way.

The German capture of the French Channel Ports enabled the Nazis to base their E-boats —they are really Schnellbootes, similar in design to but slower than our M.T.B.s— facing our South Coast, and they commenced to try to blockade this island. Hichens, and others of his breed, fought back. Slowly but surely they turned the tables upon the Nazis. The Germans have admitted that

our craft have sneaked into Calais harbour and other French ports, gunned anchored German craft and docks, and sped away before the defence booms could be dropped.

Before the war one of Hichens' greatest friends was Peter Scott, son of the famous Antarctic explorer. Scott painted wild birds and sailed yachts, and he and "Hich" had

MOTOR-TORPEDO-BOAT, one of the Royal Navy's "fly-weight terrors," moving at speed. Their quick-fire and hard-hitting raids on enemy shipping are complementary to R.A.F. bomber attacks on the enemy's land communications. M.T.B.s and their sister vessels, motor-gunboats, operate mainly off our East and South coasts from bases only 75-100 miles from the mainland of Europe.
*Photo, British Official: Crown Copyright*

much in common. War did not part these two great men; they served together with the Little Ships. Now Hichens has gone, but Lt.-Cmdr. Peter Scott is still fighting, and his great gallantry is adding glory to his flotillas.

ANOTHER who is adding to his fame with Light Coastal Forces is Lieut. Peter Dickens, D.S.O., M.B.E., D.S.C., a descendant of the great author. "Audacity" should have been his Christian name, for he has gained many victories by his complete disregard for personal safety. He is popular among his men, one of whom said to me recently: "The lads would do anything for the skipper. And it's because he's a fighter and not just a descendant of Charles Dickens." At 25 years of age this young man has gained much fame —but he prefers to be known as the son of Admiral Dickens, the Principal Admiralty Liaison Officer for the Allied Navies.

The majority of the craft attached to Light Coastal Forces flotillas are manned by either R.N.V.R. or Hostilities Only—"H.O." men in Navy language, who have joined the Senior Service since the outbreak of war. A typical example is Lieut. H. L. Lloyd, D.S.C., known in the Service as "Napoleon Lloyd" because of his hand-inside-the-jacket habit. He is said to possess the sharpest pair of eyes in the Royal Navy. On one occasion, when on night patrol in the North Sea, he told a surprised look-out that he could see an enemy convoy—about four miles off! The look-out and his shipmates could see nothing. An hour later Lloyd proved his point. A German convoy was spotted, and a sharp action took place.

Lt.-Cmdr. P. M. SCOTT, M.B.E., D.S.C.
Son of the Antarctic explorer, famous bird painter, now the brilliant commander of one of the dauntless "Little Ships."
*Photos, British Official: Crown Copyright; Associated Press*

Lt.-Cmdr. R. P. HICHENS, D.S.O., D.S.C.
Scott's close friend, recently killed in action, whose bar to his D.S.O. and triple D.S.C. proved him a great hero.

Lieut. P. DICKENS, D.S.O., M.B.E., D.S.C.
Descendant of Charles Dickens, he is an intrepid skipper serving with the Light Coastal Forces with dash and daring.

# Royal Navy Improvises as Well as It Fights

THE WANG-HO MAIN ROYAL tackle being fixed by a rating of the motor-launch. An awning, spars and boat-hooks went to the construction of this junk-like sail—an example of brilliant naval improvisation in emergency.

LITTLE SHIPS ARE DOING BIG THINGS in the war at sea. In this page we record two of their most remarkable recent exploits. First, the story of the motor-launch, one of a flotilla which set off on a 3,000-mile voyage from Britain to West Africa, and got there—under sail! Knowing they were attempting a journey which would take them to the extreme limit of their range, every expedient was tried to reduce fuel consumption to the minimum. But as they neared their destination supplies got so low that "fuel rationing" signals were made to the flotilla leader every four hours. Two days from port, the M.L. commanded by Lieut. Reynolds-Hale, D.S.C., R.N.V.R., fearing that otherwise it would have to be towed, cut down engine speed and rigged sails. With canvas awnings they fashioned a mainsail for the signal mast. With spars, boat-hooks and a smaller awning they made a sail amidships so like that of a Chinese junk that they called it the "Wang-ho Main Royal." Aft they hoisted the ordinary dinghy sail. With all sails rigged (above) the launch made 11 knots, and reached harbour on her last drops of fuel.

LIEUT J. O. THOMAS, R.N.V.R., shown above with his first lieutenant, Sub-Lieut. E. H. Whitehead, was in command of one of two motor-launches which, early on the morning of Sept. 25, 1943, intercepted a number of E-boats retreating off the East Coast. Lieut. Thomas put his helm over immediately and rammed the second boat in the enemy line. As it drew clear, both M.L.s engaged it with small guns. Then Lieut. Thomas's companion vessel rammed the enemy again, and further and heavier fire set it ablaze. Burning and abandoned by her crew—some of whom were rescued and taken prisoner—the E-boat sank after blowing up. Slightly damaged by enemy fire and the ramming, both M.L.s returned to port with casualties of only one officer and one rating slightly wounded. There they took ashore their blindfolded prisoners, including some officers (left). And there, no doubt, the personnel kicked their heels in impatience for the moment when they should slip from harbour again on the coastal patrol that goes on unceasingly. (See article in opposite page.)

 Photos, British Official

# Air Disaster Threatens Nazis as Foggia Falls

**FOGGIA FROM THE PILOT'S COCKPIT.** The highly important airfield system made available to the United Nations by the capture of Foggia on September 27, 1943—described by President Roosevelt as " one of the most important Allied successes yet "—consists of a main airfield two miles outside the town and 12 satellite fields surrounding it. As the map shows, this success gives us not only extension of air support for our armies pushing northwards in Italy, but air command of the Adriatic long-range fighter penetration into Yugoslavia, and new targets in Austria and Southern Germany.
*Photo, The Times. Map by courtesy of The Daily Sketch*

## OUR BOMBING RANGE INCREASED
### By Captain Norman Macmillan, M.C., A.F.C.

IT is no exaggeration to assert that the major victory-winning factor in this war has been proved time and again to be the possession of airfields in the correct strategic positions. But that alone is not enough. It is also necessary to have the right types of aircraft in the essential numbers to take advantage of the strategic situation ; and, when other Services are concerned in an operation, to develop to its logical conclusion the principle of the application of air power to the military object of attack so that it can be captured with the minimum loss in life and material in the shortest possible time.

The campaign in Tunisia was held up until the Eighth Army's advance provided suitable airfields whence three-dimensional war could be brought to bear upon the Axis forces which had held up the insufficiently air-supported First Army's advance from Algeria. Our airfields in Tunisia and Malta made the Sicilian operation a rapid success, with initial landings almost casualty-free.

AT Salerno we stuck our neck out farther, and had a hard fight to gain a foothold because we were so far ahead of the fighter bases. Mr. Churchill has stated that we went ahead as far as we dared. President Roosevelt's message addressed to Congress on September 17, 1943, made when the German retreat from Salerno had just begun, contained the following vital passages:

" It is now our purpose to establish bases within bombing range of Southern and Eastern Germany, and to bring devastating war home to these places by day and by night as it has already been brought home to Western Germany." Referring to the American raid on the Ploesti oilfields, he said : " We shall continue to make such raids all over the territory of Germany and the satellite countries. With Italy in our hands, the distances we have to travel will be far less and the risks proportionately reduced."

THE first of the important Italian mainland airfield areas to fall into Allied hands was Foggia, occupied by our Eighth Army on September 27. The main Gino Lisa airfield two miles outside the town is surrounded by 12 satellite fields extending outwards to 23 miles. The satellite fields have runway landing-strips of from 200 to 300 feet up to 1,700 yards, suitable for the operation of different types of aircraft.

The capture of Foggia and the two Naples airfields (which were occupied later) will enable the Allied air forces to provide the tactical air support needed by the Allied armies on the west and east coasts in order to advance north-westwards up the Italian peninsula.

But more important than the tactical support which the Foggia airfields system makes possible are the strategic opportunities which it opens up. The great industrialized area round Vienna lies less than 500 miles away. Munich is exactly 500 miles distant. When the Fortresses and Liberators bombed Munich and Weiner Neustadt from North African bases on October 1 they had to make an outward flight of 900 miles. Use of Foggia will enable them to do the same job from about half the range. When the firm of Henschel moved their Kassel aircraft factory near to Vienna they thought they were transferring to a safe area. That area is no longer safe.

ONE most important aspect of closer range bombing operation is the greater certainty of being able to select the best meteorological conditions over the targets, for weather changes are more pronounced at greater distances and reconnaissance aircraft are handicapped in reporting conditions. But at reduced ranges meteorological reconnaissance aircraft can provide satisfactory weather map data for the bombers, which may spell enormously increased success to the operation.

Budapest is but 460 miles from Foggia, and Bucharest about a hundred miles farther. The Ploesti oilfields are fewer than 600 miles away. The whole transport artery of the Danube river, from Sulina to Passau, falls within a range varying between 350 and 750 miles. Belgrade is 350 miles away, Sofia 400, Salonika 380. From Foggia the Balkans lie under enfilade air attack.

Crete, that was to have been the Nazi bastion against attack upon the Balkans, has been turned, and all the enemy from Albania to the Crimea now face the threat of dual air attack from Russia in the East and from the Anglo-American forces in the West. To Germany the loss of Foggia is a strategic air disaster, the beginning of the end of her power in the Balkans.

# 'Monty's Highway' Through Italy to Victory

ALL TRAFFIC
FOR
LONDON
STRAIGHT ON
1870 MILES

MONTY'S
HIGHWAY

FROM CALABRIA UP THE ADRIATIC COAST General Montgomery's 8th Army steadily advanced to take Foggia (see facing page) on September 27, 1943, and thereafter to split, one force keeping to the coast road, the other cutting across the Apennines to link with the 5th Army forging north to Rome from Naples. All along their victorious route Military Police have erected signboards such as this. "Monty's Highway" began at the very gates of Cairo on September 23, 1942, when the Desert Army set out on its "immortal march." *Photo, British Official*

# Guerilla Fighters Help to Free the Caucasus

MOUNTAINEERS, all of them fanatical patriots, helped the Red Army to clear the Northern Caucasus of the German invader. Honoured among these guerilla fighters is Bater-Bek (1), farmer.

Over the grave of his three brothers, who died fighting the enemy, he takes an oath to avenge them (2). His mother sees him off to join the partisans, adding to her blessing a horn of wine (3). His intimate knowledge of the countryside makes him an admirable guide (4). Though the partisan leader is worried at the rigours his men will have to undergo by the route suggested, they follow Bater-Bek with confidence (5) as he leads them through a mountain pass that will bring them face to face with the enemy.

On October 9, 1943, Moscow's victory guns saluted General Petrov's army, which by reaching the Chuska Spit opposite Kerch had finally cleared the North Caucasus of the enemy.

*Photos exclusive to*
THE WAR ILLUSTRATED

# Russians Now Stand on the Road to Berlin

SMOLENSK, once Hitler's Russian Headquarters, and the city he ordered to be held at all costs, fell to General Sokolovsky's Red Army troops on September 25, 1943. Behind the conquering Russians lay 27 months of death, torture, hunger and cold: before them the road to Berlin was opened wide.

Nazi fury at forced retreat found its usual barbarous expression in widespread destruction and plunder: deserted streets and wanton havoc confronted the first Russian patrols (1). From their cellars (4) and other places of hiding the terrorized people of Smolensk soon emerged, paying tribute to their liberators with modest posies of field-flowers (3).

Meanwhile, 200 miles farther south, the battle for Kiev raged. At Chernigov, which fell on September 21, the enemy blew up bridges (2) in vain attempt to stem the apparently irresistible Russian advance towards the Dnieper.

*Photos, Pictorial Press, Planet News*

# Army Carrier Pigeons Have Parachutes Now!

*Astonishing developments are taking place in the Army Pigeon Service. ROBERT DE WITT tells how battle training and the provision of parachutes for the nimble carrier pigeon are increasing the usefulness of these birds, indispensable when wireless or other method of communication is lacking or cannot be employed. See also pp. 122 and 686, Vol. 6.*

A SMALL group of British soldiers is isolated behind the enemy lines. Completely cut off from their main unit, a shell has smashed their portable wireless set; so no one knows of their plight. If food and supplies can be got through to them, they can hold out and act as a vicious thorn in the side of the stubbornly retreating enemy ; otherwise, the men are finished. How to send a message giving their location is perplexing them. A "runner" would have little chance.

Overhead, an Army Cooperation plane appears. They signal to it, and in response a black object falls out. After falling a few feet, the object is seen as a miniature parachute. Down it comes, with its little container. In a few minutes the soldiers have reached the container, opened it, and found a pigeon, a little surprised, perhaps, but quite ready to do its duty and fly home. In a few seconds a message giving their exact position and stating what is required has been written on the thin paper inside the small red container clipped to one of the pigeon's legs.

One of the men throws the bird into the air, and after a preliminary circle it begins to fly straight to its home at the base. It can travel at sixty miles an hour, and within the hour those vital supplies may be on their way to the isolated men.

That is a typical incident of developments in the Army Pigeon Service. In spite of wireless and many other types of signalling, there are still occasions in modern war when only a carrier pigeon can get a message through. It is impossible, of course, for every small unit to carry pigeons into battle ; therefore the Pigeon Service has worked out with Army Cooperation aircraft this method of dropping the birds where they may be required.

THE diminutive parachute and the container have been specially designed for the job. The container is made of corrugated cardboard, in the shape of a barrel, and is complete with a door ; the bird's food—the Army Pigeon Service calls the outfit "bed and breakfast "—is in a trough hooked on the door of its temporary home.

Another type of container is intended specially for use over or near water. It is waterproofed, and divided diagonally so that two pigeons can be "packed." If it is dropped in water, it floats, and the pigeons can be taken out after some time without any danger of their having had a wetting. Pigeons cannot fly if their wings have become wet : a difficulty sometimes experienced when a plane lands in the sea and the crew want to use their birds.

The Army Pigeon Service has made great advances in these matters since the start of the war, when thousands of birds were mobilized from the lofts of amateur pigeon fanciers who volunteered to cooperate. Some of these advances remain secret, but it can be revealed that pigeons are now training under battle conditions in much the same way as the men who will use them. They are accustomed to the sound of aircraft and explosive by having planes dive at them and by firecrackers exploded near.

ADVANCES have been made in training pigeons to fly after the sun has set. The instinct to alight and roost with the failing light is stronger even than the homing instinct, and it has always been taken for granted that pigeons would stop flying at sundown. But even before the war experiments were conducted at Fort Monmouth, New Jersey, in breeding and training pigeons that would fly by night. The experiments were along the lines both of selection in breeding and "conditioning" the young pigeons. For instance, their cages were darkened during the day and only lighted at feeding time in the morning and evening. They were let out for short periods at dusk, and when they arrived on the alighting board a light was automatically switched on.

The length of flights made in conditions of light that would have sent the average pigeon to roost was gradually increased, and when secrecy descended on the experiments successful night flights of some miles had been reported. They represented a tremendous triumph of patience. The value of pigeons able to carry messages by night is very great.

The stamina and skill of carrier pigeons need no emphasis to the thousands of fanciers in Britain. But this war has provided some outstanding examples. One of the pigeons attached to a headquarters in England struggled home more than 55 miles after having been hit in the air. The agonizing journey, made with a gaping wound in its side, took the bird six hours instead of the usual 70 minutes or so. Only death will make a trained carrier give up.

Pigeons which have been hurt or have made exhausting journeys are given special medical treatment, convalescence and "sick leave." Some time ago one named Faithful was just getting fit again when an urgent call came for a reliable pigeon to accompany a plane on a difficult mission. Faithful was sent. The plane came down with its wireless broken. Dispatched with a message, Faithful flew 150 miles in good time.

Pigeons seem to enjoy flying in aircraft, but when there is trouble they are as liable to "shock" and fatigue

CAUTIOUS APPROACH to capture an exhausted pigeon which alighted on a cruiser in mid-Atlantic. The bird belonged to a North of England club and was returned home via Gibraltar. *Photo, Fox*

as human beings. They are then taken off operations and given a rest. One given leave recently, named Bronzey, had been on 199 R.A.F. operations before the Halifax it was in caught fire ; and Bronzey, although unhurt, showed symptoms of shock.

Known officially as Squadron-Leader Snow White, a carrier pigeon belonging to an Australian Lancaster squadron has more war flights to her credit than 90 per cent of the R.A.F. bomber crews. Her luck in over 100 operations has been so remarkable that there is always a rush to get her after briefing.

Her airman keeper says "Snow White has bags of air sense, and always knows when an operation is pending long before we do—she gets quite excited in her cage." During a recent night raid on Berlin, Snow White laid an egg, "an occurrence which happens fairly often over enemy territory."

WHEN a carrier pigeon was released in Scotland to fly to London it flew instead to Holland and was captured there by the Dutch patriots, says Vrij Nederland, Dutch newspaper published in London. It was released by them and it returned to its owner in Scotland, who discovered an unintelligible message fastened to its leg. The message was passed on to the authorities and turned out to be a code message to the Dutch Government in England.

First news of the Dieppe raid, in August 1942, reached Britain by pigeon ; security demanded wireless silence during some phases of that expedition. In any large-scale operations against the Continent carrier pigeons would be likely to play an important part, taking news from small units to headquarters. Many of these pigeons work from the lofts of their owners, amateur fanciers who breed and train for the services. The owners have to keep a twenty-four-hour watch on their lofts when a pigeon is out on a mission. They get twopence each time one of their pigeons flies for the Army.

GOING TO BERLIN are the pigeons in these containers held by two of the crew of a Lancaster bomber which took part in a recent raid. Work and training of these indispensable message-carriers are described in this page. *Photo, L.N.A.*

## Journey's End: Spezia to Valetta

On the night of September 10, 1943, vessels of the Italian Fleet steamed silently and without pride into the Grand Harbour of Valetta, Malta. Thus ended the Battle of the Mediterranean. Admiral of the Fleet Sir Andrew Cunningham's policy of aggressiveness had indeed paid handsome dividends to the United Nations. Above, an air view of the harbour with Italian battleships and cruisers anchored side by side with their Royal Navy escorts.

335

## *They Steamed Under Royal Navy Escort—*

By September 12 most of the Italian Fleet had been accounted for. Save for the incomplete Impero, the badly damaged Conte di Cavour, Bolzano and Gorizia, and the ill-fated Roma which was sunk (3) by German Ju88 bombers soon after leaving Spezia, Mussolini's once-vaunted Navy lay under Malta's guns, or at Alexandria, Cyprus or Haifa. Ratings of H.M.S. Warspite (1) had a grandstand view as the Savoia steamed past, followed by the Venita and Italia.

Photos
Cre
Pe

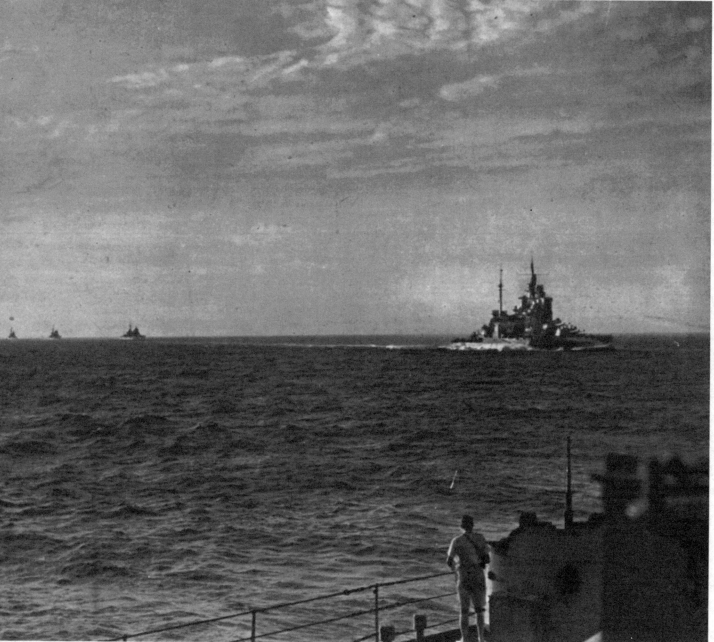

## —With a Black Flag Flying at the Masthead

An Italian Artigliere class destroyer (2), flying a black flag at her masthead in token of the "cease fire" passes the ship carrying General Eisenhower and Admiral Cunningham, who share the laurels for one of the most significant victories in British naval history. Accompanying the Warspite in the escort was H.M.S. Valiant (5), here leading two Italian battleships and five cruisers to Malta. A closer view of a Littorio class battleship is seen (4) beneath the Warspite's guns.

## This Was Malta's Greatest Hour

Photos, British Official:
Crown Copyright

On the afternoon of September 11, Admiral Romeo Oliva, Commander of the Italian Fleet, stepped ashore at the Custom House, Valetta, to be greeted by Commodore Royar Dick (bottom photograph), who conducted him to Admiral Sir Andrew Cunningham for the formal submission. It was the hour of exultation for the long-beleaguered island that so often had neared exhaustion. Italian sailors aboard the Guilio Cesare (top) looked on, smiling their own approval.

# VIEWS & REVIEWS
## Of Vital War Books

### by Hamilton Fyfe

To all but a few of us British folk Spain is an unknown land. It well repays a visit. In itself the country is not beautiful, save here and there in the south. But it is immensely interesting. The Moors during their long rule built lovely mosques, such as the one at Cordova, and almost fairy palaces, of which the Alhambra remains scarcely spoiled at all by either Time's effects or the stupidity of man.

No one who has seen the bridges at Toledo or the great cathedral of Segovia (like a ship in full sail, it has always seemed to me) is ever likely to forget them. If you have sat through the night before Good Friday to watch the processions of cowled figures carrying images through the streets of Seville, you keep an imperishable memory of what you may call either piety or superstition.

Most of us in Britain associate Spain with bull-fighting, which we shudder at as callously cruel, though hunting the fox, the stag, the hare and the otter presents scenes equally disgusting. We think of Spaniards as people who always put off till tomorrow what they ought to be doing today. We know they often say *Mañana*, which means the same as the South African Dutch expression, "There's another day tomorrow." Of their politics, their methods of government, their place in the scale of civilized nations, we know very little indeed. That was proved by the puzzlement of the British public when King Alfonso was sent packing; and later when a clique of generals and ecclesiastics started civil war and induced Hitler and Mussolini to destroy the Spanish Republic.

During the present war the position of Spain has caused equal bewilderment. We have been told—by himself and others—what fine work Sir Samuel Hoare, our Ambassador in Madrid, was doing; that he kept Franco, the dictator who governs in the interest of the Church, the army and the twin aristocracies of birth and riches, neutral or rather non-belligerent; and that we must do all we can to make him secure against the Republican masses. It did not seem to the British public that there was much to be gained by supporting a ruler who sent conscripted troops to fight in Russia against our Allies; who openly declared in his speeches that he not only hoped but felt sure Hitler would win; and who in many ways did what he could to help him defeat us when we stood alone.

How a despot who had been so brutal, so deceitful, and so warmly attached to the Nazis who flouted his Church, could be a "gallant Christian gentleman," as Lord Croft, now Under-Secretary for War, called him, or how he could, in the words of Capt. Ramsay, M.P., now detained in Brixton prison, be "fighting the cause of Christianity against anti-Christ," was hard to understand.

For enlightenment about this and other difficulties in finding answers to the Spanish riddles which have appeared insoluble to so many of us the best book I have seen is Appeasement's Child (Gollancz, 7s. 6d.), written by an American newspaper man who knows the country and other European countries well, and who shows us a Fascist State in action, giving us, as Mr. Ickes, United States Home Secretary, said about the book, "a glimpse into tomorrow towards the problems we must meet and errors we must not repeat when we win our peace."

The most dangerous error made in the past, Mr. Thomas J. Hamilton holds, was committed by the rulers of Britain, the United States and France, in allowing Hitler and Mussolini to rehearse for the present war from 1936, when the Spanish civil war began, to 1938, when the present totalitarian system was clamped upon the Spanish nation. If the Spanish Government, elected by popular vote in democratic fashion, had been permitted to purchase arms, as all Governments fighting for their lives had done in the past with the sanction of international law, we should have had Spain on our side, heartily with us and fiercely hostile to the Nazis and Fascists. This would have been of value in many ways; it would probably have shortened the war. Why, asks Mr. Hamilton, have we continued the policy of Appeasement? Why have the Foreign Offices in Washington and London supposed that by patting and stroking Franco, and letting him have supplies to pass on to Germany,

## Where Stands Franco's Spain?

and holding out hopes (as President Roosevelt did) of a vast tourist invasion of Spain after the war, we could detach him from the other totalitarian tyrants?

Since the book was written we have taken a firmer tone. Franco has now shown that he knows Hitler cannot win. Spanish newspapers, instead of abusing and sneering at the forces of democracy, fawn upon us and tell their readers what fine fellows we are. But do not let us deceive ourselves, is Mr. Hamilton's message. The Falange, on which Franco depends, may plead that it is not really Fascist, but it is so like that no difference is discernible. Franco may make changes, which will actually alter nothing. He cannot change himself; and there is abundant evidence in the book that he is a clever, cunning, opportunist politician, who will never relax his grip on power until it is forcibly wrenched from his hands.

He shows his cleverness by his skill in juggling with the conflicting interests of his supporters. Church, army, Falange, finance, big business, all have to be kept sweet, and this is far from easy. What they are agreed on apparently is that democracy is "pi'sen wherever met," and that Spain ought to be again an empire, with the South American Republics subservient to Madrid and the Roman Catholic Church linked to it for mutual aid. This megalomania has got full hold of Franco. Many Spaniards cannot see any place for them in the future, so they would like to bring back the past. They can't, but they might give trouble by trying.

If the Republic had stamped heavily on the "old gang" which worked in secret against it, it would have survived and probably prospered. No Government would, I think, ever be popular in Spain, for the people don't like being governed. They confirm in amusing fashion, and sometimes in horrifying fashion too, the saying "There's nowt so queer as folks." Where else could you find an old lady like the one, very rich and very Catholic-Conservative, who entertained a number of Red soldiers regularly, got them to play cards, and won their money by cheating? Would any of Hitler's other little helpers dare to keep the Fuehrer waiting half an hour on a railway station by being late for an appointment, then turn up smiling (as Franco did) as if he were dead on time?

When the American Red Cross took food to Spain for those who were in dire need after the civil war, they had to bribe the Fascist officials to distribute it. Customs officials also insisted on collecting duty on it. Government departments are continually at loggerheads. The police are a law unto themselves. Every business house employs a man with pleasant manners to "fix" things with the various authorities. The Auxilio Social (Social Help) was given huge amounts of money to spend and spent only a quarter of it on feeding the hungry. They did not steal the rest. They just frittered it away.

Why, you may ask, do the Spanish people put up with the incompetence and dishonesty of their government, its harshness to the poor, its toleration of *Estraperlo*, which means "racket" (as when a railway clerk says there are no tickets for the train and produces one immediately a tip is offered)? Why do they? The only answer is: "Because they don't know any better." But some day they will, Mr. Hamilton feels sure.

**IN FRANCO'S GAOLS**, of which this one at Valencia is a sample, there were in the autumn of 1939, according to an estimate by Vatican authorities, half a million political prisoners. The bulk of these were Republicans who had fought against the Nationalists—backed by Germany and Italy—in the Civil War, which lasted from July 18, 1936, to April 4, 1939. Present-day conditions in Fascist Spain are the subject of the book reviewed in this page.

*Photo, The March of Time*

# Dutch Buildings Doomed by Nazi Defence Plans

SYSTEMATIC DEMOLITION is generally heard of when an army is in headlong retreat. But from The Hague, capital of the Nazi-occupied Netherlands, come shocking reports of ruthless destruction of fine public buildings as part of the enemy's hurried preparations to stem an Allied invasion. A lyceum (modern high school) is seen in process of demolition (1), since completed. The house of the former Dutch Premier, Dr. Colijn, was not spared (2) ; and a Roman Catholic Church (4), and the Red Cross Hospital in the Sportlaan (3), shared the same fate. The site of this hospital has now been cleared.

*Photos by courtesy of the Netherlands Government Information Bureau*

# In Sight of the Enemy on the Road to Naples

**FIFTH ARMY PATROL** enters the village of Pugliano hard on the heels of the Germans retreating across the Plain of Naples. Moving ahead of our main forces, these men's job is to maintain contact with the enemy, and here the sergeant leading the patrol has paused for a moment to study the ground ahead through his binoculars. His four riflemen crouch behind ready for instant action, while, out of sight, the patrol's Bren-gun group is doubtless suitably placed to give protection by covering fire.

*Photo, British Official: Crown Copyright*

# Across the Adriatic Dalmatia Beckons Us

Advance of our 8th Army up the east coast of Italy focuses attention sharply on Dalmatia, at points only about 70 miles across the Adriatic. HENRY BAERLEIN outlines past conditions and the present strategic situation in this most turbulent country—gateway to the Balkans—where patriot bands have unceasingly harassed their Axis oppressors.

ONE presumes that King Victor Emmanuel ordered, some little time ago, that the words "Emperor of Abyssinia" should be removed from his visiting-cards ; and now, with the Allies in possession of that part of the Italian mainland sixty or seventy miles from the Albanian coast, he will, no doubt, be ready to abandon his claim to the title of "King of Albania."

After all, it was conferred on him by an arch-villain who, on Good Friday 1939, launched an unprovoked attack on a people numbering no more than a million, a people who asked only to be left alone. Every Albanian does not live in a "kula," but most of them wish they had one, a tower whose entrance can only be reached by means of a ladder which the householder then pulls up behind him. If he looks out of one of his loophole windows he may see a shepherd with half-a-dozen emaciated cows or sheep—and a rifle to prevent their loss.

Some years prior to Mussolini, Italy had been considering this rather primitive country, which in the course of two thousand years has produced one great man, Skanderbeg, who was said to be a Slav. Italy arrived with sundry loans and then pervaded the country to such an extent that the natives revolted and thrust the invaders out from every part except the lofty little island of Saseno, just off the shore, which the Italians planned to convert into a second Gibraltar. No Albanian was admitted. Afterwards came more loans and another Italian infiltration.

Now the Germans will do their utmost to keep the Allies out of Albania, not merely because their armies in Greece would be in a precarious situation, but also because the Albanian ports, ill equipped as they are, might in some degree serve the Allies as did Salonika in the last war. There are no Albanian railways, so that any troops we may land will have to overcome a German resistance far less sustained than that at Salerno. The Albanians will probably not give much assistance to either side, despite the independence that both sides will almost certainly offer.

The average Albanian, less interested in the possible liberty of his country than in his own liberty to give other Albanians a raw deal, will, however, suspend his usual fratricidal operations if more profitable ones are held out to him in the service of either the Allies or the Germans. Let our prelanding propaganda refer not much to the Atlantic Charter but to the gold and groceries that will be distributed among the deserving population. The Sons of the Eagle, as they call themselves, will then be eager to collaborate, scouting for our troops in the mountain regions and lowering the enemy's morale by a drastic treatment of stragglers.

When the Allies land in Montenegro they will, of course, have the very active support of the Yugoslav Minister of War, the heroic General Mihailovitch, who for so long has not only held out in those almost inaccessible mountains, but has inflicted serious losses among the foe. It is not always remembered that the Montenegrins are the purest of Serbs, descendants of those who, six hundred years ago, fled to the Black Mountains when the Serbian Empire was crushed by the Turks at the fatal Field of Blackbirds. The recent sufferings of the Serbs have made their Montenegrin brothers more and more

**VEGETABLE BOATS IN HARBOUR AT SPLIT, main Yugoslav seaport on the Adriatic and scene of fierce fighting between partisans and German troops in September 1943. Allied control of the Adriatic has greatly encouraged patriot uprisings throughout Dalmatia. (See facing page.)** *Photo, Mrs. Muir*

eager to help them, and here the Allies will have 100 per cent collaboration.

Winter campaigns in the Balkans are generally to be deprecated, but they are not necessarily doomed to failure. Thus, for example, as Colonel Contoleon, the Greek Military Attaché, has been reminding us, operations during the Balkan War of 1912 were continuously and effectively carried on from September to February ; one of the most important battles, the storming of Bizani, the fortress of Janina, by the Greek army taking place on February 21, in the midst of the Balkan winter.

As the Germans, far better equipped than the Yugoslav patriots, have after severe fighting captured Split, the chief Dalmatian port, and a number of others, we shall have to eject them from the entire coastal district, a more arduous operation than will be their

dislodgement from the intervening islands. Their retention of the Greek island of Corfu and of the Dalmatian group farther north will be impossible against our sea and air supremacy ; and these weapons will be very efficacious against the Germans in the narrow strip of mainland between the bleak mountains and the Adriatic. There the screen of islands, admirable for the activities of Yugoslav mariners, will greatly hamper the hostile and assist the friendly invader.

It used to be the fashion to assert that Dalmatia was impregnable because of the spine of mountains separating the coastal districts from the rest of the country. But the blocking power of mountains tends to be exaggerated. They often offer more opportunities for offensive infiltration than can be found in a closely knit web of fire in flatter country. They also handicap the defender in switching his reserves laterally in time to check a thrust up any particular valley.

From the ports of Dubrovnik and Split railways and roads run into Bosnia and Croatia. Both these provinces have provided the Axis with a good deal of trouble, whether at the hands of Mihailovitch's Chetniks or from the so-called partisans. Perfect collaboration has not always prevailed between these two, whose political outlook is respectively towards the right and the left, but both are essentially patriotic ; and even if there had not been happily brought about the present far greater tolerance towards each other—we are told that senior Allied officers have been amongst them— they will assuredly fight shoulder to shoulder against the detested German.

The partisans used to accuse Mihailovitch of sending back Italian prisoners and even Germans. But he could spare no men to guard them and, not being a murderer, he returned them — without weapons and with a certain amount of clothing—if tins of petrol were given in exchange, one for a private and up to fifty for a colonel.

In consequence of the Italian "about-turn" the Germans have had to rely more on the Ustachi, that terrorist organization on whom they conferred Croatia, where Pavelitch, their leader, used to form a political party of one person. He increased his popularity among the shadier elements by organizing the assassination of King Alexander of Yugoslavia, but when the Allies, together with Chetniks and partisans, go surging forward it is unlikely that the Germans will put themselves out to conceal him, as did the Fascists after the aforesaid assassination when Mussolini caused the Yugoslav delegates at Geneva to be told that unfortunately he had vanished. The day is not far distant when he will long to vanish again into that luxurious government-owned villa near Turin.

# Revolt Flares Up in Feud-Ridden Yugoslavia

YUGOSLAVIA is again in ferment. This feud-racked land of the Serbs, Croats and Slovenes, a product of the Treaty of Versailles, has known little internal peace since its foundation. Racial and political differences, with their resultant party squabbles in Parliament, made a mockery of Yugoslav democracy and led the people into a succession of dictatorships.

To their credit, however, it must be remembered that the revolt of March 27, 1941, was a case, probably unique in European history, of an Army rebelling against its Government in order to restore power to the people, who insisted on resisting the Axis invaders even though they were miserably unprepared.

The many recent guerilla activities of the patriots, under Mihailovitch, and the partisans, under Tito, both in collaboration with Middle East Command, prove that, though domestic differences persist, the Yugoslavs are at least united in their desire for national freedom.

KORCULA, chief town of the Dalmatian island of that name (1), which was captured by Yugoslav patriots.

The bridge in Susak (2) connecting the town with Fiume marks the old Yugoslav-Italian border. After 20 days' fighting it was announced on October 3, 1943, that the Germans had retaken the town from the partisans.

The Salcano railway viaduct (3), near Gorizia, is one of the most vital points in the German supply-line between Austria and Fiume. The Nazis have occupied the Dalmatian port of Dubrovnik, of which (4) is a street scene.

Location of heavy fighting before the Germans overcame patriot resistance was Kotor (5), naval port at the southern extremity of the Dalmatian coast. By October 13, 1943, the Germans held all the main ports and airfields of Dalmatia, while the partisans had occupied all the islands and the rest of the Adriatic coastline. See also facing page.

*Photos, Pictorial Press, E.N.A.*

# Corsica--Island Outpost of France—Free Again

**FRANCE'S MEDITERRANEAN 'HELIGOLAND'** until it was occupied by the Germans in 1940, Corsica dominated the naval bases of Spezia and Genoa from a distance of only 100 miles. With the fall of Bastia (1) on October 4, 1943, Fighting French forces which had been landing since September 20 gained complete control of the island. Citizens of the capital, Ajaccio, cheered at their liberation (4); in their town Napoleon's birthplace is still to be seen (2). It was at the storming of the Citadel of Calvi (3) in 1794 that Nelson lost an eye. Corsica is the first Department of Metropolitan France to be freed from the Nazis.

*Photos, New York Times, Mrs. Muir, Keystone. Map by courtesy of The Times*

# I WAS THERE!

## Eye Witness Stories of the War

### We Drove Along the Awesome Road of Death

Through the valley that will be remembered for years to come as scene of one of the hardest victories of the war travelled A. B. Austin, Combined British Press reporter with the 5th Army in Italy. He wrote this grimly vivid story on September 28, 1943 ; shortly after, he and two other famous war reporters lost their lives by enemy action, as told in the next page.

A. B. AUSTIN, world-famous British war reporter, whose last story from the Front appears here. He established a great reputation with his eye-witness account of the Dieppe raid on August 19, 1942.  *Photo, Topical*

ALONG the Road of Death we are driving to the Naples plain. The worst is over. We have turned the corner out of the steepest mountains at Camerelle and are heading due east for Vesuvius and Naples. For the past five days of bitter fighting I have seen a mile 'added to the Road of Death each day. I have driven so many times up and down this valley road through the mountains from Salerno, always just a fraction farther every day, as the infantry struggled ahead, that I can see every piece of ruin and decay on it with my eyes shut.

For years to come this valley will be remembered as the scene of one of the hardest victories of the war. All of us who have written about the fighting have tried to bring home to the outside world just how relentless has been the strain upon the English infantry who have stretched their energy and their courage as far as men can to force a way out of these mountains.

But the result of their fighting and of the German resistance upon the valley itself should be known too, for this is what happens in an invasion and it is not so long since we prepared for an invasion of England. This is what might have happened to any stretch of English countryside leading up from the sea. Along every mile of the lovely valley, from Salerno and Vietri to Cava de Tirreni and Camerelle and beyond, there is not a single house that has not been hit by shellfire or bombing.

WHEN you look from one of its mountain tops you see nothing but peace. The forests drop gracefully down from the high ridges to the vineyards, the orchards and the maize fields. The valley bottom looks as if it were one continuous line of pink and blue and white villas, cottages and farms, swelling every so often into villages and towns. But when you go down among the houses you find that half of them along the roadside are rubble-choked skeletons and the rest are cracked or shell-pocked.

Houses are not the only ruins. Passing along the Road of Death there is first the smashed parapet of the famous Gauntlet Bridge at Vietri. A German tank lies to one side seemingly intact, but shattered inside by the hand grenade dropped from the slope above, which killed all its crew. On the steep mountainside above, a great slash of rust runs through the green trees— the scar on the earth that the German mortar bombs had set on fire.

Every few yards there is some new sign of death and destruction : a German corpse in a ditch, badly needing burial: fallen horses swollen with death, and shattered farm carts ; a factory chimney with a shell-hole neatly drilled through it like the eye of a monstrous needle ; splintered telegraph poles dang-

ling trailing wires across broken walls; graves on high grassy shelves and in ditches—graves wherever a German or an Englishman had fallen, and there was no time to drag him out of the battle, and those are bodies that will, no doubt, be collected before long and buried, in some trim cemetery by the Mediterranean ; the crumbled ruins of futile road blocks—the kind of cement road blocks in which we once placed so much faith at home ; burnt out trucks, shell-craters ; and the rusty litter of German petrol and water cans.

THROUGH it all, up and down every day, stirring the rubble dust into clouds, flattening the shell-cases strewn on the road, bumping in and out of the shell-holes, rumbling across the sappers' bridges spanning arches that the enemy had blown up, moves the traffic of an army, the huge dust-coloured, camouflaged train of trucks and carriers and jeeps and trailers that are needed to supply any force.

Now that the tanks are moving through with all their maintenance train the traffic along the Road of Death has swelled to a roar. Luckily, past Camerelle the single road branches into several parallel roads, so that, at last, we will have elbow room and the Germans have too many different routes to mine or block thoroughly. At the head of it all slowly, methodically, painfully, moves the infantry—laden, dusty men in single file or crawling spread out over the ridges, or digging yet another line of slit trenches to hold a new position.

You come across their small headquarters in ruined houses or under bridge arches ; the Colonel or the second-in-command, unshaven and tired, sitting on the ground with his tin hat pushed back on his head, receiving a stream of messages from the signallers at their wireless sets by his side sending orders forward to his companies

and reports back to brigade headquarters. You find them, if you choose your time tactfully, always willing to explain what is happening with that patience and politeness which is most marked in the front line, probably because men cannot afford to add to the strain by losing control of their tempers.

Threading their way to and fro among all this death, destruction and physical fury are the Italian people. If to this ground struggle were added the terror of air attack this constant movement of people with their bundles and their handcarts might cause great panic and confusion. As it is they are merely a pathetic background. They move away from their homes, but however great the ruin they move back as soon as they can. Old, grey men will gravely salute you as they sit in the sun on broken chairs at the doors of roofless houses. Children run among the ruins ; swarms of children pale and ragged, too often with skin diseases. Whenever you stop small boys run up to your jeep, begging cigarettes.

Mothers sit on fallen blocks of stone to suckle their babies. Old ailing women are

LAST STAGE IN THE BATTLE FOR SCAFATI BRIDGE, which A. B. Austin and his colleagues, Stewart Sale and William Munday, saw but did not live to report. Story of how the three met their fate is in page 346. British infantrymen are here waiting for a glimpse of the enemy holding positions in houses on the other side of the river and from which machine-guns were trained on the bridge.

*Photo, British Official*

**ON THEIR LAST ASSIGNMENT,** William Munday (right background, hands on hips) and A. B. Austin (standing behind Munday) watch German prisoners—one wounded by Bren-gun fire and supported by his comrades—being brought into Scafati under guard. Shortly afterwards they and their colleague, Stewart Sale, were killed by a shell from an enemy tank, as told below by Basil Gingell, who was standing beside them but miraculously escaped. *Photo, British Official*

trundled past on handcarts wrapped in their bedclothes till they can be trundled back again in safety. Now and then someone is killed or dies in the normal way. Along the Road of Death, grotesque because it is the last thing you expect to see in a battlefield, comes the undertaker's hearse, with black hangings and plumed horses. The one thing you never find is resentment. Their homes are ruined, their lives disrupted, yet they greet you amiably, grin and wave from broken windows, talk as long as you will let them. Either life is easy to rebuild in the Mediterranean warmth or they feel our march along the Road of Death is the last battle of this war.

## I Saw a Shell Kill Three War Reporter Friends

The death by enemy action of three front-line war correspondents with the 5th Army—Stewart Sale, William Munday, and A. B. Austin (who only a few hours before wrote the story in page 345)—was witnessed, and nearly shared, by Basil Gingell, of the Combined British Press. His account of the tragedy, dated October 1, 1943, is given here.

WHEN the Italian landing was planned and Press representation was apportioned I found that Austin, Munday and myself were attached to one beach-landing party and Sale was with another party. It was therefore not until after we had set foot on Italian soil that I met Sale again, but the other two were my constant companions throughout the fighting that has taken place along that section of the Salerno bridgehead held by the British.

And I was with them when they died. With the narrow foothold such as we had at the beginning along the Gulf of Salerno, it was obvious that we were never out of range of enemy fire, for the front line was on our doorstep. Although always anxious to see battles at close quarters, it is no part of a war correspondent's job to take foolhardy risks, and all three were not only keen reporters but level-headed men.

When the break-through along the Cava Valley gained momentum Austin, Munday and myself, who knew of its imminence, joined in a procession of the armour. We reached Scafati well to the fore, but while the units pushed on over the bridge we waited behind because of snipers and machine-guns that were trained on the bridge.

We had lunch by the roadside, and while sitting there we saw Stewart Sale and Frank Gillard of the B.B.C. drive by. We hailed the new arrivals, and as the traffic moved over the bridge we decided to walk down. We had covered perhaps 200 yards, Gillard and Sale walking on ahead, and Austin, Munday and myself following. Sale stopped to look in an air-raid shelter that was in the main street, and Gillard said he was going on and crossed the road. By this time we had joined up with Sale and we stood at a street corner looking down the road. There was some general banter about the front line.

The four of us were standing in a little group in space no bigger than a hearthrug when I saw a terrific flash ahead. I heard no sound of gunfire, but the next second I felt myself bodily flung up the side of the track for more than fifty yards, while debris and dust rained down on me. I had no idea what was happening, but groping my way out I returned to the corner and there found my three companions lying as they had fallen. An ambulance attendant who darted in asked me to help him, but when he took a second glance he realized that all three were dead. He darted off to attend to others, while I stood back against the wall suffering nothing but a few scratches.

Shelling and machine-gun fire broke out, ranging on the corner where the four of us had stood. Some Italians took me to their home and there I stayed until morning. A sharp battle raged round the area throughout darkness, but in the morning my three friends were buried by the roadside where we had had our lunch on the previous day; where Austin had said that he had a story that would write itself and Munday had made his plans for the following day.

Over their graves are planted three wooden crosses made by our jeep driver, who had taken Austin, Munday and me over many miles since we landed and has himself seen more than the average share of excitement out here. There they remain, with Vesuvius in the background, until such time as all those killed in this bitter fighting in Italy can be gathered into some central resting-place.

## From England I Went East to Join Paiforce

Life on a troopship and with Paiforce (which stands for Persia and Iraq Force) is vividly described by a member of the Amalgamated Press—now L/Cpl. Lewis Hulls, of the Royal Corps of Signals. Names of places on the journey are omitted for security reasons.

WE were very crowded on the troopship—a converted liner—but not too uncomfortable. We slept in four-tiered bunks, and fed at tables seating eighteen men. The food was pretty good, the white bread and fresh butter being a particularly welcome feature. Hot sea-water showers were always available for bathing, but attempts to wash clothes in these showers ended in dismal failure; for that job we had to use our rationed supply of fresh water.

Queues were an important part of life on board; we had queues for the canteen (where such luxuries as tinned fruit and milk chocolate could be had), for baths, for barbers, for concerts, for fresh water and for meals. After settling down, we started work on a regular routine programme of training, doing P.T. and route marches along the crowded decks. In our free time we had concerts and gramophone recitals. We also had a library which included a very high proportion of first-class stuff amongst its 700 odd volumes. I had the good luck to be given the job of ship's librarian.

OUR journey took us through many different kinds of weather. Some days we shivered in our battledress, or were driven below by heavy rain and wind ; a day later, maybe, we would be sunbathing till late in the evening, finding even our tropical kit too hot. The nights often were especially beautiful and we slept on deck a lot ; in the starlight the phosphorescence on the water sparkled like hundreds of little lights flashing on and off. By day there were flying fish and porpoises to watch and an occasional albatross ; to say nothing of our companion ships in the convoy and the vigilant escort.

The journey was broken once or twice to refuel and to take on fresh water, and at one port we stayed for several days and were able to go ashore. The hospitality of the local people was quite overwhelming, and for the duration of our visit we were entertained in private homes and taken about sightseeing in cars, without needing to spend a penny ourselves. I was adopted by a very charming family who did their utmost to make my memories of their town happy and pleasant ones. Food restrictions had not yet made themselves felt there, and in those few days I gorged more oranges, pineapples, grapefruit, bananas, ice creams, steaks, eggs, and other good things than you are likely to see until the end of the war.

After more days at sea we again broke our journey. Here was a native bazaar, colourful and picturesque, with the most amazing variety of odours emanating from the district. The wares on sale were a curious mixture of trashy manufactured articles and genuine native products, such as silks, leatherwork, ivory and brass, as well as all kinds of fruit and sweetmeats. Always the authentic native article had its imported

L/Cpl. LEWIS HULLS, of the Royal Corps of Signals, gives in this and the preceding page an entertaining account of his voyage in a troopship to the Near East and his training with Paiforce (Persia and Iraq Force).

imitation counterpart, and it was not easy to distinguish between them. Prices to the white man were cheap enough, provided always that one was prepared to squat upon a bench, specially placed by the shopkeeper for the purpose, and go through the formal process of haggling. " You make bargain with me, Johnnie " was the stock phrase.

In our camp we were well served by numerous itinerant tradesmen, who would pop their heads inside our huts at the most unexpected times, offering their services. It would begin early in the morning while we were still in bed, with the " shave-wallah " who would shave you in bed—or out, if preferred—for one penny. At intervals during the day there followed others who would

crave the privilege of making your bed, cleaning your boots, bringing you fruit, or tea, or the newspaper, mending your socks, washing your clothes or curing your corns.

At last the day came to set out on the last stage of our travels, and after more days at sea, and on trains, it came as a disappointment to find we had travelled all that way just to be dumped down in the middle of a desolate expanse of semi-desert. But after a few weeks of hard work on our part a city of tents covered the wilderness for miles around ; we certainly transformed the landscape.

Our training here continues, as in England, and every now and again we disappear into the hills for a few days' manoeuvres, with only an occasional shepherd or two, dressed as in Bible days, with their shaggy flocks, for company. Recreational facilities are limited, but we can buy dates, eggs, oranges, walnuts, beer and minerals either from NAAFI or from native hawkers. There is a garrison cinema some miles away, to which they run transport for us each week. The nearest town is too far away to allow of frequent visits, but we do go in there occasionally, and last month we had a special Unit dinner at one of the few decent restaurants—a very romantic-looking " Arabian Nights " kind of building, with open courtyard and well in the centre overlooked by white stone balconies. We sat down to dinner in a long narrow room hung with rugs and tapestries. Chief items were roast turkey and pudding, washed down with beer and local wine.

OUR main occupations most evenings include reading, and cooking suppers. We can always get eggs, bread and onions, either from the canteen or hawkers, and we scrounge fat from the cookhouse. Thus provided with raw materials, we fry them in utensils made from empty tins and petrol cans ; there is a great art in making kettles, teapots, frying pans, eggslices and so on from old tins, and we have produced some excellent articles. For heat, we put sand in a tin with perforated sides, soak it in kerosene (a plentiful commodity in this land of oil) set light to it—and get on with the cooking !

# OUR DIARY OF THE WAR

**SEPTEMBER 29, Wednesday** 1,488th day
**Italy.**—Fifth Army capture of Nocera and Pompeii and collapse of German ring round Naples announced. Gen. Eisenhower and Marshal Badoglio met aboard H.M.S. Nelson off Malta to discuss use of Italian forces against Germany.
**Mediterranean.**—Yugoslav guerilla H.Q. announced evacuation of Split, on Dalmatian coast. Enemy air attacks launched against newly established British base on Cos (Dodecanese).
**Russian Front.**—Kremenchug, on the Dnieper, and Rudnya, on the Smolensk-Vitebsk railway, captured by Russians.
**Air.**—Bochum (Ruhr) heavily bombed.
**General.**—King Peter of Yugoslavia arrived in Cairo to set up his Govt. there.

**SEPTEMBER 30, Thursday** 1,489th day
**Italy.**—Eighth Army occupation of Manfredonia on Adriatic coast, and Fifth Army capture of San Severino, announced.
**Russian Front.**—Russians forced River Sozh and captured Krichev. Vitebsk, Orsha, Mogilev and Dzankhoi (Crimea) bombed by Soviet aircraft.

**OCTOBER 1, Friday** 1,490th day
**Italy.**—Naples captured by 5th Army. Fall of Avellino and Torre Annunziata announced.
**Russian Front.**—Cherikov in Mogilev area, and Berezino in Vitebsk sector, captured by Russians. Battle for Zaporozhe raging.
**Burma.**—Akyab town bombed by Wellingtons.
**China.**—Haiphong attacked by U.S. aircraft.
**Air.**—Munich region raided by Fortresses from Africa for first time ; Liberators raided Wiener Neustadt factory 25 m. S.W. of Vienna. Hagen (Ruhr) heavily bombed at night.
**Sea.**—Announced that in recent U-boat attack on convoy in N. Atlantic, six merchantmen, two escort vessels and Canadian destroyer St. Croix sunk.
**General.**—Mr. W. A. Harriman appointed U.S. Ambassador to Russia.

**OCTOBER 2, Saturday** 1,491st day
**Italy.**—Capture of San Severo and Lucera by 8th Army announced. 8th Army tanks landed behind enemy lines at Termoli on Adriatic coast.
**Mediterranean.**—Yugoslav Nat. Army of Liberation announced capture of Orahovo on River Sava.

**Australasia.** — Finschafen (New Guinea) captured by Australians.
**Air.**—Emden pounded by Fortresses ; St. Omer-Longuenesse airfield (France) attacked. Munich bombed in concentrated 25-min. attack by Lancasters at night.
**Sea.**—Revealed that British liner Ceramic was sunk off S. Africa by a U-boat in November 1942.

**OCTOBER 3, Sunday** 1,492nd day
**Italy.**—5th Army capture of Frigento and Benevento announced.
**Mediterranean.**—Enemy troops made sea and airborne landings on British-held Cos (Dodecanese), and seized several important points. Teghime Hill (Corsica), keypoint to Bastia defence, captured by Goumiers and Moroccan sharpshooters ; Furiani, Borgo, Vescovato, and Caterraggio (Corsica) taken.
**Russian Front.**—Violent battle for Zaporozhe and gateway to Crimea continued unabated.
**Air.**—Kassel, German armament centre E. of Ruhr, raided, 1,500 tons of bombs dropped ; Hanover and Rhineland objectives also attacked.

**OCTOBER 4, Monday** 1,493rd day
**Italy.**—Capture of Motta and Montemiletto by 8th Army and crossing over Calore River by 5th Army announced.

**Mediterranean.**—Bastia, last port in Corsica left to Germans, captured by French troops, and liberation of Corsica completed.
**China.**—Fresh Japanese attacks in three Chinese provinces announced.
**Air.**—Frankfurt raided by day and night ; Ludwigshafen, and other W. German targets attacked.
**Sea.**—Admiral Sir A. Cunningham appointed to succeed Sir Dudley Pound as First Sea Lord. Home Fleet, including U.S. carrier, operated against enemy shipping in Bodo area of Norway.

**OCTOBER 5, Tuesday** 1,494th day
**Italy.**—German counter-attacks at Termoli repulsed ; announced that 8th Army reinforcements landed, and important airfields of Pomigliano and Capodichino captured by 5th Army. Montesarchio taken. Bologna heavily raided.
**Australasia.**—Japanese attempt to evacuate troops from Kolombangara (Solomons) revealed.
**Pacific.**—Wake Island attacked with carrier aircraft and ship bombardment.
**General.**—Arrival of General Smuts in London announced.

**OCTOBER 6, Wednesday** 1,495th day
**Italy.**—Announced Volturno crossed by 5th Army ; fall of Aversa and Maddaloni announced.

**Australasia.**—Announced 7-mile advance by Australian troops to Dumpa, 50m. S.W. of Madang. Announced 3 Japanese warships sunk in Vella Gulf, Central Solomons.

**OCTOBER 7, Thursday** 1,496th day
**Russian Front.**—Announced new Soviet drive begun from Vitebsk to Taman peninsula ; Dnieper forced at three places ; Nevel, 30m. S.W. of Veliki Luki, and Taman captured.
**Air.**—Stuttgart bombed ; Friedrichshafen and Munich bombed by Mosquitoes and Lancasters.

**OCTOBER 8, Friday** 1,497th day
**Italy.**—Guglionesi occupied. Capture of Capua, Volturno bridgehead, announced.
**Russian Front.**—Tanks reported in action on west bank of Dnieper.
**Air.**—Day raid on Bremen. Night raid on Hanover.

**OCTOBER 9, Saturday** 1,498th day
**Italy.**—Grazzanise and Caserta taken.
**Russian Front.**—Announced all Caucasus cleared following occupation of the Kuban. Liozno, S.E. of Vitebsk, taken.
**Air.**—Anklam (Pomerania), Marienburg (East Prussia), Danzig and Gdynia day-bombed after record flights.

**OCTOBER 10, Sunday** 1,499th day
**Italy.**—Capture of Larino, Gambatesa and San Marco announced.
**Air.**—Fortresses bombed Munster (Westphalia). First raid by Fortresses on Greece : airfields at Salonika, Athens, Argos and Larissa bombed.
**Sea.**—Loss of H.M. destroyer Intrepid announced.

**OCTOBER 11, Monday** 1,500th day
**Italy.**—Capture of Pontelandolfo announced.
**Russian Front.**—Novobelitse, suburb of Gomel, occupied.
**Sea.**—Announced that on September 22 British midget submarines penetrated Altenfjord, Northern Norway, and damaged German battleship Tirpitz.

**OCTOBER 12, Tuesday** 1,501st day
**Russian Front.**—"Substantial gains," unspecified, announced in Dnieper sector.
**General.**—Announced that Portugal had agreed to grant Britain facilities in Azores to afford better protection for merchant shipping in the Atlantic.

★═══════════════ **Flash-backs** ═══════════════★

**1939**
September 29. *Poland partitioned between Germany and Russia.*
October 10. *Empire Air Training Scheme announced.*

**1940**
October 9. *Cherbourg bombarded by British warships.*

**1941**
October 2. *Hitler issued Order of Day to Germans before Moscow declaring the decisive battle was about to begin.*

October 6. *Germans launched two-pronged assault against Moscow.*

**1942**
September 29. *Germans made progress in N.W. Stalingrad.*
September 30. *Limited offensive opened by British in Egypt.*
October 4. *Sark attacked in small Combined Operations raid. Australians occupied Effogi (New Guinea)*
October 8. *British prisoners captured at Dieppe and Sark, enchained by Germans.*

# THE WAR IN THE AIR

## by Capt. Norman Macmillan, M.C., A.F.C.

THE war in the air is developing along more clear-cut lines than has ever been the case in the past. And it is striking that in such circumstances should be published the statement on Belligerent Power which appeared in The Times on October 1 under the signatures of Admiral of the Fleet Lord Chatfield, First Sea Lord 1933-38, Field-Marshal Lord Milne, Chief of the Imperial General Staff 1926-33, Marshal of the Royal Air Force Sir John Salmond, Chief of the Air Staff 1930-33, Lord Hankey, Secretary of the Committee of Imperial Defence 1912-38, and Lord Winster, a retired naval officer and a former Parliamentary Secretary to the Admiralty.

That statement is an outline of the inter-relationship as seen by the signatories of the component parts of what they call Belligerent Power, by which they mean what Hitler long ago called Total War. But what

had few friends. There were those who wanted the R.A.F. split up and handed back to the Army and Navy. There were numerous Cabinet inquiries into the subject. The Admiralty in particular was a bitter opponent of the Air Ministry.

Let us turn back for a moment to the published report of the sub-committee of the Committee of Imperial Defence, dated July 30, 1936, On the Vulnerability of Capital Ships to Air Attack. The then Sir Ernle Chatfield, as First Sea Lord, was an expert adviser to that committee presided over by Sir Thomas Inskip (now Lord Caldecote) and a strenuous champion of the battleships in whose favour the committee placed its faith.

Paragraph 34 of the sub-committee's report states : "... the Admiralty ... think that the capital ship of the future can be so designed as to distribution of her armour on

Fleet was similarly crippled in Taranto. The sea battles of the Coral Sea and Midway Island were won by aircraft, not warships. The sinking of eight enemy merchant ships in Norwegian waters on October 4, 1943, was effected by aircraft.

How much more is required to prove the truth that naval power as a fighting force is at the end of its long history, and is approaching the era when ships will provide a transport service protected by aircraft ? The danger implicit in this document is that a large part of our air power may be seized by the sailors to save themselves, and to preserve their warships.

THIS joint statement, issued after no fewer than four years of war, contains this passage : "... warships are not necessarily the most effective weapon against warships. The experiences of the war have proved that a squadron of torpedo-bomber aircraft can in certain circumstances have a greater influence on sea power than a flotilla of destroyers or even larger warships. A score or two of aircraft, particularly if shore-based, can at times outmatch a powerful battleship escorted by cruisers and smaller craft. It must be remembered, however, that navies readapt themselves in the light of experience and the danger to warships from air attack may diminish."

Here lies the pill within the sugar of the document. Give the Navy shore-based aircraft ? Where can they come from ? Only from the R.A.F. But that would be a fatal blunder, for a large part of our national air power would then be expended to protect redundant warships. Already aircraft have forced navies to use battleships costing up to £10,000,000 as escort vessels, because of their heavier armour and greater fire-power for defence against air attack. Nor has this experience been one-sided. Our own aircraft based on besieged Malta forced the Axis to employ battleships to escort their convoys between Italy and North Africa.

## WHY the Aircraft Carrier Has No Useful Future

The aircraft carrier is a temporary stop-gap for naval war. But its life is doomed because it imposes and will continue to impose too many restrictions on aircraft (which must be made to fit the ship) to compete in future with shore-based aircraft, the largest of which will carry their own fighters with them.

It is dangerous to believe that the risks which warships run from air attack may diminish. The development of warships will lag behind that of aircraft. We are only at the beginning of powerful developments in aircraft. Their striking range will increase. All the oceans will be covered by shore-based aircraft. Their hitting weapons—bombs, torpedoes, and guns—will become not less but more efficient. They will always outmatch the ship and the ship's readaptation will never catch up.

AIR power is already the deciding factor in war at sea. Tomorrow it will dominate all the oceans and all the continents. Its power lies in its capacity to surmount all terrestrial obstacles. And the fountain-head of the strength of that power is the unity of the national air force.

An island people must be supreme in the air. All their shore-based aircraft must belong to one Service so that the full power of their air strength can be concentrated upon the main objectives. The British people can never permit the adoption of a part of the R.A.F. by another Service, save at the national peril. Undivided air power must come first ; all other considerations must follow upon that main principle. If the thesis contained in Belligerent Power were to be accepted by the British people, their future world safety would be jeopardized.

'EYES OF THE ARMY' is the apt nickname of the Taylorcraft Auster III, a two-seater R.A.F. plane able to take off in the astonishingly short distance of 50 yards and to land even in a roadway, a performance which makes it specially useful for military observation work. Its wingspan is only 36 feet, length 23 feet, height just over 6 feet. Top speed is 125 miles per hour. One is shown above in a steep climb over another of the same type.

*Photo, Keystone*

the signatories do not say is that the one factor which has produced Total or Belligerent War is Air Power. All the other factors are as old as war itself. What they are really discussing, then, is the position of Air Power in modern war.

NOW, it is an established if unwritten principle of British politics and institutions that an upstart should, if possible, be summarily rejected. If, however, the upstart is strong enough to survive repression—and any thing or person surviving continual repressive measures must be strong—it is eventually adopted as a comrade by its former opponents, as an act of self-defence upon their part. But if the upstart be adopted, let it take heed for its future, and beware of smooth words, for it has been adopted not for what it is but for what it has.

Right through the years between the wars the Air Ministry and the R.A.F. had an up-hill fight against reactionary forces. The older Services seized the larger shares of the annual Treasury allowances. The Air upstart

decks and sides, and as to interior sub-division, that she will not be subject to fatal damage from the air." Paragraph 35 condescendingly dismissed the critics with : "These views, of course, are not those of the critics of the capital ship, who maintain that a concentrated air attack on ships at sea or in harbour will be so effective that they cannot survive. It is a point of view that has yet to be tested." It has been tested now.

The pre-war programme of new battleships was proceeded with. Among them was the Prince of Wales—sunk by air attack off Malaya in a matter of minutes. The Roma, a recent Italian battleship, was sunk by air attack off Sardinia. The Bismarck, then Germany's latest battleship, was discovered by air in the Atlantic and so crippled by air-launched torpedoes that one relatively small British warship was able to go close alongside and complete the sinking by gun-fire. The American Pacific Fleet was crippled by air attack in Pearl Harbour, the Italian

# Japanese S.W. Pacific Line Is Moving Back

FROM NETHERLANDS EAST INDIES TO GUADALCANAL runs the Japanese line. On February 10, 1943, Guadalcanal was cleared of the enemy; on June 30 Rendova Island fell; by August 30 New Georgia was invested. On September 14 Salamaua was captured, and Lae two days later. Thus Rabaul was menaced from two quarters (see also page 323).

WOUNDED NEAR SALAMAUA are assisted to a regimental aid post by an Australian officer. It was an Australian militia unit which took Salamaua, New Guinea, held by the enemy since March 19, 1942.

AMERICAN MOUNTAIN BATTERY in action in the Mt. Tambu-Komiatum area, south of Salamaua. Such guns as this had to be carried in parts of 100-250 lb. over the precipitous Lababia Ridge from Nassau Bay (see map in page 323).

SHIPPING IN WEWAK HARBOUR is a regular target for our bombers (left: circled) as we advance in New Guinea. Above, casualties in the Salamaua fighting are taken in litters to barges for transport to hospital.

*Photos, Sport & General, Associated Press. Map by courtesy of News Chronicle*

# These Are the 'Busters' that Rock the Reich

BRITAIN'S 4,000-lb. " block buster " is one of Bomber Command's most shattering gifts from the Royal Ordnance factories. Four people could stand inside the casing (1), which takes from two to three days to fill with the explosive. Devastation caused in Berlin, Hamburg and other German cities testifies to the tremendous damage-capacity of this bomb.

After mixing, the explosive is dried in large rotating drums (4), then placed in the casing, which is taken by travelling electric crane (2) to the cooling pits (3). The bomb is then ready to be fitted with its " tail."

" There is not likely to be any shortage," it is officially stated, " of these or yet bigger bombs for continuing our air offensive over Germany." See also page 312.

*Photos, British Official: Crown Copyright*

# Editor's Postscript

HERE is a little pen portrait (or perhaps I should say caricature) of a man you know, which I came across in a copy of the Pall Mall Magazine for September 1905, and which I am sure my readers will be interested to have brought to their notice.

"He walks with a stoop, his head thrust forward. His mouth expresses bitterness, the light eyes strained watchfulness. He talks as a man of fifty talks—a little cruelly, slowly, measuring his words, the hand for ever tilting the hat backwards and forwards, or brushing itself roughly across the tired eyes. Essentially a tired face, the expression one of intellectual energy, which has to be wound up by a rebellious consciousness. And yet it is only ten years ago that he left Harrow for Sandhurst. He is twenty-nine—separated from his boyhood by five campaigns, a Parliamentary election, and a budget of speeches. . . ."

It is almost comic to think that just forty years ago that could have appeared in a "character sketch" of Winston Spencer Churchill! (The writer was Harold Begbie, who was nearly three years older than his subject, and who died fourteen years ago). Tired at twenty-nine—tireless at sixty-nine! There is a providence that shapes the man of destiny beyond all the guesswork of the character-sketcher.

THE new kind of senior Army officer, the colonels and majors, are of very different type from those of the last war, who mostly belonged to the past and dated back almost to the time of the captain made fun of by Punch for saying, when he was asked his regiment: "It's got gween on the cuff, don't you know, and you go to it from Waterloo." But there are some of the old sort left. One made himself ridiculous lately by putting up this notice:

### DISCIPLINE

N.C.O.s and men must at all times recognize the KING'S COMMISSION. In future all ranks entering the C.O.'s office will, in his absence, salute his desk. Failure to obey the above instructions will entail severe reprimand.

Now that sounds like a joke, and you might think that if it was meant seriously it must be one martinet's whim. You might even imagine that the ancient warrior who put it up was thinking of the salute given by naval officers, petty officers and ratings when they step aboard the quarter-deck of a man-o'-war. But that had its origin in the fact that a crucifix in Catholic times hung over the deck. The salute was an act of reverence to it, and was kept up when, at the Reformation, crucifixes became in the eyes of Protestants "unholy images." But the idea of saluting a desk as if it were a colonel wearing the King's uniform is no comic flight of one disordered imagination; it seems to be fairly prevalent! Furthermore, I am told that N.C.O.s and men are supposed to salute a C.O.'s car in the street even when the great warrior is not himself in the car! Yet we laugh at the Huns greeting each other with "Heil, Hitler!"

PUBLISHERS say British authors' books are not selling in the United States as they did before the war. My friend Sir Norman Angell's latest work is an exception. It is called Let the People Know, its object being "to answer the questionings, doubts and misgivings which are present in the minds of immense numbers of average Main Street

Americans." One of the Book Clubs over there took it up and twelve thousand copies were quickly sold. It is being bought steadily still. "Why has it not been published here?" you may ask. Because it is addressed to Americans. But, having read it, I am of opinion that it might do just as much good here as it is doing on the other side. Sir Norman is in England after more than three years' absence, during which he has done excellent work in many American States, making known what Britain thinks and has been doing, and explaining the international point of view. From the windows of his rooms in the Temple he looks out on a sorry scene of devastation caused by bombing, and he cannot stay at his tower on an

**MAJ.-GEN. H. B. KLOPPER**, Commander of the South African 2nd Division at the time of the surrender of Tobruk, June 1942, who on September 29, 1943, reached the British lines near Foggia after a three weeks' trek to freedom from a prisoner-of-war camp in the mountains of Italy.
*Photo, Sport & General*

island in an Essex estuary since that got a hit some time ago and, though fortunately not destroyed, was made uninhabitable for the time being. He means to go back to the States before long to resume his teaching as a professor at Kansas State University.

WAR certainly stimulates medical discoveries. The latest is that of a drug, which is given to sufferers from shell-shock. It has a hypnotic effect. While under its influence the patient can be induced to reveal what was the cause of his trouble. This almost always turns out to be mental rather than physical. It is the emotions, not the nerves, which have usually been responsible for the distressing symptoms. Probably a man who has, in the heat of battle or in the midst of a shower of bombs, gone through some agony of mind, for the sake of a comrade perhaps, or through thinking of the effect his death would have on his mother or wife, forgets all about it when danger is past. He may have no idea what started the shock to his system which incapacitates him for any kind of duty. The new treatment enables this to be traced

and then recovery is as a rule rapid. Rest, sedatives, and mind-healing have effected cures in a few days. The fear that shell-shock was a permanent condition, which made doctors during the last war think nothing could be done to get rid of it, has passed away as a delusion—and a snare.

I HAVE sometimes watched the reactions of various types of men and women to the sight of the sentries outside Buckingham Palace stamping their feet as they turn in their monotonous tramping to and fro. I have seen looks of blank astonishment, of profound admiration, of amused contempt. A well-known surgeon, Sir L. Cheatle, who has been observing the ritual prescribed by the Guards' drill-book, now comes out with a solemn warning that this practice of stamping, which he calls "fantastic and rather ridiculous," may have, and in all probability does have, unfortunate results on the health of soldiers. For one thing, he says, it is very likely to cause varicose veins. Also the jars to the system repeated every few minutes for no reason must, the doctor fears, have a bad effect on the nerves. This is a matter that should be inquired into. The stamping is a Prussian trick, imported along with so many others by our Hanoverian kings. If you have ever seen the parade called Trooping the Colour, which used to take place annually, you have seen a performance borrowed straight from Prussia, goose-step and all. Sentries themselves were instituted by the Prussian king known as Frederick the Great, though Frederick the Scoundrel would be more accurate.

I WAS talking to a seaman about after-war prospects and he overflowed with what Homer called "winged words" about "all this planning that's so much talked about." I mildly suggested that something of the kind was necessary if we wanted a better life for everyone. "Yes," he agreed, "but do you mean everyone? What about us? What about merchant seamen? Why don't they plan for better ships? Better for us in the fo'c'sle, I mean. They improve design, if it makes for speed, and they try to get space for as much cargo as possible. But they don't ever seem to think of making us comfortable." I asked him what he would suggest for a start. "Give us a bit more room in the fo'c'sle," he said. "Give us a better chance to clean ourselves. How would you like to wash in a pail after you've been in a coal bunker? How would you like to try to wash your underclothes without any proper arrangements for simple laundering? Then look at the distance between our quarters and the cook's galley. If you want a cup of tea on a cold night you must go half the length of the ship. Put us nearer the galley and the officers' quarters too, though there may be objections raised to our being closer together. But it 'ud help to make happy ships." Not unreasonable demands it seemed to me.

RUMOUR is "fuller of tongues" today than it was when Shakespeare wrote his Henry the Fifth—since there are more tongues to spread it. The exaggeration of harm done by enemy action is both silly and dangerous. A stray bomb fell the other day on a south-coast resort. It injured three people. Next morning the story went round that twelve had been killed. There are too many of us who enjoy, as the Fat Boy in Pickwick did, "making your flesh creep."

PAGE 351

# Vigilance the Price of Our Convoys' Safety

*Photo, Fox*

**WATCHING THE SKIES** for enemy aircraft, scouring the seas for lurking U-boats, Royal Navy ships on convoy duty maintain eternal vigilance that no harm may befall our ocean transports. They share in the honour of the "altogether unprecedented" achievement remarked upon by Mr. Churchill —not an Allied vessel was sunk by U-boat action in any part of the world during the first fortnight of September 1943.

Printed in England and published every alternate Friday by the Proprietors, THE AMALGAMATED PRESS, LTD., The Fleetway House, Farringdon Street, London, E.C.4. Registered for transmission by Canadian Magazine Post. Sole Agents for Australia and New Zealand: Messrs. Gordon & Gotch, Ltd.; and for South Africa: Central News Agency, Ltd.—October 29, 1943. S.S. *Editorial Address:* JOHN CARPENTER HOUSE, WHITEFRIARS, LONDON, E.C.4.

Vol 7    *The War Illustrated*    N° 167

SIXPENCE    Edited by Sir John Hammerton    NOVEMBER 12, 1943

**JEEP-TURNED-AMBULANCE** is carrying a wounded German prisoner to the rear of the 5th Army during fighting in the heights around Salerno. This was no mechanized warfare country. Ousting the enemy from the shrub-covered, Italian mountainsides involved slow and systematic combing. Gradients were so steep, defiles so narrow and tortuous, that even jeeps could manage only part of the way. Numbers of them were put to ambulance work in the back areas.    *Photo, British Official: Crown Copyright*

NO. 168 WILL BE PUBLISHED FRIDAY, NOVEMBER 26

# Our Roving Camera Visits Busy War-Workers

WOMEN ENGINEERS help to repair electric cables alongside a railway line, damaged during a recent air raid in the London area. Few indeed are the war-jobs which women are not tackling successfully.

N.F.S. MEN of the London region (above) with the flag presented to all National Fire Service stations to commemorate the second birthday of the organization, August 18, 1943. The flag was designed by Sir Gerald W. Wollaston, Garter King of Arms, advised by Home Office officials.

ROSE HIP SYRUP, high in Vitamin C content, is now being manufactured in a plant (left) which once specialized in ice-cream making. The freezers have been adapted to remove the seeds, for later planting, and leave only the fruit from which the health-giving syrup is produced.

SEA-HARVEST thanksgiving service was held at the Congregational Church, Mevagissey, Cornwall. The church was decorated with nets, creels, ships' lamps, and samples of catches. Fishermen—seen below putting finishing touches to the decorations—attended the service in workaday jerseys and knee-boots.

SPINNING WOOL is a recreational occupation taught at Rolleston Hall, Leicestershire, one of the many English country houses converted into Red Cross convalescent homes for Service men.

*Photos, Keystone, Topical Press, L.N.A., Daily Mirror*

BATTLE FOR GOMEL, northernmost key-point in the Dnieper front extending south to Kremenchug, has resulted in many such scenes as this. While German dead, and wrecked artillery, dot the marshy ground, swarms of carrion birds hover overhead, impatient for the moment when the tumult of battle will cease and they may pounce on their prey. The fall of Gomel, which was besieged by October 29, 1943, would rob the enemy of an important communications centre and separate his Ukrainian armies from his central Dnieper forces. *Photo, News Chronicle*

# THE BATTLE FRONTS

## by Maj.-Gen. Sir Charles Gwynn, K.C.B., D.S.O.

A GREAT deal has been written about the vital importance of cooperation between the Services and between the various arms of the Services. There is no doubt that a very high standard has been reached. Yet even now there is a regrettable tendency to make extravagant claims for the results that can be produced by specific services or arms, ignoring the essential assistance given by cooperative action.

There is plenty of evidence to show that members of the fighting Services directly engaged in the war fully appreciate the value of cooperation, and they have been chiefly responsible for the improved standard that has been attained. It is the critics who appear to cling too tenaciously to preconceived theories regarding the potentialities of individual services or arms and the role that should be assigned to them.

Unfortunately it is the critics who have the best opportunity of impressing their views on the public, and there is always a danger that its members, especially those engaged in munition industries, should gain the impression that the weapons they are producing are either of minor value or are being misused. I admit that between the Services and between the arms of the Services there is always a certain degree of rivalry, and that up to a point it is a healthy rivalry; but what I deprecate is that it should be expressed in propaganda which gives the public distorted views on the conduct of war—views which may be adopted even by Members of Parliament and Ministers of the Crown.

IT is natural that each Service and arm should wish to be given a role in which its most destructive functions can be brought into play; but, to secure cooperative action, it is essential that each should be prepared at times to carry out what may seem a part detrimental to producing the maximum effects of which it is capable. Cooperation does not imply the parallel and simultaneous exercise of power but the correct adjustment of potentialities in combined action.

The Navy, no doubt, would still like to develop its maximum power in a great fleet action, but recognizes that opportunity for that, in modern warfare, may never occur, and it is content to carry out its main role of controlling sea communications, either by destroying the enemy's ships piecemeal or by purely protective action—a laborious and unending duty on the faithful fulfilment of which the other Services, and the economic life of the nation, depend. In that task it employs every weapon it possesses, including

its long-range air weapon; and it rightly demands the cooperation of the still longer range and more powerful aircraft which can operate only from shore bases.

The Army, too, would wish to crush the enemy's power of resistance by defeating him in decisive battle, but it may have to be content to fight to gain bases from which the Navy or R.A.F. can operate with greater advantage. For example, the 8th Army, by protecting the Navy's base at Alexandria and by securing air bases along the coast of North Africa from which in turn the R.A.F. could operate with the Navy, achieved more important results than the actual damage it inflicted on Rommel's Army. In carrying out its task the Army depended greatly on air cooperation on the actual battlefield to add to the power of its own weapons and for protection from the enemy's aircraft; while at the same time air action continuously operated against the enemy's supply lines. Yet air power alone could not have assumed the functions of the Army. It could not have halted Rommel's advance nor have driven him finally from the territory required to furnish bases for naval and air control of the sea route. Every extension of air action required, in fact, to be preceded by an advance of the Army to secure new air bases.

### SACRIFICES Called For Between Service Arms

Within the Army itself there is an endless necessity for cooperation between its components and its weapons, often entailing roles in which maximum individual power cannot be exercised. Formations or units may be called on to attack parts of the enemy's position where no outstanding success is possible simply in order to reduce the enemy's power of resistance at a more vital point. Artillery may be ordered to fire smoke shell, practically without destructive effect, in order to cover the advance of tanks or infantry. The unpleasant task of the sappers in clearing minefields under fire is purely altruistic.

The tank man's highest ambition is probably to break through or round the enemy and play havoc with his rearward service and control organization; but he is often required to make sacrifices in direct support of infantry action. The infantry soldier's ambition is to close with the enemy in order to destroy him or to force him to surrender, but he may only be given the task of opening the way for a tank break-through. In the last war the function of tanks was to open

the way for the infantry, but the development of mines and the increased range of the tank has reversed these roles.

I have suggested that critics tend to be obsessed by the potentialities of particular weapons, and I was interested to read lately an article by a well-known writer, who roundly criticized the use Montgomery made of armour and his great reliance on artillery—a reversion, he said, to 1917 ideas. I cannot help feeling that this critic had ignored the changes in conditions that extensive minefields and anti-tank guns have made. Certainly Montgomery, if he errs, errs in good company, for the Russians owe their success largely to reliance on artillery, and the Germans have been compelled to modify their panzer tactics.

THE R.A.F. admittedly entered the war in the belief that independent air action, the bombing of the enemy's war industries, would be the chief instrument in achieving decisive results. Cooperation in land and sea warfare was given a very subsidiary place. That belief still has its supporters, but fortunately the importance of cooperation has been fully recognized—somewhat grudgingly by certain writers, who tend to look on all diversion of air power to cooperative functions as postponing the full development of its independent action. Those critics, to my mind, seem to ignore the fact that an immense proportion of the enemy's war industries is devoted to the production of equipment needed in land and sea war. Moreover, if the Allies did not develop their power in those elements, not only could a much higher proportion of German industry be devoted to aircraft production, but our own aircraft production might be seriously affected by the enemy's sea and air action.

WE claim, justifiably, that our air attacks on Germany have assisted Russia by forcing the enemy to divert a high proportion of his fighter aircraft and of his man-power and industries to defence against air attack. But I think we are apt to forget how much the R.A.F. owes its present strength and effectiveness to the Russian Army. When Germany invaded Russia she almost simultaneously suspended bombing attacks on England. If Russia had collapsed we can hardly doubt that intensive bombing on England would have been resumed, with serious effects on our aircraft production.

Moreover, there can be no doubt that Germany's bombing-aircraft design and production would have rapidly advanced, and that she would have been able to exploit the advantages of bombing at shorter range. We should not, therefore, forget the immense influence the achievement of the Russian Army has had on the development of our air offensive, even if it was the result of indirect rather than direct cooperation.

# In the Footsteps of Garibaldi the Liberator—

ITALIAN BATTLE-LINE as it was on October 22, 1943. By October 31 Allied troops were on the move in three sectors : over the Volturno and the Trigno, and in the Vinchiaturo—Isernia area.

ANTI-TANK OBSTACLES had to be removed before the Volturno river bank could be reached, and these lusty British Tommies (above) got down to the job with vigour. Such delaying tactics by the enemy, together with appalling weather conditions, made progress difficult : "hard slogging the whole way" was one commentator's summary. Road mines, too, slowed the pace of the advance, Gen. Alexander declared on October 23, 1943.

SHORE-LANDING DECKCRAFT, built and manned (right) by British Army engineers, moves across the Volturno River near Castello Volturno. This craft was used to ferry reinforcements, carriers, ammunition and food over the river, which varies in width from 100 to 600 feet between banks ranging from 10 to 15 feet high. While at places the river could be waded normally, the heavy rains had swollen it very considerably.

WITH A 105 mm. HOWITZER, American artillerymen (right) went into action against enemy positions across the river. Meanwhile, some 85 miles across country as the bomber flies, their Canadian comrades of the 8th Army (above) were clearing out snipers' nests south of the River Trigno, where on October 23, 1943 Gen. Montgomery forced a bridgehead.

*Photos, British, Canadian and U.S. Official. Map by courtesy of Evening News*

# —the 5th Force the Volturno, Rome-ward Bound

CROSSING THE VOLTURNO RIVER, British infantry of the 5th Army make use of a pontoon bridge built by their comrades-in-arms, American engineers. The Volturno battle began on October 12, 1943, but it was not until the morning of October 15 that this crossing was possible. By October 17 General Clark's men had driven the enemy from most of their positions on the Volturno line, which extended 17 miles from the coast to Capua. Thus, almost to the day, they repeated the triumph of Garibaldi the Liberator, who, 83 years ago, forced the Volturno against 40,000 Bourbon troops, to open the road to Rome, some 80 miles to the north.

*Photo  British Official: Crown Copyright*

# THE WAR AT SEA

### by Francis E. McMurtrie

WHAT is there left for the German Navy to do ? As pointed out in my last article, in page 327, there is no longer a harbour left in which it can consider itself safe from attack, whether that attack comes from the air or from beneath the sea. Of its larger units, the biggest lies disabled in a harbour in the north of Norway, and others are under repair at Gdynia or other ports in the Baltic. Only one important vessel is known to be in seaworthy condition, the battleship Scharnhorst. It is still believed by a few people that, as a desperate resort, the remnant of a fleet that remains to Germany will be ordered to proceed to sea to do what damage it can to our commerce. A careful examination of the facts tends to discredit this belief.

It is two and a half years since the battleship Bismarck, in company with the heavy cruiser Prinz Eugen, sallied out into the Atlantic to add her weight to attacks being made on shipping by the U-boats. At that time we were still short of escort and patrol vessels, and indeed of ships for all purposes. Nor had we enough aircraft to perform the many tasks required of them. Yet the departure of the two enemy ships was promptly reported to the Commander-in-Chief of the Home Fleet by a reconnaissance plane of the Fleet Air Arm. Immediate warning was sent in every direction, and the Bismarck and her consort were intercepted as they passed through the Denmark Strait, between Iceland and Greenland. Though touch was temporarily lost with the foe as the result of bad weather, it was regained in time for the Bismarck to be brought to action and sunk before she could reach Brest, the nearest port of refuge available to the ship after she had been damaged by torpedo attack.

THIS lesson has not been lost on the enemy. Today there are at our disposal a great many more ships and aircraft of every type, and the chances of a large German warship putting to sea and remaining there for any length of time without being brought to action are far poorer than in 1941. If in spite of this daunting situation the rash decision was taken to send ships to sea, which units would be selected ? They would need to be of similar speed and characteristics, able to act together with effect. Now the Scharnhorst's speed is 27 knots ; that of the pocket battleship Admiral Scheer, also believed to be in Norwegian waters, is 26 knots. Practically all British cruisers are capable of 32 knots or more, while the modern battleships of the King George V type are equal to 30 knots. Thus the two German

ships would be in a position of greater disadvantage than the Bismarck and Prinz Eugen, capable of 30 knots without parting company.

The only fast ships of any importance of which the Germans can dispose are the heavy cruisers, Admiral Hipper and Prinz Eugen, and it is not certain that the latter is ready for sea. With a speed of 32 knots, they might take some time to hunt down, but even so their prospects of survival would not be great. It is therefore probable that, if any enemy ships do make a sortie, it will be a very short one, designed to raise the spirits of the German public, who are in need of cheering news. It was with some such object that the dash to Spitzbergen and back was undertaken by the German squadron in Norwegian waters a few weeks back. It is noteworthy that this took them in the only direction in which British warships were unlikely to be encountered.

### EDICT of Berlin Resulted in High Seas Fleet Mutiny

It may also be recalled that in October, 1918, when things were going badly for Germany, it was sought to send the High Seas Fleet to sea to do as much damage as possible, in the hope of gaining time for the sorely tried land forces of our foes. This order was not executed, for the crews of the battle squadrons, already discontented, broke into open mutiny when their officers endeavoured to carry out the edict of Berlin.

It has already been mentioned, in a previous article, that crews of the German squadron in

SIR DUDLEY POUND, late Admiral of the Fleet, who died on October 21, 1943—Trafalgar Day—at the age of 66. He was First Sea Lord of the Admiralty and Chief of Naval Staff from June 1939 till October 1, 1943.
*Photo, Pictorial Press*

Norway are in a much more unhappy position than those of the ships at Kiel and Wilhelmshaven in the last war. It is scarcely likely, therefore, that they would feel any enthusiasm for an expedition that could have only one end. Almost certainly they would demand instead that they might return to home waters, as the Lützow did at the end of September.

This seems to exhaust the possibilities of action by the German surface fleet ; for the smaller craft, such as destroyers, motor-torpedo-boats, minesweepers, and so on, are already hard put to it to maintain coastal patrols in the face of Allied activity. In October Norwegian light forces raided the " leads," or inshore channels behind the islands fringing the coasts of their own country ; British and Allied motor-gunboats and motor-torpedo-boats carry out attacks on enemy coastwise traffic in the North Sea and Channel almost nightly ; and our aircraft strew mines plentifully off the enemy shores in the Baltic and North Sea, causing many more casualties than are likely to be reported until long afterwards.

### ACOUSTIC Type Torpedo Fails to Achieve Success For Nazis

Thus the Germans are forced to fall back once more on their chosen sea weapon, the submarine. In recent months the U-boats have suffered severe defeats in every attack they have made upon convoys. An effort to spring a surprise by the use of a new type of torpedo, said to be of an acoustic pattern which is attracted to propellers, failed to achieve the success hoped for in the latter part of September. In all previous attempts by the enemy to gain a commanding advantage by the use of some novel weapon, the antidote has been devised so rapidly that the advantage has been merely transient ; and this fresh effort is unlikely to do any better.

Meanwhile, the submarine losses must be a drain on the skilled personnel available, for expert seamen, and especially technicians, cannot be trained so quickly as U-boats can be turned out by mass production methods. There is reason to believe, moreover, that the output of German submarines has sensibly declined owing to the number of engineering works put out of action which formerly supplied essential plant and equipment for U-boats. Submarines passing through the Bay of Biscay on their way out and home run the gauntlet of ceaseless attacks by our aircraft. To counter this, enemy planes have done their best to drive our machines away, but it is doubtful if the Germans can spare enough of the Luftwaffe to do more than make an occasional demonstration in this direction. In general, therefore, the outlook for the German Navy does not seem any brighter than the future of the German Army.

GREEK SUBMARINE KATSONIS, the sinking of which was announced on October 6, 1943, played a great part in her country's fight for freedom. Operating mainly in the Aegean and Adriatic seas, the Katsonis scored many successes, sinking or damaging thousands of tons of enemy shipping

*Photo, Greek Official*

# 'You Will Never Lack Friends,' said The King

BACK AGAIN IN BLIGHTY, assured by the King and Queen that "while you are in these Islands, you will never lack friends," are the first consignment of Empire repatriated prisoners of war. They reached the quayside at Leith on October 25, 1943, borne by tender (above) from the mercy ships Empress of Russia and Drottningholm. In all 3,351, they had come via Gothenburg from Continental camps as a result of the first prisoner-exchange of this war. The following day the Atlantis docked at Liverpool with 764 disabled heroes whose long night of Nazi captivity was over     *Photo, G.P.U.*

# Neutral Portugal Tries Out Her Defences

OUR ALLY FOR 400 YEARS continuously, Portugal is neutral in this war; though her recent concession to Britain of bases in the Azores (see facing page and page 383) shows where her sympathies lie. Portugal has always been on the alert against Nazi encroachment, and now with Germany reeling under the blows of the United Nations, Dr. Salazar's Government has realized the necessity for even greater vigilance, lest in his desperation Hitler should try some move in the Iberian Peninsula. And so, at dawn on Oct. 11, 1943, military manoeuvres on the largest scale began throughout the country. Lisbon had a black-out and civil defence exercises were carried out.

Petrol is rationed, and tram-cars are overcrowded (1). Barricades and air-raid shelters are going up (2), Youth Corps are in training (4), searchlights comb the Lisbon sky (5) and Portugal's modern army stands to its A.A guns of the latest pattern (3).

*Photos, Planet News*

PAGE 360

# Azores are New Atlantic Bases for the Allies

CLUSTER OF ISLANDS which form a natural cross-roads for Transatlantic communications are the Azores (see map above), where harbour and air-base facilities have been granted to Britain by the Portuguese Government (see photograph in p. 383) under a treaty dated 1373. The islands, which are 800 miles from Lisbon, are spread over a distance of 400 miles and have a total area of 922 square miles. São Miguel is the largest, Corvo the smallest, of them.

The Azores now provide for the Allies an excellent outpost for anti-U-boat operations and afford more extensive air cover for our convoys. Horta, Island of Fayal (1), is the Pan-American Clipper base. At Ponta Delgada, São Miguel—(2) is a view of its historic Collegio Cathedral—there are good harbour facilities for destroyers and other escort craft. Allied troops have already landed on Terceira Island, principal town of which is Angra do Heroismo (3).

*Photos, E.N.A., Black Star. Map by courtesy of News Chronicle*

# Air Transport Is Rivalling Wartime Shipping

Arrival of the first plane-and-carrier air-train ever to cross the Atlantic was reported in this country on July 5, 1943. The towed glider was loaded with war and medical supplies. As HAROLD A. ALBERT explains below, possibilities in this direction are tremendous. He tells something also of today's transport pilots of the skies. See also facing page.

B Y the end of 1943 the Allies will be using so many military cargo planes that air transport will approach parity with wartime ocean shipping; so predicted the U.S. Aeronautical Chamber of Commerce recently. Of late, according to their report, one-fifth of all multiple-engined plane production in America has been devoted to cargo-carrying aircraft, and this proportion is due to rise to 30 per cent shortly.

BADGE of British Overseas Airways Corporation: silver-winged lion, gold crown and oak leaves. *Photo, Topical Press*

The practical outcome was seen when Squadron-Leader R. G. Seys and Flight-Lieut. W. S. Longhurst brought the first plane-and-glider air-train across the Atlantic in 28 flying hours (see pictures in page 152). Squadron-Leader F. M. Gobeil, the co-pilot of the glider, had never flown the Atlantic before. Flight-Lieut. C. W. H. Thomson, the co-pilot of the towing plane, was posted to Canada some time ago for specialist navigational duties on the Atlantic Ferry. But it is no secret now that their Atlantic trip was the crowning triumph of many unheralded and unremarked—though record-breaking—glider trips.

One triangular-course flight, for instance, was staged from and back to Montreal by way of Newfoundland and Labrador through some of the worst weather recorded in those parts for fifty years. Another flight, southwards from Canada, covered 1,177 miles non-stop at an average speed of 150 m.p.h. As a result, Mr. O. T. Larsen, the vice-president of Trans-Canada Air Lines, is studying the possibilities of towed passenger gliders which could be dropped off individually over their respective destinations. The air-train age is near.

As many as a hundred aircraft in one day, too, have left a great northern Atlantic air base bound for Britain. One of the "train drivers," Captain William S. May—a veteran of five years' bush-flying in Western Canada —travelled practically the whole course in dense cloud and set up a new journey-time record of 7 hours 40 minutes, beating the previous eight - hour performance achieved by a Hudson bomber fourteen months before.

A WEEK later, Captain Sam Buxton, a graduate from the Britain-India service, surpassed this Atlantic feat with a new record of 7 hours 16 minutes. He "hadn't been trying." He had not faced cloud, but he had had to contend with forty-three degrees of frost. It is a disciplinary offence for transport personnel—unless under special orders—to attempt to beat previous best flying times. They have their flight plans regulating the routes, zones, altitudes and engine speeds for each mission and they attempt to stick to them. Glamour, but scant publicity, attaches to their ferry work. Yet some of these men have

crossed the Atlantic scores of times. Captain J. T. Percy, formerly one of the youngest air-liner commanders ever to be seen at Croydon, has over fifty such flights to his credit. He looks forward to piloting 100-seater planes: it is amusing to reflect that he once set up a Croydon to Paris record flight of 53 minutes.

Then there is Captain L. V. Messenger, O.B.E., a Londoner who has logged his sixtieth crossing; and a colonel who came across with a consignment of 200 bullfrogs. They were needed for experimental laboratories over here; and they made such a croaking that the colonel declares you could hardly hear the noise of the engines.

One transport pilot, Flight-Lieut. L. L. "Slim" Jones, has even flown the Atlantic three times within 56 hours. He flew an aircraft from Newfoundland to Britain, returned to Montreal as a passenger during the night, and there learned that his brother was missing from a bomber raid on Germany. Normally such swift recurrent crossings are unusual; but in order to be with his mother, Flight - Lieut. Jones took charge of another ferry plane and re-crossed the Atlantic.

As officials of Transport Command have told me, one can pay too much attention to the Atlantic routine and miss the amazing performances that have been set up between Britain and Africa or on the ferry runs to Russia, India and beyond to China. Last year 21,600,000 tons miles capacity were provided by British Overseas Airways alone, before some of the services were submerged in Transport Command.

Captain F. Dudley Travers, with a flying log of more than 16,000 hours, has flown the

Capt. W. S. MAY
Veteran "air-train driver," he established a record for the Newfoundland - Britain flight.

Capt. J. T. PERCY
He has made over 50 Atlantic crossings. Once he did the Croydon—Le Bourget trip in 53 minutes.

Capt. L. MESSENGER
Has to his credit 25 Atlantic crossings in 10 months. One trip, of 3,000 miles, occupied only 16¼ hours.

*Photos, British Official: Canadian Official*

equivalent of more than eighty times round the world. At the age of 19 he destroyed twelve enemy planes, in the old R.F.C. (Royal Flying Corps) days. Now, piloting flying boats between Britain and South Africa, he finds that every year brings a higher mileage than ever.

C APTAIN E. S. ALCOCK, too, has flown over 2,000,000 miles, a striking one-man feat when you realize that the whole of Transport Command flew only 1,100,000 flying miles in provisioning Malta before the fall of Tunisia and Sicily cleared the route for Allied convoys. His reliability in getting transports to a destination dead on time may more than once have turned the tide of victory, and this is no idle thought. In one engagement a transport pilot tipped the scales by delivering sorely-needed anti-tank ammunition on time and in time. Only air transport could have done it.

Again, when R.A.F. Signals were putting the Western Desert, Tripoli and Tunisia on the telephone, to link all arms for immediate cooperation—the prelude to Sicily—an SOS to Transport brought key equipment from England in 24 hours. Another flyer, Flying Officer R. C. Watson, has flown scores of laden planes across the Niger-Nile routes of West Africa, across the lush river jungle, the equatorial scrub waste and mountains.

He was once forced down by a sandstorm and set out to walk 127 miles to the nearest outpost. Losing his way, he staggered on for ten days till his water supply gave out. He had already lost consciousness and lived through a day or so of semi-delirium when he found himself surrounded by a company of curious but friendly bush negroes.

The transport pilot knows his world. He may find himself facing a gale in mid-ocean and must fight and beat it. His airfield may have a covering of ten feet of snow in winter, and his aircraft—probably a plane he has never flown before—may have to be serviced at thirty degrees below zero. Or he may have a run through tropical heat, carrying reinforcements, supplies, ammunition, food, even water, or blood for transfusion. It is interesting to note, by the way, that the first tug-and-glider train was loaded with vaccines for Russia.

'ABLE-SEAWOMEN' of British Overseas Airways Corporation make fast their launch preparatory to assisting stevedores with the unloading of a flying boat. Girls and women play an important part in the flying-boat service between this country and Lisbon, Africa and America. *Photo, Topical Press*

# R.A.F. Runs Biggest Airline Service in the World

**R.A.F. TRANSPORT COMMAND,** under Air Chief Marshal Sir Frederick Bowhill, from a West Country headquarters (2) controls all sorts and conditions of planes (1) all over the globe, including such craft as the Douglas Skymaster (4) which has carried President Roosevelt, Queen Wilhelmina, the Crown Prince of Norway, and other high personages on momentous journeys: here it is seen unloading freight. Among Transport Command's jobs are flying U.S.-built planes to Britain (3) and delivering supplies (5) to the Allied forces in Italy, a job it tackled directly the first airfield was taken. See also facing page.

*Photos. Topical Press, Pictorial Press, Sport & General, Associated Press*

# On a 2,000-Mile Front the Russian Battle Rages

WOMEN IN THE FRONT LINE are a commonplace of the fighting along the whole 2,000-mile Russian front. Corporal Klavdia Danilova (I) is an air-gunner who has been in over 100 battles. Senior Sgt. Valentina Ponomareva (2) is a field nurse; she is seen tending a casualty in the Kiev front line. In the same sector riflemen wait in ambush (5). To a village near Poltava return peasants (3) with their cattle. · North-west of Smolensk a column of American trucks loaded with munitions (4) moves up to the Vitebsk front.

PAGE 364

*Photos. Pictorial Press*

# Soviet Scythe Swings South From Kremenchug

**WITH BANNER PROUDLY FLYING,** Red Army troops march through Kremenchug (1), strong German bridgehead on the left bank of the Dnieper, taken on September 29, 1943, after three days' hard fighting. Soviet tactics included building a pontoon bridge (2) in the darkness and the use of pontoon rafts (3) to ferry artillery across. Twenty days later, on October 19, the Soviet offensive was resumed on a mighty scale; south-east of Kremenchug (see map) they broke through the German lines, thus exposing to annihilation the enemy forces—estimated at 50 divisions—in the Dnieper bend, in the Melitopol area and in the Crimea.

*Photos, News Chronicle, Pictorial Press. Map by courtesy of News Chronicle*

# Hungary—Axis Hyena—Fears the Reckoning

There is panic in Budapest. The fall of Mussolini, first European statesman to express open sympathy with Hungarian expansionist aspirations, came as a shock to the ruling clique, under Admiral Horthy, who had banked on an Axis victory. HENRY BAERLEIN shows how the Horthy regime, is trying to back out of the war without paying the penalty for its crimes.

His Serene Highness Nicholas Horthy has for a considerable time been very unhappy.

His hawk-like features always remained grim when foreigners expressed their surprise that a country should insist on calling itself a kingdom and all its legations abroad proclaim themselves "Royal Hungarian Legations" although the feudal regime in Budapest insisted that there should be no king but merely a regent, Horthy himself, who is also an admiral in a country which possesses no seaboard. He realized that it is much worse to have no friends.

In the early years of this war he imagined that Germany must win, and he was glad that he had already caused a biggish square in Budapest to bear the name of Hitler.

Germany "for the sake of European peace," the Hungarians, most chivalrous hyenas, grabbed what the Germans did not want. However, there was always the friendship with Italy, and this resulted in the Vienna Award whereby Hungary, through Ciano's insistence, was given a great slice of Transylvania populated by far more Rumanians than Hungarians. Germany acquiesced in this transaction on the understanding that a large Hungarian army would go to Russia.

Events in Russia began to undermine Horthy's faith in the German triumph. These doubts were shared by his son and successor-designate, Stefan, who was thereupon invited to visit Hitler at the Eastern front; but on August 20, 1942, it was announced that Stefan had been killed in action.

waiting in Budapest to travel, is one Bornemicza, a lesser nobleman, a member of what they call the "seven-plum-tree nobility." Meanwhile he has been given the status of Minister of Industry.

We are having a foretaste of the speeches that Bornemicza will in due course make to the Allies in The Pester Lloyd, the Government's official mouthpiece. It is declaring that although in 1942 82.17 per cent of Hungary's exports went to the Axis countries, and although she had notably increased her production of iron, steel, bauxite, etc., the goods she sent to Germany had nothing to do with the prosecution of the war. Her railways, says The Pester Lloyd, have been exclusively engaged in the "seasonal transport of grain and timber." Horthy has been wondering whether the tanker-wagons from the Rumanian oilfields, whose continued passage through Hungary is essential for the Nazis, can be made to look like wagons that are carrying grain!

So desperate has the Horthy regime become in its efforts to persuade the Western Democracies of its innocence that it is now using The Népszava, the Social Democratic party's official organ (so often threatened with repression for its outspokenness), and The Népszava, rather astonishingly, has lent itself to this manoeuvre. After forty years of protesting that in this most reactionary of European countries the workers have practically been slaves, The Népszava now asserts that "the workers of Hungary were always in the first ranks of the front of freedom. Therefore, they are entitled to raise their voices for their country and their capital."

ADMIRAL NICHOLAS HORTHY, Regent of Hungary, with Ribbentrop, German Foreign Minister, Keitel, Hitler's Chief of Staff, and Bormann, successor to Hess as Deputy Leader of the Nazi Party. All was fair on the Axis horizon when this cheerful picture was taken at Hitler's H.Q. on the Eastern Front. But now Italy has become an Allied co-belligerent and the Russians are decimating the German armies still on Soviet soil. The article in this page discusses how Horthy is facing up to the changed situation.
*Photo, Keystone*

This was rather forced upon him, since the finest square of all had already been dedicated to Mussolini. For Italy was the Great Power to which Hungary attached herself; Italy would, it was hoped, restore Hungary to the comparative greatness she enjoyed before the Treaty of Trianon after the last war. Italy would be grateful because Hungary, like Germany, Austria and Albania, had not protested when Abyssinia was invaded.

So, with Italy and Germany at her back —although to have Germany there was not very comfortable—Hungary thought that she could with impunity lose the friendship of her neighbours, even of Yugoslavia, with whom she concluded a treaty of eternal friendship. When the Nazis struck at Yugoslavia, Hungary seized the opportunity of also marching in and murdering many Serbs in cold blood, particularly at Novi Sad. All the Hungarian Premier had to say then was that he was sorry—the troops of his country had a little forgotten themselves.

Czechoslovakia's friendship, too, was lost when, with the little Republic sacrificed to

Hitler had not been mollified by the recollection that the Hungarian Government, before his own, had established concentration camps for political opponents and with their "numerus clausus" had blazed the anti-Semitic trail.

It then occurred to Horthy that it would be as well to make some contact with the Allies, and his wife's kinsman, Tibor von Eckhardt, an elegant person, was sent to America, where he had a pronounced success in social circles. However, in the course of a speech devoted to his and Horthy's love for democracy, a former Eckhardt victim mounted the platform and displayed terrible scars on his body, received when confined in a camp of which Horthy's emissary had been the commandant. The unhappy Eckhardt fled to South America!

Admiral Horthy has now found a new exponent of his utterly democratic sentiments, for the world has by now, he hopes, forgotten the many hundreds whom he, as chief of the White Terror, caused to be drowned in the Danube or hanged. His new spokesman, now

There follows a demand that Budapest, which for the last four years has been humming like a beehive with the production of Nazi-Fascist-Hungarian armaments, has every right to be considered an open city. "The workers desire that this should be understood," says Népszava, "not for the sake of Budapest, but for the sake of Europe, especially Southern Europe." Between the two wars Hungary spent on airing her grievances, sums so vast that if she had diverted even a quarter of them to social purposes her governing classes would now have to face far less internal discontent, of which Népszava until recently was such a clamorous voice.

The 2,500,000 landless peasants, who live in shameful conditions, are still well aware of the Agrarian Reform that was introduced in the Succession States, making the Hungarians who remained in those regions far better off than those still included in the realm of St. Stephen. They are also aware that the secret ballot, practised in only some Hungarian towns, was opposed by the ruling classes, including Count Bethlen, who during 1921-31 held office and hopes to do so again. So as Admiral Horthy tries to steer the Hungarian ship of state he will probably have to call to his side various leaders of the Peasants' Party, and Peyer, head of the Social Democratic opposition. Whether it will then be possible to prevent a German occupation of the country remains to be seen.

## Prelude to a Fortress Raid

" To destroy factories and transport and weapons of the Germans so that our invasion casualties will be cut down " is the " stern assignment " outlined for this winter by Lieut.-Gen. Ira C. Eaker (right), commanding United States Army Eighth Air Force. Four-engined Flying Fortresses are already operating with deadly effect to that end, their daring daylight raids fitting admirably into the Allied round-the-clock programme designed to give the Nazis minimum rest from punishment. Below, a Fortress crew listens intently to last-minute instructions before setting out to the distant target.

## Take-off at Dawn for the Day's Stern Task

Photos, U.S.
New

Preliminaries completed, Fortresses await the arrival of trailers laden with one-ton bombs (1). With their loads aboard, one by one the great engines of destruction head down the runway (2) for the take-off. Airborne (3), each takes up its appointed position in the formation, which is soon above the clouds (4) and headed for a German industrial centre—without an advance-guard of planes mounting anti-aircraft guns, as the Nazis fancifully declare !

## Dead on the Target the Bombs Rain Down

Enemy planes sighted, a Fortress waist-gunner goes into action (5) and at least one would-be interferer is blasted out of the skies. Five miles above the target an oxygen-masked bombardier (7) calls over the intercom, "Bombs away!" A glance downward, and he gives the American counterpart of the thumbs-up sign. Smoke and flames from the target— the 100-acres FW 190 factory at Marienburg, 200 miles beyond Berlin—soar high as the last Fortress turns for home (6).

## Homeward Bound With Headline News

Photos, Associated
Press, Keystone

Success of the day's operations will be added to the achievement on October 8, 1943, date of the great Bremen raid, when 855 planes were employed, air crews numbered over 5,000 men, and 1,116 tons of bombs were dropped; the planes used 1,000,000 gallons of petrol and 25,000 gallons of oil, and together flew 8,500 miles. Fortresses returning (1)—with an escorting Thunderbolt fighter below—"peel off" for landing over a British Stirling bomber which raided Germany overnight (2): a crew indicate smilingly (3) that no casualty is to be regretted, whilst one displays his armoured apron (left).

# VIEWS & REVIEWS Of Vital War Books

*by Hamilton Fyfe*

WHY do the Germans make war more capably than other nations? If you doubt the accuracy of the statement that they do, I appeal to Capt. Cyril Falls. He is military correspondent of The Times, a recognized authority, one of the best of our war commentators. In his new book, Ordeal by Battle (Methuen, 6s.), he takes up this position all through.

It is not entirely, not indeed chiefly, about the operations and campaigns of the past four years that he has written. "I have," he says, "maintained my resolution to write of 'war' rather than purely of 'the war' or even of 'modern war.'" His object is to "combat the theory that there is no utility in considering the past, and that the present war may be divorced from all past wars or from war as a whole." It would not be unfair, I think, to credit him with the ambition, reasonable and in his circumstances praiseworthy, that the volume may be used as a text-book to educate officers for future wars.

He does not want wars in the future. He is aware that "if we do not master war it may end in throwing the whole world into chaos, so great has now become its disruptive strength." He sees that the barriers still existing between total war and total barbarism are few and flimsy. They may have to be broken down by dire necessity. If they are, "so much the worse." Capt. Falls is no Blimp. He does not consider war either desirable or unavoidable. But it is plain that he is not very hopeful about the prospect of chaos and eclipsed civilization being taken to heart after this war any more than it was between 1919 and 1939. There are now, as there were at the beginning of that period, "high, even extravagant hopes" of lasting peace. Again "the folly of mankind may cause the warning to be disobeyed and forgotten." We must, therefore, he evidently thinks, prepare ourselves for wars to come, and the best way to do that in his opinion is to study those of the past, including that which is now in its fifth year and has caused us so many staggering surprises.

THE German generals have not shared in those surprises. They prepared them. The reason why they were prepared so skilfully and so often succeeded is, Capt. Falls says, that they were "permeated by and grounded in the thought of Clausewitz." At a certain stage of the French Revolution Danton said to Robespierre, who was getting up a tremendous ceremony of worship to a new kind of Almighty God invented by himself: "You are beginning to bore me with your Supreme Being." I confess that Capt. Falls begins to bore me at times with his Clausewitz. It would be foolish to deny that the German military historian brought to bear on his subject a first-class brain. But has he really very much to teach us today about the winning of battles?

Capt. Falls says "Yes." He maintains that "it is the grounding of Germans in the philosophy of war which has rendered modern Germany so formidable a warrior nation, which has

enabled German military thinkers to analyse so much more thoroughly than any others the First World War and to develop from it—by realizing exactly what it was and why—a new form of warfare." But the belief that we must attribute German cleverness in planning battles to philosophy—the very idea that there can be a philosophy of war—seems to be blown sky-high by two short sayings of two of the world's most competent war-makers.

NAPOLEON said the secret of success was to have one more man than the other side. Wellington said you could always win a battle "if you knew what was going on behind that hill over there."

What they meant was that greater numbers and a perfect Intelligence system were the essentials in the warfare of their time. That

---

## Background of the Battle Fronts

time was a good deal more than a century ago, but one of Capt. Falls's assumptions is that in all ages battles have been won or lost in much the same ways. So if what Napoleon and Wellington said were true, it must still be true now. Rommel, admittedly an extremely able commander, was beaten because we had more armour and more men. In the last war Ludendorff had his Clausewitz by heart; intellectually he was miles ahead of Foch and Haig, who beat him because they had good information about the state of mind of the Germans, including the army, and struck just at the right moment to topple over the swaying enemy morale.

Furthermore, if all war is, as Capt. Falls admits, a gamble, what can philosophy have to do with it?

Just as the poker player who never takes a risk will never have a good win, so the commander who consistently plays for safety will lose opportunity after opportunity. Failure to gamble on occasion may indeed involve more than such negative disadvantages; it may lead to positive misfortunes.

Many books have been written about whist. There is, one might say, a philosophy of whist. But I never saw any book that claimed to offer a philosophy of poker. Nor can this notion of a "philosophy of war" square with one of Clausewitz's pet reflections. He spoke of Friction being an element of chance which was potent in war. He meant by Friction unforeseen accidents, uncontrollable forces. Among the latter he listed Weather. Nowadays, says Capt. Falls, this has been fully recognized and the weather is studied scientifically.

The combatants will endeavour to receive reports and prognostications from stations many hundreds of miles from the scene of action, and each will strive to prevent their reaching the other. Yet still a shift in the wind may upset the best-laid plans and change the fate of great battles.

Or else "the breakdown of a vehicle which blocks a road through a cutting, the loss of a message, or the death of a leader at a critical moment, may seriously affect the conduct of an operation."

No matter how steeped in Clausewitz the German generals may be, they are not able to learn from him how to fight Nature, nor does he teach them how to insure against chance mishaps which may spoil plans carefully laid in accordance with the best principles.

That these principles might be studied by British staff officers more than in the past can readily be conceded. When the Germans drove us back in Libya during the early summer of last year, they employed the "accepted German framework" of methods. British commanders might have parried their thrusts if they had recognized them for what they were. That they did not do so "was due to lack of study of the material which was ready to their hands." There we have the reason, never officially stated, for the change made by Mr. Churchill in the commands of the 8th Army and the whole Desert Force.

AGAIN Capt. Falls regrets that some of our generals are not yet accustomed to making quick changes of plan while moving at speed. The greatly increased rapidity of movement in the field puts a strain on "the soldier of past wars who has been used to making up his mind and commanding while moving at a fraction of the present speed."

How many of us, driven through unknown country and seeking one turning among many, have cursed the impetuous chauffeur who would not slow down enough for us to collect our thoughts or pick out the correct road on the map. With a few more seconds we should be sure of it—at the pace he goes we are in doubt.

That is a brilliant example of what theologians call "exegesis"—interpretation, making plain. Everybody can see from it how a general, with his troops either advancing or retreating at a speed he never dreamed of when he was a young soldier, is liable to get flustered and to find the making of rapid decisions very difficult. It is Capt. Falls's outstanding merit that he writes in a way all can understand. He drives home the need for more flexibility both in our large aims and our methods of achieving them with homely illustrations that make his meaning perfectly clear.

FIELD-MARSHAL ERICH ROMMEL. A "tough, hard man," according to his former prisoner, Maj-Gen. H. B. Klopper (see p. 351), he is typical of the Nazi school of able, ruthless commanders who, steeped in the teachings of Clausewitz, made the word "blitzkrieg" a reality. Rommel is seen here arriving at Salonika to review his troops, before he was transferred to Northern Italy. PAGE 371 *Photo, Keystone*

# Our 17-Pounder Anti-Tank Gun Kills 'Tigers'

**TERROR OF 'THE TIGER,'** Germany's mammoth tank, is the British 17-pounder gun (above), whose long barrel is being finish-turned (below, right) in a Ministry of Supply armament factory.

*Photos, British Official: Crown Copyright*

ASTONISHING ACCURACY is one of the special points of Britain's 17-pounder anti-tank gun, designed in 1941 to counter the heavier German tanks which War Office experts then anticipated. It has proved its great worth in the Mediterranean theatre of operations. It can knock out the most heavily armoured enemy tanks at 1,000 yards range. It is the complete answer to the formidable German "Tiger."

First in action in the Western Desert and North Africa in the early part of 1943, recent reports tell of its successful use in the Termoli (Italy) fighting. While normally it would take two years to produce a gun of this type from the time its manufacture was decided on, the Ministry of Supply achieved the miracle of producing the first specimen in only five months. Since then the 17-pounder has been in large-scale production and there are now enough in service to meet all present requirements. Mr. Makin, Australian Minister for Munitions, announced on October 11 that it is also in production in Australia.

The 17-pounder measures just over 24 feet from muzzle to end of trail. It has a semi-automatic breech action which makes it possible to maintain a very high rate of fire, and it is fitted with a muzzle "brake" which absorbs much of the recoil and stabilizes the carriage. It fires "fixed" ammunition—the shell and cartridge are fitted together, as in the case of a rifle cartridge and bullet.

There is widespread testimony to its exceptional accuracy and it has been called "a magnificent tank killer." Strangely enough, the 17-pounder first went into action on the same day as the new German tank with which it was designed to deal. The first report received stated, "Seventeen-pounder had only once been fired in anger and on that occasion the third shot blew the turret off the tank at about 1,500 yards. It is said that the sole remaining occupant realized something had hit him but could not make out what it was!"

# These Are Days of Reckoning in Nazi Germany

THIS GRIM PROCESSION passing along a ruin-lined street in northern Germany illustrates the retribution now being visited upon the German people for such atrocities as Rotterdam and Coventry, perpetrated by the leaders they elected and still maintain in power. Homeless, hopeless, but still dumbly obedient, these bombed-out citizens trek to what they are told will be sanctuary. But as the Allied Nations' bombing range and power grow daily, fewer places remain where such devastation as this is not possible.

*Photo, Keystone*

AIRCRAFT FACTORY 'COUNCIL OF WAR' in session at a plant which turns out Lancaster bombers. The manager, Mr. A. Ainsworth, seen at the head of the table, with his foremen and members of various works committees elected by their mates, confer each day on how best to increase production in order to satisfy the R.A.F.'s demand for more and yet more machines for the pounding of Germany. To such conferences are brought all the problems—of labour, materials, methods of production—that inevitably arise almost hourly in a great and busy concern. Solutions are found by the pooling of opinions based upon up-to-the-minute information.

*Photo, Fox*

# THE HOME FRONT

## by E. Royston Pike

OF our prison population of about 13,000 rather more than half are now doing useful work for the War effort. This eminently satisfactory fact was revealed by the Home Secretary, Mr. Herbert Morrison, in a recent talk at the Ministry of Information. The prison workshops are as busy as can be. In the four years ended last March a range of 160 articles, some seven million units, was undertaken by prisoners for the fighting services ; the value of this output was about £920,000. In addition, a range of 240 articles, with an output of nine million units, was undertaken for other Government departments, representing a value of nearly £2,000,000, and there was the normal very large output of clothing, furniture, and other prison stores.

As farmers, too, the men and youths in prisons and Borstal have done splendidly. Some 5,000 acres are now under their cultivation ; and as well as providing nearly the whole of the vegetables required for the prisons and Borstal institutions, national food production has been helped to the extent of 8,200 head of cattle, 2,400 tons of fruit, 600 tons of sugar beet, and 60 tons of tomatoes. A party of convicts from one prison has been employed during the past year on War Office land some distance from the prison making military roads, etc., thereby saving many thousand man-hours of soldiers' time. Boys from a Borstal institution have been similarly engaged on work for the Army and Navy. In 1940 they worked many a time under machine-gun fire from enemy planes and suffered some casualties. But they carried on, and the degaussing apparatus that they produced sufficed to fit out 325 ships. Nor have the Borstal girls been behindhand ; the nimble fingers which in peacetime were sometimes a little too clever are now engaged in making parts for planes and tanks.

DO you know what the Fiduciary Issue is ? In an explanation issued on the occasion of the Issue being raised to the new highest level of £1,050 millions the Bank of England tells us that it is the total of the notes which the Bank of England is authorized by Parliament to issue against Government debt and securities, as distinguished from notes issued against gold (precious few nowadays !). One reason for the latest increase is the carrying of unnecessary notes by private individuals. Notes should not be hoarded but paid into a bank. " Many minor tragedies (we are told) occur every year through the loss or destruction of hoarded notes ; and on grounds of safety alone, it is in every one's interest to pay all the money they do not require for immediate use into a bank or savings bank."

But hoarding is not a complete answer to the question, Where do the notes go to ? The amount in the bank tills is known, and also the amount paid out in wages weekly. The amounts in the shopkeepers' tills, in the pockets of the people, and used as petty cash by business houses, are also capable of approximate estimation. But the difference between all these added together and the amount of notes in circulation is far too large to be accounted for by " hoarding." Where are the missing notes ? It sounds like a financial thriller ; and indeed, if we could give a proper answer to the question we should be led into many an exciting by-path of strange and occasionally nefarious activity in wartime.

Still the coal situation is the only piece of Home Front news to claim the right to appear on the front page of the newspapers side by side with latest cables about the fierce struggles on the Dnieper and the Volturno. Early in October the Ministry of Fuel asked the Mineworkers' Federation to agree to the working of a full Saturday shift each week in every coalfield, to make arrangements to ensure that the coal face should be cleared at the end of every shift so that the new shift can start without delay, and to agree that, in certain circumstances, a coal-getting shift should be put on one Sunday in four. The miners' leaders received these suggestions coldly enough. They estimate that 4,200,000 tons a week is the minimum output required to meet the nation's needs, and that 3,750,000 tons is the maximum that may be expected from the industry under existing conditions. With the present man-power of approximately 705,000, producing at the rate of 5¼ tons for each person a week, an additional 85,000 men would be required to produce the extra 450,000 tons a week. But the Federation is of the opinion that it is impossible to raise the man-power above 720,000, with a liability to make good the wastage of 30,000 a year.

Given 720,000 men, could the industry increase their weekly output by 10 cwt.

for each worker ? Yes, says the Federation—provided that the Government assumes full financial and operational control of the mines, so that colliery managers and technicians may become the direct servants of the State ; that pit committees are strengthened ; that mechanization is accelerated and equipment improved ; and that the minimum wage for men working underground shall be £6 a week, and for adult surface workers, £5 10s. (The present minima are 83s. and 78s. respectively.)

For two days (October 12 and 13) the House of Commons debated the situation. Major Lloyd George, Minister of Fuel and Power, stated that though 60,000 ex-miners had been returned to the mines—48,000 from industry, 9,600 from the Army, and about 1,600 from the R.A.F.—and a considerable number of volunteers had come forward, it was clear that it would now be necessary to call men up for the mines just as they were called up for the armed forces. Mr. Will Lawson, most prominent of the miner M.P.s, alleged that the extent to which miners had been kept in the forces doing practically nothing was a scandal ; he knew of miners who had done little beyond peeling potatoes and cutting grass . . . The real truth of the matter was that the miners had lost confidence in the future of the industry.

ON the second day of the debate Mr. Churchill himself defended the Government's policy. There could be no nationalization of the mines without a general election, he said, and that would be harmful to the war effort. He refused to take a gloomy view of the outlook. " We survived last winter ; not a single factory has had to stop for lack of fuel, and our stocks are higher now than last year. We are told of the great unrest in the mining industry. I think that is a little unjust to the miners. Only 750,000 tons of coal have been lost during the last 12 months by strikes, out of upwards of 200,000,000 that have been produced. Loss by strikes and stoppages has been not more than two-thirds of half of one per cent." As the House looked puzzled, the Premier went on:

"If you like, make it ·05—two-thirds of ·05 . . ." But then, since the matter was still not clear, Mr. Churchill turned to his colleagues, and in an aside that all could hear asked, "That's right, isn't it ? Neither I nor my father was ever any good at figures." The House roared its appreciation, recalling the oft-told story of Lord Randolph Churchill's query, "What's the meaning of these damned dots ? " made when he, forty years before his son, was Chancellor of the Exchequer. So in a spate of good humour the coal situation was left where it was—in the hands of the consumer.

# They Put Up Flak that Rakes London's Skies

BOFORS GUN CREW (3) is just one of the many who put up London's deadly flak barrage against Nazi intruders. Sited on the outskirts of the capital amid fields, their noisy activities are now such a commonplace to the cattle (1) that these munch placidly as the gun crew get to work on their elevated concrete platform. Contact with other posts is maintained by telephone : an officer makes a communication (2) while above him the spotter scans the sky for enemy aircraft. This post is on the bank of a river, and supplies must be ferried across to it (4) and carried up the steep flight of steps.

*Photos, Sport & General*

# With Giraud's Men in Emancipated Corsica

**CORSICA WAS FREED** by island patriots aided by landings of French and American Commandos. Seaborne Commandos approach the hill-protected harbour of Ajaccio, the capital (1), the streets of which, by September 20, 1943, were resounding to the tramp of Goums (2), desert-trained Algerian warriors. Anti-tank obstacles had to be removed (3) to permit the advance of Gen. Giraud's men. The Germans abandoned much armour (4). Patrimonio citizens (5) greet their liberators. See also page 344.

*Photos, Service Cinématographique de l'Armée, U.S. Official*

# I WAS THERE! Eye Witness Stories of the War

## My Battlefront Tour With Gen. Clark in Italy

*Before the crash of battle resounded along the Volturno front (the big "push" commenced on October 12, 1943), Noel Monks, war reporter for the Combined British Press, accompanied Gen. Mark Clark, C.-in-C. 5th Army, on a brisk tour of inspection. Here is Monk's revealing story.*

**Pte. WILLIAM REILLY, of Newcastle-upon-Tyne, only known survivor of three soldiers of a North Country regiment who escaped from Cos by swimming to another island. Reilly tells his story below.** *Photo, G.P.U.*

CLARK had already been up two hours, breakfasting and attending to multitudinous routine affairs connected with the Fifth Army, when I called at his tent at 8 a.m. He always insists that his Headquarters be housed under canvas during a campaign, no matter what town or city happens to be occupied, in preference to luxury hotels or buildings with modern conveniences, his axiom being " Live hard and be hard. War is a hard thing."

Before we climbed into the open jeep which carries Clark's three stars of rank on a plate in front, the General introduced me to his military policemen, " Limey," British army, and " Yank," U.S. army, who always precede the General in a jeep, clearing traffic and checking doubtful roads. Both were six feet, and the familiar " Red Cap " was wearing U.S. sergeant's stripes, while the American M.P. wore three British stripes. " They trade stripes just to show there's no rivalry between them," I was told. Clark proudly proclaimed them to be " the best two M.P.s in the business."

After a few brisk last minutes with his Chief of Staff, ever-smiling, alert-minded Major-General Gruenther, U.S. Army, we set off for the front. The sun was shining after two days of incessant rain, and the General was impatient to give the order that would start the Fifth Army on its way across the muddy Volturno. This would be one of his last visits to the front before issuing that order, setting in motion the operation that would be a real test of his leadership in getting his Army across the river that through the centuries has caused many militarists, including Hannibal and Garibaldi, to have sleepless nights.

After weeks of fighting my way past endless convoys to the front, the drive to our first stop, a British Command Post, was a distinct pleasure. The Anglo-American M.P. team in front cleared everything in our path. Driving through British sections Limey would take control, and in American sections Yank held sway. They made a perfect team—just another unit in this Fifth Army that has been welded into one grand fighting outfit.

A British General was surprised to see a war correspondent leap from the jeep alongside the C.-in-C., and eyed me suspiciously, but in his easy boyish manner Clark included me in his confidence with a wave of his long arm, and the two Generals went into conference. It was a brief conference, and Clark returned to the jeep. The driver had the engine running as soon as he caught sight of the General's figure emerging from the tent.

WE were well up towards the Volturno front now, and salutes came by the score as we sped along the road that a week ago, when I first travelled over it, was heavily mined. Many mines were still there and Tommies clearing them paused to salute their American chief, while Doughboys repairing the demolished canal-passes saluted, with mud falling like scales from their hands. The General returned all salutes. At times he relieved cramp in his long legs by stretching them across the bonnet of the jeep.

The next post we visited was only two miles behind the front line, and after the usual conference the General came striding to his jeep with " Now for a climb. We are going up to an observation post on the top of the mountain here. I want to get an actual picture of this crossing in my mind." We had to park our jeeps after our short drive. It was a climb all right. An officer told us shells had been falling around the post not long before our arrival.

Clark pushed on up the steep incline as though he hadn't heard. Half-way up he pointed across to an adjoining mountain where a large house stood out clearly against the skyline. "I suppose the Germans are in there." The officer grinned and said, " Yes, sir." We were within easy rifle fire. From the observation post the Volturno Valley lay directly beneath us. The post itself actually protruded over no man's land. We had five flights of stairs to climb on top of the mountain, but Clark spoke with even breath to three Generals awaiting him. " A grand spot you've got here, by golly ! " he said.

The battle area for the forthcoming crossing of the Volturno lay before us as perfectly and as clearly as though we had a complete scale model in a room. Super-lensed glasses brought details startlingly close. Each General pointed out to Clark where his particular command was going to attack. The Volturno wound like a light brown scarf down the valley. From the observation post the whole operation looked as though it would be the easiest thing in the world. There was no sign of life in the valley. Everything was still and quiet. Clark turned and remarked to me, " There's no place in the world quieter than a battlefield—before battle." One of his generals said, " There'll be a heap of noise down there soon, sir."

One of the observation officers pointed out to us enemy machine-gun positions across the river, also some trenches that seemed to be occupied by troops. The officer told me that just before we arrived he ordered a couple of rounds of artillery fire on a suspicious-looking haystack a half-mile back from the river bank. Shells fell close enough to set the stack on fire—and sure enough a German " Tiger " tank suddenly emerged from the smoke and went careering down the valley. After a long searching look from the post, Clark remarked to me, " Wouldn't Mister Churchill be tickled to death to be up here ! Trouble is, we'd never get him down—at least, not until the battle was over ! " It certainly was an O.P. to delight the heart of a military strategist. In farewell to his generals, Clark said, " Hit them hard, boys—damned hard ! " With one voice they eased his mind on that score !

## I Swam For 22 Hours to Escape From Cos

*After German reinforcements had landed on the island of Cos, in the Dodecanese, twenty-four-year-old Private William Reilly made an extraordinary last-minute escape. His remarkable story, as he told it to Norman Smart, is given here by arrangement with The Daily Express.*

WHEN out of ammunition, Reilly and two other soldiers of a North Country regiment decided to swim for it rather than be captured. Reilly, who is in hospital suffering from exhaustion, told me three of them started swimming at 6 p.m. on October 5. One of the men could hardly swim, but he managed to keep going for seven hours, and then the other two lost sight of him. The man remaining with Reilly kept going by hanging on to a door—found on the seashore—which he pushed before him. They swam for a point between two lighthouses. Reilly continues the story in his own words.

" The other man got cramp, and the last I saw of him he was shouting to a small boat for assistance. I went on, doing every kind of stroke I could think of—sometimes just resting on my back—until I reached a rock at noon.

" I was so exhausted I just fell asleep. When I awoke it was nine o'clock and the moon was up.

" I could see the land. It seemed only about 400 yards away. Had I known it was a mile and a half I don't think I should have tried it.

" But I pushed off again, and at 1 a.m. I reached the beach and fell asleep again. I awoke at sunrise, and walked about two miles over rocks which cut my feet up, until I got help."

---

**Gen. MARK CLARK, C.-in-C. of the Anglo-American 5th Army in Italy, whose brilliant generalship resulted in the Volturno River victory after five days' bitter fighting, October 12-17, 1943. See story in this page.**
*Photo, British Official* PAGE 377

**PRESENTATION OF RELICS OF AN ME 109G**, by the G.O.C. Anti-Aircraft Command, Gen. Sir Frederick Pile, as souvenirs to Major A. M. Stuart (centre) and Major E. B. Williams (right), whose batteries brought it down at Portsmouth, on August 16, 1943. Major Stuart's own story of the brilliant forty-seconds action is given below.
*Photo, Central Press*

## We Smashed a German Spy Plane 7 Miles Up

Here is the story (world copyright) of the recent destruction of an Me109G, Germany's latest spy plane. It is told by Major A. M. Stuart, R.A., who commands one of the two A.A. batteries responsible for this splendid achievement. See souvenir-presentation photograph above.

SIRENS were howling as the gunners and A.T.S. girls jumped to action posts around the four 4·5 guns. It was 6.25 p.m., a fine, late-summer day; not a cloud in the deep blue sky, not a ripple on the wide stretch of Channel beyond Portsmouth Harbour and naval base.

I saw a far thin wisp of white vapour very high up. Lt. Bob Dowling, my Gun Position Officer, had his binoculars turned that way. He told me that one of the enemy trio coming in was an Me109G. This was exciting news. The Me109G was—and is—the Luftwaffe's latest, smallest, and swiftest plane. Fitted with racks to carry two 500-lb. bombs, it could fly at more than 400 miles an hour.

But this one had maybe 20 m.p.h. more speed, for it carried no bombs. In its slim belly, Zeiss lens down, was a reconnaissance camera. It was a spy plane, escorted by two heavily-armed Focke-Wulf 190s. If it got away it would carry back a beautifully detailed panorama picture of the Portsmouth naval base and everything in and around it.

From the Command Post came a yell. "On target!" We had the height. It was terrific. Thirty-six thousand feet—seven miles up. Guns had shot at planes flying at that sub-stratosphere height before. None

had ever scored a hit for the record. Voices bawled and repeated the fuse number. The fuse caps on the noses of the 86-lb. rounds were twisted to near the extreme limit of range.

"Fire!" The guns crashed, the shells screamed away, flying up seven times faster than the target plane was flying along.

We were shooting approximately five miles ahead of the target. What we calculated was that the spy plane and at least one of the shells would collide neatly at that rendezvous. Our shells would reach the spot 40 seconds after leaving the guns.

I SAW the first shell-bursts make a perfect chequer-board pattern into which the target plane seemed to be flying. The second flock exploded in tiny white puffs ahead of the first.

It smeared, and the smear was turning dark. A flicker of orange fire jetted out of it. And the vapour trail turned down, and it was black now. The spy plane was falling, a smoking wreck, to earth.

The gun action had lasted less than a minute. But into those 40 odd seconds was packed the training of years for the oldest members of the integrated gun team, and twelve months at least for the youngest.

## I Was In Singapore When the Japanese Swooped

This story of dreadful last days on the invaded island of Singapore has been specially written for "The War Illustrated" by Flying Officer William Furneaux, Royal Australian Air Force. At the time of the incidents narrated he was a member of the Malayan Volunteer Air Force, attached to the R.A.F. He left with other evacuees two days before the island capitulated on February 15, 1942.

AFTER being bombed out of our Singapore airport my unit was stationed at the Bukit Timah racecourse, where we were unmolested from the air. But when Tengah aerodrome, a few miles away, was attacked we seemed to be right in the circuit of low-flying Japanese aircraft operating against it, and it was a marvel they did not notice our planes and attack us, but we had hidden them well among the trees.

About the time the Johore Causeway (linking Singapore Island to the Malay Peninsula) was blown up, we, the M.V.A.F., were ordered to move bag and baggage to

Sumatra. By February 8, 1942 most of the machines had gone off to Palembang, Pekanbaroe, and even as far as Batavia in Java. I was one of a few officers left behind to conduct the embarkation of the ground staff and stores, equipment, etc., and if possible to fly over to Palembang a machine which was then being repaired. A terrific artillery barrage was going on across the Strait of Johore and we were expecting Japanese parachutists at any time.

We were also expecting vast reinforcements, and even when the Japs were actually

on the island (they made their first landing on Feb. 9), most of us did not think it possible they could take it and finish us off. We were having a devil of a time with our heavy stores; we took them down to the docks several times, but had to bring them back owing to a flaw in the shipping arrangements. On the night of February 10 we were given the order to embark.

The racecourse—our station—was now the fighting front, Tengah aerodrome was lost, and an English artillery company was bravely battling its way up the Bukit Timah road towards the enemy, to try to make a stand at Bukit Panjang Village—while other troops were coming in disorder down the road towards Singapore. I saw all this at about 2 a.m. the following morning, while struggling to get my convoy through to the docks; it took me five hours, a journey of about five miles. I cannot tell you all I saw and did that ghastly night, but it did occur to me that the British Tommy is amazing in emergency. The spectacle of a diminutive Cockney handling a demoralized mob was an eye-opener to me, and the "half-pint bloke" with a North Country accent who dug the business-end of a gun into my neck and wanted to know who I was, will live long in my memory.

Having got my trucks to the docks, I went back to the racecourse to see that everything had been cleaned up, and also to get my car. I found a corporal of the R.A.S.C. with a platoon of men whose unenviable job it was to hold the racecourse against all comers. He was all against my going up to the end of the track where I had left my car among the trees, but I promised to do a bit of reconnaissance for him at the same time, so he agreed not to shoot me when I came back. It was about three-thirty in the morning, and I did not believe there were any Japs there yet. I imagined our gunners had held them up at Bukit Panjang. But I was wrong.

THERE were dozens of them. They must have carried out a very smart outflanking movement through the jungle in this part of the island. They must have noticed me, for I saw them stop and stand perfectly still on the top of a small hill against the glow in the sky—coming from an oil fire at the Naval Base—but they did not fire, in order not to reveal their presence, I suppose. And so I backed my car out of the trees and drove up the track, sweating at every pore. I said good-bye to the corporal and his men, and pushed off back to the docks again. Having decided not to wait there till morning in the hope of getting our one remaining plane away (it had been damaged again that day by an A.A. shell-splinter), I went on the ship with our ground staff and other personnel.

Things had begun to look so serious that the European women who had previously refused to leave Singapore were being

**F/O WILLIAM FURNEAUX, R.A.A.F.,** who served with the Malayan Volunteer Air Force at Singapore until February 13, 1942, two days before the island fell. Here he recounts the grim scenes immediately preceding the capitulation.

**SINGAPORE FLASH-BACK.** In one of the fine docks of the great Malayan port a freighter slowly settles down after being hit in the non-stop bombing raids which preceded the capture of the city by the Japanese on February 15, 1942. In this and the preceding page Flying Officer William Furneaux gives a vivid first-hand account of the last hectic week before the capitulation, justifying the " overwhelming sense of disaster " which then oppressed everyone ; the tragedy and infinite pathos of those heart-rending scenes are vividly portrayed.
*Photo, Associated Press*

ordered to go to the docks and harbour and board any ship that was leaving. We had already got about 20 on our boat. We stood off in the Roads for three days, coming into the dock each morning, but no one was there to tie us up. We were supposed to be taking some more cargo aboard for the Air Force, and I went ashore each day we were waiting to leave and saw dreadful panic scenes among the natives. I went along to my office, where most of them seemed resigned to the inevitable ; others still had faith in the arrival of British reinforcements.

The Jap pressure was growing every hour. They were now shelling the town, and air raids were continuous. By the morning of February 13 things looked really grim. An overwhelming sense of disaster oppressed everyone. The raiders came down to two or three thousand feet now, and there was occasional dive bombing. In the harbour we had been getting plenty, and this day they seemed to bomb us every hour. The town was covered with a vast pall of smoke, for everything of military importance had been set on fire. The great pillars of smoke, the shells and bombs falling around, the frantic women we were picking up out of sampans, all these horrors put out of my mind any idea of taking photographs, and all the time

there was buzzing in my head the ragtime we used to play, "Singapore Sorrows."

The skipper of our ship decided to sail at four o'clock in the afternoon, by which time we had taken on a fair load of refugee women, with the result that most of us—Air Force personnel—had to quarter ourselves on the open deck. And it rained every night of the four-day trip down to Batavia. The night of February 13 passed without any particular incident. Next morning everyone trotted around the deck with a cheerfulness which was astonishing ; we weren't to know what was in store for us during the next few days !

*F O Furneaux's story will be concluded in No. 168.]*

# OUR DIARY OF THE WAR

**OCTOBER 13, Wednesday** *1,502nd day*
**Italy.**—Badoglio Govt. declared war against Germany ; title of co-belligerent approved by British, U.S. and Soviet Govts. Troops landed north of River Volturno by Royal Navy.
**Mediterranean.**—Tirana airfield (Albania) bombed.
**Russian Front.**—Announced Soviet troops fighting in streets of Melitopol. Great air battles raging over Kiev.
**Australasia.**—New Zealand troops in action on Vella Lavella (Solomons).

**OCTOBER 14, Thursday** *1,503rd day*
**Italy.**—Fall of Gildone to 8th Army and Guardia to 5th Army announced. Terni marshalling yards raided.
**Russian Front.**—Zaporozhe captured by Soviet troops. Stubborn battle continued for Melitopol.
**Australasia.**—Entire New Georgia group of islands in Allied hands.
**Air.**—Schweinfurt ball-bearing works, 65 m. E. of Frankfurt, bombed by Fortresses : 104 enemy planes destroyed ; 60 bombers lost.

**OCTOBER 15, Friday** *1,504th day*
**Italy.**—Fall of Cascalenda, and establishment of several 5th Army bridgeheads across the Volturno, announced. U.S. troops seized ground N. of Capua.
**Mediterranean.**—Salonika (Greece) airfields raided.
**Russian Front.**—Kiev and Gomel battles continued. Plavni, in Zaporozhe sector, captured.
**Australasia.**—Allied shipping in Oro Bay (New Guinea) bombed by Japanese.
**General.**—Admiral Sir John H. D. Cunningham succeeded Admiral Sir Andrew B. Cunningham as C.-in-C. Mediterranean.

**OCTOBER 16, Saturday** *1,505th day*
**Italy.**—Capture of Campobasso, Vinchiaturo and four other towns announced ; battle for Capua bridgehead continued.
**Russian Front.**—Yantsykrak, 20 m. S.E. of Zaporozhe, captured by Russians.
**Australasia.**—104 Japanese aircraft destroyed over New Guinea in this and previous day's fighting.
**Burma.**—Japanese H.Q. at Kalemyo bombed.

**OCTOBER 17, Sunday** *1,506th day*
**Italy.**—Announced 5th Army had driven enemy from majority of Volturno positions, and general advance westward made by 8th Army.

**Russian Front.**—Strong enemy force on right bank of Dnieper S.E. of Kremenchug smashed by Russian break-through.
**Air.**—Mosquitoes made 83rd raid of the war on Berlin.

**OCTOBER 18, Monday** *1,507th day*
**Italy.**—Occupation of Cancello and Morrone by 5th Army announced.
**Mediterranean.**—Skopje rail junction (Yugoslavia) heavily raided by escorted Mitchells.
**Russian Front.**—Fighting in Kiev, Gomel, and Melitopol areas continued.
**Air.**—Hanover raided at night. Berlin bombed.
**General.**—Announced that 5,000 disabled Empire and U.S. prisoners-of-war to be exchanged for equal number of German wounded in Allied hands. Lord Wavell, Viceroy-designate of India, arrived in New Delhi. Mr. Eden and Mr. Cordell Hull, British and U.S. Foreign Secretaries, arrived in Moscow for 3-Power Conference.

**OCTOBER 19, Tuesday** *1,508th day*
**Italy.**—Capture of Montecilfone by 8th Army, Gioia and Liberi by 5th Army, announced.
**Russian Front.**—Vital 25 m. stretch of railway line from Dnepropetrovsk to Znamenka cut by Russians.
**General.**—Moscow Conference began.

**OCTOBER 20, Wednesday** *1,509th day*
**Italy.**—Capture of Petacciato by 8th Army, Dragoni and Roccaromana by 5th Army announced.

**Russian Front.**—Melitopol battle continued ; three stations S. of Kremenchug captured by Russians ; bridgeheads across Dnieper N. of Kiev and over River Sozh S. of Gomel extended.
**Air.**—Duren metal works, 25 m. from Cologne, and Dutch airfield of Gilze-Rijen, bombed by escorted Fortresses. Leipzig raided by Lancasters in city's first heavy raid. Mosquitoes bombed Berlin.
**General.**—Lord Wavell installed as Viceroy of India.

**OCTOBER 21, Thursday** *1,510th day*
**Mediterranean.**—Marshalling yards at Nish and Skoplje (Yugoslavia) raided ; Rhodes bombed for third successive night.
**Russian Front.**—Centre of Melitopol cleared of enemy ; Russians advanced into Dnieper Bend south of Kremenchug.
**General.**—Ships carrying British and German prisoners to be repatriated left Gothenburg (Sweden). Admiral of the Fleet Sir Dudley Pound died.

**OCTOBER 22, Friday** *1,511th day*
**Italy.**—Fall of Piedimonte d'Alife and Alife announced.
**Russian Front.**—Verkhnedneprovsk, S.E. of Kremenchug on west bank of Dnieper, Vozok and Gorodok, captured by Russians. Announced that Red Army reached Vladimer Hill, overlooking Kiev.
**Australasia.**—Japanese positions near Finschafen (New Guinea) heavily raided.
**Air.**—Kassel, German arms city, plastered with over 1,500 tons of bombs. Mosquitoes raided Cologne.

**OCTOBER 23, Saturday** *1,512th day*
**Mediterranean.**—Reported that Greek partisans had severed rail links between Athens and Salonika.
**Russian Front.**—Melitopol, German bastion protecting the Crimea, captured by Soviet troops. Znamenka and Fastov raided by Red Air Force.
**Sea.**—Cruiser Charybdis and destroyer Limbourne sunk in naval clash off Ushant (France).

**OCTOBER 24, Sunday** *1,513th day*
**Italy.**—Establishment of 8th Army bridgehead across River Trigno announced. Capture of Baiae Latina announced.
**Mediterranean.**—Tirana airfield (Albania) raided. Capture of Kotor announced by Yugoslav guerilla H.Q.
**Russian Front.**—Lozovatka, 10 m. N. of Krivoi Rog, captured by Russians.
**Sea.**—Four out of thirty E-boats attacking convoy off East Anglian coast at night destroyed.
**Air.**—French airfields of Beauvais-Nivellers, St. André-de L'Eure, bombed by U.S. Mitchells. Targets in S. Austria raided by heavy bombers.

**OCTOBER 25, Monday** *1,514th day*
**Italy.**—Capture of Sparanise announced.
**Russian Front.**—Dnepropetrovsk and Dneprodzerzhinsk-Kamenskoye captured by Russians.
**Australasia.**—Announced 123 Japanese aircraft destroyed in recent raid on Rabaul.
**General.**—British prisoners of war disembarked at Leith, from ships Empress of Russia and Drottningholm.

**OCTOBER 26, Tuesday** *1,515th day*
**Italy.**—Fall of Fracolise, Raviscanina, and Roccheeta to 5th Army, Boiano, Spinete, Petrella and Palata to 8th Army announced.
**Mediterranean.**—Evacuation of Cos (Dodecanese) by Allied troops announced. Salonika airfields (Greece) bombed.
**Russian Front.**—Rail stations of Matovo, Klarnavatka, 2½ miles from Krivoi Rog, captured by Red Army.
**Australasia.**—American troops landed on Mono Island, S.W. of Shortland, in the Solomons, in face of Japanese opposition.
**China.**—U.S. aircraft bombed Haiphong.
**General.**—Hospital ship Atlantis arrived at Liverpool with 764 repatriated wounded. Lord Wavell, Viceroy of India, arrived in Calcutta to visit Bengal famine area.

## ★ Flash-backs ★

**1940**
October 21. Mr. Churchill broadcast to France calling on all Frenchmen to re-arm their spirits before it was too late.

**1941**
October 14. Russian troops evacuated Mariupol.
October 16. Rumanian troops entered Odessa.
October 21. 50 French hostages shot by Germans for assassination

of a German officer at Bordeaux.
October 25. President Roosevelt and Mr. Churchill issued declaration condemning Nazi atrocities in Occupied Territories.

**1942**
October 17. Schneider works at Le Creusot wrecked in daylight raid by 94 Lancasters.
October 23. Great night offensive launched by 8th Army against Rommel's positions at El Alamein.

# THE WAR IN THE AIR

### by Capt. Norman Macmillan, M.C., A.F.C.

ONE of the most significant statements in the communiqués from the Eastern Front mentioned that, during a recent period of bad weather in South Russia, German aircraft were grounded while Russian airmen continued to fly over the area around Melitopol, a few hundred feet above the ground, with Stormovik ground attack aircraft prominent among them.

Until the whole story of the Russian counter-advance against the German invaders is told it will be impossible to allot full credit to the Red Air Force for the part it has played in the tremendous battles to recover the lost territory. We know how great was the part of the Royal Air Force, the Fleet Air Arm, the United States Army Air Force, the

navies or between both. The fact that one side—that which has gained the initiative in the air—can then employ its air power to aid its surface forces gives the combined forces of that side a measure of strength denied to their opponents, a measure of strength which the experience of the 1914-18 war and every war since has shown to be a decisive factor in battles on land and sea.

THE victorious and swift overrunning of all Europe by German armies was accompanied by the great air superiority which the Luftwaffe in 1940-41 possessed over its combined enemies. But the story of Germany in this war is the tale of the prodigal. The German Army leaders expended German air powe

So, when the Germans were forced to use their Army-prejudiced aircraft to fight for air mastery they came up against the products of an air theory of a different kind. The independent Royal Air Force had been designed from its beginning in 1918 to fight for and obtain air superiority and finally air mastery as the overlying principle of its existence. Other aspects of air power were kept in mind and additional Commands provided to deal with them. But the first object of the British Air Arm was to inflict decisive defeat upon the Air Arm of its opponents, and it was only because of the acceptance of that cardinal principle that the Royal Air Force preserved Britain from invasion and, in spite of its diminutive size, fought on until it had gained parity and then numerical superiority over the technically inferior Goliath of German air power.

American air outlook was keyed to a strategic conception of air war similar to the British. The instruments of American air power were different, owing doubtless to great geographical variations in the conditions which faced the two nations before the war began. So, the American heavy bombers were designed to operate over great distances (San Francisco to Honolulu is 2,400 miles across the ocean) ; they were designed to fly high (American mountain ranges are far higher than European), and elevations from which the aircraft might have to take off imposed special considerations in engine design ; and their long-range bombers were heavily armed and armoured and were thus able to fight their way through to their pre-arranged destinations.

### OUR Most Critical Stage in the War is Now at Hand

The British and American conception of the theory of air power was the same, but the application of the theory to types of aircraft was affected by the different geographical conditions facing each nation. That is why air defeat has been imposed upon Germany *and* Japan. That is why the process of conquest has ended, and the process of reconquest has begun. For the initial victory of the global war—the air victory, without which no other victory could be possible—has been won by the United Nations in every theatre of war. It is now necessary to profit by that victory, and to apply the advantage of superior air power to the attainment of final victory over Germany and Japan.

This is now our most critical stage in the war. The British Air Marshals and American Air Generals have done their initial part. It is now the turn of the ground Generals. Will the Anglo-American ground Generals employ the air power which is available to them to the best advantage, to gain victory in the shortest time, and with the fewest casualties among our troops ? Do they know enough about the application of air power ? Or should a fully qualified Air Officer of high rank be given exceptional powers of co-ordination to ensure that the air power available to us is really employed to the fullest possible advantage ?

RED AIR FORCE PLANES attached to the Soviet Northern Fleet are here seen putting " paid " to the account of a U-boat. From the White Sea to the Black Sea, Russian airmen have taken the initiative against the Luftwaffe. The strategic consequences, so advantageous to the Allied Nations, are discussed in this page.
*Photo, U.S.S.R. Official*

South African Air Force, the Royal Australian Air Force and other Allied air forces in the continuous 2,000 miles advance that drove the Germans (and the Italians) out of North Africa ; that cleared them from Pantelleria and Sicily ; and that carried the Anglo-American forces into Southern Italy.

### CHALLENGED and Forced to Decisive Aerial Combat

It is not too much to say that without air power that great feat of arms might never have been accomplished. Why ? You may well ask. For this reason. There can be no consolidation of positions in the air. There can be only the combat that is decisive. If there are aircraft in the air they can be left there to carry out their tasks, challenged and forced to fight to execute what they have been ordered to do, or destroyed and the remnants driven back whence they came.

Air power does not acknowledge a war of position. There is no such thing as a defensive war in the air when aircraft fight aircraft. The initial object of air power is to attain mastery of the air. When that has been achieved it becomes possible to use aircraft freely for purposes connected with surface actions—between armies or between

for their own ends and failed to understand that they could gain eventual victory only by crushing the air power of their enemies and preventing it from being resurrected. They believed that the Army was all-powerful (as could be expected from the descendants of the incredibly cruel Teutonic Knights who pillaged north-eastern Europe centuries ago in the perverted name of honour) and that the Luftwaffe was but an auxiliary to it. In modern war the decisive arm is air power, for without it no ground or sea force can prevail against an opponent who possesses it, as has been amply proven.

To the providential blinding of the German generals to the staringly obvious values of air power we must in the first instance ascribe the failure of German arms to achieve absolute victory in this war. Among other things —and it was only one of their mistakes —they built the wrong types of aircraft to achieve air mastery because they were required primarily for close cooperation with the Army. They failed to see that if they once attained to complete air mastery it would be possible to utilize the aircraft which had gained that air superiority to deal effectively with the needs of their ground forces.

MEANWHILE, the Red Air Force has the initiative. Climatically they were always handicapped, even in peacetime. This is now their great ally, and they have shown that they can exploit its value, for the handicap that they have always had to fight is now imposed as rigorously upon the German Luftwaffe. And it may prove, in time, that in this lay the great secret of the success of Russian winter offensive battles even before the Red Air Force had air superiority. But, today, with the attrition of the Luftwaffe through the Allied air offensive, and the supply of British and American aircraft in addition to their own output, the Russians have air superiority at their command. And that, perhaps, explains their recent continuous and sensationally successful advances and the defeat of German arms.

# Smashed-Up Lancaster Gets a New Lease of Life

BACK FROM A BIG RAID with undercarriage smashed, an engine burnt out and propellers twisted, "T for Tilly" crash-landed on the home aerodrome. Cranes hoist it on to a tractor (1), for delivery to the dismantling squad (2). In sections, the down-but-not-out Lancaster, preceded by R.A.F. motor-cycle police (3), is moved to the repair shop (4) for high-speed renovation which, successfully completed, enables it to take to the skies again (5), fit and ready to drop more bombs where these will do most good to the Allied cause.

*Photos. Keystone*

# Peril They Scorned—There Were Lives to Save

**Cpl. EADIE HATFIELD, B.E.M.**
This W.A.A.F. rescued 10 of her comrades from a half-demolished and burning dance hall, target of a high-explosive bomb.

**MISS CELIA JENKINS, B.E.M.**
A Post Office worker, she rescued two people from a bombed and burning building, one of them from a cellar on the brink of collapse.

**DR. M. THOMSON, M.B.E.**
Herself wounded, hungry and without proper medical supplies, she saved many lives during the Japanese invasion of Singapore.

**MRS. DOROTHY HIDE, B.E.M.**
Civil Defence worker, she showed "devotion to duty, conspicuous efficiency and powers of leadership in emergency."

**SISTER MURIEL MYERS**
Of Queen Alexandra's Royal Naval Nursing Service, Sister Myers was awarded the Associate Royal Red Cross medal for "outstanding zeal, patience and courage."

**NURSE M. FERRO**
She is seen receiving from Lord Gort, Governor of Malta, at an investiture in Palace Square, Valetta, her award of the Associate Royal Red Cross medal for "meritorious conduct in the wards during air raids at the General Hospital, Imtafa."

**MISS DOREEN FERRINGTON**
Member of the Women's Land Army, she helped to drag dead and injured airmen from a crashed plane. Alone, she brought a heavy gate to the scene for use as a stretcher.

**Pte. SONIA STRAW, G.M.**
This member of the A.T.S. was the first woman to be awarded the George Medal, for courage and service to others during air-raids.

**1st Off. M. R. RATHBORNE, M.B.E.**
Of the W.R.N.S., she received her Membership of the Order of the British Empire for zeal and wholehearted devotion to duty.

**Pte. M. D. STANNARD**
Member of the A.T.S., she received the Royal Humane Society's Certificate for rescuing a non-swimmer, who had already gone down twice.

*Photos, British Official; L.N.A., News Chronicle, Planet News, Keystone, The Daily Mirror, Topical*

IF Rome had a personality the city would be recalling just now the number of times it has been approached by armies, besieged, stormed, sacked, ravaged with sword and fire. There have been times when it almost ceased to exist, when grass grew in the highways, and a scanty population sheltered in ruined palaces. How Nature treats a city that falls into a condition like that is shown by the depth at which the Roman Forum was found. Imperceptible dust falls day by day, year by year, and the surface of the soil is raised higher and higher. Sometimes, when I look at the ruins of our British cities, especially London, where the remains are curiously like those of ancient Rome and Pompeii and Herculaneum, I wonder whether they will some day far in the future be excavated and exhibited to tourists from Kamchatka or Tierra del Fuego. The Forum is Rome's most interesting antiquity by a long way, in my opinion. St. Peter's is more like a huge railway station than a church. The Seven Hills are very tiring; they have always seemed to me to number seventy and seven. There is no society to speak of, owing to the cleavage between Church and State. In the streets there are always troops of priests.

STATEMENTS repeated several times lately in radio news that the weather on the Italian front was too unfavourable for flying carried my mind back to the very early days of aviation when no machine left the ground unless the air was perfectly still. At the first aircraft competition meetings—there was one in 1909 at Rheims, then one at Doncaster and another at Blackpool —the most daring pilots of that time used to wait till the flags drooped down their staffs before they would venture up. Quite right they were, too, for the planes of those days were ramshackle contraptions, with motors of what seems now ridiculously puny power. I remember seeing A. V. Roe, now Sir Alliott and a leading manufacturer, trying to get into the air with a triplane that had a nine horsepower engine. Of course it would only hop. Another famous pilot, Hubert Latham, took the first big risk in a high wind. I saw him at Blackpool, surrounded by friends and well-wishers, imploring him not to; he waved them aside with his slow, tired smile. Graham-White was the first airman to fly in the dark. I was there, too, and recall the farewell his mother took of him just before he started. He is going strong still, I am glad to hear.

FOREIGN Offices have a lot in common wherever they may be situated. You might expect the Moscow one to be different, but it isn't. The earliest Bolshevik Foreign Minister, Tchicherin, used to surprise his colleagues in diplomacy by his very careful turn-out in evening dress. But he only wore the ordinary trousers and tails with white tie. Now, according to regulations just issued by Mr. Molotov, Russian diplomats and Foreign Office functionaries are to appear in double-breasted black tunics with white shirts, having starched fronts, collars and cuffs (with mother-of-pearl links, if you please), trousers with broad black bands down the sides and gold piping, black silk socks and elastic-sided boots, such as Punch used to call "Jemimas." Gold braid will appear also on the tunics. I don't know that this is worse than what is called "Windsor uniform" which Ministers had to wear in this country until the present reign, but it must seem to many of us incongruous under a Socialist system. Socialists, however, are quite as fond of dressing-up as other people, sometimes more so (as Ramsay MacDonald), so it is really a normal development.

THE "old sweat" of last century's wars, even of the South African War, used to attach great importance to medals. The soldier of today, it seems, is inclined to laugh at them and to think they had better be abolished. This is symptomatic. For one thing, since the great majority of men who are of an age to go into one of the Services are serving in one of them, the

**Dr. ANTONIO D'OLIVEIRA SALAZAR, Prime Minister and virtual dictator of Portugal since 1932. A professor of economics, he achieved and still holds power not by violence but by invitation. On October 12, 1943, Dr. Salazar announced to the Portuguese National Assembly in Lisbon his decision, based on a 570-year-old treaty, to extend to Britain facilities in the Azores (see pages 360-361) for increased protection by air and sea of Allied merchant shipping.**
*Photo, New York Times Photos*

wearing of a medal in years to come would confer no dignity. If it did, unfairness would be caused to the men who did equally important work in factories, shipyards, coalmines and so on, and who would have received no recognition. For another thing, the Servicemen of the present do not want any reminder of the war in which they took part. There is quite enough for them to remember it by without medals. As for other distinctions, there is some feeling against them, too, due to the knowledge that they are often awarded very much at haphazard. Many go to men who are not necessarily braver or more skilful in leading than the rest, but to those who happen to attract notice. The silliness of foreign decorations, which was a joke last time, has faded out in this war. They used to be taken round in trays.

I WANTED to look up something in one of Trollope's novels and went to the shelves at the London Library where the great Victorian story-teller's works used to be ranged. To my surprise the shelves were almost empty. I asked one of the librarians if the volumes had been sent to be rebound. "No," he said; "they are out. There is a run on Trollope just now. I suppose our members like his tales because there is such a quiet, peaceful atmosphere in them. It takes their minds off the present turmoil and bloodshed and uncertainty." I asked him, "What about Thackeray? Is he sharing in the boom?" He smiled pityingly. "Oh dear no," he replied. "Nobody reads Thackeray now. He has quite gone out of fashion." That is easily explained. "Thack," as Mr. Archedeckne, the original Harry Foker, would call him, could do a big scene far better than Trollope. But he was a bad storyteller because he put in so much cheap moralizing. Trollope stuck to his characters and plot. I see the Oxford University Press are adding to their World's Classics his novel called Is He Popenjoy?—a poor title for a capital mystery tale. It is not so well known as the Barchester series.

PSKOV is attracting attention for the second time in its history. It became a short time ago, in newspaper language, one of the many "key-points" on the Russian Front. (Like "bridgehead," the term "key-point" is generally used without any regard to its meaning.) Its earlier leap into front-page news was in 1917. Gen. Russky, one of the Tsar's army commanders, had his headquarters there. He and the other leading generals had decided that there must be a change in the Russian system of government. They could not win the war, they had become convinced, if the nation was excluded by the bureaucrats from taking full part in it. The autocracy, which was really a bureaucracy, must go. There must be a ministry responsible to the Duma, an elected body which could be turned into a Parliament. Russia must be governed on constitutional lines. Well, early in March 1917 the Tsar left his headquarters at Mogilev (also prominent in the news of late) for his home at Tsarskoe Selo. His train was stopped and sent to Pskov. There Gen. Russky told him he must abdicate. He tried to offer concessions and was told "It is too late." The Tsardom was over. It ended at Pskov.

PROSPECTS of peace after the war are not so rosy. As the fate of Hitler grows more certain and the liberation of the Nazi-occupied countries draws nearer, the people of several of those countries have already begun fighting each other over questions of post-war settlement. In Greece there are some who want the king back and some who say "Never!" They are not merely arguing about it; they are at war. Then in Yugoslavia the Mihailovitch army is accused by the other patriot partisans of treachery, while in Czechoslovakia the mass of people are said to be strongly in favour of alliance with Russia, and complaints are made that obstacles are raised to this by the Foreign Offices in London and Washington under the influence of "reactionary Polish circles." Dr. Benes was to have gone to Moscow to make some arrangement months ago. He was held back. Then his journey was fixed for last month, but postponed indefinitely, not by his own wish, because of the Three-Power Conference. The Poles themselves appear to be deeply divided. Many careful observers think there is almost bound to be something like civil war in France. Have we got to keep armies all over Europe to preserve order? I sincerely hope we shall do nothing of the kind.

# Men of the 5th on the Last Lap to Naples

**SEARCHING FOR SNIPERS IN TORRE ANNUNZIATA,** Bay of Naples port, capture of which was reported on October 1, 1943, this tank-load of British infantry of the 5th Army passes a street sign indicating the road to Vesuvius. Only 12 miles to the north, beyond the famous volcano, lies Naples, which our men occupied a few hours later after soma skirmishing.

*Photo, British Official: Crown Copyright*

Printed in England and published every alternate Friday by the Proprietors, THE AMALGAMATED PRESS, LTD., The Fleetway House, Farringdon Street, London, E.C.4. Registered for transmission by Canadian Magazine Post: Sole Agents for Australia and New Zealand: Messrs. Gordon & Gotch, Ltd.; and for South Africa: Central News Agency, Ltd.—November 12, 1943.    S S    *Editorial Address:* JOHN CARPENTER HOUSE, WHITEFRIARS, LONDON, E.C.4.

Vol 7 — The War Illustrated — N° 168

Edited by Sir John Hammerton

SIXPENCE

NOVEMBER 26, 1943

**CHEERFUL TANK DESTROYER OF THE RED ARMY,** seated in one of his captures, is Senior Lieut. Savikov, commander of a company of anti-tank riflemen who have a highly creditable record of destruction of enemy armour, including formidable 60-ton Mark VI Tigers. Savikov is one of the men who have made possible the historic Russian counter-offensive which, beginning on July 13, 1943, had by November 14 taken the Red Army into the Dnieper Bend and the Crimea, and well beyond Kiev.

*Photo, Pictorial Press*

NO. 169 WILL BE PUBLISHED FRIDAY, DECEMBER 10

# Our Roving Camera Reviews the Food Front

BOTTLING FRUIT at a Maidenhead, Berks, factory these girls of the A.T.S. volunteered their services for this essential job. Working from 7.30 to 10 each night, they were remunerated with 4s. 6d. and their supper—earning more in their spare time than they get for a week's hard work at the depot.

BACK TO THE FARM, the bumper potato harvest gathered in, go land-girls and troops of Eastern Command who responded to a Ministry of Agriculture appeal for volunteers in view of the great shortage of farm labour.

FROM CAULDRON TO TROLLY (left), and from trolly to jars, go thousands of tons of jam each year at this factory, mainly for issue to the Forces.

(Above) Dehydrated cabbage is Canada's latest contribution to Britain's wartime larder; here cabbages are in the shredded state prior to the dehydration process. Great value of dehydration is that it enables much shipping space to be saved.

'ONE WON'T BE MISSED!'—not when you are helping to move 10 tons of freshly lifted, juicy carrots to the canning factory, like this aproned and booted girl (above).

(Left) Experts demonstrated ways of decontaminating "gassed" food before 800 specialists from Britain, the Dominions and the U.S. at Hurlingham Polo Ground on October 31, 1943.

*Photos, British Official, Daily Mirror, L.N.A.*
PAGE 386

# THE BATTLE FRONTS

## by Maj.-Gen. Sir Charles Gwynn, K.C.B., D.S.O.

**RUSSIAN FRONT, November 4, 1943. The Red Army was advancing on three fronts: from Nevel to Gomel; round Kiev (which fell on November 6); and in the Dnieper bend.**
*Courtesy of The Daily Telegraph*

WHEN I last discussed the situation on the Russian front the Germans had just completed their withdrawal behind the middle Dnieper and had established a strong defensive position east of the lower Dnieper, running from the bend of the river at Zaporozhe through Melitopol to the western shores of the Sea of Azov. This latter sector provided a shorter front and covered exits from the Crimea, from which, however, there were no signs of withdrawal.

It was not, therefore, merely a rearguard position but one intended to be held indefinitely. It was still a matter of speculation whether the Germans meant to stand on the Dnieper and on the Melitopol position for the winter, or whether they proposed only to hold the line as an intermediate position to cover a deliberate withdrawal at a time when mud or snow would check Russian pursuit. It is still impossible to be certain which course the Germans intended to take; but it seems probable that it was the former, in order to retain the Crimea, the abandonment of which would increase Rumania's alarm and give the Russians valuable air and naval bases.

They certainly had no intention of continuing their retreat immediately, and in particular had fortified the Melitopol line elaborately and were holding it in force. Personally, though I did not expect that the Germans would have much difficulty in holding the river line as an intermediate position, I doubted if it would be a sound position on which to meet a winter offensive.

It seemed hardly possible that, before the river froze, the Russians would be able to cross it and establish a bridgehead large enough to permit the deployment of a strong force, especially in view of the distance they

**DNEPROPETROVSK Railway Bridge, spanning the Dnieper river, was demolished by the Germans in their headlong flight from the great industrial centre which was retaken by the Russians on October 25, 1943.**
*Photo, U.S.S.R. Official*

had advanced from their original base, their lack of good communications and exhaustion caused by their previous exertions. It seemed probable that they would be satisfied to gain the east bank of the river and reorganize and rest their armies before renewing the offensive in the winter.

In the meantime, they might be expected with their usual enterprise to secure minor footholds across the river at favourable points, and also to make a determined attack on the Melitopol position if autumn rain did not make conditions too difficult. Remembering, however, how often the Russians had achieved the unexpected I ended my article by suggesting that they might not allow the Germans choice of policy. Again they have exceeded all expectations.

Almost at once they secured footings across the Dnieper, including one at Kremenchug, though not on a scale that alarmed the Germans. Then, after the shortest of pauses,

the general offensive was renewed. The Kuban was finally cleared, the Melitopol line was attacked in strength; a footing was obtained in that town, and Zaporozhe, the northern bastion of the line, captured. It seemed at first as if Kiev might be the main objective, for bridgeheads from which vigorous attacks were made were established north and south of the town. On the upper Dnieper there were heavy attacks too, and in the Veliki Luki region Nevel, which had often resisted attack, was captured. Only on the middle Dnieper, between Kiev and Zaporozhe, was there no marked activity, and it looked as if in this sector the river was too formidable an obstacle to be attacked in strength. Kiev has fallen, with amazing results, but before that it became evident that Stalin's object was not the recapture of cities, however important, but decisive defeat of von Mannstein's southern armies.

### KREMENCHUG Breakthrough a Complete Surprise

The attack on the Melitopol line was pressed relentlessly, and obviously if a breakthrough occurred there the Germans in the Crimea and those protecting its exits would have little chance of retreat without disaster. The Germans fought fiercely to hold the line, even bringing up field divisions from the Crimea as reinforcements. It was evidently no rear action but a real trial of strength. Then came the news of the breakthrough from the Kremenchug bridgehead.

THE surprise of the breakthrough was complete and its success immediate. The advance was rapid, and the main line of retreat for the troops about Dnepropetrovsk was cut. It was evident that the thrust was aimed at Krivoi Rog, the capture of which would have made the escape of the Germans within the Dnieper bend almost impossible.

The German situation had become critical in the extreme, but von Mannstein, acting with characteristic executive speed and skill, rushed all his available reserves to the danger point at Krivoi Rog. In that he was no doubt helped by the convergence of railways on this region. Naturally it was his reserves of armoured and motorized divisions that he concentrated most quickly, and it is probable that he withdrew some of those detailed for the defence of Dnepropetrovsk and neighbouring towns, trusting that the Russians would not be able to make further crossings of the Dnieper in face of the troops he had left to hold it. He may even have withdrawn some Panzer Divisions in the Melitopol line in view of the initial failure of the Russian attacks to make decisive progress.

The Russian thrust from Kremenchug had penetrated deeply but on a narrow front, and was certainly for a time exposed to counterattack. No doubt von Mannstein intended to take advantage of the opportunity and to repeat, if possible, his successful counteroffensive manoeuvre of the preceding spring, which recaptured Kharkov. But this time he had not a compact body of reserves in readiness, and the situation was so serious that he was bound to counter-attack in a somewhat piecemeal fashion before his concentration was completed. The counter-attacks succeeded in so far as they brought the spearhead of the Russian drive to a standstill, but Russian reserves were used to widen the wedge and to protect its flanks.

As reserves on both sides continued to arrive a prolonged and furious armoured battle developed around Krivoi Rog of much the same character as that in the Kursk salient in the summer. The Russian right flank was heavily threatened, but its defence

was stubborn, both sides having heavy losses. At first the Germans claimed successes and spoke of a counter-offensive which would drive the Russians back across the river. Meantime, however, the Russian left was pushing steadily on towards the line of retreat from Dnepropetrovsk, and an astounding surprise crossing of the river overwhelmed the weakened garrison of the town.

WHETHER von Mannstein had had more ambitious hopes or not, the primary object of his counter-attacks was now to hold Krivoi Rog at all costs as a bastion protecting the whole German force in the Dnieper bend from encirclement. While this situation was developing on the west bank of the Dnieper the Russians broke through the Melitopol line, and by an amazingly swift blitzkrieg pursuit broke the 6th German Army into fragments and isolated the Crimea. The whole structure of the defence of von Mannstein's group of armies was shattered, and the one and only hope of saving them from even still worse disasters lay in the outcome of the Krivoi Rog battle.

Once again the Russians have out-fought the Germans, and, Marshals Stalin and Zhukov, by an astonishing display of the arts of generalship, have out-manoeuvred their opponents. The concealment of their intentions, the coordination of their various attacks, the speed with which preparations for attack were carried through, and the rapid exploitation of success were outstanding features of their achievements. The forcing of the Dnieper line and the destruction of the 6th Army are outstanding in military history.

# Stiff Resistance Overcome in the Push to Rome

TWO ALLIED ARMIES in Italy, the 5th under General Clark and the 8th under General Montgomery, linked to effect the capture of Isernia (see map), central hinge of the German defence line, on November 4, 1943. The 5th had forged north from Naples through Aversa and across the Volturno river, its right flank pressing inwards to meet the left flank of the 8th, advancing northwards from Termoli to cross the Trigno river.

North of Termoli (1) a wrecked tank and a German's grave symbolize the stiff resistance overcome by Montgomery's men. Between Naples and Rome (2) the 5th were hampered by road destruction; here sappers are doing necessary repairs. Outside Aversa, capture of which was announced on October 6, an enemy prisoner-of-war camp was taken over; a final pocket-search (3) takes place before Nazi prisoners are dispatched to North Africa. At Grazzanise, on the Volturno, this Sherman tank (4), too heavy for our improvised bridges, found a crossing point where the water was shallow.

*Photos, British Official. Map by courtesy of News Chronicle*

# Tragedy Stalks in the Wake of the Vanquished

WAR'S DESOLATION is tragically mirrored in these pictures of the Italian scene as the Germans fled before our armies. A Tragone urchin (1) sits on the door-step of her shattered home, her wailing little sister on her knees; just behind them is the lifeless body of their mother, victim of the Nazis. At Baja e Latina, near Caserta, the church (2) was dynamited to block the road and thus gain time for the enemy in their with-drawal to the north.

Systematic demolition of bridges was also resorted to by the fleeing enemy to stem our advance; near Liberi (4) American trucks detoured by way of a creek bed. As the enemy passed on, wretched villagers, like these old folk of Raviscanina (3), returned to their humble dwellings, praying that even a few of their poor belong-ings would have survived; while more able-bodied civi-lians (5), like those of Pied-monte, cleaning up debris in a street, cooperated with our forces in restoring some semblance of order to the Nazis-produced chaos.

By November 11, 1943, the Allies had advanced as far as Cassino, some 70 miles from Rome.    *Photos, U.S. Official*

# THE WAR AT SEA

### by Francis E. McMurtrie

THERE is evidence that the Germans are seeking desperately for any small success they can snatch at sea, capable of being distorted into the semblance of a victory for the benefit of the German public, whose discontent and dismay at the bad news accumulating from every quarter require assuaging. This is the explanation of the apparent renewal of activity in the English Channel and North Sea by enemy light forces, mostly craft of the motor torpedo-boat and motor gunboat types. These are commonly referred to, loosely and inaccurately, under the term " E-boats," a corruption of " enemy boats."

It was on the night of October 24-25, 1943, that these vessels made their most daring

**PASSING MAILS AT SEA.** H.M.S. Devonshire, in Eastern waters, draws alongside her sister cruiser, H.M.S. Mauritius, to effect the exchange of eagerly-awaited letters from home. Over the fo'c'sle of the Devonshire flashes a rocket—here it looks like a flag—bearing the communicating line. Along this line, when made fast aboard the Mauritius, the bags of mail will be swung.
*Photo, British Official : Crown Copyright*

attempt to achieve an advantage. Some 30 of them, in separate divisions, concentrated at a point in the swept channel off the East coast, not far from Lowestoft. It was evidently their intention to surprise a coastal convoy ; but fortunately our own forces, comprising destroyers and motor gunboats, were on the alert, and able to give the intruders a warm reception. Four German m.t.b.s were destroyed and six or seven received damage of a more or less serious character. We sustained no losses and but few casualties. Thus the raid completely failed in its object, the Germans being obliged to admit in their own broadcasts that some of their vessels had been sunk.

OUR own light craft visit enemy waters on the far side of the Channel and North Sea practically every night, and on occasions even go so far afield as the coast of Norway. To venture so far from a base is of course a hazardous operation ; and on October 24 one of our m.g.b.s was so badly damaged in action with German aircraft off the Norwegian coast that she had to be sunk by our own forces. Her crew returned in a Nor-

wegian consort, which had been standing by her. A number of enemy coasting steamers had been attacked in the course of this patrol, at least one of them being sunk.

In the small hours of November 3 the Germans again tried to intercept one of our coastal convoys, this time off the South coast, between Dungeness and Beachy Head. Though they were able to escape with less loss than in the previous encounter, two of the attacking craft were damaged and a third almost certainly sunk in action with a destroyer of the escort, H.M.S. Whitshed.

These minor engagements have been described in some detail, as the war in European waters seems to be degenerating into a series of small ship encounters, any occasional small gain in which is likely to be exaggerated by the enemy out of all proportion to its real significance. This is due to the elimination of the Italian fleet from the ranks of our foes, and the reduction of German strength in battleships and cruisers to a few scattered and mostly disabled units.

BY the time this article appears it is possible that the Soviet Black Sea Fleet may have been given an opportunity of striking a blow at the retreating Germans. With the cutting of all lines of retirement by land, the garrison of the Crimea, composed partly of German and partly of Rumanian troops, will be obliged to evacuate its positions by sea, the obvious route being from Sebastopol to Odessa or the Danube estuary. Provided the Russians are able to supply adequate air cover, their naval forces should be able to inflict severe losses on the enemy during their withdrawal.

In order to effect this evacuation, the Germans will need to collect every available ship capable of being used as a temporary

transport. In the Rumanian and Bulgarian mercantile marines there were, before the war, about 50 vessels aggregating nearly 130,000 tons gross, all of which should be more or less suitable for the purpose, in view of the short distance to be covered. From Sebastopol to Odessa is 170 miles ; to Sulina, at the mouth of the Danube, is a trifle less. In fine weather flat-bottomed barges from the Danube could be filled with troops and taken in tow ; but weather in the Black Sea is notoriously fickle, gales springing up with little warning.

Novorossisk, 217 miles from Sebastopol, is the nearest Soviet naval base. Already ships from there have been active in covering the landing of Russian troops near Kerch, in the Eastern Crimea. Very little is known about the present strength of the Russian Black Sea Fleet, official information being practically nil. There were four or five cruisers originally, but one or two of these are suspected to have been lost. There is also an old battleship, the Pariskaya Kommuna, still useful for bombardment purposes, at least 20 destroyers, and a large number of m.t.b.s, motor launches and submarines. A small seaplane carrier is also believed to exist.

Such a force should be able to inflict heavy damage on evacuation craft, especially if well supported from the air. Against it the Germans can muster but a motley assemblage of warships of different nationalities. These comprise two or three Rumanian destroyers, a small number of motor torpedo-boats originally belonging to Rumania, Bulgaria and Italy, but now probably German-manned ; three Rumanian submarines, believed to have been reinforced by others brought down the Danube from Germany ; three gunboats, a minelayer, and sundry smaller craft of little fighting value belonging to the Rumanian and Bulgarian Navies. That the question of finding trained personnel for this heterogeneous armada is giving the enemy trouble there can be no doubt. Submarine losses have been a constant drain on Germany's naval personnel ; the quality of Rumanian and Bulgarian naval officers and men cannot be expected to be high, and their enthusiasm for an obviously lost cause may well be questioned.

WITH the publication of the joint Anglo-American announcement on November 10, it became plain to the world that for six months the U-boats in the Atlantic had been waging a losing war. How heavily they have lost may be realized when a comparison is made with the last war. In the six months from May to October last, 150 enemy submarines were destroyed. During 1914-1918 the heaviest losses sustained in any period of six months amounted to no more than one-third of this figure ; and in the whole of the 4½ years of the last war, only 178 U-boats were sunk—a total which must have been exceeded in this present year alone.

It should be emphasized that the wastage of trained personnel involved is even more serious for the Germans than the loss of U-boats. In 1918 this proved an important factor in the defeat of the enemy submarine campaign, veteran crews of the older U-boats having to be broken up to provide a nucleus of experienced hands for the complements of new submarines. There is reason to suspect, moreover, that the ablest and most daring U-boat captains have been killed or captured, leaving less enterprising men in command of the submarines that remain in service.

# Allies Prepare for Landing at a Japanese Base

BOUND FOR LAE, capital of New Guinea, this Allied troopship is packed with our men and their supplies. The latter are expertly arranged on the deck and protected by tarpaulins, ready to be unloaded without delay as soon as the landing is made. Transports such as this, bearing Australian troops, played a vital part in the brilliant air-land-sea operation (see page 269) which led to the capture of Lae on September 16, 1943. " A victory," declared Gen. MacArthur, " which is a serious blow to the enemy. With God's help we are making our way back!"   *New York Times Photos.*

# Game as Terriers are the Navy's Destroyers

First out of port when the call comes, first in the fight, the last to return to the home base—such is the glorious tradition of the "trouble ships" of our Fleet, some of whose astonishing adventures and feats of endurance are narrated by MARK PRIESTLEY. See also facing page.

IN four years of war the destroyer H.M.S. Foxhound has steamed 240,000 miles over most of the oceans of the world. It is—claims her commander, Cmdr. C. J. Wynne-Edwards, D.S.C.—a record unequalled by any other ship of the Allied Navies or Merchant Fleets.

She has fought everywhere, from one of the earliest U-boat kills off the Orkneys to playing her share in Italian waters in recent months. She has sailed to Norway, Malta, Iceland, Madagascar, New York, Oran, Cape Town, Sardinia and India, and was bombed in the London docks at the height of the Battle of Britain. Her history, in fact, is one of months of seagoing in every kind of weather, interspersed with only short periods in harbour and, once a year, the essential refit. Fourteen hundred and twenty-six days of non-stop vigilance, with "Action Stations" always just around the corner, and constant careful tending of high-powered machinery, are only a part of the achievement of her crew ; and her story is not unique in the annals of the salt-encrusted "trouble ships" of the Fleet.

Traditionally, the destroyer is the first of all fighting ships to leave port, the first to fight, and the last to return to the relative inactivity of an anchorage. There is the vivid instance of H.M.S. Vimy, which lost a screw when ramming a U-boat—and escorted a convoy 6,000 miles to North Africa before putting in for repairs. Again, there is the amazing mileage of the old Windsor, one of the first destroyers to reach Dunkirk (for the evacuation of our troops from France). In eight months she steamed 30,000 miles, and in one month completed 4,060 miles. In 1941 a six months' commission involved 16,000 miles, and in 1942 she logged another 24,000.

ONE of her sister ships, H.M.S. Woolston, celebrated her twenty-fifth birthday by escorting a troop convoy towards the landing beaches of Sicily. " The Army is dependent upon us. We will not let them down," Lieut. F. W. Hawkins had told his ship's company. For nine days the Woolston patrolled for lurking U-boats off Sicily, brought enemy planes crashing in flames, and of 62 days she spent 60 at sea.

Consider, also, the feat of the Lamerton, one of the Hunt class destroyers which kept up a shuttle service to the firing courses off Salerno. Leading up to the invasion and escorting the first Allied landings in North Africa, H.M.S. Lamerton convoyed 150,000 troops from point to point along the coast, and in one period of 61 days spent 56 at sea. Her gunnery officer, Lieut. A. G. Gardner, has been mentioned in dispatches for sinking an Axis submarine with his second salvo.

The Kelvin and the Javelin together sank eleven ships in three hours in attacking an

**AN OFFICER OF H.M.S. FOXHOUND** watches a British base come into sight. As soon as this destroyer drops anchor she will have completed the astonishing distance of 240,000 miles, on most of the Seven Seas.
*Photo, British Official : Crown Copyright*

enemy coastal convoy. The Kelvin's first salvo sank one of the ships. Simultaneously, the Javelin was staging what the Admiralty has since described as one of the most spectacular close-range sinkings of the Mediterranean war. Dashing across the bows of an enemy corvette at only ten yards range, the Javelin's gunners hurled two depth-charges, one on each side of her. Set at the minimum depth, the charges blew the enemy out of the water.

So it goes with the "terriers," feats and adventures piling together and record eclipsing record. H.M.S. Boreas, commanded by Lieut.-Cmdr. E. L. Jones, D.S.C., steamed 183,244 miles with the same ship's company between December 1941, and the Sicilian landings in 1943. The "go anywhere, do anything" spirit of her kind was epitomized in 439 days under way in the South Atlantic and elsewhere, and particularly when she found herself steaming inland up the Congo River at 22 knots. When she had been abroad for 14 months she arrived at Plymouth from Gibraltar. Within 24 hours she had sailed again—back to the Mediterranean.

There is the endurance feat of H.M.S. Offa, one of the destroyers which helped to

pile Atlantic U-boat sinkings last May up to the grand record of thirty or more. In the 21 months since her commissioning she has steamed 80,000 miles, 8,000 of them in 25 days. Another ship, H.M.S. Matchless, in a similar period, has escorted at least three Russian convoys, survived 269 air raids at Malta, acted as a screen to units of the Home Fleet, and at one time picked up more than two hundred survivors—more than the number of her own crew. Forty officers, at a tight squeeze, were quartered in her wardroom.

NATURALLY, the destroyer's role has its lighter side. Talking in a wardroom recently I was told of the laugh at the expense of H.M.S. Churchill when during darkness she imagined the 200-foot length of La Sola Island could be nothing but a U-boat, attacked it with depth-charges, and then tried to sink it by ramming. The officers of H.M.S. Tanatside, too, had a shock when they took evasive action against two torpedoes approaching to starboard. Lieut.-Cmdr. F. D. Brown, in command, immediately swung around, but to his amazement the torpedoes also turned on their course and continued to skim towards the destroyer. "There was nothing we could do," Sub.-Lieut. K. W. Rymer told me. " We watched the torpedoes getting nearer and nearer and were all ready for the impact. Suddenly they turned right about and disappeared. They were two porpoises ! "

Believe it or not, another destroyer, H.M.S. Ripley, when shrouded in fog off the East Coast, nosed her way into a cave from which, local superstition avers, no ship aground is ever refloated. But the Ripley was refloated ; it takes more than a cave to sink a destroyer.

In last year's Atlantic gales—the worst of a century—the Witch, Vanessa and Skate were all dismasted by the weight of ice forming overnight on their crosstrees. The Shikari, with her commander, Lieut.-Cmdr. Derek Williams, lashed for five days and nights to the bridge, lost a funnel. But all returned safely, after innumerable personal hazards faced by every man of the crews.

I can conclude on no more typical note than the story of an episode aboard H.M.S. Oribi. While the destroyer laboured through heavy seas, a young sub-lieutenant was sitting in the wardroom. There came a fearful roll, and the young officer was pitched through the air to crash head first against a bulkhead thirty feet away. His skull looked like an egg hit by a spoon. With the gale still at its height and six inches of water swilling around in the wardroom, the young ship's doctor—Surgeon-Lieut. Thomas Smith—lashed his patient to a settee, and operated while ratings steadied doctor and patient. This amazing scene lasted for over an hour, and the young officer's life was saved.

**TWO OF THE NAVY'S 'TERRIERS'** with notable records. (Left) H.M.S. Matchless, commissioned in February 1942, in her first year at sea three times ran the gauntlet with convoys to Russia, met the Italian fleet in battle, and survived 269 air raids at Malta. She has acted as a screen to units of the Home Fleet, and once picked up more than 200 survivors. (Right) H.M.S. Vanessa, which with H.M.S. Hesperus rammed a U-boat to destruction in the early part of this year.

*Photos, British Official : Crown Copyright*

# Mascots are Prized in our Famed 'Trouble Ships'

H.M.S. FOXHOUND'S BELL has its clapper appropriately adorned with a "brush" (1), gift of a fox-hunting officer of the destroyer. Lively ornament of the Kelvin's bell (2) is Splinters the cat. Peanut the monkey (3) is the agile mascot of the Witch; this destroyer claims to have aboard more veteran seamen than any other ship of her size in the Royal Navy. Mascots may or may not bring good luck; the navigating officer places more reliance in the Pelorus Sight (4), an instrument on the bridge for taking bearings. A good "pull up" is the depot ship (5), where minor repairs can be executed and supplies obtained. See also facing page.

*Photos, British Official: Crown Copyright*

# Scene of Contrasts is Unconquerable Leningrad

**SECOND CITY OF THE SOVIETS,** the northern citadel which the Germans could not reduce even after 16 months' siege, Leningrad today presents strange contrasts of peacetime calm and wartime activity. A Red Army girl (1) reads a poster-poem of exhortation, entitled "Kill him!" while workmen (2) complete the filling of a bomb crater. Under escort, Nazi prisoners (3) are marched along a crowded street. By the Neva, A.A. guns (4) are on the alert, while youngsters contentedly fish (5) ; in the background is St. Isaac's Cathedral.

*Photos Exclusive to* THE WAR ILLUSTRATED

# Orphans of the Siege Now Wards of the City

**THESE LENINGRAD KIDDIES,** who lost their parents during the long and memorable siege and are now the especial care of the city authorities, know exactly what to do—young as they are—when an alert sounds or a shell comes whistling over. Their home is close to Leningrad's famous landmark, the tall-spired old Admiralty Building (in background) at the end of the main thoroughfare, the Prospect of October 25, and overlooking the trees of The Garden of the Toilers.

*Photo, Pictorial Press—Exclusive to* THE WAR ILLUSTRATED

# Unity in War and Peace Pledged at Moscow

Cartoon by Low; courtesy of The Evening Standard

**R**ESULTS OF THE CONFERENCE of the Foreign Secretaries of the United Kingdom, the U.S.S.R. and the U.S.A., which took place at Moscow, October 19-30, 1943, were announced on November 1. Major decisions were:

### THE WAR IN EUROPE

Closest military cooperation in future between the three Powers, aimed at shortening the war by compelling the unconditional surrender of Germany and her satellites. Three-Power Commission to be set up in London to advise on European questions arising as the war develops.

### POST-WAR SECURITY

Close collaboration thus pledged to be continued after hostilities cease, for the organization of peace and security. A general international organization, based on the sovereign equality of, and open to, all peace-loving states, to be set up as soon as practicable. Armaments to be regulated by agreement. [China joined the Three Powers in this declaration.]

### FUTURE OF ITALY

Fascism to be utterly destroyed. Fascist officials suspected of being war criminals to be handed over to justice. Prisoners of the Fascist regime to be released with full amnesty. Freed Italy to choose her own form of government. An Advisory Council, to co-ordinate Allied policy on day-to-day Italian non-military questions, to be set up with Fighting French (and possibly Greek and Yugoslav) representation.

### FUTURE OF AUSTRIA

Independence of Austria to be restored. Account to be taken, in final settlement, of her own efforts towards liberation.

### ATROCITIES : WAR CRIMINALS

Germans implicated in atrocities to be taken to scene of their crimes, there to be dealt with according to local laws. Germans whose offences have no particular geographical location to be punished by joint decision of the Allies.

**COMPLETE SUCCESS** of the Three-Power Conference —unity in war and peace—is symbolized in the cartoon (top left). At Moscow airport M. Molotov, Soviet Commissar for Foreign Affairs, met Mr. Anthony Eden, British Foreign Secretary (above), and Mr. Cordell Hull, American Secretary of State (centre left). Round the conference table (left): 1, M. Molotov ; 2, Voroshilov ; 3, Sir Hastings Ismay; 4, Sir A. Clark Kerr; 5, Mr. Eden; 6, Mr. William Strang ; 7, Maj.-Gen. John R. Deane ; 8, Mr. James Dunn ; 9, Mr. Averell Harriman ; 10, Mr. Cordell Hull ; 11, Mr. Green Hackworth ; 12, M. Litvinov ; 13, M. Vyshinski.

Marshal Stalin, President Roosevelt and Mr. Churchill have all expressed great satisfaction at the results of the Conference.

*Photos, Pictorial Press*

# Two Red Armies Rout Mannstein's Million

TWIN SOVIET THRUSTS, launched from Kremenchug (see page 365) on October 19, 1943, and from Melitopol four days later, in a fortnight demoralized Field-Marshal Mannstein's million-strong 6th German Army in the Dnieper Bend and the Nogaisk Steppe, and bottled up his Crimean forces by the capture of Perekop on November

General Malinovsky (3) led the 3rd Ukrainian Forces of the Red Army to take Dnepropetrovsk (2), great engineering town and military stronghold in the north-east corner of the Dnieper Bend, on October 25. General Tolbukhin (1) commanded on the 4th Ukrainian Front, which crumbled following the taking of Melitopol on October 23, after ten days' fierce fighting by such as this gun crew (4), and this Russian infantry patrol (5) warily stalking the enemy. After Melitopol, the Red Army surged westwards across the Nogaisk Steppe, its formidable and victorious armour including camouflaged tanks (6). (See map in p. 387).

*Photos, U.S.S.R. Official, Pictorial Press, Planet News*

# Hitler Plans to Prevent a German 'Badoglio'

No one has studied more closely the fall of Mussolini and the rise of Badoglio than Hitler and the Junker generals. In this article Dr. EDGAR STERN-RUBARTH discusses the rivalry between the Leader of the Nazis and the Prussian military clique, and shows how Hitler has been attempting to forestall a move to replace him in order to sue for peace.

WHATEVER blunders Hitler has committed, nobody can deny that he has shown skill and cunning in dealing with his underlings. He has played one against the other—never granting his full confidence to any one of them; consistently encouraging their rivalries; always assuring that their powers overlap; carefully preventing the formation of one or several groups likely to become the nucleus of a rebellion against his own rule.

The haughty, aristocratic, ice-cold Prussian officers, hard set in the traditions of the great Emperor Frederick, were always the greatest danger. So he pampered, promoted, decorated and flattered them. As long as " his " war seemed an unlimited success, they might grumble about this and that—such as old lags and gangsters among Hitler's Black Guards being forced into their exclusive corps, or their own advice despised by the " inspired " ex-lance-corporal when he played the strategist—but they went on obeying.

When it happened that a leading general became too unruly about some such point,

under, to put it mildly, mysterious circumstances—such as Col.-General Ernst Udet, the air ace; Col. Moelders, his Roman Catholic runner-up; Field-Marshal von Reichenau; and, quite recently, Col.-General Hans Jeschonnek, Chief of Air Staff, and General von Chamier-Glyszinski, the "secret weapons" expert.

This list is far from complete, but it provides a startling commentary on the favours bestowed upon his generals by the victorious Fuehrer: fifteen Field-Marshal's ranks—as against Wilhelm II's total of seven, during the last war, of which three were mere courtesy titles for princes of ruling royal houses—and oak leaves and knight's crosses galore! No fewer than ten, among these fifteen Field-Marshals, by the way, belong to the Prussian nobility, the "Junkers." They represent that tradition of which the poet Chamisso sang, nearly 120 years ago:

*Und der Koenig absolut*
*Wenn er unseren Willen tut*
(Grant the King omnipotence
If to our will he bends).

They always were, and are today, successful plotters, taciturn, race- and caste-proud, staunch patriots in their own medieval way and, unlike the German man-in-the-street, wholly unsentimental. Bock is perhaps their most characteristic representative—a spare, tough man of 65, the last survivor of Hindenburg's staff, a general whom even in peacetime his troops called *Der Sterber*—the "die-er"—because he always told them that their task in life was to die on a battlefield. This Pomeranian baron is, undoubtedly, the leading figure of the generals' "Junta" which during the past two years has developed inside Hitler's European fortress.

HIGH-RANKING GERMAN OFFICERS who have disappeared mysteriously include Col.-Gen Hans Jeschonnek who until his death (announced on Aug. 21, 1942) had been Chief of Air Staff. He was succeeded by Gen. Korten (right), seen here in conference with Field-Marshal Goering, German Air Minister (left) and Gen. Doerzor (centre). *Photo, Fox*

usual, sneering army-slang, more than once within the clandestine conventicles of that half-dozen or so Junker generals who, regardless of Himmler and his recently increased powers over life and death, in fact control Germany's fate. It was they who inspired the plan of a withdrawal from the far-flung borders of Hitler's "Fortress Europe" to the walls of their "Citadel Germany." And it was they who launched the slogan "Hitler's Secret Weapon is—a separate peace with Russia "!

For months they tried hard enough to make that dream come true. They had to use devious ways in approaching their Russian counterparts, via Stockholm, Ankara, or even Tokyo. They had to use shady go-betweens. But they were inspired by an idea: beyond their respective national interests there was a professional one, a military-caste solidarity, and in the event of a victory of the Allies the role of that caste might be abolished, and not only in Germany!

THEY had powerful contacts, for because of the Versailles restrictions the republican Reichswehr had for years tried out all its new armament gadgets on Russia's vast fields and in cooperation with her air force. General von Niedermeyer, then a "professor" of military history at the Berlin University, had for years been head of that unofficial cooperation department and gone to and fro between Moscow and Berlin.

Of course, Germany would have to pay a price—the Nazi government system would be eliminated and a semi- or pseudo-Bolshevist regime under close military control established. And not only would Germany consent to return to her 1939 frontiers, she would lend technical and material help for Russia's reconstruction. But think of the prospects: while the concentrated power of Germany, no longer engaged against Russia, would smash the "plutocracies," Moscow could direct the Red Army southward, to gain ports on the shores of the Indian Ocean!

Almost needless to say, this Junkers scheme never got very far in the Kremlin. Its basic idea, however, has not been abandoned—the generals are prepared to sacrifice their "Supreme War Lord" and all he stands for if it offers them the slightest chance of retaining thereby their own social and professional privileges. They would like to effect a deal with whoever is prepared to bargain, and they have carefully watched the Badoglio business. The Allied treatment of the first Axis power to surrender they have considered a test case, a guide for their own future action.

THEIR attitude is no longer a secret even to the Nazis, some of whom have for the last few months tried hard to get into the fold of the Junta—Hermann Goering hardest of all. It is proof of the generals' solidly established power outside the Nazi Party machine that they are unafraid of Himmler and his new powers, so ruthlessly exercised on German civilians as well as on other peoples.

Such Hitler yes-men as Jodl, Zeitzler, Doenitz and Keitel have no access to their inner circle. And so when early in October Hitler suddenly got a new inspiration and surprised the army leaders in the East with a visit and a "stand-fast order" the event may have had particular significance. He apears to have ceased interfering with strategy. Possibly having heard of the plotters' disappointment over the Russian campaign, he may have thought it wise to show them a friendly grin when their fortunes were lowest. He, too, has had an eye on recent events in Italy!

Hitler would fall into an opportune hysteria and thereby force him to resign. Witness his C.-in-C., von Brauchitsch, early in the winter of 1941, when he insisted upon withdrawing the forces in Russia into well-prepared winter quarters. Or von Bock—at the same period, for not smashing his way into Moscow; then, after being re-employed for the 1942 summer campaign, for calling the Stalingrad-Caucasus adventure what it was, a suicidal madness. Or Field-Marshal von Leeb, because he could not vanquish indomitable Leningrad, first in April, 1942, and after having agreed to try again this spring.

ONE of the first seven Field-Marshals Hitler created after overrunning France, Blaskowitz, seems to have anticipated that development; he put his new baton in a cupboard, bought himself mufti, and stayed as a civilian in Paris!

Others were disfavoured under less publicized circumstances—Col.-General Franz Halder, Chief of General Staff and Germany's outstanding strategist; Guderian, creator of Hitler's tank-arm; Admiral of the Fleet Erich Raeder, to quote only the best-known of them. Or they lost their lives

veloped inside Hitler's European fortress.

Field-Marshal von Brauchitsch is its politician. Smooth, clever, be-monocled, with cynical smile, he never completely fell out with Hitler. Since losing his supreme command, he allowed himself to be nominally registered with the High Command's Reserve of Army Leaders, as did a number of his comrades-in-disgrace, unlike implacable Field-Marshal von Leeb, a stubborn Bavarian. Brauchitsch knows how and when to drive home the fact that, contrary to Hitler's famous "intuition," his own knowledge of strategy always proved right, as when in early autumn 1941 he built the Dnieper winter line; or when he urged for motorized infantry and mobile supply columns; or when he wanted more fighter-cover and not so many of the vulnerable Stukas. Brauchitsch would have listened to well-nigh infallible, self-effacing Halder, and to Guderian, expert in tank-warfare—but Hitler did not and paid dearly for it. Or rather, the German people paid for his madcap adventures and megalomaniac dreams. And therefore . . .

That sentence has not been completed, as yet. It may have been rounded off, in their

## Free Again in a Free Land

"The way in which you have kept up your morale is in accordance with the best traditions of the fighting Services!" were the memorable words added by Gen. Sir Ronald F. Adam (top), Adjt.-Gen. to the Forces, to their Majesties' warm message of welcome which he conveyed to repatriated troops at Leith on October 25, 1943. With self-provided music and with broad smiles men crowd to disembark, and one at least knows what to do with an outsize British sandwich. (See also illus. page 359.)

*Photos Keystone*

## For This They Longed and Dreamed—

First to set foot ashore, one-armed Rev. A. Drummond Duff (in left-hand circle), Senior Chaplain to the 51st Division of glorious renown, has great stories to tell of fighting at St. Valery, France. So has the lance-corporal, though at the moment he has no thought but for Mother, and for Dad's back-pat. Gentle hands of the Red Cross guide uncertain feet, and a crippled officer is relieved of burdensome crutches by a private: in such moments all men are brothers.

## —Through Months and Years in Nazi Camps

The mere feel of a home newspaper but an hour or two old is a joy indeed. Troubles are forgotten. Even the hobblers make light of their handicap, and if a peg-leg needs adjusting there's ready help at hand. Some can't even hobble; for these there is sisterly attention and skill. Prone or walking, their destination is a hospital, with all its comfort and care, or a rest centre; and in due course Home to relatives and friends they hold most dear.

## For Them War Is Over

No heart-tearing lament the pipers played, but exultant skirl as to the landing-stage at Leith slid one crowded tender. Next day the hospital ship Atlantis (top) arrived at Liverpool with a further 764 disabled men. Boys in the Red Cross ambulances cannot see waving hands along the route, but with a catch in the throat they hear the welcoming roar. Worst of their anguish lies behind; ahead, a new and brighter chapter opens in their lives. (See also illus. page 416.)

*Photos, G.P.U., P.N.A. Daily Mirror*

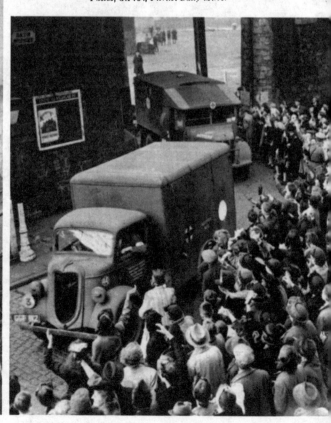

# VIEWS & REVIEWS
## Of Vital War Books

### by Hamilton Fyfe

It used to be supposed in this country that German army training made men into blindly obedient automata, incapable of more or less independent action, helpless if they were not told exactly what to do. That delusion was exploded for me, at any rate, in 1918, when I discovered by unpleasant experience how clever small parties of the enemy with machine-guns under command of sergeants or corporals could be in pushing forward—we called it then " infiltrating "—and breaking into our positions. The old idea that Germans could advance only in solid masses, shoulder to shoulder, blade by blade, had to be scrapped. The Kaiser's army had altered its methods to meet changing needs.

But how are we to reconcile the new idea with the mass surrenders at Stalingrad and (even more astonishing) in Tunisia? In droves the enemy gave themselves up; whole companies, battalions, regiments, surrendered in blocks; marched in good order to the rear, made no attempt to keep up the struggle, even when they found themselves in immensely greater strength than their guards. Alan Moorehead, in his new book The End in Africa (Hamish Hamilton, 10s. 6d.), tells how at one place there were not more than thirty British soldiers looking after about 5,000 prisoners. At another place a small contingent of our men " was completely surrounded by prisoners, and more coming in every minute." " God knows where they are supposed to go," a British sergeant said. " I just put 'em on the road and tell 'em to keep going! "

In a little seaport Moorehead and another correspondent ran into " a great crowd of Germans stranded there with their vehicles. They were entirely free to pick up the rifles they had laid down and shoot us. But they did not seem to be even morose or resentful. They were eager to be pleasant. . . . Their attitude was: ' Well, it's finished for me now. I don't have to fight any more. I can relax a bit.' " They were all sick and tired of army life, Moorehead says. But they would have obeyed, all the same, if they had been ordered to resist to the last man.

Rommel has shown that the Germans will go on fighting against impossible odds and take impossible risks so long as they are well controlled and officered.

They will keep at it if they are never given time to wonder how things are going. After Generals Alexander and Anderson had split the enemy force in two, half on Cape Bon Peninsula, half outside it, the German High Command was isolated from its troops, " who were for ever in doubt, and doubt created despair." This would have happened to any army in the last war. Now our battle training schools teach men independence in crises. It was not shown at Tobruk, but the troops there had not been through battle schools, which came into existence after their time of training.

In the absence of any battle plan, in their complete ignorance of what was happening and because they did not know when to fire or in which direction, the Tobruk garrison was mopped up piecemeal by the German forces and surrendered in one single day.

That was, fortunately, on a smaller scale than the Tunisian surrender, but they were both due, Moorehead says, to the same causes. That, it seems to me, should make the Allied commanders anxious to practise swift, ingenious tactics which will puzzle the German generals, cut them off perhaps from contact with their armies, reduce those armies to the condition of helpless uncertainty in which they were ready to give themselves up in Tunis. If such tactics had not been practised there, the bulk of the Nazi forces would have got away.

Moorehead's descriptions of the battles which led up to their annihilation (for prisoners are discounted equally with the dead) are, like those in his Year of Battle, vivid and brilliantly clear. These battles were altogether different from the desert

---

## Nazi Nemesis in North Africa

engagements, which covered enormous spaces of sand and consisted usually of a series of small encounters seeming to have little connexion. In Tunis the advances were made up mountain valleys, mostly narrow. You could stand on a mountain and watch the infantry going forward, then the tanks rolling up, then the enemy tanks emerging. You could follow every phase of the struggle. You could understand, as few people here at home seem to, why progress in these conditions must be slow; why " if you advance a thousand yards, it is considered a great achievement."

The men who make these day-by-day pushes that appear insignificant to those who do not know the obstacles they have to surmount, the opposition they must overcome from Nature as well as from Hitler, are brought before us as plainly as the scenes of battle. No use picturing them as " immaculate and shining young heroes agog with enthusiasm for the Cause. They have seen too much dirt and filth for that. They hate the war. They know it . . . They fight because they are part of a system,

part of a team. It is something they were obliged to do, and now they are in it they have a technical interest and a pride in it. They want to win and get out of it—the sooner the better."

That is why they, too, are impatient, as some folks are at home. They want to know what is being done by others. " How's the war going, mister? " they would ask, " bitter and contemptuous." . . . " Is there anyone doing anything besides us? " or " Where's the Eighth Army? Aren't they doing anything? "

Of many stories told by Moorehead to illustrate the demoniac dash and toughness of our men I have been thrilled especially by that of the major in the Argylls who led the final attack on Longstop Hill (you remember it?) and took this vital position, enabling General Alexander to prepare the crushing blows which followed. He stared in the dark up the first slopes. All that could be known about the enemy was that they were somewhere above. That was made clear by the fire and the flares that came down. The major stood up, waved his revolver, shouted to his men. " They swarmed up after him, as men will when they find a leader. He ran straight through the minefield and up through the darkness to the points where the yellow streams of bullets were coming out. He and his men yelled and screamed as they flung themselves upward. They got caught in barbed wire and clawed it aside. They jumped down into the dugouts on top of the Germans, firing as they jumped. That was one hill. Sheer rage carried them up the next slope, and again they broke through the wire and killed with the bayonet." Then a third time they swept on and up, and were successful once more.

It was near here that a young British gunner officer had his gun position overrun by the enemy. He put an Arab cloak over his uniform, hitched a plough on to his gun-towing tractor, and spent all that day ploughing round and round the field among the Germans. Night came, and in the darkness he coupled up one of his guns to the tractor and drove back to the British lines. So inextricably were the pursuits of peace mixed up with the operations of war in those fertile glens!

Whole-hearted is Moorehead's admiration for the men who fight—only one-fifth of the army, he reminds us, the four-fifths being occupied in keeping up the ceaseless flow of supplies. Not less comprehensive is his dislike of politicians, the men who talk. He was in Algiers about a year ago, after Darlan had been assassinated and when the quarrels between the de Gaullists and the Giraudists were most bitter. He thinks the United States Foreign Office made a great mistake in putting all its support behind Giraud and snubbing de Gaulle. It seems to have recognized this itself now. Moorehead hated Algiers then because of

the atmosphere of suspicion and bickering argument, the endless ferment in the streets, and the feeling that the intrigues (of French politicians) were a mean and petty betrayal of the men at the front, who were fighting for something quite different.

The position has been clarified to some extent by the recent announcement from Algiers that de Gaulle has now assumed full, undivided presidential control of the French Committee of National Liberation, Giraud remaining C.-in-C. of the Fighting French Forces.

**MASS CAPITULATION** in Tunisia, described in the book reviewed in this page, resulted in such curious situations as this: a German staff car is seen speeding towards Tunis to surrender, while Italian prisoners of war are marching away from the city to wired-in desert camps awaiting them. Once " registered " in Tunis the Germans would make a similar pilgrimage, this time on foot. PAGE 403 *Photo, British Official*

# How France Raised A Secret Desert Army

Behind the achievements of North African native warriors in the Tunisia and Sicily fighting, and in the freeing of Corsica, is a remarkable story of French resourcefulness in defeat, related here by ANDREW STEWART. He tells how, under the very noses of the Germans, France began to rebuild her shattered military forces in preparation for her revenge.

WHEN Goumiers entered Bastia, northern port and former capital of Corsica, on the morning of October 4, 1943, fourteen days after the first French Commandos had landed to join the island patriots, they enabled French High Command to announce: "The liberation of Corsica is achieved."

Thus they added further laurels to the reputation of doughty and fearless fighters which they had won during the Tunisian campaign and in Sicily. But what still is not generally known is how they and their North African comrades in arms—the Tabors of Morocco and the Maghzens of Tunisia—were welded into a secret army of some 50,000 men right under the noses of the Germans, from the time of the Armistice in France, June 21, 1940, to the Allied landing in North Africa, November 8, 1942.

During the agonizing months of May-June 1940, submerged by the German tide of metal, the French Government had called on all available reinforcements from North Africa. The bulk of the North African army of 10,000 officers and 400,000 men was sent to France, and of them only an insignificant number escaped to North Africa after the collapse—with no war material.

But under the Armistice Convention a small army of 120,000 men, armed with obsolete weapons and not permitted tanks, was conceded to France for the governance of her Empire. Immediately, the French Command in North Africa decided on a three-point policy: to make an *élite* of the authorized troops; to organize into police forces and labouring gangs as many native troops as possible; and to camouflage what unused military stores there remained—and what would in due course be forthcoming from Britain and America—so as to be able to change these undeclared troops into a regular, army when the moment came to strike again at the enemy.

So well were these secret plans prosecuted that when the great Allied landing of November 8, 1942, took place, France was able to place in the field, alongside 122,000 "authorized" Empire troops (negotiations had resulted in an increase of 2,000 in the Armistice Convention allotment), a body of some 60,000 fully armed and practised soldiers, consisting of 10,000 troops brought from Syria and 50,000 secretly-raised men comprising Goums, Maghzens and Tabors. In addition were some 1,500-2,000 volunteers, who had never been enrolled in the regular army before the collapse and who had not been declared to the Germans; 4,600 natives who.

camouflaged as "workers," had been drilled and armed; and 10,000 officers who had been disguised as Civil Servants.

To maintain so many men in arms without the knowledge of the supposedly vigilant enemy was no mean task. After all, the Germans were masters themselves of this art of raising secret armies. For it was by such camouflage that between 1920 and 1935 they built up their own Wehrmacht in defiance of the Treaty of Versailles. But the French did it. First they destroyed all documents relating to military material existing at the time of the defeat. Then all armaments remaining in North African dumps were dispersed and hidden in mountain caves, mine-wells, garages and houses.

Some 20,000 tons of actual metal of military value was also hidden. Part of it, according to sound detective story theory, was scattered on railway tracks in full sight of the enemy, if only he had eyes to see—molybdenum, aluminium and nickel amongst it.

ALMOST overnight, tanks, planes, machine-guns, mortars and cases of ammunition disappeared. Only one of the many secret dumps was ever discovered, and that was in the private house of a French officer. No higher tribute than this can be paid to the loyalty of the natives, thousands of whom

necessarily knew of the various secret *caches*. This loyalty to a stricken France is one of the outstanding features of the Goumiers. It is understandable enough. Loyalty among these people takes a personal form: when an officer has lived for a time in one district he wins the undying adherence of the natives under his charge.

Since a handful of first-class French officers with desert experience survived the collapse of May-June 1940 and returned to North Africa the Goums were sure to survive under them; but the problem was, how to maintain these groups of tribesmen-warriors in full training and competently equipped without the supervising Germans knowing.

WHAT was done with documents and material has already been described. The problem of personnel was tackled in equally efficient fashion. Officers resigned their commissions and took over jobs as native overseers and what not. Natives were enrolled as policemen and in work gangs. And an elaborate technique of using authorized troop-training facilities for the irregulars was planned. For example, a regular troop would forget to carry off its weapons after target practice. Curiously enough, a detachment of Goumiers would pass that way soon after and indulge in practice until such time as the regulars remembered to return for their arms! Suspicions grew. The Nazis demanded the dispersal of the native "police" units. French cunning triumphed.

"If you knew the country," they protested to the German High Command, "you would know that of late the tribes have been very restive. Remove those police detachments and you will require ten or fifteen divisions to restore order. Can you really afford that?"

"But," the Germans insisted, "who commands these forces?"

"Civilian controllers."

"Who appoints them?"

"The Director of Political Affairs. Which is to say, the Resident-General. That is the Sultan."

"Not the Army?"

"Of course not!"

"But look here," the Germans argued, "you have three sorts of Goums, which you call A, B and C. Now, why?"

This was very embarrassing to the French, for in fact the three types of Goums corresponded to three types of military detachments.

"Oh, there are three types of rebel native tribes," they urbanely explained. And they got away with it. Later, one of the regular Moroccan regiments was disbanded by the Germans. But that just meant that they became "workers" once again—and the building of the secret army went on!

SOLDIERS OF FREE FRANCE'S AFRICAN ARMY, a Goumier sharpens his bayonet in readiness for the attack. Though he has left his village, family and flocks for the battlefield, he still clings to his traditional robe, seeing nothing incongruous in the contrast it makes with his modern helmet, equipment, and rifle. PAGE 404 *Photo, Planet News*

# Valiant Goums in their Age-Old Battle Garb

**DESERT WARRIORS OF FIGHTING FRANCE**, the Goums include some of the most picturesque figures in the Ballied Armies. This Goumier (3) has a distinctive hair-style. His comrades (2), here being inspected by General Giraud, Free French C.-in-C., go into battle in their tribal garb. The Goums, who are officered by Frenchmen, were trained in the desert (see facing page). They march past their commanders (1). They fought magnificently in Tunisia and Sicily, where they marched (4) side by side with their American allies, sharing supplies and the hazards of battle, and they played a great part in the liberation of Corsica.

PAGE 405 *Photos, Service Cinématographique de l'Armée, Keystone*

# No 'Hitler Youth' Is the Army Cadet Force

One way of entering the British Army is through the Army Cadet Force. How widely severed in ideals of service this Force is from the Hitler Jugend, and how sane is the training given these Cadets, is explained here by Capt. J. D. Gruban, Regimental Physical Training Officer to the 61st (Mdx.) Cadet Regiment, R.A., in an interview with Capt. MARTIN THORNHILL, M.C.

BOYS of the Hitler Youth, with their "Hitler Jugend" membership labels still in their pockets, have been identified among Kesselring's troops in Italy. These youngsters, after steeping for ten impressionable years in the perverted Nazi ideology, are emerging to take their place as serving soldiers of the Reich. They are trained to Nazi perfection in all the brutal savagery and regimented ruffianism which are the basis of this Hitler-sired movement. But although fed since kindergarten days on lies, viciousness, arrogance, hardness of heart and Hitler-worship, strangely allied with physical excellence, these fanatic youths are not shaping as the first-class Nazi-pattern soldiers their trainers predicted. Faced with the hard knocks of battle, they are surprised to find that the "contemptible" foe, waiting, as they had been led to believe, browbeaten, to be robbed and butchered, has instead a healthy come-back which hurts.

For this surprising foe has been nurtured on ideals too—sound ideals having fundamentals of courtesy and chivalry, courage and a corporate spirit which long since set standards for British youth. They come largely from the Hitler Youth's opposite number, the British Army Cadet Force, which provides the raw material for our own fighting service—material which combines four essentials that make the best fighting man: true comradeship, training, discipline, and leadership.

For over fifty years the Army Cadet Force has sought to fulfil this task, under its Colonel-in-Chief, the King. During that period the training has been so systematized and improved that at the end of it cadets now enter the Army as potential N.C.O.s and officers. That the Force is achieving its objects is proved by the Government announcement on Nov. 9, 1943, that it (and other pre-service cadet organizations) would be continued, on a voluntary basis, after the war.

THE eligible-age span of our Army Cadet Force is from 14 to 17 years. Having taken Certificate A (part 1), at the age of 15 a cadet is tested as to his proficiency in, particularly, fieldcraft. If found satisfactory, he proceeds to part 2—the "Leaders' Section"—and to pass this requires a high standard of knowledge and efficiency. War Office policy directs that no part of the training we give shall go to waste, so commanding officers in the fighting forces are constantly reminded that Army Cadets with Cert. A and a good report from their own C.O. should be singled out for further leadership training. Thus, always at Army call is a constant flow of young, qualified men with years of pre-service, ready for further training to make them eligible for junior leadership.

I am frequently asked if the Junior Training Corps and the Senior Training Corps are a part of the Army Cadet Force. In the eyes of the War Office they are one. The distinction, if any, is purely domestic. Briefly, the J.T.C. and the S.T.C. are school units, and as their aggregate is relatively small they are administered directly from the War Office. The A.C.F. proper is directed through the County Cadet Committees, who, in turn, receive instructions from the War Office.

THESE "open" cadet units cater for boys from anywhere—boys still at school (but with no school unit), and youngsters who, covered by the call-up of young age-groups, are already on national service. That, however, and the fact that thousands of them work eight hours every day, does not deter large numbers from joining the A.C.F. Mere boys, they acquit themselves like men. They work like men, they train like men, and soon they may be wanted to fight like men.

And well the Army Cadet knows it. It is this spirit—the zealous will of the cadet to

GERMAN SEA-SCOUTS, part of the Nazi Youth organization "Hitler Jugend," inspected by Admiral Doenitz, who, on January 30, 1943, succeeded Admiral Raeder as C.-in-C. of the German Navy. The fundamental differences between the Nazi and British ideals and methods of training youth are made clear in the authoritative article in this page. *Photo, Keystone*

prepare and perfect himself for Army leadership—that keeps the whole organization alive; it is the hidden power that has hoisted the movement to the pitch of vast national importance. All—officers and cadets—are volunteers; there is no compulsion of any kind from any quarter. The officers hail from all walks of life, and they combine many qualities. Their particular job is to see that the training syllabus as laid down by the authorities is carried out.

Nearly all these officers enjoy the full confidence of those they teach. For the most part they are natural-born instructors; among them are many fine physical training leaders, fully trained in Swedish P.T. and Commando-like practice with ropes, scales and other equipment for the crossing of rivers and all kinds of obstacles. All are, in short, leaders of youth who realize the urgent need to pilot the young into manhood that is strong in body and mind, with an awareness of country and Empire, and proud enough of it to be ready to fight for it if they have to. It may be news to some of the critics of modern youth that, to the great majority of young and ardent sons of our old democracy, "For King and Country" is a deeply cherished motto and not a cheap slogan.

We of the Army Cadet Force are fully aware that it will be up to us to take a major part in the work of reconstruction for lasting peace after our fathers and brothers have

laid its foundations through force of arms. With the help of our brothers and sisters of Allied nations we shall also set to work to reshape the minds of the unfortunates who have been victims of the criminal misguidance of Hitlerism.

Time marches on—so does the Army Cadet Force. And as it comes more and more into the forefront, open appraisal is expected. Constructive criticism—safety valve of the true democracy—is helpful. But already there are some who accuse us of regimenting the boys on the model of the Hitler Jugend. To these I would say that there was an Army Cadet movement in Britain while Adolf Hitler was still on the bottle. Baldur von Schirach, Chief Youth Leader, hadn't even reached that stage.

The Hitler Jugend was, and still is, a political expedient—political progression from Nazi theology to Nazi warfare. It starts, in fact, in the kindergarten. Children too young for admission to the Hitler Youth join the "Jungvolk," where the same doctrines are taught. Well knowing the susceptibility of young minds, Hitler, assisted by his team of political, physiological and psychological experts, set to work to shape a new Germany which would offer itself, without reserve, to the Fuehrer and his direction. Fanatical—that has been Hitler's favourite word in all references to the motive power of his movement, and, indeed, of the Third Reich generally. It typifies the spirit that actuates practically all Germany's youth today.

This is no ill-considered indictment. Individuality of thought and action has not been tolerated since the Hitler debut. Individuality, as we know and encourage and practise it, never at any time really existed in Germany—least of all in Prussia, the seat of all things characteristically German. But it was when the old Republican flag was replaced by the swastika banner that the mantle of leadership began to fall not on the senior, not on the meritorious, but on the bully and the cad. For brute strength was to play the big, the only part in the nation-wide expansion and perfection of the rising Youth Movement.

WITH this concept firmly in mind, Reichs Sports-Fuehrer von Schammer-Osten began the job of preparing and maintaining the biggest scheme of national physical training the world has ever known. No effort or expense was spared in the Reich-wide campaign to build up the new Hitler Jugend. Was it not to recruit the ranks of Germany's all-powerful army of tomorrow, and, in particular, to furnish its invincible leaders?

The physical destruction of this still mighty army, incorporating Nazism, Prussianism, and a score of other military "isms" with a Fascist sting, is a matter for the Allied armed forces. Germany will admit no other form of defeat. And when that has been achieved, so far from ever having had the slightest ideal in common with the Hitler Youth, Britain's Army of Youth may yet be the moral force that will set doubts tingling in the tight-locked minds of young post-war Germans.

# Learning to Be Soldiers on the A.C.F. Plan

PRE-SERVICE TRAINING for some 180,000 boys is now provided by the Army Cadet Force (see facing page). For over 50 years this organization, of which H.M. the King is now Colonel-in-Chief, has groomed boys of 14-17 intending to make the Army their career. Now that all youths aged 18 may be called up for national service, there has been a great extension of the organization to cater for those who desire to be " broken in " before their time comes. This year some 100,000 such lads attended camps, where they heard lectures, saw demonstrations and engaged in actual field exercises. From reveille (4) to lights-out they lived as soldiers. Here some of them are watching a mortar being fired (1), scaling a wall (2) in true Commando fashion, and enjoying cookhouse fatigue (3).

*Photos, British Official: Crown Copyright; L.N.A., Topical Press*

# Allies Guard Oil in Netherlands West Indies

Photos, Exclusive to THE WAR ILLUSTRATED

PRECIOUS OIL REFINERIES in Curaçao and Aruba, Netherlands West Indies (see map), are guarded by Anglo-American and Dutch forces. U.S. troops (1) are on duty at the enormous Lagoen plant, Aruba. This Javanese marine (2) is one of the Dutch garrison on Curaçao, where also are men of the Shropshire Light Infantry (5), here seen on manoeuvres, in Suffisant. Commanding the Dutch forces is Col. C. J. van Asbeck (4, right), seen here with Rear-Admiral Robinson, C.-in-C. Anglo-American forces. Coastal batteries (3) command the sea approach to Curaçao, largest of this island group in the southern Caribbean.

# I WAS THERE! Eye Witness Stories of the War

## I'm Home After Three Years in Prison Camps

With the repatriated prisoners of war who reached Britain from Germany on October 25, 1943, the Rev. George Grundy, Church Army Chaplain, who was captured at Boulogne in May 1940. Condensed from an interview with W. A. Nicholson, and published by arrangement with The Daily Mail, this story of the padre's adventures begins in France at the time of the great retreat.

DAY after day I saw women and children mowed down by Nazi machine-guns. I grabbed children and pulled them to safety off the roads as enemy planes skimmed the hedge-tops. Dunkirk was about to begin. For a long time, while the roads of France were jammed with fleeing refugees, I looked after the children. At one time I gathered together 4,000 refugees.

After five days of this wondering what was happening, where it was all going to end, I commandeered a convoy of ambulances and tried to get some of these people to safety. I had gone to France to help organize Church Army work there. Soon I was in the thick of the retreat. German bombers howled above us. There was panic in the air. We had yet to come face to face with the Germans themselves.

At last they came. They came in tanks, and just outside Boulogne we saw them. Our convoy drew up by the roadside and waited. Two of my ambulances were shot off the road. Two others managed to get away. Two remained. Refugees swarmed past us, thousands of them pouring this way and that down the roads leading from Boulogne—anywhere to escape the deadly machine-gunning and the bombs. I had intended taking my convoy through to the hospital at Boulogne, where a battle was raging between the fort there and the incoming Nazi tanks.

I could not drive, but to wait seemed idle. Men were dying around me. Somehow I had to get through. Driver or no driver, I must get these wounded chaps to hospital. As I got some of them into the ambulances a German tank officer came to me. "What are you doing?" he asked. "One or two of these men here are dying," I said. He looked coldly at me. "Wait there," he said. "If you move off I will shoot." Putting his feet on the bodies of two men by the roadside, he said, contemptuously: "They are dead. They are no good."

Fifteen minutes later the tanks were ordered to move towards Le Touquet. I bundled the rest of the wounded into the ambulances. Then I looked at the bodies. To my relief, one of the men fluttered an eyelid. So I bundled him in too. Then I drove—for the first time in my life—the ambulance. At the 17th/21st General Hospital in Boulogne the most seriously wounded men were on the operating table within nine minutes. Not one man died, though many had to receive blood transfusions. By this time nearly all the doctors and chaplains had been evacuated. Only a handful were carrying on the job. Many of the wounded were told they would be evacuated soon. Time passed, but they were not.

I believe I was the only chaplain in that area. Men were dying everywhere: bodies lay unburied. Severely wounded civilians were arriving—civilians who had been machine-gunned. The officer commanding the hospital (Major Tucker) requisitioned my services as chaplain. After five days the Nazis took over the hospital. On the seventh day a German high officer—a major-general, I think—informed me it was his duty to take down the British flag from the hospital flagstaff. All the doctors were inside the hospital having a meal at the time.

HANDING the flag to me, the German officer said: "You can use this as long as you need it for funeral services." Many funeral services I had to conduct while I was there—the funerals of British Tommies who had been killed or had died from wounds. There were never enough men to carry the bodies to the graves. I had to bury the men with my own hands.

Many of the wounded were sheltering in the hospital basement. When they were told they were not going home, they were grievously disappointed. On May 20, 1940, I was officially "captured." Everybody in the area was to be marched off. As padre I volunteered to march with them. They were taken in lots of 800 at a time. I was given a liaison pass by the Gestapo. By a mutual agreement, all sick, wounded, or other men I might find hidden in private houses I was to invite to go to the English hospital and give themselves up.

REV. GEORGE GRUNDY—recently returned from Germany—narrating in this page some of his adventures, vividly describes a poignant scene in connexion with a repatriation that was cancelled. *Photo, Daily Mail*

I was also told this agreement covered escaped prisoners and all wandering soldiers. The Germans gave me a Red Cross armlet. The Gestapo told me they would ask only two questions of the men—their names and numbers. I organized a Women's Civilian Internment Camp. These poor women arrived in a terrible condition—old and sick women many of them. Later their conditions were improved. There were many English civilians too old to be interned. I did my best to console them, conducted services, organized and arranged burials, and looked after the wounded.

Six months after my capture—in November 1940—I was sent to Germany. On the way across Belgium to the Reich I contracted a bad dose of dysentery. Nuns looked after me and other people similarly stricken—57 of us altogether, all in a terrible state.

DURING a spell in hospital I lost 5½ st. When convalescing I got out of bed to take Sunday Services and administer the Sacrament to solace the wounded and the dying. There was a dark time in the experience of prisoners in Germany. It was when arrangements were made for us to be repatriated—the repatriation that never happened. Never will I forget the drama of it. Picture the scene.

In the centre of a market square was a table at which was seated a Nazi officer with papers before him. Lined around the square were 1,700 men, some on crutches, others blind. Many of them were men who have come with me this very day. All we were waiting for was a little bit of paper that would bring us back to Britain. As we stood there in suppressed excitement a Highlander with a wooden leg came into the square leading a blind Highlander. They appeared to be lost. We cheered when we saw them. It was a great moment to see these two brave men hobbling, groping their way into the square. Still we waited.

There was a rustle of papers in the German officer's hands, a faint breeze blew across the square. A hum of conversation went right through the ranks. Then the bitter truth came, with all its disappointment and anguish, in a brief message from headquarters. The German officer announced: "The repatriation will not take place. You will return to camp."

I looked around the crowd and saw the stunned disillusion on the faces of the men. I wondered how they were taking it. Then a voice told me. Someone shouted: "Oh, to —— with the —— war. Let's get back to our baseball." Baseball has become the greatest organized game in the German prison camps today.

Now, how runs life in the prison camps? The men are called at 6.30, and roll-call is at seven. In my camp there were 600 officers. The camp was originally meant to

BOXING CONTEST IN A P.O.W. CAMP in Germany—one of the most popular sports organized by the troops themselves, to while away weary hours of enforced idleness behind barbed wire and keep their minds and bodies alert and fit for the day of liberation. Equipment for this and other sports and games is sent to them by the Red Cross.

*Photo Daily Mirror*

house 250, so we had to take our meals in two shifts. Rations amounted to about five slices of bread a day, but our chief diet was potatoes. With these we had to eke out 1½ oz. of meat per week. That weight included bone, too. We turned it into a watery sort of soup.

Breakfast—between seven and eight o'clock —usually consisted of bread and margarine. Lunch was a mixture of maize or barley meal, plus soup. Some days we had meat roll : one-third of a tin heated up or fried with potatoes. At night they gave us a third of a tin of fish. The bulk of this tinned food came from our Red Cross parcels.

But for the Red Cross parcels many of us would never have seen this happy day, and but for the clothing sent from Britain we should have been in rags. I have seen officers going about in tatters. I myself often conducted services with trousers that were split and showed gaping holes. The rest of my clothing was in rags.

We came through Berlin on our way home ; but they would not allow us to see anything of the damage Allied bombs have done to the capital. We travelled at night. Our men still left behind will stick it out. They know what they have to endure is only a fragment of Britain's responsibility and that one day a British victory will give them their longed-for freedom.

Pte. J. O. CHADDOCK, Queen's Own Cameron Highlanders, whose story of night-battle in Sicily is given in this page. We are indebted to Pte. Chaddock's father for this extract from a front-line letter home.

## With the Camerons I Fought at Four Hills

*To the thunder of guns by the hundred, the 8th Army in Sicily launched a near-midnight attack against the Four Hills, at the beginning of August 1943. How his battalion waited for the crucial moment and then went into battle is told by Pte. J. O. Chaddock, of the Cameron Highlanders*

ZERO was at 23.50 hours, and we lay in the darkness waiting for the barrage to open. Our positions lay in a ridge of hills. The next ridge was held by the enemy, the Hermann Goering Panzer Grenadiers—one of Hitler's crack divisions. There were also some Eyetyes of the Napoli (Naples) division. Between these two main ridges was a large valley through which ran a road and railway, and we held as far as the railway line.

We were badly overlooked—we had held the place a few days previously, and couldn't move out of our holes for any reason whatsoever. The slightest movement and down would come a concentration of six-inch mortars. The start line for the attack was 300 yards on our side of the road and railway. The barrage, a "rolling" one, was laid on for 23.50 hours, and was to come down on the road for ten minutes and then move forward, lifting 100 yards every five minutes.

Then, after the attack was successful and all objectives taken, a defensive barrage was to come down on the F.D.L.s (Forward Defence Localities) to pin down any possible counter-attacks. Our two forward companies were to clear the two ridges, then proceed down to the next road 1,600 yards beyond, clearing the ground and then back again, finally consolidating on our side of the ridge before first light.

IT was a dark night with no moon. We lay silent, looking at the stars and watching the faint outline of the road. Watch fingers crept round—quarter to twelve, five minutes to zero, one minute . . . suddenly the hills behind glowed as hundreds of guns thundered, ripping the silence to shreds. Then the whine of the shells and the whole length of the road, 300 yards in front, erupted in smoke and flame. Simultaneously our heavy machine-guns opened up, firing from both flanks to keep German heads down, although surely no human would have his head above ground in that terrible barrage.

We went forward as the barrage lifted. A Bofors light ack-ack gun was firing tracer shells up our axis of advance to help us keep direction in the dark and the fog of the shell smoke. The first part went off O.K., although we were mortared when crossing the road and railway. The two forward companies reached their objectives, but got shot up on the trip down to the road and back, where the Boche had his main positions on the reverse side of the ridge.

A favourite trick of these Huns was this : as the boys were approaching a Spandau nest, the Jerries would shout "Kamerad !" so putting some inexperienced lads off their guard ; then would follow a vicious burst of tracer at point-blank range, and someone would be found with his insides blown through his back. When we found this was happening, very few prisoners were taken.

Perhaps one of the reasons I am still alive is because I learnt at El Alamein never to pass an empty trench without putting a few rounds in each of the dark corners. It's safe enough taking risks with the Eyetyes, although they are very treacherous sometimes ; but usually they have all their kit packed up waiting only for the barrage to pass over them. As soon as they see bayonets gleaming in the moonlight, it is "caputo" ! With Jerry, your safe plan is to shoot first and ask questions after—if you have any desire to go on living.

## We Sailed From the Terror That Was Singapore

*When the Japanese overran Singapore in the early weeks of 1942, Flying Officer William Furneaux, now of the Royal Australian Air Force, then of the Malayan Volunteer Air Force attached to the R.A.F., assisted at the evacuation of ground staff and stores. This account, which he has written specially for " The War Illustrated," tells of the sea journey from the ill-fated island and concludes the narrative he began in page 378.*

AT about 7.30 on the morning of February 14, 1942, an aircraft appeared from the East. It flew at about 200 feet above and around our ship, and when we saw a red spot on the top side of the wing as it banked to turn we opened fire with a twin-barrelled Lewis gun we had rigged to a rail forward— our only armament ! I don't know if we registered any hits, but the Jap pilot decided to fire also. He turned on the heat in no uncertain manner, which had us all scampering hot-foot for the hatches. It was a reconnaissance plane, and in due course his pals the bombers came to visit us—18 at a time. We saw three formations that day.

We were now in the Banka Strait, which became known as " Blitz Alley " and the channel in some places is so narrow that ships cannot zigzag to avoid attack. All ships escaping from Singapore to Java had to pass through this strait, and you can imagine what the score was. They were completely undefended and had no escort. Even when night came there was no respite, for submarines were busy. A ship about five miles ahead of us was sunk on the second night out. I was asleep in the rain on a hatch cover at the time, or rather trying to sleep, when suddenly, at about midnight, I heard a man's voice shouting for help.

WE dashed to the side, and although it was a dark night we saw someone hanging on to a piece of wreckage and being swept past us by the swift current. Lifebelts with flares attached were at once thrown overboard. The ship behind us, which had had her compass put out of action by a near miss earlier and which had been following us by visual means, suddenly loomed up out of the darkness, not knowing that we had slowed down, and slithered dangerously along our starboard side. It was just one darned thing after another.

All this time I, as ship's adjutant, was having my work cut out trying to make everyone as comfortable as possible, and providing food by commandeering private stocks brought aboard by some of the refugees—until I discovered, quite by accident, vast quantities of tinned meat and fruit in the lower hold forward. I also arrested a fifth columnist whom I found taking notes when a British destroyer came alongside just outside Batavia calling out through a megaphone which courses we were to take through the minefields into the port.

When we got into the harbour there were no less than a hundred and sixty ships of all sizes waiting for attention by the port authorities. We stood off for two days before we were allowed to come alongside. The Dutch harbour authorities handled the confusion very well, and in about a week they got rid of every ship, having received a warning that the port would be a trap for any vessel still there when the Japs had completely taken Sumatra, since the Sunda Strait, between Java and Sumatra, would be the only means of escape, the waters north of Java being now completely under the control of the enemy.

We established a headquarters in Batavia, and our people of the detached flights in Sumatra came drifting in one by one, some having experienced the Japanese paratroop attack on Palembang. Others had got to Padang on the west side of Sumatra and were picked up by British warships. Our C.O., Group Captain Nunn, was on a ship that was sunk in the Banka Strait, coming out of Singapore. About sixty nursing sisters from the Singapore General Hospital were on the same ship and most of these were killed when a bomb struck her. Also there were about twenty children, and these were loaded into the only lifeboat ; when the bombers came back for a second run their bombs wiped out the youngsters and fell among the people struggling in the water. They had had to jump overboard because the ship had caught fire.

The survivors of this ghastly scene scrambled on to an island, where they spent an agonizing four days. Then they were picked up by a Dutchman in a motor launch and taken to the Sumatra coast. You can well imagine the harrowing circumstances of those four days with so many terribly wounded people for whom there was neither morphia nor iodine. From the Sumatra coast they managed to struggle across to Padang, where they were picked up by a ship the name of which is not known, but which is known to have been sunk two days out of Padang bound for Colombo. There was one survivor, a Malay, who was rescued from a raft in mid-ocean.

When all our people had turned up in Batavia, or those we knew could turn up, we found we had only five aircraft left—out of the original forty-odd ! There were rumours that we were to be re-equipped by the Dutch, who had a number of training Tiger Moths. But after a couple of weeks the Dutch Government ordered us to leave Java at once, as we were without aircraft and equipment and therefore of no operational value. Some of our men—two officers and three sergeant pilots—elected to stay behind to use the five remaining aircraft, and they are still there. They did very good work, and were the only means of communication the Dutch army had at the end.

The rest of us were entrained for a place called Tjilatjap, on the south coast of Java. We arrived there on the day the Java Sea battle began. It seemed to be the port for loading personnel of Air Force squadrons who had lost their aircraft, including British, Australian and American. The ship we were put on sailed with 2,200 men of assorted R.A.F. and R.A.A.F. personnel, and we certainly overcrowded it. The holds were chockful of men, right down to the bottom of the ship, and if we had been sunk there would have been little hope of

**NEARING THE END IN SINGAPORE.** Though the swiftness of the Japanese advance on the island of Singapore in the early days of February 1942 precluded the possibility of everything likely to be useful to them being destroyed, many scenes such as the above were witnessed : a British resident's car being jettisoned lest it fall into the invaders' hands.
*Photo, Keystone*

rescue, for there were only four lifeboats. Three men died of fever, and we buried them at sea. Others were in bad condition, having made their way through the terrible Sumatran jungle for a week or more previously.

The trip to Colombo, where we finally fetched up, is one I shall not forget. Army biscuits and jam with tea once a day is not so

bad. But sleeping on the hard deck with no pillow to prop one's head up cannot be reckoned as comfort, especially when it rains most nights. It was no reluctant farewell I bade to the ship at Colombo when at last we arrived there, and a little judicious interviewing secured me a passage to Australia on repatriation in a luxury troopship.

# OUR DIARY OF THE WAR

**OCTOBER 27, Wednesday** 1,516th day
**Italy.**—Enemy shore batteries in Miturno area bombarded by U.S. ships.
**Russian Front.**—Red Army broke through German front S. of the Dnieper and advanced up to 18 miles.
**General.**—Exchange of Allied and German prisoners of war carried out at Barcelona.

**OCTOBER 28, Thursday** 1,517th day
**Italy.**—Capture of Torella, Castelmauro, Mafalda, and Riardo announced. Gen. Giraud flew to Italy to inspect battle front.
**Russian Front.**—Russians continued pursuit of enemy in Lower Dnieper ; Novo-Alexandrovka and Nizhnie Syerogozy captured ; Surazh-Vitebski taken in Vitebsk area.
**Australasia.**—U.S. paratroops landed on Choiseul Is. (Solomons).

**OCTOBER 29, Friday** 1,518th day
**Italy.**—Capture of Montefalcone announced. Savona iron and steel works, marshalling yards at Genoa, Imperia and Porte Maurizio, bombed by Fortresses.
**Burma.**—Myingyan and Akyab bombed by Wellingtons.
**Australasia.**—Vunakanau airfield (New Britain) bombed : 45 Japanese machines destroyed.
**China.**—Quongyan smelting plant and Kwangchow airfield raided by U.S. aircraft.

**OCTOBER 30, Saturday** 1,519th day
**Italy.**—Genoa marshalling yards bombed by Liberators. Fall of Pietravairano and Mondragone announced.
**Russian Front.**—Genichesk and Shchovsk taken by storm by Russians.
**Air.**—Cherbourg docks raided by Typhoons and Whirlwind bombers. Kassel still burning after raid on October 22.
**General.**—President Roosevelt announced " tremendous success " achieved at Moscow Conference.

**OCTOBER 31, Sunday** 1,520th day
**Italy.**—Enemy counter-attack from San Salvo on 8th Army bridgehead across River Trigno failed.
**Russian Front.**—Great air and tank battles raged at Krivoi Rog.

**NOVEMBER 1, Monday** 1,521st day
**Italy.**—Taking of Frosolone, Cantalupo and Teano announced.
**Russian Front.**—Soviet troops sealed German Crimea escape route by capture of Perekop and Armiansk. Kairi Zapadnye,

Lyubimovka on the Dnieper, Gromovka and stations south of Solkovo in Lower Dnieper, taken by Russians.
**Australasia.**—U.S. troops landed on Bougainville Island (Solomons).
**General.**—Details concerning decisions reached at Moscow Conference released : full agreement on measures to hasten defeat of Germany ; European Advisory Commission to be set up in London ; post-war collaboration between Britain, Russia, and China pledged ; Austrian independence guaranteed ; war criminals to be tried in the country wherein their " abominable crimes " were committed.

**NOVEMBER 2, Tuesday** 1,522nd day
**Italy.**—Capture of Casanova in German Massico defence line announced.
**Mediterranean.**—Durazzo (Albania) bombarded from the sea.
**Russian Front.**—Kakhovka, on Dnieper above Kherson, captured by Red Army.
**Australasia.**—Rabaul (New Guinea) heavily raided ; 94,000 tons of Japanese shipping sunk.
**Air.**—Wiener Neustadt Messerschmitt factory 25 miles south of Vienna attacked by American bombers.

**NOVEMBER 3, Wednesday** 1,523rd day
**Italy.**—Fall of Pratella and Gallo announced. Castelpetroso captured by 8th Army. Enemy positions north of San Salvo bombarded by Royal Navy.
**Russian Front.**—Bolshoy Kopani and

Chalbas captured by Soviet troops. Red Air Force bombed Dnieper crossings left to the Germans.
**Air.**—Heaviest bombing of Germany ever ; 4,000 tons of bombs dropped in 24 hours. Over 1,000 U.S. aircraft attacked Wilhelmshaven and French airfields. Cascade raid on Düsseldorf at night : more than 2,000 tons of bombs dropped in 27 mins. Cologne raided.

**NOVEMBER 4, Thursday** 1,524th day
**Italy.**—Isernia, central pivot of enemy positions, captured by 8th Army.
**Russian Front.**—Aleshki, 5 miles from Kherson, captured by Russians.

**NOVEMBER 5, Friday** 1,525th day
**Italy.**—Vasto captured by 8th Army. Vatican City bombed by unidentified plane.
**Burma.**—Akyab raided.
**Air.**—Gelsenkirchen and Münster, capital of Westphalia, attacked by over 1,000 U.S. bombers and fighters.
**General.**—Cairo talks between Mr. Eden and Turkish Foreign Minister, M. Menemenioglu, began. President Roosevelt announced that British, U.S., and Chinese military leaders had successfully completed discussions in Chungking. French National Committee declared itself not bound by decisions reached concerning Germany to which France was not a party.

**NOVEMBER 6, Saturday** 1,526th day
**Italy.**—Fall of Venafro to U.S. troops

of 5th Army announced. British patrols across River Garigliano.
**Russian Front.**—Kiev third city of Russia and capital of the Ukraine, captured from the enemy. Vasilkov taken. 20 salvos of 324 Moscow guns fired in honour of Russia's greatest victory yet. Announced that Russian troops had established a bridgehead on the Kerch Peninsula.
**Australasia.**—Japanese fleet of 53 warships, transports and cargo vessels, heading for Rabaul (New Britain) attacked by hundreds of American aircraft. Japanese troops landed on American bridgehead at Empress Augusta Bay, Bougainville Is. (Solomons).
**Sea.**—Disclosed that Capt. C. P. Clarke, of Somerset, had been Director of Operations in the anti-U-boat war for two years.
**General.** — Announced that Mr. Churchill had appointed Lt.-Gen. A. Carton de Wiart to be his special representative with Generalissimo Chiang Kai-shek, Lt.-Gen. H. Lumsden with Gen. MacArthur.

**NOVEMBER 7, Sunday** 1,527th day
**Russian Front.**—Fastov, 40 miles south-west of Kiev, taken by Russians.
**Home Front.**—Considerable casualties caused in London area when bombs demolished a dance-hall, wrecked a milk-bar, furniture shop and public house.
**Air.**—Duren, 25 miles south-west of Cologne, raided by Fortresses.

**NOVEMBER 8, Monday** 1,528th day
**Italy.**—Turin attacked by U.S. bombers. Capture of Carunchio, Casalbordino and Scerni announced. Revealed that Indian troops were in action.
**Russian Front.**—Makarov, Byshev, Obukhov, Gornostaypol and Privetz captured in rapid Russian advance westward from Kiev.
**General.**—Hitler addressed the Nazi Party in Munich ; he said that the hour of retaliation would come and that Germany would never capitulate.

**NOVEMBER 9, Tuesday** 1,529th day
**Italy.**—Capture of Torino and Paglieta by Gen. Montgomery's troops announced.
**Russian Front.**—Germans rolled back west of Kiev ; Borodianka captured by Red Army.
**Sea.**—Announced that during Aug.-Oct. 60 U-boats destroyed, making total of over 150 in last six months ; toll of U-boats destroyed exceeded losses of Allied merchant shipping.

★━━━━━━━━━━━━━ *Flash-backs* ━━━━━━━━━━━━━★

**1940**
October 28. *Italians bombed Patras (Greece) in first day of Italo-Greek war.*
November 5. *H.M.S. Jervis Bay (Capt. Fogarty Fegen, V.C.), sunk whilst defending Atlantic convoy against enemy surface raider.*

**1941**
October 28. *Germans reached Volokolamsk, 75 miles north-west of Moscow, in drive eastwards.*
November 2. *Simferopol, capital of the Crimea, captured by Germans.*

**1942**
October 31. *Advanced Australians troops established positions behind Germans at El Alamein.*
November 2. *Kokoda (New Guinea) recaptured from strong Japanese forces.*
November 4. *Great victory won by 8th Army in Egypt. Axis retreat westwards began.*
November 8. *U.S. and British troops under Gen. Eisenhower invaded French North Africa. Algiers captured.*

# THE WAR IN THE AIR

### by Capt. Norman Macmillan, M.C., A.F.C.

It may seem a peculiar stroke of irony that as the ring tightens more closely around the Nazi war machine, now driven out of Kiev, and within forty flying miles of Odessa, with the British and American armies slowly but persistently progressing north-westwards up the Italian peninsula, the development for operational purposes of larger and longer-range aircraft is almost within reach. The situation is almost akin to that in the last war, when the four-engined Handley Page bombers were produced and stood all ready to bomb Berlin when the Armistice intervened and the intended raid upon the German capital was never performed.

Apart from a few bombs dropped by the Polish Air Force in September 1939, the first bombs fell on Berlin in the summer of 1940. Twenty-two years passed between the first British readiness squadron for the bombing of Berlin and the first British bombs to fall upon that city. Those were the years that (I think it was) Sir Thomas Inskip used to refer to as the years that the locust had eaten. I hope we shall never again have such a large plague of locusts descend upon Britain.

By next spring, when the new Boeing B-29 super-heavy bomber (whose advent, it is said, will push the present Fortress back into the class of the medium bombers) is expected to be in action, it is reasonable to expect that the amount of " lebensraum " left to the " herrenvolk " will have shrunk still further. What part in such a reduced mileage war will such super-heavy bombers play ?

With every bomber there is a limit to the load of bombs it will carry. For two reasons. One reason is that there is a maximum weight of bombs which can be lifted ; it varies in relation to the amount of weight carried in the form of petrol and oil. The second reason is that there is a maximum cubic space load which a bomber can carry. Either reason may limit the maximum bomb load.

There is, therefore, a definite maximum performance characteristic for any heavy bomber, at which the maximum possible bomb load is transported for the maximum possible distance. Any reduction in distance cannot in these circumstances produce a bigger bomb load figure, for the simple reason that the bomb bays are all full and no more stowage is available. Any extremely heavy bomber is designed to fly for considerable distances, and must therefore carry fairly large-size petrol tanks. To take off with only partly filled tanks can aid the solution of the problem of reduction in weight, but can add nothing to the aircraft's cubic capacity for transporting bombs.

Airfields in the United Kingdom, Italy and Russia make it possible at this moment to reach every part of the territory occupied by the Germans. With the further shrinkage in the extent of the enemy-occupied territory which ought to have taken place by next spring it should become possible for almost every bomber flight to be made at full bomb capacity even with the bombers we now possess. (It has sometimes been necessary to reduce the maximum possible bomb load to about half load to enable the total fuel required for the journey to be carried without exceeding safe weight limits for take-off.)

What, then, of the new super-bombers which will operate with their full permissible bomb loads at ranges in excess of those which presumably will be required for action against European targets ? What purpose will they serve ? We must remember that some areas of the war are still of immense extent. The war at sea covers vast areas of ocean. The distance from the nearest base in Australia to the nearest base in Burma is greater than the distance across the North Atlantic ocean.

## ROOSEVELT'S Promise that Japan Shall Be Bombed

To attack a target from either of these bases involves a flight the equivalent of a trans-Atlantic crossing, if the target lies somewhere in the zone midway between Burma and Australia. Undoubtedly, the largest possible bombers will be invaluable in such an area, for a relatively small number of aircraft will be able to produce a proportionately greater amount of damage by each attack. The reduction in the number of aircraft will make it possible to effect surprise attacks in such circumstances with greater ease, in spite of increased size of the individual aircraft.

Then, again, there is the promise made by President Roosevelt that Japan proper shall be bombed. But our nearest base to Japan in the territory reconquered in New Guinea still lies some 3,000 miles away from Tokyo, and a lot more reconquering lies ahead before we can hope to do to Japanese industry in Japan what we have done to German industry in Germany. Meanwhile, Japan has time and opportunity to strengthen her defences against air attack—although there is every indication that the greatest strength lies in dispersion, and where can the Japanese disperse within Japan proper ?

**THIS WAS AN ME 410.** Shot down by A.A. fire during a raid on this country on October 31, 1943, all that was recognizable of the enemy machine was part of one of the airscrews, here being examined by a soldier.
*Photo, British Official : Crown Copyright*

The nearest points to Japan proper which still lie in the hands of the United Nations are on the mainland of China. The distances are great, greater than any which have been required to be flown against Germany during any period of the war. They will involve round flights of at least 3,600 miles as things stand today, and there is no certainty that these distances will be much altered between now and next spring.

Here, then, is an outlet for the operations of super-long-range heavy bombers. And it seems to me that we cannot get them into that particular war zone too soon. At present General MacArthur's forces fighting gallantly under the awful conditions prevailing in New Guinea and the Solomon Islands—no one who has not lived in the tropics can properly understand what fighting in these areas means—are fighting with only tactical air support ; for even the excellently executed raids upon Japanese naval and merchant shipping, and upon Japanese naval and military bases, are in reality tactical attacks.

The conditions, too, that the troops there will have to face will continue to be tough until we can get a bombing offensive under way against Japanese industry in Japan proper. It is that undermining of the German effort in Germany which has so seriously crippled the German effort on the war fronts ; and it will be the undermining of the Japanese in a similar way which will bring about their more rapid collapse on the fighting fronts.

So get a hustle on with the big bombers, the only types of aircraft which can hit Japan proper ! Do not imagine it can be done by aircraft carriers. The carrier that took Doolittle's Mitchells to bomb Japan was supposed to carry the aircraft to a point four hundred miles from Nippon for them to nip off from. But a sudden hint of a Jap fleet in the offing caused the aircraft to be launched when eight hundred miles away. That was why so many did not get through to Chiang Kai-shek's China, and a safe landing.

The solution of the breaking down of Jap resistance in the Far East with a reasonable casualty list for our men lies in the introduction of bigger bombers into that war zone at the earliest possible moment. The early duellists used to say : " Gentlemen, choose your weapons." That is what we should say to ourselves today. Upon our choice depends in great measure which side has to suffer most of the killing. In the Far East we must choose big bombers. No other weapon is strategically so important against Japan.

**THE AVRO YORK,** new British 50-passenger plane, is a civil transport version of the famous Lancaster bomber. The York's wing-span is 102 feet, its overall length 78 feet. Powered by four Rolls-Royce Merlin liquid-cooled engines, main external differences between the York and the Lancaster are shape of fuselage and the introduction of a triple tail-unit in the civil plane.
*Photo, British Official : Crown Copyright*

# Water Turns to Steam as 'Illustrious' Blazes

**BRITISH AIRCRAFT-CARRIER ILLUSTRIOUS** was hit in a heavy dive-bombing attack while escorting a convoy west of Malta on January 10, 1941. In this photograph—reproduced from Fleet Air Arm (H.M. Stationery Office, 1s. 6d.)—her flight-deck is seen pierced by bombs. Stores, stowed in the roof of the hangar below, are ablaze. Smoke pours through the jagged edges of a bomb hole, and the nearly red-hot deck turns the hose-water into steam. Fire-fighting continuously, the Illustrious reached harbour at Malta six hours later.     PAGE 413     *Photo, British Official ; Crown Copyright*

# Sanctuary in Sweden From Quisling's Terror

ACROSS THE FRONTIER formed by the rugged Kjolen range of mountains, thousands of Norwegian patriots have escaped to sanctuary in hospitable Sweden from Quisling, Norway's Nazi-maintained ruler, and his Gestapo.

Once over the frontier they are welcomed by their fellow Scandinavians, the Swedes, but before they are allowed to take part in Sweden's economic and social life, they must spend several days under supervision in a camp at Kjesater Manor.

Greeted on arrival (1), a Norwegian refugee's first job is to hand over his identity papers (2); Nazi spies are soon detected. Everyone gets a number and is allotted room (3) in one of the huts, each of which is named (4) to commemorate some great event in Norwegian history. Meals reminiscent of old days at home are provided (5), and for the first time in years the patriot can openly honour his national flag (6). Work of the Kjesater camp is financed by the Norwegian Government in London, which spends in Sweden nearly 1,000,000 kroner a month.

A LOT of amusement has been caused among British and American troops and war correspondents in Naples by a phrase-book for their use rushed out by an enterprising publisher. It has, like almost all the phrase-books I have ever seen, a curiously out-of-date air. I have often wondered why someone does not do in this line what Baedeker did so well in the guide-book business—produce something really good, and revise it every few years. I picked up one not so very long ago in Rumania which made the visitor to Bucharest inquire of his hotel-keeper, "At what time do you keep your ordinary?" and told how to ask for a boot-jack, and for a nightcap to wear in bed. Another, compiled by a Frenchman, evidently a fault-finder, as Frenchmen are apt to be when they leave their own country, complained of everything. At dinner the traveller is expected to have occasion for the phrases:

"This soup is cold."
"This plate is not clean."
"This knife does not cut well."
"This fish stinks."

When you ask your way to, let us say, the cathedral, you want an answer such as "Second on the left," or "Straight on." This book makes the person whom you have addressed say, "It is not far from here, sir or madam, but will you not take a slightly circuitous route and pass some of the principal shops? I am going in that direction myself and, if agreeable, I will accompany you." Again, the book made the user of it go into the bootmaker's shop and ask fatuously, "Have you any boots?"

THE latest kind of queue I have seen is formed by people taking boots and shoes to be mended. Inside the shop the cobbler had in front of him a rampart of footwear waiting to be attended to, which almost hid him from view. He was telling everybody, "Must be several weeks, I'm afraid, before I can hope to let you have them." He said it so apologetically and with so genial a smile that nobody seemed to mind. I have been told of a queue lined up to hand betting slips to a street bookmaker, but that I did not actually see. The latest wartime ramp I have heard of is the selling of Christmas cards sent last year as if they were new. You will no doubt have noticed that these cards usually have a doubled sheet of paper inside thin board covers; in this sheet is the greeting and the name of the sender. The dodge is to remove it and print some words on this board itself. Then you ask sixpence for a secondhand card.

POPPY Day has come and gone again. Although they were "austerity" or "utility" poppies, they sold as briskly as ever. Nobody could be seen without one, and the fact that the stalks were of cardboard instead of wire didn't matter in the least. If it were not that certain charities benefit by the observance of this anniversary, it would be better to drop it. The Armistice Day celebration has been washed out, and will never be reinstated. There may be another Armistice to commemorate, but the old Eleventh of November one will live only in the recollection of those who took part in its wild rejoicing. I doubt whether the excitement will be so great when this war ends. We know too well, as we did not know in 1918, what "the blessings of peace" are liable to be. I heard a thoughtful news-

paper editor (they aren't all, you know!) say the other day that he would not be surprised if a Day of Prayer for the continuation of the war were to be ordered, seeing how much more difficult life would be when peace comes. Absurd exaggeration? Yes, of course. But there is a germ of reality in the suggestion that we ought to bear in mind and think over.

SURPRISING the flare-up on the island of Cos. You wouldn't think it could be of much value to either side. Perhaps Goebbels fancied he could offset the disastrous defeats suffered by the German forces in Russia by playing up in Germany a "great victory" over a few hundred British troops

Actg. Maj.-Gen. R. E. LAYCOCK, D.S.O., Royal Horse Guards (The Blues), who—it was announced on October 23, 1943—succeeds Admiral Lord Louis Mountbatten as Chief of Combined Operations. Aged 36, he has seen Commando service in Cyrenaica and Crete, and he took part in the sortie on Rommel's Libyan H.Q. in 1941, from which only he and a sergeant returned. His D.S.O. was awarded for gallant and distinguished services in Sicily.
*Photo, Associated Press*

in the Aegean. Cos is one of the Grecian isles—"Lily on lily that o'erlace the sea," as Browning described them. Very lovely they look as you steam through them. Their rocky coasts and hills glitter in the sun and glow in the sunset. For all their rockiness they have fertile patches. Cos produces fine grapes, figs, olives, melons, and other crops, including that of the Cos lettuce, which every British gardener and allotment cultivator knows so well and which takes its name from the island. The inhabitants are Greeks, Turks, and Cretans; rather more of them follow Islam than Christ. The chief "sight," I am told (I never landed there myself, though steamers can anchor in the roadstead), is a sanctuary dating back to B.C. and connected with the physician Asclepius (or Aesculapius). Another medical authority whose name is

associated with Cos is Hippocrates. A huge plane tree in the market-place of the town is said to have been planted by him. Anyway, it has been there a long time, for it measures thirty feet in circumference.

WHILE women are generally thought to devote rather too much time to clothes, men are supposed to be loftily superior to fussiness about what they wear. Yet many men are not less fussy than women. Some still resent not having their trousers made with turn-ups, which is, of course, now against the regulations. Others say they cannot do without any of the pockets they have been used to. These should number ten in all, say the tailors. Two trousers pockets at the sides, one at the back. Five in the jacket—breast inside, handkerchief, sides and ticket. Two in waistcoat. Formerly there were four in waistcoats and frequently two at the back of trousers, which made thirteen. But the legal maximum is now eight—three in jacket, two in waistcoat and three in trousers. Yet women manage without any pockets at all. They carry bags, it is true, and thus make it easier to lose their purses, cigarette cases, and what not. But these bags have gone up tremendously in price. Five or six pounds must be paid now for a leather one of any lasting quality. So women's pockets may come in again. But they certainly won't want ten! Men do not really need that number, but they can't bear changing their habits. Not all, of course, but a good many.

I HAVE not seen any naval officer wearing the naval battle-dress which has been approved by the Admiralty, after much shaking of heads. It will not, I understand, be worn much on shore, except in dockyards and naval bases. Even at sea its use is optional. No officer need be seen in it unless he prefers it to his "monkey jacket," or receives an order to put it on. Most officers will, I imagine, prefer it when there is dirty work (dirty in the physical, not the moral, sense) to be done. The men have a suit for such occasions; it is known as "Number 9's." Naval battle-dress must not be worn on leave, which indicates that the authorities do not think it adds to the dignity or pleasing appearance of a man. It is made like the military battle-dress, but in navy-blue material. Not more than half a century has passed since naval officers and men began to wear regular uniforms. Before that they wore pretty much what they could get hold of, if they were poor; or what they fancied, if they were well off. Army officers, too, could please themselves as to their costume—in the higher grades. Only after the Napoleonic wars did "sealed patterns" of uniforms for both Army and Navy come into force.

A PRIVATE soldier wants to know why Army cooks have so much of their time taken up by parades, kit inspections and other spit-and-polish duties instead of being allowed to devote themselves to making the soldier's food appetizing. Often, avers complainant, soggy messes are served which are not fit to eat. He contrasts this with the meals that American soldiers get, "good enough for Presidents or Premiers," and attributes the difference to their cooks being "given a free hand." By that I suppose he means being treated as cooks rather than as soldiers.

Readers of THE WAR ILLUSTRATED who have difficulty in obtaining regular copies are advised to place an order with their newsagent immediately.

# Return of a Hero to the Land He Served

Photo, Planet News

**OVERJOYED TO BE HOME AGAIN,** and delighted at the warm welcome he received, is this Tommy, stepping ashore at Liverpool on October 26, 1943. He was one of the 764 who sailed in the Atlantis from Gothenburg, where the Swedish Red Cross supervised the first exchange of wounded prisoners-of-war between Germany and the Allies. See also pages 359 and 399-402.

*Photo, Planet News*

Printed in England and published every alternate Friday by the Proprietors, THE AMALGAMATED PRESS, LTD., The Fleetway House, Farringdon Street, London, E.C.4. Registered for transmission by Canadian Magazine Post. Sole Agents for Australia and New Zealand: Messrs. Gordon & Gotch, Ltd.; and for South Africa: Central News Agency, Ltd.—November 26, 1943. S.S. *Editorial Address:* JOHN CARPENTER HOUSE, WHITEFRIARS, LONDON, E.C.4.

Vol 7 # The War Illustrated N° 169

*Edited by Sir John Hammerton*

SIXPENCE

DECEMBER 10, 1943

JOSEPH VISSARIONOVITCH STALIN, undisputed leader of the Russian people since 1927, whose inspired generalship has resulted in unprecedented Soviet successes following the launching of a counter-offensive against the Germans on July 13 1943. He is depicted here by the Russian artist Karpov wearing the uniform of Marshal of the Soviet Union, to which rank he was appointed, on March 7, 1943, by the Presidium of the Supreme Soviet. His decorations include the gold medal of a Hero of Socialist Labour and the Order of Lenin.

NO. 170 WILL BE PUBLISHED FRIDAY, DECEMBER 24

# Allies' Activities Seen by Our Roving Camera

AMERICA ensures that her men of the U.S. Army in Britain have, like our own troops, realistic training before they engage in actual combat with the enemy. Invasion rehearsals in which live ammunition is used are intensively carried out, and here a flame-thrower team is going through its paces at a recently established Assault Training Centre.

NORWAY has given many splendid men to the Allied cause, most of them as seafarers. This 2nd Officer of an oil tanker is using an Aldis lamp to signal to other ships in his convoy.

NETHERLANDS airmen have mustered from homeland and colonies a Mitchell squadron which goes on operational flights with the R.A.F. One of the planes (above) is named "Margriet," after the youngest daughter of Princess Juliana and Prince Bernhard.

CZECHOSLOVAKIA was founded on October 28, 1918. At 25th anniversary celebrations in Britain, President Benes took the salute at a parade of Czechoslovak troops; the leader of the Bren-carriers dips his standard on passing the saluting base.

BELGIUM is represented in this parade of minesweeper crews by the officer shaking hands with H.R.H. the Duke of Gloucester, who recently inspected them at an East Coast base. It was announced on Nov. 15, 1943, that the Duke had been appointed Governor-General of Australia, as from July 1944.

POLAND has for her national emblem a defiant, white eagle. It is featured on this ensign, fluttering bravely in the breeze, as men of the Polish Navy (consisting of 12 ships and personnel of 2,600) take their turn at patrolling the Channel in quest of the common enemy of the Allied Nations.

*Photos, British Official: Crown Copyright; Keystone, Planet News, Central Press*

# THE BATTLE FRONTS

## by Maj.-Gen. Sir Charles Gwynn, K.C.B., D.S.O.

WHEN the map shows the enemy occupying a pronounced salient defensively, it is obvious to the least expert eye that a blow delivered at the base of the salient would threaten to cut his communications and line of retreat. There is, therefore, a prima facie opportunity of isolating the force in the salient with the possibility of annihilating it completely, and I have seen it suggested that the Russians have lost several such opportunities. Actually the situation is far from being as simple and straightforward as the map suggests.

It must be remembered that the enemy does not present an immobile and impotent target, but is capable of evasion and of delivering counter-blows, for both of which the mechanization of modern armies gives great facilities. Failure to exploit the possibilities of the situation to the utmost cannot therefore fairly be termed a lost opportunity. That reproach would only be justified if no attempt had been made to take advantage of the situation, or if an attempt had been made ineptly.

There are many factors which may prevent the best planned attempts being brought to fruition, and they are well illustrated by the numerous occasions on which the Russians have failed during the last year to accomplish all that was perhaps too sanguinely expected, or to repeat the complete success they achieved at Stalingrad. The enemy may, if he acts promptly and moves quickly, evade the blow by retreat covered by flank defences. Falling back on organized lines of communication and depots, he has fewer supply difficulties than the attacking force.

### ENCIRCLING Moves Made With Great Power and Speed

Retreat, of course, involves the abandonment of territory and probably the loss of much material, but if there is room to retreat and no dangerous defiles have to be passed even a beaten army has an excellent chance of escaping complete disaster. The failure of the Russians to intercept the retreating Germans from the Caucasus, though a strong attempt was made, provides an example.

When, on the other hand, the enemy delays or refuses to give ground the difficulties of rounding him up are of another order. They depend on the strength and fighting power of the force that is within the salient, and still more on the strength and mobility of reserves behind its base. The length and quality of the respective communications of the defending and attacking armies are also of vital importance. The success of the manoeuvre that isolated the 6th Army at Stalingrad was largely due to its being initiated from nearby well-established bases. This not only facilitated surprise, but enabled the encircling moves to be made with great power and speed. Furthermore, the Germans had no reserve forces immediately available to strike at the outer flanks of the Russians, and had only limited railway facilities for their movement.

When a counter-attacking force was eventually concentrated it was too weak and met with heavy defeat. In its retreat, however, it protected the flank of the army retiring from the Caucasus, and though it could not stop the Russians' vigorous attempts at interception it was able to delay them. It cannot be said that the Russians lost an opportunity of exploiting to the full their great initial success, but rather that the Germans, by capable leadership and rapid decisions and movements, were able to extricate themselves from a dangerous predicament in the Caucasus. Later in the winter campaign, when they stood to defend the Donbas and the Russian drive farther north was threatening Kharkov, the Germans were again in a dangerous salient.

The Russians made a most daring attempt to take advantage of the situation and to cut the German line of retreat, but the ever lengthening lines of their communications and lack of railway transport were a heavy handicap, made all the heavier by the fact that the enemy had an invaluable network of railways at his service. The encircling drive that the Russians attempted under the circumstances could not be made in great force and was bound to have supply difficulties. Obviously, too, it would be exposed to counter-attack. Moreover, the Germans had had time to bring up reserve divisions from the west, which gave them a compact striking force.

In spite of these unfavourable factors it seemed for a time that the attempt might succeed through its sheer daring. Then, however, an abnormally early thaw not

VICTOR OF KIEV, General Vatutin, commander of the Red Army on the First Ukrainian Front, is in the foreground of this group of officers at an observation post not far from the city, which was liberated on Nov. 6, 1943. Speed of Vatutin's army has earned him the nickname " Lightning Vatutin." *Photo, Pictorial Press*

merely brought the Russian mechanized drive to a standstill, but placed it in a dangerous situation. It was the turn of the Germans to seize the opportunity which possession of good railway communications and fresh reserves gave them. The Russians were driven back suffering a severe reverse, though they escaped complete disaster. Here again it is unjust to talk of the Russians losing an opportunity, which under unforeseeable circumstances in fact never really existed, in spite of the evidence of maps.

A VERY similar situation occurred when after the failure of the German Kursk offensive the Russians broke through at Byelgorod and recaptured Kharkov. The maps showed that the Germans in the Donbas were again in danger of encirclement. But they still had the advantage of better communications. The Russians again attempted to exploit the opening, and again the Germans counter-attacked ; but this time, without the assistance of the weather and without a fresh and compact striking force, they had only temporary success, and in the end only succeeded in establishing a

defensive flank to cover their retreat to the Dnieper. That sufficed to allow them to extricate themselves from a difficult situation.

When the Germans rallied behind the Dnieper and the Melitopol lines the map suggested that the Russians had two opportunities of effecting encirclement. By breaking through the Melitopol position there was a chance of cutting off the force holding it from retreat across the unbridged lower Dnieper, and also of isolating the force in the Crimea. That opportunity had in fact to be created by a successful penetration of the Melitopol position. That it was created and fully exploited was a great achievement.

THE other opportunity suggested by the map was the possible encirclement of the German forces within the great bend of the Dnieper. But obviously here the difficulty of making the opening from which opportunity would arise was immense. A wide, strongly defended river had first to be crossed and room secured to admit the deployment of an adequate encircling force. Moreover, even if the initial difficulties could be overcome, the difficulty of bringing up supplies and reinforcements through the bottleneck formed by temporary bridges remained. These difficulties seemed insuperable, especially as they would be increased by the enemy's air action.

Nevertheless, the Russians, undaunted, made the attempt, and, by their supremely daring Kremenchug thrust, again made an opening. Delivered on a narrow front and penetrating deeply and rapidly, the thrust obviously invited counter-attack by an enemy served by an adequate railway system in full working order. As the military correspondent of The Times remarked, the Russians had stuck out their neck and it seemed hardly possible that they could bring up their hands to protect it. In fact, for a time von Mannstein's counter-attacks placed them in a critical position, and though they stood their ground at Krivoi Rog it was probably only the Kiev breakthrough that prevented von Mannstein renewing his counter-attacks in greater strength.

WHAT I have tried to show is that in war apparent opportunities are often little more than openings which a good player will always try to exploit, sometimes at considerable risk, and will always be ready to seize. As at football, however, an opening does not always lead to a try or a goal, and in the majority of cases a good opponent can save the situation. Spectators may be disappointed when no definite result is achieved, and are apt to be more critical of the players who fail to score than of those who may have missed openings by being caught flat-footed. Spectators who have been players are probably less critical, unless the attack has been lacking in determination or adroitness. They are satisfied with the improvement effected if it opens the way for renewed attacks. What has been attempted often deserves applause more than the actual results achieved, and it is the determination of the Russians to miss no opening, and willingness to accept risks, that I think we should specially appreciate at their full worth. (Consult map on page 421.)

# Russia Triumphant in Assault and Defence

PETLYAKOV-2, Soviet dive bomber which is also used as a light reconnaissance bomber, gets under way south-west of Voroshilovgrad, in the Donbas. Russian air supremacy over the Luftwaffe has played a mighty part in recent successes, and the contribution of the PE-2 is substantial. It has a maximum speed of some 300 m.p.h. and can carry a bomb load of 1,300 lb. Russians regard it as their equivalent of the British Mosquito.

WOMEN SNIPERS of the Red Army are R. Shrypnikova (right) and O. Bykova, seen here returning from an assignment. Women fight side by side with men on the Russian front.

WOODEN RAILS had to be laid by the enemy in some parts of the Eastern Front to overcome difficulties created by soggy ground. Terrain of this type is the country lying between Gomel-Chernigov and the 1938 Polish-Russian frontier. This German fatigue party is laboriously carrying supplies to the front line along one of these wooden tracks.

VANDALISM IN KIEV, which was such a grim feature of the German retreat from the town, is symbolized by the ruins of Pechersk Abbey, one of the lovely cathedral churches of Russia's city of shrines destroyed by the enemy. The Abbey was in the monastery district of the city and was among the first to be founded in Russia.

ACROSS THE KERCH STRAITS, narrow stretch of water separating the Kuban from the Crimea, stream German troops and equipment by way of a ferry which is reputed to have made 2,000 trips during the enemy's retreat from their last footholds in the Caucasus. On October 9, 1943, the Russians announced that the Kuban had been cleared. In the final battle on the Taman Peninsula 20,000 Germans were killed and 3,000 taken prisoner. Thus the way was opened for a frontal assault on the Crimea from the east.

*Photos, U.S.S.R. Official, Planet News, Associated Press*

# Panorama of Victories on the Eastern Front

LIMIT OF GERMAN ADVANCE, DEC, 1941
LIMIT OF GERMAN ADVANCE, DEC. 1942
RUSSIAN FRONT, FEB, 1943.
RUSSIAN FRONT (APPROX.) NOV. 22, 1943.
SHADED AREA – TERRITORY REOCCUPIED
BY RUSSIA, 1943 (SUMMER OFFENSIVE).

0  25  50  100  200
*Miles*

**MILESTONES IN THE WAR** on the Eastern Front are plotted on this map.  It was in June 1941 that the German High Command launched its blitzkrieg against the Soviet Union.  Its aim was the destruction of the Red Army and the harnessing to the German war machine of the coal and iron of the Donbas, the wheat of the Ukraine, the oil of the Caucasus and the whole of Russia's diversified industry.  By December Leningrad was surrounded, Moscow besieged and the Ukraine and Donbas invaded.  A year later the enemy had broken through to Stalingrad and attained the foothills of the Caucasus.  In January 1943 the Russians hit back, and in one magnificent year's campaigns they have retaken Stalingrad, cleared the Caucasus, the Soviet Ukraine and the Donbas, invested the Crimea, raised the siege of Leningrad and swept the enemy back along the whole length of the 2,000-mile front.  By November 22, 1943, the foremost Soviet spearhead, thrusting from Korosten at the very heart of the enemy along the highway to Warsaw and Berlin, was within 50 miles of the old Polish frontier.

# THE WAR AT SEA

### by Francis E. McMurtrie

OFFICIAL excuses for the loss of Cos and Leros bear too close a resemblance to German explanations of retreats in Russia to be entirely convincing. It may be true that German losses in retaking these Dodecanese islands exceeded our own, but this does not alter the fact that the victory was an enemy one. Unquestionably the initial error was to trust the Italians in Rhodes to hold that island for the Allies, a task they proved incapable of carrying out when attacked by an inferior force of German troops. As soon as it was clear that Rhodes was firmly in enemy hands, any attempt to hold Cos, Leros and Samos was an obvious gamble. To set off the German advantage of a first-class military and air base in Rhodes, it was attempted to hold the small airfield on Cos, which could take but a limited number of planes. Once the enemy had overwhelmed Cos the end was in sight, and it would have been wiser to have evacuated Leros before incurring further losses in its defence.

Only one thing could have justified continuance of the attempt to hold either island or both. That would have been the certainty that Turkey would immediately enter the war on the side of the Allies, giving them the benefit of bases from which the whole of the Dodecanese and the other enemy-held islands of the Aegean could speedily have been reduced. Without Turkish bases the Allies had to make the most of Cyprus, 250 miles to the eastward of Rhodes—a distance beyond the effective range of fighter aircraft.

Though it differs in degree from the attempt to hold Crete in the face of enemy air superiority, this gallant adventure resembles it in certain other respects. Of such an enterprise it might be said, as of the charge of the Six Hundred and other operations undertaken with totally inadequate forces, " It was magnificent, but it was not war."

NATURALLY the Germans have made the utmost capital out of this small success in their ocean of troubles. Their claim to have sunk nine destroyers is obviously a gross exaggeration, but it is hardly to be expected that we sustained no naval losses in such a hazardous undertaking. Ships such as H.M.S. Echo, which right up to the last contrived to creep into a tiny bay to pick up those it had been decided to evacuate, at the same time intercepting and sinking a number of German landing craft, once more proved that the Navy never hesitates to attempt the impossible when circumstances demand it.

With the collapse of the submarine campaign against shipping, the Germans are casting about in every direction for some other means of striking at Allied sea communications. Though nothing has been heard lately of raiders disguised as merchantmen operating against commerce, it would not be surprising if the enemy were to resuscitate this method of attack upon trade; indeed, absence of news on the subject is no guarantee that it has even been suspended.

DURING 1941 quite a number of enemy raiders of this character were at sea, judging from the cases of interception that were reported. In May of that year two were accounted for in the Indian Ocean—the Coburg by H.M.S. Leander and H.M.A.S. Canberra, and the Pinguin by H.M.S. Cornwall. In November there was the remarkable duel between a heavily armed raider, the Kormoran, and H.M.A.S. Sydney, in which both ships were destroyed. Exactly what happened has never been explained, as there were no survivors from the Sydney, but it has been suggested that she closed the range with the object of finishing off the German ship before darkness fell, and was torpedoed by her adversary. In the same month H.M.S. Devonshire sank the raider Atlantis in the South Atlantic; and in December H.M.S. Dorsetshire disposed of another in the same area. An Italian raider, the Ramb I, was sunk by H.M.S. Leander in the Indian Ocean in March 1941.

### CLASHES Between Light Forces in Channel Islands Area

There has been no official reference to enemy surface raiders for a long time past, though in January last a report appeared in the Press of one having been scuttled to avoid capture by ships of the U.S. Navy in the South Atlantic. It is possible that recent clashes between light forces in the Channel may have been caused by enemy endeavours to screen the movements of raiders in passage. Brest and Cherbourg are geographically well situated as bases for such vessels; and it is noteworthy that there have been several encounters lately between light forces in the vicinity of the Channel Islands, lying between those ports.

Though they may be utilized as material for exaggerated stories of commerce destruction, produced for the benefit of the credulous German public, it is manifestly impossible for raiders of this type to accomplish any serious damage. But in the last war, when we were not so well equipped as today for dealing

**FATHER AND SON**, who serve aboard the same ship, Kharkov, in the Soviet Black Sea Fleet—Maxim Petrovitch and Ivan Sheherbina. Both have been twice decorated for gallantry. *Photo, U.S.S.R. Official*

with these pests, several more or less successful cruises were made by the German raiders Möwe, Wolf and Seeadler, the last-named a sailing vessel fitted with an auxiliary motor. Typical of these was the first sortie made by the Möwe, a former fruit carrier, at the end of 1915. She returned to Germany early in the following March, having captured or destroyed 15 vessels. Others were lost through striking mines laid by raiders, the most notable instance of this being the battleship King Edward VII in January 1916.

All three of the foregoing raiders were merely ordinary merchantmen, with nothing distinctive in their appearance. Of different type were the Norddeutscher Lloyd liners Kronprinz Wilhelm and Prinz Eitel Friedrich. With easily recognizable characteristics, added to the former's high speed of 23 knots, these two ships really came into the category of armed merchant cruisers. Though they did a fair amount of damage to unescorted shipping in 1914-15, fuel shortage and the impossibility of effecting permanent repairs at sea led both to internment in an American port in April of the latter year.

All such raiders suffer from certain inherent disabilities. It is impossible for the raider to attack any ships except those that sail unescorted. For a convoy to be molested would ensure engagement by the escorting warships, a conflict which could have but one termination. To keep at sea for any length of time fuel supplies have to be renewed; and since it would be suicidal to advertise the raider's movements by entering a bunkering port, the fuel must be obtained from a prize. This is not so easy when practically all Allied merchant vessels are armed and likely to fight if attacked. Moreover, fuelling at sea is a difficult and dangerous practice, through which more than one raider sustained damage during the last war.

ADMIRAL KOICHI SHIOZAWA, whose death is reported from Tokyo, was Japanese Naval Attaché in London about 16 years ago. In January 1932 he was in command of the Japanese squadron which shelled the forts at Shanghai while aircraft dropped bombs on the city. When Admiral Sir Howard Kelly, the British C.-in-C. on the China Station, arrived in H.M.S. Kent, Rear-Admiral Shiozawa made the customary official call upon him, only to be told: " If Japanese aircraft do not stop flying across my flagship, I shall be obliged to open fire upon them." Paying a hasty farewell, Shiozawa at once issued the necessary order, and as a result was superseded.

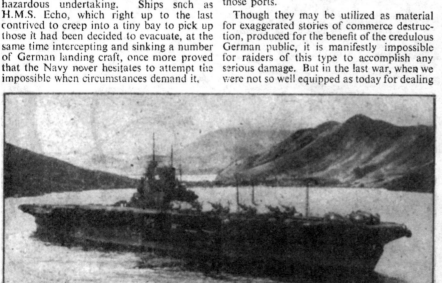

**H.M.S. VICTORIOUS**, British aircraft carrier, veteran of war in almost every sea, until recently has been operating with the U.S. Pacific Fleet. Here she is seen at anchor in a South Pacific harbour, her decks lined with U.S. Navy fighters and torpedo bombers. These machines were manned by American airmen, while the Victorious's own flying crews were based on an American carrier—a fine example of Allied cooperation. *Photo, Keystone*

# Honoured Fearnoughts of the Submarine Service

MEN OF THE UMBRA recently awarded the D.S.M. are Ldg. Telegraphist P. J. Murray (above) and P/Os Tom Jennings and R. S. Pert, 1st and 4th in the group (right). In centre of group are Ldg. Signaller J. Smith, of the Truant (left), and Chief P/O S. Kay, of the Turbulent, also awarded the D.S.M.

HEROES OF H.M. SUBMARINE UNBROKEN are Lieut. A. Mars, D.S.O. (above), awarded the D.S.C., and Ldg. Telegraphist G. Cryer (below), D.S.M.

WITH THEIR JOLLY ROGER bearing insignia denoting various "kills" are Lieut. J. G. Y. Roxborough, D.S.O., D.S.C., R.N., Commanding Officer, and his crew of H.M. submarine United, just back to a home port after service in the Mediterranean, during which the United sank 16,000 tons of enemy shipping. Bars on her flag denote ships sunk; daggers are for "special operations"; and an egg-timer recalls an occasion when the United had to lie submerged for 36 hours, whilst being hunted by enemy destroyers.

PAGE 423

# Street by Street We Go Forward in Nazi Italy

HARD STREET-FIGHTING lies behind recent Allied communiqués announcing the capture of villages and towns in Italy. It is heavy going all the way for both the 5th and 8th Armies, fight ng as they are now in mountainous country where the enemy can hold out with the minimum of men, and delayed at almost every step by systematic demolition and road mining. In Campochiaro — between Isernia and Campobasso—these Canadians (1) had a score to settle with a nest of German snipers entrenched in a house. An accurately placed Mills grenade did the trick. Sparanise, a small village some 8 miles north-west of Capua, was for several days the scene of skirmishes between 5th Army patrols and the enemy, before British troops finally captured it on October 23, 1943 ; here one of our men (2) is engaged in " mopping up "—note use of rifle from left shoulder. Teano, on the road to Sessa Aurunca, important West Italian road junction, was taken on Nov. 1. Forward units enter the town (3) in street-fighting formation.

Arrival of big Canadian reinforcements was followed by the announcement of the capture of Castel di Sangro on November 23.

*Photos, British Official: Crown Copyright; New York Times*

# Multi-Purpose Reindeer in Red Army Service

RUSSIA'S FAR NORTH, from the Kola Peninsula to Kamchatka, land of the Lapps, Samoyeds, Yakuts and other hardy peoples, is also the land of the reindeer. On this animal the possibility of human life in these regions very largely depends ; and this war has given even more importance to reindeer in the Kola Peninsula. Troops, ammunition, and other supplies are being transported to the fighting zone by reindeer sleigh convoys. Moreover, the venison is a welcome addition to Northern Russia's wartime larder, while the hides are especially useful in the making of airmen's uniforms.

Saamis, as the reindeer owners are called, bid farewell to their families (1) on leaving for active service. The reindeer teams keep to tracks (2) alongside smoothly-rolled motor roads through the snow ; ambulance work (3) and dispatch carrying (4) are included in their activities. Under the Soviet regime the perfecting of stock and training of the reindeer has been encouraged, foresight rewarded by the contribution this hardy animal is making to the Red Army's achievements.

*Photos, Exclusive to* THE WAR ILLUSTRATED

# Young and Old Forge Russia's Mighty Armour

SOVIET INDUSTRY has made a tremendous contribution to the great successes on the Eastern Front. The Soviet people, declared Marshal Stalin on November 6, 1943, working in difficult conditions, succeeded so well in supplying the Red Army that the enemy's superiority in tanks, aeroplanes, mortars and tommy-guns had been liquidated.

Feature of Russian industrialism is allotment of responsibility on ability alone. Children from the age of 14 upwards work side by side with older folk. 18-year-old Nikolai Yerofeyev (4) is a foreman in an aircraft factory; 17-year-old Nina Monakhova (3) left her typewriter to make mortars: under the Stakhanovite record-breaking system she can rise to almost any position. A damaged tank (1) did not require to bear the honoured name of Suvarov to get the most careful attention from young repair-workers. "All-in effort" includes public and private savings-for-victory schemes: here (2) delegates of a factory hand over to crews a number of tanks they had saved to pay for.

*Photos, Pictorial Press*

# Leningrad Steel a Source of Soviet Triumphs

**POURING MOLTEN METAL** into moulds at a Leningrad steel factory. Leningrad, with a normal population of 3,200,000, is an electrical engineering and machine-tool centre. Its shipbuilding includes steamers, ice-breakers and timber vessels. At the outbreak of this war it ranked second only to Moscow in the production of electric power. Strategic withdrawal of Russian centres of production to the Urals, Siberia and Central Asia has diminished Leningrad's industrial importance, but it is still the chief Baltic outlet of the U.S.S.R. and is connected with the White Sea by the Stalin Canal. See also p. 564, Vol. 6 : pp. 394, 395, Vol. 7.

*Photo, Pictorial Press*

# Ceylon is Well Prepared for Japanese Raids

PIVOT OF S.E. ASIA COMMAND, to which Lord Louis Mountbatten was appointed on August 25, 1943, Ceylon has raised its civil defence services to a high pitch of efficiency. Tamil Red Cross nurses (1) and doctor in a casualty ward, tend a lad who is a rehearsal air-raid victim ; while there is an Anderson quality about this shelter (4) in the compound of a public building. Ceylon Information Department's propaganda (6), too, has the 1943 note, whilst the porker (5) displays an anti-Goebbels slogan. The tom-tom beater (2) announces air-raid practice, and the attendant mounts to his bell (3), Cingalese counterpart of our siren.

# Lord Wavell Takes Over as Viceroy of India

FAMINE in India, mainly in Bengal, was the urgent problem facing Lord Wavell when he arrived on October 17, 1943, to be installed as Viceroy in succession to Lord Linlithgow, who, with Lady Linlithgow, greeted him at Viceroy's House, New Delhi (right). Principal causes of the famine were soaring prices of food and other goods, shortage of grain crops in stock, export of food to meet Allied war needs elsewhere, and lack of shipping to rush supplies to stricken areas when the crisis came. In Calcutta alone 8,000 people had died from starvation and attendant diseases between August 15 and October 15, 1943.

Lord Wavell acted with military resource and speed. "Like another great soldier before him," declared Mr. Amery, Secretary of State for India, on November 4, "Lord Wavell came, saw for himself and took action." Installed in office with the minimum of ceremony on October 20, he toured Calcutta and Midnapore on October 26–27 : below he is seen with Sir Thomas Rutherford, Acting Governor of Bengal, watching service of meals to the needy at a free kitchen. On October 28 he called in the Army, of which he had been so recently C.-in-C., to set up relief camps and get food moving from military and other stores to the afflicted areas.
*Photos, British Official ; Keystone*

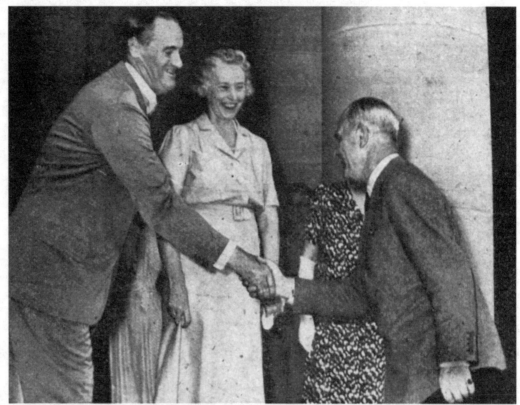

# How Hitler's Canals Help the Nazi War Effort

When the R.A.F. struck at the Dortmund-Ems Canal in 1940, and later bombed the ship elevator at Henrichenburg, they demonstrated that the tremendous importance to Germany of her inland waterways was not to be overlooked by our strategists. How specially vital are Hitler's numerous "Wasser-strassen" is here explained in detail by W. WERTH.

WITH the Allied forces steadily closing in on the citadel of Hitler's so-called European fortress the inland transport problem becomes daily of increasing importance to Nazi strategists. A short while ago Harry Hopkins, first adviser to President Roosevelt, drew special attention to Germany's traffic on inland waters, estimated today to exceed 120 million tons a year.

Ever since the Reich's foundation the great rivers Rhine, Weser, Elbe, Oder, Main, Neckar and Danube have been dredged and made usable to shipping; and a most intricate system of canals has been initiated. Today they are the most up-to-date waterways in the world, excelling even those of the Low Countries and France. And with thousands of barges confiscated from Holland, Belgium, France and the Balkan territories, Germany's inland fleet is greater than ever.

In a class of its own is the Kiel Canal, lifeline of the German Navy, connecting the Baltic with the North Sea.

All the great navigable rivers in Northern Germany run, more or less, in a south-north direction. The general plan for inland traffic by water required the construction of a water highway across the North-German plain, connecting the inland ports of the Rhine and the industrial areas there and on the Ruhr with the harbours on the North Sea and the Baltic shores, and at the same time with Berlin and other great inland cities and industrial centres, such as Magdeburg, Hanover, and Leipzig. In this way ore from Hamburg and Sweden via Stettin could be brought directly to the furnaces, and in the opposite direction coal, coke, cement, potash and other heavy goods; also foodstuffs could be conveyed to the great central markets.

Many locks overcome differences of

**NETWORK OF WATERWAYS** mapped here plays a great part in solving Germany's internal transport problems. The enemy's river-canal system is acknowledged to be the most modern in the world. See table on left for key to numbers.
*Specially drawn for THE WAR ILLUSTRATED*

altitude, and by special bridges canals are led across rivers. One can sometimes see two different "trains of ships" one above the other. Some years ago enormous ship-elevators were built—one in the west, near the river Lippe, and the town of Henrichenburg, another between Berlin and Stettin at Niederfinow. A lift carries 1,000-ton barges in five minutes to a height of 110 feet from the level of the Hohenzollern Canal to the river Oder, thus rendering a series of locks unnecessary.

Big canals demand extensive harbour installations, cranes, warehouses, granaries, tanks, and similar equipment, and the much-bombed city of Duisburg is one of the largest ports in the world. Berlin, where various canals meet—crossing the city or by-passing the outskirts—has various harbours, and a very considerable part of the capital's great industries is supplied by barge traffic.

Of a different type is the inland shipping in Southern Germany, involving use of the rivers Main and Neckar. Originally, in both rivers a heavy iron chain of more than 100 miles in length was sunk, and specially constructed tugs without propellers or paddles crawled along this chain,

which was wound over the tug. To a certain extent this system is still in use, but since 1921 so-called "Staustufen," that is "dam-steps," have been constructed; these make a river into a kind of huge staircase for shipping. At certain distances the water is dammed up by gigantic movable cylinders, which can be adapted according to the water-level.

Thus various purposes are fulfilled: the rivers, which often overflowed in winter and nearly dried up in summer, have now a constant water-level; a sufficient depth of water is secured for barges up to 1,000 tons; and overflow is used by huge power stations supplying electricity to industrial undertakings in the surrounding districts.

Modern locks lift a ship step by step. The industrial heart of Württemberg, around Stuttgart, is thus directly connected with the coal mines of the Ruhr. The linking up of the Rhine and Main with the Danube right through the industrial area round Nuremberg has been achieved by the modernizing of the hundred-year-old, small Ludwig Canal. Oil from Rumania, previously shipped to Regensburg on the Danube only, together with rich products of the Balkans, can now be transported directly to all centres in Germany proper.

There is another group of shipping, no less important, connecting the Upper Oder with the famous coal mines and factory districts in Upper Silesia; it was Rudolf Hess (now a prisoner in England) who opened the Adolf Hitler Canal in 1940. A curiosity worth mentioning is the connecting of lakes in East Prussia by transporting small steamers on specially designed railways across intervening stretches of land.

The Germans have aimed at a standard-type barge of 1,000 tons for most of their inland water traffic. Canals near the Rhine and Ruhr carry 1,250-ton ships. These are driven by their own Diesel engines or towed by tugs. Some of the most important waterways are provided with electric locomotives running along a tow-path, thus accelerating otherwise slow goods traffic. A "train" of four or five large barges is equal to the load capacity of a sea-going merchant vessel. It also equals about 50 heavily-laden goods trains, thus relieving pressure on railways.

THE time is approaching when Hitler, faced with new fronts, will have to move his divisions very quickly indeed to danger spots. His autobahnen (motor roads) will eat overmuch petrol; but canals will greatly help the railways, congested as they are, and short of rolling-stock and locomotives. Doubtless more attention will be paid by Allied bombers to Hitler's canals when the time is ripe.

Possibilities of devastating floods, causing enormous industrial dislocation, are also borne in mind by the R.A.F., as was demonstrated on May 17, 1943, when Lancaster bombers in a daring low-level attack breached three vast dams serving the Ruhr industries (see pp. 24-25, Vol. 7), a feat described by Air Chief Marshal Sir Arthur Harris as "a major victory in the battle of the Ruhr, the effect of which will last until the Boche is swept away in the flood of final disaster."

| GERMANY'S GREAT INLAND WATERWAYS | | |
|---|---|---|
| CANAL | BARGE CAPACITY (Tons) | DETAILS |
| 1. Kaiser Wilhelm (North Sea-Baltic Sea) | Over 1,200 | Opened 1895. Length 61 miles. Draught 36 feet. Surface width 112 feet; bottom-width 48 feet. Double locks at both ends. Traffic up to 22 million tons (1930). |
| 2. Dortmund-Ems | Over 1,200 | Length 166 miles. 20 locks, with ship-lift at Henrichenburg. Length 41 miles. 7 locks. |
| 3. Elbe-Trave | Over 1,200 | Length 41 miles. |
| 4. Lippe | Over 1,200 | 2 locks. |
| 5. Rhine-Herne | Over 1,200 | Length 23½ miles. Communication: Ruhrort-Herne, then Dortmund-Ems and Midland Canal. 8 locks. |
| 6. Main-Danube (Under reconstruction) | Over 1,200 | Originally the Ludwig Canal, 108 miles. In 1921 modernization started; including the river Main from Aschaffenburg, about 175 miles. 24 locks; dam near Passau. |
| 7. Neckar | 600-1,200 | Using the river by "dam-steps"; about 125 miles. 26 locks. |
| 8. Midland | 600-1,200 | Started 1905. Many short branch-canals to industrial centres as: Bernburg-Stassfurt, Leipzig-Kreypau Rhine-Herne, Lippe, etc. 4 locks. |
| 9. Ihle-Plauer | 600-1,200 | Connecting rivers Havel and Elbe, 41 miles. Double lock, ship-lift. |
| 10. Koenigsberg-Sea | 600-1,200 | Connecting Koenigsberg with Baltic Sea, 20 miles. 2 locks. |
| 11. Hohenzollern (Berlin) | 250-600-1,000 | Connecting rivers Havel and Oder, part of the "Great Ship Way" Berlin-Baltic Sea. Length 63 miles. 7 locks; ship-lift at Niederfinow. |
| 12. Teltow (Berlin) | 250-600-1,000 | Connecting rivers Spree and Havel, Southern Berlin. Length 24 miles. 1 lock. |
| 13. Oder-Spree (Berlin) | 250-600-1,000 | Connecting rivers Oder and Spree. Length 56½ miles. 7 locks. |
| 14. Ems-Jade | Under 250 | 7 locks. |
| 15. Adolf Hitler (Oder-Upper Silesia) | 600-1,000 | Constructed during this war. |

## Historic Kiev Restored to Soviet Russia

In German hands since Sept. 22, 1941, Kiev, capital of the Ukraine, was successfully stormed by Soviet forces on Nov. 6, 1943, after operations claimed to be unequalled for speed and intensity.   Whilst a smoke-pall still hung low over the once beautiful city (3), and Soviet tanks rumbled along Kreschatik Street (2), inhabitants were thanking Gen. Vatutin's troops, near the famous Opera House (1).   A pyrotechnic display in celebration of the victory lighted the Moscow sky (4) that night.

## Sweeping the Hun From the Northern Caucasus

Final clearance of the Germans on October 9, 1943, from the Northern Caucasus was due to the brilliantly combined fighting of Soviet troops, sailors and airmen. Ground crew overhaul the armament of a Red Air Force fighter (1). Marines of the valiant Black Sea Fleet go in with the bayonet to " winkle " the enemy out of a rocky coastline position (2), while Red Army reinforcements march tirelessly along a mountain highway (3) to join their comrades in the fighting line.

## *The Rising Tide of Victory Amid the Snows*

Prone in the snow, invisible to enemy planes, Red Army snipers (5) picked off unerringly stragglers from the fleeing Nazi forces as these trudged despairingly along almost impassable mountain roads, menaced at every step by avalanches, dogged by violent storms. Two Soviet pilots (4), well content after a triumphant dog-fight, land in brilliant sunshine, to be greeted with congratulations and regaled with a welcome drink by a smiling girl from a near-by collective farm.

## *At the Heroic Heart of the Soviets*

With the failure of the last German attempt to take Moscow, in March 1942, life in the Russian capital resumed its normal
course.   This girl (1) controls bridge traffic over the Moskva River;  a militiaman (3) does similar duty in Red Square,
with walls of the Kremlin on the right, St. Basil's Cathedral in background.   On Jan. 18, 1943, siege of Leningrad was
raised after a bloody crossing of the Neva, on whose embankment a field gun (2) is mounted.   (See also illus. pp. 394 and 395.)

# VIEWS & REVIEWS

Of Vital War Books

## by Hamilton Fyfe

WHAT sort of people are the Japanese? I remember during the war they fought with Russia there was a popular song called "Pansy Faces," and a verse was introduced about the "little Japansy faces" which "looked up at me and smiled." We were allies of the Japanese for many years. We were told what a delightful race they were, so artistic, so neat and tidy in their homes, so anxious to be up to date in everything, such admirers of our ways that, in the words of another song popular at the time, "if they couldn't be like us, they'd be as like us as they were able to be!"

When we think now of Japanese faces we don't think of them as smiling; we think of them as distorted with malignant cruelty. We hate the thought of their slant-eyes, yellow skins, straight, black hair, tight lips. How can we account for this change in them? Were they always ready to indulge in atrocities if they got the chance, and to follow leaders with crazy aims of Pacific dominion and no more honour than—indeed, not so much as—bandits or burglars? Or was what we were ordered by our Foreign Office, working through the Press and Parliament, to believe about them substantially true? Is their behaviour at present a mere temporary aberration, a madness that will pass away?

WELL, my theory about masses of people, whatever their race, colour, or creed, is that they can be made to behave decently if decency is urged upon them by leaders whom they trust, or made to act like devils if their leaders are of the devilish sort. I do not believe that masses of people have wills of their own. As individuals, yes; as mobs, no. The origin of the term "mob" was, you know, the Latin *mobile vulgus*, the herd that can be driven this way or that, "like a feather in the wind," as the writer of the song La Donna è mobile in Rigoletto put it. Democracy, is in my view of it, not government by mobs without wise guidance, but government according to the wishes of nations instructed and inspired by those with trained intellects, wide knowledge, and noble characters.

Now, in those days when we were told to respect and like the Japanese, they had such men to lead them. Since then the power over them has passed to thugs, whom Prof. John Morris, author of Traveller from Tokyo (Cresset Press, 10s. 6d.), calls "military gangsters"; they have inflamed the minds of a people who were not long ago peace-loving, kindly, wishful to be friends with all the world. Even now, Mr. Morris tells us, those who were his intimates when he was a professor in Tokyo are still like that.

"THE majority were intellectuals, many would have done anything to prevent this war and were profoundly shocked when it came." They had been too lazy, or too timid, or too much occupied with their private interests and studies, to make any serious attempt to save their country from the generals and admirals who are actuated not by a desire for the well-being of the people, but by their own lunatic ambitions and lust of domination.

The army now, Prof. Morris says, has complete control of the government. "In fact, it is the government. Every branch of the national life—education, industry, commerce, even religion, all are subject to its will, and it is committed to a plan of almost unlimited aggression." Mr. Morris does not believe the Ministers of the Mikado knew about the attack on Pearl Harbour until after it took place. In the Foreign Office the day the news of that shameful act of treachery

reached Tokyo he found the officials "just as much surprised and stunned as the ordinary man in the street." He suggests that the gangsters acted as they did without letting the Ministers know what they had planned. "I think it not unlikely that the attack on Pearl Harbour was launched by the Armed Forces without the previous sanction of the Government."

That is a startling suggestion. It may be sound. But I would put forward another, based on some knowledge of what Japanese Jingoes can do in the way of mystifying world opinion. They may have argued in this way: We had better leave a door open through which we might escape from the consequences

## Military Gangsters Sway Modern Japan

of our making war, if it should go badly for us. In that event we could let the politicians tell Britain and the United States, "We were not to blame, so you can make peace with us."

I have in mind many instances of such double-crossing by Japanese statesmen, military leaders, and business men. When peace was made after the Russo-Japanese War, President Theodore Roosevelt played the part of mediator. He told me the Japanese got what they wanted by asking for much more than they wanted, and withdrawing their demands for what they did not want at the last moment so as to appear reasonable, even generous, and secure what they really cared about.

THIS low kind of cunning does not appear from Prof. Morris's book to be general among the Japanese, whether they are intellectuals or not. He "grew extremely fond of them." After Japan came into the war Britons were regarded with suspicion by the police, who seem to be as bad as Hitler's Gestapo, but "not one of my Japanese friends ceased to visit me and I even made a few new friends. Some of them went to great personal trouble to keep me supplied with food. I shall never forget their kindness or the risks they took; in a country with so

vicious a system of police spying, it requires considerable courage to pay regular visits to an enemy alien in wartime."

IT is not easy to look at other nations' habits and customs without making odious comparisons, without abusing or making fun of them because they are not like our own. As I read Prof. Morris's amusing and informative pages, I could not help thinking of Alice's Wonderland. Take their system—or lack of system—in numbering their houses.

Every street is divided into blocks. The houses in a block are numbered as they are built, irrespective of their position in it. Should the block happen to be large, the house numbered One may be at this end of the street and that numbered Two at the other end.

Moreover, should several new houses be built on a site formerly occupied by one, each retains the number assigned to the original house, so that it is common to find several houses in one street all with the same number. A friend of mine lived in a street in which eleven other houses had the same number as his own.

On the other hand, when one house has been built on a site formerly occupied by several, you get the opposite result. Another friend lived in a house numbered 25-30. To add further to the confusion, the arrangement of the blocks themselves does not conform to any plan; one often finds Block Number Six, for instance, adjacent to Block Number Ten.

But when you do find the house you want, it always has a garden and is always detached. "The rows of sordid little houses or semi-detached villas that so disfigure our towns are unknown in Japan."

ANOTHER topsy-turvy method is connected with the telephone service. Instruments are very hard to get; you may have to wait four or five years. Therefore anyone who has a telephone is expected to let all his neighbours use it. Not only to call people themselves, but to be called! "There were times when the queue in my small study was like one outside a public call-box, and the cook would often have to run down the street to summon someone when she was in the midst of preparing a meal." Prof. Morris even found that one of his neighbours "actually had my telephone number printed on his card."

In restaurants the Japanese get more pleasure out of the artistic surroundings and the dainty way food is served than out of eating it. The author confesses that some of their favourite dishes made him literally sick. What meals they get now are of poor quality, so lacking in nourishment that "it is bound in time to undermine the health of the rising generation." But they "will not crack; they will support the army to the end." And the army "must conquer or perish."

**PRELUDE TO PEARL HARBOUR.** Japanese pilots being briefed for the treacherous attack on America's great Pacific naval base while Japanese envoys were still discussing "peace" in Washington, December 7, 1941. This photograph is a "still" from an enemy news reel now in the possession of the U.S. Government. The Pearl Harbour incident is discussed in the book reviewed in this page.

PAGE 435

*Photo, Associated Press*

# Dashing D.R.s of the Royal Corps of Signals

His motor-cycle isn't the only accessory with which the Dispatch Rider must be familiar.
Indispensable to every military formation, as explained here by JOHN FLEETWOOD, he is a man
of many parts and of hard and specialized training, and resourceful withal. See also facing page.

SOLDIER, signaller, secret agent, scout, King's messenger, Commando . . . . even that is not a full summing-up of the work of dispatch riders of the Royal Corps of Signals. Every military unit or formation has a dispatch rider section, and if it hails from the official Corps so much the better, for none are so fully trained and equipped as the men from the R.C.S.

Probably more than any other campaigner, the D.R. must be a man of scores of parts. True, he must be soldier first—the swift tempo and varied needs of mechanized total war demand that. But before he is ready to take the road as dispatch rider there is a course of some months, suitably reduced and compressed to meet increasingly heavy demands on the Corps. He fills every second of it.

It begins, as you might expect, with machine maintenance, and if—usually as

almost at a glance how much enemy cable to rip up, how much to take away, in order to make the line useless.

Uninterrupted communications are vital, and it is the D.R.'s task to fight the interruptions. Malta provides a vivid illustration. The power behind the island's communications was Lt.-Col. Ellis of the R.C.S.

"DURING the blitzes," he said, "our biggest job was to keep the telephone wires, which carry our service all over the island, intact. Often they provided the only means of transmitting essential information throughout the island—sometimes the only way to issue air-raid warnings. But they seemed to have a fatal attraction for bombs and shell fragments. The moment we knew a wire was down we sent out to repair it. These men would race death a score of times

obstacles. Most of them considered it almost elementary compared with problems met with on active service. Travel by night across the desert meant ability to read the stars. Without a perfect memory the D.R. would be useless ; how would he commit to memory long, intricate messages which, written, might fall into the hands of the enemy ? He must know map-reading from A to Z, even be able to memorize from a map any 40 miles of untravelled road. To recognize all unit signs and flashes, and know upon whom to make his calls he must have a thorough knowledge of army organization.

"Here," said the examiner at one of the schools, "is an imaginary road-block—a large hole. How would you get across ?" "With an imaginary plank," replied the humorist of the class. The actuality is not so humorous. Time and again dispatch riders have had to negotiate huge crater pools with planks. This fact underlines one of the basic qualities of D.R. make-up—resourcefulness, the attribute which operates as when Signalman Chalker was escorting a D.R. truck carrying important dispatches from Harrar in Abyssinia. About 20 miles out progress was impeded by a flooded river four feet deep. Hurling the dispatches across to a South African officer who had a motor-cycle on the opposite bank, Chalker persuaded some coloured boys to carry his own machine across. Farther on he overtook the officer, whose machine had broken down, and, without stopping, collected the mailbag as he passed. Shortly after, his own cycle failed him. Nothing daunted, Chalker commandeered a supply lorry going the other way, turned it round and reached the aerodrome just in time to clear the mail by aeroplane.

INGENUITY flowed freely when D.R.s of the desert Reconnaissance Corps, badly needing more bikes, raided the Hun lines and captured nine brand-new machines. And there is infinite resource in the army courier's quick-time methods of mending a puncture. One is to stuff up the hole with grass !

Other attributes officially tagged to D.R.s are energy, initiative and cunning. And the greatest of these, the older hands will tell you, is cunning. On patrol with our cars in Tunisia, a Recce D.R.'s motor-cycle broke down. The enemy was so near that he had to leave it in a ditch in no man's land. Later, he set out with a 15 cwt. truck to retrieve it. Near his cache he spotted two German soldiers settling down for a nap in a farmyard by the roadside. Stopping the truck, and equipped only with a revolver—sole official armament of the D.R.—he crawled forward and captured both men as they dozed, thus acquiring valuable identifications of the enemy units confronting our troops.

That was cunning allied to courage. Often by such acts and by closely observing enemy movements, a D.R. may be a commander's important source of information. Frequently he may be the sole means of communication, as at El Alamein when all radio communication was ordered to be suspended for security reasons, and tank commanders picked up with nets the urgent dispatches that D.R.s held aloft on sticks as they roared by.

And let us not forget the signals girls of the A.T.S. Their work is on the home front, but it is none the less vital. Generally, their function is as Signals Operators ; and a fine example of it was when sneak raiders' bombs wrecked an A.T.S. billet in an East Anglian town last May. Though a number of their colleagues had been killed outright, four surviving girls in a nearby house hardly turned a hair ; they just carried on.

ROUGH GOING is all in the day's work of a Royal Corps of Signals dispatch rider even when, as here in North Africa, the terrain is reminiscent of pre-war Isle of Man T.T. trials. Bulk of the Army's correspondence, marked maps, the most important operational orders and secret messages which cannot be entrusted to wireless, are carried by these devil-daring and superbly enterprising motor-cyclists.
Photo, British Official : Crown Copyright

ex-motor mechanic or cognate trade—the practical experience the applicant brings to the job is insufficient, intensive training makes good what is lacking. Before he graduates he knows his machine inside out. The knowledge is a vital necessity both to him and his job, since his trusty motor-cycle must—literally—never fail him.

IF, despite all he can do, it does fail him, then he must complete his task by seizing another machine or an enemy vehicle, or by getting a lift in a truck or lorry, or finishing the journey afoot—the last and degrading extremity. No matter what problems confront him, he must reach his objective. That is the cardinal feature of a dispatch rider's training. But even 100 per cent efficiency in "keeping himself on the road" would be useless without tip-top proficiency in a score of other directions.

In the fullest sense he is a signaller. When training is over, there isn't much he cannot tell you about that. As well as the laying and repair of field telephone lines and communications of all types, he can smell out breaks in lines outwardly perfect. He must know

to restore a cut line, and no one will ever know the full story of the heroic linesmen who strove, not merely between raids, but literally between bombs, to keep the lines up."

If it isn't ground and overhead lines, it is dispatches personally carried ; and the Big Blitz was as much a major operation for the Signals boys as for the A.R.P. and fire-fighting services. With telegraph and telephone communications down, dispatch riders fought their way at top speed through the scorching, screaming hell with urgent dispatches to rail termini and signal stations.

Uninterruptedly the service was maintained along the roads—for there was no other way—though these were often made impassable by piles of red-hot debris and huge tongues of flame from burning buildings on both sides. Black-out added to the difficulties. It was no picnic, when fire-bombs gave place to H.E.s, riding the roads without lights at the risk of diving headlong into craters and unlighted roped-off road sections.

All the same, this was no novelty for the experienced D.R., trained to overcome all

# They Keep Open the Line From H.Q. to Front

THE ROYAL CORPS OF SIGNALS, formed June 28, 1920, to deal with the study and practice of signal communications, has developed into a highly specialized and technically skilled body responsible for the operation of all the Army's systems of communications. Means employed by the Corps include the radio, the telegraph-line and dispatch riders (see opposite page). Latest acquisition of the radio section is the " Golden Arrow," a mobile, high-speed wireless station (1) to keep field armies in contact with H.Q. A radio operator (2) gets down to the job as British troops pass through Belpasso, Sicily. Cadet-linesmen (3) learn maintenance details from models, in preparation for work under all conditions of war and weather (4, 5 and 6).

PAGE 437

*Photos, British Official : Crown Copyright*

# THE HOME FRONT

## by E. Royston Pike

By the end of the year we shall have gathered the greatest harvest that the country has ever known. So announced Mr. R. S. Hudson, Minister of Agriculture, in a recent broadcast. It is a striking fact, and all the more remarkable in that the huge amount of food has been grown on the smallest acreage of land devoted to our agriculture since official records have been kept—this because every month of the war we have had to give up more and more land for aerodromes, battle-training grounds, and other martial purposes. Farmers and their men, their wives and the women and girls of the Land Army, between them have astonished the world ; and grateful thanks are due, too, to the great body of volunteers who have spent much of their holiday periods on the land, helping the harvesters of grain and roots. Fortunately, the weather has been kind—at least in most parts, although in the West Country and in the north persistent rain drenched the crops and laid them low, so that farmers and farmworkers had to stand by helpless for several weeks, watching their precious produce spoil.

So far as can be estimated we are likely to get one million tons more bread-corn and over a quarter of a million tons more potatoes than last year—and last year was a record one. That in itself, said the Minister of Agriculture, means a saving of enough ships to transport overseas vehicles, supplies, guns, ammunition and equipment for some eight to ten divisions. "And that is merely this year's increase over last year's. So you can picture for yourselves what last year's prodigious total means, and can see that the fields of England have had quite a lot to do with the collapse of Italy." In years gone by Michaelmas used to be the traditional end of the farming year. But things are very different today. Now a start is made with sowing for next year while this year's stooks are still standing in adjoining fields ; and in the depth of winter the farmworkers are busy in the fields, ploughing and planting so that next year's harvest shall surpass the one that has just been gathered and garnered.

Because of the fertile cooperation of man and Nature we—the forty-five millions whose homes are in this little island—are the best-fed people in Europe ; but at the same time we must recognize that this happy state of affairs would not have been possible but for the careful planning and foresight of the Ministry of Food. Lord Woolton has triumphed in a position that has proved the grave of more than one good man's reputation ; and just because he has been so successful he is now being transplanted to a fresh field of effort. On November 11 it was announced that he had been appointed Minister of Reconstruction with a seat in the War Cabinet—in other words, he is entrusted with the task of implementing what Mr. Churchill in his Mansion House speech of November 9, 1943, described as " a vast and practical scheme to make sure that in the years immediately following the war there will be food, work and homes for all." To provide these things is a simple duty, went on the Premier, and " no airy visions, no party doctrines or party prejudices or vested interests shall stand in the way."

### THE New Britain Plans Are Now Lord Woolton's Responsibility

Lord Woolton is not a party politician in the usual sense ; he has let it be inderstood that he has no political ambitions, but intends, after the war to return to the world of business in which he was so successful in the years gone by. (Of his chairmanships the most important was that of Lewis's, the departmental stores that are so prominent a feature of the northern cities ; and he was once warden of a university settlement in Liverpool). His new appointment may lead him to change his mind and his plans. The new Britain is now his responsibility, and the measure of his success will be reflected in the lives of us all. Obviously, the Prime Minister could not have made a better choice ; and it is generally anticipated that the reports of Beveridge and Barlow, Scott and Uthwatt will be retrieved from the pigeon-holes in Whitehall and some at least of their proposals included in the reconstruction programme.

Other Cabinet changes were announced at the same time as Lord Woolton's appointment. Mr. H. U. Willink, K.C., M.P. for Croydon N., became Minister of Health in succession to Mr. Ernest Brown, who received in exchange the Chancellorship of the Duchy of Lancaster. Mr. Willink is a newcomer as M.P.s go—he was elected only in 1940 ; but he has been highly commended for his work as Special Commissioner for rehousing in London following the great air raids. Lord Woolton's place at the Ministry of Food is filled by Col. J. J. Llewellin, who for some time past has been British Minister Resident in Washington for Supply and Chairman of the British Supply Council in North America. The new Minister in Washington is Mr. Ben Smith, a Labour member who can look back upon a varied career, in which he has been lower deck boxing champion in the Royal Navy, a driver of horse cabs and taxis, an organizer of the Transport and General Workers Union, and Treasurer of the Royal Household. Then Mr. Duff Cooper, lately Chancellor of the Duchy, goes to North Africa as the British envoy to the French Committee of National Liberation ; and Mr. Lennox Boyd succeeds Mr. Ben Smith as Parliamentary Secretary to the Ministry of Aircraft Production.

So few and scattered have been the raids of late months that there has been voiced in some parts a suggestion that the Civil Defence volunteers might be released from some of their duties. Mr. Herbert Morrison, Home Secretary and Minister of Home Security, is convinced, however, that the time has not yet come when we can safely relax our precautions. "If Hitler thought that his bombs would be greeted by incompetence and muddle," he said on November 18, " he would certainly risk more of his planes more often. Civil Defence personnel and Fire Guards who do duty and training on a raid-free night should consider that they have won a victory, not that they have wasted time." Mr. Morrison then referred to a recent incident, in which a crowded London dance-hall had received a direct hit from a German bomb. Very largely, he said, it was a job for the Rescue Service, but all the Civil Defence services, the W.V.S. and the N.F.S., put up a great show. "We had come to expect that of them, but a new point was the way in which a number of the Fire Guard won their spurs that night."

When such an incident as this occurs, the Wardens and their comrades come into their own. But really they are doing a fine piece of social service, every day and everywhere. "Down our street we've got a utility lady warden," said Anthony Gordon in a broadcast a short time back. "In addition to her ordinary jobs of looking for bombs, mending gas-masks and collecting old iron, she looks after all the kids in the neighbourhood. She tells them when their teas are ready, ties their bootlaces, wipes their noses, gets their balls down off roofs. And if two of them start fighting she stops it by the simple method of clipping the bigger one's ear. She's a boon to the children, but a bigger one to the mothers who want to get on with their work ; and I suppose by stopping the children fighting, she does a lot towards stopping their parents getting at it too . . ."

**LORD WOOLTON, C.H.**
Minister of Food since April 1940, his new appointment as Minister of Reconstruction was announced on Nov. 11, 1943. He is an administrator of outstanding ability.

**COL. J. J. LLEWELLIN, M.P.**
Succeeded Lord Woolton as Minister of Food. Was Minister Resident for Supply in Washington ; prior to that was Minister of Aircraft Production.

**BEN SMITH, M.P.**
New Minister Resident for Supply in Washington, with Cabinet rank. Was formerly Parliamentary Secretary to the Ministry of Aircraft Production.

**H. U. WILLINK, K.C., M.P.**
Minister of Health in succession to Mr. Ernest Brown. Formerly Special Commissioner for air-raid homeless in the London Civil Defence Region. Now becomes a Privy Councillor.

*Photos. Topical. Barratt's*

# R.A.F.'s Speedy Succour for Crashed Flyers

RESCUE IS THE JOB of the new R.A.F. Mountain Service, which brings expeditious aid to airmen crashed in hilly areas where an ordinary ambulance tender would be unable to go. Each rescue unit has a powerful four-wheel-drive ambulance fitted with medical, rescue and radio apparatus, and a jeep to act as tender. The ambulance having been brought as far as possible (1), members of the unit—equipped with head torches and wireless sets, and attired for mountain climbing—make for the scene of the disaster, while others (3) set up an emergency tent. One Welsh unit has as M.O. a skilled mountaineer, Flt.-Lt. G. D. Graham (2, wearing woollen helmet). He leads his men to the spot, and the injured airman is lowered (4), strapped to a stretcher. *Photos, Fox, Planet News*

# Busy Port of Algiers Now a Vital War Centre

ALGIERS TODAY presents a spectacle of military and political bustle. It is the administrative and commercial centre of North-West Africa, and through its port (4) pass men and material vital to the war; these are Britain-bound passengers waiting for their transport to back in. Allied sick and wounded patients convalesce here: special recuperative exercises (1) are included in the treatment. Generals Giraud, de Gaulle and Catroux (2—l. to r.) faced the first session of the provisional Consultative Assembly of France on November 9, 1943. Tommies on leave rove the bazaars for gifts to send home; like this one (3) bargaining for a tiny garment (held up by the seller)—maybe for the baby he has not seen for many months, if at all.

*Photos, British & U.S. Official*

# I WAS THERE!
### Eye Witness Stories of the War

## With the Soviet Troops I Entered Burning Kiev

*All night the battle raged at the city walls. Flames seethed and hovered over it ; the German incendiaries were working feverishly. In the morning, Nov. 6, 1943, the Russians regained the city by storm. Major H. Bukovsky, of the Red Army, who entered with the conquerors, sent the following vivid dispatch to the Soviet War News. See also illus. page 431.*

FROM our observation post it seemed that Kiev was one sea of flames. I could see the eyes of our men fill with tears at the sight of the burning city. They had seen so much already. It would not have been strange if they had forgotten how to weep. But they wept for Kiev.

Our troops did all they could to save Kiev. Day after day they pounded away at the Germans' formidable defences. Then they executed a bold manoeuvre in the rear of the Nazi garrison. For brevity and speed the Red Army's Kiev operation has no parallel in history. All arms—artillery, infantry, tanks and air force—distinguished themselves equally. The enemy was overwhelmed and annihilated ; the woods beyond Pushcha-Voditsa are littered with hundreds of wrecked guns. The charred carcasses of scores of his Panzers lie around Priorka and Svyatoshinv.

On November 6 Lieutenant-Colonel Ponomartsev's Red Banner Guards Regiment burst into Kiev from one end, fought its way to the centre, and began to clear a path to the opposite end. At the same time Capt. Chumachenko's tank battalion, together with infantry under Hero of the Soviet Union Capt. Ivanin, invaded Kalinin Square.

I overtook these troops in the morning in Kreshchatik Street, Kiev's main thoroughfare. The tanks were moving forward illuminated by the rays of the rising sun and the glare of a burning house at a street corner. As I watched, the partition wall collapsed and long tongues of fire shot across the street.

We drove through a pall of smoke to the Regional Soviet building. Farther along the smoke cleared, but the streets were in ruins. All the way to the suburb of Bessarabka we saw nothing but a chaos of destruction, traces of barbarity unequalled since the times of Batu. In Kreshchatik Street we halted and bared our heads. A grave opened before us in a lawn near the Regional Soviet building. Junior Lieut. Sheludenko's scouts were burying their fallen commander. Near the grave stood a girl holding a wreath. The Lieutenant

had been killed just as his troops burst into the city streets.

From Kreshchatik Street we swerved to the right—everywhere fires, debris, ruin. We reached the monastery of caves, the ruins of the Cathedral of the Assumption, which the Germans blew up two years ago, and the wrecked City Museum buildings. Here we met one solitary person—Sergei Emelyantsev, senior mechanic of the Kiev waterworks. He was an old man, but he was desperately eager to be allowed to come along with us. "Let me join you, if only in a supply column," he pleaded. "I'll show you where there are German tommy-gunners beyond the waterworks, firing at our troops on the Dnieper."

Entering a liberated city with the army is a heart-rending experience. In Priorka and in Podol weeping women embraced the tired, smoke-stained soldiers, who were still feeling the strain of the recent battle. Glass splinters crunched under their feet as they marched. I sensed their mingled elation and grief, their poignant pity for the women, old men and children who came forward to meet them, the people of Kiev, with faces ravaged by torment and long-deferred hope.

KIEV was half empty when our troops entered it. The Germans had evicted all the inhabitants from the centre, from Podol and the monastery district, and proclaimed the city a military zone. Long before the battle the compulsory deportation of inhabitants to Germany began. We were told of frightful scenes enacted at Kiev station only a couple of days ago. The Germans had herded the people into goods wagons, crowded almost to bursting. Those who could not be packed in they shot on the spot.

It is still too early to say how many inhabitants are left in Kiev. Lenin Street is deserted. Near one burning house we saw three women trying desperately to save some furniture. They had hurried here from the outskirts, only to find their homes in flames. Novokaravayevskaya Street, far out in the suburbs, swarmed with women weeping with

**MAJ.-GEN. LODYGIN,** Divisional Commander of Soviet infantry, at his observation post outside Kiev just before the Russians recaptured the city.     *Photo, Pictorial Press*

joy. They were the people whom the Germans had evicted from the centre of the city. At No. 14 they told us how the evictions were carried out. German soldiers armed with bottles of petrol entered the houses and ordered the tenants to leave. If anybody refused, the Germans drenched the beds and furniture with petrol and set fire to them. Before they retreated they blew up a water main, so many streets were without water.

We met a man who declared he was the sole surviving Jew in Kiev. He led us to the Jewish cemetery. This was the site of the awful tragedy of September 1941, when tens of thousands of Jews—men, women and children—were shot. Even after that the Germans continued to exterminate anyone whom they took a fancy to class as a Jew.

We climbed Vladimir Hill. Before us lay the Dnieper. The last of the troops from Trukhanov Island were being ferried across. To the left lay the vast district of Podol. Endless columns of tanks, artillery and rifle regiments wound along its streets, to disappear down the high road, where the receding battle thundered. At midday we took off from the airfield. An unforgettable sight unfolded before our eyes. There lay the vast, inexpressibly beautiful city of Kiev, wrapped in smoke and flames. After excruciating torments, it was awakening to bright day.

**BURNING KIEV** (left) was a pyre of German hopes in the central sector of the Russian front. One of Russia's oldest cities, it has been laid waste many times—notably in 1240, by the Tartars — only to rise again, as assuredly it will under the Soviets.
*Photo, Pictorial Press*

## I Saw Nazi Paratroops Attack in Leros Battle

Sole war correspondent on Leros, L. Marsland Gander witnessed severe fighting between Allied and German forces for possession of this island in the Dodecanese. He left only two days before the exhausted garrison, after prodigies of endurance and courage, was compelled to capitulate, Nov. 16, 1943.

DARINGLY landed on a rocky hillside yesterday, Nov. 13, a force of German parachutists was strengthened at dawn today by reinforcements dropped through the furious fire of many machine-guns. The Germans suffered numerous casualties. I saw a Junkers transport plane, hit squarely by a Bofors A.A. gun, fall into the sea.

Creeping into Alinda Bay in the half-light, a landing craft was heavily machine-gunned and bombarded from the overlooking height. The air was full of red streamers of tracer. Men were seen scrambling ashore from the craft, which eventually blew up with a great mushroom explosion.

The parachutists' plan was to cut the island in two halves, seizing the wasp waist between Alinda Bay and Gurna Bay. These bays separate the two main rocky humps of the island. Having shipped the cordon, the craft landed reinforcements on the northern shores. There have been no further landings of German troops this morning.

THE garrison was greatly encouraged in its stern fight by the appearance of a formation of Beaufighters, which interrupted the strafing of the enemy fighters and the constant dive-bombing of the Stukas. Nine German planes, it is claimed, have been shot down to date by one Bofors A.A. gun alone.

Leros is only eight miles long and you must watch your step in moving about, since the air is full of bullets, and bombs fall with monotonous regularity. Though attacked by Stukas for three solid days, the Italian batteries are still firing.

The previous day, Nov. 12, German Junkers in groups of four to seven attacked at intervals of a quarter of an hour or so in an effort to crack the Leros defences by bombing. They did not succeed, as was shown by their reception. After a night of alarms I was finally awakened at four o'clock by an orderly saying, " An invasion fleet reported near the island, sir ! "

I climbed to the top of a hill and watched seven invasion craft behind a smoke-screen creeping southward past Alinda Bay. On being shelled by our shore guns they sheered off and circled the island. Five landing craft attempted to enter Della Palma Bay, but three were hit by shells and one sank.

Another enemy group which got ashore

near Appelici was pushed back to the beach again. Near my vantage point was an Italian light A.A. gun which gave one group of dive-bombers a nasty surprise by putting a good burst straight into the leading Ju 87, thus diverting the bomber's attention to itself. A most determined attempt by enemy invaders came this afternoon, when a couple of dozen troop-carriers swooped through machine-gun fire to drop parachutists on the island.

As I write, Stukas are beginning their customary contest with our land batteries. Hungry for prestige, the Germans are making every effort to capture the island. They are

not bothering about losses. These days remind me of the siege of Tobruk. Holes in the ground, tunnels between rocks are our homes. Everyone in the garrison is in strangely high spirits, but all wish we had fighters. Despite the tough time they are having, they are cheerful and giving a good account of themselves . . .

Once again our forces were fighting without adequate air cover, as in Norway, Greece and Crete. This time, however, it was not a shortage of aircraft pilots which brought about such a disastrous situation, but merely the geography and distance of our nearest fighter bases from the scene of action.

In fairness to the R.A.F. it must be said that gallant efforts were made to reach the island with all the available long-range fighters. These R.A.F. sorties, which had to bypass enemy fighter fields on Rhodes, Crete or Cos were almost quixotic.

## I Took the First Churchill Tanks into Action

Suitably adapted to the terrain, Churchill tanks went into action for the first time in North Africa, near Sbiba. Their baptism of fire is here vividly described for " The War Illustrated " by Sergt. G. Powell, who was awarded the Military Medal for his gallantry and resource on that occasion.

IT was on a Sunday, February 21, 1943. We had just come to the end of a journey of 108 miles non-stop ; no food, no sleep, and no maintenance, which must be considered excellent for a forty-ton tank. At 16.00 hours I was ordered to have my troop all set and ready to go into action by 17.00 hours. Without any grumbling from my boys, there's no need to say that we were all keyed up and ready at the appointed time.

But things do go wrong sometimes. I was approaching the Guards positions when my tank just packed up. With so little time before zero hour I had no alternative but to ask for another tank. We soon had the new one ready for action, and the next thing was for me to try to get further details of what part my troop was to play in the action.

I was told that in front, 400 yards away, were a range of mountains with a road running through them. I was instructed to keep off the road (which was quite natural because Jerry was slinging his big mortars about), so there was no choice but to go over the mountain, which is not a pleasant feeling for the tanks. The only information I could obtain was that over the far side of the mountain there were two or three Arab huts which Jerry was using as machine-gun nests. My job was to wipe these out. "A bit of cake," we all called it. I was also taking in with me a platoon of Coldstream Guards.

When we arrived at the summit of the hill (I should say mountain) I couldn't see any of the enemy, but I felt something hit my leg and also noticed that my wireless operator had been hit. When we finally got over the top of the mountain, I could see my objective—about twenty Jerry tanks all lined up with a row of anti-tank guns at the back and a battery of machine-guns behind them!

I just turned my head for a split second and saw my other two tanks getting blown to "hell." Making a quick decision, I decided to charge the enemy, as it would have been suicide to try anything else. Jerry hit me about twelve times, making my tank useless for firing as he had already hit both of my guns. But I could now see the Germans getting out of their tanks and bolting. Giving orders to my driver to turn around, imagine my surprise to find German infantry not more than five yards to my front.

Sgt. G. POWELL, M.M., who was in the thick of the fighting round Sbiba, Tunisia (see map), in February 1943, when the new Churchill tanks went to the support of the Guards during Gen. Alexander's counter-stroke against Rommel. Their first appearance in battle was crowned by the taking of Kasserine on March 1, giving control of the vital Pass. See also p. 645, Vol. 6.

But we scraped them out for the count.

At this point I began to feel just where I had been hit ; I couldn't stand, but was just hanging up by the handlebars of my cupola. On the way back I started to look out for any of my boys that might have been lucky enough to jump out of their tanks when they went up. I found three of them ; two were badly burned (they died later) and the other was just shaken up. I also discovered a Guardsman who had been badly hit. So with my tank loaded up, I returned to our original starting point.

I was told later that the enemy retreated for about fifteen miles shortly after that engagement, and I think it made it easier for our boys to take the Kasserine Pass.

LEROS, Dodecanese island which, with adjacent Cos and Samos, was occupied by British troops on September 25, 1943. Strong German forces were landed on November 12 and the island capitulated four days later.
*Map by courtesy of Daily Telegraph*

# I Crashed and Was Lost in the New Guinea Jungle

*A young American fighter pilot, Capt. C. P. Sullivan, was flying over the Ramu Valley, on a mission to Wewak, when one engine of his Lightning cut out. A Japanese fighter forced him into the clouds—a second engine failed, and he went down. Here he tells of his thirty days' adventure.*

I SPENT the first night propped against a tree, listening to the noises of the jungle. On the third day an Allied bomber flew over, but failed to see me. I then set out along a native path. I made a raft of three logs, and floated down the river until the raft hit the bank and capsized. Then I went into the mountains. I had only ration chocolate to eat, and was getting weak. Suddenly a black face popped up, and I raised a hand and said " Hi ! " It belonged to a native. He gave me a banana and I went with him to a village where I was given some pig and sweet potato.

I slept that night in the village, and next day my host, whose name sounded like Sego, agreed to come part of the way to Bena Bena. The head man of the village came along. Presently we fell in with a party of hostile natives, from whose demeanour I suspected treachery. The moving spirit in the second party was a pretty mean-looking guy who answered to the name of Addi. Sego and Addi began to argue, and Addi got mad. They were obviously arguing about me. We went to another village where another man and Addi sat down uncomfortably close to me. I went and sat with Sego, but Addi objected and there was a lot of bow and arrow and knife rattling. Addi wanted me to lie down in a hut and go to sleep.

It looked too much like a trap, so I went out and put a slug into the breech of my forty-five. I sat down where I could see them all, and told them if they did anything to me

our bombers would come and get them. All but Addi looked impressed. The head man wanted to move round behind me, but I flicked my gun at him and made him sit down. I told them I would shoot them if they made me move. Addi jumped up and came at me yelling, and grabbed my arms, and I had to shoot him. Then the head man rushed at me and I shot him, too. I felt pretty bad about it after, but there was nothing else I could do. The rest ran away and I ran, too. I lay hidden, and presently some women came and wailed over the bodies.

I LEFT just before dawn. I took off my boots so that I could move quietly, but they rattled against the trees, so I left them. That was a big mistake. I went up and down ridges barefooted for sixteen days ; I kept a little stick and cut a notch on it for each day. After I left the natives I had only four pawpaws and maybe a dozen each of passion fruit and bananas, with a lot of black seeds in them. Every night I got wet, but always managed to keep my gun dry. I tried eating grass, but it was awful.

I had only six matches, and took almost a day collecting dry stuff for a fire. No one came, so next day I made a really big one. Still nothing happened, so I decided to go on. It was tough walking barefoot on burnt stubble. About noon I saw the reflection of something on a hill. It took me until next morning to reach it, and I found it was an Aussie camp. I couldn't say anything for a while, but they were just swell to me, and

**WEWAK, vital Japanese supply base in New Guinea, is the scene of this swoop on an enemy freighter by a U.S. Army Air Force medium bomber, which skims the water to drive home its attack.** *Photo, Planet News*

their officer, Lieutenant Jim Harper, of Melbourne, cut my hair and gave me food and clothes and boots, and even took me to a creek and washed my back. This was the twenty-fourth day after I crashed. After three days I went down to Dumpu, where they put me in a little runabout plane. But that crashed, too, though the pilot and I weren't hurt. I finished the journey by transport plane to hospital, where I am rapidly recovering strength.

# OUR DIARY OF THE WAR

**NOVEMBER 10, Wednesday** *1,530th day*
Italy.—Fall of Castiglione to 8th Army announced. Fierce enemy counter-attacks against Americans at Venafro and British at Calabritto repelled.
Russian Front. — Ivankovo and Gribenki captured by Soviet troops.
Australasia.—Rabaul (New Britain) heavily attacked at night by 200 Allied aircraft.
Air.—Modane, French Riviera frontier town near mouth of Mont Cenis tunnel, heavily bombed at night.

**NOVEMBER 11, Thursday** *1,531st day*
Italy.—Air reconnaissance revealed Germans scuttling ships at Leghorn and Pisa.
Mediterranean. — Annecy (France) ball-bearing works and rail yard bombed by Liberators.
Russian Front.—Radomesl, Brusilov, and Kornino in the Zhitomir region captured by Russians.
Australasia.—Announced that U.S. troops, their task accomplished, had withdrawn from Choiseul Is. (Solomons). Japanese cruiser and two destroyers sunk in Allied carrier attack on Rabaul (New Britain).
General.—War Cabinet changes announced ; Lord Woolton appointed Minister of Reconstruction ; Col. Llewellin, Minister of Food ; Mr. H. U. Willink, K.C., Minister of Health ; Mr. Ernest Brown, Chancellor of the Duchy of Lancaster ; Mr. Ben Smith, Minister Resident in Washington. Martial Law proclaimed in Lebanon Republic ; the President, Prime Minister and chief ministers arrested by French troops.

**NOVEMBER 12, Friday** *1,532nd day*
Mediterranean.—British-held island of Leros (Dodecanese) invaded by Germans ; Italians fighting side by side with British.
Russian Front.—Zhitomir captured by Red Army ; Korostyshev taken.
General.—Announced that Admiral Sir J. C. Tovey, G.C.B., K.B.E., D.S.O., promoted to succeed Sir Dudley Pound as Admiral of the Fleet. French troops cleared barricades in Beirut (Lebanon).

**NOVEMBER 13, Saturday** *1,533rd day*
Italy.—Allied and German troops in fierce battle for Mount Camino ridge, S.W. of Mignano.
Air.—Bremen bombed by U.S. Fortresses and Liberators.

**NOVEMBER 14, Sunday** *1,534th day*
Italy.—Capture of Atessa by 8th Army, Filignano and Pozzili by U.S. troops, announced.
Mediterranean.—Sofia bombed by U.S. Mitchells.
Russian Front.—Chepovichi, 20 miles S.E. of Korosten, taken by Russians.

**NOVEMBER 15, Monday** *1,535th day*
Mediterranean. — Announced that Greek paratroops landed on Samos (Dodecanese) to strengthen British garrison.
Russian Front. — Kaganovichi, in Kiev sector, captured by Red Army ; Soviet troops cut vital Gomel-Rezhitsa railway.
China.—Hong Kong and Kowloon bombed by U.S. Liberators.
General.—Duke of Gloucester appointed to succeed Lord Gowrie as Governor-General of Australia as from June 1944. Gen. Catroux arrived in Beirut (Lebanon) to deal with crisis.

**NOVEMBER 16, Tuesday** *1,536th day*
Mediterranean.—Leros, overwhelmed by German bombers, capitulated to the enemy.
Russian Front.—Fierce enemy counter-attacks S.W. of Kiev salient repelled.

Pacific.—Japanese aerodrome of Jaluit (Marshall Islands) bombed by Liberators.
Air.—Knaben molybdenum mines and Rjukan power station (Norway) bombed by U.S. Fortresses.

**NOVEMBER 17, Wednesday** *1,537th day*
Russian Front.—Korosten and Rezhitsa captured by Russians. Chernobyl, on lower reaches of River Pripet, taken. Enemy gained ground in Zhitomir region.
Australasia.—Japanese air bases on Buka Island, N. of Bougainville bombarded by U.S. naval task force.
Air.—Ludwigshafen bombed by Lancasters and Halifaxes.
General.—The Emir Feisal and Emir Khalid, sons of the king of Saudi Arabia, arrived in England.

**NOVEMBER 18, Thursday** *1,538th day*
Mediterranean.—Allied Air Forces attacked Eleusis airfield (Athens).
Russian Front.—Heavy enemy counterattacks repelled at Zhitomir and Korostyshev.
Air.—Kjeller, Luftwaffe depot 11 miles N.E. of Oslo, Norway, raided by U.S. Liberators. Berlin (350 block-busters dropped in 30 minutes) and Mannheim-Ludwigshafen heavily bombed in great

double attack ; largest number of heavy bombers ever sent to Germany took part in raids.

**NOVEMBER 19, Friday** *1,539th day*
Russian Front.—Ovruch seized by Russians. Dnieper forced in Cherkasy area. Soviet troops abandoned Zhitomir.
Air.—Fortresses attacked Western Germany. Leverkusen, near Cologne, heavily attacked at night.

**NOVEMBER 20, Saturday** *1,540th day*
Russian Front.—Russians defeated German thrusts at Korostyshev.
Australasia.—U.S. Marines and troops landed on the Makin and Tarawa atolls (Gilbert Is.).

**NOVEMBER 21, Sunday** *1,541st day*
Russian Front. — Russian troops reached bank of Beresina, N. of Gomel.
General.—Mr. William Strang chosen to be British representative on the European Advisory Commission. French National Committee decided to reinstate M. Khoury as President of the Lebanese Republic and liberate other ministers ; negotiations on independence to be opened with Syrian Government and later with Lebanese Government.

**NOVEMBER 22, Monday** *1,542nd day*
Italy.—Announced that considerable Canadian reinforcements had arrived.
Russian Front. — Enemy counterattacks in the Korostyshev and Chernyakhov sectors repulsed.
Air.—Berlin received its heaviest raid to date ; 2,300 tons of bombs dropped.
General.—Mr. Duff Cooper appointed British representative on French National Committee. Lebanese demonstrators occupied the Chamber seat of the government, and the police headquarters.

**NOVEMBER 23, Tuesday** *1,543rd day*
Australasia. — Disclosed that U.S. troops landed recently on Apamama atoll (Gilbert Is.). Announced Makin Island (Gilberts) captured by U.S. troops
Mediterranean. — Revealed that British, Greek and some Italian troops evacuated from Samos (Dodecanese).
Russian Front.—Bragin, in district of lower Pripet, occupied by Russians. Soviet troops forced to give ground south of Kiev salient.
Air.—Berlin heavily raided for second successive night ; 5,000 tons of bombs dropped on the capital in last week.

## ★ Flash-backs ★

**1939**
November 23. German magnetic mines laid in East Coast estuaries.

**1940**
November 11. First large-scale Italian air raid on Britain.

**1941**
November 16. Germans captured Kerch in the eastern Crimea.
November 17. British Commandos raided German H.Q. in Libya.
November 19. H.M.A.S. Sydney sunk in action with German raider Steiermark, which was also destroyed at the same time.

**1942**
November 10. Oran (French North Africa) captured by U.S. troops.
November 11. German troops entered Unoccupied France. Casablanca and Bougie capitulated to U.S. and British troops.
November 12. British First Army occupied Bône in Algeria.
November 13. 8th Army captured Tobruk and Gazala in Cyrenaica.
November 15. Contact made between Allied and Axis forces 12 miles N.W. of Jadeida, Tunisia.
November 20. Benghazi (Libya) occupied by British 8th Army.

# THE WAR IN THE AIR

## by Capt. Norman Macmillan, M.C., A.F.C.

THE greatest difference between surface war and air war lies in the association in each case between strategy and tactics. In surface war, both on land and at sea, strategical situations can be created by the grouping of armies or of navies with the possession of adequate lines of communication, ports, and supply facilities. Tactical actions in the face of the enemy are the products of the strategical situation.

It is usual for opponents in war so to manoeuvre that the strategical situation falls favourably before one side or the other strikes. This applies both in advances and retreats, and in the present war it has been seen more often with greater skill during the retreats than during the advances. It must be assumed that during her present great retreat in Russia, and from Africa, Germany has planned to gain by those manoeuvres a strategical situation more favourable to her than the position she held before the retreats began. Let us examine this point more closely, for it is an important one in the war at the present time, and the lessons that can be learned from it are pointers to operations on an ever-growing scale against Japan.

The all-important factor to be borne in mind is the different relationship between air strategy and tactics. The strategic situation in surface war, as we have just observed, is contained in the latent strength of the forces in the dispositions they hold before they strike. It is, indeed, a situation of threat and not of action. In such circumstances, when tactical situations follow, the forces are not always fully locked in battle; an example of reaction from a strategic situation was the inconclusive battle of Jutland in the last war, when the British Commander-in-Chief naval forces decided that the favourable strategic situation was more important than the uncertainty of establishing a successful tactical result. Nothing of this kind can happen in air war.

AND that is the principal reason why this war, and its actions, differ from previous wars. Failure to recognize that cardinal change in the principle of war has cost Britain and her Allies dearly enough. The change of principle has been unobserved or ignored by many generals and admirals, and regarded as a method, with unfortunate results in numerous actions fought all over the world.

The strategic air situation results in constant action, action even more continuous than the tactical air war over the fields of surface actions by land and sea. In air war you cannot hold a great air fleet leashed without striking. The policy of Jellicoe, at Jutland, could not possibly be that of the leaders of R.A.F. Bomber Command, or the U.S. Army Eighth Air Force, or the Mediterranean Strategic Air Force. It was possible to dominate the sea in 1914-18 by holding a Battle Fleet in strategic reserve in Scapa Flow. That is no longer possible.

We dominate the sea mainly by superior air power. Battleships are used as escort vessels, anti-aircraft ships to provide gun-fire power for the local protection of merchant ships. Their former strategic threat has been reduced by the air weapon to a faint shadow of its former glory, a shadow that falls mainly from the past. The German capital ships, far fewer than in 1914-18, were not knocked out by Britain's superior fleet, nor did this keep them in harbour.

They have been crippled by the air weapon, kept in port by the air weapon, and because the Germans knew the power of the air weapon and made the most extensive preparations for its use before 1939 they built their capital ships to stand against it better than we had done, and so their ships were harder to sink than ours. But, even so, with all the ingenuity of a people who intended to subjugate the world by the use of excess air power, their ships have failed lamentably because they have been continually restrained by the air weapon.

THE fleets of Britain, Japan, America, and Italy have all felt the effects of this new weapon. It has changed the character of naval war. Because of this there are sailors of high rank who contend that the aeroplane is not more than a gun, a weapon, and that Air Power is not a basic condition of war demanding the backing of a separate Service to secure its full use. They are wrong. The aeroplane is but at the beginning of its development. The most successful single-seat

fighters of the last war had engines which developed between 130 and 180 horse-power.

Such fighters today have engines of some 2,300 horse-power. Two machine-guns have been augmented to twelve. Cannon guns, then almost unknown, have been developed increasingly to the size of efficient anti-tank shell-guns. Bombs outweigh the greatest naval shells by nearly four times. The aircraft that are used today are not weapons, they are vehicles for weapons, shells, bullets, torpedoes, bombs, as surely as ships are vehicles for weapons. And they are the enemies of ships, the very enemies that have reduced the former strategic grandeur of navies—that lasted from Philip of Spain's day to Jellicoe's—to that of vessels of tactical value, unable to operate save in dire peril until the army and the air force clear the littoral for them, and by divesting the enemy of his striking airfields make passage safe for ships under cover of our own-held airfields.

AIR Power's Decisive Part in Atlantic Submarine War

The demonstration in the Mediterranean was the forerunner of the domination of the oceans in the future by air-power. Indeed, who can deny that air power has played the decisive part in the submarine war in the Atlantic? We were steadily losing it until aircraft of sufficient range and carrying power were employed so that only a small gap was left, which in turn was sealed with short-range Swordfish from small aircraft carriers. Soon there will be no gap. There will be no need for the short-range Swordfish. The land-based aircraft will be the supreme power over all the seas and oceans.

The strategic air forces batter Germany and occupied Europe. They cut the railway lines leading from Germany to Italy. They destroy ball-bearing manufacturing plants, chemical manufacturing plants, mines in Norway, railway yards in Sofia. The naval strategy of 1914-18 could not have starved out Germany in 1939. Only air strategy can do that; not by sitting in port, but by hitting again and again, ever harder and harsher blows.

THE whole war is keyed upon air power. Whosoever possesses it in sufficient proportions will knock the keystone out of the enemy's arch and his whole military edifice will fall. It will happen in the big scale as in the small. Our own loss of Leros is a pointer to the principle which some generals and many admirals overlooked and overlook. Troops cannot without very great risk be placed beyond the reach of our own air protection even if we have naval supremacy.

Nothing can take the place of air power either in strategy or tactics. To place troops beyond the air cover of the most efficient fighters is to fight this war on the principle of 1914-18. That was why we lost in Norway, France, Greece, Crete, Singapore. That was why Germany lost at El Alamein, Nofilia, Tunisia, Pantelleria, Sicily. After all these lessons why should we stick our troops in Leros (see eye witness story in p. 442), Samos and Cos? Only to lose the islands and most of the troops. Are we blind, or, in the American sense, merely dumb?

CAMOUFLAGED JAPANESE STEAMER on a river between Kyaukpadaung and Muale, Burma, is squarely hit by an R.A.F. Beaufighter. Bombing has gone on right through the monsoon season and our ever-growing air strength is seriously weakening Japan's long, narrow and exposed supply-lines through Burma, the north-eastern limit of Lord Louis Mountbatten's South-East Asia Command.

*Photo, British Official: Crown Copyright*

# Sky Trails of Two-Ton Bomb Load Fortresses

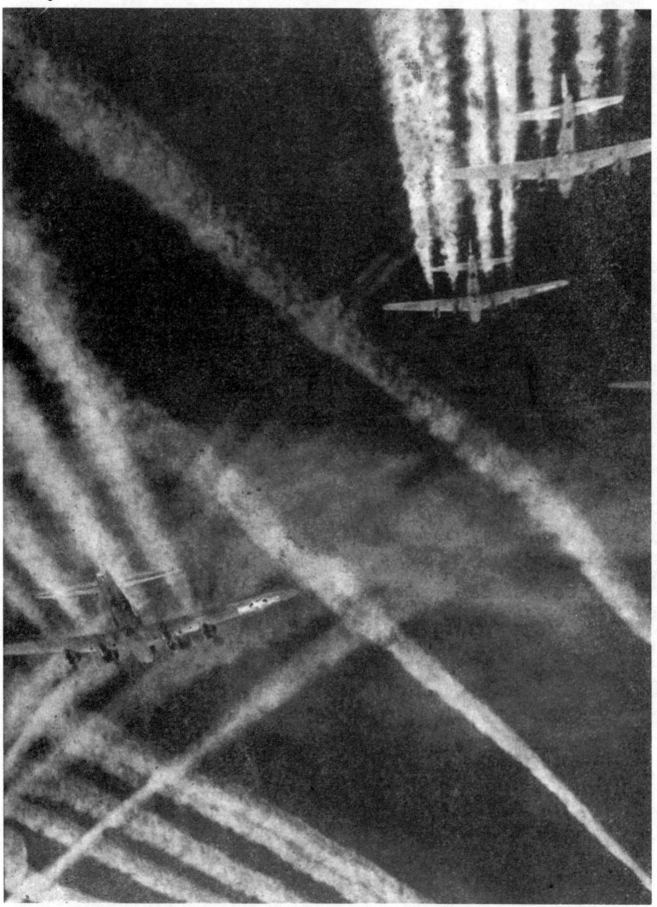

**WRITING IN THE SKY,** spelling the doom of Nazism in Europe, comes from four-engined Flying Fortress bombers for U.S. Army 8th Air Force. The machines leave a four-plumed wake behind them when operating at high altitudes. Their trails are clearly distinguishable from the single wakes streaming from single-engined fighters which have swooped into the attack and the tell-tale tracks of which traverse the photograph from left to right. Flying Fortresses have a ceiling of 40,000 ft. and a range of 2,500 miles, and can fly at 290 m.p.h. with a bomb load of over two tons. Long-range Thunderbolts escort them all the way to the target.

*Photo, U.S. Official*

# From Jungle Bases They Fly to Fight Japanese

IN THE WILDS OF NORTHERN AUSTRALIA are stationed men of the Royal Australian Air Force who are playing a vital part in the Battle of the Pacific. From an improvised control tower (1) an officer gives the "okay" to a homing machine, while a Beaufort bomber (4) taxies to a narrow clearing from which it can take off. Splendid performances are to the credit of both men and aircraft; this Avro 10 Fokker-type plane (2) has made many pioneering flights over wild New Guinea country, and W.-Cmdr. Clive R. Caldwell (3, right) has earned the nickname "Killer" for bringing down 20 Japanese planes.

*Photos, British Official: Crown Copyright*

THE Dutch are a canny folk, rather like our Northumbrians. They pursue their objects with a quiet steady persistence that often deludes observers imperfectly acquainted with them into the belief that they are not really doing anything out of the ordinary. The Nazis in Holland have been learning a lot about this Dutch characteristic. Civil servants, for instance, appear to be getting on with their work as usual, not hurrying, but not slacking either. What they are doing very often is filling up forms incorrectly, passing documents on to the wrong departments, or putting important papers which may be called for at any moment into drawers or pigeon-holes where no one would think of looking for them. This slows down, if it does not derange altogether, the business of the public offices. Private offices contribute also to the bemuddling of the hated German invaders. Merchants and distributors are obliged to have dealings with the enemy, but they do their best to confuse and puzzle and delay. These tricks are the more maddening because it is hard to detect exactly where they have occurred. They worry the Huns a lot!

THE public are reproached by the Ministry of Transport because there has been more travelling by train this year than was customary in peacetime. But if they reflected for a little while, the complainants would see that there is a simple and sound reason for this. Large numbers of people had got into the habit of travelling by coach. The coaches which ran out of London for ten, fifteen, twenty miles to the dormitory towns and villages of Surrey and Kent, used to be full always in the morning and evening. Now all those who preferred the coach to the train are obliged to travel by railway. It is this rather than disregard of the injunction to consider "Is your journey really necessary?" which accounts for the increased numbers the railways now carry. At least, that is the explanation which seems to me to fit the case. Of course, there are plenty of unnecessary journeys being made, but not nearly so many as the figures might suggest.

WE shall probably hear a good deal about the Italian port of Leghorn, on the Mediterranean, during the next month or two. I wonder—I long have wondered—how its name came to be spelt and pronounced that way in English. It is in reality Livorno, and unless it had made a speciality of making straw hats it might have been unknown in this country except to sailors and travellers on the Mediterranean coast. Last century its name became very well known here by reason of those straw hats made at Livorno becoming fashionable for Englishwomen's wear. And somehow the pronunciation and spelling came to be Leghorn. I once passed through its railway station in company with an English lady who looked out, saw the boards with Livorno on them, and said : "I never heard of this place before." I said : "Oh yes, you have!", and explained to her how we had altered the name. She asked me : "Why cannot places be called everywhere as they are called by those who live in them?" I said : "Ask me another!"

THE League of Nations would have done a most useful piece of work if it had dealt with this. Why should Venezia (Venetzia) be Venice in England, Venise in French, Venedig in German? Why do we spell Basel

in Switzerland Basle, while Italians call it Basilea, and the French Bâle? Why need we be puzzled by Geneva, Genf, Ginevra and Genève being variants of the same place-name? Not only is it bewildering when you are trying to learn geography. It has more practical drawbacks. Long ago I remember sitting one sunny autumn day in the railway station at Bellinzona, on the frontier between Italy and Switzerland, waiting for a train to Milan, for which the Italian is Milano. In came one with a placard bearing the word "Mailand" attached to the wagons. I was almost tempted to sit on, not knowing that this was the German spelling (the train had

FEODOR GUSEV, appointed Soviet Ambassador to Britain in succession to M. Ivan Maisky. The announcement was made on August 1, 1943. Aged 39, M. Gusev entered the Russian Foreign Commissariat in 1937 and became head of the Second European Department in 1939, there making a special study of British institutions. Until his appointment to London he was Soviet Minister to Canada. He speaks English fluently.    *Photo by Karsh, Ottawa*

come from Germany), but I guessed that it might be so and, a friendly porter confirming my guess, I speedily got in. I dare say French visitors to England have missed trains because they will spell our capital "Londres" instead of London. Here is a job for the new council of Nations recommended by the recent and highly successful Moscow Conference.

WE must all call that by the same name. We did not do so when we had the League of Nations ; the French called it Society of Nations, though they have the word "Ligue," pronounced like our "League" and frequently used in their language. A friend of mine, keen "internationalist," is circulating a pledge, which he would like people in all countries to sign, of support for the "International Authority" which is to be set up. "This will never do!"

I have told him. Impossible to work up enthusiasm for an institution with a name like that! No thrill in it, nothing to stir emotion or kindle the fire of imagination. My friend is particularly anxious to get young people interested. That won't be possible unless we make them feel warmly as well as think deeply. "International Authority" would leave them cold. Perhaps we ought to have a new League, different from the old in many ways, of course. Not so diplomatic, nor so dominated by politicians. A League of Peoples rather than Governments, of countries rather than States.

COUNT SFORZA surprised many people, even people who knew him, by the strong line he took, on his return to Italy from exile in the United States, against King Victor Emmanuel. Personally, he is an aristocrat of aristocrats. He comes of a very old and very historical family. That he should have turned against the Italian monarchy shows how deeply the iron of Fascism entered into the soul of all true Italians. What the king really felt about Mussolini we may never know. Some indication was given when he told a friend : "If there is anything you want to let me know privately, come and say it. Don't write. If you do, others will know what it is." The old Count (he is 70) is being reproached with having broken promises and gone back on his word in the days when he was a Cabinet Minister. But "why drag that up?" a good many are asking. Cavour, the statesman who worked for and won Italian freedom from Austria, said once : "If we did as private citizens what we do as public men, we should be called scoundrels, and rightly." There ought to be no difference, but I fear there often is.

DO you ever look through old volumes of Punch? I do often, and fascinating I find it. I learned a great deal about the 19th-century history of Europe from Punch while I was at school, and I like reviving memories of events by seeing how they struck people at the time. I turned the other day to the volumes for 1854 and '55, the years of the Crimean War, when we laid siege to Sebastopol and our soldiers suffered so badly from the cold. It was an unusually hard winter. Sometimes on the Black Sea there is hardly any severe weather. But when it does snow, it snows for days at a time ; and when it freezes, the thermometer drops to thirty or forty below zero. British troops were sent out on the assumption that the winter would be a mild one. They were not provided by the War Office with warm clothing or warming rations. The Punch pictures show how the war changed Britain from an island of clean-shaven to whiskered men. If this year is like 1854-55, the Nazis also will be letting their hair grow.

MENTION in the news from India of Manipur as one of the native States very active in support of the war sent my mind back a long way. In 1891 the newspapers were full of this small mountain principality. There was a quarrel about its rulership, and several British civil servants and army officers were murdered. The remainder were besieged in the Residency, among them a Mrs. St. Clair Grimwood. She behaved with so much pluck and good sense that, when they escaped and got back to England, she was given the Royal Red Cross.

# Moscow's Watchful Night Patrol Rides Home

*Photo, Pictorial Press*

**'OUR MILITIA'** is the affectionate way in which Moscow citizens refer to their civil security force, a mounted contingent of which, coming off duty after a night patrol, is here seen passing the Kremlin, on the bank of the Moskva River. The Militia fulfil the duties of policemen, A.R.P. leaders, traffic controllers and passport inspectors. Girls (see page 434) have replaced many of the younger men.

Printed in England and published every alternate Friday by the Proprietors, THE AMALGAMATED PRESS, LTD., The Fleetway House, Farringdon Street, London, E.C.4. Registered for transmission by Canadian Magazine Post. Sole Agents for Australia and New Zealand : Messrs. Gordon & Gotch, Ltd. ; and for South Africa : Central News Agency, Ltd.—December 10, 1943.   S.S.   *Editorial Address :* JOHN CARPENTER HOUSE, WHITEFRIARS, LONDON, E.C.4.

Vol 7

# The War Illustrated

Nº 170

*Edited by Sir John Hammerton*

SIXPENCE

DECEMBER 24, 1943

**HAPPY WITH MOUNTS AGAIN** are these members of a British mechanized cavalry regiment in Italy. Major M. Lindsay, of Fife, Scotland, surveys the landscape during reconnaissance in the Italian mountains, where the horse has come into its own once more in war; standing by is Lieut. J. Richardson, of Northumberland. As our men advance through country normally difficult for mechanized traffic, they commandeer local mules and horses accustomed to this treacherous terrain.

*Photo, British Official*

**NO. 171** WILL BE PUBLISHED FRIDAY, JANUARY 7, 1944

# Our Roving Camera Visits Occupied Europe

NORWEGIAN VILLAGERS in the Hardanger area staged this mock funeral march when they obeyed a German order to surrender their wireless sets : a dramatic demonstration that they had preserved their sense of humour under oppression. With a wagon for a hearse, and a fiddler playing melancholy music, the villagers lumped their doomed radios together and fell in behind the " hearse " in the customary style of a funeral cortège. Such sturdy spirit cannot be quenched even by the ruthlessness of Nazi rule.

KANDANOS, VILLAGE IN CRETE, once stood where this board is erected. The inscription records an act of German savagery : "As a reprisal for the foul murder of German soldiers by armed men and women the village of Kandanos·was destroyed." Kandanos is but one of 200 villages in Crete and Greece known to have been wiped out since the German occupation, which began in April 1941.

RIGOURS OF THE WARSAW GHETTO in Poland are illustrated by this pathetic queue of Jews seeking water. It was in this ghetto that thousands of Jews were massacred in March-April 1943, following their revolt against appalling conditions imposed on them by the Nazis. Some 1,000 German troops were killed in the riots, and in retaliation the enemy bombed the ghetto and then sent in S.S. and S.A. units backed by strong army formations to restore order among those already mercilessly oppressed.

ON THE MEDITERRANEAN COAST OF FRANCE (above) anti-invasion exercises staged by the Germans prove the enemy's fear that Sardinia and Corsica, now in Allied hands, may be springboards for a sea and airborne assault on the Riviera. To the east they have entrenched themselves in Northern Italy, and in Venice they have established a base for motor-torpedo boats operating in the upper Adriatic ; one is shown (left) in harbour, in St. Mark's Canal. The picturesque building in the background is the famous Doges' Palace.

*Photos, Greek Official, Norwegian Official, Planet News, Keystone*

# THE BATTLE FRONTS

## by Maj.-Gen. Sir Charles Gwynn, K.C.B., D.S.O.

THE capture of Kiev by Soviet forces and rapid exploitation of success westwards as far as the lateral railway across the Pripet Marshes produced an extraordinarily tense and interesting situation on the Russian front. The capture of Zhitomir on this railway, although it opened possibilities of a further drive towards the south-west which would cut the German main railway communications between Poland and the Ukraine, marked, however, the limits to which, for the time being, the Russian thrust could safely be carried.

Before a further advance could be made it was essential that the salient that had been created should be widened and consolidated, in view of the certainty that German counter-attacks would soon develop. The tip of the salient was quickly widened by the capture of Korosten and Ovruch, thus making secure the Russian grip on the lateral railway, and the base of the salient was extended on both flanks. The Germans, as was expected, soon commenced a series of counter-attacks, and at first they were directed towards Fastov, near the base of the salient on its southern side. If this attack had met with success it would probably have compelled the Russians to withdraw and abandon most of the ground they had won. But Vatutin had taken precautions, and though the Germans battled fiercely they failed to make progress.

TAKEN by surprise, von Manstein had been unable to assemble a strong enough force, and the most this counter-attack achieved was to prevent a junction between the Russian bridgehead at Kiev with one previously established at Pereyaslavl farther down stream. This may have been a danger that von Manstein feared, but his chief concern must have been for the safety of his communication with Poland. He therefore shifted his counter-attacks farther west against the south-western corner of the Russian salient, where the proximity of his main railways enabled him to concentrate large forces quickly. The urgency of the situation may have forced him to open his counter-offensive in a somewhat piecemeal fashion ; nevertheless, relying mainly on his highly mobile armoured troops and motorized infantry, he was able rapidly to stage very formidable attacks.

Although his primary aim was to protect his main railway communications, he probably hoped to inflict a defeat on the Russians which would seriously cripple their offensive plans. But the Russians fought a magnificent defensive battle, in spite of having had little time to consolidate their positions or to develop communications. For about a fortnight the struggle continued with an intensity greater than any since the battle of the Kursk salient. Both sides had immense losses, and as fresh German reserves arrived they were thrown into battle in attempts to break through the Russian defences. Eventually the Russians were forced to give ground, evacuating Zhitomir and Korosten successively. But the defence never lost its cohesion, and this limited success fell far short of fulfilling von Manstein's hopes.

He had, it is true, for the time at least, secured the safety of his communications with Poland, but he had failed to reopen direct lateral communications with the Upper Dnieper and Vitebsk front. Moreover, he had signally failed to disturb the rhythm of the Russian offensive as a whole, and by concentrating such a large proportion of his mobile and armoured reserves for his effort he had weakened his front elsewhere.

UNDETERRED by the critical situation at the head of the salient, the Russians continued to develop their offensive plans. They maintained heavy pressure from their Kremenchug salient southwards towards Nikopol and Krivoi Rog, making steady if slow progress ; and northwards, from the base of the salient, they operated towards the lateral railway running through Znamenka and Smyela on which the Germans, still holding the stretch of the middle Dnieper between Kremenchug and Pereyaslavl, depended. They also, by a characteristically bold and ingenious operation, established a bridgehead near Cherkasy, the principal German stronghold on this section of the front, and rapidly initiated operations for the encirclement of that town.

It was, however, to the north of the Kiev salient that the development of the Russian plans was most sensational. From the first, after his breakthrough at Kiev, Vatutin began to widen the base of the salient, driving north-westward up the Pripet River and northwards along the west bank of the Dnieper to link up with the southern flank of Rokossovsky's army which, on the opposite bank of the river, was enveloping Gomel. This enabled the latter to cross the Dnieper and swing northwards, cutting the main communications of Gomel with the

west and leaving the defenders of that hedge-hog stronghold with only a single avenue of retreat to the north-west. The situation of Gomel, therefore, became more than ever precarious and the capture of Rezhitsa, a subsidiary stronghold on the Dnieper west of Gomel, opened the way for the more complete encirclement of the southern defences of the latter.

But the Germans still clung stubbornly to Gomel, the defences of which were too strong to be carried by assault, and it was not till Rokossovsky, on Nov. 25, opened a new offensive north of Gomel and broke through the German defence line on the river Sozh that a belated decision to evacuate the town was taken, in order to escape another Stalingrad. This fresh blow had taken the Germans completely by surprise, for it was delivered on a front where, by all standards, marshes seemed to make the ground impassable. The defence was overrun and Propoisk, the main stronghold on the Sozh, was taken, opening the way to the upper Dnieper and the strongholds of Mogilev, Rogachev and Zhlobin on its banks.

EVENTS now followed in quick succession. On Nov. 26 the evacuation of Gomel was announced. Rearguards left in the city were overcome, and the Russians closed in on the retreating columns, assisted by guerilla parties which had been waiting their chance. How far the retreat was a rout is not yet known, but it certainly was not conducted in good order, and masses of equipment were abandoned. By demolitions and the use of mines direct pursuit was delayed, but meanwhile the Russians carried out enveloping operations north-westwards up the Dnieper towards Zhlobin and up the Beresina towards Bobruisk, as well as westwards to Kalinkovichi and Mozyr on the Pripet.

It seems certain that the Germans will fight desperately to hold these places, for they form bastions on the southern flank of the Vitebsk-Mogilev position, which is exposed now that the Russians have turned the line of the upper Dnieper and the Beresina. If, as seems not improbable, the Russians open a major offensive on the Vitebsk front the turning of these river lines would obviously be a factor of great importance in its development ; and the capture of Gomel removes the block on the railways and roads required for the communications of an enveloping attack.

It should be noted that the lateral communications across the Pripet Marshes are at present blocked to both sides. The Russians block the line on the south at Ovruch and on the north between Kalinkovichi and Zhlobin ; but they cannot use the intermediate line while Kalinkovichi and Mozyr hold out. At the time I write it would seem that von Manstein has fought his troops to a standstill and is bogged down by autumn mud ; but it is possible that, with his good communications, he may be able quickly to make good much of the loss of equipment he has suffered. When the ground freezes he may renew his onslaughts and might be able to reopen contact with Mozyr.

The Germans are now in three loosely connected groups, and it seems possible that, rather than await attack in defensive positions, their object will be to draw the Russians into mobile operations.

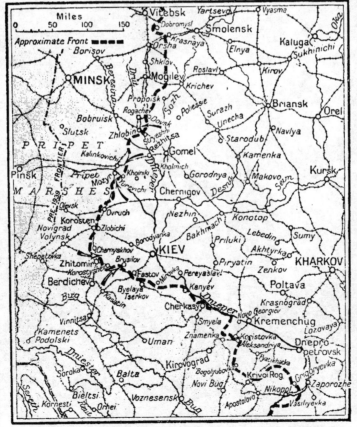

**RUSSIAN FRONT, Dec. 3, 1943.** North-west and south-west of Gomel, which fell on Nov. 26, battles were raging for Zhlobin and Mozyr. There was stalemate in the Korosten-Zhitomir sector. A Soviet thrust from Koristovka menaced Kirovograd.   PAGE 451   *Courtesy of The Times*

# New Zealanders Rejoin the Famous 8th in Italy—

VETERANS OF NORTH AFRICA FIGHTING, rested and re-equipped, New Zealanders are again actively on the warpath. On Nov. 30, 1943, it was announced that they had crossed the Mediterranean for the first time since they landed in Greece 2½ years ago, and are now with the 8th Army in Italy. Commanded by Lt.-Gen. Sir B. C. Freyberg, V.C. (5), they are the first battle-experienced infantry to fight in American tanks, one of which (2) is being hoisted on to a transport. They had lunch on the wharf (1) before carrying their kit aboard (3). Shortly afterwards they were marching through Taranto (4), northward bound.

*Photos, Sport & General*

# —And Help Deal 'Colossal Crack' at the Enemy

ACROSS THE SANGRO RIVER, eastern sector of the enemy's intended winter line, Gen. Montgomery, on Nov. 28, 1943, launched his 8th Army, strengthened by fresh New Zealanders (see facing page) and Indian troops, in a large-scale offensive aimed at dealing the Germans what he called " a colossal crack." From forward observation posts, such as this farm building (1), scouts recorded the enemy's dispositions, while a sentry (2) kept watch outside. Men of the Punjab (3) shared in preliminary reconnaissance work. Possession of the heights (4), especially the 1,000-ft.-high Santa Maria ridge, was a primary objective, and it was announced on Nov. 30 that success had been attained.

*Photos, British Official : Crown Copyright*

# THE WAR AT SEA

## by Francis E. McMurtrie

IN the intervals between threatening air reprisals at some vague date in the future and trying to persuade the enemy public that U-boats are still sinking shipping in large quantities, the German propaganda machine has recently been making much of an alleged secret weapon, said to be so terrible in its effects that the Allies would willingly call off their bombers rather than have it used against them!

This is rather too transparent an artifice to deceive anyone outside Germany. It must be obvious to most people that if the enemy were in possession of any such weapon as they hint at, no time would be lost in making the utmost use of it. Its non-appearance in action can only mean either that it has no existence or that it has not been brought beyond the experimental stage. In the past several novel weapons have been employed by the Germans. First of them was the magnetic mine, which caused much destruction of shipping until Lieut.-Commander Ouvry dismantled an intact specimen found on the beach at Shoeburyness (see story, p. 124). Once its principle was understood, science very quickly provided an antidote in the shape of the " degaussing " girdle, fitted to all ships passing through waters likely to be mined.

Next, the enemy tried the acoustic mine, detonated by the vibration of a ship's engines, conveyed through the water by the propeller. This was also speedily countered, as were sundry variations of the two types. An acoustic torpedo was another surprise, but it seems to have been overcome in a short time.

Lately a good deal has been heard of the rocket-glider bomb, released from an aeroplane which controls and directs it towards the target by wireless. So far as can be gathered from reports which have appeared, it consists of a bomb with a rocket in the tail, attached to a small glider, the whole apparatus being steered by wireless until it comes into contact with a ship and explodes. The purpose of the rocket is to give it greater acceleration. So far this ingenious device has had nothing like the success of the torpedo discharged from aircraft, or even of the ordinary type of bomb. This is scarcely surprising when it is considered that wireless impulses are capable of deflection by a stronger current from another station. As the missile gets farther from the controlling aircraft, the wireless impulse governing it becomes weaker and can be more easily countered by a stronger one, either from the vessel attacked or from some other ship.

It may be imagined that the Germans are experimenting with various forms of wireless waves in an endeavour to find one that is proof against interference. Possibly they still hope for success, and are boasting on the chance of it. But up to now they have not succeeded in inventing anything which our own scientists have failed to overcome by a counter-device.

As a result of the Cairo Conference, the Japanese have been left in no doubt that retribution is coming to them. How, when and where, they are at liberty to guess. Their greatest asset is the geographical situation of Japan, separated by thousands of miles of sea to the south and east from Allied bases. To the westward is the vast mass of China, large tracts of which are occupied by the Japanese armies ; and to the north is neutral Siberia. It has been urged that war in the Pacific is largely a matter of supply. This might equally be said about modern warfare generally, since the nature of its weapons is such as to require abundant renewal of munitions and spares for guns, tanks, aircraft, etc. It would be more correct to say that war in the Pacific is mainly an affair of

bases, upon the loss or retention of which the fortunes of the combatants depend.

At the outset of hostilities Japan's first step was to secure the principal bases in the Far East and Western Pacific. One after the other Guam, Hong Kong, Singapore, Surabaya and Manila fell into enemy hands, in the absence of Allied naval forces strong enough to defend them. Pearl Harbour, the principal American base, was rendered temporarily impotent by the lightning air attack of Dec. 7, 1941, that sank or put out of action seven out of the nine battleships then comprising the U.S. Pacific Fleet ; only one at Pearl Harbour escaped serious damage; the ninth was under refit elsewhere.

IN addition to the bases occupied in the early months of the war, Japan already possessed the fortified group of islands known as Truk, which in configuration bear a general resemblance to Scapa Flow. This unique harbour was practically presented to Japan when the mandate for the ex-German Caroline group, of which it is a component, was conferred upon her at the end of the last war. It is now believed to be the headquarters of the enemy's main fleet and is thus one of the principal objectives of the Allied forces in the Pacific.

An advanced enemy base now seriously threatened is Rabaul, capital of the large island of New Britain. This and its companion island. New Ireland, are dependencies of New Guinea, an ex-German territory mandated to Australia over 20 years ago. Rabaul is the ultimate goal of the steady advance which has been made through the Solomons since American Marines first landed in Guadalcanal in the summer of 1942. Island after island has fallen to the Allies, until the northernmost, Bougainville (named after the French navigator), has now been invaded. Already Rabaul is under frequent air attack, many ships in its harbour—formerly known as Simpson Haven—having been sunk or damaged. Of late the Japanese have found its use so expensive that they have been diverting their transport to Kavieng, in New Ireland, some distance to the northward. In the New Year the invasion of New Britain itself may be confidently expected.

Simultaneously, Australian troops continue to advance along the coast of New Guinea. Salamaua and Lae, the enemy's advanced bases, fell some time ago; and the Huon peninsula is now nearly cleared of Japanese. Most important of the remaining New Guinea bases is Wewak, which is also being raided more heavily now that Allied airfields are nearer. At sea, the U.S. Pacific Fleet has landed an expedition in the Gilbert Islands, a British group seized by the Japanese early in the war. These islands are believed to have been garrisoned by picked troops, who fought to the last. U.S. Marines landed under heavy fire, and lost, in round figures, 1,100 killed and 2,700 wounded before resistance was overcome. (See account in p. 474.)

After the Gilberts, the next group to be attacked was the Marshall Islands, another ex-German possession for which Japan was given the mandate. Japanese warships, supply ships and aircraft again suffered heavily in this affair. From the Marshalls and from New Ireland, when both are conquered, simultaneous thrusts could be directed at Truk. Increasing inferiority in the air is likely to make it difficult for the Japanese to ascertain from which of these points the attack is likely to come ; nor is it easy to see how, without bringing their main fleet into action, they can effectively repel it.

**H.M. SUBMARINE TAKU, claimed to be the most relentlessly hunted vessel in the Service. Off the Norwegian coast and in the Aegean she has had hairbreadth escapes, on one occasion surviving " a perfect avalanche " of depth charges, and on another having to lie submerged for 36 hours. Oldest man aboard is only 31, and the average age of the crew is believed to be the lowest in the submarine branch of the Royal Navy. Taku is a vessel of 1,090 tons, with a normal complement of 53.**
*Photo, Planet News*

# Americans Blast Japanese From Vella Lavella

Photo, Keystone

DEATH BY NIGHT at Vella Lavella, northernmost island of the New Georgia group in the Central Solomons (see map, p. 474), invaded by U.S. forces on August 15, 1943, and finally evacuated by the Japanese on October 9. During this period of struggle the enemy tried several times to land reinforcements, but Allied air and sea vigilance and strength prevented this. Above, a destroyer hurls fire and metal against Japanese bombers after the ship's speed and manoeuvrability had been affected by engine-room damage.

# Brains Behind Our Big Ships' Roaring Guns

No casual rule-of-thumb affair is the gunfire of a British cruiser when she goes into action, all nine 5·5-in. guns belching. The "chain of fire control" is a wondrous thing, as is explained by CAPT. FRANK H. SHAW in this vivid description of the complicated organization of specialists and mechanism that makes astonishingly accurate long-distance shooting possible.

FROM the pregnant moment when the masthead lookout, raking the horizon with powerful binoculars, reports: "Enemy smoke in sight !" the cruiser hums like a hive. "Action stations !" sounds; every man, whether on immediate duty or below at ease, speeds to his station. Although the ship is kept in readiness for instant action, there still remains much to be done. The captain takes the bridge.

His secretary, the Paymaster-Lieutenant, accompanies him ; not only to take precise notes of the action, but also to broadcast a running commentary through the cruiser's loud-speakers to the crew, who would otherwise be ignorant of events. Nothing heartens waiting men like knowing what portends.

The masthead lookout reports the position of the suspicious smoke. The range-finding officers and crews instantly apply themselves to their complicated instruments, bringing dual images of the smoke into one, reading the range in thousands of yards. The captain orders course to be altered to close the distance. The ship, quickened to fullest speed, races towards the foe, whose size is not all at once ascertainable. She might be a battleship, a heavy cruiser, or something small. In any case she will certainly be tackled.

THE gunnery officer is in his control, surrounded by instruments to record speed, deflection, atmospheric conditions, quality of light, and a score of other details necessary to the intricate science of gunnery. Down below the engine-room staff are alert ; orders may come down at any moment to "make smoke" —a useful screen, in case the enemy is a top-weight. Any moment might bring a high explosive shell of a ton weight crashing into the complicated compartments that make up a cruiser's engine-room. But the Black Squad (the stokers) work on unperturbed ; if the sides gape open to admit a greedy sea in Niagara-like torrents, it is just too bad.

Each gun-turret has an officer in charge. Each magazine is controlled by a petty officer. Ammunition-passers are stationed handily. The cruiser is armed with nine 5·5-in. guns, in three turrets. The turret-control officers await the word to describe the type of target ; this determines the kind of projectile to be used—armour-piercing, common, shrapnel, or whatever circumstances may dictate.

In a room deep in the ship's bowels, below the waterline, is another group of specialists, calculating the effect of present atmospheric conditions on flight of shell and quality of explosion of propelling charges. Weather affects cordite quite a bit. The paymaster beside the captain begins his commentary. Probably the captain inspires it. The lookout, backed now by a second man, scrutinizes the stranger closely.

"Battleship, sir, moving this way !" he reports by telephone.

"Armour-piercing !" dictates the captain to his mouthpiece, who repeats it to the gunnery officer, prefacing the command with :

"Bridge to Gunnery officer," so that no false orders can be transmitted. Gunnery control speaks to turrets : armour-piercing shell comes up from the deep magazines. Breech-blocks clash open, and from the trough into which each heavy shell is placed that shell slides into the barrel of the gun, with the quick punch of a mechanical ram to seat it firmly and engage the driving band in the rifling. The bags of cordite follow, the breech slams shut, the priming tubes are inserted by the gun-captain, who wears a belt full of them.

" No. 1 gun ready ! No. 2 gun ready ! " Each gun-captain reports to the turret officer who reports to gunnery-control who reports to Bridge—that is, the captain. And it is the captain's responsibility as to whether he shall fight his ship against overwhelming odds.

This captain elects to fight. If he can close

IN THE AFTER 14-in. GUN TURRET of H.M.S. King George V during a practice shoot. Nearest man is at the controls of the shell hoist from the magazine. Communications "number" is seen in the background, receiving directions from the gunnery control points.
*Photo, British Official : Crown Copyright*

the range his lighter guns might well prove a match for the heavy stuff carried by the enemy. He speaks to gunnery-control. "Open fire when in range ! " he orders. The rangefinders double their intent observations. They know the extreme range of the 5·5s, know that at that range the shell will fall more vertically than horizontally. The gunnery officer hears their chanted alterations and mentally applies them to his problem. He wants to be sure of hitting quickly ; the stunning effect of a correct broadside ought to be enough to disorganize completely the enemy's controls and morale.

THEREFORE it is advisable to put a different range on each gun, so that when all are fired, simultaneously, one shot at least will hit. This is known as laddering ; and it means that each gun must have its own observer, who, calculating the time of flight of the shell at specified range, can identify his own splash. Quick comparison by the spotters finds the precise range. Half the shells might overshoot, half might undershoot, but so long as one hits—and a dull red flash instead of a high white splash indicates a hit—an accurate range is found.

There are countless calculations. The two ships are steering different courses, probably

at an angle to each other ; deflection to right or left must be compensated. An appreciable number of seconds passes between a gun being fired and its projectile reaching a destination ; during that interval the target ship must have altered her position. There are the comparative speeds of the two ships, too, to be taken into account. But the complicated organization below the waterline takes care of all such details ; automatic calculators subtract, multiply and divide. And the result—the precise range to be put on the sight—is transmitted to the controls.

" Twelve thousand—closing ! " instructs the gunnery officer.

" Twelve thousand, closing—set ! " is reported by the sight-setters. There is a buzzing scream overhead, another, another. Three huge white splashes climb from the sea astern the cruiser. But before the water foams, the masthead lookout, eyes glued on the enemy, has seen the flashes and reported : "Enemy opening fire ! " The secretary transmits this to all action stations, adding his own comments— usually jocular. The fire and wrecking parties stand by, knowing that the next instant may bring them into brisk action—or leave them splashed in death along the steel decks.

" MAKE smoke ! " says the captain. In the boiler-rooms the leading stokers make precise adjustments to the burners, so that too much oil mingles with the compressed air ; instantly the funnels pour out a mighty cloud which, drooping to the water, rising to hide the masts, forms an effective screen. There is no longer a point of aim for the enemy gunners. But the cruiser's gunner has already selected one on *his* target. "Conning tower and waterline " has been his order. That means the guns train on an imaginary point where two lines would intersect.

The captain takes the microphone. His ship is smeared everywhere in thick, oily smoke that fouls everything. Down below is even worse than on deck, as the intakes of the ventilating gear draw in the thick, choking stuff. " I'm leaving the screen on a course of seventy ! " he states. Then, suddenly : " Stop making smoke ! " The cloud diminishes, vanishes.

" You may open fire ! " says the captain, quietly. A cascade of enemy shell falls far wide of the cruiser ; the smoke-cloud has baffled the enemy gunners. " All guns— fire ! " says the gunnery officer. The ship leaps as if torpedoed. Nine flame-tongues lick out ; the spotters can see the projectiles climbing on a high trajectory and then vanish.

" Splash ! Splash ! Splash ! " Each turret gunner watches for his own timed splash. So does the gunnery officer. " Hit at eleven thousand five hundred, sir ! " he reports. " Go into rapid independent, please ! " says the captain. And three times each minute the nine guns belch, recoil, run out to be reloaded. Action is definitely joined. The chain of fire control has worked without the suspicion of a hitch.

# Far Over the Sea the Shells Go Screaming

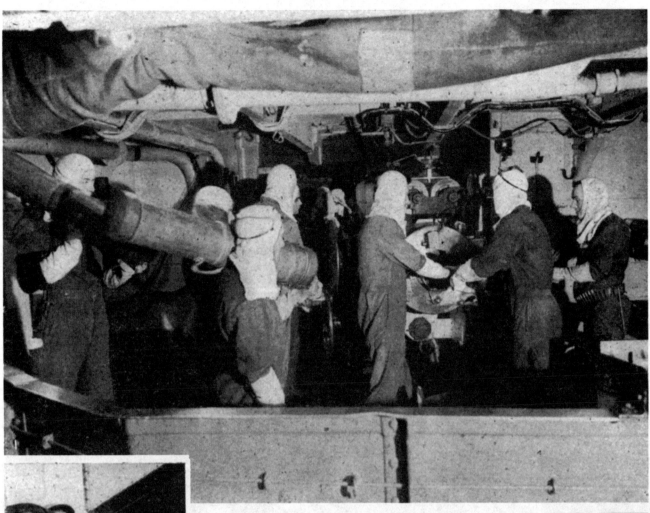

BIG GUNS of our fighting ships form the pivotal feature of the ship's construction; they are the supreme consideration. And in time of war life in the Royal Navy afloat is dictated by the necessity of keeping the great weapons ready for instant battle. Aboard the 31,100-ton battleship H.M.S. Malaya (1) the crew of a 6-in. gun battery are in action; note their protective anti-flash headgear and gauntlets. A gunnery officer aboard a cruiser (2) telephones orders during an action in which a convoy was pursued from the Bay of Biscay to the open Atlantic by U-boats and Focke-Wulf bombers. H.M.S. Rodney fires her secondary armament of 6-in. guns (3). Note main fire control tower top right. Rodney's displacement is 33,900 tons. See also facing page.

*Photos, British Official; Crown Copyright; Fox*

# Soviet Sequence: Enacted Countless Times

ON THE EASTERN FRONT at the beginning of December 1943 fighting raged most fiercely in three river sectors: in the Lower Dnieper zone, where the Soviets were beleaguering Cherkasy; in the Upper Dnieper-Sozh area, where Zhlobin was menaced; and in the Lower Pripet, where the rail junction of Mozyr was the Russian objective. (See map p. 451.) Machine-gun carts (1) escorted by cavalry move up to the front. Battle joined, Red Army men (2) pass a burning German tank. The enemy routed, liberated villagers (3) return to their homes. *Planet News, New York Times Photos*

# Guerillas Hamper German Efforts West of Kiev

Photos, Pictorial Press, Planet News

**INTO THE WESTERN UKRAINE** swept the Red Army after the fall of Kiev on Nov. 6, 1943 : Soviet tanks (1) are shown passing through a Ukrainian village. Enemy resistance—symbolized by this knocked-out tank (2)—stiffened on the Korosten-Zhitomir line (see map, p. 451). Brilliant commander on the Ukrainian front during the retreat of 1941, Marshal Budenny (3—left) revisited the battle area recently : he is seen with Lt.-Gen. Batov. Guerillas, first organized by Budenny, harass the enemy by sowing minefields in their path ; German sappers (4) are kept busy maintaining a constant and vigilant search to clear them.

# Tough 'Recces' Race Ahead As We Invade

One of Britain's newest and most formidable units is the Reconnaissance Corps. For reasons given here by JOHN ALLEN GRAYDON, these eyes of the Army, the "Recces," whose battalions—one to each infantry division—have a scale of armaments and a degree of mechanization unprecedented, are considered the world's finest exponents of open warfare today.

A TERRIFIC punch is packed by each battalion of the Reconnaissance Corps. Each has some 250 mechanized vehicles, including Bren-carriers, armoured cars with high road-speed, troop-carrying trucks, and motor-cycles. Armament includes anti-tank artillery and grenades, also batteries of mortars, and a high proportion of tommy-guns and light machine-guns.

The Recces were prominent in the Sicilian campaign. For reasons of security the full story of their exploits cannot be placed on record at this stage of the war, but by forging ahead of the main forces they were able to secure vital information which played a big part in the moulding of our plans for such a lightning capture of that Mediterranean island.

Since they arrived in the Middle East theatre and took part in the termination of the North African campaign, fighting with the First Army, the Recces have rarely ceased to be in the forefront of our land forces.

They were the first men of General Anderson's army to meet the Germans, and, although heavily outnumbered and outgunned, caused the enemy a great deal of trouble. Later, in the winter of 1942-3, they gained their initial fame by being the first British troops to enter, and hold, Goubellat, Pont du Fahs, Bou Arada, El Aroussa, Zaghouan, Enfidaville, and Depienne. One sergeant, who earned the D.C.M. during this great series of attacks, said, "And we even poked our cocky faces into Cheylus and Bir Meherga!"

THE first month of the Recces in action will live for ever in the annals of the Corps, for great feats of arms were so frequent that they became commonplace. For instance, on December 4, 1942, when headquarters were at Medjez el Bab, the order came to Sloughia to extricate the personnel of a parachute battalion who had been landed to raid the enemy airfield at Oudna, and had afterwards fought their way back across the hills. The entry in the War Diary runs :

"11.50 hours. Enemy contacted Ksar-Tyr area. In action all day, but not much success against heavier armour. 150 personnel of Para. Bn. found west of Medjez and 37 extricated from operational area . . . 5th Sweep with U.S. Recce Coy. to Ksar-Tyr area drew blank. Three Mark IVs and three 8-wheeled armoured cars seen by B squadron on south, enemy making for Pont du Fahs. 18 parachutists of Para Bn. collected during the day . . . 6th B and C squadrons with supporting arms contact enemy near Bir Meherga. Mortar troops fired 68 bombs over farm where German armoured cars were lying. Germans appeared vastly annoyed . . . 7th C squadron

dive-bombed by Ju88s, lost 4 armoured cars, 1 carrier; truck damaged near Goubellat."

Three days later the rains came; and undaunted, but very tired, exulting but inevitably limping from loss of men and material after nearly a month of incessant adventures in no man's land, the regiment was taken back to refit and to rest awhile before going out to the front again.

The Recces, whose prime task is to find out the enemy's secrets, more often than not have to fight for the information they seek. Sometimes they operate miles behind their opponents' front line. It should be stressed

that this Corps includes in its ranks some of the most intelligent, and toughest, men in the British Army. The job for which they have all volunteered calls for quick thinking, initiative, and daring. With these facts in mind one is not surprised to find that the "Mobile Commandos," as they have been so often called, include many schoolmasters and journalists.

R ADIO is the life-blood of the Recces as they operate so far from their headquarters, and their signallers, after three months of training, can master three different types of wireless set. Every man, before "passing out," must be able to transmit on the Morse buzzer 12-15 words a minute. Often, too, they pick up information being sent by British planes many miles away. There have been instances of Recce units acting on information received in this manner and

causing the enemy severe casualties. Among their other duties, they have to discover where anti-tank guns are placed, locate and map-out strong points, and take care to find where Axis minefields have been sown.

THE crews of the numerous vehicles used by the Recces are first-class engineers and map-readers, and possess a knowledge of field engineering and demolition. Lately mine-clearing has also been included in their training; and their achievements reveal that they are indeed proving wonderfully adept at every form of tactical warfare.

Already these men have shown that they are able to deal with enemy aircraft that might attempt to interfere with them while at work. Just before the Tunisian collapse a German fighter attempted to shoot-up an armoured car belonging to the Reconnaissance Corps. The gunner, holding his fire until he felt certain of a "kill," shot down the machine, and its crew of two were taken prisoner by the Recces.

Even when in training the men are encouraged to show their initiative. During one important exercise a carrier driver discovered his fan belt was broken. He pulled off his braces and made a temporary belt for the carrier. This enabled him to reach base. Later he received a new pair of braces—and the hearty congratulations of his commanding officer!

THE assault infantry, who speed ahead of the main forces in their tough little trucks, are the real Commandos of the Recces. As brave as lions, these troops, before being sent to line units, are given a rigorous course. Part of their training includes fending for themselves—"living on the land"—for two days and nights. And this appears to have stood them in good stead. For these men, in the course of their ever-dangerous work, have been known to leave base and not return for over a week! These specialist soldiers, who combine brain with brawn, are among the élite of the British Army. No matter where an Allied army may be advancing, the Recces race ahead of the leading troops, probing and fighting for details of the enemy's strength, gun positions, intentions.

This Corps, whose chief function is fighting for information, accomplished three other major tasks during the Tunisian campaign: it gave protection to the main flank of our forces; actually took and held ground required for the advance of our divisions; and maintained constant and far-reaching patrols to give adequate warning of any enemy advance. The Corps also captured many German parachute troops in Tunisia. The Army has learned to admire and rely on the superb work of the Recces.

EYES OF THE ARMY are the men of the Reconnaissance Corps, whose work is described in this page. Here one of them, skilfully camouflaged against the light and shade of a rickyard background, scans the country for sign of enemy movement. *Photo, Keystone*

# Mobile Commandos of the Reconnaissance Corps

'OUR PATROLS have been active.' Behind the familiar, terse announcement in the official communiqués lies unceasing work of men of the Army's Reconnaissance Corps, one of the most important units in our military organization. Men of the Corps, popularly known as Recces, are not only skilled in their own field, but are as tough as Commandos. (See facing page.)

A party of Recces cross a river in rubber boats (1), their Bren gunners at the ready. Bren-gun protection is also afforded to this armoured car commander (2) out on patrol. Men of the Recce Regiments have distinguished themselves in North Africa, Sicily and Italy. Indeed, first men of the 8th Army in Italy to reach the bank of the Sangro were Recces; two are seen at practice, in the Sangro area, with a two-inch mortar (3).

In Tunisia, Recces sometimes probed as much as 40 miles ahead of our main forces; having dispersed a small centre of opposition, Bren-carriers (4) pursue the retreating survivors.

*Photos, British Official: Crown Copyright; Keystone*

# Frontiers of the Future: More Balkan Problems!

As Allied control of the Adriatic makes increasingly possible an assault from the west on enemy power in the Balkans, and the Russians sweep on from the east, attention is here focused by HENRY BAERLEIN on the knotty problems of frontier adjustments in this stormy corner of Europe. These vexed questions will have a prominent place on the peace conference agenda.

ONE does not envy the statesmen whose task it will be to settle the frontiers of Central and South-eastern Europe after the war. So many considerations will have to be taken into account, and if any super-Solomons are available for the job they will inevitably be torn between perfect justice to all and preference to those whose copybook has come unblotted out of these strenuous years.

Yet, in order to avoid that simmering discontent in the new and better world we hope to build up, there must be a sincere effort to deal as fairly as possible with such countries as Bulgaria, Hungary and Rumania, despite the fact that, in comparison with Czechoslovakia, Yugoslavia and Greece, they deserve so little.

Of course, it will not be possible to prevent the presence of minorities in every country.

of their officials departed from Užhorod, the Ruthenian capital, at the beginning of the last war. When he returned with the Hungarian army in 1939, and saw what tremendous improvements had been brought about by the Czechs, he exclaimed that they should be asked to administer the whole of Hungary for twenty years!

Just as little right have the Hungarians to most of Slovakia, though it may be that various frontier rectifications can be made; and no doubt the Czech statesmen will be more disposed to agree to this if a more democratic regime is installed in Budapest. There was a violent contrast between the powers enjoyed by Hungarian electors and deputies in Czechoslovakia and those of the Slovaks in Hungary. As an example of Czech tolerance there is Ruthenia, where five-sixths of the provincial income was expended on schools,

region a river which marks the boundary between Italians and Slavs, very few of the latter living to the west and equally few of the former to the east of it.

Fiume, of course, must be allocated to Yugoslavia, the whole of its hinterland being Slav; while the absurdity of leaving Zara to the Italians must not be repeated, though I saw the other day that an M.P. advocated that, after being demilitarized, it should remain Italian. I do not know whether this gentleman has visited Zara, where the Allies in 1919 found Italian being spoken—for the simple reason that Austria-Hungary established various languages as the official ones in various provinces.

ZARA was an enclave in Yugoslavia with not even its own water supply, so that in the event of a siege it would have had to fall back on the local maraschino. The population fell from 35,000 to about 7,000, and the harbour was so empty between the two wars that when Mussolini sent a crane to be set up, the people said that in the absence of merchandise to be raised from the ships it had presumably been sent to raise Zara's morale.

The Dalmatian islands have a Yugoslav majority of about 98 or 99 per cent, and not one of them should be allotted to Italy. Sagacious Italians, such as Professor Salvemini, put forward this opinion, and were for that reason sent by Mussolini to the Lipari Islands; former Italian convict settlement. Farther down the Adriatic is Albania, whose frontier with Yugoslavia is satisfactory to both parties; that with Greece is open to discussion.

But it will be no acrimonious discussion if the Albanians continue the good work of cooperation with Greek guerillas on which they are now embarked. At Debar, to the north of Lake Ochrida, they have successfully joined forces with the Yugoslavs against the Germans, while in the Valona area the guerillas have driven the enemy from Drashovica into the hills. So far,

**ADRIATIC COASTAL RADIO STATION** in enemy-held Albania squarely hit by R.A.F. Spitfires of N.W. African Coastal Air Force, guided to the target by a Marauder from which this photograph was taken. Formerly a Turkish dependency, Albania became an independent state in 1912, suffered the ravages of war 1914-18, was reorganized by King Zogu in 1925, and annexed by Italy in April 1939. Proudly jealous of her freedom and independence, Albania is of great strategic importance in the Balkans and Adriatic. *Photo, British Official*

The remedy of transplanting populations cannot be applied in all cases. For example, in the east of Transylvania, a predominantly Rumanian province, there is a solid Hungarian block which has been settled there for centuries. Even if similar soil were to be had elsewhere, these people would be very reluctant to be moved, but fortunately they —at any rate, the large peasant majority— were well content under the Rumanian regime, with its Agrarian Reform, which was scarcely introduced into Hungary. There will be no question, therefore, of transplanting these "Szeklers," and in Transylvania, restored to Rumania, there will probably only have to be slight rectifications in the west.

IT is obvious that the territories overrun by the Hungarians with the acquiescence of Hitler will have to be abandoned. They have not the remotest right to Ruthenia, the most easterly part of Czechoslovakia, which is inhabited by the smallest group of the Slav peoples. It is true that this region was under the Hungarians for many centuries, during which they entirely neglected it. One

and the State supported more Hungarian schools than in former years had been supported by the Hungarians themselves.

In the north of Czechoslovakia are the so-called Sudeten Germans, who, so Hitler used to scream, were horribly maltreated by the barbarous Czechs. The truth is that those who voted for the Reich were very soon disillusioned and, in the vast majority, they will welcome with open arms the return of the Czechs. Naturally, every case must be judged on its merits, and those whose conduct during the war has been inimical to Czechoslovakia must be asked to depart. Generally speaking, it looks as if the old frontier of Bohemia will be restored—it was such an excellent one that the German army would have found it a hard nut to crack if the Czechs had been allowed to fight.

Yugoslavia should see herself augmented in the north-west, because it is admitted by every righteous person that the Slovenes who languished for more than twenty years under Italy will have to be reunited to their brethren. Fortunately, there is in that

efforts at quelling the uprising have been unsuccessful, though the Germans have sent two fresh divisions into the country.

IN Albania, as elsewhere, there have been quislings, and now it has been demonstrated in that country how such scoundrels should be treated; in Tirana, the capital, where sabotage is less easy than in the mountains, Mustafa Kruja, a former puppet premier, was attacked and wounded, his son and his chauffeur being killed. The more Albanians resist those who have invaded their country, the more amicable will they find the Greeks in the delimitation of the frontier.

As for Bulgaria, the ideal solution would be for her to remember that she is a Yugoslav land and ask for union with Yugoslavia. This would be well received by Slovenes and Croats, as well as by Serbs. And it would at last bring peace to Macedonia, that province inhabited by Slavs who, mostly, do not know whether they are Bulgars or Serbs. For both countries have claimed them, and have not always used very gentle means in their proselytizing efforts.

## *Fighting Leader of China's 450,000,000*

For more than thirty years a power behind China's struggle for unity and freedom, and Generalissimo since Japan declared war on his country in July 1937, Chiang Kai-shek became President of the Chinese Republic on Oct. 10, 1943—thirty-second anniversary of the Revolution, in which he played a conspicuous part in the overthrow of the Manchu dynasty. On Nov. 22, 1943, he met Churchill and Roosevelt in North Africa to plan the final overthrow of Japan.   See also p. 476.

Photo
Ke-

## *Building a New Allied Lifeline to China—*

Along the Salween River, on the Burma-Yunnan border, and in the Hupeh-Hunan region north and south of the middle Yangtze-Kiang, fighting is fiercest in this seventh year of China's war. Vital to these campaigns is the new Ledo Road under construction from Assam into Northern Burma, there to link with the Burma Road supply-line denied to her since the Japanese invasion. (1) Chinese troops shore-up with logs a river bank alongside which the new road must run.

## —While On Two Fronts the Battles Rage

China's " back door " is the Salween front, where commanders (4) plan destruction of the enemy in jungle country in which the wearing of hoods (3) as protection against malaria-carrying mosquitoes is imperative. Close behind the line nurses tend the wounded (5). On the Hupeh-Hunan front was fought from May 25 to June 6, 1943, the great battle of the Upper Yangtze-Kiang, in defence of the gateway to Chungking, the wartime capital ; troops (2) move up to the fighting-line.

## How America Is Helping China's Army

Photos, Keystone,
Pictorial Press

Under Lt.-Gen. J. W. Stilwell, C.-in-C. of U.S. Forces in China, Burma and India, schools have been established for training Chinese troops in modern offensive warfare ; signalling with flags (left), and a mortar demonstration (below).   Chinese soldiers (above) cheerfully haul a heavy roller consolidating a new airfield runway, whilst a bomber of the American China Air Task Force prepares to take off.

# VIEWS & REVIEWS

### by Hamilton Fyfe

WHEN I think of Spain I think of bare mountains, brown soil, parched crops, treeless plains, the sun a tyrant rather than a friend. Not that Spain is all like that. The south is better, greener, less harsh. But in general the Spanish landscape is repellent because it is arid, burned up.

Portugal, now so often in the news, is strangely different—I say "strangely" because you wouldn't think two countries lying together on one peninsula could be so unlike. The smaller one has been called, says Col. F. C. C. Egerton in his biography, Salazar, Rebuilder of Portugal (Hodder and Stoughton, 15s.), "the garden of Europe." Why this contrast? Because the west winds, bringing rainclouds across the Atlantic, strike the mountains of Portugal and drop abundant moisture. The soil is fertile, the air humid, everything grows in profusion. Those winds stop when they have performed this service for the Portuguese. Spain across the frontier is left dry.

Yet cultivation is not so easy as you might suppose. In some districts irrigation is necessary to produce good crops. And the peasant holdings of land are many of them so tiny that it is impossible to get out of them enough for a family to live on. The father must go to work for someone with a bigger farm, and he gets very small wages, a shilling to one-and-threepence a day.

"THE standard of living is extremely low," says Col. Egerton, "and the percentage of illiteracy is extremely high. Only one person in five can read and write. Fifteen hours is the peasant's usual working day. They live on bread, dried peas, figs, and, as an occasional treat, a little dried cod." They make up at least three-quarters of the population, which is estimated at between seven and eight millions. There do not appear to be any exact figures. As Col. Egerton remarks, the nature of the mass of people does not show much change from what it was when their monarchy was one of the leading Great Powers. That was some five centuries ago.

The character of the townsfolk, on the other hand, has, the author suggests, altered a great deal. He calls them unstable, sensual idlers. He quotes other writers who say that in their cafés Portuguese talk for the pleasure of hearing themselves ; that they lack constancy, tenacity of purpose ; that they "make promises on the generous impulse of the moment, but do not always remember to keep them." The change in these city-dwellers is attributed to abandoning the Portuguese tradition, to which the country people have remained faithful ; and to the passionate eagerness of the educated to get into a government post, "to which no responsibility is attached and in which there is no incentive to any action, still less to any protracted effort."

THE present rulers, with Salazar at their head, are trying to break "this new and utterly objectionable tradition," which accounts for the Lisbon cafés being crowded at almost all hours of the day with men who seem to have nothing particular to do. Salazar has spoken of "changing the mentality of the Portuguese people." He himself has a mind which is the opposite of that which has been described.

He comes of a family of peasants. His father belonged to the middle class of cultivators, had just enough land to keep his wife and children in fair comfort. Below this class are those who have to hire themselves out, and above it those who can afford to hire, because their farms are large—too large for them to work entirely themselves. The future ruler of his country was a studious lad and became a professor of economics at an early age—he began university teaching in 1914, when he was twenty-five. Being interested in politics, he gave lectures on the measures which he thought should be adopted to get the nation out of difficulties caused by the incompetence of its kings and the hasty rehash of its institutions by Republicans after the monarchy had been abolished.

HE was especially emphatic about the possibility of democracy being harmonized with Roman Catholicism, but he has always, we are told by Col. Egerton, had his own definition of democracy. If it means that the poor and weak should be taken care

---

## Portugal and Her Peasant Premier

---

of, that everyone should have "at least as large a share as they need of the common wealth, that the masses should be assisted by education to reach a higher stage of culture and well-being, and that all positions should be open to merit"—then he approves of it. But he does not consider equality possible, and he condemns democracy if it confers privileges on any section or class.

As a professor, he did not mix up politics with his teaching. He had no wish for political power, he always said. But he became very well known in Portugal for his views both on economic and on constitutional matters ; and in 1926, when the nation's finances were in a bad way, the Army leaders who then governed asked him to become a Minister and try to put them straight. He accepted the call, but remained Minister only a few days. His colleagues found he had made up his mind as to what needed doing, and was determined to do it—without compromise or concession. They declined to work with such a man.

Exactly what happened then was not officially explained ; it never has been. Col. Egerton says Salazar has kept the secret to himself. But his colleagues didn't ; and what they say helps one to understand why, less than a week after his appointment, Salazar, putting a call through from his house to his office, was answered by someone who said : "Yes, what is it? Minister of Finance speaking." Salazar replied quietly : "Indeed, I thought I was the holder of that post. I see I was wrong." Then he went back at once to his University chair. The military dictators felt they had made a mistake in asking him to leave it.

But in less than eighteen months they had made things so much worse that they were compelled to beg him to come back—this time with a free hand. He showed at once that he understood what was required to put Portugal on its financial feet. He risked unpopularity, but for that he cared little. He still cares so little that he will seldom consent to be photographed ; few people know him. When the financial position had been righted, the highest place was open to him. He took it, and since 1932 he has been nominally Prime Minister, but really sole ruler, with a shadowy President in the background, who would take the count if by any chance Salazar were to be knocked out. At present there does not appear to be any likelihood of that happening.

His system is not democratic. Salazar said himself it is "anti-democratic." He does not allow freedom of speech or writing, political parties or strikes. The National Assembly consists of Government nominees. Criticism of the Government is a criminal offence. Salazar says this is the only system by which the Portuguese can be kept in order. He may be right. He did not impose himself on them. He was invited to rule. If his mother had been alive, he would not have accepted the invitation.

"I COULD not have taken up the burden," he once said, "if she had been anxious." What sort of man he is the book does not reveal, but he seems to have a sense of humour. When a critic of his measures, also a professor, went, as he thought, too far, he asked him to take over the department complained of. The professor demurred. He was also a bank director and the salary offered him was small. But Salazar made him accept the post, and must have been rather disappointed when the professor made a success of it !

DR. SALAZAR, Prime Minister of Portugal since 1932, is the subject of the book reviewed in this page. He is here seen—in centre, wearing black trilby hat—with his Under-Secretary for War, Capt. Santos Costa, inspecting Portuguese troops before they left to reinforce the Azores garrison in April 1941. *Photo, Associated Press*

# Small Aegean Islands Lost to Allies for a Time

FALL OF COS AND LEROS, British-held Dodecanese islands, followed the capitulation to the Germans of the Italian garrison of the adjacent island of Rhodes, on Sept. 8, 1943. The enemy invaded Cos on Oct. 3 and by Oct. 26 had overcome Allied resistance, claiming 600 British prisoners: some are seen (2) landing at a Greek port. Leros was invaded on Nov. 12. an enemy equipment barge (1) on fire in Alinda Bay (see map in p. 442). The defenders were forced to give in four days later after the most intense bombing (3), which, because of geographical conditions and great distance of our fighter bases, the R.A.F. was unable to counter.

*Photos, British Official: Crown Copyright: Associated Press*

# Crisis in the Lebanon Flares Up and Fades Out

T HE LEBANON was from Nov. 11 to 24, 1943, the scene of serious crisis, imperilling Allied security in the Middle East. On Nov. 11 the French Committee of National Liberation suspended the Lebanese Constitution, abolished the Chamber, arrested the President, M. Bechara Khoury (1), and all but one of the Cabinet, installing a temporary Government. Deadlock had been reached between French and Lebanese over the latter's determination to make their independence — promised by Gen. Catroux on behalf of Free France in June 1941 — a reality. Demonstrators (2) marched in protest to the British and American Legations. Motor cyclist patrols (5) stood ready outside the Town Hall in Beirut, the capital. On Nov. 13 Mr. R. G. Casey (4—2nd from right), flew to Beirut to confer with Maj.-Gen. Sir E. Spears, British Minister to Syria and Lebanon (2nd from left). Two days later Gen. Catroux (3, taking salute) arrived ; on Nov. 24 he announced the end of the "misunderstanding."

*Photos, British Official: Crown Copyright; Associated Press*

# Specialist Flyers Dare Death for the R.A.F.

Daredevils of the skies, with consummate skill at their fingertips, with cool nerves and tremendous courage, throw planes about in the air to test their worthiness before these go into production or are flown in battle. And they help to probe the secrets of captured enemy aircraft. KEITH COOPER tells of the risks these pilots run. (See also facing page.)

FOR reasons of security little is allowed to be said of the work carried out by Britain's test pilots. But were it not for their daring, courage, and desire to serve the men of the R.A.F., our air casualties would be far heavier than they are today. Although every possible examination of a new-type plane is carried out in wind-tunnel tests, it remains for the test pilot, when the model is turned into the real thing, to see whether or not the plane is all its designer claims it to be. And it is not always a pleasant task.

I remember when Philip Lucas, 39-year-old test pilot for Hawker's, went aloft to test the strength and power of Sydney Camm's latest product, the Typhoon. Lucas, who has been a test pilot for over ten years, took the new Typhoon high into the air and began to put the plane through its paces. Suddenly, without warning, the machine developed tail vibration and part of the cockpit cover split.

The test pilot who had never baled out of a machine would have been justified had he done so on this occasion. But Lucas determined to bring the Typhoon down in one piece. Far below, on the tarmac, no one realized what a great fight he was putting up inside the cockpit—and he brought the plane down as though nothing had happened. Quietly he explained what had occurred. Officials studied Lucas's reports and devised improvements. Then the test pilot again took the Typhoon aloft, put it through its paces, this time successfully, and it went into production. Now this wonderful plane is taking toll of the German Air Force in the West, and Lucas has been awarded the George Medal.

Jeff Quill, who tests Spitfires, is another

Capt. GEOFFREY DE HAVILLAND, son of the head of the De Havilland Aircraft Co., is one of Britain's most skilled and intrepid test pilots. Here is a recent portrait of him by Mrs. Dulcie Lambrick.  *By kind permission of the artist*

who gets great satisfaction out of making sure that the machines his firm hands over to the R.A.F. lads of Fighter Command are in the best possible condition. During the Battle of Britain Quill, who is a quiet and retiring man, "ran the rule" over most of the Spitfire machines that went into service during that momentous period.

THERE are many amazing stories told of this young man who tests enormously powerful planes with the same confidence as you and I walk. He once became mixed up in a "dog-fight" over Britain. Testing a Spitfire, he suddenly saw, just below, a squadron of German fighters, and several bombers, fighting it out with an outnumbered flight of "Spits." And Quill, so the story goes, swooped into action. Although there has never been any official record of this incident, Quill, according to pilots who took part in that battle, shot down three of the Huns before they turned for home.

The first Spitfire ever flown in this country was in the charge of Captain "Mutt" Summers, who is still on active service. A most remarkable pilot, he has flown nearly three hundred different types of plane and has spent well over 6,000 hours in the air during his near-twenty years as a flyer. On one occasion a plane he was testing broke into a million pieces and many of these fragments pierced his parachute—but Summers landed safely. Once, too, when trying out a secret fighter, he glanced out of his cockpit and found a Hun flying close, so Summers promptly disappeared with great alacrity, into a cloudbank.

These test pilots, as I have noticed when talking to them, are grave and quiet men who take a very serious view of their job, utterly different from those sometimes portrayed on the screen. And it should be noted that not all of them are young men. Captain Barnard, of the Ministry of Aircraft Production, is over 50 years of age, yet as fit and

able as most younger men. He has flown nearly every kind of plane, from a Spitfire to a Lancaster, and is a perfect example of the fine type to be found among Britain's test pilots.

As well as making sure that the products of our factories are perfect, these specialists also fly captured enemy planes and discover their strong and weak points. Such valuable aircraft as the F.W.190, and certain types of M.E.s, have had their secrets probed by these daredevils of the skies. And their reports have played a big part in assisting our fighter squadrons to take measures to overcome the power of the Luftwaffe's latest. One of the R.A.F.'s greatest experts in the flying of captured enemy machines is Wing-Commander Wilson. His experience in this direction is unequalled. It is said by his colleagues that he is more at home in a Heinkel than a Wellington—but they are only joking!

As one would expect from such a dangerous calling, many of these men pay the supreme price for their courage. Young John De Havilland, one of three pilot sons of Capt. Geoffrey De Havilland, senr. (head of the De Havilland Aircraft Co.), was killed in a collision between two Mosquitoes in the air near St. Albans, Herts, on August 23, 1943. Christopher Staniland of Fairey Aviation Company; P. E. G. Sayer of the Gloster Aircraft Company, and Captain Valentine Baker, D.F.C., of the Martin-Baker Aircraft Company, are but a few of the gallant band of daring flyers who have also lost their lives in the service of their country. When the time comes to lay down the burden other venturesome young pilots take it up, scornful of possible consequences. The debt we owe to them cannot be reckoned by ordinary standards.

Capt. VALENTINE BAKER, D.F.C., of the Martin-Baker Aircraft Co., one of the band of fearless pilots who have lost their lives in testing new types of aircraft.  *Photo, Fox*

PHILIP C. LUCAS, G.M., chief test pilot of Hawker's. For his courageous and invaluable work with the prototype of the Hawker Typhoon (see article in this page) he was awarded the George Medal.  *Photo, G.P.U.*

# Ordeal by Swift Trial for Pilot and Plane

FROM BLUEPRINT to full production of an aircraft is a long and cautious process, and possibly the most vital stage is that of the testing of the prototype. Theory and laboratory tests can go only so far; ultimately the first specimen must take to the air, there to justify its designer's hopes, or confound them in disaster and maybe death for the test pilot. Typical of these experts is Ralph Munday (2) of Hawker's. He made exhaustive try-outs of the Typhoon (1), one of the fastest fighters in the world, following the initial flight by his colleague, Philip C. Lucas (see article and photograph in facing page). Airborne, the pilot must take constant notes of such details as altitude temperatures, recorded on a wing thermometer (4). Yet another flight successfully over, Munday discusses techical progress (3) with confrère Capt. H. S. Broad (right).

*Photos, Topical Press*

# Centre of Nazi War Machine Again the Target

**HEART OF HITLER'S CRUMBLING EMPIRE,** Berlin has now the grim distinction of being the world's most bombed city, following five consecutive night attacks, Nov. 22-26, 1943. Lancasters (1) line up for the take-off. Four miles above the target (2) they are ghostly shapes amid smoke and cloud. Home again, a bomber (5) is guided up the runway. Air Vice-Marshal G. E. Brooks, A.O.C. Royal Canadian Air Force Bomber Group in Britain (4), greets returning Canadian crews. In Berlin itself Goering (3) urges calm. PAGE 472 *Photos, British Official, Associated Press, G.P.U., Keystone*

# I WAS THERE!
Eye Witness
Stories of the War

## We Stoked Berlin's Still Smouldering Fires

*Canadian-built bomber Q for Queenie took part in the great all-Lancaster assault on the night of Nov. 26, 1943, when over 1,000 tons of bombs showered down on Berlin. It was her first operational trip, described here by a Canadian Public Relations Officer who accompanied Queenie's crew of seven members of the R.C.A.F. Pathfinder Squadron.*

'G FOR GEORGIE,' a Lancaster which has taken part in 71 missions, including the Berlin raids of Nov. 23 and 26, 1943. W/O H. Carter, of New South Wales, is at the controls.
*Photo, Associated Press*

BEFORE us Berlin was marked by the white pillars of searchlights, balls of anti-aircraft fire and the dim glow of old fires which smouldered through the wreckage left by raiders during the previous two nights. Behind us, after the Pathfinders' bombs had started scores of new fires, was a ruddy glow visible from Hanover, more than 100 miles on the homeward journey.

Berlin's 35-mile area was dotted with light so that it was hard to distinguish the bursting of anti-aircraft shells below from the coloured marking flares dropped by the Pathfinders, or the results of the first bomb-bursts. Pin-pricked across were innumerable flecks of light marking the sites of incendiary bombs, and almost indistinguishable among the pyrotechnical background, were small, dull squares where fires had done their work and were burning themselves out through the skeleton of some building.

From over 20,000 feet the entire picture was dominated by numerous white flares, centred off to one side of the target area. The coloured flares of the Pathfinders stood out in sharp contrast, and new fires were neatly ringing the carefully placed flares.

The attack swept in from the south, and apparently caught the defenders by surprise. The approach was a steady movement from England to the target, but the return was a severe test of the aircraft's manoeuvrability. The pilot hurled the aircraft into an endless series of zigzags as the searchlights attempted to cone the bomber, and fighters appeared and were spotted by the watching gunners. As soon as the casual "Bombs away!" report was given, the rear-gunner cut in with, "Better get her weaving, Skipper. There's a Jerry fighter below!"

As Q for Queenie waltzed away from the bombing run a number of searchlights caught and coned the Focke-Wulf 190 below and to the port side of the bomber. So eagerly did the searchlight batteries concentrate on their own aircraft that the pilot fired a recognition flare. By the time the lights took up their probing again Q for Queenie was some distance away, and the wireless operator was muttering into his microphone, "I'll bet there's 700 searchlights there right now!"

One of the crew placed his mouth against the flap of my helmet to shout, "There goes one of ours!" He pointed to the target area, and we saw a large orange ball floating earthwards under a parachute of oily smoke. No one spoke over the inter-com. until the mid-upper gunner warned, "Jerry kite just passed overhead, starboard quarter." Soon serried rows of searchlights came into view, and the bomber, which was steadily climbing despite its gyrations, had reached over 20,000 feet when the navigator informed the captain, "The Dutch coast is now about 20 miles away."

"Coast coming up!" the bomb-aimer reported in a few minutes, and the pilot clipped, "Here we go. Watch your ears, everyone!" He pushed the control column slightly, and Q for Queenie began to gain speed on its final lap towards home. As we crossed the North Sea the sparks from the speeding engines lightly traced the shape of the wing behind each of the four engines. The voices on the inter-communication system became less clipped as the bomber reeled off the miles, although the tall crew-men, with their muzzle-like oxygen-microphone masks, loomed through the semi-darkness inside the craft like Martians, as they checked instruments and peered endlessly above and below.

### Keep Your Eyes Skinned!

"Take a look and see if everything's clear underneath," suggested the pilot to the bomb-aimer. He wanted to be sure there were no "hang-ups." A few seconds later the bomb-aimer announced: "Clean as a chicken," and someone commented: "Good show, and a darn good prang!" It was as the last possibility of aerial mishap seemed to disappear that the air-gunner disclosed that Q for Queenie had dropped more than "cookies" (block-busters) on Berlin.

Soon the searchlights of England were seen stabbing the sky, and the gunners were warned, "Possible enemy planes—keep your eyes skinned!" The course carried the bomber past the lights, and the welcome light of the home-base was seen amidst the runway markers.

"Q for Queenie calling base. May we land?" the wireless operator asked. "Okay to land, Q for Queenie. Okay to land," replied the voice of a W.A.A.F. operator, and the first operational sortie of Canada's first lady of the air ended with an absolutely perfect landing.

'D FOR DONALD,' safely home from one of the "prangings" of Berlin. Its crew's first responsibility on landing is to report, to the Engineer Sergeant of the flight, on the performance of the aircraft throughout its long and hazardous mission.

PAGE 473 *Photo, G.P.U.*

# I Left My Pots and Pans and Downed a Bomber!

Ship's cook, Petty Officer J. H. Hubbard, of the cruiser Aurora on service in the Mediterranean, had already been mentioned in dispatches when he achieved the further distinction of shooting down a German bomber. This feat, which surprised the rear-admiral, has won him the D.S.M.

THE Aurora was on harbour guard duty at Bône, North Africa. Everything was quiet, and I was among my pots and pans in the galley. Suddenly the alarm "Repel enemy aircraft" was sounded. I left everything and dashed to my action station as No. 2 Oerlikon gunner. Almost immediately a Focke Wulf 119 appeared out of the clouds on the port bow. It was followed by a second and a third.

They were diving to attack shipping in the harbour. I got the second one in my sights, followed him round, waited until he got within range, and pressed the trigger. I saw a stream of tracer bullets enter the aircraft amidships. It swerved away, lost height and crashed on land.

The whole thing was witnessed by Rear-Admiral C. H. J. Harcourt, commanding our squadron, who expressed surprise when he learned that a ship's cook had been responsible for bringing down the bomber!

Actually a cook has as much chance of success in an action like this as any other member of a ship's crew. We are all trained in gunnery, all have our action stations, and I've fired thousands of rounds at enemy aircraft, particularly during the hectic days of the 1941-42 Malta convoys.

I manned a gun during the Oran landing, and had many a showdown with enemy aircraft during the Malta blitzes. It was the experience I got then which helped me to bring down the Focke Wulf.

P/O Cook J. H. Hubbard, versatile hero of an astonishing exploit in the Mediterranean. Simply and without fuss he tells in this page how he won the Distinguished Service Medal.
*Photo, British Official*

# They Bombed Us, But We Landed Our Ammunition

Sailing in convoy to the Mediterranean, carrying 6,000 tons of ammunition, incendiary bombs and military trucks, the steamship Empire Brutus was attacked and hit by German bombers. Her skipper, Capt. C. J. B. Cornwall, tells the dramatic story (given here by courtesy of The Daily Telegraph) of how she weathered the storm and won to port. The cargo she carried is now being used by us on the battlefields of Italy.

ONE bomber broke formation and headed straight for the ship. From the bridge I saw a stick of bombs falling towards us. I had no time to take avoiding action. One of the bombs struck the rail a few feet below where I was standing, glanced off, and burst alongside at water level.

The explosion rocked the ship. A gaping hole was blown in her side. Thousands of gallons of water poured into the engine-room. The stokehold filled with coal-blackened water. The bulkhead between the engine-room and No. 3 hold collapsed. The hold flooded.

As we appeared in imminent danger of breaking up, I gave orders to abandon ship. The crew took to the boats, rowed to a safe distance, then sat at their oars for half an hour, watching the ship. The commander of a corvette was standing by to pick us up. He shouted through his loud-hailer, "What are you going to do, captain?"

"I'm going back," I replied. I asked for volunteers. Every man agreed to return. I chose 23 men. An Admiralty tug took in tow the Empire Brutus, which was now heavily water-logged. All that night, with the ship groaning beneath them, the crew stood to their posts. The next morning my crew climbed into the flooded bunkers, filled buckets with the coal, and passed it aloft to be dumped aboard the tug.

A German plane flew overhead. An hour later a Liberator appeared and stayed with us for the rest of the day. Empire Brutus and the tug continued in this way for five days and nights. Several times I was afraid she would break up, but eventually, after travelling 210 miles at an average speed of just over two knots, we brought her triumphantly into port.

The port authorities asked me to beach her on a sandbank. I refused. I told them that if the ship had stayed afloat so long she would keep up a bit longer! We discharged the cargo into another ship.

# I Saw the Japanese Annihilated on Betio Island

War Correspondent Henry Keys saw from start to finish the savage battle of Betio, in the Gilberts—saw how this Japanese stronghold in the Pacific was won from them in desperate and costly fighting from Nov. 20 to Nov. 23, 1943. His story is given here by arrangement with The Daily Express.

I SAILED with the greatest armada America has ever set afloat to see this battle from start to finish. For four days appalling punishment was rained on the 4,000 defenders of Betio Island, but they fought back all the time. Warships of all types, from 16-in. battleships to destroyers, delivered more than 2,200 tons of shells on the 540-acre atoll.

Aircraft plastered it with 700 tons of bombs, many of them 2,000-pounders, and strafed it with a million rounds of 50-calibre explosive bullets. A little palm-covered Pacific isle was turned into a hell on earth. And the Japs never gave in. They were annihilated.

In peace or war Tarawa has been the most important in the chain of the Gilbert Archipelago. Betio is a chop-shaped island at the west end of the chain, about 4,000 yards long. It is 400 yards wide at one end and tapers to a narrow point. It averages six feet above sea level, and is nowhere more than 12 feet. On it the Japanese built their only airfield in the Gilberts, and fortified it to such an extent and with such military excellence that they can be forgiven for thinking it was impregnable.

The American Command believed it to be good too. For this reason battleships, carriers, cruisers and destroyers were sent to escort the transports and to bombard the atoll mercilessly. Within a few minutes of the enemy's first fire the 16-in. guns of the flagship from which I watched the battle roared in reply. The muzzle blast of the giant guns was fiercely hot, and the fumes of cordite burned our faces, while, involuntarily, we bent at the knees from the shock of the terrible concussions.

Our success was almost immediate. An enormous fire started in the centre of the island, bursting into explosions every few seconds. We had hit an ammunition dump. A few minutes later we knocked out one of the enemy batteries. Two other battleships, as well as cruisers and destroyers, moved into position for a planned bombardment, and for the next four hours naval guns poured a stream of glowing shells on the island.

The flagship moved in to 5,000 yards. Even at that distance it was possible to feel the shock of the explosions on Betio transmitted through the water and the structure of the heavy ship. By dawn many fires on the atoll glowed redly into rolling masses of black smoke.

## 2,000-Pounders Rained Down

Our fire slackened only a few minutes before the dive-bombers were due. This was to allow the smoke and dust to clear away so that the pilots could see the targets. The first bombers carried 2,000-pounders. One after another, in a seemingly endless chain, they peeled off and shot to earth, pulling out only a few hundred feet above the ground. After the bombers came the strafers, and then the bombardment was resumed.

Lieut.-Commander R. A. Macpherson, flying the flagship's observation plane, reported the utter destruction in the key areas, and that the further shelling of them was pointless. The beaches where it was proposed to land received most attention. An area a mile long and 50 yards deep received a bombardment equivalent to 20 lb. of explosive per square yard. As the warships continued the monotonous pounding, armoured landing vessels with the first wave

BETIO ISLAND, in the Gilberts, was the scene of one of the bloodiest Allied victories during the whole Pacific campaign, as is made evident by the personal story on the right.
*Map by courtesy of News Chronicle*

of assault troops moved on Betio; literally hundreds of these vessels dotted the water. They seemed a formidable yet a forlorn force at one and the same time. Then the shelling suddenly ended. The landing craft negotiated the reef against only light enemy fire. But once ashore the Marines found that the Japanese had recovered quickly. Solidly entrenched in coral and concrete dug-outs, pillboxes and blockhouses, behind 5-ft.-high parapets along the beaches, they opened fire with automatic weapons.

### Mowed Down the Marines

The Marines had no cover. Second waves encountered even greater difficulty from heavy cross-fire. One 75-mm. gun, which was still working, totally destroyed several landing boats, while light and heavy machine-gun fire mowed down the Marines as they floundered 800 yards through the surf to the shore. It was some hours before they could penetrate beyond the Japanese parapets. Though many of the enemy had been killed and his major gun positions destroyed, Saturday's advances were so small and the position of the Marines so insecure that by nightfall the situation was obviously critical.

We were not going to win, if we won at all, without very heavy casualties. However, although the Marines barely had a toehold, the Japanese were scarcely fit to counter-attack. Saturday night they remained below ground, enabling the Marines to maintain their positions.

This led to a wave of optimism on Sunday morning. But a few hours later the situation was again critical. A Jap counter-attack had partially succeeded. By noon the Marines staged a recovery. They drove across the centre and western end of the island, and took part of the airfield. But

**INCENDIARIES ARE LOADED** on a U.S. bomber whose appointed target is installations on one of the Tarawa islands, in the Gilbert group, South-west Pacific (see map in facing page).
*Photo, U.S. Official*

few of the Japs could be got at. They were up to their old tricks of sniping from the trees and from heavily protected machine-gun nests. To advance at all the Marines had to dig out the enemy with grenades.

This was laborious and costly. All Saturday and Sunday the Marines had the fullest support of naval and aerial bombardment on request. From dawn till dusk the planes bombed and strafed. Destroyers closed in to automatic weapon range. By Monday morning, though still dangerous, the position had crystallized, and it was clear that we should get control.

When I landed on Betio yesterday the island looked ghastly and bizarre. Nowhere did there seem to be an inch not struck by shell or bomb. Then last night the Japanese counter-attacked again. Leaving their holes at the eastern end, a large number tried a wild yelling bayonet charge along the south beach. It lasted but a few minutes. The enemy reeled back madly under devastating Marine artillery fire. Other troops tried yesterday to wade from Betio to the next atoll of Bairiki, two miles away.

### Enemy Completely Annihilated

They found themselves under fire of the Marines, who had landed on Bairiki, and the automatic weapons of the destroyers standing by for that purpose.

Driven back into the hell of Betio, they fought like rats in a trap, and fought as only desperate, well-trained men can fight. General Smith announced early this morning that complete annihilation of the enemy could be expected by afternoon. He was right. Around noon word went over Betio that the island had been officially declared "secured." But even then snipers still fought on.

# OUR DIARY OF THE WAR

**NOVEMBER 24, Wednesday** 1,544th day
**Italy.**—Announced that Alfedena occupied by 8th Army.
**Russian Front.**—Anufrievka, in Kremenchug region, captured by Russians. Germans launched fresh assaults on Kiev salient.
**Australasia.**—Announced four Japanese destroyers sunk in recent naval battle off the Solomons.
**Pacific.**—U.S. escort carrier Liscombe Bay sunk off Gilbert Islands.
**Air.**—Ludwigshafen attacked by Halifaxes. Mosquitoes bombed Berlin.

**NOVEMBER 25, Thursday** 1,545th day
**Italy.**—8th Army crossed the Sangro and established substantial bridgehead. Gen. Montgomery in Order of the Day to his troops declared that the Germans would be dealt a "colossal crack."
**Russian Front.**—Propoisk, on River Sozh, taken by Red Army.
**Air.**—Frankfort-on-Main raided. Berlin attacked by Mosquitoes.

**NOVEMBER 26, Friday** 1,546th day
**Italy.**—8th Army consolidated newly-won gains across Sangro River.
**Russian Front.**—Gomel taken by Soviet troops.
**Australasia.**—Sattelberg, New Guinea, captured by Australians.
**Pacific.**—Revealed very heavy casualties suffered by U.S. troops in Gilbert Is.
**Air.**—Berlin (over 1,000 tons of bombs dropped) and Stuttgart heavily raided at night. Heaviest U.S. air attack of war on Bremen.
**General.**—Three-Power Conference held in N. Africa between British, U.S. and Chinese representatives, headed by Mr. Churchill, President Roosevelt and Generalissimo Chiang-Kai-shek, ended after five days of discussion beginning Nov. 22. Measures decided upon to intensify war against Japan and liberate territories she has occupied.

**NOVEMBER 27, Saturday** 1,547th day
**Russian Front.**—Soviet troops steadily advanced into White Russia, last Soviet Republic east of Poland.
**Sea.**—Admiralty announced loss of the submarine Trooper.

**NOVEMBER 28, Sunday** 1,548th day
**Italy.**—8th Army launched offensive across Sangro River under air cover.
**Russian Front.**—German attacks in Brusilov, Korosten and Chernyakhov areas repulsed. Cherchesk, Rogin, Pruda and Velsk seized by Russians.

**General.**—Mr. Churchill, Marshal Stalin, and President Roosevelt met at Teheran (Persia) to discuss next phase of war with Germany and problems of post-war world.

**NOVEMBER 29, Monday** 1,549th day
**Italy.**—Announced that in fresh 8th Army offensive bridgehead across Sangro at Archi secured, and gap torn in German winter defence line.
**Mediterranean.**—Serajevo (Yugoslavia) raided by Allied bombers.
**Russian Front.**—German offensive persisted S. of Kiev salient in Korosten, Chernyakhov and Brusilov areas.
**Australasia.**—Announced fresh Japanese counter-attacks repulsed at Sattelberg (New Guinea).
**China.**—Japanese entered Changteh.
**Pacific.**—Announced Vice-Admiral Kindaid to command Allied naval forces in S.W. Pacific.
**Air.**—Bremen heavily attacked by escorted U.S. Fortresses.
**General.**—Mr. Churchill presented Marshal Stalin with the Sword of Stalingrad, at Teheran.

**NOVEMBER 30, Tuesday** 1,550th day
**Italy.**—Stated that all high ground commanding the Sangro valley in British hands. Santa Maria, Mozzagrogna and Romangoli captured. New Zealand troops rejoined 8th Army.

**Mediterranean.**—Durazzo (Albania) bombarded by British destroyers.
**Russian Front.**—Russians announced withdrawal from Korosten, captured by them on Nov. 17.
**Air.**—Solingen, 14 miles E. of Düsseldorf, attacked by escorted Fortresses.

**DECEMBER 1, Wednesday** 1,551st day
**Italy.**—Announced that Castel di Frentano, and Casoli, taken by 8th Army. British troops advanced beyond Rocca San Giovanni. Turin ball-bearing works bombed.
**Australasia.**—Announced Australians had taken Bonga (New Guinea).
**Air.**—Solingen attacked for second successive day by Fortresses.
**General.**—Teheran Conference ended : plans for the destruction of the German forces concerted ; responsibility for an enduring peace assumed by the three Powers.

**DECEMBER 2, Thursday** 1,552nd day
**Italy.**—Capture of Fossacesia-Romangoli ridge completed after heavy fighting. 5th Army launched offensive, preceded by barrage of 650 guns.
**Mediterranean.**—Marseilles submarine pens attacked by Fortresses.
**Russian Front.**—Zavad and Buda, in River Pripet area, occupied by Russians.
**Air.**—Berlin (1,500 tons of bombs dropped) heavily raided.

**DECEMBER 3, Friday** 1,553rd day
**Russian Front.**—Dovsk and Sversken, N.W. of Gomel, Koristovka and Novo Georgiev, S.W. of Kremenchug, captured by Red Army.
**China.**—Japanese captured Changteh.
**Air.**—Leipzig bombed in concentration attack ; 1,500 tons of bombs dropped.

**DECEMBER 4, Saturday** 1,554th day
**Italy.**—Capture of Treglio, Lanciano and Orsogna by 8th Army announced.
**Russian Front.**—Gorodets, in Rogachev region, and Khalch in Zhlobin sector, taken by Soviet troops.
**Pacific.**—Kwajalein and Wotje atolls (Marshall Islands) attacked by U.S. aircraft carrier task force.
**General.**—Mr. Churchill, President Roosevelt and Mr. Ismet Inonu, President of Turkey, met in Cairo to discuss general political situation and examine policy to be followed.

**DECEMBER 5, Sunday** 1,555th day
**Italy.**—Announced San Vito captured by 8th Army.
**India.**—Calcutta raided by Japanese for first time in daylight.
**Pacific.**—Mili atoll (Marshall Islands) raided by Liberators.

**DECEMBER 6, Monday** 1,556th day
**Italy.**—Announced that 8th Army had reached line of Moro River.
**Mediterranean.**—Recent successes by H.M. submarines in this theatre announced ; 17 enemy ships sunk.
**Russian Front.**—Aleksandriya, S.W. of Kremenchug, captured by Russian troops. Announced that German and Finnish guns were shelling non-military objectives in Leningrad.
**Sea.**—Announced that destroyer Hursley and 4 corvettes handed over by Royal Navy to Greek Navy.
**General.**—Third phase of Allied conferences in Middle East successfully concluded ; conversations with Turkish President said to be "most fruitful." Gen. Smuts arrived in Cairo.

**DECEMBER 7, Tuesday** 1,557th day
**Italy.**—Revealed that 8th Army troops had crossed the Moro River ; fighting on Monte Maggiore and Monte Camino.
**Russian Front.**—Pantayevka in Kremenchug region captured by Red Army ; certain localities yielded to Germans in Chernyakhov area.
**Sea.**—U.S. battleship Wisconsin (45,000 tons) launched at Philadelphia Navy Yard.

## ★ ═══ Flash-backs ═══

**1939**
November 30. *Helsinki bombed in first day of Russo-Finnish war.*

**1940**
November 30. *Pogradets captured by Greek troops.*

**1941**
November 27. *Italian garrison of Gondar (Abyssinia) surrendered to British and Ethiopian troops.*
November 28. *Rostov-on-Don retaken by Russians.*

November 30. *Tobruk-Sidi Rezegh corridor broken by German assault.*
December 2. *H.M.S. Prince of Wales arrived at Singapore.*
December 7. *War with Japan began. Libyan tank battle resumed at Bir-el-Gobi.*

**1942**
November 27. *German troops entered Toulon. French warships in harbour scuttled by crews.*
December 7. *Allied armour forced German withdrawal at Tebourba.*

**EAST MEETS WEST IN PACIFIC VICTORY CONCLAVE.** The Conference, which ended on Nov. 26, 1943, after five days' minute examination of the strategic approach to the complete defeat of Japan, had the Mena House Hotel, near Cairo, for its setting. It was attended by Marshal Chiang Kai-shek, President and Generalissimo of China (see illus. p. 463), Mr. Roosevelt and Mr. Churchill, and their advisers. Mme. Chiang Kai-shek acted as interpreter for her husband. Composition of the delegations showed that the conference was mainly of a military character, and the official announcement of the conclusions reached, made in Cairo on Dec. 1, revealed complete unanimity among the Allies. Pressure on Japan is to be increased and sustained until she has disgorged all the territories " she has taken by violence and greed." Korea, Manchuria, Formosa, the Pescadores and the Pacific islands occupied since her treacherous swoop on Pearl Harbour on Dec.7, 1941, are notably listed for redemption. This happily informal conference photograph shows : Front row, l. to r., Marshal Chiang Kai-shek, Mr. Roosevelt, Mr. Churchill, Mme. Chiang Kai-shek ; back row, l. to r., Sir A. Cadogan, Mr. Eden, Mr. L. Steinhardt, Mr. J. G. Winant, Mr. H. Macmillan, Dr. Wang Chung-hui, Mr. R. G. Casey, Lord Killearn, Maj. Desmond Morton, Mr. A. Harriman, an unidentified delegate, and Lord Leathers.

*Photo, British Official: Crown Copyright*

# THE WAR IN THE AIR

### by Capt. Norman Macmillan, M.C., A.F.C.

THREE important developments have occurred in the air war which are, curiously enough, representative of the all-embracing nature of air power. In Germany, Berlin has been heavily bombed. In Italy, the Eighth Army's attack on the Sangro front broke through the strong German winter defence line carved out of rock, after artillery and air bombardments of which it was stated that the air element was not much less effective and accurate than the gunnery element. In mid-Pacific, some of the Gilbert Islands were occupied by a United States amphibious task force after an air bombardment of the Japanese holding force as great as one of the bombardments of Berlin (see story in page 474).

Here are illustrated the three sides of air war—the independent strategic action, the preparation for the advance of an army, and the preparation for the employment of a naval amphibious force. There is no other service capable of this universal action.

No force but an independent air force could bomb Berlin as Bomber Command bombs it (see pages 472-473). The United States Army Eighth Air Force based in Britain for the bombing of Germany and occupied Europe is an independent strategic air force, too, detached from the army. The difference between Bomber Command and its American opposite number is that the British force is organized and provided for by a separate Ministry, whereas the American force is organized and provided for by the War Department. In action there is no difference, and in this war the U.S. Air Force is moving towards a separate air force organization, despite the opposition of those whose interests or inclinations are of a contrary tendency.

It was Britain's failure to produce a separate strategic striking force in the early part of the 1914-18 War that brought the Smuts Report to the War Cabinet into the political arena of those days and created the requisite conditions for the establishment of

PRESSING THE BUTTON that unloads death-dealing steel. This is a Mark IX bomb-sight and release in a British Lancaster bomber.
*Photo, British Official: Crown Copyright*

the separate Royal Air Force. If we had not taken that step then, and, against the cruellest opposition, afterwards upheld the policy of an independent air force, reactionary interests would have carved the Royal Air Force into two and handed one part to the Navy and the other part to the Army; and there would have been no adequate force to bomb Germany, nor would there have been a sufficient or rigorously-enough trained fighter force to have won the Battle of Britain, the initial victory from which all other Allied victories in this war have sprung. And so this still greater war might possibly have been already lost to us.

## POLICY Which Saved Britain and Helped Turn the Tide

Even as things turned out, the power of the strategic independent bombing force was delayed because of the demands made upon the Air Force by the other services on land and at sea who, before the war, fought tooth and nail to secure the largest shares in the defence votes, and by that very action were responsible for the inability of the Air Force to do more than it was feasibly able to do during the early part of the war.

Yet the technical deficiencies in the land and sea forces were greater than in the Air Force. The British Expeditionary Force went to France without a single gun-tank, parachute troops, or tommy-guns. What use were the Prince of Wales and the Repulse, or the guns of the naval defence of Singapore? Why did the Hood blow up when the Bismarck was so difficult to sink? What proportion of Italy's navy was crippled by aircraft, and what by ships? Why was Germany winning the submarine war at sea until the Air Force really got cracking on the job? And what could the Army have done if the Air Force had not won the Battle of Britain?— an army, as Mr. Churchill said, bereft of its equipment, with few tanks, and few guns. If there is any policy which can be said to have saved Britain in this war and brought about the turning of the tide, it was the policy of the independence of the Air Force.

The guns of the present-day British army are extremely accurate. They are numerous. It is a remarkable statement that the barrage provided by the Air Force was almost as effective and accurate as that of the massed guns upon the Sangro front before the Army broke through. Those who have been closely associated with the development of air power have never doubted that the accuracy of air bombardment would eventually equal that of gun bombardment. But here is the evidence of groundsmen in support of the belief of those who know the air.

But there is more in air bombardment than that. The aeroplane is the most mobile of all weapons. No army can retreat fast enough to escape it. They may pull out of range of the guns until they decide again to stand, but they cannot pull out of range of air bombardment. Thus, taken in the aggregate, before, during and after the battle, the tactical air force must be at least as great as, if not greater than, the artillery in its effect upon the enemy. And that does not take into account the field strategical air force, which, before the action, began to cut the lines of communication with the enemy army by its attacks upon railway bridges and junctions, ports, ships, locomotives and rolling stock, and factories and dumps. Nor does it take into consideration the accurate photography from the air which makes the whole plan of action possible, and which

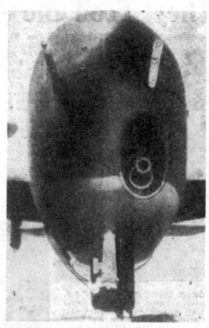

NOSE OF A MITCHELL B-25, American medium bomber, now fitted with 75-mm. (3-in.) cannon, equivalent to a powerful field gun—probably the most sensational development in aircraft armament revealed since this war began. *Photo, Keystone*

reveals in detail the enemy machine-gun nests and strongly defended points.

The work of the Air Force under Tedder and Coningham has shown that the independent air force represented by the R.A.F. is the finest field air force in the world, and that all the ancient claptrap of the need for an air force in khaki is just the wind of propagandists. If Malaya had been the defence responsibility of the Air Force instead of the Navy, we might never have lost Singapore. At least, the Japanese Air Force would have been decimated as was the German Air Force in the Battle of Britain, and it would have been unable to blast a way through for the oncoming Japanese Army.

## PUNISHED As No Islands Have Ever Been Dealt With Before

In the American occupation of the Gilbert Islands we see the procedure in reverse. A great air force swoops upon the selected islands and blasts them as no islands have ever been pounded before, except perhaps Pantelleria and parts of Sicily. The air forces hold off the enemy warships, prevent them from getting near the scene of action, the landing forces go ashore, and four days later an aerodrome is crushed flat out of the coral rock of the atoll and the aircraft begin to land. Here again the aeroplane is the core of the whole action, forming at once an attack, holding and occupying weapon, without which no operation in modern war can be sure of success, and with which, in adequate numbers and types of aircraft, no operation in modern war need fail.

But are we sure that in these great diversions of the use of air power in modern war on land and sea we are pursuing the best policy? Is it not certain that if we were to concentrate our bombing resources on bombarding Germany the war would be immeasurably shortened? The most efficient distribution of air power to wreak the maximum destruction upon the enemy will help determine the length of the war and the duration of the subsequent peace—for air power is the best form of military power to enforce conditions which guarantee peace. That is why the Air Force must ultimately become the leading service. The air arm is *a priori* the victory-winning arm. Must we wait until a third world war before it is given its opportunity?

# They Trod the Path of Duty to its Glorious End

F/O L. R. TRIGG, D.F.C., R.N.Z.A.F. (above) awarded the Victoria Cross for an exploit cited as "an epic of grim determination and high courage." In Aug. 1943 he undertook, as captain and pilot, a patrol in a Liberator, a type of machine new to him, and attacked a surfaced U-boat, his aircraft receiving many hits from the submarine's A.A. guns. With his plane in flames he skimmed to within 50 feet of the enemy craft and so effectively bombed her that she sank in 20 minutes. Trigg and his gallant crew are missing, believed killed.
*After a British Official photo*

Pte. ERIC ANDERSON, of the East Yorkshire Regiment (below), stretcher-bearer hero of the Wadi Akarit, Tunisia, fighting. On April 6, 1943, his battalion was making a dawn attack on a strongly held enemy position, when the advance company suddenly came under intense and accurate machine-gun and mortar fire, being compelled to withdraw behind the crest of a hill, and unavoidably leaving behind a few men who were wounded and pinned to the ground by the strafing.

Anderson went forward alone and, single-handed, brought back one of his comrades. Again and yet again he entered the hell that was no man's land, carrying two more of the wounded to safety. A fourth time he went out alone, still regardless of his own safety, and as he was administering first-aid preparatory to making the return journey he was hit and mortally wounded. Posthumously awarded the V.C., "his example was an inspiration to all."

**VICTORIA CROSS** highest British Empire award For Valour

Acting F/Sgt. A. L. AARON, D.F.M., R.A.F.V.R. (above), posthumously awarded the V.C. for "an example of devotion to duty which has seldom been equalled and never surpassed." On the night of Aug. 12, 1943, Aaron was captain and pilot of a Stirling bomber detailed to attack Turin. Devastating bursts of fire from an enemy fighter met them as they approached to attack. Three engines were hit, the windscreen shattered, front and rear gun turrets put out of action and elevator control damaged, rendering the Stirling unstable and difficult to control.

The navigator was killed and members of the crew wounded. Aaron himself was badly hit in the face and wounded in the lung, and his right arm was rendered useless. Unable to speak, by signs he urged the bomb-aimer to take over control and set course southward in an effort to fly the crippled bomber to Sicily or North Africa. Aaron was assisted to the rear of the bomber and treated with morphia, but, mindful of his responsibility as captain, he insisted on resuming control, and was assisted into his seat and had his feet placed on the rudder bar.

But his weakness was so great that he was persuaded to desist. Though nearing complete exhaustion and in great pain he helped to get his machine home—by writing instructions with his left hand. Five hours after leaving the target the flare path at Bône airfield was sighted, and he summoned his remaining strength to direct attempts to land the damaged craft in the darkness. Nine hours after the bomb-aimer achieved the landing Aaron died.

F/Lieut. W. E. NEWTON, R.A.A.F. (above), in 52 operational sorties over New Guinea, from May 1942 to March 1943, provided "many examples of conspicuous bravery," culminating in the feat of valour which earned him the V.C. On March 17, having bombed his objective, his aircraft burst into flames. He kept calm and turned his machine away towards the shore, finally landing on the water. Two members of the crew managed to extricate themselves and were seen swimming to the land; their V.C. captain is missing, having done all he could to keep his comrades out of enemy hands, regardless of risks he himself ran.

*Photos, British Official : Crown Copyright; L.N.A., Daily Express*

ONE of the favourite arguments of those who used to admire Hitlerism and Fascism of the Mussolini brand was that under absolute rulers government was so much more competently carried on, the real interest of the population better served, the best men picked to serve it. I have known firm believers in democracy say there was "something in that argument." I never fell for it, and now it has been completely exploded, not only by revelations as to the corruption and incompetence of Fascist administrators in Italy, but by the retention in office by Hitler of the man who has been the most complete and utter failure of the whole war. In any democratic country Hermann Goering would have been sacked long ago, if he had ever been appointed Air Force Chief, which I do not think he would have been, seeing that he never showed any sign of real ability. He has done nothing that he boasted he would do. He promised Germans victory in the Battle of Britain. They were beaten. He assured them they need not fear bombs on their cities. One by one those cities are being reduced to ruins. Yet he sticks to his job. Nothing could more plainly show what poor boobs the German people are.

DID the tremendous explosion of public anger provoked by the release of Mosley and his wife come as a surprise to the Home Secretary and the Government in general? I must say it astonished me. When I read the first bald announcement that he was about to be set at liberty for reasons of health, I thought, "This will mean questions in the Commons." But the instant flaring-up of indignation all over the country and among all classes was something for which I can hardly recollect a parallel in the last fifty years. The Hoare-Laval agreement caused something of the kind, but not nearly so widespread. When the Tsar of Russia's fleet on its way to Japanese waters during the Russo-Japanese War sank British fishing-boats in the North Sea as a result of sudden panic, a howl went up which might have carried us into the conflict, if statesmen had not handled the incident wisely. But that was more a newspaper outcry than an outburst of popular rage. This Mosley episode was gingerly dealt with by the Press. The howl came from the public, and it seemed to me that all sections of the public were thinking alike in a most unusual way.

THE latest report of a cure being discovered for the "common cold" could not have been circulated at a moment more certain to ensure interest in it. Launched in the summer it would have received little notice. Just at the beginning of winter there is always a lot of coryza, as the doctors call it when they want to make patients believe they are suffering from something rather important! All the unfortunates who were sneezing or sniffing, coughing and blowing their noses, seized on this piece of news with gratitude and hope. My hope is that they will not expect anything to come of it. In my time there have been so many statements that diseases have at last been overcome: I ceased long ago to believe in any of them. The truth about colds is that no remedy can remove them; they have to take their course. They are a sign that something has gone wrong in our bodies and that "something" can be removed with care and perseverance. If you merely take a medicine that lessens the symptoms of your cold, you drive them elsewhere and very likely the change is for the worse.

I DO not travel about the country much these days. When I do, I can answer with a firm "Yes!" the query "Is your journey really necessary?" Wherever I go I notice disregard by farmers of the warning given by the Ministry of Agriculture against building hay-stacks or wheat-stacks close together. The customary way is to put them in a rickyard. That was also the sensible way—once. Now that high explosive and incendiary bombs are liable to fall at any moment on any part of the country it is the reverse of sensible to place ricks in a bunch, so that if one catches fire they must all be destroyed. This seems so obvious that one can hardly understand why farmers do not act upon it. But they are hard to detach from traditional methods. They are inclined, many of them, to snort with disdain at advice from the Ministry of Agriculture. They keep to their old habits, and in far too many cases one sees groups of stacks literally "asking for it." The County Agricultural Committees should take the matter in hand, using compulsion if necessary. For the loss, when ricks burn, is not the farmer's only, but the nation's

WHAT we are too much inclined to forget just now, it seems to me, is that Man is not by nature a planning animal. He does not, in most circumstances, plan for himself and he dislikes very much being planned for by other people. Each of us has individual tastes, preferences, and ideas of how we like to live; we want to arrange our lives as far as we can for ourselves. There has been an amusing illustration of this. At a Practical Planning Exhibition in Westminster there was on show a model kitchen. A practical housewife went to see it, and wrote to a newspaper to say it was all wrong. It wasn't the sort of kitchen any woman would like. Who could have designed it? Some man, she supposed, who knew nothing about kitchen labours. She was wrong. The design was concocted by six working women who live on Birmingham City Council Estates. It was set up for criticism in Birmingham, and many other women gave their views. It was modified in accordance with some of these. So it does embody the ideas of housewives. Yet other housewives don't approve of it at all. Well, there you are! Tastes differ, and opinions vary. Planning is a tricky business. We must go at it with a lot of care.

IN the congratulatory articles about the hundredth anniversary of the founding of Macmillans, the great publishing firm, there has been reference not only to the famous authors whose merit it perceived while they were young and unknown, but also to some whom it declined to publish and who became famous nevertheless. One of these was Bernard Shaw. He offered his early novels to the firm, and had them returned with thanks. I have seen it suggested that this was an error of judgement. With that I do not agree. Those novels are included in the complete edition of Shaw's works, but they are curiosities even now, and at the time they were written, more than fifty years ago, they were certainly not the sort of fiction for Macmillans to accept, and they failed at first to find acceptance from any publisher. Shaw has the good sense and generosity to recognize this himself. He has been unusually quiet of late. That is due partly, no doubt, to his being only three years off ninety. But he admits that the complexities of this war puzzle him; that is one reason why he has not written as frequently about it as he did about the conflict of 1914-18.

AT one period of the Napoleonic Wars there was a heated controversy about sailors' pigtails, which used to be the only style in the British Navy. Now there is going on a discussion about soldiers' pyjamas, which may seem a trifle compared with the tremendous issues still trembling in the scales of Fate, but it has a very real interest for millions of our fighting men. Not so much when they are actually fighting, for then there is not much chance of sleeping in beds and taking off day-clothes to put on nightwear. But when they are living through intervals between engagements, and especially when they are at home on leave, they do like to enjoy as far as they can the amenities of peacetime. Very few are able to get sleeping-suits. They are not part of the clothing issue. The War Office expects soldiers to sleep in their day-shirts. And the men have not enough coupons to buy pyjamas, even if they are procurable at a moderate price. The matter keeps on bobbing up in the House of Commons, but evidently we are short of pyjama materials and shall be for a considerable time to come.

**AIR COMMODORE D. C. T. BENNETT, C.B.E., D.S.O.,** commanding officer of the Pathfinder Force, which by laying marker flares guides R.A.F. bombers to their targets, is an expert in astro-navigation, a pioneer of flying, former Mercury "pick-a-back" aircraft pilot, and co-organizer of the Atlantic Ferry Service. Pathfinder's gilt eagle badge is seen under his "wings."
*Photo, British Official: Crown Copyright*

# Ready for Battle They Drop from the Sky

Printed in England and published every alternate Friday by the Proprietors, THE AMALGAMATED PRESS, LTD., The Fleetway House, Farringdon Street, London, E.C.4. Registered for transmission by Canadian Magazine Post. Sole Agents for Australia and New Zealand : Messrs. Gordon & Gotch, Ltd. ; and for South Africa : Central News Agency, Ltd.—December 24, 1943.

**POLISH PARACHUTE TROOPS** train to take their place in the great all-out Allied offensive against the common enemy.   Having safely landed from the troop-carrying plane and disengaged themselves from their descent apparatus, they rush to where the big container, borne on its own parachute, has fallen.   Packed in the container are weapons, arranged for swift assembly, plus ammunition and other items essential to the previously planned operation, which, all going well, can be embarked upon within a minute or two of touching earth.

*Photo, Keystone*

S.S.   *Editorial Address :* JOHN CARPENTER HOUSE, WHITEFRIARS, LONDON, E.C.4.

Vol 7    The War Illustrated    Nº 171

Edited by Sir John Hammerton

SIXPENCE                                            JANUARY 7, 1944

**ON HIS WAY TO N. AFRICA** for the historic Three-Power Conference at Cairo (Nov. 22-26, 1943) Mr. Churchill spent two days at Malta. He is here seen amid the ruins of the much-bombed Valetta dockyard area, where he received a tumultuous welcome. It was with the utmost concern that the people of the United Nations learned on Dec. 16 that the Premier was seriously ill with pneumonia, but by Dec. 23 it was stated that he was well on the way to recovery.    *Photo, British Official: Crown Copyright*

NO. 172 WILL BE PUBLISHED FRIDAY, JANUARY 21

# Sidelights of War Seen by Our Roving Camera

ARAB GIFT TO MR. CHURCHILL. Two Arabian princes, the Emir Feisal and the Emir Khalid, sons of King Abdul Aziz of Saudi Arabia, visited No. 10, Downing Street on Dec. 6, 1943, and on behalf of their father presented Mrs. Churchill with a jewelled Arab sword. The Premier's wife is here accepting the sword from Prince Emir Feisal in her husband's absence in the Middle East (see p p. 495-499). On the extreme left stands Sheik Hafiz Wahba.

HISTORIC CITY CEREMONY. The City of Chicago flag was exchanged for that of the City of London, and the Union Jack for the Stars and Stripes, at an impressive exchange of standards at London's Mansion House on Nov. 9, 1943. Gen. Devers, commanding U.S. Army in Europe, talks to H.A.C. (Honourable Artillery Company) pikemen in 17th-century uniform.

GAS TEST ON THE SOUTHERN RAILWAY. At an extensive demonstration and exercise held by the Southern Railway in a Kent district recently, lengths of rail were taken up, a crater dug and mustard gas sprayed in the area. Signal and telegraph departments went into action, and in a short time trains moved over the decontaminated section of the line. A decontamination squad (above) is hard at work clearing away contaminated sleepers and rails. Right, Water ambulance launch now in use by Combined Operations is fitted to carry six cot patients, here seen in their well-protected bunks.

*Photos, British Official: Crown Copyright; New York Times Photos; Topical Press*

# THE BATTLE FRONTS

## by Maj.-Gen. Sir Charles Gwynn, K.C.B., D.S.O.

**ITALIAN FRONT, Dec. 15, 1943.** Right flank of the 8th Army was menacing strongly fortified Ortona, and Orsogna by Dec. 22. A 5-mile bridgehead had been established across the Moro. *Courtesy of The Times*

By the end of Nov. 1943 it had become clear, from the marked and continuous fall in Allied shipping losses over a period of months, that the battle of the Atlantic had for all practical purposes been won. The striking victories gained by aircraft and escort vessels in the first half of December, over U-boat packs making desperate attempts to revive their menace, gave further proof of the efficiency not only of defensive measures but of our counter-offensive. Proof had also been given of the value of our new bases in the Azores.

With the immense economies effected by reopening the Mediterranean route, and with new construction vastly exceeding losses, it is evident that our power of multiplying offensive fronts, and of enlarging the scale of operations, will rapidly increase. It will be seen, therefore, that the winning of the battle of the Atlantic not only implies that our offensive action against the U-boats has gained the upper hand, but that increased offensive power all round results from it. I doubt whether the Teheran Conference, and the subsequent Cairo Conference in which Turkey took part, could have been conducted in such an atmosphere of confidence if the situation in the Atlantic had imposed limitations on what the Anglo-American representatives could safely promise to undertake.

The progress of the Italian campaign is bound to be slow, so long as the enemy is determined to fight hard for every foot of ground that gives him such ample opportunities for delaying and defensive action. Anything like a sensational break-through on either the 8th or 5th Army front obviously cannot be expected ; and, in the uncertain weather conditions of winter, amphibious operations to turn the enemy's positions must present few attractions.

On small-scale maps the day to day progress of the armies may seem insignificant ; but from the beginning of October, when Naples had just been captured, to the middle of December the 5th Army advanced some 30 miles in the coastal region through appallingly difficult country and under desperate weather conditions.

It had not broken through the position on which the enemy had apparently hoped to stand for the winter, but had broken into it and secured a number of important tactical features. On the Adriatic coast the 8th Army's advance in the same period had covered about 60 miles and had definitely broken through the enemy's winter position on the Sangro, though without being able to prevent his retirement in good order.

These may seem small gains for 2½ months of hard fighting when compared with the great areas that have changed hands rapidly in Russia, France and Poland ; but they should be compared rather with the advances made in the offensives in the last war. When the enemy stands to fight with determination only a very deep penetration or outflanking of his position will compel him to carry out a long strategic withdrawal ; and neither was feasible in the Italian theatre where the terrain provided natural opportunities for defence in great depth. In the mountainous central sector of the front the advance has actually covered longer distances during the period. The enemy, owing to indifferent communications, could only hold the ground lightly and there were in consequence greater opportunities of employing infiltration tactics.

The Allied troops have evidently fought magnificently throughout, and have inflicted very heavy losses on the enemy, compelling him to employ more of his reserve divisions than he had probably ever intended. In the long run this may prove to be of more importance than a rapid advance.

It is unfortunate, though perhaps unavoidable, that in armies composed of elements drawn from many quarters the part played by British troops should be somewhat obscured. Although General Clark commands the 5th American Army, there is in it, I understand, actually a majority of British troops and they have certainly taken a full share in its operations. Being an American army, however, American war correspondents are naturally drawn to it and take a special interest in American exploits.

The 8th is, of course, a British Army, but obviously, both for clarity in description and in justice, the splendid New Zealand, Canadian and Indian Divisions, which do not bear British distinctive numbers, must be mentioned by name. British Divisions are at times mentioned by their numbers, but since that might give useful information to the enemy this is not generally permitted. It is consequently not easy for correspondents to indicate how many British Divisions have actually been engaged. One thing those of us who have friends or relatives fighting in Italy may be sure of is that if they belong to infantry or R.E. units they are playing a dominant part in the battle. Splendidly as the artillery, aircraft and, where practicable, tanks have cooperated, it has been, and probably will continue to be, essentially a campaign for infantry with the Engineers as an indispensable adjunct.

In Russia, as I write in mid-December, the drawn-out autumn battles are approaching their end and winter operations of a different order are due to begin. The crisis in the Kiev salient has not yet passed, but with every day that Vatutin's army continues to retain its cohesion the chances that Manstein's counter-offensive will achieve a major success diminish. Up till now he has had the immense advantage of possessing good railway communications behind him, whereas the Russians have had none west of the Dnieper. But when frost hardens the ground, permitting motor transport to function more efficiently, this advantage will have less value, and already Von Manstein must have expended most of his reserves.

The Russians have, during the last month, fought a magnificent defensive battle in the Salient under most unfavourable conditions. If it can be successfully maintained for a few more days it may prove of even greater importance than the victories gained in offensive battles farther south in the bend of the Dnieper.

In his counter-offensive Von Manstein gambled with high stakes and if, as seems probable, he has lost, the expenditure of his reserve power may prove more disastrous to him than the loss of his positions in the middle Dnieper and of the lateral railway through Znamenka. Nevertheless, the loss of the latter will make the task of maintaining supplies for his troops in the Dnieper bend exceedingly difficult ; already he is reported to be using air transport to supplement other means of communication.

**SOVIET MILITARY MISSION TO ITALY**, it was revealed on Dec. 13, 1943, was headed by Maj.-Gen. Vasiliev, victor of Perekop, capture of which on Nov. 1, 1943, bottled up forces in the Crimea. Gen. Vasiliev (centre, wearing glasses) is seen with two of his officers during a tour of inspection of the Monte Camino sector. PAGE 483 *Photo, British Official: Crown Copyright*

# Sword of Honour City: Stalingrad Resurgent

A MERE 3,000 CITIZENS REMAINED ALIVE among the ruins when Stalingrad was liberated by Soviet forces on Jan. 31, 1943. Refugees then began to return, and by November 10,500 reconstructed or newly-built residences, mostly huts, had been occupied. Lessons are resumed in a renovated classroom (1) of the battered Lenin School (3), whilst the upper storeys are made usable again. Citizens combine to repair a settlement (4), and tanks are once more produced in the tractor plant (2), where Rashida Shakirova (5) is leading electrician. See p. 495.       PAGE 484       *Photos, Pictorial Press*

# Germans Use Rocket Shells in Russia and Italy

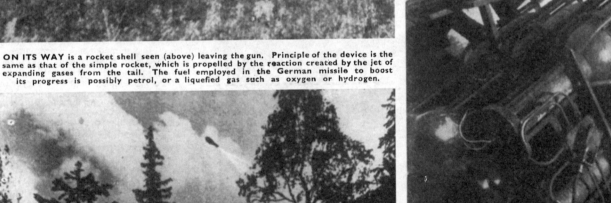

FIRED FROM ITS CRATE is this type of German incendiary rocket, (known as the 32 cm.) here seen held in the firing position by U.S. soldiers who captured it intact during the fighting in Italy.

ON ITS WAY is a rocket shell seen (above) leaving the gun. Principle of the device is the same as that of the simple rocket, which is propelled by the reaction created by the jet of expanding gases from the tail. The fuel employed in the German missile to boost its progress is possibly petrol, or a liquefied gas such as oxygen or hydrogen.

ROCKET-PROPELLED shells and bombs have featured prominently in recent enemy "secret weapon" propaganda. It has even been reported that 15-ton rocket shells have been employed against Leningrad from German bases over 100 miles away! Photographs have been released by the enemy through neutral channels to give credence to Nazi claims that multiple rocket guns (rear view above) are being used on the Eastern Front; six shells are fired in quick succession, and in the photograph one of the gunners is seen sighting the weapon, whilst another bends down (bottom left corner) to adjust the last of the six detonators. Left, two rocket shells hurtling high above a Russian forest.

*Photos, U.S. Official, Keystone*
*Associated Press*

# THE WAR AT SEA

## by Francis E. McMurtrie

At first sight readers may think our naval and air critics are encroaching on each other's ground in this number. But in fact Mr. McMurtrie deals interestingly with air power from the seaman's viewpoint whereas Capt. Macmillan (in page 508) gives an airman's comments on the sea war.

MORE than once in these pages I have expressed the opinion that the German Navy will never again proceed to sea as a fleet or squadron, except possibly on some evasive enterprise in which it could scarcely be intercepted, such as the dash to Spitzbergen. It was recently revealed that last summer the Home Fleet, under the command of Admiral Sir Bruce Fraser, in conjunction with a task force of the United States Navy under Rear-Admiral Olaf M. Hustvedt, practically trailed its coat outside the anchorage in which the German fleet lay in Northern Norwegian waters. So cautious was the enemy response that only a reconnaissance aircraft ventured to approach the Allied force : and as the result of the Fleet Air Arm's vigilance, it failed to return to its base.

IT has since been the turn of the Japanese to be treated to a similar demonstration. During the second week in Dec. 1943 a strong force of the United States Pacific Fleet, comprising battleships, aircraft carriers, cruisers and destroyers, cruised within a comparatively short range of Truk, the island stronghold which is the principal Japanese naval base in the Pacific. Though it has been stated that the main enemy fleet is stationed there, it gave no sign of its presence on this occasion. Yet it has been suggested that the importance of Truk is such that the Japanese would be likely to fight a major action, throwing in all their naval resources, were it to be threatened.

Having regard to the recent tendency of our Eastern enemy to husband his resources in heavy ships, it seems doubtful if Truk would be regarded as worth a supreme gamble. Rather does it seem likely that the main fleet will continue to be held in reserve, to be risked only in the last resort. A serious assault would probably find only subsidiary naval vessels at Truk, which would endeavour to escape if complete investment of the group were threatened.

PARTICULARS released in Dec. 1943 of a successful action against U-boats in the North Atlantic by the Royal Navy in conjunction with Coastal Command aircraft included the mention of a new class of frigate, known officially as the "Captain" class. There appears to be a very large number of these useful craft, all of which were constructed in the United States. The first few were launched in U.S. Navy Yards in 1942, but recently the names of a great many more have been reported in the Press on both sides of the Atlantic as having been launched from private shipyards in America. These include such names as Berry, Blackwood, Bligh, Bullen, Capel, Duff, Foley and Louis, all of whom fought under Nelson at the Nile, Copenhagen or Trafalgar ; Stayner, who was Blake's right-hand man at Santa Cruz de Tenerife in April 1657 ; Drury, who was with Admiral Duncan at Camperdown ; Calder, who was captain of the fleet under Jervis at St. Vincent ; Bentinck and Thornbrough, who were amongst Howe's captains at the Glorious First of June 1794.

According to particulars published in the American Press, these vessels are identical in type with those known in the United States Navy as "destroyer escorts." The latter displace about 1,300 tons and are 300 feet in length with a beam of 35 feet. They are armed with three dual purpose guns of 3-in. calibre, together with two 40-millimetre Bofors pieces and four 20-millimetre Oerlikons. Machinery varies in different ships, some having turbine engines, others triple expansion and still others Diesel motors. Horse-power is stated as 5,400, equal to a speed of over 21 knots, or sufficient to overtake any U-boat. Judging from the particulars given these little ships are making a useful contribution to the Allied victory in the Battle of the Atlantic.

CREDIT has also to be accorded to the increasing number of escort aircraft carriers which are employed to bridge the mid-Atlantic gap, between the effective ranges of shore-based planes. According to statements made in America, the United States Navy now includes over 40 of these valuable vessels, many of which have been improvised from merchant ship hulls, though some of the more recent have been specially built for the purpose. The earlier ones were named after sounds, the later ones after bays, e.g. Long Island, Copahee, Barnes, Core, Hamlin ; and Natoma Bay, Fanshaw Bay, Kadashan Bay, Nehenta Bay ; but a few of the latest type have been given battle names, a privilege hitherto reserved for the big fleet aircraft carriers. Instances of the latter class of name are Casablanca, Guadalcanal, Tripoli, Corregidor and Wake Island.

Though fewer names have been published, it seems reasonable to conclude that British escort aircraft carriers must by this time be almost as numerous. Names that have actually been released on this side of the Atlantic include Archer, Attacker, Battler, Biter, Fencer, Hunter, Ravager, Stalker, Searcher, Tracker. According to the American Press, one named Chaser was launched in June 1942 and a sister ship, the Pursuer, in the following month. Two named Striker and Trailer had gone afloat in the previous May. This year the launch in the U.S.A. of an escort carrier for the Royal Navy named Ameer has been announced. From her name she would appear to be of a different type from the others mentioned.

AMERICAN escort carriers appear to vary in displacement from about 7,700 tons to fully 10,000 tons. Their complement of aircraft may be as many as 30, and their armament includes light guns on high-angle mountings, ranging from machine-guns to 3-in. or 4-in. weapons. In some cases Diesel motors are used for propulsion ; in others geared turbines, supplied with steam by watertube boilers of the Foster-Wheeler pattern. There is no doubt that the very considerable number of aircraft carriers now available for service, not only in the Battle of the Atlantic but also in other spheres of operation, has greatly relieved the pressure on the Allied Navies. At Salerno, aircraft from carriers of this (escort) type proved invaluable in affording continuous cover to the invading troops while land-based planes refuelled.

One of the results of a more plentiful supply of carriers has been the discarding of seaplanes as an item of equipment by the majority of cruisers. There is obviously little need for a seaplane's services if a carrier is within reach ; while the considerable amount of deck space occupied by an aircraft and the necessary catapult can ill be spared. There is also the added danger of fire from the petrol that has to be carried. Judging from recent official photographs the heavy 10,000-ton cruisers, which are liable to be detailed to distant waters in quest of raiders, are almost the only ones that now carry seaplanes.

**LAST MOMENTS OF A U-BOAT,** one of six destroyed by Coastal Command aircraft in a sea-and-air action fought around a N. Atlantic convoy. A Liberator, it was announced on Dec. 5, 1943, accounted for this one, which lay half-submerged long enough for its crew to inflate their rubber dinghies.

*Photo, British Official*

# U.S. Naval Task Force Aids British Home Fleet

**NAVAL COOPERATION OF BRITAIN AND AMERICA** is demonstrated in the top photograph, where destroyers of the U.S. task force in company with British destroyers form a protective screen for battleships. Below, Bofors guns of an American battleship go into action. Inset, Adm. Stark (right), commander of U.S. naval forces in Europe, and Mr. A. V. Alexander, First Lord of the Admiralty (left), inspect a guard of honour at a Northern base where they recently visited units of the U.S. Fleet now operating with the Royal Navy.

*Photos, British Official*

# Our Monitors Help the Land Fighting in Italy

Seldom in the news, but doing a magnificent and highly important job, the Navy's monitors are specialized warships with a single purpose the smashing of land targets. How these vessels, armed with 15-in. and smaller guns but not equipped to fight other warships, carry out their great task is described by ALEXANDER DILKE.

IN the Italian campaign monitors have come into their own. Geography dictated that much of the fighting should take place on the coastal plains; where that is the case, monitors are able to bring their 15-in. guns to bear on vital targets in the enemy lines and well behind them. How many of these specialized warships are now engaged must remain a secret. The only name which may be mentioned at present is H.M.S. Roberts.

But it is no secret to the Germans that the devastating shells from the batteries of these ships played a decisive part in the critical battle of Salerno when the whole fate of the Italian invasion hung in the balance. While the guns of the destroyers steaming close to the shore engaged the German tanks trying to sally out of the ravines, the heavier guns of the monitors and battleships were ranged on the German heavy batteries farther inland, and on German communications and similar targets. Wherever the fighting goes in the " leg " of Italy, the monitors will find targets. There is no other part of Europe

and was back again in a few weeks bombarding the same targets. The Germans had to wait nearly 25 years to get her. She was sunk in February 1941 off the North African coast, but only after three bombs and two mines had broken her back.

H.M.S. TERROR played a considerable part in the first Libyan campaign, where she was part of the "Inshore Squadron" to which General Wavell alloted such a generous share of the victory. When war broke out she was in the Far East, but was brought to the Mediterranean. Her first task was one very much out of the line of a monitor—anti-aircraft defence of Malta in the first weeks of the war with Italy, when no other defence was possible. She survived further bombardments in Suda Bay, was attacked by E-boats while bombarding Sidi Barrani in the opening stages of the campaign, and then incessantly attacked from the air.

But the Germans did not get her until she had poured hundreds of rounds into vital

a single shell completely destroyed a chemical factory, and a salvo on Spaccaformo, twelve miles inland, was sufficient to force the garrison, which had been putting up a hot resistance, to surrender. There were many instances of enemy batteries being put out of action or coming out to surrender after one or two near misses.

Monitors are equipped with elaborate ranging apparatus, but wireless and the new style of amphibious operations have opened up fresh possibilities to them. In Italy they have been working with the aid of observers on the land as well as with " spotting planes." They are thus able to fire at targets completely out of sight with great accuracy, and even to fire through a smoke-screen.

At the opening of the present war, as at the beginning of the last, the Royal Navy was poorly provided with monitors. In 1914 Britain had no true monitors, but, chiefly under the inspiration of Lord Fisher, sixteen were built in record time, of which H.M.S. Terror and H.M.S. Erebus became the most famous. The latter, incidentally, survived a devastating blow amidships by a small boat laden with high explosive. Four were sunk in operations, and all the rest but three were scrapped during the period of disarmament. Of these three, one became the hulk Drake, at Plymouth, her guns being mounted on H.M.S. Erebus.

THOSE scrapped monitors would be worth almost their weight in gold in the amphibious warfare we are now undertaking, but their places have been taken by new vessels to an extent which must remain secret. One of the difficulties in building monitors is that the huge guns with their accompanying ranging apparatus cannot be produced in a day or even a few weeks. It is a lengthy and highly specialized job for which only a few establishments are equipped.

A monitor has a remarkably shallow draught — perhaps 11 feet, compared with 27-28 feet of a battleship carrying comparable guns. Her armour is generally limited to about 4 inches, with heavier armour on the gunhouse. The Royal Navy is now the only one to possess monitors. This is in accordance with a long tradition of amphibious warfare. The monitor as a type dates back to the 17th century, but the name itself comes from the famous " Monitor " built by Ericsson for the Federals in the U.S. Civil War.

THE duel between the Monitor, which was virtually a floating 11-in. gun battery, heavily armoured, and the Merrimac, built by the Confederates, is a classic of naval history. It was indecisive, in a sense, since neither ship was sunk, but it established the turret mounting of heavy guns and led to the construction of " monitors " along very different lines from those of the " bomb ketches " of the 17th century. The United States did not continue the construction of monitors after the 1914-18 war, presumably not envisaging amphibious warfare under conditions when they would be effective—as now.

H.M.S. ROBERTS, renowned British monitor referred to in this page, whose guns played a decisive part in smashing rail and road communications in Sicily and destroying enemy coastal batteries on the Italian mainland. Her two formidable guns are here seen in their forward turret, a feature which characterizes the monitor's design. The Roberts has distinguished herself in many daring operations in the Mediterranean.
*Photo, British Official: Crown Copyright*

where this type of warship could be used over such a long period.

THE monitor is a specialized warship with a single purpose—the bombardment of shore targets. It is not equipped to fight other warships, and Allied naval supremacy is a condition for it going into action. It is defensively armed, and able to take punishment, but otherwise everything is subordinated to the two great guns in a forward turret which are characteristic of its design. Its shallow draught enables it to approach closer to the shore than a battleship with a comparable armament, and its guns are mounted so that they can fire at a high angle, with a maximum range of 40,000 yards. At the long ranges the shell plunges on its target almost vertically, doing greater destruction to land targets than a shell fired at a low elevation, and having a more demoralizing effect, since the shell gives no audible warning of its approach.

Of the ability of the monitor, with its extensive torpedo bulges, to take punishment, the case of H.M.S. Terror is the classic. When bombarding German positions on the Belgian Coast in the last war she was hit by three torpedoes simultaneously. She reached port,

targets behind the enemy lines, playing a big part in turning defeat into rout. Whenever the enemy showed signs of stubborn resistance along the coastal road, as at Bardia and Tobruk, the guns of the Terror ranged on them and helped them to change their mind.

Enemy aircraft made such a dead-set for her that, in the absence of an air " umbrella," her end at some time was almost inevitable. It came through a near-miss from a bomb off Benghazi. She tried to make Tobruk, but two mines flooded more compartments, and another near-miss flooded her engine compartment and she had to be abandoned. Thus ended a great career, in which her guns had pumped hundreds of tons of high explosive on the enemy in two wars.

The work of H.M.S. Roberts in recent months has been equally devastating. She followed the enemy all the way up the east coast of Sicily, remaining in action for ten weeks, with only two days on which the crews were not closed up at action stations. Her most spectacular feat, perhaps, was blocking the road at Taormina. A few well-directed shells started a landslide of rock which completely blocked the road and railway in the enemy's rear. On another occasion

# Monty's Men Push on Along the Road to Rome

DRIVE BEYOND THE SANGRO enabled the 8th Army to reach the outskirts of Ortona and Orsogna by Dec. 22, 1943 (see p. 483). 1, German mortar bombs burst among Sherman tanks, Bren carriers and anti-tank guns. 2, Gen. Montgomery passes a bogged Sherman tank and hands cut cigarettes. 3, Indian troops escort a batch of German prisoners. 4, British infantry climb a steep rugged slope. 5, Bren gun group in a hillside slit trench picks off its Nazi targets.

*Photos, British Official*

# Fire Mud and Snow Fail to Stop Our Advance

MOUNTAIN VILLAGES BLAZE as the Germans, forced from their defensive line across Italy, from the Sangro to the Garigliano, adopt a " scorched earth " policy. During mid-November 1943 the 5th and 8th Armies captured several of these villages in a series of progressive pushes, and the above drawing shows a night scene on the road to Alfedena (announced captured by the 8th on Nov. 24). In the middle distance the townlet of Rionero burns ; the sky and the intervening valleys are lit up by fires in other villages as the Allies advance from the south.

WINTER'S APPROACH IN THE APENNINES inevitably slowed down Allied progress ; yet despite difficult conditions successes in some mountain districts were scored along the line occupied by the 5th and 8th Armies. Monte Meta, 6,700 ft. high (see map, page 483), here towers in the background. Snow and rain have churned the precipitous track into a morass over which slither tanks and pack-mules in their long, arduous ascent. Many tracks deteriorated into creeks of deep mud. *Drawings by E. G. Lambert and W. G. Whitaker, by courtesy of The Sphere*

# Colossal Task for R.E.s of the 8th Army in Italy

**MASTERS OF DEMOLITION,** the retreating Germans blew up this important Italian road bridge N.W. of Vasto, captured by the 8th Army on Nov. 5, 1943. Royal Engineers are shown repairing the huge gap in order that supply lines to our forward troops can be maintained. Vasto is a small port between Termoli and Pescara on the Adriatic coast : its capture was followed by further successful attacks by the 8th Army, enabling the latter to command the road S.W. from that town to Castiglione. the fall of which was announced on Nov. 19.　PAGE 491　*Photo, British Official*

# Dodecanese Islanders Gain Sanctuary in Egypt

GREEK REFUGEES, plunged into the front line of war and driven from their homes with the fall of the islands of Cos, Samos, and Leros in the Dodecanese (see illus. p. 468), escaped in what small craft they could find. Many waited on rocks off their island-coasts until Allied ships could give them passage to freedom and safety.

A party of refugees crowds aboard a rescue ship (1), and starving members of a Greek family look forward to a meat meal as they rest on deck (2). Another family (3) resolutely faces the future as father, mother and child arrive at a temporary camp in Egypt, where food, clothing, and medical supplies are distributed by the U.S. Red Cross and the British-operated Middle East Refugee Relief Association; a substantial meal is in progress (4).

*Photos, British Official : Crown Copyright; U.S. Official*

# Turkey Affirms Her Friendship with the Allies

READY FOR ACTION, if required, are Turkey's highly trained parachute troops (1). In Ankara, the capital, members of a " Hunter's Club "—an organization that popularizes hunting in Turkey and now trains its members for Home Guard duties—are on the march (2), and mechanized troops and transport are assembled (3). Soldiers unpack bombs delivered under Lease-Lend from U.S.A. ; they are being reloaded (4) into freight-cars at Iskenderun (Alexandretta) for shipment to air bases. A Turkish "Magister " training plane about to be tested (5). *Photos, Sport & General, Keystone*

# Praise the Men Who Pass the Ammunition

Victory demands not only men and guns in the correct place and at the right time, but adequate supplies of ammunition, which dictate the course of battles. DONALD COWIE explains the difficulties and narrates the triumphs of those whose task it is, under front line fire, on communication lines, on the High Seas, on the home front, to keep well fed our insatiable guns.

WHO saved Egypt—and possibly the world—in the summer of 1942? Some say General Auchinleck and some the South Africans ; others argue about Sherman tanks and 25-pounder guns. No one mentions the ammunition men of the Eighth Army. No one ever does . . .

But consider how our retreating remnants stopped at last to dig themselves in at El Alamein. Only a screen of a few 25-pounder guns held the rocky line as the wearied troops sorted themselves out. Rommel's tanks continually pressed forward ; our guns just contrived to hold them at bay. Then it was revealed that ammunition was very nearly exhausted and the nearest dumps were far off in the Nile Valley.

Part of that last supply was rushed to the railway, transported to a section of the track near Alamein, transferred into R.A.S.C. lorries, and then—Axis bombers came over. The Luftwaffe and Regia Aeronautica had always appreciated a sitting target. Those lethal-laden lorries were straddled again and again with bombs as they lurched forward across the rocks and the rubble. Meanwhile, our distant gunners were anxiously handling their last shells. Even more urgent S O Ss came through, and the Cockney drivers of the lorries swore as dispatch riders came alongside on motor-cycles, urging speed.

A DIVE-BOMBER swooped, and both lorry and motor-cycle disappeared in a flash of flame. A load of ammunition is easily destroyed. Yet the convoy went on, swerving to avoid the burning hulks of its more unfortunate vehicles. Now, over to the guns.

The gunners knew they could not last much longer. Always they turned to look for the delayed supplies. The view was obliterated by dust and smoke. Then a little convoy of vehicles emerged from the inferno, driving at high speed over the rough ground. Some of them had partly-smashed cabs, and many had Bren guns spitting against the sky. One was actually on fire as it plunged ahead. This was a real case of running the gauntlet, especially as Rommel's own field guns now had the range of the ground over which the lorries were travelling.

But the foremost vehicles were already disgorging grim men with cases of shells in their arms. The men were running to the guns, which, replenished, drove back the nearest German tanks, and began to silence the German batteries. Egypt was saved. And who had been responsible?

That story was worth telling in detail because it epitomizes many similar cases in this war when all depended upon the gallantry of a body of men who have received less than their due in publicity. Once workers of this kind on the communication lines had a relatively soft job. But under modern conditions the ammunition bearers not only play a vitally important part, they often have to take risks which the most seasoned front line troops would be loath to face.

THE point is that while more ammunition than ever is needed by the multifarious engines of war of today—guns, automatic arms, tanks, armoured cars—the speed of spearheads makes it necessary for the " ammo men " to be equally mobile and ready to expose themselves.

Admittedly there has been a great development in methods whereby the guns, tanks and forward troops can carry a certain amount of their own ammunition. Caissons, those trailers behind the guns, run on pneumatic tires and the whole outfit is self-propelled. Every available inch of space within tanks is decorated with clips of big shells, mortar bombs, smoke candles, and small-arms cartridges for machine-guns and rifles. When the " tankee " takes a nap within his mobile fortress a rack of shells hangs above his head. The forward troops twist belts of ammunition round their bodies like snakes.

Now consider how many rounds are fired in the shortest battle. The machine-gun or quick-firing principle has revolutionized fire-power. In five minutes the Bren gun will exhaust the .303 ammunition supply of 750 riflemen. For six hours' intensive bombardment per mile of front in the last war British guns required 67,700 shells. But modern artillery fires much faster, and it can rarely be reached by permanent, well-protected communication lines.

From the anchored supply ships off the Sicilian shore to the open beaches of the invasion's beginning, a chain of men continually stood waist-deep in the water. They were passing shells from hand to hand. As it happened they had to suffer little more than muscle-strain, but they might have had to do that job under fire.

Which introduces yet another aspect of this work, unknown to the general public. Ammunition is abnormally sensitive, not only to bombs but also to atmospheric conditions. " Keep your powder dry " has been the wise commander's cry throughout the ages. This is sufficient of a problem for the " ammo men " in hastily-constructed dumps.

Continual greasing of the shells and small-arms belts, careful attention to waterproofing of roofs and fixing of tarpaulins are principal methods. But imagine the worry of safeguarding those temperamental cargoes during combined operations or forward pushes in bad weather, or when supplies have to be brought up under fire to the front line.

Here is another example of how ammunition supply dictates the course of battles. Dumps of shells for the B.E.F. in 1939-40 had been prepared behind their lines, but within a few days after the German invasion these were behind the *German* lines. It was quite impossible with our resources then to provide all the retreating units with ammunition. The gallant 51st (Highland) Division was eventually forced to capitulate because it did not have a single round left.

IT is now the enemy's turn to be parted fatally from his ammunition. We captured hundreds of thousands of rounds from the Germans and Italians in North Africa and Sicily. Afterwards it was the " ammo men's " Herculean task to collect and make an inventory of this booty, assigning part of it to arms factories for breaking down and re-manufacture, and the other part for use in captured guns and small arms.

And one should not forget the railwaymen of countless British sidings, junctions and stations during air raids, the seamen on innumerable shell-laden ships sailing through U-boat and aerial attacks, the munition workers themselves at dangerous factories, all risking their lives that the guns may not be idle. They are the third line, as the R.A.S.C. men are the second, of those who know that it is good to praise the Lord but essential also to pass the ammunition.

**FEEDING THE GUNS IN ITALY is a task that might daunt the most indomitable. Yet these 8th Army men, leading a mule train laden with ammunition, can find time to grin as they pass a Sherman tank being dug out of the mud as men and animals move towards forward positions on the Sangro River front. Hazards and difficulties engendered by the enemy and the weather in Italy are further exemplified in illustrations in pp. 490-491. See also story in p. 505.**

*Photo, British Official : Crown Copyright*

## King George's Sword for Russia's Man of Steel

Highlight of the Teheran Conference was the presentation in the Soviet Embassy of the Sword of Stalingrad by Mr. Churchill (on behalf of H.M. the King) to Marshal Stalin. Facing the Sword, in its case on the table (below), the two great leaders salute during the playing of their national anthems. On his way to the Cairo Conference, which preceded the Teheran meeting, Mr. Churchill called at Malta, where he is seen (top) with Field-Marshal Lord Gort, Governor of the Island.

## 'Our Nations Shall Work Together in War and

In Persia's capital, Teheran, there met for the first time the leaders of the three greatest nations. Nov. 28, 1943, also marked the occasion of Stalin. Above, President and the two Premiers are seated on the steps of the Soviet Legation. Behind, left to right, are Field-Marshal Si Sir Alan Brooke and Admiral Leahy. In every corner of the world will be felt the consequences of this meeting, at which it was declar destruction of the German forces." The conferences were summed up by Field-Marshal Smuts as "the most significant gathe

*Photos. British Official : Crown Copyright*

ting between Roosevelt and
Marshal Voroshilov, General
concerted our plans for the
undred years."

## Many Happy Returns!

Our indefatigable Premier celebrated, and had celebrated for him, his 69th birthday during the conference in Teheran. Numerous gifts included a specially made hat (top) presented to him on behalf of representatives of the British Press. Below, Mr. Churchill is greeted by the Shah of Persia.

## Chungking Comes to Cairo

The complete defeat of Japan was planned at the first Cairo Conference. While in Africa, Generalissimo Chiang Kai-shek, accompanied by his charming and talented wife, found time for a short sightseeing tour of the city. Accompanied by Sir Robert Greg, K.C.M.G., they are seen (top) leaving the Ibn Tulûn Mosque, and (below) hand-in-hand they survey enthralled from the high vantage point of the Mehemet Ali Mosque places of interest pointed out by Sir Robert, who knows Cario as the Generalissimo and Madame Chiang Kai-shek know their own native cities. See article in facing page.

*Photos, British Official : Crown Copyright*

498

# Friends in Fact, in Spirit and in Purpose

Momentous decisions, of which no man can yet grasp the real magnitude or gauge the final consequences, were taken when Allied leaders met in a series of conferences commencing November 22, 1943, to plan next steps in the prosecution of the war. A brief background outline is given here by E. ROYSTON PIKE. See illus. pages 495-498.

SOMEWHERE in North Africa—later it was revealed that the scene was the Egyptian desert hard by the Pyramids at Gizeh—the supreme heads of the great democracies of Britain, the United States and China met to discuss and plan the military ruin of Germany and Germany's oriental jackal, Japan.

First to arrive and pass through the heavily-guarded, barbed-wire barriers into the enclosure dotted with the villas of the meeting-place was the valiant Chiang Kai-shek, generalissimo of Free China. He flew from Chungking in four days, reaching Cairo on November 21, and with him was his wife to act as his interpreter and guide in a strange new world.

"Madame" was a charming figure, in her long black Chinese dress, slit at the sides, her black high-necked mandarin coat, green jade earrings and light straw hat; while as for her husband, he was the man whom everybody wanted to see and greet, so that, as the correspondents put it, China "stole the show." When the official photographs were taken, Mr. Churchill (who went by sea, accompanied by his daughter Mrs. Sarah Oliver, arriving also on November 21) invited Marshal Chiang to "Come and have the seat of honour. This is your conference!" With true Chinese courtesy the Marshal declined, and sat on one side of President Roosevelt (who arrived by air on November 22), with Mr. Churchill on the other.

FOR five days the statesmen were in conference, while the British, American and Chinese Chiefs of Staff and the numerous advisers who had accompanied the world leaders conferred as to the steps that would bring the enemy peoples to their knees. The talks ended on November 26, but it was not until 12.30 a.m. on December 2 that a special communiqué was published, telling the world of the conference and its momentous decisions. "The three great Allies," it read, "expressed their resolve to bring unrelenting pressure against their brutal enemies by sea, land and air. The pressure is already rising . . ." Then came passages which must have caused unease in Tokyo. Japan, it was declared, is to be stripped of all the islands in the Pacific she has occupied since 1914, of all the territories she has stolen from the Chinese—Manchuria, Formosa, Korea . . .

When this "Pacific Charter," as it has been called, was issued, Marshal Chiang was back in Chungking and Mr. Churchill and President Roosevelt were just concluding a visit to Teheran, whither they had repaired on the conclusion of the Cairo meetings.

It was on Saturday afternoon, November 27, that the President and the Premier touched down in Teheran, having made the journey with their staffs non-stop in ten large passenger transport planes. An interesting detail—another was that the two great ones had paid a visit to the Pyramids and listened perforce to a dragoman's 15-minute description of the Sphinx—was that the President's plane made a detour over Jerusalem so that he might catch a glimpse of the Holy City.

At Teheran they found the master of a sixth, the Socialist sixth, of the world waiting to hail them. Marshal Stalin had arrived by plane from Moscow the preceding day, and had taken up his residence in the grounds of the Russian Embassy, converted (together with its not distant neighbour, the British Legation) into a fortress-like area, ringed with cordons of troops, police, and G.P.U. agents.

Stepping from their planes, Mr. Roosevelt and Mr. Churchill had their first sight of the Red Army in the very personable guard of honour lined up at the Teheran airport. Sir Reader Bullard, the British Minister, and Gen. Selby, Acting G.O.C. Persia-Iraq Force, met Mr. Churchill and drove him to the British Legation. The President similarly went to the residence of Mr. Louis Dreyfus,

THREE GREAT LEADERS CONFER AT CAIRO. This radio photograph shows President Inönü of Turkey seated between Mr. Roosevelt and Mr. Churchill outside the house where the Premier stayed during the third Three-Power Conference, held near Cairo on Dec. 4-6, 1943. Behind the Prime Minister stand Mr. Eden and Sir Knatchbull-Hugessen, British Ambassador in Ankara.
*Photo, British Official : Crown Copyright*

the U.S. Minister, for the night; but the next day (Sunday) he accepted the personal invitation extended to him by Marshal Stalin to make the Soviet Embassy his headquarters. Hardly had he arrived there when the Marshal, dressed in the beige-coloured uniform of a Marshal of the Soviet Union, with the ribbon and star of a Hero of the Soviet Union on his breast, walked down the garden path from his villa and visited the President in the free-and-easy fashion of one calling upon a friend and neighbour. After an hour and a half of conversation, the two were joined by Mr. Churchill. Soon the conference had begun in real earnest and, with the staff talks, it continued throughout Monday and Tuesday with hardly a break.

On the Monday afternoon there was an impressive little ceremony in the conference room of the Russian Embassy when Marshal Stalin accepted from the hands of Mr. Churchill the Sword given by the King to "the steel-hearted citizens of Stalingrad." As the Marshal received it, he solemnly kissed the naked blade and then passed it to Marshal Voroshilov, who in turn handed it to a young lieutenant to hold and guard. Then after the President had handled it, too, and

read the inscription—"Truly, a heart of steel," was his comment—the Sword was proudly borne out, and those within heard the ringing words of command as the guards presented arms in homage.

THE next day (Nov. 30) was Mr. Churchill's 69th birthday, and he was the proud recipient of a number of gifts, while in the evening there was a dinner party at the British Legation, at which the Premier was host and President Roosevelt and Marshal Stalin were the guests of honour. Of the thirty-four present, only one was a woman—Mrs. Oliver. In the middle of the table was the birthday cake—not very large, but bearing a prominent "V" and surmounted by 69 candles.

The proceedings were described as gay and cordial. Marshal Stalin, we are told, was the life and soul of the party, rising to every toast, moving about the room to clink glasses with the person toasted, and in speech after speech expressing his friendship for the President and the Premier. "Roosevelt the Man," proposed Mr. Churchill. "My fighting friend," gave Mr. Stalin, turning to the Premier; and "Stalin the Great" was the happy Churchillian response.

Wednesday, December 1, was the last day of the conference, and after the final session the three leaders sat down to put their signatures to the Declaration of the Three Powers.

"Our Nations shall work together in war and in the peace that will follow," ran one sentence. "We have concerted our plans for the destruction of the German forces" was another. "No power on earth can prevent our destroying the German armies by land, their U-boats by sea, and their war plants from the air. Our attacks will be relentless and increasing." And so to the conclusion : "From these friendly conferences we look with confidence to the day when all peoples of the world may live free lives untouched by tyranny and according to their varying desires and their own consciences. We came here with hope and determination. We leave here friends in fact, in spirit and in purpose."

After President Roosevelt had visited the American troops at Amirabad, and Mr. Churchill had reviewed some units of "Paiforce," the conference broke up. Marshal Stalin returned to Moscow, and the President and Premier flew back to Cairo.

Here they engaged in another series of talks, this time with President Inönü of Turkey and his Foreign Minister, M. Menemenjoglu (see illus. in p. 511). The communiqué issued after their conference stated that "the study of all problems in a spirit of understanding and loyalty showed that the closest unity existed between the U.S.A., Turkey and Great Britain in their attitude to the world situation." Another participant in these talks was Field Marshal Smuts, who called at Cairo on his return journey to South Africa from London; and it was he who most fittingly summed up the conferences as "the most significant gatherings for a hundred years," a sign and indication that the greatest Powers in the world are now "absolutely undivided for final victory."

BRITAIN'S GREAT 'LITTLE SHIPS' on night patrol sight a convoy in the North Sea. This graphic drawing (which is among the illustrations in the book reviewed in the facing page) shows a flotilla of motor gunboats of the Nore Command at a dramatic moment. On the extreme right a convoy is seen faintly outlined in the moonlight as it returns to its base just before dawn. The gun crews of the M.G.B.s man their weapons, captains and coxswains stand by alert while recognition signals are exchanged. On Oct. 24-25, 1943, some 30 German E-boats attempting to attack a convoy off the East Coast were driven off with loss by M.G.B.s.

*Drawn by C. E. Turner; by courtesy of The Illustrated London News*

# VIEWS & REVIEWS

### Of Vital War Books

### by Hamilton Fyfe

"LIGHT Coastal Forces." We have heard much of them lately. They have been doing grand work. Though manned almost entirely by crews drawn from factories, offices, shop counters, warehouses, "the professional skill of both officers and men has maintained the great tradition built up by many generations of British seamen," to quote the Prime Minister's words of some six months ago.

They must not be confused with Coastal Command, which is an aircraft force. The two often work together. Indeed, some of the most highly successful operations against U-boats have been the result of their united efforts. But they have no permanent connexion, and it is a pity their titles are so much alike, causing many people to get them mixed up.

In his most readable and informative book, The Little Ships (Hodder & Stoughton, 7s. 6d.), Mr. Gordon Holman explains the nature of the three main types of vessels included in Coastal Forces. First, there are the M.G.B.s—the motor-gunboats—which have been called the Spitfires of the sea. All ships of war are uncomfortable. At least, that is my experience ; but the M.G.B.s are apparently like sardine tins for discomfort. "The head-space in the engine-room does not permit even a short man to stand upright, and there is hardly room to set one's feet to do any standing." In order to watch over "the enormous horse-power in his charge the all-important engineer must sit astride part of the driving system. When an adjustment or emergency repair is called for, he may have to lie down at full length to reach the affected part."

EVERYTHING else is on the same miniature scale. "Quite apart from the fighting, a considerable measure of hardship must be faced in living in these conditions over any extended period at sea." A senior officer said that "after 48 hours, of a good doing on a longish trip you feel pretty stiff. I have never tried to ride across country for 48 hours, but I have done it for a shorter time. If you can imagine the Grand National going on for 48 hours, that would be rather like the strain you have to stand up to in these vessels."

The violence with which they plunge and roll and jump about requires in their crews "a particular quality of stomach." Men are often hurt badly by being thrown about. A First Lieutenant after going below one morning was absent for a very long time. Search was made and he was found lying stunned "and looking the most horrible green colour" in the wardroom. The boat had hit an extra large sea and tossed him over. Another was flung down so heavily that he sprained both ankles.

You would hardly think it could be possible, but space in the second kind of Coastal Force ship, the motor-torpedo-boat, is even more limited than in motor-gunboats. "The wardroom in some is so small that one long

seat is provided, and the appearance is similar to that of the odd railway compartment that has one row of seats facing a book or parcel ledge." Tedious are the many days and nights of searching for the enemy ; they may go on for weeks, even months, with scarcely an incident to break the monotony. But the excitement when an enemy ship is first sighted makes up for all that. Sometimes action follows instantly ; at other times the victim has to be stalked with the greatest patience. So cleverly is this stalking performed that there have been occasions

## Fighting Midgets of the Great Waters

when Nazi ships have been sunk by torpedo without knowing what hit them, probably imagining they had struck a mine.

THIRDLY come the motor-launches, which are built in Canada, Australia, South Africa and India, as well as in Britain, on what is inelegantly called the "pre-fabrication" system, which means that separate parts can be shipped to any port and the vessels assembled there. "Launches" does not describe them at all. They are fine sea boats, average about 110 feet in length, and have petrol engines. They escort convoys hugging our coasts, they keep off E-boat attacks, they lay mines off enemy coasts. They may be called on to join in such desperate adventures as the destruction of the lock gates at St. Nazaire. Of this exploit Mr. Holman gives a vivid eye-witness account.

It was a grand success so far as doing what

**IN THE WARDROOM OF A MOTOR-GUNBOAT.** Despite cramped conditions it contains a cushioned settee, folding table and sleeping berth. These light craft that guard our waterways are dealt with vividly in the book, The Little Ships, reviewed in this page. Another illustration from the book is in facing page. PAGE 501 *Drawn by C. E. Turner ; by courtesy of The Illustrated London News*

had to be done was concerned, but the losses were so heavy that I can't help wondering if the damage to the U-boat lair in the French port right up the River Loire was really worth what we suffered. I certainly did not realize until I read this story of the exploit, in which Mr. Holman shared, what it meant to run up the river lined on each bank with German batteries.

ONE young seaman had told his mother, who was worried about him, "because I am the only one," that he had got "a nice, safe job," keeping near the coast, so she felt he was fairly secure. But he had been twice torpedoed ("a whacking great explosion and then you start swimming," he described it), and at St. Nazaire he was wounded. But he was not in the least downhearted and declared that his luck had held, for "with all that going on," not to be killed was "the best bit of luck of all." That is the spirit of the men in the motor-launches, Mr. Holman assures us.

We have had luck too—in getting time to organize the Coastal Forces so as to give the Germans a surprise when they found out that our slackness before the war had been compensated by rapid action. "I shall not be popular if I say that we had been caught mildly napping," says Mr. Holman cautiously. He might have given his statement much more emphasis.

At the beginning of the war "the enemy enjoyed undoubted supremacy in the field of light craft." The value of such craft and the urgent need for them were not grasped. "I have it on very good authority that officers of accepted capacity in important commands asked 'What the hell are all these motor-boat flotillas being formed for ?'" In the course of a few weeks, "or months at the most, they were asking, 'Why the hell cannot we have more of these Coastal Forces flotillas ?'"

Admirals were, some of them, inclined to rate the Little Ships as foolishly as did the high-up army general who was conducting manoeuvres some time *after* Dunkirk and, when Mr. Holman asked him about air reconnaissance, replied, "Oh, yes, they've put some planes at my disposal, but weather and all sorts of things can upset those fellows in the air, so I prefer to rely on my own ground reconnaissance."

THAT sort of stupidity is less common in the Navy, Mr. Holman thinks, than it is in the Army—or was, let us hope, before men like Gen. Montgomery began telling the War Office and the General Staff what warfare today is really like. But even the Navy "is too steeped in tradition to step out briskly after new and untried things."

Happily, there are brains at the Admiralty and among our admirals, and once these had been convinced of the vastly important part the Little Ships had to play in the war, the building of them and the training of their crews proceeded with great speed. The results could scarcely have been better.

It is worth noting that like the Dominions and Colonies, our Allies are making a substantial contribution to the manning of the Little Ships fleet.

# New Zealanders Land to Battle in the Solomons

OFF VELLA LAVELLA, northernmost island of the Central Solomons group (see also illus. page 455), New Zealand landing-craft (left) make for the shore. Empty craft are seen returning to the transports for more men; a very efficient shuttle service between the ships and the island beaches was maintained. This landing was achieved on Sept. 17, 1943.

MAJ.-GEN. C. E. BARROW-CLOUGH (below, left), commanding New Zealand troops in the S. Pacific, in conversation with Col. E. E. Brown. The latter is in command of the U.S. infantry whom the New Zealanders reinforced. The island was invaded by the Americans on Aug. 15.

CAMOUFLAGED for jungle warfare this New Zealander (above) leaps ashore with a heavy load of kit. He and his comrades played a great part in the taking of the island. Hours after our troops had landed enemy aircraft came over but were intercepted before they could attack the ships. The Vella Lavella victory loosened Japanese hold not only on the Solomons and New Guinea but also on the Netherlands East Indies.

READY TO ATTACK, New Zealanders disembark (right) from their craft upon the densely wooded beach at Baka Baka on Vella Lavella. By Oct. 9 the island had been finally evacuated by the enemy after weeks of some of the bitterest fighting that had yet taken place in the Pacific.

*Photos, Central Press*

# Bloody Struggle for Tarawa in the Central Pacific

FIERCE BATTLES on Tarawa and Makin, outer Japanese defences, raged from Nov. 20-23, 1943. Above, U.S. troops pause after fighting their way ashore at Tarawa. Left, knocked-out U.S. tank surrounded by fuel-drums used by enemy planes.

TARAWA ATOLL was the chief Japanese air base in the Gilberts, and there U.S. forces struck the first blow of a long-term offensive in the Central Pacific. This photograph shows one of many smashed enemy pill-boxes, tribute to the Allies' terrific fire-power. Two U.S. Marines on the extreme left look at fallen Japanese under a broken palm.   (See eye-witness story in page 474).     *Photos, Associated Press, Keystone*

# France's Richelieu is at Sea with the Allied Fleets

VALEUR

**GIANT FRENCH BATTLESHIP,** the Richelieu recently returned to Oran from New York to join Allied naval units under direct command of the Royal Navy. Disabled by British naval aircraft on July 8, 1940, at Dakar, this 35,000-ton vessel was repaired in America, where she arrived last February (see page 617, Vol. 6). 1, One of her Bofors A.A. gun platforms with the exhortation "Valeur" beneath; such plaques are a feature of French warships. 2, Looking down on the 15-in. guns and foredeck. 3, Entering Oran harbour.     PAGE 504     *Photos, British Official*

# I WAS THERE! Eye Witness Stories of the War

## I Baled Out Over Bomb-Battered Pantelleria

After terrific Allied naval and aerial bombardment lasting 13 days, the Italian island of Pantelleria, in the Sicilian Channel, surrendered on June 11, 1943 (see pages 70-71). One of our airmen who took part in the aerial assaults relates his thrilling mishap in a letter home. He is Flt.-Lieut. Fry, with many successful sorties over enemy-occupied Europe to his credit.

**B**ECAUSE of weather conditions we were forced to attack fairly low, and we were hit by flak and set on fire. After some difficulty in clipping on my parachute, due to the smoke and flames, and in opening the front escape hatch, on which I had been lying and which had been damaged by flak, I baled out, followed by the pilot, the others leaving by other exits. I can remember most distinctly my thoughts at the time, such as "So you've bought it at last!" and "It's too bad; shortly I shall be blown to hell when we 'prang.' . . . If only I could open this hatch and bale out there'd be no trouble."

However, the hatch did open, and out I went, never before having been so glad to leave an aircraft. I remember no sensation in falling other than a pleasant rush of air, until I pulled the rip cord with my left hand.

As the chute opened I could see the silk blowing out. Then came a gentle tug as she opened fully and checked the fall, tightening my harness automatically. I found that swing and drift could be corrected by tugging on the suspension cords and spilling air, and I thoroughly enjoyed the descent. You can imagine my intense relief, even though it might mean being taken prisoner. As I descended I saw that if I was not careful, I should probably drift into the sea; so I spilt air vigorously, which quickened the rate of descent and, as luck would have it, I made land by about a hundred yards.

Actually I landed on a very rocky promontory, which at fifty feet up looked quite pleasant and smooth in the dim light, but at twenty feet looked, as it was, an appalling landing surface, and then the slow descent seemed to change to a rush. I pulled on the shrouds, and the next moment was on the ground without too big a bump. But the ground was rocky, and I banged my right knee, tearing a ligament, which prevented my moving far.

I scouted round for a hiding-place, and, having found one, made a bed of my parachute therein. I decided I was not going to be taken prisoner if I could possibly avoid it. I heard what appeared to be parties searching for us, but I was well hidden; and as luck would have it I was still wearing my water bottle, and I had some Horlick's tablets in my pocket. I eventually decided my position from the coast direction and stars, and settled down to enjoy the not so distant bombing, which was a fine spectacle.

With the coming of dawn, night bombing ceased, and shortly I had to hide again, as there were enemy moving not more than about fifty yards away. During the day, bombing again became intensive, and the naval bombardment was really terrifying—strong points, not so far from me, were some of the targets—and never in my life before had I been so frightened.

The surrender (of Pantelleria) came as a very welcome event and, after waiting an hour or so in case of mistake, I set off limping painfully to find our troops. The enemy appeared to be overjoyed at another successful surrender, and were now very friendly. I spoke to some, and watched them destroying some of their equipment and packing

FLT.-LT. R. H. FRY, whose graphic description of a parachute descent from a burning plane appears in this page, completed his second tour of operational flying by this 'enjoyable' experience at Pantelleria. *Photo, Carl Cloud*

their kit ready to become P.O.Ws. After about a five-mile limp up and down hill, making detours for craters, booby traps, and so on, I contacted our forces and shortly was on board one of the ships, where I received excellent attention. After this it took me three or four days to make camp by way of Algeria, where I found two others of my crew had returned. The other two were not located, and are presumed killed.

## Men, Mules and Mud I Saw on Monte Camino

One of the key heights on the road to Rome, Monte Camino enemy positions were broken into by the 5th Army by December 7, 1943. War Correspondent Alexander Clifford describes appalling conditions mastered by the foot-slogging troops, in this vivid dispatch written on the night of Dec. 4, published here by arrangement with The Daily Mail.

**T**HEY were fighting in the rainclouds on Monte Camino all today. Just because this battle is so big and serious, it is not moving fast. On paper today's results were the occupation of a few knobs and peaks and crests which have numbers, because they have never been important enough to have names.

But to get them there was expended a wealth of bravery and endurance in conditions as appalling as anything we have met in this war. As important as anything else in this battle is a path. It is a horrible, steep, twisting mule-path which climbs the barren side of the mountain. Now history is flowing along it. It is as literal a lifeline as ever existed.

BOMBS BLAST PANTELLERIA, then Mussolini's island fortress in the Sicilian Straits. It was occupied by Allied forces on June 11, 1943, at a cost of only 40 casualties, so intensive was the preliminary " softening " by air and sea bombardment. The readiness of German troops to capitulate in Tunis was duplicated by the Italian garrison of Pantelleria, when about 11,000 prisoners were taken. In his account, above, Flt.-Lt. Fry describes the enemy as being " overjoyed at another successful surrender." *Photo, British Official*

When I climbed up it this afternoon there was a yellow stream of rainwater cascading down it. The little pebbles and the large boulders seemed slippery whatever sort of boots you had on. But if you didn't walk on stones you were walking in brown mud, which might only be three inches deep but might suddenly deepen to 15 inches.

The path was so steep that you had to lean right forward to keep your balance, and in five minutes you were sweating, despite the bitter, driving rain. All day it rained with a violence that would have created records in England, but the supply column moved steadily like an endless band. Everything depended on it.

Bowed men in tin hats and greatcoats splashed to the waist in mud, with 40 lb. boxes of rations on their backs. Their faces dripped with rain and sweat. Sometimes they stumbled on slippery rocks and dropped to their knees in the stream. But the check was only momentary, and none seemed to stop for rest. Other men were festooned with ammunition. Others had big, blue haversacks filled with all sorts of odd spare parts which were needed.

There were mules scrambling up laden with blankets. They were driven by blasphemous British troops who went past grumbling softly that they were hired as soldiers, not muleteers ; someone had to drive the mules !

Most men had bulky shapeless gas capes against the rain. Some wore sacks over their heads like coalheavers to keep the rain from running down their necks. It wasn't a well-dressed army, but it was a very efficient one. Every so often they had to clamber aside and lodge themselves against some boulder to let the down traffic pass, including wounded borne shoulder-high on stretchers by four men each.

One moment the column stopped with a jerk and all heads swung up to the cliff top. The Germans had begun to lob mortar shells over. But there was nothing much anyone could do. You could lie face downwards

against the banks if you liked, but it didn't protect you much, and you got up dirtier and wetter than before. The best thing was to climb on. The men, fighting in the swirling mists at the top were living the life supplied to them by that one mule track. Everything they ate was cold and rain-sodden. Only an idiot could be cheerful in these conditions. No one could enjoy doing these things. Yet the grumbling one heard was not sullen or bad-tempered. Men didn't seem to suggest that too much was being asked of them.

Scattered round in barns and stables and wine cellars, unit headquarters were fighting to keep the battle going. I suppose half a dozen times today I heard conversations like this : ''Number Nine have pinched four of our mules ? . . . That's a bloody bad show.

You'd better pinch some from someone else. . . . Listen, I've got to have those mules ; we've got to get greatcoats and mortar-bombs up quickly . . . Yes, both coats and bombs ; they're calling out for them . . . That's right up towards the convent, but it's a monastery, not a convent—can't you tell the difference ?''

It has been an unceasing strain to keep this battle supplied. But the battle itself has started very well. It is a fight for one isolated hill, a hill so formidable that it was a major problem even getting on to it to meet the Germans. It seems that our concentrated artillery smoothed the path for the initial assault, but the enemy is holding on with skill and tenacity, and every yard is being contested. Monte Camino will be remembered as one of the big battles of the campaign.

## How We Escaped the Gestapo Drag Net in Oslo

*This story of the German mass arrests of Oslo University students on November 30, 1943, is told by two students who, warned in time to evade the Nazi net stretched across the city, reached Sweden after a 23-hour journey on skis. Deportations to Germany commenced on December 8.*

It all began on November 8, when about 2,000 of us Oslo University students sent in our letters protesting against the arrest of eight of our professors and many students. These arrests followed immediately after protests had been made by the faculties, and the action was supported by everyone. Apart from the handful of Nazis, no one intended to support the new regulations which had given the Nazi rector, Hoel, power to admit whom he wished to the University, regardless of qualifications other than political ones. Afterwards, a travel ban was imposed on all the students. Before any of us could leave Oslo we had to make a special application to the Nasjonal Samling (Quisling Party) Youth Service, who then referred it to the State Police. They usually refused to issue a permit.

Fourteen days before the big German drive was made, however, the travel ban was lifted. Everything now seemed to be all right. A

few students went to their homes in various parts of Norway, but the majority stayed in Oslo. Then the Nazis began attempts to get all the students to withdraw their protests. The ''authorities'' published a ''law'' regarding the detention of people who were considered ''dangerous,'' namely those who were opposed to the Germans and their lackeys, the quislings. As this did not have any effect, a printed form was distributed to all students. On it we were asked to state whether we thought our protest was ''in order.'' This did not result in anything.

Then, in the early hours of Sunday morning, November 28, the fire which precipitated matters broke out in the great Aula Assembly Hall in the University. The fire brigades were called out by an anonymous person, and the whole affair was shrouded in mystery. On Monday morning Norwegian police guards appeared at the University, and took up their places, and inspected all students' identity cards. Then our suspicions that something was about to happen were confirmed. Nothing more happened that day, however, except for the Nazi Press campaign blaming the fire in Aula on ''communistic elements,'' but on Tuesday the rumour went round that students should keep away from the University. Most of us, however, believed that this was only an attempt from unauthorized quarters to provoke a students' strike, or that the Nasjonal Samling were about to make one of their usual manœuvres.

Later in the day the story went round that there were to be mass arrests of students, and that they would be deported to Germany. Many of us—particularly those who had been engaged on opposition work—took heed of the warning and kept away from the University. Most students, however, believed that this was a false alarm, or that it had been circulated by the Germans in order to create confusion.

We two met in Oslo soon after 10.30 that morning. We saw lorries loaded with German and Norwegian police being driven in all directions. We made our way to Marjorstua, where we met other

STRETCHER BEARERS move towards the front line on the 5th Army's Camino sector. They are shown passing through the ruins of San Clemente at the base of the famous Monastery Ridge, where fierce fighting resulted in the announcement of an Allied victory on Dec. 8, 1943. The rigorous conditions imposed by rain and mud are described by an eye witness in this and the preceding page.　　PAGE 506　　*Photo, British Official.*

science students, who told us that the arrests had already begun at the Natural Science Department of the University at Blindern (just outside the city), but some had managed to get away. It was difficult to know what to do. We did not dare to go to our homes, because we knew the police would be looking for us there. We just wandered around the town for a while, and then realized that we had to get out of Oslo before the Gestapo's control became absolutely effective.

We took a tram, and as we passed Karl Johan (the main street) we saw great crowds in front of the University buildings. The students were being brought in in batches. The police were using all kinds of vehicles—lorries, cars, motor cycles and combinations. We travelled to a suburban railway station by tram, and while making the journey could see the Germans driving outwards to occupy all the road junctions and bridges round Oslo. We took a train without difficulty, travelled a little way and then changed to another one. Up to now the Germans were only covering the roads. On the train we talked to a Norwegian who had just been visiting the State Hospital in Oslo. He told us that the hospital had been occupied by the Germans, who had placed machine-guns in the doorways and corridors. Many of the medical students, he told us, had heard the rumours and had kept away from the hospital.

When we were some miles out of Oslo we continued our journey on foot. We were, of course, going east towards Sweden. On the way we were helped by good people, and among other things were given skis. When darkness fell we took our direction from the stars, as we had no compass. About 11 o'clock that night we reached a lake where, fortunately, we found a boat. We clambered aboard, and as there were no oars we used our skis as paddles. It was freezing hard,

**OSLO STUDENTS being addressed by their Rector, Prof. Didrik Arup Seip, on Matriculation Day, 1939, a few months before the Germans invaded Norway (April 9, 1940). Rector Seip was arrested and taken to Germany soon after the Occupation was completed. His defiant spirit remained with his students, many of whom, as is told here, have been rounded up and sent to join him in captivity. Some have since been released.** *Photo, Royal Norwegian Government*

and when we reached the other side our skis were coated with ice which made the going difficult on the other side.

All night we kept going, and at 8.20 in the morning we reached the frontier. It was another hour and a half before we reached a Swedish town, after having walked and skied for the best part of 23 hours. We were given a terrific welcome, and the best meal we had had for years. Then we were able to read in

the newspapers the great reaction the mass arrests had caused in Sweden. Judging by what we saw and heard in Oslo when we left, we estimate that about 1,000 men students and about 500 women students escaped the German drag net. Some 4,000 students were actually enrolled at the University, but about 1,000 of them were engaged on agricultural work. Only 1,500 of the remaining 3,000 were rounded up on November 30.

# OUR DIARY OF THE WAR

**DECEMBER 8, Wednesday** 1,558th day
**Italy.**—Announced Monte Camino captured by 5th Army.
**Russian Front.**—Yelisavetgradka district, centre of Kirovograd region, taken by Russians. Heavy German losses in battle S. of Kiev bulge.
**General.**—Mr. Roosevelt visited Malta. Oslo University students arrested on November 30 deported to Germany.

**DECEMBER 9, Thursday** 1,559th day
**Italy.**—Desperate fighting took place on Adriatic front for Orsogna.
**Russian Front.**—New Russian drive brought Red Army to within 17 m. of Kirovograd.
**China.**—Changteh recaptured by Chinese.

**DECEMBER 10, Friday** 1,560th day
**Italy.**—Announced 5th Army had cleared Monte Camino and Monte Maggiore ridges.
**Russian Front.**—Znamenka, in Dnieper Bend, captured by Russians.

**DECEMBER 11, Saturday** 1,561st day
**Russian Front.**—Mass panzer attacks S. of Kiev bulge held by Russians.
**Air.**—Luftwaffe lost 138 fighters during raid on Emden by escorted Fortresses and Liberators.
**Sea.**—Announced recent Atlantic convoy battle resulted in destruction of 5 U-boats by Coastal Command Liberators and naval vessels.
**General.**—Mr. Eden and Mr. Winant, U.S. Ambassador, returned to Britain.

**DECEMBER 12, Sunday** 1,562nd day
**Italy.**—Announced San Leonardo captured by 8th Army, and second bridgehead across Moro River secured.
**Russian Front.**—Chigirin district, centre of Kirovograd region, captured by Red Army.
**General.**—Treaty of "amity, mutual aid and collaboration after the war," signed in Moscow between Soviet and Czech Governments.

**DECEMBER 13, Monday** 1,563rd day
**Italy.**—8th Army steadily pushed back Germans between Majella mountains and Adriatic Sea.
**Russian Front.**—Russian troops entered outskirts of Cherkasy.
**Sea.**—Revealed that in May last, task force of U.S. Navy commanded by Rear-

Admiral Hustvedt operated with British Home Fleet off Norway.
**General.**—Announced that President Roosevelt flew to Sicily on his return from Cairo and Teheran.

**DECEMBER 14, Tuesday** 1,564th day
**Russian Front.**—Fall of Cherkasy, last German Middle-Dnieper bastion, announced. Radomysl, S. of Malin, evacuated by Red Army.
**Australasia.**—Announced that Australians on Huon Peninsula (New Guinea) had crossed Sewi River with tanks. U.S. heavily raided Arawe (New Britain).

**DECEMBER 15, Wednesday** 1,565th day
**Italy.**—Capture of Caldari by 8th Army announced.
**Mediterranean.**—Eleusis, Kalamaki, and Tatoi airfields (near Athens), and the Piraeus, raided by over 300 bombers and fighters. Innsbruck and Bolzano, key towns on Brenner Pass, heavily raided.
**Russian Front.**—Mogailovka and Beloziere, S.E. of Cherkasy, taken by Soviet troops.
**Australasia.**—U.S. troops of Gen. Krueger's Sixth American Army landed in New Britain at Cape Merkus between Gasmata and Cape Gloucester. Preliminary naval and air bombardments softened up the area preparatory to seaborne attack. Australian troops captured Lakona (New Guinea).

**DECEMBER 16, Thursday** 1,566th day
**Italy.**—Fall of Berardi to Canadian troops of 8th Army announced. Fierce fighting continued in the Ortona-Orsogna sector. Revealed that on December 2,

nearly 40 German bombers sank 17 Allied merchantmen in Bari harbour.
**Russian Front.**—Novoseltsy, 35 m. S.E. of Cherkasy, taken by Red Army.
**Air.**—Berlin heavily raided ; 1,500 tons of bombs dropped.
**General.**—Announced that President Roosevelt had returned to United States.

**DECEMBER 17, Friday** 1,567th day
**Russian Front.**—German counter-attacks in Kirovograd sector defeated.
**Australasia.**—Japanese bombers and fighters raided Arawe (New Britain).

**DECEMBER 18, Saturday** 1,568th day
**Italy.**—Fierce tank battle raged on 8th Army front. New Zealand troops cut the Orsogna-Ortona road.
**Mediterranean.**—Two enemy destroyers engaged by patrol boats and light craft of Royal Navy and U.S. Navy near Elba.
**Russian Front.**—Germans fought to a standstill in their Kiev offensive.
**Australasia.**—Announced that U.S. troops had captured Arawe peninsula (New Britain).

**DECEMBER 19, Sunday** 1,569th day
**Italy.**—Fall of San Pietro to U.S. troops of 5th Army announced.
**Mediterranean.**—Innsbruck and Augsburg (S. Germany) bombed by Fortresses.
**Russian Front.**—Announced that troops of the First Baltic Front under General Bagramyan had launched an offensive near Nevel ; breach of 19 m. deep and 50 m. wide made in enemy's defences. Yezersishche, Gribachi and Bytikha taken. Four war criminals (3

German and 1 Russian) hanged in Kharkov public square before 40,000 people.
**Australasia.**—Arawe aerodrome (New Britain) occupied by Americans.
**Pacific.**—Taroa Island, in Marshall group, bombed by U.S. aircraft.
**S.E. Asia.**—Bangkok, capital city of Thailand, attacked by R.A.F. and U.S. bombers in first long-distance raid since creation of Eastern Air Command.
**General.**—Announced all combat units of R.A.F. and U.S.A.A.F. in the S.E. Asia theatre to be united into single air force, the Eastern Air Command, under Air Chief Marshal Sir Richard Peirse.

**DECEMBER 20, Monday** 1,570th day
**Italy.**—Fall of Consalvi to 8th Army announced.
**Mediterranean.**—Rail yards at Sofia (Bulgaria), and airfields at Eleusis, near Athens, bombed.
**Russian Front.**—Soviet troops captured 70 places W. of Nevel.
**Air.**—Bremen (1,200 tons of bombs dropped) bombed by Fortresses and Liberators ; 50 enemy fighters destroyed in day's attacks. Frankfurt very heavily raided at night : over 2,000 tons of bombs, including 8,000 and 4,000 pounders, dropped in 30 minutes by force of Lancasters and Halifaxes. Mannheim-Ludwigshafen attacked.
**General.**—Revealed that recently discussions had taken place in Alexandria between representatives of Marshal Tito's Yugoslav partisan forces and those of British and U.S. fighting forces, concerning the implementation of Allied military support. Full agreement was reached. Military coup d'état overthrew Bolivian Govt. under Gen. Enrique Peñaranda.

**DECEMBER 21, Tuesday** 1,571st day
**Italy.**—8th Army further improved its positions in prolonged fighting in area between Ortona, on Adriatic, and Orsogna at foot of the Majella mountains.
**Russian Front.**—S. of Nevel, Russian troops captured over 100 places, including Rassiliki and Gribali (20 miles W. of Vitebsk). Germans renewed their Kiev and Kirovograd counter-offensives.
**Air.**—Military installations in Pas de Calais area of N. France heavily attacked by hundreds of Allied bombers.
**General.**—Announced several prominent Frenchmen, including M. Flandin, M. Boisson and M. Peyrouton, arrested by French National Committee on charges of treason.

★ ═══════ *Flash-backs* ═══════

**1940**
December 11. *Sidi Barrani captured in General Wavell's Western Desert offensive.*
December 12. *Germans heavily raided Sheffield at night.*

**1941**
December 9. *Indian and S. African troops reoccupied El Adem (Libya) and raised the siege of Tobruk.*

December 17. *Japanese landed in N. Borneo, from which British troops had withdrawn previously.*

**1942**
December 14. *American forces captured Buna village (New Guinea) from Japanese.*
December 16. *Russians opened offensive in Middle Don area on front of over 60 miles.*

# THE WAR IN THE AIR

### by Capt. Norman Macmillan, M.C., A.F.C.

THE difference between the air and the sea methods of warfare was well illustrated by the report of the sweeps of a combined British and American fleet to an area within the Arctic Circle and some 200 miles off the Norwegian coast, operations made some months ago, although revealed only in December 1943.

These naval sweeps were apparently made to entice the German warships Tirpitz, Scharnhorst, Gneisenau and Lützow to come out and fight. They did not appear. One German aircraft flew over the Anglo-American armada, and was shot down.

Conrad tells in his book, The Raider, the Frenchman's view of the blockade of Toulon by Horatio Nelson. The French ships just do not come out to meet the British ships

superior force (for if it was not a superior force, what was the point of sending it there ?). With the experience of the 1914-18 war and of the present war to demonstrate naval methods, was there any reason to expect that the enemy naval force would come out and fight ? Surely we know by now that the metier of battleships is to stay in harbour as the kings of the chessboard of war—the most precious but least manoeuvrable of all the pieces, the ones that stick it out to the end of the game—and then assume the titles of winner and loser.

### VICTORY Over the Submarine Won by Superior Aircraft

Wars are won most quickly by concentrating force to do the most damage to the enemy will and power to wage war. Is this

and everywhere to provide picturesque sweeps that can have no effect upon the enemy's conduct of the war, and make no impression upon his power to wage the fight? If the effort which was expended upon this naval gesture (for surely that is all it was?) could have been accorded to the manufacture of bombs and bombers, the training of aircrews, and the multiplicity of industrial requirements that lie behind every large raid on Germany, a still greater air blow might have been struck at the enemy's power to continue the war.

THE very fact that the enemy warships were so far from west central Europe is in itself significant. The weapons that drove them out of the ports of France and Germany were the bomber and the torpedo-bomber. These are the weapons that will continue most to harry them wherever they are to be found. If the Navy had proceeded to the Arctic zone with a sufficient fleet of aircraft of the kind required for attack upon the enemy vessels, something might have been accomplished. But naval air power had handicapped itself by the choice of aircraft of too-short range, carrying bombs and torpedoes of too-small size, to do the destructive work that might have been effected by quite different aircraft.

It has not been officially disclosed, but perhaps one of the manoeuvres of this armada within the Norwegian Sea was concerned with the attack of the miniature submarines on the enemy Tirpitz and other small craft in Altenfjord, near Hammerfest, on September 22, while another was possibly an escort to the attack of a number of aircraft from a U.S. aircraft carrier upon eight merchant supply vessels in Norwegian coastal waters. Even if this were so the result is small compared with the energy put out by the two nations to effect it. Again, recently the United States sent a naval task force close to Truk, the Japanese naval base in the Caroline Islands, in the expectation that part of the Japanese fleet might be enticed out to fight. But the enemy failed to respond.

Large naval ships cannot guarantee an engagement with the enemy's opposite numbers. They dare not proceed within striking range of the enemy ships when the latter are in harbour. Into the engagement must go submarines or aircraft. What then is the purpose of these floating big gun batteries, that seldom get a chance to fire a shot in anger, that are targets for underwater and aircraft, and that absorb such a large amount of the war effort to build, equip, munition, provision, man, and maintain ?

THE Committee that reported on the Vulnerability of Capital Ships to Air Attack (see p. 348), stated in one part of their report : "The advocates of the extreme air view would wish this Country to build no capital ships (other Powers still continuing to build them). If their theories turn out well founded, we have wasted money ; if ill founded, we would, in putting them to the test, have lost the Empire." How much of the Empire have we temporarily lost, and must fight hard with the help of air power to regain, through ignoring the views of the practical commonsense air-minded realists of the twentieth century? That Committee and the Admiralty had their way. We now know that capital ships alone failed to give protection to the lost lands.

WORLD'S LARGEST FLYING BOAT, the Martin Mars, seen here during its final tests, has been handed over to the U.S. Naval Air Transport Service, it was announced on Dec. 3, 1943. The Mars will be used to convey men and materials to distant war theatres. It is a 70-ton plane with a wing-span of 200 ft., carries 15-20 tons of cargo and has sleeping accommodation for 32 men. It has four 2,000 horse-power engines, and has flown 4,375 miles non-stop, in 34 hours 17 minutes. *Photo, Planet News*

that haunt the blue seas like white ghosts on the horizon. A fast British frigate—captured from the French—sails close inshore seeking information, giving rise to the traditional navy phrase " eyes of the fleet." The French want to get rid of the encompassing ships of the blockading force. An old French seaman gunner called Peyrol, a former member of the brotherhood of the coast, does the trick at the cost of his life by planting false dispatches into the hands of the captain of the frigate, and on this information Nelson sails off on his vain chase to the West Indies, to return later to fight the Battle of Trafalgar.

THE naval method does not change. We have today the same methods as Nelson —with this difference, that the ships cannot sail so close to the enemy coastline because of longer-range guns and the still longer range threat of bomber and torpedo aircraft. Nelson did not have to lie 200 miles off the French coast, as the Anglo-American warships lay off the Norwegian coast.

Now, just what was the point of this display of modern naval power ? Could anyone really believe that the German ships would come out and fight what was presumably a

principle followed by sending a powerful battle fleet to sea with the object of enticing an enemy fleet to come out to fight ? How much fuel was used in this operation? How much man-power (perhaps our scarcest asset in this war) was deflected into a manoeuvre which could achieve nothing? Have we not already seen in the Far East that the victory-winning weapon is the aeroplane, and that when allied with ground forces it can sweep the enemy before it?

Has it not been demonstrated that sea power as formerly known is dead, and that the principal place of sea power today is to transport men and materials to enable soldiers and aircrews to fight together on land, and to enable aircrews to fight over the sea? Is there anyone who doubts that victory over the submarine has been largely won by the use of aircraft, whose superior manoeuvre, speed, and vision have done so much to oust that terror of the oceans?

Why then must the navy continue to conform to its ancient pattern of waging war, burning up fuel, and employing man-power in the factories dockyards, harbours, railways

*Apropos Capt. Macmillan's comments on the war at sea, readers are referred to the editorial note on p. 486.*

# U.S. Airmen Strike at Japanese in New Britain

**RABAUL, VITAL ENEMY BASE IN NEW BRITAIN,** captured by the Japanese early in 1941, was heavily attacked by the 5th U.S.A.A.F. on Nov. 2, 1943, when 3 destroyers, 8 cargo ships, aggregating 50,000 tons, and 4 coastal vessels were sunk. The enemy lost 67 fighters. 1, Blazing and sinking ships in the harbour. 2, U.S. dive-bomber reaches its carrier with engine on fire. 3, Parachute bombs falling on enemy airfield ; note protective revetments round bombers, and crashed fighter on left. See also map in page 109. PAGE 509 *Photos, U.S. Official, Keystone*

# Disillusionment Spreads with Debris in Berlin

**WIDESPREAD DEVASTATION** was caused by the six big R.A.F. raids on Berlin Nov. 22-26 and Dec. 2, 1943 (see p. 472), and ensuing street scenes such as these are shot with grim irony for the people of Britain. Bombed-out Berliners queue at an emergency food centre (1); others besiege an improvised market (4). Members of A.R.P. Luftwaffe unit (2) remove furniture. From the Heroes' Hall, porters carry away art treasures (3). The British Embassy was damaged; German firemen find Sir N. Henderson's car (5) still flying its flag. Tackling a fire (6)  *Photos, Associated Press, Keystone, Planet News.*

THERE are only two ways in which the Germans can be forced to give in. One is breaking up their war effort by persistent bombing so that they cannot produce enough planes and tanks and ammunition to make good their wastage and keep near the Allied output. In this connexion we must keep in mind what Mr. Ernest Bevin pointed out not long ago—that the Nazis can use the labour of 130 millions of people, while we have only 17 million workers. True, there are vast numbers in the United States, but even so our total hardly comes up to that of all the Nazified countries put together. Unless large numbers refuse to work for Hitler, he can go on for a good long time yet. The other possible ending might come through the German army declining to fight any longer a war it cannot win. Last time it was the generals who decided to throw up the sponge. How near they may be to that today we cannot even guess. The broadcast warnings which their fellow-generals in Russia (as prisoners of war) are giving them as to the war being lost may have some effect. It is a clever move by the Russians anyway.

I HAVE always welcomed the end of a year. Partly because as a child I found the days after Christmas dull and eventless by comparison with the jolly, exciting joys and presents of Christmas Day. Also because with the turn of the year one could begin to look forward to " the flowers that bloom in the spring." Now under the nuisance of the black-out the prospect of lighter mornings and evenings, though still far off, fills us with pleasurable anticipation. Surely that is something to make us feel more cheerful. Whether the wave of hopefulness about the finish of the war, which began in November and has not yet subsided, is likely to be justified no one can tell. There is no extra charge for hoping. Only it is best not to expect too much.

IT is said that Mr. Bernard Shaw is leaving the bulk of his fortune, which must be very large, to be spent on making the spelling of English more phonetic than it is and so inducing more people of other nationalities to learn our language. If this be true, it seems likely that the money will be wasted. Changes in language do not come in that way. They occur gradually, imperceptibly. You cannot alter spelling any more than we can add cubits to our statures by "taking thought." We do spell in an irrational way. Take the number of different combinations of letters we employ to represent the sound of "e" as in "bed." I have put down nine right off and composed a rhyme of them.

> Lying in bed
> I called to my frend
> And gest :
> Are you at rest
> Or have you lesure
> To take any plesure
> In the tale of a shepherd
> Attacked by a lepard ?
> He beried his hed.
> Oh, shut up ! he sed.

In a reverse way there are many pronunciations of the letters "ough." Here is a sentence containing them :
Though the tough cough and hiccough plough me through,
O'er life's dark lough my journey I pursue.
Illogical ? Yes. But isn't life illogical too ?

EVERY soldier has a number. That is a sound plan. No one objects. Every motor-car has a number. Everybody sees how necessary that is. Why, asks a friend of mine, should not the whole population be numbered ? Not in the sense of the word which implies counting. We do that ; we have had censuses for a very long time. What my friend means is that we should each of us have a number, as each soldier has, and should be called on to produce it whenever we have dealing with public offices or come into contact with the police, whether making complaint or having complaint made against us. This mode of identification would be useful in many ways. I have even heard it suggested that every person ought to have an identity book, in which the main

**M. NUMAN MENEMENCIOGLU,** appointed Turkish Foreign Minister in August 1942. He accompanied President Inönü to Cairo for the Three-Power Conference, December 4-6, 1943, where he had important discussions with Mr. Anthony Eden. He was born in 1890. *Photo, New York Times Photos*

features of his or her life would be on record. Would there be any great objection to this, except on the part of people who had something to hide ? We do not mind having our present identity cards and being asked to show them when we have any official business to transact. "Why not keep the system which war has introduced and extend it when war ends ?" my friend asks.

AMONG my friends are several professional men in the thirties who have recently been receiving their calling-up notices for the Services. Eight or ten days would seem to be the average time allowed them before having to report to their units, which is little enough to set one's affairs in order, I think. Though naturally it is a bit of a wrench to change one's occupation at this stage in life, I find that, on the whole, they face the immediate prospect with little grumbling. They are wise as probably it will do them a great deal of good. Physically they should certainly be the better for an open-air life and plenty of hard exercise. They will benefit mentally as well. Their outlook will be widened.

They will learn more about life than books have ever taught or could ever teach them. They will be able to study human character at close range and in wide variety. I won't go so far as to say that I envy them, but I do rather wish that, when I was their age, such a change had occurred in my life. At any rate it would have been an experience very interesting to look back on—assuming, of course, that I had come through it alive.

MANY people ask me if I can tell them why this war has produced no songs to compare with Tipperary, Keep the Home Fires Burning, Pack Up Your Troubles, and others that are still sung today after a quarter of a century, in default of any good new ones. I have no reason to suggest, except that the craze for crooning seems to have made all tunes sound alike—and all equally dreary, and that song composers seem to be afraid of melody and well-marked rhythm. The same lack of war ditties is complained of by Germans. They have not even got their Hymn of Hate, which they used to roar out lustily in the last war. It was forbidden because a Jew wrote it, and another was published in the obscene weekly edited by the Jew-baiter, Julius Streicher ; but this revised version never caught on. Its refrain :

> England is the curse of the world ;
> She knows but greed and hate and gold

is poor stuff after the concentrated venom which the Hebrew writer of the original Hymn of Hate got into his vigorous lines.

ONE of the many changes that this war has seen is the disuse of the monocle, even by the Prussian officers who used to wear it almost as part of their uniform. Every picture of a general or colonel would show the single eyeglass, without cord or rim, held firmly in the eye. I can't imagine Rommel with one. Rushing about as he does, he would never be able to keep it fixed. As for the monocle in our own Army, where it was pretty popular at one time, it has disappeared. I saw a man in the Strand wearing one, and for a moment I could not think what it was. It had a gallery to it and was therefore easier to retain in position than the rimless glass of former days. What a curious fashion it was ! Mostly the eyeglass was worn for swank, because it seemed to give the wearer an advantage over other people. It did not always do that. I once saw a young exquisite drop his monocle in his soup. He wiped it and put it away !

WAR may foster heroic virtues ; it certainly increases the prevalence of petty vices. I was told in a shop the other day, one of those shops where the articles for sale are displayed on counters all over the floor, not merely round the sides, that a great many small things were stolen nowadays, far more than used to be the case. The pilferers were difficult to detect. For instance, a schoolboy, evidently from a respectable home, was suspected of having taken two pocket-knives, but not until he was seen to pocket a third could anything be done. Then he was told he must give the knife back. He declared he had not got it, but a threat of fetching a policeman made him produce it and stammer the excuse that he took it for a friend. Nothing was said about the other two knives he probably stole nor were his parents informed of his delinquency which they should have been.

# Captive From the Land of the Rising Sun

Printed in England and published every alternate Friday by the Proprietors, THE AMALGAMATED PRESS, LTD., The Fleetway House, Farringdon Street, London, E.C.4.

**SCANTILY DRESSED JAPANESE PRISONER**, wounded in the right leg, marches before two men of the U.S. Marine Corps. He is one of the very few survivors of the enemy garrison of some 4,000 on Tarawa in the Gilberts. The Marines landed on the Tarawa and Makin atolls on Nov. 20, 1943, and three days later the costly fighting ended with the capture of both these places. (See page 503.)

*Photo, Associated Press*

Printed in England and published every alternate Friday by the Proprietors, THE AMALGAMATED PRESS, LTD., The Fleetway House, Farringdon Street, London, E.C.4.
Registered for transmission by Canadian Magazine Post. Sole Agents for Australia and New Zealand: Messrs. Gordon & Gotch, Ltd.; and for South Africa: Central
News Agency, Ltd.—January 7, 1944. S.S. *Editorial Address:* JOHN CARPENTER HOUSE, WHITEFRIARS, LONDON, E.C.4

Vol 7    # The War Illustrated    N° 172

*Edited by Sir John Hammerton*

SIXPENCE    JANUARY 21, 1944

**INDIAN MULETEERS IN ITALY** are here bringing in 8th Army wounded during the fierce fighting on the Sangro River front at the beginning of Dec. 1943 when General Montgomery's forces pierced the German winter line. The Bengal Lancers, 15th Punjabis and 5th Gurkha Rifles—serving with the Indian Division of the 8th Army—played a brilliant part in the Sangro battle ; and in the capture of Villa San Tommaso, west of Ortona, announced on Jan. 2, 1944, Indian troops again distinguished themselves.    *Photo, British Official*

NO. 173 WILL BE PUBLISHED FRIDAY, FEBRUARY 4

# Our Roving Camera Visits Women Workers

BEHIND THE RAILWAY FRONT, this goggles-protected metal-worker in a big L.N.E.R. locomotive works is skilled in handling her tube-grinding machine. She was formerly a warehouse assistant.

ROYAL OBSERVER CORPS women share duty with men at certain stations. Posts are situated throughout the country and are staffed continuously for the purpose of functioning as "eyes and ears" of the R.A.F.—identifying by sight or hearing every type of aircraft, Allied or enemy, approaching each position.

UTILITY UNIFORMS recently introduced for nurses are designed to save materials and laundry work ; free of pleats and tucks they can be entirely machine-laundered. Aprons have no strings ; they are fastened with unbreakable and detachable buttons. A pioneer in war-time reform of nurses' uniforms is Miss Clare Alexandra, Matron of The London Hospital ; she enlisted the aid of a West End designer.

WRENS on foreign service are doing yet another job formerly performed by men. Right, a Wren Boarding Officer descends a merchant vessel's ladder to a boat after having collected confidential documents from the captain.

AIR STEWARDESSES attend to the comfort of passengers taking long trips on urgent official business in aircraft of British Overseas Airways. These young women wear dark blue and white uniforms, with rose-coloured epaulettes. After the war they look forward to working on Transatlantic and European Air services.

A.T.S. GIRLS (right) at an Ordnance Depot in the Home Counties clean a 17-pounder anti-tank gun—Britain's shattering answer to the vaunted Nazi Tiger tank ; fighting in North Africa saw its first battle-test (see page 372). Specially trained in the technical intricacies of the work, selected members of the A.T.S. also check repaired guns for the accuracy of the firing instruments before the guns are reissued to artillery units at home or abroad.

*Photos, British Official : Crown Copyright ; Keystone, Fox*

# THE BATTLE FRONTS

### by Maj.-Gen. Sir Charles Gwynn, K.C.B., D.S.O.

**GENERAL EISENHOWER** (facing camera) greeted by Gen. Montgomery when he arrived by plane recently at the 8th Army Tactical H.Q. in Italy. *Photo, British Official*

THE last ten days of 1943 brought many signs that the climax of the war was close at hand. The Russian winter offensive opened in earnest. And, even more significant, the announcement of the names of the principal American, British and French commanders who will be in executive control in the decisive effort gave clear indications that the full power of the Allies would shortly be released. The long, and, no doubt for many, boring period of preparation and training is practically over ; and with prospects of action all talk of staleness can be dropped.

The team of leaders President Roosevelt and Mr. Churchill have chosen must give general satisfaction and inspire confidence. General Eisenhower has proved himself a supremely good mixer who can inspire his subordinates with the same quality—if necessary, by showing his teeth. I have always argued that great military forces must necessarily be composed of average human material. The test of the really great leader is his power of getting something more than average results from the average man. · A commander, himself endowed with many of the qualities of genius, may by intolerance upset the balance of his machine.

Star performers will always emerge from the mass, but it is on the average man that the bulk of the work will fall. Treated with sympathy and understanding he will often develop unsuspected qualities and the general average will reach astonishing heights. Impatience and intolerance, on the other hand, tend to induce an inferiority complex in the less gifted, lowering the general standard and often giving rise to friction and jealousies. If I mistake not, both General Eisenhower and General Alexander to a remarkable degree possess the power of getting the best out of their subordinates of all grades and of all standards of natural attainment, encouraging initiative and avoiding over centralization of control.

The appointment of General Alexander as C.-in-C. in Italy is, I think, to be welcomed, not only in the interests of operations in that theatre but because it is the best assurance to the armies there that the importance of their role has not diminished. It may, in fact, indicate that Italy will provide a base for more extended operations. General Wilson's appointment to succeed General Eisenhower in the Mediterranean theatre may have surprised the general public, but it is a sure sign that he has retained the confidence of the Army and of the supreme directorate of the war. Both he and General Paget, who succeeds him in the Middle East, have had plenty of experience of being called on to make bricks without straw, and it is to be hoped that they have now come into a land of plenty.

OF all the appointments, that of Air Chief Marshal Tedder to be deputy to General Eisenhower is perhaps the most interesting and significant. Ever since the fall of France it has been obvious that it would be impracticable to open a second front in western Europe except under cover of decisive air superiority, properly applied in closest combination with the Navy and Army ; not merely during the initial landings but throughout the more critical stage in which the enemy's major counter-attacks may be expected. An immense degree of superiority is now assured, but in order to make the combined effect of sea, land and air effort irresistible it may be necessary for the air arm to forgo for a time what normally is the most effective role of its giant long-range aircraft. There almost certainly would be occasions on which interference with the movements of the enemy's reserves and with his communications would justify suspension of attacks on his armament industries.

To be fully effective, attacks on movements and communications require maximum concentration and continuity of action, otherwise the result produced is short lived. At Salerno, Tedder used every available aircraft to deal with the critical situation, and we may be confident he would not hesitate to do so again in operations on an immensely greater scale and in a more prolonged crisis. The opening of a second front will not have been fully achieved until the armies landed, in combination with the air as a single entity, are in a position to take the offensive. Before that stage is reached there may be much bitter defensive fighting.

## RUSSIA

The actual events of the last days of 1943 were immensely encouraging. In my last article I suggested that von Manstein's gambling counter-offensive in the Kiev bulge was in sight of a failure that might prove disastrous. I had in mind the possibility of a riposte by the Russians, similar to those delivered last winter against von Hoth's attempt to relieve von Paulus at Stalingrad and against the German offensive in the Kursk salient last summer. But I did not expect the riposte would come so quickly or with such devastating effect.

It was one of those occasions where it was sufficiently obvious that should the German offensive exhaust itself, there might be an opportunity for a counter-stroke. But the opportunity would not in reality exist unless the Russians were in a position to seize it promptly. And that, I thought, must be extremely doubtful ; for it must be remembered that for some weeks they had been engaged in a desperate defensive battle which absorbed reserves as they arrived and made immense demands on supply services, handicapped by weather conditions and indifferent communications.

Clearly, immense credit must be given to Vatutin for using his reserves economically, and he must evidently, from the beginning of the defensive battle, have kept the possibility of a counter-stroke in view. But even more credit must, I think, be given to his administrative services, which, in spite of appalling difficulties, not only kept the defensive battle supplied, but built up the reserves of material without which a counter-stroke would have been impossible, however tempting the opening for it might appear. The days have passed in which the Russians could with justification be accused of lacking administrative and organizing capacity.

THE offensive north of the Pripet marshes has also gone amazingly well, and the great German bastion at Vitebsk stands, as I write, in imminent danger. Here again the Russians have shattered widely held expectations by breaking through the reputedly impregnable Todt defences under conditions which appeared to make it impracticable to use the heaviest weapons against them. It is evident that, both in attack and defence, the Russians have exploited the power of artillery to a degree never before reached ; and it has been as the result of bold changes in organization adapted to the development in the technique of control of artillery fire.

But, although their artillery is probably the basic weapon on which their tactics rely, the Russians appear also to have shown great versatility in the employment of other weapons ; adapting their methods to the actual problems presented by ground and weather conditions and the enemy's tactical dispositions. In contrast the Germans, in spite of their skill and high standard of training, seem increasingly to rely on text book methods which have become stereotyped.

In the bend of the Dnieper they are fighting hard to retain their position, but the counter-attacks they are delivering with great violence give little prospect of recovering ground of importance and must prove desperate expensive. If, as seems probable, the Russians renew their offensive on a major scale in this area when the freezing of the Dnieper presents them with new openings, the Germans may pay for a profligate use of their reserves.

**IN THE KIEV SALIENT** Russian counter-blows had developed into a mighty offensive by the end of 1943 ; arrows show directions of the Soviet advance. See also p. 523.
*By courtesy of The Daily Telegraph*

# Nazi Defence Line Key-town Falls to the 8th

REPORTED TO EQUAL THE FURY OF STALINGRAD, the struggle for Ortona, key-town to the enemy's Adriatic defence line, ended in triumph for the 8th Army on Dec. 28, 1943. Nazi suicide squads lowered tanks into house basements and fired the guns through windows ; nevertheless, yard by yard the Canadians advanced, whilst Bren carriers (3) battled through the wrecked streets. A stretcher case arrives at an advanced dressing station (1), and prisoners are brought in (2) over masses of rubble. See story in page 537.

See story in page 537.

*Photos, British Official : Crown Copyright*

# First Shells of a Fierce Barrage at Conca Casale

OPENING CHORUS of a hail of shells on the small Italian town of Conca Casale is watched by U.S. infantrymen of the 5th Army. Smoke of the first explosions rises from a German observation post tucked away among buildings smashed by previous bombardments. When the barrage lifts infantry will advance for the bayonet-point assault. Scene of this engagement is near Venafro, announced captured on Nov. 6, 1943, whence forces pushed on towards Cassino : by January 4, 1944 they had reached San Vittore, north of the road to Rome.

*Photo, U.S. Official*

# THE WAR AT SEA

## by Francis E. McMurtrie

**Capt. J. HUGHES HALLETT, D.S.O., R.N.** (left) of H.M.S. Jamaica, whose torpedoes finished off the Scharnhorst. Right, Cmdr. M. D. C. Meyrick, D.S.O.,R.N., led destroyers to the attack.
*Photos, Bassano, Daily Mirror*

SELDOM has an enemy loss given greater satisfaction to the Royal Navy than the sinking of the Scharnhorst in a night action. It is not generally appreciated that she was the ship which, in company with the Gneisenau, destroyed the armed merchant cruiser Rawalpindi to the south-east of Iceland on November 23, 1939. At the time this was credited to the "pocket battleship" Deutschland (afterwards renamed Lützow) and another unidentified warship ; but it has since been fairly well established that the ships actually concerned were the two 26,000-ton battleships of the Scharnhorst class. Thus the odds against Rawalpindi were even heavier than originally supposed.

On June 8, 1940, the same two enemy battleships surprised the aircraft carrier Glorious while she was evacuating British planes from Northern Norway. The destroyers Ardent and Acasta, which were in company, did their best to protect her, but the odds were too great, and all three ships were sunk. As Admiral Sir Bruce Fraser was captain of the Glorious from May 1936 to December 1937 he must have felt peculiar satisfaction in putting an end to the career of the Scharnhorst. On two previous occasions the latter vessel was chased by British capital ships which failed to overtake her, evidence that her actual speed was considerably greater than the 27 knots for which she was officially supposed to have been designed.

ON April 9, 1940, the battle cruiser Renown, wearing the flag of Vice-Admiral Whitworth, was engaged for a short period with the Scharnhorst and Gneisenau off the Norwegian coast not far from Narvik, the former ship being hit at least once before she disappeared to the southward, a smoke screen laid by her consort covering the retreat. This brief action took place in a snowstorm, with a gale blowing, the opponents opening fire upon each other at a range of 18,000 yards.

Towards the end of 1940 the Scharnhorst and Gneisenau were sent out into the Atlantic to act as commerce destroyers. They seem to have confined their attentions to unescorted ships, but even so sank a good many. In March 1941 two which had been captured, the Bianca and San Casimiro, were intercepted with prize crews on board, who promptly scuttled both ships when H.M.S. Renown approached. On the afternoon of March 8, H.M.S. Malaya was escorting a north-bound convoy between the Canaries and the Cape Verde Islands, with a Swordfish aircraft scouting ahead. This plane sighted the two German battleships, and reported to the Malaya, which did her utmost to make contact. Every preparation was made to open fire at long range, but it proved impossible to bring them to action before dark.

A little over a fortnight later the Scharnhorst and Gneisenau took refuge in Brest, in which port they were blockaded for nearly a year. Their sensational dash up Channel and through the Dover Straits on their way back to Germany in February 1942 was less successful than it seemed at the time, for the Gneisenau has never been to sea since. It is believed she received such structural damage from British torpedoes during the passage that she has had to be completely rebuilt.

### INTO a Trap the Scharnhorst Sailed from Altenfjord

It may be inferred that on December 26, 1943, the Scharnhorst fell into a skilfully baited trap. On how many previous occasions our convoys had passed round the north of Norway in tempting fashion without evoking interference from the German Navy is not known ; but last month the hours of darkness were at their maximum, and the opportunity must have seemed to the enemy too good to be missed. When the Scharnhorst sailed from the Altenfjord (where her crippled consort, the Tirpitz, is still lying) she is reported to have been accompanied by a flotilla of destroyers ; but these were not with her when she was sighted by the convoy escort. A westerly wind of almost gale force appears to have been blowing, and it may be presumed that the destroyers found the head sea that confronted them when they emerged from the shelter of the islands fringing the coast to be more than they could face. Thus the Scharnhorst had to proceed without her protecting screen of destroyers.

At 9.35 a.m. the cruisers Belfast (flagship of Vice-Admiral R. L. Burnett), Norfolk, and Sheffield, which were protecting the convoy on its starboard flank, sighted the Scharnhorst in what is well described as "the half-light of an Arctic dawn." Fire was at once opened on the intruder, which was hit by an 8-in. shell from the Norfolk, the guns of the other two cruisers being of 6-in. calibre. Though her main armament comprised nine 11-inch guns, the Scharnhorst did not stay to fight it out, but disappeared to the north-eastward at high speed. No more was seen of her until 12.30 p.m., by which time it was getting dark. Another exchange of gunfire took place, H.M.S. Norfolk being hit aft, but again the Scharnhorst evaded closer contact, turning south towards the Norwegian coast.

In the meantime another British formation under the immediate command of Admiral Sir Bruce Fraser, Commander-in-Chief of the Home Fleet, with his flag in the battleship Duke of York, had been moving up from the south-westward. At about 4.15 the Scharnhorst was sighted ahead of the Duke of York, which at once altered course to bring her broadside to bear, and obtained a hit almost at once. In view of the fact that the enemy can only have been seen by the light afforded by star shell, this must be reckoned extraordinarily good shooting by the Duke of York's 14-in. guns. The Scharnhorst turned first north and then east, hoping to get out of range before she could be hit again : but a shell from the Duke of York entered below the waterline, slowing her up.

THIS also gave the opportunity for a torpedo attack by two divisions of destroyers, comprising the four new sister ships Savage, Saumarez, Scorpion, and Stord (the last-named belonging to the Royal Norwegian Navy) ; the Matchless and Musketeer, both of 1,920 tons, the Opportune and the Virago, of which no particulars have been published. All have been completed since war began. Three torpedoes are believed to have hit the Scharnhorst, whose plight thus became desperate. Closing the range, the Duke of York opened a destructive fire that within about 20 minutes had reduced the enemy ship to a blazing wreck. H.M.S. Jamaica, a cruiser which was in company with the Duke of York, was then ordered to sink her with torpedoes, and she disappeared at 7.45 p.m. There were only 36 survivors.

Apart from the hope of intercepting a convoy with valuable munitions for Russia, the Scharnhorst's sortie was probably undertaken with the object of strengthening the morale of the German Navy, which has suffered seriously from the effect of spending long months in harbour far from home. Its disastrous termination must have produced precisely the opposite effect, besides advertising to the world the ineffectiveness of German arms at sea. This bad impression was heightened two days later by the complete rout of German forces in the Bay of Biscay (see pp. 532, 540) by H.M.S. Glasgow and Enterprise, and aircraft of Coastal Command, three out of 11 enemy destroyers being sunk.

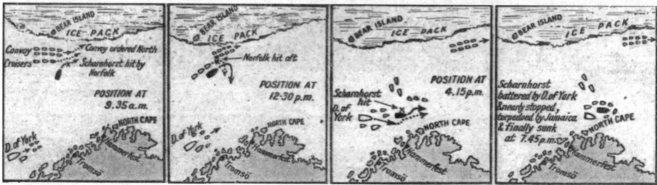

**SINKING OF THE SCHARNHORST**, phase by phase : (l. to r.) at 9.35 a.m. on Dec. 26, 1943, convoy turns north as cruisers Belfast, Norfolk, Sheffield, open fire on the German battleship, which is hit by Norfolk ; at 12.30 p.m., after again having tried to close with convoy, and Norfolk being hit, Scharnhorst turns south ; at 4.15 p.m. the Duke of York, accompanied by Jamaica and destroyers, registers a hit. Pursued, Scharnhorst is pounded by the Duke of York at 7 p.m., and at 7.45 sinks after attack by Jamaica. See facing page and p. 520.

*By courtesy of The Daily Telegraph*

# This Was the Scharnhorst: Late of Hitler's Navy

**A**FTER A 12-HOUR CHASE IN ARCTIC GLOOM the 26,000-ton German battleship Scharnhorst, enticed from her lair in Altenfjord, Northern Norway, by the sight of a Russia-bound convoy, was trapped and encircled by Home Fleet units and sunk off the North Cape on Dec. 26, 1943 (see pages 518 and 520). Launched in 1936, she bore the name of the founder of the Prussian Army and of a cruiser sunk at the Battle of the Falklands, Dec. 8, 1914. Like her sister ship, the Gneisenau (now under complete reconstruction), Scharnhorst carried a complement of 1,461; her length at the waterline was 741 ft. 6 ins., beam 98 ft. 6 ins., draught 28 ft. 8 ins. Armament consisted of nine 11-in. guns, twelve 5·9-in., fourteen 4·1-in., and sixteen 37-mm. A.A. guns; four aircraft and two launching catapults.

Details in the above drawing show (A) main armament of 11-in. guns; (B) secondary armament of 5·9-in. guns; (C) 4·1-in. A.A. guns; (D) catapults; (E) reconnaissance aircraft and (F) aircraft hangar; (G) cranes; (H) range-finding towers; (J) fighting tower; (K) ship's boats; (L) 12-in. belt of armour amidships.

Interception of the Scharnhorst by Vice-Adm. R. L. Burnett, commanding the 10th Cruiser Squadron, opened the action. Engaged by the cruisers Norfolk, Belfast (in which Adm. Burnett flew his flag) and Sheffield, she was forced under the guns of Duke of York, which scored an underwater hit. This slowed her up and enabled a destroyer force under Cmdr. M. D. C. Meyrick, R.N., in the Savage, to reach a position in which they could attack. Shortly afterwards Musketeer, Matchless, Opportune and Virago attacked. Damage inflicted enabled the Duke of York to close the range. "I was able to observe definite hits, which showed dull red glows," said Paymaster Lieut. T. B. Homan, R.N., later. "The enemy appeared to be slowly circling, and a cloud of thick smoke was hanging over her." The cruiser Jamaica delivered her torpedoes, and then, "It only remained to carry out a search for survivors," said Adm. Sir Bruce Fraser, C.-in-C. Home Fleet, "and this resulted in Matchless picking up six and Scorpion 30 from the sea." To the C.-in-C. Mr. Churchill sent the message: "Heartiest congratulations to you and Home Fleet on your brilliant action. All comes to him who knows how to wait." Awards in connexion with the action include the K.B.E. for Adm. Burnett, and the D.S.O. for Cmdr. Meyrick.

*Specially drawn for* THE WAR ILLUSTRATED *by Haworth*

# They Rounded-up the Scharnhorst for the Kill

FIRST HIT OF THE BATTLE which resulted in the sinking of the Scharnhorst (1) was scored by the 8-in. guns of the 9,925-ton cruiser Norfolk (3), Capt. D. K. Bain, awarded D.S.O. Closing in for the kill, the 35,000-ton Duke of York (2), flagship of Adm. Sir Bruce Fraser (see illus. page 543), crashed salvo after salvo from her ten 14-in. guns into the trapped enemy, which was sent to the bottom by the torpedos of the 8,000-ton cruiser Jamaica (4), Capt. J. Hughes-Hallett, awarded D.S.O. See also pages 518, 519, 540. PAGE 520 *Photos, British Official; P. A. Vicary*

# Air Battles Higher Than Man Has Yet Fought

Pilots are testing the possibilities of aerial combat and bomber flight more than seven miles above the surface of the earth. JOHN FROMANTEEL explains this latest grim phase in the duel for air supremacy, with all the known and unknown perils to be faced by the pioneers who are not hesitating to prepare the way. See also story in page 221.

"PATROL base at 35,000 feet," said the controller. "Patrol base at 35,000 feet." Then he had abruptly cut off. Now the lone fighter-recco aircraft is circling in great sweeps ten miles across, and all that the onlooker from the ground can see is its fine white trail. The aircraft itself is out of sight, heading for the stratosphere.

Far below, nearly six miles down, a thick floor of cloud hides the earth. It is not long past dawn, and where the light of the half moon touches the peaks of swirling vapour they are tipped with silver, and long shadows lie along the valleys.

The lone pilot is an advance guard of the fighters that will soon patrol the skies, not only in the stratosphere but even in the troposphere, seven miles above the earth's surface. "The reason for going ever higher," an aircraft designer tells me, "is that air battles cannot be as decisive at 10,000 and 15,000 feet, where they have been fought since the war began."

Our technical superiority depends upon the ability to fly high. If bombers can fly at 35,000 feet at speeds of over 300 miles an hour with full bomb load, they will not only be practically immune from night attack en route to their targets but should also be able to raid in daylight. Our fighters, too, must be able to fly high to counter the enemy in the six- and seven- mile troposphere limits which they are trying to make their own. We have good reason to believe that under Prof. Messerschmitt the Germans have made great strides in high flying, particularly in their fighters and fighter-bombers. German fighters have been encountered above 35,000 feet. In the grim fight to retain technical superiority in the air they constitute a real menace.

"IT is difficult enough to build an aircraft which will fly in the troposphere," says this aircraft designer. "But it is even harder to train a breed of pilots who can live and work at such a height, even if they fly in oxygen suits or in pressure-cabins like a flying submarine." The chief obstacles to troposphere flying are cold, "aeromebolism" (a mild form of diver's "bends," caused through pressure changing) and altitude sickness. The greatest is altitude sickness—oxygen starvation.

At 25,000 feet death results in about 20 minutes if an oxygen mask fails. And oxygen masks are effective only up to about 36,000 feet. Even the best pilot, with the best apparatus, reaches the ceiling of safe human flight around 38,000 feet. Strangest symptom of this troposphere altitude sickness is the victim's unawareness of peril. In fact with some pilots the more severe the attack the better they feel—for a time; and aeromedical experts are still struggling to discover why this is so.

The classic account of the results of exposure to troposphere altitude was written nearly 70 years ago by the French meteorologist Tissandier. With two companions he made a balloon ascent. They had oxygen but, feeling fine, failed to use it in time. Tissandier's companions died.

He wrote of his experiences : "I now come to the fateful moment when we were overcome by the terrible action of reduced air pressure. At 22,900 feet torpor had seized me. I wrote, nevertheless, though I have no clear recollection of writing. At 24,600 feet the torpor that overcomes one is extraordinary. But there is no suffering, nor thought of danger. On the contrary, one feels a sort of inward joy. At 26,000 feet I felt so weak I could not even turn my head. I wanted to call out, but my tongue was paralyzed. All at once I fell down powerless and lost all further memory."

The inexorable limit of man's endurance can best be understood by considering the cocoon of atmosphere that surrounds our globe to a depth of about 100 miles. At sea-

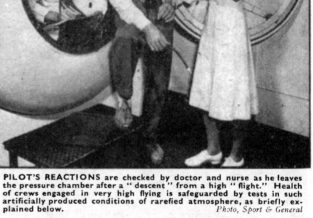

PILOT'S REACTIONS are checked by doctor and nurse as he leaves the pressure chamber after a " descent " from a high " flight." Health of crews engaged in very high flying is safeguarded by tests in such artificially produced conditions of rarefied atmosphere, as briefly explained below.
*Photo, Sport & General*

level the 14.7-lb. per sq. in. pressure drives oxygen through the walls of the lungs and into the blood-stream for distribution in the body. But as altitude increases pressure drops, and in the troposphere not even breathing 100 per cent oxygen will save the pilot.

LACK of pressure has other effects. Formation of bubbles of nitrogen begins in the spinal fluid at 18,000 feet, and in the blood at 30,000 feet. This is the " aeromebolism" —resembling the "bends" which afflict tunnel workers and divers from the opposite cause—and is the result of too great blood pressure. If the pilot doesn't come down out of the troposphere when first attacked, aeromebolism may cause paralysis and even death.

Another effect of low pressure is that the gases in the pilot's stomach and intestines expand and may cause severe cramp. Troposphere pilots are put on a special diet of foods that are non gas-forming. There is also the risk that bloating will force the diaphragm upward against the heart and cause fainting.

Pressure-chamber tests are made with all pilots who want to try seven-mile-high flying—the present limit reached for troposphere work. There is a telephone headset inside the dome-shaped chamber, and the pilot is encouraged to keep talking while the air pressure is cut down.

" That's how it feels at 35,000 . . . at 38,000 . . ." jabbers on the pressure operator, and the pilot—who can be seen through a double plate-glass window—keeps on talking. The pressure has to be brought back so slowly that it takes nearly eight minutes—and if the pilot stopped talking suddenly through the "bends" it would be too late to save his life.

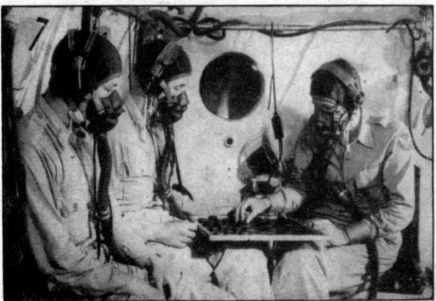

GAME OF DRAUGHTS is played—to show how comfortable they are—by these pilots using oxygen apparatus in the pressure chamber (on the ground) in which breathing would otherwise be extremely difficult if not impossible, because the air has been purposely " thinned " to reproduce high-flying conditions
*Photo, U.S. Official*

# Czech-Soviet Mutual Aid Pact Signed in Moscow

AT THE KREMLIN, on Dec. 12, 1943, was signed the Czech-Soviet treaty "of amity, mutual aid and collaboration after the war"; watched by (4, r. to l.) Marshal Stalin, Dr. Benes, President Kalinin, and Marshal Voroshilov, M. Molotov adds his signature.

Dr. Benes arrived in the Soviet capital (1) on Dec. 11; r. to l., the Czech President, Marshal Voroshilov, M. Molotov, M. Lozovsky. (2) Dr. Benes (left) is seen with Marshal Stalin, and later (3, second from r.) he inspects a captured German mortar. During his visit he stated: "The day of retribution will come, and our much-suffering peoples will have won a new solid and lasting peace." M. Molotov replied: "Our Army is fighting for all peoples under the yoke of German occupation."

*Photos, Pictorial Press*

# Russians Smash on Over the 1939 Polish Frontier

**CAPTURE OF ZHITOMIR** on Dec. 31, 1943 by troops of the First Ukrainian Army under Gen. Vatutin followed the forcing of a 180-mile wide breach in the Kiev bulge, in which 8 enemy tank divisions, including the Adolf Hitler and Reich divisions, and 14 infantry divisions, were routed. Above, a Soviet anti-tank unit in action. Below, Zhitomir occupied by German infantry before the big push which carried the Russians, by Jan. 6, 1944, 12 miles across the 1939 Polish frontier.

*Photos, Pictorial Press, Planet News*

# Just Who Is Fighting Whom In Yugoslavia?

Always the Balkans have had a reputation for fierce politics and bloody strife, and today, as is described in this article by E. ROYSTON PIKE, the cauldron is once again boiling over. General Mihailovitch and his Chetniks were the subject of an article in p. 499, Vol. 6 ; and reference should also be made to pp. 342-343; p. 222, Vol. 5 ; and pp. 386 and 470, Vol. 4.

ARE you for General Mihailovitch or for Marshal Tito ? This is the question that is being put to the Yugoslavs, both inside their country and outside it. A thousand pities that it should be so, when Yugoslavia is still squirming beneath the Nazi boot. One would have thought that a common oppressor would have made all Yugoslavs brothers. But in the Balkans old memories are a long time dying, ancient feuds poison the lives of new generations, jealousies and rivalries are the very body and spirit of politics. Yugoslavia is a very young country, we should remember ; and in the earlier part of its brief life of little more than twenty years it was known officially not as Yugoslavia but as the Triune Kingdom of Serbs, Croats, and Slovenes. In those three words lie the roots of the present tragedy.

The new state that was brought into being in 1919 was predominantly Serb, for it was built around the old kingdom of Serbia which, after being overrun by the Germans in 1915, had a glorious resurrection in the great and victorious company of the Allies three years later. The throne was occupied by the royal family of Serbia, the political generals were nearly all Serbs, the governing classes were Serb. From the very beginning the Croats and Slovenes complained bitterly of their subordination ; particularly the Croats, who had for many years boasted of a material culture far superior to that of their new fellow-citizens whose headquarters were in Belgrade. The fact that the Croats are Catholics while the Serbs are Greek Orthodox in religion was another barrier to a full and proper understanding.

FOR years the struggle between the races continued within the Yugoslav state. The Croats demanded a measure of home rule, but the Serbs turned a deaf ear to every suggestion of local autonomy, and intensified their policy of centralization. So bitter was the conflict that the parliamentary regime collapsed under the strain. The Croat leader, Stephan Raditch, and his brother were shot dead in the Yugoslav parliament by a Serb M.P. in 1928, and in the following year King Alexander made himself dictator, ruling with firm ruthlessness and suppressing all opposition, both racial and democratic, until in 1934 he, too, was

murdered—as he was driving down a street in Marseilles. The assassin was a Croat, a member of a terrorist organization known as the Ustachis and led by one Pavelitch. Alexander's son Peter, a boy of eleven, was proclaimed king, but Prince Paul, Alexander's brother, was regent, and under him the old warfare of Serb and Croat went on.

For a brief moment in the spring of 1941 the men of every race seemed to remember that they were Yugoslavs before everything else. Paul was kicked out because of his truckling to the Axis, and young Peter assumed the royal power. But the pitifully weak army of the little country was no match for von List's panzers, and in a fortnight the country was overrun. Then the old divisions bore horrible fruit. Yugoslavia was dismembered. Much of Slovenia went to Italy; Croatia was proclaimed a kingdom, under Italian protection, and Pavelitch and his gangsters indulged in an orgy of brutality and murder ; while as for Serbia, it was reduced to its old-time limits and in Belgrade the Serb general Neditch ruled as a Nazi quisling.

This is where General Mihailovitch comes in. He, too, was a Serb, but no quisling. He played a gallant part in the open war of April 1941, and then and for some time afterwards he maintained armed resistance on a considerable scale against the invaders. Chetniks (patriots) his men were called, and they made themselves a nuisance to the Nazis. And to the Italians too ? That is not quite so certain. The General's foes—and he has many—declare that after a while he came to an understanding with the Italians (who may have been jealous of their German allies) and received from them arms and stores. With these (so it is alleged) he waged war not so much against the Germans as against the Croats and the bands of nationalist fighters who were now coming into prominence under the name of Partisans.

From the first—from, that is, the autumn of 1941—it was widely believed that the Partisans were Communists, receiving not only their inspiration but something much more tangible from Moscow. Whatever the source of their arms, they knew how to use them ; and such was their policy of continuous aggression that before long they constituted the head and spear of Yugoslav resistance.

Their leader was a mysterious figure whose name was not made known for a long time ; and then it was not at once revealed that "Marshal Tito" was Josif Broz, a Croat workingman of 53 who deserted the Austrian army in 1915 (like so many more of the Austrian Slavs), spent two years in Russian prison-camps, joined the Red Army and fought in the

Civil War, and then, returning to his own country, became a trade union leader. Five years in a Balkan prison did not break his health or his spirit. Broz went underground and sapped and mined at the foundations of Alexander's dictatorship. He had a part—how big we do not know—in the Spanish Civil War, and what he learnt in Spain has evidently profited him since he became a leader, soon *the* leader, of the Partisans.

Today he is reported to have an army of 200,000 men under him, as compared with a

**Brig. F. H. R. MACLEAN, M.P.** (left), is Tito's right-hand man and leader of the British military mission in Yugoslavia. Marshal Tito (right), Yugoslav leader and commander of the National Army of Liberation and the Partisan Detachments, in Dec. 1943 set up his own Council and thus aroused the antipathy of the Royal Yugoslav Government in Cairo.
*Photos, Universal Pictorial Press, The Daily Mail*

tenth of that number left to Mihailovitch. This figure is probably greatly exaggerated, but it is stated that Tito is at present occupying twelve Axis divisions. His forces are known as the National Army of Liberation and the Partisan Detachments of Yugoslavia : the former being troops organized on the model of a continental army, while the latter are guerillas, civilians one day and doughty warriors the next.

So successful has Marshal Tito been that he has been recognized by the Allies, on Dec. 22, 1943, as a comrade-in-arms. As long ago as last spring a British military mission, under the leadership of Brigadier F. H. R. Maclean, M.P., was sent to him in his mountain fastness, and military aid has also been rendered on the largest scale possible.

BUT unfortunately Marshal Tito is not persona grata with all the Yugoslavs. To the government-in-exile in Cairo his name is like a red rag to a bull, and we have had the decidedly unpleasant spectacle of the Cairo royalists denouncing Tito and his followers as " impostors, brazenly attacking the legal monarchy," and claiming that for two and a half years the Serbs have continued the struggle alone, and have sacrificed more lives in proportion to their population than Russia ; while Tito for his part has set up a National Council of Liberation, which has forbidden King Peter to return to Yugoslavia until after its complete liberation, when the question of the monarchy will be reconsidered, and has accused Mihailovitch of organizing the mass extermination of Moslems, Croats, and Serbian patriots with the aim of creating a "Greater Serbia."

All this is very confusing, and much of it is deplorable. Britain and her allies are openly supporting Tito in the field, while still extending diplomatic recognition to King Peter's Government in Cairo. Such a situation cannot endure for long.

**KING PETER II OF YUGOSLAVIA** greets officers of the Royal Yugoslav Guard ; he is shaking hands with the Brigadier. On extreme left is Gen. Zivkovitch, Yugoslav C.-in-C. and a former premier under King Alexander.
*Photo, British Official*

# Here Under Tito's Banner Yugoslavs are Free

YUGOSLAV PARTISANS, under Marshal Tito (see facing page), now control a large part of the Dalmatian coast. When a British ship called at a Dalmatian port, the crew journeyed through wild country to visit Tito's H.Q.; led by one of their officers (1), they were cheered by village children (2) wearing national youth badges. On a house wall (3) a slogan reads: "Long Live Brother Stalin." After a Nazi raid on the Partisans 24 German soldiers were killed, and were accorded by the invaders a "heroes' funeral" (4) in Belgrade. *Photos, British Official; Keystone*

# Non-Belligerent Turkey in the Allied Camp

Implications of Turkey's friendliness to the Allies are weighed by SYED EDRIS ALI SHAH;
he examines the possibilities of her active participation in the war—unity and understanding
having been achieved in the three-day conference at Cairo, December 1943, between her President,
Ismet Inönü, President Roosevelt and Mr. Churchill.   See also pages 527-530.

WHEN the Turkish Foreign Minister agreed with newspapermen who suggested that Turkey could be said to have entered the Allied Camp "without being belligerent," he expressed the whole truth. For Turkey all along has had decided leanings towards the cause for which the United Nations are fighting. And at this point of the war it is pertinent to consider what the value of Turkish help to the Allies might be, and its nature.

First of all, we must look at Turkey's technical position in this conflict. Under what circumstances would she actively line up with the other democracies, and are there any treaties binding her with the Allies? Turkey has, since the 1914-18 war, stood for stability in all political affairs, both internal and international. She was the instigator of the Balkan Entente, and a signatory of the Saadabad Pact between Iran, Iraq, and Turkey and Afghanistan. She has a pact of friendship with Russia.

But perhaps most important of all is her Treaty of Mutual Assistance with Britain. This pact, signed in 1939, with France as the third party, provided for full mutual assistance between the contracting parties. Why then, it may be asked, did the Turks not join the Western Democracies during the first few years of this war? International treaties of this type have always to be considered in the light of the circumstances prevailing at the moment when they should become operative; as it happened, the Allies did not press the Turks to discharge their obligations at the beginning of the war. The Turkish Army was not fully equipped, and was certainly

Anatolian mainland, Allied war material and supplies could travel to Russia.

Secondly, European Turkey could be used as the bridgehead for the invasion of South-Eastern Europe: from here, United Nations troops, with air support from the Turkish mainland, could assail Hitler's back door by way of Bulgaria and Greece, forming part of the Russian advance from the East. In this way the Dodecanese could be overwhelmed by that superior air power which was not available to complete the conquest of Cos and Leros; such support would certainly prove decisive here. The British and United States troops now in Italy might cross the Adriatic to link up with the guerilla forces of Albania and Yugoslavia, and form the third prong of the drive to eject Germany from the Balkans.

LASTLY, there are the Turkish Armed Forces, if she decided on complete participation in the war. The Turkish Army comprises at least 25 Infantry Field Divisions, three Cavalry Divisions, such as the Russians have used with great success, and one Armoured Brigade. The active strength of this force is half a million, which expands to over two millions on mobilization. The Turkish Air Force a year ago consisted of 36 squadrons, since when it has been expanded and largely re-equipped with Hurricanes. The Navy includes eight modern destroyers, thirteen submarines, and the refitted battle-cruiser Yavuz, formerly the German Goeben.

Against this Turkish force, and the Anglo-American-Russian troops that would be fighting with it, let us consider what the

Germans can muster. There are probably eighteen German Divisions in the Balkans at present. In addition, there are the armies of the second-class satellites: the Bulgars have 25 divisions, the traitor Croats (Ustashis) have three or four, and the Rumanians about twelve. Although the nearest Allied bases are 1,200 miles away in Syria, and the Syria-Iskenderun (Alexandretta) railway would cut this to 800 miles, by the time Turkey joined in the Allies would have considerable forces massed within striking distance.

The Dodecanese would have to be cleaned up quickly, as the Luftwaffe would be using them as air bases for attack upon the Turkish shipping, harbour installations and communications, as well as troop concentrations and open towns. As soon as hostilities broke out, the Germans would try to forestall the Thracian bridgehead by over-running Thrace, and possibly Asiatic Turkey as well. Within Bulgaria, most likely place to become a battleground, all seems to be confusion. In March 1941 German troops first used her territory as a base of operations against Russia. In December 1941 Bulgaria became an enemy of Britain and the United States. But she is not yet officially at war with Russia, and diplomatic connexions have not been severed. By lining up with the Axis, Bulgaria was given slices of Yugoslavia and Greece, while the astute Boris sat on the throne in Sofia, juggling with his Axis masters to keep out of the fighting as much as possible.

SINCE the death of King Boris, however, the position has been steadily deteriorating, and the present Bulgar Government is completely in Germany's pocket. Her army of half a million, however, is intact, having only to fight the Greek and Yugoslav guerilla forces; and Bulgaria trembles at the thought of the approach of the death-knell of her imperialistic ambitions. However much the quisling Bulgar leaders may play the tune about "traditional Turko-Bulgar friendship," Turkey is not in the least deceived. Yes, Turkey is ready and willing to pull her weight in the struggle against evil; and when the time comes—and it is not far off—when they are asked to share the burden the heirs of Ataturk will prove themselves fully equal to the task.

**BRITISH PLANES** are helping to swell Turkey's Air Force; above, a Turkish pilot adjusts his parachute before taking off in a British-built Bisley. Headed by Gen. Omurtak a Turkish military mission recently visited the British Mediterranean Battle Fleet; right, Gen. Omurtak (2nd from right) inspects the flagship.  *Photos, British Official; Central Press*

unprepared for aerial attack. Even today the Turks cannot fight unless they are guaranteed adequate supplies of arms and ammunition regularly, as well as fighter and bomber support. At one time Britain was unable to provide this aid; thus Turkey waited until she should be able to throw into battle a force worthy of her traditions.

The Turkish Government might decide to give certain concessions to Britain, short of actually entering the war, much as has been done by Portugal. Many advantages could accrue from this, chief of which are the following: firstly, access to the Black Sea, which would stop the German transports and ammunition ships plying through the Dardanelles, to and from the Aegean. By this route, as well as overland through the

## Ataturk Still Dominates His Capital

In the forecourt of the Turkish People's House in Ankara (formerly Angora) stands the commanding figure of the late Kemal Ataturk (top left) who, as Turkey's first President, guided the new republic to her place among the modern democracies. He had great regard for his Premier and successor—the present President, Ismet Inönü. Affairs of government are conducted from Ankara, capital since 1923; (top right) view from railway station, and (below) the Ministerial quarter.

Photos, B.
New

## *As Echoes of War Resound on Her Frontiers—*

Developments in modern warfare are of necessity very closely followed by those responsible for the efficiency and immediate readiness of Turkey's armed forces.  Army training includes captive-parachute jumping from a tower (1), carried out
assiduously by embryo parachute troops, and theory goes hand in hand with practice in the air force ; a class at the Eskeshir
Air College receives aero engine instruction (2).   Cadets of a Naval College vie in smartness on the drill ground (3).

## —Turkey's Armed Forces are Trained and Alert

The national hero, Kemal Ataturk (Gazi Mustafa Kemal Pasha), effected radical changes in Turkey's defences in the course of his presidency, October 29, 1923 to November 9, 1938, and today her powerful army numbers over 2,000,000 when fully mobilized. During large-scale manoeuvres in 1943, field artillery move up to forward positions (5), while infantry divisions make full use of mechanized transport. a column of which is being piloted by a dispatch rider (4).

## *Istanbul—City of the Sultans*

Photos, Pictorial Press.
Paul Popper

Famous for centuries as capital of sultan-ruled Turkey, Constantinople—now known as Istanbul—guards the mouth of the Bosphorus. Significant of close pre-war relations existing between Great Britain and Turkey, battleships of both countries rode side by side (top) in the Bay of Istanbul on the coastline of the Sea of Marmara. Below, viewed across the stretch of water known as the Golden Horn, is a panorama of the Stamboul district. See also page 526.

# VIEWS & REVIEWS
## Of Vital War Books

### by Hamilton Fyfe

THEODORE ROOSEVELT once said to me, a trifle bitterly, "The American people are ready enough to build arches of triumph for popular rulers, but directly the rulers have passed under them they are liable to be pelted with the bricks the arches were made of." We were on a Nile steamer at the time. He was on his way back to the United States after the hunting trip in Africa which followed his term as President. I went with him and took part in his reception at New York. Never, I think, have I seen such enthusiasm. The arch of triumph could not have been more magnificent or, seemingly, more solid. Yet in a couple of years he had lost his popularity and sank gradually into an embittered, discontented man.

Much the same thing happened to Hoover, who was hailed with the loudest cheers when he was elected President and who left office amid a chorus of "good riddance!" from every side. And Woodrow Wilson, too, had his triumphal arch with the pelting of bricks afterwards that broke his spirit and brought on his body a paralytic stroke. With these examples from recent history in mind, Franklin Roosevelt must sometimes ask himself how permanent his hold will be on the fickle affections of the mob. Already the mass confidence which has given him three terms of office (twelve years) is diminishing. He will almost certainly stand for a fourth term this year. My own opinion is that the American people would be wise to re-elect him. But a great deal depends on what may happen between now and next November.

SOME close observers, who are honestly eager for that "better world" we hear so much of, think it would be more advantageous to have Wendell Willkie as President with the full support both of the Senate and the House of Representatives, rather than Roosevelt with majorities in both Houses against him. In such a case Roosevelt could get nothing done, whereas Willkie, whose ideas (as he proclaims them) are very much the same, might be able, if he stood up to Wall Street, to do a good deal.

It is that "standing up to Wall Street" which makes me feel Roosevelt would be the safer choice —safer, I mean, from the point of view of the "better world" crowd. He has done it already. Not always successfully, but on the whole with enough encouragement to make him go on doing it. Whereas with Willkie one can't tell. He might or he might not. Even if he did, Wall Street would find him a less formidable champion than Roosevelt with his immense world prestige.

"If," writes Compton Mackenzie in his biography of the President which has just appeared, Mr. Roosevelt (Harrap, 17s. 6d.), "democracy can still be acclaimed as the political ideal of all humanity, it is due supremely to him."

The Vatican trusts Roosevelt. Jewry trusts Roosevelt. Tormented France trusts Roosevelt. Greece, glorious in her chains, trusts Roosevelt. Martyred Poland trusts Roosevelt. Dogged Holland trusts Roosevelt. China, risen from a sleep of centuries, trusts Roosevelt. Latin America, so long a suspicious neighbour, trusts Roosevelt. Even the poor poisoned heart of Italy beats feebly for Roosevelt, and we in Britain and the Dominions of the Empire trust the man who, speaking in our common tongue, first gave us the assurance of victory

when adamantine Churchill had pledged our honour and committed us to the proud defiance he knew we desired to offer.

Allowing for some inflations of sentiment, some over-emphasis of language, that is the truth about the President's position in the world today. He proved himself a consummately skilful politician when between September 1939 and December 1941 (Pearl Harbour was attacked then and war forced on the American nation by Japan) he led his people step by step away from neutrality and

## Roosevelt—the True Heir of Washington

ranged them almost alongside Britain in the struggle against Fascism. The gift of destroyers, which he made without consulting Congress; the Lease-lend arrangement; the protection by American warships of convoys carrying munitions to Britain; the conception of the Atlantic Charter—these stand out as great actions, the actions of a statesman put through with the ability of a political genius.

WOODROW WILSON had a statesmanlike mind, but he was not politically ingenious. That caused his downfall. He was more of an "intellectual" than Franklin D.; less of a believer in the rock-bottom good sense and decency of his fellow men. He had nothing like such a persuasive radio voice and style. These gifts have helped the President enormously. His broad, smiling, frank, open features also contributed to make the mass of people feel sure he has led them well. He speaks, too, in a language that the least literary, even the illiterate, among his hearers can understand.

Mr. Mackenzie calls him "the man in the street one turning ahead." A clever phrase, but inadequate, it seems to me, as a final summing-up of the man whom the author

**PRESIDENT ROOSEVELT, whose return to America from the 3-power conferences in the Middle East was announced on Dec. 16, 1943, is here seen relaxing for a brief while in his study. Compton Mackenzie's graphic biography of the President is reviewed in this page.**   PAGE 531   *Photo, Keystone*

himself describes as "the true heir of Washington," who has "illuminated the ancient word with his own vitality so that it glows again as warmly on his lips as upon the lips of Pericles in the market-place of Athens 2,400 years ago." If Roosevelt has the mental calibre of Washington and the eloquence of Pericles, he can hardly be as near to the man in the street as Mr. Mackenzie suggests.

THE main fault of the book is its turgidity. Take this passage about the severe test of character which F.D.R. had to face when he was attacked by infantile paralysis at the age of 39.

Infantile paralysis threatened him with permanent unemployment. Infantile paralysis foreclosed upon the farm of his ambition. Infantile paralysis made away with the savings of his experience. Infantile paralysis deprived him of his purchasing power from life. Infantile paralysis taught him as hard a lesson as poverty can teach.

I would offer the suggestion that probably the long rest from the pursuit of his profession (the law) and the seclusion which his illness made necessary were of the greater value to him. What a difference it might have made to many of us if at 40 we had been for a time withdrawn from active life, given opportunity to reflect, to read, to dream! Roosevelt emerged from that seclusion a man of greater power, of finer character, of more penetrating mind. He certainly faced his ordeal with firm endurance, even with humour, but I should put his wife's courage above his—and I think he would too.

In the winter of 1921-22 she had her husband at home after his long stay in hospital. Her mother-in-law fussed a great deal, thought she was not doing the right thing in letting the invalid see visitors, wanted to override the doctor's decisions. There was one nurse in the house, but Mrs. Roosevelt did a great deal for the patient herself. "His legs were in plaster casts to stretch the muscles, and every day a little bit had to be chipped out at the back, which was torture for him"—and for her. At last the strain proved too great. One afternoon she suddenly began to sob, and could not stop sobbing. This went on until the evening. Then, instead of going to bed and sending for the doctor and making a second invalid in the house, she rose up, said "This won't do!" mopped her face with a towel soaked in cold water, and resolutely went about her duties again. She said sarcastically later on "it requires an audience as a rule to keep on these emotional jags." She got rid of hers by the one effort of will, and was not troubled again. That was real heroism.

THE President has been lucky in his wife—or perhaps, one should credit him not with luck but with good judgement in selecting her. He had plenty of choice, for he was lucky in most other ways. He had good looks, he was well off, he knew all "the best people," he had been to the right school and the right university. When I met him first at Alice Roosevelt's wedding in New York, I could see he had everything in his favour. Like our own Winston, he was given a good start in life's handicap. But in neither case could they have reached high positions but for their industry, patience and seeking after knowledge of every kind that could be useful.

"Seest thou a man diligent in his business? He shall stand before kings; he shall not stand before mean men." That is true of both the national leaders. They were diligent in all they undertook. We must congratulate ourselves on having had their leadership in very difficult hours.

# Two Ships Attack Eleven in Big Sea-Air Battle

BAY OF BISCAY BATTLE on Dec. 27 and 28, 1943, resulted in the destruction of a 5,000-ton armed enemy blockade runner (see page 540) and the sinking of three German destroyers ; others were damaged. The enemy force consisted of five modern Narvik class destroyers, each mounting five 5·9-in. guns, and six Elbing class destroyers, each mounting four 4·1-in. guns. H.M. cruisers Glasgow and Enterprise opened fire on the enemy ships and a running fight ensued ; a number of hits were scored by our cruisers. Halifaxes and a Sunderland of Coastal Command with U.S. Liberators joined the battle, while Beaufighters and Mosquitoes provided air cover for the British cruisers. The blockade runner, making for a French port, was shadowed by the R.A.F. and R.C.A.F. and was sunk by a Liberator.

AFTER ACTION IN THE BAY some of the triumphant crew (1) of H.M.S. Enterprise (2) are back in a British port ; displacement 7,580 tons, complement 572, Enterprise (Capt. H. T. W. Grant, R.C.N.) took part in the 1940 Norwegian operations. Capt. C. P. Clarke, R. N. (4) is commander of the 9,000-ton Newcastle class cruiser Glasgow (3), complement 700 ; she brought Norway's King Haakon to Britain in 1940. Both Captains have been awarded the D.S.O. for their achievements in the battle described above. PAGE 532 *Photos, G.P.U., Wright & Logan, Daily Mirror, Central Press*

# Americans Storm Fiercely Blazing Makin Atoll

SAVAGE BLOWS WERE STRUCK at the Japanese in the Central Pacific when, on Nov. 20, 1943, American troops landed on Makin and Tarawa atolls in the Gilberts (see illus. p. 503, and map in p. 474). Men of the 165th Infantry advance hip-deep through the surf (top) towards Butaritari beach at Makin, which is shrouded in a heavy smoke pall after the terrific U.S. naval bombardment. Landing effected (bottom), a bulldozer is ready to carve a road for vehicles, while enemy oil-dumps burn in the background. Within 48 hours Makin was taken. *Photos, New York Times*

# At Hell-Fire Corner: Britain's Front-Line Town

In the shadow of Dover Castle high up on the famous white cliffs, constantly threatened by German guns just 73 seconds' shell-flight across the Channel, live and work gallant folk of the type that has made our country so truly great. JOHN ALLEN GRAYDON pays tribute to their outstanding bravery and devotion—especially when we stood alone. See also facing page.

OVER three years ago, on August 12, 1940, German shells fell for the first time "in the vicinity of Dover." Since then the Nazis have spent many thousands of pounds in lobbing more than 1,700 shells across the Channel; but the value of their attacks, from a military angle, is small. If they planned to shatter the morale of the people of Hell-Fire Corner, as I first named it, the Germans have been beaten, for in this front-line town of Dover I have always been impressed by the citizens' sheer courage and determination.

Although on a clear day one can see the French coast with the naked eye—some locals often wisecrack: "The Fatherland looks good this morning!"—the Doverites do not allow the enemy to upset their enjoyment. In the local Hippodrome, which stands on the front, and can be seen by German patrols with the aid of field-glasses, they still have their twice-nightly shows: "And we've given them with but one or two exceptions all the time the shells have been lobbed over," Mr. H. R. Armstrong, the manager, told me. "And," he added

LACONIC NOTICE above proclaims the Dover Hippodrome's sentiments; the manager assures residents, and members of the Services, of their due ration of first-class entertainment, bombardment or no bombardment. And though the shelling warning is in operation (right) buses continue to run.

*Photos, Keystone, Topical*

with a smile, "I think the Service lads enjoy it." I have been to shows at the Hippodrome, and can testify to the entertainment given to the men in the front line.

ALTHOUGH Dover has suffered because of its geographical position, being but 73 seconds "as the shell flies" from the muzzles of the German guns on the French coast, the town is not the heap of rubble many think it must be. Her wounds are varied and many, but to live among these wonderful people, and their Mayor, Alderman J. R. Cairns, is a

tonic. The comradeship of the people of Dover is a credit to them, while their understanding of little difficulties has impressed itself upon me for ever. In addition, it is one of the most orderly towns in the country.

I visited the A.R.P. control-room, among the finest I have ever seen in my travels around Britain. The controller showed me a map of the town on which is indicated every shell and bomb that has landed in the area. A book, kept in the control-room, interested me. It contains the reports from patrols that spend every night on top of the hills on either side of Dover. They watch for the area in which shells or bombs fall. Sometimes these brave folk have been injured while watching for shell-bursts. In the book I read of one man who reported he had been hit but asked if he might continue; the book states that permission was given!

## UNDERGROUND Restaurant for Dover Straits Fighters

Most popular meeting-place in the town is The Crypt, the "front-line" underground restaurant: the crypt of the old Flemish church of St. Nicholas. It is over 400 years old. The church, which was demolished in 1836, was once used by refugees from Flanders as a secret place of worship. Now, after a century, refugees from the twentieth-century terror—fighting men who take part in the "Battle of the Dover Straits"—often go to the Crypt for a meal after hitting hard at the Hun in the Channel

"We have dozens of famous people visit us here," Mr. W. J. Evans, the manager and son of a former Trinity House pilot, told me. "Among the celebrities who have lunched here are Sir Malcolm Campbell and Sir Roger Keyes." When Sir Roger visited The Crypt a waitress asked him for his autograph. The former chief of the Commandos ran through the autograph book, pausing for a

moment at one page. Then, turning to the waitress, he said: "I see you have here the signature of one of my first Commandos." He then wrote his own signature, adding the sentence: "We'll see it through . . ."

NEAR to The Crypt is St. Mary's Parish Church, where the Rev. Purcell, young priest-in-charge, conducts most interesting services. I glanced through a record he keeps and noticed that on more than one occasion he has been interrupted by air-raids and shell-fire warnings. Once, when about to conduct a wedding, a shell warning went. Promptly donning his tin-hat he became Warden Purcell and hurried off to his post.

When the bombardment eased for a while he returned to his beloved church to see if everything was in order—and found a sailor, looking extremely unhappy, sitting in a pew. The sailor did not seem to realize that shells had been whining over the church; what worried him was the fact that his bride had not arrived. It was explained to him that she was in an air-raid shelter, putting the finishing touches to her dressing. When the all clear sounded the padre removed his tin-hat, slipped on his robes, and the wedding ceremony was solemnized.

THE other day I had the rare opportunity, for a journalist, of visiting the "Gateway to England"—Dover Castle. From the ancient Keep it was possible to see France as if it were but two or three miles away. And all the time I sensed that Dover Castle really was "something"—in other words, this was England! And I say that without wishing to hurt the feelings of my friends in Wales, Scotland, and Ireland. Within this ancient pile are men and women belonging to all Services, working upon tasks, deep beneath the ground, about which I am not allowed to say anything.

I went into the Port Wall Signalling Station, whence the men on duty have a perfect view of shipping passing through the Straits. While I was in the Station a flotilla of motor launches were returning, their signalling lamps winking as they made contact with the men standing by my side. "We've seen some very exciting actions from here," one officer told me. "One night we saw what must have been an enemy tanker go up in flames. It really lit up the Channel."

The magnificent work of the Dover Fire Brigade during heavy aerial bombardments of the town has not escaped the notice of H.M. the King; the minutes of the Dover Council include the record that his Majesty " had been graciously pleased to award the George Medal to Executive Chief Officer E. H. Harmer, Second Officer C. W. A. Brown, and Section Officer A. E. Campbell, in recognition of their gallantry on the occasion of a fire, caused by enemy action, in Dover Harbour." These men " volunteered to return to a blazing ship containing high explosives, in which they fought fires while enemy aircraft were still in the neighbourhood."

# Dover's Defiance Continues Whatever Betides

THERE'LL ALWAYS BE AN ENGLAND while the spirit displayed by Britain's front line citizens at Hell-Fire Corner continues to survive. This Dover street (1) testifies to the town's long and grim ordeal of enemy bombing and shelling. But they are still cheerfully busy at the appropriately named bookshop (2). With Dover Castle in the background, a Canterbury-bound bus picks up passengers at a shattered "stop" (3) ; and Inspector Webb, of the local R.S.P.C.A. (4) plucks from raid-debris a stray cat. See also facing page. PAGE 535 *Photos, Keystone, Topical Press*

# SUBMARINE DEPOT SHIPS

*Specially drawn for*
*THE WAR ILLUSTRATED*
*By Haworth*

SUPPLYING THE MANY NEEDS of H.M. submarines, depot or "parent" ships perform indispensable service in the war at sea. When a submarine returns from a lengthy patrol its crew needs rest and relaxation and a brief change from cramped living conditions; their vessel requires revictualling, refuelling and re-arming, perhaps minor repairs or a general overhaul. These requirements are administered by a depot ship, as and when necessary.

Somewhat staid in appearance but costly to construct, these specialized ships are splendidly equipped with workshops for on-the-spot repairs of submarines as these come alongside. For the submarine crews there are comfortable quarters, including recreation-rooms, bars, a well-stocked library and even a cinema.

Above, a submarine is seen moored alongside, and the business of rearming it with torpedoes is in progress. Taken from the depot ship's store, torpedoes are charged with compressed air (providing the motive power), and the explosive heads are fitted; they are then swung outboard by electric crane (A) and lowered for stowage by members of the submarine's crew (B); others are attending to the gun (C).

Returning to the depot ship, (D) is the fire-director tower, (E) chart-house, (F) periscope derrick, (G) searchlight tower, (H) multiple A.A. guns, (J) galley, (K) dual-purpose guns, (L) cabins, (M) heavy electric crane, (N) motor-boats. These ships, of which the above is a typical example, vary from some 5,000 tons displacement to over 12,000 tons, with a speed of from 14 to 17 knots. In addition to carrying supplies, and spares for effecting repairs, it has on board trained men for the replacement of any submarine crew members who may be sick or injured as a result of an action.

# I WAS THERE! Eye Witness Stories of the War

## Ghastly Road of the Five Graves Led to Ortona

For days the 8th Army fought doggedly for the town and port of Ortona on the Adriatic coast of Italy. A British United Press War Reporter wrote the following dispatch on Dec. 22, 1943, when savage street fighting was in progress. On Dec. 28 Ortona was reported evacuated by the enemy.

I HAVE just travelled down the "Road of the Five Graves" into the battered bomb-shattered town that once was Ortona. The "Road of the Five Graves" is the Eighth Army's name for the shambles of a highway that leads to the gates of the town. A few hundred yards from the first white-walled cottages overlooking the grey Adriatic lie the remains of a Sherman tank, split wide open by a mine.

On the right of the road beside it there are five fresh graves, each with an unpainted cross at its head and a handful of wild winter flowers laid on top. The five British soldiers who lie in them took their toll of the enemy before they were stopped within sight of their goal, and the remains of German guns, tanks, and men are strewn out all along the road that leads along the last mile to the town.

That last mile might well be called the road of a hundred and five graves. It is a very grim mile. The pleasant countryside looks as if a bloody steam-roller had passed over it. What were once orchards are blackened ruins, and what were farms are heaps of rubble. When I got to the gates of Ortona after that death-haunted last mile, street fighting was still going on in the town. Some Germans were holding out in houses converted into blockhouses, and Nazi tanks were still posted at the street corners.

We passed the first houses. They looked as if a wrecking squad had just finished working on them. A few yards along the main street the rattle of machine-gun fire made us halt, and a car came racing down the road towards us. The driver was a young Welshman, Driver John Nugent, of Llanelian Road, Colwyn Bay, who explained that he had gone into the town to set up an observation post, but the Germans had opened fire at him from the upper storeys of houses they still held. "They caught me by surprise, but I turned the car round and got out through their fire safely," he said.

Canadian troops were meanwhile entering the town from the coast road with tank reinforcements, and were already winkling out the remaining groups of tough Nazis still resisting. Ortona itself looked as though squads of saboteurs and wreckers had used it as a practice-ground, but the sight lost a lot of its impressiveness when you remembered that long mile leading into the port.

British and German dead lie huddled in what were once orchards. Cattle and sheep lie rotting in the fields on either side of the road, unnoticed almost since the barrages of both sides first began to sweep across the ground. Even the farmhouses seemed to convey the same message of death, with their sides ripped open by shells, and their interiors revealing furniture splintered by explosions, floorboards ripped up, and all the everyday things of farm life strewn about the ground.

The trees here have been clipped down to their stumps by the barrages. Haystacks have been reduced to black lumps. Vineyards are pitted with craters, while lying by the roadside at one point is a German self-propelling gun, a fiery tomb for the occupants who failed to get out. In among the wreckage of the roads—twisted guns, broken rifles, discarded helmets, empty cartridge and shell-cases—are the dead monsters that were Mark IV Specials, the German tanks second in German estimation only to the Tigers.

CAPTURED NEAR ORTONA by Indian units, these German prisoners were among those who put up fierce resistance against the 8th Army in heavy fighting for possession of the Adriatic port in Dec. 1943. *Photo, British Official*

The country leading to Ortona is a graveyard of them ; they loll with shattered tracks in gullies and ditches, their 10-ft. gun barrels still looking menacing. In spite of all this destruction, it is the five graves by the side of the Sherman which have given the road its name. The tank had gone through a day's hard fighting and was within sight of its objective when it was finally smashed.

"It must have taken 300 pounds of explosives to do that job," a young Canadian engineer told me. "It lifted the tank from one side of the road to the other, slicing it open at the same time !"

## Our Seven Weeks' Nightmare as Arctic Castaways

Swept ashore on a barren island, within sight of several wooden huts, members of the crew of a British ship sunk in the Arctic Circle were rendered great service by three of their comrades—Peyer, Burnett and Whiteside, gunners of the Maritime Royal Artillery, who have been awarded the B.E.M. The story is told by one of the men and by the Master.

THE following morning, when it was light enough to investigate, we found one of the huts was quite habitable, and the remaining twenty-three of us moved in. There was a small coal stove in which we soon made a fire, for there was plenty of wood and some coal. There was not a tree in the place, but plenty of driftwood and old boxes. Before the end of our stay we demolished one of the huts for firewood.

After we had slept that first night we all felt a little better. We collected the remainder of the lifeboat rations and at once made ourselves hot drinks, melting the snow for water. This revived us considerably and we all became terribly hungry. The lifeboat rations lasted us a long time and we found some tins of corned beef and biscuits in one of the huts, so we managed very well, but most of our thoughts were concentrated on food, and we planned the

**GUNNER WHITESIDE, B.E.M.,** Member of the Maritime Artillery, was a gunner in the torpedoed ship whose crew suffered an open-boat ordeal lasting seven days. Their subsequent adventures are told here.
*Photo, Associated Photos Ltd., Liverpool*

kind of meals we would like to have—I think we even dreamed of food.

As long as we had food for tomorrow we never looked further ahead. I never doubted we should be rescued or somehow come through alive. The Master encouraged us to take exercise each day, but after a time most of us were suffering so much from frost-bitten feet that it was impossible.

*Continuing the story, the Master said :*

The Army gunners were practically unaffected by frost-bite and it was really due to them that we survived at all. One man, Whiteside, was a really tough guy—a Liverpool docker in peacetime, only 4 ft. 11 ins., and he suffered no ill effects at all. Sergeant Peyer was also fairly well most of the time, and these two, assisted by Burnett, looked after us, nursing the men who were ill, going out to collect firewood, and generally running things. The Third Officer and Sergeant Peyer made the first two attempts to try to fetch help. They were unsuccessful in their efforts. It was such a rock-strewn, barren place, broken up by ravines, with large stretches of snow and ice, that they returned each time completely exhausted.

Thirteen men died during the first three or four days from frost-bite and from exhaustion and exposure. I believed right to the end we should come through, and often talked things over and made plans with the Third Officer, who was quite cheerful until he became seriously ill towards the last.

**DEVASTATED** Russian territory as seen from the air is described in this page by a war correspondent who recently concluded a 1,000-mile flight over former battlefields. Retreating Germans left Karachev (right) razed to the ground; the site was recaptured by Soviet forces on **August 15, 1943.**
*Photo, U.S.S.R. Official*

A third sortie to try to find help was made by Whiteside, Peyer and another man. They discovered a small hut in which was a sack of flour and some tins of corned beef and cocoa, which they brought back with them. We were coming to the end of our lifeboat rations and the flour kept us alive for three or four weeks. We mixed it with water, cooked it and ate the small cakes.

There were dozens of boxes of matches in the hut, fortunately for us, and two primus stoves. There was little oil for these, but Whiteside and I managed to get the petrol tank out of the lifeboat. There was quite a lot of petrol left, as we could not use it when the motor froze up. We had hot drinks three times a day and looked forward to them very much, although towards the end the coffee and cocoa ran out and we had to make do with hot water, with occasional drinks of malted milk made from a few tablets. We also found some tins of what proved to be whale blubber preserved in oil, and we lived on that for about five or six days, each man having a small portion. We drank the boiled oil, although it was not particularly nice . . . .

*The Master and Whiteside made yet a further sortie to try to find help, again without success. By this time the situation was becoming desperate as most of the men were in a very bad condition. The Master continues :*

I decided to make a final attempt to get help, or die in the effort. Whiteside, Peyer and myself set out. We had covered a good distance when Whiteside, for the first time, fell down. We turned back, but it was as much as we could do to reach the hut. We collapsed on arrival. A few days later Whiteside went out to collect firewood, but came running back into the hut, leaving the door open, absolutely terrified. I could get nothing out of him, and we thought we were about to be attacked by bears.

A little later two figures appeared wearing white, camouflaged suits. They were from a camp twelve miles away, out on a patrol and trapping expedition. They divided the food in their rucksacks between the nine of us, also cigarettes, then set off to fetch help. They were accompanied by Whiteside, who walked the entire twelve miles back without assistance, and Burnett. The latter was not in such good condition and had to be carried the last part of the journey.

A rescue party returned to the hut with two sledges, provisions and clothing. We were all in pretty bad condition now, as we had not sufficient energy to exercise ourselves any longer. The three most serious cases were taken to the camp at once, leaving five of us still in the hut. A doctor and two of the rescue party stayed with us, looking after us as well as they could . . . .

*The next day, nearly seven weeks after the men had been cast ashore, a party of men with four sledges arrived at the hut and that same night the remaining five men arrived safely at the camp. All the party were kept in bed for about two months and remained at the camp for nearly six months before they eventually returned to this country.*

# I Flew 1,000 Miles Over Battle-Torn Russia

Vast pitted areas where fighting has swayed to and fro for two and a half years now present an eerie and awe-inspiring spectacle, declares Duncan Hooper, Reuters Special Correspondent, after a sensational flight of inspection over some of the worst-scarred Soviet territory.

WITHIN less than an hour's flight from Moscow I began to note bomb and shell craters pitting fields now far from the sound of guns and dotted with stacks of fodder gathered in the third wartime harvest. But in the broad belt of territory which up to a few months ago was still under German occupation the scars of more recent conflicts are deep and heavy. Here there is no sprouting autumn-sown wheat to lighten the countryside with patches of green, and there are many more roofless buildings than smoking chimneys. Seen from a height of 200 feet the earth is criss-crossed with trenches and strewn with the grey, cindery patches of villages which the

war has ploughed up with high explosives. Passing over the Steppes where the hulks of German tanks are still rusting, it is easy to reconstruct the battles that led to the expulsion of the invaders. Over the approaches to the road and rail junctions I saw one line of zig-zagging trenches after another, then perhaps some ruined village straddled with bomb bursts.

At some points the earth had been churned and rechurned until it resembled a huge over-turned anthill. Over the wrecked towns the names of which once figured in the Soviet communiqués for weeks at a time, it was easier to count roofed than unroofed buildings.

### Moonlight on Blackened Rafters

There were many signs of swift reconstruction work, in new wooden bridges thrown across rivers and black patches marking filled-in bomb craters on the roads. But rebuilding and repopulation of these war cities will take years, even when Russia is able to throw in her whole energies.

I landed near Kursk and drove in after dark. Even today it looks like a front-line city, with fire-blackened, boarded windows looking on to the streets and neat holes drilled by anti-tank shells in garden walls.

Numbers of large buildings were apparently intact, but a second glance revealed empty husks with moonlight slanting through blackened rafters.

Once a flash lit the sky and the boom of an explosion rolled across the countryside. Another German mine had gone up. Hundreds of miles behind the present front line, long forgotten mines and unexploded shells are still claiming their victims. Sometimes it is a peasant who strikes an unfamiliar metal object with his tractor blades as he ploughs or harrows the former battlefield. Sometimes it is a luckless vehicle which

AMIDST THE RUINS OF HOME to which she has just returned this Russian woman relates to Soviet troops a story of horror during the German occupation of the village, when she and her children existed in an orchard hiding-place.
*Photo by courtesy of Soviet Embassy*

bumps over a spot where the button of a detonator has been resting unsuspected a few inches below the surface for several seasons. Nearer the front, in wrecked villages, after two years of German domination, children scatter immediately at the sight of an unfamiliar motor-car. Fields are unkempt. Almost every family has lost one or more of its number to German deportation gangs.

# OUR DIARY OF THE WAR

**DECEMBER 22, Wednesday** 1,572nd day
Russian Front.—Continued progress made by Russian tanks and cavalry in the advance on Vitebsk ; 128 German tanks destroyed.

**DECEMBER 23, Thursday** 1,573rd day
Air.—Hutted camp near Merlimont (France) and two rail junctions bombed by Allies. Berlin (1,000 tons of bombs) heavily raided at night. Total of 200,000 tons dropped on Germany to date.
General.—Announced that Gen. de Lattre de Tassigny had escaped from a French prison camp and placed himself at the disposal of Gen. de Gaulle.

**DECEMBER 24, Friday** 1,574th day
Russian Front.—Gorodok, S.W. of Nevel, stormed by Soviet troops.
General.—Names of Allied commanders for Second Front invasion armies revealed : Gen. Dwight D. Eisenhower to be Allied Supreme Commander of combined British and U.S. expeditionary forces in Gt. Britain ; General Sir B. Montgomery to command British Group of Armies under Gen. Eisenhower. In the Mediterranean, Gen. Sir Henry Maitland Wilson to assume post of Allied Supreme Commander, and Gen. Sir H. Alexander to be Allied C.-in-C. Italy. U.S. Strategic Bombing Force operating against Germany to be led by General Carl Spaatz.

**DECEMBER 25, Saturday** 1,575th day
Russian Front.—Red Army captured 200 inhabited localities in Vitebsk region. Zaluchye, Kurino and Novka taken.

**DECEMBER 26, Sunday** 1,576th day
Russian Front.—Russians recaptured Radomysl in recently launched offensive W. of Kiev.
India.—Japanese raided Chittagong.
Australasia.—U.S. Marines landed at Silimati Point, E. of Cape Gloucester, New Britain.
Sea.—German battleship Scharnhorst sunk off North Cape, Norway, by Home Fleet units.

**DECEMBER 27, Monday** 1,577th day
Australasia.—Australians on Huon Peninsula, New Guinea, took Pimple Hill.
Sea.—Enemy blockade-runner sunk in Bay of Biscay by Coastal Command aircraft.
General.—Air Chief Marshal Tedder appointed Deputy Supreme Commander of Allied invasion forces under Gen. Eisenhower.

**DECEMBER 28, Tuesday** 1,578th day
Italy.—Ortona cleared of the enemy by Canadian troops of the 8th Army.
Russian Front.—Korostyshev reoccupied by Red Army in Russian counter-offensive S. and W. of Kiev.
Australasia.—Announced that three Japanese counter-attacks in Arawe area of New Britain repulsed.
Pacific.—Nauru Is., 400 miles W. of the Gilberts, attacked by U.S. aircraft.
Sea.—In Bay of Biscay, cruisers H.M.S. Enterprise and H.M.S. Glasgow sank 3 out of a force of 11 enemy destroyers.
General.—Appointments to U.S. commands in Allied invasion forces announced : Lt.-Gen. Jacob Devers to command U.S. forces in the Mediterranean and to be Deputy Supreme Commander under Gen. Sir H. Maitland-Wilson ; Maj.-Gen. James Doolittle to command 8th U.S. Air Force in Britain ; Lt.-Gen. Ira C. Eaker to command Allied Air Forces in the Mediterranean ; Lt.-Gen. Nathan Twining to command 15th U.S. Air Force in the Mediterranean.

**DECEMBER 29, Wednesday** 1,579th day
Russian Front.—Korosten (occupied by the Germans on November 10) and Chernyakhov recaptured by Russians ; also Lozvida, Skvira, Turchinska and Belopolye.

Announced fresh Soviet offensive had begun in Dnieper Bend W. of Zaporozhe.
Air.—Berlin (over 2,000 tons of bombs) heavily raided. Revealed that Ascension Is. had been used for months past as a stage in the passage of 5,000 aircraft from U.S.A. to Africa.
General.—Appointments announced : Admiral Sir Bertram Ramsay to be Allied Naval C.-in-C. under Gen. Eisenhower, and Air Marshal Sir Trafford Leigh-Mallory to be Allied Air C.-in-C.

**DECEMBER 30, Thursday** 1,580th day
Russian Front.—Marshal Stalin in Order of the Day to Gen. Vatutin announced that Russians in Kiev salient had advanced between 30 and 60 miles in five days over a 180 mile front and defeated 8 German tank and 14 infantry divisions. Soviet troops captured Kasatin.
Australasia.—U.S. Marines captured Cape Gloucester aerodrome, New Britain.
Air.—Greatest number of bombers and fighters ever dispatched by U.S. Air Force from Britain attacked targets in S.W. Germany.

**DECEMBER 31, Friday** 1,581st day
Russian Front.—Zhitomir recaptured by troops of the First Ukrainian Front under Gen. Vatutin. In the battle for

Vitebsk, Red Army cut important Vitebsk-Orsha road.
Pacific.—Parashumir, Japanese base in Kurile Islands, raided by U.S. aircraft.
India.—Thirteen Japanese aircraft destroyed off the Arakan coast.
Air.—Two ball-bearing factories at Paris attacked by Fortresses and Liberators. Château Bernard aerodrome at Cognac also attacked.

**JANUARY 1, Sat., 1944** 1,582nd day
Russian Front.—Belokovorichi, 27 miles from old Polish frontier, taken by Gen. Vatutin's First Ukrainian Army.
Air.—Berlin bombed (1,000 tons) by Lancasters in first great raid of 1944.
General.—Gen. Carl Spaatz, commanding U.S. Strategic Bombing Force arrived in London.

**JANUARY 2, Sunday** 1,583rd day
Italy.—Announced that Canadian troops of 8th Army had captured Villa San Tommaso.
Australasia.—U.S. troops under Brig.-Gen. C. A. Martin landed at Saidor, on N. coast of New Guinea, 55 miles from Madang ; harbour and airfield occupied.
Air.—Bomber Command aircraft dropped 1,000 tons of bombs on Berlin.

**JANUARY 3, Monday** 1,584th day
Italy.—Bitter struggle continued N. of Ortona as 8th Army pressed forward.
Russian Front.—Novgorod-Volynsk, on main Kiev-Warsaw railway and 15 miles from 1939 Polish frontier, Olevsk, Djerzhinsk and Ostraya Mogila, fell to swiftly advancing First Ukrainian Army.
General.—Announced that Gen. Sir Bernard Montgomery had arrived in England to take up his new post as Commander of British Group of Armies under Gen. Eisenhower.

**JANUARY 4, Tuesday** 1,585th day
Italy.—5th Army launched strong attack along 10-mile front on road to Rome.
Mediterranean.—Announced that Marshal Tito's Yugoslav partisans had captured town hall and prison of Banjaluka, Central Bosnia.
Russian Front.—Byelaya Tserkov, 40 miles S.W. of Kiev, taken by Red Army ; also Pliska, district centre of Vinnitsa region, and Stavishch, district centre of Kiev sector. Russians crossed 1939 Polish border E. of Olevsk.

★ **Flash-backs** ★

**1940**
December 27. British-held Pacific island of Nauru heavily shelled by unidentified German raider.

**1941**
December 23. Revealed that Mr. Churchill and Service chiefs had arrived in Washington to discuss measures for Allied co-ordination.
December 26. Mr. Churchill addressed both Houses of Congress, avowing that the British and American peoples would walk together "in majesty, in justice, and in peace."

December 29. British troops withdrawn from Ipoh, Malaya.

**1942**
December 24. Admiral Darlan assassinated in Algiers.
December 29. Kotelnikovo, S.W. of Stalingrad, captured by Russians.
December 31. Zimovniki captured as Nazis fled from Kotelnikovo, towards Rostov-on-Don.

**1943**
January 1. Veliki Luki, Nazi defence bastion, taken by Soviet troops.
January 4. Caucasian centre of Nalchik liberated by Russians.

# THE WAR IN THE AIR

### by Capt. Norman Macmillan, M.C., A.F.C.

I⊤ might at first sight appear that the entirely naval action in which the Scharnhorst was sunk off the North Cape (see pp. 518-520) was an incident in the war so completely maritime as to refute by its mere occurrence the arguments on air power which I have recently put forth in these columns. But a moment's reflection will show that this is indeed not so, although I do not doubt for an instant that naval protagonists will long point to the Scharnhorst action as the perfect case for the absolute indispensability of the capital ship.

But the battle in which the Scharnhorst was sunk did not commence with the departure of an escorted convoy bound from Britain (presumably) for North Russia. That action had its roots in the German invasion of Norway that was sprung upon a

the western seaports of Norway, from Kristiansand North to Narvik. The very gallant naval battle of Narvik followed. The expeditionary forces that were dispatched to Central and Northern Norway were hastily scratched together and escorted to Norway by warships. Anti-aircraft ships were supposed to be able to provide the necessary anti-aircraft defence for the small ports left to us. The whole of that story has never been told, but the fact is that the Norwegian expeditions were a failure. They were inadequately equipped for modern war, and could not have hoped to succeed. After a brief experience of German methods of warfare the Allied forces which pushed up the Gudbrands Valley demanded air support. (All that the R.A.F. had been able to do up till then was to bomb aerodromes from Denmark to Trondheim, and that by puny forces only).

was to play in modern war, but its lessons were known only to the few and were unappreciated by the public generally. It took Dunkirk to teach the British people as a whole their lesson. If Britain had possessed adequate air power in 1940 the German forces could not have trampled over the Scandinavian kingdom so swiftly and might have been denied the country altogether. But primarily because we lacked air power Norway was lost, and as a result it became possible for German warships to use the Norwegian fiords and ports, and continue to use them because only there could they get out of the reach of our present superior air power.

I⊤ has been amply demonstrated that German naval ships cannot now safely use bases anywhere between the Bay of Biscay and Central Norway, mainly because of the range, flexibility and striking power of Allied air strength. The former German naval ports of Kiel and Wilhelmshaven are almost useless to them. American aircraft by day and British aircraft by night hammer them unmercifully. There can be no doubt that if we had had adequate air power at the beginning of the war it would not have been possible for Germany to deploy her naval striking forces, and the submarine menace would have been curtailed from the very start.

### BLOCKADE Runner Sunk by Aircraft Without Ship Assistance

If we are persuaded by the sinking of the Scharnhorst that the naval tradition of things still holds in the world today we shall do a grave injustice to the coming generation. If this action, for the skill of which as a tactical evolution I have no words but praise to offer, were to be taken as a future model, we should place their security in jeopardy. We must see that the Scharnhorst action was the result not of foresight but of the very opposite, and that if we are to be secure in the future, we must organize our air power and the bases which it can use so that such threats can be crushed at source instead of being allowed to continue to cause an immense diversion of our true offensive against the enemy, as the extraordinarily few German heavy warships have been able to do. Indeed, the inadequacy of naval methods alone in dealing with such enemy weapons is apparent from the time it has taken to accomplish the liquidation of the Scharnhorst, and the tremendous national effort which Britain has had to make to deal with four German capital ships, two of which are still not sunk. Air power can alter that.

It is notable that the German merchant ship which tried to reach a Bay of Biscay port was sunk by aircraft without surface ship assistance on December 27, 1943, when weather over the Bay was notoriously bad; and that it was the initial intelligence from and subsequent shadowing by long-range land-based aircraft and the air cover of shore-based Mosquito fighters which enabled our two cruisers to close with the eleven German destroyers (who came out, too late, as escort to the blockade-runner) and, assisted by aircraft, to sink three.

GENERAL Sir Bernard Montgomery, the British general who has most skilfully employed the aid of the air in land battles, said recently that " the air battle must be won before the land or sea battle is begun. This is the first great principle of modern wars." That is the principle which surface soldiers and sailors have had to accept after three years of war during which a bitter lesson was learned from a series of defeats that were saved from disaster only by the few hundred pilots who fought—almost all single-handed —in the Battle of Britain. If those boys had not won that fight the Duke of York would never have been in the Arctic to sink the Scharnhorst, for the safety of naval bases is entirely consequent upon air defence.

**BAY OF BISCAY BLOCKADE RUNNER.** This fast German merchant ship of about 5,000 tons was intercepted and sunk on Dec. 27, 1943. This hand-camera photograph, taken by one of the crew of the attacking Liberator which effected the sinking, shows the first bomb explosion on the enemy's deck. See also p. 532.
*Photo, British Official*

surprised Britain and France in April 1940. The purpose of the German invasion of Norway was not then clear. It was generally suggested that it was intended to deny to us the iron ore which we had been receiving from the Swedish mines through the port of Narvik, and to secure all the ore and the use of that ice-free port for the German war machine. We know now that that was merely a subsidiary reason for the invasion; the real purpose was to guard the northern flank of Western Europe against the time when Germany was to invade Russia.

### TWO Aircraft Squadrons Against a Thousand German Planes

Britain and France were unprepared for the invasion of Norway. The mines that were laid in Norwegian territorial waters by British naval ships were laid too late to stop the German naval units from moving into

So No. 223 Squadron, R.A.F., was sent to Norway in an aircraft carrier from whose deck eighteen pilots flew their Gladiator biplanes and landed on a frozen lake inland from Aandalsnes, only to be bombed out in twenty-four hours. There was no aerodrome available in Central Norway, and because our fighters could not intervene from British bases, the surface forces, both land and sea, were compelled to withdraw. Two air squadrons then went to the Narvik area; their Gladiator and Hurricane fighters staved things off for a brief space. But what were two squadrons of aircraft against a thousand German planes? Narvik was evacuated in early June 1940, and the German forces soon afterwards captured the two most northerly provinces of Norway.

The campaign in Norway was Britain's first awakening to the part that air power

# R.A.F. Now at Battle-Stations in Azores Outpost

MID-ATLANTIC AIR BASE, the Azores, 400-mile long island chain about 800 miles due west of Portugal, was garrisoned by Allied sea, air and land forces in Oct. 1943 (see pp. 360-361). The result has been catastrophic to U-boats in the Atlantic; protection is given to Allied shipping in the south similar to that which Iceland provides in the north. The Allied use of harbours, airfields and flying-boat bases closes the Bay of Biscay gap.

Flying Fortresses of R.A.F. Coastal Command at their dispersal points (1). A Canadian radio operator has a rough-and-ready shave as he chats to an air-gunner (2). Arriving at Terceira Island to take up duties are (3, l. to r.) Commodore R. V. Holt, Air Vice-Marshal G. R. Bromet and Wing-Cmdr. B. D. S. Tuke with the ship's captain. This R.A.F. mechanic servicing a Wellington (4) has become accustomed to unusual traffic on the airfield.

*Photos, British Official: Crown Copyright*

# Latest Warplane News from the World's Skyways

IT is undeniable that the youth of Britain is more air-minded than it has ever been and possesses a wide practical knowledge of wartime aircraft. Every editor has had this demonstrated to him: if the slightest slip in the technical description of aircraft is made in his pages, the morning after publication sees the inevitable correction from two or three schoolboys. As this note is written a letter arrived from a boy of 8¼ years which pointed out a mistake in a pre-war publication and claimed that he could identify 300 British, American and German aeroplanes.

For schoolboys, air cadets, R.A.F. and Royal Observer Corps members, air correspondents and war editors, a better guarantee against error or a greater wealth of reference could hardly be found than in Aircraft of the Fighting Powers, of which the fourth annual volume (titled 1943 Aircraft) has just been issued by the Har-borough Publishing Co. Ltd. Produced by Aircraft (Technical) Publications, Ltd., at the moderate price of one guinea, it is edited by D. A. Russell, M.I Mech.E., and, with its earlier volumes, provides a comprehensive chronological record of the development and use of military aircraft in the Second Great War. The mass of valuable information given, for which a necessarily high standard of accuracy is claimed, includes scale drawings, specifications and all known armament and performance figures with operational histories of every one of the aircraft described. This 1943 volume includes no fewer than 76 aircraft, of which 17 are British and 47 American, an indication of the mass of new U.S. production. It also gives useful notes on military aircraft markings and colour schemes for Great Britain, U.S.A., Russia, Germany and Japan.

AMONG the six British fighters described is the new version of the Hurricane, the II D which, with its 40-mm. shell gun, at long last supplies the need for an anti-tank plane ("The War Illustrated" recorded the urgent need for a "tank buster" as far back as Feb. 10, 1942, p. 474, vol. 5); also the Spitfires V and IX (R.R. Merlin 61 engine). Others that have big names here presented in full detail are the Hawker Typhoon (speed said to exceed 400 m.p.h.) and the ubiquitous, versatile and ever-successful Mosquito, "the best all-round two-motor fighter in the world." Special types of baby two-seaters only recently heard of are the lively little British "air jeep," the Taylorcraft Auster, and the Wicko Warferry. The Auster can climb at 1,000 ft. a minute, and land in any flat field. It was on communications service in Holland in 1940 and will doubtless be heard of again in civilian flying. Another machine of topical interest is the Airspeed Horsa I, a heavy glider transport which carries a crew of two and 25 troops and all their equipment, a valuable craft for invasion work.

Of the American machines it is noticeable that the 1943 list includes no fewer than 27 trainers of different types with three training gliders and—a little surprising—five biplanes. Details of the new type Fortress were not released in time for this book, but the Consolidated Liberators III and IV are included. Their normal bomb load is now eight 1,100-lb. bombs. The Liberator III is on service with the R.A.F. (Coastal Command); the IV was built by Fords. Other Americans of high reputation on this side here described are the Lightning, Mustang, Marauder and Avenger.

ENEMY planes include the Messerschmitt 109G (analogous to the Spitfire IX) and the 210, the latest twin-motor fighter, the Heinkel 177 (Germany's largest bomber before the Ju90 and delayed by the great Rostock raid), the Junkers 90 and 87D, the D.F.S. glider (shot down in dozens in Crete) and the very odd Blohm and Voss 138B flying boat.

**NEW GIANTS FOR OLD.** Aircraft are always being improved, as the book reviewed in this page amply demonstrates. Top right, the amphibian Catalina III, with a range of 3,750 miles, speed 185 m.p.h. at 10,000 ft., span 104 ft., bomb load 2,000 lb. Among a number enlarged or improved even since the book was published are the new Fortress II, B-17 G, carrying extra 1,000-lb. bombs, extra chin turret similar to the tail turret seen above, with two 0·5 machine-guns, span 103 ft. 9 in.; and (bottom right), the six-engined Me 323, largely used by the Germans in Tunisia and elsewhere for heavy transport; a cannon and tractor are being loaded into the plane.

*Photos, British Official; Associated Press*

THE New Year has found most people optimistic about the war coming to an end soon. Perhaps it is just as well they should be; it may help them to go cheerfully through whatever 1944 has up its sleeve for us. For myself, I like better to be prepared for the worst. If it doesn't happen, I've lost nothing; if it does, I am ready for it. No need to be gloomy, or even grim. Having "a heart for any fate" should not mean anticipating disaster, or even momentary set-backs. But I do find it hard sometimes to understand why people suppose peace is just round the corner at this stage. One acquaintance of mine explained that "we are all getting very tired of it." But he had no reply to my "So what?" Another quoted the result of a Gallup-poll. So many men and women had given their opinions as to how long it would last. It seems to me silly to take polls of that kind. If the popularity of a politician or the efficacy of a law is in question, some guidance as to public opinion can be obtained by asking all and sundry how they feel about it or what their experience has been. But no one on earth can offer an opinion worth anything on the duration of the war. No one, I repeat.

LETTERS from soldiers fighting in Italy speak with furious disgust of the Italian mud. Many of them complain that their ordinary service boots, with the small ankle-gaiters now in use, are quite unfit for squelching about in such conditions. The Americans appear to be better equipped. They have high boots which reach well above the knees. Surely somebody in the War Office might have known what autumn and winter are like in the Apennine country. Was it expected we should just rush through it and be in Rome well before Christmas? "The clerk of the weather" is apt to make us pay for that sort of optimism. Another advantage the Americans have over British troops out there is in army lorries. Ours get bogged often, the others very seldom. Here again there would seem to have been lack of foresight on somebody's part. "Somebody" ought to be made to suffer for it.

IN several pictures of famous men and reporters reproduced in newspapers lately the reporters have had notebooks and pencils in their hands. This is a change from the days when I was on a daily paper in Fleet Street. We should have been ashamed to show a notebook when we were interviewing anyone or conversing in a group with a public personage who had information to give us. In my experience a pencil is fatal to an interview. The interviewer is hampered by it; the interviewee is alarmed and begins at once to think "Shouldn't I be wiser to say nothing?" Talk must be free and without restraint or it will give very poor results. Not less ruinous to newspaper men's chances of getting a "story" is to surround the man who can, if he chooses, provide it and let him see that his very words are going to be taken down. He is reminded instantly of the proverb, "least said, soonest mended" and instead of talking easily in a friendly way, he becomes stilted and cautious. To advertise the fact that you are a reporter is the worst way to get news.

OF all the many wonders promised to us for "after the war" none is more attractive than those which are to be achieved (perhaps) by plastics. There was a wireless talk on the subject not long ago from which it appeared that this material for use in literally endless ways can be made from almost anything, and now an Australian, who owns a factory for making it, says the housing problem can be solved by it. Millions of people are going to want houses—in many parts of the world. Both labour and materials will be in short supply. If we stick to our old building methods, it will be a quarter of a century, so experts predict, before the deficiency is made up. Suppose we could, as this enterprising Australian suggests, have rooms stamped out with openings for doors or windows to be fitted, and then put together to form a dwelling, large or small as might

Adm. SIR BRUCE AUSTIN FRASER, G.C.B., K.B.E., renowned as the Navy's greatest gunner and authority on air-sea warfare. His appointment as C.-in-C. the Home Fleet was announced on March 23, 1943. Units under his command sank the German battleship Scharnhorst, for which he was promoted to G.C.B. See illus. page 519.
*Photo, British Official*

be required. Nothing could be simpler or quicker, or cheaper, for Mr. Milton says £200 would pay for a home with a living-room, two bedrooms, kitchen and bath, while half that sum would furnish it—in plastics too. It sounds like Paradise Regained !

QUEEN VICTORIA's first Prime Minister, Lord Melbourne, once said to his Cabinet after a discussion on some public matter of great interest at the moment: "Now, gentlemen, it doesn't matter what we say about this, but let's all say the same thing." We were told in one of the "B.B.C. Close-ups" that news announcers are trained to pronounce names of places in a uniform manner as near as possible to the way they are pronounced in the country where they are. But they do not all profit by this training. Some, for example, sound the G in Gomel and Mogilev on the Russian front, others make it an H, which is correct. There is not a G at the beginning of the one or in the middle of the other. The letter stands for a guttural H. Both Russians and people of other nationalities get mixed up over this. A ship's captain once greeted a friend of mine who was leaving Leningrad by ship for England with "Going for a goliday? Where's gusband?" It does not matter much how the B.B.C. announcers pronounce Russian words, but they should all do it the same way.

WHY a printing firm in Glasgow should be allowed to use paper for a large pamphlet on the subject of Regulation 18B, which is priced at a shilling, it is hard to understand. If paper is really needed urgently for munitions, as we are constantly told, this and many other purposes to which it is put can hardly be in the national interest. I don't like this regulation which suspends the Habeas Corpus Act and enables the Home Office to detain anybody without trial or accusation. I don't think anybody who believes in democracy likes it. But the more it is argued against, the more I feel it was, and may still be, indispensable to our war effort. The pamphlet is entitled It Might Have Happened to You, which is most misleading, for detention under this power has not happened to anybody who had not incurred suspicion in some way. Where Fascism is concerned, to be like Caesar's wife is the only sensible course—"above suspicion."

I HAVE been looking through some numbers of the 8th Army's weekly paper, called The Crusader, and amusing myself by noticing how small and very large issues are mixed up in its pages—quite rightly, for the journal has to appeal to many different interests. Complaints about the cigarettes supplied to the troops (which have been mentioned in Parliament) are next to articles on the post-war world. Demands for more and better chocolate are sandwiched between an explanation of the split among Yugoslav patriots and a report of Field-Marshal Smuts's speech which stirred up such heated controversy. A parachute officer urges the need for changes at home and begs soldiers to acquire the knowledge that will enable them to take part in making these wisely. A gunner pleads for the retention of many institutions and habits which are dear to him and many others. Letters about emigration from Britain are often printed. Some want to go to South Africa, others to Australia. The Crusader shows that men on active service find time to think a good deal on a wide variety of subjects.

IT may seem to some people almost frivolous that Paris, under German domination, with so many major woes to afflict the population, should be so much disturbed about not being able to enjoy its usual meat meals. But no one acquainted with the habits of Parisians will feel any surprise. French people do not habitually eat much meat, but their traditional lunch, an omelette and a cutlet, means a great deal to them. A cut off the joint they would not care about. The large, rather over-cooked steaks and chops, which used to be the staple fare in our restaurants and hotels, would scarcely appeal to them. But they were very fond of their dainty cutlets, lamb for choice. Once they could not imagine lunch without them. Now this dish is rarely seen, and the small round pieces of underdone steak on toast (tournedos) are even less frequently seen. Seven departments in what was Unoccupied France have been told by Vichy they must spare some of their meat, which is abundant, for the capital. But will they be likely to obey ?

# Crossing Monte Camino's Rugged Slopes

Photo, British Official: Crown Copyright

**A KEY HEIGHT ON THE ROAD TO ROME,** Monte Camino towered jaggedly before the 5th Army. But in a final grim assault the summit was successfully stormed. Following up this magnificent achievement the infantry, expert in mountain warfare, descended the western slope and took three villages and an important highway. It was announced on December 10, 1943, that both Monte Camino and Monte Maggiore had been cleared of the enemy. See story in page 505.

*Photo, British Official: Crown Copyright*

Printed in England and published every alternate Friday by the Proprietors, THE AMALGAMATED PRESS, LTD., The Fleetway House, Farringdon Street, London, E.C.4. Registered for transmission by Canadian Magazine Post. Sole Agents for Australia and New Zealand: Messrs. Gordon & Gotch, Ltd.; and for South Africa: Central News Agency, Ltd.—January 21, 1944. S.S. *Editorial Address:* JOHN CARPENTER HOUSE, WHITEFRIARS, LONDON, E.C.4.

Vol 7 · The War Illustrated · Nº 173

*Edited by Sir John Hammerton*

SIXPENCE

FEBRUARY 4, 1944

**GENERAL SIR BERNARD MONTGOMERY, K.C.B., D.S.O.,** surveys the shell-torn ruins of Fossacesia behind the Allied lines on the Italian front. Now in Britain in his new post of C.-in-C. of the British Group of Invasion Armies under General Eisenhower (announced on Dec. 24, 1943), he has handed over the Eighth Army, which he commanded in North Africa, Sicily and Italy from August 1942, to Lieut.-General Sir Oliver Leese (see illus. p. 554), one of his Corps Commanders.
*Photo, British Official*

NO. 174 WILL BE PUBLISHED FRIDAY, FEBRUARY 18

# Home Front Revisited by Our Roving Camera

SIR WILLIAM BEVERIDGE explains his social security plans, in a talk on "Security and Adventure," to schoolboys and girls at Central Hall, Westminster, London, on Jan. 5, 1944. The meeting, attended by more than 2,000, was arranged by the Council for Education on World Citizenship.

PUBLIC HEALTH emergency laboratory units are being established at strategic points in Britain to prevent, or combat, wartime epidemics. Bacteriologists and their staffs, complete with all necessary medical equipment, arrive speedily at the scene of operations.

U.S. ARMY TRANSPORTATION CORPS and British R.E.s work together (left) at this busy depot assembling vital rolling-stock for future military operations. Outcrop coal, to supplement mined supplies, so very necessary to the war effort, is obtained without shaft-sinking ; in Yorkshire it is being lifted by mechanical shovels (right) at the rate of thousands of tons a month. Airborne troops' supplies are contained in light hampers (in circle, above) specially manufactured for the purpose.

*Photos, New York Times Photos, Planet News, Central Press*

# THE BATTLE FRONTS

## by Maj.-Gen. Sir Charles Gwynn, K.C.B., D.S.O.

WHEN the Russians were approaching the Dnieper, I discussed (page 291) the question whether the Germans would attempt to hold the river as a winter defence line or only as an intermediate position pending further withdrawal. I thought, in view of the obvious objections to the Dnieper line that they would adopt the latter alternative, but apparently Hitler decided to insist on the former. The Dnieper position has been shattered, but the Germans are clinging obstinately to the fragments that remain—on the Upper Dnieper from Vitebsk to Zhlobin, on the Middle at Kanyev, and on the Lower from Nikopol to the Black Sea.

In the centre, Vatutin's offensive has driven them back well beyond the line on which I thought they might have established a winter front, and they have lost the only two lateral railways across the Pripet Marshes. The net result is that their front, previously overlong, has been greatly lengthened, and their northern and southern armies are separated by the marshes and are connected only by roundabout lateral communications. Their situation is, of course, still further worsened by the heavy losses they have sustained ; and by the fact that the considerable forces in the Crimea and on the Leningrad front on their flanks can exercise no influence on the major operations and make little demands on Russian resources.

Obviously, the general strategic situation is desperately unfavourable for the Germans, particularly on the southern half of their front. If they attempt to withdraw from the Dnieper bend now, while the ground is hard, they would be hotly pursued by the 3rd and 4th Ukrainian Armies at present facing them on the Dnieper ; while Koniev's 2nd and part of Vatutin's 1st armies could operate on the flanks of their retreat. Moreover, the main part of Vatutin's army threatens to close the avenue of retreat towards Poland and to interpose between that portion of von Manstein's southern armies which is attempting to keep the avenue to Poland open, and the portion which is still clinging to the Ukraine.

So far as I can judge, the Germans have only two hopes of escaping from their predicament without complete disaster. They may, on the one hand, hope to retain their positions in the Dnieper bend until the spring thaw, when Russian pursuit would be practically impossible, and when their possession of intact railways would still make a deliberate withdrawal practicable. In the meantime, they may hope that the momentum of the Russian offensive may be reduced by exhaustion of the troops and difficulty of maintaining supplies over ever-lengthening and indifferent communication lines.

Clearly, much depends on whether the spring thaw comes early, since that would shorten the critical period in which the Russian offensive must be checked or slowed down if a forced retreat is to be avoided.

The winter has so far been abnormally mild and this, it is said, is generally followed by an early spring. The other hope the Germans may have is that von Manstein will not only succeed in keeping open communication between the Ukraine and Poland, but may, if he can be strongly reinforced from central reserves, be able to throw back Vatutin's main offensive thrust and recover lost ground. If these are the German hopes it may be interesting to consider how far the course of events, since I last wrote a fortnight ago, suggest that they may be fulfilled.

At that time Vatutin's renewal of the offensive after the seven weeks of defensive battle in which he had fought von Manstein to exhaustion had only been in progress for a

**MOVES ON THE RUSSIAN FRONT, January 14, 1944, indicated by arrows.** Following the capture of Kalinkovichi and Mozyr, in White Russia, on that date, Soviet forces made a new twin thrust towards Pinsk, tearing apart the middle Pripet Marshes and the Zhlobin-Bobruisk supply line. On the Vinnitsa and Uman sectors battles of great violence were in progress. *By courtesy of The News Chronicle*

week. He had recovered Korosten and Zhitomir, and at Kasatin had cut one of the two railways from the Ukraine to Poland ; but the German stronghold of Berdichev, on the same line, appeared likely to be a formidable obstacle in his advance to the second. It was, however, soon apparent that Vatutin's offensive had amazing weight, despite the difficulty of its long lines of communication. His main front of attack extended over 100 miles, facing towards Shepetovka in the west and Vinnitsa in the south, thus threatening Berdichev in the centre with encirclement.

AFTER being driven out of Zhitomir, Manstein apparently retreated towards the south-west, presumably hoping to rally on the Shepetovka-Berdichev line where he might receive reinforcements from reserves in Poland. But this gave Vatutin the opportunity of outflanking Berdichev on the east ; resulting first in the capture of Kasatin and, later, to the outflanking of Vinnitsa. On Jan. 5 Berdichev itself was captured by storm, and by the middle of the month the Russians were getting close to Shepetovka

on the right, and had by-passed Vinnitsa on the left, reaching the line of the Upper Bug. Here they were only some 20 miles distant from Zhmerinka on the last railway between the Ukraine and Poland.

MEANWHILE, however, von Manstein had received substantial reinforcements and, fighting stubbornly, was able to slow down the advance of the Russians towards Shepetovka and south of Berdichev ; while counter-attacking fiercely, though without much success, their salient east of Vinnitsa. His counter-attacks, however, seem to be defensive in character and there are no signs that he has been sufficiently reinforced to stage another large-scale counter-offensive. The ranks of his depleted units have no doubt been refilled and his losses of tanks made good from depots in Poland ; but it seems improbable that he can have been given a sufficient number of divisions from the German central reserve to enable him to embark on ambitious operations. It is very doubtful whether, in fact, the Germans still have as strong a central reserve as they are sometimes credited with.

Vatutin, in addition to his main drive, has been able with his right wing to attack westwards along the south side of the Pripet Marshes, and, by capturing Sarny, has cut the second railway across them. This is an important success which must greatly add to von Manstein's difficulties ; and it has been made all the more important by Rokossovsky's capture of Mozyr ; for the two armies can now co-operate closely and threaten the important centre of Pinsk.

It would seem that von Manstein is under such heavy pressure from Vatutin's main force and right wing that he has little prospect of saving Vinnitsa or of keeping the railway through Zhmerinka open indefinitely. It is evident that Vatutin has immense forces at his disposal, for he has been able with his left wing to strike south, in yet a third direction in order to co-operate with Koniev's army against the German pocket on the Middle Dnieper at Kanyev. After capturing Byelaya Tserkov this thrust has made rapid progress, cutting all direct railway connexions between the Middle Dnieper and the Polish frontier while, at the same time, Koniev, after capturing Kirovograd and inflicting a heavy defeat on the Germans there, threatens to cut the railway from Smyela to Odessa.

THE Germans in the pocket are obviously in a desperately precarious position although a counter-attack in the Uman region has temporarily relieved the situation. Their withdrawal or annihilation would enable Koniev and Vatutin to advance on a long front to the Bug, threatening the line of retreat of the armies behind the lower Dnieper to an extent that would almost certainly entail their early withdrawal. Incidentally, the elimination of the Middle Dnieper pocket would open a new line of communication for the Russians through their Cherkasy bridgehead, which would help greatly to maintain the momentum of an advance to the Bug. It would seem that neither of the suggested hopes the Germans may have is likely to be fulfilled, and that they will be in still greater trouble before the spring thaw gives them a respite.

# In Mud and Misery German Grenadiers Retreat

**WAR-TIDE IN RUSSIA FLOWS AT LOW EBB** for Germany's vaunted panzer grenadiers (below) clinging to a mud-clogged tracked car in retreat from the Nevel front, which commenced early in October 1943. In victorious contrast is the Soviet cavalryman (top) in camouflage-cloak and armed with automatic carbine ; Cossacks were the first to cross the Polish 1939 frontier, on Jan. 4, 1944, in advance of infantry and mechanized divisions of Vatutin's First Ukrainian Army.

*Photos, Planet News, New York Times Photos*

# Rapidly Vatutin Moves the East Front West

**' THE EAST FRONT IS COMING NEARER HOME ! '** wailed a Wehrmacht spokesman in a broadcast on Jan. 12, 1944, on which day the Soviet First Ukrainian Army under General Nikolai Federovitch Vatutin striking westward along snowy roads (1) on an 80-mile front into Poland captured the large railway junction and important German stronghold of Sarny. Germans surrender to a Russian outpost (3) ; two camouflaged enemy machine-gunners use tracer bullets by night (2) against a Russian advanced position.

*Photos, Planet News, Pictorial Press*

# THE WAR AT SEA

## by Francis E. McMurtrie

ONE of the secrets of the success with which the Scharnhorst was first repelled, kept within reach and finally engaged and sunk, is now known to have been very careful advance planning by the Commander-in-Chief of the Home Fleet and his staff. Every possibility was taken into consideration, and the various ships concerned in the action had all rehearsed, in a series of exercises, the parts they were likely to play. In these rehearsals one of our own ships acted as though she were a German attempting an attack on a convoy. H.M.S. Jamaica, it is stated, was the dummy Scharnhorst in one of the most recent of these exercises, and carried out manoeuvres very similar to those of the German battleship on

been sunk, as the Soviet Navy claims that a ship believed to be a cruiser was destroyed in the Gulf of Finland a couple of years ago.

THERE are also the battleship Gneisenau, of 26,000 tons, sister to the sunk Scharnhorst, and the aircraft carrier Graf Zeppelin. When last seen the Gneisenau was undergoing complete reconstruction, as the internal damage done by Allied bombing at Brest and by a torpedo hit on passage from there to Germany was very extensive. Owing to shortage of material, it is believed that such of the Gneisenau's equipment as had remained intact was taken from her to replace corresponding gear which had been destroyed or damaged in the Scharnhorst, in order that

1940-41. (See illustration in p. 134, Vol. 2.) What is the reason for this concentration of the heavier German warships in the Baltic ? Possibly the success of British midget submarines in penetrating such a remote anchorage as the Altenfjord may have had something to do with it ; but the governing factor may well be the desire of the German Army, which carries much more weight than the Navy in the counsels of the High Command, to have under its control a sufficient reserve of naval material to counterbalance anything the Russians may bring out from Kronstadt in the spring.

At present the Baltic is frozen up, and ships can only get out of port with the aid of powerful icebreakers. In March the ice should begin to melt, by which time the German armies may well be retreating through Estonia and Latvia, with the Soviet forces pressing them hard. Their flank would then be exposed to attacks from the Red Fleet if the latter were not faced with serious opposition at sea ; and it would be possible for guerilla forces to be landed in the rear of the retreating Germans.

So far as is known, the Soviet fleet at Kronstadt includes two old battleships, the Marat and Oktiabrskaya Revolutia ; a heavy cruiser, the Petropavlovsk, acquired from Germany early in 1940 and possibly still incomplete ; and two or three cruisers of the 8,500-ton Kirov class. Many destroyers, submarines, motor-torpedo-boats and minesweepers should also be available.

Doubtless the Germans may consider their two old coast defence ships, the Schlesien and Schleswig-Holstein, of 13,040 tons, to be worth using in support of military operations. Though they are nearly 38 years old, their armour is still sound, and they mount four 11-in. and ten 5·9-in. guns. They are inferior on paper to the Marat and Oktiabrskaya Revolutia, which are 10,000 tons heavier, and mount twelve 12-in. guns each as main armament.

IN the meantime, a third naval Power in the Baltic is taking no chances of being caught napping in the event of war touching her territory. This is Sweden, a neutral whose sympathies earlier in the war seemed

PACKED WITH GERMAN SURVIVORS from the Bay of Biscay action on Dec. 28, 1943, when three of a total force of 11 enemy destroyers were sunk by the cruisers H.M.S. Glasgow and Enterprise, a lifeboat heads for the rescue ship. Aircraft of Coastal Command, first to spot the enemy force, took part in the action, and it was from an Australian-manned Sunderland that this photograph was taken. On the previous day a 5,000-ton enemy blockade-runner was sunk by a Liberator. See also p. 532.
*Photo, British Official : Crown Copyright*

December 26. Thus when the real operation had to be carried out, every move was made with such precision that the action is likely to go down in naval history as a model of its kind. (See story in p. 570 ; also pp. 518-520.)

THERE are now no German ships of any size in Norwegian waters, except the 40,000-ton Tirpitz, which is lying crippled in the Altenfjord. There she is guarded against air attack by the 46-year-old Norwegian coast defence ships Harald Haarfagre and Tordenskjold, which the Germans have renamed Thetis and Nymphe respectively, and rearmed with high-angle guns of various calibres.

All the other enemy warships of any importance that were formerly in the Altenfjord and other Norwegian anchorages appear to have returned to the Baltic. They include the 10,000-ton "pocket battleships" Admiral Scheer and Lützow (the latter is believed to have been damaged by torpedo attack from our midget submarines in September), the 10,000-ton cruisers Admiral Hipper and Prinz Eugen, and the smaller cruisers Nürnberg, Leipzig, Köln and Emden, of which little has been heard for a long time. It is possible, indeed, that one of them may have

the latter might sooner be made ready for sea. Thus the Scharnhorst was partly composed of material removed from her sister ship.

As for the Graf Zeppelin, it is rumoured that she has been disarmed in order that her guns may be utilized for other purposes. When this ship was launched, her design was acclaimed by admirers of Germany as superior to anything built by the Allies. The extensive range of her armament, which included no fewer than sixteen 5·9-in. guns, ten of 4·1-in. calibre and twenty-two of 37 mm., was extolled as being superior to that of most cruisers, so that she would be better able to defend herself against surface vessels than other ships of her category. In fact, it was merely a proof that the Germans were inexperienced in aircraft carrier design, for a carrier's own aircraft are her best defence against other ships, and any guns except high-angle ones merely add weight and occupy valuable space without conferring any corresponding advantage. It was for this reason that the 8-in. guns formerly carried as primary armament by the U.S. aircraft carriers Saratoga and Lexington were removed when those ships were refitted in

likely to be attracted more by Germany. Nazi cruelty in Norway and Denmark has now produced a great change in Swedish feeling, and the swing-round has even affected the amount of iron ore which Germany is being permitted to purchase from the Grangesberg mines this year. The Royal Swedish Navy today comprises seven coast defence ships of between 3,400 and 7,300 tons ; one fairly modern cruiser and one older, but modernized ; 21 modern destroyers ; two minelayers ; 28 submarines ; and a considerable number of torpedo-boats, minesweepers and smaller craft. This efficient little fleet would be a hard nut for even the German Navy to tackle, now that the latter has suffered so many losses. Under construction are two cruisers and two large destroyers.

FROM a reply to a question in Parliament, it seems that Spain is being asked to release a number of Italian ships which have been lying idle in Spanish harbours for a considerable time past. Being merchant vessels, their case is quite different from that of the cruiser Attilio Regolo, which, together with three or four smaller craft, was interned last September at Mahon, in the island of Minorca.

# How Mighty Duke of York Prepared for Victory

BEFORE HER GREAT TRIUMPH in the Scharnhorst battle, Dec. 26, 1943 (see pp. 518-520 and 570), H.M.S. Duke of York refits in dry-dock. Prior to smashing the German battleship, she carried Admiral Sir Bruce Fraser, C.-in-C. Home Fleet, on a good will visit to Vice-Admiral Golovko, C.-in-C. Soviet Northern Fleet. It was the first occasion on which a Home Fleet flagship had entered a Russian harbour. The Vice-Admiral and his officers were profoundly impressed during their tour of inspection of this colossal ship of war.      PAGE 551      *Photo, Keystone*

# He Sails With 10,000 Lives Dependent on Him

The liner-turned-troop-transport carries multitudes of battle-trained men over the seas to reinforce our armies or take part in invasion plans. Its master is numbered among the finest seamen in the world, and CAPT. FRANK H. SHAW further describes him as "the man who has forgotten what peaceful sleep is—who eats his meals on the bridge." See also facing page.

THE man with most responsibility in the whole Merchant Navy is the master of a big troop-carrying transport. His task requires almost superhuman ability and courageous resourcefulness. A ship of the Queen Mary type is a big enough responsibility for any one individual even in peacetime, when there is a staff trained to a hair to share the burden with the man on the bridge; his chief concern then is to keep the passengers safe and entertained.

Now he is required to carry some ten thousand human beings, each man a highly-trained soldier, through seas full of death

may fall or a torpedo skim across his course. Naturally, the big transport is heavily armed. She bristles with guns of every kind, from lean 6-in. pieces capable of fighting-off a light cruiser or a pack of destroyers, to high-angle "Chicago pianos" for dealing with diving aircraft. The defence of his ship against all forms of attack is the captain's affair. He has to save his packed masses of efficient manhood by every possible means.

The Navy might keep down the U-boat packs by distant attack; the R.A.F. might lend a useful hand, not only against submarines but against air-assaults; but there

are completely unfamiliar with the geography of a ship, no matter what theoretical embarkation training they have had. There is an inevitable mêlée, each unit's commanders demanding the best accommodation and special favours. The captain has to behave like Solomon at his best to placate hot, hurried warriors. He also has to see that meals are arranged for, well in advance. Long before the last drafts are up the gangway the first-comers are starving with hunger. The men, already trained to a hair, must be kept fighting-fit, and in the long run the captain, through his staff, is entirely responsible.

Although there is an O.C. Troops with staff aboard, the actual discipline, as affecting the ship's routine and safety, is the captain's affair. If there are "crimes" he must arrange for the detention of the defaulters, and that they get adequate exercise; also that they are not overlooked if disaster comes.

MORE than likely the transport will proceed out of convoy, perhaps even without an escort, relying on her speed to outpace U-boats or surface-raiders. She is a target for every form of enemy frightfulness, and the captain must steer courses that keep him clear of trouble. If his cruiser escort lags, or fails through engine-trouble, he must go on alone, with added responsibility. Even with the most trustworthy officers this burden is hard to bear; the main strain rests on his shoulders

There are so many things to be considered. Sanitation and bathing facilities—probably the ship's swimming-pool is now functioning as an ammunition magazine; such trifles as forbidding the whole complement to rush to this side or that if a strange object is sighted, for such a sudden alteration of weight might affect his ship's stability; adequate boat-drill, so that, if hit fatally, the ship can be abandoned in orderly fashion with a minimum of human loss. These are only a few of his responsibilities.

Although the actual invasion may be carried on by invasion-barges and light craft when

**FIGHTING MEN ARE NOW HER PASSENGERS.** The Queen Mary, Britain's 81,235-ton peacetime luxury liner, speed 30 knots, now in drab war-paint and heavily armed, has been transporting Allied troops to battle-fronts throughout the world. In pre-war days she twice won the Blue Riband for the fastest Atlantic crossing, in 1936 and again in 1938.

*Photo, Associated Press*

and danger, and land them at an arranged destination in condition fit, if necessary, for instant battle-service. His ship has lost its sleek beauty. She is now purely utilitarian. Handsome panelling is either torn down or screened against damage; the ameliorations of sea-life are forgotten until the war ends and civilization regains its sanity.

The transport captain's main responsibility in war is not only his ship. The result of a battle might well depend upon him; for if his human freight is not delivered to schedule defeat might result. The Royal Navy and the R.A.F. give the trooper protection; but the enemy spares no effort to destroy it. Speed alone cannot be of much aid; the maximum speed of the ship is some thirty knots, whilst that of an Axis bombing plane may well be almost 300 m.p.h. Ability to manoeuvre with lightning-like promptness is one of the main qualities of such a shipmaster—a veteran of the sea with an acquired intuition which tells him just when a bomb

is always the odd chance of the enemy eluding such defences or desperately driving through them to concentrate on the big, packed ship whose value in the war-effort may not be estimated. Think of it—10,000 men complete with equipment, stores and ammunition, sent to the bottom at one blow.

WITHOUT in any way belittling the courage and efficiency of every Merchant Navy captain under war conditions, full marks must in fairness go to the cool, resourceful man on the ex-liner's bridge—the man who has forgotten what peaceful sleep is, who seldom sits to a meal but eats it from a tray on the bridge whilst keeping every faculty alert for the unforeseen contingency. Ten thousand men look to him for continued existence, for a chance to prove themselves heroes. He dare not let them down.

When troops first embark the ship becomes a bear-garden. Most of her new passengers

the real issue arises, the transport must naturally enter the danger-zone, and the nearer she can attain to the enemy coast the more valuable is her service; for her high speed helps in that element of surprise which is so essential in modern war. The nearer her approach the greater her risk, as she comes in range of dive-bombing attacks, which, until the Air Forces gain supremacy, are bound to be fierce and frequent.

The successful outcome of our invasion plans has been due in large measure to the skill, courage and endurance of the masters of Merchant Navy transports. The finest merchant seamen in the world are in command of these leviathans. They have been trained to face any eventuality with coolness and skill, for new circumstances are bound to arise with every new adventure and split-second decisions must oft be made and acted upon. The world owes more than is realized to her merchant shipmasters—not only to feed and equip the world but also to save it.

# In an Allied Troopship Bound for Distant Battle

ARE WE DOWNHEARTED ? Cheerful warriors provide the answer as the packed troopship (4) moves off on her long voyage. Excitement of departure subsided, a sergeant (1) takes the first opportunity to squat on his kitbag and write a letter home. On the High Seas, ship's surgeon and hospital staff (3) carry out an urgent operation. An operation of a very different kind is Crossing the Line : a nurse (2) receives King Neptune's boisterous attentions. See also facing page.

*Photos, British Official ; Crown Copyright ; Topical Press*

# House by House Ortona Fell to Monty's Men

DEEP MUD NOTWITHSTANDING, 8th Army guns in Italy (5) softened-up the Ortona defences preliminary to tanks and infantry gaining entrance to the town (1). Prolonged street-fighting followed (2). Well wrapped up against the bitter weather in warm comforts from Home (3), our men completed mopping-up operations by Dec. 28, 1943. Successor to the 8th's beloved General Sir Bernard Montgomery, Lieut.-General Sir Oliver Leese (4) assumed command in Italy on Dec. 30, 1943. See Ortona story in page 569.

*Photos. British and Canadian Official*

# Fighting France Beats Nazis on Italian Soil

**VETERANS OF THE TUNISIAN CAMPAIGN,** French troops now on the 5th Army front in Italy have scored important successes, notably the capture of Acquafondata and San Elia, announced on Jan. 15 and Jan. 18, 1944, respectively. Great skill in mountain warfare earned them these triumphs in the difficult northern sector. General Clark, 5th Army Commander, commenting on these achievements in a message to General Giraud, stated: " Every day the French forces under General Juin are adding a new glorious page to their distinguished record." PAGE 555 *Photo, British Official*

# Planning to Regain the Key to the Orient

First step towards fulfilment of the recent Cairo Conference decisions (see p. 499) for the liberation of all territory occupied by Japan during a 50-year period of aggression is the reconquest of Burma, cornerstone of Japan's illgotten empire. A Special Correspondent throws light on the tasks confronting Lord Louis Mountbatten as Supreme Allied Commander S.E. Asia. See also facing page.

OCCUPYING a highly strategic position in the Far East, the reconquest of Burma, the Key to the Orient, will be the first Allied objective on the Asiatic mainland. For this purpose, powerful land and air forces are concentrated in India, and strong naval units in Ceylon, possibly in preparation for operations against the Nicobar and Andaman Is. Though simultaneous attacks may be carried out against the Burmese-Javan arc of islands, the main task of Lord Louis Mountbatten is the conquest of Burma and the opening of the Burma Road. With Burma once again under the control of the Allies, not only would the Chinese armies be able to receive heavy equipment and other vital war material in quantity, but Japan's position in South Eastern Asia would become extremely precarious. From Burma thrusts could be developed into Siam and French Indo-China which would completely paralyze the enemy's hold on the Indies and Malaya.

The immediate problem confronting the South-East Asia Command, then, is the wresting of Burma from the Japanese. Separated from India by jungle-covered mountain ranges and the Bay of Bengal, the reconquest of Burma will be a hard task. As a result, the offensive against the Japanese in Burma will have to be launched from more than one direction and across more than one element. From Assam and Manipur overland thrusts into Northern and Upper Burma can be expected, coupled with naval landings along the west coast and in Lower Burma.

ALREADY, American trained Chinese troops have forced their way into Northern Burma. In their wake a motor road known as the Tokyo Road is being constructed. This runs from the railhead of Ledo in Assam and crosses the Patkai Range into the Hukong Valley, jade mine district of Burma. The Chinese intend to link this road with the Burma Road at Paoshan, running via Maingkwan, Myitkyina and Tengchung (Tengyueh). Another important road has recently been built from the Indian State of Manipur towards the Chindwin Valley. These roads are likely to be the most important invasion routes in Upper Burma.

However, as the Burmese west coast is shut off from the interior of Burma by the Arakan Yoma mountain range, Rangoon, which is the gateway to Burma and the Burma Road, is the most important objective in the country. Thus, for the Allies it is desirable that landings from the sea should be carried out as near as possible to the Burmese capital of Rangoon, situated on the Irrawaddy Delta. But landings on the Delta with its mangrove swamps would be difficult.

Further, with the Japanese still in full control of the naval and air bases in the Andaman Islands, attempts to land men and material on the Delta without first gaining control of the Andamans may prove to be hazardous. Therefore efforts to seize

these islands, just over a hundred miles away from the Burmese coast and some 900 miles away from Ceylon, may first be made. With the Andamans in the hands of the United Nations landings could also be made near Moulmein. This would enable the Allies to cut Japanese overland communications with Siam running across the Dawna Range through the Kawkareik Pass.

At present most of the land activity on the

BURMA FRONT. Reopening of the Burma Road would enable vital war supplies to reach Chinese armies. Meantime, Chinese troops are building the Tokyo Road, from Ledo railhead, Assam, across the Patkai Range into the Hukong Valley, eventually to link up with the Burma Road. See also illus. page 464. *Specially drawn for THE WAR ILLUSTRATED*

Burmese war zone is confined to the Arakan front. Though the Burmese coastal province of Arakan is not strategically vital to the forces of the United Nations, that is if a direct landing can be effected in the neighbourhood of Rangoon, control of Arakan with its important air base and capacious harbours at Akyab and Kyaukpyu would nevertheless be of great advantage. Its occupation would pave the way for a thrust into the heart of the country. The 100 mile long Taungup-Padaung motor road, across the Arakan Yoma mountain range via the Taungup Pass linking the Burmese west coast with the Irrawaddy Valley, has been greatly improved by the Japanese, who have been using it as the main supply route for their forces in Arakan. They are, however,

now finding it increasingly difficult to move traffic freely owing to the frequent Anglo-U.S. air attacks on supply dumps near Taungup and on motor convoys along the Taungup-Prome road itself. As proved in last winter's campaign, the Arakan coastal strip can only be successfully occupied by combined sea and land operations. Thus, landings along the Burmese west coast, near Taungup in particular, may be made with a view to a drive into the interior through the Taungup Pass.

REALIZING that Burma will be the first Allied objective on the Asiatic mainland, the Japanese High Command have also been making military preparations to counter the Allied threat. Improvement of communications in and between the countries her armies have occupied seems to be the essential feature of Japanese preparations. Though the Shanghai-Singapore rail link is still an ambitious dream, Burma has definitely been connected with Siam by a good military road running through the Kawkareik Pass, while the Rangoon-Bangkok railway on which British prisoners of war have been put to work is still under construction. The projected railway is to run from the southern Burmese rail terminus of Yé, 220 miles south of Rangoon, through the Three Pagodas Pass. Recently large stocks of material which the Nipponese had accumulated at Thanbyuzayat, south of Moulmein, for the construction of the Rangoon-Bangkok railroad, were bombed by the United States Tenth Air Force operating from airfields in India.

Japanese military preparations in Burma, therefore, have not been allowed to continue unhindered. Throughout the monsoons, U.S and British Air Forces incessantly bombed railway connexions and dock installations including key bridges like the 3,940 feet long Ava Bridge near Mandalay, which is the main link in the rail connexion between Lower Burma and the regions threatened by the forces of the United Nations from Assam.

DESPITE difficulties, the Japanese have been steadily reinforcing their forces in Burma under the command of Lieutenant-General Matakasu Kawabé. According to Chinese reports the strength of the Japanese army in Burma is put at ten divisions, with reserves in Siam and Indo-China, while a large proportion of the Nipponese Air Force is based on Chiengmai in Siam. Thus the fight against the Japanese in Burma will be hard, but everything is being done to ease the lot of our men engaged. For example, British troops fighting in Arakan are now getting fresh wholemeal bread, supplies reaching the most advanced positions every 24 hours from field bakeries set up at strategic points and staffed by bakers of the R.I.A.S.C. From these working depots the bread, baked in clay ovens, is distributed to strong-points in the jungle hills overshadowing the main battle fronts. Mobile canteens penetrate even the jungle trails, see photograph on opposite page.

# Our 14th Army is Now on the Move in Burma

**WITH THE RECAPTURE OF MAUNGDAW,** Burma key-point 60 miles up the coast from Akyab, by the 14th Army (reported on Jan. 11, 1944), and advances on the central part of the Burmese front, Cairo Conference decisions are being implemented. A British advanced post (4) menaces Japanese patrols; communication is by field telephone (3); an officer seeking unit identifications (1) scrutinizes articles from Japanese casualties. Freight train (2) is shot up by a Beaufighter. Convoy men (5) stop for tea at a mobile canteen.

*Photos, British and Indian Official*

# Maps for Battles to Come Prepared at Top Speed

Army cartographers not only record hour-to-hour changes in the battle zones for the information of our commanders; they plot the ground where future battles are likely to be fought. In this article HARRIMAN DICKSON outlines the astonishing organization which has contributed so greatly to our successes in the field and which is indispensable for the achievement of victories to come.

Tucked away behind G.H.Q. in Italy are a handful of trucks which, but for their very elaborate camouflage, might pass unnoticed by the casual visitor. The camouflage experts spent some time on the job. It was a particularly vital one. For from these trucks come up-to-the-minute maps which go straight to the front-line troops. In previous wars you studied your map at leisure, several days before the battle. Today maps are issued with the same high speed and efficiency as newspapers.

A big offensive is about to begin. Reconnaissance planes get pictures of the enemy's forward areas. They show considerable changes of gun positions, minefields and trenches. The information is rushed back to the Mapping Unit, who are specially equipped to deal with stop-press details. All the alterations in the German dispositions are quickly recorded on fresh maps. Then the printing machines begin to turn over. They are capable of printing thousands of maps in several colours, and they can complete a full-scale job in a few hours.

Four hours after receipt of details of the new enemy dispositions, brand-new maps are leaving the Mapping Unit again for dispatch to the fighting forces. Tank commanders, ready to go into action, get their copies. Commandos, about to launch a surprise attack, see from the new and revised map that they must switch their area of operations. It may mean hundreds of men spared from annihilation. Certainly hundreds of casualties are saved through this service. The Germans have a very healthy respect for our map-making units. On at least three occasions they have issued to their own men copies of our maps taken from prisoners.

The British staffs of the mapping units are highly specialized men who know every trick and turn of the "trade." Their work does not stop between battles; a lull in the fighting may give them more work than ever, for the enemy begins to change his dispositions during the lull, and our experts have to survey and prepare maps of the area which looks like being the next centre of fighting. There are several map-making units at the battle fronts, and on occasion they come in for their full share of actual warfare. The map-making unit in France had a warm time during the Dunkirk operations, and in the North African campaign a unit was strafed from the air for several hours. Map-making is not the easiest thing to do under fire. The ground may heave under you, just as you are touching - in the most tricky corner of, say, the toe of Italy, but as every moment is vital there must be no letting-up.

It has long been recognized in military circles that if your maps are more accurate and up-to-date than the enemy's, then you start the battle with a distinct advantage over him. The battle of Alamein was clear evidence of this; our maps of the enemy's lines were astonishingly complete. Every battery was carefully marked. Officers knew just where the trouble would start. Similarly, the infantry had close-ups of minefields ahead and knew just how to enter them. Those maps were not only very detailed and accurate, they were completed only three days before the battle began. Thousands of them were then rushed through the printing presses of the Eighth Army Survey Units into the hands of front-line troops.

The number of maps required for any major operation today gives some idea of the scope of the map-making units. For the invasion of Sicily, over 3,500,000 maps were printed. In Italy that number has probably been doubled. The Sicilian maps were prepared from large numbers of air photographs taken of the coast defences. They had to be flown to Cairo, printed and flown back to the invasion Armies; and these maps showed every one of the details taken only three or four days before.

The basic maps required by our forces in the Mediterranean are prepared by the Army Survey Directorate in Cairo. They also produce the maps and charts for the Navy and the R.A.F. More than 2,000 men are employed day and night translating every new move on the battle fronts into mapping terms. Beginning, sometimes, with a few scrawled lines set down on paper by a lance-corporal, they produce, in a few hours, a beautifully coloured map, complete in every detail. And that map may influence the whole course of a new campaign. Issues are not confined to overseas forces, of course. During one month alone—November 1943—no less than 1,031,776 maps were issued by the Army Survey Department to troops stationed in the United Kingdom.

MOBILE MAP-PRODUCING UNIT equipped to accompany a main body of troops. It comprises a printing press, with personnel of surveyors, cartographers and draughtsmen skilled in rapid and accurate production of entirely new maps or the last-minute improvement of existing ones for speedy issue in the field. *Photo, Fox*

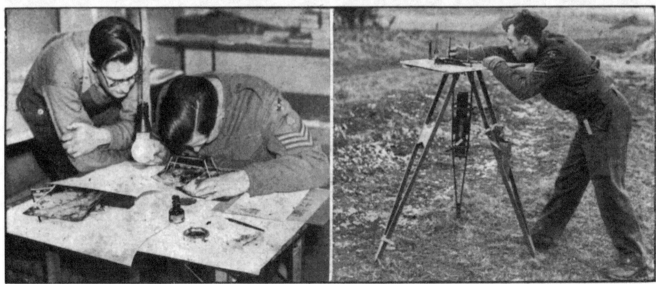

FROM AERIAL PHOTOGRAPHS studied through a magnifying glass (left) army experts prepare data for a new map. A Royal Engineers surveyor (right) uses his plane instruments to make an accurate land survey. Combination of these air and land efforts makes possible a minutely detailed map of any given area not actually in enemy hands or under fire. Panorama photographs of enemy-held territory are naturally lacking in certain details, which can be determined only from ground level.

*Photos, Fox*

## *No Enemy Bombs Will Fall on the Reich!*

Thus Goering boasted to the German people. The weapon the Nazis used so ruthlessly against defenceless cities and hamlets has been turned against them, and no capital in the world has suffered such devastation as Berlin. Between the start of the Battle of Berlin, Nov. 18, 1943, and Dec. 16, six major raids resulted in complete destruction of 1,300 acres of buildings; in four later raids 5,000 tons were dropped. Here, at the Brandenburg Gate, women prepare to serve food to the bombed-out.

### As the Hour of Final Reckoning Nears—

The strains of a Nazi military band (1) marching down Berlin's bombed Unter Den Linden, past debris at the corner of Friedrich Strasse, may or may not cheer the sinking hearts of those quaking under shattering blows from Britain. From the tubes, night-shelterers emerge (2), and queue for water—the R.A.F. having cut off the main supply—from an old street-fountain erected in pre-mains days (3). A wrecked shoe shop (4) announces that business will be conducted in the basement.

Photos

## —From 'Europe's Aircraft Carrier' Britain

With Gestapo chiefs and high Nazi officials in attendance, Goering strives to infuse hope into the homeless (6); not their homes but war factories of the Reich were the R.A.F. objectives. In the Wittenbergplatz district (5) of Berlin demolition squads have been active. Foreign workers and war-prisoners are no longer set to this task; as bombing rises to a climax they are worked still harder in the factories. The labour of clearing-up now falls compulsorily upon the bombed-out.

## Berlin's Evacuees Wait—and Wonder

Photo, Keystone

Fervently they hope the present peace of the East Prussian countryside where they and their belongings are lined up to await transport to an unspecified destination will not be shattered.    They are leaving for good, they trust, the panic atmosphere and acute food problems of the capital and other big towns, intensified now by the inadequacy of rail and lorry traffic to such an extent that tens of thousands of bombed-out civilians stand perforce in long queues for hours for doled-out soup.

# VIEWS & REVIEWS Of Vital War Books

*by Hamilton Fyfe*

WE have not heard nearly as much about General MacArthur, now in command of all military forces engaged against Japan in the S.W. Pacific, with his headquarters in Australia, as we have about the war leaders on this side of the world. There is a vivid and most heartening sketch of him in Mr. Clark Lee's book, They Call It Pacific (John Long, 12s. 6d.), a freshly-observed and largely new account of the loss of the Philippines by the U.S.

MacArthur was made responsible for their defence, but he was not given anything like the materials or the men to put up adequate resistance to the furious Japanese onslaught. But he certainly made the most effective use of the means he had at his disposal. Above all he inspired his men. "He never allowed himself the luxury of letting down," which means that he never relaxed ("letting down" with us has a different meaning).

He always kept his shoulders back and his chin at a fighting angle. He always looked serenely confident, even at the blackest moments. He spoke to privates always with a word of praise or cheer, as readily as he spoke to the members of his staff. His hair grew long, but his trousers retained their crease and his shoes their polish. It was part of his code to keep them that way.

He thinks of warfare, Mr. Lee says, in terms of offence. He plans to strike blows, not to parry them. He never thinks, "as some commanders did, in terms of what he might lose." The French generals especially were obsessed by fear of losses.

MacArthur's orderly and personal servant, a Filipino and a good soldier, as most of the Filipino troops are, in the author's opinion, says of him he is "always in tip-top condition, walks, walks, walks constantly, does callisthenics, no drinks. Always leaves parties at 11 p.m." He is "a soldier and a man of culture, whom some men hate because he is both prophet and poet and a master of the English language, who can tell you the details of every great battle in history, whose incisive brain and great military knowledge," Mr. Lee suggests, "ought to have been employed in planning great battles, massing hundreds of thousands of men and thousands of tanks and planes, to attack, not to defend."

MR. LEE charges his country with having failed the Filipinos as Britain is blamed for losing Singapore and the Dutch Government is considered to have left Java and Sumatra without proper protection. "We told them we were big and strong and powerful and would take care of them, and they believed us." But when the Japs attacked there were not enough men to make that boast good. "Gen. MacArthur did not have even enough troops to hold an unbroken line across the fifteen-mile-wide peninsula of Bataan and he had to leave part of the mountainous area in the centre undefended. The Japs quickly found that out."

As for air defence, there was almost none. The principal military airfield was bombed while "the pilots had come down to eat and to refuel their planes all together, instead of a few at a time." The machines were caught on the ground and destroyed, "lined up in straight rows and not dispersed, because our fliers had not had any experience and did not understand the necessity for dispersal. Underground hangars were being built, but were not yet finished. Radio detecting equipment was inadequate." So the Americans suffered "one of the most crushing blows in the whole Philippines campaign." The enemy was able to bomb undisturbed. "Why doesn't our Air Force knock them out?" the Americans in Manila and elsewhere kept on asking each other. They only learned afterwards there was no Air Force to do it.

That undoubtedly made the Japanese programme of Asia for the Asiatics appeal to the Filipinos more than it would have done

## MacArthur of the Unpacific Pacific

if the United States had kept its promise to defend them with its might and power. "Such a programme," a shrewd Filipino told Mr. Lee, "has a terrific pull for lots of Oriental people." He pointed out that the Americans and the natives of the islands lived in two different worlds, and "so long as Americans insist on living in their own and keeping us in ours, the spiritual and psychological differences between us will continue to exist and to grow deeper. And if America doesn't send us help, who knows . . .?"

But America will send help. MacArthur

**GENERAL DOUGLAS MacARTHUR, hero of Corregidor, victor of the Bismarck Sea battle, Allied Supreme Commander in the S.W. Pacific since March 1942. He is responsible for directing Allied thrusts against the Japanese in New Guinea and the Solomons. A vivid sketch of this 63-years-old campaigner is given in the book reviewed here.**
PAGE 563                                        *Photo, Pictorial Press*

has made up his mind to go back to the Philippines and he can return only as conqueror. He knows all the obstacles. He does not underrate them. "The Jap is a first-class fighting man," the General says. "Their troops facing me on Bataan may not have been as good as the best troops in the (First) World War, but it would take the best troops to beat them.

"THEIR officers spend lives heedlessly, even for unimportant objectives. The individual Jap is a fanatic. He will throw himself on a land mine to explode it and clear the way for others. He will fling himself on barbed wire and let those following him climb over his body." A Japanese general said his country's rulers were prepared to lose ten million men in the Pacific war. Consequently Gen. MacArthur's view is, "The only way for America to win is to kill Japs, kill more Japs, and kill still more Japs." Not a pleasant prospect for either side !

MacArthur knows why the Japs drove the U.S. and Great Britain and the Netherlands out of the Far East and conquered a vast and rich empire containing all the natural resources needed to make Japan the world's most powerful nation. It was by reason of their very careful planning and their bold, fearless attack. "Mostly they won," declares Mr. Lee, "because of the indecision and slowness of the United States." American forces in the Pacific were too small, merely "token" forces. The reaction after Pearl Harbour was too slow. With air control established in their favour, the Japanese drives could not be stopped. The Japanese Air Force was the decisive factor everywhere. It "operated like a smooth, first-class machine." Army and Navy "worked perfectly together as a single team." Their preparations were amazing, and they knew every foot of the ground they were to fight over, since their spies had for years been laboriously gathering the information they would need.

ALL this MacArthur knows and takes fully into account. At this moment he is making his plans—plans that will be no less thorough and perfect than those of the enemy—with every difficulty charted, every eventuality foreseen. When the time comes, he will put those plans into operation and will be on his way back to the Philippines. That will be his supreme testing-time. In the Battle of Bataan he did the utmost that could be done with what he had. "It may have given the United States sufficient time to recover from the Pearl Harbour disaster and to build up its Pacific forces to an extent that the Jap advance was finally stopped—at Coral Sea and Midway."

Those naval victories and the successful challenging of Japanese superiority in the air point the way to the triple power that MacArthur will be able to deploy. But even when he has used it and Japan has been utterly beaten, there will still be another war to carry through. That the Japs are brutal we know. One little example Mr. Lee gives almost without comment; it is so familiar. Jap sentries in Shanghai frequently slapped or clubbed foreigners for smoking as they passed, this being an insult to their emperor through his representatives—themselves ! But what about the "amiable-looking British business-men who in Hong Kong pushed Chinese off sidewalks or hit rickshaw-pullers with a cane?" And the American woman in Manila who, being refused a drink after closing hours, called out, "You Filipinos are dirt. We are the ruling race here." Unless we can "live in the same world" with the people we live amongst, we shall have fought the war and won it all in vain.

# Battle of Communications on the Karelian Front

RUSSIAN TROOPS on the Karelian Front, Finland, are alert in intercepting enemy attackers of vital railway communications, and any disruption caused is set right in the minimum of time. As marauders appear, A.A. crews of an armoured train (2) stand to their guns, awaiting the fire order from their commander. The enemy driven off, damage is repaired by the train crews themselves (4), who replace blasted track with new rails, while linesmen (3) rapidly restore telegraph wires by the track-side. Red Army sappers (1) strike back, mining a railway bridge essential to the enemy's needs ; its destruction aided the Soviet High Command's strategic planning.

Most important region of the Karelian front is the rich industrial Karelian Peninsula, ceded to Russia by Finland on March 12, 1940, but re-occupied by Finnish troops in the autumn of 1941. Recently launched Soviet offensives in the Leningrad and Volkov areas threaten to outflank the whole Karelian Isthmus from the sea.

*Photos, Pictorial Press*

# The Soviet Sharpshooter Learns to Get His Man

SCHOOL FOR SNIPERS in a Russian forest trains Red Army marksmen who take such heavy toll of the enemy; here also, battle-skilled troops have refresher courses during lulls in fighting on their particular sectors. Sergeant Andrei Lavenko, chief instructor, who has 40 Germans to his credit, is coaching one of his pupils, who will become still more adept at picking off Germans at long range—for which purpose the rifles are fitted with telescopic sights.

*Photo, Pictorial Press*

# Behind the Scenes with Showmen of the Services

*Between spells of activity overseas, and in intervals of hard training, boredom can be one of the worst afflictions. How this is dispelled by the well-organized machinery of Services entertainments, and, all else lacking, how men are encouraged to amuse themselves, even in the most unpromising circumstances, is explained by CAPT. MARTIN THORNHILL, M.C.*

WAR is not the dismal affair it used to be. When the troops move on, the Show moves on too. Established troupes of showmen are literally a branch of the Services now, keeping serving men entertained, maintaining good cheer and morale among millions of troops in training and reserve, overseas and at the fronts.

Welfare in the Forces began with "Comforts," an ambiguous term which covered all army welfare, such as it was, in the war days of the near past. Apart from a few local amateur shows provided by kindly civilian well-wishers, the efforts of a few hard-working padres, conscientious colonels and a handful of local welfare officers, there was nothing except table games in the canteens, and what the soldier himself could cram into his leaves.

All the same, it was directly on those modest early efforts to ameliorate the soldier's lot that the Government, the War Office and the show world have built their vast contemporary schemes of Forces welfare and entertainment. The platoon subaltern was always responsible not merely for the training of his men but for their general welfare. If a soldier got into trouble, his subaltern put in a word for him; he visited him in hospital, saw that all his men were suitably provided for in off-duty hours. In short, every subaltern was his men's unofficial welfare officer.

## Just Short of Going Crazy

But there were obvious limits to what a junior company officer could do, virtually without funds and with no official entertainment schemes. For thousands of soldiers quartered in outlying districts, in camp or on active service, canteen draughts and dominoes, an occasional game of football, an amateur show or two, just about kept the men from going crazy—little more. Boredom set in. Something had to be done about it.

And it was—if slowly. Early in the war county and local welfare officers were appointed, and units were encouraged to detail an officer to co-operate with them. Each was responsible for seeing that the men of his unit received books, comforts, handicrafts and lectures. ENSA (Entertainments National Service Association) was formed to distribute professional entertainment to all Commands. Soon the allocation of ENSA parties was something like 20 per Command, producing about 150 performances a week.

So far so good. ENSA and its companion body—CEMA (Council for the Encouragement of Music and the Arts), and the rest—had been doing a fine job of work. But the Forces now numbered several millions, and there was not nearly enough entertainment to go round. So the War Office encouraged units as far as possible to provide for their own entertainment. Keen comb-outs revealed enlisted professional entertainers. After that it was a short jump to bands, orchestras, concert parties, choirs, theatrical companies.

And that, broadly, is the point to which Forces entertainment has now advanced. The soldier-entertainer and his troupe of showboys is now officially recognized, modelled—be it noted—on those few but fine, hard-working divisional concert parties of the 1914-1918 war: the Roosters, Splinters, Balmorals, Rouge et Noir. This unit-supplied material is at the complete disposal of District Entertainment Officers, who distribute it with the single aim of keeping every unit in their territory constantly supplied.

Every D.E.O. is a regimental officer specially selected for his job, with funds at hand and stage properties available from central supply stores. With the help of an assistant Entertainment Officer in each unit who voluntarily undertakes the task in addition to his normal duties, the function of the District Officer is to see that the Forces in his region are willing and able to entertain themselves, he himself filling the multiple role of general manager, film renter and distributor, censor, legal expert, transport wizard, and solver of other problems.

A C.O. asks for the Sunday opening of a cinema in his area to be arranged. The E.O. attends to it. Can the E.O. provide producer, props, curtains, footlights, spotlight, for a troops show during a particular

**ENTERTAINMENT FOR THE TROOPS** by the troops not infrequently reveals unexpected talent among amateur performers. There may be a star of the future among the members of this concert party who are busily sorting costumes. *Photo, Fox*

week? He can, and he does. A unit E.O. wants to outfit a new concert party; how about clothing coupons? The D.E.O. contrives that too. There's some privately donated equipment—a film-projector maybe: what is the best use that the E.O. can make of it? Why, there is probably an isolated A.A. battery out on the Lincolnshire Fens—the very place for it.

IF entertainment for the troops by the troops is a major part of the Army show game today, don't imagine that, in these critical times when shortage of man-power and troop concert parties skip parades and cut the fighting. True, there is a War Office Central Pool of Artistes—a limited number of onetime professionals, some unfit for strenuous war service, the others serving soldiers who report back to their units for training every three months. Like ENSA, the C. P. of A. provides a shuttle service of entertainers purely supernumerary to units' own entertainment efforts; their main function is to step in where unforeseen circumstances forecast a blank week, or to supply artistes for isolated batteries and detachments which cannot provide their own entertainment.

But, like his counterpart in Russia, where

the soldier-performer scheme is also popular, our khaki showman is a soldier first, entertainer afterwards. His filling of that role does not exempt him from swapping his saxophone for a Bren gun. The need arises quite frequently on active service; and even troupes of civilian show-makers have had some exciting moments.

While the Eighth Army was on the move from El Alamein there was little time for organized entertainment, but once General Montgomery had gained the coveted goal, Tripoli, there was some breathing space. A few days after the last enemy truck had rolled westward out of the city, the largest welfare convoy ever assembled in the Middle East began its journey across 1,500 miles of dreary desert from Cairo.

IT had been smaller "mobiles" like these that braved bombs and shells to give the troops entertainment during the siege of Tobruk. In tunnels and hide-outs within the beleaguered garrison, one tireless organizer saw to it that the shows went on throughout the siege. And when the port was at last relieved this showman led the cinema cavalcade on to Derna, then to Benghazi. There his car was blasted by a bomb, which severely wounded him, forcing him to relinquish his job to another.

## Dispersed by Tanks and Shells

This man was the shows hero of Tobruk, even if his fun fare was only films. But in the view of the Directorate of Army Welfare it is invidious to mention names, for in all the theatres of war there are scores of outstanding yet unsung members of troupes who work unceasingly to keep the troops in good heart. Often their shows are forced by bombing and shell-fire to disperse, only to reform as soon as it seems reasonably safe to carry on. Once at least, when enemy tanks made a sudden appearance, troupers have found themselves well and truly in the front line, with barely five minutes in which to seize suitcases and get out.

India, where there are more troops than ever before ready for large-scale invasion of Burma, has its ENSA too: ACES, for short—Amenities, Comforts and Education for the Services. A knotty problem in a country 17 times the size of the U.K. is the travel question, so in India units are encouraged to furnish their own fun. And between them they are staging many a show that brightens the lives of troops in lonely jungle outposts on the Burma border, as well as in Burma itself.

IN bamboo thickets and jungle glades, by rugged mountain passes, on the edges of dangerous swamps, the war's showmen bring popular fun to some of the world's most appreciative audiences. Night after night, the stage as often as not a giant ant-hill levelled off at the top by willing hands from the audience, with oil lamps as footlights, the tropical moon a spotlight, little bands of entertainers play to off-stage accompaniments by roaring tigers and laughing hyenas, the dismal howl of the jackal, chattering monkeys and the non-stop drone of clouds of mosquitoes like the hum of distant planes.

There are plenty of critics of the quality of entertainment provided for the Forces, cynical comments on the lack of shows at places where they are most needed. But make no mistake about it, the stuff they give the troops—and the stuff the troops give themselves—to keep boredom at bay, is getting bigger and better.

# Inside a Fifty Miles-per-Hour Churchill Tank

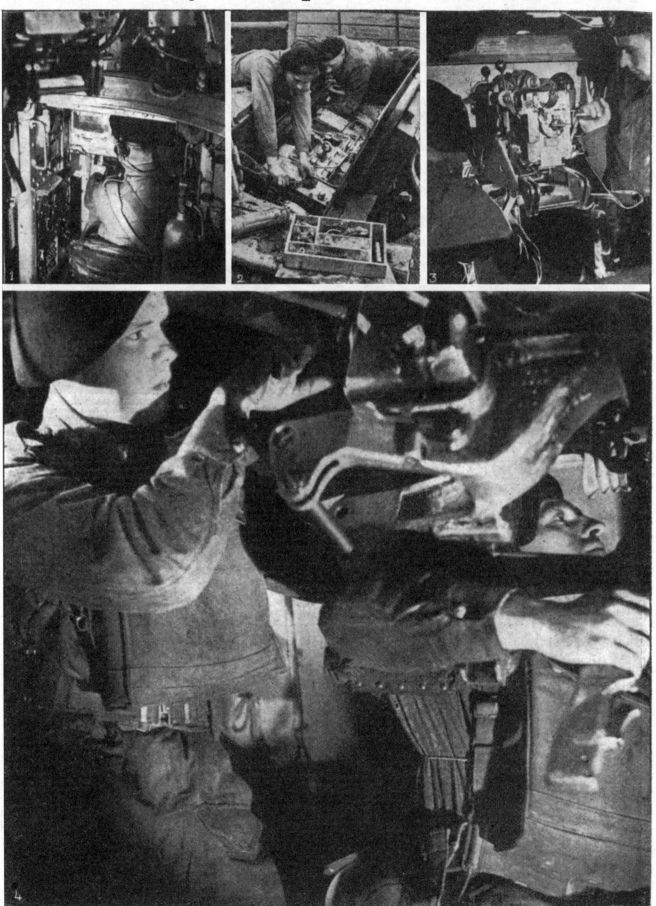

MAZE OF MACHINERY leaves little room for the crew of a Churchill tank, as is obvious from the positions of the driver (1) at his steering lever, the gunner (3, left) and the wireless operator (3, right) who also acts as gun-loader. The gunner (4, right) assisted by the wireless operator who is attending to the gun's breech is seen from another angle. Royal Armoured Corps men adjust the engines (2). The weight of a Churchill is 28-30 tons, and its speed up to 50 miles per hour.

*Photos, British Official : Crown Copyright*

# Tenacious Devotion to Duty Gained These Awards

Lieut. T. W. DOWNING, G.M. (left) and Capt. E. M. KETLEY, O.B.E.
These officers were members of a small party of the Royal Army Ordnance Corps who volunteered for the dangerous task of dumping overboard from a ship's hold 50,000 rounds of ammunition. It was liable to explode at any moment, but they continued operations until it was disposed of, June 8—11, 1943.

Pte. R. KELLIHER, V.C.
During an attack by his platoon on a strongly defended Japanese position at Nadzab, New Guinea, on September 13, 1943, when heavy machine-gun fire from a concealed post only 50 yards distant had stopped the advance, causing several casualties, Pte. Kelliher, Australian Military Forces, suddenly and on his own initiative rushed the post with grenades, killing some of the gun-crew. Returning to his platoon for a Bren gun he again advanced and finally silenced the post. Again he dashed out, to rescue his wounded section-leader, and returned safely.

Sapper R. SOUTHALL, M.M.
Searching for enemy mines north of Enfidaville, Tunisia, Sapper Southall stepped on one. To save comrades from injury he continued to stand on it until his foot was blown off.

Fusilier T. MOORE, M.M.
At Lemon Bridge in the Catania Plain (Sicily), July 1943, a heavy German counter-attack developed, and in the face of devastating fire Fusilier Moore withdrew some of his battalion's guns.

Major F. G. DELFORCE, D.S.O.
Commanding a mixed force, Major Delforce, Royal Fusiliers (smoking pipe in group above) received the D.S.O. for his part in holding St. Lucia, keypoint of the Salerno bridgehead, loss of which would have had serious consequences, on Sept. 15, 1943.

Sgt. J. STEWART, M.M.
Of the Queen's Royal Regiment, this sergeant received the M.M. for conspicuous gallantry displayed during the fighting in Tunis, May 7—8, 1943, when he prevented the destruction of an important bridge.

*Photos, British Official Crown Copyright; Sport & General, G.P.U.*

# I WAS THERE! Eye Witness Stories of the War

## Japanese Night-Prowlers Routed in the Solomons

New Zealand and U.S. troops landed on Mono Island (known also as Treasury Island) in the Solomons, S.W. of the Shortland Islands, on October 26, 1943, and were in complete occupation by November 3—after extraordinary incidents such as related here by a N.Z. Official War Correspondent.

AT times a score or more Japanese prowled among our lines and foxholes, chattering among themselves, singing sometimes and conducting themselves with a strangely carefree abandon that suggested a queer twist of psychology, or, what might well have been possible, over-indulgence in their alcoholic saki, many bottles of which were found in camp sites.

They sat on fallen trees and felt gingerly for men's heads in foxholes (three coconuts and pieces of coral placed here and there !) and clicked signals to each other with wooden sticks. Four sat for two hours within a yard of a wounded New Zealander, but they never saw him. One poked a skinny hand under the log roof of a big foxhole and was riddled with a tommy-gun burst.

There were occasional interchanges of fire through one night, but no enemy were killed. Four lay dead after the second night. It turned out that they had a purpose, for from trees along the beach came snipers' fire, and on the following day at least nine snipers were found. They had been eliminated by spraying the tree tops with bullets.

One battalion has this story about "The Corpse that Walked," which has the testimony of the commanding officer as a guarantee of veracity. Late one afternoon there were shots from tree-tops and coconut palms which whizzed close to a private's head. He turned his automatic rifle into a palm, and was rewarded by the falling of a sniper's rifle and the slumping of a barely discernible body amongst the greenery. The Japanese had been tied to the tree and the body stayed where it was. Dusk was falling and the body was left alone. In the morning it was gone.

Referring to another night incident, a South Island corporal now knows what it feels like to have his steel helmet lifted slowly back while he slept in a foxhole. He woke to semi-consciousness one night as his hat was being pulled gently upwards. Not realizing what was happening he drowsily pulled it back on his head. Next moment a hand jerked it up again, and the truth then dawned upon the corporal that someone was trying to lift his chin and expose his throat. The corporal did not drowse any more. He lashed out with his fists, and a dark form slid off in a hurry. With this blood-curdling lesson of night-risks in mind it is perhaps needless to record that the corporal slept no more that night, nor the night after !

## Our Captors Became Our Prisoners at Ortona

Captured during the street-fighting in Ortona, Italy, 15 Canadian soldiers of the 8th Army were rescued from a house by a patrol from their own battalion. Two of them tell their stories here, in an Associated Press dispatch from Douglas Amaron. See also pages 516, 537 and 554.

WHEN the rescue patrol arrived, the Germans, under the command of a young parachute troop lieutenant, surrendered their weapons and left the house as the prisoners of their erstwhile captives. One of the captured Canadians, Sergeant John Elaschuk, known throughout his unit as the "immortal sergeant," said :

There were twice as many Germans in the building as Canadians. The only order given to us was to keep quiet and muffle any coughing. None of the Germans was more than 24 years old, and one of them was not a day over 17. An officer, who spoke French and English, was about 21. The Germans, who had just returned from leave, were wearing spotlessly clean, well-pressed uniforms. They tried hard to pump

**TO THIS PALM-FRINGED BAY OF MONO ISLAND** New Zealand troops rushed supplies and equipment from their armed invasion craft. Japanese strove desperately to prevent the landing on Oct. 26, 1943, using heavy guns, but these were quickly put out of action by a naval bombardment. Deadly night skirmishes were a feature of the battle for this island which now forms an important base for further Allied progress in the Solomons. See story above, descriptive of the first three nights spent by the New Zealanders on Mono.

*Photo, Keystone*

us for information, using indirect methods of questioning which, however, had little effect on us.

They asked us about Sherman tanks, and we told them we knew nothing. We gave them the same answer when they wanted to know how many Canadians had been killed in Ortona. They were particularly keen to hear the true story of Hess. They wanted all the details, but as I did not know much about him I could not give them the information, even had I wanted to.

The Germans, who all carried pictures of Hitler, had not much to say about the war, except for the comment of one officer, who said, "Win or lose, you Canadians can return to Canada and be happy—if we lose, we lose everything!" Some of the Germans who were in good spirit whistled bars of the Lambeth Walk, and I was almost tempted to join in myself.

*Private Wilfrid Haimes, another Canadian, said that his captors had asked him where his section was quartered :*

I told them I didn't know. After they had finished with me they took me to a back street. We passed a house, and one German wanted to throw a grenade through the door, but another stopped him and shone a torch in instead. Just then a gramophone in the house started playing a record from the opera Carmen, and the door opened. A Canadian corporal came out, and the Germans grabbed him and took us both back.

About noon Canadian troops in the town went into the attack again and approached our building. One of the German officers took me aside and told me that the men must keep "very quiet." Then he went upstairs, and as soon as he had gone all the other Germans in the room turned their weapons over to me. Things began to

**FROM A SHELL-HOLED HOUSE IN ORTONA** Canadian Pte. George Cunningham emerges, to be congratulated by one of the men who rescued him after six hours in German hands. Later, Pte. Cunningham had the joy of helping his rescuers to capture eight Germans. See story commencing in previous page.
*Photo, British Official : Crown Copyright*

happen fast then, with the Canadians in the street letting loose with everything they had into the house. Elaschuk and some of the others started shouting, and only their yells prevented us from being mortared by our rescuers. The Jerries were just as anxious to get away as we were, and they were genuinely glad to become our prisoners.

a ring-side seat. Before darkness came on I had a very good view of the Battle Ensigns being hoisted in Duke of York—two at the foremast and one aft—a grand sight.

As we gradually closed the range after contact had been made in the dark, it was difficult to realize what was about to happen before my eyes. Then the cruisers which had shadowed Scharnhorst during the day fired their star shell to illuminate her—and the party was on. The star shell burst and hung in the sky and seemed to light up the whole horizon, but it was not until Duke of York had fired her star shell that I was able to pick out the Scharnhorst steaming at high speed, about 7 miles away. Then Duke of York fired the first salvo of her 14-in. guns. There was no warning buzzer and I was temporarily blinded by the flash, which seemed to roar all around me.

## We Saw the Scharnhorst Hit in North Cape Battle

The shelling and destruction of the German battleship on December 26, 1943, is graphically described by Leading-Seaman R. Daly, Able-Seaman Litton, and Paymaster-Lieut. T. B. Homan, R.N., all of the victorious Duke of York. They gave these personal accounts when their ship returned to base after the memorable action. See also pages 518-520 and 551.

THE first indication we had that we were nearing the enemy was when we saw a star shell fired by the cruiser Belfast in the distance (said Daly). Soon we turned and fired star shell too. Our star shell fell right over the Scharnhorst and for a time I could see her very plainly travelling at full speed. Our 14-in. guns then opened up, but our first salvo fell short. With the second salvo, however, I distinctly saw four hits, which showed up as four huge red flashes along the length of the ship.

As our job was look-outs against enemy destroyers coming in to make torpedo attacks we had to shut our eyes every time we heard the "Fire" bell ring, otherwise we would have been temporarily blinded by the flash. Immediately we heard the guns go off, however, we looked up, and it was amazing to see our shells racing through the sky, just like shooting stars. The shells from the Jamaica we could follow all the way from ship to target.

WITH every salvo I said, "Let's hope she gets this lot bang in the middle !" At times we could hear the Scharnhorst's shells whistling overhead, and I noticed that during the first part of the action white smoke could be seen where they had hit the water, but later on all we could see was black smoke. We heard our foremast being hit, and a shower of shrapnel descended all over the deck. We all ducked down just in time as the shrapnel bounced off the bulkheads just above us.

After a time (said Litton, taking up the

story) there was a lull in the action, and we were told that our destroyers had gone in to make a torpedo attack. A short while after this I saw two huge flashes and our ship shook with some explosion. Some of the chaps said "We've been hit on the catapult deck !" but I said, "No, we've tin-fished her. Well done the 'boats,' that shook her !" I could see the destroyers coming out from the attack and the enemy certainly sent out something at them, thousands of tracer bullets and shells seemed to be flying at them at the same time. The destroyers let go too.

And then I saw a big white flash which lasted for a minute or two and I thought that one of our boats had been hit, which later proved to be correct. A short while after that, our 14-in. and 5·25-in. guns opened up again and the cruiser astern also began to fire. Fire seemed to be coming from the other side of the enemy, which indicated that the three cruisers who had been shadowing her during the day were also making contact. We got many hits, and I saw a great fire break out on board her and noticed that she was only firing from her after turret and trying to put up a smoke screen. The next we saw was two destroyers lighting up the area with their searchlights, picking up survivors, and then we began to draw away.

I WAS fortunate (said Paymaster-Lieutenant T. B. Homan, R.N.) in having an action station on the wings of the Admiral's bridge in Duke of York, and as the light H.A. armament was not manned I was able to watch the whole action from what might be termed

AFTER my eyes had cleared and the smoke of our guns had passed, I was able to follow the 14-in. "bricks" flying through the night sky towards the enemy. More star shell lit up the scene, and then five minutes or so later Scharnhorst fired her first broadside from her 11-in. guns. After that the air seemed full of gun flashes, the deafening roar and acrid fumes of our guns, shells streaking across the night sky and the stabs of the enemy's guns as she returned our fire.

I was able to see Belfast and the other two cruisers firing at Scharnhorst in the distance. Now and then there would be a very short period of absolute silence whilst guns were reloaded and range corrected. Then the overwhelming noise would start up again.

I felt at times that I was witnessing one of Hollywood's gigantic productions and it seemed impossible that this was the real thing—a night action at sea. The sound of Duke of York's guns, shattering as it was, was an inspiring and comforting sound. But the whine of the Scharnhorst's shells and the sight of the fountains of water thrown up around Duke of York, as they landed just off our bows and what seemed to be only a few yards off our beam, were sufficient to remove any ideas that my berth was at all comfortable, or that the fight was all one-sided. Duke of York was undoubtedly lucky but was masterfully handled by the Captain to whom a lot is owed for bringing us through undamaged.

Shrapnel clattered on the masts and funnels now and then and made me duck. I

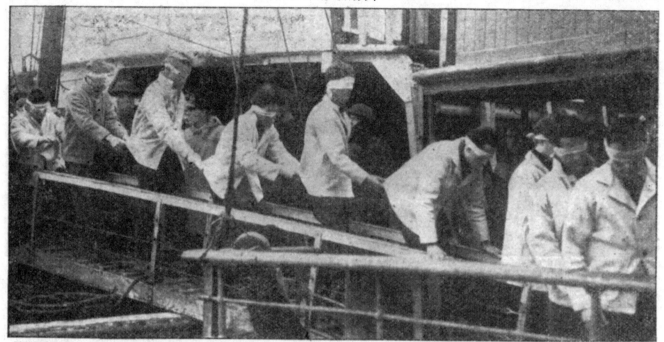

**BLINDFOLDED SURVIVORS OF THE SCHARNHORST,** sunk in the action off North Cape on Dec. 26, 1943, were landed at a British port on their way to internment. H.M. Destroyers Scorpion and Matchless picked up 36 Nazi seamen and transferred them to the Duke of York (see illus. p. 551), whose broadsides crippled the German vessel. Majority of the survivors were aged between 19 and 21, and for some it was their first sea trip. Stories of the action are related in this and the previous page.

*Photo, British Official : Crown Copyright*

should have ducked a considerable amount more had I known of the hole which had appeared in the port support of the foremast about 20 feet away from my position. I found this out next day—and swallowed hard. When the destroyers went in later in the action the enemy opened up with his lighter weapons and they seemed to be going into a hail of tracer shell streaming toward them.

When Duke of York closed the range a second time I was able to observe definite hits on the Scharnhorst which showed several dull red glows. Her firing was now fairly erratic, although even now an occasional spout of water would mark her shells landing uncommonly close. At the end, the enemy appeared to be slowly circling and a cloud of thick smoke was hanging over her.

Jamaica left us to go in and fire her torpedoes, but I could not see the Scharnhorst now as the smoke from her fires obscured the view. The cruisers played searchlights over where she was last seen, and the action was over. Again, all was very dark and very quiet. It was difficult to realize what a tremendous scene had just been enacted before my eyes out there in the darkness.

# OUR DIARY OF THE WAR

**JANUARY 5, Wednesday** *1,586th day*
**Italy.**—Announced that Lt.-Gen. Sir Oliver Leese appointed commander of 8th Army in succession to Gen. Montgomery.
**Russian Front.**—Berdichev captured by Red Army. Soviet forces launched offensive in Kirovograd region.
**Australasia.**—Revealed that on Jan. 4 600 Japanese killed in battle at Cape Gloucester, New Britain.

**JANUARY 6, Thursday** *1,587th day*
**Russian Front.**—Rokitno, 12 miles over Polish frontier, Chudnov and Goroditsa, captured by First Ukrainian Army.
**General.**—Gen. Sir Harold Franklyn appointed C.-in-C., Home Forces.

**JANUARY 7, Friday** *1,588th day*
**Russian Front.**—Break-through 25 miles in depth by Second Ukrainian Army under Gen. Koniev on a 60-mile front in the Kirovograd region ; Novgoradka captured. Klesov, district centre of Rovno area 12 miles from Sarny, and Yarnushpol, taken.
**Air.**—Revealed that a fighter plane operated by jet-propulsion, invented by Group-Captain Frank Whittle, R.A.F., would soon be in production.

**JANUARY 8, Saturday** *1,589th day*
**Italy.**—Capture of San Vittore by 5th Army announced.
**Russian Front.**—Kirovograd captured by Soviet troops ; 8 German divisions routed.
**General.**—Appointments announced : Air Marshal Sir John Slessor to be deputy Air Commander in Mediterranean area under Gen. Ira. C. Eaker ; Air Chief Marshal Sir Sholto Douglas to be his successor as C.-in-C. Coastal Command.

**JANUARY 9, Sunday** *1,590th day*
**Russian Front.**—Polonnoye captured by Russians.
**General.**—Lt.-Gen. J. A. H. Gammell appointed Chief of Staff in the Mediterranean. Maj.-Gen. Bedell Smith, U.S. Army, appointed Chief of Staff to Gen. Eisenhower.

**JANUARY 10, Monday** *1,591st day*
**Italy.**—Capture of Catena Vecchio by 5th Army announced. Bridgehead across. River Pecchia forced.
**Mediterranean.**—Sofia, Bulgarian capital, bombed by Fortresses.

**Russian Front.**—Lyudvipol and Berezno across 1939 Polish frontier ; rail link between Smyela and Krisinovka cut.

**JANUARY 11, Tuesday** *1,592nd day*
**Mediterranean.**—Piraeus, port of Athens, heavily bombed.
**Russian Front.**—Soviet troops launched offensive in the Mozyr direction and on Sarny front forced a crossing of the River Slucz. 40-miles Red Army front established to date in Poland.
**Burma.**—Capture of Maungdaw, 60 miles N.W. of Akyab, announced. Revealed that British force in action on the Burmese front was the 14th Army.
**Air.**—Over 700 escorted Liberators and Fortresses bombed Oschersleben, Halberstadt and Brunswick fighter-aircraft assembly plants.
**General.**—Count Ciano and 4 other ex-members of the Fascist Grand Council executed in Verona.

**JANUARY 12, Wednesday** *1,593rd day*
**Italy.**—Capture of Monte Caparo by U.S. troops of 5th Army announced.
**Russian Front.**—Sarny rail junction, first major town across Polish frontier, captured by Red Army.
**General.**—Mr. Churchill and Gen. de

Gaulle met for discussions at Marrakesh (Morocco), where the Prime Minister had been convalescing.

**JANUARY 13, Thursday** *1,594th day*
**Italy.**—Fall of Cervaro to U.S. troops of 5th Army announced. French troops under Gen. Juin launched an attack S.W. of Rocchetta.
**Russian Front.**—Korets, district centre of Rovno region, captured by Russians.
**Australasia.**—Announced that Australian troops had reached Gniesenau Point, 5 miles from Sio, New Guinea.
**General.**—Revealed that shortly before sinking of the German battleship Scharnhorst, Adml. Sir Bruce Fraser, C.-in-C. of the Home Fleet, had paid a visit in the Duke of York to a Russian naval port.

**JANUARY 14, Friday** *1,595th day*
**Italy.**—Announced fierce enemy counter-attacks launched at Cervaro repulsed ; U.S. troops crossed Rome road in direction of Monte Trocchio.
**Russian Front.**—Mozyr, Kalinkovichi, Klinsk, Kachury and Kozenki in White Russia, captured by Soviet troops.
**Burma.**—Capture of Kanyindan and Dilpara by 14th Army announced.
**Air.**—Brunswick (2,000 tons dropped) heavily bombed.

**JANUARY 15, Saturday** *1,596th day*
**Italy.**—Fall of Acquafondata to French troops of the 5th Army announced ; Montefero, Montepagano, and Monte Pile heights stormed. U.S. troops seized Monte Trocchio.
**Russian Front.**—Gen. Rokossovsky's Army reached a point 25 miles west of Mozyr. Soviet troops under Gen. Govorov launched an offensive in the Leningrad area, south of Oranienbaum and Pulkovo.

**JANUARY 16, Sunday** *1,597th day*
**Italy.**—Capture of Cardito, Monte Croce and Vallerotonda, by French troops of 5th Army announced.
**Mediterranean.**—Klagenfurt Messerschmitt factory in Austrian province of Carinthia bombed by Fortresses.
**Russian Front.**—Revealed that Russian forces had broken enemy defences N. of Novo Sokolniki. Kostopol, 35 miles S.W. of Sarny, captured by Soviet troops.
**General.**—Revealed that Gen. Eisenhower had taken up his post in the United Kingdom as Supreme Commander of the Allied Expeditionary Forces.

**JANUARY 17, Monday** *1,598th day*
**Italy.**—Announced forward 5th Army troops had reached the River Rapido. British troops of the 5th Army forced three crossings of the Garigliano River at Argento, Sujo and near Minturno.
**Russian Front.**—Tulchin, in Rovno region, occupied by Red Army.
**Australasia.**—Announced Sio (New Guinea) taken by Australians.
**General.**—Lt.-General Omar Bradley appointed to command U.S. Army in the Field under Gen. Eisenhower.

**JANUARY 18, Tuesday** *1,599th day*
**Italy.**—Announced that French troops of the 5th Army had captured San Elia.
**Russian Front.**—Announced that two fresh offensives recently launched by Red Army had carried them beyond enemy fortified defences of the Leningrad front, and had pierced fortifications north of Novgorod on the Volkhov front. Russian troops captured Slavuta and cut the rail connexion between Shepetovka and Rovno, S.W. of Novigrad Volynsk.
**General.**—Mr. Churchill returned to England from N. Africa.

★━━━━━━ *Flash-backs* ━━━━━━★

### 1941
January 5. *Bardia surrendered to Gen. Wavell's 8th Army. 30,000 Italians made prisoner.*
January 18. *Dive-bombing attacks on Malta commenced. Aircraft-carrier Illustrious in Valetta harbour enemy's main objective.*

### 1942
January 12. *Attack on Halfaya (Egypt) began by British and Imperial troops.*
January 17. *Halfaya garrison surrendered to South Africans.*

### 1943
January 5. *Tsimlyanskaya on Don front taken by Red Army troops.*
January 12. *Conquest of Fezzan by Free French troops under Gen. Leclerc completed.*
January 14. *President Roosevelt and Mr. Churchill, accompanied by the combined Chiefs of Staff, met at Casablanca, French Morocco, to plan the enemy's "unconditional surrender."*
January 15. *Gen. Montgomery's 8th Army opened an offensive at Buerat (Tribolitania).*

THE NEW MUSTANG P51 B single-engined fighter which acted as escort during the war's greatest air battle when some 1,200 Allied planes, including over 700 Liberators and Fortresses, successfully attacked vital German aircraft plants at Halberstadt, Oschersleben and Brunswick, on Jan. 11, 1944. The improved Mustang is Anglo-American, built originally in U.S.A. from British specifications. Speed is said to be over 400 m.p.h., and auxiliary tanks under the wings give it the longest range of any single-seat fighter in the world.

*Photo, Associated Press*

# THE WAR IN THE AIR

### by Capt. Norman Macmillan, M.C., A.F.C.

THE war in the air is playing a far more important part in the whole war than the average person with whom I come into contact realizes. And I am going to present to readers my view of the far-reaching nature of the effects of the air war, and of some of the disadvantages we have encountered through the unimaginative misemployment (I purposely use this strong word) of air power.

By the time this article is published the large-scale raids made on German targets by Bomber Command will have been proceeding for about eleven months. The attacks made earlier—the first of the 1,000-bomber raids on Cologne, the Ruhr and Bremen—were experimental try-outs of the new method of bombing which has since achieved such remarkable results. Those early raids were made with twin-engined bombers forming the major part of the formations engaged, and it took about 90 minutes to unload about 1,500 tons of bombs. Now, employing four-engined bombers, it is possible, as in the recent raid on Brunswick (Jan. 11, 1944), to decant 2,000 tons of bombs in 23 minutes.

What, you may ask, is the reason for the concentration of effort in modern bombing? Why do we not do as the Germans did when they attacked our cities and maintain a steady attack throughout the night, dropping bombs at a slower pace, but keeping on dropping them for the ten hours of darkness? There are several reasons, not just one, and they concern both the flying conditions and the surface conditions.

### CONFLAGRATIONS Beyond Control of Nazi Civil Defence Services

In flight there is the obvious need to avoid unnecessary casualties among our aircraft, and the shortest possible time spent over the target exposes them to the least possible risk from enemy night fighters and flak, while reduction in the time spent over the target means that a greater load of bombs can be carried, because of reduction in weight of petrol.

On the surface, the great concentration of bombing produces within an extremely brief period a conflagration so great that the German civil defence services are powerless to control the flames within the target area. The most they can do is to work to prevent the fires from spreading to other areas. In this way the target area marked out for

attack is devastated by one successful assault, and the same area need not be again dealt with on the grand scale; any isolated targets that may have survived within the area can be of small value to the enemy, but, if it is desired to deal with them, this can be done by American bombers operating in daylight, or by British Mosquito bombers flying either by day or night.

OF course, some target areas are better protected from attack because they are dispersed. A notable example was Essen, where industry sprawled widely over a large zone. That was why repetitive raids were required to be launched against this area, but even in this case the devastation was but a question of time. What is important is this : *any war industrial area can be devastated so that it is useless to the German war effort.* And without industry Germany can no longer maintain either her armies in the field or her civilian population in the Reich. Her whole effort would inevitably collapse.

What has already been achieved ? Bomber Command and the American bomber force in Britain working together by night and day dropped 157,000 tons and 55,000 tons respectively on enemy targets during 1943. In that first year of real bombing Bomber Command dropped 136,000 tons on Germany alone. Twenty-seven per cent of all Germany's built-up area has been devastated, covering an aggregate area of about 40 square miles, and Germany has been forced on to the defensive because she has suffered a reduced production of all-important weapons. She has been compelled to give priority to 'defensive' weapons. Fighters have taken precedence over bombers, and probably over other surface and sea weapons. The measure of German fear of the bombing battle of Germany is evidenced in her production of fighter aircraft in such quantities that the Luftwaffe first-line strength is numerically 1,000 aircraft greater than it was a year ago.

THIS does not mean that she has as great an aircraft industry, for it must be remembered that it is possible to build at least three fighters for every bomber, so that the replacement of a bomber programme by a fighter programme automatically increases the output of aircraft even from a depleted industry. Remember, too, that it is only in recent

months that we have attacked the fighter aircraft factories. The continuation of the bomber offensive will have such an effect upon the German aircraft industry that Germany will not be able to maintain her production of fighter aircraft. Then, with the bomber offensive growing and the German fighter defence diminishing, the end would be near.

If we and the Americans had achieved the bombing strength we should have had, the effect upon German industry would by now have been much greater than it is. Germany would not have had her present increase in fighter strength. Her armies would have been depleted of still more weapons. Her soldiers would have been up against the wall. The great mass of her civilian population would have been homeless and unable to sustain their industrial efforts.

### WOULD Germany Welcome an Invasion of Europe?

Why have we failed to accomplish this ? Because we have not concentrated our force at the vital point. We have followed devious war trails. Our bombers have been employed for extraneous purposes. What we have been expending in a winter mud-crawl up the Italian peninsula could have been better employed against German industry. Germany wants us to fight her armies; they are still her best weapons. She would welcome a premature invasion of Europe. It is the one way she might hope to win this war, and if we had made the attempt too soon we should have lost our opportunity to defeat her by air power, for our already partially dispersed bomber force would then have been almost wholly dispersed.

BUT, you may ask, what proof is there that bombing will defeat Germany? Well, it is known that it is the weapon Germany fears most. Those who really know what the Luftwaffe did here, and what we are doing to Germany, know the effect of bombing on us and its effect on Germany. The retreat of the German armies in Russia is the direct result of the destruction of German industry. The victorious Russian armies advance in the rear of an army forced by Bomber Command to retire to a line which it believes it can maintain with the industry it now possesses, with something substantial left over to oppose invasion. If our bombing is maintained and increased the Nazi line will be too long to hold, and battered German industry will bring Hitler's downfall because it will be unable to give him arms. We can win the war by bombing. We might lose it through premature invasion. If we invade too soon it will cost us dearly.

# Shooting Japanese Planes out of Pacific Skies

**ACCURATE ALLIED FIRE** plays havoc with Japanese aircraft over Pacific waters. Tribute to a Liberator's marksmanship is this shattered wing-tip (1) falling into the sea ; an enemy transport plane (2) believed to be carrying Japanese officials, is another victim. A Zero torpedo-bomber (3) which had attempted to attack one of the American aircraft carriers raiding the Marshall Islands on Dec. 4, 1943, is blown apart by the carrier's guns. In the Rabaul area alone, during intense air activity the Japanese lost, between Dec. 24, 1943, and Jan. 6, 1944, nearly 200 planes, heartening indication of the constantly increasing toll being taken by our fighters.

*Photos, Keystone*

# Ice-Chamber Tests Make High Flight Possible

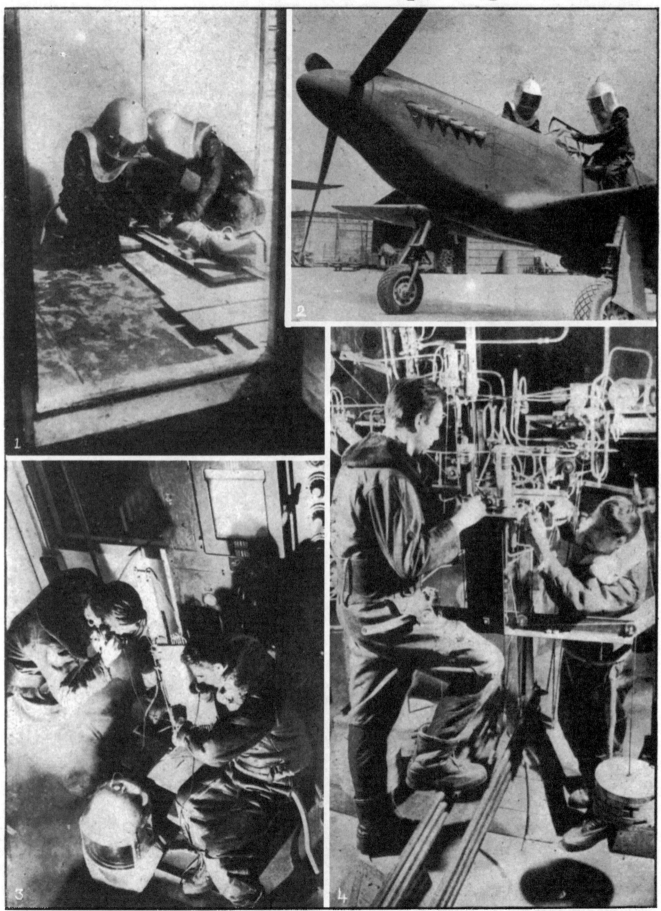

AT 70 DEGREES BELOW ZERO, approximating to a height of 35,000 feet, the atmosphere in this pressure chamber (1) necessitates warm suits made of horsehide lined with wool, and aluminium helmets welded to padded shoulders : the men are undergoing a working-test in stratosphere and Arctic conditions without leaving the ground ; contact with observers outside is maintained by telephone (3). Low temperature affects planes too; a component is removed (2) for testing in the chamber, and a plane's hydraulic system (4) follows it. See p. 521. PAGE 574 *Photos, Keystone*

PROPHECIES during this war have seldom been fulfilled—so far. Certainly Hitler's have not. Nor was Mr. Chamberlain any more fortunate when he said the future would show that Hitler in 1940 "had missed the bus," though this phrase was alleged to have been first used by a high-ranking officer in this connexion. Unluckily it was broadcast on the eve of the series of colossal blows by which the Nazis brought the Continent and a large part of Scandinavia under their temporary domination. But one prediction I can remember reflects credit in a high degree on the man who uttered it. Mr. Ernest Bevin declared a long time ago, when we were getting the worst of the air raids, that in course of time we should drop five tons of bombs on Germany for every ton they dropped here. That has come true already. Indeed, we have done better than that. And as the months go by we shall increase the weight of our attacks. Two years before war began, in 1937, Hitler said meditatively and with a melancholy air to a Rumanian politician who visited him, "What an appalling thing to picture London and other cities destroyed by bombs!" He was thinking, the visitor believed, of German cities being treated in the same way. But was he? When he threatened to "erase" ours, he had such superiority in the air that such a possibility as the obliteration of Berlin could not occur to him. Goering assured him that no bombs would ever fall on the Reich (see pp. 559-562). Of all war prophecies that is the one which will be pilloried in history as the most fatuous of all.

NOT many people are aware of the large number of Irish men and women who have been imported to work for us in war factories and in constructing airfields. There are about 80 girls from Eire in what used to be a college for training Church of England clergymen not far from Oxford. The other day an organizer for the Workers' Educational Association went to this college to see if a course of lectures would be welcomed. He sketched the sort of subjects that could be dealt with and then asked "What subject would most of you prefer?" The reply was a shout of "Men!" He said he never felt so much at a loss. He departed without arranging anything.

IS there more crime of the mean and petty kind in wartime than at other times, or is it merely that we hear more about it? One certainly does notice a larger record of really revolting sneak-thefts. As bad a one as any I heard of a few days ago. An old lady travelling by train (journey strictly necessary!) in a first-class compartment went out for a few moments, leaving her bag very carelessly on her seat. When she opened it again, she found all her clothing and ration coupons had been taken out, together with a valuable gold-bound morocco wallet (which was empty). Her identity card had been left, fortunately. What ought to be done to the incredibly caddish offenders who are guilty of acts like that—if they can be caught? I believe making them wear a distinguishing mark and having a statement of their offence displayed outside their houses would have more of a deterrent effect than any fine or imprisonment. Public opinion might do a lot towards decreasing crime.

I HAVE made a discovery. I am a rack-renter! Do you know what that is? I have had to look it up in the dictionary. I had a dim memory of the term being applied to Irish landlords in the days long ago when the Rent War was going on across St. George's Channel. It was then supposed to mean an unjust, grasping landlord. The dictionary supports that. It says rack-rent is "a rent stretched to the utmost, an exorbitant rent." Now it happens that a house of mine is being used by the military, having been requisitioned for a staff headquarters. The Army authorities have sent me an agreement to sign and in this I am described as a "person receiving the rack-rent of the land or a person who would receive the rack-rent if the land were let at a rack-rent." That sounds like Alice in Wonderland. War Office documents often do. I haven't the slightest idea what it means, nor, I would venture to bet, has the official who signed it. I am receiving far less rent than the house is worth, therefore I am not, according to the dictionary, a rack-renter. Why should the War Office call me one?

THEY might, now I come to think of it, have discovered its significance from Shakespeare. In Much Ado About Nothing the Friar says wisely:

It so falls out,
That what we have we prize not to the worth
Whiles we enjoy it; but, being lack'd and lost,
Why, then we rack the value, then we find
The virtue that possession would not show us
Whiles it was ours.

There the word is used in its right sense. Shakespeare was saying that when we have lost a possession, we strain its value, exaggerate it, set an exorbitant price upon it. That use of the expression has gone out, except in the compound "rack-rent," which, as the above instance shows, may not be quite clear even to officials who employ it.

Its original meaning survives in rack-stick, a stick used for stretching a rope. All meanings seem to have developed from the rack on which unfortunate victims of tyranny were tortured by being stretched. A hat-rack, a luggage-rack, a newspaper-rack, all bear some slight resemblance to the instrument of torture. But why the piece of ice used for curling should in Scotland be called a rack, I cannot imagine. I might add that some very expensive linoleum could not be removed from the house in question as it was pasted to the floor boards. In the event of its being damaged I am to be compensated to an amount not exceeding eighteen-pence per yard!

HOW would you say the war has affected the dog population in this country? Most people think it has gone down very much, that the increased difficulty of buying dog food, meat especially, must have made a number of dog-owners reluctantly part with their four-footed friends. Yet the figures show that the difference is not really great after all. There were in 1939 two million eight hundred thousand dogs. The latest estimate is that there are now two million four hundred thousand. There is an inclination to think even that is too many. The Government must decide this. I read a long time ago that the Germans had been forbidden to keep dogs. I didn't believe it at the time, and I don't now. They have not been as short of meat as we have. Yet it is pretty certain their drop in dog numbers has been heavier in proportion than ours, because they take more careful precautions against future risks. However, as our statistics mean that we have no more than one dog to every sixteen or so of our human population, it can't, I think, be called excessive, even in present circumstances.

THREE letters I read in a daily paper from men in the Army or Air Force about what they call excessive "spit and polish," unnecessary cleaning, exaggerated regard for appearances, made a letter I received myself from Persia particularly interesting. It was from a young officer friend of mine. "I have," he told me, "received a formal reprimand in writing for having the badge on my hat three-eighths of an inch out of place." Now what possible justification can there be for such old-maidish fussiness as that? What a shock the writer of the reprimand would receive from "Monty's" beret, stuck all over with badges! And here is another gem. Before an inspection men of a unit were told "every man must see that his trousers are properly ironed!"

THERE are names in the news from the Italian front which must give all who read Browning (and anyone who does not misses a lot of interest and pleasure) a painful jolt. Fano, for instance—when I read of this little town by the sea being a target for attack from the air, I hoped the church with the picture by Guercino in it had escaped. This picture gave the poet the idea for "The Guardian Angel," in which occur the often-quoted lines:

O world as God has made it! All is beauty:
And knowing this, is love, and love is duty.
   What further may be sought for or declared?

As God made it! What would Browning have said of the world today, as Man is making it? Nothing very comforting!

**WITHSTANDING THE STORM**
*"Storms Make Oaks Take Deeper Root"*
Originally published in The Sun, Sydney, Australia, on Aug. 27, 1940, this cartoon was reprinted as tribute to the spirit of Britain on Sept. 3, 1943, the fourth anniversary of war with Germany.

# Tedder's Carpet will Pave the Allied Way

**AIR CHIEF MARSHAL SIR ARTHUR WILLIAM TEDDER, K.C.B.,** on the balcony of Air House, his former Cairo home as A.O.C.-in-C. Mediterranean Air Command. On December 27, 1943, he was appointed Deputy Supreme Commander, under General Eisenhower, of the Allied forces which will invade Western Europe from these shores : indication that fullest use will be made of the Allies' air might to prepare our way. Air Chief Marshal Tedder is the creator of the famous "carpet" or pattern bombing technique. *Photo, British Official*

Printed in England and published every alternate Friday by the Proprietors, THE AMALGAMATED PRESS, LTD., The Fleetway House, Farringdon Street, London, E.C.4. Registered for transmission by Canadian Magazine Post. Sole Agents for Australia and New Zealand : Messrs. Gordon & Gotch, Ltd ; and for South Africa : Central News Agency, Ltd.—February 4, 1944.   S.S.   *Editorial Address :* JOHN CARPENTER HOUSE, WHITEFRIARS, LONDON, E.C.4.

Vol 7    # The War Illustrated    № 174

Edited by Sir John Hammerton

SIXPENCE                                                  FEBRUARY 18, 1944

**SUPREME ALLIED COMMANDER S.E. ASIA** is Acting Vice-Admiral Lord Louis Mountbatten, G.C.V.O., D.S.O., Naval A.D.C. to H.M. the King, appointed Aug. 25, 1943. Former Combined Operations Chief, he helped plan famous raids at Vaagso, St. Nazaire and Dieppe. Aged 43, he has been in the Navy for 31 years. With him is Air Chief Marshal Sir R. Pierse, K.C.B., C.B., D.S.O. (left), who on Dec. 19, 1943, was announced commander of all combat units of the R.A.F. and U.S.A.A.F. in S.E. Asia (known as Eastern Air Command). He was A.O.C.-in-C. Bomber Command, 1940-42.        *Photo, British Official: Crown Copyright*

# Our Roving Camera Comes Back to London

AT THE COLONIES EXHIBITION opened in London on Jan. 17, 1944, Lt.-Gen. Sir William Dobbie, ex-Governor of Malta, and Lady Dobbie, visited the Malta section and inspected the George Cross, a replica of that which was presented to the Island on Sept. 13, 1942. (See pp. 586 and 587.)

AMERICAN SOLDIERS enjoy sightseeing trips and the novelty of an old-fashioned ride in this brightly-painted wagon driven through London streets by Mr. Henry Walter, 56-year-old ex-soldier wounded in the 1914-1918 war. He calls for his passengers each morning at the Washington Club, Piccadilly, in all weathers, and seldom starts without a full quota of sightseers.

AUSTRALIA DAY SERVICE for Commonwealth troops was held in the famous church of St. Martin-in-the-Fields, on Jan. 26, 1944. Royal Australian Air Force men march past Buckingham Palace (right) on their way to the service, which was also attended by the High Commissioner for Australia, The Rt. Hon. S. M. Bruce. The first contingent of Australian forces arrived in England on June 16, 1940.

GUN-SITE "EMPTIES" being collected (below) after the fierce anti-aircraft barrage of Jan. 21-22, 1944, which, with the toll exacted by our night-fighters, accounted for 16 out of some 90 German raiders on this country. Shells of all calibres fired in an average heavy barrage cost, approximately, £100,000. The empty cases can be re-charged and used again.

NATIONAL FIRE SERVICE static water tanks all over the country are being used as salvage dumps by idiotic folk whose disused fenders, old bedsteads and other oddments have to be fished out by hard-worked N.F.S. men after the water has been drained off, as above. Those who endanger the public safety in this manner are, in effect, saboteurs in their own country.

*Photos, British and Colonial News Service, Topical Press, Planet News, Fox, and Associated Press*

# THE BATTLE FRONTS

## by Maj.-Gen. Sir Charles Gwynn, K.C.B., D.S.O.

**ITALY** The Nettuno landing entirely changed the situation in Italy. It must have been generally expected that sooner or later General Alexander would employ some such manoeuvre, but winter weather conditions made it impossible to foresee when it could be attempted or how far behind the enemy's front a landing might be possible—except that after our Salerno experience the attempt would almost certainly be made within operational range of fighter aircraft. The boldness of the enterprise and the risks accepted should be fully appreciated by those inclined to wonder why such an obvious manoeuvre had for so long been delayed.

The danger that a break in the weather might leave a small force stranded, cut off from reinforcements and supplies and without full air support, was undoubtedly great. Re-embarkation might equally have been impossible and the enemy could hardly have failed to inflict on us a serious reverse. As it was, the daring of the operation no doubt contributed largely to the flying start it gained, and the weather fortunately held at the most critical stage. It seems certain that Kesselring must have been convinced that the risks of a full-scale landing in winter were too great for General Alexander to accept.

Otherwise it is inconceivable that he should not only have left the section of coastline, where a landing in fine weather might obviously be attempted, inadequately guarded, but that he should have committed the main part of his immediately available strategic reserves to operations on his land front. As a result of his wrong appreciation of General Alexander's character he was caught badly on the wrong foot, and at the time I am writing it is yet to be seen how far he will be able to recover his balance. Allied supremacy in the air and complete command of the Tyrrhenian Sea were important factors in achieving surprise, but in the main it had a psychological basis.

THE timing of the 5th Army's offensive against the Cassino position, which preceded the landing, was admirable. It tied the enemy down and caused Kesselring to commit his main reserves, though whether to strengthen his position or to deliver a major counter-attack is still uncertain. The fierce counter-attacks he actually delivered after he had news of the landing were probably intended to reduce the pressure on his southern front while he was disengaging and regrouping his forces for a counter-stroke against the Nettuno beach-head. He probably realized that he had lost all chance of delivering a rapid counter-stroke in the critical three or four days after the landing, and as a second-best course sought to deliver it in strength and after deliberate preparation.

Meanwhile, he naturally used his carefully husbanded air reserves to disturb the Allied landing operations, and probably counted on

a break in the weather which would have the same effect. The fact that the Allies were largely dependent on the small and indifferent port of Anzio obviously made it certain that some time would elapse before they could develop their full strength. Kesselring therefore had still a good chance of being able to deliver a powerful counter-stroke before the Allies could take the offensive in strength, and his chances were greatly improved by the number and strength of the positions on which the advance of the main body of the 5th, and 8th, Army could be held up. Moreover, he would probably have time to receive substantial reinforcements from Northern Italy.

IT was, therefore, clear from the beginning that although General Alexander's landing operation had achieved an amazingly good start, a crisis had still to be passed before it

**ALLIED THRUSTS FROM NETTUNO-ANZIO BEACH-HEAD,** west coast of Italy, where a landing was made on Jan. 22, 1944, and from the main Fifth Army front at Cassino, are indicated by arrows. By Feb. 7 our troops had pushed inland ten miles from the beach-head, taking Aprilia and menacing the Appian Way road to Rome. On the main Fifth Army front U.S. forces were fighting in the outskirts of Cassino, pivot of the Gustav Line.
*By courtesy of The Daily Mail*

could be certain that it would achieve its strategical purpose. Much obviously depends on whether Allied air power can decisively affect Kesselring's movements and, in that also, weather is a factor of importance. He has the advantage of interior lines with favourable conditions to delay one of the armies opposing him while he strikes at the other. It is therefore all the more important to deprive him of the mobility on which successful exploitation of interior line strategy greatly depends.

Surprise has been expressed that General Alexander did not exploit the opportunity presented by his flying start to press farther inland. But such a course might have upset the complicated disembarkation programme without compensating results. Establishment of a secure well-stocked base was of a primary importance, and I hold that he was wise to keep to prearranged plans without being drawn into doubtful pursuit.

I have before now had occasion to point out that amphibious operations must pass through three stages before they can be considered completely successful—the initial landing; the establishment of a secure beach-head base; and finally the deployment of a fully equipped and well-supplied force capable of far-reaching offensive action. The third stage may prove to be the most difficult and take the longest time to complete. The

first two stages have in this case, it is to be hoped, been successfully passed and co-operative action by the 8th and main body of the 5th Army should reduce the difficulties of the third stage. But encouraging as the success of the Nettuno landing has in many respects been it will, I hope, not lead us to under-estimate the magnitude of the task that awaits us in western Europe.

**RUSSIA** If the Nettuno landing has changed the situation in Italy the Leningrad offensive has brought about an almost equally great change in the situation in Russia. Not only has Leningrad been relieved after its long ordeal, but another great Russian force has been released for offensive operations. It always seemed probable that the Germans might be compelled to raise the siege of the city, either in order to shorten their front or because the communications of their northern armies were threatened by a Russian offensive in the centre.

Few can have expected, however, that the Russians in the course of a week could break into the great defences of the investing army and capture many of its elaborately fortified strongholds. It seemed that the utmost that could be expected from the defenders of the city would be a vigorous pursuit of a deliberate German withdrawal. The success achieved is one more sign of the immense resources and striking power of the Red Army which again the Germans appear to have under-estimated, with the result that they have again been surprised. Already they have suffered immense losses of men and material, and they are faced with the inevitable necessity of retreat under difficult, if not impossible, conditions.

It will need all their executive skill to extricate themselves without catastrophic disaster, and even should they rally on a shorter line it will not result in much economy of strength, since the Russians have gained increased liberty of action. It remains to be seen whether the German troops, which have for so long been on a static front, are in a fit condition to carry out an orderly retreat in the circumstances. The very fact that they have failed to hold the strongest defences leads one to suspect that some of them were of inferior quality, or had deteriorated greatly in a prolonged period of inactivity.

GERMAN troops on all fronts show no sign of deterioration in attack nor in defence where picked troops are involved, but there are certainly reasons to suspect that those normally used in a defensive role are becoming unreliable. Possibly the immense losses sustained during the last two years has caused a shortage of officers and N.C.O.s of the highest class, without whom deterioration of units is bound to set in.

Obviously the more completely an army is drawn into intensive fighting the more its weaknesses will be revealed, for picked troops, so effective when concentrated for offensive action or to hold particularly vulnerable points, cannot be everywhere. In the situation which now confronts them the Germans may have reason to regret that their determination to exploit offensive strategy has led them to place excessive reliance on their storm troop policy.

# 5th Army Land at Nettuno 30 Miles From Rome—

SURFRISE LANDING by 5th Army troops at Nettuno on the west coast of Italy, some 30 miles south of Rome, on Jan. 22, 1944, out-manoeuvred the Germans. By Feb. 3 the Allied beach-head, with Anzio as its centre, had been widened to about 14 miles, with an average depth of 8 miles; the spearhead of the attack extending beyond that distance, with the British forces at the north-west in the area of Campoleone, and the Americans south-east of them near Cisterna, some 10 miles from the beach-head and close to the Appian Way, westernmost of the two main roads to Rome from the south.

Troops wade ashore from landing craft (1), and more arrive in " ducks " (4). These Germans (2) were among the first prisoners taken. General Alexander, C.-in-C. Allied Armies in Italy, who personally directed the operations at Nettuno, and Admiral Troubridge, commander of naval forces engaged, watch a sapper sweeping for mines (3). See story in p. 601.

*Photos, British and U.S. Official*

# —While from the S.E. our Main Forces Hit Hard

CANADIANS of a mortar section (1) of the 8th Army fire on German positions north of the Ortona area. The 8th's new Commander, Lieut.-General Sir Oliver Leese, K.C.B., C.B.E., D.S.O., is seen (2-left) talking to some of his senior British and Canadian officers shortly after his appointment on Dec. 30, 1943 (in succession to General Montgomery).

Crew of this heavy machine-gun (3) are members of the French Expeditionary Corps which has distinguished itself in fighting with General Mark Clark's 5th Army; the British infantrymen (4) advancing over rough country in the Cassino area, where the German Gustav Line was pierced on Jan. 31, 1944, after a three-day battle, are also of the 5th. By Feb. 2, our main forces were only a mile from the German defence bastion of Cassino. See map in p. 579.

*Photos, British, Canadian and U.S. Official*

# THE WAR AT SEA

## by Francis E. McMurtrie

BRITISH submarines are now operating in the Far East. Last month one succeeded in torpedoing a Japanese cruiser of the Kuma class, of 5,100 tons, in the northern approaches to the Straits of Malacca. This does not mean that there is no longer scope for submarine operations in European waters, as illustrated by the torpedoing of the Tirpitz and Lützow in the Altenfjord, and frequent sinkings of Axis supply ships in the Mediterranean. It does imply, however, that we now possess a sufficient force of submarines to spare some for service with the Eastern Fleet.

In the Pacific the Japanese losses from the attacks of United States submarines must be causing grave concern in Tokyo. At regular intervals, and with increasing frequency, the

a point where it will no longer suffice to meet her urgent needs. Not only have her armies in Malaya, the Netherlands Indies, Indo-China, Siam and Burma to be kept supplied with stores and munitions, but the people of Japan itself need to be fed, for which a certain amount of imported rice is essential. Moreover, the maintenance of munition manufacture is dependent on the import of rubber and other necessities which the Japanese cannot, for various reasons, produce in their own country.

### DISMAL Prospect Indeed for Japan's Large Cities

Already it is believed that the rate at which Japanese shipping is being destroyed exceeds the capacity for replacement. Though Japan

**KEEPING THE SEA LANES OPEN** is part of the work of the gallant little minesweepers. Mr. A. V. Alexander, First Lord of the Admiralty, stated on Nov. 11, 1943, that they had disposed of mines sufficient to have destroyed the British merchant fleet two or three times over. In sweeping they are frequently under enemy fire. H.M.S. Dornoch (foreground) about to begin a sweep ; behind her is the Canadian-built Shippigan. *Photo, British Official*

Navy Department in Washington is able to announce the destruction of a number of enemy vessels in the course of a patrol carried out by an unnamed submarine. There are now something like 150 modern ocean-going submarines in the United States Fleet, exclusive of older craft of smaller size, suitable for coastal operations or training work. It may be estimated that from 40 to 50 of these ocean-going craft are always at sea, either operating in enemy waters or proceeding to or from their patrol stations. This number, moreover, is steadily increasing as more and more submarines are launched. Four went afloat on the same day from the Navy Yard at Portsmouth, New Hampshire, in January 1944.

A TIME must inevitably come when the mounting losses from Allied submarine attack reduce the tonnage of which Japan can dispose for supply and transport purposes to

is thought to have begun the war with fully 5,000,000 tons of mercantile shipping, the operations which she has undertaken are so far-flung that the margin available to meet losses has probably been expended.

ANOTHER method of attack which holds out a dismal prospect for the inhabitants of Tokyo, Osaka and other large cities is embodied in the orders recently placed for three giant American aircraft carriers of 45,000 tons displacement. Two were begun last year and the third is to be laid down shortly. These ships will be able to carry the largest types of bombers, involving a total weight of aircraft 50 per cent greater than in the 27,000-ton carriers of the Essex class. They will also be faster than previous aircraft carriers, and more elaborately divided into watertight compartments. It is believed that these three ships will all be in service next

year, by which time other Allied resources may also be freed for concentration against Japan. This goes far to explain the gloomy tone which recent broadcasts from Tokyo have assumed.

Apart from the coming giants, the United States Navy is already able to dispose of a very large number of aircraft carriers. There are now in commission nearly 20 fleet carriers, of which three were completed before the war. These are the Saratoga, Enterprise and Ranger. New construction includes the Essex, Yorktown, Intrepid, Hornet, Franklin, Lexington, Bunker Hill and Wasp, all ships of 27,000 tons, carrying fully 100 aircraft each; and the Independence, Princeton, Belleau Wood, Cowpens, Monterey, Cabot, Langley, Bataan and San Jacinto, of about 10,000 tons.

It is questionable whether the Japanese have more than half a dozen fleet aircraft carriers, for they lost the majority of those they originally had at the Battles of the Coral Sea and Midway. They are still believed to possess the Syokaku and Zuikaku, of 20,000 tons, both modern ships, and two older ones, the Hosyo and Ryuzyo, though there is a possibility that one of the latter pair may have been sunk.

Three or four 15,000-ton ships which are reported to have been designed on Japanese " pocket battleship " lines, with a main armament of six 12-in. guns, may have been converted into aircraft carriers instead, but until evidence of their existence is forthcoming this must be regarded as problematical. In any case, the inferiority of the Japanese in aircraft carriers is very marked, and gives them little hope of victory in such operations as are now being vigorously conducted in the Pacific.

### BASES and Airfields in the Vast Pacific Spaces

Nor do the foregoing figures take into account the large number of aircraft carriers of the escort type which the United States Navy has at its disposal. These are ships of between 7,000 and 10,000 tons, with speeds of between 16·5 and 18 knots. Though unsuitable for fleet work, they have proved invaluable in the Battle of the Atlantic. There are believed to be about 40 of them at present in service.

A fleet with such an abundance of aircraft carriers available is at a great advantage compared with an opponent less completely equipped. In the vast spaces of the Pacific, where bases and airfields may be separated by thousands of miles of sea, air reconnaissance must be undertaken by carrier-borne planes. With some hundreds of these, the U.S. Fleet is in an excellent position to launch an attack on the Japanese stronghold at Truk when the surrounding bastions, such as Kwajalein, Rabaul and Nauru, have been reduced. (See page 590.)

IN two quarters Allied Armies are advancing with the aid of Navies. The landing at Nettuno-Anzio, 30 miles from Rome, could not have been effected without naval support, both before and after the troops were ashore. In the Leningrad area the situation is similar, with the Russian warships supporting Soviet attacks on the retreating Germans.

So far the only Soviet ships mentioned by name have been the Oktiabrskaya Revolutia and the Petropavlovsk. The former is an old battleship of 23,000 tons, launched in 1912. She is armed with 12-in. guns of an obsolete pattern. Much more modern is the Petropavlovsk, this being the name given by the Russians to a cruiser acquired from the German Navy in January 1940, when Hitler was endeavouring to conciliate his future foes in Eastern Europe. She is a ship of 10,000 tons, which was designed to mount a main armament of eight 8-in. guns. It has been reported from Swedish sources that she now carries instead twelve 7·1-in. guns of Soviet manufacture.

# Royal Navy Rides Supreme in Northern Waters

SUNRISE AHEAD OF H.M.S. MILNE (3), one of the Navy's famous destroyers, from which these photographs were secured. She took part in the N. Africa landings on Nov. 8, 1942, and fought in the great convoy to Russia action in Sept. 1942, as the flagship of Rear-Adm. R. L. Burnett (see p. 317, Vol. 6). An icy scene on the deck of the Milne (2). One of the destroyers which attacked the German battleship Scharnhorst off N. Norway on Dec. 26, 1943 (see pp. 518-20) was H.M.S. Saumarez (1), here seen with H.M.S. Mahratta.

*Photos, British Official : Crown Copyright*

# Australia's Allied Works Council in Swift Action

The Japanese threat of invasion urged Australia to embark on a programme of development, the like of which no man had previously conceived. The tremendous achievements cannot yet be divulged in full, by reason of security measures ; but sufficient can be revealed for the Commonwealth's contribution to the Allied pool to be appreciated at least in part. See facing page

WITH a total population of only 7,137,220, in an area of 2,974,580 square miles, Australia's problems when war loomed on her very shores were far from simple ; they have not been lessened by the fact that 850,000 of her sons are now serving in the armed forces.

How the Commonwealth's economic, industrial and human resources were so marshalled as to ensure defence—and preparations for ultimate attack—on the most determined scale makes a success story seldom equalled. A defence programme had to be organized almost overnight. In a normal year prior to 1939-1940 development work by the Commonwealth Government amounted to a mere £2,100,000 ; from February 1942 to June 1943 no less than £56,000,000 was spent out of an authorized sum of £85,500,000 for capital works associated with defence.

This transformation in effort came about when, faced with the Japanese menace, Mr. Curtin, the Australian Prime Minister, put into motion machinery to evolve an organization known as the Allied Works Council. This was established by National Security Regulations promulgated on February 26, 1942, to provide for and carry out the colossal requirements of the Chiefs of Staff. (Hitherto, execution of the Australian defence works programme had been the responsibility of a Works Directorate, under the control of the Minister of the Interior.) At once a gigantic "behind the lines" construction effort was inaugurated. Given the task of building, extending and maintaining roads, docks, wharves, aerodromes, munition plants, ammunition depots and repair sheds, oil storage installations and pipe-lines, stores, warehouses, camps, hospitals and other war essentials, the Council went swiftly to work.

AMONG the most vital arteries of war are roads, of which in 1939 the Commonwealth had 500,000 miles ; to these have been added, in the few months since the Council's birth, some 5,000 miles of strategic highway for the speedy passage of Australian and United States troops : equivalent to a roadway from the southernmost point of the mainland to Tokyo. Vast areas which had never known the mark of a wheel resounded (and still resound) to the clangour of bulldozers and mechanical scoops gouging out pioneer trails. In their wake toil armies of workers turning the tracks into broad highways paved with gravel or bitumen.

Across the "dead heart" of the continent, a waterless desert, they drove the 400 miles Northern East-West highway, and found water, the greatest of all necessities to the "outback"; 931 miles of the Queensland Inland Road have been completed ; and the North-South Transcontinental Road, last link of 980 miles. These are three outstanding achievements in the face of obstacles including blazing desert heat, tropical disease, treacherous swamps, and floods caused by torrential rains.

Where now battle planes are lifting into the sky, and touching-down again after participation in round-the-clock attacks on Japanese positions north of the mainland, were unexplored blocks of primeval forest and almost impenetrable bushland. From these unpromising sites have been hacked out, by bulldozers and tractors, runways by the score ; and whilst the mechanical monsters did their clearing and levelling, there were run-up aerodrome buildings, complete to the last detail.

Hospitals are, unfortunately, a concomitant of war. Near cities and large towns these have sprung up in miraculous fashion, and immense healing centres have been established, even in remote and sparsely populated areas where such institutions were entirely lacking. Much of the construction is, naturally, of timber, and such is the urgent demand for wooden structures of all kinds that the development of prefabrication methods has had to be speeded up to keep pace with ever-increasing requirements. Hospitals, hangars, stores, and other great building projects for which precious steel could not be spared owe their existence now to Australia's woodmen and craftsmen.

**HON. E. G. THEODORE,** former Federal Treasurer retired from political life, undertook the great task of controlling the Allied Works Council, of which he is now the Director-General.

The provision of food for front-line troops in the Pacific is being largely solved by dehydration plants planned on a most extensive scale. Refrigeration depots have been established at strategic points. Flax mills have come into operation where previously there was no form of industry.

All this immense scheme of wartime development work, still continuing at utmost speed, hangs on a sufficient labour supply ; without organization of workers little could have been achieved. And so in April 1942 the Allied Works Council was empowered to form the Civil Constructional Corps as an emergency measure. Consisting of compulsorily called and volunteer personnel from all walks of life, the Corps now has a total membership of more than 50,000 workers.

Construction camps, forming Corps centres, now dotted all over the continent, are under the strict control and direction of the Personnel Directorate of the Allied Works Council, so this "army behind the Army" experiences very little of the rough conditions for which construction camps hitherto were noted. Not that the work is all in the "collar and tie" class, as the 2,500 men who drove 500 miles of new highway through the tropical region of northern Queensland in three and a half months will testify ; a feat all the more commendable when it is noted that 80 per cent of the workers had never before been engaged on road-making.

THEY laboured in torrential rains : a fall of 9 inches in October, 28 inches in November, 12 inches in December, 11 inches in January. A river broke its banks and spread for 28 miles. At one camp floodwaters surrounded the men for three weeks ; one workman became lost, and other members of the Corps welded together galvanized iron sheets to form a boat, and set out in search of him. Sixty hours later they discovered him perched in a tree-top which was just visible above swirling muddy water.

At another camp a worker developed appendicitis. An operation was needed to save his life. A plane used on the road work for communication and observation landed on a hastily constructed emergency runway, took the man aboard and flew him to hospital just in time.

Examples of team-work and co-operation in the ranks of the Civil Constructional Corps could be multiplied almost indefinitely : a spirit auguring well for the post-war years if it can be fostered and maintained. And in these mighty works of development and construction, enforced by total war, the Australia of tomorrow will reap advantages which should place the Commonwealth among the top-ranking nations of the earth.

**JUST ONE OF MANY RUNWAYS in North Australia built since the outbreak of war by the Allied Works Council ; in the background is an American Flying Fortress. Hundreds of strategically placed airfields and landing-grounds have been hewn out of primeval forests and bushland and buildings run up, to facilitate attacks on Japanese positions north of the mainland.**

*Photos by courtesy of the Australian Government*

# Vast Tasks of Australian Civil Construction Corps

AUSTRALIA'S ALLIED WORKS COUNCIL, through the labours of the Civil Constructional Corps, as outlined in the facing page, has effected a mighty change in the wartime face of the Commonwealth. Corps workers are seen spreading gravel over the surface of a newly constructed airfield (1), erecting the framework of an Army barracks (2), building a vast hospital for Australian and United States troops (5), and roofing a gigantic oil-storage tank (3) in Central Australia for Allied use. One of the great new strategic highways (4) for the swift movement of troops and war supplies crosses the continent from the centre to the northern coast. Eighty per cent of the Corps members employed on roads were strange to the work, yet contracts were completed in record time.

*Photos by courtesy of the Australian Government*

# Britain's Colonies in the War : No. 1—Nigeria

Photos, British Official

AT IBADAN, WEST AFRICA, Nigerian chiefs meet to discuss increased war production. The quaintly titled The One of Ife, Aderemi I, C.M.G. (2, extreme right), was elected president of the conference ; Chief Omarin of W. Urhobo (1) and The Pere of Akugbene (3) are seen arriving ; the conference in session (4). The Colony's principal contributions are rubber, and palm kernels for oil ; many recruits have been raised for the Royal W. African Frontier Force, and large sums have been collected for the purchase of planes for the R.A.F.

# Columbite from Nigeria Makes Warplane Steel

**A MINERAL NOW IN GREAT DEMAND** by our American allies, who use it in making special steels for aircraft construction, columbite (containing tantalum and niobium, found in association with tin ores) until recently was regarded as of slight commercial value. Its rise to importance for alloying steel has led to the opening of many mines in Northern Nigeria, giving employment to hundreds of natives. Labourers carrying headpans from which they have emptied rubble are seen at work at one of these mines.

*Photo, British Official : Crown Copyright*

# Bessarabia Has Its Problem for the Allies

Incorporated within the Soviet Union since June 28, 1940, Bessarabia has a population of 2,367,000, with Rumanians (1,609,000) and Russians (353,000) predominating. For years this province of 17,150 square miles, in the Black Sea region, has been a bone of contention between Russia and Rumania ; the problem is discussed here by HENRY BAERLEIN.

We have heard a good deal about countries and provinces whose misfortune it is to possess a more or less obstreperous alien minority ; and perhaps Bessarabia, of which we shall probably be hearing much in the near future, can claim in this respect a sad pre-eminence. For while in the northern half the Rumanians predominate, the southern portion is a strange mosaic of Rumanians, Ukrainians, Germans, Bulgarians, and even Poles and Swiss.

When Russia occupied the country in 1812, the Turks being driven out, the Tsar's former French master, a Swiss called La Harpe, toured the land and discovered that near the old Turkish settlement of Akkerman (Cetatea Alba) the soil, red in colour, much resembled that of his own vine-growing part of Switzerland. He obtained the Tsar's permission to secure for its cultivation some of his countrymen, and today the little town of Saba, after many vicissitudes, is still inhabited by Swiss vine-growers, who were more prosperous when their wine supplied the Russian market than when, after the last war, Bessarabia became a Rumanian province and its products had to compete with Rumania's excellent other wines.

The wisdom of that Tsar was displayed in placing the south Bessarabian villages always about fifteen miles from each other, so that, with some exceptions, they have dwelt in amity with their neighbours. And Russia, having administered the province for more than a century, does not see why this should not continue. She points out that Odessa is the natural outlet for Bessarabian cereals, fruit and cattle, while it is to Odessa that the Bessarabian railways converge. The U.S.S.R. always felt Bessarabia to be part of the old Tsarist territory, and hence did not acknowledge the decision of the Bessarabian Diet (taken in 1918) for union with Rumania.

That was a time when conditions in Russia were very liquid, when the Russian armies, devoid of discipline, were not welcome sojourners in Bessarabia, and when the local population of the whole province argued that half the three millions were Rumanians, the next largest entity, the Ukrainians, not amounting to more than one-fifth. During the interval between the two world wars Bessarabia remained in Rumania, with Russia protesting, and with the river Dniester that separates them not available for traffic. The railway bridge across the river at Tighina was destroyed by the Rumanians, while the Russians established on their side of the river a Moldavian (i.e. Rumanian) Soviet Republic ; for on the left bank of the Dniester are many folk of Rumanian origin, and it was hoped that they would be as a magnet to Bessarabia. Of course, the Government in Bucharest forbade their people in Bessarabia to cross the river ; when they

did so by night they were lavishly entertained by the Russian authorities.

Can this question, the ownership of Bessarabia, be solved to the satisfaction of both parties ? Some of the experts have suggested that the central part should go to Rumania, while Russia should have the south, giving her access to the mouths of the Danube, which she has never ceased to desire, and should also have the north of the province where the Ukrainian population is in the

NEARNESS OF RUSSIANS to Rumania brings into prominence the position of Bessarabia. Originally a province of the Principality of Moldavia, constituent part of Rumania, it was taken by Russia in 1812, returned to Rumania in 1856, lost again by her in 1878, regained in 1919, and incorporated within the Soviet Union in June 1940.
*Specially drawn for* THE WAR ILLUSTRATED

majority. Another solution consists in a transference of populations, and it is a fact that on the left bank of the Dniester there are more Rumanians than there are Russians on the right bank.

Moreover, there are people of Russian origin on the right bank, the Lipovani, who would prefer to stay where they are, not because they would nowadays suffer on account of their religious practices that were obnoxious to Peter the Great and caused them to seek refuge in these remote parts, but because their livelihood, hunting the sturgeon and producing the delectable caviar, binds them to Valcov, that second and miniature Venice. The Lipovani are so steadfast that even today they do not smoke because it was an indulgence of Peter's ; they compensate themselves by taking large quantities of vodka.

One obtains a good idea of the terrain of Bessarabia when it has rained, for when this had happened during our last night at Valcov we had to telephone to various villages on

our proposed route northwards to inquire if the roads were passable ; and our smallish American car had the high-powered engine essential to the negotiation of those soft, sandy tracks. We received reassuring answers, but we often had to desert the road in favour of the adjoining fields, the ditches of which were a trap for our springs ; and in one village, on the flat, we had to put a chain on the wheels ; in another, our skilful driver had to charge an incline three times before we conquered the mud and the vast ruts. There is no stone in Bessarabia, so that the making of good roads is always extremely costly.

In the north-west the country is traversed by well-wooded offshoots of the Carpathians. Generally, however, Bessarabia (which, of course, has nothing at all to do with Arabia, its name being derived from an important family, the Bessarabs, of other days) on the whole is an undulating, fairly fertile plain on which the breeding of cattle is the chief business, with other exports in the shape of salt, wool and tallow, while leather, soap and candles are manufactured there.

I shall not soon forget a visit to the archiepiscopal soap factory, just behind His Beatitude's palace at Kishinev (Chisinau), the capital, for I had some difficulty in declining the gift, as a souvenir, of a church candle rather larger than myself, with which I would presumably have been destined to travel until the heat of the sun had rendered it less formidable.

Kishinev (Chisinau) certainly has the air of a Russian city, with enormously wide streets and with an hotel, the Londra (i.e. London), whose corridors are almost as spacious. Everything except the prices seemed to be exaggerated, and the cosmopolitan character of the town was clear in the picture-houses, for the actors in the mainly American films spoke English (which scarcely anyone understood), the pictures had captions in Rumanian, and a blackboard at one side gave a Russian translation.

Water-melons, tobacco, barley, flax, saffron and madder are among the products of Bessarabia, whose peasants ask only to be left alone, whether a Russian or a Rumanian flag flies over them. Too often since the Turks departed—after a regime which lasted for more than three centuries and of which certain picturesque fortresses along the Dniester are reminders—has the province been assigned to this and then to that power ; the Treaty of Paris, for instance, giving it to Moldavia, the Berlin Congress of 1878 returning it to Russia. At various times the southern Danube ports have been transferred and re-transferred, so that one hopes that at last, when Europe is considered calmly after this war, a permanent solution will be found.

# Govorov's Guns Break Nazi Leningrad Line

**GREATEST BARRAGE OF THE WAR** heralded yet another Russian offensive, launched from Leningrad (announced on Jan. 18, 1944), which city the Nazis harassed with guns emplaced south of Oranienbaum. Massed Soviet artillery smashed German defences covering the approaches to the Baltic States, and on Feb. I our Ally's advancing forces captured Kingisepp, 75 miles south-west of Leningrad, and, developing their successes north and south, later crossed the Estonian frontier, while other troops menaced Luga, pivot of the entire German salient. The enemy was cleared from the whole length of coastline from Leningrad to the mouth of the Luga, which the Russians had crossed.

Guns that opened the offensive are seen (4) blasting German positions. Red Army reinforcements march through Leningrad's suburbs (1), and snow-camouflaged, self-propelled guns cross the great Strike Square (3). Commander of the victorious Russians, artillery expert Gen. Govorov (2) also broke the Mannerheim Line in Finland in Feb. 1940.

*Photos, Planet News*

# Pacific Stronghold Bases Japan Must Defend

After the Japanese struck at Pearl Harbour, on Dec. 7, 1941, the world learned with astonishment of naval and military installations in the Carolines and other Pacific island groups owned by Japan. DONALD COWIE indicates the importance of these bases, and reveals the secret construction in the Truk atoll of naval accommodation for half the Japanese battlefleet.

I WELL remember my first acquaintance with the Truk atoll. We were talking in the saloon of a ship that was carrying us through the South Seas, when one man actually claimed to have visited the mysterious interior island of the Japanese Caroline group. "It is another Wilhelmshaven," he declared, "bristling with guns, battleships in the lagoon, great air-strips and oil-tanks in the jungle." And did we laugh !

Yes, I am afraid we did (though, significantly, some of us were later refused permission by the Japanese to visit that atoll), and thus we allowed ourselves to be lulled, with the rest of the world, into a feeling of Pacific security. It was obvious enough that the Japanese would never be able to make real bases from those scanty islands, which, as mandates from the League of Nations, had been their principal reward for joining us in the 1914–1918 war.

And it has been from those bases in the Caroline, Marshall, Palau and Ladrones Islands that our enemies have successively raided Pearl Harbour, taken the Philippines and Dutch East Indies in flank, and penetrated through New Guinea and the Solomons nearly to Australia and New Zealand. We also know, with relief, that Allied amphibious expeditions have already begun to assault, in strength and successfully so far, the outer bastions of those mysterious Gibraltars, Wilhelmshavens and Portsmouths of the remote South. But what else do we know?

HERE are some of the bleak facts which tantalize Service chiefs when considering the region. The groups of Japanese islands under discussion lie, most conveniently for their owners, between Japan in the north and New Guinea in the south, between the Philippines in the west and the British-owned (and recently recaptured) Gilberts in the east. They are 935 nautical miles south of Yokohama, 1,215 nautical miles north of Cooktown, Australia, 485 nautical miles east of the Philippines, and 1,920 west of Hawaii.

They consist, in all, of some 1,400 islands, but their total land area does not exceed 1,500 square miles ; and generally they comprise a particularly useless and uninteresting type of oceanic pinprick, lacking any great mineral, agricultural or forest wealth. They are administered from Koror, an island of the Palau group in the West Carolines, and subsidiary governmental headquarters are at Truk atoll and Ponape in the East Carolines, Jaluit in the Marshalls, Yap and Palau Islands in the West Carolines, and Saipan in the Ladrones.

A dull and valueless picture? But that, as we now know, is precisely what the Japanese have desired to instil in our minds. Perhaps we would have been wiser all along to concentrate upon the weird reputation of Truk atoll for creating typhoons. Not only does this atoll (consisting of over 200 small islands) boast the largest coral reef in the world, but it has been identified by meteorologists as the birthplace of most of those great, circular wind-storms, sometimes 500 miles in diameter, which periodically sweep across the entire Pacific area. Being at the original centre of these, however, Truk is always deceptively beautiful and calm.

## Vast Construction Works

Behind the sparse guide-book facts are the certainties now that ever since the 1914–1918 war, while refusing proper inspection facilities to League representatives, Japan has been most efficiently transforming the best of those islands into formidable bases.

Strongest of all is Truk, where the vast, unrippled lagoon within the great coral reef shelters at this moment perhaps half of the entire Japanese battlefleet, hundreds of ships attended by all the clangorous facilities of yard, basin and workshop. A huge paper town, that might have been transplanted direct from Japan, covers the white-sanded land beneath the palm trees. The native Kanakas, now nearly outnumbered in all these islands by their swarming masters (the Japanese population increasing by some 9,000 a year while Micronesian statistics remain stationary), provide sullen labour for endless construction works.

Truk atoll possesses not only the great naval base but also a large military aerodrome, and seaplane anchorages, submarine shelters, storage tanks, barracks for the temporary housing of thousands of soldiers on their way south, east, west. Upon this single base rests the security of the entire Japanese position in the South-west Pacific, as that of our own position in the East Indies depended upon ill-fated Singapore. That is why the Japanese fleet sticks to the base as much as possible and has not yet been lured out to full-scale action by our tentative operations in the New Guinea and Gilberts areas. It is also why we are making every effort so to provoke a naval clinch by jabbing air-sea raids against Truk's main outliers.

There are subsidiary Japanese bases in the atolls of Jaluit and Mili (numerous islands enclosed by two big reefs) and in that of Kapingamarangi or Greenwich Island. The first two are in the east, near the Gilberts, and contain lagoons adapted for flying-boats as well as harbours for warships and merchantmen. It is probable that the aircraft and shipping have already been disturbed by the continuous, recent raids of the Americans from the Gilberts. Doubtless the next step will be to occupy Jaluit and Mili, after which there will still be a 1,100-nautical-mile journey to Truk atoll, via many other islands, notably Ponape, about two-thirds of the way : an island which has more vegetation than the others, some extraordinary monuments of the Easter Island variety dating back to an unknown civilization, and more recent Japanese efforts to intimidate aesthetic man.

THE Kapingamarangi atoll is an isolated group 420 nautical miles south-east of Truk atoll and 615 nautical miles north-east of our positions in New Guinea. As such it has proved a perfect half-way house for the Japanese coming down to Rabaul in New Britain, and as such it will doubtless be an early objective of General MacArthur's forces after Rabaul has been taken. Already the atoll has been visited by a Liberator or two ; these have done damage and brought back photographs of lagoons crowded with shipping and aircraft and of ant-like activity under the palms.

It is early yet to speak of Truk's main outliers in other directions, towards the Philippines and Japan itself, but we must be prepared to deal eventually with similar bases at Saipan and Tinian in the Ladrones Islands ("Thieves" Islands is the literal translation) which provide a series of stepping-stones to the Japanese mainland. The Palau Islands, towards the Philippines, contain the valuable phosphate island of Angaur, and bases in the islands of Yap and elsewhere. Then isolated Guam, in the Ladrones, will invite the special attention of Americans—who lost it on their entry into the war and who will require it again for its anchorage and airfield.

Is it likely that Admiral Nimitz and General MacArthur, when they have finally uncovered the secrets of these strongholds, will proceed to a direct assault upon Japan? It is not. President Roosevelt has himself pointed out that if we took an island once a month it would "take 50 years to reach Tokyo." What we want is that battlefleet at Truk. An American naval spokesman said the other day : "When Truk is threatened, I am sure the Japanese fleet will be drawn into action, which is our paramount objective."

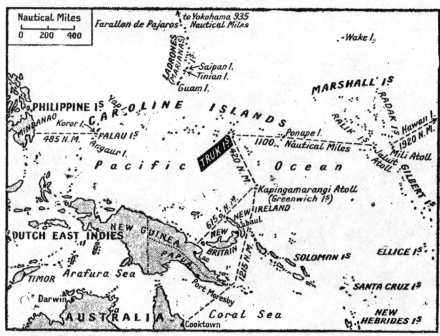

STRATEGIC KEYPOINTS are Japanese bases in the Ladrones, Caroline, Palau, and Marshall Islands ; dotted lines show the relative distances between them and Yokohama, Cooktown (Australia), the Philippines and Hawaii respectively. It was announced on Feb. 1, 1944, that the Marshall Islands had been invaded by U.S. troops ; from that position elimination of Truk could be made easier.

*Specially drawn for* THE WAR ILLUSTRATED

## Still They Call it Pacific!

Fighting one of the bloodiest engagements, so far, of the Pacific campaign, Nov. 20-24, 1943, United States Marines at cost of heavy casualties wrested from the Japanese the atolls of Makin and Tarawa, in the Gilbert Islands. Awaiting their turn to land on Makin are (1) Marines aboard a transport; pushing on after the retreating enemy they saw this derelict flying boat (3), and dummy artillery (2) constructed of palm trunks—a device of the crafty Japanese to give to distant observers a false impression of overwhelming fire-power.

*Photos, New York Times Photos, Planet News, Keystone*

## U.S. Marines Assault Bougainville Island—

Foothold gained at Empress Augusta Bay, Bougainville Island, in the Solomons, on Nov. 1, 1943, United States Marines have engaged the Japanese garrison in stern fighting throughout the ensuing weeks.  From one of the many landing craft (1), with anti-aircraft gun sweeping the sky, Marines wade landwards (2) for the initial attack, and halt for a moment on the drive inland for a refreshing drink of coconut milk (4), whilst amphibious tanks patrol the captured shore (5).

## —Last Japanese Stronghold in the Solomons

With doors gaping wide (3) a giant landing craft disgorges supplies for the invading Marines; a tractor hauls a loaded trailer from the vessel's interior, whilst other tractors move landed ammunition and stores up-beach.  A bomb-blasted area (6) near the Bougainville front lines gives to reinforcements plain evidence of the advantages of cover afforded to the Japanese defenders;  even at a short distance the Marines are scarcely distinguishable against the background of tangled foliage.

## Stars and Stripes Run Up at Tarawa

Photos, Keystone, New York Times
Photos, Associated Press

The Japanese lost their chief air base in the Central Pacific Gilbert Islands when U.S. Forces captured Tarawa, killing or capturing every enemy encountered. Naval coast defence guns (1) that had to be silenced by camouflaged Marines crawling over open ground (3), and a Japanese plane (4) shot down during the landing. A wounded comrade (5) is carried to a dressing station; whilst, marking the hour of triumph, "Old Glory" (2) flutters to a palm-tree top. (*See map in p. 474.*)

# VIEWS & REVIEWS Of Vital War Books

## by Hamilton Fyfe

WE often hear the Japanese called "double-faced." So they are. But the duplicity goes deeper than their faces; it is inherent in their whole nature. They are in their inmost being what a speaker on the air the other evening called "feudal." Their politeness when they want anything or when they are with people whose standards are different from their own is merely on the surface. Below it is the "feudalism" which keeps them narrow-minded, absurdly vain, ruthlessly cruel, and tied to a system which seems to belong altogether to a remote and disgusting past.

I say "seems" rather than "does" belong because we have seen in the last ten years that it is quite possible for this kind of system to be re-established among people supposed to have long-since outgrown it. Hitler has done this in Germany. He has rushed the nation back to the Middle Ages—or even farther back. He has made them show they are still in very truth Huns, and that in cruelty, ridiculous pride, intellectual blinkerdom, they are on the same level as the Japanese.

But I don't think "feudal" is the right word for that damnable union of detestable qualities. There was, after all, something to admire in the way many feudal lords looked after their people, and in the loyalty of tenants, retainers, serfs even, to those lords. The justice of the manor was rough and ready, but it did exist, whereas in the systems of Hitler and Hirohito it does not. The king, as the head of the feudal system, was held in honour so long as he could keep the barons in order: he was not made to seem foolish to the rest of the world by the sickening, nonsensical flattery that Hirohito, as emperor, receives.

THE whole method of government both in Germany and Japan, so far as it has any foundation at all, is based on the belief that human beings in the mass are utterly without wills of their own or sense enough to resist tyranny in its early stages, that they can be harried, driven, ill-treated, killed singly or forced to die in battle by droves, given a deal far more raw than is inflicted on any species of non-human animal. That belief is unhappily not an illusion. Both Japanese and Germans have in their own cases proved it to be the catastrophic truth. But while the Nazis make efforts to persuade the world they are not entirely without intelligence and common decent feeling, the governing Japanese exult in the total absence from their system of any features but terrorism and shameless exploitation of their dupes.

Some little time ago (p. 435) I discussed a book by Prof. John Morris, who spent several years teaching in a Japanese University. He found the colleagues he worked with and the people among whom he lived pleasant, friendly, and not inclined to take seriously all the nonsense about their divine emperor receiving advice from the Sun-goddess, or about the destiny of Japan being to dominate the entire globe—though they did not repudiate it. Now I have been reading another account of Japanese ways—this time by a Russian, who was enveigled into working for the secret service in Manchuria after it had been seized by Japan and who gives a horrifying description of the mode, both diabolically clever and savage, by which they crushed opposition, robbed, murdered, tortured, and gloried in their crimes.

The title of the book, Bushido (Hutchinson, 8s. 6d.), suggested to me at first that a contrast would be drawn between the extravagant claims of that "system of chivalry," as it used to be called here when we were making use of the Japanese as allies, and their actual behaviour. I remember reading many eulogies of Bushido and hearing it recommended for imitation by us. I remember H. G. Wells writing about the samurai as if they were like the very gentil, parfit knights of chivalrous days, and urging that we ought to have them in Britain (though I don't recollect his proposing to become one himself!) Now we are told they were gangsters of the type familiar in Chicago, serving masters who, though they owned land in vast quantities and had high-sounding titles, were only the Al Capones of an earlier time.

## What is 'Bushido'? New Light on Japanese Tyranny

The sub-title of Bushido, written by Alexandre Pernikoff, is The Anatomy of Terror. Of this anatomy the modern samurai have made a close study. There is no doubt, I am afraid, that they enjoy keeping people in a state of permanent alarm and uncertainty as much as they enjoy maltreating them physically. The reason for their enjoyment is given in the book as revenge. They know the West for a long time either despised them or looked on them as funny little folk with pretty artistic ways. They want to show the West it was wrong.

The much-talked-of Japanese equanimity is but a forced show, beneath which surge violent passions. No one in the world can take as much abuse and humiliation as a Japanese and no one resents it more. Once insulted, even slightly, a Japanese will never forget it. He will smile, yes, but the dream of revenge will long lie dormant in his soul and, when the proper time arrives, this desire will manifest itself in the most grotesque and abhorrent forms.

They are filled with hatred for the Chinese, who have held them up for so long in districts where they expected easy victory. They

**GENERAL HEDEKI TOJO;** Japan's 59-year-old Prime Minister and War Minister, typifies the cult of bushido (" the way of the warrior "), extolled to the Japanese army since 1880 and dealt with in the book reviewed in this page.
PAGE 595       *Photo, Planet News*

would like to exterminate them. There will not be any left in Manchuria in forty years, they boast; and they are doing their best to make this threat come true. In a Manchurian village Chinese seen working under the supervision of Japanese soldiers were "half-naked, unkempt, dirty, emaciated, reduced to the state of animals." The houses which had not been burned down were surrounded by barbed wire fences. Their wretched inhabitants were made "to build roads and homes for their oppressors, and used as pack animals by the army, while their own fields remained untouched. Later on they will be doomed to die of hunger, conveniently vacating their places for Japanese settlers. It is all part of the scheme."

AGAINST Russians, too, there is the same bitter resentment; they have stood in Japan's way for a long time. There were many anti-Soviet Russians in Manchuria, especially in Harbin, where the author of the book lived. The behaviour of the Japanese has forced them to "look in the direction of the U.S.S.R. for deliverance. They are ready to welcome Red soldiers as their brothers and saviours, and the Soviet regime seems to them a heavenly sanctuary. The communists are human beings, they think; the Japanese are nothing but brutal, ferocious apes without a single human quality."

That is not quite correct. They have one human quality, developed in a most unusual degree—that is, dishonesty. "The corruption of Japanese officials has reached staggering proportions. It is found more profitable to sell Government jobs to the highest bidder than to prosecute grafters." So tremendous were the amounts in bribes collected by even low-ranking officials that some positions paying fixed salaries of 1,500 to 2,000 yen a year were auctioned as high as 50.000 yen a year, payable in advance to the Military Mission, which in effect ruled the province of Manchuria.

One result of this universal bribery was that spying grew to huge proportions. "Without exaggeration at least 50 per cent of the Japanese effort in Harbin was spent on spying. We even have to watch our own agents and gendarmes," a powerful man in the Secret Service admitted; "they all come because they want to get rich quickly. Even I am watched. It's the only good system for ensuring people's honesty." The meanest tricks are practised to spy on quite inoffensive, harmless persons in their homes. Every business has a Japanese "adviser," whose salary must be paid by the firm and who is often so ignorant that he leads his employer into very serious trouble.

THEY cannot, many of them, speak the language of those for whom they are supposed to interpret and do business. "Extremely sensitive and self-conscious, the Japanese will never admit that they lack any educational accomplishment. In order to learn a foreign language they will lock themselves up in their rooms and work on it alone with the aid of text-books and dictionaries instead of enlisting somebody's help. The results are often comical." Common all over Japan, says the author, are such signs as "Boiled language today" at a restaurant, meaning boiled tongue, "langue" being French for tongue; and "This exit must only be used for coming in."

Still, though there are limits to their cleverness we must not underrate it. To us it seems senseless to instil terror into people by arresting them for "looking sad while they spoke to one another." We think it idiotic to "cultivate laughter by police enforcement" so as to spread the illusion that Manchuria is a happy land. But such methods have their effect, as this book shows. They have cowed the unfortunate population into putting up with conditions of tyranny that are almost without parallel in the records of "man's inhumanity to man."

# Allied Action and Cool Ingenuity in New Guinea

BEHIND A MATILDA TANK Australian troops move in for a dawn attack on the Japanese-held village of Sattelberg, north-eastern New Guinea. This hill-point and base dominating all the country behind Finschhafen on the coast fell to the Australians after fierce fighting on Nov. 26, 1943. Its capture was vital to the consolidation of positions in the area and to future attacks against the enemy's main operational base at Madang in the north.

FORCED DOWN IN THE JUNGLE, the crew of an American bomber operating over New Guinea devised ingenious signals to guide rescuers. Some went ahead, found a missionary settlement and blazed signs (left) for their comrades behind to follow. Later (centre) they displayed a request for coffee and cigarettes, and (right) their final " Jolly Roger " symbol is completed, timed 8 o'clock, the letter T indicating that a wounded member of the crew can be moved by plane. All were eventually rescued, one at a time. PAGE 596 *Photos, Sport & General. Keystone*

# New Zealand Warhawks in Guadalcanal Jungles

AMIDST WAVING PALMS in a jungle clearing on Guadalcanal, Warhawk fighter-bombers of a Royal New Zealand Air Force squadron prepare to take off (top). Nearby, ground crews service planes (below) whose pilots have had outstanding success against the Japanese. Warhawks are American built, armed with six ·5 machine-guns, have a speed of 355 m.p.h. at 20,000 feet, and can carry one 500-lb. bomb or an extra 33-gallon fuel tank, giving a 900-mile range. Guadalcanal was cleared of the enemy by Feb. 10, 1943. PAGE 597 *Photos, Royal New Zealand Air Force Official*

# We Are the Flying Eyes of the Heavy Guns

Aloft in a small, low-powered "Buzzard," unarmed yet in the thick of battle, getting the range for our artillery : there are hazards a-plenty in the work of this branch of the Service, outlined by a pilot of an Air Observation Post Squadron. He leaves no room for doubt that the bitter hatred felt and shown by the Nazis for these aerial spotters is fully justified !

AMIDST the wartime welter of thundering 2,000-h.p. aero-motors, and 13-gun warplanes, and machines with a wing-span of about 130 feet, my unarmed 90-h.p. machine, that comes in to land at a little over 30 m.p.h., is something to look at twice. It is not a second-rater ; it has been in front-line operations on and off since 1940. When the last salvos are fired it will probably still be cruising around overhead spotting for the guns and exchanging rapid radio badinage with the gunners.

I am not an R.A.F. man, but Army right through—member of an Air Observation Post Squadron, trained in the mysteries of ballistics and propellants, and given a movable projection of the blasted tree trunk so familiar to artillery spotters on the ground. I am expected to land beside the guns, though they may be sited in a hedge between two ploughed fields cratered by bombs, or in a scrub-oak forest clearing in Italy, or on the beach of a seaborne landing, or beside a main road in a village. In all these places I have landed : also in soft Tunisian sand-hills and on sulphurous ledges on a volcano's side.

So far I have met nothing as bad as my training landings. In a disused corner of an English aerodrome, where personnel were encouraged to tip rubbish and empty cans, logs and similar obstacles, and where the authorities kindly added a cartload of old bricks, we were expected to make perfect "three points," and the instructor who sat in the side-by-side seat was pained and vocal if he was shaken up at all. So now, in Italy, you may often see an artillery-spotting aircraft pop down in the road, or between adjoining craters in a ploughed field, or on the lawn of a big house that may be in use temporarily as "Guns" H.Q. ; and the take-off, in a fair breeze, needs a run of only about 100 feet.

Being unarmed in the thick of the battle has a queer thrill. For artillery-spotting aircraft are madly disliked by the German infantry—perhaps understandably, as our job is to heap coals of T.N.T. on their heads. As soon as we slide down out of a cloud they open up with everything they have except the tinned sausage, and whistle up any German fighters that happen to be handy. Sometimes we operate under an umbrella of Spitfires,

FROM AIR TO GROUND go messages for the Allied artillery. This wireless truck receives from the spotting plane the details which, passed on to batteries, enables fire on enemy positions to be registered accurately.

and then we take no more notice of the fighting than a high-bred duchess would do of a street-brawl. But often "Guns" requires urgent details, there are no fighters available, and we go forth alone.

I have been lucky ; I have never been attacked by more than three German fighters, and seldom by any at all. At that, dodging the flak is quite business enough. On the occasion when three were after me, I dodged round and round some tall trees that dotted the hillside where we were. It is a dangerous business for a pilot who knows that his machine will stall at anything less than very high speed to come down to ground level and shave trees by inches, as I can do while flying in perfect safety at less than the speed of a baby car, and with an aircraft that will continue to do vertical turns as required.

Over Longstop Hill, in Tunisia, two of our

"Buzzards," as they are called, operated at zero feet, under a Spitfire umbrella, until the Germans nearly went mad. Sundry Luftwaffe aircraft that came up to interfere were shot down ; one, at least, flew straight into the ground when the pilot's annoyance over-reached his flying sense.

There were some hidden German guns on that hill that no one could site. By the simple process of flying so low over them that the slipstream must have cooled the gunners' heated cheeks, we drew rifle-fire and machine-gun "measles" from the Germans, flashed back the details, and then stood off until our own heavies got the range. That settled that, and it was an obstacle that had proved a real stumbling-block to our infantry's advance.

ONE of our A.O.P.S. spotting planes was set upon recently by thirteen Messer-schmitt fighters. They carried enough metal to fill the unarmed little 100-m.p.h. machine solid. But it popped down into a very narrow and twisty valley between two hills, and there flew bumps and circuits while the thirteen enemy fighters whined and roared and dived and zoomed, their shells and bullets spattering the landscape and shooting the leaves off every tree for miles, while our spotter sent out urgent and slightly uncomplimentary messages to Spitfires about 80 miles away. It was still in its little valley doing acrobatics when the Spits arrived and chased the thirteen Messerschmitts home, shooting one down.

Several times "Buzzards" have been badly shot up, and the pilot has been knocked out, but the observer has brought the machine safely in. A spare "stick" is often fitted opposite the observer's seat, the instruments can be read from both seats, and the aircraft is wonderfully easy to handle. In addition to artillery spotting, it does spells at light transport of urgent stuff, and works as a flying staff-car when the Brass Hats want to go-see for themselves or to rush across country to conferences.

Don't forget, as you watch the Typhoons go thundering past overhead or see the Lancasters blot out the moon, that the war also has jobs for unarmed runabouts of exactly the type that civilians will go week-ending in during the happy days so soon—we hope—to come.

ARTILLERY OBSERVATION BY PLANE is part of the perfected Allied technique in air-land observation. An Auster III spotter, known as a "Buzzard," is seen taking off on a mission for the guns. In this case the pilot, in wireless communication with an Army Gun Position Officer, announces corrections as he watches the shells fall ; the G.P. officer sends these corrections on to the guns.

*Photos, British Official*

# Such is the War Harvest Now Reaped by Italians

**REFUGEES FROM ORTONA** who sheltered in a railway tunnel during the battle for their native town (see pp. 516, 537, 554, 569) trekked to San Vito, four miles south on the Adriatic coast ; there men of the victorious 8th Army, who had occupied Ortona on Dec. 5, 1943, offered them a warm welcome.   These destitute women and children, just arrived at San Vito, are buoyed up by the knowledge that they will be cared for by those who are now ridding Italy of the Hitler-Mussolini curse.

*Photo, Canadian Official*

# Bevin Boys Start Their Coal-Mine Training

**COAL SHORTAGE** prompted Mr. Ernest Bevin, Minister of Labour, to adopt a revolutionary method of recruiting mine-workers when he introduced his ballot scheme in Parliament on Dec. 2, 1943, by which many youths ready for call-up would be diverted to the mines. The first trainees were " drawn from the hat " on Dec. 14, and by Jan. 18, 1944, some were in training. Youths line up for equipment (1) at the Swinton, Manchester, training centre ; others (3) descend the shaft at the Askern Colliery. Filled tubs (2) on their way to the surface in a mine whose workers believe in record output. A 14-year-old volunteer grins broadly (4), while a group of other lads (5) emerge from the pithead at Markham Main Colliery, near Doncaster.

*Photos, G.P.U., Fox, Evening News, New York Times Photos, Keystone*

# I WAS THERE!

## How We Landed on the Beaches South of Rome

On the morning of Jan. 22, 1944, General Clark's 5th Army made surprise landings on the west coast of Italy—near Nettuno, 57 miles behind the German General Kesselring's so-called Gustav Line. The initial operations are described by war reporter Vaughan Thomas. See also illus. page 580.

**WATCHING FOR JAPANESE PLANES, U.S. troops in assault craft go in on the beaches of New Britain in the Central Pacific. See story below.** *Photo, New York Times Photos*

W E'VE landed on the beaches almost unopposed. We seem to have caught the Germans right on the hop, and so far the operation has gone almost to plan. All yesterday, under a warm sun, the great invasion fleet steamed along the Italian coast. There was an armada of little ships, of assault craft, trawlers, patrol boats, and all the new special ships that we've been building for just this sort of job. It was the most tempting target that the · Luftwaffe has had for many a day, yet not a single German aircraft appeared.

As darkness fell, the long lines of ships turned towards the shore. Our escorting destroyers melted into the darkness away to the south-east. Now, well behind us we could see flashes of light playing on the horizon. They came from the guns of the advancing 5th Army, and we got the measure from them of how far we were already penetrating past the German line.

### Ripped the Night Wide Open

Zero hour was 2 a.m. The night was perfect for the job, a calm sea, a slight mist to hide us from the shore, and just enough starlight to show us the dark outlines of our own great host of ships riding quietly only a few miles off the enemy coastline.

On the deck of our own landing craft we waited in full kit for the signal. Suddenly away to our starboard there was a vivid flash that seemed to rip the night wide open, and our little landing craft rocked with the impact of the explosion. Our own guns had opened up on the coast defences. "The party's on!" one of our signalmen whispered to me, and in the deep silence that followed that sudden outburst from our guns we heard a steady chugging of motor engines. Across our bows went a long string of dark shapes each with a little red rear light and a white wake. For one fantastic moment they looked like a string of London taxicabs moving through a fog, then they vanished towards the blurred line of the shore.

The assault craft were going in with the first wave. This was the critical moment. We watched anxiously to see how the Germans were going to react. That opening burst of gunfire must have told them we were coming in. Now was the time for them to open up, but not a sound came from that dark line of beach. It became clear that we'd caught the Germans on the hop. The beach was mined, but the sappers went to work and soon ducks and jeeps were pouring ashore.

Our turn came at dawn. Our landing craft grounded and we moved in a long procession of khaki between the carefully laid tapes out through the pine woods to the open country beyond. Then the Germans started to wake up. There was a high-pitched whine and a shell crumped down in the field beyond us. The whole procession moved rapidly after that, and now we are in our allotted positions.

Everywhere men are digging in. So far we have had no counter-attack, but it can't be long before the enemy gets over his surprise. Our own air cover has arrived, so when that attack does come we feel quite certain that we'll hold it.

## At Cape Gloucester We Crashed Our Way Ashore

, Covered by Australian and American naval units, U.S. troops effected a landing at Cape Gloucester, New Britain, on December 26, 1943. Operations were witnessed by Kenneth Slessor, Australian Official War Correspondent, who gives here an awe-inspiring account of the great assault.

F ROM the flag deck of an Australian destroyer I watched 3,000 Allied shells blasting a fringe of the coast at Cape Gloucester into a wilderness of elemental fire and earth. Australian and American warships battered a gateway for the invasion troops with 130 tons of naval high explosive. As the fog of the last shellburst curled up to meet the vertical smoke pillars from innumerable bombs, we saw the long lines of American assault craft driving to the beach.

**TOWN SQUARE OF ANZIO, Italian coastal town near Nettuno, captured by U.S. troops of the 5th Army on Jan. 22, 1944, early in the surprise Allied landing behind the German lines and between the latter and Rome some 30 miles distant. Story of our invasion armada and the landing is given above.** PAGE 601 *Photo, U.S. Official*

"Good luck to you, Yanks!" said an Australian boy next to me, hooded and helmeted at his Oerlikon gun, and that was what we were all saying in our hearts. At 7.45 a.m. a signaller with telephone clamped to his big brown ears, grinned as he said "O.K." in acknowledgment of a message. "The first wave is ashore without opposition," he told us.

It was still dark, with stabs of tropical lightning, when the guns started at 6 o'clock. The huge peak behind Cape Gloucester loomed through floating shelves of cloud like a swathed and ghostly Fujiyama. One star, as white and brilliant as a flare, made a channel in the dark water. The warships, which had been poising stealthily in their picked positions since 4.30 a.m., opened their mouths with a crash of noise and incandescence which came as a physical shock.

From my post close behind Bib, the port gun of the destroyer's forward turret, it felt as if a fist had punched me on the side of the face. It was hard to hold a pen to paper and take notes on the successive waves of explosion as Bib and Anzac and Aussie, Yvonne and Yvette, the destroyer's other guns, added their uproar.

Two American warships, outlined in black against the first trickle of dawn, were belching wisps of flame to our left, and another Australian ship lit us with sheets of intense naphtha-white to our right. In the deceptive dimness, Cape Gloucester seemed to be almost under our bows instead of six or seven miles away. The shells burst in leaping points of incandescence. Suddenly two daubs of twisting red flame licked up from the shore. Perhaps they were fuel stores or ammunition dumps; perhaps buildings; but they were only fires now. A double boom of broadsides from the cruisers came like the thump of a big drum between the sharper and more splitting bark of the destroyer's open guns. At intervals a white tracer shell went probing up the heights behind the landing area like a star torn loose.

As dawn filled the sky with a light as cold as steel, the Japanese on the shore—if any still remained—must have peered from their burrows at a terrible semicircle of fighting ships. Now it was possible to see a line of American landing craft, a whole alphabet of assault boats waiting in the distance for their moment to come surging in. They looked as tiny as water-beetles against the huge cloud-shapes which filled the sky behind them. Two cruisers began to take form in the west, their masts and turrets poking from balls of dark-red smoke. You could see the bombardment area quite clearly.

Spouts of white vapour were rising from the shellfire like a terrace of hot springs. Away on a rocky point to the east, six magical palm trees appeared, blowing and bending on stalks of smoke. With sunrise, every man in our ship glanced for a moment to where a sailor was running up the Australian battle flag, the Blue Ensign, which flies only when the guns fire. The Oerlikon gunners, hooded like Bedouins, in their anti-flash gear, nudged me and pointed at the mast. We began our second run from west to east. A double bell rang on the bridge before each salvo, giving us a fraction of a second to brace ourselves and push cottonwool into our ears before the ship plunged with the shock.

Films of smoke, as brown and transparent as tortoiseshell, blew over the flag deck. The smell was more like that of burning bones than of cordite. Soon after seven o'clock a cloud of American bombers swept high overhead as majestically as a fleet of liners. Even through the din of bombing we could hear the heavy concussion of their bombs as columns of dust and smoke swirled up from the flat undergrowth behind the beach. After them came a swarm of Mitchells swooping low over the landing area and leaving a swollen screen of smoke in their wake. I could see no sign of anti-aircraft fire from the shore.

Daylight showed the wreck of a Japanese destroyer lying on the knife-edge reefs which fringe the coast—one reason why the bombardment force did not approach closer than six miles. I pulled the plugs of cottonwool from my ears as a signaller with telephones shouted the message for which we had been waiting : " Everything going all right. No fire from shore. Landing will take place in five minutes."

The line of assault craft was moving as he spoke. I could guess what the huddled men in them were thinking as they furrowed as calmly as suburban ferries to the beach head. I remembered, too, how beautiful the destroyers had seemed as they hovered on the outskirts of the Finschhafen landing. Soon the invasion craft had raced into the distance and were visible only as grooves of foam. The guns had stopped. For a moment there

was a strange silence on sea and land. We strained our eyes into the white dazzle of haze which hung between us and the beach, trying to picture the broad snouts of the barges pushing through the sand, and the men jumping and wading and surging up that tiny arc of territory several miles away.

" First wave is ashore without opposition," said the signaller. Drifts of smoke still rolled over the beach. " Well, we will give them a nice Christmas present," said a gunner. A signaller pressed the telephone to his ears

and spoke again : " Beach wreck, second wave now landing." Ten minutes later a bombardment force turned out to sea in anti-aircraft formation, destroyers screening cruisers on each flank. The Cape, with its great hump of mountain, melted into a faraway vagueness of mist and cloud and the lingering smoke of explosions. Down on the gun decks there was a clatter of empty shell cases being collected. The Navy had done its job and departed with the happy feeling that the men on land were doing theirs.

## Our Submarine Chased and Fought Ten Enemy Ships

*Patrolling on the surface, at night, in the Aegean, a British submarine encountered ten enemy vessels—eight Siebel ferries and two supply ships ; she immediately turned to attack and engaged in a spirited torpedo action. The story is told by Lieut. J. P. Fyfe, R.N., in command of the submarine.*

As my torpedoes seemed to have caused no alarm or despondency, I altered course and gave chase at full speed. While we closed the convoy the gunlayer and trainer were kept on the bridge to accustom their eyes to the dark, so that when we opened fire they were on the target immediately. We obtained several hits on the rear * Siebel ferry, and then shifted target to the next ferry, which was hit twice. In both these shoots, some "overs" hit ships beyond the target.

The rear ferry, which was probably carrying ammunition, was now on fire, emitting showers of coloured sparks—an inspiring sight. Then the outline of a larger supply vessel was seen through the smoke. We fired one round at it and this hit. For a while we shifted target to a Siebel ferry that was coming out of the smoke, and had secured at least two hits when the supply ship also emerged from smoke and re-engaged.

It was now getting light and after we had got eight more hits on the supply ship, which was seen to be stopped and was being abandoned, we altered course and gave chase to the remainder of the convoy. When the

range had been closed again we opened fire on the smaller supply ship and got three hits. Two Siebel ferries then opened fire. We saw a Siebel ferry sink, and it is possible that at least one more sank. And then, as we withdrew, we saw shells from our own surface forces, who had apparently picked up our enemy report, bursting around the target.

I had decided to withdraw, with the intention of diving and attacking the stationary supply ship. We dived, but as we were getting into position to fire I saw through the periscope two of our destroyers closing my prey. I watched the destroyers blow up the supply ship with a torpedo, and from the size of the explosion I considered she was carrying ammunition.

As we withdrew I saw many survivors in the water, some swimming, some floating face-down and some in boats. From the position of the supply ship's sinking I concluded that most of the survivors must have come from the Siebel ferries. Then three anti-submarine craft started to hunt us. We went deep and silenced all machinery.

*\* A Siebel ferry, used chiefly for carrying men and equipment, resembles two landing craft joined together side by side.*

## They Used Glider Bombs Against Our Convoy

*An escorting Liberator's crew recently had the experience of witnessing German glider bombs being used against a convoy in the Bay of Biscay. Flight-Lieut. Hugh Sutherland, R.A.F.V.R., captain of the Liberator, broadcast this account, including details of his own attack on the enemy.*

We were patrolling within sight of the convoy. It was a quiet wintry sort of day with some broken cloud, but we were paying more-attention to the

sea than to the sky because our primary duty was anti-submarine patrol.

While we were watching, the ack-ack guns of the escort opened fire and I saw an aircraft. It was about five miles away. We immediately increased speed and made towards him. In a moment or two I recognized him as a Heinkel 177. We'd never seen one before, but there was no mistaking the high fin and rudder and the long nose. We thought it must be a reconnaissance aircraft, and decided to chase it away and if possible shoot it down.

When the range had closed to a mile, he evidently spotted us, for he turned away and headed for cloud cover, and we lost him. We turned back then to the convoy and almost at once sighted four other He. 177s in loose formation approaching the convoy from the north. They were about two miles from the convoy.

These aircraft had an advantage of about 3,000 feet over us, so we climbed straight for them. They didn't see us at first. We were not able to reach their altitude before they passed over the convoy, so we followed them through the flak that the convoy was putting up. As these Heinkels went over we saw one of them release a glider bomb. It looked exactly like a small monoplane, and performed the most unusual aerobatics ; it went all over the shop. It looked as though they were trying to steer it at one of the ships,

AFTER THE TERRIFIC BOMBARDMENT which pulverized Japanese defences on the beaches of New Britain, American troops swarmed ashore at Cape Gloucester on Dec. 26, 1943 and firmly established a beachhead. Above, Marines manhandle a jeep through shallow water after unloading it from a landing craft ; in the background is an " alligator," a general utility land-and-water transport vehicle. See story commencing in p. 601.    PAGE 602     *Photo, Keystone*

but it fell harmlessly into the sea, where it exploded and burned on the surface of the water.

All this time we were closing the range. When we had crossed right over the convoy the leader of the Heinkels turned for a second bombing run and met us face to face. I think he was surprised. We were all ready and waiting and were able to engage him, first with the nose-guns, and then with the rear-guns as he passed. The closing speed must have been somewhere about 360 miles an hour and we were about a hundred yards distant. The rear gunner observed hits. I don't think the Heinkel opened fire on us at all ; he continued his bombing run but didn't drop any more bombs. That was the last we saw of him.

We'd scarcely got rid of that one when the second pilot reported another He. 177 who had obligingly started his bombing run on a converging course with ours at the same height, and at 90 degrees to our heading. I took this excellent opportunity and dived below him, enabling the tail gunner to pump four hundred rounds into him. His starboard engines caught fire, and when we last saw him disappearing into cloud he was on fire and losing height.

As we watched him the tail gunner reported a Focke Wulf 200 closing on us. I think he was the first of the party to see us at all, and he did attempt to shoot at us, but from extreme range. It didn't take us long to shake him off. When we did come out of our evasive action we found ourselves side by side with another Heinkel. He was close enough for us to see the glider bombs tucked up under his wings. You can just see their bodies, rather like extra fuel tanks.

My side gunner opened fire, and we could see his bullets entering the aircraft, which returned the fire, but very inaccurately. Then he broke away, and as he went we found ourselves in the flak from the convoy, and we had to take evasive action.

GUIDING GLIDER BOMBS is one of the functions of this latest version of the Luftwaffe's Heinkel 177, whose maximum speed is 270 miles an hour at 19,000 feet, range 1,100 miles at 215 miles an hour, and bomb-load (according to the Germans) 17,000 lbs. Planes controlling glider-bombs by radio are comparatively easy targets for our fighters, as they are obliged to keep a steady course or lose control of their bombs. See story commencing in facing page. *Photo, British Official*

The sky now seemed to be relatively clear of Heinkels, and for about ten minutes we searched in vain. Then to our delight we discovered one beneath us. That was just what we wanted. We dived on to his tail. As the nose-gunner opened fire the Heinkel jettisoned his bombs and made off to the east. The bombs didn't perform any aerobatics this time ; they went straight into the sea about two miles from the nearest ship.

The Heinkel opened fire on us with a heavy cannon in the tail, but an accurate burst from our nose-gun silenced the cannon immediately. We were able to sit on his tail until the range was short enough for really accurate concentrated fire. This was all the nose-gunner's picnic. He raked the Heinkel from stem to stern at short range. We saw the starboard engine catch fire, and as we followed him down through the cloud the nose-gunner was still pumping away. We lost the Heinkel at sea level in a patch of low cloud.

The whole performance lasted about thirty-five minutes. My flight engineer said he wouldn't have missed it for twenty quid. Then we went back to our patrol, to the convoy which was still pursuing its steady course below us.

*Since this action Flying-Officer H. Sutherland (as he then was) has been promoted to Flight-Lieutenant and awarded the D.F.C. Two members of the crew, Flight-Sgts. A. P. Gibbs and M. N. Werbiski, both of the R.C.A.F., have been awarded the D.F.M.*

# OUR DIARY OF THE WAR

**JANUARY 19, Wednesday** 1,600th day
Russian Front.—Krasnoye Selo, 20 miles from Leningrad, and Ropsha and Peterhof taken by Gen. Govorov's armies. Many German siege guns captured.

**JANUARY 20, Thursday** 1,601st day
Italy.—Capture of Suio, Tufo, and Argento by British troops of the 5th Army announced. Loss of Minturno admitted by the Germans.
Russian Front.—Novgorod, N. of Lake Ilmen, and Ligovo captured by Red Army.
Pacific.—Paramushire, Japanese base in Kurile Islands, attacked by U.S. aircraft.
Air.—Berlin (over 2,300 tons dropped) bombed by Lancasters and Halifaxes in heaviest raid to date.

**JANUARY 21, Friday** 1,602nd day
Mediterranean.—Announced that Jajce in W. Bosnia captured by Yugoslav partisans under Marshal Tito.
Russian Front.—Mga, important rail junction 25 miles S.E. of Leningrad, Petrushino and Pavlovo captured by Gen. Govorov's Russian forces.
Australasia.—Australians made a thrust along the Faria River (New Guinea) towards Daumoina.
Air.—Magdeburg, Germany, heavily raided ; 2,000 tons of bombs dropped.

**JANUARY 22, Saturday** 1,603rd day
Italy.—Troops of 5th Army landed 30 miles south of the Tiber estuary on the Anzio Bay coastline in the Nettuno area.
Mediterranean.—Rail yards at Vrattsa (Bulgaria) and Skoplje (Yugoslavia) raided by Allied aircraft.
Russian Front.—Taitsi rail station, 18 miles from Leningrad, and Tutino, N.W. of Novgorod, taken by forces under Generals Govorov and Meretskov.

**JANUARY 23, Sunday** 1,604th day
Russian Front.—Pustynka, N.E. of Tosno, and Lelchitsy, near Mozyr, occupied by Soviet troops.

**JANUARY 24, Monday** 1,605th day
Italy.—Fall of Nettuno to 5th Army announced. Hospital ship St. David sunk in Anzio Bay by enemy bombers. Revealed that Lt.-Gen. Sir Richard O'Connor, Lt.-Gen. Philip Neame, V.C., and Air Marshal O. T. Boyd had escaped from Italian prison camps and reached Britain.
Russian Front.—Pushkin and Pavlovsk

captured by troops of the Leningrad front, under General Govorov.
Burma.—Appointments announced : Gen. Sir George Gifford, G.C.B., D.S.O., to be C.-in-C., Army group in S.E. Asia ; Lt.-Gen. W. S. Slim, C.B.E., D.S.O., M.C., to be Commander of the 14th Army.

**JANUARY 25, Tuesday** 1,606th day
Italy.—Fall of Anzio announced. Allied beach-head extended to depth of 12 miles inland. Monte Croce re-taken by French.
Russian Front.—Vladimirskaya and Frezernyi, S.W. of Pushkin, captured by Red Army troops of the Leningrad front.
Australasia.—Fall of Kankiryo (New Guinea) to Australian troops announced.

**JANUARY 26, Wednesday** 1,607th day
Italy.—Gen. Alexander, C.-in-C., Italy ; and Gen. Mark Clark, Commander of the 5th Army, inspected the Anzio Bay beach-head. Reinforcements successfully landed.
Russian Front.—Krasnogvardeisk, 20 miles south of Leningrad, captured by Russians of General Govorov's command.
Sea.—Loss of H.M. destroyer Holcombe announced by Board of Admiralty.

**JANUARY 27, Thursday** 1,608th day
Russian Front.—Tosno, important district centre of the Leningrad region, captured by Soviet troops. Volosovo, in the Krasnogvardeisk region, taken. Special Order of the Day addressed to Gen. Govorov announced that the siege of Leningrad had been raised ; 24 salvos from 324 Leningrad guns honoured the occasion ; 300,000 Germans in full retreat.
Air.—Berlin (1,500 tons dropped) raided by all-Lancaster force of bombers.

**JANUARY 28, Friday** 1,609th day
Italy.—Announced that U.S. troops of the 5th Army had crossed the River Rapido. Counter-attacks repulsed in beach-head.
Russian Front.—Lyuban, Pomeranie, Trubnikov-Bor, Babino and Torfyanoye captured by Soviet troops of the Volkhov front. Violent enemy attacks in the Vinnitsa region repelled.
Air.—Berlin (1,500 tons dropped) very heavily bombed by great force of Lancasters and Halifaxes.
General.—Announced that Lt.-Gen. Sir Francis Nosworthy, K.C.B., D.S.O., M.C., appointed to be G.O.C., W. Africa. Mr. Eden disclosed barbarous treatment of British and Allied prisoners of war by the Japanese.

**JANUARY 29, Saturday** 1,610th day
Italy.—British troops captured a bridge on the Anzio-Albano road 20 miles from Rome. Fierce air battles raged.

Russian Front.—Novo-Sokolniki, 130 miles S. of Lake Ilmen on Leningrad-Odessa railway, captured by troops under Gen. Popov ; Chudovo stormed by Red Army and Leningrad-Moscow railway freed.
Air.—Over 800 escorted Fortresses and Liberators carried out heaviest day raid of the war on Frankfurt ; 1,800 tons of bombs dropped.

**JANUARY 30, Sunday** 1,611th day
Italy.—5th Army troops captured heights beyond Cassino and the Rapido River. Heavy artillery landed in beach-head.
Pacific.—Kwajalein, Maloelap and Wotje atolls in Marshall Islands attacked by U.S. carrier task force. Wake Island bombed.
Air.—Brunswick and Hanover bombed by Fortresses and Liberators. Berlin raided at night, bringing total of bombs dropped in three nights to 5,000 tons.

**JANUARY 31, Monday** 1,612th day
Italy.—Allied Anzio Bay beach-head further extended in Carroceto region.
Mediterranean.—Klagenfurt (S. Germany) airfield bombed.
Russian Front.—Outskirts of Kingisepp, near Estonian border, reached. Malaya-Stremlenie in Volosovo area captured. River Luga forced at several points.
Pacific.—Announced that American amphibious forces had landed in the Roi and Kwajalein areas of Kwajalein atoll in the Marshall Islands and established beach-heads.

**FEBRUARY 1, Tuesday** 1,613rd day
Italy.—Announced that British troops reached Campoleone, 15 miles from Anzio ; U.S. troops reached Cisterna. Canadians of 8th Army supported by tanks and artillery attacked the Tollo-Villagrande road.
Russian Front.—Kingisepp. Important German centre of resistance in the Narva direction, captured by Red Army.
Sea.—Vice-Admiral Sir Algernon U. Willis, K.C.B., D.S.O., appointed Second Sea Lord.
General.—Announced that each of the 16 constituent Republics of the Soviet Union to have own national army, the right to negotiate and conclude agreements with foreign governments, and the right to sever relations with the Soviet Union.

★—————— *Flash-backs* ——————★

### 1941
January 19. British troops crossed the borders of Italian Eritrea in the direction of Agordat and Asmara. Sabdaret captured.

January 24. General Cunningham's troops invaded Italian Somaliland.

### 1942
January 23. Five-day Allied air bombardment of Japanese convoy in Macassar Straits (between Borneo and Celebes) began.

### 1943
January 23. Tripoli captured by General Montgomery's 8th Army.

January 29. Advance guard of 8th Army crossed Tunisian frontier.

January 30. Maikop oilfields (Caucasus) cleared of the enemy by the Russians. Mr. Churchill arrived in Turkey for two-day conference with President Inonu.

January 31. Field-Marshal Paulus and 15 German generals surrendered at Stalingrad to troops of Marshal Zhukov's command.

# THE WAR IN THE AIR

### by Capt. Norman Macmillan, M.C., A.F.C.

**THE BATTLE OF BERLIN**

| | Target | Bomb Tonnage | Planes Miss'g | Remarks |
|---|---|---|---|---|
| **1943** | | | | |
| Nov. 18 | Berlin and Ludwigshaven | 2,500 | 32 | Record force of nearly 1,000 bombers and larger force went to Berlin, dropping 350 4,000-lb. bombs. |
| Nov. 22 | Berlin | 2,300 plus | 26 | |
| Nov. 23 | Berlin | 1,500 plus | 20 | |
| Nov. 26 | Berlin and Stuttgart | 1,000 plus | 32 | All-Lancaster bomber force. |
| Dec. 2 | Berlin | 1,500 | 41 | |
| Dec. 16 | Berlin | 1,500 | 30 | |
| Dec. 23 | Berlin | 1,000 | 17 | |
| Dec. 29 | Berlin | 2,000 plus | 20 | |
| **1944** | | | | |
| Jan. 1 | Berlin and Hamburg | 1,000 | 27 | |
| Jan. 2 | Berlin | 1,000 | 27 | Germans reported 730 bomber force. |
| Jan. 20 | Berlin | 2,300 | 35 | |
| Jan. 27 | Berlin | 1,500 plus | 34 | |
| Jan. 28 | Berlin | 1,500 plus | 47 | Record all-Lancaster bomber force. |
| Jan. 30 | Berlin | 1,500 plus | 33 | |

**NOTE:** The bomb tonnages given are approximate. Air Ministry reports do not always state exactly what tonnage was dropped on the main target, and frequently there were diversionary targets and mine-laying operations. The number of aircraft reported missing cannot always be engaged in the Battle of Berlin, for all Bomber Command aircraft missing in the night's operations are reported in the casualty figure published. A total of 20,000 tons of bombs had, however, been dropped on Berlin before the end of January 1944, since the real battle opened on Nov. 18, 1943, and it is probable that not less than half of Berlin's built-up area was devastated by the former date.

I AM one of those who believe that bombing can defeat a nation at war. But I make this proviso—that the bombing must be carried out on the scale required to effect the defeat of the enemy within a given time. Nothing less than this will do the job; although the effect of bombing on a reduced scale and over a longer period will have a marked result upon the war efficiency of the bombed nation.

It requires faith to accumulate the necessary bombing force to achieve the strength and frequency of attack by which, and in no other way, victory from strategic bombing can be attained. The United Nations have not displayed that sufficiency of faith towards this redoubtable arm of war. There have been too many pulling in other directions.

The disposition of the United Nations' air forces is a matter which cannot be disclosed while the war continues. And so it is not easy to state a case. But just as Lord Dowding said that he was anxious about the drain upon the resources of Fighter Command caused by the succession of actions in Norway, the Low Countries, and France, so must the four commanders of Bomber Command have been anxious about the drain upon their Command to the Mediterranean zone, to the anti-submarine war, and to other areas of activity.

Probably the time factor is the most important in strategic bombing, for if the enemy is given no respite the cumulative effect of air bombardment snowballs so rapidly as to defy even improvisation to offset its disastrous results. But if the time element is slowed down—due to no matter what causes—the enemy is given time to act to counter the effect of the air bombardment, both on the ground, by civil defence and Government measures promulgated and carried into effect, and in the air, by the devising of new measures of defence.

IN strategic bombing the time factor is curtailed more effectively, I should say, by weight of attack. The strength of attack aircraft available to a commander of a strategic bombing force enables him to obliterate (that is the word for modern bombing) a larger target area in one blow, or conversely to smash effectively several smaller target areas in a single night or day. Time was when it needed the most favourable conditions of weather to make a bombing attack—raid was then the correct word. That time has long since gone. Thus, with weather discounted as a deterrent to air bombardment, it is possible to make use of larger forces than would formerly have been deployable.

Sir Stafford Cripps, Minister of Aircraft Production, said to the workers in a Midland aero-engine factory on January 24, 1944, that "the only thing which could prevent our finishing the war in Europe this year would be the failure of people on the factory front to provide our fighting men with the implements they needed."

This may be interpreted to mean that the United Nations have got the military personnel estimated to be necessary for the defeat of the enemy in Europe this year, but as the scale of expenditure of munitions of all kinds is likely to be very heavy to smash through modern defence works—and our experience in North Africa, Sicily, and Italy must serve as a valuable guide—the supply position is likely to be the bottle-neck the size of which will determine the rapidity of the outcome. In other words, the scale and continuity of the United Nations offensive in 1944 are the factors which will decide the duration of the war in Europe.

BUT this is not the complete picture. It is only the obverse side of war. There is the reverse side also to be considered. For events in war are never conditioned by what one side does, but by what both contestants do. Therefore, the duration of the war in Europe is dependent upon the efforts of the United Nations in relation to the effort which the enemy can bring to bear against them.

We have had it in our power for almost a year to determine to a very remarkable degree just what that enemy effort would be. I have previously pointed out (page 572) that the effect of the air bombardment of Germany had played a most important part in the retreat of the German armies before the Red armies. Indeed, it is the only pre-assault method that can affect the production rate of the enemy on any scale. Thus the rapidity of the remaining stages of the war in Europe are as much, if not more, dependent upon the efforts of Bomber Command than upon any other factor, in our factories, in the field, or on the sea.

And if Bomber Command had had the strength allotted to it—whatever that strength might be—to have completed already on the eve of the invasion of Europe its programme of the destruction of the German centres of war industry, the German armies everywhere would now be tottering, and the submarines and aircraft ending their long, over four years' run. But, unfortunately, the necessary faith was lacking. Perhaps, when the war is over, we shall learn how much that absence of faith—or perhaps predilection for other ways—cost us in time, men, and money.

On the night of January 30-31, Bomber Command made its 14th major attack in the Battle of Berlin. Here is a great engagement, being waged by a magnificently handled "army" or "fleet" of the air, bombarding the capital city of the enemy hundreds of miles inland. There has never been anything like it in the history of the world.

IT is a shattering affair, this destruction of a capital city of 4½ million people, a city spread over some 350 square miles of land. Probably an average assault means that we send between 4,000 and 5,000 men to attack. The defence sends more than 1,000 fighter aircraft up against them, outnumbering our aircraft by theirs. Hundreds of guns line the route. More than 750,000 troops oppose our few thousands. As many more civil defence workers line up for duty. The skies are lit by searchlights and parachute flares, almost as brightly as by the sun. Ground guns of all calibres fire thousands of shells. Aircraft fire rocket shells, cannon-gun shells, and incendiary and explosive bullets.

These attacks are no mere incidents of the war. They are the greatest battles that are now being fought—greater even than those being waged in the mountains and level spaces of southern Italy, opposed by far greater enemy strength, both on the ground and in the air. Yet it is probable that fewer aircraft are employed on one of its great Berlin attacks by Bomber Command than are disposed of in the Mediterranean. For more than 5,000 tons of bombs were dropped on the Anzio area alone in one week before the actual Allied landing!

It was the heavy concentration of the strategic bombers on the vital communication towns in German hands that consolidated the bridgehead at Salerno, and enabled our army there to stay in Italy and prevented them from being ousted and turned back on to the sea. When this war ends we shall come to know how we might have won it more quickly. German industry should be Target Number One.

**THE HELLDIVER, LATEST U.S. DIVE-BOMBER,** hit the Japanese hard in its first action on Nov. 11, 1943 when a squadron attacked Rabaul, New Britain, fought off some 80 Japanese Zero fighters, probably sank a heavy cruiser, a light cruiser and a destroyer and damaged another destroyer and heavy cruiser. The Helldiver, bigger and heavier than earlier dive-bombers, is an all-metal two-seater, powered by a 1,700 h.p. Wright Double-Roll Cyclone engine. PAGE 604 *Photo, U.S. Official*

# Where Hawker Typhoons Take Shape and Grow

FORMIDABLE FIGHTER, the Hawker Typhoon is a development of the famous Hurricane; it went into action for the first time early in 1942. Speed is well over 400 m.p.h. and it has alternative armaments—twelve ·303 machine-guns, or four 20-mm.-cannon. The fighter-bomber version carries two 500-lb. bombs under the wings. In impressive rows, on a factory's assembly lines, Typhoons progress towards completion (1) ; a woman electrician (2) works on a complicated instrument panel, whilst engine installation is a matter for several pairs of hands (3). A Typhoon complete and ready for action (4).

*Photos, Keystone, Topical Press*

# Spitfires at Casablanca Fly from Crate to Battle

Photos, English Official : Crown Copyright

**SEABORNE TO CASABLANCA,** important N.W. African Allied air base and one terminal of the Trans-Africa Air Route, crated Spitfire sections are seized by squads of skilled Service fitters and local workmen who rapidly assemble the engine (1), wing sections (2), and other components from the huge wooden cases. Test pilots give the planes a tryout ; then ferry pilots deliver them in full fighting trim (3) to operational bases in Africa, the Middle East and Near East; the Spitfire here seen is flying over Fez. in Morocco.

WITH a deep sigh of relief large numbers of us greeted the First of February this year. February is not a month to stir enthusiasm as a rule. "Fill-dyke" country people call it. It generally lives up to Shakespeare's description of it—"so full of frost, of storm and cloudiness." But this year the new clothing coupons (kew-pongs, if you adopt the customary pronunciation) were available on the first of the month, and many who had only just managed to hold their suits or frocks together through January rushed thankfully to buy—not what they liked, probably, but what would at any rate keep them warm. The sale of underclothing must have been prodigious. For men this is the crux of the rationing problem. I know men who, once accustomed to tear off their vests and pants and hurl them aside, often causing holes or splits, now remove them as gingerly as if they were of priceless old lace. I know others who will wear shirts for the unheard-of period of three or four days. "I daren't have a clean one every day now," one of them said to me sadly. "They would not last any time, seeing how they are treated by the laundry, and I couldn't get any more when they are gone." He actually seemed to regard this as a hardship. "Think of what men in the Services go through," I exhorted him. But he only shook his head and growled.

MY note about the danger of placing haystacks near together (p. 479), so that if one catches fire they all burn, brings me a letter from Station-Sergeant Loats, of Epping, Essex. He reads my Postscript regularly, he says, and agrees with most of it, "though with a small number of its views I do not agree." That is as it should be. Then he mentions that as long ago as 1941 the Ministry of Agriculture made it an offence to put ricks within 20 yards of a dwelling-house, or within 20 yards of one another. I knew of this Order and based my remarks on it, deploring that it was not obeyed. Sergeant Loats says the duty of enforcing it rests on the County Police and adds: "We are doing our best to keep up with the mass of legislation thrust upon us and eagerly looking forward to the day when we can welcome our victorious comrades back on the beat once more." Yes, sergeant, we all of us share that eagerness with you."

SOME folks have been moralizing over the contrast between the high prices bid for cigars at auctions in London and the very low prices pictures fetch. This is said to be evidence of an increasing unhealthy "materialism," whatever that word may mean. If it indicates a preference for good tobacco over a bad or even indifferent painting, I am a materialist all the time. During the later Victorian age absurd sums were paid for pictures. Millais could make £40,000 in a good year. Even Wilson Steer, who was a rebel against the Academy and, unlike Millais, remained so all his life, and a really fine painter in my opinion, left £156,000 when he died, last year.

WAR has always been the enemy of artists. In Anatole France's novel The Gods Are Athirst, which I have just re-read, there is an eloquent passage on this. He shows how during the campaigns of the revolutionary armies those rich people who had bought works of art were ruined, while those who made fortunes were manufacturers of arms and ammunition, proprietors of gambling shops, and speculators on the Stock Exchange. That sort of person, Anatole France wrote contemptuously, doesn't like pictures and wouldn't buy them if he did, for fear of letting the world know how rich he was !

"FIFTH-COLUMN" is generally regarded as a phrase which originated during the Spanish Civil War and was at once adopted everywhere as a particularly neat description of traitors within the gates. Its origin is well known. There were said to be four of Franco's columns advancing on Madrid at one period, with a fifth column of Franco sympathizers in the city ready to collaborate

NEW HOME FORCES C.-IN-C., Lt.-General Sir Harold E. Franklyn, K.C.B., D.S.O., M.C., succeeded Gen. Sir Bernard Paget (now C.-in-C. Middle East) in that post on Jan. 6, 1944. G.O.C. Troops in Northern Ireland since May 1941, he gained a reputation for toughening-up training schemes. He commanded the 5th Division at Arras in 1940, delaying the German advance on the Channel ports for more than two days. *Photo, British Official*

with them. Now I discover that almost the same expression was made use of by the Empress Eugénie of France just before she had to flee from Paris when revolution against Louis Napoleon's Second Bonapartist Empire broke out. This was during the war of 1870 in which Prussia and the other States into which Germany was then divided defeated France, capturing Paris and imposing what seemed then severe peace terms. The Empress remarked bitterly, no doubt repeating what someone else had said, that, in addition to the three enemy armies moving on Paris, there was a fourth hostile army in the capital working in aid of the foe.

WHY do the men who are fighting our battles put up with this sort of treatment ? A group of them returning from leave, some of them going to the Middle East, failed to find any room in third-class coaches on their train to London and got into a first. Along comes a railway official after a little while, when they had settled down in warmth and comfort, and turns them out. They had to stand all the rest of the journey in a cold third-class corridor, although the first-class remained empty. There is another side to the story, however, and that is the eagerness with which third-class ticket holders may be seen hastening into first-class compartments while lots of room is available in the third-class. Only yesterday an inspector came into the compartment in which I was travelling and quite rightly informed three or four of the eight occupants that there were lots of third-class seats farther on.

WHEN soldiers leaving England at the outset of the war sang "Good-bye, Leicester Square," that open space in the very heart of London was as they had always known it : a garden with patches of grass and flower-beds and railings round it. Now the railings have gone and there are paths all over it. Almost no traces of the garden remain. To the discussion as to whether the railings should be replaced whenever that becomes possible and the former look of the Square restored, the late Sir Edwin Lutyens, the eminent architect, who was President of the Royal Academy, contributed a good idea. He offered to prepare a new design which he would present to London and which might easily be an improvement on the old lay-out. Presumably it would still be more or less a garden, since he said he could count on the advice of the Institute of Landscape Architects. And it could be turned into a much more attractive garden than the one which was laid out seventy years ago by a financier of the day named Albert Grant, who called himself Baron Grant.

FOR a long time before 1874 Leicester Square had been a disgrace to London. It was a refuse-heap ; it was a frequent butt for the sarcasms of Punch. The owners would do nothing to it, nor would they let anybody else clean it up. That so historic a spot should become an eyesore and an offence to the nose was deeply resented. Once, as Leicester Fields, it had been a notorious place for duels (there is one in Thackeray's Esmond). Then it became a favourite neighbourhood for painters. Reynolds, Hogarth, Sir Thomas Lawrence, all lived in it. Later, the Royal Panopticon of Science and Art was built there, to become in course of years the Alhambra Theatre. There was a Panorama, too, and a Great Globe to teach geography. Towards the end of last century the Empire Theatre was built, and more recently a huge picture palace. So the Square links up the old London with the new in a most interesting fashion.

KALEIDOSCOPIC changes in the way we look at other nations have always amused cynical observers. Not very many years ago we were told to admire and like the Japanese —even after they had savaged and annexed Korea ! In the days when Finland was struggling for independence against Tsarist Russia we believed the Finns to be a highly civilized people, and sympathized warmly with their aspirations. Now they are angling for sympathy again, as they see their ally, Hitler, is bound to be beaten. But one cannot forget that little more than two years ago their Press was cock-a-hoop for Nazi victory and looking forward to Hitler's "being able to lay hands on important parts of the British Empire." And they have copied Nazi methods of treating prisoners of war and interned civilians.

# Green Howards in the Mountains of Italy

*Photo, British Official : Crown Copyright*

**UP A SNOW-COVERED HILLSIDE** these Green Howards (Alexandra, Princess of Wales's Own Yorkshire Regiment) advance to new positions. Among the first Allied troops to land in Italy, Sept. 3, 1943, the Green Howards have since been engaged in much hard fighting in the mountainous centre of the front.   The 1st Battalion took part in the Norwegian campaign in 1940, and the regiment was represented at Dunkirk, at Gazala, where it formed part of the 50th Division, and at Mersa Matruh after the fall of Tobruk.

Printed in England and published every alternate Friday by the Proprietors, THE AMALGAMATED PRESS, LTD., The Fleetway House, Farringdon Street, London, E.C.4. Registered for transmission by Canadian Magazine Post.   Sole Agents for Australia and New Zealand : Messrs. Gordon & Gotch, Ltd. ; and for South Africa : Central News Agency, Ltd.—February 18, 1944.       S.S.       *Editorial Address :* JOHN CARPENTER HOUSE, WHITEFRIARS, LONDON, E.C.4.

Vol 7    The War Illustrated    Nº 175

SIXPENCE     Edited by Sir John Hammerton     MARCH 3, 1944

**TWENTY-YEAR-OLD YUGOSLAV GIRL FIGHTER** credited with killing 20 Germans; she is standing before a portrait of her leader, Marshal Tito, while recovering in an Allied rest-camp in Italy from wounds received battling with the Nazis in Yugoslavia. Camps take many such partisans, of both sexes and all ages; restored to health, they are trained by battle experts before returning to continue the fight for liberation in their native land. Of Marshal Tito's army of 200,000 nearly a quarter are women, all fierce and fearless campaigners. See also p. 618.     *Photo, Planet News*

NO. 176 WILL BE PUBLISHED FRIDAY, MARCH 17

# Our Roving Camera Visits the War Factories

CLOGS WITHOUT COUPONS are being made for certain women war workers, a group of whom here try on their new Utility footwear. The clogs, with leather uppers and wooden soles, cost 13s. 3d. a pair, are smart in appearance and comfortable to wear. Special distribution is made to girls engaged in heavy outdoor work for which ordinary shoes prove unsuitable; the clogs are designed for abnormal conditions.

PAUSE IN PLANE MAKING for a cup of tea at a large aircraft factory where every amenity for the workers is provided; in the background is a fighter in process of assembly. Cake and tea trolleys are wheeled to every department at the 9 a.m. and 3 p.m. breaks, and the employees can buy those welcome refreshments to help them through a long and tiring shift.

ARTIFICIAL LIMBS are being made and repaired by Polish ex-Servicemen in a factory in the grounds of Queen Mary's Hospital, Roehampton, London. When the war is ended the men will return to Poland to continue in the same work. Some 3,374 artificial limbs, from all sources, have so far been supplied to Forces casualties in this war, and 1,593 to civilians.

GRINDING THE CARBON that burns in our searchlights is a specialized job in this London workshop. The emery stones used for the grinding are so hard that it is not practical to fashion each one separately, so pieces are arranged in a jig-saw pattern to form a large millstone (above), the spaces between being filled with molten spelter, a zinc alloy.

IN THE WELDING SCHOOL (left) of a large factory near London soldiers are taught to become expert workmen. Here they are using oxy-acetylene torches in the butt welding process, which entails the placing of two plates or surfaces of metal together, edge to edge, and welding along the seams. Note the goggles protecting workers' eyes from sparks and the fierce glare. The butt welding method is an effective and speedy means of carrying out many repair jobs of a military nature, and the training the men receive will provide a valuable start in a new career when they return to civil life. Men shown in the photograph are U.S. personnel.
*Photos, Keystone, Sport & General, Fox, Daily Mirror*

# THE BATTLE FRONTS

## by Maj.-Gen. Sir Charles Gwynn, K.C.B., D.S.O.

NEW MOBILE MORTAR used by Nazis on the Eastern Front. It differs from the German combination ground mortar which throws rocket shells in that it has 10 barrels instead of 6, and is mounted on a version of semi-track type lorry. *Photo, News Chronicle*

**RUSSIA** When I last wrote the Russian Leningrad offensive had for the time being diverted attention from the southern front. There the second wave of von Manstein's counter-attacks east of Vinnitsa had not only brought Vatutin's central drive towards Zhmerinka to a standstill, but had compelled it to give ground a little. Moreover, communiqués gave no information as to the situation either of Vatutin's right or left offensives, and it was generally assumed that they also had been brought to a halt.

Some critics suggested that Vatutin had made a mistake in striking in three divergent directions, instead of concentrating his blows on what appeared to be the most important objective. Personally, I believed that Vatutin was, in the circumstances, probably right; partly, because, he was adding to von Manstein's difficulty in using his reserves, and partly I thought a great concentration of Russian forces in any one direction might overtax their indifferent communications. On the other hand, I expected that Vatutin would renew his offensive after a pause to close up his reserves of men and material.

I was confident that Vatutin, a general of great capacity who has especially shown his skill in co-ordinating offensive and defensive action, had the situation in hand. What form his offensive would take was naturally speculative, but it seemed improbable that he would immediately renew his drive towards Zhmerinka, to cover which von Manstein had concentrated his reserves and where his railway communication still remained good. Co-operation with Koniev's Army against the Kanyev salient seemed to offer great possibilities. It was doubtful, however, whether on his right Vatutin would have sufficient resources to do more than maintain pressure towards Rovno, and possibly co-operate with Rokossovsky's Army in clearing the Pripet Marshes towards Pinsk.

These seemed to be reasonable expectations, but once again Vatutin has far exceeded them. The Germans, who might have taken advantage of Vatutin's pause to extricate themselves from their precarious position at Kanyev and Smyela, decided for some reason difficult to understand to chance their arm, and Koniev and Vatutin have neatly amputated it at the shoulder. It is difficult to believe that Hitler alone was responsible for the decision to hold on to Kanyev till too late. That would imply an unbelievable lack of moral courage on the part of the German General Staff. I suspect, rather, that the General Staff over-estimated the degree to which the Russians had outrun their resources and the difficulties they were in owing to abnormal weather.

Von Manstein's success in halting Vatutin's central drive may have helped to mislead them. Be that as it may, the speed with which Vatutin and Koniev carried out their surgical operation, in spite of the unfavourable state of the operating theatre, was so remarkable that it raises the question whether the Russians have evolved a technique or designed a vehicle which to some extent defeats

mud. The later success of the third Ukrainian Army at Nikopol, in which there has also been rapid exploitation, would almost suggest that they must have. If they have, German hopes of a respite during the spring thaw may prove unfounded.

It is, of course, impossible to get really reliable information as to the state of the ground. The Germans certainly complain of it, and it is adding to their difficulties; but frost at night may temporarily improve conditions and offer advantages to the Russians, who hold the initiative. What is certain is that where the Germans have lost their railway communications, as in the case of the ten Divisions of the 8th Army and of the 6th Army in the Nikopol region, they are deprived of the advantage they previously held over the Russians.

THE success of Vatutin's right-hand thrust into Poland, resulting in the capture of Rovno and Luck, was more unexpected than his co-operative offensive with Koniev. It would seem to imply that von Manstein must have denuded this part of his front of reserves for his Vinnitsa counter-attacks. Cavalry and other lightly-armed troops in this case gave the thrust mobility and power of operating off the roads, and their penetration could only have been checked by mobile troops.

The fact that reserves apparently were not available and that the defence of important key points was entrusted to Hungarian troops of doubtful reliability demonstrates the weakness of von Manstein's position. The Lvov-Odessa railway is now threatened at a new point, and even the vital railway centre of Lvov itself, with its railway connexions to Rumania, is coming into the danger zone. It seems probable that von Manstein may have to weaken his Vinnitsa concentration to meet the threat, and thus afford Vatutin an opportunity of renewing his drive towards Zhmerinka. It is evident that the whole southern front is crumbling and that the Germans, with insufficient reserves to retrieve

the situation, must pin their hopes of escaping further disaster on an early spring thaw to check pursuit of an inevitable retreat.

Meantime, in the north the outlook for the Germans is almost equally serious. They have suffered a great defeat, but at the time I am writing they may escape its catastrophic consequences if they can hold open the escape avenue through Luga a little longer and can prevent an invasion of Estonia through the Narva defile.

**ITALY** The failure of the Anzio-Nettuno landings to achieve immediate sensational results has undoubtedly caused disappointment, and there has been criticism of the Allied Command on the grounds that plans are too rigid and methods too stereotyped. But in amphibious operations plans must necessarily follow a much more rigid programme than in normal land campaigns, and they must be drawn up in detail before transports are stowed and troops embarked. Moreover, once made they cannot be radically changed without great danger of causing confusion and delays. In this case the weakness of the opposition encountered could not have been foreseen, and Kesselring's dispatch of his reserves from Rome to his southern front was not known at the time the troops embarked. Probably by changes of plan when the situation was known, temporary successes might have been achieved; but it must remain questionable whether they would have seriously disturbed Kesselring's subsequent movements.

So far, Kesselring has not been able to mount a full-scale offensive, and though he has delivered fierce local attacks, their primary object probably was defensive—the elimination of the offensive potentialities of the landed force. Naturally he must also have envisaged the possibility of gaining a decisive victory should circumstances develop favourably for him, and he evidently took full advantage of the opportunity presented when weather temporarily grounded our air-arm. He has, however, been compelled not only to commit his reserves, but to call in reinforcements from other theatres. That in itself is no mean achievement and may have been one of the main objects of the Allied landing.

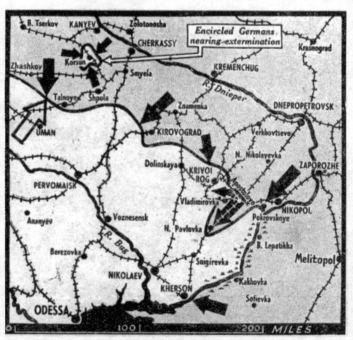

LIQUIDATION OF THE GERMAN 8TH ARMY in the Korsun pocket was completed on Feb. 17, 1944 and is indicated by converging black arrows (top left). Up to the last, German relief attempts had been maintained without success. Other important Russian movements are those shown in the Krivoi Rog and Kherson regions. PAGE 611 *Courtesy of The Daily Mail*

# 5th Army's Two Fronts in the Battles for Rome

IN THEIR ADVANCE along a road north of Anzio, shortly after the Allied landing on the west coast of Italy on Jan. 22, 1944, troops of the 5th Army were preceded by Sherman tanks, behind one of which (1) a British section moves up ; past Anzio's buildings reduced by our naval guns, Adm. Sir John Cunningham, K.C.B., M.V.O., C.-in-C. Mediterranean (2, right) picks his way accompanied by Rr.-Adm. Lowry, U.S. Navy. Key-town on the main 5th Army front and barring the way to Rome, Cassino, through which Allied troops were fighting street by street on Feb. 15, is shattered by terrific artillery fire (3).

*Photos, British and U.S. Official*

# Nazis Suffer Greatest Defeat Since Stalingrad

ROWS OF GERMAN DEAD and shattered equipment (1) belonged to 10 German divisions trapped by the Red Army in the Kanyev pocket in the Dnieper Bend; the encirclement was announced on Feb. 3, 1944; and by Feb. 17 annihilation of these divisions had been completed. Russian engineers (2) mined " escape " bridges behind the enemy, for whom supplies were dropped (3) from Nazi planes. In Estonia, Red Army patrols in winter camouflage (4) pushed on towards the Narva key-point.

*Photos, U.S. Official, Planet News*

COVERING THE FIFTH ARMY LANDING on the west coast of Italy, south of Rome, on Jan. 22, 1944, Allied warships included an improved version of the British Dido class light cruiser. She is seen (above) with her guns blazing away at the distant shore, from which dense clouds of shell-smoke rise, whilst landing craft move in to the beach. Ahead went minesweepers, clearing the sea approaches. British, American, French, Greek and Dutch ships all supported this operation, and considerable credit is due to the navigators who guided the armada of landing craft to the right places on what is a difficult stretch of coast. With little delay after the landing a smooth shuttle-service of ships, carrying more men and supplies, was in full swing. See story in p. 601.

*Photo, British Official: Crown Copyright*

H.M. RESCUE TUG FIREFLY towing a merchant vessel which has been torpedoed. When ships are in distress around our shores, or even in mid-Atlantic, the rescue tugs, which are under direct Admiralty command, go out from Britain to the rescue. They cover thousands of miles in all weathers and are often attacked by the enemy. One tug is always in readiness in each of the ports from which this service operates. *Photo, British Official*

# THE WAR AT SEA

### by Francis E. McMurtrie

Though less detailed than some previous statements, the joint announcement on the progress of the U-boat war during January, issued under the authority of the Prime Minister and President Roosevelt, was nevertheless satisfactory. Its most encouraging feature was the definite news that more enemy submarines were destroyed during January than in December, in spite of the limited opportunities afforded for encounters owing to the extreme caution exercised by the U-boats. "Unrelenting action by our surface and air forces" is given as the key to this enhanced success.

An example of this unrelenting action was furnished this month. When four U-boats emerged from French Atlantic ports recently, each was in turn located and attacked by aircraft of the Coastal Command as it traversed the Bay of Biscay on the surface. At least one of the four is believed to have been seriously damaged by depth charges dropped from the air, while the others were forced to submerge and may also have sustained injuries. This constant liability to be attacked from overhead, whenever they appear on the surface, is bound to have a detrimental effect on the morale and general efficiency of the German submarine service.

That the enemy have very deep respect for the ample protection now afforded to shipping is shown by the experience of a convoy of 148 ships that recently reached North African ports from this country without loss or damage. Apart from big troop convoys, such as those assembled for the invasion of Sicily, or for the North African landings of November 1942, this was the largest convoy that has yet been seen at sea. It covered some 70 square miles of ocean, and would thus appear to have afforded an ideal target for the German "wolf-pack" method of attack. Yet on only three occasions was there even a suspicion of U-boats being in the vicinity; and though depth charges were at once dropped by the ships of the escort in order to test the situation, no trace of the enemy was found. At one stage of the passage four German bombers made a half-hearted attack, but they were easily driven off, suggesting that the enemy's boasts of a new system of co-operation between aircraft and submarines do not amount to much.

That the Germans themselves are not insensible to these facts may be judged from the reply made by a U-boat captain to a welcoming speech broadcast as he entered an Atlantic port of France. He is reported to have declared : "We have not been spared anything on this cruise. We have had heavy seas, furious gales, enemy aircraft, bombs, depth charges and shell fire." Apparently he considered himself to be lucky to have survived all these hazards.

### ESCORT Vessels Summoned by Radio to Attack U-Boats

Nor is there any prospect of the U-boats obtaining a respite. The construction of escort ships of every description is now at the peak, including fast destroyers, sloops, frigates, corvettes, minesweepers, trawlers and the light craft which we call motor-launches and the Americans class as submarine chasers. Particulars of these types are scanty, but in speed they vary from the 36-40 knots of the destroyer to the 17 knots of the corvette or the 12 knots of the trawler. As ocean-going submarines are capable of 21 knots on the surface, the faster ships are naturally the more effective, but all have done their part nobly. In narrow waters, such as the English Channel, coastal convoys can be quite well protected by the light craft, which are unsuitable by reason of their limited fuel capacity for ocean voyages. Aircraft, either those of the Fleet Air Arm borne in carriers, or their opposite numbers of the Coastal Command based on shore, are used to patrol the area of sea through which a convoy is passing, and to attack with depth charges any U-boat that may be sighted. Escort vessels called to the scene by radio may then be able to complete her destruction if damaged, or at least ensure that she is kept below the surface and so rendered incapable of reaching the convoy. Under water, few submarines can make more than 9 knots, and this only for a limited time.

Less has been heard in this country of the Royal New Zealand Navy than of any of the other Dominion Services. Though its present title was assumed as recently as September 1941, it is over 30 years old, the original organization having been started in 1913. During the last war two small New Zealand warships, the light cruisers Psyche and Pyramus, did good work in various quarters, including the escort of convoys across the Indian Ocean, the patrolling of the East African coast and of the Persian Gulf, and the occupation of sundry Pacific islands that formerly belonged to Germany. H.M.S. New Zealand, a battle-cruiser whose cost was defrayed by the Dominion, became famous as the result of her participation in the Battles of Heligoland, the Dogger Bank and Jutland. She did not receive a single serious hit, for which immunity the ship's company gave credit to the Maori regalia worn by the captain. It consisted of a grass cloak and a stone tiki, or charm, which had belonged years earlier to a celebrated Maori chief who was regarded as invulnerable.

In the present war the R.N.Z.N. has grown in the number of its personnel from a little over 700 officers and men to the present figure of 9,000. This is the highest percentage of population of any Dominion, and is possibly due to the fact that New Zealand is an island nation. In the executive branch the majority of the officers come from the Royal N.Z. Naval Reserve or the Royal N.Z. Naval Volunteer Reserve.

A New Zealand cruiser, H.M.S. Achilles, took part in the Battle of the Plate, when the German pocket battleship Admiral Graf Spee was decisively defeated by three ships which in theory she ought to have been able to sink one after the other. Another, the Leander, participated in sinking the raider Coburg in the Indian Ocean in May 1941.

New Zealand warships have also been engaged in various actions in the south-west Pacific. It was H.M.N.Z. corvette Tui that destroyed the biggest Japanese submarine on record, a vessel of 2,563 tons, as officially announced on October 1, 1943. Another Japanese submarine was rammed and sunk by H.M.N.Z. corvette Moa off Cape Esperance.

The material strength of the Royal New Zealand Navy today is greater than it has ever been. It includes the 8,000-ton cruiser Gambia, mounting twelve 6-in. guns ; the cruisers Achilles and Leander, of over 7,000 tons, each armed with eight 6-in. guns ; the corvettes Kiwi and Tui, built at Leith and delivered since war began ; three groups of trawlers, one of the Isles type, one of the Castle type and the third built in New Zealand shipyards ; the armed merchant cruiser Monowai, a vessel of over 10,000 tons gross with a speed of 18·5 knots. Two British-built corvettes, the Arabis and Arbutus, are to be taken over this year.

# Our Underwater 'Commandos' Strike Hard Inland

Tremendously efficient are the men who "run" our submarines, and because underwater warfare is among the most dangerous of enterprises it is essentially a young man's job. Our submariners do not confine themselves to the torpedoing of enemy ships, as JOHN ALLEN GRAYDON points out. On occasion, and with great success, they shell Axis airfields, trains and viaducts.

THE Royal Navy, in the quiet manner that is theirs, have been building up one of the biggest and finest submarine fleets the world has ever seen. Every man is an expert at his task, and before being sent to a "boat" has received a training excelled nowhere for thoroughness.

It can now be revealed that R.N.V.R. (Royal Naval Volunteer Reserve) are taking charge of submarines. After serving for three years with our underwater "commandos," and learning the secrets of "The Trade," as submariners call their art, and having proved their leadership, those fortunate enough to attract official attention have been recommended for—or have taken—commands.

Many of these youngsters—the men of the "Second String" subs, as I have heard them called—have joined forces with such successful veterans as Commander Ben Bryant, D.S.O. (and two Bars), D.S.C., and Commander A. G. Mars, a "young veteran" who, over the past few months, has shown himself to be among the greatest leaders in "The Trade." Such men as these are always setting the new captains a lesson in patience, tactics, and courage. To their credit the youthful commanders and crews are quick to learn.

COMMANDER BRYANT is a great believer in the small submarine, and aboard such craft he himself has been most successful. He stated recently: "The small submarine may have a short radius of action, and be slow on the surface, but it has fine lines which tend to reduce its wake—the deadly enemy of the submarine whether on the surface, or submerged.

"It also has great tactical qualities," Commander Bryant continued. "When a submarine is submerged its speed is limited to the lowest possible. With an enemy zig-zagging at high speed you want to be able to turn quickly, too, during an attack, since the submarine is a torpedo tube which has herself to be trained on the enemy.

"I am a great believer in using the submarine as a submersible gunboat," the Commander went on, with a smile, "for in this type of action the submarine usually has things very much its own way. It can choose the range, the weather gauge, the advantage of the light, and it can exploit surprise and break off the action whenever it likes."

YOUNG commanders who have studied under Commander Ben Bryant have often put his ideas into practice, and during the Mediterranean campaign many Italian ships were known to beach themselves rather than risk running the gauntlet of our submarines.

One youthful commander chased a ship so close inshore that he ran aground and through his periscope saw a horse and trap less than fifty yards away, and the town's fire engines rushing about! The Italians even stated that our daring submariners, during the hours of darkness, sometimes swam ashore, walked around on the beach, then swam back to their "boat," as a submarine is always called in the Senior Service.

According to neutral sources, too, the German coastal defenders in Norway are now, following a certain incident, always looking out for "underwater commandos." Not so long ago, on Blekeoya Island, near Oslo, a letter to "Corporal Hitler" was found pinned by a British naval dagger to the door of a fisherman's cottage. It read: "You said we won't succeed in landing on the European mainland. Now you can see we've been here—and we can promise to come back again!" It was signed "Tommy Hawkins, submarine officer." This story was circulated all over Norway by the underground newspaper "X Y Z," and did much to put heart into those beneath the Nazi jackboot.

Sometimes our submarines have followed convoys into harbour, "rested" on the bed for some hours, then, surfacing, have taken a heavy toll of ships and surrounding harbour works. Other submarines have shelled Axis airfields, railway trains, and viaducts.

Two young commanders—I keep stressing "young" because I am referring not to the veteran aces but newcomers to this most dangerous of all war tasks—kept watch upon a line of Italian railway track that ran over a certain viaduct. Carefully they

Lieut.-Cmdr. L. W. A. BENNINGTON, D.S.O., D.S.C., R.N., who commanded a submarine of the Eastern Fleet which recently sank a Japanese cruiser of the Kuma class in the northern approaches of the Malacca Strait. Here he is seen looking through the periscope of H.M.S. submarine Porpoise.
*Photo, British Official: Crown Copyright*

compiled a time-table. Then, at the right moment they opened fire on two trains that were passing, inflicting tremendous damage on these munition carriers as well as wrecking the viaducts and firing oil storage tanks. Next morning, to make certain that the report they handed H.Q. would be accurate in every detail, the two commanders went in close to the shore and checked up details!

MANY of the young men who help to make up the crews of our submarines possess the traditional Nelson spirit, and nothing affords them greater pleasure than being a member of a boarding party. I have had the pleasure of meeting many who have taken part in our underwater sea war, and it is a tonic to hear them talk of their beloved skippers and boats.

"I remember when I went aboard a tug we had 'captured,'" a youth from Swansea told me. "When we surfaced all the Italians jumped overboard and began to swim towards us. I reckon we might have put a prize crew aboard, only enemy planes and E-boats were in the vicinity. Anyway, after making sure she would go down we returned to our boat and took aboard the Italians. And—would you believe it?—some of the

Wops were so keen at the way we worked they said they'd like to join us if the Admiralty would let 'em!"

This particular seaman, who had served aboard some of the best-known submarines in the Royal Navy, has heard hundreds of depth charges explode around him, and his views of the subject make interesting reading. "I'll confess that depth charges always give me a funny feeling in my stomach," he said. "No, I'm not exactly frightened—but I don't feel too pleased with life. Mind you, we do try to take our minds off the business. Chaps sometimes run a sweep as to the number of depth charges that will be flung at us. Others prefer to read thrillers. And, of course, we heave a big sigh of relief when it is all over. Coming face to face with death breeds a terrific respect within us all for the fellows with whom we live, work, and fight. That is why I wouldn't change from a submarine for anything."

I HAVE heard hundreds of submariners express similar sentiments, and this, as much as anything else, accounts for their high standard of efficiency.

Quite a number of our Mediterranean submarines operated from Malta. In two years one flotilla sank more than 80 Axis ships, including two battleships torpedoed; four, possibly five, cruisers were sunk and several more damaged; eight destroyers were sunk; 70 merchant ships, including six liners, were sunk and others damaged. During this period they were under the command of Captain G. W. W. Simpson, C.B.E., and altogether sank about half a million tons of supplies destined for the Axis armies in Africa.

When Malta was heavily blitzed the Germans made a point of plastering the flotilla's base, over 400 bomb-hits being registered. At this stage it was impossible to carry out maintenance, so a special squad of repair crews was formed. When a submarine returned from patrol an extra crew took over and the regular crew went to a rest camp on the George Cross Island.

The repair crew took the submarine out to sea and then, by lying on the bottom during the day and coming to the surface at night, carried out the necessary maintenance and, returning to base, handed the boat over to the regular crew when the task was completed. And the underwater offensive continued.

IT was during one of these blitzes that a British submarine commander had one of his most amusing experiences. Following the torpedoing of an armed trawler, he went up to periscope depth—and found, only a few yards away, an Italian seaman, on a raft, shaking his fist at the periscope. The submarine surfaced, took aboard the Italian, and found him to be a most "charming" person. But he did not know he had been seen threatening us with his fist. Only when he was landed at Malta was he acquainted with this fact. He almost ran into the detention camp!

Our submarines paved the way for many of our Middle East victories. And in offensives to come, when they will again be prominent, our underwater "commandos" will find their ranks swelled by more young men. As Rear-Admiral Claude Barry, Flag Officer Commanding Submarines, said recently: "In the very near future British submarines will be working in greater numbers in close association with those of the United States against the long and vulnerable sea communications of the hastily-constructed Japanese Empire." They can be relied upon.

# With Honours the Submariners Return Home

VETERANS OF THE DEEPS are H.M. submarines Seraph, Rorqual and Unrivalled. The Seraph (1) was used in the secret landing of General Mark Clark, C.-in-C. 5th Army, on the Algerian coast when he made contact with pro-Allied French leaders and prepared the way for the landing in N. Africa on Nov. 8, 1942. An Able Seaman of the Rorqual (2), helped by a Petty Officer, packs before going on leave ; Rorqual has laid more than 1,200 mines in enemy supply routes and has sunk 40,000 tons of shipping and one U-boat. London school children, who have " adopted " the Unrivalled, are seen (3) with the submarine's crew and her Jolly Roger ; among other exploits Unrivalled brought to Malta a convoy of eight Italian ships which had surrendered to her unconditionally.

'THIS SOUP'S GOOD!' says a bearded seaman to the Petty Officer cook as he tastes it hot in the galley of H.M. submarine Trident (4), just docked at a northern harbour after a 26,000 miles operational cruise, which in twelve months has taken her from the North Cape to the Malacca Straits. In Feb. 1942 she attacked and damaged the 10,000-ton German cruiser Prinz Eugen. During her last commission the Trident operated with five different flotillas and sank or severely damaged some 17,000 tons of enemy shipping ; men of varied pre-war professions were among her personnel. The First Lieutenant was a lawyer, the Third Officer an Australian medical student, the Fourth Officer a metallurgical chemist. Her total "bag" since the outbreak of war is 60,000 tons. The Trident has been "adopted" by schoolchildren of Dursley, Gloucestershire.

*Photos, British Official : Crown Copyright ; Evening News*

# Yugoslav Partisans Out-Match the Wehrmacht

IN THEIR VALIANT STRUGGLE against the Germans, Yugoslav partisans under Marshal Tito (2, left) continue to achieve triumphs of arms, retaking the two important towns of Vakuf and Kupres, near Sarajevo, Western Bosnia (reported on Feb. 6, 1944). In snow-clad mountains (1) Tito's men rest awhile ; a patrol (4) goes in search of the enemy. At an Allied camp in Italy women partisans train in realistic battle conditions (3), increasing their skill as warriors before returning to Yugoslavia. See pp. 524-5, 609.

PAGE 618          *Photos, U.S. Official, Planet News*

# Britain's Colonies in the War: No. 2—E. Africa

FINE FIGHTERS and disciplined soldiers, native troops of East Africa took a notable part in the memorable campaigns in British and Italian Somaliland and Abyssinia, and such men as these manning a heavy anti-aircraft gun (4) are now serving in Ceylon and India. At an East African Army Engineers' Training Centre courses for native recruits include barbed wire defence erection (2), bridge and road construction.

Kenya Information Officers arrange for chiefs, such as this one of the Masai tribe (1), and relatives to broadcast from Nairobi messages to those serving overseas. On the day fighting ended in North Africa, Wakikuyu tribesmen (3) from a reserve outside Nairobi came into the town ; they were especially interested in large-scale maps of North Africa and Russia.

East Africa supplies the Allies with many valuable war materials, including pyrethrum (base for insecticides used in anti-malaria work), sisal in place of Manila hemp, and cotton. Wheat, maize and barley are also supplied in large quantities. Vegetables, dehydrated on the spot, are sent to Middle East Forces.

*Photos, British Official : Crown Copyright*

# These Vital Days Before the Great Assault

*Softening-up of the enemy for the great Second Front progresses swiftly and inexorably. The nature of all our high-speed measures and preparations cannot be divulged in full, but FRANK S. STUART reveals here things the enemy already knows, and some of the results our actions have had and are having on the objects of our immediate and devastating attention.*

As the date for the Second Front draws nearer, the activity on our airfields facing the Continent becomes feverish. Daily greater numbers of fighters, fighter-bombers and photographic reconnaissance machines take off and touch down; the problem of controlling this vast traffic and maintaining contact with it during operations is providing some headaches and affording invaluable practice for future civil airport officials.

I am disclosing no secret when I say that our major effort is directed against German communications by rail, road and canal inland of the "invasion coast." When we attack, if the Germans cannot switch powerful forces of tanks, men and guns swiftly from point to point, they will have to retreat to a place where such communications exist. Obviously our plan is to disrupt such communications as far back as possible.

SPECIALIST airmen go out by day and night picking off locomotives and wrecking goods trains, tunnels, rail, road and water bridges, electric transformers, and other objects. During the past year about 1,000 enemy locomotives have been knocked out; one machine on a single sortie has often got three, and a squadron once wrecked 34 in two moonlight nights. Now our machines often have to hang about for a long time waiting for trains. Steam trains are spotted in moonlight by their plume of white smoke, electric trains by flashes from the line. The raider tries to put a cannon shell or two into the engine, either bursting the boiler or damaging some other vital part. Drivers usually slow down and jump for it immediately they hear an aircraft circling overhead.

Shells hitting electric engines or rails give off vivid flashes of coloured light. Transformers struck by a burst of fire give off violent displays of colour. Petrol trains, the raiders' favourite target, go up in a flaming rush of yellow fire. Ammunition trains break up in a long series of explosions. Anti-aircraft guns on many of the trains add to the illuminations with long streamers of coloured tracers. As it is necessary to go down to 500 feet or so to ensure hitting an engine, some risk has to be taken.

JUST when pilot and observer are watching the train, too, is a favourite second for a German aircraft to dive out of a cloud and attack from behind. Those who fail to keep a sharp lookout often don't need to watch anything any more. Fighter-bombers usually attend to bridges, perhaps with a 250-lb. bomb. Bridges are almost always heavily guarded with flak; as one needs to go low to have a fair chance of a hit, the task of attacking them is not very pleasant. Nevertheless, many enemy bridges are smashed up every month, with consequent traffic dislocation over a wide area. A tendency of hunted trains to dart into tunnels and stay there in safety has been countered recently by planes carrying a couple of medium bombs and sealing in both ends of a tunnel when the train is hiding inside.

Very great activity has been going on recently in obtaining photographs for the Second Front. As many as 10,000 aerial pictures have been taken in a single day by the Photographic Reconnaissance Units, while at home big machines run off up to 1,000 prints an hour. Experts with magnifying glasses and a lot of special apparatus then analyze the pictures and make reports on the stories these tell, before fitting them into mosaics that provide thousands of photographic maps of vital districts ready for area commanders of the Second Front attacks.

THE Germans are magnificent camouflage experts—their only fault is that sometimes they are too thorough, and make their dummy villages (that perhaps hide aerodromes) a little too truly rural, with runways as roads, hangars as hayricks or farm buildings, and real cows walking about. But even the best camouflage is hard put to it to hide tell-tale marks from modern British and

THRICE-ARMED TO CRACK THE ENEMY is this fighter-bomber version of the Mosquito, world's fastest twin-engined aircraft which already has done much to smash German rail communications, and is likely to play a considerable part in the coming great assault in the west. Nose-view shows the four 20-mm. cannon. There are four machine-guns; and two 500-lb. bombs are seen being "loaded up." *Photo, Fox*

American cameras. A dark smudge on grassland tells where marching men have passed; faint crisscross lines show bruised grass from tank-tracks or lorry wheels even after the grass has straightened up and looks normal from ground-level.

Certain cameras, if three of them are fitted to a high-flying aircraft, will photograph 20,000 square miles in three hours. Other cameras will feed a fixed negative into the observer's hand less than 60 seconds after he has clicked the shutter; so that it is possible for a picture to be taken, and a bomb to descend on a special target so disclosed, all within two or three minutes.

Detailed pictures of certain special objectives can only be obtained by a very low-level approach at "zero feet," hopping over hedges at between 6 and 7 miles a minute. The difficulty is obvious—how to guess when to click the shutter? Any error in timing the blind approach, and you might be a quarter of a mile beyond the objective in three seconds! The trick is worked by checking passing landmarks and intricate timing, but, especially in a one-man machine, it is not easy; in fact, the R.A.F., which

deplores "shooting a line," calls this low-level photography Dicing—from the cliché, "Dicing with Death." Air Commodore Boothman, the Schneider Trophy ace, is in charge of the home-based P.R.U. Wing, and speed is its watchword.

Plenty of activity is going on in the R.A.F. Regiment. Heavy work will fall upon it as soon as we have captured or set up fighter airfields, for the Germans are known to have powerful weapons and special units intended to break these up. Our weapons of defence also are very powerful, and the men who use them are selected "tough guys."

It will be vital to establish airfields at the earliest moment after troops go ashore. Sites selected must be well drained, fairly level, able to be cleared of obstructions, yet with suitable cover near for aircraft dispersal, and for bomb and petrol dumps. Immediately such sites are chosen, sometimes by officers who venture dangerously ahead into no man's land during an advance, vans and lorries roll up, great steel mesh runways are unrolled and interlocked, fire-points for defence are sited, "bottles" dug for machine-gun posts, and mobile headquarters' vans arrive capable of signalling and of controlling the movements of our fighter squadrons.

WHERE existing airfields are captured they are usually left by the enemy ploughed up; our bulldozers and rollers get to work, and portable runways are laid. Enormous quantities of replacements and repairs have to be carried forward to maintain our newly-gained airfields. In the North African advance some of our Spitfires were fitted with six successive pairs of wings. For a squadron of 12 machines, nearly 200 men and 10 tons of equipment are needed for immediate operations, and about 40 lb. per day dead-weight per man for maintenance, apart from machine requirements.

Among the special aircraft preparing to take part in the Second Front attack are certain to be tank-busters. The Hurricane with large cannon was tried out for this purpose some time ago. Latterly, the Americans have used, in the Pacific, Mitchells carrying 75-mm. guns such as would knock out even a Tiger tank.

MANY unarmed aircraft, apart from photographic machines, are certain to be present with the invasion armadas. These will include 90 m.p.h. artillery spotters whose method of escape, if attacked, is to dodge slowly in tight circles with which faster standard fighters cannot cope. Generals will be flown to key observation points by aerial chauffeurs, and also to battlefield conferences.

Huge transport aircraft and gliders are lining up ready for their part in the coming operations. More of these will be used than in any battle yet, so as to supply men, guns, ammunition, food and petrol to our advancing columns, and to carry vital material to the battlefields and bring back wounded. Such fleets of aeroplanes as have never before taken the air will be an inevitable part of the Second Front, many of them perhaps carrying parachute troops, or airborne divisions fully armed and gunned. We know that, owing to their losses and to Bomber Command's crippling blows at German production, the Luftwaffe will be devastated when General Eisenhower's whistle blows.

# Our New Projector Pierces 4-inch Armour Plate

**LATEST ANTI-TANK WEAPON** used by British infantry has proved its devastating powers in Italy. Called the Piat (Projector, Infantry, Anti-Tank) it weighs 33 lb. and fires a 2¾-lb. bomb which can stop a tank at 115 yards. Girls at one of the factories in Britain where the Piat is made are seen holding a newly-completed projector (1); an armourer (2) adjusts the sights. The Number 2 of a Piat team (3) loads a bomb, and the men assume the firing position (4). A German tank (5) receives a direct hit.

*Photos, British Official, Sport & General*

# Leningrad: A Memory of Imperial St. Petersburg

The massive grandeur of Old St. Petersburg, deriving from both East and West, suffered little outward deterioration when in the last war it became Petrograd, but when the fact that all the pomp and circumstance of Tsardom had for ever gone was finally confirmed by renaming Peter's imperial capital, Leningrad, only the material form remained, all manifestations of imperial luxury were at an end ; the palaces of the Tsars became museums for the people, in the grandiose mansions of the nobles the administrative, social and educational work of the Soviets set up their headquarters. But in the two and a half years of ineffectual siege Leningrad has gained new glory as a hero town at the sacrifice of most of its architectural splendour, and when its grievous wounds are repaired its past grandeur will be but a memory. That is why I have asked Mr. GEORGE SOLOVEYTCHIK, the eminent Anglo-Russian journalist, to write this short article recalling the city of his youth—as he knew it then.—EDITOR.

THE great battle for the complete liberation of Leningrad from the deadly grip of German encirclement is over. It was short and momentous, the Russian advance fanning out with terrific speed. This new drive came almost exactly a year to a day after the siege of Russia's second-largest city—and for over two hundred years her capital—was first partly raised, when an important but still precarious lifeline with the hinterland was established.

Now, at long last, the enemy pincers have been finally unjammed, and the many famous garden cities around Leningrad—like Pushkin (formerly Tsarskoye Selo), Peterhof, Gatchina and Pavlovsk—with their rich historical associations and famous palaces turned by the Soviet Government into museums, are once more in Russian hands. The railway line to Moscow has been cleared, which is of immense strategic and administrative importance.

I was born in Leningrad, went to school there, and spent an exceedingly happy childhood in that city. Only in those days its name was St. Petersburg, which was changed during the last war to Petrograd, and it was renamed after Lenin in January, 1924. Its liberation is naturally a great thrill to me.

Now, far be it from me to defend the Russian Tsarist regime, which was its own gravedigger. But when I think of St. Petersburg in its heyday my memories cannot but take me back to the dazzling yet tragic pre-1917 era. Englishmen, Frenchmen, Americans, Italians, Dutchmen, Belgians, Scandinavians, even Germans—all those whose large resident colonies or whose occasional visitors have known the Imperial capital of Russia in those days—can never forget its peculiar spell.

A city of sleet and gale ; a city where the springtime is enchantingly tender and fragrant ; a city whose sunsets over the vast expanse of the Neva and the golden spires, cupolas and steeples are so beautiful as to be almost unreal ; a city that is a fantastic amalgam of granite, grey skies and water ; whose buildings range from the grandiose to the depths of humility, from breathtaking splendour to miserable squalor. A city where everything seemed to have been mapped out by Peter the Great—its superhuman creator, in whom the Russians of today like to recognize the precursor of Lenin and Stalin—and a city wonderfully embellished by French and Italian masters brought there by the Great Catherine who felt she was the continuator of Peter's work.

A CITY of endless daring and unending frustration ; a city of almost uncanny realism and of dreams ; a city of ghosts and nightmares. But there was harmony in all these apparent contradictions, just as the various oddly assorted landmarks of St. Petersburg blended into one harmonious whole. The two sphinxes outside the Academy did not seem the least bit out of place in their strange Nordic surroundings ; or the two rostral columns outside the Bourse ; or again the huge Roman arch which constitutes the entrance to Peter's intended and never completed "New Holland." Within a stone's throw of each other could be seen his pathetically humble little house (one of the earliest built on this Baltic swamp-land) ; the fairly recent blue mosque with its stately minaret, and finally the two Manchurian lions—like the sphinxes, truly strange visitors in such a place.

But they were not by any means the only exotic importations that had found a permanent place in the heart of the all-absorbing and ever adaptive St. Petersburg. Thus in the shop windows of Eilers, the leading florist, you could see roses or orchids or lilies of the valley in January, when the temperature in the street outside was anything from 5 to 15 degrees below freezing point, and when —much to my joy— school was occasionally suspended because of the cold weather. In the museums, such as the world-famous Hermitage, or that of Alexander III, and in the rich, private collections, there was not only an unusually large choice of old masters and Russian artists for the student and the connoisseur to contemplate, but the treasures of Asia —both ancient and modern—were unique.

Greece and Rome ; the land of the ancient Scythians and the Eastern world of modern times ; Italy and Holland ; touches of Germany, France, Britain and Scandinavia ; and all this against the typical Russian background—moreover, somehow inseparably blended with it—such was the St. Petersburg of those days.

During the early stages of the revolution the deterioration of Leningrad was a strange, sad and yet absorbingly instructive process to watch. Here was the agony of a whole civilization, the end of an era of Russian, indeed of European, history. Then there followed a long period of adjustment, and at long last reconstruction and even expansion —though on an entirely new basis. No

longer a capital—with all that this implies, especially in a country like Russia—Leningrad became once more a great industrial and cultural centre. It was still the cradle of the revolution, a keystone in the whole of the Soviet government's intricate and powerful superstructure. Its strategic importance also remained enormous, and it was the base of Russia's Baltic fleet.

AGAIN, despite the vast industrialization work carried on under the three Five-Year Plans, with the creation of entire new economic regions in the south-eastern part of Russia or in Siberia, Leningrad has never ceased to be one of the country's principal industrial centres. Its huge naval yards, for instance, have in recent years been feverishly active ; its enormous mechanical and engineering works, its electro-technical industry and an almost endless range of other factories, big and small, have maintained or greatly increased their production.

Peter the Great considered his new capital as "a window into Europe." One of the few European capitals that have never been penetrated by a foreign invader, Leningrad has stood in proud defiance of man and nature alike. It is the symbol of the unconquerable spirit of Russia.

**AFTER ITS LIBERATION**, in January, 1944, by Gen. Govorov's troops, Leningrad commences the hard climb back to normal conditions. Across Ostrovsky Square, fronting the famous State Public Library (above), citizens walk to their daily occupations. *Photo, Planet News*

# *Peterhof Palace—Then and Now*

On the Gulf of Finland, at Peterhof, stood a magnificent palace of the Russian Tsars, famous in pre-war days (bottom) as a museum and cultural centre, its gardens a holiday resort for the workers of Leningrad. For two years—until the great drive westward by General Govorov's forces—Hitler's vandals were in occupation. Gauntly the snow-covered skeleton now rears to the sky (top), desolate background for Cossacks of the Red Army advance guard. *See story in p. 633.*

## *Only as Captives did the Nazis Reach Leningrad*

Through the city which their most savage efforts had failed to subdue files a long line of German prisoners (1), wondering, maybe, at the unconquerable spirit that had kept Leningrad's once beleaguered citizens true to the humblest tasks, such as toiling in the cabbage-patch garden facing St. Isaac's Cathedral (2). Here by the Griboyedov Canal stood for 150 years a fine house ; one Nazi bomb sufficed to destroy it (4), revealing in the distance the historic Church of the Resurrection.

## *Where the German Siege Guns will Roar No More*

Blasted back from the Leningrad defences the enemy abandoned many large siege guns; this one (3), with shells stacked at the rear, is inspected by Soviet artillerymen, whilst naval anti-aircraft gunners on the Neva (5) guard the liberated city against air attack. Fifteen miles to the south lies Pushkin (Tsarskoye Selo), freed on Jan. 24, 1944, where not a house remains undamaged; Red Army men pass before the ruins of the former palace (6) of Catherine the Great.

## Salute to Leningrad's Deliverers

Following a special Order of the Day issued by Marshal Stalin on Jan. 27, 1944, to commemorate the victory, and in honour of its complete liberation from enemy blockade, the "City of Lenin" saluted the gallant troops of the Leningrad Front with 24 artillery salvos from 324 guns; the night sky over Pushkin Square (top) during the deafening ceremony. Before the siege was raised, lorries repeatedly crossed frozen Lake Ladoga by night (left) with much-needed supplies.

Photos, Planet News, Pictorial Press

# VIEWS & REVIEWS
### Of Vital War Books

## by Hamilton Fyfe

COULD there be a comment more bitter and cynical on the value of liberty and self-government than the history of the Italian nation during the past three-quarters of a century? It is just on 75 years since Italians became a nation with a State of their own. In 1870 the sovereignty of the Pope over Rome and a large tract of territory was brought to an end. The Austrian domination over another large area had already been thrown off. The southern part, Naples and Sicily, formerly under a tyrannical king, had been liberated. Unity was at last achieved.

All lovers of freedom rejoiced. A constitutional monarchy was set up—to the disgust of some who had worked hardest for unity and a republic. The Italian people, at last masters of their fate, captains of the soul they had rhapsodized about so windily, seemed to be starting on a path of prosperity and content.

What a disillusionment awaited them—and all who had sympathized with them during their long struggle. Within a very few years the famous French novelists, the de Goncourt brothers, were noting that Rome under the monarchy was worse off materially than it had been under the Popes. Discontent spread widely. The mass of the nation remained ignorant and wretchedly poor. Politics became a scramble for hand-outs. Members of Parliament devoted their energy to getting what they could out of Governments for the benefit of their constituencies. "Parish-pump politics" this was called. To change the metaphor, the State was looked on as a milch cow, which could be milked by the deputies for the advantage of those who had voted for them.

Feeble kings, cunning politicians who baited hooks for greedy supporters, ambitious politicians who held out glowing hopes of a vast African Empire, dictatorships concealed under democratic formulae, alliance with the German Kaiser for the furtherance of plans made in Berlin for the Junker domination of Europe—by such events and personalities was the ideal of Italy that animated Mazzini and Garibaldi, and admirers of them like George Meredith, dragged down and tarnished, and, by the time the twentieth century began, completely lost sight of.

WAR in 1914 found Italy unprepared and hesitating between two courses—to play false at once with its ally, Germany, or to remain neutral and get whatever could be squeezed out of both belligerents. It chose the latter for a time, then, having broken the treaty known as the Triple Alliance, joined Britain and France. In a very short time it was clear that Italy would be more of a worry than a help to the Allies. Nevertheless, large claims were made for reward when the spoils were divided up and, because these were not all allowed, a tumult of accusation and denunciation arose. The cry went up that "Italy had been defrauded" of its rightful share in the war loot.

Italian politics, says Mr. Cecil Sprigge, a former Rome correspondent of the Manchester Guardian, in his book The Development of Modern Italy (Duckworth, 10s. 6d.), "worked up into a climax of moral and intellectual disarray," which was exploited by "the most ambitious and least scrupulous of candidates for national leadership," Benito Mussolini.

Mr. Sprigge agrees with the outline I have given of the disappointment caused by Italian failure to make good use of freedom after so many centuries of under-doggism. "A dull and tarnished epoch," he calls the period that followed unification. He does not carry the story beyond "the fine October afternoon in 1922 when Mussolini led the armed black-shirts up the Corso in Rome to the altar of the Italian fatherland" and the Roman people looked on without any opinion about it, except that it was *una*

## Variations on an Italian Theme

*bella fiesta*, a pretty spectacle. For the continuation of the tragedy into which that pretty spectacle developed I turned to another book, One Man Alone: the History of Mussolini and the Axis (Chatto & Windus, 15s.). This is by another Rome correspondent, Mr. Maxwell Macartney of The Times. His account of what happened during the twenty years of the Duce's dictatorship makes one wonder more than ever at its being brought to an end so easily—unless we adopt the explanation, which neither Mr. Sprigge nor Mr. Macartney hint at—that the Italians have as yet almost no capacity for governing themselves.

LET me explain how I arrive at this conclusion. A generation ago, we learn from Mr. Sprigge, elections were "a mere parody on representative government." In 1921 they were very little better. Free speech was prevented, meetings were broken up, voters were forcibly removed when they went to vote, voting papers "disappeared." As for the elections of 1924, they were in

**TWENTY YEARS' MISRULE ENDED.** Mussolini, here seen talking to Marshal Graziani after his rescue by the Germans, left behind as a painful heritage for the Italian people the bitter fruits of his dictatorship, as remarked upon in this page. PAGE 627 *Photo, G.P.U.*

Mr. Sprigge's words "mass terrorism." Now people who submit to that kind of violence are clearly not governing themselves. Sections of them make a lot of noise, they fill the air with complaints and lamentation. But the mass of the nation is inert.

When Crispi started the idea of a colonial empire, they nodded and said "Fine!" When the Triple Alliance was formed they thought they were secure. When it was broken they thought breaking it was wise. They sat quiet while old Giolitti played a sort of political chess, moving his pieces here and there so that he might stay in office. They put up with Mussolini, did what he ordered, let their children be taught the devil's tale of "wholesome war" and crazy nationalism; allowed him to rush them into siding with Hitler, whom they disliked and ridiculed, against us whom they have always liked and looked to as their best customers, because we spend large sums on making holiday among them; made no audible protest when he muddled the campaigns so badly that they met with nothing but defeats, and only heaved a sigh of relief and gave him a parting kick when a few men at the top had put him on the run.

GAYDA, the broadcaster who used to be so frequently in the British Press and was understood to be Mussolini's mouthpiece, was a typical twentieth-century Italian. He told Mr. Macartney once that he didn't believe what he said in his radio talks. "I regard myself," he said, "in the light of a lawyer. A lawyer is not concerned with the innocence or guilt of a man whom he is defending. I have my brief. It is my business to do the best I can for my client." Not even Mussolini was genuinely what he seemed to be. He was a play actor. "In public he was constantly posing. He swaggered and strutted," he pretended to be always in a hurry, impatient of opposition or criticism, eager for cheering crowds wherever he went. All theatricalism, Mr. Macartney says. He found the Duce, when they were alone, unaffected, natural in manner, not unready to listen to argument and criticism. He was impetuous, but behaved as a normal man—not like Hitler, who flies off the handle with only one listener and bites the carpet when he is by himself.

AND what about the man who took Mussolini's place? I have found a picture of him drawn from life in a book by two correspondents, Alfred Wagg and David Brown, about the early stages of the Italian campaign, called No Spaghetti for Breakfast (Nicholson & Watson, 10s. 6d.). Does he show signs of possessing a character more energetic, more genuine, more based on principles, less inclined to play-act? The American Army officers who went to make arrangements for Italy's capitulation thought not. He seemed feeble, timid, cunning, a procrastinator, unable to make up his mind, tearfully anxious to persuade them that he was on the side of the United Nations. The Italian people, however, seem to be quite ready to let Badoglio govern them.

Well, what is to be done about Italy? Recovery will be long and perhaps painful, Mr. Macartney fears, although "no great effort will be required for the elimination of the Fascist virus." We must be patient, we must have no illusions about the Italians wishing to be "good little Democrats" all at once. I should add that the chief need is a sound system of education and sensible honest newspapers. Those two changes might work wonders—in time. Without them Italy will go on sinking as she has sunk during the past 75 years.

# Useful Men to Have About, These Marines

In that Invasion of Europe which is prophesied for the spring, the Royal Marines will have a prominent part to play. In this article E. ROYSTON PIKE tells something of the famous Corps. Other information may be had in The Royal Marines, prepared for the Admiralty by the Ministry of Information, and published by H.M.S.O. at 9d. See also facing page, and p. 630.

USEFUL men to have about a ship, and equally useful men to have about ashore. That is as good a way as any of summing up his Majesty's Royals—the men whose motto is *Per Mare Per Terram* (By Sea, By Land) and who wear the badge of the globe encircled with laurel. As Rudyard Kipling wrote years ago :

For there isn't a job on the top o' the earth
the beggar don't know, nor do—
You can leave 'im at night on a bald man's
'ead, to paddle 'is own canoe—
E's a sort a' bloomin' cosmopolouse—
soldier an' sailor too.

Tradition is a very living thing in the armed services of the British Crown, but the Royal Marines have more of it, perhaps, than most of their comrades in blue or khaki. One of the first things a new recruit sees on entering barracks is a coloured poster depicting the uniforms, badges, and distinctions worn by the Royal Marines in their almost 300 years of very active and highly honourable activity. In nearly every war that Britain has been engaged in since 1664, when the Corps was originally founded, the Royal Marines have played their part. From the very first they have been sea-soldiers.

IT was the Lord High Admiral of England—the Duke of York, Charles II's brother and afterwards James II of not very happy memory—who raised them, and their first name was the Duke of York and Albany's Maritime Regiment of Foot, otherwise the Admiral's Regiment. They were specially enlisted and trained for military duties on board ship, which so far had been performed by troops of the line temporarily embarked.

One of their earliest and greatest achievements was their taking possession of the Rock of Gibraltar in 1704, thereby winning " an immortal honour " for themselves and a bulwark beyond price for the Empire. In 1748, after the Peace of Aix la Chapelle that concluded the War of the Austrian Succession as the history books call it, the Corps was disbanded. But seven years later it was reformed, and it has lived and flourished gloriously ever since : the laurel wreath in the Marines' badge was awarded in recognition of their fine work during the Seven Years' War, of 1756-63, when Marine detachments seized Belle Isle while the Royal Navy was blockading Brest, and held it as an advanced base.

THIS part of Europe has been frequently mentioned in this war's communiqués; it may be mentioned again, when we may be sure that the Marines will once again "be there." George III granted them the "Royal" in their name in 1802, " in consideration of their very meritorious service during the late war"—that is, the war with the French at the time of the Revolution; and later the Duke of Clarence, Lord High Admiral and General of Marines (afterwards he became king as William IV), presented the Corps, on behalf of his brother George IV, with new colours displaying the badge we all know so well today

So many were the glorious deeds that might be inscribed on the colours, said the Duke, that the King had been pleased to adopt "the Great Globe itself," encircled with laurel, as the most suitable emblem for a corps whose duties took them to all parts of the world, "in every quarter of which they had earned laurels by their valour." At the same time, the Royal Cipher (G.R. IV) was interlaced with the Foul Anchor, to show their connexion with the Royal Navy ; their proud motto remained, and surmounting the Imperial Crown on the badge was to appear the word "Gibraltar."

On 16 days in the year the Adjutant on the parade-ground reads out the names of some of the great battles in which the Corps has been engaged. Among them are St. Vincent, on St. Valentine's Day in 1797 ; the Glorious First of June in 1794, when the Admiral was the Marines' Honorary Colonel, Lord Howe ; Camperdown, in 1797 ; and Nelson's three great victories of the Nile, Copenhagen, and Trafalgar. In the 1914-18 war four battalions of Marines were employed by Mr. Churchill, then First Lord of the Admiralty, in the gallant but unsuccessful bid to hold Antwerp. The 63rd (Royal Naval) Division was formed, organized and administered by H.Q. Royal Marines Forces. Four Marine battalions fought gloriously on Gallipoli ; reduced by casualties to half, they went to France with the R.N.D. and took part in some of the bloodiest fighting.

Marine battalions fought in the battles of the Somme, before Arras and in the horrible mud of Passchendaele, in the Cambrai battle that was so nearly a break-through. Marines charged down the Mole at Zeebrugge. Marines had a part in the little wars in the African jungle, in the Balkan mountains, and in north and south Russia.

Then in this war : it would be easier to say where the Royal Marines have *not* been than to give a comprehensive list of their activities. They have fired their guns in nearly every important engagement of the war, in France and Norway, in Madagascar and Burma, in Malta and Malaya and at Dieppe. Expeditionary forces of Marines occupied the Faroes and Iceland. Two hundred Marines from Chatham, many of them pensioners recalled to the Colours at the beginning of the war, were rushed to Holland in May 1940 and saw the Queen of the Netherlands safely on board H.M.S. Hereward on the way to England. Other scratch companies from Chatham gave cover to the naval demolition parties at Calais and Boulogne.

Marines fought gallantly at Hongkong ; and survivors from the detachments on the Prince of Wales and the Repulse struggled ashore from the sunken ships and, joining what was left of the 2nd Argyll and Sutherland Highlanders, formed a composite battalion which was officially called the Marine Argyll Battalion, but will probably be always remembered as the Plymouth Argylls (the Prince of Wales, and the Repulse were "Plymouth ships"). They fought to the end in Singapore.

AND so they did in Crete. To understand their work in that tragic island we must make the acquaintance of M.N.B.D.O., which is short for Mobile Naval Base Defence Organization. Its function is to provide the Fleet with a base in any part of the world, to do it in a week, and to defend it when it has been made. The whole unit numbers about 8,000 men, and it is commanded by a Major-General of the Royal Marines. It is a body of specialists, of craftsmen trained not only to fight but in all the arts of military engineering and of mechanized war. It is carried in specially equipped merchant-vessels, and its Landing and Maintenance Group is responsible for getting the unit ashore in landing-craft, and for transporting it when landed. Then the Group builds wharves, makes roadways from the beach, and erects buildings. The unit has naval coastal guns, anti-aircraft and anti-tank guns, and searchlights. It has a Land Defence Force consisting of rifle companies, machine-gun sections and light artillery batteries.

The first of these comprehensive units, M.N.B.D.O. (1), under Major-General E. C. Weston, was sent to Alexandria in April 1941, and on its arrival was given the task of providing a naval base in Crete, to which Maitland Wilson's men were being withdrawn. It never had time to get going properly, and only some 2,200 Marines were actually landed on the island. But those 2,200 constituted the rearguard, and when Freyberg was ordered to return to Egypt, Weston took command. The losses of the rearguard were severe ; only a thousand Marines got back from Crete.

And, so runs the story in the recently published Admiralty account, The Royal Marines, 1939-43, not all who might have escaped seized the opportunity. There was one little party who refused the offer of a lift in a Sunderland. Gathering up the rations and ammunition the plane had brought, they turned their backs upon security and retired into the hills to carry on the fight. There they may be fighting yet, waiting to welcome their comrades from the sea.

IN PULLOVER AND SLACKS Gen. Sir Bernard Montgomery, K.C.B., D.S.O., inspected these Royal Marine Commandos before leaving Italy to take up his new post as C.-in-C. of the British Group of Armies under General Dwight Eisenhower. The Marines made an advance landing which greatly aided the capture of Termoli on the Adriatic coast, 17 miles ahead of the main 8th Army forces, on Oct. 2, 1943. *Photo, Associated Press*

# They Man the Forts that Guard our Shipping

OUT AT SEA is this anti-aircraft fort (3), one of several protecting our shipping in the Thames Estuary and along the East Coast. Fifty feet high, it bristles with A.A. guns manned by Royal Marines under R.N.V.R. officers. The forts, which are commissioned as H.M. ships, have destroyed numerous minelaying aircraft; a sergeant (1) marks up four. Lt.-Gen. Sir Thomas Hunton, K.C.B. (2), is the first R.M. officer to be titled G.O.C. Royal Marines: until December 11, 1943, the title was Adjutant-General.

*Photos, British Official*

# Exploits of Marines as Force Viper in Burma

ROYAL MARINES who volunteered for "special service of a hazardous nature" when the threat to Burma had grown extremely grave, became known as Force Viper. As such, they acquired a makeshift flotilla of motor-launches and motor-boats (1) for the expedition from Rangoon on Feb. 11, 1942. Each armed with a Vickers machine-gun, the motor-boats were manned entirely by Marines; the launches had Chittagonian native crews. A bearded Marine stands by the side of the native captain (3) at the controls of one of the launches.

Black smoke billows up from oil-tanks (4) at Syriam, three miles south of Rangoon, fired to prevent these falling into Japanese hands; in the foreground is a Force Viper craft covering the demolition parties. Early in May 1942 the Force aided the crossing at Kalewa on the Chindwin River of British and Indian troops of the 17th Division (2). See also pp. 628-9.

*Photos from The Royal Marines, published by the Ministry of Information*

# Allied Barrage Tears the Night Sky at Nettuno

**MEETING THE GERMAN RAIDERS,** Allied anti-aircraft guns put up a terrific hail of tracer shells over Nettuno, Italian west coast beach-head secured by the Allies on Jan. 22, 1944. Endeavouring to knock out our armada of supply ships the Germans called in bombers from as far away as Bordeaux. By Feb. 16 German land attacks against the beach-head were mainly north and west of Carroceto, some 7 miles inland. These were beaten off, while the Fifth Army gained some ground in the area west of Cisterna.
*Photo, Planet News*

# Home Guard Gunners Help Claw Down Raiders

**BEHIND THE GREAT A.A. BARRAGE** which batters German raiders over Britain thousands of Home Guards share duty with comrades of the Regular Army. These mixed batteries went into vigorous action around London on January 24, 1944. During the attack ammunition is drawn (1) to feed the gun. A Home Guard sets the 3·7-in. shell fuses (2), and others load the tray (3) which carries the shell into the breech. Loaded, a gunner (4, right) waits with hand on the firing lever. The shoot over, the crew (5) enjoy a game of cards.

*Photos, I.N.A.*

## The Nazis Bombed and Sank Our Hospital Ship

*Returning from the Anzio beach-head, west coast of Italy, with Allied wounded, the St. David was deliberately sunk by enemy planes on Jan. 24, 1944. The story by Sec.-Lieut. Ruth Hindman, of the American Nursing Corps, is given here by courtesy of The Daily Telegraph.*

WE had lain off Anzio all Monday afternoon taking off wounded. The weather was not good for small craft that day, and it was a rather longer process than we had anticipated. About 5.30 p.m. we set sail, the St. David leading, followed by her sister ships, Leinster and St. Andrew.

When we were about four miles out the black-out was lifted. This is customary with hospital ships at sea, in order to distinguish them, in the hope of avoiding enemy attack. The weather turned very rough. It must have been about eight o'clock, when we were 20 miles out at sea, that I heard a crash. We all ran up on deck with our lifebelts, and were told the ship had been hit and we must take to the boats.

We did our best with the wounded. Fortunately a good proportion of them were walking casualties. It all seemed one confused rush, and then the ship began to heel over, and we were told to jump for it.

Miss Berret jumped for one of the boats, but the boat itself was tipped over and everyone in it was tossed out into the water. I was just behind her, and I went straight down into the sea.

The whole of the time from the bomb hitting our ship to the time we had to jump into the water was only four minutes—it seemed much longer. I felt myself being sucked down under the ship. I struggled and came up twice, and each time something hit me on the head. The third time I was luckier.

All around me people were clinging to rafts and bits of wreckage. Some of them had torches with which they were signalling to the boats that had been put out by the Leinster and the St. Andrew to search for us. But the ordinary flashlight does not carry far.

We spent about an hour in the water before being picked up by the Leinster. One man of our surgical team was trying to get all the wounded off right up to the last, and instead of jumping for the boats he went back to the sick bays.

**HOSPITAL SHIP ST. DAVID**, the story of whose recent sinking by Nazi bombers is told on the left. Former G.W. Rly. cross-Channel packet-boat, the 2,702-ton St. David successfully carried hundreds of casualties from France in 1940. *Photo, Keystone*

## I Walked Through Wreckage That Was Peterhof

*After two years of German occupation, what was left of the once beautiful town of Peterhof, near Leningrad, was recaptured by Russian forces on Jan. 19, 1944. The retreating vandals left it as described by the Soviet War News correspondent, Ivan Bondarenko.*

MANY of our friends abroad have visited Peterhof, a favourite beauty spot where Leningrad people loved to spend their holidays. They will remember the "Big Cascade," the canal leading from the sea to the magnificent palace of the Russian Tsars, to the fountains of the first avenue. At the very end of this avenue stood a mighty bronze figure of Samson wrestling with the lion, from whose jaws a 60-foot column of water flung out a myriad of sparkling silver drops.

It was dear to every Russian heart, this architectural gem wrought by Peter the First, the author of Russia's great transformation.

But Peterhof exists no more. The barbarians have destroyed this wonderful town. They have well-nigh swept it from the face of the earth.

I walked through Peterhof only yesterday with some of the Red Army men who had turned the Germans out. The main palace, which was the centre of the state life of the Russian Tsars, has been utterly wrecked. Built during Peter the First's reign, it was rebuilt by his daughter Elizabeth according to the designs of the famous Rastrelli. Silken hangings, beautiful parquet floors, exquisitely-moulded ceilings, silver-framed mirrors, rich paintings—all have been plundered or destroyed.

The middle palace was burning when we entered. Everything that had survived the occupation was ablaze. "Mon Plaisir," the little palace on the seashore, where Peter lived, was a pile of ashes. Hardly a house remained standing. The ancient cathedral had been defiled. The Germans blew up the Peterhof fountains. The statue of Samson was sawn in sections and taken to Germany.

### Dead Germans in the Snow

The place that was Peterhof is a graveyard, black and dismal. In the avenues where the bees used to drone so peacefully under the age-old limes, the bodies of dead Germans lie on the smoke-grimed snow, among trenches and wrecked bunkers. Rare tapestries, pictures, chandeliers, parquet floors—all are gone. The vandals cut down ancient trees to build obstacles. They herded the people of the town into German captivity. The treasures of Peterhof, accumulated for generations, have been destroyed in two years of German occupation.

**PETERHOF IN PEACE—AND IN WAR.** In 1918 the town's magnificent palaces were transformed into museums and workers' rest homes and excursions were conducted for sightseers and holiday-makers from every part of the Soviet Union. The Imperial Palace grounds in the days before the war are seen on the left ; on the right, ruins of the Palace after the Germans had been driven far west. The story of Peterhof's desolation is told above. See also illus. p. 623. *Photos, E.N.A., U.S.S.R. Official*

## Our 3 Days' Skirmish in the Hills of Arakan

*"This story is about only one small fragment of the whole war, and means little to the world; but it is the whole war to the people in it!" declares Philip Wynter, Evening Standard war reporter, writing from the Arakan Front, Burma. See also pp. 556–557.*

WITH around him the battle noises of tanks, guns, mortars and machine-guns, a soldier on a narrow sector of the Arakan front says, "I suppose when it's all over, they'll call it a skirmish in the hills!" For three hours the noise of the guns and bursting shells has been rolling around these hills, and tanks are standing in paddy fields firing at one small conical hill 400 yards ahead of them.

Columns of dust and smoke are leaping from the hilltop just as flames leap from fire when petrol is flung on it. On the left and right and behind more shells are tearing great patches of soil and scrub from the slopes and foothills of a steep, jungle-covered range. Looking away from this scene of smoke and sound you see rows of quiet green hillocks and the blue sky without clouds.

**JAPANESE THOUGHT THEY WERE HIDDEN** in this well-camouflaged paddle-steamer which they had made their headquarters on a river in Burma. But they were not clever enough to deceive the patrolling R.A.F. Beaufighters which are ever on the alert to spot such hiding-places. A stream of cannon shells from the Beaufighter which secured this photograph set the vessel ablaze a few seconds later.
*Photo, British Official: Crown Copyright*

the infantry, whose job is to take the hill, is standing in a slit trench and talking down a field telephone.

"Tanks will give five minutes' machine-gun fire along the top of the bunker to keep their heads down, and then our men will go up," he says. His troops—men of a Home Counties regiment, many of whom come from Kent hopfields and London suburbs—are under cover at the foot of the hill. A senior officer arrives and watches the shells blasting a ridge behind the hill.

Now the infantry are going up the steep slope of the hill. They are crawling up the slope. They are near the top. The tanks are silent. It looks like a film does when the sound track stops. A group of bent figures are moving, stumbling. A few feet from the top they turn and scamper down the slope.

an hour. The radio operator at the top is still saying "Report my signals—over." There are more men this time and they are going up just as the others did. They are there on the top now. They have got it.

Wham! A column of dust leaps up on the top of the hills. A direct hit. They are all dead. No; it is a miracle, they are moving back down the slope fast. Then another shell on the hills.

The Japs have had a gun laid on there and fired as soon as the infantry got there. Nobody has the conical hill now. The officer is busy on the phone. He says: "Looks like guns near road . . . over open sights." A few minutes pass, and then all the guns in the locality start probing for the Jap guns.

Somebody is getting news from the men attacking the hill. He is repeating into the microphone as he listens. "They killed some Japs. Three Japs left ran, and they think they wounded them with grenades. The bunker has collapsed. There was no cover on top. Yes, they were shelled off the top. Tanks are coming out to rally."

The air is thick with the noise of shells again, and a fight on the left is getting noisier. There is a lot of machine-gun fire and the crack of rifles, but you cannot see what is going on at the top. Tanks are rumbling across the paddy fields between the hillocks, and a few shells drop among them from somewhere. Probably it is a parting gesture from the Japs, because someone reports hearing that the Jap guns are pulling out now.

As we go down the trail for a cup of tea we learn that the men who reached the top of the hill found six Jap bodies. Later in the day they went up again and occupied the hill. This story is about only one small fragment of the whole war and means little to the world; but it is the whole war to the people in it!

Just behind this little battle, about 2,000 yards away on a track leading to the front, there is a scene which is probably unique. There a few men, and scores of brown Arakanese children, are making the road better. The noise of battle is just over the hill. Shells are flying overhead.

Little girls and boys wearing brick-red loonghis (like sarongs) are patting the wet dirt road surface with bamboo sticks. Most of them are aged five or six, up to 10. Toddlers of two or three are naked. Here there is a little girl with a ring in her nose, wearing a red loonghi and her hair done up in a bun at the back, patting the road.

Here is another little girl, aged about three, naked, carrying an old jam tin full of water and pouring it on the road. There is a small boy, aged about seven, wearing a loin cloth, smoking a cigarette and chopping the side of the road with a mattock. His head is shaved.

Like a swarm of ants these children dodge out of the way of your truck as you come along, and most conscientiously pour water in front of you so that the truck won't raise the dust. There are only a few men among them and no women, because the Arakanese people are Moslems and the women are hidden from the world.

Over there on the right vultures are circling over something dead. The tanks have stopped firing and are sitting like a row of steel pill-boxes at the foot of the conical hill. There cannot be anyone alive on that conical hill. But there is. There is the crack of a sniper's rifle, and a burst of machine-gun fire. The Jap fire sounds more metallic than ours. The tanks fire again and the hill top is a mass of smoke and dust.

They stop again, and you notice the rushing noise of shells overhead. There cannot be any Japs left. But again there is the crackle of fire from a bunker near the top of the conical hill, and "wham"—all together go the shells of the tanks.

This is all part of a small battle which has been going on for three days now as our troops slice pieces off Japanese strong points on the perimeter of their coastal bastion, or fortress system, on the Maungdaw-Buthidaung road. These strong points dominate a cross-roads. Tanks are in action for the third successive day, and the guns have been bombarding this area intermittently for three days and nights.

We are watching today's fighting from an observation post on a ridge overlooking the conical hill, where the officer commanding

Puffs of smoke show as they run. Japs come out of a bunker and lob grenades.

I cannot see if anyone is hit; they all seem to have got down. Then the tanks fire again for some time, and you see the infantry going up again slowly, getting nearer and nearer the top. They are throwing grenades up. Then the firing starts all over again, and the top of the hill is spouting smoke and dirt into the air. More minutes pass and more shells rush overhead.

And now they try again. My watch shows this has been going on for more than

## These Thirty Women are Busy Saving Lives

*Valuable war work, without glamour or limelight, is being performed by women volunteers in an outhouse behind the Epsom High Street, Surrey. They are making camouflage netting, in eight-hour shifts, and the story of their activities is told by an Evening Standard reporter.*

THEY never sit down when on duty five days a week. They never talk—unless in muffled accents which are almost indistinguishable. Their work is dirty and fatiguing, and they have not even the satisfaction of knowing where their output goes. But the articles they fashion are saving lives in all branches of the fighting

Services. So they are cheerful and content.

They are making camouflage netting under the direction of the Ministry of Supply, which comes into the picture only at the beginning, when the material and designs are provided, and at the end, when a conveyance calls for the finished products. Each of these has its special purpose. Perhaps it is to conceal a gun, perhaps a lorry, perhaps a man. Or

A LEAF FROM NATURE'S BOOK has taught British experts how best to use camouflage in war. Netting is the base for most camouflage, and here (left) W.V.S. members who have taken over a London convent as a factory weave the deceptive patterns of coloured scrim (cloth strips made from textile scraps) which will conceal practically anything, anywhere. One of the many uses to which the camouflage netting is put is seen on the right where a 5th Army gun position on the Italian front has been skilfully screened from enemy reconnaissance. *Photos, Planet News, Keystone*

it may be an aeroplane or a searchlight or a hundred and one other things.

When I entered the premises these women, in dark overalls, were working skilfully and at high speed. Their noses and mouths were covered by cotton masks such as doctors and nurses wear in an operating theatre, to protect their throats against the dust.

They took bales of webbing, about 4 in. wide, to be wound on a machine. Next they carted them to a mechanical cutter and obtained their particular lengths. Then they stood in front of 14-ft. square frames, where the nets were affixed. And there they remained standing for hours, threading the coloured pieces in and out of the strands of the nets according to the intricate patterns allotted them.

Twenty-five nets are completed and dispatched each week. The one man who has contributed directly to the effort is the husband of one of the volunteers. He made the mechanical equipment. The men who have assisted indirectly are those whose disused razor blades have been acquired by their wives for active service in cutting odd shapes of binding.

It all began in a billiards room at the residence of Mrs. Turner, and it has been going on for two years. As the operations grew, the band of helpers moved to a barn. Now there is a bit more room. But no furniture, no comfort, no music while you work. Yet Miss M. Wilmer, who supervises the women's service, smiled happily as she praised her loyal helpers.

# OUR DIARY OF THE WAR

**FEBRUARY 2, Wednesday** *1,614th day*
**Italy.**—Announced that a breakthrough in German Gustav Line running from Adriatic coast through Cassino to Tyrrhenian coast achieved by U.S. and French troops of 5th Army.
**Russian Front.**—Vanaluka and Krivaya Luka, 11 miles N. and S. of Narva, respectively, captured by troops of the Leningrad front under Gen. Govorov.
**Pacific.**—Announced that ten landings effected in the Marshall Islands on Jan. 31, by U.S troops and Marines with powerful naval and air support. Roi Island, in Kwajalein atoll, taken.

**FEBRUARY 3, Thursday** *1,615th day*
**Italy.**—Big German counter-offensive announced against Anzio beach-head.
**Russian Front.**—Encirclement of over 100,000 Germans in Kanyev area of Dnieper Bend announced.

**FEBRUARY 4, Friday** *1,616th day*
**Italy.**—American troops reached outskirts of Cassino. Four German counterattacks against Anzio beach-head repulsed by 5th Army troops.
**Mediterranean.**—Toulon raided by Fortresses ; French battle-cruiser Dunkerque reported hit.
**Russian Front.**—Trapped German divisions in Dnieper Bend compressed by surrounding Soviet forces. Coast of Gulf of Finland up to River Narva cleared of all remaining German troops.
**Australasia.**—In two days of Allied air attacks on Wewak, Rabaul and Madang (New Guinea), Japanese lost 108 aircraft.
**Burma.**—Japanese launched attack on Arakan front and took Taung Bazaar.
**Pacific.**—Parashumir, in the Kurile Islands, heavily shelled by U.S. naval units under Rear-Adml. W. D. Baker.
**Air.**—Frankfurt raided by escorted Fortresses and Liberators.
**Sea.**—Revealed that early in January, U.S cruiser Omaha and destroyers Jouett and Somers sank three German blockade runners in the Atlantic.

**FEBRUARY 5, Saturday** *1,617th day*
**Russian Front.**—Capture by Russians of Rovno, Luck, and Zdolbunov, W. of 1939 Polish frontier, announced.
**Pacific.**—U.S. 7th Division completed capture of Kwajalein, Ebeye and Loi Islands in the Marshall group. Stated

that U.S. troops had captured 19 of the 32 islands in the Kwajalein atoll.

**FEBRUARY 6, Sunday** *1,618th day*
**Russian Front.**—Enemy LowerDnieper defence line broken by troops of the Third Ukrainian Front after four days' fighting. Apostolovo and Marganets captured. Russians cleared Germans from east bank of Narva River. Helsinki (Finnish capital) bombed by 200 Soviet planes.
**Pacific.**—Gugegwe, Bigej and Ebler islands, in the Kwajalein atoll, taken by U.S. troops.

**FEBRUARY 7, Monday** *1,619th day*
**Italy.**—Capture of Pizzoferato and Montenerodomo by 8th Army announced. Violent enemy counter-attacks in Cisterna and Carroceto areas of Anzio beach-head repulsed by Allied troops.
**Russian Front.**—Ivanovka taken by Gen. Malinovsky's troops in the Dnieper Bend. Attempts by German 8th Army to break out of Kanyev pocket failed.

**FEBRUARY 8, Tuesday** *1,620th day*
**Russian Front.**—Nikopol and Znamenka captured by troops of 3rd and 4th Ukrainian Fronts. German Nikopol bridge-head on left bank of Dnieper liquidated and seven divisions routed.

**Pacific.**—Capture of whole of the Kwajalein atoll (Marshall Islands) by U.S. troops announced.
**Air.**—Frankfurt attacked by escorted Fortresses and Liberators for third time in eleven days. Limoges aero-engine works, 200 miles S. of Paris, raided at night by Lancasters.

**FEBRUARY 9, Wednesday** *1,621st day*
**Italy.**—Announced that Formia, on Italian west coast, bombarded from the sea several times recently.
**Russian Front.**—Oredezh, district centre of Leningrad region, occupied by Russian troops. Gorodishche, N. of Zvenigorodka, captured.

**FEBRUARY 10, Thursday** *1,622nd day*
**Italy.**—Bitter street fighting raged in Cassino. Some progress made.
**Russian Front.**—German 8th Army trapped in Kanyev pocket in middle Dnieper still further compressed by surrounding Soviet armies.
**Australasia.**—Australians in New Guinea advancing from Sio linked with U.S. troops at Yagomi, near Saidor.
**Air.**—Brunswick attacked by U.S. Fortresses. Fighter airfield at Gilze-Rijen (Holland) bombed by Liberators.

★ ━━━━━━ *Flash-backs* ━━━━━━ ★

### 1940
February 12. First Australian and New Zealand troops to reach the Middle East arrived at Suez.

### 1941
February 7. Italian divisions S. of Benghazi defeated in Battle of Soluk, near Gulf of Sirte.
February 9. Genoa bombarded by powerful units of the Royal Navy.
February 15. Kismayu (Italian Somaliland) captured by South African and East African troops.

### 1942
February 15. Japanese made large-scale sea landings in S. Sumatra.

### 1943
February 8. Red Army captured Kursk in drive to Ukraine.
February 12. Krasnodar, capital of the Kuban, taken by the Russians.
February 14. Capture of Rostov and Voroshilovgrad by Generals Malinovsky and Vatutin announced.
February 15. Germans attacked the Faid Pass (Tunisia) and penetrated American positions.

**FEBRUARY 11, Friday** *1,623rd day*
**Italy.**—5th Army troops returned ot the attack at Carroceto.
**Russian Front.**—Shepetovka, 35 miles E. of 1939 Polish frontier, captured by troops of Gen. Vatutin's command.
**Air.**—Frankfurt heavily raided by escorted Fortresses and Liberators.
**Sea.**—Announced that recently a convoy of 148 ships (escort included) reached N. Africa from Britain intact.

**FEBRUARY 12, Saturday** *1,624th day*
**Russian Front.**—Batetskaya, 15 miles E. of Luga on railway to Novgorod, taken by Russian troops. Luga, important centre in enemy's northern defence positions, captured by Red Army.
**Australasia.**—Rooke Island, between Huon Peninsula and New Britain, occupied by Allied forces.

**FEBRUARY 13, Sunday** *1,625th day*
**Russian Front.**—Announced that in five days of battle along shores and E. of Lake Peipus, towns of Gdov, Polna, and Lyady captured by Russians.

**FEBRUARY 14, Monday** *1,626th day*
**Italy.**—Fortresses, Mitchells, Marauders and Allied artillery heavily bombarded ancient monastery of Cassino, used as fort.
**Mediterranean.**—Announced that Brig. E. F. Davies, chief officer of Allied military mission to Albania, captured.
**Russian Front.**—Korsun, main centre of resistance for trapped Germans in Dnieper Bend, captured. German relief attacks N.W. of Zvenigorodka drove a small wedge into Soviet positions.
**Australasia.**—Green Islands, N. of Bougainville (Solomons), captured by New Zealand and American troops.
**General.**—Appointments announced : Lt.-Gen. Sir A. F. South to be G.O.C.-in-C. Persia and Iraq ; Lt.-Gen. Sir K. A. N. Anderson to be G.O.C.-in-C. Eastern Command : Lt.-Gen. W. D. Morgan to be G.O.C.-in-C. Southern Command ; Lt.-Gen. Sir H. C. Loyd to be G.O.C.-in-C. London District.

**FEBRUARY 15, Tuesday** *1,627th day*
**Russian Front.**—Gorodets and Erebryanka, S. and S.W. of Luga, taken by Soviet forces.
**Air.**—Berlin received heaviest raid yet (2,500 tons) in history.

# THE WAR IN THE AIR

### by Capt. Norman Macmillan, M.C., A.F.C.

IN my last article (page 604) I said I believed that a nation can be defeated in war by bombing. But I made certain provisos, for it is, of course, obvious that the bombers must be able to reach the targets whose destruction is necessary to produce conditions which will bring about the surrender of the enemy. And it is also necessary that the bombing shall be carried out rapidly in sufficient strength to do what is required.

This is well illustrated in the Pacific war zone. There, Japan has been attacked once only, by the Mitchell bombers led by "Jimmy" Doolittle from an American aircraft carrier. It should be noted that Mitchell bombers were Army machines, and that Doolittle is an Army officer. In this action the U.S. Navy returned to the original role of navies,

series of stepping stones across the Pacific, the world's largest ocean, to serve as bases for the carrier force.

It is perhaps doubtful if an attack on the Marshall Islands would have succeeded so swiftly before the reconquest of Papua, part of New Guinea, the Solomon Islands, and part of New Britain. For two reasons : one, the normal one of creating a dangerous salient, and the other the direct question of balance of forces. The battles of Midway Island, the Coral Sea, and those in Melanesia have worn down Japanese sea and air strength during a period when American strength has increased with great rapidity. American air power is now so dominant over the South-West Pacific that almost any operation by sea or land is possible.

**RAILWAY MARSHALLING YARD AT VERONA,** Italy, spouts smoke in dense clouds as bombs are dropped dead on the target by Flying Fortresses of the 15th U.S.A.A.F., on Jan. 28, 1944. Verona is a vital link in the German communications system in the north-east of Italy, and Allied bombers have paid the rail yards special attention.                                   *Photo, U.S. Official*

which was to carry soldiers to sea to fight ; that is very largely the role of all navies in the Pacific zone.

The importance of bombing Japan proper as a means to winning the war over that enemy is recognized. It has been mentioned by President Roosevelt as one of the aims of the Pacific war. It was referred to by Admiral Nimitz soon after the consolidation of the American landing in the Marshall Islands. " My objective," the American commander-in-chief of the Pacific Fleet said, " is to get ground and air forces into China." The Navy will push ahead and " try to land wherever we can in China." From Chinese bases, U.S. air forces will launch raids on Japan on the scale of those against Germany.

THERE are here several important points of strategy. First is the statement that the objective of the Navy is to get land and air forces into the Chinese mainland. To do that it is essential for the land and air forces to aid the Navy to succeed. The Navy cannot in one stride achieve the objective named by Admiral Nimitz. The distances are too great. It is imperative to build up a

Japanese ships are not safe in harbour or on the sea. Even under cover of night, when formerly the Japanese thought it safe to run supplies to their forces on the islands in small craft, the enemy supply line is being steadily broken. Aircraft operating with powerful searchlights (as they do when hunting the German submarines in the North Atlantic zone) constantly seek these supply craft and destroy them. The Japanese forces in some of the islands are reported to be suffering from this blockade—in which submarines play a part—to the point of starvation and shortage of military supplies.

### AIRFIELDS Swiftly Conjured out of Virgin Territory

Thus the United Nations' commanders-in-chief in the various south-west Pacific zones can determine that the enemy will be in a difficult position to resist before an attack is launched. Success can be almost guaranteed before operations are begun, by the employment of air power in adequate strength.

It is important to observe that every move made in this area is concerned initially with

the capture of airfields or of terrain where airfields can be swiftly made. The machinery available to modern military engineering is so efficient that airfield engineers can conjure an airfield good enough for fighter operation out of virgin territory with astonishing speed. But if the enemy is in possession of an airfield it is desirable to capture it at the earliest possible moment after the beginning of an attack, because this is the best means of neutralizing his air power.

EXPERIENCE in the war everywhere has shown the need to increase the range of heavy bombers and high-performance fighters, so that strategic bombardment from the air can be applied almost irrespective of distance, and enemy air power pressed far back from any zone of surface fighting. Where suitable aircraft are not available, or where air bases are too distant from the operational zone, the solution is to be found in the employment of aircraft carriers. The aircraft carrier is, however, an incomplete answer to the problem, because it limits the size of aircraft and therefore imposes a limit upon the size of bomb that can be used.

### GETTING Our Bombers Into Position to Batter Japan

Moreover, the floating airfield is handicapped when operating against a powerful land-based air force, if only for the reason that the latter's airfields are unsinkable. That is why it is necessary to get aircraft on to shore-based airfields in China before the Japanese industrial targets between Tokyo and Nagasaki can be properly assailed from the air, with sufficient strength and rapidity to bring about the destruction of the Japanese war machine, and create the requisite conditions for Japanese surrender.

Yet we have seen how the combined aircraft and warship bombardment of the atoll of Kwajalein, the Japanese main naval and air base and administrative centre in the Marshall Islands, caused the death of half the garrison and so made its fall to the Americans with remarkably light casualties a foregone conclusion. This shows that it is possible in the present state of Japanese air strength to bring to bear against such " outposts " a concentration of sea-borne air-power sufficient to cause their fall in collaboration with the operations of sea and land forces. But it should not be forgotten that these actions are merely an opening in a longer-term strategy of getting the heavy bombers into position to bombard Japan. That is the objective. The capture of Kwajalein atoll is an incident.

THE surrender of Italy was almost directly brought about by air bombardment. It was perhaps symptomatic that our occupational forces were not ready to follow up with sufficient speed to take full advantage of the strategic opening given them by air power. I have already in these notes referred to the lack of faith in air power which has delayed the fullest possible air bombardment of Germany. Let us hope that we shall have learned our lesson by the time the bombers get into position for their master-stroke against Japan. For Japan can be beaten by air power used as we now know how to use it. Although geography demands that naval and land forces must aid the air to get into position to defeat Japan, when once that bombardment begins I do not expect that America will repeat the mistake that we have made over the strength and frequency of our attacks on Germany.

Meanwhile, Allied forces in India, Burma and China prepare to aid Admiral Nimitz's strategy. General Joseph Stilwell, commanding U.S. ground forces in India, says that transport aircraft will land supplies on new Chinese airfields for a full-scale offensive to support Nimitz's westward thrust. Dual objective—mainland air bases from which to attack Japan.

# Massed Airborne Troops Descend on England

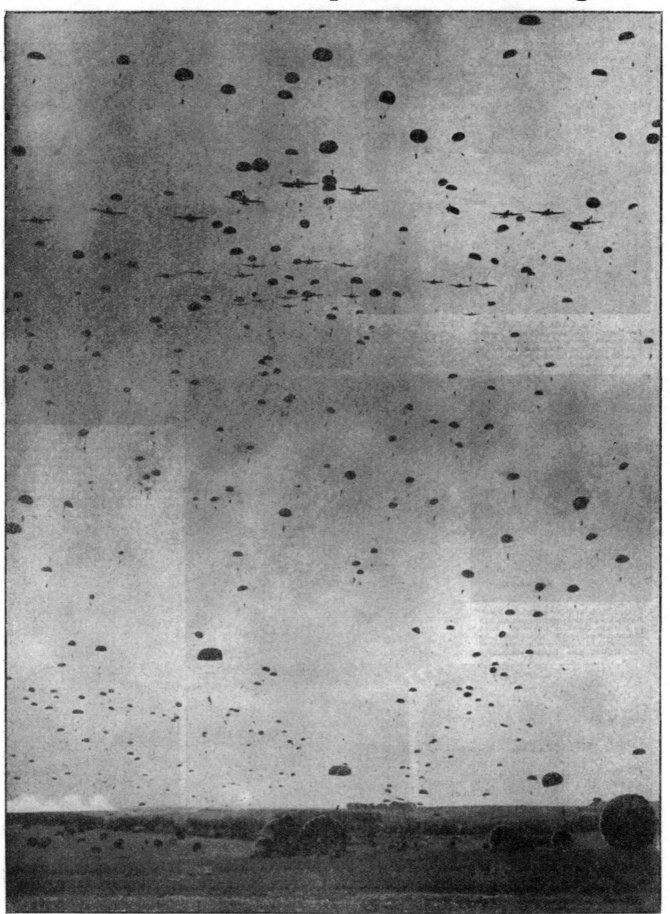

**DROPPING INTO BATTLE** from the sky came British and Canadian parachute troops during a recent great airborne invasion rehearsal in England. Amid the billowing parachutes are twenty-five planes of the U.S. Army Air Force Troops Carrier Command Squadron which dropped the men over the " battle " area. A number have landed and are preparing for immediate action. Allied parachute troops have gained distinction in several actions in the Tunisian campaign and in Italy, but mass use against the Germans has yet to be staged.    PAGE 637    *New York Times Photos*

# Decorated for Services Rendered in the Air

Actg. S./Ldr. P. J. E. RITCHIE, D.F.C., R.A.F.
For "great skill and qualities of leadership" which he displayed particularly during one operation when, leading a fighter escort to a force of torpedo-carrying aircraft attacked by enemy planes, he prevented the latter from achieving their aim of destroying the torpedo-carriers, he was awarded the D.F.C. in May 1943.

P./O. J. E. F. WRIGHT, D.F.C., R.A.F.
Aged 21, he is the first film cameraman to win the D.F.C. in this war. With 35 operational sorties to his credit, he has produced valuable film records of the Sicilian and Italian campaigns.

Actg. W-Cmdr. L. COHEN, D.S.O., D.F.C., M.C., R.A.F.V.R.
Air Liaison Officer to the Royal Navy since 1940, W-Cmdr. Cohen has taken part in many sorties, ranging from the Norwegian coast to the North African coast and has acted as air-gunner and observer. Aged 68, the D.F.C. was added to his other decorations for "his magnificent example to all."

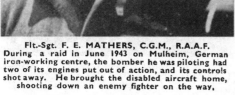

Flt.-Sgt. F. E. MATHERS, C.G.M., R.A.A.F.
During a raid in June 1943 on Mulheim, German iron-working centre, the bomber he was piloting had two of its engines put out of action, and its controls shot away. He brought the disabled aircraft home, shooting down an enemy fighter on the way.

P./O. R. C. DUNSTAN, D.S.O., R.A.A.F.
P./O. Dunstan lost a leg in fighting at Tobruk on Jan. 15, 1941. Discharged, he later joined the R.A.F. as an air-gunner, and, despite his handicap, took part in many hazardous operations.

Actg. S./Ldr. A. W. BARR, D.F.C., R.A.A.F.
"Outstanding qualities of leadership and devotion to duty" earned for him a Bar to his Distinguished Flying Cross.

*Photos, British Official ; Crown Copyright*

A PROMINENT member of the Labour Party once defined Socialism to me—I had asked him to tell me in a sentence what it meant—as "Doing Things for Ourselves." If that is correct, the British Restaurants, of which there are now over 2,000 all over the country (although a number have recently been closed), must be called a Socialistic experiment, though most of those who run them and serve in them, whether as paid or voluntary helpers, would repudiate the suggestion vehemently. They are a striking illustration of doing things for ourselves. They serve not far short of 600,000 meals a day, mostly in the middle of the day, though some open again in the evening. So far as my experience goes the meals are excellent. Naturally they are not all up to the same standard either of cooking or variety of choice. Some have tables daintily covered, with flowers on them; others are not quite so trim. But in general they could hardly be improved upon. What will be done about them after the war, many people are now wondering.

A RE Socialism and Trade Unionism opposed to one another? It looks more and more like it. Take this illustration from Russia. A young woman working in a large ball-bearing factory was constantly hearing about the shortage of labour, which is felt in the U.S.S.R. as well as here. She thought a lot about it and came to the conclusion that too many people were being employed on her particular job.

She was leader of a factory "brigade," so she reduced the number of those she led by half, and then she made this smaller force work so hard that they produced four times as much as the "brigade" had turned out before. Just think what the old-fashioned British or American trade union leader would say about that! The Russians have realized that the national interest must come before any sectional interest, even if it means doing more work with fewer workers. Some discovery!

M R. HAROLD NICHOLSON, M.P., put into circulation among his fellow-legislators an amusing story the other day. He was coming back to London in a train that was packed during an all-night journey. In the early morning he found himself in the corridor next to a Polish airman. They began to talk, and the M.P. said "Isn't it fine and rather wonderful the cheerful, good-tempered way our people suffer discomfort of this kind?" To which the Pole swiftly answered with one bitter word which he jerked out with disdainful rage: "Sheeps!"

" T HE Future of Cricket" is to be considered by a committee which the Marylebone Cricket Club has nominated. This committee consists of amateurs, or "Gentlemen," as they are called still, to distinguish them from "Players," that is, professional cricketers. This has called forth some unfavourable comment. There certainly seems every reason why those who are really most concerned in such matters as Sunday matches, one of the points the committee is to discuss, should take part in the discussion. But the exclusion of the professionals by the M.C.C. is no surprise.

The line of demarcation between Gentlemen and Players has always been insisted on firmly at Lord's (the celebrated match ground at St. John's Wood). They are an autocratic body, the governing council of the M.C.C. I have always been amused by the notices they put up on the gates, worded like Tsarist rescripts in the old days of monarchy in Russia. By the way, an exhibition game of cricket was played last year in Moscow before a large crowd of spectators. Their verdict was that as a game it was "rather too slow." Many people here think that too.

W HAT Nissen huts are like to live in now I do not know from experience, though I hear them spoken of by some men with approval. But I know what they were like when they were used first—in the last war soon after they had been invented by a serving officer of Danish extraction, Lt.-Col. Peter N. Nissen, D.S.O., of the R.E.'s. The idea seemed a good one. Instead of making

Lieut.-General **OMAR BRADLEY, D.S.M.**, whose appointment to command the U.S. Army in the Field under General Eisenhower was announced on Jan. 17, 1944. Now 50 years old, he led the American Second Corps throughout the Tunisian campaign, and it was to him that the German General Krause, Afrika Korps artillery commander, surrendered unconditionally in May 1943. *Photo, Associated Press*

a four-sided hut out of corrugated iron roofing, which involved a lot of cutting and fixing in position, Lt.-Col. Nissen took a sheet of corrugated iron, bent it into a half-circle, filled up the ends with more roofing, and there was your hut! The chief drawbacks were that it was desperately hot when the summer sun shone powerfully on it, and piercingly cold in winter. My recollection, however, is of a quarter-century ago, and I am assured that extensive improvements have now been effected in these huts, which then filled and again are filling such great and varied needs. Easily transported in sections, speedily erected and, when necessary, dismantled and removed to other positions, their utility is obvious.

W HAT a fresh torment to railway travel has been added by the station announcers whose voices rumble overhead and for the most part, in my experience, give no help at all because, perhaps, I may be going a bit deaf; their accents, sometimes hoarse and unpleasing, sometimes ladylike and mincing, but often quite agreeable or amusing, have on many passengers a merely disturbing effect. Amid the bustle and hurried coming-and-going which prevail in all big stations nowadays, the monotonous recital of the names of places, coming from the roof, creates that feeling of tension which "noises off" are always apt to produce. At one Underground station I occasionally use the loudspeaker voice almost terrifies! The novelty was introduced in order to save the station staffs from being too much interrogated by passengers about their trains. But just as many flustered men and women—especially men, I think—seem to be asking questions, often quite unnecessary questions, of the harassed porters, guards and ticket-inspectors. The good order and absence of agitation and excitement at the London termini and those in other big cities is very remarkable. People wait patiently, they move about methodically, they most of them take the trouble to look at indicator boards or posters to find out about their trains. I would have children taught to do that at school.

A TOWN near which I live received a consignment of oranges, and all the children seemed to be sucking them and throwing away the peel. I really should have liked to see a collection of it made. Now that candied peel of the sort that was so good in puddings and cakes is unprocurable, orange peel makes a very fair substitute. And although these oranges were not the kind used for marmalade of the best quality, their peel could have been used to stiffen and flavour. It went to my heart (or should I say, to my stomach?) to see this waste. The Ministry of Food advocates the use of the peel because "there is twice as much Vitamin C in the peel of an orange as in the flesh or juice."

I NCONGRUOUS are some of the contrasts between what different units of our soldiers are doing in these days of hard fighting and expectation of still more fiercely-contested engagements to come. I have had a letter from a young friend of mine who was a light opera singer and a clever actor as well. He is in South Africa, and he spends a large part of his time carrying on his peacetime occupation. Very sensible of the authorities to let him take part in entertainments, considering that there cannot be very much to do in the soldiering line out there.

I SUPPOSE it was bound to be revived—that old controversy: Are the Guards regiments really smarter in peace and better fighters in war than regiments of the Line? It always crops up in wartime. No conclusion is ever come to, the reason being that no yardstick exists by which we can measure the respective merits of the two competitors. More trouble is taken to keep Guardsmen spick and span when they are in barracks. But as to their qualities in battle, I don't believe—nor do they really believe themselves—that these are superior to the rest of the combatant forces. It is interesting that in all the countries troops known as Guards should have so high a reputation; even the U.S.S.R. is no exception to this. They were originally Household Guards, raised by sovereigns for their own protection, who picked the best they could get. So the legend started, and it survives today. Once our Brigade of Guards did require its recruits to be taller and better developed physically than the general run. But that, I learn, has been dropped for the duration of the war.

# Tight-Packed with Trouble for the Japanese

Photo, Associated Press

**CRAMMED TO UTMOST CAPACITY** with U.S. Marines, lorries, jeeps, water and water-purifying tanks, oil drums, barbed wire, rafts and food-canisters for dropping from the air, this shallow-draught, ocean-crossing L.S.T. (landing ship, tank), only half of which appears in the photograph, heads for the Cape Gloucester area, New Britain, where a landing was effected on Dec. 26, 1943. A bridgehead was established and Japanese air-strips were captured, from which to continue pounding enemy positions there and in New Guinea. See story in p. 601.

Printed in England and published every alternate Friday by the Proprietors, THE AMALGAMATED PRESS, LTD., The Fleetway House, Farringdon Street, London, E.C.4. Registered for transmission by Canadian Magazine Post. Sole Agents for Australia and New Zealand : Messrs. Gordon & Gotch, Ltd. ; and for South Africa : Central News Agency, Ltd.—March 3, 1944.     S.S.     *Editorial Address* : JOHN CARPENTER HOUSE, WHITEFRIARS, LONDON, E.C.4.

Vol 7    The War Illustrated    N° 176

*Edited by Sir John Hammerton*

SIXPENCE

MARCH 17, 1944

**THROUGH BATTLE'S SMOKE TO VICTORY** will go special Royal Marines formations as spearhead of the Allied full-scale landing in Europe. Marines are here seen training in England, charging with the new 8·5-in. triangular bayonet which now largely replaces, on active service overseas, the 17·2-in. flat-bladed type. This gallant Corps, now rich in battle honours, was formed on Oct. 28, 1664, when King Charles II sanctioned the raising of a regiment for sea service. See also pp. 628-630 and 672.
*Photo, Planet News*

# Our Roving Camera Inspects 2nd Front Stores

500-lb. BOMBS STACKED in the open, ready for use, at an Allied Ordnance Depot in England, contrast violently with the peaceful farmer and his sheep (above). More are in preparation (right) where a worker is seen removing bomb-cases from the electric annealing ovens after the heating process.

DUCKS FROM THE U.S. arrive with masses of other war material to back the Allied drive to victory. These amphibious landing craft may soon move eastward to imprint their tracks on the territory of Hitler's "fortress." See also illus. pp. 301 and 656-657.

COMPLETE RAILWAYS will go with the Allied forces: British and U.S. technicians are working 24 hours a day assembling thousands of tons of rolling stock. An American soldier, perched on top of an enormous pile of wagon wheels (right) checks the stock.

*Photos, Associated Press, Fox Photos, New York Times Photos*

# THE BATTLE FRONTS

## by Maj.-Gen. Sir Charles Gwynn, K.C.B., D.S.O.

**ITALY** Kesselring's attacks on the Anzio beach-head, which began about a fortnight after the landing on Jan. 22, 1944, are interesting to study. They started, apparently, as a number of fierce local counter-attacks, no doubt intended to secure points of tactical advantage and to disturb the organization of the forward defences of the beach-head. They may have been partly exploratory and partly defensive in character pending the arrival of reinforcing divisions. Nevertheless, about the time I last wrote, aided by bad weather which grounded Allied aircraft, they had gained a substantial amount of ground and had developed a formidable offensive operation, indicating that Kesselring had assembled sufficient forces to make a determined effort to retrieve the opportunity he had lost of counter-attacking before the beach-head could be well established.

After some days of intensive and testing fighting this first wave of the offensive was brought to a standstill, and a short pause occurred. It was quite evident, however, that Kesselring was assembling his available forces for a further effort. In due course it was made, this time as a typical blitzkrieg attempt at penetration by armour and storm troop infantry, supported by great concentrations of artillery and considerable air attacks. After some three days' desperate fighting the spearhead of the offensive penetrated the forward defences of the Allies on a narrow front, but failed to break through their main zone of resistance. Moreover, the width of the gap made does not appear to have been materially increased by the fanning out, which has always been an essential feature in German attacks after initial penetration on a narrow front.

As a consequence, the whole main thrust became caught in a pocket under the converging artillery fire of the defence, in which naval guns were also able to co-operate, and by concentrated air attack. In the circumstances the enemy must have suffered immense casualties, not only among troops actually committed to the attack but among those moving up in support, which would be particularly vulnerable to air attack. It is probable, however, that as so often has happened in Russia, artillery was the decisive weapon in checking penetration by armour. In the event the enemy failed to hold all the ground gained, and was driven back some distance by counter-attack. That the counter-attack did not regain more was probably in turn due to the enemy's artillery, which had exceptionally good observation points. I do not in any way suggest that infantry and tanks played a secondary part in the battle; they were fiercely engaged, but the conditions certainly would seem to have been such as to make artillery the decisive factor.

There can be no doubt that von Mackensen, who commanded the German Army engaged on the Anzio front, in this second attempt made a maximum effort. His army is reported to have consisted of 9 divisions out of Kesselring's total force of 18. Six of the nine he put into his main thrust, leaving only three to contain the Allies on other sections of the perimeter. In view of the losses he has sustained it seems improbable that von Mackensen with his own resources could renew his attack with any prospects of success, unless he receives large drafts to replace casualties. He may, however, by relieving the divisions on his defensive sectors by depleted divisions, and by using such drafts as he receives to strengthen the divisions which have suffered least, build up

another formidable offensive force which might be further strengthened by divisions from Kesselring's southern army.

It must be expected that after some such re-shuffling process Kesselring will order von Mackensen to renew his offensive at least once again, but it seems improbable that he will be given any more reinforcements from other theatres. He has already received one from France and one from the Balkans, the latter of inferior quality, and with the Russian front so far from being stabilized none could be spared from there or from such central reserves as exist. How far Kesselring can afford to denude his southern front is difficult to judge. He has so far successfully held the Cassino position, and there are other strong positions behind it. But his troops have been under heavy strain and need frequent relief.

**RUSSIAN ADVANCE** on the great German Baltic bastion of Pskov, Lake Peipus area, on Feb. 28, 1944, is shown by converging arrows there, and near Dno which fell to the Red Army on Feb. 24. In White Russia they were menacing Bobruisk.
*Courtesy of The Daily Telegraph*

On the 8th Army front he has latterly been under less heavy pressure, but with the prospect of improving weather it might be dangerous to weaken his defences, for the Pescara-Rome road must be more than ever an important link in his system of communication. On the whole, two or three divisions would seem to be the most that Kesselring could give von Mackensen so long as he is determined to hold his southern front in strength, and that would not provide a much stronger offensive force than had previously failed. It is possible, however, that he might decide to hold his southern front as a rearguard delaying position while he concentrated a maximum force against the beach-head. That would be a gambling course, for if the major effort failed it would probably make it difficult to re-establish as strong a defensive position as he has now.

On the other hand, if the former course were taken and Mackensen failed to achieve a decisive victory it would probably be practicable to revert to the purely defensive policy pursued before the landing, especially

if the attack reduced the offensive potentialities of the Anzio force. It is evident that Kesselring has no fear that the Allies will attempt landing in the north, because he has moved all his reserves from northern Italy, which he had retained there previously to meet that contingency.

The landing, admittedly, has not achieved its original purpose, and the enemy's reactions to it were probably not what were expected; but its effect on the general military situation is undoubtedly valuable. It has compelled Kesselring to engage his whole force with the addition of divisions drawn from other theatres, and has immensely increased the rate of his losses and expenditure of war material. That may be quite as important as the political effect of the capture of Rome.

**RUSSIA** In Russia the Red Army has maintained its amazing offensive power, and appears even to have gained fresh impetus since there has been a recurrence of more normal winter weather. The Germans on almost the whole front are in retreat, but it is a retreat forced on them by a series of defeats and not one voluntarily undertaken on a well co-ordinated plan. How far retreat will carry them, and what rallying position they hope to reach, is still uncertain. They still seem unwilling to withdraw from Estonia, presumably in the hope of influencing Finland's decision, and while they remain there they must hold on to Pskov as long as possible.

But that great key-point is threatened from north and east, and with the whole front between it and Sokolniki fluid to hold on too long might invite another disaster. In the centre of the front Rokossovsky's capture of Rogachev, probably made possible by the change of weather, seems likely to make the German position on the Upper Dnieper and at Vitebsk untenable, and it may be an opening move in another great Russian offensive.

In the south, von Manstein's abortive attempts to rescue the 8th Army in the Kanyev pocket only added to the scale of that disaster. Now Vatutin and Koniev can combine in an unhampered drive towards the Bug. The situation on Vatutin's right in the Rovno region is at the moment somewhat obscure. There may be a pause pending a further advance, for probably the Germans have brought in reserves to meet a very threatening situation. Farther south, the capture of Krivoi Rog was a notable success, and the Germans paid a heavy price for holding it so long; and though they probably extricated the bulk of their troops they are now certain to be fiercely pursued by Malinovsky's and Tolbukhin's armies. Here again there is no sign of a well co-ordinated voluntary withdrawal, but rather of a forced retreat involving heavy losses in rearguard actions demanding heavy sacrifices. As a result of their retreat the Germans may at last reach a shorter front on which to rally, but it will be with depleted divisions and without having shaken off pursuit.

It is a matter of opinion whether the Germans may in time retire to the inner citadel of the European fortress, but there are no indications that that is their intention. Personally, I adhere to the view I have previously expressed, that they will be compelled to fight to a decision on the outer perimeter. They may still hope that Russia can be fought till she is exhausted, and therefore cling to untenable positions even at the risk of disaster. Their action in Italy and the retention of the army in Norway and other outlying sectors all point to the same policy. The immensely increased weight of the Allied air offensive serves to emphasize the necessity of keeping at a distance the bases from which it is conducted, and it must be expected that the fiercest fight of all will be on the western wall of the outer perimeter.

# From Cassino Front to Beach-Head below Rome

A BIG GUN OF THE 5TH ARMY in Italy moves into position to fire, along with many others like it, on German positions at Cassino and beyond ; the gun (1) is a 9·5-in. long-range type, throwing a very heavy shell. Splinters spatter the water and a smoke column rises (2) as the enemy bombard Allied supply ships off Anzio beach-head. A snow-camouflaged New Zealander of the 8th Army goes out on patrol ; even his tommy-gun is covered with white material (3).

*Photos, British Official ; Planet News*

# Red Guards Push Westward with Colour Flying

За Родину!
За Сталина!
Огонь! По врагу

WITH THEIR REGIMENTAL COLOUR fluttering in the icy breeze, these Red Guards (1) push on in pursuit of the enemy; for their share in the relief of Leningrad they were awarded the Order of the Red Banner, which Stalin himself gained in 1919. At the commencement of the city's final liberation an armoured train (2) bore the inscription "For the Fatherland, For Stalin, Fire at the Enemy." From beneath a Nazi anti-tank gun whose crew he has destroyed, Corporal Mekhalev does further havoc with his machine-gun (3). Troops of the Leningrad front had by March 2 crossed the River Narva and were approaching the town itself some 150 miles west of Leningrad.     PAGE 645     Photos, Pictorial Press

# THE WAR AT SEA

## by Francis E. McMurtrie

RECENT operations in the Western Pacific afford an excellent example of the advantages flowing from superior sea power. On the one hand the Japanese Navy is growing steadily weaker as the result of the drain imposed by its losses in the Solomons and other areas in 1942-43, while on the other the U.S. Navy is adding to its strength almost daily by its immense programme of new construction. Thus our enemies are no longer able to withstand the fresh thrusts made at the island groups, which they had taken such pains to fortify as ramparts for the inner fortress of Japan itself.

raids on various outlying atolls in the Marshalls and on Ponape in the Eastern Carolines.

This was swiftly followed by a blow at Truk, in the Central Carolines, the main Japanese base in the Western Pacific. On February 16 hundreds of naval aircraft, launched from carriers, descended on the group and dropped bombs on all the principal islands. Battleships, cruisers and destroyers followed this up with a heavy bombardment. When reconnaissance planes had flown over the base earlier in the month there were at least 25 Japanese warships there, including a

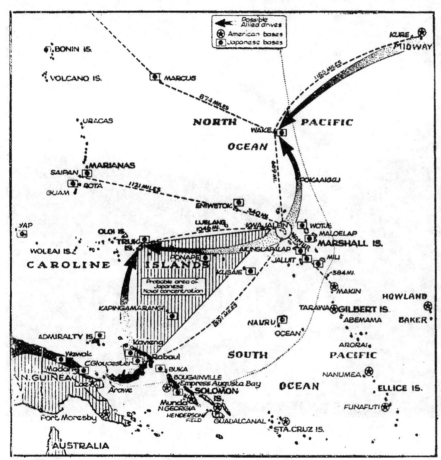

**FOOTHOLDS GAINED IN THE MARSHALL ISLANDS** recently by U.S. forces, and their subsequent successful air-sea attack on Truk, Japanese naval base, on Feb. 16, 1944, will facilitate further Allied drives from the Kwajalein atoll against Truk and Wake Island. By landing in the Admiralty Islands on Feb. 29, isolation of the enemy at Rabaul was carried a stage further. See also illus. page 660.

*New York Times*

It was at the beginning of February 1944 that Admiral Chester W. Nimitz, Commander-in-Chief of the United States Pacific Fleet, announced a new assault on the principal atolls of the Marshall Islands ; this was preceded by an intensive bombing attack by carrier-borne aircraft, and a heavy bombardment by battleships and lighter vessels. So heavy was the preliminary battering of the enemy defences that the resistance met by the Marines who carried out the landing was comparatively feeble, compared with the stubborn opposition encountered in the Gilbert Islands in November 1943. Thus, practically all objectives were completely occupied within a week, with relatively few casualties to the American forces. The whole of the Japanese garrisons were wiped out, very few prisoners being taken, and so the United States force was left free to prosecute attacks on other Japanese islands. These began on February 14, 1944, when carrier-borne aircraft delivered simultaneous

couple of aircraft carriers. Most of these had gone, but two cruisers and three destroyers were still in the area. These were sunk, together with 18 other vessels, mostly transports or supply ships. Over 200 enemy aircraft were also destroyed.

The seriousness of these losses was apparent from the fact that Tokyo admitted the above figures of warship losses, as well as the destruction of 126 planes ; evidently those caught on the ground were not included by the enemy in their figures. Moreover, the Japanese Premier, General Tojo, announced that the two Chiefs of Staff, Admiral of the Fleet Osami Nagano and General Sugiyama, had both resigned. For nearly ten years Nagano had been regarded as Japan's greatest admiral ; he represented Japan at the London Naval Conference of 1935-36, and was subsequently Commander-in-Chief of the fleet before becoming Chief of the Naval Staff. Both he and his military confrère

remain on the general board of field marshals and admirals of the fleet, which acts in an advisory capacity to the Emperor.

To land at Truk would have been a much more difficult task than the invasion of the Marshalls, which are coral atolls. The numerous islands which make up the Truk group are of volcanic formation, well wooded, and with hills rising to 1,000 feet and more. Lying in a lagoon 40 miles across, surrounded by a reef, and containing plenty of deep water, Truk is ideally situated as a fleet anchorage.

ATTENTION was first drawn to the importance of Truk in a book published in 1925, entitled The Great Pacific War, by the late Hector Bywater. In the authorship of this book the present writer had a considerable share. A careful study of charts and sailing directions had shown that as an anchorage Truk was unequalled anywhere within a very considerable radius. Its relation to Japan is similar to that of Pearl Harbour, in Hawaii, to the United States. In other words, it is an important advanced base. Though the Japanese evidently do not consider it worth the hazard of fighting a major naval action, its neutralization and ultimate loss cannot fail to weaken the enemy's main defences.

Nor did the Allied thrust stop short at Truk. Within a week, some hundreds of American planes carried out attacks on islands in the Mariana (or Ladrones) group, lying north of the Carolines, and between 1,300 and 1,400 miles from Tokyo. Guam, formerly held by the United States, and overwhelmed by a Japanese assault in December 1941, was one of the islands raided. Others were Saipan, used by the Japanese fleet as a secondary base, and Tinian.

Tinian was the landfall which H.M.S. Centurion made in August 1742, after a long and arduous passage from Acapulco, in Mexico. She was the survivor of a small squadron under Commodore (afterwards Lord) Anson, dispatched from England in 1740 to harry Spanish settlements on the west coast of South America. Having suffered greatly from sickness and bad weather, this squadron was gradually reduced to a single ship and some 250 men, but Anson's indomitable spirit carried them through many trials and dangers to ultimate success. When Tinian was reached, everyone was suffering from scurvy to such an extent that only 71 men were capable of working at all, and they were terribly enfeebled. Tinian at that date was fertile, with abundance of fresh fruit and vegetables, wild cattle and pigs, so that it proved a veritable haven of rest for the exhausted expedition.

ALL three islands are flat, without the facilities for fortification possessed by Truk. Their conquest should therefore present fewer difficulties when the time comes to follow up the preliminary attacks. With Truk, Guam, Tinian and Saipan in Allied hands, the position of Japan would be seriously compromised. Apart from air raids on Japanese cities, the seaborne trade along the eastern coast, upon which the whole life of the country is largely dependent, will be liable to attack and communications with the Philippines are also likely to be harassed. The whole series of operations was under the command of Admiral R. A. Spruance, U.S.N. Rear-Admiral Mark Mitcher, formerly commanding officer of the aircraft carrier Hornet, from which the bombing of Tokyo was carried out in April 1942, was another of the flag officers engaged.

It looks as though the enemy forces in the islands of New Britain and New Ireland, and on the neighbouring coast of New Guinea, estimated at 50,000 will now be abandoned to their fate. How long it will be before Truk is occupied depends on a variety of circumstances ; but it is unlikely to be left unmolested in the meantime.

# Going Down for the Last Time: End of a U-Boat

COASTAL COMMAND SCORES YET AGAIN in the Bay of Biscay; its prey is this German U-boat, sinking as the Sunderland which caught it circles to make another attack. It was Coastal Command's first 1944 kill. Searching for U-boats from the Arctic to near the Equator, Coastal Command, which at one time had only a limited range around the shores of Britain, has now flown 100 million miles in more than 100,000 sorties, which include attacks on U-boats and enemy shipping, and photographic reconnaissance.

*Photo, British Official*

# Royal Navy Keeps Watch Over Boom Defences

GUARDING SHIPPING at anchor in our ports, harbours and other waterways is the special task of units of the Royal Navy, who keep in repair the great boom defences around our shores. These defences consist of miles of steel anti-submarine and anti-torpedo nets and heavy wire hawsers suspended below the surface at varying depths by means of giant steel buoys, taken to the site by boom defence vessels manned by seamen, engineers, stokers and riggers.

A boom defence Maintenance Vessel (1, left), and a Gate Vessel, which opens the boom itself to allow ships to pass in and out (right), are at work hauling in a steel cable for repair ; another Maintenance Vessel (4) arrives at a boom to examine the huge buoys. Miles of lost steel cable from damaged torpedo nets have been salvaged from the sea (2) ; a punctured buoy weighing 5 cwts. (3) is brought in, one of hundreds forming a boom measuring nearly five miles in length.

*Photos, Topical Press*

# These Are Our Intrepid Midget Submarines

THE VICTORIA CROSS has been awarded, it was announced on Feb. 23, 1944, to Lieut. B. C. G. Place, D.S.C., R.N. (3) and to Lieut. D. Cameron, R.N.R. (4), for their supreme courage when, as the commanding officers of two of H.M. midget submarines, X6 and X7, they carried out, on Sept. 22, 1943, a daring attack which crippled the German battleship Tirpitz, moored in the heavily protected anchorage of Kaafjord, North Norway. Through miles of fjord patrolled and protected by anti-submarine and torpedo nets, they manoeuvred their tiny craft after a passage of at least 1,000 miles from their base, successfully dealt with their objective, and then scuttled their vessels to prevent them falling into enemy hands. The two commanders, with most of their crews, were taken prisoner.

SIZE OF THE X-BOATS may be judged from these photographs of one under way (1), with a member of the crew on deck by the periscope, and another showing the hatchway open (2) ; so small are they that there is probably insufficient room for their personnel to lie down at full length or to stand up properly. From their perilous positions within the screen of nets protecting the Tirpitz, and from a range of only 200 yards, X6 and X7 got to work. There was an enormous explosion. It lifted the huge bulk of the battleship and left her completely crippled. In the words of Rear-Admiral C. B. Barry, " It was, in fact, another answer to the ever-recurring naval problem of how to deal with an enemy ship which will not come out to sea and fight."

*Photos, British Official*

# Northern Ireland's Place in the Allied Ranks

*Where stands Ulster in the war strategy of the United Nations? Whilst Southern Ireland has preferred to remain neutral in this war, the counties of Londonderry, Antrim, Down, Armagh, Tyrone and Fermanagh, now under the jurisdiction of the Parliament of Northern Ireland, and part of the United Kingdom, are making great and vital contributions to the Allies' common pool.*

IN the period of acute crisis preceding the outbreak of war in 1939, the Parliament of Northern Ireland passed a resolution placing all the resources of the area—5,237 square miles, with a population of a little over a million and a quarter—at the disposal of His Majesty's Government. For Ulster is British to the core. Its flag is the Union Jack. Its currency is the British currency. It is part of the fiscal union of the United Kingdom of Great Britain and Northern Ireland, and it pays the same rates of national taxation.

Glowing tribute was paid by Mr. Churchill in May 1943 when, looking back to December 1940, our "dark and dangerous hour," he wrote, "We were alone, and had to face single-handed the full

From local air bases R.A.F. planes go out on patrol over the waters of the Atlantic. "The unprotected gaps in mid-Atlantic, the stretch of ocean which could not be covered by shore-based aircraft from either side, would have been far wider if it had not been for the Coastal Command bases in Northern Ireland," declared Mr. Herbert Morrison, at Londonderry, in July 1943: "similarly with the surface patrol craft whose range would have been lessened without the Ulster bases." It was from a Coastal Command station there that the German battleship Bismarck—afterwards sunk—was sighted.

Though aircraft construction is a modern development in Northern Ireland the wartime output of planes has reached enormous

Cadet Force for boys aged 14-17 has since been formed. Several men of Ulster families hold high rank in the British forces, these including Field-Marshal Sir John G. Dill ("specially employed" since Dec. 1941); General Sir Alan Brooke, Chief of the Imperial General Staff since 1941; General Hon. Sir Harold Alexander, now Commander-in-Chief of the Allied Armies in Italy; General Sir Bernard Montgomery, now Commander-in-Chief of the British Group of Armies under General Dwight Eisenhower; and General Sir Claude Auchinleck, A.D.C. to the King.

As in the rest of the United Kingdom, war production is directly under the Production and Supply Ministries of the British Government, through the various Regional Officers in Belfast. Engineering shops have been converted to the production of a large variety of munitions. Weapons and equipment produced in Ulster played an important part in the land, sea and air fighting in the Middle East and North African campaigns and now in Italy.

FROM a rope factory which is reputed to be the largest in the world, enormous quantities of that indispensable item are being produced for the Navy, Army and Air Force. The linen industry, founded in N. Ireland 300 years ago, like the heavy engineering firms, is on war service; with a reduction in peacetime requirements, thousands of women operatives in the industry have transferred their skill to the making of munitions, and others are making aeroplane fabrics, battle-dress and so on.

To feed the factories using material made from flax, the acreage under flax crops has been increased from the pre-war figure of 20,000 acres to over 90,000. With Continental supplies cut off, the linen industry would have been crippled but for this extra flax grown in the territory of Ulster.

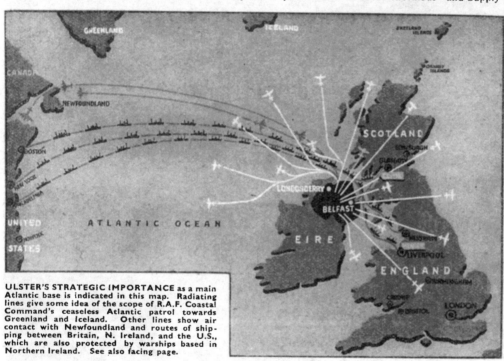

**ULSTER'S STRATEGIC IMPORTANCE as a main Atlantic base is indicated in this map. Radiating lines give some idea of the scope of R.A.F. Coastal Command's ceaseless Atlantic patrol towards Greenland and Iceland. Other lines show air contact with Newfoundland and routes of shipping between Britain, N. Ireland, and the U.S., which are also protected by warships based in Northern Ireland. See also facing page.**

fury of the German attack, raining down death and destruction on our cities, and, still more deadly, seeking to strangle our life by cutting off the entry to our ports of the ships which brought us our food and the weapons we so sorely needed. Only one great channel of entry remained open because loyal Ulster gave us the full use of the Northern Irish ports and waters, and thus ensured the free working of the Clyde and Mersey. But for the loyalty of Northern Ireland and its devotion to what has now become the cause of thirty Governments or nations, we should have been confronted with slavery and death, and the light which now shines so strongly throughout the world would have been quenched."

Not only do the ports of Belfast (the capital) and Londonderry, with their excellent sea approaches, afford first-class facilities for Allied fighting and merchant ships, but shipbuilding capacity is being employed to the fullest extent. Northern Ireland built the aircraft carrier Formidable, and H.M.S. Penelope, a light cruiser so often holed in action that she has become known throughout the Royal Navy as H.M.S. Pepperpot. From Belfast came its namesake, the heavy cruiser which, as flagship of Vice-Adml. R. L. Burnett, took part in the action that resulted in the sinking of the German battleship Scharnhorst on Dec. 26, 1943 (see pp. 518-520, 570). Before the war Belfast ship construction frequently headed the world's new tonnage lists, and now the output of craft has increased by bounds.

proportions; and Ulstermen are serving in all branches of the R.A.F., whilst plenty of youths below military age have enrolled in the A.T.C. Others have joined the Sea Cadet Corps. By a decision of the Imperial Government, conscription was not applied in Northern Ireland; but there has been no lack of volunteers for all the fighting and auxiliary Services. H.M.S. Ajax and Exeter, which took part in the Battle of the River Plate in Dec. 1939, are only two among many ships of the Royal Navy whose crews include men from N. Ireland; and the Ulster division of the R.N.V.R. is on active service.

IT is the home, also, of famous British regiments—the Royal Ulster Rifles, the Royal Inniskilling Fusiliers and the Royal Irish Fusiliers, as well as the now mechanized North Irish Horse. The R.I.F., who celebrated their 150th birthday last year, have (it was recently announced) been fighting with the Irish Brigade as part of the 8th Army in Italy; they fought with great distinction in Sicily, and in N. Africa won many laurels. Also raised in N. Ireland are the 102nd Anti-Aircraft Brigade and the 3rd (Ulster) Searchlight Regiment.

Young soldiers' battalions were formed, at the beginning of 1941, for home service with the R.U.R. and the R.I.F., and an Army

Shipments of food to Britain are on a considerable scale, agricultural production playing a most important part in N. Ireland's war effort. Agriculture is the principal industry, and in spite of the surplus produced Ulster is subject to the same controls in food rationing as the rest of the United Kingdom. Today Ulster sends us food to the value of over £11,000,000 in the year, covering such items as eggs (350,000,000 in a year), milk, fat cattle and sheep, pigs and bacon, potatoes and fruit. The canning industry has grown enormously, most of the output coming here, and the mechanization of farming has been intensified to such an extent that whereas in 1939 there were only 550 tractors in the country there are now 5,500 all fully employed.

On the financial side much also has been achieved. One instance must suffice: between April and June 1943, Wings for Victory Weeks raised well over £11,500,000. The story could be considerably extended. But sufficient has here been recorded to give background to Mr. Hugh Dalton's (President of the Board of Trade) recent declaration as to "the vitality, energy and patriotism of the people of Northern Ireland," and to Mr. Oliver Lyttelton's words: "Ulster is a sure shield against U-boat attack."

# Ulster Helps to Turn Our War Machine's Wheels

IN THIS WAR the people of N. Ireland, as explained in the facing page, are busier than ever before, in many and diverse ways. Training under realistic conditions are these A.A. gunners (1) during a recent exercise; their gun can also be used as an anti-tank weapon. G.O.C. of these and other troops in N. Ireland is 57-year-old Lt.-Gen. Sir Alan G. Cunningham, K.C.B., D.S.O., M.C. (2). In 1941 he was G.O.C. of the East African Imperial Force troops who conquered Italian Somaliland and took Addis Ababa.

Fledgling airmen of the A.T.C. (3) watch with keen interest as they are shown how to swing the prop of a plane, by a Wing Commander instructor at one of the camps attached to an R.A.F. airfield, where the boys also attend lectures and take part in many of the normal duties. Hundreds of young fellows have flocked to join the Corps; they enter on approbation at 15¼ and can be enrolled at 15½. Creation of the A.T.C. was announced by the Secretary for Air, Sir Archibald Sinclair, on Jan. 9, 1941, and it came into operation on Feb. 1. The Corps' total strength in Great Britain and Northern Ireland is approximately 200,000, this including instructors, officers and cadets.

WAR PRODUCTION in N. Ireland includes the growing of over 90,000 acres of flax, from which linen is woven and items of Service equipment are manufactured, including parachutes, harness, aircraft fabric, etc., for the R.A.F. Flax-growing and conversion to its several war uses engages the considerable attention of specialists, who are continually striving to improve the quality of the flax itself and the processes.

It is not harvested like other crops, but pulled from the ground, usually by hand. Bundled into sheaves, the flax plants are placed in small water-dams (4) for the "retting" process, which enables the fibres to be separated easily from the stems. Removed from the water, the plants are spread out to dry, then re-tied in sheaves and stacked for further drying in readiness for scutching, and then spinning before weaving.

*Photos, British Official: Crown Copyright; Pictorial Press*

# 5th Army Gets Oil by Pipe-Line from the Coast

**ACROSS LAND AND WATER** snake the pipe-lines carrying vital oil supplies to our fighting men. Above, two soldiers of the 5th Army guard a double line which engineers have slung across a river, suspended by steel wires and cradles from towers on either side ; it runs from an Italian port to a depot just behind the main Allied front. At this terminal point (below) troops load great numbers of filled oil containers on to trucks for distribution to the units in the field.

*Photos. New York Times Photos*

# Venerable Pile That Became a Nazi Fortress

MONASTERY OR MAN? was the burning question which had to be decided by the Allied Command during the attack by the 5th Army on the town of Cassino, overlooked by the great, grey monastery which the Germans, despite official Nazi denials, were using as a strongpoint to hold up our advance on Rome. The Allies had refrained from turning their artillery against the ancient and historic pile, as they might well have done at the commencement of the fight for Cassino; and still the enemy continued to direct their guns from the protection of its walls.

Mr. Frank Gervasi, Mediterranean correspondent for "Collier's Magazine," is quoted as declaring on his return to New York by air from Italy, "While the Germans were using the monastery as an observation post, I saw as many as 800 Allied soldiers go out and only 24 come back, because the Germans could see every move and turn their fire on them." Repeated warnings against this sacrilege and treachery failed to have effect, and at last, reluctantly, on Feb. 15, 1944, to save further wastage of life of our men our bombers and artillery smashed down the walls about the garrison.

Cassino Monastery, standing on top of Mount Cassino overlooking the town on the valley slope at its foot (below), as it was before the Allies were forced to neutralize it; right, obscured by the burst from one of the bombs dropped by our aircraft after a final appeal to the German garrison to withdraw had been ignored. See also p. 655.

*Photos, U.S. Official*

# 'Cloak of Invisibility' Gives Life—or Death

*In warfare today applications of the smoke screen are highly technical developments of rough-and-ready methods dating back to the early days of organized battle. In this fascinating account ALEXANDER DILKE outlines the history of smoke, for offence or defence, from the earliest recorded instance to its present status as a standardized and widely employed weapon.*

IT is almost certain that when we invade the Continent from the west smoke screens will play a big part. They saved many lives at Dieppe, where R.A.F. bombers screened the landing of numerous units.

Smoke screens laid with the precision of an artillery barrage to hide the movement of troops are a modern invention. But the use of smoke to blind an enemy is probably as old as systematic warfare. The earliest recorded instance is the smoke screen which covered the retirement of the Israelites from Egypt, recorded in the 14th chapter of Exodus. The pillar of cloud " came between the camp of the Egyptians and the camp of Israel; and it was a cloud and darkness to them, but it gave light by night to these : so that the one came not near the other all the night."

At various times during the succeeding centuries, certain individual generals utilized smoke screens, but it was not until the middle of the war of 1914-1918 that their great value in attack and defence was fully realized. Amongst the historical instances of the use of smoke screens those of Caesar and Pompey are of special interest, for they used them to cover landing operations in the same area where fighting took place in 1943.

Until the development of modern chemistry the means available for producing smoke were crude ; but it is astonishing that commanders did not make more use of the smoke screen. Drake seems to have used smoke to conceal his ship from the numerically superior Spaniards off the coast of South America, but on land we have to wait until the 17th century for further instances of the deliberate use of smoke.

PROBABLY the chief difficulty was that of enveloping the enemy in smoke instead of their own troops. To generate smoke immediately in front of the advancing forces, or for the advancing troops themselves to carry smoke-candles, was to invite disaster, for the smoke simply blinded—and probably choked—the users, and the defenders had only to fire into the smoke cloud to be fairly sure of hitting something.

The basic principle in the use of smoke is that it must be laid over or near the enemy. This was realized both by Gustavus Adolphus and Charles XII of Sweden, both of whom used smoke to enable their armies to cross rivers in the face of opposition. The problem of carrying the smoke to the enemy was solved by building special smoke-generating barges which were propelled across the river before the attack began.

In a sense, all battles that raged during the last century were fought from behind smoke screens. The powder of artillery and musket produced such a dense smoke that after the first volley both sides fought more or less in the dark, a fact which probably accounts for the remarkably few casualties considering the point-blank range and lack of cover. When smokeless powder was introduced, a few enterprising officers perceived the possibility of a deliberately placed smoke screen and experiments were actually carried out, before the turn of the century.

THE smoke candles, meant for testing drains, which were tried at Aldershot did not, apparently, give satisfaction, for the matter was dropped. Possibly the difficulty lay in finding a method of projecting the candles into the enemy lines. Not until November 1916 were the first smoke shells used, and then not until the technique of lighting candles had been tried, with disastrous results. This was in 1915, and the smoke intended to conceal the British trenches simply drew the enemy's shellfire.

## The Coming of the Tanks

Once the principle that smoke must be projected had been driven home, the British went rapidly ahead, and Arras, in 1917, saw the smoke screen laid by the artillery to blind the well-established enemy. The Germans quickly imitated the British methods ; and smoke, both for offence and defence, became a standard weapon on every battlefield. The coming of the tanks gave opportunities for new developments.

In the present war the Germans themselves have provided testimony of the effectiveness of British smoke material and technique used in conjunction with tanks. A German correspondent broadcasting on the El Alamein battle said the British used a new smoke screen of " unbelievable " efficiency. He described how the British artillery firing " artificial fog " shells laid down a milky wall of a depth, width and thickness never before seen. Out of this wall the tanks appeared right in their midst, having penetrated unseen.

THE Nazis have made considerable use of smoke for blinding the defenders of fortified positions. According to a German commentator, the smoke is provided by specially trained " fog troopers," completely motorized and organized like artillery regiments. They emphasize the " panic " effect of artificial fog on the defenders, firing at an enemy they cannot see, losing touch with even the men standing next to them.

The Nazis made great use of smoke in attacking Russian strongholds. It was probably this that gave rise to accusations of " poison gas." Whether the smoke was actually poisonous does not seem certain. At the time of the attack on the Caucasus, the Cologne Der Neue Tag published a letter from a German soldier at the front, eulogizing their new smoke screens, produced by shells from mortars. He spoke of the effect of the smoke on the eyes of the defenders, and ended, " Before we dismantle our guns we look once again at the Soviet forts. Nothing moves. The silence of the graveyards reigns everywhere. The infantry advances, and the hotly-contested point is ours." The account was remarkable in suggesting that the point was subdued by smoke without the use of explosives.

The Germans are putting smoke to another use. They have tried to screen some of their munition centres from bombing by creating smoke when the R.A.F. is signalled. The technique has not been successful. The modern R.A.F. concentrated raid does not give time for the smoke to obscure the target.

APART from the use of smoke from damped fires at sea, the generation of smoke screens by chemicals is a highly technical matter in which constant research proceeds. The requirement of countless minute opaque particles to be produced from a comparatively small amount of material is not easy to fulfil. Compounds of phosphorus are extensively used. The oxide of the comparatively rare titanium has the property of dividing into minute opaque particles—it was used for making air mail paper opaque. Smoke generators may make use of particles formed in combination with the moisture of the air.

Smoke can be projected in grenades, mortar bombs, shells and aerial bombs. Aircraft laying a smoke screen like " skywriting " have been tried, but bombs seem to be the better method. Smoke bombs were used at Dieppe, and a number of awards were made to pilots of the planes charged with the difficult and dangerous mission of laying them precisely. Wing-Commander Wilfred Surplice who was awarded the D.S.O. (see portrait p. 292, Vol. 6), made the first smoke sortie; and upon the accuracy of the smoke bomb delivery depended not only the success of the subsequent smoke-laying operations, but, to a great degree, the success of the whole combined operation.

At sea, smoke has been used not only by destroyers to cover ships they are protecting, but also by merchant ships to screen themselves. Special smoke-generators beside the stern gun were introduced on merchant ships in the last war. Many warships, especially those of the Axis, owe their survival to the fact that if air is cut off from oil furnaces dense black smoke is produced in quantities.

**ALGIERS HARBOUR BEGAN TO DISAPPEAR** as a smoke screen drifted across its length during an enemy air raid shortly after the Allies landed there on Nov. 8, 1942. In the battlefield, mortars and guns put down a screen from their bombs and shells which are usually of light or medium type. The tank has proved invaluable as a fast screen-layer. Latest improved smoke-compound to be used by British troops enables more to be packed into the container, thus producing a denser smoke.

*Photo, British Official*

## *Cassino's Sanctuary Used for Shelling 5th Army*

Perched 1,800 feet above the road to Rome, the vast, castle-like Cassino Monastery was founded by St. Benedict in the year 529. The centuries swept on, and war engulfed this shrine of learning and of faith. The Germans opposing the 5th Army made of it an observation post, and presently an armed fortress: and so that many precious lives might be saved and the advance of Deliverance no longer be delayed the Allies were compelled, in Feb. 1944, to reduce it to ruins. See p. 653.

## Sea Craft to Free the World

Flying the White Ensign of the Royal Navy, landing craft of manifold types make possible victorious advances from the sea: the climax of their usefulness will be apparent when the Allies descend in full force upon the mainland of Western Europe. On their bows is lettering to identify them: LSI (left background) are anchored landing ships from which assault craft are being lowered; LCF, major landing craft armed with A.A. guns; LCI, the latest type of infantry landing craft; LST, tank-landing ship; LCS, support craft; LCT, landing craft carrying tanks, guns and heavy equipment; LCA, landing assault craft; lower right, an amphibious duck (see illus. p. 301).

*Drawn by C. E. Turner. By courtesy of The Illustrated London News*

## Modern Frigate as Escort to Allied Convoy

Germany's wolf-packs of the underseas recognize the latter-day frigates of the Royal Navy as in part responsible for the great toll exacted of them. H.M.S. Helmsdale, representative of the River class, and here seen tossing in a North Atlantic swell, helping to protect the convoy looming dimly in the misty distance, flies the signal "VJ" (Vinegar Johnnie, in Service parlance) bidding the vessels to keep station : for the merchant ship that strays becomes an easier U-boat target.

*Drawn by C. E. Turner. By courtesy of The Illustrated London News*

# VIEWS & REVIEWS

### by Hamilton Fyfe

WE have heard a lot about the neglect of defences and precautions at Singapore. We know how the surprise attack on Pearl Harbour, in December 1941, with its disastrous consequences, was made possible by the slackness and complacency of naval officers commanding there. Less has been written about the easy wins Japan had in New Guinea and other Pacific islands. In New Guinea Diary (Gollancz, 10s. 6d.) by an Australian war correspondent, Mr. George H. Johnston, blame is ladled out to the Australian authorities with a freedom that no British or American newspaperman would adopt.

"Australians are paying dearly for their errors of the past. They say there's no sense in crying over spilt milk. But perhaps we can be permitted to shed a silent tear or two for the things we didn't do in the years that the locust hath eaten, things that could have been done but weren't and things that shouldn't have been done but were. 'Our little friends the Japanese'—the phrase was used more than once in the years before the Second World War began—are raining bombs on Australian territory and that these bombs contain scrap metal exported from Australia is . . . a probability."

There was a small outcry against letting Japan have this scrap metal. Some people thought it was for bombs which would be used against the Chinese. But the protest was disregarded. Business came first in the minds of the scrap metal merchants. "And now," says Mr. Johnston, "we're getting a few of those bombs ourselves."

THAT, he charges, was only one instance of fatuity. For years it had been known that Japan was making most careful and systematic investigation of everything in the waters of North Australia and the surrounding island groups. Every Japanese pearling lugger had a naval officer on board. A dirty little Japanese 200-ton steamer used to run regularly between Truk and Rabaul and as far sometimes as Port Moresby. "She never seemed to carry any cargo, but nobody worried very much about her. Then when Japan struck in the South Seas the Truk-Rabaul supply line became enormously valuable to the aggressors." Rabaul has been the centre of the operations against New Guinea. Truk was turned into "an immense defence arsenal for future aggression," and the base from which the enemy forces holding what they gained at the beginning have been munitioned and fed.

These places have been in the news for a long time past. Lately they have figured more prominently. But very little was said about them in the Australian Press while the Japs were charting every anchorage and every reef "and knew the defence set-up like an open book."

We pottered around, doing a little bit here and putting the rest off until the weather got cooler... It was generally agreed there would be plenty of warning when the time came. Rabaul had about a week's warning! And you can't manufacture anti-aircraft guns in a week from coconut palms. The one commanding fact of this war is that you don't get warning of what is coming."

New Guinea was called by the white people who lived there "the Land of Tomorrow." When the Spaniard doesn't feel active, he says Manana. When the Russian procrastinates he murmurs See chass. The Chinese have a word Maskee for use in lazy moods. All mean the same thing, "no hurry," as the word Dehori in the language of the New Guinea people. The white people who went to Papua adopted it and themselves lived in the spirit of it.

Papua is the part of New Guinea that was mandated to Australia. It is, according to Mr. Johnston, a very rich country, but its riches have so far been left by the Australians almost untouched. If they had been developed

---

## A Grim Chapter in Australia's War Story

---

it could be producing for Australia "almost every commodity that Japanese aggression has taken from us." Its agricultural possibilities are tremendous. Sugar, tobacco, tea, coffee, cocoa can be grown with every prospect of success. Quinine and nutmegs have been grown experimentally. Sisal for rope-making is prolific. Rubber could be cultivated on a vast scale; it grows wild there. Minerals, too, abound. There is coal in immense quantities and of proved high quality. Copper, gold, manganese, lead, iron, silver and a host of other valuable substances can be mined, including wolfram (chief ore of tungsten, which is used in making special steels, etc., and for munitions), which we are trying to stop Portugal and Spain sending to Hitler. None of these possibilities has been tapped in the twenty years Australia has had Papua to govern.

EXCUSE must be found in the climate which disinclines to activity and encourages "smug self-satisfaction." Anything that called for exertion beyond the ordinary could be put off, "and in the Tropics even thinking is sometimes arduous."

The laws of tropical behaviour ordain a great deal of "lolling back in cane chairs, sipping long drinks, and discussing hangovers of the night before." Only exceptional white people can be energetic in the tropical countries, people who take care of their health and take themselves seriously and do not take many drinks. So it came about that within a few weeks of Japan striking the first blow, only one Australian base stood between Rabaul in Japanese hands and the Australian mainland.

THIS was Port Moresby. We have heard a good deal about that too. General Morris, in command of the New Guinea Force, spoke of it as the Tobruk of the Pacific. If the enemy had taken it, it would have given them the chance to carry out direct air assaults on Australia. So long as we held it, it was a barrier to his advance. It used to be a sleepy tropical port with a splendid harbour and an inner anchorage where a big fleet can lie hidden. It had one wharf and a few small jetties where vessels loaded copra. On hills round the town, which consists mainly of grass and cane huts and a few with iron roofing, are the bungalows of the white folks, ugly, decrepit and badly needing a coat of paint. Not an attractive picture, but still less attractive was Port Moresby when it had been bombed and deserted after nightfall. "In the hotels and houses, where there was the sound of tinkling ice and swing music and laughter are heard only the buzzing of insects and the kek-kek-kek-kek of the gecko lizard."

PORT MORESBY held out, the retreat of the Allied forces came to an end, the return journey began. The newspapers and the radio used to tell us about the battles on the Owen Stanley Range, which is the backbone of the Papua part of New Guinea. We got accustomed to the repetition of the name Kokoda, though it conveyed little to our minds.

For thousands of Australians who have walked the weary sodden miles of this dreadful footpath—and these Australians are the fathers of the next generation—it will be the one memory more unforgettable than any other that life will give them.

These were the troops who climbed every inch of the agonizing track, sometimes in burning sunshine, sometimes in cold mist, who "buried so many of their cobbers and saw so many more going back weak with sickness or mauled by the mortar bombs and bullets and grenades of the enemy, men gone from their ranks simply to win a few more hundred yards of this wild, unfriendly and utterly untamed mountain." It was what General Allen called it, "the toughest campaign of the Australian troops in this or any other war." It is described by Mr. Johnston with vivid power and full appreciation of the human elements in the grim drama.

One very interesting comment he makes on the Coral Sea engagement. It was the first time ships ever engaged each other more than a hundred miles apart, the first time a naval battle has been fought with no gunfire from ships except that of anti-aircraft guns. The attacking was all done on both sides by aircraft and it was a great victory for the Allied Nations. It is bound to affect future naval strategy. It may alter the whole conception of warfare at sea.

**JAPAN PLANNED TO TAKE NEW GUINEA** before this war began, as the book reviewed in this page reveals. Over an improvised bridge Australian troops are here seen crossing a jungle torrent on the trail from Kokoda to Buna, which they captured from the enemy on Dec. 14, 1942; since then they have pushed on N.W. round the coast some 250 miles closer to Madang. PAGE 659 *Photo, Sport & General*

# First Japanese Territory Won by the Allies

ISLAND BY ISLAND we push back the Japanese in the Pacific. On Jan. 31, 1944, U.S. forces stormed the Kwajalein group of the Marshall Islands ; covering an area five times the size of Great Britain, the Marshalls were taken from the Germans by the Japanese in the 1914-18 war. American marines (top) on shell-blasted Namur, occupied by the Allies on Feb. 2 ; others, on Roi Island (below), containing the best airfield in the Marshalls, and also captured on Feb. 2, watch an enemy dump on Namur go up in smoke. (See map in p. 646.)  PAGE 660  *Photos, Planet News*

# Britain's Colonies in the War: No. 3—W. Indies

UNDER Democratic Constitution offered to Jamaica by the British Government in Feb. 1943, and which it was announced was accepted by the people on May 19, 1943, for the first time in history they will be able to have a decisive say in the government of their island : the new constitution comes into effect in 1944. The part played by the West Indies in the Allied war effort has been immense.

In addition to the supply of skilled men for the Armed Forces, many technicians have been sent to Britain to work in our factories ; hundreds more are serving in the Merchant Navy and in their own local Merchant Marine forces. When Britain's need for timber for war purposes was most great, British Honduras sent a forestry unit, consisting of expert loggers, to help fell and prepare the trees. Trinidad, now the largest oil producing centre in the British Empire, has provided considerable quantities for the Allied use. The chief mineral which the W. Indies produce is bauxite, essential in the manufacture of aluminium.

In an effort to be self-supporting, the W. Indies are using derelict sugar plantations in an intensive cultivation of foodstuffs, most of which were imported before the war. Recently the first food yeast factory to be constructed in the world was set up in Jamaica. Sugar and fruit are the main exports, Canada and America now being the chief recipients. Another recent development is the dehydration of fruits on a considerable scale.

**TAKING A CENSUS** in Jamaica (4), which will form the basis for the first election under the Colony's new democratic constitution. The W. Indian islands of St. Christopher and Nevis (of the Leeward Group) purchased these mobile canteens (1) and presented them to the people of Liverpool. Glad to be in uniform are these Jamaican girls (2) who formed the first A.T.S. unit to be founded in Jamaica in 1943. Good friends with the squadron mascot is this W. Indian Flight Sergeant (3), pilot of a Spitfire : he hails from Trinidad. PAGE 661 *Photos, British Official ; Pictorial Press*

# Will Rail Transport in Germany Stand the Strain?

Speedy movement of enemy troops and materials to oppose the coming attack on Europe from the west will depend largely upon the capabilities of the German railways. These, seriously overstrained, are presenting Hitler with problems of the first magnitude. The position is outlined by Dr. ERNEST WERTH to whose article in p. 430 reference should also be made.

Too little consideration has been given in this country to the significance of an order issued to the German railways a short while ago. Similar measures had been taken in the autumn of 1942, when the German traffic system became so overstrained that it was unable to cope with the demands of war transport. Then, as now, it was decreed that railway trucks and wagons should be overloaded by 25 per cent above their normal capacity.

But so many breakdowns and accidents occurred in consequence that a few months later the average speed of goods trains had to be reduced by about 30 per cent, thus again lowering the general capacity of transport to about 87 per cent of normal. Later on this practice had to be abandoned, because the number of broken axles, springs, and so on exceeded the possibility of repairs.

The fact that the Nazi dictator of transport, General Adolf von Schell, has once more to

At this crucial moment, when the Second Front is about to materialize, the speedy movement of troops and material—depending upon the efficiency of the railways—may become decisive. The situation is quite different from the position in the 1914-1918 war. It is true that the Germans lost the Battle of the Marne because two Army Corps, urgently needed on their right flank in France, were then on transport to Eastern Prussia; where, by the way, they arrived too late for Tannenberg. But later on, from 1917 onwards the war in the east was practically over, and German traffic was concentrated to the west and only in a minor degree to the south and south-east. Now the war of two fronts—nightmare of all German strategists—starts at a time when the principal means of movement (railways) is already in a state of advanced deterioration.

Contrary to British tradition, the railways in Germany were always the property, and

With a second front in the west, the task of military transport will be to cover distances of roughly 1,000 miles from the east to France, and 600 and more miles from Germany to Italy and the south-east. The difference from the situation in 1918 is evident; there must be a constant stream of traffic not only east-west and vice versa but north-south; and therefore great junctions and crossings like Cologne, Frankfurt, Stuttgart, Nuremberg, Leipzig, Hanover and Berlin have been constant targets for Bomber Command. Here indeed are most sensitive joints, even the temporary paralysis of which must involve grave traffic jams and hold-ups.

The German railways entered this war with a personnel of more than one million and a stock of about 35,000 locomotives, 70,000 coaches and about 75,000 trucks and wagons. The occupation of Austria and Czechoslovakia added another 13,000 miles of railways, and since then the stocks of nearly all European countries have been plundered for German military purposes. Entire lines, including the permanent way, the signal system, etc., in western countries have been dismantled and transported to the east, where the wider Russian gauge had to be changed over to the German standard.

But notwithstanding all efforts, the severe winter of 1941-1942 saw a great disaster for the German Army, mainly because the railway traffic suffered a complete breakdown. It appeared that the Central-European locomotives were entirely unsuitable for the Russian climate. Thousands of locomotives became frozen, their boilers and pipes burst beyond repair, and long rows of rolling stock, fit only to be scrapped, crowded the sidings of Poland. In this emergency German engineers hurriedly designed a so-called "utility locomotive," known as the K 42, which was to be not only cheaper and simpler for mass production, but at the same time more efficient and, in particular, "winterproof." It is, however, known that the average monthly production of that model never exceeded 200, whilst occasionally the bag of R.A.F. "locomotive-busters" in the west reached 250 machines and more. In addition to the K 42, it has lately been announced that a special goods train utility locomotive, the K 44, has been designed and will be in mass production at the well-known Orenstein and Koppel works at Berlin.

If one takes into consideration the damage that great locomotive works like the Henschel factory at Kassel, the State works in Hanover, and the famous firms Borsig and Schwartzkopf at Berlin, must have suffered in air raids, one can estimate Hitler's railway problem in the spring of 1944.

For him everything now depends on a frictionless flow of traffic. The transport of one division today requires about 60 trains, its constant reinforcements many more. A glance at the map shows that all this traffic is, in the end, confined to some 8 to 10 trunk lines in each direction. And here, particularly in the west, a special danger point arises: of some 25 bridges crossing the Rhine, about 12 are main railway bridges.

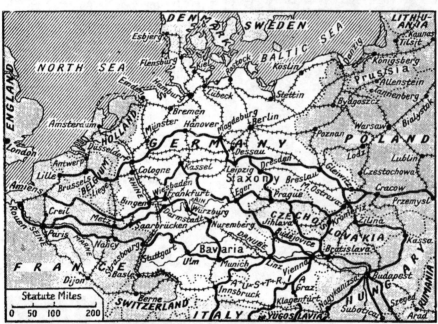

VITAL STRATEGIC RAILWAYS (shown by heavy lines) in Germany and France, Belgium and Austria, Czechoslovakia and Poland, and in part of Italy and of Yugoslavia, are now a matter of anxious concern to Hitler, who, as explained in this page, has neglected Germany's rail transport system in favour of his now almost useless motor highways. *Specially drawn for* THE WAR ILLUSTRATED

fall back on methods already proved to be dangerous, at a time when Germany is facing an invasion from the west, shows that her much advertised advantage of the "inner line of communication" may become jeopardized. Today this inner line is a problem of railways. Since 1933, when Hitler seized power, he has ignored all the warnings of experts and grossly neglected the railways. Necessary repairs to the permanent way, and replacement of rolling stock could not take place because the Fuehrer was hypnotized by his beloved "autobahnen."

These costly highways for motor traffic have become almost useless for the Nazi war effort; petrol and tires being so scarce that motor trucks and lorries, even for military purposes, have nearly vanished in Nazi-occupied Europe. For the movements of troops and the transport of reinforcements now the railways play a more important role than at any time during the war. One has only to look at the campaign in the east, where the conquest of railway junctions and the cutting of railway lines compels the Germans to give up one position after another.

under the management, of the State. There were before 1918 the Royal Prussian, the Royal Bavarian, Saxonian, and other lines, and even after their amalgamation into one huge undertaking the so-called private company was in fact under complete State control. Consequently, military influences and strategic considerations were dominant. It is significant that the military authorities, apprehending destruction of power stations, objected to electrification, although electric power from mountain rivers, artificial lakes and canalized rivers was cheap and abundant.

Of about 36,500 miles of German track only about 1,000 miles, mostly in Bavaria and Central Germany, were electrified. Moreover, lines were constructed for purely military purposes, such as that laid down in the 1914-1918 war from the military and industrial centre of Berlin via Dessau to the west and nicknamed "Kanonenbahn" or "cannon track." Between the wars, for the same reasons, a double railroad was constructed from the industrial district of Frankfurt on Main to Saarbrücken, with a huge bridge across the Rhine near Bingen.

In 1944 during and after invasion from the west, the combined Allied air forces may well be able to keep those bridges, and the railways and marshalling yards around them, under constant assault. No Atlantic Wall no newly constructed Dutch Wall or Siegfried Line, could be held with supplies from the rear interrupted by the cutting off of their life-lines. We may see in the west, as in the east, a battle for railways and communications.

# Fighting Senegalese get their Share of Jeeps

**STREAMS OF WAR MATERIALS** for the Allies include these rows of jeeps just arrived at Casablanca, North Africa, where Senegalese troops assemble them ready for the road. Fierce warriors from French West Africa, Senegalese took part in the victorious march by Gen. Leclerc's Fighting French troops from Chad Territory in French Equatorial Africa, against Italian positions in Libya more than a 1,000 miles distant, which coincided with Gen. Montgomery's drive into Tripolitania from the east. See Vol 6, p. 526. *Photo, Keystone*

# China Recaptures Burned Rice-Town of Changteh

IMPORTANT RICE CENTRE, Changteh, in the Tungting lake area, was taken by overwhelming Japanese forces on November 25, 1943, after a 15-day siege in which the Chinese garrison fought magnificently. The enemy did not hold the city for long, however. On December 9 Chinese forces recaptured it.

During the fight the city was largely reduced to ashes, as is shown by the remnants of one of the towers (4), where a small band of Chinese, under intensive artillery fire, battled on until ammunition and food were exhausted. Allied aircraft dropped supplies for the heroic defenders, in containers made of plaster and bamboo (3). Sullen and resentful are these untidy Japanese prisoners (2); the Japanese took no prisoners. After the recapture of the city the people return home, a Chinese soldier (1) carrying in a cradle slung from his shoulder an orphaned baby he has found by the wayside.

*Photos, Topical Press*

# I WAS THERE! Eye Witness Stories of the War

## They Posted Me 'Missing' When Sahib was Sunk

*Chief P/O F. R. Flack, coxswain of the submarine Sahib and one of the survivors after her sinking in the Central Mediterranean—and posted as "missing" until he was heard over the German radio telling his wife and mother and father that he was safe—tells in this Evening Standard story of the strange and adventurous journey that led him recently to Buckingham Palace, to receive the D.S.M. at the hand of the King.*

**Chief P/O F. R. FLACK, of H.M. submarine Sahib, whose D.S.M. is admired by his young son immediately after the investiture. See story on the left.** *Photo, Evening Standard*

SAHIB, as you know, was sunk. Exactly how she was sunk I cannot tell you, but at the end of the first lap of my journey I found myself swimming about in the Mediterranean with all the rest of the crew of the Sahib.

While we were doing that, the enemy came over and machine-gunned us from the air. One of my shipmates was killed. Eventually we were picked up by some destroyers. We were split into parties, and with Lieutenant J. H. Bromage, who was in command of the Sahib, the other officers and 10 ratings, I arrived at Camp 70, near Ancona.

We were there when the Italian collapse came. We were told to remain in camp and see what happened. After a couple of days 500 Germans turned up there, and some of the British naval personnel decided that it was time to leave.

I got out with Petty-Officer Boatman, of Saffron Walden, Artificer Winrow, of Liverpool, and Corporal Bode, of the R.A.S.C., whose home is at Walthamstow. For a week we managed to feed ourselves. Then we had to seek some help, so one would risk going to a farmhouse while the others watched to see what sort of reception he got. The Italians nearly always helped us.

After 23 days we slipped through the German lines and walked into a British sentry. He took us along to have the finest cup of tea I have ever tasted. The next lap of the journey was back to the base from which the Sahib had sailed. I went round and called on my brother. He had a bit of a shock!

*Then Flack came home and with two other Frederick Flacks—his father and young son—and his wife and mother he went to receive his decoration.*

## Along Ledo Road to the Northern Burma Front

*Ceaselessly men toil and sweat to keep the Ledo lifeline open. Through jungle, which was the home of tigers, leopards, black panthers and elephants, bulldozers now gouge their shattering way. Philip Wynter, Australian Consolidated Press, tells the romantic story of this great battle-track.*

I HAVE just come over the Ledo Road after some days of rain, and the men on the road were fighting a 24-hour battle to keep the road open and move the convoys through. In the spectacle of the Ledo Road to the Northern Burma front, and the people on it, you find its meaning. A road sign says: "This is your lifeline. Treat it right." Other signs are in English and Chinese characters. The military "traffic cops" are either American or Chinese.

On the road you meet Chinese soldiers going to the front, Chinese driving trucks and jeeps, American negroes driving trucks and bulldozers. You meet American engineers planning, directing and measuring; Indian soldiers heaving crowbars; hillmen from the Himalayas cutting the jungle, building camps, and local head-hunting tribesmen passing by indifferently.

You climb over the steep ranges of Northern Burma—above the clouds and into dark valleys. You pass through jungle so thick that sunlight falls only on the pathway cleared for the road, and under the roadside wall of trees, vines, ferns and palms the ground is dark like a cave. This was the home of tigers, leopards, black panthers and elephants until the clatter of bulldozers and the smell of men drove them to quieter haunts.

This was the old opium-smuggling route from China to India, and a rough track, known locally as "Marco Polo Trail," touches the new Ledo Road at many points. Along this track lie bones and skulls of thousands whom starvation and plague killed as they fled from Japanese columns in Burma two years ago.

Today the great impulses "Keep the road open," "Keep it moving forward," and "Send the supplies through," knit into one pattern the jungle, the ranges, the road and the lives of people on it. This means constant combat with the terrain, jungle, rain, mud, landslides, malaria, miteborne typhus, leeches, millions of jungle insects and heat.

And the road can be measured against the sweat and lives of the men working through daylight hours and by oil flares at night to carve a road into new country, widen and make its surface passable, to repair rain and traffic damage. For 14 months since the road first began to move from the Assam Province of North-eastern India into Northern Burma, men have done this. At the same time they kept flowing forward long columns

**WINDING THEIR WAY** along the Ledo Road are these U.S. Army supply trucks, in the rear of engineers who are building the road and troops who are clearing the way of Japanese. American-trained Chinese soldiers are under Lieut. Gen. J. Stilwell, commander of the U.S. Armies in Burma, India and China. See story above, and map in p. 556.

*Photo, Planet News*

WIVES AND MOTHERS OF NATIVE LABOURERS take head-balanced baskets of fruit and other food to their menfolk toiling on the Ledo Road which, under the supervision of U.S. engineers, is being pushed ahead in Northern Burma despite incredible difficulties. American negros, Indian soldiers and hillmen from the Himalayas are helping in the work of constructing this new life-line to China, as the accompanying story relates. See also photograph in the previous page. *Photo, Keystone*

of trucks with food, ammunition, medical supplies, petrol, engineering equipment and spare parts for the colonies of men working on the road.

All the time Chinese troops have operated in front of the jungle cutters and bulldozers at the moving roadhead. Today, reaching more than 100 miles across the frontier ranges, Ledo Road is moving deeper into Northern Burma in Hukwang Valley. It is common knowledge that the supreme aim of the road is connexion with the old Burma Road, supply route to China, when clearance of the Japanese makes it possible.

## I Went to Battle in a Tank in England

Taking part in one of the biggest invasion exercises carried out by an American armoured unit, Philip Grune, Evening Standard reporter with U.S. Forces, gives his impressions of "battle" fought with near-realism over a great area of the English countryside.

GID CARTER, from Tennessee, sat quietly at the controls of an M-4 Sherman tank, his eyes to the periscope, reacting instantaneously to the inter-com orders of his commander. He looked like an automaton as he pulled one lever, then another, as the tank swung to the right or left, accelerated or stopped dead.

As I sat beside him in the second driver's seat, I knew that Gid and his pals in this iron battlewagon—Corporal Marvin Peterson, of Virginia, the gunner, and Private "Pearly" Allen Bailey, of Virginia, assistant gunner and radio operator had been trained as thoroughly as any Flying Fortress crew. For a day I was one of the crew of this Sherman, commanded by Sergeant Lorrain Duco, of Illinois, taking part in one of the biggest invasion exercises carried out by one of America's armoured units. The rolling English countryside had been turned into a great battle area; all day the hills resounded to the roar of big guns, the whine of howitzer and mortar shells, and the shattering clatter of machine-guns.

When I climbed into the small cockpit I was told : "Once you are buttoned down you cannot get out until the exercise is over; it'll be dangerous." And what I saw through the 3-in. periscope convinced me that the officer briefing us was right. The vast area in front of us was as dangerous as no man's land in the real battle zones.

### Patterned with Bursting Shells

The plan was to capture a position which the "enemy" had occupied during the night. It was not known how strongly the position was held, but the reconnaissance unit had reported that the enemy had established themselves in a clump of trees behind a hill some four miles away. Our job was to knock out the position before reinforcements could be brought up. In our tank we waited for orders to "take off," just as bombers wait for the word from the control tower to speed along the runway.

First the 105-mm. howitzers opened the attack. I could hear the whine of the great shells as they passed over our column, and watched the live ammunition burst on the escarpment where the enemy were entrenched. The whole area was patterned with the bursting shells.

This bombardment went on for half an hour; then we got orders to move forward.

GIANT RESCUER OF DISABLED TANKS or other heavy Army vehicles is the American M.25, seen here during manoeuvres in Britain hauling a tank out of a bomb crater, while actual explosions simulate real war conditions. This tank recovery vehicle, completely enclosed in armour, has a crew of 7 highly skilled technicians; it can carry up to 40 tons at a speed of 28 m.p.h. and is armed against attack. It is equipped with comprehensive repair equipment, and can move through water. *Photo, U.S. Official*

**GETTING READY FOR THE SECOND FRONT** are these American Sherman tanks during realistic battle rehearsal in a vast training area in Britain. Just after the photograph was taken the tanks went into a live ammunition fight. The Sherman carries a crew of seven, has a cruising range of 150 miles, and is armed with a 75-mm. gun; later versions have a 90-mm. gun and four machine-guns. See accompanying story.
*Photo, Topical*

With our 75-mm. blazing and machine-guns cracking we took our position with scores of tanks pounding down on the target. I was fascinated by the tracers from our machine-guns as we weaved and turned through the downs in violent evasive action, and forgot to take notice of Sergeant Duco's order to let go the 75.

The recoil nearly broke my neck, but these boys in the tank just went straight ahead and banged away at the ridge, now quickly approaching. The shells from the howitzers and mortars still screamed overhead. Then came our order to stop. The big column, like a battle fleet at sea, lined up in position ready to advance to the next enemy stronghold, as the infantry streamed through, under cover of a smoke screen.

The results of the exercise showed that the tank guns, as well as the big fellows, had got the enemy position. The commanding general said that no quickly established enemy position could have held out against such accurate and heavy shelling. But if the reconnaissance had been inaccurate and the position was strongly held and fortified, we had reserves behind us—another great column of tanks which could have gone in behind us.

Sergeant Duco, who has seen action in Sicily and is now one of the instructors, said that the battle was as realistic as he had seen.

He lost his tank in Sicily—knocked out by a 90-mm. shell—but he got away with a few burns. Now he and the rest of the men in this armoured unit are waiting for the time when they will roll into Europe.

Until then they will be on daily manoeuvres, and beyond the red flag perched behind the thatched farmhouse, denoting "danger zone," the once peaceful country will remain a battle area. Some of the instructors of this armoured unit have been in action against the enemy. The rest are getting their first smell of powder and, with the live shells flying about, learning the hard way how to keep out of trouble when at last they encounter real conflict beyond our shores.

# OUR DIARY OF THE WAR

**FEBRUARY 16, Wednesday** *1,628th day*
**Italy.**—Germans launched heavy attack in northern area of Anzio beach-head. Total British casualties from Sept. 3, 1943-Feb. 12, 1944, announced as 36,626, including 7,635 dead.
**Russian Front.**—Zapolye, S. of Luga, taken by Russians. Helsinki heavily bombed by Red Air Force.
**Burma.**—Japanese troops captured the Ngakyedyauk Pass, and isolated the 7th Indian Division.
**Pacific.**—Truk, great Japanese naval base in the Caroline Islands, attacked by powerful U.S. naval task force.

**FEBRUARY 17, Thursday** *1,629th day*
**Russian Front.**—Liquidation of 8th German Army trapped in Korsun pocket of Dnieper Bend completed.
**Pacific.**—Two-day American assault on Truk (Caroline Islands) ended; 201 Japanese aircraft and 23 ships destroyed by air and naval attack.
**Air.**—Revealed that 9th U.S. Air Force under Maj.-Gen. L. H. Brereton had arrived in Britain.
**Sea.**—Announced that U.S. troopship recently sunk in European waters with loss of 1,000 men.

**FEBRUARY 18, Friday** *1,630th day*
**Russian Front.**—Staraya Russa and Shimsk, German bastions in the Ilmen region, captured by Soviet troops.
**Home Front.**—Germans made biggest attempt since 1940-41 to fire London.

**FEBRUARY 19, Saturday** *1,631st day*
**Italy.**—German counter-offensive on Anzio continued.
**Russian Front.**—Plyussa, 55 m. N.E. of Pskov, taken by Russians.
**Burma.**—Enemy defences W. of the Mayu peninsula raided by British troops.
**Australasia.**—12 merchantmen and three warships sunk in Japanese convoy N.W. of New Ireland, in attack continuous since Feb. 15.
**Air.**—Leipzig (2,300 tons dropped) bombed. Berlin raided by Mosquitoes.

**FEBRUARY 20, Sunday** *1,632nd day*
**Italy.**—Revealed Indian and New Zealand troops fighting in Cassino battle.
**Home Front.**—Many incendiaries and H.E. bombs dropped in London raid.
**Air.**—Leipzig, Brunswick, Gotha, Hal-

berstadt and Bernberg aircraft factories, Gutow and Oschersleben military installations, attacked by 2,000 Allied aircraft. Marauders of 9th U.S.A.A.F. in action for first time since their arrival in Britain.

**FEBRUARY 21, Monday** *1,633rd day*
**Burma.**—Fifth Indian Division cleared Japanese from commanding positions.
**Pacific.**—Japanese bombed U.S. naval task force moving to attack Tinian and Saipan Islands in the Marianas.
**Air.**—Brunswick and Hanover aircraft factories, Bramsche, Lingen, Vechte, Quakenbruck, Diepholz and Ahlhorn airfields, bombed.

**FEBRUARY 22, Tuesday** *1,634th day*
**Russian Front.**—Krivoi Rog captured by troops of the 3rd Ukrainian Front. Morino and Mihailovsky taken.
**Home Front.**—German bombers attacking London met by great anti-aircraft barrage, described as "heaviest yet."
**Pacific.**—Conquest of Eniwetok atoll (Marshall Islands) completed by capture of Parry Island. Task force of U.S. Pacific Fleet attacked Tinian and Saipan Islands.

**FEBRUARY 23, Wednesday** *1,635th day*
**Mediterranean.**—Announced that Marshal Tito's Yugoslav partisans had reached the Skoplje-Nish railway line.
**Home Front.**—London bombed for fourth night in succession.
**Air.**—Steyr aircraft works, 95 m. W. of Vienna, attacked by Liberators.

**FEBRUARY 24, Thursday** *1,636th day*
**Russian Front.**—Dno junction, on route to Pskov, captured by troops of the 2nd Baltic Front. Rogachev taken by troops of the 1st White Russian Front.
**Home Front.**—Many high explosives and fire-bombs dropped on London.
**Burma.**—Ngakyedyauk Pass cleared of the Japanese.
**Australasia.**—Announced that all western New Britain in American hands.
**Air.**—Schweinfurt ball-bearing works and Gotha aircraft assembly plant attacked from Britain, Steyr (Austria) air components factory by Fortresses from Italy.

**FEBRUARY 25, Friday** *1,637th day*
**Russian Front.**—Germans announced evacuation of Vitebsk.
**Air.**—Regensburg, Stuttgart, Augsburg, and Furth aircraft works raided in two-way blow from Italy and Britain. Augsburg (1,700 tons dropped) twice attacked at night.

**FEBRUARY 26, Saturday** *1,638th day*
**Mediterranean.**—Revealed that Capt. Randolph Churchill, the Premier's son, recently landed by parachute in partisan-controlled Yugoslavia.
**Russian Front.**—Russians freed great trunk railway from Leningrad to Nevel on a 300-mile front by capture of Porkhov, 15 m. N. of Pskov.
**Air.**—Estimated German fighter output cut by 60 per cent, bomber output by 25 per cent, as result of last week of bombing.

**FEBRUARY 27, Sunday** *1,639th day*
**Russian Front.**—Bezhakitsy, W. of Kholm, Zabelye and Putoshka, in Novo-Sokolniki region, taken by Red Army.

**FEBRUARY 28, Monday** *1,640th day*
**Italy.**—Announced that two strong-points in Anzio area captured by British troops of 5th Army.
**Russian Front.**—Karamyshevo, Sladkovichi, Pozherevichi, Toroshino, and Veshki, in the Pskov area, liberated.

**FEBRUARY 29, Tuesday** *1,641st day*
**Italy.**—German heavy guns on perimeter of Anzio beach-head opened heaviest bombardment since the first landings.
**Pacific.**—American forces landed on Los Negros Island, in the Admiralty Is.
**Air.**—Brunswick raided for third time in ten days by American bombers. Announced formation of Air Defence of Great Britain, under Air Marshal Sir R. M. Hill, K.C.B., M.C., A.F.C., to replace Fighter Command.
**General.**—Soviet armistice terms to Finland announced. Relations with Germany to be severed and all German forces interned; re-establishment of Soviet-Finnish Treaty of 1940; repatriation of Soviet and Allied prisoners and civilians; demobilization of Finnish Army, reparations, and the future of Petsamo to be discussed in Moscow.

★══════ *Flash-backs* ══════★

### 1940
February 17. *Russians forced Finns to withdraw in the Karelian Isthmus, N. of Leningrad.*
February 22. *Islands in Gulf of Finland occupied by Russians.*

### 1941
February 17. *Imperial troops crossed Juba River (Italian Somaliland) at Tonte, N. of Gobwen.*
February 18. *Large Australian forces arrived at Singapore.*
February 25. *Mogadishu, capital of Italian Somaliland, captured by East and West African troops.*

### 1942
February 16. *Formation of 10th Army in Persia and Iraq announced.*
February 23. *Dorogobuzh, on the Dnieper, 45 m. east of Smolensk, captured by Soviet troops.*

### 1943
February 16. *Kharkov, gateway to the Ukraine, taken by Red Army.*
February 17. *Medenine (Tunisia) occupied by Gen. Montgomery's men of the 8th Army.*
February 22. *Myebon, S. of Akyab on Arakan coastline, raided by Allied troops based on India.*

# THE WAR IN THE AIR

## by Capt. Norman Macmillan, M.C., A.F.C.

THE air war continues to rise to greater intensity in every theatre of war, except perhaps the Russian, where an almost steady volume of air activity appears to be maintained, particularly by the Germans, who withdraw bomber and fighter formations of the hard-pressed Luftwaffe for action on other fronts as their front in Russia contracts with the continued withdrawal of the German armies. The Germans can effect this air withdrawal without unduly reducing the proportion of their armies' air support per hundred miles of front, not only because of contraction of the defensive line but because of the shortening of lines of communication.

Length of communication lines affects air power just as it affects land and sea power. The aircraft are assembled in factories far removed from the fighting front. From these factories they have to be flown to pools, although the markings on some recently captured German aircraft have indicated that many of their machines have been flown direct from factory to first-line airfield, due to shortage of supplies relative to the demands of the fighting forces.

It must be remembered, however, that shortage of aircraft supplies is sometimes a temporary deficiency brought about by changes of production from one type of aircraft to another, or by the introduction of modifications, such as changes in engine or armament or equipment, all of which must occur from time to time to keep pace with technical developments. And it may be that these particular captured aircraft indicate simply the natural desire of the German generals to get the latest types into action without delay, while maintaining a reserve of earlier types in the pool.

This, indeed, was the method adopted by Fighter Command of the R.A.F. during the Battle of Britain, and the reserve aircraft when brought out during the closing stages of that battle were less well armoured than those that fought in the opening stages. Such occurrences are almost inevitable during defensive fighting, when generals are often forced to play their best cards first to take the attack of their more powerful opponents, with the hope that by doing so they will be able to produce a more favourable balance.

MARSHAL STALIN proclaimed in a recent Order of the Day that the Red Armies have driven back the enemy 1,000 miles. That means to the Luftwaffe 1,000 miles shorter journey to transport their bombs, fuel, lubricating oil, spares, and technical stores; and it simultaneously knocks the same distance off the journey which the aircraft ferried from factory or pool to front have to fly. All this means a saving in time and personnel, and a saving in aircraft, too, for it is known that numerous German aircraft crashed during ferry flights to the eastern front and thus were lost before they ever got into action.

It is almost certainly this combination of savings that has made it possible for the Luftwaffe to transfer not inconsiderable forces of bombers to Western Europe. Probably the main object behind this transfer was the urgency to get bomber aircraft into position to meet the threat of invasion. The German generals know now from experience gained by them in Sicily and Italy—at Salerno and Anzio—that the critical moment of any amphibious attack is when the assault forces first come in. Then the assault forces' organization to resist counter-attack is at its lowest, and must so continue until sufficient troops can be got ashore to establish positions, get guns into action, seize enough ground for armoured fighting vehicles and fighter air-

craft to deploy, and land all the paraphernalia of modern war, disperse it and get it into the fighting lines. Quick as the Germans are at moving aircraft from one front to another it is possible that the Nazi generals feel they dare not take the risk of waiting until the invasion assault begins before transferring bombers from the east to the west.

Taking this as the most probable German point of view, it is possible to read into Stalin's declaration that the enemy is still powerful and not yet beaten; consider also the Roosevelt-Churchill warnings that great battles loom ahead, the significance of the German method of retreat and sacrifice of surrounded troops.

### WORLD Has Never Seen a Bigger Defensive Action of its Kind

Germany is fighting a desperate defensive action on land, at sea, and in the air. It is the biggest action of its kind the world has ever seen. And it is being fought with skill and tenacity that display the clever marshalling of forces and the as yet unbroken will to fight of the German soldier. The fact that the present first-line strength of the Luftwaffe is about 1,000 aircraft greater than at the beginning of the war is said to be due to the increased production of fighters compared to bombers. This is reasonable, for the weight of material and the number of man-hours required for fighter production is far below that demanded for bomber production. And as the former ratio of the Luftwaffe was around 65 per cent bombers

BEFORE THE ALLIED BOMBING the Messerschmitt fighter plane plant at Gotha, north Germany, looked like this (top). When U.S.A.A.F. Liberator aircraft left it after their attack on Feb. 25, 1944, it was just another funeral pyre of Nazi hopes (below).
*Photos, U.S. Official*

ROCKET BURSTS IN THE NIGHT SKY over London had devastating effect during recent raids on the capital. Latest British A.A. weapon, the rocket gun, whose shells, or projectiles, rush into the sky with terrific noise, is the result of five years' patient secret research culminating in successful tests in Jamaica, where weather conditions permitted best observation of results. Many Nazi planes have fallen to this rocket gun. *Photo, Keystone*

and 25 per cent fighters (the remainder being marine and army co-operation and other types) there was ample opportunity to switch production priorities from one to the other; but the stress is apparent—fighters for defence. At one time we had to do the same.

While the German bombers in the west await zero hour for invasion they are employed in a renewal of the attack on Britain. London is the chief target. The attacks are made by night, for the Luftwaffe still fears the daylight assault on Britain. They have not yet, at any rate, caught up with the quality of American heavy day bombers that can fight back fighters. These interim-invasion attacks on London are a combination of reprisal, exercise, and employment of waiting forces. As the Russian front continues to shorten—the line Memel-Odessa is about 20 per cent shorter than the line Narva-Odessa—it is probable that more bombers will be released for transfer to the west, and that the attacks against Britain will be increased in weight or frequency.

To some extent these attacks on Britain are a result of the Allied policy of bombing fighter factories to clear the skies of fighters for the invasion. And it is one of the penalties that Britain has to pay for being an advanced base. For almost three years we have maintained an unbroken bomber offensive with scant reply from the Luftwaffe, and we have presumably learned more about offensive bombing than about defence against the night bomber. We have multiplied A.A. guns. But multiplied Nazi guns did not stop our bombers from bombing German targets. We need still more scientific night fighter defence. It will come with the need to provide it.

Meanwhile, in the Pacific a U.S. task force has bombed Truk, Japanese naval base in the Carolines. More bombs have fallen on the most northerly Kurile islands, on uncaptured portions of the Marshalls, and on the Marianas. Rabaul has been practically bombed into impotence; the whole New Britain area is dominated by Allied air power. The British night and American day heavy bombers range at will all over west, central and southern Europe. The air offensive never stops.

# Allied Bombers in Battle on the Italian Fronts

**AIR SUPPORT FOR THE ALLIED BEACH-HEAD** south of Rome is strikingly illustrated by these B.25 Mitchell bombers (top) of the 12th U.S.A.A.F. flying low over the Italian countryside against German positions. Besides throwing their weight into beach-head battles, our airmen strike frequently at transport well to the enemy's rear, and hinder the regrouping of troops ; bombs are leaving an R.A.F. Baltimore (below) on the way down to a target on the Rome-Pescara road. Allied air forces have flown as many as 1,600 sorties in one day. PAGE 669 *Photos, British and U.S. Official*

# Daring Skip-Bombers Surprise Japanese Shipping

PURSUING A NEW AIR ATTACK TECHNIQUE, Allied bombers in the South-West Pacific are taking increasing toll of Japanese merchant vessels and warships. The method is known as "skip-bombing," in which the aircraft comes in on its target at a very low altitude—usually about 50 feet—travelling at high speed and releasing its bombs when close to the objective; the bombs travel forward horizontally for a distance before hitting the water just in front of the vessel, then bound or skip up from the surface of the sea against it. The R.A.F. were the first to employ this ingenious plan, against land targets in Northern France, in 1941. The Americans have adopted it, experimented with it for both land and sea attack, and are now finding it successful against Japanese shipping.

In Diagram 1, attacking planes are approaching their objective low above the water, thus presenting difficult targets for enemy fire (A). In Diagram 2, the bomber pilot (B) is aiming his plane at one of the merchant vessels; it is the pilot, judging the crucial moment, not the bomb-aimer (C), who actually releases the bombs. When the appropriate striking distance has been reached, the bombs

leave the plane, hit the water's surface a glancing blow (D), then pass on into the hull or super-structure of the vessel. By this time the plane (E) has passed over the ship and is clear of the danger area. Delayed action bombs are sometimes used; these give the attacking plane more time to get away from the target before the dropped bombs explode.

Any type of aircraft may skip-bomb. Flying Fortresses have been known to carry out the manoeuvre successfully; but best for the purpose is a medium bomber, such as the Mitchell or Marauder. Bombs used range in weight up to 1,000 lb. Beyond that weight their shape alters considerably and is not adaptable to the skip-bombing technique; 250-lb. and 500-lb bombs are those most used. In misty or cloudy weather, low-level reconnaissance followed by surprise skip-bombing has proved particularly deadly. The main purpose behind this low-level method of attack is that the vessels present a bigger target than they do from a height; it is, in fact, a combination of dive-bombing and aerial torpedo attack.

**T**RYING to follow the course of operations in this war is far more difficult than it was last time. Then, and in most wars of the past, there was a "front," or, rather, two fronts facing one another. If one were dented or broken through, it meant that the whole of it felt the shock, and very likely had to withdraw—as a whole. With a map, the whole of the fighting could be understood pretty clearly. Now there are no well-defined fronts with no man's land between them. Battles go on all over the place. What have come to be known as "hedgehog" defences stand like separate fortresses, with perhaps only the slenderest of communications with the main body. These are really developments on a mighty scale of our blockhouses in South Africa (1899–1902) and the pillboxes of which so much was heard last time (1914–18), which were blockhouses more strongly fortified. The use of hedgehogs is for defence or for keeping certain territory free of enemy incursions. Attacking troops have no time for them. That is why we hear of them only on the Nazi side in Russia. We shall find a lot of them when we invade the Continent, but we have our plans for knocking them out.

**D**ID you ever see Somerset Maugham's play Home and Beauty ? I have never forgotten the roar of laughter which greeted Sir Charles Hawtrey, one of the dressiest of actors, when he entered as a soldier just demobilized in the most comically ill-fitting suit you can imagine. Sir James Grigg, as War Minister, is wisely resolved not to ask men to look like that when they leave the forces. The Austerity Clothing rule for clothing soldiers on demobilization having been relaxed, it will not be practicable to maintain restrictions for the general public. So permanent turn-ups and more pockets than are really needed will be on order again, and men who like to dress as they always have dressed will be contented. But it seems to many women that men have behaved in this matter more like "slaves of fashion" than the sex which is usually labelled in that way. Philip Snowden, when he was Chancellor of the Exchequer, once calculated that, if every Chinese coolie were to add an inch to his shirt or blouse, or whatever his upper garment is called, the cotton industry in Lancashire would be prosperous as never before. So I'm told that the extra cloth needed for turn-ups will require much more shipping space to be allotted to wool, which is not a good thing at all, if it's true ; but I hae ma doots and I seriously question if any shipping space was saved while Austerity ruled in men's clothing.

**I**T is not only Roman Catholic bishops and archbishops who are worried about the increased number of marriages the law is being asked to dissolve. At the present rate of increase the Divorce Court will soon need as many judges as the whole of the several King's Bench Courts put together. The war has something to do with it, a good deal probably. Absence does not always make the heart grow fonder. Sometimes it weakens fondness to such an extent that the heart shrinks from the thought of returning to the absent one, and starts a new adventure. This has happened to many wives and husbands during the past five years. It is all very well for the old lady of 83 who lately celebrated her sixtieth wedding-day to say that all married people would get on famously if they would only practise "give and take." Normally that is true of most marriages. But when one partner is at one end of the world and the wife or husband at the other, that formula has no validity. Letters can do a great deal to keep the tie of affection firm, if they are regular and frequent, and if written with the aim of keeping the absent one in touch with home concerns. A lot of today's divorces are due to wives not taking enough trouble in this respect.

**T**HAT "the whole wage structure" in the coal-mining industry needs overhauling and simplifying, as the Government has suggested to both owners and colliers, is

Lieut.-General W. J. SLIM, C.B.E., D.S.O., M.C., whose appointment as Commander of the 14th Army in South-East Asia was announced on Jan. 24, 1944. Aged 52, his regimental service was with the 6th Gurkha Rifles. Whilst a brigade commander in the 5th Indian Division he was wounded in the Eritrean campaign, in 1941.
*Photo, British Official : Crown Copyright*

undeniable. The way miners' wages are calculated is extraordinarily complicated. When the negotiations were going on years ago which might, if they had succeeded, have averted the nine-days General Strike of 1926 as well as the long-drawn-out misery of mining workers for several months of that year, the leaders of both sides complained in private of Mr. Baldwin's "stupidity" in not being able to follow quickly their discussions and proposals. The truth was that they were talking about terms and calculations which were familiar to them, while he was making acquaintance, for the first time, with the system which had grown up over a very long period and become almost unintelligible to anyone outside the industry. There seemed no reason then, as there is none now, why all the figuring, the adding and subtracting and percentaging, should not be wiped out and a method substituted which would be on all fours with those of other occupations. Perhaps it might even be possible to evolve a general scale of wages for the whole of the pits, not different scales for different localities. If we could get this "reformed altogether," in Hamlet's words, we should have reaped one benefit from war.

**R**UMMY is a capital card game for a number of people. I have played it often when I couldn't get Bridge, which is very much better. And I have always had a theory that Rummy was derived somehow from Poker—at a good many removes no doubt, but in a direct line of descent. Now that notion is strengthened by what came out the other day in a London police-court. The keeper of a gambling house was in the dock and it was stated by the police who raided the place that the game being played at the time of the raid was Double Rummy. Devotees of what seems to them a quiet family game, at which you can lose a few coppers, if you play for money at all, will be astonished to learn that it is in favour at gambling clubs where large sums change hands. The proprietor of the one that attracted the attention of the police was said to be making as much as £5 an hour out of it. Suppose he kept open from eight p.m. till two a.m., his income would be over £10,000 a year, more than we give our Prime Minister. It's a queer world !

**I** WONDER how mothers in Canada have taken the counsel offered them by the head of the Dominion Medical Service. He thinks they bring up boys too softly. They don't, he suggests, train them to face the hard experiences they may have to go through. They make them what are sometimes called "mothers' boys." It seems a curious charge to bring against Canadian parents. From what I have seen of life on prairie farms and in the logging camps of British Columbia, and on board the huge grain barges that ply on the Great Lakes, I should say this eminent doctor's view must be based on a few cases that have happened to come to his notice, not on a carefully conducted survey of the country as a whole. I have also memories of Canadian troops which make me certain that the accusation must lie justly against only a small number of mothers. They would all be in the cities, where, as in the United States, there is a deplorable tendency for mothers to spoil their boys by too much solicitous care, too careful watch on their health and activities, too easy giving-way to their demands. But most Canadians live away from cities and their miasmatic moral influences. So I don't think we need worry.

**I**T is very interesting to notice the difference between the praise Lord Woolton used to get from the Press when he was Food Minister and the critical tone almost all newspapers, including the heavies as well as the lighter skirmishing forces, adopt towards him as Minister for Reconstruction. He is the same man, capable, prudent, cautious. He has much the same problems with which to deal. After all, providing houses is not so very much unlike providing bread, meat and bacon. At any rate, it requires the same qualities of mind and character. How explain the change ? I think I can do it. Food Ministry headquarters are staffed by an exceedingly able set of men, and throughout the country they are assisted by experts. The nominal head, the Minister, has little to do except make speeches and answer questions in Parliament (that is so in most cases). Now Lord Woolton has at present only a nucleus staff. He must solve problems more or less for himself, and rely largely on his own judgement. Naturally he walks warily and wants time to ponder them. The critics should bear that in mind.

# For the Greatest Assault of All Time

Photo, Planet News

**PERFECTING THE HANDLING OF INVASION CRAFT** during arduous rehearsal, here are some of Britain's Royal Marines, who will be among the first to touch down on the enemy's western beaches when dawns the day of the great Allied assault. Many hundreds are completing their training as flotilla officers, coxswains and crews of these landing craft, combining admirably the skill of the sailor with that of the accomplished soldier. See also pp. 176, 628-630, 656-657.

Printed in England and published every alternate Friday by the Proprietors, THE AMALGAMATED PRESS, LTD., The Fleetway House, Farringdon Street, London, E.C.4. Registered for transmission by Canadian Magazine Post. Sole Agents for Australia and New Zealand: Messrs. Gordon & Gotch, Ltd.; and for South Africa: Central News Agency, Ltd.—March 17, 1944. S.S. Editorial Address: JOHN CARPENTER HOUSE, WHITEFRIARS, LONDON, E.C.4.

Vol 7 **The War Illustrated** N° 177

SIXPENCE · *Edited by Sir John Hammerton* MARCH 31, 1944

**LOCATING ENEMY MINES,** this Red Army sapper wriggles along over the snow, pushing his detecting apparatus ahead, seeking shallowly buried explosives left in the wake of retreating Nazis to hinder the Russian advance. Each mine as discovered will be carefully lifted and rendered innocuous. The British method consists in detecting along a "lane" marked through the minefield with tapes; sappers follow, marking each position; then come the men who unearth the mines and remove the detonators. *Photo, U.S.S.R. Official*

**NO. 178 WILL BE PUBLISHED FRIDAY, APRIL 14**

# Our Roving Camera With Britain's Transport

LADEN WITH IRON ORE is this train bound for a foundry in Yorkshire. The ore is converted into steel used in road and rail transport work and in engineering and machine construction; it is essential also for munition and armour plate making.

AN A.A. PATROL finds it hard going in the snowdrifts of Derbyshire during a recent wintry spell in the north of England. Automobile Association patrols are carrying out invaluable war tasks, helping to ensure the smooth running of road traffic.

THIS LONDON 'UTILITY' BUS, among the first of its kind, dispenses with pre-war cushioned comfort. Introduced in July 1943, it has wooden slatted seats which have not been seen in London's buses since 1925. There are 65 of these austerity vehicles in use at the present time.

COAL BARGES (above) proceed along the Regent's Canal in the heart of London—one stretch of the 2,000 miles of our inland waterways along which now travel 1,000,000 tons of cargo a year. Mainly a haunt of pleasure boats and waterfowl in peacetime, canals which had been long neglected in favour of road and rail transport have come into their own again under the stress of wartime needs.

INVASION CRAFT passes along a Manchester street (left) from works which produced it, towards the waters on which it will play its part, along with thousands of others, in gigantic operations to come. There are several types of these vessels, devised for every conceivable sea-borne attack purpose; this one is an L.C.M. (Landing Craft, Materials.) See illus. pp. 656-657.

*Photos, Fox, F. H. Brindley, Daily Mirror, Topical*

# THE BATTLE FRONTS

## by Maj.-Gen. Sir Charles Gwynn, K.C.B., D.S.O.

NATIVE troops and native communities in Africa have played a part in the war which I suggest our American friends should not lose sight of when they indulge in criticisms of the Empire and its relations with the coloured races. Their part necessarily has been small, but we should appreciate the loyalty displayed and the fact that the contribution made was of great strategical value, out of all proportion to the numbers engaged.

For example, let me take the Anglo-Egyptian Sudan, a country which I knew in the early years of its occupation after the liquidation of the Khalifa's regime, and when even the most optimistic never hoped to see it reach its present stage of prosperity, or that its occupation could ever be more than a safeguard of the interests of Egypt, especially her water supply.

When Mussolini conquered Abyssinia the strategic importance of the country increased, obviously, though it was equally obvious that so long as Britain could control the Suez Canal route there was no immediate danger, and that Italy had merely acquired a hostage to fortune. In the first year of the war that fact no doubt partly accounted for Italy's attitude of non-belligerency, and it was not considered necessary to strengthen the military forces in the country, although those forces were astonishingly small. They consisted primarily of the Sudan Defence Force.

NATIVE Sudanese troops commanded by a few British regular officers seconded for limited periods of service, but with educated Sudanese providing the bulk of the officer cadre. To give an idea of the quality of the latter, the first Sudanese to win a British decoration was a young officer of 6 months' service who, in the earlier fighting at Gallabat, was awarded the M.C. for rallying his platoon with lasting effect when it showed signs of wavering in its first encounter with bombs and other modern weapons. The force, only some 4,500 strong, though highly trained, was organized as an irregular army consisting of self-contained units of great mobility—motorized machine-gun groups and mounted infantry companies, as the nature of the districts in which they were normally stationed demanded. Essentially it was an armed constabulary available to support the civil police and to maintain order in outlying areas. In addition, at Khartoum a small number of British and Egyptian units were stationed, partly as a guard to the Headquarters of Government, but mainly as a token of the political status of the country.

## MIDDLE East Position Precarious When France Collapsed

While Italy remained non-belligerent, beyond patrolling 1,200 miles of common frontier, no action was taken and friendly relations were maintained, British officers on occasion dining with Italians and receiving invitations to visit Italian H.Q. at Asmara in Eritrea. But when the collapse of France and the entry of Italy into the war rendered our position in the Middle East precarious the Italian Army of over 250,000 men in Abyssinia became a serious menace to surrounding British possessions, and General Wavell, requiring every man he could muster for the defence of Egypt, was unable to reinforce them. British Somaliland, unless strongly reinforced, was clearly indefensible, especially when the neighbouring French Colony of Jibuti became by the Armistice terms with Italy an Italian advanced base. Its loss in August 1940 had only prestige importance.

Kenya was protected by great stretches of difficult country on both sides of the frontier, and reinforced by South African troops seemed unlikely to be seriously attacked. The Sudan, on the other hand, was specially threatened. Even if a major invasion of Egypt through the Sudan seemed to be prohibited by great distances, yet its loss might gravely affect the attitude of the Egyptian Government, and a comparatively small force might have secured control of the Nile waters by capturing the great Aswan Dam.

Moreover, Eritrea, the headquarters and base of the Italian main forces in Abyssinia, well stocked with material accumulated for the Abyssinian war, gave an easy line of approach to the Sudan at the most vulnerable section of its frontier. A glance at the map shows that Kassala, lying 40 miles from the frontier on the railway from Port Sudan to Kordofan, was the main gateway for in-

**IMPORTANCE OF SUDAN DEFENCE at the time of the Italian threat in July 1940 is shown above; the Anglo-Egyptian Sudan frontier line was within easy reach from Italian Eritrea.**
*Specially drawn for* THE WAR ILLUSTRATED

vasion, and that farther south, Gallabat, on the main route from Gedaref to northern Abyssinia and Addis Ababa, gave a subsidiary point of entry. From Kassala the invader could strike direct at Khartoum, with possibly a column co-operating from Gallabat and Gedaref.

In the dry season the River Atbara would have been no great obstacle, and with motor transport the lack of water between that river and the Blue Nile would have presented no great difficulty. For political and prestige reasons the enemy might have struck direct at the capital, but at the time I thought it more probable his main objective would be Atbara, where the river of that name joins the Nile, and where the railways from Port Sudan and Wadi Halfa meet. The capture of these railways would have meant the isolation of the whole of the Sudan and would have rendered the recapture of the country an exceedingly difficult operation.

Why the Duc d'Aosta did not seize his opportunity but waited till Wavell, having defeated Graziani in Libya, was in a position to reinforce the Sudan and to take the offensive, is inexplicable. He may have had

no heart in an aggressive war, but he was undoubtedly imposed upon by one of the greatest bluffs in military history and which became more potent when news of Wavell's victories in Libya shook Italian morale.

Immediately on their declaration of war the Italians began a series of bombing raids on Kassala, Gedaref and other centres. Their frontier posts, particularly opposite Kassala and Gallabat, were reinforced and there was a concentration at Umm Hagar which threatened an advance on Gedaref. These were indications that an invasion was contemplated, but it was unlikely it would be attempted seriously till after the rainy season, which had already started in Abyssinia and was soon to begin in the Sudan.

## DARING Desert Frontier Raids by Sudan Defence Force

Preliminary attempts to capture Kassala and Gallabat were, however, expected and though, with the weak forces available, determined resistance at either place was out of the question, in face of a strong attack there was no question of lightly abandoning them. On the contrary, adopting the same offensive policy as Wavell pursued in Libya, the S.D.F. began at once to harass the enemy, raiding across the frontier and ambushing his patrols—the motor-machine-gun group at Kassala being especially active and successful. As typical of its work, one day a patrol bumped into an Italian battalion which promptly dispersed into the bush, firing wildly. A few days later another patrol met the same battalion and, closing to 100 yards range, inflicted heavy casualties on it without loss to themselves. On another occasion an Italian cavalry force 1,200 strong was routed by a machine-gun company.

These activities soon established a complete moral ascendancy over the enemy and caused him grossly to over-estimate our strength. On July 4, 1940, however, he advanced and, supported by aircraft, occupied Kassala and Gallabat, our own troops withdrawing according to plan to previously prepared positions without losing contact or abandoning their harassing tactics. At Kassala withdrawal was in any case necessary during the rains. The enemy having occupied these frontier posts settled down into defensive positions.

UNTIL well on in autumn rains caused a lull; in October, when the enemy might be expected to make a serious attempt at invasion, offensive patrolling was resumed with renewed strength and vigour; newly recruited units had slightly increased our strength, and by constantly changing points of attack the enemy was given the impression that strong reinforcements had arrived. After changing hands several times Gallabat was finally recaptured on November 11. The enemy's morale steadily deteriorated and news of Wavell's victory at Sidi Barani, on December 11, did not improve it.

Having removed all immediate danger to Egypt at Sidi Barani, Wavell was able at last to reinforce the Sudan and to put into operation his plans for the liquidation of the menace from Abyssinia. On January 18, 1941, General Platt's campaign into Eritrea and Northern Abyssinia was launched, the Italians withdrawing from Kassala on that date. Sudan Defence Force units co-operated with distinction with the various columns of General Platt's command and with the Emperor's patriot forces. Space does not permit me to record their exploits in the campaign, but an interesting account of them will be found in the Journal of the Royal African Society of July 1942.

To give an example, however, of the tasks they carried out. When an Italian force, 12,000 strong, retired on Debra Marcos, two companies of the newly-formed Frontier Battalion of the S.D.F. totalling 300 men sufficed to pin them to their trenches.

# Unusual Weapons in Action on Italian Fronts

ONCE THE GERMANS FIRED IT, but now U.S. soldiers of the 5th Army in Italy are learning how to use this captured anti-tank gun against its former owners.

LONG TOMS were used by British troops for the first time against Chieti, south of Pescara, on the 8th Army front ; they are American 155-mm. guns firing a 95-lb. shell, and the gunners ramming the big projectile home into the breech (above) are units of a heavy artillery battery. Other batteries in the same regiment still use British artillery.

GERMAN SECRET WEAPON that did not prove effective is this radio controlled miniature tank (centre, right), packed with high explosive and used against our Anzio beach-head positions on Feb. 19, 1944 ; our gunners knocked out 14. Ready to fire on the Nazis at St. Angelo, on the main 5th Army front, are these camouflaged 75-mm. guns (bottom), mounted on half-tracks ; a half-track vehicle is one which, unlike a tank or bren-carrier, has front wheels of normal motor car pattern free from tracks.

*Photos, British and U.S. Official, Topical*

# Westward March of Russia's Battle Lines

**Statute Miles**

| 0 | 50 | 100 | 200 | 300 | 400 |

•••••• Limit of German Advance, Dec. 6th 1941
━ ━ ━ Limit of German Advance, Nov. 18th 1942
━ ∙ ━ Russian Front, March 1943
━━━━ Russian Advance, Mar. 12th 1944

Gomel  *Principal places specially honoured in Marshal Stalin's Orders of the Day are underlined*

——— Railways        ········ Canals

**IN LESS THAN A YEAR,** between March 1943 and March 12, 1944, the Red Army had thrust the Germans out of a vast area of territory (exceeding 500 miles at its greatest breadth), shown by tinted area in the centre of map above. The total advance westwards since Nov. 1942 covers 1,200 miles from the Caucasus. Comparison between these huge gains and the earlier German advances may be made by means of the symbols which outline the limit of the German advance to Dec. 6, 1941, the second limit to Nov. 18, 1942, the Russian front in March 1943, and the advance up to March 12, 1944, the dates chosen being the most critical periods in this front.

In 1942 the Russian offensive proceeded in the Lake Ilmen region until the end of March ; in 1943, on the Central Front, it ended about March 22, followed by a long lull. The present Red Army drive shows no signs of slackening, and the question giving grave concern to the German High

Command is how long it will continue. They know that, except at a few scattered points, their front line has little stability now.

Present indications are that there is little to prevent the Russians from adding to their latest triumphs. These by March 20, 1944, were the crossing of the River Dniester, the border of Bessarabia which was ceded to Russia in 1940, and the capture of the Moldavian town of Soroka. To the north-west, on the First Ukrainian Front, Red Army forces had taken the Polish town of Krzemieniec, 20 miles beyond the pre-war 1939 Polish frontier. On the Second Ukrainian Front the streets of Vinnitsa, strongest Nazi fortress of the line, had been penetrated, and a large part of the railway centre of Kovel, 40 miles north-west of Luck, was also in Russian hands.

*By courtesy of George Philip & Son, Ltd.*

# THE WAR AT SEA

### by Francis E. McMurtrie

ACCORDING to enemy reports, a force composed partly of British Commando troops and partly of Yugoslav partisan formations recently seized the island of Lissa, in the Adriatic. This is by no means the first time this island has suddenly become prominent in wartime, nor is it likely to be the last, a fact due to its strategic situation. Though only about 11 miles long from east to west, and six miles broad from north to south, it lies farther out from the mainland than the other islands fringing the Dalmatian coast, from which Lissa is distant some 40 miles. Its possession gives the Allies a useful little harbour, the port of San

scanty, comprising two ex-Italian battleships, neither of which is in seaworthy condition, and a cruiser which we put out of action as the result of an air attack on Ancona some time ago. Two cruisers which were under construction at Trieste are believed still to be incomplete. There may be a few old destroyers or torpedo boats available, as well as submarines and motor torpedo boats, but the enemy have not so far shown much disposition to be adventurous with these.

In the South-West Pacific the net continues to close round the Japanese forces in New Britain, New Ireland and Bougainville. With the seizure of the main airfield in the

are believed to have still at their disposal about the same number of submarines as at the beginning of 1943. On the other hand, it may well be questioned whether they possess an adequate proportion of experienced submarine captains, most of the more daring and skilful ones having been eliminated. One of the recent casualties is reported to be a son of Grossadmiral Dönitz, the German naval chief.

IN spite of reverses, the Germans continue to build more concrete pens for U-boats in the ports from which they operate. New weapons and equipment have been provided in an endeavour to enable the submarines to overcome the obstacles that have defeated them. Additional anti-aircraft guns mounted in U-boats have not prevented our planes from pressing home their attacks, nor has the invention of the acoustic torpedo added appreciably to the few successes the enemy have been able to score. One of the latest plans seems to have been to co-ordinate attacks on convoys by long-range aircraft with those of enemy submarines; but our escort fighters have proved equal to this fresh threat. For the development of the various measures by which the defeat of the U-boats has been achieved the First Lord paid a well-deserved tribute to the late Admiral of the Fleet Sir Dudley Pound, whose far-sighted planning was the secret of our success.

### SERIOUS Losses of Enemy Shipping

Having regard to the relative shipping resources of the Allies and of the enemy countries, there is no doubt that the latter are now suffering more serious losses than the former. British and Allied submarines (such as the Norwegian Ula and the Polish Sokol and Dzik) are constantly engaged in operations against German coastal convoys, and their efforts are supplemented by air attacks across the North Sea. In the Pacific there must come a time when the Japanese no longer have enough shipping to maintain communications with their forces overseas.

**HITLER BLUNDERED YET AGAIN** when, in April 1943 he decorated a U-boat commander, Lieut. Otto von Bülow, for "sinking" the U.S. aircraft carrier Ranger—seen above with attendant destroyer. Six months later the Ranger took part, with a British task force, in raiding enemy vessels in Norwegian waters. In that period she had sunk 40,000 tons of shipping.
*Photo, New York Times Photos*

Giorgio, on the eastern side of the Adriatic. This is important as an aid to the control of sea communications, as there is no good harbour on the opposite coast of Italy between Bari and Ancona, and the latter port is still in enemy hands.

### ONLY Scanty German Naval Forces in the Adriatic

During the Napoleonic Wars the island, which had long been a dependency of Venice, was occupied first by the French and later by the British. In 1811 a Franco-Venetian force of eight frigates, with two smaller vessels, under Commodore Dubourdieu, sailed from Ancona with the object of recapturing Lissa. Off the island this squadron was brought to action by four British frigates under Captain William Hoste, and decisively defeated, losing half its strength. In 1866, during the war between Italy and Austria, a very similar result attended the efforts of the Italian fleet under Admiral Persano, to take the island. At the Battle of Lissa on July 20, 1866, Persano lost two ironclads and had other ships disabled by the Austrian fleet under Admiral Tegetthoff, which lost no ships.

It is improbable that the Germans will attempt any kind of naval sortie to recapture Lissa. Their forces in the Adriatic are

Admiralty group, immediately to the westward of New Ireland, the United States Navy has combined a daring incursion into the harbour of Rabaul, which seems to have been left to its fate by the Japanese High Command. This port and Kavieng were the headquarters of the Japanese forces in the South-West Pacific island area, but now that communications with Japan by sea and air are practically at an end the fate of both bases is scarcely in doubt. United States Marines continue to advance along the coast from the western end of New Britain, and fresh landings may be expected to bring the threat to Rabaul closer.

WHEN introducing the Navy Estimates the First Lord of the Admiralty threw fresh light on the progress of the Battle of the Atlantic. It was already known that the tide turned dramatically against the U-boats at the opening of spring last year, though for some time heavy attacks continued to be made. Sometimes as many as 30 enemy submarines would be involved in an attack on a convoy, but increased escort forces, operating in close conjunction with aircraft from carriers or from shore bases, inflicted defeats so severe that the U-boats "virtually abandoned the North Atlantic for some months." In spite of their heavy losses, the Germans

IT was disclosed that the maintenance of the Nettuno beach-head had cost our Navy, up to the first week in March, losses which included the cruisers Spartan and Penelope, the destroyers Inglefield and Janus, and five landing craft described by Mr. Alexander as " major assault vessels." Previously the existence of H.M.S. Spartan had not been revealed, though an official photograph of a naval bombardment off Nettuno had shown in the foreground a cruiser, otherwise unidentified, which appeared to be of an improved Dido type (see illus. p. 614). It seems reasonable to conclude that the Spartan was not the only new cruiser of this design; and in due course we may expect to hear some official mention of the doings of her sister ships. Altogether our cruiser losses have amounted to 28 ships since the war began.

Mr. Angus Macdonald, Canadian Minister of National Defence for the Naval Service, has announced that the Dominion will shortly acquire two modern cruisers from the Admiralty, besides manning a couple of aircraft carriers. Other additions in 1944 will be 100 smaller fighting ships and a considerable number of auxiliary vessels. This calls attention to the phenomenal expansion which the Royal Canadian Navy has undergone. In 1939 its personnel comprised less than 4,500, including all reserves. Today it exceeds 70,000, and by the end of the year it is expected to have reached 90,000.

# Fleet Air Arm Base on the Rock of Gibraltar

H.M.S. CORMORANT II, one of the non-seagoing homes of aircraft of the Fleet, is the Royal Naval Air Station on the racecourse of the famous towering Rock. Planes from such redoubtable carriers as H.M.S. Illustrious, Indomitable and Formidable have also operated from here; others, patrolling the Straits by day and by night, have sent to the sea-bed many a Nazi submarine. Aided by a mobile crane, Service mechanics are seen putting an overhauled engine into a Beaufighter.

*Photo, British Official: Crown Copyright*

# Fishermen of Britain Fight to Bring Us Food

Enemy planes may swoop and gun them as they trawl. Mine and shell, torpedo and bomb : the hardy sons of Britain who battle for our fish must face these too, even as they combat fierce storms. A great and heroic role they are acting today, these coastal fearnoughts, as described here by JOHN ALLEN GRAYDON. See also facing page.

ON the eve of our declaration of war on Germany, in September 1939, nearly seventy per cent of our fishing fleet was called for service with the Royal Navy. As members of the Royal Naval Reserve, they expected this call to arms. After all, who knew the coastal waters around the British Isles better than they ? Who better fitted for the dangerous task of fishing for mines ? As these fishermen prepared to fight the enemy, the thoughts of others turned to the immediate future of the fishing industry. They realized that fish would now become a more essential food than ever before, but who was to take these vacant places in the hunt for fish ?

Ancient mariners and young boys, aboard trawlers that in some cases had long been laid aside as out-of-date, took up the challenge of the sea—and in so doing faced mine, shell, bullet, bomb and torpedo. But it takes more even than that to prevent mariners of Britain from putting to sea. So, despite all obstacles, the fishing fleets have brought in good supplies throughout the war, although many of their best hunting grounds are today barred, for obvious reasons.

IN my travels around the country I have had opportunities of talking with these grand men of the sea. Always do they praise their colleagues. Never once have I heard a fisherman seek praise for his own work. In Aberdeen, Grimsby, Fleetwood and Yarmouth, in Ramsgate, Deal and Dover, I have listened with interest to stories of great bravery and devotion to duty. Yet, outside the immediate circle of fishermen, few people realize to what lengths our fishing fleet goes to assure Britain's supply of fish.

These tough-as-nails fishermen, many of whom also make up the crews of our lifeboats, have produced more than one man who has been honoured. One of the most recent is seventy-year-old Skipper J. C. Locke, of the trawler Mizpah, who comes from Rye. During the First Great War he served with distinction in the Dover Patrol, and when we again went to war he offered his services to the Royal Navy once more. They told him he was too old—so back went the skipper to his fishing grounds in the English Channel.

On many occasions he has fished whilst dog-fights were taking place overhead. He must have seen as many aerial battles as any other man during the Battle of Britain. Several times German machines swooped and gunned him as he trawled, but always did they miss. Within sight of the enemy's guns, never knowing when some arm of the German war machine might attempt to end his career, Skipper Locke went about his work. Then one afternoon two German fighters, keeping clear of the R.A.F. and seeking an easy victim, turned their cannon guns upon the little Mizpah.

From mast-height they riddled the trawler. Two of Locke's men were killed by his side. He himself was wounded and lost consciousness. On recovering he observed that an incendiary bullet had pierced the boat's petrol tank and that part of the deck was on fire. Despite very painful injuries Skipper Locke successfully fought the flames and washed the burning petrol overboard. His jacket caught fire, and his left arm was severely burnt. But he again smothered the flames—and for the second time lost consciousness. Another trawler, sensing trouble aboard Locke's command, hurried to the rescue, pulled him aboard, and beached the Mizpah. Today, recovered from his injuries, Skipper Locke is once more on fishing duty.

IN the waters of the North Sea more than one Nazi, in plane or E-boat, has cause to remember the gallantry and determination of the men who go down to the sea for fish. On one occasion, when E-boats were very active off the East Coast, a trawler, setting course for the fishing grounds, found herself surrounded by four of these enemy torpedo boats. One opened fire.

The answer the enemy received, in hot lead, from the trawler, caused great confusion. One E-boat was seen to near-capsize, some men were thrown into the water, and the other craft, sensing a trap, opened fire. In the darkness, however, their fire was directed at each other ! Eventually, much to the joy of the fishermen, who were completely outgunned, the German forces fled towards the Dutch coast. To this day they probably think it was a special anti-E-boat patrol that had attempted to trap them.

Youth has played a distinguished part in this never-ceasing " Fight for Fish "—for fight it is, with the weather as the enemy's ally doing everything possible to halt the successful progress of the fishing fleet. In Grimsby I heard several people praise eighteen-year-old trimmer Cyril Rawlings, who has served aboard the trawler Chandos. The men who praised him are known for their usual lack of enthusiasm over anything —but Rawlings' pluck impressed them.

WHEN the Chandos was putting out to her fishing grounds in the North Sea, snow piling against the windows of the wheelhouse, a German plane dived from out of the grey sky and riddled the wheelhouse. The skipper was killed instantly. In his cabin the mate, wounded in the last war, stumped on the deck and, entering the wheelhouse, saw a sight that he will never forget.

Trimmer Rawlings, the boy, was showing the greatness of a fighting man. Blood was pouring down his trousers into his sea-boots ; but at the gun he was keeping up a terrific fire at the plane circling above. Twice the German dived at the trawler, guns blazing. But Rawlings, as cool as if he were at practice, returned the enemy fire. And when it had made its third dive, the boy pumped lead into the German machine's tail. Smoke suddenly streaked out, and the enemy pilot turned for home.

Then, his job completed and the Chandos safe, Rawlings collapsed. During this battle he had lost several pints of blood, but never had he taken his finger from the trigger. A little later, when the nets were hauled aboard, pieces of a German plane were found among the catch of cod. Had the youthful trimmer shot down the Nazi machine ? It is quite possible, but the fishermen made no claims. It is not their habit. They do the work and let others do the shouting. Their official records will add to the tales of the sea when the last All Clear has sounded.

**DANGERS ARE HEAVY** and the catch is sometimes considerably lighter than the North Atlantic haul seen here ; but the fishing trawlers carry on with their task of adding to our food supplies, braving man-made perils of the wartime seas and of the air, as told in this page.
*Photo, Keystone*

# This Trawler Helped to Send a U-Boat to its Doom

FISH was the quarry of H.M. trawler Imperialist before the war; now she hunts U-boats. Since early 1940, when she discarded fishing nets for guns and depth charges, the Imperialist has gained for herself a long record of achievements; she is credited with having shot down a German Condor aircraft which attempted to attack an Atlantic convoy, and with assisting at the capture of an enemy blockade runner. Her latest exploit, announced on Feb. 20, 1944, was a great part played in destroying a U-boat in the Straits of Gibraltar.

Describing this successful attack, the Commanding Officer of the Imperialist, Lieut.-Cmdr. B. H. Craig Rodgers, R.N.V.R., said : "The first salvo from our 4-in. gun crippled the enemy's forward gun. The Imperialist's smaller armament must have scored nearly a hundred hits. The U-boat submerged or sank, so we proceeded over the position and dropped some more depth charges—about four tons in all."

Built in 1939, and in peacetime sailing from Hull, she began her fighting career in the early days of the Norwegian campaign.

BEAM VIEW of H.M. trawler Imperialist (1), and at action stations (2) on one of her Bofors guns. Two seamen pass the clips, each containing four shells, to the loader who places them in the magazine. The Bofors fires 120 shells per minute ; there are two types, a light 14-mm. firing a 2-lb shell, and a 3-in. firing a 16-lb shell.

SMILING CREW of the Imperialist (3). The Commanding Officer, Lieut.-Cmdr. B. H. Craig Rodgers, is sixth from the left in the second row. The ship and her crew have been adopted by Osset Grammar School, Yorkshire, and also by the Rotary Club, Chelmsford, Essex. Armed trawlers such as the Imperialist have added greatly to Britain's naval strength. Early in the war they proved their versatility, engaging in the transport of stores, in minesweeping and convoy work. They are comparatively slow, but have great sea-range.

*Photos, British Official*

# Our Colonies in the War: No. 4—Ascension

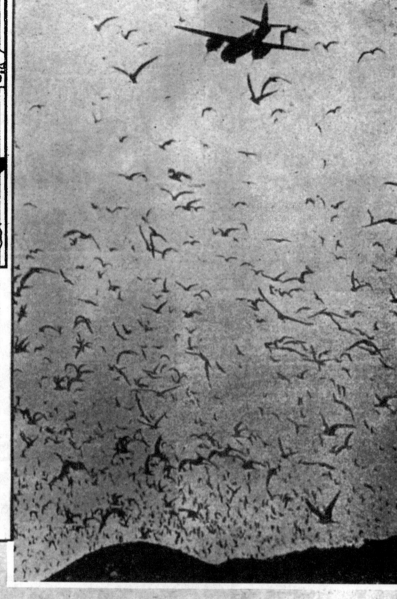

THIRTY-FOUR SQUARE MILES Ascension Island occupies an important place in the war effort of the British Empire. Discovered by a Portuguese, Joao da Nova, in 1501, on Ascension Day, it remained uninhabited until after the arrival of Napoleon as a prisoner on St. Helena, when it was garrisoned by the British Government and administered by the Admiralty, who named the island H.M.S. Ascension. In 1922 it became part of the dependency of the colony of St. Helena and passed into the jurisdiction of the Colonial Office.

Most vital role played by Ascension Island is as a wireless station relaying messages from all parts of the world. The company of Cable and Wireless Ltd. are in charge of this important work ; they control a 300,000-mile chain of telegraph routes. Except for a handful of native guano workers, the cables staff, their families and servants, are the only inhabitants : they have transformed this island of 39 craters, dominated by the 2,500-ft. Green Mountain, into a habitable link in the chain of the Empire. Position of Ascension is shown in the map above ; 2,000 miles from W. Africa, it is equi-distant between W. Africa and S. America and is 3,350 miles by air from the nearest West Indian port.

It has also become a ferry-point for Allied planes ; a U.S. aircraft (right) comes in to land through a cloud of sooty terns or Wideawake birds. Below, U.S. Army tents in an area where engineers have hacked out of the mountainous terrain runways for the planes passing through the island.

*Photos, New York Times Photos, Keystone*

# 14th Army Jungle-Fighters Wipe Out Japanese

Photos, British Official; Keystone, Planet News

IN THE BURMA WILDS British and Indian troops recently won their first big victory over the Japanese in Arakan. A strong force encircled the 7th Division of our 14th Army; supplies were flown to our men in R.A.F. and U.S. planes. Finally the Japanese, depleted in numbers, were themselves surrounded by 14th Army reinforcements and liquidated.

Three of our jungle warriors (1) rest in the undergrowth: they are (left to right), L./Cpl. W. Foskett, of a Midland regiment, who comes from Wellingborough; Major J. C. Lamb, Royal Artillery, of Chelsea; and Lieut. H. A. Vansen, Gurkha Rifles, of Teddington. On the North Burma front Chinese soldiers carry a wounded comrade (2), while others bring in blindfolded Japanese prisoners (3). A Kachin tribesman scout, one of many fighting for the Allies, takes up a sniping position in a tree (4). Adm. Lord Louis Mountbatten, G.C.V.O., D.S.O., Supreme Allied Commander in S.E. Asia, inspects Indian troops near the Arakan frontier (5). See map in p. 556.

# Gladly Would the Finns Get Out of the War

Great was the interest with which the war between Finland and Soviet Russia in the winter of
1939–40 was followed. Once again Finland is in the forefront of the world's news : not now
regarded, however, as a gallant little people defying a Goliath, but as the unhappy victim of her
own shortsighted and misguided politicians, as indicated here by E. ROYSTON PIKE.

WHEN in the winter of 1939 Finland was attacked by Soviet Russia, the sympathies of the democratic world were engaged on the side of a little nation represented as struggling to maintain its freedom against a totalitarian monster.

For a few weeks it seemed as if the impossible were about to become the accomplished. The Finns fought well, and the Red Army staggered and stumbled in the snows. In this country and in America those who still retained their anti-Bolshevik prejudices and fears openly rejoiced over the discomfiture of a country, a system of government and society, whose fall they had so long hoped for and (but with diminishing confidence) prophesied. There was even talk of sending an expeditionary force of British and French to aid the Finns.

Looking back on that time, so near if we count our days by the leaves of a calendar, so infinitely remote if we think of the immense changes that four years have brought, such talk seems just midsummer madness, although it is only fair to remember that at that time and for nearly eighteen months longer the Soviet was the partner if not the actual ally of our German foe. Fortunately for us, there was so swift a change in the Finnish war that we were not militarily involved. The Russians brought up their steam-hammer to crack the obstinately hard nut.

The nut was cracked, even crushed. Across the Mannerheim Line the Red Army poured in overwhelming strength. The Finnish towns, of wooden construction for the most part, were blistered and burnt by the Soviet bombers. The Finns threw in the towel and accepted the terms—in the world's opinion not unduly harsh—imposed by the victors. In March 1940 the peace treaty was signed in Moscow.

## A Most Fateful June Morning

But the Finns, watching the developing struggle between Germany and the Allies, hoped and worked for a *revanche*. Germany had given them no aid in their struggle, whereas Britain and France had supplied military stores and equipment and offered troops. Yet it was to Germany that the supposedly ultra-democratic Finns now tended to turn, as it became more and more apparent that Hitler was bent on taking the Moscow road. On a June morning in 1941, surely one of the most fateful mornings in the history of the world, the German armies crossed the frontier into Russia ; and Hitler's proclamation to the German people, read over the wireless by Dr. Goebbels, boasted that "the champions of Finnish liberty, commanded by their Marshal [Mannerheim], are protecting Finnish territory," and that the shore of the Arctic Ocean was manned by the German victors of Narvik and "their Finnish comrades."

THREE days later President Ryti said the Russians had made an attack on Finland (but this was denied in Moscow), and that the new war was therefore one of defence. On June 27 Field Marshal Mannerheim issued an Order of the Day to his Army in which he proclaimed a "holy war" against Russia on the side of Germany. He followed this up with another proclamation, on July 11, in which he said that a "great Finland" was their objective, and the "liberation" of the Karelian people on both sides of the isthmus.

Not long afterwards Vaino Tanner, one of the strongest of Finland's politicians and a confirmed anti-Russian, asserted that Finland

had no desire to do more than recover the territories lost in the 1939–40 war ; but though these were soon overrun by the German-Finn armies, there was no peace for Finland. Whether they wanted to or not, the Finns were irremovably fastened to Hitler's chariot wheels. Finn troops helped Dietl and his seven or eight German-Austrian divisions in their attack on Murmansk, and Finns were involved in that threat to Leningrad which came so dangerously near to success. If the attack had been launched from behind the old Finnish frontier Leningrad would almost certainly have fallen. These things are remembered by the Russians. We should remember them too.

Since then not far short of three years have slipped away. In the spring of 1944 the

**WHILE FINLAND HESITATES** the Red Army closes in on Pskov (south of Narva at foot of map), capture of which would cut off Finland from Germany and jeopardize Dietl's troops in the north.
*Specially drawn for THE WAR ILLUSTRATED*

Finns were still at Germany's side, the declared foes not only of Russia but of Britain (while the U.S.A. gave them a last warning to "get out of the war" or add America to the list of their enemies). Gladly, ever so gladly, the Finns would have "got out." But *could* they ? To Stockholm in February went old Paasikivi, former Finnish prime minister and (so it was reported) persona grata with Moscow (he conducted the negotiations which ended the war in 1940). In the Swedish capital he made contact with Mme. Kollontay, the Soviet Union's ambassador to Sweden. The old lady—as chic and charming as in the days, so long ago, when she, the daughter of a Russian Tsarist general, became a revolutionary and startled the Bolshevik world with the elegance of her wardrobe and the number and variety of her amours—acted as go-between ; and on Feb. 29 Moscow broadcast the terms handed by Mme. Kollontay to M. Paasikivi on Feb. 16 as the basis for an armistice.

They required the rupture of Finnish relations with Germany and the internment

of German troops and warships in Finland, with the understanding that if this were considered by Finland to be beyond her power, then the Soviet Union would be ready to offer her the necessary assistance with its troops and air force ; the re-establishment of the Soviet-Finnish treaty of 1940 and the withdrawal of the Finnish troops to the 1940 frontier ; and the immediate repatriation of Soviet and Allied prisoners of war and civilians in the Finnish labour-camps. The partial or complete demobilization of the Finnish army, reparations for damage done to the Soviet Union, and the future of the Petsamo area were questions reserved for future negotiation in Moscow.

PAASIKIVI was told that if the Finnish Government were ready to accept these immediately, the delegates might proceed to Moscow forthwith. " The rumours spread by some organs of the foreign press," concluded the Russian statement, " to the effect that the Soviet Government had demanded Finland's unconditional surrender and her consent to the occupation by Soviet troops of Helsinki and other large Finnish towns, are without foundation."

But the Finns professed to find some of the terms harsh and impossible of fulfilment. They were reported to have objected to the restoration of the frontier imposed following their defeat in the 1939-40 war. They resented the compulsory lease of the naval base at Hango to the Russians, and (so it was said) they jibbed at requests that the Russians should be permitted to transport their troops through Finnish territory to Hango and over the Salla-Kemi railway to the Gulf of Bothnia.

But the main obstacle was (it may well be believed) the Nazi divisions in the north, on the Murmansk front. At this time Dietl's army held a line of some 250 miles from Salla to Petsamo on the Arctic, the northern groups being based on Parkkina and the southern relying for their supplies on the Bothnian ports of Oulu and Tornio. From Tornio to Petsamo a fine new 800-mile-long highway had been constructed, and along this vital artery had been brought large masses of equipment which the Germans were naturally loth to abandon. In March the Bothnian ports were still frozen, and movement along the Arctic shore would be a hazardous undertaking, exposed as it would be to British attacks from sea and air, not to mention the bombers of the Red Air Force.

THE problem as Dietl saw it was no easy one, then. He had perhaps 100,000 men under arms—though their fighting quality was problematical after so many months, years even, in the depressing regions of the Arctic twilight. In addition there were 100,000 workers of the Todt labour organizations in northern Finland and Norway.

None of the alternatives could have seemed very attractive. He could retreat into Norway, or down the length of Finland to the Baltic, where his legions might be ferried over to Germany. He might retire on the Bothnian ports—but not until the thaws of spring cleared the channel of ice. He might submit to internment by the Finns, or the Finns and Russians combined. But that, screamed the Nazi press, was unthinkable.

In this he was aided and abetted by the Finns. They played for time. To and from Stockholm their emissaries passed, while the real facts of the military situation were blanketed by the Finn censorship. And all the time the Germans strove desperately to induce their ally to remain in the war.

# Uneasy Finland Ponders while Time Runs Short

CESSATION OF HOSTILITIES and Finland's withdrawal from the war are dependent on acceptance of Russia's terms, awaited by Juho Paasikivi (4), as peace negotiator in Stockholm in February 1944 ; these were handed to him by Soviet Ambassador Mme. Alexandra Kollontay (3). E. Linkomies, Finnish Premier (5). Pro-British feeling is suggested by this soldier (2) selecting a book from a big display of English works. After Red Air Force bombers had raided Helsinki (1), on Feb. 6, the streets looked like this. PAGE 685 *Photos, New York Times Photos, Associated Press, Black Star*

# What Exactly is Happening in Rumania Now?

Since July 1, 1940, when she renounced the Anglo-French pledge of assistance in the event of aggression, Rumania has adhered to the enemy cause. How bitterly she is repenting of that link-up is shown by HENRY BAERLEIN, who also comments upon reports of alarm issuing from the country as the Nazi grip tightens and sheer disaster threatens in the East.

WHEN the German flood swept over Rumania we had to wait a considerable time before we had any real knowledge of what was happening there. Even now the Allied bombing of the Ploesti oil refineries constitutes the sum total of what most of us know, for the German censorship has been rigorous, and to slip a message through has required a good deal of ingenuity. But now a number of interesting reports have been conveyed to this country. Some of them are sensational, but not on that account less worthy of belief ; those of which I make use here have come from the most reputable sources.

For many months bewilderment and apathy prevailed in Bucharest. A war was being waged, with numerous deaths ; thousands were being sent back, seriously wounded, from the front. But these were nearly always peasants, provincial schoolmasters and so forth. Very, very seldom did the elegant society of the capital have to deplore the loss of one of its members. Those who went came back, as a rule, in a week or two covered with decorations ; and when the War Office decided that there would be no exemptions for men over twenty years of age there resulted quite a panic, with nearly all the well-to-do families trying to have their sons appointed as instructors in depots, or, at any rate, have them entered as cadets in a military academy.

THERE was hardly any panic in Bucharest on the day when American airmen bombarded Ploesti, some thirty miles away, for this coincided with the return of white bread to the capital, and that was a source of undiluted joy. But when the Russian armies continued to advance and it became evident that the Germans were not retiring, as they had proclaimed, of their own free will, there arose the keenest anxiety to quit. Some four thousand requests for visas were made at the Swiss Legation, where a deaf ear was turned to most of them. A like number applied to the more accommodating Turks. Indignation was expressed at the departure for Istanbul of certain princesses and professors, while these were envied.

How, demanded the distracted people of Bucharest, would it be possible to free themselves from the German clutch ? It was notorious that more than one Rumanian general had been liquidated by this stern ally for having protested against the futile march into lands which never would belong to Rumania. The Germans who had originally come to Bucharest as "military instructors" were now planted on both flanks of Rumanian regiments in the east. Could not the Opposition leaders, Maniu, the revered old Transylvanian, or the Liberal Bratiano, do anything in this lamentable situation ?

Michael Antonescu, the Marshal's nephew and perhaps the most influential person under present conditions, was endeavouring to detach Rumania from the losing side. When compelled by the Germans to recall Lahovary, the Minister at Berne, whom he had instructed to act in this sense, he was able to replace him very adequately ; for Vespasian Pella, professor of law, remained a disciple of Titulescu, whose wise policy had included an understanding with Russia. Moreover, the new envoys to Copenhagen and Ankara were men who leaned more towards the Western Powers than to Germany.

THE Russians also were equally wise, for Rumanian soldiers who came back on leave or as cripples related what they had seen in the industrial regions they had invaded ; and what they had not seen with their own eyes had been explained to them—comfortable apartments, gratuitous heating and cinema performances, excellent clothing and nourishment provided, kindergartens, and so on. All this and more compared most favourably with conditions in Rumania. The Russians were, indeed, less to be dreaded than the Germans.

But the Germans cannot yet be spurned with impunity, as was discovered by Tudor Arghezi, the best of contemporary Rumanian poets and a talented journalist. In the newspaper Informatia on October 1, 1943, he published an article entitled "Baron" which was obviously aimed at Baron von Killinger, the German Minister. As an exercise in humorous invective it would have gratified Rabelais ; so that Killinger, white with rage, rushed to see Michael Antonescu, and Arghezi had perforce to leave for a concentration camp.

But Antonescu refused to celebrate the Tripartite Pact in the fashion laid down by Ribbentrop. Not a word did he utter of the peril of Bolshevism or of the "imminent victory of the Axis." Rumania, he said, had turned to the one country which, in the actual circumstances, could stand in the way of a Russian expansion. He added, also, that Gafencu, the Rumanian Minister in Moscow, had been instructed to explain to the

**MICHAEL ANTONESCU,** Rumanian Deputy Prime Minister since Jan. 27,1941,and Minister for Foreign Affairs and Propaganda. The photograph was taken at a reception in the Kaiserhof Hotel, Berlin. *Photo, Associated Press*

Kremlin that adhesion to the Germans did not imply hostility to the Soviet, with whom they were always ready to normalize their relations.

Here let me insert that, according to the latest information, it has been decided by the Rumanian authorities to defend the Dniester which separates Bessarabia from Russia. This is mainly due to lack of a political solution after the Moscow and Teheran conferences ; it is to be deplored, because it means strengthening the Germans and exposing the nation to ruin. How much better it would be if negotiations with the Kremlin could be opened up, knowing as one does that Russia will certainly not keep her hands off Bessarabia. From that province with its variegated population, and from Bukovina, where are many Ukrainians, there has suddenly grown an intense desire on the part of the Rumanian civilians to fly to Bucharest ; but they are being told that their journey is not really necessary.

A certain Allied personage, for the time being a refugee in Rumania, has been suggesting that the young King, now staying at a hunting-box near Arad in the far west of the country, should seek refuge with the Allies, and with their help and a Rumanian Legion assembled abroad endeavour to liberate his country from the Germans to whom he has always been opposed. But such a step would be premature and would cause the Nazis to take more drastic measures. Himmler is said to have visited Rumania.

ONE can understand the bitterness of Rumanians who realize that their losses in Russia have been much greater than those of Hitler's other satellite, Hungary, for there is a reckoning in prospect with that country on the subject of Transylvania. By the Vienna Award the entire north and east of this fair province were allotted to Hungary, mainly owing to the insistence of her patron Italy. By the way, it is known that after Mussolini's rescue by the Germans he telephoned to Bova Skopa, Italian Minister at Bucharest, saying that he counted on him.

Skopa replied that his oath had been to the King, and so Mussolini appointed in his place the very Germanophil Trandafilo, for many years Stefani's agent and cordially detested by the Rumanians for his arrogant behaviour. The Marshal has been obliged, by German orders, to recognize him ; but Bova Skopa and his staff come and go as they like.

The Italian troops who happened to be in Rumania have been disarmed and left at liberty ; some in Moldavia have sought refuge with the Jews. If the Rumanian people could seek refuge in the Allied camp they would do so today.

Significant of this desire was the announcement on March 14, 1944, that Prince Barbu Stirbey, 70-year-old statesman in close touch with Rumania's political leaders, was on his way to Cairo to contact British, American and Russian representatives. That Antonescu knew of this intention and permitted him to go, suggests that it had at least nominal Government approval.

**80 MILES TO GO**—and then Rumania. By March 17, 1944, the Red Army was reported within 12 miles of Nikolayev, Black Sea port 160 miles from the Rumanian border, while other forces advancing from the north-east had cut the Warsaw-Odessa railway only 80 miles distant. Map shows Bessarabia and Moldavia, final bulwarks against the Red Army march. *Specially drawn for* THE WAR ILLUSTRATED

## Life-Savers in Action in Italy

Front-line R.A.M.C. personnel are saving hundreds of lives by giving our wounded blood transfusions (1), fortifying the patient against the shock of the journey to the Casualty Clearing Station, to which he may be transported by Duck (2) if a river crossing is involved. From the C.C.S. he travels to an airfield, and is placed aboard an ambulance plane (3) for passage to hospital (4), whence, if necessary, he is flown to N. Africa, particulars of his case being recorded on the way (5).

## 5th Army Scenes of Triumph

In Nettuno town, taken in the Allied beach-landing south of Rome on January 22, 1944, a British infantryman on patrol pauses to wonder at the peace which has descended on this old castle (top left). In a fierce night battle commencing on February 7 a handful of Grenadier Guardsmen—clerks, batmen, cooks and supply column drivers—held our positions on the Buono Riposo (Sweet Repose) ridge in the Anzio beach-head against an all-out attack. After 18 hours of fierce fighting the enemy's objective of isolating this sector was frustrated; Guardsmen are seen (right) preparing to leave their rocky bivouac and move forward. On the 5th Army's main front, a gun manned by French artillerymen (above) fires at German concentrations beyond the hills at Acquafondata.

*Photos, British and U.S. Official*

# *The Human Story Behind the Lines*

*Photos, British and New Zealand Official*

Regimental bootmender Lance-Sgt. Harding, with a captured German police dog on his knees (1), obviously has no complaints in respect of his job in an Anzio beach-head sector ; whilst front-line barber Pte. Sneath ministers to the requirements of a field communications unit (2). Strange location this (4) for a sewing-machine ; tents are being repaired for New Zealanders on the 8th Army Front. Direction boards (3) bring a touch of home to the 5th Army's main front north of the Garigliano.

# VIEWS & REVIEWS Of Vital War Books

### by Hamilton Fyfe

Long ago—it was during the South African War—the first impression I got of the Army Nurses was that they had an ugly uniform which made them look unattractive, hard-faced and unsympathetic. That silly notion soon went. I found out how wrong I had been in my hasty judgement. I still think the uniform was ugly; it is much better now. But I know that underneath it were the kindest of hearts, the stoutest of courage, the most self-sacrificing devotion to duty. I saw these qualities again during the First Great War. Now I have been reading a book which shows me they are equally conspicuous in this.

The book is called Grey and Scarlet (Hodder and Stoughton, 6s.); it contains letters written from and diaries kept in various parts of the world where Army nurses in their grey and scarlet have served. Miss Ada Harrison has edited them and made a very wise choice among the mass of material she must have had to go through. No more vivid or informative picture of the life of these " ministering angels " could be drawn, and, though they draw it themselves, there is not a word in the whole book which suggests they are doing anything out of the common, anything for which they deserve to be called heroines. Yet to my mind these are heroic stories, if the word has any meaning at all.

Take the account which is given of the trips made by one of the diarists between Dover and Dunkirk, taking off men wounded during the evacuation. You might call it monotonous, this record of "Sailed for Dunkirk . . . Sailed for Dover . . . Sailed again for Dunkirk," and so on for a whole week, going or returning the whole time. Not a word about the weariness of it, scarcely a word about the incessant dangers. They were so fully occupied with looking after their patients that "literally one did not realize the aerial battle that was going on all the time." The same note is sounded in a diary of a nurse on an ambulance train in France during the 1940 disasters. While they were loading stretcher cases, "patients straight from the casualty clearing stations," there was "a tremendous bombardment overhead, but we were too busy to take a great deal of notice."

Just like that! "Oh, do go away! Can't you see we've got a job of work to do? No time for you!" What a contrast between the way the nurses made the best of everything and uttered no complaint, and the peevish, utterly selfish and stupid grumbling of the passengers on one of the ships that brought to Britain refugees from the south of France, where they had been living as tax-dodgers very likely. "They made me sick!" one of the contributors to the book admits frankly. "Though they were being taken home safely at no expense to themselves, they did nothing but grumble, each trying to seize the best place for him or herself." The staff "seemed to be run off their legs trying to deal with their woes and complaints. They seemed to think the nurses were 'universal aunts' with free stocks of everything on board for their benefit. As we had only our own very limited supplies of clothes, soap, etc., it was impossible to provide everyone with washing materials, towels, night-clothes, face creams, underwear, as well as medical equipment!"

Not less troublesome, though far more to be pitied, were the streams of refugees on the roads in France during those calamitous weeks of 1940, when the French army collapsed and the Germans advanced rapidly, meeting with no opposition. At Albert an ambulance train was waiting to get to the coast when

"the station began to fill up with refugees—tragic and pathetic figures—nearly all old people, or mothers with families and babies in arms,

---

## Grey and Scarlet In Praise of War Nurses

---

all laden with suit-cases and bundles . . . Trains came in crowded to suffocation point and frightened and hysterical people pushed and fought to get in while the people in the train were equally determined to keep them out. We three sisters and the orderlies helped the old people and held babies while mothers pushed their way in wherever possible. Our acting C.O. was very apprehensive in case we should be left with babies on our hands ! "

There are illuminating sidelights on the French mind in two of the nurses' stories. One says : "I still think the working people of France believe that their country had to lay down arms because the English ran away"; and the other tells how in the Military Hospital at Jerusalem, "while a whole ward of Indians was especially remarkable for the quiet and patient manner in which they bore suffering, in direct contrast was the behaviour of our French patients, of whom some were De Gaullists, whilst others were prisoners, allied to the Vichy Government, sent to us during the Syrian campaign. Their excited talk and fierce arguments made it necessary to transfer the Vichy men to another hospital."

None of the nurses had more perilous and harassing duties than those which fell to them in Singapore. "In spite of large red crosses on all the buildings and barrack-square the Japs dive-bombed and machine-gunned us frequently. It was terrible to see the shell-shocked patients and hear their screams as the bullets fell around us." No screams from nurses, however, though "all sisters donned tin hats and, if bombs were dropping too near, dived under the beds."

"I can see the matron now, after one of the worst raids, jumping up from under a bed and rushing out into the open, with bombs still dropping, the air so thick with smoke and the smell of cordite, that it was impossible to see more than a few inches ahead, to find out if the night sisters had been hurt, as their house was some distance away. We could see the flames and the planes diving down and machine-gunning, but that made no difference to her. On she rushed and later returned to say they were all right, in spite of their house being half on top of them, and were on the way up to join us and have some tea, which we all badly needed."

It sounds a delightfully feminine touch, that last about the tea. But it isn't really. Nowadays men are just as anxious as women for tea after they have been through hell.

Unhappily there was no tea in the lifeboat which for twelve days and nights was afloat in the Atlantic after a ship had been sunk by a submarine's torpedoes. There were 52 men in her, and one woman—the nurse who tells the story. Two meals a day they had, if they could be called meals—one at 7 a.m., the other at 6 p.m. They consisted of a spoonful of a meat extract, two ounces of water, two biscuits, three chocolate squares and three malted milk tablets. Yet "we felt grand after breakfast," says the narrative. But as the days went by, and the men grew weaker, they talked about food incessantly. The men's thoughts dwelt on beer, though one little chap said always, "Never mind, Sister, we'll have a cup of tea." And at last they got it, after they had been sighted by a plane and picked up by a corvette. Their legs were "terribly wobbly" by then, and the writer confesses that in the lifeboat "we were so weak and so snappy by the time we were rescued that I had a few little weeps to myself under the blanket at night."

The Army of today is a very different Army from that I used to know. They were a bit helpless. They expected everything to be done for them, and it was done. They did not have to improvise and invent, as our troops did, for example, when they went into Tobruk after it had been smashed up. Now they are self-reliant. The Australians used to say last time that, if you gave a lot of hungry Tommies a sheep they wouldn't know what to do with it. Now they would know all right. It's the same with the Army nurses. Now they have learnt to scratch up what is required when it hasn't been provided.

The clever way they rigged up operating theatres in the most difficult conditions wins my admiration. In Iceland the authorities were not very helpful (the Goebbels propaganda had a good deal of influence all through the country), but "with a little improvisation" they made "a workable little place." In Malta they started with one small theatre and soon had a larger one in addition. They even managed to instal one on board a not very large ship. Nothing daunts them ; they never seem to be discouraged by hardships or obstacles. These modest cheery records of brave competent women make me feel proud to be their fellow-countryman.

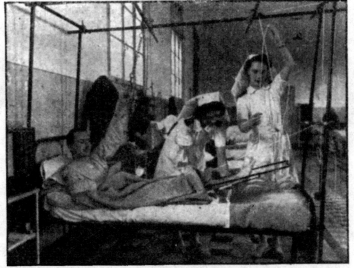

**IN A NORTH AFRICAN HOSPITAL for wounded Service men, Nursing Sisters of the R.A.F. are seen adjusting a leg-cradle to aid the recovery of an injured limb. Noble work of the war nurses is dealt with in the book reviewed in this page. See also p. 687.** PAGE 691 *Photo, British Official*

# Stalin's Great Airmen Pick their Nazi Targets

ON EVERY SOVIET FRONT the Red Air Force, with generous backing by British and American machines, continues to drive the Nazi invader from Russian soil. From the commencement of the treacherous German attack, on June 22, 1941, when Marshal Stalin's sky-fighters were none too numerous, to these present triumphant days of aerial conquest, to the best of her astonishing ability Russia has smitten the foe in the air. Well and truly are the tables now turned : for today Russia's aircraft production about equals Britain's—which far exceeds that of Germany.

Russian Petlyakov-2 reconnaissance and dive bombers, skilfully hidden from enemy observation within a wood (1), stand ready for action, whilst the airmen gather around maps (2) to complete the plan of attack ; now the planes prepare to take off (3) and soar into the clouds (4) en route to the appointed targets.

*Photos, Pictorial Press*

# Troops of the Red Army Rush to their Tanks

wide open Red Army tankmen are here seen clustering, to continue the push that daily takes the valiant Russians nearer to Berlin. In the development of military technique Soviet factories are excelling; from the great Kharkov tank plant, transferred to the rear when the Nazi

AGAINST REELING GERMANS the great Soviet winter offensive continues. To snow-camouflaged battle-machines that crack Nazi defences wide open Red Army tankmen are here seen clustering, to continue the push that daily takes the valiant Russians nearer to Berlin. In the development of military technique Soviet factories are excelling; from the great Kharkov tank plant, transferred to the rear when the Nazi threat became tense, ever more powerful models are rolling out. See p. 310,

*Photo, U.S.S.R. Official*

# How We Speed the Training of a £5,000 Pilot

Without leaving the ground, yet in most realistic conditions, new R.A.F. pilots destined to bomb German targets are now having their flying training time speeded up by weeks, and at the same time thousands of pounds and the lives of many trainees are being saved. This ingenious cyclorama method of putting the final polish on our future airmen is described by W. J. BENTLEY.

"YOU'RE coming in too close . . . keep her nose up, you'll hit the edge of the airfield . . . For Pete's sake, keep your motors running or you'll prang, and you've still got your full bomb load!" The instructor's metallic voice through the microphone rose to a strident pitch as the pilot fumbled at the controls. "No time now to do another circuit. This means hitting the deck!"

A sudden silence—and then the budding bomber pilot took off his headset and his leather helmet, and said: "I'm very sorry, sir. Let me start again; I think I've got the feel of the controls now."

He makes himself cosy once more in the seat of the cyclorama peep-show—a Link Trainer (dummy aeroplane) on the ground, standing in the middle of a brilliantly-lit circular screen on which is painted a most realistic scene of the ground from 2,000 feet up. On the other side of the room, indignantly barking into the microphone, is the instructor who had tried to prevent the bomber boy from pranging only a moment or two ago.

The instructor's microphone is linked to head-telephones in the pilot's helmet, and as the controls of the youngster's dummy plane are connected by electric cables with a recording machine, every movement, every last-minute manoeuvre, is traced on a rolling strip of paper like a player-piano roll by a stylus.

THEY have only to look at the graph thus drawn to see that, had a real machine been handled in the way this young pilot had just worked stick and rudder-bar, an aircraft would have crashed by coming in too low at the edge of the airfield, and the pilot would have had no chance to bale out.

A man's life, as well as some thousands of pounds, is saved almost every hour in the cyclorama peep-show—the new way of training budding bomber heroes. Yet every time you see an R.A.F. bomber in the sky you can reckon that at least £5,000 has been spent on the pilot's training. This amount invested by you (through the R.A.F.) in every young pilot represents his Service pay (actually one of the smallest items on the bill), the pay and expenses of his instructors, the fuel used in training planes and their use and upkeep during the time the pilot is in training.

SINCE this war began we have been speeding up his training time, and now they do formation landing and advanced aerial battle tactics weeks before they did in peacetime training. The Nazis have speeded up their training, too, and their average total figure spent on training per head in the Luftwaffe was some £2,800. So when you read of "five more Messerschmitts down" you can, if they are, say, Me.110s (which have a crew of three—pilot, radio-op. and rear-gunner), add another £8,000-£9,000 per plane to the

total loss, for the money invested in training.

The Link Trainer itself is not new. Even before the war the Link was used both by the R.A.F. and the Luftwaffe for training in blind flying. With a hood drawn over the cockpit of the dummy plane, the pilot "flew" a prescribed course through various weather conditions. And all the time he moved the controls a pneumatic pump rocked his cockpit just as a real plane would rock and roll, and the stylus traced out on a map the actual course he would have followed in a real flight.

A HARBOUR FROM 2,000 FEET UP is the impression given to the trainee pilot by this realistically painted scene, photograph of which was taken from the cockpit of the Link Trainer, looking towards the tail (foreground). The Link Trainer is actuated mainly by electrically operated bellows beneath the floor on which it stands. See also facing page. *Photo, Pictorial Press*

This was all right from a technical point of view, but sitting in a dummy plane in an empty room, or in a cold hangar, gave little realism. Although as you kicked the rudder-bar you "turned," and as you pulled the stick you "climbed," it was quite impossible to imagine yourself in a real bomber at 20,000 feet, with engines roaring and the grey clouds swirling through the prop arcs.

And then at one airfield the instructors had a good idea. They carried the Link trainer into the officers' mess, painted the distempered walls with scenery representing landscape as it appears at some 5,000 feet (an artist who in peacetime draws back-

cloths for pantos did this piece of daubing!) and fitted a theatrical "rain-effect" disc to the light, giving a magic-lantern effect of bad weather. A peep-show, but it worked.

From this the R.A.F. has developed the "cyclorama," in which each one of the £5,000-brigade does many hours "flying" before going up to copy those tactics in a real bomber. Real flying is sandwiched with hours of training in the peep-show, so that often a pilot, engrossed in some air-battle stunts, almost forgets whether he is flying a real aircraft 20,000-feet up or if he is in the cyclorama only six feet from the ground!

Each peep-show is in a fabric tower on wooden supports, looking like nothing but the "Wall of Death" towers in which stunt motor-cyclists ride. Inside, the whole fabric is painted with a landscape scene, as seen from, say, 2,000 feet. Each cyclorama drum has a different scene, and in the complete training unit there are at least three drums, covering up to high bomber altitudes. In the middle of each is a stubby little wooden cockpit with fore-shortened wings and tail-plane. As you sit down in the cockpit you face a big semi-circle of barely-transparent celluloid—giving the optical illusion of looking straight ahead through a whirling prop.

READY for action? The motor is switched on, and at the slightest finger-touch of the stick or throttle or rudder controls the cockpit will buck and turn—and every movement will be recorded on the paper graph strip now running under the stylus. The lights are turned almost out, and the projector-lantern high above, in the centre of the cyclorama, gives a wonderfully realistic effect of rain, mist or heavy cloud. Cross lights begin to flash on the celluloid, just as they flash on a whirling propeller.

"You're still not flying level," barks the metallic voice through the headset. "Bank over towards the church steeple. That's your course. Now follow the river." The lights go dim, as you run into a bank of heavy cloud, and now there's only the compass-dial to guide you. The stick's too far over; you're side-slipping, losing height—and just as you begin to feel in a hopeless muddle with all the controls the light mercifully goes up again, and there's the painted church steeple still almost straight ahead. Yes, this time you've stuck to your course.

Another half-hour of this and you feel like radio-ing back to the instructor: "Got any hot coffee? It's cold up here at five thousand!" Though actually your "horizon" is a painted bit of scenery in a peep-show exactly 6 ft. 8in. from the floor. Make-believe? Ask any pilot who has experienced this tremendous aid to the acquisition of skill and he will bid you try it for yourself and see!

# He Learns to Fly High 6 Feet from the Ground

**IN THE COCKPIT** of a Visual Link Trainer sits a pupil (1) in telephonic contact with an instructor (left), while three other learners watch, near the cyclorama circular screen. Whatever movement the pilot makes he has an aerial landscape before—or rather, through optical illusion, beneath—his dummy plane (2). The instructor explains the Link's controls (3), gives the pupil flying directions by microphone (5), and checks his reactions by meters corresponding with those in the Link (4). See also facing page.

PAGE 695     *Photos, Pictorial Press*

# They Gained these Awards for Heroism at Sea

Lt.-Cmdr. ARMITAGE, G.C., G.M.
He gained the George Medal "for gallantry and undaunted devotion to duty in the face of the enemy." This bust of Lt.-Cmdr. Armitage is by John Skeaping.

Ldg. Seaman F. BANNER, D.S.M.
"For leadership, skill and devotion to duty" aboard H.M. destroyer Tartar, during an action off North Africa in May 1943.

P/O G. E. SHEPHERD, D.S.M.
While taking part in convoying merchantmen to N. Russian ports through violent attack, Petty-Officer Shepherd, a gunner, showed great endurance.

Chief Stoker J. R. CARTER, D.S.M.
He received the D.S.M. from H.M. the King at a recent investiture, for gallantry at Narvik, Apr. 13, 1940.

Ldg. Seaman L. SORRELL, D.S.M.
Gun-layer on a tanker in the Mediterranean when enemy aircraft attacked, he helped to bring one down and damaged another.

Lt. M. KRISHNAN, D.S.C.
Serving in the Royal Indian Navy, he won his award in operations in the Persian Gulf, when he boarded an enemy tug with a small party and by threatening the German and Italian crew with an imaginary bomb captured 50 of them.

Able Seaman H. J. YEATS, D.S.M.
Wounded by a bomb during the North African landings in Nov. 1942, Able Seaman Yeats insisted on carrying out his duties. He was awarded the D.S.M.

Srgn.-Lt. P. EVANS, G.M., R.N.V.R.
Although injured in both legs he had himself carried around on a chair for 12 hours to attend to the wounded survivors from a Canadian corvette.

*Photos, British Official. Crown Copyright; Associated Press, Planet News*

# I WAS THERE!

## We 'Recce' Men Raided the Nazis at Anzio

*For a week during the Germans' first heavy attack against the west-Italy beach-head a British " thin red line " was strung out along two miles of the perimeter defences. As related here by their Colonel, a Malay-born Irishman, those 172 men of the Reconnaissance Corps, by aggressive night patrolling caused great chaos and confusion in the enemy camp, whilst holding off at least two German battalions.*

WE knocked a hole in the kitchen wall of a farmhouse to make a gun slit, and into that kitchen we drove an armoured car. We had our mortars too, and twelve anti-tank guns with a field battery of 25-pounders we could call on if we were in trouble. They were to stand us in good stead. Our first worry was a wood 150 yards ahead.

We sent a patrol out on the first night we were in our unaccustomed role as troops of the line. They found a tank harbour, but no sign that there were any enemy in the wood. What puzzled us was the amount of fire movement by day from the wood. Mortar fire was particularly troublesome and we couldn't make it out how the wood became alive with Germans during the day. At night we covered the approaches, and nothing could get into it in daylight without being observed. So Sergeant William Parker —his home is at 10, Crowhurst Road, Colchester, Essex—took a daylight patrol into the wood, killed three and brought three back as prisoners. These turned out to be the enemy's mortar observation post crew, and we had no more bother from mortars.

There was sniping, however, from the forward edge of the wood. They wounded a dispatch rider who was crawling up one hundred and fifty yards away. But there was no more accurate fire after that. We decided to do some aggressive night work, but before we could jump off we were attacked by an enemy force two companies strong. We called on the gunners and they stopped the attack in its tracks. Two hours later the enemy tried again and got within fifty yards of us. The position was serious, so we asked the gunners if they could do a map shoot. " Yes," they said, " if we didn't mind ten per cent casualties." The

barrage came down, but was so accurate that we had no one so much as scratched.

The enemy withdrew, and the day was quiet after that. That night we decided to try to clear out four farmhouses which the enemy held in strength behind the wood. The leading assault troop cleared out the first house without much trouble, although the Germans tossed hand grenades at us from the upper windows. The next farmhouse was twenty yards away and a machine-gun, firing on a fixed line about two feet off the ground, pinned down the assault party.

The fire from this machine-gun annoyed Lieutenant John Alexander McNeil, of Linn Drive, Muirend, Glasgow, so he collected a Bren gun and walked calmly forward firing it at everything and then running the last 50 yards. He spotted the slot the machine-gun was firing through and rolled three hand grenades into it. A trooper with a two-inch mortar gave them bombs as well. That stopped the machine-gun. Just as they were getting in the front door they spotted reinforcements coming down a side road. With four Bren guns they waited until the Germans were within 20 yards. Then they let them have it—and none arrived. Next, fire came at Lieut. McNeil's troop from the wood between their position and our lines. It

**HERO OF THE SOVIET UNION, fighter-pilot Lieut. V. D. Lavrinenkov, who has brought down 30 enemy planes, tells below the remarkable story of his escape from the German lines.** *Photo, Pictorial Press*

wasn't until we sent a patrol in that we found out how the enemy got there. In a big hole in the ground covered with corrugated iron and undergrowth 100 Germans lived by day, watching our patrols trying to solve the mystery of the empty wood that filled with Germans at night.

## I Rammed a German Plane—and Walked Home

*Famous air-ace Vladimir Lavrinenkov, Hero of the Soviet Union, was shot down over the German lines some months ago, just after his 30th " kill "— a F.W., which he destroyed by ramming. He escaped, and with the aid of guerillas made his way back to Soviet-held territory. Here is his sensational story, reproduced by courtesy of the Soviet War News.*

I RAMMED the F.W. while we were on patrol covering an advance by our land troops. When my machine began to fall, I pushed

back the hood, baled out, and hit the ground before the parachute was fully open. For a moment I lost consciousness, then felt a sudden sharp pain in the shoulder, and heard German speech.

When I opened my eyes I saw I was the centre of a crowd of German soldiers. One was unstrapping my parachute, another was going through my pockets, and a third was standing over me with his rifle at the ready. Just then one of our fighters roared low over the ground, its machine-guns spitting. The Germans threw themselves flat, but were back a minute later.

I had no papers on me except a ration card, which recorded my status as a Hero of the Soviet Union and a senior lieutenant in a Guards regiment. The Germans put me into a side-car and took me to a village. They let me lie down on some ammunition cases, and a German officer came up. He asked in excellent Russian : " How did you happen to get shot down ? " At first I thought I wouldn't speak, but at his next question I changed my mind. "Are you a Communist ?" he asked me.

Not wanting him to get the idea I was afraid, I said yes, I was a Communist. Then he offered me a cigarette. I refused. I had my own tobacco. So I wiped the blood off my face and began to smoke. Then the Nazi said : "We're going to take you to Germany."

I told him not to bother. They could shoot me right where I was. But he said there wasn't any point in shooting a flyer like me in a hurry. Then I knew why they weren't beating me up. They considered me quite an important prize, I suppose, and wanted to keep me intact for a bit.

The officer disappeared into a hut. Some

**A BRITISH ' RECCE ' SERGEANT stands in his Bren carrier, examining a map in the possession of two American anti-tank officers of the 5th Army. Exploits in the Anzio beach-head of the Reconnaissance Corps (which was placed under Royal Armoured Corps directorate on January 1, 1944 are narrated above.** *Photo, British Official*

women and children were standing a few yards away behind a fence. One of the women whispered : "Will the Red Army come soon ?" I told her in about five days. My chest had been hit, and I was coughing up blood. They put me back in the side-car. The motor-cycle bumped badly over the rough road, and that seemed to make the bleeding worse.

Late that night I was called out for questioning. The interpreter told me I was at the headquarters of a Luftwaffe Corps. So I told him how sorry I was I hadn't known their address before. Then the German asked : " Have you got many planes ?"

"Oh, enough to be getting on with," I said.

"How many aircraft have you shot down ?"

"Quite a few." I was just about done in. The inspector offered me some food, but I refused. The cross-examination was cut short. I was taken to another room and allowed to lie down on the floor. But I couldn't sleep, although I was dead tired. I couldn't stop thinking about Smolensk and my young brother.

In the morning they gave me some thin soup and a piece of bread. Then I was put in a lorry, and an officer told me he'd shoot me if I tried to jump out. The warning was really quite unnecessary. Two toughs sat on each side of me, with their fingers on the trigger. We drove into a town, and I was pushed into a small cell with iron gratings. The walls were covered with inscriptions. I remember one of them was : "A captain awaited his fate here." I broke off a piece of lime and wrote : " Vlad. Lavr."

### I Planned to Kill the Pilot

I had a visit from a hefty German with a bruised face. He turned out to be the pilot of the F.W. I had rammed. He was quite talkative about the affair. It appeared that his navigator had been killed, the gunner wounded, and the machine was a total loss. I told him I was delighted to hear it, and refused further conversation.

The next day, as I was marched along a street, women ran up and thrust apples into my hands. A boy dropped a cigarette and several plums into my pocket. I spent the night in the commandant's headquarters, and the next morning, with two wounded Red Army men, I was put aboard a plane. I was scared we might be bound for Germany, and was planning how I could kill the pilot and the guards before we got to the frontier. But we landed quite soon. It looked like Dnieprodzerzhinsk.

I was brought again for questioning. Two officers from the Luftwaffe intelligence department were sitting behind a table. Before long, the talk turned to politics. "What are you fighting for ?" they asked me. I told them it was for our land, for our country. "Well, who do you think will win ?"

"We will," I said.

"Why do you think so ?"

"In our country everybody thinks so."

"But the German army is invincible," they said at the finish. But I told them even they didn't believe that any more. That evening I and my two comrades were put aboard a train at a small station near Dnieprodzerzhinsk. We were accompanied by two officers with innumerable bags and sacks crammed with stolen goods. The carriage was crowded with officers of all ranks, representatives of German firms and Gestapo men hurrying to get away before they were caught by the Soviet offensive.

THIS scene of the German retreat gave me a great kick, of course. I began to have a look round. There were two doors opening on opposite sides of the carriage. I tried one with my foot. The two officers were sitting at a small table. drinking brandy.

We decided to make a dash for it. The next day would be too late—they were taking us to Germany. When the train stopped at one of the stations and the officers went out for a walk we decided on our plan. At about nine the train would be going up a gradient. Karyukin and I would jump through one door, and Korolev through the other.

Soon it was dark. Rocking slightly, the train was going at medium speed. We pretended to be asleep. I snored peacefully, but in fact I was trying to gauge the speed of the train. At last the train slowed down and began to labour up the gradient. I nudged my comrades, put out my leg and pressed the door. It gave way. I leapt, and Karyukin jumped after me.

We both rolled down the embankment and felt no pain at the fall, although it was later discovered that Karyukin had sprained his arm and I had bruised myself badly. We heard shots. Korolev was nowhere about. Evidently he had no time to open the door. Karyukin and I clasped hands so as not to lose each other in the darkness, and set off.

Just before sunrise we came on a rick, and went to sleep in the straw. When we awoke we saw an elderly peasant working in a field nearby. He was frightened at the sight of us, but we managed to calm him down, and got him to give us some old clothes and food. We walked for six days in the direction of Poltava. I figured it was the shortest way to the front line. We got to the Dnieper, and a boatman rowed us across. By that time the corns on my feet were giving me such hell I could hardly move.

I collapsed about 200 yards from the river bank. Karyukin dragged me behind some bushes. After a time I managed to get up, and with great difficulty we reached Komarkovka, where an old peasant called Ivan Shevchenko gave us shelter. We slept in a rick. Shevchenko's wife cut my corns, rubbed my feet with ointment and bandaged them with rags.

WE asked the old man whether there were guerillas in the neighbourhood. He was evasive at first, but then told us to walk towards Bakhmach to a point where the wagon ruts turned off into a wood to the right of the road. "Walk along the tracks," he said. We took his advice, and soon were stopped by a patrol. We were taken to the commander of a partisan detachment, who questioned us closely and then said : "O.K., lads. We'll take you along."

For several days both of us rested. Then the commander—he turned out to be Ivan Kuzmich Primak, of the Chapayev Detachment—gave us each a carbine and a pair of hand grenades. In the next few weeks we took part in many guerilla operations, blowing up bridges, sinking barges laden with grain, capturing herds of cattle that the Germans were driving westward, freeing captive Soviet people, wrecking cars and firing supply trains.

In one of the skirmishes Karyukin was killed. The partisans buried him under a tall oak tree in the forest. At last the Chapayev Detachment joined up with regular Red Army troops on the offensive, and soon I was back with my unit.

## First British Link with Tito in Yugoslavia

*The first members of the British Military Mission to the People's Army of Liberation in Yugoslavia parachuted into a field near the partisan head-quarters in May 1943. Here is the story of Lieut.-Col. F. W. D. Deakin, D.S.O., who led the Mission, as told to Eric Gray, Daily Express correspondent by one of Marshal Tito's staff officers who accompanied the British.*

TITO had been expecting the mission for several days before its members landed. They had been delayed by bad weather. Word had gone round among the farmers near our headquarters—" The Englishmen are coming ! " A peasant ran out to meet them, crying " Our Allies have come at last ! "

The six men—Captain Deakin, as he then was, another officer and four radio operators—were taken first to the farm, where women brought them milk and eggs. Then, at daybreak, they set off on foot for Tito's headquarters. These were a few miles away in the forest, on the shore of Lake Crno Jezero, the Black Lake, one of the most beautiful in Yugoslavia, 5,000 feet above sea level.

**Lieut.-Col. F. W. D. DEAKIN, D.S.O., ex-don of Wadham College, Oxford, who as head of the British Military Mission to Marshal Tito's partisan army in Yugoslavia, in 1943, experienced an adventurous journey, the high-lights of which are related here.** *Photo, News Chronicle*

The mission arrived about 8 a.m. and spent most of that first day talking with Tito and his staff officers. The mission had arrived in the middle of the fifth great German offensive against the partisans, which was to last all through the summer of 1943. Seven Axis divisions were fighting us at that time. The number has doubled since then. Enemy forces were, in fact, only a few miles from our camp, and we had to move that night. It was pouring with rain as we set off on one of the worst journeys in partisan history.

We had to cross Mount Durmitor, which rises 7,500 feet behind the lake, and we walked all through the night. I admired the endurance of the Englishmen who had not slept for 24 hours, and who marched with the best of us. They refused to ride. I heard Deakin say to his assistant : " I don't think we ought to take the horses from these people. They have been fighting for two years and are underfed. They ought to ride before we do." That first night's march was typical of our life for the next three months. The Germans were attacking furiously all the time, and we never slept twice in the same spot.

We had a few hours' sleep in the daytime and moved by night. For food we had a little bread, a small bowl of gruel which the Englishmen said was like porridge, and a small ration of horse meat. But for two months we had no bread at all, and no gruel.

I showed Deakin and his men which were the best herbs to eat in the forest. Beach leaves are best if you can find them—they taste rather like spinach when boiled. The Germans reconnoitred our position from the air every day. It was easy for them because we were never far from one of the main groups of armies which Tito commanded personally.

We were attacked constantly on the ground and from the air. The Germans

**MARSHAL TITO'S MEN TAKE TO THE WATER,** carrying out a strategic move across one of the many inland lakes which dot the mountainous regions of Yugoslavia (right); the flag of the Yugoslav partisan army is flying. A detachment of the Nazi troops they battle against are seen here (left) using a field wireless set to keep in contact with other groups in the same area. See accompanying story of the first British Military Mission's arrival at the partisan headquarters.

*Photos, U.S. Official, New York Times Photos*

dropped anti-personnel bombs. We had neither anti-aircraft guns nor fighters. They bombed low all the time.

On June 6, 11 days after the mission had arrived, Deakin's brother officer was killed. We had been attacked all day from the air. The Germans probably knew that the partisan headquarters were in that area, because they went through the forest like a fine comb, bombing and machine-gunning every patch. At the same time we were surrounded by enemy ground forces. We saw the flashes of their guns all around us

at night, unpleasantly encircling our position.

We were near the height known as Mount Milinklada, on the Bosnia-Montenegro frontier. Our troops forced a passage about a mile wide through the German ring, and the whole army marched through it. Troops ahead were throwing hand grenades into the snipers' nests as we went along. Tito and Deakin marched in front. When the bombing became very bad we lay flat under the trees.

Tito and Deakin were both hit by bomb splinters—Tito in the left arm, Deakin on the left leg. One day when we were lowest for

food Deakin opened his last tin of bully beef and shared it with us. We were delighted when he got his promotion to major. He had been married about a fortnight before coming out to us, and he was anxiously awaiting a letter from his wife. He got the first one when another group of British officers joined the mission.

They, too, landed by parachute in the night. The Germans were only a few miles away, and when we moved we left an empty British canister behind just to make them furiously angry.

# OUR DIARY OF THE WAR

**MARCH 1, Wednesday** *1,642nd day*
**Italy.**—Revealed that Germans were using remote-controlled explosives-filled miniature tanks.
**Russian Front.**—Announced that Germans' Narva defence line S. of the town broken, and Narva-Tallinn railway cut.
**Sea.**—Loss of H.M. destroyer *Warwick* announced by Board of Admiralty.

**MARCH 2, Thursday** *1,643rd day*
**Air.**—Albert (France) industrial plants attacked with 12,000 lb. bombs.

**MARCH 3, Friday** *1,644th day*
**Italy.**—Collapse of enemy's third major assault on Anzio beach-head announced.
**Russian Front.**—Markovo captured by Russian troops in Pskov region.
**Burma.**—British troops E. of Kalapanzin occupied Japanese positions N.E. of Buthidaung.
**Pacific.**—Japanese attacked U.S. positions on the air strip of Momote, Admiralty Islands. Ponape and Kusaie (Caroline Islands) bombed.
**Air.**—U.S. daylight offensive reached Berlin. Lightnings made wide sweep over the German capital.

**MARCH 4, Saturday** *1,645th day*
**Italy.**—Announced three fresh attacks by German infantry defeated at Anzio.
**Russian Front.**—Troops of the First Ukrainian front under command of Marshal Zhukov launched an offensive on a front 110 miles wide and 15-30 miles deep. Izyaslavl, Shumsk, Yanpol, and Ostropol taken in the drive.
**Burma.**—Walawbum and Maingkwan fell to Chinese-American drive in N. Burma.
**Air.**—Berlin raided for first time by American heavy bombers in daytime.

**MARCH 5, Sunday** *1,646th day*
**Italy.**—Announced enemy attack at Cisterna repelled by U.S. troops.
**Air.**—Cognac and Bérgerac, French air bases, bombed by Liberators.

**MARCH 6, Monday** *1,647th day*
**Russian Front.**—Odessa-Lvov railway, German southern supply route, cut by Soviet capture of Volchisk.
**Air.**—Berlin attacked in daylight by strong force of U.S. heavy bombers; 176 enemy aircraft destroyed for loss of

68 bombers. Rail yards at Trappes, 15 miles S.W. of Paris, raided at night by Halifaxes.
**General.**—Appointments announced: Air Vice-Marshal S. P. Simpson, C.B.E., M.C., to be A.O.C. a Coastal Command group ; Air Vice-Marshal William Elliot, C.B., C.B.E., D.F.C., to be A.O.C., R.A.F. Station, Gibraltar.

**MARCH 7, Tuesday** *1,648th day*
**Mediterranean.**—Toulon naval base heavily bombed by Liberators.
**Sea.**—Loss in Anzio beach-head operations of cruisers *Penelope* and *Spartan*, destroyers *Janus* and *Inglefield*, and five major assault craft, announced. Revealed convoy losses now less than one ship in every thousand.

**MARCH 8, Wednesday** *1,649th day*
**Russian Front.**—Cherni-Ostrov, 11 miles N.W. of Proskurov, occupied by Russians.
**Air.**—More than 350,000 incendiaries and 10,000 H.E. bombs dropped on Berlin in great U.S. daylight raid. Erkner ball-bearing factory hit.
**General.**—Appointments announced: Lt.-Gen. Sir E. L. Morris, K.C.B., O.B.E., M.C., to be G.O.C.-in-C., Northern Command ; Lt.-Gen. J. G. des R. Swayne, C.B., C.B.E., to be Chief of Staff, India ; Lt.-Gen. E. C. A. Schreiber, C.B., D.S.O.,

to be G.O.C.-in-C., Southern Command ; Major-Gen. D. G. Watson, C.B., C.B.E., M.C., to be G.O.C.-in-C. Western Command.

**MARCH 9, Thursday** *1,650th day*
**Russian Front.** — Staro-Konstantinov captured by troops of the First Ukrainian front. River Ingulets forced and Dolinskaya-Nikolaiev railway cut by General Malinovsky's forces.
**Air.**—Berlin again raided by day by escorted Liberators and Fortresses. Marignane aircraft factories near Marseilles bombed by Lancasters.

**MARCH 10, Friday** *1,651st day*
**Russian Front.**—Announced that after five days' fighting, troops of the 2nd Ukrainian front under Marshal Koniev had advanced from 25 to 44 miles. Uman, Kristinovka, and Zvenigorodka occupied. 14 German divisions routed. Krasilov and Novo Konstantinov taken in Proskurov region.
**General.**—Rejection of U.S. note delivered to Eire on Feb. 21 requesting removal of Axis consular and diplomatic officials, announced.

**MARCH 11, Saturday** *1,652nd day*
**Italy.**—Florence and Padua bombed by Fortresses and Marauders.

**Mediterranean.** — Toulon heavily raided by Liberators of the 15th U.S. Air Force.
**Russian Front.**—Troops under Marshals Zhukov and Koniev and General Malinovsky continued to advance. Berislavl, Ladyzhenka, Zlatopol, Novo Mirogod, Belshaya-Viska and Marzhanovka taken.
**Air.**—Munster and military targets in the Pas de Calais area attacked by Fortresses, Liberators and Marauders. Mosquitoes over Hamburg at night.
**General.**—Pierre Pucheu, ex-Vichy Minister of the Interior, sentenced to death in Algiers. King Peter of Yugoslavia and his ministers arrived in England.

**MARCH 12, Sunday** *1,653rd day*
**Russian Front.**—Dolinskaya, on River Bug, captured by Red Army.
**Burma.**—Buthidaung (Arakan) captured by British troops of 14th Army.
**Pacific.**—Occupation of Wotho atoll, 75 miles N.W. of Kwajalein in the Marshall Islands, announced.
**General.**—Announced that as from March 13 all travel to Northern Ireland and Eire from Great Britain suspended for military reasons of " paramount importance."

**MARCH 13, Monday** *1,654th day*
**Russian Front.**—Kherson, on the mouth of the Dnieper, captured by forces of Gen. Malinovsky's command. Russians passed to the offensive at Vinnitsa.
**Air.**—French rail targets at Le Mans bombed by Halifaxes, and Frankfurt attacked by Mosquitoes, at night.

**MARCH 14, Tuesday** *1,655th day*
**Russian Front.**—Several German divisions trapped in Bereznegovati sector by troops of the 3rd Ukrainian Front. Proskurov offensive continued.
**Home Front.**—Phosphorous bombs and high explosives dropped on London in large-scale fire-raising attack.
**Burma.**—Announced that columns of the 14th Army had entered Upper Burma and crossed River Chindwin.
**Australasia.**—Defeat of Japanese attack on Bougainville Island announced.
**Pacific.**—Announced that Hauwei and Butjoluo Island in the Admiralties occupied by Allied troops.

★━━━━━ *Flash-backs* ━━━━━★

**1940**
March 12. *Russo-Finnish peace terms signed in Moscow.*

**1941**
March 9. *Italians launched offensive against Greeks in Albania.*
March 14. *Clydebank and Glasgow heavily bombed for second night running by more than 200 planes.*

**1942**
March 8. *Japanese troops landed*

*at Lae and Salamaua (New Guinea) and seized airfield.*
**1943**
March 3. *Rzhev, W. of Moscow, stormed and captured by Red Army forces.*
March 4. *Two-day battle of Bismarck Sea ended. Entire Japanese convoy bound for New Guinea sunk by the Allies.*
March 12. *Vyazma, on Moscow-Warsaw main line, taken by Soviet troops.*

# THE WAR IN THE AIR

## by Capt. Norman Macmillan, M.C., A.F.C.

A GOOD idea of the immensity of the background to air war is obtainable from the words spoken on February 29, 1944, by Sir Archibald Sinclair, Secretary of State for Air, when introducing, in the House of Commons, the Air Estimates for the ensuing year. The Air Secretary said: ". . . Before rearmament started the vote for air supplies was about seventeen million pounds per year, that is, about half of the then Army vote, and a little more than one-third of the vote for the Navy. Today the man power allotted to the Ministry of Aircraft Production is larger than the whole labour force in the Ministry of Supply, which in its turn is greater than the man power allotted for shipbuilding, both for the Navy and for the Merchant Service."

It could scarcely be expressed in fewer words how blind the British people were, before the war rearmament programme began, to the overwhelming part that the air would play in the coming war, and how enormous is the effort that has since been made to bring our air power to the scale required to beat the German war machine. It must be remembered, too, that that effort remained on a comparatively puny scale until the German assault was launched on the Low Countries and France. For it was not until after that attack had begun that the Ministry of Aircraft Production was formed.

IT is to that blindness that we owe in great measure the long-drawn-out nature of the present war compared with the war of 1914-18. It was German air power—then in its zenith—that drove us out of Norway, and contributed in decisive measure to our withdrawal from Belgium and France. German air power forced us to leave Greece, and ousted us from Crete. Japanese air power carried the Japanese armies to the very gates of India. Truly we had many lessons to teach us how wrong-headed we had been before the war rearmament began. But there is no race that learns its lesson more thoroughly than the British. And so, today, we have gained great superiority over both German and Japanese, even when the Royal Air Force and the Dominion Air Forces alone are considered. When the American and Russian Air Forces are added to them, the superiority is far greater than was ever enjoyed by our enemies.

Sir Archibald also said: "Of the resources allotted to the air war, the largest share is given to Bomber Command." That is to be expected, for the official communiqués make it patently clear that Bomber Command suffers the heaviest casualties and therefore needs the greatest number of replacements. In addition, Bomber Command transports the heaviest loads and therefore needs the greatest labour force to produce those loads. Moreover, heavy bombers require more man-hours to produce than do fighters, and so, even if the casualties were equal, the proportion of the aircraft industry allocated to Bomber Command would have to be greater.

But it is curious, is it not, that the Air Secretary should go out of his way to draw attention to this apparently obvious allocation of man power. It can mean but one thing: that Bomber Command did not always have this priority. There must have been a time when other air interests took priority, even as the Army and still more the Navy took priority in the Service Votes in the years that Sir Thomas Inskip (as he then was) referred to as those "that the locusts" had eaten.

It is clear what those other air interests were—the Battle of Britain, the war in North Africa, and the anti-submarine war. The first may be over, the second is over, and the third appears to have been substantially won, although it cannot end until the war ends. These priorities having presumably been satisfied, Bomber Command now has its turn. What a pity that turn came so late. The war might have been finished, so far as Germany is concerned, if it had been possible to give Bomber Command the opportunity earlier to "get there firstest with the mostest men" as Mr. Churchill quoted as a reason for our North African successes.

But as with the pre-war blindness about the power of the air, there has also been war blindness about the power of the bomber. Not so very long ago there were controversies raging in the Press and in books about the relative methods of employing air power. There were those who denied to the air its place as a separate service, who said that every aircraft should serve the Navy or the Army direct in the field of war on sea or on land, and who pooh-poohed the strategic employment of bomber forces operating independently. The critics would have closed down the Air Ministry and divided up the R.A.F. into naval and military portions to be handled by the Admirals and Generals.

But this war has proved these critics to be wrong. The strategic air forces have been the deciding factors time and time again. They paved the way for the successive advances of the Eighth Army, they smashed Pantelleria, they brought about the easy landings in Sicily, they smashed the enemy air power in that island, they saved our bridgehead at Salerno, and they have done much to hold our beach-head at Anzio. The strategic air forces in the Pacific have smashed the Japanese maritime lines of communication, and have aided landings on one island after another. They have fetched and carried guns and stores of all kinds.

The Japanese—who have a two-Service air force organization—used their air strength strategically to strike at Pearl Harbour and to break our naval defence in the Malayan area of the Far East. The Americans—who also have a two-Service air organization—are now in process, due to their enormous production of over 100,000 aircraft a year, of outvying the R.A.F. in the strategic employment of

| THE BATTLE OF BERLIN (Continued from page 604). B=Bombers. F=Fighters. | | | | | | | |
|---|---|---|---|---|---|---|---|
| Date 1944 | Target | Bomb Tonnage | Planes Missing | | Planes D'stroy'd | | Remarks |
| | | | B | F | By B | By F | |
| Feb. 15 | Berlin by night with diversionary attack on Frankfort - on - Oder, by Bomber Command, R.A.F. | 2,500 plus | 43 | — | — | — | Record force of over 1,000 sorties. |
| Mar. 3 | U.S. Fighter Sweep sent first U.S. planes over Berlin, on diversionary sweep. | — | — | — | — | — | Only previous recorded day raid on Berlin by Mosquitoes was on Jan. 30, 1943. |
| Mar. 4 | Berlin bombed by U.S. 8th Air Force bombers escorted by fighters of 8th and 9th U.S. A. A. A. F. and R.A.F. | ? | 14 | 23 | 6 | 9 | First heavy bomber raid on Berlin by day. |
| Mar. 6 | Similar attack by force of 1,500 bombers and fighters. | 1,400 | 68 | 11 | 93 | 83 | First main day attack. |
| Mar. 8 | Similar attack by 750 bombers and 800 fighters. | 1,400 | 38 | — | 42 | 83 | Second main day attack. |
| Mar. 9 | Berlin and Hanover American attack by day. | ? | 7 | 1 | — | — | Weather heavy clouds. No fighter opposition. |

**NOTE:** R.A.F. new 12,000-lb. bomb used for the first time against Gnome-Le-Rhône aero-engine works at Limoges on the night following Feb. 8, 1944. Used again on night following March 2 against FW190 factory at Albert.

military aircraft in huge independent fleets of bombers and fighters. These forces are as independent as Bomber Command.

ONE day it will be known how great has been the contribution of the R.A.F. to the winning of the war at sea. It will be known how terrific was the destruction caused by Bomber Command in the submarine industry in Germany, how great was the part played by Coastal Command, yet how futile were the raids against submarine pens, bomb-proof and blast-proof, and what a waste of effort these raids were. You will notice we do not make these raids today. This is another lesson we have learned.

Perhaps that is why Bomber Command now has priority in the labour force that feeds the maw of war. For since Bomber Command began to make its terrific raids on German targets, the German armies in Russia have been unable to withstand the Red Armies' pressure, the Luftwaffe and the submarine have suffered—although their dragons' tails can still thresh—and German power to maintain the offensive has steadily declined. Bomber Command put Germany on the defensive. Our leaders know that now. That is why the American air forces are now striking hard upon the same strategic note.

**R.A.F. RANGE OF BOMBS** from the 500-lb. to the latest, the 12,000-pounder: the enormous size of the latter may be gauged from the R.A.F. men standing behind it; the 8,000-lb. bomb is not shown. See also p.p. 701 and 702.

*Photo, British Official*

# U.S. Bombers Blast Berlin in Daylight Raids

FIRST DAYLIGHT bombing raid on Berlin by U.S. crews took place on March 4, 1944. Two days later the visit was repeated, this time on a colossal scale : hundreds of bombers of the U.S. 8th Air Force setting out to smash factories, airfields and other military installations in the Berlin district, Fortresses and Liberators having as escort and support Mustangs, Lightnings and Thunderbolts. Of these, 68 bombers and 11 fighters failed to return, but 176 enemy aircraft were destroyed. Thus are the United States Strategic Forces supplementing by day the shattering night attacks by the R.A.F.

Opposition was first encountered 100 miles west of the city, and air battles were continuous over the remainder of the distance and for part of the journey home. Hedge-hopping back after the bombs were dropped, one Fortress roared so low over the main street of one German town that its crew were able to whistle and wave to cyclists below ; hit by flak, one engine went dead, but the Fortress carried on, skimmed a bare 10 feet above the North Sea and reached its base in Britain with only one casualty—a minor cut on the tail gunner's left hand.

Outnumbering the biggest Luftwaffe formation that has ever attacked an English city, this mighty bomber force successfully delivered in full daylight an attack the weight of which was heavier than anything Britain has known. Allied blows have yet to reach their peak, as stressed by Mr. Churchill when, in his review of the war on Feb. 22, he said, "Scales and degrees of attack will be reached far beyond the dimensions of anything which has yet been employed or even imagined."

THROUGH A FLAK-FILLED SKY went these Flying Fortresses (above) of the U.S. 8th Air Force, high over the Greater Berlin area during their large-scale daylight attack.

HOME AGAIN THOUGH BADLY HOLED is this Fortress (centre) ; a member of her crew thought little of the damage as he viewed his airfield again. Lightnings head back to base (below) ; these, with Mustangs and Thunderbolts, escorted the great bomber armada out to Berlin and back again.

*Photos, U.S. Official, Associated Press, Planet News*

# R.A.F. Drops 5½-ton Bombs—with This Effect

SELECTED TARGETS OF GREAT SIZE are now being dealt with by special British bombs of huge weight and enormous power. One of these 12,000-lb. "factory-busters" has such devastating effect that the flash of the explosion turns night into day. Describing how the aircraft, relieved of such a tremendous weight in a split second, leaps upward, one of our airmen said, "When you release the bomb it feels like pressing the button of a lift and finding yourself ten storeys up before you can take your finger off the button."

This latest air weapon was used by a small force of Lancasters on the night of February 8, 1944, to smash the large Gnome-le-Rhône aero-engine works at Limoges, in France, and again on March 2 to shatter the vast German aircraft factory at Albert, Northern France.

The Gnome-le-Rhône factory before the R.A.F. dropped their 5½-tonners is seen on the right ; and, below, when the bombers had departed. All the machine shops, the boiler house and the transformer stations were destroyed or severely damaged ; of 48 bays 21 were totally destroyed. Built in 1939 as one of the main repair depots of the French Air Force, it was later producing engines for Nazi aircraft. Now, indeed, has it felt the awesome weight of our mighty air arm.

The extra heavy, or "block-busting" type of bomb was first used in an attack on Naples, on October 21, 1941, when 4,000-lb. bombs. were dropped. Germany got her first 4,000-lb. pounding on July 8, 1942 ; Wilhelmshaven was the target. Two months later 8,000-lb. bombs rained down on Karlsruhe. And now this 12,000-lb. bomb . . . Crews who sally forth with such a cargo have strict orders to make sure of hitting the target or bring the bomb back for use on another occasion. See also pp. 700 and 701.

*Photos, British Official*

I HAVE sometimes said in the past, "There are too many Flag Days." But there is one coming on Tuesday, April 4, which has my very heartiest good wishes. A number of sailors' aid societies are going to collect money to provide more hostels for sailors when they are ashore. In ordinary times men who are too far from their homes or have no homes to go to nearly always go to the same place where they are known, where they meet acquaintances, where they can pick up news that interests them. Now these hostels are often too full up to take in their "regulars," who find themselves at a loose end. The number of seafaring men has greatly increased and the need for more accommodation is urgent. No one better deserves help of the kind. A chaplain of a hostel tells me many stories of the dogged devotion to duty shown by the men he comes across. One old fellow of 72, who had been seven times torpedoed, was asked if he didn't think of retiring. He retorted angrily, "Don't the women and children want the stuff we bring?" A boy of 17, torpedoed on his first voyage, had to lie up for a bit, but when someone inquired, "What shall you do when you're well again?" he just said simply, "I shall get another ship." Don't forget: April 4, and give as generously as you can.

THE case for the small trader is very persuasively put in the pamphlet which Mr. Erskine-Hill, a Conservative M.P., has published with the approval of Conservative Party headquarters. If these little shopkeepers were right in supposing that Board of Trade inspectors are specially down on them for small infractions of the law, mere technical offences, they would certainly receive public sympathy in even greater measure than they do now. But this wants a great deal of proving before it can be accepted as fact. It is, of course, always the hope of an inspector, whatever he inspects, to justify his existence by catching someone doing what he "didn't oughter." It would be very dull, going round day after day and never finding anything wrong. Also, it might suggest to the authorities that inspection was not, after all, necessary. But the Board of Trade people are not likely to be more generally in favour of the multiple stores and the big establishments than they are to be friends of the small trader. The whole question is difficult. The little shop does useful work. Many prefer its homely atmosphere. The big place offers a wider choice. But there ought to be room for both.

SOME people I know are inclined to treat the American Presidential Election preliminary skirmishes more seriously than they need. The New Statesman calls it "a major disaster, like the fall of France" that the United States should be torn in the middle of the war by this orgy of the worst kind of political intoxication. So it looks to those who are far away and who have never been in America while a Presidential struggle was in progress. On the surface there appear to be signs of disunity on every subject ; of utter dishonesty in the tossing to and fro of accusations and abuse ; of the most important issue (in this case the War) being lost sight of in the pursuit of trivialities. But below the surface the national mind works much as usual. I do not believe the will to victory will be in any serious degree impaired. There is acute danger, however, for the will to lasting peace in such an appeal as Thomas Dewey is making to German-Americans. Peace terms, he urges, "must not be too rigid." That is an open bid for the German-American vote, which is large in many States of the Union. Is it any wonder some Russians should be asking whether they are to take Allied assurances at their face value ?

ANOTHER plea to us "not to be beastly to the Germans," as Noel Coward put it in that satirical song of his, is put forward by Mr. Brailsford in a Penguin booklet on Our Settlement with Germany, which has been denounced strongly by The Spectator, usually on the same side as the author of Scarlet and Steel and so many other works of very great value and interest. He now

AIR MARSHAL SIR R. M. HILL, K.C.B., M.C., A.F.C., whose appointment, at the age of 49, as A.O.C. of the Air Defence of Great Britain—an organization replacing Fighter Command—was announced on Feb. 29, 1944. Previously he was A.O.C. No. 12 (Fighter) Group, R.A.F. *Photo, British Official*

says "the Germans need a psychiatrist rather than a policeman," meaning that they are not really responsible for their crimes and bestialities and should be treated like hospital patients, not as criminals. That sort of appeal may have some effect on people who have not experienced German cruelty and harsh contempt, but it will not prevent the Germans from being regarded with detestation, and despised as well for their folly in worshipping creatures like the Kaiser and Hitler, for a great many years to come. It will hardly be safe for them to leave their own country and, as civil war is almost certain to rage there, it won't be very comfortable for them to stop at home. Whether the United Nations will really send "policemen," that is, armies of occupation, to try to hinder Nazis and anti-Nazis (of whom there will be plenty when they are soundly beaten) from destroying each other, is doubtful, I fancy.

WHEN a question was asked in the House of Commons the other day about delay in clearing up ruins after air raids, and the questioner, Lt.-Col. Astor of The Times, referred to this delay as reminding him of "If seven maids with seven mops swept it for half a year," it occurred to me that scarcely any book is so frequently quoted as Through the Looking Glass. Why, that very poem in which the above passage occurs bulges with lines that are continually heard. The Walrus and the Carpenter are two of the most familiar figures in our minds. This is an interesting illustration of the unexpectedness of literary fame. Recently the B.B.C. Brains Trust was asked a question: Could they say what books would be still read 100 years hence ? Of course they couldn't even make a guess. When Lewis Carroll published Alice's Adventures in Wonderland, in 1865, and its continuation, Through the Looking Glass, seven years later, no one—probably least of all Carroll himself (or Charles Lutwidge Dodgson, to give him his correct name)—could have imagined that these stories written by a mathematician for children would take a permanent place in literature.

ONE of my most unforgettable cinema memories is that of Emil Jannings as the magnificent hotel porter in The Last Laugh—I think that was the title of the film in which that gorgeously attired personage was degraded to wearing ordinary clothes, in which he seemed to dwindle and collapse, and then at last he was restored to his glory and looked more resplendent than ever. I thought of him when I read that in New York there are to be women hotel porters, because of the scarcity of men. Can women ever really take the place of those most useful as well as most impressive guides, philosophers and friends to the hotel guest ? Whatever you wanted to know, the hall porter would know it. You asked him about trains, about plane routes, about the best shops, about the amusements to go to. He was always helpful, affable, slightly condescending, but cheerfully reassuring whatever difficulty you might be in. He was not so prominent a figure in English hotels as in those abroad; and as in the United States the duties of the hall porter on the Continent were divided up between two or three lesser luminaries. So perhaps New York will not feel the change so much as would, say, Nice or Genoa, Scheveningen or Copenhagen.

WHY do so many of us like noise? When we rejoice, it seems as if we must do it noisily. If we want to honour a man, we cheer and sing For he's a jolly good fellow. When we part after a festive gathering in the hope that it may be followed by many more, we roar out Auld Lang Syne. In Moscow every Soviet victory (and they happen pretty often) is announced by salvos of cannon fire. This is a curious survival for a State that claims to be in the front rank of progress and culture : a survival of an instinct that was strong in the very earliest men. Whether they were glad or frightened, they felt they must create an uproar to relieve their exuberance or raise their courage. The Chinese in quite recent times let off fire crackers to scare away evil spirits. Mexican soldiers fire their rifles in the air—or did, at any rate, during their last war with the United States, believing that a loud report can be as efficacious as bullets in driving off the enemy. Beating huge drums is a method used by many African tribes to celebrate a victory or inspire warriors with determination to avenge a defeat. Many people, both in and out of the Forces, find the noisiness of this war one of its most disagreeable features. Tanks make a more hideous din than anything did before they were invented. The London A.A. barrage is something never heard in the world before.

# Our Fire-Fighters Beat the Fire-Raisers

*Photo, Keystone*

**FLAMES LIGHT UP A LONDON BUILDING** and reveal the men fighting the conflagration during one of the Luftwaffe's recent intensified night attacks on the Capital. The average Nazi-raised fire is short-lived, thanks to co-operation between the National Fire Service and the street fire parties. Well trained in the breathing space since the 1940-41 attacks, they help to cope now heroically with all that Germany can send down in the incendiary line. More than 30,000 instructors are responsible for the coaching of over 5,000,000 men and women fire guards.

Printed in England and published every alternate Friday by the Proprietors, THE AMALGAMATED PRESS, LTD., The Fleetway House, Farringdon Street, London, E.C.4. Registered for transmission by Canadian Magazine Post. Sole Agents for Australia and New Zealand : Messrs. Gordon & Gotch, Ltd. ; and for South Africa : Central News Agency, Ltd.—March 31, 1944. S.S. *Editorial Address :* JOHN CARPENTER HOUSE, WHITEFRIARS, LONDON, E.C.4.

Vol 7 # The War Illustrated N° 178

Edited by Sir John Hammerton

SIXPENCE

APRIL 14, 1944

ON GUARD IN THE AZORES, Allied mid-Atlantic air base, this corporal of the R.A.F. Regiment strikes a modern note against the ancient stone sentry-box of his observation post. " By means of aircraft operating from the Azores," said Mr. Churchill and Mr. Roosevelt in a joint statement, " we have been able to improve the protection to our convoys and to diminish the area in which enemy U-boats were free from attention by our forces." See also p. 541. *Photo, British Official: Crown Copyright*

NO. 179 WILL BE PUBLISHED FRIDAY, APRIL 28

# Our Roving Camera Inspects Air Raid Fighters

SEARCHLIGHT projector operator (left) is a member of the A.T.S. Girls snap into action to illumine the targets for the A.A. guns. A.T.S. also serve at fire control instruments, command posts and plotting rooms.

WOMEN SWITCHBOARD OPERATORS at the London Region Fire Control Room, headquarters of the N.F.S. This switchboard is the nerve centre through which the operations officer receives reports of fires and through which he issues his fire-fighting orders.

CIVIL DEFENCE PERSONNEL labour doggedly, with a mobile crane, to clear away debris after a direct hit. Folks may be trapped beneath the rubble masses : men of the Rescue Service attend to these when contact has been made.

ROCKET GUNS of the multiple-barrelled type being unloaded (above) for swift assembly ; on its mobile mounting (left) one hurls salvos of rockets into the night sky. Large numbers of batteries are now operating, mostly manned by Home Guards. In its original form the rocket weapon was designed for defence against the low-flying dive-bomber. Salvos were then fired, experimentally, at high-flying night raiders ; the first battery went into action in the spring of 1941, and now rocket guns are used with outstanding success against targets whose speed sometimes exceeds 400 miles per hour at 25,000 ft. The propellant, developed in Britain, is also in production in the Middle East, and its secrets have been made known to U.S. Army Ordnance by the British authorities. It is in use in various theatres of operations.

*Photos. British Official, Fox, Associated Press*

# THE BATTLE FRONTS

*by E. Royston Pike*

**RUSSIA** A thousand days of the Russian war! Did Hitler realize the sinister significance of March 18, 1944, as he dropped the calendar-leaf into his waste-paper basket? If so, what thoughts of the "might have been" must have surged through his tormented brain, what a load of bitter disappointment and falsified hopes must have weighed down his spirit! A thousand days of fighting, of vast conquests, of tremendous victories: his troops almost within sound of the Kremlin's bells, within sight of the peaks of the Caucasus.

Then the dreadful débâcle of Stalingrad, the beginning of the retreat (of course, then, it was easy to make out that it was just a retirement "according to plan"), the abandonment of the Donetz, the retirement to the Dnieper. And now the guns of Moscow were booming for yet another Russian victory, the greatest of the campaign, perhaps the greatest of the war, a victory which must find a place in any future collection of "decisive battles of the world."

Up to the beginning of March 1944 the Germans in Russia were retreating in good order. Every mile of ground was stubbornly contested, and though Nazi losses were terrific it was unfortunately all too certain that the Red Army too was losing the cream of its young fighting strength. The German commentators breathed an almost audible sigh of relief—"The front of Von Manstein stands firm."

THEIR satisfaction was short lived. On March 4 the 1st Ukrainian Front group of Russian armies under Marshal Zhukov delivered a terrific punch from the direction of Shepetovka. In 24 hours the Russians advanced 30 miles; by March 7 they had reached the suburbs of Tarnopol and had cut the supremely important Lwow-Odessa railway along a 12-mile stretch at Volochisk. Here for the time being the advance was slowed up, though not stayed. Somehow Von Manstein scraped up some reserves from Lwow and pushed them into the gap.

Practically simultaneously another great Russian offensive was launched four or five hundred miles away to the south-east. Here

the attackers were General Malinovsky's 3rd Ukrainian Front; and a week's battle, of furious swirling movement, brought them into the Black Sea port of Kherson.

Still the amazing Russians had not shot all their bolts. Another group, the 2nd Ukrainian Front under Marshal Koniev, on March 10 attacked the Germans in the Uman sector, about half-way between the other two offensives, and in a series of forced marches swept through Uman, abandoned by the Germans in what was described by the Russians for the first time as a panic flight, to the banks of the Bug.

Here Manstein's men might have been expected to halt and recover. The river was broad, and swollen with spring floods. On every side the black earth district was a morass of mud, and military commentators spoke knowingly of difficulties engendered by the thaw. But the Russians showed that they had taken the measure of "General Mud." Driving their tanks and transports through the squelching mass, they covered a dozen or even twenty miles a day, driving the enemy before them. They reached the Bug, they crossed it on March 15, they pursued the broken foe beyond it to where the Dniester suggested another line on which some sort of stand might be made.

From the Bug to the Dniester is a matter of fifty miles. The Russians covered the distance in a couple of days. The fact speaks

**VICTORY FLAG OVER SATTELBERG, New Guinea, Japanese stronghold captured by the Australians on Nov. 26, 1943. Hoisting the flag is Sgt. T. C. Derrick, V.C., D.C.M., who silenced 10 enemy machine-gun posts and made this victory possible. His V.C. is the 14th to be won by an Australian in this war.**
*Photo, Sport & General*

OUR *distinguished military commentator, Maj.-Gen. Sir Charles Gwynn, K.C.B., D.S.O., has unfortunately had to undergo an operation recently which must, for a time, prevent his maintaining his regular contribution to our pages. We hope, however, that after the lapse of a few issues he may be able to resume that long series of authoritative reviews on the War situation which has become an established and greatly appreciated feature of* THE WAR ILLUSTRATED.—Ed.

volumes as to the wholesale rout of Manstein's divisions, their disorganization, perhaps even their disintegration. But not, it would seem, their collapsing morale. The number of prisoners claimed by the Russians was significantly small. The Nazis, or most of them, were still resisting fiercely, though their resistance was that of men who have no longer any hope of victory, but who fear defeat more than death. All the same, the Russians captured 200 tanks intact, which suggests that for a time at least the enemy thought only of flight.

MARCH 18 was the 1,000th day of the war, and the Russians were in jubilant mood as they announced from Moscow another series of tremendous victories. Koniev's 2nd Ukrainian Front had captured Yampol on the northern bank of the Dniester, and looked across the 400 yards of river to the cottages of the Bessarabian villages on the farther bank. Malinovsky's 3rd Ukrainian Front had completely smashed the German 6th Army—reformed since Paulus' surrender at Stalingrad a year earlier. Marshal Zhukov's 1st Ukrainians had taken Zmerinka, on the Odessa-Lwow railway, and in honour of their victory Moscow guns fired a dozen salvos. During the preceding fortnight the German casualties (said Moscow) totalled almost a quarter of a million, of whom 100,000 were dead.

It was indeed a great victory, and the Russians were swift to exploit it. The Germans attempting to cross the Dniester

were mercilessly harried, and their massed transport, awaiting their ferries, was bombed and bombed again by the Stormoviks. Then, on March 19, the Red Army crossed the river in strength, some of the bridges having been captured intact before the German demolition squads could get to work. Koniev got his tanks across, and within a few hours they were deep into Bessarabia.

WHEREUPON all Hitler's satellites in the Balkans shivered with apprehension. Rumanian quislings started packing their bags. Pro-ally—or so they would. like it to be deemed—Rumanians and Bulgars and Hungarians got ready to depart on peace missions to the Allies. Hitler found his south-eastern wall collapsing, the battle for the Danube about to begin; and on March 21 his troops converted Hungary and her neighbours into militarily occupied countries such as France had been since 1940. March 21—another fateful anniversary. It was on that day in 1918 that the Kaiser's hosts plunged through the mists on the Somme to overwhelm General Gough's Fifth Army and, so the Germans boasted, win the war. But November 11 was only eight months ahead.

**BURMA** While the world-shaking battle was raging across the plains of southern Russia a very different struggle was developing in the Burmese jungles. In March both the Japanese and the Allies were making offensives, although in widely separated zones. From the north, Gen. Stilwell's little army of Americans and Chinese was developing a pincer movement down the Hukawng valley against Myitkyina, the Japanese key base on the Irrawaddy. About a hundred miles to the south a force of British airborne troops was endeavouring to get astride the railway and river communications of Myitkyina (see p. 708 for Burma front illustrations).

In the Chin hills, still more to the south, the Japanese were hitting at British and Indian forces guarding the approach to India. Judged on the scale of the Burma campaign this was a major offensive; but many more troops were fighting near Cassino in Italy than there were in the whole of Burma.

**Lieut.-Gen. H. D. G. CRERAR, C.B., D.S.O. (left), now commander of the 1st Canadian Army (in succession to Lieut.-Gen. A. G. L. MacNaughton), seen in Italy with Lieut.-Gen. E. L. M. Burns, O.B.E., M.C., one of his Corps commanders.**
*Photo, Canadian Official*

# With Our 14th Army in Japanese-Held Burma

JUNGLE AIR BASE and Army stronghold for the Allies were established when an airborne force seized Japanese-occupied territory in Upper Burma, it was announced on March 17, 1944. Air Marshal Sir John E. A. Baldwin, C.-in-C. Tactical Air Force of Eastern Command (1, right). A Vengeance dive-bomber returns to its Arakan base (5). Ghurka riflemen (3) who escaped from a Japanese ambush and saved the battalion treasure chest. Men of the 1st Punjab Regt. in a forward position (2). A casualty is carried aboard a hospital sampan (4). *Photos, Indian Official and Keystone*

# Bloody is the Fighting for the Ruins of Cassino

IN THE STREETS and in the hills around Cassino, on March 29, 1944, the 5th Army were fighting with utmost gallantry against an enemy fanatically defending a position which, after weeks of battle, had on March 15, 1944, been pounded to a mass of rubble by our bombers and artillery in attacks of a scale unprecedented for a target of comparable size. Cassino, strategically placed and well adapted for defence, has long held up the Allied forces. Beyond it lies the road to Rome.

Chief among the German troops whose lives are daily being thrown away in its defence, are the men of the 1st Parachute Regiment, whom our Forces first encountered at Ortona, in Italy. There they put up a house-to-house defence when they were assailed by the 8th Army in December 1943. Now their numbers are dwindling—and they are soldiers of a quality which cannot be replaced from the Nazi reserves.

In the words of one of our war correspondents in a recent cable home : " Dogged resistance and skill of concealment are part of the German parachutist's make-up. They are street-fighting specialists. Here are two examples of the kind of fight they put up : " One German unit was buried in a cellar on the day of the great Allied bombardment. It took them four days to extricate themselves. Instead of retiring exhausted, they set about building a strong-point in the rubble in which they had been buried . . . A New Zealand unit took 50 German prisoners from a house in Cassino. When they returned to the house after handing over their prisoners, they found another 50 Germans in possession."

Prolongation of the bitter fighting is due in large measure to lengthy tunnels deep beneath the town, some of these forming connexions between series of strongpoints among the rubble and all of them providing the Nazi troops with protection against even our heaviest bombardments.

**EVERY UNIT OF ALLIED AIR POWER** in the Mediterranean area was concentrated in the greatest air attack ever delivered against so small a target when they shattered the city of Cassino (below). Immediately after the bombing, British and U.S. artillery added a terrific barrage to complete the destruction of the ancient stone buildings which still concealed and protected enemy gun emplacements. Into the maelstrom went these Allied patrol vehicles (above), among which were Red Cross units bearing their flag of mercy.

*Photos, U.S. Official*

# THE WAR AT SEA

### by Francis E. McMurtrie

SEVERAL weeks after the completion of the operation, the Admiralty released particulars of the destruction of six U-boats in the Atlantic by the Second Escort Group. This group comprised the war-built sloops Starling, Kite, Magpie, Wild Goose and Woodpecker, under the command of Captain F. J. Walker, R.N., as senior officer (see page 711). Before the war Captain Walker was in command of the experimental anti-submarine establishment at Portland, and the theories which he then formed have been carried into practice with great success in the past eighteen months, more U-boats having been destroyed by the Second Escort Group than by any other.

Over a period of 20 days the sloops repeatedly made contact with U-boats before these could attack the convoys they were

of warship construction that has been in progress in this country and the United States for three years past. All the time these vessels are increasing in numbers, whereas the destruction of U-boats during 1943 was so considerable that the total available remained more or less stationary.

### HEROIC Son of a Naval Captain Proves that Heredity Counts

Furthermore, personnel of the escort craft have continued to gain valuable experience during this time. That they have thus reached a very high standard of efficiency in submarine hunting is illustrated by the latest exploits of the Second Escort Group, as briefly related. Captain Walker, whose fine record of service has gained him the C.B. and the D.S.O., is in his forty-eighth year.

States Navy's submarine flotillas cannot be considered unduly heavy. Up to the time of writing they include 23 units, all but four of them of modern design.

Since the number of new submarines launched last year from American shipyards was about sixty, there is little consolation to be found by the enemy in the destruction of about one-third of that number in a space of over twice that period. No doubt General Tojo had these facts in mind when he told Parliament in Tokyo on March 22, 1944, that the situation had become "extraordinarily acute." He had just learned of the annihilation of yet another convoy of reinforcements and supplies dispatched to Wewak, the main Japanese base in New Guinea. At this rate it will not be long before that port will be in as hopeless a position as Rabaul in New Britain, and Kavieng in New Ireland, both of which are now cut off from succour and are under frequent bombardment by the Allied fleet. When these strongholds are eliminated, it will be the turn of Truk. Now that the Japanese airfield at Lorengau, in the Admiralty group, has been taken, and the remaining atolls in the Marshalls are falling one by one, it should soon be possible to bring Truk under attack by shore-based aircraft as well as carrier-borne planes.

### SHIPS Built in Britain and U.S. for Transfer to Red Fleet

A good deal of interest was aroused by the report that the Soviet Government was about to take over one-third of the Italian fleet now operating with the Allies. This appears to have arisen through a misreading of some remarks by President Roosevelt, who actually intended to imply that the Red Fleet was to be reinforced by a quantity of fresh tonnage, built in British and American yards, equal in the aggregate to about one-third of the Italian total. Already a number of mine-sweepers, motor-torpedo-boats and sub-marine chasers have been transferred to the Russian flag from the United States Navy, and more ships will follow in the near future.

It would seem that the question was raised in the first instance by the Soviet Government, which is anxious to replace its naval losses. No official statement of these has appeared, but there is reason to believe that the cruiser Krasni Krim has been sunk in the Black Sea ; and it is possible that her sister ship, the Chervonaya Ukraina, has also been lost. A good many destroyers and submarines have also become casualties, and the enemy have claimed that two of the cruisers in the Baltic have been sunk.

THERE are three old battleships, the Marat, Oktiabrskaya Revolutia and Pariskaya Kommuna, dating from 1911, which are long overdue for replacement. The first-named is believed to have been badly damaged by German air attacks on Kronstadt during 1942. In these circumstances it may well have been suggested that three Italian battleships, of approximately the same age and displacement, but reconstructed and modernized throughout, should be earmarked for replacement of the three old Russian ships. These three Italian vessels are the Andrea Doria, Caio Duilio and Giulio Cesare, all of which submitted to Allied control at Malta last September.

At the moment there does not appear to be any particular use for battleships in the Soviet Navy, except for bombardment of German-held coasts in the Gulf of Finland or in the Black Sea ; and for such purposes the Italian ships could hardly be made available while Denmark and the Aegean islands remain in enemy hands. Actually, the principal Russian need at the moment would seem to be for vessels capable of aiding in the escort of convoys to the White Sea, such as cruisers, destroyers, sloops, frigates and minesweepers.

**A HANDSHAKE FROM THE COMMANDER** of the sloop H.M.S. Aberdeen obviously pleases the dog, which was found floating on timber miles out in the Atlantic after the French merchant vessel which had owned it had been torpedoed. Adopted by the Aberdeen as ship's mascot, it was promptly christened " H.M.V.," as when rescued it was sitting in the same position as the well-known gramophone record advertisement dog. *Photo, British Official*

guarding. In five instances persistent depth charging resulted in the destruction of the enemy submarines under water, evidence in the shape of wreckage and bodies being seen floating. In the sixth case, the submarine was forced to surface after five and a half hours of depth charging and was engaged by the guns of the Starling, Captain Walker's vessel. Her crew at once abandoned ship, the U-boat sinking stern first immediately afterwards. Altogether 51 survivors were rescued and made prisoners. H.M.S. Woodpecker was hit by a torpedo, and afterwards foundered ; but not a casualty was incurred.

SUCH successes as these illustrate the results of the system which is now employed to repel submarine attacks on shipping. Though it is partly the fruit of experience, it could not be carried into effect were it not that an ample force of escort vessels—destroyers, sloops, frigates and corvettes—is now available, as the result of the immense programme

He is the son of a captain in the Royal Navy, evidence that heredity sometimes counts.

FORTUNATELY, Japan is in no position to build warships in such large numbers as the Allies have done, She is thus constrained to watch her fine mercantile fleet gradually dwindling as the result of the excessive demands made on it by war in the Pacific and Indian Oceans. Had it remained intact, the task of maintaining communications with the Dutch Indies, the Philippines, Burma, Siam, Malaya, and the various island groups seized by the Japanese in 1941-42, would still have taxed its capabilities. As it is, the losses inflicted by Allied surface warships, submarines and aircraft are believed to have reduced the total tonnage available by at least one-third ; and as time goes on Allied naval and air strength expands, causing the rate of loss to rise. For such important results the losses sustained by the United

# 5 British Sloops Sink 6 U-Boats in 20 Days

MOST TRIUMPHANT U-BOAT HUNT OF THE WAR recently ended with a tremendous welcome home for the sloop H.M.S. Starling (1), whose Captain Walker, C.B., D.S.O., R.N., is seen on the bridge taking a hasty snack whilst in action (3, right). Four other sloops of the Second Escort Group, commanded by Capt. Walker, assisted in the sinking of six U-boats within 20 days; an exploding depth charge from H.M.S. Kite throws up a great column of water (4), and the crew of H.M.S. Wild Goose display their battle-flag (2). See p. 710.   *Photos, British Official : Topical*

# The Fleet Oiler Waits On Our Fighting Ships

Her cargo is crude oil for the big ships' furnaces, and petrol for the planes they carry, or for the brood of an aircraft carrier. A warship may be stranded without fuel, unable to steam, steer, or anchor—a sitting shot for the enemy ; all its hopes are then placed in the speedy services of one of these Handmaidens of the Navy, whose work is described by CAPT. FRANK H. SHAW.

THERE is one type of ship which seldom gets the credit she deserves, although without her the Navy would be to all intents and purposes immobilized. The role played by the Fleet Oiler is unique, for she differs considerably from the coal-burning Navy's colliers. Seldom was the necessary fuel transferred from ship to ship in open sea ; coaling was a laborious, messy and difficult task at anchor ; at sea, with a wind blowing, it was practically impossible.

The oiler has changed all that. By her sturdy work she enables the fighting ships to perform exceptional voyages, lengthens their capacity of action, and generally keeps them tended. Her 12,000 tons of invaluable oil is always at the Navy's service ; and if the battleships, cruisers and destroyers cannot break off their duties to come to her, she simply lifts her anchors and goes—at full speed—to them.

Normally she lies, well-hidden, in some lonely loch or fjord with a perpetual brood of hungry vessels nuzzling at her, for all the world like a sow with her litter. She is officially listed as a Fleet Auxiliary, being both Royal Navy and Merchant Navy, and her crew is hand-picked, because specialists are needed to perform the oiler's onerous tasks. It is man's work to bring a laden oiler alongside a towering battleship in a seaway, when both vessels are sheering awkwardly under helm, and high seas are doing their utmost to frustrate the necessary union.

Yet the warships must have oil—not only heavy oil to feed their furnaces, but high octane spirit to fill all the tanks of the planes carried. Or an aircraft carrier may demand attention. Also the oiler acts to some extent as general supply ship to the mobile fleet : she serves as mail-boat, beef-boat, canteen filer. Also, possessing as she usually does, a commodious sick-bay with an adequate personnel of doctors and sick-berth stewards, she can, on occasion, serve as a useful clearing hospital for casualties which need more specialized care than is obtainable aboard a fighting ship liable to meet hot action every time smoke is spotted on the skyline.

AN oiler's existence when at her moorings in shelter can be prosaic and monotonous. For lonely harbours are usually selected, so that refuelling warships can come and go without interfering with normal traffic ; but there is always the variety of some ship, great or small, appearing out of nowhere with a peremptory demand for the precious fluid that is the Navy's life-blood. And the people of such client-ships usually have interesting stories to tell, of breathless attacks from the air, of bombardments of enemy coasts, of sorties on stealthy convoys, of pitched battles between giant-ship and giant-ship off Norwegian coasts.

The close-packed crews of destroyers and corvettes like to clamber aboard and stretch their cramped legs in the spaciousness of the oiler, although her lean, low decks are hampered by countless gadgets designed for quick action in refuelling. Although, when moored, immune from the actual hazards of seagoing, the daily—sometimes hourly—arrivals bring the tang of spindrift with them ; as often as not they are ice-coated and bleached from constant battling with unfriendly seas, and every man-Jack aboard the visitors is eager for mail. So that a friendly atmosphere prevails all around. There is a sort of motherliness about the oiler, offering a cordial welcome home.

There is nothing outstandingly beautiful about these glorified tankers. Indeed, with engines and funnels aft, a long expanse of deck, broken only by the midships superstructure of the bridge and officers' accommodation, she is ugly, looking draggled and sluttish alongside the sleek, razor-lined craft that come to her. She is strictly utilitarian. But her crew know their job inside out, by day and by night, for when a warship needs fuel she usually needs it in a hurry. And, as Nelson said, five minutes might spell the difference between defeat and victory. Lights may not be exhibited ; the coupling of oil-hose has very often to be done in black darkness, with rain sluicing like Niagara, or snow falling almost impenetrably.

## Decks too Hot to Walk Upon

The atmosphere aboard the oiler is close and oppressive, especially below, for, as any moment might bring a call for what she carries, the liquid fuel must be kept liquid by the steampipes interspersing the giant tanks. For crude oil such as is used in ships' furnaces solidifies if not kept at a certain temperature ; and it can happen that the decks are actually too hot to walk upon. Refuelling whilst at anchor is a simple matter in many ways : it merely means that the linking hose-pipes must be attached to the warships' intakes, and the pumps set going for as long as is necessary to rebunker.

There is, of course, a constant liability to attack from the air, since the enemy's reconnaissance aircraft are over quite often. If an oiler can be sunk, it means delay in the movements of the ships dependent on her. And during that delay, commerce-raiders might break through the cordon and escape to open sea, where an infinite amount of damage can be wrought. So the oiler is well-armed, though her guns seem as if fitted as an afterthought ; they do not blend into her outlines in the same way as do those of fighting ships. But they are not the less efficacious

on that account ; they have brought down diving raiders wholesale.

It is frequently necessary for the fleet oiler to leave her moorings and steam to a busier port to replenish her supplies and be overhauled. She needs to go warily on such voyages, for the lurking U-boat is very watchful, and she would be a good prize for the scurrying E-boats that are always waiting on opportunity. Since the oiler usually owns a good turn of speed, escorts are not considered essential ; and in case of attack she occasionally has to fight her own way through such hazards as may offer.

THE fact that enemy surface ships are more or less penned in to close waters limits the oiler's activities. To maintain the tireless patrol of the misted Northern seas demands much steady steaming ; but not much of it is performed at high speed, for high speed devours oil greedily. The great battleships and the tiny corvettes alike can usually manage to make port before supplies run out. But it can happen that a warship, detached on duty, runs short of fuel ; and when that happens the fleet oiler has to go to the customer.

The fleet oiler's navigation staff is superexcellent. They must be so, to locate that trivial pinpoint presented by a small ship in the middle of a mighty sea. For the most part wireless silence must be maintained, in case the location of the warship is betrayed to the enemy ; at night time " darken-ship " is the order. Only infinitesimal lights may be shown at the best of times. Once the " dry " ship is spotted, expert seamanship is necessary to bring the two alongside ; and mooring gear of superior quality must be employed to hold them together, with great fenders dropped between hull and hull to take the chafe of the rubbing, grinding sides.

It is when sea-warfare finds wider fields than the narrow waters of the North that the fleet oiler shows her outstanding value. It often happens that a fleet of big ships must steam many thousands of miles at high speed to perform a vital mission. She must accompany the fleet or steam out from harbour to intercept it at a signal ; and she must, ranging alongside ship after empty ship, replenish their stores. Such a task means long working hours for the crew. In occasional instances the battle formation of the fleet cannot be disturbed, and the refuelling must take place at night, in total darkness, with the ships reeling drunkenly. Crude oil for the fires, refined petrol for the aircraft : no wonder the oiler is called the Handmaiden of the Navy.

**THROUGH FEED-PIPES** connecting the fleet oiler and H.M.S. Warspite (right) the life-blood of the Royal Navy flows. On the services of the tanker the several successes of the Warspite have depended, as is the case with other of our fighting ships in this war.

*Photo, British Official*

# Beaufighters Blast Enemy Merchant Shipping

CENTRE OF CONCENTRATED CANNON FIRE from Beaufighters of R.A.F. Coastal Command escorted by Spitfires of the Air Defence of Great Britain, this enemy merchantman (1) is one of several attended to off the Dutch coast on March 1, 1944 ; near misses are registered (3) as torpedo-carrying Beaufighters take up the attack; later, two torpedoes struck home. In the Aegean also our Beaufighters are busy ; a well-aimed bomb has wiped this vessel (2) off the active list.

*Photos, British Official*

# Britain's Colonies in the War: No. 5—Fiji

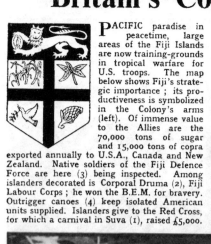

PACIFIC paradise in peacetime, large areas of the Fiji Islands are now training-grounds in tropical warfare for U.S. troops. The map below shows Fiji's strategic importance ; its productiveness is symbolized in the Colony's arms (left). Of immense value to the Allies are the 70,000 tons of sugar and 15,000 tons of copra exported annually to U.S.A., Canada and New Zealand. Native soldiers of the Fiji Defence Force are here (3) being inspected. Among islanders decorated is Corporal Druma (2), Fiji Labour Corps ; he won the B.E.M. for bravery. Outrigger canoes (4) keep isolated American units supplied. Islanders give to the Red Cross, for which a carnival in Suva (1), raised £5,000.

# Australians Ejected the Japanese From These Hills

NEW GUINEA NATIVES, with sure-footed care for the casualties they carry, act as stretcher-bearers down the slopes of Shaggy Ridge in the Finisterre Range ; far below is the Faria River, with Ramu Valley beyond. Australian forces driving on from Sio, on the Huon Peninsula, which they captured on Jan. 16, 1944, threw out the Japanese from their Finisterre strongholds and by Feb. 10 had joined up with U.S. troops near the American beach-head at Saidor, 55 miles south-east of Madang.

*Photo, Australian Official*

# Mighty Sky-Freighters Sway the Fortunes of War

The entire picture of military operations has been transformed by transports of the air. They take to the Allied front lines the requirements of battle—men, guns, ammunition, food and water—and race back with the wounded. They can turn a last desperate stand into a resounding triumph, as MARK PRIESTLEY vigorously recounts in this article.

SOME of the fighting officers of R.A.F. Transport Command call the giant Avro York "Noah's Ark." They watch jeeps drive up the gangway of the 30-ton freighter plane and pack two by two into the plane's long interior. Smoothly the flying pantechnicons take to the air, cruise at 275 m.p.h., and presently land their cargoes at airfields that only a short time before were held by the enemy.

**Capt. RICHARD ALLEN**
Piloting a Liberator run by British Overseas Airways Corporation and carrying a maximum load, he reduced the record of flying time from Montreal to Britain to 11 hours 35 minutes.

**Wing Cmdr. LANCE WADE**
Before his death in Italy, on Jan. 1, 1944, in a communications aircraft, he had destroyed 25 enemy planes. His decorations include the D.S.O., D.F.C., and two bars.

*Photos, British Official: Crown Copyright; Planet News*

Air superiority is now a phrase implying far more than fighting supremacy. It stands for war strength in sealed packages, for guns and ammunition, crated Spitfires, and even aero engines flown direct to the battle line. In every theatre of war today Allied transport planes are delivering armies and keeping them supplied, carrying everything from water to love-letters, whisking up reinforcements and racing wounded back from the forward areas.

The American landings on the Marshall Islands were backed by a flood of such mighty freighters as the wooden Curtis Caravan, four-engined Lockheed Constellations and 70-ton Mars cargo flying boats. The landings on Italy were speeded directly and indirectly by transport aircraft. When Air Force Signals were putting Tripoli and Tunisia on the telephone to link all arms for immediate co-operation, key equipment was flown from England in 24 hours. Communications were established and forward squadrons and ground forces gained an advantage that has paved the road to Rome.

In these and many other ways the new era of troop and supply transport has recast the entire military picture of war. In a recent engagement, a transport pilot tipped the scales by delivering sorely needed anti-tank ammunition on time and in time. Only air transport could have done it.

In New Guinea the scene was changed over-night when every plane that could fly was ordered to the rescue of Kokoda. Outnumbered five to one, the battered but valiant 39th Battalion of Australians was making its last stand when air transport turned the tide. Guns and mortars, tins of beef and crates of blood plasma, boxes of ammunition and bundles of brown mosquito netting were dropped to the fighters on the ground. The tide of battle turned; within a month the Japanese advance had ended.

On the day the Australians took Gona village at bayonet point, hundreds of Americans were flown in to back them. One tiny strip of jungle averaged 59 transport landings a day. And the planes never returned empty. But for aircraft, wounded men would have taken two months to reach Port Moresby from the Buna front and many would have died on the way. The transports switched the wounded of the dawn attacks into modern operating theatres before midday.

The casualties removed from Italy by air constitute a high proportion of the total (see illus. p. 687). It is now no secret that R.A.F. Transport Command conveyed 14,898 patients from Sicily in a month. Many of the planes were air ambulances proper, others were twin-engined transports fitted with removable racks for stretchers. Outward bound the planes fly food, equipment and even oil to the front lines; homeward bound they evacuate sick and wounded men with organized and in all ways admirable efficiency.

On one occasion, 21 R.A.F. nursing sisters were moved 500 miles by "airmail" to render them available for a new hospital. Mobile field hospitals, complete with staff and equipment, are commonly flown across the Mediterranean. Air transport has cut the route back to Britain from Egypt or Africa by 6,000 miles, and the York aircraft which recently flew from the United Kingdom to Cairo in 18 hours was no more than making a routine flight.

Airmail alone to the Army Post Office in North Africa totalled 36,000 lb. last Christmas—enough to stuff six Fortresses—besides 1,500,000 airgraphs to the U.K. and over 3,000,000 from home. It may look easy when you see the transport pilot make a perfect landing dead on time after a 2,000-miles run, yet the task obviously has its dangers. "Wild-Cat" Wade, the Spitfire ace with a record of 25 enemy aircraft downed by his guns, was killed in a communications aircraft miles behind the line in Italy; and the transport planes often deliberately face higher hazards.

It is not generally known—although the fact has been disclosed by the U.S. Office of War Information—that compact aluminium printing presses and other goods, and messages of encouragement, have been dropped by parachute over enemy-occupied territory and even over Germany itself. Nor did a B.24 Liberator—in the hands of Captain Richard Allen and carrying a maximum load—make any fuss about clipping 21 minutes off the fastest Atlantic record.

THE transport flyer may face an airfield that has acquired an overnight covering of ten feet of snow, and his aircraft may have to be serviced at thirty degrees below zero. He may merely be shifting mails or he may help in the movement of squadrons and of troops. It is nothing, as Squadron-Leader Ernest Murray told me, to have to land in the dark with only car headlights providing an uncertain flare path.

Transport reliability may turn threatened defeat into victory. There is the example of the Indo-China wing of the U.S. Transport Command: more supplies have been ferried to China over the 17,000-foot hump of the Himalayas than were ever hauled along the Burma Road at the peak of its traffic. As a result, air attacks on the Japanese in China have been doubled and redoubled. In a practically non-stop stream of planes the pilots in December 1943 carried ten times more tonnage of vital supplies than in December 1942.

The Indo-China wing even has its own efficient rescue squadron. It seldom happens, but when plane crews are forced to jump or crash in wild country rescue planes are always ready. This minor detail alone is significant of the transport transformation. Coming over the horizon are such giants as our 32-ton Tudor and the 70-ton flying boats, larger than any aircraft yet made in this country, being built by the British firm of Saunders-Roe. The war is pulling into shape the new world of air transport. And our sky-freighters are making peace dawn all the sooner.

**JEEPS PACK INTO IT TWO BY TWO,** so they call R.A.F. Transport Command's four-engined Avro York the "Noah's Ark." It can carry 10 tons of war freight, has a 3,000-mile range and a speed of over 300 miles per hour. Alternative load is 50 passengers. See also illus. p. 412. PAGE 716 *Planet News*

# These Flying Pantechnicons Deliver War Goods

SKYMASTER IS THE NAME of this Douglas C.54 transport plane (1), which carries its own crane for loading and unloading supplies. Another of the 16 types used by America is this high-speed Lockheed Constellation (3). An Alaskan transport's engines are warmed up by the use of hot-air machines (2) before it takes off ; while in kindlier climate, another wings its way over Egypt's pyramids (4). A U.S. freighter on the India-China route (5); native cattle lie down in its welcome shade.

# Workshop for Germany: Switzerland's Dilemma

*As the waves of war advance, the neutral Swiss look over their ramparts. Compelled by force of circumstances to realize that their country is far more valuable to the Nazis as a workshop than it would be as a battlefield, what prospect do they now see? JOHN ENGLAND explains what the present holds for this peace-loving people and suggests what the future may bring.*

FOR three hundred years no foreign soldier has stepped on Swiss soil to wage war. For three hundred years no Swiss army has left its mountain home to wage war abroad. Yet despite this apparent immunity, the Swiss government decided in 1936 that the condition of Europe warranted a vast scheme of rearmament and general preparation for defensive war.

When I visited Switzerland in 1939 I was told that in the three preceding years this little republic of a mere four million people had sunk the enormous capital sum of £46,000,000 in arms. Not only that. The age limits for military service had been changed to rope in all men between 18 and 60. The annual period of training had been increased from three to four months, and the systematic exercise in marksmanship had been brought to a higher standard of efficiency. In addition, nation-wide organization of all the auxiliary services, A.R.P., Fire Service, Red Cross, and so on, had by that date been perfected, so that no citizen was without his or her assigned post against the possibility of invasion.

On the side of material, the modernization of this peace-loving State under the stress of the increasing threat of war was even more impressive. All types of arms and armaments had been modernized with a complete disregard of cost, from small arms and the ordinary soldier's equipment to the guns which today, invisible and rock-protected, give the vast wall of concrete and steel which stretches from Geneva to the Jura Mountains its offensive sting.

This defence system of concrete walls, pillboxes, machine-gun posts, and blockhouses, is Switzerland's first line of defence. Her second line is the ramparts of the Alps. And between these two every bridge and every highway is mined. In the Zurich district I saw something of this fine protective system and learned something, too, of how Switzerland stands prepared for the coming of any aggressor. I was told, for example, that complete mobilization could be carried out throughout the Confederation in forty-eight hours. I was told that within one hour every post of the outer defence system could be manned. And every man knows precisely what is his military task, and how to perform it without detailed orders.

SWITZERLAND is the only country that has kept her citizens armed and equipped for war through periods of peace. Then, as today, every Swiss of military age had in his own home rifle, ammunition, and uniform. Cavalrymen are given their own horses and have them at hand in their own stables. The order for mobilization finds the army virtually at battle stations. The alarm of invasion might, within sixty seconds, find every road and bridge blown sky-high. A single button controls the whole system.

Such, in brief, are the measures Switzerland has taken to preserve her neutrality. It is fair to ask: What obstacles would the invader meet? There are, first of all, the apparent obstacles—the mountains, the passes of which are covered by artillery. No doubt a military machine, such as Germany's, could, caring nothing for the cost in men and materials, force a way through. But there are limits to what the invader can do. For example, the bridges of the mountain roads,

and most of the highways themselves, are incapable of supporting the weight of heavy tanks, a circumstance which would restrict, too, the transport of artillery units—in the event of the system of defence by mines having broken down.

ON the air side, the Confederation has prepared itself thoroughly. Anti-aircraft defence naturally plays a more important role than fighting aircraft and bombers. It is, indeed, the central characteristic of the Swiss rearmament that it could never be taken for anything but a defensive machine. It could not be used for offence, for it lacks all those adjuncts which an army designed for movement in remote terrains finds to be absolutely essential.

**SWISS APPEAL FOR AID** for war-stricken children of the Occupied Countries, at a Red Cross exhibition in Lausanne, met with the sympathy of the citizens and resulted in substantial contributions. Work of the Red Cross among interned British and Empire troops in neutral Switzerland is mentioned in this page. *Photo, New York Times Photos*

What has transpired since Italy's fall to bring this four-year-old system of defensive measures in a neutral State into the news? The answer is simple. There are two routes by which the Germans were able to move men and war materials between Germany and Italy. The first was the Brenner. But the Brenner is a single-track line, and is not adapted to heavy war traffic of this kind. The other route is via the Simplon and St. Gotthard systems, with their tunnels (which have now been mined at both ends).

Switzerland is in a very difficult position. She is today virtually enclosed in the heart of continental Europe; and the envelope that encloses her is the military might of Nazi Germany. All her foreign trade is cut off, and at her frontiers Gestapo agents in civilian dress watch her customs officers and sometimes even interfere with them.

Like ourselves, Switzerland imports food and all her raw materials. It is quite wrong to envisage this lovely land as one wherein yodelling herdsmen roam the mountains in the wake of bell-tinkling cattle. Only 21 per cent of the population is on the land; no less than 44·6 per cent is employed in industry. At the time I was in Switzerland

I was told that the contingency that has now befallen had been provided against by the accumulation of vast stores of raw materials of all kinds, and of all essential foods.

It is these materials which have kept the wheels of Switzerland's industry turning—for Nazi Germany. Here she had no choice, since there was for her, ringed about as she has been, no alternative customer. From Zurich and the other great industrial centres, Switzerland has been pouring into Germany the precision instruments which are the natural transition of the watchmaker's craft to war work. As for food, it is upon the stocks of accumulated staple foods that the country has been feeding. Even so, there is no meat in Lausanne, or in Geneva, and precious little anywhere else.

Naturally that food shortage affects also the thousands of British and Empire soldiers who escaped from captivity after Italy capitulated and are now interned in Switzerland; they are, however, being looked after, so far as is possible, by the International Red Cross. They are allowed by the Swiss Government to be at liberty in towns and villages in about 20 centres, where their daily routine is a fairly rigorous one. Just now boredom is one of their chief handicaps, but this the Red Cross is trying hard to dispel by providing the officers and men with occupations and educational interests.

IF one considers Switzerland today from the Nazi standpoint it is plain she is far more valuable to the Germans as a workshop than as a battlefield. Faced by the terrible dilemma of risking war by closing her transport systems to all transit traffic, Switzerland has taken no action in the face of the plain Nazi threat and the overt hostile act of closing the Swiss-Italian frontier. The collapse of Italy and the occupation of the northern part of the "leg" by the Nazis and their puppet Italian government, has created a situation crucial for Switzerland, for German customs officers control all outside world openings and thus maintain what is, virtually, a state of blockade. What do the Swiss think of the Nazis and of the Democratic Nations in arms? In the 1914-18 war the line-up was one that followed the logic of language: German-speaking Swiss were pro-German, the French-speaking were pro-Ally. When I was in Zurich and Berne I found everywhere a complete detestation of all that Hitler's Germany stands for. I never met, or heard of, a single Swiss Nazi sympathizer. But since then Dr. Goebbels has been very active. His high-powered propaganda has been worked with skill and thoroughness. So far, in face of it, we have done nothing by way of counter-propaganda. The fact, therefore, has to be faced—the inevitable has happened: there has been some lapse here and there towards the Nazi view, evidenced from the pages of the Gazette de Lausanne, and La Suisse.

By and large, I think it may be taken as fairly certain that Switzerland has an overwhelming majority in favour of those things for which the United Nations stand and for which they are fighting. But, as Professor von Salis put it: "Part of the ransom which the Swiss people must pay for their policy of *stillesitzen* (neutrality) is to endure without hope of recompense or benefit great military, financial and personal sacrifices."

**SERVICING A LIBERATOR**  Charles Cundall, A.R.A.

**PARACHUTE DROP**  Henry Carr

## War Depicted by the Artist's Brush

CELEBRATING its fifth year of activity, Britain's War Artists' Advisory Committee has placed on view at The National Gallery, London, new oil paintings, water colours and drawings covering every aspect of the war in Europe, from N. Africa, Malta, Sicily and Italy to as far north as Iceland, and ranging from the picturesquely vigorous to the grimly dramatic. In this and the following pages is a selection of striking examples of the work of artists who have contributed to this display. There are eight official artists, appointed by the Committee, now attached to the Armed Forces.

*Exhibited at The National Gallery, London, Spring 1944. Crown copyright reserved.*

**A PATHFINDER**　　　　　　　　　　　　**J. Berry**

**HEAVY A.A. AND VALETTA IN DISTANCE DURIN**

**R.A.F. AIR SEA RESCUE LAUNCHES ; THE FISH QUAY BEYOND**　　　　　**Stephen Bone**

**MINES STORED IN MELI**

*Exhibited at The National Gallery*

Leslie Cole

**BRIGADIER DE LA BERE (MALTA)**

Leslie Cole

CILY

John Worsley

**WOOLWICH ARSENAL, 1943**

Robert Austin

**REFITTING H.M. SUBMARINE SHAKESPEARE**

Sir Muirhead Bone

**THE SINKING OF THE SCHARNHORST**

*Exhibited at The National Gallery, London, Spring 1944. Crown copyright reserved.*

Charles Pears

# VIEWS & REVIEWS

Of Vital War Books

by Hamilton Fyfe

WHY is the Eighth Army famous beyond any other army in the war? What gave it the bold spirit, the unflagging energy, the dogged determination to go through, which its commander praised so warmly when he left it? Why, when we see a book called I Was an Eighth Army Soldier (Gollancz, 4s. 6d.), do we feel sure there will be something in it that isn't in in other war books?

Well, if you are in doubt as to the answers to those questions, you will find yourself wiser when you have read the account Driver R. J. Crawford, of the R.A.S.C., gives of his experiences in the Desert. He did not write them himself. He narrated them to a R.A.S.C. major, who used to be on the Daily Express, and knew how to put them into the right words and sentences. The result couldn't be improved on. No collaboration was ever more successful. The pages from beginning to end tingle with life. They bring the sand and the brassy sun and the hot blue sky and the pests and the perils so vividly before us that even the most stay-at-home readers will feel they have been there. The nature of the fighting is not described so much as shown in the clear little pictures that emerge from the narrator's memory.

BUT first let us see why the Eighth Army was different (is still, perhaps—I don't know). Was it General Montgomery's doing? In large part, yes. His name became known as the names of Bonaparte and Garibaldi were known to their troops; it had the sound of a bugle-call; it made every man feel as if he were under the eye of the commander himself. He is, as I have said before on this page, an unusual man to be a general in any army—and most unusual to be one of the supreme leaders of our British forces. Plumer was popular, Allenby was popular, but to nothing like the same extent. Montgomery is admired and loved and trusted ("loved" is not too strong a word) because he is utterly unlike the ordinary British general, because he has a personality which compels respect as well as affection, because he seems to the troops to be always among them—in spirit, if not in body; always inspiring, encouraging them, not as a far-off brass hat, but as one of themselves.

You may call that "legend." But no legend ever grew up without some foundation on fact; as a rule legends have a pretty solid foundation. The idea the soldiers have of Montgomery is the right one. It couldn't be otherwise. An army does not make a hero of its commander without good reason. But that is not the whole story. We must go behind the popularity of the General and ask what it is founded on. Quite certainly, I think, it is founded on his being different, and on the difference being specially attractive to the troops. "Only a 'human general' could succeed in the Desert." Australians and South Africans took to him from the start. Indians, who are commended as the best night fighters ever, saw in him a man after their own hearts.

We British arrived in the Desert rather timorous and a little worried. We were very much "Hollywood" in our ideas. We pictured harems, swaying-robed Arabs on sleek Arabian horses, long lines of British soldiers tramping endlessly through the waterless sand, dropping by the wayside as thirst weakened and finally halted their faltering steps! It was all very Beau Geste and Foreign Legion!

But all that quickly wore off. They got to know the Desert. They "settled down to it with a sense of humour. They made the best of every bad situation." They were not, like the Italians, frightened of it. They did not even dislike it, as the Germans did,

## Revelations of an 8th Army Soldier

never feeling sure of themselves, never comfortable. They grinned and bore it. They made a joke of its discomforts. They said it wasn't such a bad old Desert after all. At Tobruk, when Crawford was drafted in there, after it had been battered by the enemy for more than half a year, they found nothing but "a shambles of stone and ironwork. Our job was to make a home for ourselves." They did it too. They found old bedsteads. A derelict rubber horse once used by sea-bathers was converted into a "li-lo." A camel skin served for a bedspread. On an ancient kitchen range they cooked. From a dump of German car batteries they rigged up their electric light.

FOOD abounded in certain "caches" stocked by the garrison as reserves. "We dug up cases of beer, Italian cheeses, tins of fruit, bottles of whisky, and hundreds of other luxury items." They built a dance hall. They gave dinner parties. "Invitations would be carried out with style and dignity, the host visiting his guests in their dug-outs and ceremoniously requesting their presence at, say, 7.30 p.m. It was this kind

of play-acting and humour that saved us from going mad." What drove them nearly crazy were the pests of the Desert rather than the attentions of the Hun.

At least the human enemy did have to rest occasionally. The flea was the torturer supreme and never rested. No matter what we did, it was always with us.

SOME relief was obtained by keeping tame mice. The fleas seemed to prefer them. The mice "became great companions and, apart from their flea-collecting propensities, we trained them into doing all kinds of tricks." Lizards they liked because they made war on flies, "easily the most dangerous of all our enemies."

Beetles were amusing. Scorpions and centipedes were not. They produced more casualties than the Germans. Most of us ate meals with a handkerchief or piece of paper in one hand and our food in the other. While we tried to get the food to our mouths free from flies, we waved the other hand about wildly; even so we ate many hundreds of flies. They settled on food like a cloud and no amount of waving disturbed them. They could clean jam and butter from a slice of bread much quicker than we could eat it . . . Several men actually lost their reason because of flies. Their unending presence was nerve-racking to the strongest of us.

Kites had a maddening trick of swooping down and snatching up food, but you had to laugh at them sometimes. At first mysterious disappearances of dinners caused puzzlement and alarm. Theft was suspected, practical joking, ill-will. Then the birds, "vultures of the Desert," were caught dropping swiftly and picking up food which they ate, as they flew away, in the air.

One day I saw one of our drivers smack another under the jaw for stealing his dinner, as he thought. Some of us had seen the kites pick up the dinner and the affair was amicably settled after our explanations.

As for sandstorms, well, no one who has been in one will think Crawford exaggerates when he says "words can hardly describe the experience." It is bad enough when you can keep inside a house or when you are on a train (on the line from Atbara to Khartoum I was once in a very thick one): when you have to keep on driving a lorry through it, the misery is trebled. Pace was reduced to a crawl. Visibility was often only two or three yards. Not only were eyes filled with sand, but it got through clothes and, as the heat caused violent perspiration, it entered the pores of the skin. If it was not scrubbed out soon, it brought on boils or eczema. As for making tea for the mid-day meal in a sandstorm, it generally ended as half tea and half sand. "Every mess-tin had at least a quarter of an inch in the bottom of it when the remnants were poured away."

Yet, even when they had to retreat before Rommel's advance, there was no feeling that they were beaten, that they had better chuck it. "Never once did I hear a man want to give in." Sometimes they were stunned and lifeless after heavy defeat, but "there was never a whimper, no one bemoaned his fate." Those are not mere heartening phrases. Crawford is always genuine. That is the value of the book. Revealing how the 8th Army was moulded (as the Foreword says) into the finest fighting machine in the world, through the eyes of this one soldier is mirrowed the soul of that great army.

8th ARMY TANK COMMANDERS exchange good luck wishes as they set out from besieged Tobruk in November 1941 to make contact with Imperial troops at Sidi Rezegh, where quantity of British tanks brought victory. When quality was added to quantity, as at El Alamein and Mareth, the German panzers were finally defeated. An 8th Army soldier makes absorbingly interesting disclosures in the book reviewed in this page.    PAGE 723    *Photo, British Official*

# Manstein is Sacked from South Russian Front

LOSS OF TEN DIVISIONS in the Korsun "pocket" and several more north-west of Nikolayev, led to Field Marshal von Manstein being replaced as Supreme Commander of the German armies on the southern Russian front by Field Marshal von Kleist. Manstein, whose name is linked with retreats—he was beaten at Stalingrad and on the Don—inspects his troops (1) before handing over.

German tanks hastily abandoned will doubtless be employed by the Russians against their former owners, for these tanks (3) are in thoroughly sound condition. Ten-barrelled rocket guns (2) are being used by the Nazi army. Swift-moving motor-sleighs (4) carry Russian shock-troops over frozen marsh-land to attack enemy positions at Pskov, on the northern front. See map in p. 677.

*Photos, Planet News, Associated Press, Pictorial Press*

# This Monster Will Roar No More for Germany

**ONE OF THE WEHRMACHT'S HEAVIES** was this huge siege mortar captured by the Russians; it is believed to be either a 240-mm. or 305-mm. piece. In Moscow it was examined by members of the Soviet Supreme Command; left to right are Adm. Kuznetzov, People's Commissar for the Navy; Marshal Voronov, in charge of Red Army artillery; Marshal Zhukov, Deputy Supreme Commander; and Marshal Voroshilov. Comparable British weapon is the 9·2-in. gun which fires a 390-lb. shell a distance of 20,000 yds.

*Photo, Keystone*

# This Soviet Plane Turned Nazi Jeers to Fears

One of the earliest aircraft ever produced by the Soviet, the plywood-and-fabric Yu.2 was almost a museum piece. Normally this two-seater would be obsolete by now; but the impossible has happened, and Russian airmen are today maddening the Nazis with it. Achievements of this astonishing old-timer are here narrated by the Soviet writer KONSTANTIN SIMONOV.

THE Germans called the Yu.2 "Russ-plywood." These aircraft are made of wood and linen. Their speed is only 60-70 miles an hour, and they make a noise like a motor-cycle on a bad road. What a queer notion to send people in such rickety affairs to drop bombs by hand out of the cockpit on to the German positions!

But Russians are obstinate people, and if they once get a good idea into their heads they will carry it out, sooner or later, on a grand Russian scale. Before long, bomber detachments of "Russ-plywood" were pounding the Germans with hundreds of tons of bombs. The Germans stopped making jokes about our Yu.2s.

At Stalingrad, as soon as it was dark and the first white glow-worms of signal rockets marked the forward positions, the sky began to growl softly over the German positions. German searchlights groped, German A.A. guns fired at random, and vari-coloured threads of machine-gun bursts converged from all sides on the queer sound. The gurgling and rumbling went on. The Yu.2s were abroad.

Here and there they would suspend flares like lamps over the ground itself, drop small bombs into gullies crowded with German troops, on roads along which columns were marching, into houses where the Germans had their Headquarters.

After a lot of hard work, the German A.A. gunners did finally get the measure of the "Russ-plywood." So our pilots adopted new methods. They climbed to the limit, took aim at their targets, glided over soundlessly and dropped their cargoes in dead silence. About this time fantastic hints concerning some strange new Russian aircraft with noiseless engines, or with none at all, appeared in German soldiers' letters from the front . . .

ON autumn nights the steppe is pervaded with the scent of wormwood, and a chilly ground-wind blows from the Dnieper. The cloudy, starless sky is black, remote, impenetrable. But away to the left a broad crimson glow stretches for many miles where Stalingrad burns. We are crossing a flying-field, and somewhere close at hand invisible aircraft hum in the air. Fifteen or twenty kilometres away a searchlight swings its blade in our direction, and goes out.

"Our men are coming back. They're preparing to land. The searchlight's showing them the right direction," my companion explains. After half an hour's tramp we reach the command-post. From above this is only a huge haystack, just like thousands dotting the steppe. We stoop and squeeze through a little door curtained with two tent-cloaks. Within, we find quite a big room. Two tables are placed to form the letter "T." The commander and detachment commissar are seated close to a lantern on the table.

WE have arrived at a busy moment; crews come in to report and then go out to take off. The freshness of the night air and the fragrance of hay fill the room.

Tonight the crews are going to bomb a settlement around an airfield not far from Stalingrad. The Germans broke into it and stationed large units there, so for the past few days it has been subjected to a severe pounding. Many of the Yu.2 pilots used to live in that settlement. That was where they learned to fly. So today's tasks are particularly exact and reports very detailed.

"What were you pounding just now?" Captain Ovodov asks a tall airman just back from a sortie.

"Number Three."

"That was the house you used to live in, wasn't it?"

"No, I was in Number Four. There are fires here and here, and right in this spot."

"Just here?" the commander asks, growing thoughtful. "Yes. In short, my cottage is either occupied or burned down. Well, that's that."

Every night means seven or eight hours in the air, every night means fifteen sorties, every night these little "Russ-plywood" aircraft drop tons of bombs on the enemy. Sometimes they beat the heavy bombers at their own game.

"We rarely have a day off," Captain Ovodov says, "particularly in summer. Unless, of course, there's a terrific fog. Then we're free."

Just as the tommy-gun cannot really replace the rifle in an experienced sniper's hands, the old leisurely Yu.2 proved irreplaceable. Its deficiencies, such as its slow speed, became advantages. At Stalingrad, where the front line passed from house to house, from village to village, in zigzags, wedges and tongues, not one contemporary night-bomber could have tackled the jobs the Yu.2 could do. It could bomb the German half of a block while the other half-block was still in Soviet hands. Its low speed and ideal bombing-aim enabled it to hang over the target and strike unerringly. It bombed places where the German pilots would not risk operating for fear of dropping their loads on their own troops.

The Yu.2 pilots loved their planes for their serviceability, the simple way you could take off and land in them, and for the fact that though they looked so flimsy they were really one of the grimmest of weapons. They could stand six night flights in any weather, go wherever they were sent. The pilots knew that the infantry down below were fonder of these planes than of any other. They called them affectionately the "foresters," or the "cornflies," according to the landscape.

ALL the pilots were experienced night-flyers, who rarely suffered losses. During six months only two failed to return from their mission. They took off and landed in pitch darkness. Never once had the Germans been able to bomb their aerodrome: all the lighting allowed was a couple of lanterns. Yu.2 pilots boasted that they themselves could land by the light of a cigarette.

This is a great day for the detachment: pilots and navigators are to receive rewards for their work. The best receive the Order of Lenin. Now, just before daybreak, they are making their second sortie.

An hour later they return, rubbing their eyes, red from sleeplessness and wind, and shivering in the sharp morning air. Some day, when the history of this war is written, the names of these obscure heroes will be remembered; they are the hardworking, manly, modest young fellows who responsible for altering the significance of the nickname "Russ-plywood" from the absurd to the grim.

AERIAL RECONNAISSANCE is the immediate job of this low-flying Yu.2. Tomorrow it may be doing particularly useful work in connexion with communications and supplies for guerilla forces in the rear of the German lines; the next day it may be dropping bombs. Several Guards bomber regiments of the Russian Air Force are equipped with this old and slow-flying, but amazingly efficient, plane which has gained the wholesome respect of enemy A.A. gunners after having been regarded by them as a harmless joke. See also facing page.

*Photo, Pictorial Press*

# Old-Timer of the Red Air Force Fights On

YU.2 BIPLANE BOMBERS of Russia's sky armoury stand motionless (top), but ready for action in the dusk on a snow-covered Soviet airfield, their undercarriages replaced by skis to enable them more easily to negotiate treacherously slippery ground. Below, they drop their flares on German front line positions to light the way ; in spite of the fact that they first took the air 15 years ago they are still remarkable for accurate night precision bombing.  See descriptive account in facing page.

*Photos, Pictorial Press*

# 'Golden Arrow' Will Flash Home Victory News

FROM BATTLEFIELD to Britain, when our western offensive begins, will come news of the Forces' progress flashed direct to London by mobile wireless transmitting and receiving units named " Golden Arrow," after the famous peace-time boat train.

A unit consists of seven vehicles, including two Diesel power-generators (one a spare) mounted as trailers towed by the lorries, and the section commander's small utility truck ; each section has an officer and 22 operators, instrument mechanics, electricians, and drivers of the Royal Corps of Signals, and a cook of the Army Catering Corps with petrol-burning stove.

A complete Golden Arrow unit is seen on the road (1). A corporal adjusts the tuning coils (2) ; a signalman replaces a transmitter valve (3). Inside the wireless station vehicle (4) ; a dispatch rider, in the background, is delivering messages for transmission.

*Photos, Associated Press, G.P.U.*

# I WAS THERE!

## How We Cracked the Pill-Boxes at Kwajalein

Capture of Kwajalein, in the Marshall Islands, completed on Feb. 5, 1944, involved plenty of Japanese pill-box cracking, a grim operation with a technique of its own and described here by Howard Handleman, Daily Express correspondent in that area of the Pacific. See also illus. p. 660.

WHILE leaning on the side of a concrete pill-box in which Private First Class John Garrison had just bayoneted a lone Jap, I had a close-up view of the technique of pill-box busting. The Americans were cleaning-up on this Jap-held island in the Pacific. The Jap pill-boxes were close together. Old-fashioned they were, with gun-slots facing the Pacific Ocean, and foot-thick reinforced steel doors, which do not crack at all easily.

Pill-box cracking is a job for all kinds of specialists—riflemen, grenade-throwers, flame-throwers, tanks and engineers with " satchel charges " filled with T.N.T. Our men moved slowly from pill-box to pill-box, sweating in the sun as they lugged heavy equipment. A sergeant with camouflage and war-paint sweating off his face, reported : " Two pill-boxes cleared, three full of Japs. That's what is holding us up." He sent a runner back for the tanks, and it was comforting to see them.

Tank No. 13, with a pretty girl and the words " Miss Friday " painted on the side, rumbled through the jungle with a 37-mm. gun moving from the turret. The tank blasted two heavy explosive shells into a pill-box at less than 15 yards, crumbling the concrete. A flame-thrower began jetting two sheets of solid flame into the box. A great cloud of black smoke poured out.

A squad moved to the next box, hopping forward with the movement of men in fear of being shot. I ducked forward with them. The next few minutes gave a blue-print of anti-pill-box technique. Staff-Sergeant Jack Martin and another rifleman ran close to the pill-box and poured a stream of rifle bullets at it to keep the Japs under cover, while Private Edgar Johnson moved up with a flame-thrower.

The riflemen ran back as the flame-thrower moved into position all alone before the pill-box. Johnson squirted the sheet of flame directly at the door, another obliquely at the door, and a third at the concrete wall. The fuel consumed, he dropped back a few paces to refill. Asked if he got his Japs, he said, coolly enough, " I think so, sir, but I wouldn't want to say."

Then the soldiers moved forward to the next pill-box, which was the toughest of all. Tank No. 13 threw a few 37s at the box. The flame-throwers were refuelling, so they were not used. The riflemen shot lots of rounds. A machine-gun, newly arrived, covered the slot of the pill-box with steady fire. Grenades were thrown. No. 13 continued to fire its vicious 37-mm. gun.

Finally an engineer, with spectacles, trudged up with T.N.T. wrapped in gun-sacking, and bound with wire. This is the " satchel charge." Under fire and machine-gun cover, Corporal Chester Gibson crouched low, and moved as close as he possibly could to the box.

The sergeant shouted : " Everybody down ! " and everyone hugged the earth as Gibson threw the charge at the box, and grabbed the earth himself. The charge which blew up the pill-box stunned everyone in a wide radius as the ground shook, and ears tingled. It sounds easy. It is not.

## I Walked Out of the War into Liechtenstein

The only country in Europe which has not a single soldier or a single gun : such is the remarkable little principality recently visited by Frederick Gleaner, Daily Express representative. He gives here the intriguing story of his interview with its ruler, Prince Franz Joseph, on March 14, 1944.

AT 11 o'clock this morning I crossed the River Rhine and walked right out of the war. By showing my passport to a Swiss guard at the frontier station of Buchs and crossing the ancient stone bridge, I stepped into the only country in Europe which has not a single soldier or a single gun—Liechtenstein, the tiny neutral principality on the borders of Nazi-land.

I was there to call on its ruler, 38-year-old Prince Franz Joseph II, who, with his fair-haired 23-year-old consort, lives in his small domain, simply and inexpensively. A smart grey-blue bus drove me past snow-covered farms into the capital, Vaduz.

At the main gate of Liechtenstein Castle four old cannon pointed their muzzles across the wide Rhine valley towards Switzerland. " You will notice the birds' nests in the muzzles of these old relics," said my guide. Inside, the castle breathed an air of solid, Victorian comfort. The walls of the main hall, with its open fireplace, were hung with priceless Van Dyck and Brueghel canvases. Packets of English and American cigarettes were on a table.

The door opened, and Prince Franz Joseph came in. He is a tall, youthful-looking man, dressed in tweed jacket and golfing trousers. His eyes are dark, he has a well-trimmed black moustache and the heavy lower lip of the Hapsburgs. He speaks German with an Austrian accent, and uses his hands frequently when talking. (He succeeded his great-uncle, Prince Franz Joseph I, in 1938.)

The Prince offered me an English cigarette as we sat down in a window seat and talked informally. He began by saying : "So far the Germans have not interfered with either my country or myself. I am able to travel wherever I wish on a German visa, and frequently visit my estates in Vienna and Czechoslovakia."

He did not agree that life was either lonely or monotonous in Liechtenstein. "We receive guests frequently," he said. "Then there is mountain climbing, chamois hunting and trips to Zurich. We enjoy English movies like In Which We Serve and Mrs. Miniver, which the Swiss cinemas are now showing."

Prince Franz said his country had no outstanding international problems, except the possibility that the tiny principality (its total area is 60 square miles, population 10,000) may one day be swamped with hordes of refugees. "We have anticipated this," he said, "by increasing our regular police force from seven to 87. We believe this force

FLAME-THROWERS were used by American Marines to destroy this Japanese strongpoint on Namur, one of the islands of the Kwajalein atoll. Dynamite, bayonets, bombs and shells all featured in the great clearance. How enemy concrete pill-boxes were dealt with, one by one, in the furious battle of the Marshall Islands is told above.

*Photo, Planet News*

will be sufficient to cope with the refugee problem should it arise.''

But though Liechtenstein is neutral in practice, she is still technically at war with both Germany and Italy. In 1866, together with her big ally Austria, she declared war on Prussia and Italy. She furnished one officer and 58 sharpshooters to the joint war effort : but when Austria made a peace treaty with her enemies, Liechtenstein was not included. And a separate official peace treaty was never made.

None of Liechtenstein's £100,000 budget has to be spent on war needs. Very little is required for the maintenance of law and order. The police force's last big job was in autumn 1939, when a score or more of Nazi thugs staged a ''march on Vaduz,'' with the declared intention of liberating the population from the princely yoke. Sergeant Joseph Brunhart, chief of police, quickly handled the situation by clapping four ringleaders into gaol, sending the rest home to mother.

Lt. A. A. Duff, D.S.C., R.N., captain of H.M. submarine Stubborn, was on his first voyage as her commander (although he had sailed in her before) at the time of the exciting incidents which he relates below. *Photo, British Official*

## This is the Fire-Raked Cockpit of Anzio

'' The whole compact and ferocious bag of tricks is contained in a cockpit less than the area bounded by Battersea, Marble Arch, Holborn, and Southwark,'' declared an observer who recently returned from the beach-head in Italy and gave the following impressions to a Reuter correspondent. Stories of the beach-landings on the morning of Jan. 22, 1944, and the magnificent work of the Reconnaissance Corps in that area, are in pp. 601 and 697.

TAKE a large London suburb, fill it with some of the finest Allied troops and drop it in the middle of enemy territory, and you have some idea of what is going on at Anzio. Every acre can be swept by enemy gunfire. The Fuehrer sees an immense political prize in throwing the attack back into the sea.

The Allies, with the possiblity of gaining another foot in the door of Europe, know that the eyes of the world are on this splintered wicket gate. The most murderous entertainment being dished out on the beach-head is exported to Jerry.

The German prisoners are a strange crew. They are for the most part either extraordinarily young or obviously too old. They are made up of divisions from widely scattered parts of Europe. There is a tough backbone among them, but the usual run of customers in the prisoner of war cages are anything less than Herrenvolk.

All the prisoners of war look as if they had '' had it '' when they were nabbed. They have the effusive relief of men who have been suddenly released from the hail of shells, bombs and mortars. Those that I saw were young, dishevelled loons—disillusioned clods whom five years ago I saw at Nuremberg.

Men who have accounted for about one in seven of the enemy regard this as the bloodiest affray since the Fuehrer '' put on that coat which was most dear to him.'' The Reconnaissance Regiment, Guards, infantry, gunners and all the rest of them have fought

through the horror and filth of this campaign with the fury and courage that in wartime comes from our cities, our shires and our hills in such abundant measure.

If Barnum and Bailey, Von Moltke, Cecil B. de Mille, Ludendorff, Genghis Khan and Charles B. Cochran got together for a warlike conference, maybe they could stage an Anzio in the heart of England. It would smash half the country to a solid pulp. It would bring ammunition dumps, wagon lines, gun parks, prisoners of war cages, petrol points and graveyards. It would bring misery and death.

But the scale of this terrific fight would be wrenched from the comparative serenity of newspaper headlines and brought out into its proper perspective.

## Four Times Our Submarine Bumped the Sea-bed

H.M. submarine Stubborn has returned safely after one of the most remarkable patrols of this war. She is commanded by 24-year-old Lieut. A. A. Duff, D.S.C., R.N., and this is his story, told on his arrival back at the home port, where he and his crew were given a tremendous welcome.

WE had torpedoed two of a convoy hugging the enemy coast. This convoy, which was escorted by four trawlers, a minesweeper and another patrol vessel, was the second large one we had successfully attacked on the patrol. The first lot of depth charges didn't worry us much, but the large number which came hurtling down in the next fifteen minutes were much too close. Our after-hydroplanes—used for obtaining the desired depth—were jammed at hard-a-dive ; the starboard propeller was put out of action, and a tank which is used for quick diving was inadver-

tently flooded. We went whistling down and were dangerously deep before I could pull up by blowing main ballast and regain trim by rushing all hands aft to bring up the bow.

One after another the hands scrambled through narrow openings in watertight bulkheads and down the shoulder-wide alley, until they were heaped like a collapsed Rugby scrum in the aftermost compartment. Then, for some unknown reason, the submarine rose to the surface. Nothing could stop her, and we lay for a brief period in sight of an armed patrol vessel. Then we went into another steep dive, which I again managed

ON THE ANZIO BEACH-HEAD, day and night, showers of anti-personnel bombs sent down by the Luftwaffe failed to shift these British gunners, who had dug for themselves holes to which, with the unfailing humour of our troops, they gave such names as '' Sea View '' (left). One of the many guns (right) which, with a concentration of fire seldom equalled in this war, smashed the German attacks ; it is a 5·5 in. manned by the Royal Artillery. See story above.

　*Photos, British Official*

to check when we were very deep indeed — and more depth charges came down.

We corrected the trim, with most of the crew placed forward this time, and the Stubborn, proceeding on her port motor, with her bow up at an angle of 25 degrees, was headed to make a rush through the minefield. We got along like that for a time, until the rate of rise got out of control, and we broke surface again. This time we were seen by the minesweeper which was only a mile and a half away. We dived with the utmost speed and went down and down, out of control. The ultimate figure on the depth gauge was passed ; the needle stuck, and we were still going down.

And here the Guardian Angel stepped in and provided an entirely unexpected sea bottom. A study of the chart shows no shallow patch in the deep waters anywhere in that vicinity. But we had no doubt that we had touched bottom, because the Stubborn bumped on the sea-bed four times before she came to rest with a nine degrees bow-down angle. Many more depth charges were dropped very close, so that the boat was lifted off the bottom by the force of the explosions, but that was the last we heard of the enemy . . .

*Lieutenant Duff waited until it was dark before he tried to move, and then it was found that the Stubborn was firmly stuck. The after-hydroplanes had fallen off, but the starboard propeller had freed itself. Attempts were made to get her off stern first and rock her free by running the crew about, but all failed. By now the pressure of air inside the submarine was abnormally high, and Lieutenant Duff decided to run his main air compression, drawing air from inside the boat—a very unusual procedure. In this way he pumped up an air group to 3,000 lb. per square inch and was able to pull the submarine off the sea bed. Continuing his story:*

She shot up at an angle of 70 degrees. I was lying flat on the conning tower ladder. Everyone was slung in a heap. But we surfaced all right and steamed as fast as we could away from the enemy coast. The ordeal was by no means over. On the

H.M. SUBMARINE STUBBORN lived up to her name in one of the most remarkable patrols of the war. She is here seen coming home, escorted by the Norwegian destroyer Narvik, passing a cheering crowd of sailors aboard her depot ship H.M.S. Forth. See facing page for the story of her adventures.
*Photo, British Official*

following afternoon her rudder suddenly failed to answer the wheel. She lay helpless in enemy-patrolled waters, and it was blowing a gale. The boat lay beam on to the sea, rolling horribly. I ordered a sail to be rigged to the periscope standard, hoping that would bring the ship's head to sea. But in a few seconds the canvas was torn to ribbons.

*Only at this stage did the Stubborn send a signal for help. Destroyers were sent immediately, but the weather was so bad that it was two days before they* were able to sight the stricken submarine. Then, for six hours, they could not take her in tow because the weather was too bad. They had to wait until it moderated sufficiently to get the tow line made fast. Eventually, this was done after dark—a fine feat of seamanship by both craft—and they steamed away from the danger zone. When the Stubborn had been in tow for eight hours the cable parted. But now Lieut. Duff's experiments in steering without a rudder were rewarded, because the Stubborn was able to proceed under her own power at about 7½ knots and carry out an efficient zig-zag as though under continuous helm. She steamed thus for about 300 miles and then she was taken in tow again and brought safely home.*

# OUR DIARY OF THE WAR

**MARCH 15, Wednesday**     1,656th day
**Italy.**—Cassino attacked with 1,400 tons of bombs ; every unit of Mediterranean Air Force in action.
**Russian Front.**—Kalinovka, Turbov, Voronovitsa, Trostinets, Obodovka, and Olgopol in Vinnitsa sector captured by Russians.
**Australasia.**—American troops landed on Manus Island in the Admiralties.
**Air.**—Brunswick bombed by Fortresses and Liberators for seventh time. Stuttgart and Munich attacked by over 1,000 aircraft at night.

**MARCH 16, Thursday**     1,657th day
**Italy.**—Three-quarters of Cassino occupied by 5th Army troops. Castle Hill, N. of the town, captured.
**Russian Front.**—Vapnyarka taken by troops of 2nd Ukrainian Front. Nemirov, Voroshilovka, and Bobrinets captured.
**Air.**—Clermont-Ferrand, 30 miles S.W. of Vichy, attacked at night with 12,000-lb. bombs. Amiens raided.

**MARCH 17, Friday**     1,658th day
**Italy.**—Cassino railway station captured by New Zealand troops of 5th Army.
**Russian Front.**—Dubno, Demidovka, and Targowica captured by Marshal Zhukov's troops.
**Burma.**—Announced landings made by British airborne troops in N. Burma and by British and W. African troops on coast of Arakan, 15 miles below Razavil. Chinese operating under Gen. Stilwell captured Tingkawk Sakan.
**General.**—Finnish Government rejected Russia's armistice terms.

**MARCH 18, Saturday**     1,659th day
**Russian Front.**—Zhmerinka, on Odessa-Lwow railway, captured by 1st Ukrainian Army. Yampol and Pomoshnaya taken by 2nd Ukrainian Army. Liquidation of German Sixth Army on Lower Bug Front announced.
**Australasia.**—Lorengau, Japanese base on Manus Island, taken by U.S. troops.
**Air.**—Oberpfofenhoffen, Lechfeld, Landsberg, Friedrichshafen and Augsburg hit in great day attack by over 1,500 U.S. bombers and fighters. At night, 1,000 bombers went to Frankfurt and Bergerac.
**Sea.**—Loss of destroyer Mahratta announced by Board of Admiralty.

**MARCH 19, Sunday**     1,660th day
**Russian Front.**—Krzemieniec, 20 miles inside 1939 Polish frontier, captured by troops of 1st Ukrainian Front. River Dniester forced along a stretch of 30 miles by Marshal Koniev. Soroka and Zhelanets occupied.
**Australasia.**—Emerau Island, 84 miles N.W. of Kavieng, invaded by U.S. troops.
**Burma.**—Announced that major offensive launched by Japanese troops in the Chindwin Valley along Indian frontier.
**Sea.**—Announced that in recent operations extending over 20 days in N. Atlantic six U-boats sunk by five British sloops under command of Capt. F. J. Walker, C.B., D.S.O. (two bars).

**MARCH 20, Monday**     1,661st day
**Russian Front.**—Mogilev-Podolski, on the Dniester, and Vinnitsa, on the Bug, captured by Marshals Koniev and Zhukov.
**Australasia.**—Occupation of Emerau Is., N.W. of Kavieng, New Ireland, completed by American assault troops.
**General.**—Pierre Pucheu, former Vichy Minister of the Interior, executed.

**MARCH 21, Tuesday**     1,662nd day
**Russian Front.**—Cernauti-Balti railway cut in Red Army southern offensive.
**Home Front.**—Many incendiaries dropped in fire attack on London.
**Burma.**—Fall of Jambubum and Sumprabum in northern Burma announced.

**MARCH 22, Wednesday**     1,663rd day
**Russian Front.**—Pervomaisk, on River Bug, captured by 2nd Ukrainian Front troops.
**Air.**—Berlin attacked in daylight by Fortresses and Liberators. In greatest raid of the war, 3,000 tons dropped on Frankfurt at night by Lancasters and Halifaxes.
**General.**—German occupation of Hungary, reported to have begun on March 19, completed. Resignation of Hungarian Govt. announced. Hungarian Ambassador in Berlin, A. Sztojay, appointed Premier.

**MARCH 23, Thursday**     1,664th day
**Russian Front.**—Kapuchnitsy and Tremblova taken on the southern front.
**Air.**—Hamm rail-junction, Achmer and Handorf air bases, Munster and Brunswick factories, bombed by over 1,000 U.S. planes. Rail targets at Laon, and objectives at Lyons raided at night. Mosquitoes attacked Dortmund.

**MARCH 24, Friday**     1,665th day
**Italy.**—Announced Germans had regained a quarter of Cassino.
**Russian Front.**—Announced that in five days' fighting troops of the 1st Ukrainian Front had broken German defences in the Tarnopol-Proskurov sector and advanced up to 60 miles. Czorkov, Gusiatyn and Zaleszcyk taken.
**Home Front.**—Intense flak barrage defeated enemy incendiary raid on London.

**Air.**—Schweinfurt and Frankfurt industrial targets, French airfields of Nancy and St. Dizier, raided by Fortresses and Liberators. At night Berlin (2,500 tons) had its heaviest raid to date.

**MARCH 25, Saturday**     1,666th day
**Russian Front.**—Proskurov, great German bastion in western Ukraine, fell to Marshal Zhukov. Fifty mile stretch of River Dniester reached above Mogilev-Podolski.
**Burma.**—Capture of Shaduzup in the Mogaung Valley by U.S. and Chinese troops announced.
**Air.**—Aulnoye rail targets (N. France) and objectives in Lyons area attacked at night. Berlin bombed.

**MARCH 26, Sunday**     1,667th day
**Russian Front.**—Troops of 2nd Ukrainian Army reached the State frontier of the Soviet Union with Rumania, the River Pruth, on a front of 50 miles. Balti and Kamenets Podolski captured.
**Air.**—Military installations in Pas de Calais and Cherbourg areas, and E-boat nests at Ymuiden (Holland) bombed. At night, Essen subjected to saturation attack ; Hanover and Courtrai (Belgium) attacked.
**General.**—Mr. Churchill said that the "hour of greatest effort and action is approaching."

**MARCH 27, Monday**     1,668th day
**Russian Front.**—Soviet troops entered suburbs of Nikolayev. Gorodenka taken.
**Burma.**—Announced that Allied troops were in rear of enemy in Upper Burma, under command of Maj.-Gen. O. C. Wingate.
**Air.**—Nine airfields in central and S.W. France attacked by Fortresses and Liberators. Tours marshalling yards raided.

**MARCH 28, Tuesday**     1,669th day
**Russian Front.**—Nikolayev, important Black Sea naval base and German strongpoint on the southern Bug, captured by 3rd Ukrainian Army. Slobodka, on main line from Odessa to Zmerinka ; Gvozdets, district centre of Stanislavov region ; Minkousti, and Chelmenti in Cernauti area, taken by Soviet troops.
**Air.**—French airfields of Dijon, Chartres, and Chateaudun bombed.

★ ═══════════ *Flash-backs* ═══════════ ★

### 1940
March 15.   Finns ratified peace terms with Russia at Helsinki.

### 1941
March 16.   Berbera, capital of British Somaliland, recaptured.
March 20.   British Somaliland cleared of Italian troops.
March 27.   Harar, Abyssinia, taken by 11th African Division.

### 1942
March 22.   Three-day Axis sea and air attack on Malta-bound convoy in Mediterranean commenced.

### 1943
March 15.   Russians evacuated industrial city of Kharkov.
March 20.   Assault on Mareth Line positions by 8th Army.
March 27.   Fondouk, Tunisia, taken by American troops.
March 28.   Mareth, Toujane, and Matmata captured by 8th Army.

# THE WAR IN THE AIR

### by Capt. Norman Macmillan, M.C., A.F.C.

No operation in this war has been more novel and spectacular than the dispatch of a strong force by air into the heart of Northern Burma, where it alighted behind the Japanese "lines" within the area under "control" of the Far Eastern enemy. The operation was carried out by towed gliders and troop transport aircraft. This form of attack was strategically first employed by the German Army during the offensive against Holland and Belgium in 1940. The scene of the first glider attack was the fort of Eben-Emael, which the Belgians had built during the years between the wars to cover the approaches to the three vital bridges that spanned the Albert Canal.

As with the British defences at Singapore, the Belgian defences of fort Eben-Emael anticipated attack from a certain direction. Both these great fortresses were built before the rapid development of air power which followed the tremendous technical advances made during the past decade. And both fell to attack from the quarter whence it had been supposed not to be possible.

### GLIDER-BORNE Troops Landed on Fort-Top

The Belgian fort was put out of action within thirty-six hours of the beginning of the main German assault upon the Low Countries and France by glider-borne troops who descended in the night behind and even on top of the fort and who were reinforced by parachute troops. The bridge guards were attacked not from the front but from the rear. The German armies poured over the bridges and the great, or rather supposedly great, bastion of the Albert Canal proved almost valueless, due to the employment of new strategical and tactical methods of war.

But nothing of any importance in modes of war has been introduced by the Germans which has not swiftly been seized upon by the Allies and bettered. The Germans failed because they did not believe sufficiently in their new methods. One can perceive in case after case that the torpid mind of military orthodoxy interfered with the more advanced thinkers in the German military hierarchy. It is well for the world that it was so, or we should not now have turned the tables on our foe; there would have been no time to do so.

AND so the Germans who first used the glider as a means of taking troops into battle made provision for this form of military transport on so small a scale that their victories won by novel methods left them dry of resources sufficient to sweep them on to complete victory. What would have been the fate of Britain in 1940 had Germany possessed a great fleet of gliders that could have alighted in the darkness in numerous parts of Britain? It is sheer speculation to guess at the effect, but undoubtedly the war would not have gone as it has gone for us. We should have known the meaning of fighting in our own homeland.

Now nearly four years later, a great air-borne force was landed within the heart of Northern Burma by gliders, complete with all sorts of equipment for turning fields marked out for the initial landings into airfields suitable for the use of troop transport aircraft. And that meant no small parcels of equipment. Troop transport aircraft require considerable fore-and-aft and lateral room to alight. The approaches to the actual alighting area must be reasonably good, especially for night landings, for no air

**BACK FROM ATLANTIC PATROL,** aircraft of R.A.F. Coastal Command get routine inspection; here the tail unit of a Liberator is being overhauled. American-built, its wing span is 110 ft., length 64 ft., height 17 ft. 11 ins. Its speed is 335 m.p.h. at 16,000 ft. and its range 3,000 miles. The bomb load is 8,000 lbs.
*Photo, British Official: Crown Copyright*

commander wishes unnecessarily to have excessive crashes which cost lives and block the runways and approaches with wreckage which takes time to remove, and in Burma may set the jungle alight from petrol fires and throw well-laid plans awry.

A MODERN military airfield is not just simply a place to land. It must have proper control over flying with signals organization, lighting for night landings, radio communication with bases and with aircraft in flight, telephone communication between one part and another of the widely dispersed area (so dispersed for security against bomb attacks), and runway surfaces which will carry modern aircraft weighing anything up to twenty tons. These cannot be conjured out of the jungle. The materials and appliances to create the airfield must be transported to the spot. And that was done in the case of General Wingate's airborne expedition in Northern Burma.

If for any reason such an expedition were to fail to provide itself quickly with an efficient airfield, it would be so severely handicapped as to jeopardize its capacity to hit the enemy, or even to survive. For, surrounded by enemy forces, it depends upon air transport for its supplies of food and ammunition, weapons, medical requirements, evacuation of wounded and sick, and all the hundred-and-one details of a modern military command. Such supplies cannot continue to come in by glider; for there is a limit to the number of gliders that may be used in one operation, because the gliders can only return whence they came if air-tugs can get down to tow them off again, or unless the runways are of sufficient length and width to enable tugs to hook up the gliders from the ground while on the wing. But even the last-named method does not solve the problem, for it is certain that in air operations of this kind a large number of gliders will be damaged in landing and so cannot be returned to their starting points by air.

### CRASH-LANDING Safely in Confined Spaces

It is imperative to get an airfield into operation with the minimum delay and to provide for the adequate protection of that airfield. This means that a fighter force must fly in as soon as possible to give air cover, for in the case of the Burma air expedition, the scene of operations was too distant from airfields in India for adequate air cover to be provided from them. Soon one airfield is not enough. Satellite airfields are required to allow for dispersal in the event of enemy air attack succeeding in breaking through the fighter screen, so that the temporary damaging of one airfield will not hold up the stream of supplies and reinforcements. In this way, by the use of air transports, a really big army can be built up in an area where the enemy may have hoped that he was in occupation.

Why, it may be asked, are gliders used for the initial operation? Why not use air transports straight away? The answer is that gliders can be crash-landed in comparatively small spaces with relative safety to their occupants. They have no hot engines and lubricating oils or petrol to catch fire when they crash-land. They can be more lightly built, so that if they begin to disintegrate there are fewer heavy parts to cause injury to the occupants. And they are far easier and quicker to build than air transports, requiring a relative handful of man-hours for their production compared with a power-driven air transport. Moreover, two or more gliders can be towed by one air-tug, so that a large force can be flown in quickly. And the gliders can get down in rapid succession one after another.

OUR admiration should go to the pilots who steered their gliders through the night skies over the jungle hills of Burma, for flying a towed glider is no easy ride. The glider strains and yaws on the end of its silk nylon rope as it follows the wake of its tug, heaves in the air, and makes great lunges about the sky. It is in no way a "willing" tow. It is so much dead-weight, a troop-packed engineless aircraft the safety of whose freight is absolutely dependent on skilful handling. Pilots have to work hard to keep them on their course. Certainly these glider pilots who landed in Burma have made their mark in military history.

# Corsair is the Fleet Air Arm's Latest Fighter

THE CORSAIR PILOTS had put in months of hard training for the great day when their squadron should join the carrier. Some had carried out deck-landing training at an airfield in America, then perfecting landings on the flight-deck of a carrier before returning to England to start their operational careers in real earnest.

The plane that crashed (1). The pilot was unhurt and his aircraft was removed by the self-propelling crane seen in the background. A Corsair on the deck-landing area (3) starts to taxi away; folding its wings (2), it will then enter the lift which will bear it down into the hangar.

*Photos, British Official*

LATEST ADDITION to our air striking power at sea is the American-built Vought-Sikorsky Corsair aircraft, a single-seater ship-board fighter powered with a 1,850 h.p. Pratt-Hind Whitney Double Wasp engine; wing-span 40 feet, length 30 feet.

A notable event was the day recently on which a complete squadron of these planes joined a British aircraft carrier off the north-west coast of Scotland: the first operational Fleet Air Arm squadron, equipped with the new Corsairs, were to make their first landings on a British flight-deck. The superstructure and gun wells of the carrier were crowded with officers and ratings as the leading Corsair came in to alight. Apart from one which crashed on the flight-deck as the result of a miscalculation on its pilot's part, all made perfect landings.

# Rumania and Hungary Now in Parlous Plight

GERMAN MILITARY OCCUPATION of Hungary, reported to have begun on March 19, 1944, was complete by March 22. In Rumania, German forces were considerably strengthened from Austria. To the east, the Red Army were over the Dniester and had reached points less than 25 miles from the Rumanian frontier.

Gains secured by Hungary at the expense of Rumania, Slovakia and Yugoslavia as reward for her participation in Germany's war are now of no account; her fate is comparable with that of Rumania, whose men were sacrificed before Odessa, Sebastopol and in the Caucasus.

Concrete fortifications along the Hungarian frontier (3) are today of as little value to Hungary as was the Maginot Line to France. On the lower Dniester, 32 miles east of Kishinev, the Tighina Bridge (1) links Bessarabia with Russia; at Tiraspol, 8 miles from Tighina, this Rumanian sentry (2) keeps anxious watch. See map in p. 677.

*Photos, Muir*

**B**ASIC English is receiving a very considerable amount of attention at present, thanks to Mr. Churchill's interest in it, and I think that from the point of view of international relationships it is most desirable that this should be so. I would point out, however, that Basic English can be of no conceivable use to an Englishman who has learned his native tongue in the natural way that all native tongues are learned, and it would be a truly terrifying prospect for English literature if our schools were to teach British boys and girls only the limited vocabulary which the inventor of Basic English has contrived for the expression of all ordinary thoughts on the common affairs of life. On the other hand, the study of foreign languages—and here again more from the commercial point of view than the literary—presented on the principles of Basic English is going to be of immense importance in the future and might well result in making the English, who are not notably gifted in foreign languages, quite a polyglot people. I cannot imagine, however, that Basic English will ever be popular with the coloured citizens of the United States, who have a passion for using long and sonorous words. A friend of mine tells a story of travelling in the Southern States and having some doubt about arriving at a junction in time to catch another train. He discussed it with the Negro conductor, who set his mind at rest with these consoling words. "Believe me, Sah, you can eliminate the possibility of any such contingency occurring."

**I** HOPE everyone who reads this is doing all he or she can do to make the "Salute the Soldier" weeks surpass in their financial result the efforts that were so successful in providing money for ships and aircraft. A good start has been made and the collection will go on until July ends. We must make the total a lot higher than the earlier drives for the war fund yielded, satisfactory though they were, all things considered. Now we have an incentive to invest in War Savings of all kinds which did not exist before. We can feel it is the last effort we shall have to make before the enemy's strength is broken in Europe. After that there will be Japan, it is true; but victory on this side of the world will release enormous quantities of men and women and armaments, and the cost of the war will be somewhat less burdensome. Apart from the sums that will be raised to meet this burden, it is a very good thing that the Army should be publicized a bit more than it has been during this war. We used in the past to hear only of Tommy Atkins. The Navy was the "silent Service." The Air Force didn't exist. Now both the sailors and the airmen tend to overshadow the soldier. It is time the balance was restored.

**I** HAVE known British generals with all sorts of queer habits—or I should say habits that seemed queer in British generals. I never knew one who learned poems and enjoyed repeating them to himself. That is Field Marshal Wavell's hobby, and he has let us know what are the poems he likes best by publishing a book of them. It is not surprising that he rates Kipling very highly among his favourites, but it is surprising that he admits to not caring for Tennyson. I should have thought anybody who liked the one Victorian poet would be keen on the other. They had much the same qualities, metrical perfection among

others, and a sort of super-Man-in-the-Street mentality. You may wonder at my calling Kipling a Victorian. But if you look back over his work, you will see that he made his name during the reign of the old Queen, and it was just about the time she died that he had his very dangerous illness in America and only just scraped through, with the result that never afterwards did his work appear to have quite the same vigour and distinction. His "Soldiers Three" were soldiers of the Queen, and his finest poem, "Recessional," was inspired by his reflections on her Diamond Jubilee. I hope the Viceroy of India (Lord Wavell assumed this appointment on Oct. 20, 1943) does not recite Kipling to Indians, by the way!

**Lieut.-General SIR THOMAS RALPH EASTWOOD, K.C.B., D.S.O., M.C.,** arrived at Gibraltar on Feb. 27, 1944, to assume his new duties as Governor and C.-in-C. of the " Rock." Born in 1890, he was Director-General Home Guard 1940-41, and G.O.C.-in-C. Northern Command from 1941. He is 53 years old, and fought in Samoa, Egypt, Gallipoli and France in the 1914-18 war.
*Photo, British Official : Crown Copyright*

**I** DON'T know how it is now, but in the old Tsarist Russia there used to be Black Markets for all kinds of things, long before we heard of them here. If you wanted tickets for the Imperial Ballet, for instance, you were often told at the box-office that none were to be had ; but they could always be bought just round the corner from a speculator. Same with railway reservations. At the station ticket-offices you would be told no places were vacant, but there were people ready to sell you what you wanted at a slightly increased price. Now I am told by a friend just back from America that this bad practice which once flourished in a despotic State has invaded the most democratic of countries. Pullman sleepers are cornered and sold by outside speculators because there is such a run on them. Trains are crammed, a large proportion of the travellers being men in uniform, though that was not true of the crowd marooned in Florida, rich holiday-makers who had to queue up day after day for weeks and return in conditions they described as "horrifying."

If you have a long distance to go, you must have a Pullman or else arrive utterly worn and weary at your destination. And the Pullmans are being taken off many trains to save space.

**W**HETHER hospitals "supported by voluntary contributions" will keep going when the new Health scheme promised by the Government comes into force seems to be doubtful. Those who have been the most liberal subscribers to them in the past are not likely to be able to afford that luxury in the future. The New Rich do not support charities as the Old Rich did. For the inheritors of wealth it was a tradition that they should set aside a certain sum every year for "charities." Those who have made fortunes seldom feel any urge or obligation to do that. A few like Lord Nuffield give enormous amounts, but generally speaking the charities find it more and more difficult to collect money. Those whom they succeed in tapping are for the most part a stage army. Their names figure in a great many lists and they are continually approached by the compilers of other lists who want them to extend their benefactions. It is a "vicious" circle, if I may so describe it without decrying the objects on which the money is spent. The appearance of your name in one or two annual reports leads to your being urged to figure in a lot more. I have experienced this myself. Evidently the supporters of charities are very limited in number and becoming more so.

**O**NE of the military terms that have come into general use of late, as "terrain" did during the last war, is "logistics." This hideous monstrosity of verbiage comes, I believe, from the French originally. The derivation is from *loger* and it means anything to do with the lodgment of soldiers. The smaller Oxford Dictionary says "The art of moving and quartering troops." I suppose it is useful to have a portmanteau expression of this nature to hold what might otherwise have to be a bulky string of words, but I wish we could hit on something more in keeping with our own language. The equivalent might seem to be "quartering," since the French for our "quartermaster" is "maréchal de logis" ; but that would not include the movement of troops, and usually that is what logistics has to do with in the writings of military correspondents. Not many people who come across it can have any idea of its meaning. Perhaps that is why there are some writers who like to use it as often as they can.

**T**HE M.P. who wants the Army to be supplied with mackintoshes ought to be told that these garments are called "waterproofs" in War Office parlance—or at any rate used to be until a short time ago. Probably the reason is that they existed and were worn by soldiers of high rank before the term "mackintosh" came into circulation. It was in 1823 that a Mr. Charles Macintosh (spelt without the "k") hailing from the Scottish Highlands, patented the rubberized coat or cloak which is supposed to keep out even heavy, persistent rain. It was called after him, as the sandwich took the name of the earl who first had slices of meat put between slices of bread, and the Garibaldi biscuit that of the Italian patriot general who kept his troops going strong on raisins sandwiched between pieces of hard baked maize flour.

# They Will Help Naples to Rise Again

**SCHOOL ONCE MORE** has become part of the everyday lives of these kiddies, shepherded by their teacher through a ruin-bordered street of Naples, which the 5th Army cleared of the enemy on Oct. 1, 1943. With textbooks supplied by the Allied Military Government, schools in all liberated Italian towns and cities are resuming the education of the rising generation; this time with instruction founded on sane lines, untainted by those insidious doctrines formerly taught.

*Photo, U.S. Official*

Printed in England and published every alternate Friday by the Proprietors, THE AMALGAMATED PRESS, LTD., The Fleetway House, Farringdon Street, London, E.C.4. Registered for transmission by Canadian Magazine Post. Sole Agents for Australia and New Zealand: Messrs. Gordon & Gotch, Ltd.; and for South Africa: Central News Agency, Ltd.—April 14, 1944. S.S. *Editorial Address:* JOHN CARPENTER HOUSE. WHITEFRIARS. LONDON. E.C.4.

Vol 7  # The War Illustrated  Nº 179

*Edited by Sir John Hammerton*

SIXPENCE

APRIL 28, 1944

**HANDLING HER BOAT-HOOK** like a professional bargee is this girl now training under a Ministry of War Transport scheme designed to make still greater use of our inland waterways for carrying vital supplies when the Allied Western offensive opens. Barges work in pairs, with a crew of three each; six pairs of boats on regular runs are now operated by women. An average round trip takes 16 days, and crews sometimes work a 16-hour day.

*Photo, Associated Press*

NO. 180 WILL BE PUBLISHED FRIDAY. MAY 12

# A Homeland Tour With Our Roving Camera

VISITING TROOPS in Yorkshire, our indefatigable Prime Minister, during a recent extensive tour, inspected an armoured formation and took keen interest in a tank demonstration. He is seen (left) driving in a half-track car along a line of Sherman tanks and their crews—all impatient for action in Western Europe.

BRITAIN'S LATEST TANK, the Centaur (below), incorporating new features, has recently been taken off the secret list, though doubtless the enemy is well enough acquainted with it and is regretting its appearance at the battle fronts. It is a cruiser tank, mounting a 6-pdr. gun and described as having a three-man turret. The average British cruiser tank's weight is 14-17 tons, and speed 25-40 miles per hour, the crew numbering four or five. Armament of earlier cruiser types was usually a 2-pdr. gun.

IDENTITY CARD CHECK-UP by police is to ensure that new coastal area restrictions, imposed early in April 1944 for operational security reasons, are complied with. Everyone over 16 in the " regulated " areas must be able to produce their card to any constable or member of the Allied forces on duty.

THE 100,000th Rolls-Royce Merlin aero engine is being finished off (above) by two workers who have had many years service with the firm ; they helped to build the first Rolls-Royce engine ever produced. Now the most famous in the world, the Merlin has been fitted to 14 different types of operational aircraft.

FAMOUS VICTORIES, such as the Battle of Britain and of Malta, are commemorated by these tablets around the 36-foot base of the famous yew tree (left), reputed to be 2,000 years old, in the 12th-century St. Helen's Churchyard, in Darley Dale, Derbyshire.

*Photos, British Official ; Planet News, Fox, F. H. Brindley*

# THE BATTLE FRONTS

### by E. Royston Pike

**ITALY** In the encyclopedias Cassino's claim to fame is the possession of a Benedictine monastery founded by St. Benedict himself in A.D. 529. In the history books of the future, however, Cassino will have a place because of the furious and bloody battles that were waged in and about it during the spring months of 1944.

By the middle of January the massive rock on which the monastery was perched, and the town in the valley below, had come within range of the 5th Army's guns. Regardless of the fact that Cassino was one of the holy places of the Catholic world—why, indeed, should the exponents of German paganism have concern for such sentimental trifles ?—the Nazis made the monastery hill and its surroundings one huge strongpoint, scored with trenches and gun-pits and tunnelled through with galleries in which men and guns might lie hidden, out of reach of bomb and shell.

The first attempt to take the place by flanking movements and by frontal assault failed. The general opinion of men on the spot seems to have been that the occupation by the enemy of the monastery as an observation post was largely responsible for the failure of the Allied operations ; and at length, but only after prolonged deliberation and much discussion of the right and wrong of bombing so holy a place (during which time many valuable lives were lost), the word was given to bomb. On February 15 much of the monastery was blown to bits. But the bombs had little if any effect on its value to the enemy, and the battle continued, rising to a fresh pitch of violence.

A MONTH after the monastery's formidable walls it was the turn of the town to be bombed. "Between breakfast and lunch today," wrote Christopher Buckley, Special Correspondent of The Daily Telegraph, on March 15, "in brilliant weather, I saw Cassino flattened from the air by persistent, almost ceaseless bombing over a space of four hours . . . The bombing, intended to reduce the German strongpoints to rubble, was followed by a terrific artillery barrage from massed Allied guns, after which the infantry went forward to the assault." It was a terrible and impressive display. Never in the whole history of war had a more intense load of bombs been put on to so small a target ; and to the observers watching from a hillside two miles away nearly all the bombing seemed to be of remarkable accuracy. (See illus. p. 709.)

Later it was discovered that only something in the neighbourhood of 40 per cent of the bombs had fallen within the target area—and this in bright sunshine, with practically no opposition—and the artillery bombardment was also ineffective in crushing the enemy powers of resistance. As soon as the guns ceased and the infantry moved forward, "from the rubble (reported Christopher Buckley) machine-gunners sprang to life. From caves and tunnels on the hillside, many of them prepared or enlarged during the week's lull caused by the weather which had prevented air operations, the enemy emerged. They came from the cellars of houses in front of and behind our advancing infantry. Three-quarters or more of Cassino was cleared ; and then, with the impetus of our attack partly lost, the enemy began to counter-attack."

So once more on that blasted mountainside there was failure. Why ? asked Buckley ; and answered his own question. We overestimated the probable effects of air-bombing : because half the town had been blotted

out it was fallaciously assumed that the garrison was either dead or demoralized. (In fact, many of them survived, and the prisoners taken were reported to be still "fighting fit.") Then there was the intensely heavy rain on the following night preventing the attack on Monastery Hill developing with its full force. Finally, the German parachute troops forming the garrison put up an extremely tough resistance, as determined as anything we have met with so far in this war.

What, then, ought to have been done ? Should the bombing have been more intensive, delivered by even more planes than the 500-odd that were engaged ? Scarcely, since

**DRIVING ON IN RUMANIA, Russian troops were by April 12, 1944, five miles east of Jassy, dominating the road to the Galatz Gap and the Ploesti oilfields; they were also hammering at the Tolgyes Pass in the Carpathians.**
*By courtesy of News Chronicle*

"the heavier the bomb load you put down in advance the more you obstruct the subsequent advance of your own forces." As it was, the craters in Cassino were so numerous that only two tanks were able to get into the town on the day of the assault ; and a town that has been laid in ruins is a hardly less formidable obstacle than one in which every house in a street is a potential machine-gun nest. Perhaps, then, more infantry ought to have been employed ? (Better troops could hardly have been put into the battle, since the New Zealanders were there in force.) But Christopher Buckley scouted the view that reversion to the Somme tactics of the last war, mass infantry assaults following gigantic bombardments, represents the solution of Cassino's problem.

**RUSSIA** As March drew to a close the Russians surged on with hardly a check. All along the vast front from just south of the Pripet marshes, opposite Lwow, to the estuary of the Bug at Nikolayev, the German armies under Manstein and Kleist were engulfed or swept away or pushed back by the flood of Russian tanks and apparently inexhaustible hosts of men.

In the north Marshal Zhukov's 1st Ukrainian Front smashed the German lines in and about Tarnopol and developed a threat to Lwow. On March 19 Moscow's guns saluted the capture of Kremenets ; and in the next four days the Russians made an advance of 40 to 60 miles to reach the Dniester at Zaleschiki, some 63 miles south of Tarnopol. Crossing the river they roared on to the Pruth. Cernauti (Czernowitz) was their primary objective ; and on March 30 they were fighting their way through the suburbs of this, the chief town of Bukovina. At the same time they stormed Kolomyja, 45 miles to the north-west, on the upper reaches of the Pruth ; and very shortly a great stretch of the river's eastern bank was in Russian hands. Here Zhukov's men were in the foothills of the Carpathians ; and at night the peaks of the whole mountain chain were reported to be ablaze with beacons lighted by the guerillas to guide their liberators by little-known tracks through the difficult countryside.

SENSATIONAL as was the advance of the 1st Ukrainian Front, it was paralleled, perhaps surpassed, by their comrades of the 2nd Ukrainian Front under Marshal Koniev. In a week the Russians in this sector covered a hundred miles from Uman, reached the Dniester and crossed it on a broad front. Bessarabia became a battlefield as with swift, savage thrusts Koniev drove across the lowlands separating the Dniester from the Pruth. There he linked up with Zhukov on his right ; and together the two great Red Army groups crossed yet another river which only the strategists had thought to be a grave obstacle in the Russians' path. Pontoons brought up by the marvellous supply trains, boats of every description, barrels, doors, bundles of reeds—everything and anything was used to get the men across. Their élan was terrific. The Germans, battered and bewildered, hastened westward.

Meanwhile, Malinovsky's 3rd Ukrainian Front had been fighting its way through Nikolayev (captured on March 28) towards the Black Sea shore to within little more than 20 miles of Odessa. On April 2 great columns of smoke rising from the city spoke of German attempts to destroy their stores and installations before the Russians pierced their defences. The city fell on April 10.

RUMANIA proper was invaded on April 2 ; that night Mr. Molotov, Soviet Foreign Commissar, issued a warning to the Rumanians that the Red Army would pursue their troops until they should decide to abandon the Germans who had brought upon them such disasters and humiliations. Russia sought no territorial conquests nor did she seek to make social changes in Rumania ; but she would continue the war until the enemy's complete rout and capitulation.

Historians and novelists have found in Napoleon's retreat from Moscow a theme calculated to arouse their utmost powers of description. For all we know, there may be some new Tolstoy in the ranks of the Russians pursuing Hitler's shattered legions ; but as yet we must rely upon tantalizingly scrappy accounts of what is beyond a doubt one of the greatest events of the present century.

But in imagination we may stand amongst the wondering peasantry on the Rumanian pathways, watching a ragged and wearied horde, sweating and swearing, caked with dust, with bloodshot eyes, wounds bandaged with dirty rags, some without boots, but many carrying bags of loot, pouring along the same roads down which in 1941 the German army had marched so confidently, so cheerfully, so gloriously, to smash the Russian army and state. What the winter's snows did to Napoleon's Grande Armée, the armoured might and native valour of Stalin's Russia have done to Hitler's war machine.

# Interludes of War on the Main 5th Army Front

REST AND RELAXATION are provided for some of our men on the main 5th Army front in Italy by a mobile tented "circus" controlled by the Expeditionary Force Institute, as the N.A.A.F.I. is known overseas; in a barber's tent (1) they enjoy their first comfortable hair-cut for weeks. To our forward infantry frequent change of socks is vital to good health; at a battalion H.Q. hours are spent washing and darning them (2). Pack mules which carry supplies to 5th Army forward positions are tended by Italian soldiers (3). On their way to firing positions at Cassino Sherman tanks cross a repaired bridge (4). Keeping in touch with New Zealand, Indian and British troops on the hills above Cassino are these field radio operators (5).

*Photos, British Official; Associated Press, Planet News*

# No Rest for the Westward-Driven Wehrmacht

LED BY RUSSIA'S ABLEST COMMANDER, Marshal Zhukov (2), the 1st Ukrainian Army reached the frontier of Czechoslovakia on April 8, 1944. Columns of retreating Nazis head westwards on a snow-covered Russian road (1); lacking adequate motor transport, the Germans make use of horse-drawn vehicles, and across the Pripet River enemy troops are evacuated in rubber dinghies (3). A shell (4) is raised into the breech of a Soviet long-range gun on the White Russian front (5) to batter a distant position.

*Photos, Keystone, Pictorial Press*

# THE WAR AT SEA

## by Francis E. McMurtrie

SINCE she was disabled by torpedoes from British midget submarines last September, little had been heard of Germany's largest warship, the 45,000-ton Tirpitz. It had been reported from Swedish sources that other vessels were constantly alongside her, presumably engaged in the patching of the damage. To effect more than temporary repairs to so large a ship would be impossible without putting her in dry dock; and there is no dry dock big enough to take her nearer than Kiel.

In March the Hamburg-Südamerika liner Monte Rosa, of 14,000 tons gross, was reported to be in Kaafjord, the inlet at the farther end of Altenfjord where the Tirpitz has been lying for many months past. On

forecastle. Sixteen bombs struck her in all. Large explosions were seen near the mainmast and on the forecastle. Anti-aircraft fire was met from the Tirpitz and from shore batteries throughout the operation, but when the last aircraft went in, the battleship had stopped firing. When last seen the Tirpitz was on fire amidships.

A GERMAN account of the operation alleges that 16 British aircraft were brought down, a gross exaggeration. In fact, only three Barracuda bombers and one fighter failed to return to the carriers, a low price to pay for the disablement of the enemy's most important fighting ship. A further enemy claim to have sunk 14 British escort vessels

Escorting fighters included Seafires (a naval variety of the famous Spitfire), Corsairs, Hellcats and Wildcats, the three latter being of American build and design, though flown by British naval airmen.

It is just four years since the last successful dive-bombing attack was delivered by British naval aircraft against a German warship in Norwegian waters. On April 9, 1940, the cruiser Königsberg was sunk in Bergen harbour by Skua aircraft.

Admiral Sir Bruce Fraser has received congratulations from the King and from the Prime Minister on the success of this operation. Since he became Commander-in-Chief of the Home Fleet a year ago the Tirpitz has been put out of action twice; her consort, the battleship Scharnhorst, has been sunk; and a number of convoys have been escorted to North Russia without serious loss.

It may be questioned whether the Tirpitz will ever see Germany again. Should Finland drop out of the war, as seems probable, the German grip on North Norway will soon have to be relinquished, and if the great battleship cannot be brought away she may have to be scuttled, like the Admiral Graf Spee in the River Plate in 1939.

## RESERVES for Drafting to New U-Boats

Germany's few remaining surface warships comprise the dismantled battleship Gneisenau, which can be written off for practical purposes; the two "pocket battleships," Lützow and Admiral Scheer; and six cruisers, the Admiral Hipper, Prinz Eugen, Nürnberg, Leipzig, Köln and Emden. There is also the aircraft carrier Graf Zeppelin, but she has never been to sea. All of these are believed to be in the Baltic, where their inactivity gives rise to the suspicion that their complements are being used as a reserve from which officers and men can be drafted to man new U-boats commissioned to replace the heavy casualties of the past fifteen months.

IN the Pacific the tide continues to run strongly against the Japanese. It is considered that some 100,000 Japanese troops in New Guinea, New Britain, New Ireland, the Admiralty group, and Bougainville have been abandoned to their fate by the High Command in Tokyo. It is merely a question of time before all of them are wiped out or left to starve, in the absence of reinforcements and supplies. Occupation of more and more of the various groups of islands lying to the northward make more remote any prospect of relief. Most of the Marshalls have now been taken by United States forces, leaving in enemy hands only four islands of any importance in this group.

A BARRACUDA, the new Fleet Air Arm torpedo-bomber, is here seen flying across a destroyer's stern. A perfectly timed surprise attack by Barracudas, on April 3, 1944, left Germany's sole remaining capital ship, the 45,000-ton Tirpitz, ablaze in Altenfjord. The Tirpitz was also the target, in Sept. 1943, of our midget submarines (see p. 649).

*Photo, British Official*

March 30 the Monte Rosa sailed for Germany taking with her, it is suspected, the salvage equipment and skilled workmen who had been engaged in making the battleship ready for sea. On her way south, not far from the Norwegian port of Stavanger, the Monte Rosa was attacked by Beaufighters of the Coastal Command. She was torpedoed twice, the second attack being made after midnight, March 31–April 1, by units of a New Zealand air squadron. Though the ultimate result could not be observed, there is no doubt the liner was sunk.

AFTER the departure of the Monte Rosa, the Tirpitz prepared to follow her. As she was about to get under way, towards dawn on April 3, successive attacks were made on her by two forces of Barracuda aircraft of the Fleet Air Arm, flying from carriers of the Home Fleet. These carriers were supported by other ships under Vice-Admiral Sir Henry Moore, the second-in-command of the Home Fleet.

In the first attack the Tirpitz was hit by heavy and medium-sized bombs at points near the bridge, amidships, and forward; in the second, an hour later, hits were scored near the after turret, amidships and on the

may also be regarded as a ludicrous falsehood.

Swedish reports suggest that the Tirpitz incurred some 300 casualties, which may well be true, since she was apparently engaged in unmooring ship, and would therefore be likely to have her full complement on board with many of them on the upper deck. Though it is improbable that injuries sufficient to prevent the ship from steaming can have been inflicted, it may be assumed that the gunnery control system was put out of action, and other serious damage done that would reduce her fighting power very considerably.

This is the first time that Barracuda aircraft have taken part in an operation of first class importance, though it is known that they have been coming into service with the Fleet Air Arm for some time past. This new type can be used for either bombing or torpedo attack, as well as for reconnaissance, or gunnery spotting. In the present case it seems probable that dive-bombing was the method employed, for not only would the cliffs of the Altenfjord interfere with high level bombing, but the latter form of attack could scarcely have produced so many hits.

FREQUENT attacks were made by the U.S. Pacific Fleet during March and April on atolls in the Caroline, Mariana and Palau groups. In the course of these operations, which included naval bombardments and air bombing, two Japanese destroyers and another warship were sunk, and a battleship was damaged by a torpedo from an American submarine.

The most important Japanese strongholds in these groups are Truk, Yap, Guam, Saipan, Tinian and Babelthuap. Of these, the last-named is distant only 600 miles from the Philippines, and if occupied by American troops and used as an airfield and naval base might prove a thorn in the side of the Japanese garrisons. That this possibility is already causing alarm may be inferred from the fact that an air-raid warning is reported to have been given in Manila, capital of the Philippines, early in April.

# Pontoons Linked Landing Craft with Kwajalein

**SEA TOO SHALLOW FOR LANDING CRAFT** assailing Kwajalein, in the Marshall Islands in the Pacific, on January 31, 1944, was bridged by sectional pontoons, across which U.S. troops poured to beat the Japanese. Transport of bulky pontoon components, of which there are several types, and speedy assembly at the spot required is the concern of Army engineers ; to the labours of the latter, under fire, spectacular triumphs of the fighting men not infrequently are due. See also illus. p. 660. *Photo, New York Times Photos*

# Little Rescue Tugs are Winning Big Victories

In accordance with traditions of the great Silent Service, the tug fleet of the Royal Navy pursues its work of saving stricken ships and their cargoes with the minimum of talk. Seldom do the achievements of the men who so daringly serve aboard these craft come to light : the following account, by HOWARD JOHNS, is therefore of especial interest. See also facing page.

FOR reasons of security little is ever said of the great work being carried out by salvage tugs of the Royal Navy. One chance word might give the enemy a line to work upon and result in our losing a valuable ship, trained seamen, and a cargo worth thousands of pounds. Thus the "little tough guys" of the sea work hard and often, in fair weather and foul, with even less

H.M. TUG GROWLER, ocean-going rescue vessel, powered with Diesel engines, has a cruising endurance of over 50 days. Her sleek build is specially designed to withstand the roughest weather. All tugs are armed in wartime as protection against enemy interference with their rescue work.
*Photo, British Official*

praise than is bestowed upon other branches of the Senior Service.

Under the command of Captain C. Walcott, C.B.E., Captain-in-Charge Rescue Tugs, some of the greatest sea victories of this war are being won. Not only are the men of the tugs fighting a ruthless enemy, the elements also sometimes seem to side with the Germans. But by reason of grim determination and tremendous skill they seldom know defeat. Scores of Allied ships claimed by the enemy as sunk by either submarine or air attack have reached port and been repaired, thanks to our quick-thinking tug skippers.

Before the war Holland specialized in salvage work and owned a fleet of tugs that were in great demand. Many, I am told, came to this country when Hitler invaded Holland. Since 1940 the tug fleet of the Royal Navy has been developed and many new units added to the sturdy "toughs," including the 16 knot Brigand type with 3,000 h.p. engines. When things were very black, America sent over tugs to assist our hard-pressed fleet ; one of them starred in the famous film Tugboat Annie. When the film had been completed the tug was sunk ; she was refloated to come to our aid and has been very successful off the East Coast of England, especially in "E-Boat Alley."

THE men of the tugs come from the ports around Britain, from the large and the small rivers. The last few years have blended them into a perfect team, and in the course of extensive travel rarely have I met a happier set of men than those who serve aboard the tugs. One of the best-known leaders is Lieut.-Commander Harold Osbourne, O.B.E., R.N.R., Senior Master of Tugs. In the last four years at sea he has salvaged 40,000 tons of shipping and saved cargoes worth many thousands of pounds.

In the course of his valuable and daring work the Commander has had some unusual tows. For example, on one occasion he was sent out to the assistance of a Sunderland flying-boat believed to be in distress. He

located the plane, as it was being tossed about by Atlantic waves. Quickly Lieut.-Commander Osbourne secured a "tow," and for 230 miles hauled the flying-boat back to port. Today it is once more on operational duty. On another occasion he towed back to base a tanker, the after-part of which was under water. His skill resulted in the saving of 10,000 gallons of petrol.

Another tug, the Samsonia, received a signal to go to the assistance of a "plane that is adrift." When he received the message the skipper was rather surprised—but orders are orders. Eventually he located the plane, a Lockheed bomber, lashed to a raft. Apparently it had been resting on the deck of a ship that had been torpedoed. Anyway, after three days of towing through heavy seas they reached Britain with the plane whose only damage was a dented nose.

Some of the cargoes saved by our tugs have been worth a small fortune. H.M.S. Dexterous, under the command of Sub-Lieutenant Ronald Fletcher, R.N.R., a thirty-year-old salvage expert, went 270 miles out into the Atlantic in heavy weather to the assistance of a vessel known to be carrying cargo essential to the war effort. And the Dexterous brought back to Britain a ship carrying a cargo worth £250,000.

ONE of the great salvage jobs of the war was completed by the tug H.M.S. Saucy. She towed a bottomless ship nearly 1,000 miles from Iceland to this country. The vessel had been on the rocks for nearly twelve months, but was still packed with a cargo. Temporary repairs were made and two tugs commenced the long haul to base. Bad weather was encountered and one of the tugs broke away. It was essential that the cargo should not roll, or the vessel would capsize. A signal was sent to the Saucy that the bulkheads were giving way. There was nothing to do but heave-to for the night while further temporary repairs were carried out.

"Waves were breaking over the cargo ship," said the C.O. of the Saucy, "and at times she was like a breakwater. They had to keep shoring up her decks, using nearly 1,000 feet of timber. At one time we had to pump 84 tons of precious oil on to the water to prevent the ship rolling. But we finished the job after one of the most exciting tasks I have had for years." Note the remark : "But we finished the job." That is a fact of which our tugs are justly proud, for they overcome very great difficulties to keep this record.

A typical example is the tug H.M.S. Bustler. Exchange of engine parts enabled her to bring a 14,000-ton merchant ship safely to port over miles of ocean. The Bustler was towing a bomb-damaged ship in the Mediterranean when she herself broke down. The merchant vessel had most of her stern missing and was drawing 52 ft. of water by the stern and 47 ft. by the head. Most of the time the tug was working on alternate engines. Then her

engineer officer had an idea. The ship in tow had similar engines to those in the tug, so the merchantman was boarded, parts collected and exchanged, and adapted to the tug's engines. After that everything went according to plan ; when the Bustler reached port they had voyaged nearly 1,500 miles.

Sometimes failure to bring a stricken ship home is accompanied by immense credit to the rescue tug crew concerned, as when the effort has been truly tremendous. Witness, for example, the endeavour of the tug Stormking which tried so valiantly to bring to port the sloop H.M.S. Woodpecker—one of the five sloops which shared in the sinking of six U-boats (see p. 711). Crippled by a torpedo, the Woodpecker was towed for eight days, a distance of 600 miles, the last part of the way by the Stormking—only to capsize and sink in heavy weather, with her ensign flying, when 40 miles from land.

"IT was a bitter blow," said Lieut. L. Colmans, R.N.R., the Stormking's commanding officer. "But it would have been impossible to tow the sinking sloop any farther as she might have plunged to the bottom at any moment. We had to slip the tow-rope." Said Sub-Lieut. A. C. Hooper, R.N.R., also of the Stormking, "Twice during the tow part of the complement of the Woodpecker was taken off. A skeleton crew was retained on board. Then we had a signal to expect a north-easterly gale. Immediately Commander H. L. Pryse, R.N.R., her commanding officer, decided that the Woodpecker could not live through a gale and he ordered 'Abandon ship.' The ship's company watched the end of their ship from the decks of the corvettes H.M.S. Azalea and H.M.C.S. Chilliawack."

The gallant little Stormking, with several salvaged ships to her credit, celebrated the first anniversary of her commission in March 1944, and her commanding officer, who took part in beach operations during the N. African landings, at the age of 25 is the youngest captain in the rescue tug service.

HIT BY A TORPEDO, the sloop Woodpecker (in background) was photographed from the deck of H.M. tug Stormking which had her in tow before she foundered and sank, as related above. See also pp. 710-711.
*Photo, British Official*

# They Salvage Torpedoed British Merchantman

SALVAGE OFFICER AND TUG CAPTAINS go into conference (1), planning to the last detail how to save a torpedoed cargo vessel. Operations agreed upon, a pilot rope is thrown from the wreck to a rescue tug (2) where the massive tow rope is hooked into position (3) and then prepared for casting off (4). Once again the little tugs of the Royal Navy have justified themselves : that which was a wreck (5) will sail another day. See narratives in facing page.

*Photos, Keystone*

# Street Fighting Taught Amidst Italian Rubble

LESSONS IN STREET FIGHTING in Ortona, Italy, which was captured on Dec. 28, 1943, by the 8th Army after days of bitter house-to-house combat, are now part of routine training. Part of the town, a few miles behind the present front line, has been turned into a "school" where veterans of this type of warfare pass on their hard-won practical knowledge to the less experienced : a signpost (1) proclaims the fact ; it also warns trainees against imaginary mines. A section advances from behind the cover of a battered wall (2) and picks its way to the first house.

U.S. TROOPS CO-OPERATE with British in similar training in England. "Entrymen" about to clear a house (3) ; at a street corner a British Bren-gun group (4) repels a counter-attack, while another Bren is taken to the top floor of a house by a soldier who uses ropes and grappling-irons to scale the wall (5), and an American follows him up (6). This method of climbing is known as "fly-walking." A house is usually cleared from the top downwards, if practicable.

*Photos, British Official ; F. H. Brindley*

# Britain's Colonies in the War: No. 6---Trinidad

IMPORTANT CONTRIBUTOR to Allied war supplies pool is Trinidad, separated from Venezuela, S. America, by the Gulf of Paria, which forms an almost land-locked harbour capable of containing all the navies of the world. Trinidad was discovered by Columbus on his first voyage in 1498 ; it became British in 1797.

Chief help to the war effort is oil, of which Trinidad is the British Empire's leading producer ; in 1940 there were some 2,416 wells producing over 20,219,000 gallons a year. Pitch, from which asphalt is made, is also produced in large quantities ; pre-war figure was 127,859 tons annually. Other important commodities, pre-war figures for which give a guide to the amounts supplied, are sugar 270,000.000 lb. ; cocoa 43,000,000 lb. ; copra 9,500,000 lb. Some 2,500,000 coconuts are produced, and thousands of gallons of rum, most of which goes to the Navy. Trinidad has given many men to the Forces, and they serve all over the world. Decorations gained by men of the island include the M.C., two D.F.C.s and a D.C.M. There is a local Defence Force, and Trinidad women have formed A.T.S. and W.A.A.F units.

One of the oil-wells (1) producing to capacity for the United Nations, and the largest sugar refinery on the island (2). Down a rope cradle-way (3) to ships waiting at the jetty go barrels of valuable pitch-asphalt from the famous pitch lake in S.W. Trinidad —144 acres in extent. Hoisting the R.A.F. standard at a commemorative service to the Battle of Britain held at Piarco airfield (4) is Acting Governor A. B. Wright.

*Photos, Lubinski, Sport & General, E. P. Smith*

# Honoured Rest at the Last for the Fallen

The last rites that it is in the power of the Authorities to accord to those who have given their lives in the war are the responsibility of the Graves Registration Service and the Imperial War Graves Commission. ALEXANDER DILKE explains here the work of the special units concerned with interment, and the marking and maintaining of the last hallowed resting places.

B Y 1914-18 standards our casualties in the present war have been "light," though many thousands of soldiers, sailors and airmen from the Empire lie buried in Britain or "some corner of a foreign field that is for ever England." The burial of these men who have given their lives, and the marking of their graves, is receiving the same reverent care as the similar sad task during and after the last war, a task which was only just completed before the outbreak of the present war.

In Madagascar, North Africa, Sicily, Italy, New Guinea and in Britain itself new cemeteries have been designed according to the very high standards set in 1918. As the fighting front has moved forward, soldiers specially trained for the work begin the task of bringing the men from their scattered graves and burying them in these cemeteries with the temporary standard cross to mark

are being laid out and during the coming months some will be handed over to the Imperial War Graves Commission.

The choice of a site for a military cemetery is never simple, for ease of access and maintenance as well as military association and environment have to be taken into consideration. The work of locating the scattered graves of men who fell in the many battles in Africa is now going on apace. It is difficult and sometimes dangerous work. Millions of mines were sown in the desert. Although it is now over one and a half years since Alamein, and the front line is thousands of miles away, unexploded shells, booby traps and mines remain. Rommel's booby-traps tied to our dead or littered near their temporary graves in the desert still wait for the unwary. Six officers and men of the Graves Registration Service have been killed

In Madagascar the work of making permanent cemeteries is progressing. In Abyssinia the Foreign Office last year opened negotiations with the Ethiopian Government concerning the care of British war graves. In Palestine and in Syria new cemeteries have been opened. Some of the dead of the present war have been buried in the British Naval Cemetery at Tripoli (Syria) where lie men from H.M.S. Victoria and H.M.S. Camperdown, killed in 1893.

F ROM Burma and Malaya there is no news, and it does not seem likely that there will be until the Japanese have been driven out. From the countries of Occupied Europe, reports of burials during the present war are received through the International Red Cross. Belgian patriots recently placed new crosses on the graves of Allied soldiers who fell during the 1940 campaign, at the cemetery at Blankenberghe. Friendly Danes have planted British graves in their country with roses and tulips.

News from the Continent of cemeteries containing the graves of the last war indicates that there has been no vandalism, although (necessarily) some neglect. Where headstones have been damaged or destroyed by battles or bombing they have been replaced by the Vichy authorities with wooden crosses. Men to the number of 157 employed by the Imperial War Graves Commission in looking after the cemeteries and memorials have been interned.

Because of the air war, many men engaged on active service have died in Britain. The Commission is responsible for all war graves in Britain and has marked with wooden crosses those in over 1,000 Service plots and privately owned graves in cemeteries and churchyards. The majority of men of all nationalities lie in Brookwood, where there is a U.S. Military Cemetery, and a Canadian Section where 50 Canadians brought back from Dieppe were buried with maple leaves from the tree in the centre of the 1914-18 Canadian plot. There are new sections for Belgian, Czechoslovak, French, and Polish graves.

SALUTE TO AMERICAN ARMY DEAD is fired by a guard of honour over the burial place of troops who fell during the fighting for Kwajalein Island, in the Pacific Marshalls group (see story in p. 729 and illus. p. 743). Painstaking search for the bodies of those as yet unburied will be carried out as in other theatres of war, as explained in this page.                    *Photo, Associated Press*

the grave. Full details are most carefully recorded, and in due course the temporary cross will be replaced by whatever form of permanent headstone is agreed upon.

On the overseas battlefields, the work of marking and maintaining graves is carried out by the Graves Registration Service of the Army. When circumstances permit, the Imperial War Graves Commission takes over responsibility. Shortly after the Germans had been driven from North Africa, the Army requested the Commission to take over responsibility for permanent maintenance and construction of the graves of soldiers who fell in the East African campaigns and the many campaigns in the Desert and in Tunisia and Algeria.

T HE Commission created a new administrative area and appointed Col. R. H. Hoffman, formerly of the Staff of the Union of South Africa Defence Force, to take charge. As Assistant Director of Graves Registration and Inquiries in the Middle East for a year, he had great experience of the special problems involved. Mr. J. Hubert Worthington was appointed Principal Architect for North Africa. Seventeen to nineteen permanent cemeteries for those who fell in the Western Desert and North Africa

lately. Shifting sands of the desert make maps obsolete and may obliterate a grave where a man was hastily buried in the heat of battle. Yet all these graves are being located by special units, going out with lorries into the desert and searching several days, perhaps, for a single grave.

The soldiers carrying out this work feel a special responsibility and are determined that no comrade-in-arms shall lie in an unmarked grave. if persistence and the skilful use of recorded information and knowledge of the ways of the desert can prevent it. When all the men who fell at or near Alamein are brought in, they will lie in a cemetery approached at both ends through triumphal arches, and the desert site will be beautified with grass and shrubs.

It was not until fifteen years after the Cease Fire in 1918 that the Imperial War Graves Commission was satisfied that every fallen soldier who could be identified had been given a grave. Years after the end of the war, the finding of a cigarette case or a chance remark, resulted in identifications being made and another headstone being erected. We may expect the same thing to happen after the end of the present war.

I N Service plots, marked in the same way, are the graves of Nursing Services, W.R.N.S., A.T.S. and W.A.A.F. They have not been grouped separately, and the Commission has found that this absolute equality of treatment has the full approval of the Services and of the relatives.

The nature of this war has led to more civilians than Servicemen being killed in Britain. About 50,000 men, women and children have been killed by bombs. The Imperial War Graves Commission does not mark their graves, but it records each one, and with the aid of relatives has compiled a list, county by county ; three leather-bound volumes with names and details have been deposited in Westminster Abbey. Copies are available for the consultation of the public in London, Edinburgh and Belfast.

At the end of the 1914-18 war the Imperial War Graves Commission was faced with the gigantic task of finding permanent resting places and memorials for 1,100,000 dead who were buried in 100,000 different places. Now, under the Vice-Chairmanship of Major-General Sir Fabian Ware, K.C.V.O., they have the advantage of experience, and we may be confident that when temporary crosses are replaced by permanent memorials, and the planting of the cemeteries has been completed, these will be worthy of the cause for which the fallen gave their lives.

# Here Repose the Brave Who Gave Their All

A SIMPLE STONE marks the valorous deeds of men of the 8th Army who fell and were buried at Mozzagrogna (1), important Italian village on the River Sangro, captured on Nov. 30, 1943. On the 5th Army Garigliano front, steel helmets and rifles belong to three British soldiers who gave their lives (4). In the Tunisian campaign, a British Parachute Brigade fought with great distinction between November 1942 and April 1943 on every sector of the 1st Army front; on the site of one of the Brigade's battles a sergeant pays homage to fallen comrades (2). A Canadian padre holds a drumhead service at a cemetery of the Canadian Seaforth Highlanders of the 8th Army (3).

*Photos, British Official*

# How Do We Stand in the Burmese War Zone?

Fighting in the Far East flares up and increases in tempo. For the Japanese in Burma this has meant determined Allied offensives in the north and the south, while they have launched an attack on the Indian frontier State of Manipur. In this article a Special Correspondent of THE WAR ILLUSTRATED reviews the somewhat confused position.

DURING the past month the Allied and Japanese forces in the Burmese war zone have been very active. For in some six weeks, with the commencement of the monsoons, the campaigning season in Burma will have come to an end. It is now evident that, while an invasion of German-occupied Western Europe is still pending, a large scale "aero-naval" offensive against the Japanese in Burma and the Burmese-Javan chain of islands is not possible.

Instead, early in December 1943, American-equipped and trained Chinese forces under General Joseph Stilwell launched an offensive across the Patkai Range and forced their way into the Hukawng Valley. Their immediate object is to clear Northern Burma of the Japanese by capturing their main base at Myitkyina, the terminus of the railway from Mandalay and Rangoon, while the ultimate aim is to link the Burma Road with Ledo in Assam by means of a motor road. The airfield at Myitkyina is also of immense value to the China Air Ferry Command.

In this attack the Chinese have met with a fair amount of success. Their main line of advance has been down the Hukawng Valley, crossing the Patkai Range via the Paungsoe Pass. The town of Maingkwan in the valley is now in their hands and they are operating in the neighbourhood of Shaduzup, which is occupied by the British. From Shaduzup a fairly good metalled road, 68 miles long, runs to Mogaung, which is on the Mandalay–Myitkyina railway. To the north of Myitkyina a British column composed of Gurkhas and Chin levies is advancing from Sumprabum towards Myitkyina.

It must be remembered that Northern Burma is a mountainous and sparsely populated country, and even after Burma was overrun the Japanese were never able to clear this part of Burma entirely of British and Indian forces, who held strong positions in some sectors.

To prevent hard-pressed Japanese forces in the Mogaung-Myitkyina area from receiving reinforcements from Mandalay by rail, British and American airborne troops (complete with arms and supplies), under the late Maj.-Gen. Orde Wingate, were dropped, according to the Japanese, near Katha, 100 miles south of Myitkyina, where the British also managed to construct an air strip right in the centre of Northern Burma. This daring move on the part of the Allied forces placed the enemy in a precarious position. But these military operations in Northern Burma cannot be interpreted as being part of any major campaign to reconquer Burma. Their main aim is, perhaps, to open up communications with China.

On April 3, 1944, it was announced that the Japanese had launched their expected counter-attack against the airborne Allied troops and the air strip which had been established 200 miles behind their lines. An attacking force of 200 of the enemy took up positions a short distance north of the landing strip, which was used by Dakota transport planes bearing supplies for the Allied columns. Early in the fight, which lasted throughout three days, the Japanese gained control of the light plane dispersal area, but were later driven out. Only one small plane was found not to have been destroyed or rendered non-airworthy by the withdrawing Japanese. British and American wounded were assisted into the plane, and a Polish sergeant took off safely amid a hail of bullets from the enemy. The Japanese were eventually routed

with the aid of Allied fighters, and the danger of losing the air strip was averted.

It is quite probable that the Japanese High Command, fearing that the British and Indian troops would develop simultaneous thrusts from Manipur towards the Chindwin Valley, decided to forestall any such projected offensive by themselves invading India. At this late stage of the campaigning season it is unlikely that the present Japanese attack is part of any grandiose military offensive against India.

IN their drive against Manipur State the Japanese made three separate assaults: one from Tiddim in the Chin Hills, the second from Tamu on the Burmese-Indian

NORTH OF IMPHAL, on April 12, 1944, Japanese troops were near the 14th Army's railhead at Dinapur, while Gen. Stilwell's Chinese troops were advancing towards Mogaung and the enemy key air base of Myitkyina, Burma railway terminus.
*By courtesy of News Chronicle*

frontier in the Kabaw Valley, and the other from the neighbourhood of Tamanthi across the Naga Hills towards Kohima. It was the last of these thrusts, striking north-west into

India in the direction of the vital Assam-Bengal railway, forming the main supply route for General Stilwell's American-equipped Chinese troops in Northern Burma, which seemed to constitute the greatest danger. If the railway should be cut, supplies could be flown to General Stilwell, but the pressure on the Japanese on that front would be considerably relieved. Imphal itself, the capital of Manipur State, was directly menaced by this northern drive.

THE Seventeenth Indian Division, who were in Tiddim when the Japanese began an outflanking movement, moved out twenty-four hours ahead of programme. They made a successful fighting withdrawal into the Imphal plain with all their wounded and the bulk of their transport, clearing Japanese road blocks on the way.

The very difficult nature of the country will be appreciated. There is but one good road in the Manipur frontier region, and it leads from Tamu to Manipur Road Station, near Dinapur. This road crosses the Letha range, 3,000 feet above sea-level, and continues up the Manipur River Valley to Imphal, 52 miles from Tamu. Another, poorer, road connects Imphal with Silchar, a town on the branch of the Assam-Bengal railway.

Climatic conditions are extremely bad; the country surrounding Imphal is very malarious, while the rainfall during the monsoon season is between 200 and 300 inches. Part of the Japanese plan may well be to seize strategic points inside the Indian frontier, which they can hold during the rainy season, thus forestalling the Allies from preparing for an attack on Burma from Assam.

In the Burmese maritime province of Arakan, though Maungdaw and Buthidaung are in British hands, the presence of strong Japanese forces in the Mayu Hills has prevented British forces from advancing southwards. Nevertheless, Kyauktaw, due east of Buthidaung, was recently captured by British troops. The Province of Arakan is cut by a maze of rivers and tidal creeks and covered with a series of low-lying, wooded hills, which send out spurs and sub-spurs almost to the sea coast. Thus an overland drive towards Akyab is very slow and difficult. Arakan can only be occupied by a combined sea and land offensive, and obviously the South-East Asia Command do not consider this isolated province of sufficient strategic importance to warrant such an attack at the present stage.

## JAPANESE IN TUNNELS HELD UP OUR ADVANCE

IT may appear from outside that the Arakan campaign in Burma is making painfully slow progress. It appears that way, too, from inside (writes Geoffrey Tebbutt, Evening Standard war correspondent on the Arakan front). Contributing factors were two Japanese tunnel positions on an abandoned railway line between Maungdaw and Buthidaung where the road corkscrews through the wild precipitous gorges of the Mayu range.

The Japanese have been there some months, and it was necessary for us to secure them to maintain the wet season supply line to Buthidaung. One, the most westerly, was taken during the last week in March 1944.

THIS tunnel is 150 yards long, 8 to 10 feet high and 11 feet wide, and had been attacked for several weeks. A handful of Japs held it desperately. There is a mountain of earth above the tunnel, and shells and bombs apparently did not affect it. The paths by which British troops approached the defences are steep and narrow.

This is what happened just before the capture. A three days' artillery mortar bombardment pre-

ceded an attack by three British companies, which, operating from two directions, gained with difficulty three more of the features surrounding the tunnel. The Japanese had only a little light artillery around the tunnel, but they tossed grenades down as the attackers climbed.

THE British company had to use scaling ladders to climb a 50-foot brick retaining wall in the railway cutting, and observation of the enemy's movements during the preliminary bombardment was almost impossible through the clouds of dust as the shells burst.

It took a day to bring direct fire to bear on the tunnel entrance, then Sherman tanks were able to send a few rounds near the tunnel entrance.

They also used searchlights in a vain attempt to penetrate the dust and observe the enemy's defences near the tunnel mouth, while the Japanese, withdrawing from one bamboo covered hill to another, further delayed the capture of the tunnel itself. It will long be remembered by the succession of units assigned to it as among the hardest and ugliest tasks they have had.

Photos, Indian Official, Keystone

# *Through the Green Hell of Burma*

Jungle horrors are increased by extreme difficulties of terrain encountered by our forces now engaged in Burma. Rivers may help to solve transport problems: a supply barge (top) navigated by native boatmen plies between densely wooded shores. Water, too, is on occasion the best path to follow: jungle-wise Kachin scouts (bottom) wade knee-deep on the trail of the Japanese. They are led by a U.S. sergeant, left foreground. Regular Allied troops follow the scouts.

751

# New Roads for the Jungle Fighters in Arakan

Indian Air Force co-operates with the R.A.F. in support of troops : Sqd.-Leader Mehar Singh (1) shows a photo-mosaic of enemy territory, prepared by his squadron, to Air Marshal Sir John Baldwin.   Engineers have succeeded in rebuilding or improving a number of roads in Arakan : laden carriers (4) move up with war essentials and return with Allied wounded.
Chinese warriors are inspected by Admiral Lord Louis Mountbatten (2, centre) and Generalissimo Chiang Kai-shek.

Photos
Paul P

## *Supplies Arrive by Air for Guerilla Columns*

Playing a significant part in the jungle campaigns in Northern Burma are airborne troops; their brilliant commander, Maj.-Gen. Orde Wingate, was killed in a plane crash on March 24, 1944. Where other means fail, food and ammunition are taken to the Allied guerilla columns by air and dropped by parachute (5). Commander of the 5th Indian Division on the Arakan front is Maj.-Gen. H. R. Briggs, D.S.O. and bar (3), seen studying a map on the steps of his caravan headquarters.

cial,
tone

## *Tanks and Mules Move up on the Burma Front*

Photos, Indian Official

British and Indian troops of the 14th Army scored a signal success when they turned encirclement of the 7th Division by Japanese in the Ngakyedauk Pass area into a great victory, on Feb. 24, 1944: a Gen. Grant tank (top) manned by the 25th Dragoons which helped to blast enemy positions.    The steep pass is surmounted by a mule convoy (bottom) which delivers urgently needed stores, including radio sets whereby communication is maintained between widely separated columns.

# VIEWS & REVIEWS
## Of Vital War Books

### by Hamilton Fyfe

WE talk a lot about terrifying developments in machinery for killing that have made warfare today something totally different from what it used to be. Why shouldn't we think sometimes about the change in the way the wounded are looked after, the vast improvement in the treatment of wounds, the rapidity with which the injured are taken back from the front and, by various stages, each most carefully thought out and systematized, landed in a first-class hospital, where they have every chance to recover? I want you to think about this side of warfare as it is revealed in a very readable, instructive and also entertaining book called R.A.M.C. (Hutchinson, 6s.) by Major Anthony Cotterell, who amused us with What! No Morning Tea! and has another book about Army life, An Apple for the Sergeant, coming out soon.

One statement in it will probably surprise you. Disease and illness give the Army doctors far more work than do wounds. In the 1914-18 war twice as many men went down "sick" as were casualties in the fighting. In the Pacific islands the ratio is no doubt higher; there malaria claims many victims. In Burma and Malaya climate accounts also for many casualties of the "non-battle" order.

One of the worst causes of sickness in the Army is dyspepsia. Though the author does not say so, the main reason for this is bad cooking. The food is excellent; never has it been better or so varied. But the standard of cooking is still low. Major Cotterell says soldiers who suffer from acute indigestion "were usually suffering from the same thing in civil life," or it is due to "the change to a new environment." I am afraid this will not explain the fact that "in a large hospital 15 to 20 per cent of the cases will be dyspeptic," or that "one in eight of the B.E.F. cases evacuated home from France up to the end of April 1940 was a case of stomach trouble."

ON the other hand, no one is likely to contest the assertion "in North Africa the R.A.M.C. probably provided a better medical service than any army ever had before." Indeed, most of us who know how good it was would take out the "probably." For the first time parachute surgical units were used in this war area. "Of course, only the barest essentials, in their most compressed and capsule form, could be taken"; but all the same, the articles dropped with the surgeon, the anaesthetist and their orderlies, included operating table, plaster of paris, blood plasma, sterilizer, anaesthetic equipment, drugs, medical comforts, bedpan. Beds, blankets and operating theatre had to be improvised on descent.

In the desert this was difficult enough, but the jungle is worse. In Abyssinia one such theatre was a thatched hut built by muleteers.

It was about 9 feet by 12 feet and 8 feet high. The roof leaked wickedly, and the bitterly cold winds shrieked through the walls, however thickly they had been thatched. They tried lining the walls and roof with their mackintosh ground-sheets, but on battle days these had to be taken down and used to cover the patients waiting outside for treatment. Channels were dug at the foot of the walls to drain the rainwater. They were not dug deep enough at first and the surgeon had to operate with his feet astride a growing stream. His hands became stiff with cold. He had to keep on washing them in hot water. They became chapped and raw.

That illustrates one aspect of the work the army surgeons do; taking it all as it comes, keeping a cheerful countenance to encourage their patients, and working sometimes till they literally drop with fatigue. Another

side of their work—or rather that of the administration staff—is the organization necessary for the evacuation of, say, 20,000 battle casualties after an engagement or, more likely, while one is still going on. To clear off that number, seventy-eight trains are required at a time when every railway is jammed with the urgent confusions of battle.

These trains must be organized to arrive at the right place at the right time, and get their highly perishable cargoes away quickly. They must run to a perfect timetable, and yet not interfere with the delivery of supplies and reinforcements. Meanwhile, the enemy is doing his best to prevent anything arriving anywhere. The lines or, worse still, the solitary line is being attacked wherever possible.

Through all this the casualties must be nursed and comforted with dressing, drugs, and skill. All this must be organized. Even to provide 20,000 men with cups of tea and cigarettes takes a bit of thinking out, and the doctors themselves must eat.

And, after all, the casualties, which have been reckoned by the staff at 20,000, may by misfortune be turned into 40,000. "It is then

## The Wonderworking R.A.M.C.

necessary to perform miracles." To the everlasting credit of the R.A.M.C. these miracles are always forthcoming. They were in France, when the retreat was so rapid that there was scarcely ever time to settle down and work on the wounded. They were in Malaya. They were in all the African campaigns. They were when we slipped up so badly at Salerno.

In the R.A.M.C. they are now ('twas not ever thus!) more open to new ideas than the general run of doctors in private practice. They have, for example, taken up psychiatry, which has knocked out the delusion, prevalent during the last war, that abnormal behaviour was due to "shell-shock," a term used to cover almost all types of psychological illness caused by battle conditions. Now that theory has been abandoned. It has been realized that the trouble originates

### A FIELD SURGICAL UNIT AT WORK

FACTS and figures recently published (in the Evening News) are striking testimony to the efficiency of the R.A.M.C. In nine months in North Africa, Sicily and Italy, one Field Surgical Unit dealt with 1,400 cases, only 5·5 per cent of which proved fatal—about one in twenty. During battles, this particular unit was in operation for 16 hours out of every 24.

In North Africa some 60 per cent of the wounds were caused by mortar fire. In Italy a greater proportion were caused by high explosive shells. Limb wounds formed the greatest part of the surgical work. Of the soldiers suffering from these, a considerable number will, after complete treatment, be classed as Category A fighting men.

The knee, 44 per cent, and the elbow, 29 per cent, were the joints most frequently injured. Of a thousand major battle casualties, flesh wounds accounted for 40 per cent, bone and joint injuries 30 per cent, abdominal wounds 8 per cent, penetrating chest wounds 4 per cent, and penetrating head wounds 2 per cent.

inside the man rather than outside. He has had something that was in his mind or character stirred up by what he has been through. The psychiatrist tries to make him a useful member of society again.

WE did not for some time after the war began—two and a half years, to be exact—adopt the German system of finding out by careful examination of recruits what work a man is specially fitted to do and what he could not possibly do. One in every ten men "needs special consideration as to how he should be employed." If they don't get it, they are a nuisance, possibly a danger. They are liable to break out in all sorts of ways in "the gruesome stress of battle," though they may do so without going into battle at all. The R.A.M.C. finds them something to do that is within their powers.

Another problem for the R.A.M.C. which has been a headache of this war is that of wounded men in tanks. It is particularly difficult to get them out. You cannot have stretcher-bearers. "The wounded are either carried back by tank or else by the medical officer who careers round the battlefield in his scout car followed by an ambulance." First-aid equipment of tanks now includes small chloroform flasks which can be crushed in cotton wool and held to a wounded man's mouth, so as to give him unconsciousness while he is being lifted out. After that, if he is lucky, he will get back to base and so, if he is badly hit, home. A Scottish soldier wounded on a Wednesday in North Africa was by Friday in a hospital twenty miles from Glasgow, where he lived. That is what the Royal Army Medical Corps can do, with the aid of the R.A.F.

THE FLAG OF MERCY, carried by a British medical orderly, goes forward amidst the rubble of Cassino on the main 5th Army front in Italy. The Red Cross was first adopted as a world symbol for healing in 1864. In that year, too, it was agreed that medical personnel of all nations at war were to be regarded as non-combatants. The wonderful story of the Royal Army Medical Corps in this war is told in the book here reviewed.

*Photo, British Official*

# Sweden Looks Anxiously to Her Home Defences

KINGDOM OF SWEDEN, sandwiched between Occupied Norway and pro-Nazi Finland, possesses vast timber resources and an annual iron ore production of 14 million tons, both long desired by the Germans. Should the latter violate her neutrality, Sweden's ports will be blocked by sunken ships. Backing Sweden's attitude is a modern army 600,000 strong, a Home Guard of 300,000, and a Navy and Air Force of considerable striking power.

STREET FIGHTING IN STOCKHOLM, Sweden's capital, carried out as an exercise on March 12, 1944, was closely watched by Minister of Defence Dr. Skold (2). Home Guards and regular troops participated: a Home Guard is ready with a sub-machine gun at a vantage point (1), and regulars advance behind the cover of a tank (3). House-to-house fighting occupied certain members of the Home Guard, who sniped from house balconies (4). A bridge is held against the "enemy" (5), and A.R.P. personnel rescue a "casualty" from a bombed building (6).

*Photos, Pictorial Press*

# Aircraft Supply 7th Division on Arakan Front

**REMARKABLE AIR SUPPLY FEAT** was performed when the 7th Division of the 14th Army was cut off on the Arakan front in Burma. Until it was relieved and the Japanese defeated, on Feb. 24, 1944, R.A.F. and U.S.A.A.F. transport planes dropped tons of supplies to the Division. Some of the parachuted stores are seen on the ground in a jungle clearing, while one of the transports which dropped them is discernible against the background of dense forest. See also p. 753.

*Photo, British Official*

# How 40,000 Civilian Sky-Watchers Aid the R.A.F.

Following their usual civilian occupations when off duty, donning blue battledress and beret when their turn comes, members of the Royal Observer Corps—whose motto is "Forewarned is Fore-armed "—render to Britain indispensable front-line service that never ends. In every type of weather, frequently in circumstances of great personal danger, this round-the-clock vigilance proceeds unfailingly, as described below by KEITH COOPER.

From lonely hilltops, headlands and other strategic points, the "Eyes and Ears of the R.A.F." operate without intermission: checking by sight or hearing the movements of all aircraft, friendly or hostile, over Britain. Working in closest co-operation with the R.A.F., by the efficiency and courage of its 40,000 members the Royal Observer Corps has saved very many lives and enabled our fighter pilots and ground defences to take heavy toll of the enemy in the air.

Formed nearly 30 years ago, the Observer Corps received the title of Royal in April 1941 in recognition of its magnificent work. At various times under the Admiralty, the War Office, or the Police, this civilian organization is today R.A.F. controlled, with its headquarters at R.A.F. Fighter Command : the latter, it was announced in February 1944, now replaced by an organization called the Air Defence of Great Britain, under the leadership of Air Marshal Sir Roderic Maxwell Hill.

The present commandant of the R.O.C. is Air Commodore Finlay Crerar, C.B.E., who before taking up this post was Deputy-Director of R.A.F. Welfare. Recruits to the Corps come from many walks of life. Mostly they are part-time watchers, men receiving payment of 1s. 3d. an hour, women 10d., girls 6d., boys 9d. Full-time men observers receive from £2 12s. to £3 18s. 6d. for a 48-hour week; women from £2 8s. 6d. to £2 15s.

Trained to identify by sight or hearing every type of aircraft—and there are nearly 300 kinds of friendly and hostile planes —the Corps operates about 1,500 posts, each of these constantly manned by two observers. There is nothing elaborate about the posts: they may be huts, or sand-bagged shelters, affording a clear view of the sky. Here continual watch is kept, by day and night, by each "crew" with its binoculars, headphone and mouthpiece, map, and an instrument for ascertaining the height of any aircraft located.

By permanent telephone line each post is linked to a centre, of which there are 40, strategically placed, and during a normal day over 1,500,000 messages originate at the posts, these comprising details — identification, height, speed, direction —of every outgoing or in-coming aircraft that may be seen or heard. At the centres to which these messages go direct the details are recorded, and there the course of planes reported upon is plotted on large squared maps. Posts are also con-nected to their neighbours by phone, so that the course any aircraft takes can be followed (and duly plotted) from one end of the country to the other.

Each centre is responsible for passing on all this information to Fighter Command (now, as previously mentioned, known as Air Defence of Great Britain), and in response fighter planes go up to intercept and do battle with intruders, ground defences are warned, and air-raid warnings sounded. Radiolocation now assists, but during the Battle of Britain the Observer Corps was the sole means of tracking enemy aircraft.

When Rudolf Hess deposited himself by parachute in Scotland, in May 1941, and, as Hitler's deputy, brought with him a peace plan the "rejection of which would be followed by the utter destruction of Britain," it was the R.O.C. who followed the course of his Me. 110 from the moment this was sighted off the coast until it crashed.

The Nazis realize to the full the value to our defence system of these." Eyes and Ears," and on more than one occasion the crew of an observation post have had a narrow shave. On one occasion a Messerschmitt dived at a hill-top post and opened fire. The post was riddled by bullets. Death stared the two watchers in the face. But they phoned to their centre details of the enemy, and this information resulted in the German fighter being destroyed.

In the log-books of the posts you will find pencilled entries forming the core of many an interesting story. There is, for example, brief data of one observer on duty on the East Coast. Glancing out to sea, at midnight, he saw a merchant ship drifting on to the rocks. At once he raised the alarm: coast-guards and a rocket life-saving squad were called to the scene. The ship's lights were failing, and promptly the observer suggested the calling-up of a mobile searchlight. Thanks to his action nearly all the crew were saved.

To him, this sort of thing was just part of his recognized work, as is reporting the efforts and progress of a maimed Allied bomber or fighter limping home from battle on the Continent in the darkness of a stormy night, or co-operating with the Air-Sea Rescue Service whereby ditched airmen are saved from a watery grave, or logging through strenuous hours the departure or arrival of hordes of bombers or fighters, Allied or enemy. Nothing mechanically winged is missed, but recorded in such detail as time permits.

It is essential that an observer shall be kept up to scratch in his or her knowledge of aircraft development and tactics ; therefore an examination must be passed at intervals of six months ; silhouettes of planes must be identified with absolute certainty, and the incidentals of reporting and route-plotting must be to them as easy as A B C. A constitution that stands up to prolonged nerve-strain and to the rigours of winter nights spent mostly in the open is as necessary as all this skill.

Proud are they of the metal badge worn on the blue beret, depicting an Eliza-bethan coast-watcher holding aloft a flaming torch. For in that badge is an echo of Armada days and nights, when other observers kept grim watch and ward, but unbeset by the perils these modern counterparts cheer-fully and most valiantly accept as part of the price of citizenship today.

Proud also are they of the praise bestowed upon them by the R.A.F. fighter pilots ; for of the Royal Observer Corps the fighters say: "They point 'em out and we knock 'em down !"

IN A ROYAL OBSERVER CORPS CENTRE, plotters seated around a large-scale table-map move counters over the face of the map in accordance with reports coming in from the neighbouring posts. This enables tellers, in the balcony overlooking the table, to phone minute-by-minute accounts of the progress of reported planes to an R.A.F. centre.

*Photo, British Official*

# On their Eyes and Ears Our Country Depends

TELEPHONE REPORTS from Royal Observer Corps observation posts guide this woman member at a report centre (1) in charting a plane's course on a squared map. Off-duty after a four-hour spell of watching and listening, an observer makes tea for himself and colleague who is still on the job (2). A roof-top post (4) in a suburb offers more comforts than usually come the way of observers. Commandant of the R.O.C. since June 23, 1943, is Air-Commodore Finlay Crerar, C.B.E., aged 40 (3). His is the honour of directing the activities of the 40,000 boys, girls, women and men who constitute this great Corps and whose invaluable aid to the R.A.F. is the subject of the article in the facing page. Air-Commodore Crerar (then Wing Commander) organized the County of Aberdeen R.A.F. Squadron in the 1940 air battles over Britain.

*Photos, British Official ; Keystone*

# By Air and Land They Proved Themselves Men

**Flt.-Lt. W. REID**

In a night raid on Düsseldorf on Nov. 3, 1943, his bomber was attacked by an enemy fighter. Wounded in the head, shoulder and hands, he concealed the extent of his injuries and continued on his course. Soon afterwards another Nazi plane attacked, the bomber's navigator was killed, the wireless operator fatally injured and the mid-upper turret oxygen system destroyed. Flt.-Lt. Reid was again hit and was supplied with oxygen from a portable supply.

Having memorized his course, he went on to bomb the target effectively. Weak from loss of blood, with a crippled and defenceless plane, he reached a home airfield and landed safely. For "devotion to duty beyond praise" he won the V.C. Flt.-Lt. Reid is 23, enlisted in 1941, trained as a pilot in America, and has taken part in ten raids.

**Actg. Major P. TRIQUET**

The V.C. presented to him only a few hours after he had flown to London from Sicily, Major Triquet gained his award for superb leadership of a Canadian force in action on Dec. 14, 1943, when they withstood overwhelming odds during an 8th Army attack on the village of Casa Berardi, vital to the capture of the Ortona-Orsogna key road junction. With disregard for personal danger, Major Triquet rallied his men until the point was taken.

**Lt. A. G. HORWOOD**

First British officer of this war to gain the V.C. on the Burma front, Lt. Horwood's posthumously awarded decoration was for "calm, resolute bravery." At Kyaukchaw, on Jan. 17, 1944, he went with a forward company of the Northamptonshire Regiment into action against a Japanese position. Throughout the day he lay in an exposed position, constantly fired upon, returning at night with valuable information. On Jan. 19 he made another attack, carried out personal reconnaissance along and about a bare ridge, and deliberately drew the enemy fire to discover their positions.

On the 20th he volunteered to lead yet another attack, and while standing up directing his men he was mortally wounded. Lt. Horwood, who was 30, won the D.C.M. in France, where he was taken prisoner but escaped and reached Dunkirk.

**Havildar GAJE GHALE**

Of 5th Royal Gurkha Rifles, Havildar Ghale (above) commanding a platoon ordered to take an important point in the Chin Hills, Burma, was wounded in the arm, chest and leg, but led his men forward in furious assaults, stormed the enemy position and held it until it was consolidated. Havildar Ghale received his V.C. decoration from Lord Wavell, Viceroy of India, at Delhi Fort, on Jan. 1, 1944.

**Sgt. THOMAS C. DERRICK**

His V.C. was awarded for "outstanding leadership and devotion to duty" during the final assault by Australian troops on Sattelberg, New Guinea, in Nov. 1943, when he was in charge of a platoon attacking a Japanese position. Ordered to withdraw, Sgt. Derrick (left) begged a last attempt to take the position. Heading his men, he hurled grenades, drove the enemy out and enabled the company to gain a firm hold. Alone he destroyed 10 enemy posts.

**Actg. Major W. P. SIDNEY**

On the night of Feb. 7-8, 1944, Major Sidney (right) commanding a support company of a Grenadier Guards battalion in the Carroceto-Buono Riposo Ridge area of the Anzio beachhead (see illus. pp. 688-689) won his V.C. for leading an attack against German infiltration, fighting single-handed, and although wounded holding on until the position was restored.

*Photos, British, Australian, Canadian and Indian Official; P.N.A. and G.P.U*

# I WAS THERE! Eye Witness Stories of the War

## With the 'Bats o' Hell' I Flew to Los Negros

Landing was made on Los Negros Island, in the Admiralties, on Feb. 29, 1944, and its capture was announced on March 8. Dickson Brown, News Chronicle war correspondent, who accompanied the air-cover bombers, wrote this vivid dispatch from the most advanced fighter and bomber airfield in New Guinea after six hours' successful flying.

IN torrential rain today I descended in a jeep the precipitous track from the commanding officer's newly erected hilltop shack to this, the most advanced fighter and bomber airfield in New Guinea. I was to join a mission of Mitchell medium bombers which had been ordered to cover the landing in the Admiralty Islands of the American First Cavalry Division (Dismounted).

The territory was not new to the American fliers. They had been several times to the Admiralties, bombing and strafing, during the past fortnight. At the usual briefing of the men detailed instructions were given, as this was the unit's first co-ordinated mission involving the covering of naval and landing operations.

The flight leader was youthful Lt. Richard Reinbold, from Newark, Ohio, who explained the mission, the landing points, and so on. In his final chat he said: "Boys, the weather's as bad as it can be, but we've got to make it. This morning we're accompanied by a war correspondent, and this fellow is British. I want you to show him what the Bats o' Hell can do when they get going!"

make a run on the selected strip to get the full benefit of the eight guns in our nose. We swoop fast to tree-top height, and the guns send streams of lead along the path. Then we make a second run as the navigator reports he has spotted a machine-gun post. Down we come. There is more strafing, and three 500-pounders drop around the machine-gun nest.

Our turret gunner, observing the result, says the thing has disappeared. We keep on circling low, watching the destroyers disgorge the troops into small boats which then make shoreward. Everything seems to be moving smoothly. The landing point is immediately

ANOTHER SHOCK FOR THE JAPANESE came from these U.S. troops (left) as they landed on Los Negros Island, Admiralty group, on Feb. 29, 1944. Map shows position of the Admiralty Islands in relation to other operational spheres.

north of Momote airfield, on Los Negros Island.

This airfield is small and probably unusable at present by modern aircraft. But I noticed several small shacks which had hitherto been "installations," but which now were mangled ruins, and a Jap bomber in pieces at the end of the runway. Although I kept my eyes

"Bats o' Hell" is the unit's nickname, scribbled across the noses of its aircraft. Our target, pin-pointed on the map, is Los Negros, in the eastern Admiralties, and we are to bomb and strafe the area immediately in advance of the point at which the troops are to be landed. That is at least 400 miles from the take-off.

Two hours' fast flying through alternating heavy shower clouds and bright sunshine finds us nearing the islands, and I pick out the remnants of a smokescreen—probably the result of a naval shelling on the Los Negros shore. Unlike the landings on Arawe, New Britain, on December 15, and Cape Gloucester on December 26, there is no sign of heavy landing craft. This time faster moving destroyer craft are being used.

Speed is essential to success, owing to MacArthur's and Kenney's desire to take full advantage of the apparent lack of Japanese aircraft and warships in this theatre. Reinbold comes low, circles around the proposed landing point and has a look for Japs.

Then we climb 2,000 ft. and prepare to

Gen. DOUGLAS MacARTHUR, Supreme Commander in the S.W. Pacific (left), personally directed the Los Negros landing (story in this page). With him are Lt.-Gen. W. Krueger, U.S. 6th Army commander, and Vice-Adm. Kinkaid, commander of Allied naval forces. *Keystone*

skinned for Japs, I saw none. But the communiqué reports light resistance, which was quickly overcome, and a sharp counter-attack on the airstrip, which was also repulsed with negligible losses. During the whole mission there has been no sign of Japanese aircraft or surface vessel.

Apparently, as on many similar occasions in the past, the Japs have been entirely hoodwinked, believing the Allies would attack Wewak or other parts of the New Guinea coast rather than the Admiralties, as reconnaissance has reported a gradual building up of aircraft in those areas.

Reinbold makes a last circle and sets course for home. "Sorry there wasn't more fun," he says, "but I guess it's good that the Japs appear to be on the run." Back in the mess hall, after six hours' flying, our crew of six drink to the day when the Mitchell "Bats o' Hell" get over Tokyo.

## I Saw a Japanese Legend Die in Burma Jungle

"Looks tame enough, doesn't he? All the same, a vicious type!" The speaker was a British officer, the object of his remarks a Japanese prisoner bowing low and grinning obsequiously. This surprising prison-camp story comes from Graham Stanford, Daily Mail correspondent on the Arakan front.

IN barbed-wire enclosed pens, guarded by stocky Gurkha sentries, I saw today a group of prisoners from General Tannabashi's army. It was a surprising experience. There were nearly 30 of them, all but one—the only silent member—only too ready to talk of their sufferings and terror under intensive R.A.F. bombing in the jungle.

Since this war began we have heard a good deal about the super Jap. But here was a group of very cowed little men, demoralized, bitter against their commander, talkative—and far from thoughts of hara-kiri. They tell us resentfully that when they went into battle they believed they had air supremacy, but they seldom saw their own planes.

Hungry, wounded, and generally battle-weary, they poured out their hearts to the British troops around them without reserve. One of them recognized a British officer as a one-time patron of his café in a Japanese city. He and most of the prisoners expressed decided opinions about their "crack" commander Tannabashi, who launched this

offensive with the intention of driving the Fourteenth Army into the Bay of Bengal.

They hated Tannabashi. They said he was a fat, overbearing man, a stickler for discipline who gave his troops no consideration. They were sent into battle with short rations. They were hungry all the time and many were sick. And all the time there was the bombing. They had no loyalty to Tannabashi, and pretended none. Not one of these malaria-ridden, ragged troops bore any resemblance to the legendary Jap superman who, it is said, even when captured, retains his dignity and arrogance.

These half-starved men bowed low when British officers approached, and grinned quickly back if they saw one of their captors smile. They were obsequious, only too ready to please. As soon as one was captured he asked, "Well, when do I start to work for you?" Another said he would like a job acting as interpreter. Two were appointed orderlies to their wounded comrades and today they were cheerfully working under the supervision of the British doctor.

JAPANESE PRISONERS brought in for interrogation on the Burma front. At the commencement of Japan's bid for power few prisoners were taken by the Allies : the enemy's "religion" proclaimed it a disgrace to be captured alive. Now, both in the Pacific and Burma, that idea has undergone a fundamental change, as revealed in the accompanying narrative. *Photo, Indian Official*

I saw them have their food. They tore into large platefuls of rice, and said that it was the first real meal they had had since the battle started. Some had even been reduced to eating monkeys.

The more intelligent of the prisoners discoursed quite readily on the war—one expressed the view that Japan knew now that she stood alone ; that it was only a matter of time before Germany was out of the war. Even so, he insisted that it would be three years before his country was beaten.

The first Japs captured in the Pacific theatre tried hara-kiri. If they failed, they closed their mouths. But these men made no effort to join their ancestors. They shuffled about their compound in all humility. One in particular bowed low every time he was addressed.

" Looks tame, doesn't he ? " said a British officer, as the Jap's face wreathed in a smile to reveal a row of broken, discoloured teeth. " All the same, a vicious type. This is how they get these days when they're captured."

## Last Voyage of Armed Merchantman Breconshire

For 19 months the 10,000-ton Breconshire had ferried supplies from Alexandria to Malta. On March 20, 1942, carrying fuel oil and aviation spirit, she set out on what was to be her final adventure. The great story of her sensational last hours is here condensed from a recent broadcast by Petty Officer A. Francis-Smith, by courtesy of the B.B.C.

A T last Malta came in view through the mist, six miles away, and we felt that our job was almost finished But hardly had the protecting Hurricanes left us when three Messerschmitts, flying at mast height, appeared and dropped bombs. One of them penetrated our engine-room and put the ship completely out of action. We took the tragedy with a smile, and commenced to lower the collision mat over the hole and sent signals for help, floundering the while in very heavy seas, lying helpless, a sitting target for this determined enemy. Our guns were now constantly in action as waves of bombers continued to attack us. Ammunition was running short, and what did remain above water was distributed to the guns.

Some of the bombs had sprung the plates, and the oil from the tanks made a thick film on the surface of the water. The auxiliary dynamo was put out of action, and all mess decks, food stores, and refrigerators were under water, thus limiting our food supplies. We were without

light and means of cooking. Two of the crew, however, got a small forge and, with coal from the cargo, boiled eggs, meat and vegetable hash. We didn't worry if the tea was made with the water in which the eggs had been boiled.

At last, in the distance, pitching on heavy seas, came the cruiser Penelope. We managed to get a large steel hawser aboard. This was rather a feat, as our winches were out of action. She commenced to tow, but the heavy weather and the additional weight of the ship broke the hawser and damaged the cruiser. The Penelope returned to Grand Harbour, leaving us drifting shorewards. We dropped both port and starboard anchors and sat there waiting—waiting to make harbour or meet our doom.

We passed a quiet night, mostly in talk and sleep. Speculations of success or failure—how long it would take for repairs . . . Tuesday morning dawned cheerless. Our water was almost exhausted and breakfast was cold tinned fish and army biscuits—but how we enjoyed it ! The day was spent in getting ready to receive tugs that were coming out that night in an endeavour to tow us to safety. The enemy still attacked us during the day, but with small formations.

T HE next morning, Wednesday, the tug Ancient, with Capt. Nicholls of the Penelope in command, took charge and we commenced to move. Ropes broke and were replaced, and we moved slowly but surely towards safety. This fact added enthusiasm and heart to the then very tired officers and men. Slowly we moved round Delimara Point into Kalafrana Bay and moored to a buoy. Later that afternoon 16 Stuka bombers attacked us ; we damaged a number, but they scored near misses which opened up more plates on our side, causing a list to port.

The German air force decided to make a last determined effort to complete our destruction and sent thirty Ju 88s to finish us off. These aircraft aimed and dropped more than 120 bombs, only one of which hit us, in the after-hold, which set us on fire, and a near miss exploded alongside and opened up the ship. Yet there's always something to cause a laugh—in this particular case, the guns' crews near the hold were covered in coal, wheat and condensed milk, which shook them considerably but gave the rest of us a real good laugh.

We managed to get the fire under control, but next morning she turned over on her side and sank, leaving about eight feet of hull sticking up above the water. Immediately salvage operations were begun. Holes were drilled in the side, and 5,000 tons of fuel oil was pumped out—1,000 tons of which enabled the damaged Penelope, who was dependent on us for this oil, to make a dash for Gibraltar and then America, where she was repaired. Salvage operations continued until the remains of the serviceable cargo had been delivered to their destination—Malta !

H.M.S. BRECONSHIRE, 10,000-TON MERCHANT SHIP converted to an anti-aircraft armed merchantman, played a grand part in the defence of Malta. To the very end she managed to " deliver the goods," and part of her thrilling story is told here. Above, the Breconshire, in wartime camouflage, is seen on one of her earlier voyages, arriving in Malta's Grand Harbour with troop reinforcements.

*Photo, British Official*

# On a Mine-Laying Raid with a Polish Squadron

The heavily loaded Wellington flashes over tumbled seas on one of those dangerous missions whose successful completion is summarized in news broadcasts as "Mines were laid in enemy waters." This operational account by a Polish correspondent is the story behind the familiar phrase.

I STOOD glancing down for a sign of enemy shipping, but there was none to be seen. It was silent inside the plane, the crew busy keeping the course and watching the sea. Presently the pilot's voice came through: "Attention ! Going down !" The speed increased. Far below three or four lights winked—lighter buoys, perhaps. The dim shape of land could be seen. Flying low, we drove straight over an enemy port. The ground had now come to life and was preparing a lively welcome for us with search-lights and A.A. fire.

Far to right and left lights flashed, as though announcing the arrival of the Wellington. It seemed as though the black land were waiting to swallow us up. Fire was coming up from the flak-ships below. We seemed in a tight spot and I could not help wondering what was going to happen next. Suddenly the plane was flooded with a bright glare from nose to tail. For a minute we were blinded. I thought a searchlight had got to us, but no ; it was bursting A.A. shells from the shore batteries.

The pilot dived sharply, out of range, but they were still after us. Shells burst all around. The Wellington pushed stubbornly on to the target. There was no time for fear ; I could only admire the Polish crew who flew straight down that lane of fire to prevent the movement of German shipping by dropping their mines in exactly the position indicated. A sharp order through the intercom. and the plane lifted slightly.

The mines were away ! A sharp turn and we were speeding back the way we had come. They lost us as we turned, but the flak was still very heavy. Another dive and we were out of it. Not until then did we realize what a blaze of light the Germans had made in the Wellington's honour. The coast was like a rainbow.

We flew in curves close to the surface. The fire and searchlights disappeared from sight. The nearer we drew to England, the worse became the weather ; we were flying through cloud again and kept on until we came to the coast. We spotted the dark line of cliffs. We began to talk, and drink our coffee. Suddenly the weather cleared and we could see a number of outward-bound planes. They called us from below, giving the order in which we were to land. We turned, and followed a lane of flickering light. We rolled towards the place from which we had set out six hours before . . . The next morning I heard that while I had been out on the raid my flat in London had been bombed !

MINES BEING LOADED INTO THIS STIRLING are for the obstruction—or destruction—of hostile shipping. During March 1944, Bomber Command aircraft laid mines in enemy waters on 14 nights. These operations—one is described in this page—are carried out in accordance with carefully laid plans, and in strictly defined areas only.
*Photo, Sport & General*

# OUR DIARY OF THE WAR

**MARCH 29, Wednesday** 1,670th day
**Russian Front.**—Link-up of troops of the 1st and 2nd Ukrainian Fronts announced. Kolomyja in Carpathian foot-hills captured by 1st Ukrainian Army. River Pruth forced by troops under Marshal Koniev.
**Burma.**—Announced reverse suffered by 14th Army in Ukhrul sector of Manipur.
**Pacific.**—Palau Islands, in the Carolines, attacked by U.S. Pacific Fleet.
**Air.**—Brunswick raided in daylight by escorted Fortresses and Liberators.

**MARCH 30, Thursday** 1,671st day
**Mediterranean.**—Sofia rail yards (Bulgaria) attacked by Fortresses and Liberators based on Italy.
**Russian Front.**—Cernauti, regional centre of the Ukraine and economic centre of N. Bukovina, stormed and captured. Storozhinets and Lipkani taken.
**Australasia.**—Japanese air base of Hollandia, Dutch New Guinea, heavily raided.
**Air.**—Great night attack on Nuremberg by Lancasters and Halifaxes ; 94 Allied planes lost.

**MARCH 31, Friday** 1,672nd day
**Russian Front.**—Ochakov, 40 miles E. of Odessa, captured by Gen. Malinovsky's 3rd Ukrainian Army.
**Australasia.**—Hollandia, Dutch New Guinea, attacked ; 189 Japanese planes destroyed in this and previous raid.
**Pacific.**—Wolfi Islands (Carolines) attacked by U.S. Pacific Fleet.

**APRIL 1, Saturday** 1,673rd day
**Italy.**—Capture of Monte Marrone, 14 miles N.E. of Cassino, announced.
**Russian Front.**—Podhajce, 28 miles S.W. of Tarnopol, captured by Red Army. Marshal Zhukov's 1st Ukrainian Army reached Yablonica Pass.
**Australasia.**—Ndrilo and Koruniat Islands in Admiralties taken by U.S. troops.
**General.**—Announced that Maj.-Gen. O. C. Wingate, D.S.O., commander of British forces behind Japanese lines in Burma killed in plane mishap on March 24.

**APRIL 2, Sunday** 1,674th day
**Mediterranean.**—Steyr (Austria) ball-bearing factories attacked by U.S. bombers.
**Russian Front.**—Announced that troops of the 2nd Ukrainian Front had entered Rumania at several points.

**Air.**—Announced that 9,100 aircraft were produced in March by the U.S.A.

**APRIL 3, Monday** 1,675th day
**Mediterranean Front.**—Budapest, Hungarian capital, bombed for first time since Sept. 1942 by Fortresses and Liberators. At night, Wellingtons and Liberators raided the city.
**Sea.**—German battleship Tirpitz, in Alten Fjord, N. Norway, attacked by escorted Barracuda dive-bombers of the Fleet Air Arm ; 16 direct hits obtained.

**APRIL 4, Tuesday** 1,676th day
**Mediterranean.**—Bucharest, Rumanian capital, raided by American bombers.
**Russian Front.**—Germans trapped in Skala area defeated in their attempts to break out. Russians occupied most of Tarnopol.

**APRIL 5, Wednesday** 1,677th day
**Mediterranean.**—Ploesti oilfields raided by large American bomber force.
**Russian Front.** — Razdelnaya, junction on main railway from Odessa to the west, captured by Gen. Malinovsky's 3rd Ukrainian Army.

**APRIL 6, Thursday** 1,678th day
**Russian Front.**—Gen. Malinovsky's troops reached a point 13 miles N.E. of Odessa.
**Australasia.**—Hollandia, Dutch New Guinea, heavily raided by Allied bombers.
**Air.**—Hamburg bombed by Mosquitoes at night.

**APRIL 7, Friday** 1,679th day
**Russian Front.**—Desperate German attempts to break out in Tarnopol and Skala areas smashed. More enemy troops surrounded near Razdelnaya.
**Burma.**—Capture of the eastern tunnel on the Maungdaw-Buthidaung road by the 14th Army announced.

**APRIL 8, Saturday** 1,680th day
**Russian Front.**—Announced that Red Army had reached the Czechoslovakian frontier. Czechoslovak Govt. in exile summoned people to rise against Germans. Sereth, 21 miles N.E. of Cernauti, Botsani

**Burma.**—Announced that Japanese held 15-mile stretch of Imphal-Kohima road, 40 miles inside India.
**Air.**—Toulouse aircraft factories attacked by Lancasters at night.

and Doroka, 50 miles W. of Rumanian frontier, occupied. German "pocket" at Razdelnaya liquidated.
**Air.**—Brunswick and aerodromes N. of the Ruhr attacked by Fortresses and Liberators.

**APRIL 9, Sunday** 1,681st day
**Russian Front.**—Announced that Marshals Zhukov and Koniev in co-ordination had cleared province of Bukovina of the enemy. Front of 180 miles from Yablonica Pass to a point 50 miles N.W. of Jassy established by combined armies.
**Burma.**—Evacuation of Tamu, in the Kabaw Valley, by 14th Army announced.
**Air.**—Poznan, Gdynia (Poland), Marien-burg (E. Prussia), Tutow and Warne-munde (Germany), attacked by escorted Fortresses and Liberators. Hasselt (Belgium) rail objectives bombed. Lille (N. France) and Villeneuve St.-Georges (near Paris) raided by Lancasters, Stirlings and Halifaxes.

**APRIL 10, Monday** 1,682nd day
**Russian Front.**—Odessa, important political and economic centre of the Soviet Union, and great Black Sea naval base, captured by troops of the 3rd Ukrainian Front. Revealed that offensive against the Crimea recently launched by Gen. Tolbukhin's 4th Ukrainian Army group ; Armyansk taken.
**Sea.**—Announced two Japanese block-ade-runners sunk in Indian Ocean.
**Air.**—Rail yards and depots at Ghent, Tours, Tergnier, Aulnoye and Laon, heavily attacked at night ; 3,600 tons of bombs dropped in record raid. Mosquitoes bombed Hanover.

**APRIL 11, Tuesday** 1,683rd day
**Russian Front.**—Announced that Gen. Tolbukhin's troops in the Crimea had crossed the Siwash Sea and captured the important rail junction of Zhankoi. Troops of the Maritime Front under Gen. Eremenko seized Kerch. Germans recaptured Buczacz, relieving troops trapped in Skala area.
**Pacific.**—Capture by Allies of Ailuk, Likiep, Rongelap, and Utrik atolls announced.
**Air.**—Oschersleben, Bernberg, Rostock and Arnimswalde raided by over 1,600 American aircraft.

★ ═══════ *Flash-backs* ═══════ ★

### 1940
**April 9.** Germans occupied Copenhagen and Oslo ; landings were made at Narvik, Bergen, Trondhjem and Stavanger.

### 1941
**March 29.** Diredawa (Abyssinia) occupied by South Africans under Gen. Cunningham.
**April 9.** Salonika (Greece) captured by German motorized forces after fierce fighting.

### 1942
**April 3.** Mandalay, in Central Burma, set on fire by Japanese bombers ; 2,000 people killed.

### 1943
**March 29.** Gabès and El Hamma taken by Gen. Montgomery's 8th Army in Tunisia.
**April 7.** Rommel's defences along Wadi Akarit broken by 8th Army. Contact made with U.S. troops at El Guettar by forward 8th Army troops.
**April 10.** 8th Army occupied Tunisian port of Sfax.
**April 11.** British 1st Army captured Kairouan. Contact established with 8th Army near Fondouk, which fell April 9.

BOMB DOORS STILL OPEN after releasing its load during a recent raid on an airfield at Gael, near St. Malo, France, this R.A.F. Mosquito veers away from the scene of its successful attack. Claimed to be the most versatile aircraft in service anywhere in the world, the Mosquito has now been adapted to carry a 4,000-lb. bomb.

*Photo, British Official*

# THE WAR IN THE AIR

## by Capt. Norman Macmillan, M.C., A.F.C.

As the war in the air increases in ferocity the facts associated with it become more difficult to comprehend unless one maintains the closest possible watch over every aspect of this branch of military power. Those with reactionary outlook, who dislike to see the older Services displaced in any degree by the newer Service of the air, seize quickly enough upon any apparently adverse effect of air action and say with emphasis that air power is overrated and that it is merely an auxiliary to the Army and Navy. Now the air can, of course, be used as an auxiliary to the older Services, and it can also be employed as an independent arm of war ; in either case it can fail if it is used wrongly or over-optimistically. Did not the Luftwaffe fail in its independent attempt to defeat Britain in 1940 ? Did not the Allied air forces fail to dislodge the German troops from Cassino on March 15, 1944 ? Can Bomber Command continue to afford such heavy losses as those incurred when in the attacks on Leipzig on February 20, Berlin on March 24, and Nuremberg on March 30, 1944, the aircraft that failed to return numbered 79, 73 and 94 respectively ? Do not these air facts disclose that offensive air power is meeting its match in the air and on the ground ? Has too much been expected from the air and must we reorientate our views ?

All these conflicting elements of evidence of the value of air power need sorting out. They cannot be measured without something to measure them by. Bomber Command's attacks on German towns are measured against the result of the Luftwaffe raid on Coventry on November 14, 1940. Coventry was a target which we knew. It was the object of one isolated large-scale (for those days) attack. The number of bombers used against it was assessed accurately. The weight of bombs that fell on the Midlands town was known within a small margin of error. So in that one foul night the Luftwaffe generals, believing that they were defeating Britain, were, in fact, preparing the yardstick by which their own ultimate defeat was to be measured.

Judged by the measuring scale of Coventry there is no doubt about the effectiveness of the independent air attacks against German towns, although there may, indeed, must be changes in the relative weight of bombs required to destroy any one square mile of built-up area. For in Europe one urban area is not identical with another. Medieval and subsequent town-planners made great variations in the densities of their built-up areas, due in many cases to the war needs of the time at which places were built, or to the commercial transport aspect then appertaining. But already sufficient evidence has been accumulated to make it possible to state with sufficient accuracy what weight of bombs will be required to destroy any given town to such an extent that its value as a war centre to Germany becomes negative.

### ASSESSING Damage Inflicted on the Enemy by Air Attack

What is not yet fully known is how long it will take for this method of total war attack to make the whole war edifice of the enemy crumble so that he is no longer able to maintain the effort required to oppose the will of the nations arrayed against him. It is probable that it will not be possible fully to estimate this until the war has ended and direct evidence is forthcoming from those in Germany whose tongues and pens are at present unable to say and write what they know. Nor indeed, until that time, will it be possible for the people of Britain to know the full effect of the German air assault on them, for undoubtedly there is much which is still undisclosed even of the 1940-41 assault against us.

Without the remarkable development of air photography, and the possession of long-range, very swift, photographic reconnaissance aircraft which can appear over a target and photograph it from a great height before any enemy aircraft can get up to drive them off, it would be impossible to assess the actual damage inflicted by independent air attack. But with this asset of the camera and the stereoscopic method of examination of air photographs which was first developed for peaceful aerial survey and mapping organizations it is impossible for the enemy to hide the result of bomb damage on urban areas. But it still requires older methods of intelligence to find out what the enemy has done to counter the effect of the attacks—what he has done for the evacuation of the civil population, for the reconstruction of factories destroyed or damaged, how far he has been able to salvage useful materials or tools for use elsewhere, and where the people and materials have been removed for re-employment. And the psychological effect of the attacks on the civil population and on

their will to maintain the struggle is a factor of immense importance, and will have a great bearing on the rapidity with which the enemy structure collapses, despite all statements that the attacks are directed (as they are) to the destruction of the enemy's power to produce physically the weapons of war. Victory is won when the will of one side crumbles before the will of the opposing side. Victory is spiritual not material, and nothing that anyone can say can alter that. The alternative to defeat may be death, but death is not defeat. And it is because of this psychological factor that the air attacks upon German towns constitute a great but at present unassessable feature of the war. How much is it playing and how much has it played in the retreat of the Germans in Russia ? There are those who say its contribution in those bloody fields is enormous.

Thus the losses of Bomber Command, rising occasionally to high figures, and percentages greater than the average, should not cause undue alarm. It is the average that counts, and that average has kept around four per cent for a long time, and was lower in March than in a lengthy period preceding that month. Nevertheless, these occasional high losses indicate that there are conditions when the German night defences prove themselves to be more formidable than usual, probably due to a combination of suitable visibility, weather handicaps for the bombers, increasing offensive fire-power on the part of night fighters, and the employment of larger numbers of these defence aircraft.

The failure of the bombers to defeat the enemy at Cassino in one blow after the ground forces had tried unsuccessfully for many weeks to capture the town is but an incident in a great war. It is and must always be possible to find terrain where no form of weapon can destroy the enemy there dug in except the primitive method of man against man. War then returns to the war of siege. The use of the bomber for direct assault is then probably an incorrect application of air power, and quicker (even if to begin with apparently more protracted) results may be gained by siege warfare, using the bombers to isolate the force and starve it out. But if the direct method is to be used it must be borne in mind that all through this war the tendency has been to underestimate the weight of bombs required to achieve any given result, and that the estimate first thought of in every case may be wrong through underestimation. In the battle of Germany the crucial factor is now the capacity of the enemy to maintain his fighter strength ; we shall make a cardinal mistake if we underestimate that. Bomber Command losses give the best evidence; they are more important than the Cassino stoppage.

# Allied Air Arm Stretches Far Over the Reich

ROUND-THE-CLOCK BLOWS by the R.A.F. and U.S.A.A.F. bombers steadily wear down the German war machine. Co-operation is the keynote; a U.S. Fortress captain (inset) explains the controls to a visiting R.A.F. Lancaster pilot. A Fortress with open bomb doors (top) just before its load crashed down on Hitler's domain. R.A.F. station commander and officers watch from the control tower (below) for planes returning from the great raid on Nuremberg by Lancasters and Halifaxes on the night of March 30-31, 1944.　PAGE 765　*Photos, British and U.S. Official, Barratt's*

# Up and Down with Our Parachute Troops

**READY FOR THE BREATH-SNATCHING DROP** is this parachute trooper (1). With his comrades he listens to a detailed briefing (2) before entering a plane bound for "enemy" territory during a rehearsal in Britain. The pilot warns them that they are near to the dropping zone (3); one by one they perch on the brink (4), eyes directed at the signal-light overhead, before leaving the aircraft (5). Down to earth, and in a minute or so he and the others will be ready for action (6).

*Photos, Keystone*

AMERICA does everything on a larger scale than other countries. Therefore it is not surprising to hear that 300 million pounds (not dollars) is being spent yearly in the various Black Markets which have sprung up there since rationing began. One-twentieth part of the petrol purchased is handed over without any coupons changing hands, so an official of the Office of Price Administration asserts, adding that, if this could be stopped, the regular ration could be made a quarter larger than it is at present. Nearly the same proportion of the nation's food is dealt in by Black Marketeers and their clients. Other things that are being sold on the sly at prices far higher than they are worth are clothes, furniture, refrigerators and car tires. We often hear that democracy has so far been a failure. The reason usually given is that which G. K. Chesterton offered for the failure of Christianity—"it has never been tried." Now that is not true. Many shots have been made at workable democratic systems. Not one has hit the mark. Why? The reason seems to me plain. It is contained in the complaint that everywhere people try to get the better of one another and secure selfish advantage for themselves when they are asked to make little sacrifices for the benefit of the community. There can be no rule of the people by and for the people unless all the people share and share alike willingly, unless community interest prevails over individual gain.

SILVER fox farms were pretty numerous not long ago. I suppose not many of them have survived the war. But why not start a cat farm? This would once have seemed a ridiculous suggestion. Cats were plentiful, far too plentiful. Kittens had to be drowned by the thousand, if not the million, every year. But today, like so many other things, this has been changed completely. Cats have become so scarce that for a quite ordinary kitten you are asked to pay as much as 12s. 6d., while a half-Persian costs a guinea at least. For pedigree Persians and Siamese six to eight guineas is nothing out of the way. And this at a time when there is more work for cats to do than ever before. Mice have increased enormously; rats are a worse pest and peril than they were in the years of peace. Not many cats will tackle a rat, it is true; but on the other hand the mere presence of a cat tends to keep rats away, as it certainly does scare mice, if the cat is active on its feet.

THERE is a well-known hymn which speaks of "knitting severed friendships up where partings are no more." A great many relationships which have never been cut short, because they were unrecognized, have been knitted up by the war. Numbers of people in this country have been made aware of them by young relatives in the Forces who have come from Canada or Australia or New Zealand and have been very glad to look them up. An acquaintance of mine told me the other day she had two cousins of different families staying with her in her small London flat, of whose existence she was ignorant until they appeared on her threshold and announced themselves. In a train the other day I was talking to a Canadian from Saskatchewan, who said what a godsend it had been to him to find he had relations in England and Scotland, who had made him more than welcome. He said this gave him quite a new feeling about "the Old Country," and he knew a great many others were like him. Such meetings, which ripen often into affection, are a very good thing for both the visitors and the hosts. They really do tighten those "bonds of Empire" which are much talked about by politicians, but have not meant a great deal to ordinary folk.

COMPLAINTS reach me sometimes about the slowness of promotion in the Army for men who are said to be doing really exceptionally good work and ought to have larger scope for their initiative and vigour. How far these have any justification it is very hard to judge. One could get at the truth only by close investigation of each individual case. But it is noticeable that some

Maj.-Gen. ORDE CHARLES WINGATE, D.S.O., lost his life in a plane crash in Burma on March 24, 1944, aged 41. Intrepid leader of jungle fighters, he perfected a penetration technique which he had already proved in Abyssinia, and in Burma early in 1943 when he led a raiding column 1,000 miles through Japanese-held territory (see pp. 46-49). *Photo, Associated Press*

Army officers who are not taking active part in the war manage to go up the ladder of regimental rank with remarkable rapidity. I have been particularly struck by the transformation of M.P.s and others who were captains only a little while ago into majors and colonels. Some who have been at Whitehall all the time, doing useful work, I have no doubt, but not always military work, have attained these two "steps" in a couple of years or so. It would be very interesting to know why. Many members are in favour of military titles being dropped in the House unless they apply to retired officers. Some drop them gradually of their own free will. Mr. Attlee, for example, used to be called Major Attlee, and Mr. Eden Captain Eden.

WHAT is it makes most men still dislike the sight of a woman smoking in the street? They don't object to women enjoying a cigarette after dinner in a dining-room or restaurant, nor does smoking by women in a cinema, theatre, or train disturb them. But somehow to see a woman with a cigarette in her mouth in the street does arouse in most men a feeling that it is unbecoming in both senses of that word, that it is out of keeping with the womanly character and that it diminishes the attractiveness of woman. I have been putting these queries to myself after reading the regulations about A.T.S. girls and their cigarettes. Why should it be permissible by Army rule for a soldier to smoke anywhere and forbidden to the service-woman in uniform to do the same? Suppose they are waiting together to go into a cinema: the man may smoke, the woman may not, says the War Office, though inside they both can. I should have said, in spite of the irrational sentiment I have mentioned as affecting the majority of men, that it would have been better to make a rule that all A.T.S. members must have their hair cut short. To see fluffy curls under a service cap, as one does frequently, suggests the comic opera chorus. It is a glaring incongruity.

IT happened in a seaside town. The conductor was hurrying passengers off at a stop. An old lady had some difficulty in getting up from her seat. "Now, come on, missis," the conductor urged. "You need a bit of yeast to help you rise!" She looked at him with scornful dignity. "And if you were given some," she told him, "you would be better bred!"

"JUVENILE delinquency" is an expression often on the lips of those who like long words and enjoy thinking that morals are declining and "boys not what they used to be when I was young." That a good deal of mischief is done by boys is true. Partly that is due to there being fewer policemen about. But there is another, even more potent, cause, and that is adult delinquency. Boys are imitative creatures. Set them a good example (so long as you don't do it in a priggish way) and they will follow it; but let them see their elders stealing and wantonly destroying other people's property, and they are quick to do the same whenever they get the chance. How appalling the increase in these offences has been during the war years is shown by the loss incurred by one railway company alone of as much as £2,000 worth a day from railway carriages. Besides the wrenching off of electric lamps and ripping of cushions, there is perpetual pilfering from freight wagons. I see that a German convicted of stealing from a store where goods intended for public use were kept has been sentenced to death and executed. I also see that railway chiefs are calling for more severe punishment of railway thieves. This will have to come.

ONE of the commonest sights in Russia used to be a man or woman—but usually a man—sitting on a seat in a public park with the ground all about the seat strewn with sunflower seed husks. These were chewed as much by Russians of the poorer classes as gum is by American office-boys. The slightly sweet content of the seed was swallowed and the husk rejected. Everywhere you went you saw sunflowers growing, the huge kind that have never seemed to me to suit British gardens. They were grown not for their appearance but for their seeds. Now it seems the cultivation of this species is to be recommended to agriculturists in this country. They have been studied for some years past by the Science Department at South Kensington, and it is believed they could be grown in South and East England for the production of an edible oil, also useful as a lubricant.

# Wounded in Battle for Anzio Beach-head

Photo, Keystone

**ROWS OF STRETCHERS,** each containing a wounded American soldier of the 5th Army, wait for landing-barges which will transport them to hospital ships outside Anzio port. Medical personnel, some of whom are seen above, do a magnificent job, dealing with each case in the speedy and efficient manner made possible by modern equipment. See pp. 687 and 755.

Printed in England and published every alternative Friday by the Proprietors, THE AMALGAMATED PRESS, LTD., The Fleetway House, Farringdon Street, London, E.C.4. Registered for transmission by Canadian Magazine Post. Sole Agents for Australia and New Zealand: Messrs. Gordon & Gotch, Ltd. ; and for South Africa : Central News Agency, Ltd.—April 28, 1944. S.S. *Editorial Address* : JOHN CARPENTER HOUSE, WHITEFRIARS, LONDON, E.C.4.

Vol 7 · *The War Illustrated* · Nº 180

*Edited by Sir John Hammerton*

SIXPENCE

MAY 12, 1944

NEW ZEALAND PATROL, seeking out Nazis, probes hiding-places in the much-battered town of Cassino. Originally on the 8th Army front, it was announced on Feb. 18, 1944 that New Zealand units had been transferred to the 5th Army sector near Cassino, where they formed the spearhead of the Allied thrust into the town after it was bombed on March 15. They have also campaigned with very great distinction in Libya, Egypt, Crete, Greece and the S.W. Pacific. *Photo British Official Crown Copyright*

NO. 181 WILL BE PUBLISHED FRIDAY, MAY 26

# Back to the Land Goes Our Roving Camera

HOLIDAY-MAKERS help wartime agriculture. Hundreds of men and women, such as these threshing on a Bedfordshire farm, spend breaks from their own war job doing yet another.

WINDMILLS ARE SAVING FUEL while helping to produce the nation's bread. Many hitherto useless, although picturesque, windmills have been repaired and are again doing the task for which they were originally intended. The vanes of Saxtead Mill in Suffolk (centre, left) turn for victory now, while its owner (above) releases a sack of grain from the hoist inside the mill. Much credit for the rehabilitation of these old mills is due to the Society for the Protection of Ancient Buildings.

R.A.F. GARDENS, counterparts of civilian allotments, established on unused ground at airfields all over the country, in 1943 produced food for their own messes to the value of £285,147; the acreage under cultivation was 6,041. Both the R.A.F. and W.A.A.F. do this sparetime work—a grand contribution to Britain's agricultural effort. Above, ploughing at an R.A.F. station under the nose of a Lancaster bomber.

GRAIN STORAGE is one of the problems which harvest brings each year in Britain. To cope with it, silos, for drying and storing grain, like this one (left) have been built. The central tower houses the drying machinery which takes the moisture out of the grain before milling and reduces its bulk. Twelve 65-ft.-high bins on either side of it have a storage capacity of 5,000 tons.

*Photos, British Official; Fox, Topical Press, J. Dixon-Scott*

# THE BATTLE FRONTS

## by Maj.-Gen. Sir Charles Gwynn, K.C.B., D.S.O.

General NIKOLAI VATUTIN, late commander of the 1st Ukrainian Front, who died after a serious operation in Kiev on April 14, 1944. General Vatutin specially distinguished himself at Stalingrad, in the great Byelgorod-Kursk battle in July 1943, and in the capture of Kiev on Nov. 6, 1943. His successor is Marshal Zhukov. *Photo, Pictorial Press*

BY the end of February the Russian northern offensive had reached the limits imposed by the approach of spring and the nature of the terrain. The Germans had rallied on the line that some months ago I suggested they might withdraw to as a winter position. Meanwhile, in spite of the great successes it had achieved in liquidating the German Korsun pocket and in capturing Shepetovka on the one flank and Nikopol on the other, it seemed that the Russian southern offensive might have exhausted itself and been brought to a standstill by spring mud and difficulties of communication. The great river lines of the Bug, the Dniester and Sereth, in any case, seemed to offer the Germans great possibilities of carrying out a deliberate withdrawal if that were their intention.

They still retained their hold on the Lower Dnieper and, although it was threatened, the main lateral railway between Odessa and Von Manstein's concentration in the Vinnitsa area remained open. Moreover, Von Manstein in the latter area had first-class railway communication with Germany through Poland, and could therefore quickly receive reinforcements and be kept well supplied with munitions. This gave him undoubted offensive potentialities and great advantage over the Russians, whose immensely long lines of communication, almost entirely served by motor transport, were bound to be affected by the thaw.

In these circumstances the Germans, despite the mauling they had received, may well have thought that they had survived the worst of the Russian winter offensive without a complete disruption of their plans and might count on a respite at last. There is good reason, therefore, to believe that the resumption of the Russian southern offensive in the first week of March came as a strategic surprise of the first order. Zhukov's great drive between Tarnopol and Proskurov dislocated German strategic dispositions and threatened Manstein's powerful defensive group at Vinnitsa with the fate of Von Paulus' army at Stalingrad, cutting its communications with its base at Lvov.

IT is probable that Manstein's troops had exhausted their strength in their counter-attacks to arrest Vatutin's previous drives towards Zmerinka and in their unavailing efforts to rescue the 8th Army at Korsun. When Koniev at Uman attacked the force that had attempted that rescue, German troops for the first time gave way to panic and were unable to recover sufficiently to carry out a co-ordinated withdrawal. Koniev's rapid advance across the Bug and Dniester brought him up in line with Zhukov's army to form the great Russian wedge which split the German front line into two irretrievably separated groups, crossed the Pruth and Sereth into Rumania and reached the Hungarian frontier, although Von Manstein did in the end succeed in saving the remnants of the 15 divisions in the Skala pocket.

Von Kleist's southern group was in a more precarious situation. Its communications with Germany were long and circuitous and were soon to suffer from the bombing attacks of the Allied Mediterranean Air Forces. Moreover, a considerable part of his force was composed of Rumanian troops of doubtful reliability. His army, which had clung so long to their positions in the Dnieper bend and on the Lower Dnieper, were in a great salient and had already suffered heavily from the attacks of Malinovsky's 3rd Ukrainian Army. It was now faced with the necessity of carrying out a difficult and

belated retreat in which its northern flank was threatened by the southwards advance of Koniev's left wing. Nikolayev was lost, but for a time Malinovsky was checked on the line of the Bug. Von Kleist also used his best reserves to check Koniev's advance southwards, covering the withdrawal from the Bug and preventing the junction of the two Russian armies.

MALINOVSKY was not, however, to be denied, and by the end of March he had forced the line of the Bug while Koniev, meanwhile, in spite of strong resistance, had forced Von Kleist's left back to the line Jassy, Kishinev, Tiraspol. Here it stood firm and it looked as if, with the flank protection given it, the force retreating from the Bug might rally to cover Odessa. But by a lightning stroke which captured the important railway junction of Razjelnaya, Malinovsky thrust a wedge between the two German wings and surrounded and annihilated a strong force which attempted a counterstroke. The force retreating from the Bug, disrupted and demoralized, failed to rally and the way to Odessa was opened. Whether the Germans had intended to cling

OUR 14th ARMY, striking hard from strongly-held positions at Dimapur (Assam) had, by April 24, 1944, completed the relief of the beleaguered British garrison of Kohima, 44 miles to the S.E. On the Imphal sector, north-east of the town itself, further advances were being made. *By courtesy of The Times*

to Odessa may be doubtful, but it is unbelievable that its hurried and disorderly abandonment was in accordance with plan.

These events, and in particular the loss of Odessa, may have convinced the Germans that they must attempt to evacuate the Crimea. It would seem that some preparations to do so had been belatedly made when Tolbukhin's devastating attack was launched. It had been long prepared, and its timing was perfect to take advantage of the moment when the morale of the garrison might be expected to be at its lowest, and when its hopes of either evacuation or reinforcements had been reduced to a minimum. Tolbukhin's amazingly swift and complete success recalls the cat-like strategy that brought about the Stalingrad disaster (see map in p. 778).

By the middle of April the Russian offensive had thus achieved the liberation of all Russian territory south of the Pripet marshes,

except the south half of Bessarabia, and had penetrated into Rumania, making substantial progress towards capturing the passes of the Carpathians. Even more important, it had inflicted immense losses of men and material on the enemy. This despite the fact that seasonal conditions were unfavourable and that the enemy still possessed railway communications to facilitate retreat, and natural and fortified defensive positions.

To what can we attribute these latest amazing achievements of the Red Army, which have so far exceeded the expectations of the most optimistic commentators? Primarily, credit must be given to the astonishing endurance and high morale of the Russian soldiers, who have proved capable of such great efforts after months of intensive fighting, and to the high standards of tactical skill they have attained; secondly, to the organization which, in spite of all difficulties, never allowed the armies to run short of food and munition supplies.

But the best troops in the world could not have accomplished so much if the higher control of their efforts and strategic planning had not been bold, far-sighted and supremely well directed. How far Marshal Stalin has been responsible for the planning and strategy of the campaigns one does not know, but evidently he has exercised immense influence and must possess military acumen of the highest order. That he has been amazingly well served by his advisers and generals is undoubted, but I should be surprised if the patience displayed in Russian strategy and selection of the moment to strike should not be credited to Stalin himself. That patience, so remarkably displayed when Stalingrad seemed almost lost, is still well in evidence.

The admirable co-ordination of Russian offensives has been outstanding, and this may have in part been due to the apparent absence of jealousy or friction between Russian generals. If there has been friction nothing has been heard of it, in contrast to the many rumours which have been current of jealousies between German commanders and of friction between generals in the field and the higher command. Perhaps the policy adopted by Stalin of promptly broadcasting his appreciation of the achievements of individual bodies of troops and their commanders has had its moral effect. It curiously contrasts with our own practice which so often, for reasons of secrecy, leaves us in ignorance of the names of divisions and their commanders taking part in operations.

# Allied Leaders of the S.E. Asia Command

NEW LEADER OF THE CHINDITS, in succession to the late Maj.-General Wingate, under whom he served, is Maj.-General W. D. A. Lentaigne, D.S.O., seen (2, right) with Field Marshal Lord Wavell, during an inspection of a Gurkha regiment; Major-General Lentaigne is an expert in jungle fighting. With U.S. sharpshooters, General W. J. Stilwell, Deputy Supreme Commander S.E. Asia Command (5, seated centre), watches his American-trained Chinese troops driving Japanese across the Tanai River in North Burma. Brig.-General F. Merrill cooks for himself in the jungle (1); one of the youngest U.S. Army generals, he commands an Allied column ("Merrill's Marauders") in Upper Burma.

COMMANDER OF THE 7th INDIAN DIVISION in the Arakan is Maj.-General F. W. Messervy, C.B., D.S.O. (3); veteran of the African campaign, during the Japanese offensive in the Arakan in February 1944 his leadership was instrumental in saving a dangerous situation. Colonel P. G. Cochran (4), 33-year-old U.S. air ace, on March 5, 1944, led the Allied airborne force which landed behind enemy lines in North Burma; later, he commanded glider reinforcements. At bottom centre is the badge of the famous 14th Army in Burma commanded by General W. J. Slim; the letter "S" forming the hilt of the sword stands for his name and the sword's position, hilt uppermost, means offence. (See illus. 671.)

*Photos, British and Indian Official, Keystone, Planet News*

# Move and Counter-Move on the Burma Fronts

**NARROWNESS OF THE MOGAUNG VALLEY** hindered the full use of General Stilwell's American and Chinese forces pushing on towards the Mandalay Railway by way of the Hukawng River in the northern section of Burma and threatening the Japanese 18th Division holding Northern Burma in the Myitkyina area. U.S. troops (" Merrill's Marauders," see pp. 772 and 800) were making for Mogaung itself, while another commando force of Gurkhas and British-trained Katchin tribesmen, overcoming enemy resistance, were proceeding down the Mali Valley. The activities of the British force which crossed the Chin Hills and Chindwin River (announced on March 14) are closely related to Gen. Stilwell's southward drive.

**STEPS IN THE FIGHTING** in the Manipur State and immediate territories linked in this particular struggle between the Allies and the Japanese are indicated in this view of the terrain, from Tiddim looking northwards to Manipur. The enemy attacks, in three or possibly four prongs, on Assam had as their objective the isolation of Imphal, capital of Manipur State and main Allied base in the region, by cutting the roads converging on the city. The Japanese forces which branched off towards the Tiddim road, where they placed road blocks, made only little progress. British forward units formed themselves into the defensive box system, used so successfully in Arakan, and held the Japanese. In the Tammu area, where the second enemy prong was operating, the Allies were gaining ground (see also map, p. 771).

*Drawings by H. P. Burton and E. G. Lambert by courtesy of The Sphere*

# THE WAR AT SEA

## by Francis E. McMurtrie

SINCE the Japanese Navy made brief incursion into the Indian Ocean in April 1942, resulting in the loss of H.M. aircraft carrier Hermes and the cruisers Dorsetshire and Cornwall, it has been content to confine itself to covering the route from Singapore to Rangoon and Akyab, in Burma. When Lord Louis Mountbatten transferred the headquarters of the South-East Asia Command to Ceylon, in which island the British naval base of Trincomalee is situated, the enemy should have been on the alert. Yet they were obviously taken completely by surprise when the blow fell.

A force mainly British, though it included American, Dutch and French warships, all under Admiral Sir James Somerville, Commander-in-Chief of the Eastern Fleet, proceeded to execute a lightning attack on Sabang, at the northern end of Sumatra. This port is a well-known fuelling station in peacetime, but has been used as an advanced base by the Japanese since they occupied Singapore and the Dutch Indies. On April 19 the attack was brought off exactly as planned. Flights of Barracuda, Dauntless and Avenger torpedo-bombers were flown off from British and U.S. aircraft carriers, covered by Hellcat and Corsair fighters. All returned undamaged except one Barracuda, which was slightly damaged by its own bomb burst, and an American fighter which came down in the sea. The pilot of the latter was rescued by a British submarine, a remarkable incident which has added to the keenness of Anglo-American co-operation.

DESTRUCTION done at Sabang was considerable. Two 5,000-ton Japanese supply ships, two destroyers and sundry other craft were bombed and set on fire in the harbour. The power-station, wireless and radio-location buildings, barracks and coaling wharf were all hit. Eighteen enemy aircraft were destroyed or set on fire on the ground, and the oil tanks were left ablaze with columns of smoke rising to 7,000 feet.

With this successful stroke it may be said that the offensive has now definitely passed to the Allies in the Indian Ocean, as it already had in the Pacific. Whether as a result the Japanese will consider it worth while to reinforce their South China Sea Fleet, based upon Singapore, remains to be seen. The attack on Sabang has proved to them that sea communications with their armies in Burma can no longer be considered safe, in spite of their possession of the Andaman and Nicobar Islands, lying between Sabang and Rangoon. Though otherwise unimportant, these islands possess some useful harbours, and the time will doubtless come when an expedition for their recovery will be undertaken. That is not likely to be just yet, as the approach of the monsoon is bound to delay operations in the Bay of Bengal for a time. Nothing is known of the strength of the Eastern Fleet, but enemy accounts say that it includes battleships, aircraft carriers, cruisers, destroyers, submarines, and ancillary craft of all descriptions.

## GREAT Resources of Sebastopol will be Reorganized

By the time these comments appear it is highly probable that Sebastopol will have fallen, thus completing the Soviet reconquest of the Crimea (see map in page 778). Apart from the high strategic value of this great peninsula, which projects southward a long distance towards the centre of the Black Sea, Sebastopol itself is the only first-class naval base in the south of Russia. Novorossisk, at the western end of the Caucasus range, is of only secondary importance, and Batum is a smaller place still. Odessa has always been a commercial port ; and Nikolayev, though it possesses important shipbuilding yards, is too far up the estuary of the Bug to be of much value for naval purposes.

White buildings and plant may be destroyed, dry docks and basins are not so easily put out of action, and the Russians may be trusted to reorganize the resources of Sebastopol by clearing the harbour of wrecks and tidying the dockyard as one of the first tasks to be undertaken. It must be a couple of years since there was any opportunity of docking the larger ships of the Soviet Black Sea Fleet, Sebastopol being the only port with a dry dock capable of taking battleships or heavy cruisers. There was formerly a large floating dock at Nikolayev, but that is believed to have been destroyed or rendered useless.

Before the war the Black Sea Fleet comprised one old battleship of 23,256 tons, the Pariskaya Kommuna ; the cruisers Krasni

Kavkaz, Chervonaya Ukraina and Krasni Krim, of 8,030, 6,934 and 6,600 tons respectively ; about 30 modern destroyers ; four older destroyers ; 40 or 50 submarines ; and a considerable number of patrol vessels, motor torpedo-boats and other small craft. There is also a small seaplane carrier, converted from a merchant vessel.

Owing to her low speed—probably under 16 knots—and obsolete design and armament, the Pariskaya Kommuna cannot be reckoned of much fighting value, though her 12-in. guns are said to have carried out some useful coastal bombardments in support of the Red Army. The three cruisers are worth more, but the Germans claim that both the Chervonaya Ukraina and Krasni Krim were sunk during 1942. Though this may prove to be true of at least one of them, a recent message from Moscow mentioned the Krasni Krim as having been in action off Sebastopol last month. Two new cruisers, the Molotov and Voroshilov of 8,800 tons, are reported to have been launched at Nikolayev during 1939-40, but it is questionable whether they have been completed. They are believed to have been saved from capture when the port was evacuated, and may now be lying in Batum or Novorossisk. The hulls of a new 35,000-ton battleship, the Krasnaya Bessarabia, and of four destroyers and two submarines, were demolished on the slips so that they might not fall into enemy hands intact. (See illus. p. 129, Vol. 5.)

APART from the doubtful mention of the Krasni Krim, little has been heard for some time of the larger Russian ships in the Black Sea. Destroyers, motor torpedo-boats, submarines and aircraft appear to have been kept busy, interfering with the escape of German troops from the Crimea. Various enemy transports and smaller craft have been sunk or damaged. The best chance of escape from Sebastopol would appear to be by small fast craft during the hours of darkness.

Enemy naval strength in the Black Sea is not great. The Rumanian Navy originally possessed four destroyers, three submarines, a minelayer or two and three motor torpedo-boats, besides sundry vessels of less importance. At least two, and possibly all, of the destroyers have been sunk ; so have a couple of the motor torpedo-boats. Bulgaria has a still smaller navy, two motor torpedo-boats being the only modern units. Some Italian submarines and motor torpedo-boats which were transported overland are believed to remain in enemy hands ; and there may also be a few German submarines and light craft, which proceeded down the Danube. With Sebastopol once more in Russian hands, the Black Sea Fleet could be used to disrupt communications between Rumanian and Bulgarian ports and the Bosphorus, and to support advance of the Soviet armies by bombarding enemy coast positions.

**ON THE WAY BACK TO SEBASTOPOL** to join other units of the Soviet Black Sea Fleet engaged in preventing enemy evacuation, is this submarine which has already sunk four loaded German transports. A radio order from Moscow called upon this Fleet to stop the Nazis attempting to escape from the Crimea (see map in p. 778). PAGE 774 *Photo, Planet News*

# Human Torpedoes Add to Royal Navy's Triumphs

LEGENDARY DARING OF THE ROYAL NAVY was typified in one of the war's most amazing sea actions when—as can now be revealed—"Human Torpedoes," manned by Submarine Branch personnel, penetrated the strongly defended enemy harbour base at Palermo one night in January 1943, sank the Italian Regolo class cruiser Ulpio Traiano, and severely damaged the 8,500-ton transport Viminale. The human torpedo which sank the cruiser was manned by Lieut. R. T. G. Greenland, R.N.V.R (2), who, it was announced on April 19, 1944, was awarded the D.S.O., and Ldg. Signalman A. Ferrier (5), who gained the C.G.M. Sub-Lieut. R. G. Dove, R.N.V.R. (3), and Ldg. Seaman J. Freel (4), crew of the craft which damaged the Viminale, gained the D.S.O. and C.G.M. respectively. With others who took part in the operations they were made prisoners of war.

Human torpedoes are approximately the same size and shape as ordinary torpedoes, 21 ins. in diameter, 18 ft. long, are driven by electric batteries and manned by a crew of two who wear diving-suits and sit astride the body of the torpedo. Approaching the target at slow speed, they dive below it, detach the explosive head from the main body and fix it to the bottom of the enemy ship. Time fuses are set, and the human torpedo, now minus its warhead, is driven away in order to be clear of the target-area before the explosion occurs. An officer in his diving-suit (1). Mr. A. V. Alexander, First Lord of the Admiralty, watches a member of the crew going aboard his craft (7). A human torpedo under way (6). PAGE 775 *Photos, British Official: Daily Mirror*

# Barracudas Caught Germany's Largest Warship—

**FLEET AIR ARM BARRACUDAS**—named after a vicious, predatory 5-foot fish found in the southern seas—in a brilliant surprise attack on April 3, 1944, severely damaged the German 45,000-ton Tirpitz, in Altenfjord. One of the attacking torpedo-bombers (2) soars at a steep angle, then dives targetwards from above the clouds (3); and smoke from a direct hit rises from the stricken warship (1); beyond can be seen the wake of a motor-launch departing hurriedly from her side. See also pp. 742, 777 and story in p. 794

See also pp. 742, 777 and story in p. 794

*Photos, British Official; Charles E. Brown*

# —And Ravager's Fighters Helped to Smash Her

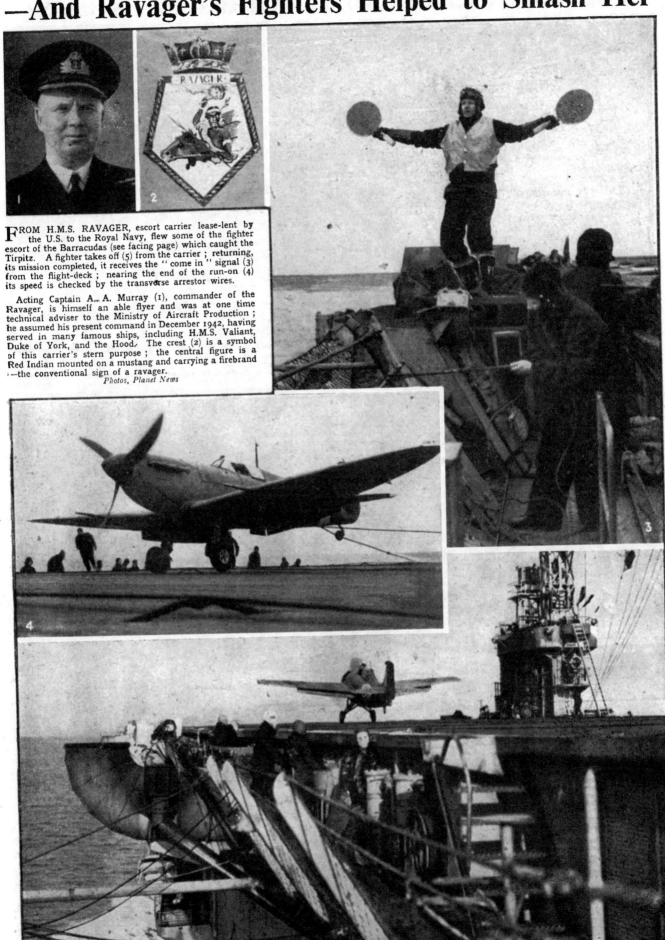

FROM H.M.S. RAVAGER, escort carrier lease-lent by the U.S. to the Royal Navy, flew some of the fighter escort of the Barracudas (see facing page) which caught the Tirpitz. A fighter takes off (5) from the carrier; returning, its mission completed, it receives the "come in" signal (3) from the flight-deck; nearing the end of the run-on (4) its speed is checked by the transverse arrestor wires.

Acting Captain A. A. Murray (1), commander of the Ravager, is himself an able flyer and was at one time technical adviser to the Ministry of Aircraft Production; he assumed his present command in December 1942, having served in many famous ships, including H.M.S. Valiant, Duke of York, and the Hood. The crest (2) is a symbol of this carrier's stern purpose; the central figure is a Red Indian mounted on a mustang and carrying a firebrand —the conventional sign of a ravager.

*Photos, Planet News*

# The Last Crimean Battle Draws to its Close

THRUSTS OF THE RED ARMIES in the Crimea are shown in the above map, which records the push of the 4th Ukrainian Army, commanded by General Tolbukhin, down from the Perekop Isthmus to Sevastopol and the co-ordinated drive by General Eremenko's independent Maritime Army from the Kerch peninsula, which began on April 10, 1944, round the Black Sea coast to the same goal. By April 20, massed Russian artillery and aircraft were bombarding Sevastopol, the only city on the peninsula left in German hands.

*Specially drawn for* THE WAR ILLUSTRATED *by Félix Gardon*

ODESSA, on the Black Sea coast, wrecked and ruined by the Nazis, withstood the horrors of 30 months' occupation (see facing page). One of the largest transport centres of the Soviet Union, through it flowed supplies of grain, timber, oil and coal. An important industrial city, it possessed huge flour mills, sugar refineries and shipbuilding yards. A centre of science and culture, before the war thousands of patients visited its sanatoria and rest homes; population in 1939 was 604,000.

The Germans shattered the progressive life of Odessa, but not the spirit of its people; these citizens (1) are demolishing one of the Nazi street defence works after the Red Army had arrived. The enemy seized everything of value they could lay hands on, including these pianos (2) from the Conservatory of Music, but their plans went awry, thanks to the victorious Soviet troops (3), whose welcome in Odessa streets was warm reward for valour.

*U.S.S.R. Official, Pictorial Press*

# Odessa in the Hands of Russia Once Again

**GREAT BLACK SEA PORT** and naval base of Odessa fell to the Russian 3rd Ukrainian Army on April 10, 1944. For two and a half years it had been an important German base, but during the last fortnight of enemy occupation 10,000 Russian guerillas swarmed out of its 100 miles of catacombs, 80 to 100 feet below ground, to dominate the city by night. Above is seen the imposing flight of steps, long known as the Richelieu stairway, leading from the water front to the spacious boulevard 150 feet above. (See also facing page.)

*Photo, Planet News*

# What Happens when the Enemy is 'In the Bag'

A problem confronting the Allies is what to do with large numbers of the enemy when these are rounded up. They have to be sorted, fed, reclothed, given hospital treatment if necessary, transported to some place of security, and generally cared for in accordance with international law. How this works out in practice is explained by WALLACE FORD.

THREE British officers at an Italian port—and scores of others elsewhere—are preparing for one of the biggest jobs of the war: the reception and transfer of a million German prisoners. For that is the number they must expect to handle when our full-scale assault on Hitler-held Europe gets under way. As the tide of victory turns, the flood-mark of " p.o.w. " inevitably becomes higher.

An expert in dealing with prisoners of war in North Africa, Major Joseph Goldware thought he was handling an immense and complex job when he was told to prepare for 10,000 prisoners. The first 100 came through with disappointing slowness. They had three guards to a prisoner and so many blankets that they could heap them on their cots like mattresses. Then, less than two months later, the great round-up started and prisoners poured in by the hundred thousand.

Anyone who lived through those amazing days will never forget the scenes on the Cape Bon Peninsula. Enemy companies, hundreds strong, stopped isolated Allied soldiers and asked to be disarmed and meekly said that they " hadn't been captured yet." Thousands sat around unfenced posts which had been hurriedly marked as reception centres. Those already in lorries shouted jokes to their stranded comrades. Prisoners had to be put in charge of prisoners. Fussy enemy officers who wanted priority of treatment sometimes made a nuisance of themselves.

WHAT happens to prisoners once they fall into Allied hands ? Most people know that treatment is prescribed under international law, but very few probably realize the thoroughness and intricacy of the 97 articles of the 1929 Convention. It seems paradoxical, for instance, that the most severe disciplinary punishment for a refractory prisoner is imprisonment ; yet this distinguishes between confinement in cells and the ordinary mild rigours of life in an internment camp.

Prisoners must never be insulted or ill-treated. A questioned p.o.w. is under an obligation to tell the truth concerning his name, rank and number, if indeed he gives them. On the other hand, he need not reply, and he can try to lead an interrogator up the garden path in army matters. This may be difficult, for many interrogator-officers have been lawyers, schoolmasters or business managers in civil life and have considerable tact in handling men. Some prisoners, distrustful at first, have afterwards relented so considerably that they have wept on leaving the reception ports. One Nazi at a camp near Oran even had a wedding party recently when he was married by proxy, through the Swiss government, to his sweetheart in Germany. Another qualified by post as a German solicitor, and has now applied to study English law. Perhaps he feels, after all, that Nazi law will not be so useful in the post-war world.

THE self-reliance of p.o.w. is proverbial. Sometimes, as in invasion, the vital priorities of war supplies upon shipping space necessarily mean initial shortages of equipment for prisoners. Near Algiers, when the droves of captives swept aside all prearrangements, our prisoners made their own dishes out of gallon cans, beat out spoons on wooden moulds, set up their own tailor shops and shoe-repair shops out of salvage, made their own soap and built their own ovens for bread, and set up a complete hospital camp with a German medical staff.

Then, extending activities, they built a prison city of adobe barracks with walls 18 inches thick, a complete camp capable of housing 30,000 prisoners. Africa alone has many such camps today. Scores of others are scattered through Britain, Canada, South Africa and the United States. " We can move out 25,000 prisoners in a day," one commanding officer of a p.o.w. division told me, "and we've never lost a prisoner yet between the camps and the boats."

Attempted escapes are rare. One prisoner, a former U-boat rating, attempted a novel break when he scrambled through a porthole while his prison-ship was going up the

BRITISH GUARD brings out a Nazi prisoner on the Anzio front. Five feet in height, 18 years old, he has been a soldier for only a few months. Now, for him, the war is over and good food and comparative comfort will be his lot as an enforced " guest " of the Allies.
*Photo, British Official*

St. Lawrence, but he was caught at the United States border. When three others escaped from a North of England camp and built themselves a fire in a moorland cave where they hoped to spend the night, they were discovered and rounded up by three schoolboys. At one time there was an alarm that eleven had broken out of a camp in one of the north-western counties. Two were caught by a middle-aged gardener ; the others were discovered hiding between the ceiling and roof of their dormitory.

Perhaps one of the most spectacular attempts of all was when 98 prisoners planned to seize a camp near Schreiber, 400 miles east of Winnipeg, and storm another camp not far away. With tools made from old tin cans they constructed a tunnel 120 feet long, from which smaller tunnels radiated to every individual hut. Deep below ground they constructed a workshop safe from the eyes of guards, where they made and collected equipment. No detail had been overlooked, yet a trivial accident at the last moment gave the whole show away. A prisoner stumbled over a pail in the darkness and the clatter was heard by a sentry.

THEN there was the amazing episode—staged before our precautionary measures were fully complete—when two escaped German airmen prisoners strolled on to an airfield and almost commandeered a plane. They told a groundsman to prepare a Miles Magister. While the petrol tanks were being filled the escapees drank tea with the station adjutant. He was suspicious that the two were not the " Dutchmen " they purported to be, and then suddenly he detected that their ersatz uniform buttons were made of silver paper.

Prisoners in Allied hands have scant cause for regrets. The rations they receive are equivalent to those of the British army ; their pay is regularly made up ; two or three letters and four postcards a month soften the barbed wires. Tattered and forlorn "tramps" in North Africa were given natty American uniforms ; men saved from the sea are given secondhand civilian clothing. It is surprising to discover that in camps on British soil the prisoners assemble every morning to salute a large portrait of Hitler and are under the control of Nazi officers ; we permit this in strict accordance with the laws protecting prisoners.

DEJECTED JAPANESE captured during the fighting for Kwajalein Island in the Pacific, which fell to U.S. troops on Feb. 5, 1944 ; the island is the largest in the Kwajalein Atoll, strategic heart of the Marshall Islands. Wounded prisoners received the same expert medical care and attention as the American forces, whose casualties during the battle were few. Japanese losses were very heavy.

*Photo, Paul Popper*

# 'Mikes' Sound-Range for Our Gunners in Italy

THE RUMBLE OF ENEMY GUNS is picked up by concealed microphones, and graph films are made recording the firing positions. At an advanced Allied post (1) the sounds are reported by telephone. A "mike" (2) is positioned between that post and headquarters, where the reports are received by wireless (3) and recording machinery is switched on to catch the microphone-transmitted rumbles. Resulting graphs are then read (4), enabling exact positions of enemy guns to be plotted (5) for the guidance of our own artillery.

PAGE 781

*Photos, British Official*

# Watch Himmler! Wiliest of Nazi Gangsters

Since Himmler came into authority as Gestapo head, police chief and leader of the S.S. he has, with one eye on the Fuehrer he is supposed to serve, steadily increased his own grasp on Nazi Germany with a ruthless cunning seldom surpassed even in Germany. His progressive seizure of the reins of control is described here by Dr. EDGAR STERN-RUBARTH.

BEHIND the dramatic events of the land, sea and air war other moves are evident which, ultimately, may prove no less momentous. Such moves started inside Germany early in Hitler's career when the powers that made him began their fight for supremacy; they were going on all through the intervening years; and the most sinister of them won the game only a few weeks ago—the fight of the Party against the traditional supreme power of the Army.

The first Nazi leader who undertook it, Captain Ernst Roehm, creator of Hitler's Brownshirt and Black Guard forces, paid for his temerity ten years ago, with his own and a thousand or so other lives, during a "purge" in which many rancours and rivalries were given vent, but by means of which the Junker generals made their fortress safe from intrusion by Party rabble for many years.

Himmler succeeded, as Chief of the Police, the Gestapo and the S.S., systematically converted into a fully armed and militarized body, blindly obedient and immunized against any kind of moral scruples. Originally trained as a civil war army, the S.S., for political as well as military reasons, had to be split, early in the war, into two distinct categories, the major one, the Waffen- (or fighting) S.S. about 40 divisions strong, being fully invested in the fighting forces, on an equal footing with the regular army.

Yet they were not entirely equal. Himmler had first choice in selecting his men, and was permitted to offer them better equipment, better pay, better food, better quarters and prospects of advancement—in future civilian life as well as in the field.

He promoted strong-arm men of the early Party days, gangsters and gaolbirds many of them, to exalted rank. He assimilated their ranks to those of the regular army, by giving them each a second, a police rank as majors, colonels, generals of police or Waffen-S.S. But as yet they still remained outsiders, not officially recognized by, and frequently at loggerheads with, the regular officers who had won their promotion by hard work and long years of service. In the fierce battles in Russia in 1943 many an S.S.-division fell victim to the caste-proud army commanders who, consciously or unconsciously, ordered them to the most dangerous sector of the line.

HIMMLER, however, kept silent, utilizing his Guards' sanguinary sacrifices for propaganda. He knew of his unbreakable hold over Hitler, for whose protection he had early been granted an entirely free hand; he even advised against drastic measures when, on an occasion late in 1943, his spies brought details of a "generals' plot" the failure of which, due to lack of response in the Allied camp, he foresaw.

But when the Junker-strategists came back into the Fuehrer's fold, when their centuries-old supreme instrument of power, the General Staff, was abolished, and the whole direction of the forces welded into the new "Wehrmachtstab" headed by Hitler's yes-men, Jodl and Zeitzler; when another Nazi, Rommel, was made Inspector-General of Defences, and

a suddenly resurrected Supreme War Lord made examples of Field Marshals von Kuechler and von Kluge, commanders respectively in North and Central Russia—as well as a number of other minor generals—Heinrich Himmler saw daylight.

Whether Hitler is aware of that sinister figure's real aims it is impossible to say; but even the most omnipotent of Caesars might well have doubts, remembering the fate of other dictators at the hands of their lieutenants. Having nominated, as his successor in case of his sudden demise, Reich

HIMMLER WATCHES OPERATIONS—he is on Hitler's right—at recent S.S. manoeuvres; 43 years old, son of a secondary school-teacher, in 1928 Heinrich Himmler became Reich Leader of the S.S., in 1934 chief of German police and Gestapo, and in August 1943 he was appointed Minister of the Interior. Himmler's rise to power is described in this page.     *Photo, Keystone*

Marshal Goering, Hitler was, however, more seriously concerned about his eventual succession. He decreed a Directorate of Three—Goering, Field Marshal Keitel, and either his Deputy Martin Bormann, or Heinrich Himmler, whose power, a short while ago, he had multiplied by making him Minister of the Interior. Which of these other three Himmler wishes to see eliminated, in order to inherit that third of Hitler's power which, in his crafty hands and backed by his Black Army, should soon become a one-man rule of his own, nobody could safely predict.

Himmler has frustrated all efforts at re-establishing the Brownshirt organization, unreliable as compared with his Black Guards. Their leader, Victor Lutze, died in an "accident," like so many obstructionist army leaders before and since: von Fritsch, Udet, von Reichenau, Jeschonnek, Moelders, von Chamier-Glyszinski and others. He has

created what amounts to Foreign Legions on a gigantic scale, with so-called "Volksdeutsche"—foreigners of allegedly Germanic descent—Estonian, Latvian, Lithuanian, Dutch, Wallonian, Galician and other S.S.-divisions which he uses respectively in countries other than their own in order to save his own cut-throats.

On similar lines he is building up what he calls a Pan-European Police under S.S.-control. He multiplies the tank divisions among his own army so that already they amount to nearly one-third of the army's total; and of late he has got hold of the whole Italian Fascist forces to be reconstructed under direct German—that is, Himmler's—command.

HIS big stroke was the recent overpowering of his old enemies, the proud and noble army chiefs. When they ate humble pie once more with Hitler, Himmler made him sign a whole sheaf of orders. By these, officers of the Waffen-S.S. might be transferred to any army unit, automatically gaining the army rank of their S.S. appointment; the first case in point was S.S.-Obergruppenfuehrer Krueger's recent appointment as General Commanding the 1st Tank Division, succeeding the wounded General von Wietersheim. All officers' messes of army and S.S. can be used indiscriminately by officers of both forces.

S.S. officers may be placed in key positions controlling the granting of army commissions, promotion, training and so on, such as the Army Personnel Board, the National Political Educational Institutions (replacing the former Cadet Colleges, now for some time Nazified) to which Chief Himmler's right-hand man, S.S.-Obergruppenfuehrer Heissmeyer, was appointed at the beginning of 1944, as well as Military Propaganda organizations.

The whole previous basis of professional officers' selection was abolished by a new rule, under which every recruit or volunteer, irrespective of education or social standing, can apply, and if found suitable must receive officer's training and, after two courses of from four to six months each with an intervening half year's active service, is eventually granted a commission.

THERE is one order Himmler has not yet "arranged": that by which the widespread Military Intelligence organization, built up by Admiral Canaris, and frequently fought by Himmler's espionage network, is handed over to him wholesale. Apart from it he has firmly established his own gangster organizations as Germany's fourth arm. It now ranks with the Army, the Navy, and the Luftwaffe—with a claim of being "The Guards"—nearly a million of them. They owe allegiance to Adolf Hitler; but Heinrich Himmler, ex-chemist, ex-poultry farmer, torturer and executioner, who has just ordered half a million of his "friendly" smiling portraits to be displayed in offices everywhere, thus equalling Hitler's own conceit, actually commands them. Latest, and perhaps most significant, Himmler move is indirect control of home propaganda. Tacitly, or otherwise, Goebbels bends to the S.S. leader's direction.

## Mobility and Fire Power in Italy

Speed of movement adds enormously to artillery value. Accompanying and guarding 8th Army supply convoys are self-propelled Bofors A.A. guns. Mounted on a Morris chassis, with a 70 h.p. engine, the 40-mm. Bofors (above, camouflaged) has a speed up to 40 m.p.h. It can throw 2-lb. shells to a height of 9,000 feet at 120 per minute; the new Stiffkey Stick sight provides a simple method of assessing the difference between the point where the target is and where it will be by the time the shell has reached it. A makeshift field-kitchen provides the gunners with a meal, eaten in shifts so that the Bofors remains manned. 194-mm. railway guns recently went into action on the Cassino front; manned by Italians (right) one is lobbing shells to a distance of 10 miles.

*Photos, British Official:
Crown Copyright*

## *Life and Death Close Neighbours in Cassino*

Constantly under shell and mortar fire the ruins of Cassino afford first-class concealment for snipers of both sides ; the commander (1) of a New Zealand platoon waits for an incautious movement to provide him with a Nazi target.   The panorama (2) of the Cassino front shows, in addition to Monastery Hill, Mount Trocchio (left) with the shattered town of Cervaro in the foreground.   On the Anzio beach-head a stretcher case is lowered (4) into a Regimental Aid Post.

Photos, British Crown Copyright